A Dictionary of Irish Saints

A Dictionary of Irish Saints

SECOND EDITION

PÁDRAIG Ó RIAIN

FOUR COURTS PRESS

Typeset in 10.5pt on 12pt DantePro by
Carrigboy Typesetting Services for
FOUR COURTS PRESS LTD
7 Malpas Street, Dublin 8, Ireland
www.fourcourtspress.ie
and in North America for
FOUR COURTS PRESS
c/o IPG, 814 N. Franklin St, Chicago, IL 60610

First edition 2011
Second edition with additions and corrections 2025

A catalogue record for this title is available
from the British Library.

ISBN 978-1-80151-162-9

Printed in England
by CPI Antony Rowe, Chippenham, Wilts.

For Amelia, Charlotte, Isolde, Ailbhe, Eluisa, Méabh, Íde,
Max, Sasha and Felix

CONTENTS

PREFACE TO THE SECOND EDITION

In the thirteen years since its publication by Four Courts Press in 2011 *A dictionary of Irish saints* has rarely been far from my desk. Beginning with notes added to an interleaved copy, followed by entries in an online copy generously provided by Four Courts Press, I have since assembled a large selection of additional material which was published separately by Four Courts in 2022 in *A supplement to a dictionary of Irish saints* and is here incorporated into this Second Edition of the *Dictionary*.

In addition to those named in the original work, some of whom, and especially my colleagues in the Locus Project: Kevin Murray and Emma Nic Cárthaigh, have continued to assist in identifying the locations of churches associated with saints, the following have also provided valuable further information: Cormac Bourke, Jeremy Cunningham, Fidelma Maguire, Joseph Mannion, Pádraig Ó Cearbhaill, Conchubhar Ó Crualaoich and Laurence Walsh OCSO. As heretofore, Dagmar Ó Riain-Raedel, and our son, Diarmuid, have continued to encourage my work on the *Dictionary*. Finally, I owe a continuing debt of gratitude to the staff of Four Courts Press for the care with which they have brought this new edition of the *Dictionary* through the press.

PREFACE

In his *De arte poetica* (ll. 386–90), Horace advised readers that a written work, having first been read by critics, should then be kept for at least nine years before being published, for 'a word once sent does not know the way back'. Although this dictionary was begun many more than nine years ago, I fear that I may have failed Horace on other counts. The kernel of the dictionary dates to the 1970s, when I first became aware of the importance of saints' genealogies through a study of *Buile Shuibhne*, published in *Éigse* 15 (1974). At that point, I began to bring together background material for an edition of the corpus of saints' genealogies that was completed and published in 1985 under the title *Corpus genealogiarum sanctorum Hiberniae* (*CGSH*). My notes on the genealogies, collected in two large manuscript volumes, have served as a basis for a large proportion of the entries presented here. However, due to other commitments, work on the dictionary was set aside for almost twenty years until after my retirement in 2002. Drafting of entries began in earnest in 2006; a first version was completed by 2009 and, following several re-readings and numerous additions and corrections, the work was finally handed to outside readers during 2010.

The idea of a dictionary had been conceived sixty years earlier by the eminent Bollandist, Paul Grosjean, who, in an article published in *Analecta Bollandiana* 69 (p. 86) in 1951, stressed the need for a summary biographical dictionary of Irish saints, containing information on such matters as feastdays, localizations, chronology and genealogies. Although Grosjean was eminently qualified to undertake a work of this kind, he appears not to have done so, and the only other attempt to provide a dictionary that I know of was unfinished when its author, the noted historian and archaeologist, Liam de Paor, died in 1998. Unfinished surveys of Irish saints are, of course, nothing new. The *Acta sanctorum Hiberniae*, begun by the Franciscan John Colgan in the early seventeenth century under the auspices of his order, was published up to the end of March only, while his late nineteenth-century successor, the secular priest, John Canon O'Hanlon, succeeded in bringing his monumental *Lives of the Irish saints* as far as the month of October.

Both Colgan's *Acta* (*ASH*) and *Trias thaumaturga* (*TT*), and O'Hanlon's *Lives* (*LIS*), receive regular mention in the references to sources in the present dictionary. Moreover, each in its own way has heavily influenced my work. The 1948 reprint of Colgan's *Acta* was still in print in the early 1960s, when I procured a copy at the original price of five guineas. Due to the loss of several manuscripts used by him, Colgan's work has become an indispensable primary source of information on many saints. O'Hanlon's *Lives*, an almost complete set of which I had the good fortune of acquiring in 1968, contributed greatly to my abiding interest in the records of the saints.

I owe a debt of gratitude to numerous colleagues and friends who have provided assistance during the preparation of this work, not least to the many local informants met in the course of visits to sites associated with the saints. I am especially indebted to my colleague in the *Locus* Project, Diarmuid Ó Murchadha, who read the work in its entirety and provided a regular (and very welcome) stream of corrigenda and addenda. Sadly, Diarmuid died as this book, which owes so much to him, was in press. My other colleague, Kevin Murray, who read substantial parts of the dictionary, also drew my attention to numerous improvements that needed to be made to the original draft. I have received valuable additional information on individual saints or places associated with them from, among others: Pádraigín Clancy, James Dollard, David Dumville, Hugh Fogarty, Senan Furlong, Karen Jankulak, the late Ailbhe MacShamhráin, Luke McInerney, Michael MacMahon, Bernadette Moran, Colmán Ó Clabaigh, Seosamh Ó Dufaigh, Kenneth Nicholls, Pádraig Ó Macháin, Nollaig Ó Muraíle, the late Pádraig Ó hIceadha of Cullen, the late Pádraig Ó Riain (no relation) of Kilbrin, the late William O'Sullivan, and Emer Purcell.

In preparing this work, I've had the good fortune of easy access to several libraries, well endowed with sources of information on Irish and universal saints. 'Special Collections' in the Boole Library of University College Cork, formerly under the direction of Helen Davis, now cared for by Mary Lombard and her colleagues, has been a constant support. I've also been made welcome in the library of the Royal Irish Academy, in the Manuscripts Room of Trinity College Dublin, and especially in the Franciscan library in Killiney, where Fr Ignatius Fennessy could not have been more hospitable. Further afield, I've had the good fortune of being able to avail of the magnificent collections in the Historical and Theological libraries of the University of Bonn, and in the library of the Max Planck Institute in Göttingen, while this was still devoted to the subject-area of history.

My work on the dictionary has received constant encouragement from my family, from my wife Dagmar (who read and commented helpfully on many entries) and from our four children (Hilda, Kathi, Diarmuid and Elsa). To these and to all who have helped, through acts of kindness or encouragement, I offer my heartfelt thanks.

Finally, I wish to thank Four Courts Press for agreeing to publish this book, and to acknowledge the contribution of Michael Potterton, who carefully copy-edited the entire text and made many very helpful suggestions. Generous financial support towards the defrayal of the costs of the dictionary was received from the Publications Committee of the National University of Ireland.

Pádraig Ó Riain,
Cill Chúile, Corcaigh
25.07.2011
(Féil Bhairre agus Neasáin)

SOURCES

(The abbreviated titles used here follow almost entirely the system adopted by the editors of the *Historical dictionary of Gaelic placenames* (*HDGP*))

AAR *Calendar of Archbishop Alen's register, c.1172–1534*, ed. C. McNeill, indexed L. Price (Dublin, 1950).

AB *Analecta Bollandiana* (1882–).

AbEMLS *Above and beyond: essays in memory of Leo Swan*, ed. T. Condit & C. Corlett (Dublin, 2005).

ACE *Archdiocese of Cashel and Emly: Pobal Ailbhe*, C. O'Dwyer (Strasburg, 2008).

ACDS *Ancient church dedications in Scotland: non-scriptural dedications*, J.M. Mackinlay (Edinburgh, 1914).

ACL *Archiv für celtische Lexikographie*, 3 vols, ed. W. Stokes & K. Meyer (Halle, 1898–1907).

AClon. *Annals of Clonmacnoise being the Annals of Ireland from the earliest period to AD1408*, ed. D. Murphy (Dublin, 1896).

ACoC *The antiquities of County Clare: John O'Donovan, Eugene Curry*, ed. M. Comber (Ennis, 1997).

ACon. *Annála Connacht: the Annals of Connacht (AD1224–1544)*, ed. A.M. Freeman (Dublin, 1944).

ACoK *The antiquities of the county of Kerry*, J. O'Donovan (Cork, 1983).

AcS 'Acallamh na Senórach', ed. W. Stokes, *IT* iv, 1, 14–438.

AD *Aithdioghluim dána*, 2 vols, ed. L. McKenna (ITS 37, 40; London, 1939–40).

AdB *Adomnán at Birr, AD697*, ed. T. O'Loughlin (Dublin, 2001).

AF *Airne Fíngein*, ed. J. Vendryes (*MMIS* 15, Dublin, 1953).

AfL *Archiv für Liturgiewissenschaft* (1950–).

AFM *Annála ríoghachta Éireann: Annals of the kingdom of Ireland by the Four Masters*, 7 vols, ed. J. O'Donovan (Dublin, 1848–51; 2nd ed. 1856; facs. repr. with introduction and appendix by K. Nicholls, Dublin, 1990).

AgS *Agallamh na Seanórach*, 3 vols, ed. N. Ní Shéaghdha (*LóL* 7, 10, 15, Dublin, 1942–5).

AH *Archivium Hibernicum* (1912–).

AHHS *Armagh, history and society: interdisciplinary essays on the history of an Irish county*, ed. A.J. Hughes & W. Nolan (Dublin, 2001).

AHP *Adomnan and the holy places: the perceptions of an Insular monk on the locations of the biblical drama*, T. O'Loughlin (London, 2007).

AHWD *Ancient and holy wells of Dublin*, G. Branigan (Dublin, 2012).

AI *The Annals of Inisfallen (MS Rawlinson B 503)*, ed. S. Mac Airt (Dublin, 1951).

AICK *Archaeological inventory of County Cork*, 5 vols, comp. D. Power, E. Byrne, U. Egan, S. Lane & M. Sleeman (Dublin, 1992–2009).

AICW *Archaeological inventory of County Carlow*, comp. A. Brindley & A. Kilfeather (Dublin, 1993).

AIFJC *The Annals of Ireland by Friar John Clyn*, ed. B. Williams (Dublin, 2007).

AIGY *Archaeological inventory of County Galway*, 2 vols, comp. P. Gosling, O. Alcock & K. de hÓra (Dublin, 1993, 1999).

AIH *Ancient Irish histories: the works of Spencer, Campion, Hanmer and Marleburrough*, 2 vols (Dublin, 1809).

AIKY *Archaeological inventory of County Kerry*, I, comp. E. Byrne, A. McQueen & R. Cronin (Dublin, 2009).

AILC *Adomnán of Iona: Life of St Columba*, trans. R. Sharpe (London, 1995).

AilIM *Ailerani interpretatio mystica et moralis progenitorum Domini Iesu Christi*, ed. A. Breen (Dublin, 1995).

AILM *Archaeological inventory of County Leitrim*, comp. M.J. Moore (Dublin, 2003).

AILS *Archaeological inventory of County Laois*, comp. P.D. Sweetman, O. Alcock & B. Moran (Dublin, 1995).

AIMA *Aquitaine and Ireland in the Middle Ages*, ed. J.-M. Picard (Dublin, 1995).

AIMN *Archaeological inventory of County Monaghan*, comp. A.L. Brindley (Dublin, 1996).

Ainm *Ainm* (1986–).

AIOY *Archaeological inventory of County Offaly*, comp. C. O'Brien & P.D. Sweetman (Dublin, 1997).

AIRV *Anglo-Saxon/Irish relations before the Vikings*, ed. J. Graham Campbell & M. Ryan (Proceedings of the British Academy 157; London, 2009).

AISO *Archaeological inventory of County Sligo*, comp. U. Egan, E. Byrne & M. Sleeman (Dublin, 2005).

AITLP *Adomnán of Iona: theologian, lawmaker, peacemaker*, ed. J.M. Wooding, R. Aist, T.O. Clancy & T. O'Loughlin (Dublin, 2010).

AITY *Archaeological inventory of County Tipperary*, I (N. Tipperary), comp. J. Farrelly & C. O'Brien (Dublin, 2002).

AIWD *Archaeological inventory of County Waterford*, comp. M.J. Moore (Dublin, 1999).

AIWX *Archaeological inventory of County Wexford*, comp. M.J. Moore (Dublin, 1996).

AJ *Ardmore Journal: Irisleabhar Áird Mhór* 1 (1984) –10 (1993).

ALC *Annals of Loch Cé: a chronicle of Irish affairs from AD1014 to AD1590*, 2 vols, ed. W.M. Hennessy (Rolls Series, London, 1871; repr. Caisleán an Bhúrcaigh, 2000).

AMBR *Ancient Meath according to the Book of Rights*, P. Walsh, Leaves of History, ser. 1 (Drogheda, 1930).

AMC	*Aislinge Meic Conglinne: the vision of Mac Conglinne*, ed. K. Meyer (London 1892; repr. Felinfach, 1999).
AMME	*Aided Muirchertaig Meic Erca*, ed. L. Nic Dhonnchadha (*MMIS* 19, Dublin, 1964).
AMW	Archives of the Marquis of Waterford, Curraghmore House.
AmraeCC	*Amrae Coluimb Chille: a critical edition*, J. Bisagni (Early Irish Text Series 1; Dublin, 2019).
ANA	*The Anglo-Norman advance into the south-west of Ireland, 1185–1221*, G. Cunningham (Roscrea, 1987).
Anecd.	*Anecdota from Irish manuscripts*, 5 vols, ed. O.J. Bergin, R.I. Best, K. Meyer, J.G. O'Keeffe (Halle/Dublin, 1907–13).
AnH	*Analecta Hibernica* 1 (1930–).
AnnU	*De annatis Hiberniae: a calendar of the First-fruits' fees levied on papal appointments to benefices in Ireland, AD1400–1535*, I (Ulster), ed. M.A. Costello & A. Coleman (Dundalk, 1909; repr. Maynooth, 1912).
AntB	*The Antiphonary of Bangor: an early Irish manuscript in the Ambrosian Library at Milan*, 2 vols, ed. F.E. Warren (HBS 4,10, London, 1893, 1895).
ApalF	*Apalóga na bhFilí, 1200–1650*, L.P. Ó Caithnia (Leabhair Thaighde 45, Dublin, 1984).
ARos.	'The annals of Roscrea', ed. D. Gleeson & S. Mac Airt, in *PRIA* 59C3 (1958), 137–80.
AS	*Acta sanctorum quotquot toto orbe coluntur*, ed. J. Bolland et al. (Antwerp/Brussels, 1643–). [volumes cited by month – Ian., Feb., Iun., Iul., Nov.].
ASCD	*Archaeological survey of County Donegal*, comp. B. Lacy et al. (Lifford, 1983).
ASE	*The Blackwell Encyclopaedia of Anglo-Saxon England*, ed. M. Lapidge, J. Blair, S. Keynes & D. Scragg (London, 2001).
ASH	*Acta sanctorum veteris et majoris Scotiae seu Hiberniae ... sanctorum Insulae*, I, ed. J. Colgan (Louvain, 1645; repr. Dublin, 1947).
ASHCS	*Acta sanctorum Hiberniae ex codice Salmanticensi nunc primum integre edita*, ed. C. de Smedt & J. de Backer (Edinburgh & London, 1887).
ASI	'Anglo-Saxon Ireland: the evidence of the Martyrology of Tallaght', P. Ó Riain, *H.M. Chadwick Memorial Lectures*, 3 (Cambridge, 1993).
ATig.	'The annals of Tigernach', ed. W. Stokes, in *RC* 16 (1895), 374–419, 17 (1896), 6–33, 119–263, 337–420, 18 (1897), 9–59, 150–97, 267–303; repr. 2 vols (Felinfach, 1993).
AU	*Annála Uladh: Annals of Ulster*, 4 vols, ed. W.M. Hennessy & B. Mac Carthy (Dublin, 1887–1901; facs. repr. with new intr. by N. Ó Muraíle, Dublin, 1998); *The Annals of Ulster (to AD1131)*, ed. S. Mac Airt & G. Mac Niocaill (Dublin, 1983).
AurÉ	*Auraicept na n-éces: the scholars' primer*, ed. G. Calder (Edinburgh, 1917; repr. Dublin, 1995).
BAd.	*Betha Adamnáin*, ed. M. Herbert & P. Ó Riain (ITS 54, London, 1988).

BAil. *Beatha Ailbhe: the Life of Saint Ailbhe of Cashel and Emly*, ed. P. Ó Riain, ITS 67 (London & Dublin, 2017).

BB *The Book of Ballymote*, Photo-lithogr. facs., with intr. by R. Atkinson (Dublin, 1887).

BBa. *Beatha Bharra: Saint Finbarr of Cork. The complete life*, ed. P. Ó Riain (ITS 57, Dublin, 1994).

BBL *The Black Book of Limerick*, ed. J. MacCaffrey (Dublin, 1907).

BBR Brussels Bibliotheque Royale.

BBr. *Bethu Brigte*, ed. D. Ó hAodha (Dublin, 1978).

BCC *Betha Colaim Chille Life of Columcille compiled by Manus O'Donnell in 1532*, ed. A. O'Kelleher & G. Schoepperle (Chicago, IL, 1918; repr. 1994).

BCLMA *St Bernard of Clairvaux's Life of St Malachy of Armagh*, ed. H.J. Lawlor (Translations of Christian Literature, ser. 5, London, 1920).

BCML *Betha Colmáin maic Lúacháin. Life of Colmán son of Lúachán*, ed. K. Meyer (TLS 17, Dublin, 1911).

BCOC *Bernard de Clairvaux: Ouevres complétes XXXI, Éloge de la Nouvelle Chevalerie; Vie de Saint Malachie*, ed. P.-Y. Emery (Sources Chrétiennes 367, Paris, 1990).

Béaloideas *Béaloideas: the Journal of the Folklore of Ireland Society* (1927–).

Bech. *Bechbretha*, ed. T. Charles-Edwards & F. Kelly (EILS I, Dublin, 1983).

BEH *Bede: Ecclesiastical history of the English people*, ed. B. Colgrave & R.A.B. Mynors (Oxford, 1969).

BFen. *The Book of Fenagh*, ed. W.M. Hennessy & D.H. Kelly (Dublin, 1875; repr. Dublin, 1939).

BFen. (supp.) Book of Fenagh (supp. vol.).

BGBR *Beiträge zur Geschichte des Bistums Regensburg* (1967–).

BHJ *Bandon Historical Journal* (1984–).

BHL *Bibliotheca Hagiographica Latina*, 2 vols, ed. Socii Bollandiani (Brussels, 1898–9).

BiblSS *Enciclopedia dei Santi: Bibliotheca Sanctorum*, 14 vols (Rome, 1961–70).

BK *The Book of Kells: proceedings of a conference held at Trinity College Dublin, 6–9 September 1992*, ed. F. O'Mahony (Dublin, 1994).

BLCat. *Catalogue of Irish manuscripts in the British Library (formerly British Museum)*, 2 vols, S.H. O'Grady & R. Flower (London, 1926; repr. Dublin, 1992).

BLec. *The Book of Lecan: Leabhar Mór Mhic Fhir Bhisigh Leacain*, collotype facs., with intr. by K. Mulchrone (Dublin, 1937).

BLH *Britain, 400–600: language and history*, ed. A. Bammesberger & A. Wollmann (Heidelberg, 1990).

BLis. *The Book of Mac Carthaigh Riabhach otherwise the Book of Lismore*, collotype facs., with intr. by R.A.S. Macalister (Dublin, 1950).

BLM	*The birth and life of St Moling*, W. Stokes (London, 1907).
BLSP	*The book of letters of Saint Patrick the bishop: Liber epistolarum Sancti Patricii episcopi*, ed. D.R. Howlett (Dublin, 1994).
BM	British Museum.
BMag.	*The Book of Magauran: Leabhar Méig Shamhradháin*, ed. L. McKenna (Dublin, 1947).
BMG	*Bláithfhleasg de mhílseáinaibh na Gaoidheilge*, ed. P. O Briain (Dublin, 1893).
BMisc.	*A bardic miscellany: five hundred bardic poems from manuscripts in Irish and British libraries*, ed. D. McManus & E. Ó Raghallaigh (TIS 2, Dublin, 2010).
BNCS	*Beatha Naoim Chiaráin Saighre: Life of S. Kiaran (the Elder) of Seir*, ed. D.B. Mulcahy (Dublin, 1895).
BNÉ	*Bethada náem nÉrenn: lives of Irish saints*, 2 vols, ed. C. Plummer (Oxford, 1922).
Bod. Cat.	*Cataloguc of Irish language manuscripts in the Bodleian Library at Oxford and Oxford College Libraries*, 2 vols, B. Ó Cuív (Dublin, 2001–3).
BOI	*The Book of Inishowen: a guidebook and conspectus relating to the barony of Inishowen, County Donegal*, H.P. Swan (Buncrana, 1938).
BOM	*Book of obits and martyrology of the cathedral church of the Holy Trinity, commonly called Christ Church, Dublin*, ed. J.C. Crosthwaite & J.H. Todd (Dublin, 1844).
BP	*Bethu Phátraic: the Tripartite Life of Patrick*, ed. K. Mulchrone (Dublin & London, 1939).
Breifne	*Breifne: Journal of the Cumann Seanchais Bhreifne* (1958–).
Brendaniana	*Brendaniana: St Brendan the voyager in story and legend*, D. O'Donoghue (Dublin, 1893).
BrevA	*Breviarium Aberdonense*, 2 vols, W.J. Blew (London, 1854).
Bruchst.	*Bruchstücke der älteren Lyrik Irlands*, ed. K. Meyer (Preuss. Akad. der Wissensch. 7, Berlin, 1919).
BS	*Buile Shuibhne*, ed. J.G. O'Keeffe (*MMIS* 1, Dublin, 1952); *Buile Suibhne (The Frenzy of Suibhne)*, ed. J.G. O'Keeffe (ITS 12, London, 1913).
BUPNS	*Bulletin of the Ulster Place-name Society*, 1st ser. 1 (1952) –5 (1957); 2nd ser. 1 (1978) –4 (1981–2).
CA	*Cáin Adamnáin: an Old-Irish treatise on the Law of Adamnan*, ed. K. Meyer (Oxford, 1905).
Cal.PR	*Calendar of patent rolls.*
CAn.	*Cóir Anmann: a Late Middle Irish treatise on personal names*, 2 vols, ed. S. Arbuthnot (ITS 59–60, London, 2005–7).
Carloviana	*Carloviana: Journal of the Old Carlow Society* (1947–).
CarmG	*Carmina Gadelica*, 2 vols, A. Carmichael (Edinburgh, 1900).
CasaIt.	*Casa Italia III: Gemellaggi tra Italia e Irlanda* (Dublin, 2004), 108–12.
CathA	*Cath Almaine*, ed. P. Ó Riain (*MMIS* 25, Dublin, 1975).

CB *Catholic Bulletin* (1911–39).

CBC *The Compossicion Booke of Conought*, ed. A.M. Freeman (IMC, Dublin, 1936).

CBR *Curadán Boniface and the Early Church of Rosemarkie*, A. MacDonald (Alness, 1992).

CC *Caithréim Cellaig*, ed. K. Mulchrone (*MMIS* 24, Dublin, 1971).

CCBI *The Celtic Church in Britain and Ireland*, H. Zimmer (London, 1902).

CCC *Caithreim Cellachain Caisil: the victorious career of Cellachan of Cashel*, ed. A. Bugge (Christiana, 1905).

CCCD *Christ Church Cathedral, Dublin: a history*, ed. K. Milne (Dublin, 2000).

CCDK *Cenél Conaill and the Donegal kingdoms, AD500–800*, B. Lacey (Dublin, 2006).

CCH *Cardiganshire County History* I, ed. J.L. Davies & D.P. Kirby (Cardiff, 1994).

CCLC *Clonmacnois – the church and lands of St Ciarán: change and continuity in an Irish monastic foundation (6th to 16th century)*, A. Kehnel (Münster, 1997).

CCS *Colmán of Cloyne: a study*, P. MacCotter (Dublin, 2004).

CCSt. *County Clare studies*, ed. C. Ó Murchadha ([Ennis], Co. Clare, 2000).

CCT *Camchuairt Chonamara Theas*, L. Mac Con Iomaire (Baile Átha Cliath, 2002).

CDI *Calendar of documents relating to Ireland, 1171–1307*, 5 vols (London, 1875–86).

CDKL *Collections relating to the dioceses of Kildare and Leighlin*, i, M. Comerford (Dublin, 1883).

CE *Cambrensis Eversus seu potius historica fides in rebus Hibernicis Giraldo Cambrensi arrogata ... ostendit Gratianus Lucius, Hibernus*, 3 vols, ed. M. Kelly (Dublin, 1848–51).

CECW *Celtic and Early Christian Wexford, AD400 to 1166*, E. Culleton (Dublin, 1999).

CEIS *The church in early Irish society*, K. Hughes (London, 1966).

CéliD *Céli Dé in Ireland: monastic writing and identity in the early Middle Ages*, ed. W. Follett (Woodbridge, 2006).

CeltC *Celtic connections: proceedings of the tenth International Congress of Celtic Studies*, I, ed. R. Black, W. Gillies & R. Ó Maolalaigh (Phantassie, 1999).

Celtica *Celtica* (1946–).

CeltL *Celtic Leinster: towards an historical geography of early Irish civilization, AD500–1600*, A.P. Smyth (Dublin, 1982).

CeltM *Celtic mythology*, P. Mac Cana (London, 1968).

CeltT *Celtic theology: humanity, world and God in early Irish writings*, T. O'Loughlin (London, 2000).

Census 1659 *A census of Ireland, circa 1659, with supplementary material from the Poll Money Ordinances (1660–61)*, ed. S. Pender (IMC, Dublin, 1939).

CGG *Cogadh Gaedhel re Gallaibh: the war of the Gaedhil with the Gaill*, ed. J.H. Todd (London, 1867).

CGH *Corpus genealogiarum Hiberniae*, I, ed. M.A. O'Brien (Dublin, 1962).

CGSH *Corpus genealogiarum sanctorum Hiberniae*, ed. P. Ó Riain (Dublin, 1985).

CH *Collectanea Hibernica* (1958–).

CHSC *Celtic hagiography and saints' cults*, ed. J. Cartwright (Cardiff, 2003).

CI *The Chronicle of Ireland*, 2 vols, T.M. Charles-Edwards (Liverpool, 2006).

CICI *Cultural identity and cultural integration: Ireland and Europe in the early Middle Ages*, ed. D. Edel (Dublin, 1995).

CIIC *Corpus inscriptionum Insularum Celticarum*, 2 vols, ed. R.A.S. Macalister (Dublin, 1945–9; vol. 1 repr., Dublin, 1996).

CínCC *Cín Chille Cúile: texts, saints and places: essays in honour of Pádraig Ó Riain*, ed. J. Carey, M. Herbert & K. Murray (Aberystwyth, 2004).

CJRI *Calendar of the justiciary rolls, or Proceedings in the court of the justiciar of Ireland ... [1295–1314]*, 3 vols, ed. J. Mills, H. Wood, A.E. Langman & M.C. Griffith (Dublin, 1905, 1914, 1952).

CKHS *Cork, history and society: interdisciplinary essays on the history of an Irish county*, ed. P. O' Flanagan & N. Buttimer (Dublin, 1993).

CKV *Clerics, kings and vikings: essays on medieval Ireland in honour of Donnchadh Ó Corráin*, ed. E. Purcell, P. MacCotter, J. Nyhan & J. Sheehan (Dublin, 2015).

CL *A carnival of learning*, ed. P. Harbison & V. Hall (Roscrea, 2012).

ClavP *Clavis Patricii Ï: a computer-generated concordance to the Libri epistolarum of Saint Patrick*, K. Devine (Dublin, 1989).

CLCP *Cummian's letter 'De controversia Paschali'*, M. Walsh & D. Ó Cróinín (Toronto, 1988).

ClLTÁ *Logainmneacha na hÉireann III: cluain i logainmneacha Contae Thiobraid Árann*, P. Ó Cearbhaill (Baile Átha Cliath, 2010).

CLMH *Cinq leçons sur la méthode hagiographique*, H. Delehaye (Brussels, 1934).

CLPD *Connemara: the last pool of darkness*, T. Robinson (London/Dublin, 2008).

ClRec. *Clogher Record* (1953–).

CLTÁ *Logainmneacha na hÉireann II: Cill i logainmneacha Contae Thiobraid Árann*, P. Ó Cearbhaill (Baile Átha Cliath, 2007).

CLuim. *Cathair Luimnighe*, 2 vols, G. Mac Spealáin (Dublin, 1948, 1950).

CM *Crede Mihi: the most ancient register book of the archbishops of Dublin before the Reformation*, ed. J. Gilbert (Dublin, 1897).

CMCS *Cambrian* (formerly *Cambridge*) *Medieval Celtic Studies* (1981–).

CMIS 'On the colophons and marginalia of Irish scribes', C. Plummer, in *PBA* 12, 11–44.

CMR *The banquet of Dun na nGedh and the Battle of Magh Rath, an ancient historical tale*, ed. J. O'Donovan (IAS, Dublin, 1842; repr. Felinfach, 1995).

CnM *Cathair na Mart: Journal of the Westport Hisorical Society* (1981–).

CoC *Conntae an Chláir: a Triocha agus a Tuatha*, S. Ó hÓgáin (Dublin, 1938).

COD *Calendar of Ormond Deeds, 1172–1350*, ed. E. Curtis (IMC, Dublin, 1932).

COL 'The Columban onomastic legacy', N. Ó Muraíle, in *Studies in the cult of Saint Columba*, ed. C. Bourke (Dublin, 1997), 193–228.

Colk.Cat. *Trinity College library Dublin: Descriptive catalogue of the medieval and Renaissance manuscripts*, M.L. Colker, 2 vols (London, 1991).

CorcaD *Corca Dhuibhne i Aos Iorruis Tuaiscirt agus Uí Fhearba*, D. Ó Conchúir (Dublin, 1973).

CorkD 'The Cork decretal letter of 1199', ed. D. Ó Murchadha, *JCHAS* 106 (2001), 79–100.

CornS 'Cornish saints', ser. 1–48, G.H. Doble (Shipston-on-Stour et al., 1923–45).

CPCR *Calendar of patent and close rolls of chancery in Ireland, Henry VIII to 18th Elizabeth*, ed. J. Morrin (Dublin, 1861).

CPL *Calendar of papal letters relating to Great Britain and Ireland* (1893–).

CPNS *The history of the Celtic place-names of Scotland*, W.J. Watson (Edinburgh & London, 1926; repr. Dublin, 1986).

CPPI *Church and polity in pre-Norman Ireland: the case of Glendalough*, A. MacShamhráin (Maynooth, 1996).

CPR *Clerical and parochial records of Cork, Cloyne and Ross*, 3 vols, W.M. Brady (London, 1864).

CR *Celtic Review* 1 (1904) –10 (1916).

CrC[1] *Crichad an Chaoilli, being the topography of ancient Fermoy*, ed. P. Power (Irish Historical Documents 2, Cork, 1932).

CrC[2] 'The ancient territory of Fermoy', ed. J.G. O'Keeffe, *Ériu* 10 (1928), 170–90.

CS *Chronicum Scotorum: a chronicle of Irish affairs from the earliest times to AD1135*, ed. W.M. Hennessy (Rolls Series, London, 1866).

CSax. *Celt and Saxon*, ed. K. Jackson, P.H. Blair, B. Colgrave, B. Dickens, J. Taylor, H. Taylor, C. Brooke & N.K. Chadwick (Cambridge, 1963).

CSI *Church and settlement in Ireland*, ed. J. Lyttleton & M. Stout (Dublin, 2018).

CSGMA *Councils and synods of the Gaelic early and central Middle Ages*, D.N. Dumville (Cambridge, 1997).

CSMA *Chartularies of St Mary's Abbey, Dublin … and Annals of Ireland*, 2 vols, ed. J.T. Gilbert (London, 1884–6).

CSPI *Calendar of the state papers relating to Ireland*, 24 vols (London, 1860–1911).

CSt *Clonmacnoise studies*, 2 vols, ed. H.A. King (Dublin, 1998, 2003).

CT *Caithréim Thoirdhealbhaigh: The triumphs of Turlough*, 2 vols, ed. S.H. O'Grady (ITS 26, 27; London, 1929).

Cymmrod. *Y Cymmrodor* (1877–).

DA	*Donegal Annual: Journal of the County Donegal Historical Society* (1947–).
DAMC	*Dánta Aindréis Mhic Cruitín*, ed. L. O'Looney (Ennis, 1935).
DD	*Dioghluim dána*, ed. L. Mac Cionnaith (Dublin, 1938).
DDé	*Dán Dé: the prose poems of Donnchadh Mor O Dálaigh, and the religious poems in the duanaire of the Yellow Book of Lecan*, ed. L. McKenna (Dublin, n.d.).
DDSC	*Davnet and Dympna: a single cult*, S. Ó Dufaigh (Castleblaney, 2021).
Decies	*Decies: Journal of the Waterford Archaeological and Historical Society* (1976–).
DEPPP	*Diocese of Elphin: people, places and pilgrimage*, ed. F. Beirne (Dublin, 2000).
DERMB	*Duanta Eoghain Ruaidh Mhic an Bhaird*, ed. T. Ó Raghallaigh (Galway, 1930).
DIB	*Dictionary of Irish biography from the earliest times to the year 2002*, ed. J. McGuire & J. Quinn (9 vols, Dublin / Cambridge, 2009).
DIL	*Dictionary of the Irish language based mainly on Old and Middle Irish materials* (compact ed., Dublin, 1983).
Dinn.	*Dinnseanchas*, 1 (1964) –6 (1975).
DiocCl.	*Diocese of Cloyne, AD2002: a glimpse of our Christian heritage* (Rome, 2002).
DiocL	*The diocese of Limerick, ancient and medieval*, J. Begley (Dublin, 1906).
DisSP	*Discovering Saint Patrick*, T. O'Loughlin (London, 2005).
DK	*The diocese of Kilmore: its history and antiquities*, P. O'Connell (Dublin, 1937).
DKil	*The diocese of Kilmore 1800–1950*, D. Gallogly (Cavan, 1999).
DLHS	*Donegal, history and society: interdisciplinary essays on the history of an Irish county*, ed. W. Nolan, L. Ronayne & M. Dunlevy (Dublin, 1995).
DLS	*Adamnan's De locis sanctis*, ed. D. Meehan & L. Bieler (Dublin, 1958).
DLTC	*St Dunstan: his life, times and cult*, ed. M. Ramsay, M. Sparks & T. Tatton-Brown (Woodbridge, 1992).
DMU	*Duanaire Mhéig Uidhir: the poembook of Cú Chonnacht Még Uidhir, lord of Fermanagh, 1566–1589*, ed. D. Greene (Dublin, 1972).
DMW	*Dublin in the medieval world: studies in honour of Howard B. Clarke*, ed. J. Bradley, A.J. Fletcher & A. Simms (Dublin, 2009).
DNHS	*Down, history and society: interdisciplinary essays on the history of an Irish county*, ed. L. Proudfoot (Dublin, 1997).
DOH	*Derry: an outline history of the diocese*, B. Bonner (Dublin, 1982).
DPH	*De praesulibus Hiberniae*, 2 vols, ed. J.F. O'Doherty (IMC, Dublin, 1944).
DQE	'De quibusdam episcopis, Bodleian MS Rawlinson, no. 480', trans. D.H. Kelly, *PRIA* (Irish MSS Series 3), 82–133.
DTUH	*The death-tales of the Ulster heroes*, ed. K. Meyer (TLS 14, Dublin & London, 1906).

DUPN *A dictionary of Ulster place-names*, P. McKay (Belfast, 1999).

DYHS *Derry and Londonderry, history and society: interdisciplinary essays on the history of an Irish county*, ed. G. O'Brien (Dublin, 1999).

EA *Ecclesiastical antiquities of Down, Connor and Dromore, consisting of a taxation of those dioceses, compiled in the year MCCCVI*, ed. W. Reeves (Dublin, 1847).

EarlyCI *Early Christian Ireland*, M. de Paor & L. de Paor (London, 1958).

ECI *Early Christian Ireland*, T.M. Charles-Edwards (Cambridge, 2000).

ECIM *Early Christian inscriptions of Munster: a corpus of the inscribed stones*, E. Okasha & E. Forsyth (Cork, 2001).

EH *Expugnatio Hibernica: the conquest of Ireland, by Giraldus Cambrensis*, ed. & trans. A.B. Scott & F.X. Martin (Dublin, 1978).

EHR *English Historical Review*.

Éigse *Éigse: a Journal of Irish Studies* (1939–).

EIHM *Early Irish history and mythology*, T.F. O'Rahilly (Dublin, 1946).

EIL *Early Irish lyrics: eighth to twelfth century*, ed. G. Murphy (Oxford, 1956).

EILI *Early Irish laws and institutions*, E. Mac Neill (Dublin, 1935).

EILS Early Irish Law Series.

EIM *Early Irish metrics*, G. Murphy (Dublin, 1961).

EIMP *Extents of Irish monastic possessions, 1540–1541, from manuscripts in the Public Record Office, London*, ed. N.B. White (IMC, Dublin, 1943).

EIRD *Ex ipsis rerum documentis: Beiträge zur Mediävistik*, ed. K. Herbers, H.H. Kortüm & C. Servatius (Sigmaringen, 1991).

EMH *The early medieval hand-bells of Ireland and Britain*, C. Bourke (Dublin, 2020).

EMMAHS *Early medieval Munster: archaeology, history and society*, ed. M.A. Monk & J. Sheehan (Cork, 1998).

Ériu *Ériu* (1904–).

ESSH *Early sources of Scottish history, AD500 to 1286*, 2 vols, ed. A.O. Anderson (Edinburgh, 1922; repr. Stamford, 1990).

ÉtC *Études Celtiques* (1936–).

EWGT *Early Welsh genealogical tracts*, ed. P.C. Bartrum (Cardiff, 1966).

FAI *Fragmentary annals of Ireland*, ed. J.N. Radner (Dublin, 1978).

FC *Famulus Christi: essays in commemoration of the thirteenth centenary of the birth of the Venerable Bede*, ed. G. Bonner (London, 1976).

FDG *Fled Dúin na nGéd*, ed. R. Lehmann (*MMIS* 21, Dublin, 1964).

Feasta *Feasta* (1948–).

FEMN *Féil-sgríbhinn Eóin Mhic Néill: essays and studies presented to Professor Eoin MacNeill DLitt. on the occasion of his seventieth birthday*, ed. J. Ryan (Dublin, 1940).

FFÉ *Foras Feasa ar Éirinn: the history of Ireland by Geoffrey Keating DD*, 4 vols, ed. P.S. Dinneen & D. Comyn (ITS 4, 8, 9, 15, London, 1902–14).

FG *Folia Gadelica: essays presented by former students to R.A. Breatnach*, ed. P. de Brún, S. Ó Coileáin & P. Ó Riain (Cork, 1983).

FHHS *Fermanagh, history and society: interdisciplinary essays on the history of an Irish county*, ed. E. Murphy & W. Roulston (Dublin, 2004).

FIO *Fursa's Irish origins: Munster, Connacht or Ulster?*, P. Ó Riain (Fursey Occasional Paper 6; Norwich, 2015).

FKHS *Indogermanica et Caucasica: Festschrift für Karl Horst Schmidt zum 65. Geburtstag*, ed. R. Bielmeier & R. Stempel (Berlin & New York, 1994).

FL *The festival of Lughnasa*, M. Mac Neill (Oxford, 1962).

FLK Cat. *Catalogue of Irish manuscripts in the Franciscan library, Killiney*, M. Dillon, C. Mooney & P. de Brún (Dublin, 1969).

FLLSP *Four Latin lives of St Patrick*, ed. L. Bieler, (*SLH* 8, Dublin, 1971).

FMA *La femme au moyen-âge*, ed. M. Rouche & J. Heuclin (Maubeuge, 1990).

FNCC *Family names of County Cork*, D. Ó Murchadha (Dún Laoghaire, 1985).

FourIM *Four Irish martyrologies: Drummond, Turin, Cashel, York*, ed. P. Ó Riain (HBS 115, London, 2003).

FPM *Ildánach ildírech: a Festschrift for Proinsias Mac Cana*, ed. J. Carey, J.T. Koch & P.-Y. Lambert (Andover & Aberystwyth, 1999).

FranC *Franciscan Cork*, ed. J. O'Callaghan (Cork, 1953).

FSHIM *Feastdays of the saints: a history of Irish martyrologies*, P. Ó Riain (*SH* 86, Brussels, 2006).

FSPP *Five seventeenth-century political poems*, ed. C. O'Rahilly (Dublin, 1952).

FTorna *Féilscríbhinn Torna: essays and studies presented to Professor Tadhg Ua Donnchadha (Torna)*, ed. S. Pender (Cork, 1947).

Gadelica *Gadelica: a Journal of Modern-Irish Studies*, ed. T.F. O'Rahilly (1 vol., Dublin, 1912–13).

GBLMM *Geoffrey of Burton: life and miracles of St Modwenna*, ed. R. Bartlett (Oxford, 2002).

GCG *Glendalough, city of God*, ed. C. Doherty, L. Doran & M. Kelly (Dublin, 2011).

GCL 'Geinealach Chorca Laidhe', ed. J. O'Donovan, in *Miscellany of the Celtic Society* (Dublin, 1849).

GELB *Fil súil nglais: a grey eye looks back: a Festschrift in honour of Colm Ó Baoill*, ed. S. Arbuthnot & K. Hollo (Scotland, 2007).

GILSL *Gaelic Ireland (c.600–c.1700): lordship, saints and learning*, ed. L. McInerney & K. Simms (Dublin, 2021).

GJ *Gaelic Journal: Irisleabhar na Gaedhilge* 1 (1882) –19 (1909).

GNA *Gildas: new approaches*, ed. M. Lapidge & D.N. Dumville (Woodbridge, 1984).

GPN *Gaelic personal names*, D. Ó Corráin & F. Maguire (Dublin, 1981).

GRSH *Genealogiae regum et sanctorum Hiberniae by the Four Masters*, ed. P. Walsh, *AH* 5–6 (1916–17) and separately (Maynooth & Dublin, 1918).

GT *Genealogical tracts*, I, ed. T. Ó Raithbheartaigh (IMC, Dublin, 1932).

GUH *Gleanings from Ulster history*, S. Ó Ceallaigh (Cork, 1951).

GYHS *Galway, history and society: interdisciplinary essays on the history of an Irish county*, ed. G. Moran (Dublin, 1996).

HADDC *An historical account of the diocese of Down and Connor, ancient and modern*, 5 vols, J. O'Laverty (Dublin, 1878).

HADK *The history and antiquities of the diocese of Kilmacduagh*, J. Fahey (Dublin, 1893).

HADO *The history and antiquities of the diocese of Ossory*, 4 vols, W. Carrigan (Dublin, 1905).

Harl. Harley Manuscripts, British Library, London.

HB *Hail Brigit: an Old-Irish poem on the Hill of Alenn*, ed. K. Meyer (Halle & Dublin, 1912).

HBS Henry Bradshaw Society.

HCAD *History of the Catholic diocese of Dublin*, ed. J. Kelly & D. Keogh (Dublin, 1999).

HCI *The high crosses of Ireland*, 3 vols, P. Harbison (Bonn & Dublin, 1992).

HCIC *Historiae Catholicae Iberniae compendium ... a D. Philippo O'Sullevano Bearro, Iberno*, ed. M. Kelly (Dublin, 1850).

HCK *A history of County Kilkenny*, O. O'Kelly (Kilkenny, 1969); repr. in 1985 as *The place-names of the county of Kilkenny*.

HCM *The history of the county of Monaghan*, E.P. Shirley (London, 1879).

HDA *History of the diocese of Ardagh*, J.J. MacNamee (Dublin, 1954).

HDC *An historical account of the diocese of Down and Connor, ancient and modern*, J. O'Laverty (Dublin, 1878).

HDCK *A history of the diocese of Cork from the earliest times to the Reformation*, E. Bolster (Shannon, 1972).

HDF *History of the diocese of Ferns*, W.H. Grattan Flood (Waterford, 1916).

HDGP *Historical dictionary of Gaelic placenames / Foclóir stairiúil áitainmneacha na Gaeilge*, ed. Pádraig Ó Riain, Diarmuid Ó Murchadha & Kevin Murray (London, 2003–).

HDK *A history of the diocese of Killaloe*, A. Gwynn & D.F. Gleeson (Dublin, 1962).

Hereditas *Hereditas: tráchtais agus aistí in ómós don Ollamh Séamus Ó Duilearga*, ed. B. Almqvist, B. Mac Aodha & G. Mac Eoin (Dublin, 1975).

Herm. *Hermathena* (1873–).

HibM *Hibernica minora, being a fragment of an Old-Irish treatise on the psalter*, ed. K. Meyer (*Anecd. Oxon.*, *MMS* 8, Oxford, 1894).

HIC *A history of Irish Catholicism*, 6 vols, gen. ed. P.J. Corish (Dublin 1967–72).

HK *History of Kilsaran union of parishes in the county of Louth*, J.B. Leslie (Dundalk, 1908).

HOI *The heart of Ireland*, P.A. Sharkey (Boyle, 1927).

HMDC *A history of the medieval diocese of Cloyne*, P. MacCotter (Dublin, 2013).

HookP *The Hook Peninsula, County Wexford*, B. Colfer (Cork, 2004).

HSCT *History of Sligo county and town*, 3 vols, W.G. Wood-Martin (Dublin, 1882–91).

HTCC *The history and topography of the county of Clare*, J. Frost (London, 1893).

HTN *Historical and topographical notes etc. on Buttevant, Castletownroche, Doneraile, Mallow and places in their vicinity*, J. Grove White (Cork, 1905–25).

HWI *The holy wells of Ireland*, P. Logan (Gerrard's Cross, Bucks, 1980).

IA *Irish antiquity: essays and studies presented to Professor M.J. O'Kelly*, ed. D. Ó Corráin (Cork, 1981).

IARP *Irish art in the Romanesque period (1020–1170)*, F. Henry (Chatham, 1970).

IAS Irish Archæological Society.

IB *Immram Brain: Bran's journey to the land of the women*, ed. S. Mac Mathúna (Tübingen, 1985).

IBP *Irish bardic poetry*, ed. O. Bergin, comp. & re-ed. D. Greene & F. Kelly (Dublin, 1970).

IBVSH *Irlande et Bretagne: vingt siècles d'histoire*, ed. C. Laurent & H. Davies (Rennes, 1994).

IC 'The Irish "charters"' in P. Fox (ed.), *The Book of Kells, MS 58, Trinity College Library Dublin: commentary* (Luzern, 1990), 153–65.

ICCH *Irish castles and castellated houses*, H.G. Leask (Dundalk, 1964).

ICCS International Congress of Celtic Studies.

ICF *In Conall's footsteps*, L. McGill (Dingle, 1992).

IChr. *Irland und die Christenheit, Bibelstudien und Mission: Ireland and Christendom, the Bible and the missions*, ed. P. Ní Chatháin & M. Richter (Stuttgart, 1987).

ICT *The Irish comic tradition*, V. Mercer (Oxford, 1962).

IEKF *Irland und Europa, die Kirche im Frühmittelalter: Ireland and Europe, the early church*, ed. P. Ní Chatháin & M. Richter (Stuttgart, 1984).

IEME *Ireland in early mediaeval Europe: studies in memory of Kathleen Hughes*, ed. D. Whitelock, R. McKitterick & D.N. Dumville (Cambridge, 1982).

IER *The Irish Ecclesiastical Record*, 5 (*recte* 4) ser. (1 (1865) –12 (1876); 1 (1880) –17 (1896); 1 (1897) –32 (1912); 1 (1913) –110 (1968)).

IETC *Ireland and Europe in the twelfth century: reform and renewal*, ed. D. Bracken & D. Ó Riain-Raedel (Dublin, 2006).

IETÜ *Ireland and Europe in the early Middle Ages: texts and transmissions/ Irland und Europa im früheren Mittelalter: Text und Überlieferung*, ed. P. Ní Chatháin & M. Richter (Dublin, 2002).

IHS *Irish Historical Studies* (1938–).

IIAM *L'irlanda e gli irlandesi nell' alto medioevo*, Settimane di Studio lvii (Spoleto, 2010).

IKD *Iona, Kells and Derry: the history and hagiography of the monastic familia of Columba*, M. Herbert (Oxford, 1988).

IKHK *Irish kings and high-kings*, F.J. Byrne (London, 1973; repr. with add. notes & corrigenda, Dublin, 2001).

ILL *Irish leaders and learning through the ages*, P. Walsh. Essays collected, ed. & intr. N. Ó Muraíle (Dublin, 2003).

ILSC *Irish life in the seventeenth century*, E. MacLysaght (Cork & Oxford, 1950).

IMC Irish Manuscripts Commission.

IML *Irish men of learning*, P. Walsh (Dublin, 1947).

Imm. *Immrama*, ed. A.G. Van Hamel (*MMIS* 10, Dublin, 1941).

IMN *Irisleabhar Muighe Nuadhat* (1907–).

IMPAL *Inishmurray: monks and pilgrims in an Atlantic landscape*, ed. J. O'Sullivan & T. Ó Carragáin (Cork, 2008).

InaF *Iomarbhágh na bhfileadh: the contention of the bards*, 2 vols, ed. L. McKenna (ITS 20–1, London, 1920).

Innes Review *Innes Review* (1950–).

INP *The origin and history of the Irish names of places*, 3 vols, P.W. Joyce (Dublin, 1869–1913).

InsT *The Insular tradition*, ed. C.E. Karkov, M. Ryan & R.T. Farrell (New York, 1997).

Iona *Iona: the earliest poetry of a Celtic monastery*, ed. T.O. Clancy & G. Márkus (Edinburgh, 1995).

IOS *The Irish Ordnance Survey: history, culture and memory*, G.M. Doherty (Dublin, 2004).

IP *I, Patricius: the Roman history of an Irish saint*, P. Colling Egan (Maysville, MO, 2020).

IRC *Irish royal charters texts and contexts*, M.T. Flanagan (Oxford, 2005).

IrL *Irish litanies*, ed. C. Plummer (HBS 62, London, 1925).

IrM *Irish Monthly* 1 (1873) –973 (1954).

IrP *The Irish penitentials*, ed. L. Bieler (Dublin, 1975).

IrR *Irish Rosary* (1897–).

IrT *Irish texts*, 5 vols, ed. J. Fraser, P. Grosjean & J.G. O'Keeffe (London, 1931–4).

ISEVA *Ireland and Scandinavia in the early Viking Age*, ed. H.B. Clarke, M. Ní Mhaonaigh & R. Ó Floinn (Dublin, 1998).

IsPatrick *Island of Saint Patrick*, ed. A. MacShamhráin (Dublin, 2004).

IT *Irische Texte mit Übersetzungen und Wörterbuch*, i–iii, ed. W. Stokes & E. Windisch (Leipzig & Berlin, 1880–1909).

ITS Irish Texts Society.

IV *Ionae vitae sanctorum Columbani, Vedastis, Iohannis*, ed. B. Krusch, Scriptores Rerum Germanicarum in usum scholarum ex Monumentis Germaniae historicis separatim editi (Hannover & Leipzig, 1905).

IVN *Leabhar Breathnach annso sis: the Irish version of the Historia Britonum of Nennius*, ed. J.H. Todd (IAS, Dublin, 1848).

IWMA	*Ireland and Wales in the Middle Ages*, ed. K. Jankulak & J. Wooding (Dublin, 2007).
JACAS	*Journal of the Ardagh and Clonmacnoise Antiquarian Society*, 2 vols in 12 (1926–51).
JCHAS	*Journal of the Cork Historical and Archaeological Society* (1892–).
JCKAS	*Journal of the County Kildare Archæological Society* (1891–).
JCLAS	*Journal of the County Louth Archaeological Society* (1904–).
JCS	*Journal of Celtic Studies* 1 (1949) –3 (1981–2).
JEH	*Journal of Ecclesiastical History* 1 (1958–).
JGAHS	*Journal of the Galway Archæological and Historical Society* (1900–).
JIA	*Journal of Irish archaeology*, 1 (1983–).
JKAHS	*Journal of the Kerry Archaeological and Historical Society* –30 (1968–97); ser. 2 (2001–)
JNMArchS	*Journal of the North Munster Archaeological Society* 1.1 (1909) –3.4 (1915).
JRSAI	*Journal of the Royal Society of Antiquaries of Ireland* (1849–). This incorporates all versions of the journal which are listed in sequential order in the foreword to the 1997 reprint to vol. 1.
JWAS	*Journal of the Waterford and South-East of Ireland Archæological Society* 1 (1894) –19 (1920).
JWWHS	*Journal of the West Wicklow Historical Society* 1 (1983–4).
Keimelia	*Keimelia: studies in medieval archaeology and history in memory of Tom Delaney*, ed. G. Mac Niocaill & P.F. Wallace (Galway, 1988).
KeltRh.	*Kelten am Rhein: Akten des dreizehnten Internationalen Keltologie-kongresses: proceedings of the thirteenth International Congress of Celtic Studies*, vol. 2, ed. S. Zimmer (Beihefte der Bonner Jahrbücher 58; Mainz, 2009).
Kenney	*The sources for the early history of Ireland (ecclesiastical)*, J.F. Kenney (Records of Civilization 11, Cornell 1929, repr. Dublin, 1979).
KLT	*The kingship and landscape of Tara*, ed. E. Bhreathnach (Dublin, 2005).
KSS	*Kalendars of Scottish saints, with personal notes of those of Alba, Laudonia & Strathclyde*, A.P. Forbes (Edinburgh, 1872).
Laud Misc. 615	Bodleian MS Laud Miscellany 615.
LB	*Leabhar breac, the Speckled book, otherwise styled Leabhar mór Dúna Doighre …*, lithogr. reprod., with preface by S. Ferguson (Dublin, 1872–6).
Lbran.	*Leabhar Branach: the Book of the O'Byrnes*, ed. S. Mac Airt (Dublin, 1944).
Lbret.	*Lebor Bretnach: the Irish version of the Historia Britonum ascribed to Nennius*, ed. A.G. Van Hamel (IMC, Dublin, 1932).
LC	*Lebor na cert: the Book of rights*, ed. M. Dillon (ITS 46, London, 1962).
LCAB	*Leabhar Cloinne Aodha Buidhe*, ed. Tadhg Ó Donnchadha (IMC, Dublin, 1931).

LCC *Léachtaí Cholm Cille.*

LDHS *Longford, history and society: interdisciplinary essays on the history of an Irish county*, ed. M. Morris & F. O'Ferrall (Dublin, 2010).

LegSS *Legends of Scottish saints: readings, hymns and prayers for the commemorations of Scottish saints in the Aberdeen Breviary*, ed. A. Macquarrie (Dublin, 2012).

LF 3 *Lost and found III: rediscovering more of Ireland's past*, ed. J. Fenwick (Dublin, 2018).

LG *Lebor Gabála Érenn: the Book of the taking of Ireland*, 5 vols, ed. R.A.S. Macalister (ITS 34–5, 39, 41, 44, Dublin & London, 1938–56).

Lgen. *Leabhar mór na ngenealach: the Great book of Irish genealogies, compiled by Dubhaltach Mac Fhirbhisigh*, 5 vols, ed. N. Ó Muraíle (Dublin, 2003).

LH *The Irish Liber hymnorum*, 2 vols, ed. J.H. Bernard & R. Atkinson (HBS 13–14, London, 1898).

LHEB *Language and history in early Britain*, K. Jackson (Edinburgh, 1953).

Lia Fáil *Lia Fáil* 1 (1925) –4 (1932).

LigeG *Lige Guill: the grave of Goll: a Fenian poem from the Book of Leinster*, ed. D. Ó Murchadha (ITS 62, Dublin & London, 2009).

LIS *Lives of the Irish saints*, 10 vols, J. O'Hanlon (Dublin, 1875–1907).

LisL *Lives of the saints from the Book of Lismore*, ed. W. Stokes (*Anecd. Oxon.*, Oxford, 1890).

LL *The Book of Leinster formerly Lebar na Núachongbála*, 6 vols, ed. R.I. Best, O. Bergin, M.A. O'Brien & A. O'Sullivan (Dublin, 1954–83).

LLLSK *The life, legends and legacy of Saint Kerrill*, J. Mannion ([Galway], 2004).

Llog. *Liostaí logainmneacha*, arna ullmhú ag Brainse logainmneacha na Suirbhéireachta Ordanáis (Baile Átha Cliath, 1991–).

LM *An leabhar Muimhneach maraon le suim aguisíní*, ed. T. Ó Donnchadha (IMC, Dublin, [1940]).

LME *Logainmneacha Mhaigh Eo*, 10 vols, F. Mac Gabhann (Baile Átha Cliath, 2014).

LnaÉ *Logainmneacha na hÉireann* 1 (*Contae Luimnigh*), ed. A. Ó Maolfabhail (Dublin, 1990).

LnaL *Lorg na leabhar a festschrift for Pádraig A. Breatnach*, ed. C. Breathnach, M. Ní Úrdail & G. Ó Riain (Dublin, 2019).

Logainm.ie www.logainm.ie.

LóL *Leabhair ó Lámhsgríbhnibh.*

LOSB *The legend of St Brendan: a critical bibliography*, G.S. Burgess & C. Strijbosch (Dublin, 2000).

LSC *Adomnán of Iona: Life of St Columba*, trans. R. Sharpe (London, 1995).

LSHS *Laois, history and society: interdisciplinary essays on the history of an Irish county*, ed. P.G. Lane & W. Nolan (Dublin, 2000).

LSLC *Local saints and local churches*, ed. R. Sharpe & A. Thacker (Oxford, 2002).

LSP *Libri Sancti Patricii: the Latin writings of Saint Patrick*, ed. N.J.D. White, *PRIA* 25 (1905), 201–326.

LSS *Legends of saints and sinners*, D. Hyde (Dublin, 1915).

LSUC *Leabhar Sheáin Uí Chonaill*, S. Ó Duilearga (Dublin, 1948).

LU *Lebor na hUidre: Book of the Dun Cow*, ed. R.I. Best & O. Bergin (Dublin, 1929).

LUM *The Book of Uí Maine otherwise called 'the Book of the O'Kellys'*, ed. R.A.S. Macalister (Facs. in collotype 4, Dublin, 1942).

LWS *Lives of the Welsh saints by G.H. Doble*, ed. D. Simon Evans (Cardiff, 1971).

MakS *The making of a saint: Finbarr of Cork, 600–1200*, P. Ó Riain (ITS, Subsidiary Series 5, London, 1997).

MartA *Le martyrologe d'Adon: ses deux familles, ses trois recensions, texte et commentaire*, ed. J. Dubois & G. Renaud (Paris, 1984).

MartD *The Martyrology of Donegal: a calendar of the saints of Ireland*, ed. J.H. Todd & W. Reeves (IACS, Dublin, 1864).

MartFC *A martyrology of four cities: Metz, Cologne, Dublin, Lund*, ed. P. Ó Riain. (HBS 118, London, 2008).

MartG *Félire hÚi Gormáin: the Martyrology of Gorman*, ed. W. Stokes (HBS 9, London, 1895).

MartO[1] 'On the Calendar of Oengus', ed. W. Stokes, *Transactions of the Royal Irish Academy* 1 (1880), 1–32, i–ccclii.

MartO[2] *Féilire Oengusso Céli Dé: the Martyrology of Oengus the Culdee*, ed. W. Stokes (HBS 29, London, 1905; repr. Dublin, 1984).

MartR *The martyrology of the Regensburg Schottenkloster*, ed. P. Ó Riain (HBS 124, London, 2019).

MartT *The Martyrology of Tallaght*, ed. R.I. Best & H.J. Lawlor (HBS 68, London, 1931).

MartU *Le martyrologe d'Usuard: texte et commentaire*, ed. J. Dubois (*SH* 40, Brussels, 1965).

MB *Mil na mbeach: sliocht de sheinleabhraibh ... iarna chur in eagar ... do Chuallacht Chuilm Chille ... ag Maigh Nuadhat* (Dublin, 1911).

MCMHW *Miscellanea Celtica in memoriam Heinrich Wagner*, ed. S. Mac Mathúna & A. Ó Corráin (Acta Universitatis Upsaliensis Studia *Celtica* Upsaliensia, Uppsala, 1997).

MD *The metrical dindshenchas*, 5 vols, ed. E.J. Gwynn (TLS 7–12, 1906–35; repr. Dublin, 1991).

Mdub. *Medieval Dublin*, 10 vols, ed. S. Duffy (2000–10).

MedAE *Medium Aevum* (1932–).

MedI *Medieval Ireland: territorial, political and economic divisions*, ed. P. MacCotter (Dublin, 2008).

MedT *Medieval Trim: history and archaeology*, M. Potterton (Dublin, 2005).

MFCJ *Mallow Field Club Journal* (1983–).

MGF *Me Guidhir Fhearmanach: the Maguires of Fermanagh .i. Maghnus agus Giolla Íosa 'dhá mhac Dhuinn Mhóir mic Raghnaill'*, ed. P. Ua Duinnín (Dublin, 1917).

MGH.PL	*Monumenta Germaniae Historica (Poetae Latini)*, vol. 1, ed. E. Dümmler (Berlin, 1881).
MGH.SRM	*Monumenta Germaniae Historica (Scriptores Rerum Merovingicarum)*.
MGH.SS	*Monumenta Germaniae Historica (Scriptores)*.
MHA	*Medieval hagiography: an anthology*, ed. T. Head (London, 1999).
MHDI	*Mary: a history of devotion in Ireland*, P. O'Dwyer (Dublin, 1998).
MHH	*Miscellanea hagiographica Hiberniae*, ed. C. Plummer (*SH* 15, Brussels, 1925).
MIA	*Miscellaneous Irish annals (AD1114–1437)*, ed. S. Ó hInnse (Dublin, 1947).
MIAS	*Miscellany of the Irish Archæological (and Celtic) Society* i, ed. J. O'Donovan (IACS, Dublin, 1846).
MIDS	*Medieval Irish Dominican studies, Benedict O'Sullivan OP*, ed. H. Fenning (Dublin, 2009).
MIL	*Medieval Irish lyrics: selected and translated*, J. Carney (Dublin, 1967).
MÍOB	*Maol Íosa Ó Brolcháin*, M. Ní Bhrolcháin (Maynooth, 1986).
MirL	*A miracle of learning: studies in manuscripts and Irish learning: essays in honour of William O'Sullivan*, ed. T. Barnard, D. Ó Cróinín & K. Simms (Cambridge, 1998).
MISL	*Medieval Irish saints lives: an introduction*, R. Sharpe (Oxford, 1991).
MISM	*Medieval Ireland: saints and martyrologies*, J. Hennig (Variorum Collected Studies, CS 298; Northampton, 1989).
MKM	*Miscellany presented to Kuno Meyer ... on the occasion of his appointment to the chair of Celtic philology in the University of Berlin*, ed. O. Bergin & C. Marstrander (Halle, 1912).
MM	*The manuscript materials of ancient Irish history*, E. O'Curry (Dublin, 1861; repr. Dublin, 1995).
MMIS	Medieval and Modern Irish Series.
MMN	*The monastery of Saint Mochaoi of Nendrum*, H.C. Lawlor (Belfast, 1925).
MMS	Medieval and Modern Series.
MMTEIW	*The medieval mystical tradition: England, Ireland, Wales*, ed. M. Glasscoe (Woodbridge, 1999).
MMUC	*Measgra i gcuimhne Mhichíl Uí Chléirigh .i. Miscellany of historical and linguistic studies in honour of Brother Michael Ó Cléirigh OFM, chief of the Four Masters, 1643–1943*, ed. S. O'Brien (Dublin, 1944).
MOC	*Michael O Cleirigh, chief of the Four Masters, and his associates*, B. Jennings (Dublin & Cork, 1936).
Molaise	*Molaise, abbot of Leighlin and hermit of Holy Island: the life and legacy of Saint Laisren in Ireland and Scotland*, C. Kenny (Killala, 1998).
MP	*Mayo places: their names and origins*, N. Ó Muraíle (Dublin, 1985).
MPA	*Medieval province of Armagh, 1470–1545*, A. Gwynn (Dundalk, 1946).
MPPP	*The medieval pilgrimage to St Patrick's Purgatory Lough Derg and the European tradition*, ed. M. Haren & Y. de Pontfarcy (Enniskillen, 1988).

MRHI	*Medieval religious houses: Ireland*, A. Gwynn & R.N. Hadcock (Longmans, 1970).
MS Bollandien	Manuscript 452 in the Library of the Bollandists, Brussels.
MSNAF	*Mémoires de la Société nationale des Antiquaires de France* 1 (1872).
MSPAG	*Medieval studies presented to Aubrey Gwynn SJ*, ed. J.A. Watt, J.B. Morrall & F.X. Martin (Dublin, 1961).
MT	'The monastery of Tallaght', ed. E.J. Gwynn & W.J. Purton, in *PRIA* 29C (1911), 115–79.
MWPSS	*Medieval Welsh poems to saints and shrines*, ed. B. Lewis (Medieval and Modern Welsh Series xiv; Dublin, 2015).
NCHC	*The antient and present state of the county and city of Cork: in four books*, C. Smith (Dublin, 1750).
NCHK	*The antient and present state of the county of Kerry*, C. Smith (Dublin, 1756).
ND	*Nua-Dhuanaire*, 3 pts, ed. P. de Brún, B. Ó Buachalla & T. Ó Concheanainn (Dublin, 1971–8).
NHI	*A new history of Ireland*, 9 vols, ed. T.W. Moody, F.X. Martin, F.J. Byrne, A. Cosgrove, W.E. Vaughan, J.R Hill & D. Ó Cróinín (Oxford, 1976–[2005]).
NL	*Northern lights: following folklore in north-western Europe*, ed. S. Ó Catháin et al. (Dublin, 2001).
NLA	*Nova Legenda Angliae*, 2 vols, ed. C. Horstmann (Oxford, 1901).
NLI	National Library of Ireland.
NMAJ	*North Munster Antiquarian Journal* (1936–).
Nomina	*Nomina: a Journal of Name Studies Relating to Great Britain and Ireland* (1977–).
NotesEHDT	*Notes on the early history of the dioceses of Tuam, Killala and Achonry*, H.T. Knox (Dublin, 1904).
NSB	*Navigatio Sancti Brendani*, 2 vols, ed. G. Orlandi (Milan & Varese, 1968).
NSBA	*Navigatio Sancti Brendani Abbatis*, ed. C. Selmer (Notre Dame, IN, 1959).
NSW	*The North Sea world in the Middle Ages: Studies in the cultural history of north-western Europe*, ed. T.R. Liszka & L.E.M. Walker (Dublin, 2001).
OÁr	*Oileáin Árann: stair na n-Oileán anuas go dtí 1922*, A. Powell (Dublin, [n.d.]).
OC	*The Other Clare* (1977–).
OCBG	'The O Clery book of genealogies', ed. S. Pender, *Analecta Hibernica* 18 (1951), i–xxxiii, 1–198.
OCL	*Oidhe chloinne Lir: the fate of the children of Lir*, R.J. O'Duffy, Society for the Preservation of the Irish Language (Dublin, 1883).
ODCC	*The Oxford Dictionary of the Christian Church*, ed. F.L. Cross & E.A. Livingstone (Oxford, 1997).
ODS	*The Oxford Dictionary of Saints*, D.H. Farmer (Oxford, 1978).

OFWC *A chorographical description of west or h-Iar Connaught, written AD1684 by Roderic O'Flaherty Esq.*, ed. J. Hardiman (IAS, Dublin, 1846; repr. Galway, 1978).

Ogma *Ogma: essays in Celtic studies in honour of Próinséas Ní Chatháin*, ed. M. Richter & J.-M. Picard (Dublin, 2002).

OH *Offaly Heritage: Journal of the Offaly Historical and Archaeological Society* (2003–).

OKR *Old Kilkenny Review* (1946–).

OldI *Old Ireland*, ed. R. McNally (Dublin, 1965).

OLL *Ossory, Laois and Leinster* (2004–).

OnomG *Onomasticon Goedelicum locorum et tribuum Hiberniae et Scotiae: an index, with identifications, to the Gaelic names of places and tribes*, ed. E. Hogan (Dublin & London, 1910).

OSL Ordnance Survey Letters.

OV *The Otherworld voyage in early Irish literature*, ed. J. Wooding (Dublin, 2000).

OYHS *Offaly, history and society: interdisciplinary essays on the history of an Irish county*, ed. W. Nolan & T.P. O'Neill (Dublin, 1998).

PABD *Place-names and antiquities of the barony of Duhallow*, M.J. Bowman (Duhallow, 2000).

ParB *The parish of Ballinasloe: its history from the earliest times to the present day*, P.K. Egan (Dublin, 1960).

PBA *Proceedings of the British Academy.*

PCNT *The parish churches of north Tipperary: commemorating a two-hundred-year heritage*, W.J. Hayes & J. Kennedy (Roscrea, 2007).

PCV *Acts of Archbishop Colton in his metropolitan visitation in the diocese of Derry, ADMCCCXCVII, with a rental of the see estates at that time*, ed. W. Reeves (IAS, Dublin, 1850).

PÉ *Príomhshruth Éireann*, M. Ó Braonáin, ed. S. Mac Muirí, M. Seoighe & P. Breatnach (Limerick, 1994).

Peritia *Peritia: Journal of the Medieval Academy of Ireland* (1982–).

PHCC *Proceedings of the Harvard Celtic Colloquium* (1981–).

PIBA *Proceedings of the Irish Biblical Association* 1: *Biblical studies: the medieval Irish contribution*, M. McNamara (Dublin, 1976).

PilgI *Pilgrimage in Ireland: the monuments and the people*, P. Harbison (London, 1991).

PIM *The place-names of the Isle of Man with their origin and history*, J.J. Kneen (The Manx Society, Douglas, 1925; repr. 1979).

PLPS *The priory of Llanthony Prima and Secunda in Ireland, 1172–1541*, ed. A. Hogan (Dublin, 2008).

PLSS *Pinkerton's Lives of the Scottish saints*, 2 vols, ed. W.M. Metcalfe (Paisley, 1889).

PMIS *Progress in medieval Irish studies*, ed. K. McCone & K. Simms (Maynooth, 1996).

PML	*Poems on marcher lords, from a sixteenth-century Tipperary manuscript*, ed. A. O'Sullivan & P. Ó Riain (ITS 53, London, 1987).
PnaB	*Párliament na mban*, ed. B. Ó Cuív (Dublin, 1952).
PNB	*Historical notes on Laois and place-names of Ballyroan*, S. Mac Cába (1962).
PNCL	*Notes on the place-names of the parishes and townlands of the county of Londonderry*, A. Moore Munn (Derry, 1925; repr. 1985).
PNCW	*The place-names of County Wicklow*, 7 vols, L. Price (Dublin, 1945–67).
PND	*The place-names of the Decies*, P. Power (Cork, 1952).
PNNI	The Place-names of Northern Ireland Series.
PNW	*The place-names of Westmeath*, P. Walsh (Dublin, 1957).
PPPMI	*Princes, prelates and poets in medieval Ireland: essays in honour of Katharine Simms*, ed. S. Duffy (Dublin, 2013).
PR	*Poems on the O'Reillys*, ed. J. Carney (Dublin, 1950).
PRC	*Pipe roll of Cloyne (rotulus pipae Clonensis)*, ed. P. MacCotter & K. Nicholls (Cloyne, 1996).
PRIA	*Proceedings of the Royal Irish Academy* (1836–).
ProphB	*Prophecy of Berchán*, B.T. Hudson (Westport, CT, & London, 1996).
ProphSS	*The prophecies of saints Colum-Cille, Maeltamlacht, Ultan, Senan, Bearcan and Malachy*, N. O'Kearney (Dublin, 1856; repr. 1925).
Propug.CV	*Propugnaculum catholicae veritatis, libris X. constructum*, A. Bruodinus, 2 vols (Digitized copy of Prague, 1669 edition).
PSICCSO	*Proceedings of the Seventh International Congress of Celtic Studies, Oxford, 1983*, ed. D.E. Evans, J.G. Griffith & E.M. Jope (Oxford, 1986).
PSP	*The problem of St Patrick*, J. Carney (Dublin, 1973).
PTBA	*The Patrician texts in the Book of Armagh*, ed. L. Bieler (*SLH* 10; Dublin, 1979).
RC	*Revue Celtique* 1 (1870) –51 (1934).
RClon.	'Dubaltach mac Firbhisigh's Translation of "The registry of Clonmacnoise"', ed. J. O'Donovan, *The Journal of the Kilkenny and South-east of Ireland Archæological Society* 1 (new ser., 1856–7), 444–60.
RD	'The prose tales in the Rennes Dindshenchas', ed. W. Stokes, *RC* 15 (1894), 272–336, 418–84, & 16 (1895), 31–83, 135–67, 269–312.
ReisIrl.	*Reisen in Irland oder Irland in historischer, politischer und sozialer Beziehung*, J. Clement (Kiel, 1845).
Rep. Nov.	*Reportorium Novum*: Dublin Diocesan Historical Record (1955–).
RIA 23N10	*Facsimiles in collotype of Irish manuscripts VI MS 23N10 (formerly Betham 145) in the library of the Royal Irish Academy*, intr. R.I. Best (Dublin, 1954).
RIA	Royal Irish Academy.
RIGI	*Royal inauguration in medieval Ireland* c.*1100–1600*, E. Fitzpatrick (Woodbridge, 2004).
RIM	*Registrum Iohannes Mey: the register of John Mey, archbishop of Armagh, 1443–1456*, ed. W.G.H. Quigley & E.F.D. Roberts (Belfast, 1972).

RIW *Relics and the Insular world, c.600–c.800*, Julia M.H. Smith, Kathleen Hughes Memorial Lectures 15 (Cambridge, 2017).

RM *Ríocht na Midhe* (1955–).

RNF *Register of Nicholas Fleming, archbishop of Armagh, 1404–1416*, ed. B. Smyth (Dublin, 2003).

ROLN *Registrum Octaviani alias Liber Niger*, 2 vols, ed. M.A. Sughi (Dublin, 1999).

RSC *Relics of Saint Cuthbert*, ed. C.F. Battiscombe (Oxford, 1956).

RSLD *Rhigyfarch's Life of St David*, ed. J.W. James (Cardiff, 1967).

RSTA *Register of the abbey of St Thomas the Martyr, Dublin*, ed. J.T. Gilbert (London, 1889).

RT *The rule of Tallaght*, ed. E. Gwynn, *Hermathena* 44 (1927).

SACCL *A survey of the ancient churches in the county of Limerick*, T.J. Westropp, *PRIA* 25C (1905), 327–480.

SacE *Sacris Erudiri* (1948–).

SacH *Sacred histories: a festschrift for Máire Herbert*, ed. J. Carey, K. Murray & C. Ó Dochartaigh (Dublin, 2015).

SaintP *Saint Patrick, AD493–1993*, D.N. Dumville, T.M. Charles-Edwards, K.R. Dark, K.L. Maund, A.P.McD. Orchard, L. Abrams & A. Corrêa (Woodbridge, 1993).

SaintPMN *Saint Patrick*, E. MacNeill [ed. J. Ryan] (Dublin, 1964).

SAL *Stones of Aran: Labyrinth*, T. Robinson (London, 1995).

SAM *Seanchas Ard Mhacha* (1954–).

SATDF *Some account of the territory or dominion of Farney, in the province and earldom of Ulster*, E.P. Shirley (London, 1845).

SATM *Stair Aos Trí Muighe (i gContae Luimnigh)*, G. Mac Spealáin (Dublin, 1967).

SBDeer *Studies on the Book of Deer*, ed. K. Forsythe (Dublin, 2008).

SBK *Saint Brigid of Kildare: life, legend and cult*, N. Kissane (Dublin, 2017).

SCJ *Studia Celtica Japonica* (1988–).

SCO *Sancti Columbani opera*, ed. G.S.M. Walker (*SLH* 2; Dublin, 1957).

SCorn. *The saints of Cornwall*, N. Orme (Oxford, 2000).

ScriptOralia 68 *Text und Zeittiefe*, ed. H.L.C. Tristram (Tübingen, 1993).

Scriptorium 1 (1946–).

ScrV *Scripturus Vitam: Lateinische Biographie von der Antike bis in die Gegenwart: Festgabe für Walter Berschin zum 65. Geburtstag*, ed. D. Walz (Heidelberg, 2002).

SCSW *The settlements of the Celtic saints in Wales*, E.G. Bowen (Cardiff, 1954).

SD *Seanchas Duthalla: Duhallow Magazine* 1 (1974–).

SeanC *Seanachas ó Chairbre* I, ed. D. Ó Cróinín (Folklore Studies 13, Dublin, 1985).

Seanchas *Seanchas: studies in early and medieval Irish archaeology, history and literature in honour of Francis J. Byrne*, ed. A.P. Smyth (Dublin, 2000).

SeanM	*An seanchaidhe Muimhneach .i. Meascra de bhéaloideas ilchinéal ó 'An Lóchrann'*, ed. An Seabhac (Dublin, 1932).
SeánR	*Seán na Ráithíneach*, ed. Torna (Dublin, 1954).
SeaS	*The seafaring saint: sources and analogues of the twelfth-century Voyage of Saint Brendan*, C.S. Strijbosch (Dublin, 2000).
SexAM	*The Irish sex aetates mundi*, ed. D. Ó Cróinín (Dublin, 1983).
SG	*Silva Gadelica (I–XXXI)*, 2 vols, ed. S.H. O'Grady (London, 1892).
SGS	*Scottish Gaelic Studies* (1926–).
SH	*Subsidia Hagiographica*.
SHK	*A short history of Kinsale*, M. Mulcahy (Cork, 1966).
SIB	*Schottenklöster: irische Benediktinerkonvente im hochmittelalterlichen Deutschland*, H. Flachenecker (*Quellen und Forschungen aus dem Gebiet der Geschichte* 18, Paderborn – Munich – Vienna – Zürich, 1995).
SIHI	*Les saints irlandais hors d'Irlande*, L. Gougaud (Louvain & Oxford, 1936).
SLH	*Scriptores Latini Hiberniae*.
SLJF	*The saints' lives of Jocelin of Furness: hagiography, patronage and ecclesiastical politics*, H. Birkett (Woodbridge, 2010).
SML	*Saint Moling Luachra: a pilgrimage from Sliabh Luachra to Rinn Ros Broic above the stream-pools of the Barrow*, M.B. de Paor (Dublin, 2001).
SnaS	*Saoithiúlacht na Sean-Ghaeilge*, P.L Henry (Dublin, 1978).
SourcesC	*Sources chrétiennes*.
Speculum	(1926–).
SpesS	*Spes Scotorum: hope of Scots: Saint Columba, Iona & Scotland*, ed. D. Broun & T.O. Clancy (Edinburgh, 1999).
SPOC	*Saint Patrick: his origins and career*, R.P.C. Hanson (Oxford, 1968).
SPW	*Saint Patrick's world: the Christian culture of Ireland's apostolic age*, L. de Paor (Dublin, 1993).
SS	*Studies in Irish hagiography: saints and scholars*, ed. J. Carey, M. Herbert & P. Ó Riain (Dublin, 2001).
SSS	*Sages, saints and storytellers: Celtic studies in honour of Professor James Carney*, ed. D. Ó Corráin, L. Breatnach & K. McCone (Maynooth Monographs 2, Maynooth, 1989).
StC	*Studia Celtica* (1966–).
StH	*Studia Hibernica* (1961–).
StMull.	*St Mullins illustrated: a local history and the life of St Moling*, P. O'Leary (Graigue-na-Managh, 1913).
StonyA	Stonyhurst College, MS A II 20 (smaller vol.).
StonyB	Stonyhurst College, MS A II 20, i & ii (larger vol.).
StoryM	*The story of Mellifont*, C. Conway (Dublin, 1958).
Studies	*Studies: an Irish Quarterly Review* (1912–).
SZ	*Selections of the Zoilomastix of Philip O'Sullivan Beare*, ed. T.J. O'Donnell (IMC, Dublin, 1960).

TBB *Trí bior-ghaoithe an bháis Séathrún Kéitinn do sgríobh*, ed. O. Bergin (Dublin, 1931).

TBF *Transitus beati Fursei*, O. Rackham (Norwich, 2007).

TC *Tiarnach of Clones*, S. Ó Dufaigh (Mullaghmurphy, Co. Monaghan, 2018).

TCCD *Triocha-chéad Chorca Dhuibhne*, ed. P. Ó Siochfhradha (Baile Átha Cliath, 1939).

TCD Trinity College Dublin.

TCHyF *The genealogies, tribes and customs of Hy-Fiachrach, commonly called O'Dowda's Country*, ed. J. O'Donovan (IAS, Dublin, 1844).

TCHyM *Tribes and customs of Hy-Many, commonly called O'Kelly's Country*, ed. J. O'Donovan (IAS, Dublin, 1943; repr. Cork, 1976).

TCR *The twelfth-century reform*, A. Gwynn (*HIC* 2, Dublin, 1968).

TD *Téada dúchais: aistí in ómós don Ollamh Breandán Ó Madagáin*, ed. M. Ó Briain & P. Ó Héalaí (Indreabhán, 2002).

TDall *A bhfuil aguinn dár chum Tadhg Dall Ó hUiginn: the bardic poems of Tadhg Dall Ó Huiginn (1550–1591)*, 2 vols, ed. E. Knott (ITS 22–3, London, 1922–6).

TDH *The Derrynaflan Hoard, I: a preliminary account*, ed. M. Ryan (Dublin, 1983).

TDI *A topographical dictionary of Ireland*, 2 vols, ed. S. Lewis (London, 1837; repr. New York, 1970).

TEAB *The end and beyond medieval Irish eschatology*, 2 vols, ed. J. Carey, E. Nic Cárthaigh & C. Ó Dochartaigh (Aberystwyth, 2014).

TEHS *Tyrone, history and society: interdisciplinary essays on the history of an Irish county*, ed. C. Dillon & H.A. Jefferies (Dublin, 2000).

TEI *Tales of the elders of Ireland (Acallam na Senórach)*, trans. A. Dooley & H. Roe (Oxford, 1999).

TEP *Two epistles of St. Patrick the bishop*, P. Colling Egan (Maysville, MO, 2021).

TG *An cantaire siúlach: Tadhg Gaelach*, ed. Ú. Nic Éinrí (Dán agus Talann 8, Dingle, 2001).

TH *Toponomia Hiberniae*, 4 vols, B. Ó Cíobháin (Dublin, 1978–85).

The Fold *Diocesan Monthly Magazine of Cork and Ross* 1 (1953) –50 (2003).

The Past *The Past: Journal of the Uí Cinsealaigh Historical Society* (1920–).

THEH *Giraldi Cambrensis opera*, vol. 5: *Topographia Hibernica et Expugnatio Hibernica*, ed. J. Dimock (Rolls Series, London, 1867).

Thes. *Thesaurus Palæohibernicus: a collection of Old-Irish glosses, scholia and verse*, 2 vols & suppl., ed. W. Stokes & J. Strachan (Cambridge, 1901–3, 1910; repr. Dublin, 1975).

Thought 5.1 (New York, June 1930), 22–41.

TIC *The transformation of the Irish church in the twelfth and thirteenth centuries*, M.T. Flanagan (Studies in Celtic History 29, Woodbridge, 2010).

TIS Trinity Irish Studies/Léann na Tríonóide.

TKAS	*Transactions of the Kilkenny Archaeological Society* 1 (1849) –3 (1855).
TLS	Todd Lecture Series.
TLSP	*Two lives of Saint Patrick: Vita secunda and Vita quarta*, F.J. Byrne & P. Francis; repr. from *JRSAI* 124 (1994), 5–117.
TMD	*Tales of medieval Dublin*, ed. S. Booker & C.N. Peters (Dublin, 2014).
TMIH	*Three Middle-Irish homilies on the lives of saints Patrick, Brigit and Columba*, ed. W. Stokes (Calcutta, 1877).
TNW	*Logainmneacha na hÉireann iv: townland names of co. Wexford: ainmneacha na mbailte fearainn co. Loch Garman*, ed. C. Ó Crualaoich & A. Mac Giolla Chomhghaill, 2 vols (Dublin, 2016).
TOAS	*Transactions of the Ossory Archaeological Society* 1–3 (1874–83).
TP	*Topographical poems*, ed. J. Carney (Dublin, 1943).
TPat.	*The two Patricks: a lecture on the history of Christianity in fifth-century Ireland*, T.F. O'Rahilly (Dublin, 1942).
TRIA	*Transactions of the Royal Irish Academy* 1 (1787) –3 (1907).
Triads	*The triads of Ireland*, ed. K. Meyer (TLS 13, Dublin, 1906).
TromG	*Tromdámh Guaire*, ed. M. Joynt (*MMIS* 2, Dublin, 1931).
TT	*Triadis thaumaturgae seu divorum Patricii, Columbae et Brigidae, trium veteris et maioris Scotiae seu Hiberniae, sanctorum Insulae, communium patronorum acta*, ed. J. Colgan (Louvain, 1647; repr. Dublin, 1997).
TTS	*Ten thousand saints: a study in Irish and European origins* (Kilkenny, 1972).
UCA	*Uí Cairbre Aobhdha (i gContae Luimnighe)*, G. Mac Spealáin (Baile Átha Cliath, 1960).
UCC DP 2002 Thor.	*The Lives of St Carthage of Lismore*, ed. & trans. D.J. Thornton (UCC, PhD, 2002).
UCC	University College Cork.
UíR	*Uí Ráthach*, An Seabhac (Dublin, [n.d.]).
UJA	*Ulster Journal of Archaeology* (1st ser. 1 (1853) –9 (1862); 2nd ser. 1 (1895) –17 (1911); 3rd ser. 1 (1938–)).
UL Camb.	University Library Cambridge.
Ulidia	*Ulidia: proceedings of the first International Conference on the Ulster Cycle of Tales*, ed. J.P. Mallory & G. Stockman (Belfast, 1994).
ULS	*Ulster Local Studies: Journal of the Federation for Ulster Local Studies* (1975–).
UrS	*Urkeltischer Sprachschatz*, W. Stokes & A. Bezzenberger, Vergleichendes Wörterbuch der Indogermanischen Sprachen 2 (Göttingen, 1894).
VB	*Venerabilis Baedae historiam ecclesiasticum gentis Anglorum Historiam abbatum epistolam ad Ecgbertum una cum historia abbatum auctore anonymo*, ed. C. Plummer (Oxford, 1896).

VC[1] *The life of St Columba, founder of Hy, written by Adamnan*, ed. W. Reeves (Dublin & Edinburgh, 1857).

VC[2] *Adomnán's Life of Columba*, ed. A.O. Anderson & M.O. Anderson (London & Edinburgh, 1961; rev. ed. Oxford, 1991).

VCol. *Ionae vitae sanctorum Columbani, Vedastis, Iohannis*, Scriptores Rerum Germanicarum in usum scholarum ex Monumentis Germaniae Historicis separatim editi (Hannover & Leipzig, 1905).

VFBA *The Vita Fursei and its Use by Bede and Aelfric*, A. Casey (Fursey Occasional Paper 5; Norwich, 2010).

ViewIL *A view of the Irish language*, ed. B. Ó Cuív (Dublin, 1969).

VisTnug. *Die Vision des Tnugdalus' Alber's von Windberg: Literatur und Frömmigkeitsgeschichte im ausgehenden 12. Jahrhundert*, ed. B. Pfeil (Frankfurt, 1999).

VP *Vita prima* of Brighid (= *TT* 527–45).

VPH *De vita S. Patricii Hiberniae apostoli libri II*, R. Stanihurst (Antwerp, 1587).

VSB *Le vies des saints de la Bretagne Armorique*, ed. A.-M. Thomas & J.-M. Abgrall (Quimper, 1901).

VSBG *Vitae sanctorum Brittaniae et Genealogiae*, ed. A.W. Wade-Evans (Hist. & Law Ser. 9, Cardiff, 1944).

VSHH *Vitae sanctorum Hiberniae e codice olim Salmanticensi*, ed. W.W. Heist (*SH* 28, Brussels, 1965).

VSHP *Vitae sanctorum Hiberniae*, 2 vols, ed. C. Plummer (Oxford, 1910; repr. 1968).

VT *The Tripartite Life of St Patrick with other documents relating to that saint*, 2 vols, ed. W. Stokes (Rolls Series 89, London, 1887).

WatLis. *Waterford & Lismore: a compendious dictionary of the united dioceses*, P. Power (Dublin & Cork, 1937).

WBP *The writings of Bishop Patrick 1074–1084*, A. Gwynn (Dublin, 1955).

WGK *The world of Geoffrey Keating: history, myth and religion in seventeenth-century Ireland*, B. Cunningham (Dublin, 2000).

WLC *Wilde's Loch Coirib: its shores and islands, with notices of Loch Measga*, ed. C. O Lochlainn (Dublin, 1955).

WSZL *Walahfrid Strabo: Zwei Legenden. Blathmac, der Martyrer von Iona (Hy). Mammes, der christliche Orpheus*, ed. M. Pörnbacher (*Reichenauer Texte und Bilder* 7, Sigmaringen, 1997).

WWHS *Wicklow, history and society: interdisciplinary essays on the history of an Irish county*, ed. K. Hannigan & W. Nolan (Dublin, 1994).

WWRJU *The whole works of the most reverend James Ussher*, 17 vols, ed. C.R. Elrington, H. Todd & W. Reeves (Dublin, 1847–64).

ZCP *Zeitschrift für celtische Philologie* (1899–).

ABBREVIATIONS

add.	added / additional
app.	appendix
b. / bb	barony / baronies
c.	*circa*
cat.	catalogue
cf.	compare
Co. / Cos	County / Counties
col. / cols	column / columns
comp.	compilation / compiled by
E.	east(ern)
ed.	editor / edited by
et al.	et alii
facs.	facsimile
fl.	flourished / floruit
fo. / fos	folio / folios
gl.	gloss(ed) / glossing
ind.	index
intr.	introduction / introduced by
inq.	inquisition(s)
l. / ll.	line / lines
lithogr.	lithograph(ed)
Lr	lower
marg.	margin
MS / MSS	manuscript / manuscripts
n. / nn	note(s) / footnote(s)
N.	north(ern)
n.d.	no date
NE	north-east(ern)
NW	north-west(ern)
p.c.	personal communication
proc.	proceedings

repr.	reprint(ed)
reprod.	reproduce(d)
S.	south(ern)
s.a.	*sub anno*
ser.	series
SCO.	Scotland
SE	south-east(ern)
SS	saints
St	saint
SW	south-west(ern)
tl.	townland
trans.	translation / translated by
Upr	upper
v.l.	*varia lectio*
W.	west(ern)

PROVINCES & COUNTIES

Provinces

CONN.	Connacht
LEIN.	Leinster
MUNS.	Munster
ULST.	Ulster

Counties

AH	Armagh
AM	Antrim
CE	Clare
CK	Cork
CN	Cavan
CW	Carlow
DB	Dublin
DL	Donegal
DN	Down
DY	Derry
FH	Fermanagh
GY	Galway
KE	Kildare
KK	Kilkenny
KY	Kerry
LD	Longford
LH	Louth
LK	Limerick
LM	Leitrim
LS	Laois
MH	Meath
MN	Monaghan
MO	Mayo
OY	Offaly
RN	Roscommon
SO	Sligo
TE	Tyrone
TY	Tipperary
WD	Waterford
WH	Westmeath
WW	Wicklow
WX	Wexford

INTRODUCTION

Sources of entries

Early sources

Material for the entries in this dictionary has come from a variety of mainly pre-Reformation sources, including Lives of the saints, martyrologies, genealogies of the saints, shorter tracts on the saints (some of them available only in manuscript), annals, annates and other papal documents, which often name the patrons of churches. The occurrence of a saint's name in any one of these sources does not guarantee inclusion in the dictionary. Reference to the Index of Feastdays will reveal, for example, gaps on certain days, where insufficient material was to hand to justify the insertion of a saint's name. Although by no means followed strictly, the normal requirements for inclusion here have been those adopted as essential *coordonnées* by the Bollandists, records of the saint's feast and known place of burial or worship, augmented, whenever available, by information on the saint's pedigree. As my previous work has focused mainly on Lives, martyrologies and genealogies of the saints, these sources have received the closest attention.[1]

Saints' Lives

Although relatively few in number, and largely confined to patrons of substantial churches, saints' Lives have proven to be of inestimable value. This is not because they throw much light on their subjects but, paradoxically, because they reveal how the traditions surrounding the saints could be used to great effect in the protection and promotion of the interests of the communities that held them in high regard. Typically, Lives appear to have been compiled against a background of change, which may explain why, judging by the extant corpus, their production was periodic. Thus, after four Lives had been compiled in the period 650 to 700 – two of Patrick, one each of Brighid and Colum Cille – there was a long interval of well over a hundred years, until the first half of the ninth century, when one Latin Life (Brighid's so-called *vita prima*) and two vernacular Lives – one each of Brighid and Patrick – were produced.[2] Thereafter, for almost three hundred years, either the conditions for hagiographical activity in Ireland were unfavourable or (much less likely) the record then produced has vanished without trace. Among the very few hagiographical texts written during this long period, again by writers

1 *CínCC* xi–xvi. **2** *PTBA*; *TT* 518–45; *BBr.*; *BP*; *VT*. The view taken by some scholars that the so-called O'Donohue Lives, a collection of mainly Midland texts, were compiled in the period 750–850 is not accepted here. As is argued in the relevant entries, there are many pointers in these texts to a much later date of composition.

from the three chief ecclesiastical communities of Armagh, Kildare and Kells (which had taken over the leadership of the Columban community from Iona), were vernacular Lives of Patrick, Brighid and Adhamhnán.[3]

The fifty-year period that followed the beginning of the English conquest of Ireland in 1169 was, by any standard, one of intense hagiographical activity. In fact, the bulk of the surviving record of the Irish saints, liturgical and literary, was written during this period, only to be followed by a trough of inactivity that lasted well over a century. Then, as the fourteenth century waned, new collections began to be made of earlier Lives, with some rewriting, and some new vernacular Lives were composed.[4]

Martyrologies and calendars

The compilation of the extant Irish martyrologies and calendars of saints, the earliest of which date to the first half of the ninth century, was also periodic in character. About 830, an abbreviated version of the Hieronymian martyrology, received from Northumbria and previously used in the churches of Iona and Bangor, was considerably enlarged at the monastery of Tallaght, mainly by reference to patrons and founders of churches associated with the *céili Dé*.[5] About this time also, an Irish calendar, possibly compiled in Glendalough, was brought to the monastery of Reichenau on Lake Constance, from where it eventually reached its present repository in the Badische Landesbibliothek, Karlsruhe.[6] The ninth-century Tallaght martyrologies, one in prose, the other metrical, went on to serve as the basis for the entire subsequent Irish corpus of texts of this kind. However, new martyrologies begin to appear only in the late twelfth century in northern churches associated with the canons regular of St Augustine.[7] A final (pre-Reformation) phase of martyrological activity may be dated to the period 1350–1450, when several copies were made of the Tallaght metrical text.

Dates of manuscripts

Users of pre-Reformation Lives and martyrologies should bear in mind that, with the notable exception of the early Lives of Patrick, Brighid and Colum Cille, these texts survive almost exclusively in manuscripts dating to the fourteenth or fifteenth century. The transmission of the Martyrology of Aonghas, the most popular of all Irish texts of this kind, may serve as a useful example. Of the first phase of the text, completed at Tallaght about 830, no manuscript evidence whatsoever survives. Nor are there many traces of its influence on other texts up to the second half of the twelfth century, at which point it received a new lease of life at Armagh in a much enlarged version, with prose preface, glosses and extensive commentary. Once more, however, there is no surviving manuscript copy of the text from this period. A third and final phase, begun about 1400 when Renaissance fashions were in the air, finally produced copies of the late twelfth-

3 *TMIH*; *BAd*. Proposals of dates outside these parameters are discussed in individual entries. **4** For example, the Lives in *MHH*. See *Bréifne* 11, 533–56. **5** *FSHIM* 1–118. **6** *AfL* 31, 33–78. **7** *FSHIM* 119–224. **8** Ibid. 173–204.

century augmented version, of which eight have survived.[8] Ironically, the production of the Renaissance versions appears to have had little to do with the essentially liturgical inspiration of the first and second phases of the text. The surviving copies were made for patrons, ecclesiastical and lay, whose main interest lay in possessing in their book-presses copies of a text which had allegedly been written in remote antiquity.

Much the same applies to most Latin, and all vernacular, Lives of the Irish saints, none of which is preserved in a manuscript datable to earlier than the fourteenth century. Brighid's ninth-century vernacular Life, for example, which is rightly described by its editor as 'the earliest surviving saint's Life written largely in Irish', survives in a manuscript written shortly before 1500.[9] The same manuscript contains a copy of the ninth-century vernacular Life of Patrick, and the version preferred by the modern editor of this text is only twenty years older, dating to 1477.[10] In both cases, the copies of the Lives were written for lay patrons, Renaissance lords, unconcerned with the preservation of the tattered and blackened exemplars.

Saints' genealogies

It is usually held that the further west one goes in Europe, the more medieval genealogies one finds. Michael O'Brien's *Corpus genealogiarum Hiberniae*, which was to be one only of several projected volumes, probably contains more medieval texts of this kind than are to be found in the entire remaining European record.[11] Within Ireland, the surviving collections of pedigrees, mainly preserved in the great manuscript miscellanies of the twelfth and later centuries, appear to derive ultimately from a corpus brought together in an early eleventh-century (no longer extant) Munster manuscript known as *Saltair Chaisil*, 'The Psalter of Cashel'.[12] The assembly and updating of secular genealogies continued until the mid-seventeenth century, when the Ó Cléirighs and their colleagues made compilations of both secular and saints' pedigrees, and Dubhaltach Mac Fhirbhisigh, from Lackan in Sligo, brought together in his *Leabhar mór na ngenealach* what Eugene O'Curry has described as 'the greatest national genealogical collection in the world', certainly in the western world.[13]

The surviving pre-Reformation manuscripts that contain collections of saints' genealogies include two from the twelfth century, namely the Book of Glendalough (part of Rawlinson B 502) (*c.*1130) and the Book of Leinster (*c.*1160–70), four from the late fourteenth century, namely the Book of Ballymote, the Book of Lecan (*c.*1397), the Book of Uí Mhaine and Rawlinson B 486, and one from the fifteenth century, Laud 610 (1453–4). As reported in a seventeenth-century description of the manuscript, the early eleventh-century *Saltair* contained 'a pedigree of our principall saincts, Patrick Brigid Colu[m]ba Ailbeus Ruadanus Declanus, etc'.[14] Most of the surviving collections similarly lead off with the pedigrees of the three national saints. However, in keeping with its

9 *BBr.* ix; *Bod. Cat.* i, 234. **10** *BP* v; cf. *VT* x–xiv. **11** *CGH*. **12** *Éigse* 23, 107–30; *Peritia* 17–18, 295–337. **13** *Lgen.; MM* 228. **14** *Éigse* 23, 122.

Munster provenance, the *Saltair* gave subsequent precedence to three southern saints, connected with Emly (Ailbhe), Lorrha (Ruadhán) and Ardmore (Déaglán). The tendency to award pride of place to saints from the compiler-editor's part of the country, immediately after the national saints, is characteristic of most collections. Saints of the Fothairt of north Leinster, more specifically of the Kildare area, are given this honour in the Book of Leinster. Similarly, the successors of Colum Cille on Iona and in Kells are given precedence in the Book of Glendalough version (probably originally from Kells), whereas saints associated with churches in north Tipperary and Clare, within the diocese of Killaloe, are placed first in the Lorrha manuscript (Rawlinson B 486).[15] This also applies to the early seventeenth-century collection in *Genealogiae regum et sanctorum Hiberniae*, compiled by the Four Masters, which accords precedence to the saints of Ceinéal Conaill.[16]

Local bias also manifests itself in individual pedigrees, which often reflect the interests of families associated with the churches in which the saints were venerated. As the saints were thought to have lived in the remote past, native historians and genealogists were prone to reshape their histories, and pedigrees proved particularly susceptible to localization and manipulation.[17] In this way, an originally unified cult, such as that of Fionnbharr (alias Finnian), might acquire six or more different statements of the saint's descent, depending on the locations and governance of the churches that had adopted the saint as patron.[18] Each such statement clearly implied a total claim to the saint, who was provided with several possible backgrounds, none of which may reflect his or her true origins. This tendency also explains why two or more alternative pedigrees are sometimes recorded for individual saints. Molua of Clonfert, for example, and Caimín of Inishcaltra are each provided with three alternative descents.[19]

Despite their unreliability as genuine statements of origin, saints' pedigrees can be useful indicators, both of the spread of cults and of the local interests to which they regularly fell prey. As such, they are deserving of the respect shown to them, not only by the native genealogists, but also by such modern commentators as the Bollandist, Paul Grosjean, who treated them as a *coordonnée hagiographique* equal in value for Irish saints to the two *coordonnées* – day of death and place of burial – established by Hippolyte Delehaye for the saints of the universal church.[20]

Modern sources

In addition to pre-Reformation sources, extensive use has been made here of later (mainly oral) tradition, as preserved in collections, journals of folklore and local historical journals. In this regard, the material collected in the 1830s in the course of the Ordnance Survey of Ireland has proved particularly useful.[21] Travelling, often with great difficulty, to every parish in Ireland (except those of Cork, where

15 *CGSH* pp 1–4, 337, 342, 344. **16** *GRSH* 37–43. **17** *Nomina* 7, 23–9; *CGSH* xiii–xiv. **18** *MakS* 1–29. **19** *CGSH* §§116, 290. **20** *CLMH* 13–7; *AB* 76, 389n. **21** References are to manuscript page numbers, as provided in typescript by M. O'Flanagan in 1927–8, and in printed form by M. Herity in his *Ordnance Survey Letter* series, published by the Four Masters Press, Dublin (2000–10).

financial considerations unfortunately brought this part of the survey to an end), John O'Donovan, Eugene O'Curry, Thomas O'Conor and others endeavoured to systematically collect information on local devotion. Despite his jaundiced (if also very discerning) view of the value of the written sources of information on the saints, O'Donovan's observations on these matters are of particular interest. When finishing his letters from Co. Offaly, he had this to say:[22]

> I have been very severe on the saints all along, for no other reason … but because I am (not) a saint myself, for if I were I would hide their faults as well as the pious Butler, who has omitted to relate … the silly part of their conduct, and has holden up the heroic and noble part, as an example to the faithful. He has manufactured his lives of the saints well & so as to suit the feelings of the pious believers of his own age. Jocelyn has done the same, and so had our honest Colgan; but unfortunately the saint of Jocelyn and the saints of Colgan would not be saints at all to the readers of Butler, and we must not therefore condemn that amiable Christian philosopher for rejecting those narrations which would offend the belief and religious feelings of the present day.

These perceptive comments are followed by others, which, while thoroughly sensible and indeed modern in their evaluation of the texts, might have left O'Donovan open to severe clerical criticism, had they been published in 1838. He continues in much the same vein:

> The principal fault which I reprehend in the writers of our hagiology is their making their Christian heroes too fond of duplicity & equivocation … which … savour more of the tricks of the arch rebel than of the pure doctrines … but as these have passed the crucible of doctors of divinity, I should be very timid in pronouncing any opinion … further than this, that I believe them to be the productions of an ulterior age and therefore rather to be considered as the … fabricated stories of ignorant bards and ecclesiastics, than as containing the sentiments of the original teachers of Christianity in Ireland … fabrications of the middle ages when … the ecclesiastics made use of the lowest and basest cunning to terrify the … chiefs to obedience and make them render the church its due support.[23]

In propagating the view that hagiographical writings were relatively late fabrications, designed to protect and promote the interests of the communities that produced them, O'Donovan was far ahead of his time. Moreover, despite his

22 OSL OY ii, 202. Alban Butler's celebrated *Lives of the saints*, first published in the early eighteenth century, was reprinted on numerous occasions. Jocelin of Furness, a Cistercian monk, was the author of several saints' Lives, most notably that of Patrick, which was written about 1185 (*SLJF*). John Colgan's *Acta sanctorum Hiberniae* (*ASH*) and *Trias thaumaturga* (*TT*), were published in Louvain in 1645 and 1647 respectively. O'Donovan (OSL DL 5) elsewhere aptly described Colgan as 'the most remarkable Milesian that Ireland ever produced'. **23** OSL OY 203.

poor opinion of the writings of earlier hagiographers, he tended to be at his most impatient with informants who could tell him nothing about traditional local patterns of devotion or, as he put it himself, 'ould saints'.[24] Thus, arriving in the Meath parish of Emlagh, he found that the ancient patron of the parish, Beagán by name, 'had been dethroned' and replaced by the 'more illustrious' feast of the conception of the Blessed Virgin, a very common practice in the early nineteenth century, which, as O'Donovan stated, had the effect of hurling Beagán 'into the gaping gulf of blank oblivion'.[25] Much of the blame for this lay with the priests who, 'inclining very much … to Protestant notions', were putting an end to the venerable old customs.[26] O'Donovan wished they had delayed their 'reformation' until he had their territories traversed.[27]

Notwithstanding these impediments to his work, O'Donovan and his colleagues did the history of Irish devotion to the saints a huge service by making a habit of enquiring after local patrons, whenever and wherever the opportunity presented itself. Particularly valuable in this regard are the descriptions thus provided of practices at annual patterns, when the saint's relic, if still preserved locally, was put on display. At Inishkeel in Donegal, for example, we learn that the saint's bell, known as the *Bearnán Conaill*, still remained in the custody of its traditional keepers, the Uí Bhreisléin (O'Breslens), of which family the saint was reputedly a member. During the annual pattern, locally called a *turas*, the 'Senior' of the O'Breslens sat or stood or knelt at a sacred rocky place called 'Conall's bed' and, praying in Latin, held forth the bell to be kissed by the pilgrims, for which office it was a part of the ceremony that he receive 'more or less [payment] from each of them'.[28]

The conservatism of local practice in this instance is shown by the saint's genealogy, which attaches him to the Uí Bhreisléin.[29] Moreover, the rituals of the *turas*, then common throughout Ireland, seem to have changed but little from much earlier practice, as is shown by a passage from the vernacular Life of Forannán of Alternan in Sligo, which was possibly compiled in the early sixteenth century. Taken from a manuscript in the possession of Forannán's coarb or successor, the Life asserts that the saint had attached many virtues to a water-filled vessel in which those attending the annual pattern at his well were invited to bathe, with a guarantee of being cured of whatever ailments affected them, provided their 'clothes or raiments of penance' (*éadach agus eirreadh an aithrighe*) – or whatever alms penitents from outside the area might offer – were left with the saint's successor.[30] Moreover, the curses of the clergy, their churches and bells, and of all the saints of Ireland, together with shortness of life, were promised to those reckless enough to refuse to pay a due tax and levy to Forannán's successor. 'St Arnon's (Ernan's) Holy Well', as it came to be known locally, continues to be frequented, as does that of Conall in Inishkeel, although now bereft of the saint's

24 OSL MH 6. Cf. OSL WW 111: 'I hate to describe places with which no historical associations are connected'. OSL LD 60: 'I never saw a county less interesting than this; the people have forgotten everything about its ancient state'. **25** OSL MH 153. **26** *IOS* 137. **27** Ibid. **28** OSL DL 202; *DLHS* 106–7. **29** *Lgen.* 158.6.7. **30** *Anecd.* iii, 5–6. **31** *TDI* i, 594; *HWI* 151–2.

bell and the O'Breslen family member who held it up to be kissed, against payment.[31]

The remarkable tenacity of Irish folk memory, as revealed by the Ordnance Survey Letters, is also shown by O'Donovan's account of a visit to the Monaghan church of Muckno, near Castleblayney, in 1835.[32] By then, an origin legend had gained currency locally that described how Muckno had been founded at a place identified for the saint by a (heavenly) pig that swam across the nearby lake. Although the swim was based on the erroneous belief that Muckno derives from *muc-shnámh*, 'pig-swim', the presence of an animal, usually wild, often formed an integral part of foundation stories.[33] More significantly, O'Donovan was also told by locals that the patron of Muckno, Maol Dóid, belonged to a family named Hanratty. This affiliation is again borne out by an early genealogy which presents the eponymous ancestor of the O'Hanrattys, a man named Ionnrachtach, as a great-grandson of the saint's brother.[34]

Diocesan histories also figure prominently among the sources extensively used here. If published before 1922, when many of the documents kept in the Public Records Office were destroyed, these histories can be useful primary sources. On the whole, however, Irish diocesan histories are of an uneven quality, with some paying little attention to local saints. Among notable exceptions are William Carrigan's *History of the diocese of Ossory* and James O'Laverty's *History of the dioceses of Down and Connor*, both of which have proved very useful. The series of *Archaeological inventories*, in course of production by the Stationary Office, Dublin, which regularly contain sections on holy wells and early ecclesiastical monuments, have also provided numerous references.

Finally, historical, archaeological and antiquarian journals have been combed for information on dedications to saints and surviving traditions concerning them. Early issues of some of the more prestigious journals, such as those published by the Royal Society of Antiquaries of Ireland (earlier the Kilkenny Archaeological Society), the Cork Historical and Archaeological Society, the Galway Archæological and Historical Society, the Kerry Archaeological and Historical Society, the County Kildare Archæological Society, the County Louth Archaeological Society, the North Munster Archaeological Society, and the Waterford and South-East of Ireland Archæological Society, were sources of much valuable information, often drawn from documents since lost. More recent journals, such as *Seanchas Ard Mhacha*, the *Clogher Record* and *Innes Review*, feature regular contributions on saints and their churches, as do journals specifically concerned with place-names, such as *Dinnseanchas* and *Ainm*.

32 OSL AH/MN 77–8. **33** *VSHH* i, cxliv–v. Cf. entries below on Bearach; Feadhbhair; Fiontan of Doon; Gobnaid; Maol Dóid; Mochuille; Muireadhach of Banagher. **34** OCBG §1672.

Editorial policy

In presenting this dictionary to its users, I am conscious not only of the imperfections that attend all such endeavours, but also of the limits that I have felt obliged to attach to it. It includes only those saints whose cults were native to (and largely confined to) Ireland and – to a much lesser degree – Scotland. Irish saints venerated on the Continent are accepted only when devotion to them was also well established at home. Thus, while Fursa of Péronne and Faolán of Aachen are admitted, Columbanus of Bobbio is not. The cults of Fursa and Faolán flourished in Ireland, most notably in the Galway churches of Killursa and 'Killilan' in Cahertinny townland, parish of Kilconickny, where they appear to have benefitted from an association with Bréanainn of Clonfert. Furthermore, only those saints who died before 1200 are included. This means that while room is found for Maol Maodhóg (Malachy) who died in 1148, and Lorcán Ua Tuathail (Laurence O'Toole) who died in 1180, none of those who gained sanctity through martyrdom at the hands of over-zealous reformers in the sixteenth or early seventeenth century is included.

An immediate problem faced by the compiler of a dictionary of this kind is the fact that the change of language, from Irish to English, which began in earnest in the seventeenth century, affected the names of local saints, many of which were altered almost beyond recognition. In deciding to use Classical Irish forms as headwords in the vast majority of cases, I have been guided by an instinct similar to that which prompted Paul Walsh, in his edition of the Ordnance Survey Letters for Westmeath, to restore Irish forms of names where John O'Donovan, who wrote most of the letters, had used anglicized forms.[35] Unlike Walsh, however, who wrote at a time when 'brighter hopes were entertained' about the future of the Irish language, I have adopted the Irish forms mainly because the traditional approach in compilations of this kind in most cases requires me to do so. I have failed, for example, to find Hugh of Rahugh (here presented as Aodh of Rahugh) under the anglicized form of his name, by which he came to be known locally, in any previous dictionary or index of saints' names. He invariably figures as 'Aed(h)', sometimes accompanied by the patronymic 'Mac Bricc', son of Brecc, or some closely related form, based on usage that dates back to the Old Irish period.[36] Indeed, the most authoritative of all modern dictionaries of saints, the *Bibliotheca Sanctorum*, or *Enciclopedia dei Santi*, published at the Vatican between 1961 and 1970, renders the name as Aido, from Old Irish Aíd combined with the Italian masculine ending *o*, and much the same applies to Aidano (Old Irish Aídán) and Ailbeo (Old Irish Ailbe), which are followed in the *Enciclopedia* by such Old or Middle Irish forms as Ailerán, Airennán, Brénainn, Caemhan, Caemhog, Coemgen and Oengus, to name a few examples only.[37] Contributors to the *Enciclopedia* included such scholars as the Franciscans, Cuthbert Mág Craith and Fergal Grannell (who also used mainly Old Irish forms in his contributions to

35 *PNW* vii. 36 ODS 4. 37 *BiblSS*. Although this saint is omitted from *DIB*, the most recent dictionary to contain entries on Irish saints, Áed is also the form of the name preferred by its editors.

the *Dictionnaire d'histoire et de géographie écclesiastiques*) and the late Vatican librarian, Leonard Boyle. While I remain conscious, therefore, of the displeasure that users of my dictionary may sometimes feel on finding such well-established forms as Brendan or Kevin passed over in favour of Bréanainn and Caoimhghin, I am consoled, not only by the practice of previous authors, but also by the dangers that sometimes attended the adoption of anglicized forms of the names.

An example is provided by the unfortunate Maol Ruain of Tallaght, one of the more influential of the early Irish saints, who founded in 774 the monastery of Tallaght, a focal point of the anchoritic revival associated with the so-called Culdees or *céili Dé*, and a centre of scribal activity.[38] Maol Ruain's feast of 7 July continued to be observed at Tallaght up to the late nineteenth century, by which time, however, the saint, now called Mollroone (Mollroony), had come to be regarded as a female, whose loaf and griddle – the base of a high cross and a hollowed out stone – were pointed out in the local graveyard.[39]

Partly guided then by the dangers inherent in using modern anglicized forms, I show a general preference here for Classical Irish forms of the saints' names. The Classical Irish standard is adopted because it represents a happy mean between Middle and Modern Irish, not far removed from the earlier forms preferred by previous commentators, yet easily recognizable by those proficient in Modern Irish. Besides, the use of Classical Irish forms is also the norm in the *Historical dictionary of Gaelic placenames*, currently being prepared by the *Locus* Project in University College Cork, and published by the Irish Texts Society.[40] And finally, the anglicized forms will also be found here in their appropriate places, accompanied by cross-references to the Classical Irish forms.

There are a few exceptions to the above rule, including the anglicized form Patrick, which is preferred over Pádraig for several reasons. Firstly, the saint's cult has by now assumed global proportions under the guise of Patrick. Secondly, of all the saints included in the dictionary, Patrick the Briton is one of very few non-natives of note. Finally, the anglicized form, which is arguably closer to the original Latin name *Patricius*, is also favoured by the compilers of the *Enciclopedia dei Santi*, albeit under the Italian guise of *Patrizio*.[41] My use of the form Finnian (instead of Finnia), which is based on the Latin form *Vinnianus* (*Finnianus*), for the patrons of Clonard and Movilla, also forms an exception, not least because the saint, like Patrick, may have been born in Britain.

Patrick's church of Armagh also forms an exception to the general rule of pinpointing the locations of saints' churches at the beginning of entries, in townland (wherever relevant), parish, barony and county. Located in the county and barony of the same name, Armagh was felt to be sufficiently well known to be left without further qualification, and this also applies to other major church sites.

38 *CéliD* 173–4; *AFM s.a.* **39** OSL DB, 57. **40** *HDGP*. **41** *BiblSS* x, 396–408.

Indexes

The indexes of place-names are designed to cater to both local and scholarly interest in the saints and, as in most historical surveys of this kind, the separately indexed civil parishes are preferred to modern denominational divisions. An index of feastdays is also supplied to cater to those interested in saints associated with particular days. An index of subjects, although far from complete, may prove of interest to those concerned with particular aspects of devotion to the saints. Finally, while also cited in their appropriate alphabetical places in the body of the dictionary, a list of alternative (mainly anglicized) forms of names is added for convenience and ease of reference.

Conclusion

In most cases, the information provided in this dictionary is quite limited; little beyond names of saints and their churches, augmented perhaps by names of parents and dates of feasts, can now be recovered from the available sources. In some cases, where more extensive sources are available, possibly including Lives, attention is drawn to the saint's genealogy, reputed actions during life, encounters with other saints, diffusion of cult, alleged date and day of death, relics and miracles performed after death, as far as possible in that order. Sources are cited for all the information provided. Users of this information should bear in mind at all times that the documentary remains almost always date to several centuries after the reputed lifetimes of the saints. For this reason, terms like 'reputed, alleged, supposed' will be found in almost every entry and, even if absent, no less caution is to be observed in accepting or rejecting traditions of the saints. Everything that has been recorded in writing of the saints is worthy of attention, but almost always only in relation either to the hand that wrote it or to the vested interests that encouraged its confirmation in writing.

At the beginning of his book on 'Ten thousand Irish saints', Hubert Butler stated that he could count at least fifty churches within ten miles of his home in Kilkenny, and that what he could do every Irish person could do.[42] Scarcely a single parish in Ireland is without one or more dedications to native saints, in the form of churches in ruins, holy wells or other ecclesiastical monuments. This dictionary is intended to serve as a guide to the (mainly documentary) sources of information on Ireland's local saints for those who have an interest in them, scholarly or otherwise. As such, it will hopefully serve to stimulate rather than entirely satisfy the curiosity of its readers.

42 *TTS* 13–14.

DICTIONARY OF IRISH SAINTS

A

Abán of Adamstown, formerly Moyarney (Magh Arnaidhe), barony of Bantry, Co. Wexford, and of Killabban (Ceall Abáin), barony of Ballyadams, Co. Laois. The saint's pedigree, which names his father as Laighneach (Laighnéan) of the Uí Chormaic (Dál gCormaic) of Leinster, reflects the location of his church in Laois.[1] His mother, Mealla (alias Míolla), is said by one source to have been a sister of Caoimhghin, which may imply some form of association between Glendalough and Abán's church in Laois, whereas other sources, which sometimes give her the name Caineach Abadh, describe her as a sister of Iobhar of Begerin, near Wexford town.[2] The saint's name – also written Eibbán, Moab(b)a, Latin Abbanus and, in anglicized form, Abban – has been taken to mean 'little abbot', from Irish ab, 'abbot', but it is far more likely to have been a hypocoristic or pet form of Ailbhe, with characteristic doubling of the medial consonant (*Abba*).[3] An awareness of this equivalence may be contained in the assertion that Ceall Ailbhe, now perhaps an ecclesiastical site in the Meath parish of Kilshine, was among the churches founded by the saint.[4]

Beginning with a general description of Ireland, apparently aimed at an Anglo-Norman audience, the saint's biographer – whose work survives in two Latin redactions and a vernacular adaptation – attributed to Patrick a prophecy of the birth of three sons of Leinster 'of eternal life', Abán, Caoimhghin of Glendalough, and Moling of St Mullin's, the last of whom is also associated with the abbacy of Ferns.[5] Baptized by Iobhar and sent to Begerin for his initial schooling, Abán is shown walking Christ-like on the water in order to join his maternal uncle on a pilgrimage to Rome.[6] En route, in a ploy probably designed to counter the English allegation that the conquest of Ireland resulted from the need 'to spread the faith', the saint is said to have converted a British (read English) king and his people from paganism, before founding the church of Abingdon, near Oxford, whose name is spuriously derived from *Abbaindun vel Dun Abbain,* 'Abán's dwelling'.[7] The author of the saint's vernacular Life chose to place these events in Padua in Italy, famous for its association with St Antony, which indicates a Franciscan provenance for this version of the text, probably the friary at New Ross in Wexford, where there was a dedication to the saint.[8]

Back in Ireland, the saint is brought on a journey countrywide, but especially in south Munster, where he is said to have founded several churches: Ballyvourney (Boirneach) – later, according to local tradition, the location of his grave – which he allegedly surrendered to Gobnaid; 'Killagh Abbey' (Ceall Achaidh Choinchinn), near Milltown in Kerry, where he prophesied the advent of Fíonán, the church's patron; Coole Abbey (Cúil Chollainge), near Castlelyons, and Kilcrumper (Ceall Chruimhthir), near Fermoy in Cork; Toureen, alias Peakaun (Cluain Aird Mobheagóg), in the Tipperary parish of Killardry, where a vivid description is given of the church; and the Éile / Fir Cheall area on the marches of

Munster and Leinster, where he is said to have effected the conversion of a local man of royal descent whose son he baptized.[9] His probable biographer, Albinus Ua Maoil Mhuadh (O'Molloy) (†1223), bishop of Ferns, was a native of this area, and possibly spoke of himself when he asserted, using the first person: 'I who gathered together and wrote the Life am a descendant (Latin *nepos*) of that son'.[10]

Finally brought back to Leinster, Abán is shown founding his two main churches there in quick succession, at Killabban in Laois and at Adamstown in south Wexford, together with several other foundations *per circuitem*, 'roundabout', doubtless named with a view to defending local property interests.[11] A concern with property, probably under serious threat from Anglo-Norman encroachment, permeates the remainder of the Life, the saint being called upon to make successive miraculous interventions, most of which no longer held any interest for the author of the vernacular Life who either condensed or omitted them.

Among other saints introduced into the Life were Colum Cille, who is shown petitioning Abán to obtain heavenly assurance that his own prayers would be answered, and Bréanainn, who is asked by Abán to give an account of his recent sea-voyage.[12] On the saint's death, his *praepositus*, 'provost', allegedly a native of Killabban, having arranged to steal Abán's remains, and take them on a wagon driven by oxen to his church in Laois, had his plans for sole possession of the remains thwarted by the appearance of a duplicate wagon and pair of oxen, which carried the remains back to Adamstown.[13] By means of this *topos*, what must have been rival claims to the location of the saint's burial – not to mention his supposed grave in Ballyvourney – were cleverly satisfied by the saint's biographer.

The saint is featured in two other Lives; that of Finnian of Clonard which awards him the considerable distinction of baptizing the infant subject of the Life; and that of Molua of Clonfertmulloe which refers to Abán's founding of the church that gave name to New Ross (Ros Mhic Threóin).[14] The saint's cult appears to have spread also to Doonane in the parish of Rathaspick, adjoining Killabban, Leixlip in Kildare, where a church was named after him, and to Kirk Braddan parish on the Isle of Man.[15] In keeping with the double location of his remains, Abán was remembered on two feastdays, 16 March and 27 October, but his day had been forgotten in Killabban by the early nineteenth century.[16] The March feast found its way, under the guise of Albanus, into the copy of the Martyrology of Usuard prepared by Grevenus of Cologne in the late fifteenth century.[17] Finally, it has recently been shown that a quatrain in Irish cited in the saint's Life, which is preserved separately in a manuscript copied in Waterford in the thirteenth century, was regarded as a charm to ensure safe passage for marine travellers.[18]

1 *CGSH* §287.1; *GRSH* 85; *Lgen.* 450.12, 727.9; *DIB* i, 1–2. **2** *CGSH* §287.3; *CPPI* 183; *VSHP* i, 3–33 at 4 §3; *VSHH* 256–74, at 256 §2; *BNÉ* i, 3–10, at 3 §1; *CGSH* §722.79. **3** *GPN* 11; *VSHP* i, 23 §32; *VSHH* 268 §26. **4** *HDGP* iii, 123. **5** *VSHP* i, 3–4 §§1–2; *VSHH* 256 §1; cf. *ZCP* 8, 110. **6** *VSHP* i, 7–10 §§8–12; *VSHH* 258–60 §§5–6; *BNÉ* i, 4–5 §8–10. **7** *VSHP* i, 10–12 §§13–14; *VSHH* 260–2 §§7–10; *PSICCSO* 165. **8** *BNÉ* i, 5–6 §§11–15; *PSICCSO* 162. **9** *VSHP* i, 17 §22; *VSHH* 264 §17; *BNÉ* i, 8 §24; *JCHAS* 57, 29–30. **10** *VSHP* i, 19–20 §§25–6; *VSHH* 265–6 §§18–20; *PSICCSO* 159–70, *PPPMI* 333–7; *LnaL* 100. **11** *VSHP* i, 20–1 §§27–8; *VSHH* 266–7 §§22–3. **12** *VSHP* i, 28–9 §§45–6; *VSHH* 271–2 §§40–1; cf. *IrL* 60.

13 *VSHP* i, 30–2 §§49–52; *VSHH* 272–4 §§43–6. **14** *VSHH* 96 §2; *VSHP* ii, 220 §39. **15** *JCKAS* 3, 489; *PIM* 188. **16** *MartT* 24–84; *MartO*[2] 82, 219; *MartG* 56, 204; *MartD* 76; OSL LS ii, 6. **17** *AS*.Iun. vi, 158. **18** *LnaL* 95–112.

Abban. *See* Abán.

Abeogus. *See* Dobheóg.

Abigail (Abby). *See* Gobnaid.

Acobhrán of Achadh Rathain. *See* Acobhrán of Kilrush.

Acobhrán of Kilrush, barony of Moyarta, Co. Clare, or of Kilrush, barony of Offaly West, Co. Kildare. This saint's name may derive from *acobhar*, 'desire'. In the early martyrologies, the notice of the saint's feast (28 January) is not accompanied by the name of a church.[1] In the later martyrological record, he is assigned to Ceall Rois 'in the termon of Inis Cathaigh', now Kilrush near Scattery Island in Clare.[2] A note added to the seventeenth-century Martyrology of Donegal links the saint, however, to 'Ros Mucrois', three miles from Kildare, which points to the nearby Kilrush, one of the churches subject to Brighid.[3] As the saint's feast fell close to that of Brighid (1 February), this seems a more appropriate association. Some martyrologies commemorate a nominally different saint named Acobhrán son of Bóchra on 28 November, attaching him to the unidentified church of Achadh Rathain in or near the Cork barony of Imokilly.[4] In the tract on the mothers of the saints, which names Bóchra's husband as Feidhlimidh, the saint's name is rendered 'Aodh Chobhrán'.[5] Acobhrán is reputedly among the Irish saints whose cults spread to Cornwall. Attested in medieval documents as *Achobhran* and *Achebrannus*, the Cornish saint of the name is now the eponymous patron of the parish of S. Keverne near the Lizard.[6]

1 *MartT* 13; *MartO*[2] 38. **2** *MartG* 24; *MartO*[2] 54. **3** *MartD* 354; *CGSH* §670.53. **4** *MartO*[2] 237; *MartG* 228; *MartD* 320. **5** *CGSH* §722.36. **6** *CMCS* 12, 47–8; CornS 29, 27–8.

Ádhamair. *See* Aodhamair.

Adhamhnán of Iona (Í), Scotland. Although used of more than one saint, the name Adhamhnán – possibly from *adhomhna*, 'great fear/awe', and commonly written Adomnán (Adamnán) or, in anglicized form, Eunan – almost invariably refers to the eighth and most celebrated successor of Colum Cille as abbot of Iona.[1] The saint's pedigree assigns him to the Ceinéal Lughdhach, a branch of the Ceinéal Conaill in the later barony of Kilmacrenan, who were also Colum Cille's kindred, and among the Donegal churches associated with him are Drumhome (Druim Thuama), where he appears to have spent part of his youth, and Raphoe (Ráith Bhoth), the seat of a diocese of which he is still patron.[2] This latter church lay within the territory of Ceinéal Éanna, a segment of Ceinéal Conaill in the barony of Raphoe, and this may explain why his mother, Rónaid daughter of Séighín, who is said to have been remembered on 3 May or 5 August, is attached to that family.[3]

Adhamhnán's biography of Colum Cille is regarded as the most accomplished of the seventh-century Lives of Irish saints.[4] There is no denying the saint's wide learning, sophisticated style of writing, and capacity for subtle argument, exemplified by his use of the circumstances surrounding Colum Cille's death to impress on his community that Eastertide was an occasion of joy and not of sorrow or controversy.[5] But Adhamhnán was also a slave to convention, as when he allowed the age of his sainted predecessor to be 77, composed of 43 years in Ireland and 34 in Scotland.[6] As the number seven (4+3; 3+4) stood for completeness and perfection, Adhamhnán showed an awareness of the science of numerology, which later also led to the assertion that he himself died at the age of 77.[7] A dependence on oral tradition is reflected, among other ways, by Adhamhnán's failure to distinguish between Colum Cille and his likely Ossory double, Cainneach of Aghaboe.[8]

Adhamhnán also composed a work on the holy places (*De locis sanctis*), for which he was deemed 'illustrious' outside Ireland and Scotland.[9] His description is not based on personal experience, as he had never travelled further than Northumbria, but allegedly, since this may have been merely a literary fiction, on an account given him by Arculf, a Frankish pilgrim shipwrecked off the coast of Scotland.[10] As Adhamhnán's narrative has been shown to have influenced the Venerable Bede's work on the same subject, the saint may have brought a copy to Northumbria on one of his two journeys there from Iona, made in the hope of negotiating the return of a (human) prey taken by Saxon raiders from Ireland.[11]

Also associated with the saint's name is his celebrated *cáin* (law), one of the four chief laws of Ireland, which was first proclaimed in 697 at Birr in Offaly in the presence of many kings and prelates.[12] Otherwise known as *lex innocentium* (law of the innocents), the *cáin* was designed to protect non-combatants and especially women from the effects of battle. The text of the *cáin*, together with a list of those that witnessed it by their presence, has been preserved in what is sometimes regarded as a contemporary text.[13]

Alone among Irish biographers of saints, Adhamhnán himself not only attained saintly status, but was also made the subject of a vernacular biography, written at Kells about 960–75, which survives in a single manuscript, transcribed in 1628–9 by the indefatigable Franciscan, Míchéal Ó Cléirigh.[14] By the middle of the tenth century, Adhamhnán's memory had begun to rival that of Colum Cille, as is shown by the tendency to describe abbots of Kells as coarbs of both saints.[15] The Life, which is tendentious, bears no comparison, however, with its subject's Life of Colum Cille. It is essentially an essay on ecclesiastical relations with the secular authority, as seen from a Kells perspective. One part of the text, consisting of ten episodes, comments on mid-tenth-century Irish politics, and especially on the misbehaviour of Conghalach (†964), king of Tara.[16] A second part, principally comprising four episodes located on Iona, deals with attributes of the good and virtuous abbot.[17] An Office Life of the saint, which arguably depends on his vernacular biography, has been preserved in the Breviary of Aberdeen, and a set of *mionannála*, 'minor annals', relates how, as a youth, the saint foretold the accession of his *anamchara*, 'soul-friend', Fionnachta *Fleadhach* 'of the feasts' († 695), to the kingship of Tara, before later foretelling the dire consequences of the king's failure to observe his summons to a meeting.[18]

The *fís*, 'vision', credited to Adhamhnán, which is now held to have been composed by an Irishman resident in Lorraine, has been described as a 'minor masterpiece of medieval literature'.[19] An episode in the *Monastery of Tallaght*, which shows Adhamhnán appointing an abbot at Clonmacnoise, ties in with an account in his Life of Colum Cille of how Colum was greeted on his arrival at the church, as if he were 'an angel of the Lord'.[20] In addition to some *canones*, mainly dealing with alimentary regulations, several poems have been credited to Adhamhnán, including one in praise of Colum Cille and another on the contents of his own reliquary, but despite the opinions of some scholars, none of them is likely to have been composed by him.[21] A number of prophecies have been ascribed to him.[22]

Besides Raphoe, Drumhome – perhaps also the nearby Skreen – in Donegal, and Skreen (Scrín Adhamhnáin) in Sligo, the saint, who was likened in manners to Pope Silvester, was patron of several churches in the diocese of Derry.[23] These included Dunboe, Errigal (which was shared with the apostle Paul), and Bovevagh, shared with Eoghan of Ardstraw.[24] The saint's shrine was kept at the Monaghan church of Donaghmoyne, and his bell, known as the *Dubh Díoghlach*, may have been kept at Skreen in Co. Sligo.[25] At Syonan (Suidhe Adhamhnáin) in the Westmeath parish of Ardnurcher, he preached to the populace, according to local tradition.[26] At least twenty Scottish churches also commemorate Adhamhnán.[27] Born, according to the annals in 624, the saint died in 704 and his feast, which fell on 23 September, found its way into several external martyrologies.[28] It was also recorded, albeit on 25 September, in an early ninth-century calendar kept by an Irishman on the Reichenau in Lake Constance.[29] The day observed at Raphoe was 7 September.[30] Adhamhnán's relics were brought to Ireland in 727, when his Law was renewed, and brought back to Iona in 730.[31] A relic of the saint, accompanied by relics of Colum Cille and Finnian of Movilla, had reached Saint-Maurice d'Agaune in the Swiss canton of Valais by the second half of the eighth century.[32]

1 *VC*^{2} 92–3; *Ériu* 11, 120–1; *AB* 78, 375–9; *DERMB* 433; *DIB* i, 25–6; *BiblSS i*, 199–201; VC^1, xl–lxviii. **2** *CGSH* §340; *GRSH* 37; *Lgen*. 697.6; cf. *AITLP* 20–35. **3** *CGSH* §722.21; *GRSH* 52. **4** *VC*^{1}; *VC*^{2}; *AILC*; *Peritia* 1, 160–77; ibid. 3, 50–70; ibid. 6–7, 141–57; ibid. 17–18, 154–82. **5** *VC*^{1} III.23 (228–9); *VC*^{2} 124b–125a (516–18); *AILC* 225; *AU s.a.* 704. **6** *SCJ* 5, 7–18. **7** Ibid.; cf. *UJA* 6 (1st ser.), 24–5. **8** *FG* 20–35. **9** *DLS*; *AHP*; *Peritia* 10, 98–122; *Ériu* 51, 93–106; *Innes Review* 46, 1–14; *AITLP* 162–204. **10** *AHP* 61–3; *Ériu* 52, 25–52. **11** *AHP* 188–97; *VC*^{1} II.46 (186); *VC*^{2} 103b (460–2); *AILC* 203; *AU s.a.* 687. **12** *Ériu* 2, 190; *AU s.a.*; *ZCP* 21, 338; *AdB*. **13** *CA* 14–20 §28; *Peritia* 1, 178–215. **14** *BAd*.; *IKD* 151–79; *StH* 27, 155–8. **15** *BAd*. 3; but cf. *AITLP* 112–13. **16** *BAd*. 8–31. **17** Ibid. 31–41. **18** Ibid. 36–41; *BrevA* pars aest. 114v–115; cf. *IKD* 170–4; *Innes Review* 51, 36–9; *LegSS* 232–3, 318–20; SG i, 403–6. **19** ITS *SS* 20, 45; p.c. (John Carey); *StC* 12/13, 77. **20** *MT* §84; *VC*^{2} 214–16. **21** *Celtica* 15, 25–41; *Ériu* 1, 225–8; *LH* i, 184; *Kenney* 245. **22** *Éigse* 5, 86 §39; cf. *TBB* 168–9. **23** *CGSH* §712.30; *DOH* 82–3. **24** *Celtica* 1, 82; *DLHS* 195 **25** *AU s.a.* 832; *JRSAI* 134, 37–42; *UJA* (2nd ser.) 2, 153, 155; *EMH* 483 §219. **26** *PNW* 18. **27** *CPNS* 271–2; *KSS* 265–6; *ACDS* 56–60; *CarmG* ii, 221; *Innes Review* 48, 60–2, 63–8; COL; *SpesS* 62–70. **28** *AU s.a.*; *ZCP* 5, 496; *MartT* 73; *MartO*^{2} 196; *MartG* 182; *MartD* 254–6; *AS*.Iun. vii, 554; *FSHIM* 138. **29** *AfL* 31, 59. **30** *VC*^{1} 257; OSL DY 73. **31** *AU s.a.* **32** *RIW* 13, 32.

Ádhán of Imleach Tuaiscirt. This man, also known as Ua an Éigis, 'descendant of the poet', is included in a list of saints subject to Brighid of Kildare, which places him, together with a female companion named Afraic, in the unidentified church of Imleach Tuaiscirt.[1] He does not appear to be connected with Onchú, another poet's descendant, who was a noted collector of relics. The saint's name may be a variant of Aodhán.

1 *CGSH* §670.76.

Adhlann daughter of Rónán. *See* Osnad.

Adhlann of Derry. According to one notice of his death, Adhlann (†950) son of Éigneachán, abbot of Derry, was the Guaire Aidhne of the clergy of Ireland, which means that he was noted for his hospitality.[1] His pedigree, which is found only in later recensions of the corpus of saints' genealogies, attaches him to the Ceinéal Lughdhach branch of Ceinéal Conaill, and makes him a brother of Domhnall, eponymous ancestor of the O'Donnells (Uí Dhomhnaill).[2] He reputedly lived, therefore, at a time when this family, which held the equivalent of the barony of Kilmacrenan, was beginning to attain the status that eventually led to its position as the most powerful group in Ceinéal Conaill. No feastday is known for the saint.

1 *AFM s.a.* 950. 2 *CGSH* §662.22; *GRSH* 38; *Lgen.* 698.6.

Ádhnach of Leitir Dalláin, probably in or near the townland of Kildallan (Ceall Dalláin), parish of Kildallan, barony of Tullyhunco, Co. Cavan.[1] The saint's pedigree attaches him through his father Urchaol (Earc) to a branch of the Ceinéal Mic Caorthainn of the territory known as Oirghialla, later approximately the equivalent of the diocese of Clogher.[2] The saint's name may derive from Aodh, and the proximity of Kildallan to the adjoining parish of Drumlane, a centre of the cult of Maodhóg (from *Mo-Aodh-óg*), suggests that Ádhnach's cult originated as a localization of that of his better-known namesake. The saint's feastday has not been recorded.

1 *CGSH* p. 327; *Lgen.* Iv, 462. 2 *CGSH* §57; *GRSH* 66; *Lgen.* 713.12; *CGH* 141a51.

Adomnán. *See* Adhamhnán.

Adhuar of Ossory. Were it not for a single annal for the year 810, which credits Adhuar with a law concerning cattle, promulgated in Munster, the genealogies would be the only source of information on this saint.[1] The connection with a law named after him is borne out by a marginal gloss added by the Book of Leinster scribe to the entry on Adhuar in the Osraighe (Ossory) section of the secular genealogies, which reads: *Adhuar ... qui fecit an cháin*, 'Adhuar who made the law'.[2] The saint's Osraighe descent provides him with a father named Eichean(n) and attaches him to a family which held lands in Uí Fhairchealláin, now Offerlane in Laois.[3] The Laois connection is confirmed by a second pedigree which makes him a nephew of Adhuar, eponymous ancestor of Síol Adhuair (seed of Adhuar), a branch of the local ruling family.4 The saint's name probably derives from *adh* + *uar*, 'very cold'. Neither his church nor his feastday is known.

1 *AI s.a.* 2 *CGH* 129a29; *Celtica* 21, 562–6. 3 *CGSH* §277; *GRSH* 93. 4 *CGH* 127b5.

Áed / Áedán. *See* Aodh / Aodhán.

Áedgein. *See* Aoidhghin.

Afraic of Clonfad (Cluain Fada i nUíbh Cuilinn), parish of Offerlane, barony of Upperwoods, Co. Laois. A daughter of Cumhlachtach, this saint is twice mentioned in the list of persons subject to Brighid of Kildare.[1] In one case, she accompanies Ádhán, descendant of the poet, at the unidentified church of Imleach Tuaiscirt; in the other, she is one of several saints attached to Clonfad. The name, also written Af(f)rica, and presumably a borrowing of Latin *Africa*, was otherwise borne by the only two abbesses of Kildare to have adopted non-Irish names, one of whom died in 743, the other in 834.[2] One of these was probably the daughter of Cumhlachtach.

1 *CGSH* §670.47.76; *DIB* i,40. 2 *AU s.a.*

Aghadán. This saint was one of seven sons of Aonghas, said to have come to Ireland from Scotland, and in keeping with this tradition, his pedigree attaches him to the tribal grouping of Dál Riada which had settlements in both countries.[1] Various churches, mainly located in the Midlands, are assigned to the seven brothers, with that of Aghadán, an (unidentified) *díseart*, 'hermitage', lying on the river Inny in Westmeath. Aghadán's feast of 12 June is recorded only in the seventeenth-century Martyrology of Donegal, where he joins three of his brothers, Torannán, Mochuille, and Troscán.[2] As a poem on the brothers is attributed to Colum Cille, the proximity of their feast to that of Colum (9 June) points to a possible association of churches. The saint's name, diminutive in form, is otherwise unattested.

1 *CGSH* §§209, 701.5; *GRSH* 80; *Lgen.* 721.8; *Ériu* 32, 95–114, at 106–7, 112. 2 *MartD* 166–8.

Aghna of Drumadart (Druim Dá Dhart), parish of Inver, barony of Banagh, Co. Donegal. The patron of this parish was Náile, but neither Aghna nor either of her two sisters, Caisin and Laoighseach, is mentioned in this saint's Life.[1] All three siblings were remembered, however, at Drumadart on 22 May, and recalled with them on this day was Conall, patron of the adjoining parish of Inishkeel.[2] A second saint named Aghna, commemorated on 18 May, probably echoes, as has been suggested elsewhere, an entry in the corresponding list of Hieronymian saints.[3] In a note to the index provided by Míchéal Ó Cléirigh to his martyrology, John Colgan described this latter Aghna, whom he evidently took to be Irish, as a daughter of Eoghan son of Tál.[4]

1 *MHH* 97–155. 2 *MartG* 102. 3 *MartG* 330. 4 *MartD* 354; *GRSH* 105.

Aghorogus of Ballybogan. *See* Ciarán of Errigal.

Aidan. *See* Aodhán; Maodhóg.

Aídbe. *See* Aoidhbhe.

Aifín of the now obsolete 'Killafeen' (Ceall Aifín) in the townland of Laragh, parish of Mullinacuff, barony of Shillelagh, Co. Wicklow.[1] Aifín's church is featured in the vernacular Lives of Caoimhghin as a place of assembly, allegedly often visited by Caoimhghin, which implies that it belonged to the *paruchia* of Glendalough.[2] Aifín is also included, under the guise of 'Affinus, a Frank', among the forty saints said by a litany to have been with Caoimhghin at Glendalough.[3] In the list of those commemorated on 3 June he is accompanied not only by Caoimhghin, but also by Glúnshalach – a reformed outlaw likewise associated with Glendalough – and Moninne of Killevy (Ceall Shléibhe) whose main feast fell on 6 July.[4] Aifín and Glúnshalach are again brought together by Conchobhrán, Moninne's biographer, who credits the patron of Killevy with the saint's conversion.[5] Far from being a Frank, Aifín was, according to Moninne's biographer, Glúnshalach's nephew, in which case he would have belonged, like his uncle, to the tribal grouping of Dál nAraidhe of north Down and south Antrim. The saint's name is sometimes written Aiféan.

1 *HDGP* iii, 122; cf. *PNCW* 36. 2 *BNÉ* 129 §3, 149–50 §16, 162–3 §§27, 29; *CPPI* 119, 188. 3 *IrL* 56. 4 *MartT* 47; *MartG* 108; *MartD* 144. 5 *PRIA* 28C12, §§10–11; *CGSH* §119; *Celtica* 5, 48.

Aighleann of Killiney (Ceall Inghean Léinín), barony of Rathdown, Co. Dublin. This saint was one of seven daughters of Léinín, the others being Machain, Luidhean, Druighean, Luiceall, Rímhtheach, and Brighid.[1] Her much better-known brother, Colmán, was patron of the church and diocese of Cloyne. Together with her sisters, Aighleann was patron of Killiney. Unlike her sisters, however, who are said to have remained virgins, Aighleann reputedly gave birth to three sons of Eacha of Ceinéal Laoghaire (now approximately the Meath baronies of Navan), namely Fiontan of Slanore, Colum (Colmán) of Myshall, and Lughaidh of Teernacreeve.[2] Aighleann and her sisters were commemorated on 6 March under the collective guise of Ingheana Léinín.[3] One of her sisters, Brighid, is locally regarded as patron of two ecclesiastical sites in the diocese of Cloyne: *Teampall Brighde* in the Cork parish of Buttevant, a few miles from the church of Kilmaclenine which takes name from Brighid's brother, Colmán son of Léinín; and Britway in the barony of Barrymore.[4] Another sister, Machain, alias 'Machua', is described as patron of Shanagarry in the parish of Kilmahon (probably from Irish Ceall Mhachain) in a late eighteenth-century list of Cloyne parishes.[5]

1 *CGSH* §§160.1.2, 215.2. 2 Ibid. §722.31. 3 *MartT* 21; *MartG* 48; *MartD* 68. 4 *CCS* 126; *PRC* 28, 50. 5 *CPR* i, lxviii; *HMDC* 10.

Ailbhe of Emly (Imleach Iobhair), barony of Clanwilliam, Co. Tipperary. As patron of Emly, Ailbhe son of Olc Náis (Olga) was attached to Munster's most important early church, and was thus the southern province's premier saint, whence the saying: *Mumha uile … iar gcúl Ailbhe*, 'all Munster … behind Ailbhe'.[1] With the establishment of dioceses in the early twelfth century, and the rise to ecclesiastical prominence of Cashel, he was adopted as patron of the archdiocese of Cashel and Emly.[1] Despite being referred to as *alter Patricius*, 'second Patrick', Ailbhe – whose real origins are obscure and probably pre-Christian – ranked among the so-called pre-Patrician saints who, apparently because of Munster pretensions to ecclesiastical primacy, were held to have already evangelized the south of Ireland before Patrick's time.[2] Much of the saint's record reflects southern ecclesiastical politics. His pedigrees variously attach him to the Dulraighe and Taograighe, both of which were hereditary ecclesiastical families at Emly, and among his immediate ancestors was a son of Dail (Dula) named Olga Cráibhtheach, 'pious'.[3] His mother Sant is said also to have given birth to Colmán, a son of Aonghas son of Nadh Fraoich, king of Munster.[4] His paternal family was provided with a remote descent from the Dál nAraidhe of Ulster, possibly based opportunistically on the similarity between this tribal name and Araidh, which was used of a people and territory close to Emly.

The saint's Life, which survives in both vernacular and Latin versions, likewise attributes to him a visit to Dál nAraidhe, where he is said to have founded his first church at Kilroot (Ceall Ruaidh) in Antrim.[5] The version of the saint's Life in the *Codex Salmanticensis* forms part of the so-called O'Donohue Lives which are considered by some scholars to date to 750–850, or even earlier.[6] This dating is not universally accepted, however, and the saint's alleged visits to Rome and Wales, which account for eighteen of the Life's fifty-five chapters, argue against an early date.[7] Several episodes contain details that appear to reflect familiarity with the corpus of Irish saints' pedigrees, whose manuscript transmission begins with the Psalter of Cashel in the early eleventh century.[8] The choice of the two Irish saints selected to meet Ailbhe in Rome, Déaglán of Ardmore and Colmán son of Daráine, may depend on an assertion in the surviving corpus that one of these two 'brothers' was also regarded as a uterine sibling of the Emly saint.[9] Finally, while in Wales, Ailbhe is said to have prophesied David's sanctity when the latter was still in his mother's womb, arguably borrowing in the process a motif that occurs in Rhygyfarch's Life of David, which was written shortly before 1100.[10]

Back in Ireland, while first settled in his 'ancestral' Dál nAraidhe, Ailbhe is seen to perform a series of miracles, somewhat clumsily knitted together in the Salamancan text, which involved visits to the Liffey plain, among other places, and encounters with Brighid of Kildare.[11] A return to Munster follows, beginning with a visit to Cashel, where the saint meets several noted persons. These include: his maternal relative, Aonghas son of Nadh Fraoich, who appoints him as 'father' of all the men of Munster, a situation first brought about historically by his patronage of the archdiocese of Cashel and Emly in the twelfth century; Bishop Iobhar, who shows deference to him, presumably out of regard for Iobhar's perceived place in the name (Imleach Iobhair) of Ailbhe's principal foundation; Éanna, whom he assists in obtaining permission from Aonghas to settle in Aran, evidently on the assumption that the island lay within the jurisdiction of the king of Cashel; and a certain Bishop Cianán, apparently of Duleek, with whom, in accordance with angelic instructions, he chooses the place of his resurrection at Emly.[12]

The remainder of the Life revolves around the saint's relations with mainly Munster churches and their saints, such as Mac Reithe, described as his 'pupil', Sciath of Ardskeagh, Moghobóg of Kinsale, and Neasán of Mungret, who, in a show of deference that would be unexpected in an early text, visits Ailbhe.[13] He is also brought outside of Munster to Connacht, where his cult was represented by his namesake and double, Ailbhe (Oilbhe) son of Rónán, patron of the Sligo church of Shancough, and in one short chapter, reference is made to a prospective ocean-voyage to the island of Thule (Tele) for which, perhaps in line with the notion of the *stabilitas* required of monks, not to mention the requirement to be 'steady, not restless' in the rule attributed to the saint, he is here refused permission by Aonghas, king of Cashel.[14]

Ailbhe's reputation as a pilgrim to the 'Land of Promise' is otherwise attested in the so-called second litany of Irish saints, in the Life of Mac Reithe, and in the secular tale of the voyage of the Uí Chorra.[15] No doubt because of the importance of his churches, first Emly, then Cashel – which is shown among many other ways by the proclamation of his *cáin*, 'ecclesiastical law', over Munster in the late eighth century – the saint also figured prominently in other saints' Lives, at home and abroad.[16] Patrick's circuit of Munster, as reported in his ninth-century Tripartite Life, brought the Armagh saint to Emly, where he is said to have involved Ailbhe in one of his miracles.[17] Rhygyfarch, the late eleventh-century biographer of David of Menevia, who was probably aware of the leading role of Ailbhe's successors in the preparations for the twelfth-century reform in Ireland, assigned to the 'bishop of Munster' the symbolically important task of baptizing David.[18] The monks of the *Schottenklöster* in Germany and Austria, who were predominantly recruited in Munster, also took an interest in Ailbhe's cult, germanicizing his name as Albert, in which guise he was later brought back to Ireland to join Ailbhe as co-patron of the archdiocese of Cashel and Emly.[19] The saint's biographers etymologized his name as a compound of *ail*, 'rock', and *beo*, 'live', and it has been suggested more recently that the root element may be Celtic *alb^{h}o*, 'white'.[20] Locally, the name was anglicized as 'Elly' and 'Ailbe' (pronounced 'Ale-bee').[21]

Ailbhe is said to have died in either 527, 534 or 542, supposedly on the same night as Tuathal Maol Garbh, king of Tara, and about the same time as several other saints.[22] His feastday oscillated between 10 and (principally) 12 September.[23] As Albert, he was, however, remembered at Cashel on 8 January in line with his place in the Great Austrian Legendary.[24] After death, Ailbhe was thought to have remained efficacious, as is shown by the vengeance he allegedly wrought in 1123 on a person who stormed his church at Emly and burnt his gapped bell-shrine, the *Bearnán Ailbhe*.[25] His name is invoked in both Stowe Missal litanies, and his role as defender of Munster is exemplified in a prophetic poem, which describes how he expels hordes of Saxons.[26]

1 *CGSH* §729.3; *BiblSS* i, 635–7. **2** *SSS* 376–99; cf. *SGS* 3, 75 §2. **3** *CGSH* §135; *GRSH* 110; *Lgen.* 731.7; *CGH* 119a13, 326h8. **4** *CGSH* §722.59. **5** *VSHH* 118–31, at 123–4 §22; *VSHP* i, xxviii–xxxi, 46–64, at 53–4 §20; *IrR* 16, 814–16; *SPW* 227–43; *Kenney* 527; *BAil.* 72 §22. **6** *MISL* 329, 390; *PMIS* 79–90; *CeltC* 182. **7** *VSHH* 119–23 §§4–21; *VSHP* i, 47–54 §§4–19; *BAil.* 60–72 §§4–21. **8** *CGSH* xiii–xlvii. **9** Ibid. §§107, 722.59. **10** *VSHH* 123 §21; *VSHP* i, 53 §19; *VSBG* 152 §5; *BAil.* 70–2 §21. **11** *VSHH* 124 §§23–7; *VSHP* i, 54 §21; *BAil.* 72–4 §§23–7. **12** *VSHH* 124–6 §§29–34; *VSHP* i, 54–8 §§22–30; *Éigse* 9, 18–29; *BAil.* 74–8 §§29–34. **13** *BAil.* 78–86 §§36–50; *VSHH* 126–30 §§36–50; *VSHP* i, 58–62 §§31–42. **14** *LSLC* 291–302; *VSHH* 129 §49; *VSHP* i, 61 §41; *Ériu* 3, 96 §7; *BAil.* 86 §49. **15** *IrL* 62; *MHH* 17–18 §§16–19; *Imm.* 108 §21; *CeltC* 182–9. **16** *AI s.a.* 784; *AU s.a.* 793; VSHP ii, 69–70 §§21–2. **17** *BP* 2331–3; *VT* 198.

18 *VSBG* 153 §7. **19** *EMMAHS* 21. **20** *VSHH* 118 §2; *VSHP* i, 47 §1; *GPN* 16; *BAil.* 58 §2. **21** OSL TY iii, 122. **22** *AU s.a.*; *IrT* iii, 84 §5; *LUM* 154rb 29–30. **23** *MartT* 70; *MartO*² 194; *MartG* 174; *MartD* 244–6; OSL TY iii, 182. **24** *IER* (2nd ser.) 4, 90. **25** *AU s.a*; *EMH* 484 §220. **26** HBS 32, 14–15; *EAB* 719 §§15–16.

Ailbhe of Shancough (Seanchua), barony of Tirerrill, Co. Sligo. This son of Rónán is described by Tíreachán, the seventh-century biographer of Patrick, as the first priest to have been ordained west of the Shannon.[1] The holding of the pattern-day at 'Tobar Eilibh', the well of Ailbhe (locally thought to have been a female) in the townland of Derrysallagh, near Shancough, on 10 September implies, however, that he was ultimately identical with Ailbhe of Emly.[2] This is supported by the fact that Mac Treana, patron of the neighbouring parish of Kilmactranny, is provided with a genealogy that likewise associates him with the church of Emly.[3]

Some time after its foundation about 1215, the Premonstratensian priory of Holy Trinity on Lough Key was given possession of the churches of Shancough and Kilmactranny, together with the more important Kilronan, and the management of these churches and their lands was entrusted to the hereditary erenagh family of Uí Dhuibhgeannáin (O'Duignans) of Kilronan.[4] Despite its early importance, Shancough in Tirerrill appears to have been the least of the three church properties held by this family, as is shown by the fact that the O'Duignan Life of Lasair of Kilronan, although finding room for Mac Treana, ignores both Shancough and its saint.[5] In keeping with the tendency of the O'Duignans to establish the best possible connections for the churches under their care, Ailbhe of Shancough eventually acquired yet another identity. In a note to Patrick's Tripartite Life, John Colgan identified the saint as a son of Rónán, otherwise recorded both in the metrical recension of the genealogies of the saints and in *Genealogiae Regum et Sanctorum Hiberniae*.[6] This latter descent had the effect of attaching Ailbhe to the line of Conall Gulban, ancestor of 'Muintir Dhomhnaill', the O'Donnells of Donegal, the second most important branch of the whole northern nobility.[7]

The annals date the saint's death to 542, and a feastday of 30 January, already associated with the cult of a priest named Ailbhe in an early martyrology, was assigned to the son of Rónán in seventeenth-century sources.[8] In the saint's guise as a female, she assumed traits associated with Brighid of Kildare, including the plucking out of her eyes to dissuade a suitor.[9] 'St Eliva', who is venerated at Toberelva in the Roscommon parish of Baslick, probably also represents this cult.[10]

1 *PTBA* 138 §19.5. **2** OSL SO 237. **3** *CGH* 326h16; *AnH* 12, 107, 109. **4** *MRHI* 205; *CBC* 129, 154. **5** *Ériu* 5, 90–2. **6** *TT* 89, 113; cf. pp 183, 226; *CGSH* §662.18; *GRSH* 38. **7** *LSLC* 291–302. **8** *MartT* 13; *MartG* 26; *MartD* 30; *GRSH* 38; ATig. *s.a.*; *Ériu* 48, 108. **9** *Béaloideas* 2, 56–7. **10** *OSL RN* i, 165.

Ailearán. *See* Oilearán.

Ailfinus of 'Tegnagomark' (Teach na Comairche), the now obsolete name of a church in the parish of Clonleigh, barony of Raphoe, Co. Donegal. This man is known from two sources, one of which appears to derive from the other. The earlier source, a litany of Irish saints, describes him as a holy pilgrim (*oilithir*) at Teach na Comairche.[1] Its probable derivative, a miscellaneous entry in the corpus of saints' genealogies, locates Teach na Comairche in Maigh Íotha, now the part of Raphoe barony containing Clonleigh.[2] The saint's name, which is Latin in form, may derive from Ailbhe. The Emly saint of this latter name was also a noted pilgrim and, as is shown by the history of Ailbhe son of Rónán, the cult of the southern saint appears to have spread northwards, at least as far as north Connacht. An early seventeenth-century description of the diocese of Derry names the patron of the Donegal church as 'Aghenagus'.[3]

1 *IrL* 62, 64. 2 *CGSH* §171. 3 *AnH* 12, 107, 109.

Ailill. *See* Oilill.

Aillén. *See* Oilléan.

Ailtín. *See* Eiltín.

Ainmhire. Several minor saints of this name figure in the record, with feastdays accorded to four. These are attached to the following sites: Oileach (10 June), possibly at or near the royal residence of the Uí Néill in the parish of Clonmany, barony of Inishowen, Co. Donegal; Cluain Fada (15 September), now Clonfad in the parish of Killucan, barony of Farbill, Co. Westmeath; Ros Ó gConna (25 September) in Mughdhorna, now Cremorne barony, Co. Monaghan; and Ráith Nua (2 November), now probably Rathnew, barony of Newcastle, Co. Wicklow.[1] The last-mentioned is attested only in the seventeenth-century Martyrology of Donegal, which tended to draw identifications from the annals, in this case possibly from an entry for 779 which notes the obit of Ainmhire, abbot of Rathnew.[2]

1 *MartT* 71; *MartG* 114, 176, 184, 210. 2 *MartD* 164, 248, 258, 292; *AU s.a.*

Ainmhire of Kilroe (Ceall Ró), parish of Killala, barony of Tirawley, Co. Mayo. This saint was one of seven sons of Draighean, the others being Eothach, Mac Earca (Ciair), Drugán, Fíonán, Faolán, and Meachar.[1] Though no location is provided for Ainmhire, he and his brothers are said to have been baptized by Patrick when the latter was in Tír Amhalghadha, now approximately the Mayo barony of Tirawley.[2] One brother (Mac Earca) is singled out for special mention in the same passage in association with the church of Kilroe, and it is to this church that the sons of Draighean as a group are attached on their feastday of 15 April.[3] Elsewhere, in a text dealing mainly with north Connacht, two of the brothers (Eothach and Meachar) are cited in a passage that outlines agreements made by Cormac of Killala, and in the same text the brothers as a group are said to have given their blessing to Killala Bay.[4] Ainmhire may be the same as his namesake in Uí Oilealla (whence the Sligo barony of Tirerrill, adjoining Tirawley), who is said to have offered himself and his *reigléas*, 'church', at Drumcolumb (Druim Eidir Dhá Loch) to Finnian of Clonard.[5]

1 *CGSH* §364. 2 *BP* 1609–13; *VT* 140. 3 *MartT* 33; *MartG* 76; *MartD* 102. 4 *IrT* iii, 4, §9, 6 §16. 5 *LisL* 2696–704.

Aithche. Having misread the phrase *agus a itche*, 'and his prayer', in a gloss to his exemplar at 15 January, Míchéal Ó Cléirigh created a bogus saint named Aithche whom he located at Ceall Aithche in Caonraighe (whence the barony of Kenry) in the diocese and county of Limerick, allegedly the scene of an annual feast and pattern.[1] It is not possible to say which place in Kenry is intended.[2] Ó Cléirigh is known, however, to have visited friaries near this area, such as Ennis and Quin in Clare, and he may have had in mind Íde of Killeedy whose feast fell on this day.[3]

1 *MartG* 16; *MartD* 16, 360. 2 *HDGP* iii, 125. 3 *MOC* 138–9.

Aíthghin. *See* Aoidhghin.

Aithmhead of Clochar. The martyrologies, which notice this saintly bishop at 2 February, assign him simply to Clochar, now possibly the Tyrone church of Clogher.[1] A priest of the name, and a bishop who used the diminutive form, Aithmheadán, are recorded in the lists of Irish priests and bishops.[2]

1 *MartT* 14; *MartG* 28; *MartD* 36. 2 *CGSH* §§704.232, 705.67.

Aithneann of Killannin (Ceall Aithneann), barony of Moycullen, Co. Galway. Seventeenth-century sources describe Aithneann as a virgin who enjoyed a popular feast at her church and nearby well.[1] Though the pattern was held on 18 January, there is no trace of the name in the lists of saints commemorated on this day, unless she is identical with Ana, one of four sisters commemorated at a place called Cluain Greanaigh (Greancha), now possibly Clonygrange in the Meath parish of Killaconnigan.[2] Against this, a note added to the list in the Martyrology of Tallaght for 3 September assigns Ana, together with Bláth(nad), who is also her companion at 18 January, to Slanore (Snámh Luthair) in the Cavan parish of Kilmore.[3]

1 *MartD* 360. 2 *OFWC* 54; *WLC* 175; *MartT* 9; *MartG* 18; *MartD* 20. 3 *MartT* 116.

Albert. *See* Ailbhe.

Amhaill. While in the Westmeath parish of Kilcumreragh, John O'Donovan noticed a holy well called *Tobar Amhaill*, at which stations were performed on Fridays, and especially on Good Friday.[1] Although thought by locals to be a saint, the patron of the well is otherwise unattested.

1 *PNW* 19.

Ana. *See* Aithneann.

Anfadhán. Saints of this name (also written Amphadán) are recorded in the martyrologies, in association with Glendalough (11 January), Taghmon (21 October), and Roscrea (19 December). Two of the name are also in the lists of bishops and priests preserved in the Book of Leinster.[1] A note to the variant form 'Amphadan', apparently added by John Colgan, speculatively suggested a Latin equivalent *Amphianus*.[2]

1 *MartT* 7, 82, 87; *MartG* 14, 242; *MartD* 12, 342. 2 *CGSH* §§704.194, 705.83.

Angais of Killart (Ceall Aird) in the townland of Oldcourt, parish of Kilberry, barony of Narragh and Reban West, Co. Kildare. Among the saintly virgins subject to Brighid of Kildare were three daughters of Aodh son of Eirnín, named Angais (perhaps more correctly Anghais), Dairtinne and Brónach, all of whom were attached to Killart.[1] Though Angais is not known from any other source, her sister Dairtinne is among those commemorated by the martyrologies in the list for 3 July, at Ceall Aird in Uí Earcáin, doubtless the same as Killart.[2] It was to her family (Fothairt) that Brighid also belonged. As this family gave name to the Wexford barony of Forth, the seven daughters of Aodh, who were patrons of a chapel in the parish of Ballybrennan, may also represent this cult.[3] One of the seven, Sineach (Innick) by name, was also patron of the adjoining Wexford parishes of Killinick and Kilscoran.[4] A namesake of Angais, described as a daughter of Breasal and located in the unidentified church of Cruach Angais, was remembered on 12 November.[5]

1 *CGSH* §670.9; **2** *MartT* 53; *MartG* 128; *MartD* 186; *HDGP* iii, 124. **3** *The Past* 2, 59. **4** Ibid. **5** *MartG* 216; *MartD* 306.

Angán of Míleac Fiaich. Patron of an unidentified church, possibly in Laois, this saint is one of seven children credited to Damhradh daughter of Oilill Fionn, whose father (Aodh Rón, king of Uí Fhailghe) was slain in 604.[1] The other sons were named Cuán, Conbhran, Colmán, Cas, Tnuán, and Mobheagóg. The Uí Fhailghe held lands mainly in east Offaly and west Kildare, but also in north Laois, where there are three townlands named Meelick. Angán's church must have been a place of some substance in which, according to a litany, there were seven holy bishops, probably the seven sons of Damhradh.[2] The first-named of Damhradh's seven children, Cuán, may be the same as Mochua of Míleac, who is mentioned in a note to the *Leabhar Breac* version of the Martyrology of Aonghas.[3]

1 *CGSH* §722.83; *AU s.a.* **2** *IrL* 68. **3** *MartO*[1] l.

Aodh. There are numerous saints of this name, in one or other of its variant forms, including Aodhán, Aoidhghin, Maodhóg, Taodhóg and, probably, Ádhán, Ádhnach, and the feminine Aodhamair (Ádhamair). The most common forms of the name when used of saints are, however, Aodh, Aodhán, and Maodhóg. As the name derives from Celtic **aidos*, 'fire', a meaning still preserved in Early Irish *áed*, the origins of the cult associated with it lie in pre-Christian times.[1] The Celtic Aedui of Gaul were named after their ancestral fire-god, and many Irish deities bore the name, including Aodh of Síodh Aodha, at Ballyshannon in Donegal, Aodh son of the Daghdha, chief of the Tuatha Dé Danann, Aodh son of Aodh of the same group, and Aodh (alias Goll) son of Morna. One (ultimately pre-Christian) bearer of the name, Aodh Eangach, the long-awaited saviour of Ireland, who is already mentioned in the Old Irish tale, *Baile an Scáil*, is said to have bestowed land in the territory of Uí Néill on Aodh of Rahugh.[2] As this saint had a close association with Slieve League in south Donegal, his origins were probably linked to the ancestral divinity of this area, reflected locally not only in the name Síodh Aodha at Ballyshannon, but also in Tír Aodha, now Tirhugh barony. Many saints of the name are distinguished only by their churches.

1 *EIHM* 148, 320; *VSHP* i, xxviii. 2 ITS 58, §62.

Aodh of Aghadooey (Achadh Dumha), parish and barony of Burrishoole, Co. Mayo, and of Glenavy (Lann Abhaigh), barony of Upper Masserene, Co. Antrim. A son of Colga, this saint is known both from the list of homonymous saints and – under the guise of Taodh (Taodhóg) and Aodhán – from two separate entries in the martyrologies, at 31 January and 6 November.[1] As Aodh's January feast coincides with that of Maodhóg of Ferns, it may be inferred that the saint's cult was a localized version of that of his south Leinster namesake. The cult appears later to have been supplanted at Aghadooey by that of Bearóg, who was remembered locally at a well (*Tobar Bhearóige*) and bed (*Leabaidh Bhearóige*).[2] Despite being treated as a female in Aghadooey, the latter saint is probably the same as Dobhearóg, patron of Kildavaroge in the neighbouring parish of Crossmolina, who may have been ultimately identical with Bearach of Kilbarry in Roscommon.

1 *CGSH* §707.25; *MartT* 13; *MartG* 26, 212; *MartD* 32, 298. 2 OSL MO ii, 8.

Aodh of Aughrim, parish of Dysert, barony of Inchiquin, Co. Clare. A church in the townland of Aughrim was named *Teampall Aodha mhic Conaill*, but no local memory of the patron survived.[1] As churches sometimes took their names from secular rulers – for example, Cormac's Chapel on the Rock of Cashel – the person intended here may be Aodh son of Conall of Dál gCais, coincidentally the first of that sept said to have gone to Cashel.[2]

1 OSL CE, 54. 2 *CoC* 14.

Aodh of Drumkerrill. *See* Maodhóg of Ferns.

Aodh of Drumshinny. *See* Maodhóg of Ferns.

Aodh of Eachradh. *See* Aodhán of Eachradh.

Aodh of Forenaghts, barony of South Salt, Co. Kildare, which may represent an earlier Imleach Fornochta. Aodh son of Cormac of Imleach Fornochta and his son Iollann figure in the list of saints said to have been subject to Brighid.[1] He may be identical with Aodh of Rahugh, likewise an associate of Brighid, whose father's name was also rendered Cormac Breac, and whose feast of 4 May was within the octave of the feast of Aodh of Forenaghts (10 May).[2]

1 *CGSH* §670.62; OSL KE i, 66. 2 *CGSH* §9; *MartT* 41; *MartG* 94; *MartD* 124; *CGSH* §670.62; *VSHH* 168–9 §§3–7.

Aodh of Foyran (Faoibhréan), barony of Fore, Co. Westmeath. The feast of this son of Raoi is recorded in the martyrologies at 1 November.[1] As the patron of the parish was Aodh of Rahugh, whose Life brings him to the area about Foyran, the two are almost certainly identical, as is also suggested by the proximity of their feasts, with that of Aodh of Rahugh falling on 10 November.[2] Locally, the saint of Foyran was also known as Aodhán (Edan).[3]

1 *MartG* 208; *MartD* 292. 2 *VSHH* 176 §§29, 31. 3 *PNW* 48–9; *ILL* 247.

Aodh of Inis Beoaidh (perhaps also Inis Beoáin), parish of Feighcullen, baronies of Connell and East Offaly, Co. Kildare. A son of Foirtchearn, this saint, together with three others (Cairbre, Pól and Deineath), is said to have been subject to Brighid at Inis Beoaidh.[1] This place was close to Kildare, and even closer to the church of Kilmeage (Ceall Maodhóg, earlier Cluain Domhail), which took its name from Aodhán, a probable double of Aodh son of Foirtchearn.[2]

1 *CGSH* §670.39. 2 Ibid. §230; *CathA* 3 §4, 37.

Aodh of Kilcrow (Ceall Chraoi), parish of Churchtown, barony of Narragh and Reban West, Co. Kildare. A son of Criomhthann, this saint is one of a group of six attached to the church of Kilcrow.[1] Other members of the group were Crotha daughter of Brión, Cormac the deacon, Gobán son of Cormac, Conmhac son of Criomhthann (probably Aodh's brother), and Crunnmhaol son of Rónán, the only one otherwise attested.

1 *CGSH* §367.1.2; *HDGP* iii, 150.

Aodh of Killare. *See* Aodh of Rahugh.

Aodh of Killeenmore (Ceall Iain Mhóir), parish of Whitechurch, barony of Naas North, Co. Kildare. Allegedly a bishop, Aodh is said to have been one of fourteen children (seven sons and seven daughters) of Muireadhach son of Foirtchearn of the Déise Breagh, a group that gave name to the Meath baronies of Deece.[1] The sisters are unnamed, but the saint's brothers are variously called Mainchín, Diarmuid, Taircheall, Faobharchú, Cainne, and Mac Laisre. The three churches assigned to members of the family were located in the north-east corner of Kildare, close to the southern boundary of the barony of Deece Upper, at Killeenmore, Killeenbeg (Ceall Iain Bhig) in the parish of Kill, and Oughterard (Uachtar Aird).[2] Eithne daughter of Ian, eponym of Killeen (Ceall Iain), is said to have dwelt at Oughterard.

1 *CGSH* §88.1.2; *CGH* 144c6; *GRSH* 76; *Lgen.* 718.10. 2 *CGSH* §§87, 88.2.

Aodh of Killerrig. *See* Aodh of Sleaty.

Aodh of Kilmeage. *See* Aodhán of Kilmeage.

Aodh of Lisgoole (Gabhal Mhucraighe/Lios Gabhla), parish of Rossorry, barony of Clanawley, Co. Fermanagh. A son of Guaire and reputedly a bishop, this saint is first in the list of those belonging to the Clann Lughdhach, whose patrimony is said to have stretched from Lough Erne to Slieve Bloom.[1] Aodh's church at Lisgoole, near Lough Erne, was later the site of a Franciscan friary.[2] The saint's feast of 25 January is shared by Fuinche, and it may be no coincidence that a saint of the latter name was attached to the neighbouring church of Rossorry.[3] On 31 January, within the octave of Aodh's commemoration, fell the feast of a much more important representative of the cult, Maodhóg of Ferns, who had many associations with the area about Lough Erne.[4] Aodh son of Guaire is thus likely to have been a localized version of Maodhóg. In his own right, however, he was possibly invoked, as Bishop Aodh, in a poem on Oirghialla, a territory approximately the equivalent of the later diocese of Clogher, unless, as has also been suggested, this was Aodh of Rahugh.[5]

1 *CGSH* §690.1; *BB* 87eb. **2** *MRHI* 254. **3** *MartT* 13; *MartG* 22; *MartD* 26; *CGSH* §690.2. **4** *BNÉ* ii, 357n. **5** *Ériu* 16, 183 §42; *KLT* 138 §42, 220.

Aodh of Rahugh (Ráith Aodha), barony of Moycashel, Co. Westmeath, and also patron of both Killare (Ceall Áir), barony of Rathconrath, Co. Westmeath, and Slieve League (Sliabh Liag), parish of Glencolumbkille, barony of Banagh, Co. Donegal. In line with the location of his principal church at Rahugh, Aodh is provided through his father Breac (Cormac Breac) with a descent from Fiacha (son of Niall Naoighiallach), eponym of the Ceinéal Fiachach of Moycashel, with the added distinction of being the only saint attached to this group.[1] His connection with Donegal led, however, to his occasional inclusion among the saints of Ceinéal Boghaine (whence Banagh barony), and from this may also derive the tradition of a close relationship between him and Colum Cille, eponym of Glencolumbkille.[2] In the corpus of saints' pedigrees, Aodh's descent follows immediately on that of Colum Cille, who is elsewhere said both to have directed the saint to his Donegal church and also to have miraculously learned of his death.[3] Given the presence of Síodh Aodha (at Ballyshannon) and Tír Aodha (Tirhugh) at no great distance from Slieve League, the saint's more remote origins probably lay in a pre-Christian ancestral role.[4]

Aodh's church of Rahugh was the only one of his foundations to command the attention of the annalists, who cover its activities in a number of entries, extending from 776 to 1246, one of which refers to the holding there in 859 of a *ríoghdháil*, 'royal assembly', of the nobles of Ireland, attended by both king of Tara and abbot of Armagh.[5] The text of the saint's Life, which is preserved in three Latin collections, also underlines Rahugh's importance by giving it the distinction of being the only one of Aodh's churches to receive coverage of its origin legend.[6] In the Salamancan collection, the saint's Life is among the so-called O'Donohue Lives which some recent opinion is inclined to date to as early as the period 750–850.[7] Earlier opinion, however, considered Aodh's Life to be as late as the twelfth century and not to have been compiled in the saint's own church.[8] This is also the view taken here, not least because there are features of the O'Donohue Lives that point to the influence of the canons regular of St Augustine whose first foundation in Ireland dates to no earlier than the 1130s.[9] The locations of Aodh's two principal churches, at Rahugh and Killare, respectively within a few miles of the Augustinian priories of Durrow and Ballymore, point in the same direction.[10] Durrow was founded in the 1140s by Murchadh Ua Maoil Sheachlainn, *ardrí*, 'high-king', of Midhe (mainly Westmeath) who died there in 1153, and this may explain why Aodh's biographer attached the saint to the Uí Néill rather than to the more local dynasty of Ceinéal Fiachach.[11]

In keeping with an assertion that the saint's mother Eithne belonged to the Múscraighe Tíre of Ormond in north-west Tipperary, Aodh, having been born according to another source at Killare, is said by his biographer to have spent his youth with her, in the process meeting with two other patrons of Augustinian priories, Cainneach – whose own Life features an encounter with a much more mature Aodh – and Bréanainn, before returning to his *patria* at the church of a man named Iollann, probably at Ráith Liphitean, now Rathlihen in the Offaly parish of Killoughy, where he performed a number of miracles.[12] Leaving Iollann, he founded his first church at a place called Eanach Midhbhréan, *in terra Munnensium* (recte *Mumensium*), 'in the lands of the Munstermen', now possibly Annagh in the parish of Dorrha, close to Lorrha, the site of an Augustinian priory.[13] With his church apparently lying just south of the line thought to have divided Ireland into two halves, Aodh's early interventions at several locations south and north of the line involved tensions between Munster and the Uí Néill.[14]

Some of the miracles attributed to the saint can be traced to the influence of other sources. Aodh's reputation as a leech, for example, which is independently attested both in an early prayer against headache invoking his name and in an episode in the ninth-century vernacular Life of Brighid of Kildare, is exemplified here by reference not only to an unnamed local, but also to his cure of Brighid (now patron of Killare) whose well at the base of the Hill of Ushnagh adjoins the remains of Aodh's church.[15] The saint's next intervention, which brought about the birth of Aodh Sláine, head of a powerful southern Uí Néill dynasty, to a previously barren queen of Tara, is elsewhere attested in additions to a birth-tale preserved in the late eleventh- or early twelfth-century codex *Leabhar na hUidhre*.[16] This manuscript was compiled and kept for some time at Clonmacnoise, the location of a house of canons regular from the mid-twelfth century onwards.[17]

The remainder of the Life widens the scope of the saint's activities to accommodate numerous other locations, mainly in the Midlands, but also in adjoining parts of Leinster, Connacht and Munster, all of them probably chosen on the basis of property interests that required protection. Several episodes focus on the district about the river Inny and Lough Leane at the northernmost tip of the present county of Westmeath, where Aodh (locally known as Aodhán/Edan) was associated with the church of Foyran (Foibhréan).[18] The saint's encounters with Ríóg of Inchbofin on Lough Ree and Éanán (alias Éanóg) of Drumraney probably reflect the proximity of the churches of both to Aodh's church of Killare.[19] Towards the end of the text, Aodh is brought on a visit to Molaise at Devenish, the site of a priory of canons regular founded about 1130–40, and the saint spends his last days at Rahugh *in orientali parte Midi*, 'in the eastern part of Midhe'. His death which (despite the tradition that he was 'undying') is assigned to the year 589, is said to have become immediately known to Colum Cille on Iona.[20]

A late poem attributed to Colum Cille refers to Aodh as a bishop *ón tsliabh*, 'from Slieve (League)'.[21] Some traditions of the saint survived until the early nineteenth century at Killare, especially in connection with the circumstances of his birth, allegedly on a hollowed stone 'in the shape of a head'.[22] The presence of a well named *Tobar Maodhóg* in the townland of Carn, parish of Conry, adjoining Killare, would suggest that Aodh was also patron of this parish.[23] Aodh died, according to the annals in 589 and, although 10 November appears to have been the saint's principal feastday, he was also commemorated on 28 February, 4 May and 16 November.[24] A late tradition asserts that he was buried along with Tasach of Elphin at Racoon Hill in the Donegal parish of Drumhome.[25] He may also have been remembered, as Mac Bric, in Scotland.[26] Aodh's crozier is now in the National Museum.

1 *CGSH* §9; *GRSH* 56; *Lgen*. 705.1; *KLT* 219–20; *BiblSS* i, 628–9. **2** *BB* 85ba. **3** *VSHH* 181 §52; *ZCP* 12, 394 §35. **4** *EIHM* 148, 320; *VSHP* i, xxviii. **5** *AU s.a.*776, 859, *ACon*. 1246.3. **6** *VSHH* 167–81, at 180–1 §48; *VSHP* i, xxvi–xxviii, 34–45, at 44; *AS*.Nov. iv, 495–531 §34. **7** *MirL* 91–100; *MISL* 297–339; *PMIS* 79–90. **8** *Kenney* 393. **9** *MRHI* 146–56; cf. *CSI* 17–31. **10** *MRHI* 160, 174. **11** ATig. *s.a.* **12** *VSHH* 167–9 §§1–6, 190 §32; *VSHP* i, 34–6 §§1–4, 162 §27; *AS*.Nov. iv, 504–6 §§1–6; *MartD* xli. **13** *VSHH* 169 §7; *VSHP* i, 36 §4; *AS*.Nov. iv, 506 §7; cf. *MRHI* 405. **14** *VSHH* 169–73 §§8–16; *VSHP* i, 36–8 §§5–12; *AS*.Nov. iv, 507–10 §§8–16. **15** *LisL* 324; *AS*.Nov. iv, 503, 510 §17; *VSHH* 173 §17; *VSHP* i, 38–9 §13; *BBr*. 9 §26; *VSHH* 29–30 §§62–4; *ASH* 423 (31); *PNW* 21. **16** *VSHH* 173 §18; *VSHP* i, 39 §14; *AS*.Nov. iv, 510 §18; *LU* 4243–5. **17** *MRHI* 165. **18** *VSHH* 173–6 §§19–31; *VSHP* i, 39–41 §§15–23; *AS*.Nov. iv, 510–13 §§19–31; *PNW* 48–9. **19** *VSHH* 180 §§45–6; *VSHP* i, 43–4 §§31–2; *AS*.Nov. iv, 515–16 §§45–6. **20** *VSHH* 180–1 §§47–52; *VSHP* i, 44–5 §§33–6; *AS*.Nov. iv, 516–17 §§47–52; *AU s.a.*; *BL Cat*. ii, 471; *AB* 55, 285–95. **21** *ZCP* 12, 394 §35. **22** *ASH* 422 (5); *PNW* 20–2. **23** Ibid. 23. **24** *MartT* 19, 39; *MartO*^{2} 233; *MartG* 90, 214; *MartD* 120, 302, 310–11n; *AU s.a.* **25** *Béaloideas* 6, 149. **26** *CPNS* 166.

Aodh of Sleaty (Sléibhte), barony of Slievemargy, Co. Laois. This saint is distinguished as much by his apparent historicity as by his Patrician connections. The notice of his death in 700 described him as an anchorite, but the martyrologists, who commemorated Aodh at 7 February, afforded him the title of bishop.[1] The latter title is also supplied by Patrick's biographer Muirchú, who avowedly wrote 'at the request of Aodh, bishop of the see of Sléibhte'.[2] He is said to have brought his testament to Patrick's successor Séighín (†688), bestowing his church in Leinster on Armagh 'till Doom'.[3] This action has been variously interpreted: as an attempt to win over the northern church to Roman practice respecting Easter; as an indication that Armagh had already adopted Roman practice under Séighín; or simply as an assertion of Sleaty's independence of Brighid's *paruchia* in Leinster.[4] Aodh is also included among the church dignitaries who, led by Flann Feabhla, bishop of Armagh, endorsed the Law of Adhamhnán.[5] The popularity of the saint may have led to the localization of his cult at other churches, such as Killerrig (Ceall Deirge Daimh), not far from Sleaty, in the barony and county of Carlow, whose patron was also named Aodh.[6] The saint's feast, as already stated, fell on 7 February. Aodh's genealogy, which names his father as Brocán, attaches him to the Uí Bhairrche of north Carlow.[7]

1 *AU s.a.*; *MartT* 15; *MartG* 32; *MartD* 40; *DIB* i, 29; *BiblSS* i, 629–31. **2** *PTBA* 66. **3** Ibid. 1. **4** *CEIS* 115–20; *ECI* 261–2, 428–9; *CeltT* 88. **5** *CA* 16 §28; *Peritia* 1, 192. **6** *CGSH* §707.32; *HDGP* iii, 163. **7** *CGSH* §245; *BiblSS* i, 631.

Aodh of Slieve League. *See* Aodh of Rahugh.

Aodh of Teach Mic Bhric. *See* Aodh of Rahugh.

Aodh of Trim. *See* Aodh Beag of Trim.

Aodh of Uí Dhúnlainge. *See* Maodhóg of Clonmore.

Aodh son of Brocán. *See* Aodh son of Maol Odhráin.

Aodh son of Eirnín. *See* Angais.

Aodh son of Eoghan. *See* Maodhóg of Clonmore.

Aodh son of Fínghin. *See* Maoldóid of Muckno.

Aodh son of Maol Odhráin (Brocán), bishop. While differing as to the name of this saint's father, the relevant sources agree in assigning him to the Uí Bhairrche, who held lands in parts of counties Carlow and Wexford, including the area about Carlow town.[1] His attachment to this group, together with his description as bishop, suggest that he may have been a localized version of Aodh of Sleaty in Laois, a few miles north of Carlow town.

1 *CGSH* §245.

Aodh son of Miodhghna. *See* Momhaodhóg of Fiddown.

Aodh son of Mursan. This man is known from two sources, the list of homonymous saints and, under the guise of Maodhóg son of Mursan, the record of those commemorated on 17 December.[1]

1 *CGSH* §707.31; *MartT* 86; *MartG* 240; *MartD* 338.

Aodh son of Séadna. *See* Maodhóg of Ferns.

Aodh son of Seanach. A man of this name is listed among the saints of the Uí Mhaine who, reportedly at the request of Colum Cille, joined forces against Diarmuid son of Cearbhall, king of Tara, in the lead-up to the battle of Cúil Dreimhne.[1] An ostensibly different saint of the name accompanied Moling as part of a deputation from the Leinstermen to Fíonnachta Fleadhach, king of Tara, in quest of a remission of the *bóramha* tribute.[2] Despite Míchéal Ó Cléirigh, who opted for the latter, it is impossible to say which of the two was commemorated on 22 September.[3]

1 *IMN* 22, 5. 2 *SG* i, 382. 3 *MartT* 73; *MartG* 182; *MartD* 252.

Aodh the martyr. *See* Aodh Deochain.

Aodh Beag, 'little', of Trim (Áth Truim), baronies of Lower Moyfenrath and Upper Navan, Co. Meath. Both Aodh Beag (son of Fearghas) and his brother Aodh Mór are associated with the church of Trim.[1] As this church was among the offerings of Feidhlimidh son of Laoghaire (eponym of Ceinéal Laoghaire in the Meath baronies of Navan) to Lomán and Patrick, the two brothers are doubtless identical with the two bishops (Aodh *magnus* and Aodh *parvus*) who are said to have formed part of Feidhlimidh's ecclesiastical succession at Trim.[2] Their father Fearghas was thought to be Feidhlimidh's son, and their sister Lasair was attached to Clonlyon (Cluain Laighean) in the Meath parish of Kilmore.[3] Because of their identical names and church, it has been suggested that both brothers were originally one and the same.[4] Together with Lomán, the brothers were commemorated on 17 February and, according to some seventeenth-century sources, the feast of their sister fell on the following day at Clonmethan (Gleann

Meadhóin) in the Dublin barony of Balrothery West.[5] One of these sources also suggested the possible identity of this Lasair with the like-named patron of Ceall Archalgach, now perhaps an ecclesiastical site in the townland of Collinstown in the Westmeath parish of St Feighins.[6]

1 *CGSH* §690.9; *Lgen.* 707.11. 2 *PTBA* 168–70. 3 *CGSH* §690.11. 4 *JEH* 1, 165–6. 5 *MartT* 17; *MartG* 38; *MartD* 52; *GRSH* 52. 6 *GRSH* 52; *MartT* 64; *MartG* 160; *MartD* 224; *HDGP* iii, 128.

Aodh Caol, 'slender', of Trim (Áth Truim), baronies of Lower Moyfenrath and Upper Navan, Co. Meath. This son of Fearadhach was assigned, like Aodh Beag and Aodh Mór, to the church of Trim. Unlike these, however, Aodh Caol is said to have descended from Éanna son of Laoghaire, Feidhlimidh's brother.[1] Though the early ninth-century Martyrology of Tallaght allows for three saints named Aodh at Trim in its list for 17 February, Aodh Caol was remembered five days earlier, at 12 February, together with the like-named and probably identical Aodhán of Clonard (Cluain Dartadha), townland of Tullygorey in the Kildare parish of Kilberry.[2] Aodhán was reputedly accompanied at Clonard by 'Romans'.[3] In line with the tradition that represented a number of Trim ecclesiastics as married men and ancestors of other saints, Aodh Caol is said to have fathered several children.[4]

1 *CGSH* §73; *GRSH* 49; *Lgen.* 707.2. 2 *MartT* 16–17; *MartG* 34; *MartD* 46. 3 *IrL* 64. 4 *CGH* 144g45; *IA* 329.

Aodh Cobhrán. *See* Acobhrán.

Aodh Deochain, 'deacon', of Magheraculmoney (Cúil Mhaine), a parish touching Lough Erne, in the barony of Lurg, Co. Fermanagh. Aodh's attachment through his father Maine to the Colla Uais branch of the Oirghialla, as well as the location of his church, leave little doubt but that he was identical with Maodhóg of Ferns, who enjoyed a similar descent and was said to belong to the Fir Luirg (whence Lurg) on Lough Erne.[1] Aodh is assigned two feastdays, 10 July and 31 August (the same day of the month as Maodhóg's 31 January), the second of which he shares with two others of the name, an otherwise unknown Aodh the martyr and Aodhán (Aidan) of Lindisfarne.[2]

1 *CGSH* §§58, 63; *Dinn.* 2, 79–80. 2 *MartT* 55, 67; *MartG* 166; *MartD* 192, 230.

Aodh Fionn, 'fair', of Cloonard (Cluain Aird), parish of Tibohine, barony of Frenchpark, Co. Roscommon. This saint was attached through his father Caol to the Uí Oilealla, who held lands corresponding approximately to the present Sligo barony of Tirerrill.[1] Aodh Fionn and his six brothers, Seanach, Fionnoll, Dreamhan, Colmán, Fearadhach, and Feadhbhar, were known as the sons of Caolbhadh, and they are said to have occupied two churches, Cloonard in Ciarraighe Airtigh, and Imleach Gaileang in Luighne, now perhaps Emlaghfad in the Sligo barony of Corran, adjoining Leyny. The group of brothers may be identical with the sons of Caolbhadh noticed in the martyrologies at 24 April.[2] The parish named Kilcolman, adjoining Tibohine, possibly retains the name of Aodh Fionn's brother Colmán.

1 *CGSH* §393; *Lgen.* 712.2. 2 *MartT* 36; *MartG* 82; *MartD* 110.

AODH MÓR, 'great'. *See* Aodh Beag.

AODHAMAIR. This saint's name, also written Ádhamair, Éadhamair, Íomair, and anglicized Imor, probably derives from *Aodh*, with feminine suffix *–am(m)air*. The saint's father is variously named Aodh and Eoghan, which would suggest that the cult underwent at least two localizations.[1] As daughter of Eoghan, the saint was placed among the Conmhaicne of Cúil Toladh, in the present Mayo barony of Kilmaine, in line with the location of one of her churches at Killimor in the parish of Ballinchalla. Elsewhere, under the guise of Ádhamair, she figures among the saints of Uí Mhaine (a territory principally in east Galway and south Roscommon) who are said to have joined forces with Colum Cille against Diarmuid son of Cearbhall, king of Tara, in the lead-up to the battle of Cúil Dreimhne.[2] This accords with the Galway locations of three other churches named for her: Killimorbologue, barony of Longford; Killimordaly, barony of Kilconnell; and an ecclesiastical site at Killaughan (Ceall Aodhamair Shoghain) in the parish of Ballymacward, barony of Tiaquin.[3] At Killimorbologue, Aodhamair apparently underwent a change of sex. According to a story based on a poem recorded in 1837, Imor's conversion to the service of God came after *his* wooing of a girl already loved by another from across the river Shannon in Ely of the O'Carrolls, who died because of the struggle between the two suitors.[4] Colgan's suggestion that the saint may be identical with a Ceachtamair mentioned in Patrick's Life is without foundation.[5] Her feast, which is recorded under the guise of Aodhamair daughter of Aodh, fell on 18 January.[6]

1 *CGSH* §§389, 708.10*add*; *GRSH* 105; *Lgen*. 729.12. 2 *IMN* 22, 5. 3 *HDGP* iii, 128. 4 OSL GY ii, 72–4. 5 *TT* 112 §82. 6 *MartT* 9; *MartG* 18; *MartD* 20.

AODHÁN. Saints bearing this diminutive form of the name Aodh are found throughout Ireland and the Gaelic-speaking area of Scotland. Its best-known bearers were Aodhán (more commonly Maodhóg) son of Séadna of Ferns – who also brought the name into Welsh usage as Aeddan (Maidoc) – and Aidan, first bishop of the see of Lindisfarne, who evangelized Northumbria. As in the case of Aodh, many saints of the name are otherwise known by little more than by reference to their churches and feasts. Originally lenited, the medial consonant *d* subsequently underwent delenition to give the modern form Aodán.

AODHÁN of Bovevagh (Both Mheadhbha), barony of Keenaght, Co. Derry. An entry in the tract on the genealogies of kings and saints (*Genealogiae Regum et Sanctorum Hiberniae*) compiled by the Four Masters, although absent from the earlier corpus of pedigrees, assigns Aodhán son of Fiontan to the Cianachta of Derry, very much in line with the location of his church.[1] Colgan took the saint to be identical with Aodhán *monachus*, 'the monk', a son of Colum Cille's sister Sineach, who was mother, according to Adhamhnán, of the 'men of Maca Céin' (alias Cianachta) of Cúil Uisce, an unidentified site, probably in the barony of Keenaght.[2]

1 *GRSH* 122. 2 *TT* 478 (5); *VC*[2] 548.

Aodhán of Clonard (Cluain Dartadha), in the townland of Tullygorey, parish of Kilberry, barony of Narragh and Reban West, Co. Kildare.[1] This saint is included with his namesake and probable double, Aodh Caol son of Fearadhach, in the list of those commemorated on 12 February.[2] An early litany describes him as surrounded by *Rómhánaigh*, 'Romans', who were probably clerics following Roman practice on the question of how to calculate the date of Easter.[3]

1 *CGSH* §707.12, p. 318. 2 *MartT* 16; *MartG* 34; *MartD* 47. 3 *IrL* 64.

Aodhán of Clonkeen. *See* Aruin.

Aodhán of Clonoghil. *See* Aodhán of Templeshanbo.

Aodhán of Cluain Tarbh. Attached to a place called Cluain Tarbh in the list of saints of the one name, this man may be the same as the person commemorated on 3 August at a church variously named Cluain 'Tarbhfheithe' and Cluain Cairbre.[1] There are two Mayo townlands named Cloontariff, in the parishes of Aghamore and Knock, and both share a boundary with Killedan (Ceall Aodháin) which may take name from this saint.[2]

1 *CGSH* §707.13; *MartT* 60; *MartG* 148; *MartD* 210. 2 But cf. *MP* 60.

Aodhán of Eachradh (Eachaireadh). Also known as Maodhóg and Aodh, this man is included, among many others of the name, in the list of homonymous saints.[1] According to his so-called *vita prima*, 'first Life', Molua of Clonfertmulloe, apparently then in north Munster, visited a certain Maodhóg at a place named 'cella Echairith', miraculously causing an apple-tree to grow in front of its church.[2] This may have been in the area now comprising two adjoining townlands, Killahara (from Coill Eachra) and Kilkillahara (Ceall Choill Eachra) in the Tipperary parish of Loughmoe West.[3] Alternatively, the reference may be to the Laois townland of Agharra in the parish of Erke.[4] Aodhán was remembered on 11 April, together with his namesake and probable double, the better-known Maodhóg of Clonmore.[5]

1 *CGSH* §707.11. 2 *VSHH* 144 §66. 3 *PML* 26, 28, 40; *CLTÁ* 96–7. 4 Logainm.ie 'Agharra'. 5 *MartT* 32 (Aodhán); *MartG* 76 (Aodh); *MartD* 100 (Aodh).

Aodhán of Glendalough, townland of Sevenchurches, parish of Derrylossary, barony of Ballinacor North, Co. Wicklow. This man's mother, Brígh daughter of Cobhthach, is said to have had four sons by Maine son of Fearghas, including three saints – Séighín, probably of Rathvilly, Bishop Aodhán, and Bishop Éidchéan of Clonfad – along with one king, Aodh son of Ainmhire.[1] Brígh's father Cobhthach was a son of Criomhthann son of Éanna Ceinsealach, progenitor of the Uí Cheinsealaigh, the ruling dynasty of South Leinster. Aodhán's paternal descent attached him to the Dál Meisin Corb, which means that he was also regarded as a kinsman of Caoimhghin of Glendalough.[2] The saint figures prominently in a section of the tract on the *bóramha* tribute which deals with the attempt by the saint's uterine brother, Aodh son of Ainmhire, king of the northern half of Ireland, to take revenge on the men of Leinster for the killing of his son Cumascach.[3] Brannabh son of Eacha, king of Leinster, is said to have persuaded Aodhán to act as a messenger to his brother and, following Aodh's death in the ensuing battle at Bealach Dúin Bholg, the bishop reputedly arranged to have the king buried at Glendalough.

1 *CGSH* §§380.1, 722.64. 2 *CGSH* §181.13; *GRSH* 85; *CPPI* 119. 3 *SG* i, 370–81; *Éigse* 7, 95–111; *Ériu* 47, 57–62.

Aodhán of Inis Lothair. This man is said to have been born to Lubaid, Patrick's sister, through an illicit liaison with Colmán son of Oilill of the Uí Bhreasail of Armagh, which allegedly resulted in the punishment and death of Aodhán's mother.[1]

1 *BP* 2774–87; *VT* 234.

Aodhán of Iorluachair, a large tract of land in west Munster, comprising the hilly region north of Killarney and adjoining parts of Cork and Limerick. Although this saint has the distinction of being first in the list of homonymous saints, little else is known of him.[1] He may have been the saint named Aodhán (Aidanus) from the banks of the river Maine, to the west of Iorluachair, who figures in the Life of Mochuda of Lismore.[2] If so, he was probably also identical with the Aodhán of Corca Dhuibhne remembered on 8 April, which fell between the feasts of his namesakes (Aodh Oiléin, 'of the island', and Aodhach of Maca Eilich), and seven days after the feast of Aodhán 'in Ulster'.[3]

1 *CGSH* §707.1. 2 *VSHP* i, 171 §6; ITS 16, 76. 3 *MartT* 31; *MartG* 72; *MartD* 96–8.

Aodhán of Kilmeage (Ceall Maodhóg/Cluain Domhail), barony of Connell, Co. Kildare. Designated a bishop, Aodhán is said to have been a son of Toirdhealbhach of the leading line of the Dál gCais of Thomond, and thus a brother of Flannán of Killaloe.[1] While the evidence of the list of those 'in union' with Maol Ruain of Tallaght provides Flannán with a notional floruit in the period about 800, Aodhán, the *clamh*, 'leprous one', is said to have been maltreated by the forces of Fearghal son of Maol Dúin almost one hundred years earlier, during the events that preceded the battle of Allen in 722.[2] With six other (unnamed) bishops, Aodhán of Kilmeage is also invoked in the second litany of Irish saints.[3] He was still remembered as patron of Kilmeage in the early seventeenth century, albeit under the guise of Maodhóg.[4] A namesake and probable double, Aodh son of Foirtchearn, was venerated at Inis Beoaidh, apparently in the parish of Feighcullen, which adjoins Kilmeage. The feast of the saint, whose name was also written as Aodh and Maodhóg, fell on 2 June.[5]

1 *CGSH* §230; *GRSH* 119; *CGH* 152b23. 2 *CathA* 3 §4; *CGSH* §§713.5; 724.5. 3 *IrL* 68. 4 *Dinn.* 2, 31. 5 *MartG* 108; *MartD* 142; *GRSH* 119.

Aodhán of Kilmore (Ceall Mhór, alias Ceall Mhór Aodháin), a parish in the county and barony of Monaghan. The genealogists attached Aodhán son of Aonghas (or Fearghas), who is also included in the list of homonymous saints, to the Ceinéal Eichin branch of Ceinéal Eoghain, which appears to have held lands in the Bréadach on the east side of Inishowen.[1] Though Patrick is alleged to have proclaimed the attributes of *claoine* (crookedness) and *costadhaighe* (constancy) for the descendants of Aodhán's grandfather Eichean, neither the saint nor his uncle (Maine son of Eichean) appears to have been unduly affected by the former characteristic.[2] Aodhán's church was deemed worthy of a visit from Colmán of Lynally, who availed of the opportunity to enforce there the practice of resting from manual work on Sundays.[3] Apart from his alleged occupancy of the see of Clogher, little else is known of the saint, but the occurrence of his feastday on 2 November, the day after that of Aodh of Foyran, and eight days ahead of the feast of Aodh of Rahugh, would suggest that he was a localized version of the latter saint.[4] An association with his church at Kilmore was also attributed to Aodhán of Lindisfarne.[5]

1 *CGSH* §§29, 707.3; *GRSH* 44; *Lgen.* 149.7; *HDGP* ii, 173. 2 *BLec.* 58Vab. 3 *VSHH* 213 §11; *VSHP* i, 262 §12. 4 *MartG* 210; *MartD* 292; *Cl.Rec.* 7, 380. 5 *ClRec.* 7, 380; *DPH* i, 179, 188.

Aodhán of Lindisfarne, England. First bishop among the people of Northumbria, and described by Bede as a 'man of outstanding gentleness, devotion and moderation', Aodhán (anglicized Aidan) came from Iona in 635 at the invitation of King Oswald, who had previously spent years of exile on the Scottish island.[1] Given a bishop's see on Lindisfarne by Oswald, who had a royal seat nearby at Bamburgh, and who also occasionally acted as interpreter, Aodhán preached extensively, thus laying the foundation for the emergence of Northumbria as a vibrant centre of Christianity in western Europe.[2] Although he must have maintained close contact with Iona up to his death in 651, which is noted in the Irish annals, there is no record of an involvement with Irish affairs after his move to Northumbria.[3] Following his death, his remains were translated to Lindisfarne and, as befitted a person held to be a saint, were subsequently placed on the right side of the altar of a new church built on the island.[4]

Through the transmission of the martyrology later kept on Lindisfarne to Iona, Aodhán's feast of 31 August entered the Irish record in first place among additions to the basic Hieronymian text.[5] The feast also found its way to the Continent, where it was added to the Calendar of Willibrord at Echternach.[6] A mention of the feast of 'Aidanus' in the ninth-century Life of Fiontan of Rheinau, although sometimes thought to refer to the patron of Lindisfarne, more probably relates to Maodhóg (alias Aodhán) of Ferns, as his day (31 January) was immediately followed by that of Brighid (1 February), whose festival is also featured in the Life.[7]

The use of the Irish name for Lindisfarne, viz. Inis Meadhchóid, in the early martyrologies led in the later record to confusion with Scattery Island (Inis Cathaigh), off Kilrush in Clare.[8] Among other Irish churches claiming to be connected with Aodhán is the Derry church of Magilligan, the location, according to local tradition, of the saint's tomb and holy well, and the Monaghan church of Kilmore (Ceall Mhór Aodháin), from where, having allegedly spent some time as bishop of Clogher, he is said to have travelled to England.[9] Some Scottish churches were also dedicated to him and a short office Life is contained in the Breviary of Aberdeen.[10]

1 *BEH* 219; *DIB* i, 38–9; *BiblSS* i, 625–7. 2 *BEH* 231. 3 *AU s.a.* 4 *BEH* 265. 5 *FSHIM* 57–74; *MartT* 67; *MartO*[2] 179. 6 HBS 55, 10. 7 *MGH.SS* 15.1, 506 §§9–11; *SIHI* 2. 8 *MartG* 166; *MartD* 230. 9 *PNCL* 230; *ClRec.* 7, 380; *PNCL* 230, 236. 10 *KSS* 269; *LegSS* 208–11, 321–2.

Aodhán of Lismore (Lios Mór), barony of Coshmore and Coshbride, Co. Waterford. This saint, also known as Maodhóg, is noticed in the annals under 768, the year of his death.[1] Assuming that the same person is intended, the martyrologies, which describe him as both abbot and bishop, notice Aodhán on three days, 16 March, 19 July and 29 December.[2]

1 *AU s.a.* 2 *MartT* 2, 56; *MartG* 56, 138, 248; *MartD* 76, 196, 350.

Aodhán of Mullenakill. *See* Aodhán Laoch.

Aodhán of Templeshanbo (Seanbhoth), barony of Scarawalsh, Co. Wexford. Together with Colmán son of Eacha, an associate at the church of Templeshanbo, Aodhán was attached to the saints of Uí Fhiachrach in Connacht.[1] His branch of the Uí Fhiachrach was known, according to Dubhaltach Mac Fhir Bhisigh, as Uí Eachach of the river Moy and, together with the Uí Shuanaigh, these are said to have been children of Fearamhla daughter of Díoma Dubh.[2] Though also attached to the church of Clonoghil (Cluain Eochaille) in the Sligo parish of the same name, Aodhán travelled, according to the same author, from north Connacht to the banks of the Cashen river in Kerry in pursuit of his stepbrother Triallach, who wished to escape from worldly things.[3] Aodhán died, according to the annals, in 563 (or 570) and John Colgan suggested, speculatively, that his feast fell either on 1 January or 9 October.[4]

1 *CGSH* §662.77; *GRSH* 61. 2 *Lgen.* 253.1; *IrT* iii, 5 §11. 3 *Lgen.* 253.1. 4 *GRSH* 61; *AU s.a.*

Aodhán Laoch, 'layman'. Besides being included in the list of saints of one name, Aodhán the layman is also commemorated in the Martyrology of Tallaght at 1 April.[1] Later martyrologies located him in Ceall Aodháin *i nUltaibh*, 'in east Ulster', now perhaps an old graveyard in the townland of Corporation, parish of Killyleagh in the Down barony of Dufferin.[2] Together with Aodhán of what may be Mullenakill in the Armagh parish of Killyman, whose feast fell on 29 March, he probably represented a north-eastern localization of the same original cult.[3]

1 *CGSH* §707.16; *MartT* 29. 2 *MartG* 68; *MartD* 92; *HDGP* iii, 127. 3 *MartT* 28; *MartG* 210; *MartD* 293; *AHHS* 304, 326.

Aoibhinn daughter of Ainmhire. *See* Éanna of Inishmore.

Aoidhbhe of Terryglass (Tír Dá Ghlas), barony of Lower Ormond, Co. Tipperary. The martyrologies record the feast of this saint, whose name derives from Aodh, at 24 May, describing him variously as bishop and abbot.[1] He is not among the abbots of Terryglass recorded in the annals, and notes added to the Martyrology of Aonghas in the late twelfth century associate other churches with him, including a hermitage in the Galtee mountains, south of Emly, and a church named Bréachmhagh in Ceara which gave name to the townland and parish of Breaghwy in the Mayo barony of Carra.[2]

1 *MartT* 45; *MartO*[2] 126; *MartG* 102; *MartD* 138. 2 *MartO*[2] 136; DQE 90; *HDGP* ii, 172.

Aoidhghin of Ardlonan (Aird Lonáin), parish of Kilbeg, barony of Lower Kells, Co. Meath. Aoidhghin's church was probably situated in the present townland of

Kilbeg Upper, which adjoins Ardlonan.[1] Although remembered by the martyrologists on 18 December, nothing else is known of the saint.[2]

1 *HDGP* i, 38. 2 *MartT* 86; *MartG* 240; *MartD* 340.

Aoidhghin of Bodoney (Both Domhnaigh), an ecclesiastical site in the townland of Glenlark, parish of Bodoney Lower, barony of Strabane Upper, Co. Tyrone. According to the list of those in orders with Patrick, Aoidhghin (also written Áithgein and Áithgne) son of Lughar (alias Aol/Daol) was the Armagh saint's cook, a not inappropriate role for a man whose name literally means 'born of fire'.[1] Although one of his two pedigrees attaches him to the Clann Cholmáin of Westmeath, the other – which assigns him to the Oirghialla – would place his lifetime much later than that of Patrick.[2] The Oirghialla pedigree, which also establishes a relationship for the saint with the ruling family of the Farney/Cremorne area in Monaghan, at some distance from his church, shows that he was considered to be a brother of Ceanannán, patron of a church named Domhnach Coinre in the Antrim barony of Cary.[3] Aoidhghin is also said to have had a saintly sister named Curcach of whom little else is known. An alias Cormac is attested in some sources.[4] The saint's feastday, which is recorded only in the early ninth-century Martyrology of Tallaght, fell on 3 May, the vigil of the feast of Aodh of Rahugh and two days later than that of a namesake and probable double, Aoidhghin of Fore.[5] According to a 1607 survey, Patrick was then patron of Bodoney.[6]

1 *BP* 3130; *CGSH* §671.8; *BiblSS* i, 646–7. 2 *CGSH* §§43, 61.1; *Lgen.* 739.4.5. 3 *BP* 1896–7. 4 *CGSH* §61.1 (Lb); *GRSH* 73. 5 *MartT* 39; *GRSH* 73 §1. 6 *DYHS* 196.

Aoidhghin of Fore (Fobhar), now the name of a townland in the parish of St Feighins, barony of Fore, Co. Westmeath. This saint's feast fell on 1 May, two days ahead of that of Aoidhghin of Bodoney.[1] Though Aoidhghin of Fore is provided with an obit of 771, the two may have been identical, especially in view of the Clann Cholmáin (Westmeath) pedigree sometimes attached to Aoidhghin of Bodoney.[2]

1 *MartT* 38–9; *MartG* 88–90; *MartD* 116, 120. 2 *AU s.a.*

Aoidhghin of Teach Deireascain, an unidentified church near the (equally unidentified) well of Tiobra Sabhraille.[1] Aoidhghin son of Fidhghin Liaigh, 'the leech', and his two brothers, Fuireamhain and Trostán, are among those said to have been subject to Brighid of Kildare.[2] His brother Trostán may be the saint after whom was named the Roscommon parish of Kiltrustan, which lies between two townlands called Kilbride (Ceall Bhrighde). There are also places called Trustan and Trustan Glebe in the Fermanagh parishes of Killesher and Aghavea, whose patron Lasair daughter of Rónán, was connected with the Roscommon church of Kilronan, near Boyle.

1 *CGSH* §670.60. 2 Ibid.

Aoileann. *See* Faoileann.

Aolchú. *See* Pupa.

Aona of Clonmacnoise (Cluain Mac Nóis), barony of Garrycastle, Co. Offaly. The obit of this saintly abbot, whose father is variously named Bearach and Eoghan, is recorded in the annals for 570, with the Annals of Tighearnach, kept at Clonmacnoise, declaring that he held the abbacy for twenty-six years.[1] Bearing a name that is also written Aonghas and Éanna, the saint is taken to have been the immediate successor of Ciarán, founder-patron of Clonmacnoise, and to have belonged to the ruling segment of the Laoighis, known as Laoighis Réada.[2] Probably because of his position as Ciarán's first coarb, Aona figures in other saints' Lives, including that of his predecessor. While in Inis Ainghin, now Hareisland on Lough Ree, or in Inis Clothrann, now Inchcleraun on the same lake, Ciarán is said to have foretold how 'Aonghas', then an unruly adolescent, would one day succeed him.[3] Perhaps connected with this tradition is the 'strict penance' enjoined on Aona by Ciarán, according to the Old Irish Table of Commutations.[4] The biographer of Íde of Killeedy, who is said to have died in the same year (570 or 570) as Aona, describes how, just before her death, she blessed water for messengers from Clonmacnoise in the fruitless hope that it would cure their infirm abbot, again called Aonghas.[5] Other Lives that feature Aona (alias Aonghas) are those of Colum of Terryglass and Daigh of Inishkeen.[6] A separate tale relates how he liberated the son of a widow imprisoned by Guaire Aidhne, who was allegedly Aona's *anmchara*, 'soul-friend'.[7] The saint's feast of 20 January is recorded in most martyrologies.[8] Ciarán's shrine was profaned on Hare Island in 894.[9]

1 *CGSH* §144; *GRSH* 102; *Lgen.* 731.9; *AU*[1] *s. A.* 570, 576; ATig. *s.a.* 2 ATig. *s.a.*; *NHI* 9, 246; *FEMN* 493; *LSHS* 58; *AB* 69, 98–9. 3 *VSHP* i, 210 §26; cf. *MartO*[2] 48–50; *Ériu* 19, 64 §25. 4 *Ériu* 19, 64 §25. 5 *VSHP* ii, 130 §35; *AU s.a.* 6 *VSHH* 233, 392; *VSHH* 232–3, 392. 7 *ACL* iii, 1–2; *SG* i, 401. 8 *MartT* 10; *MartD* 24. 9 *AFM s.a.*

Aonghas. Although several saints of this name, a derivative of *aon* + *gus*, 'singular valour', are included in a list of bishops preserved in the twelfth-century Book of Leinster, none of these appears to be otherwise attested.[1]

1 *CGSH* §704.124–8; *Celtica* 12, 193–5.

Aonghas of Aharney (Achadh Toghartha), barony of Galmoy, Co. Kilkenny. This saint's church, now known as Barony, was located in the townland of Ballyconra, parish of Aharney.[1] Unsurprisingly, as the parish was dedicated to Brighid of Kildare, it is in her company, together with that of her aunt Cuman and some other saints, that Aonghas was assigned to his church.[2] A pattern in honour of Brighid was held on 1 February at a well south of the church.[3]

1 *HADO* ii, 308–12; *HDGP* i, 23. 2 *CGSH* §173; *Lgen.* 751.4. 3 OSL KK i, 95.

Aonghas of Burt (Beart), barony of Inishowen West, Co. Donegal. Having left Domhnach Mór Maighe Tóchair (whence the name of Donagh parish in the Inishowen peninsula), Patrick entered, according to his Tripartite Life, a nearby territory named Bréadach that belonged to the family of Oilill son of Eoghan.[1] There, in a place named Domhnach Bile, which John Colgan, a native of this area, took to be another form of the name Magh Bhile (now Moville in the barony of Inishowen East), Patrick is said to have ordained Aonghas son of Oilill.[2] Colgan also states that Aonghas, reputedly a bishop, was attached to an 'old chapel' named Druim Bearta, near an Ó Dochartaigh castle, presumably the seat of the famous Cathaoir Ó Dochartaigh at Burt.[3] Although a similar place-name (Druim Beartach) figures in the list of names commemorated on 18 February, Aonghas is not attached to it.[4] The latest of the martyrologies, that of Donegal, assigns him to a church named Druim Rátha, now perhaps Drumrat in the parish and county of Donegal.[5] A new church, built in Burt in 1967 on the model of the nearby Grianán of Aileach, but in modern architectural style, is dedicated to Aonghas, whose pedigree is recorded on a stone-panel forming part of a decorative wall in front of the building.

1 *BP* 1822–6; *VT* 156. 2 Ibid.; *TT* 181 §177; *Lgen*. 702.3. 3 *TT* 181 §178; OSL DL 107–9; cf. *HDGP* ii, 139. 4 *MartT* 17; *MartG* 38. 5 *MartD* 52; *GRSH* 44.

Aonghas of Clonmacnoise. *See* Aona.

Aonghas of Connor. *See* Mac Nise of Connor.

Aonghas of Rathaspick (Ráith na nEasbag), barony of Forth, Co. Wexford. This saint is known from two sources, martyrologies and secular genealogies, of which one includes Aonghas among those commemorated on 16 February, while the other describes him as a descendant of Daigh son of Dubhthach of the Dál bhFiatach.[1] Because of the saint's descent, his church is usually thought to have lain in east Ulster, possibly at Tullinespick (which may derive from Tulach na nEasbag) in the Down parish of Bright, but the Wexford church of Rathaspick is more likely for three reasons.[2] First, Aonghas' descent provides a possible link with Munna of Taghmon, whose (confused) pedigree also includes the names Daigh son of Dubhthach, and whose church gave name to a parish close to Rathaspick.[4] Second, Aonghas' feast fell on the vigil of the feast of Fiontan of Clonenagh, who belonged to the Fothairt, the group that gave name to the barony of Forth. Third, the local well and church at Rathaspick are said to have been dedicated to Brighid of Kildare, chief saint of the Fothairt.[5]

1 *MartT* 17; *MartG* 36; *MartD* 50; cf. *GRSH* 93; *Lgen*. 493.6. 2 *CGH* 330b38; *Lgen*. 493.6; *ZCP* 8, 328. 3 *ZCP* 13, 334; cf. *EA* 168. 4 *CGSH* §155. 5 *CECW* 212; *The Past* 2, 57.

Aonghas of Tallaght (Tamhlachta), barony of Uppercross, Co. Dublin. A bishop and noted *céile Dé*, 'client of God', this son of Aonghobha is one of the few early Irish saints whose personality can be glimpsed, however dimly, in the prologue and epilogue of his best-known work, the metrical martyrology known in Irish as *Féilire Aonghasa*.[1] Martyrologists usually required skill in the science of *computus*, but piously, Aonghas attributed his book to the inspiration of the host of saints whose feasts decided its arrangement 'by their perfect deaths'.[2] Warming to his theme, he contrasted the abiding glory of his saints with the forgotten state of their tormentors, and compared the decline of such pre-Christian centres of authority as Tara with the flourishing state of churches such as Armagh.

In the epilogue to his hugely influential work, which survives in more copies than any other Irish martyrology, Aonghas describes himself as both *páipearán*, 'mendicant', and *deidhbhléan de thuaith Íosa*, 'a poor man of Jesus' family', before making an appeal to the 'thousands and thousands that had gone to heaven every day from the earth' – headed by his teacher Maol Ruain, founder of Tallaght – for assistance in attaining his own salvation and the privilege of dying at Easter or during Lent.[3] A poem composed some centuries after his death states that he died on a Friday, but offers no information on the time of year. His name was, however, added to what has been shown to be his other great work, the Martyrology of Tallaght, at 11 March, which would place his death during Lent.[4] As bishop, a title accorded him in the notice of his feast, Aonghas would have had primary responsibility for the liturgy at Tallaght, and he may have compiled his two martyrologies in response to a decree promulgated at a council held in Aachen in 817, which required that a reading be made from a martyrology each day at the beginning of the monastic chapter, immediately after the office of Prime.[5] Despite his boast of having drawn on many authorities, the sole source of his metrical text seems to have been his other work, the prose Martyrology of Tallaght, which itself was an abbreviated copy of a Hieronymian text, originally drawn up in Northumbria and brought to Tallaght via Iona and Bangor.[6]

The preface added to the metrical martyrology in the late twelfth century purports to record incidents in the life of the saint which bring him from a church named after him at Dysert (Díseart Aonghasa), near Croom in Limerick, to Coolbanagher (Cúil Bheannchair), a little north of Dysartenos (Díseart Aonghasa), in Laois, where he allegedly began his metrical martyrology, and thence to Tallaght, where he completed it.[7] The saint's genealogy attached him to the Uí Eachach Cobha of south-east Ulster.[8] His obit is not recorded, but he appears to have died shortly after he had completed his two martyrologies, about 830. Since John Colgan, the so-called second litany of Irish saints has been attributed to Aonghas, but there is no manuscript evidence to support this.[9] A late (perhaps twelfth-century) poem states that he was reared at Clonenagh (Cluain Eidhneach) in the Laois barony of Maryborough West, and later buried there.[10]

1 *MartO*[2] 17–31, 264–88. 2 Ibid. 269 (l. 107). 3 Ibid. 282 (ll. 396, 408), 288 (ll. 561–4). 4 *MartT* 22. 5 *DIB* vii, 448; *FSHIM* 96–7. 6 Ibid. 99–118. 7 *MartO*[2] 2–15. 8 *CGSH* §118; *GRSH* 98; *Lgen*. 732.7. 9 *IrL* xx. 10 *MartO*[2] xxiv–xxvi.

Aonghas son of Faibhreach. *See* Mac Nise of Connor.

Aonghas Láimhiodhan of Moyne (Maighean), parish of Kilmacar, barony of Fassadinin, Co. Kilkenny. Bearing the epithet *Láimhiodhan*, 'pure-hand', and the alias, Muicín (Mainchín, Latin Moginus/Moganus) son of Moiche, this saintly son of Bairrfhionn was attached to the Uí Dheagha branch of the Osraighe that gave name to the barony of Ida in the same county. Two versions of his pedigree are preserved under the two separate forms of his name, Aonghas and Muicín, both of them providing him with an Osraighe lineage.[1] His mother was named Díognad daughter of Gaibhrín, a sister of Fiontan of Clonenagh.[2] The saint is also mentioned under both forms of his name in two poems ascribed to Moling of St

Mullin's, as Muicín of Moyne, one of six saints of Uí Dheagha, and as Aonghas Láimhiodhan, entrusted with the care of Moling's books, which were carelessly placed in the cave of Dearc Fearna, thereby causing them to be damaged by floodwater.[3] Despite its identification as a cave near Ferns in Wexford, this is probably Dunmore Cave in the parish of Mothell (not far from Moyne), which continued to be known locally as Dearc Fearna until the late nineteenth century.[4] The saint was venerated in three other Ossory churches, Killermogh, Kilderry, and Sheepstown (parish of Knocktopher).[5] His principal church was, however, at Moyne in the deanery of Odogh, and he was remembered annually on 4 March, vigil of the feast of Ossory's patron, Ciarán of Saighir.[6]

Colgan mistakenly identified Aonghas Láimhiodhan as the like-named patron of Rathaspick, and a second saint named Muicín, commemorated in the Martyrology of Tallaght at 20 March, has been shown to be in mistake for a Hieronymian saint named Mucius.[7] The *sanctorale* of TCD MS 78 (ff. 130–77) contains an entry on Muicín under the guise of 'Mokyn'.[8]

1 *CGSH* §§182, 278; *CGH* 129a12; *Lgen.* 727.2. **2** *CGSH* §182.2. **3** *Anecd.* ii, 36–8; *JCS* i, 227–31. **4** *OnomG* 342; *HADO* iii, 459. **5** Ibid. ii, 204–6. **6** Ibid.; *MartT* 20; *MartG* 48; *MartD* 62. **7** *GRSH* 93; *MartT* 25; *RSC* 147–8. **8** *Colk.Cat.*, i, 122–5.

Araght. *See* Athracht.

Arannán. *See* Forannán of Alternan.

Artach. The secular genealogies, which assign Artach to the Uí Eachach of Sliabh Breagh, appear to be the only authority for this saint.[1] The hilly area represented by Sliabh Breagh is taken to have extended from Meath into the southern part of Louth.[2] Nearby, in the parish of Mayne, is a church named Killartery, presumably from Ceall Artraighe, 'church of the Artraighe'. Artach may reflect, albeit corruptly, the eponym of this church.

1 *Lgen.* 1051.3; *BLec.* 77va. **2** *HDGP* ii, 174; *OnomG* 605.

Aruin of Clonkeen (Cluain Caoin), barony of Ardee, Co. Louth. The martyrologies commemorate a bishop of this name at 1 August, assigning him to a church named Cluain Caoin.[1] In a note on the saint, Míchéal Ó Cléirigh locates his wonder-working bell five miles from 'Athriagh', which appears to be a corrupt form of Áth Fhir Diadh, now Ardee.[2] This would point to the church that gave name to Clonkeen parish in the barony of Ardee, about five miles from Ardee itself, but the original patron of this church was named Aodhán, and the local parish church was dedicated to him under the guise of Maodhóg (Medocus).[3] The saint's name, which is otherwise unattested, has been taken to represent Aaron.[4]

1 *MartT* 59; *MartG* 148; *MartD* 208. **2** *MartD* 354; *HDGP* i, 133; *EMH* 479 §203. **3** *CSMA* i, 153, 161; *ROLN* §115. **4** *MartD* 354.

Asach (Assicus). *See* Tasach.

Asán. *See* Osán.

Asnad. *See* Osnad.

Asúrnaidh. *See* Sárnad daughter of Aodh.

Athchaoin of Colp (Inbhear Colptha), barony of Lower Duleek, Co. Meath, near the mouth (*inbhear*) of the river Boyne. Athchaoin is one of a large number of children credited to Eithne daughter of Conchraidh.[1] Among the saint's siblings were Mochob of Kilmore, who mentioned in the Life of the Welsh saint Cybi, Earnán of Tory Island, Sciath daughter of Meachar, the seven Neamhainn of Druim Leathan – who may be the same as the seven holy bishops of Druim Leithinn (Leithlinne), mentioned in a litany – and Colmán of Reachra, now probably Lambay Island off the Dublin coast.[2] Whereas Mochob's feast fell on 12 November, both Athchaoin and Colmán are featured in the list of those commemorated on 16 June.[3] According to the Ordnance Survey of 1836, the patron of Colp, thought by some to have been a Scot named St Colpa, was considered by others to have been Colum Cille, whose feast fell seven days before that of Athchaoin.[4]

1 *CGSH* 722.98. 2 *IrL* 68; *EA* 292; VSBG 240 §1 UJA 78 (202, 270). 3 *MartT* 50, *MartG* 116, 216; *MartD* 170, 306. 4 OSL MH 128; *Dinn.* 1, 55.

Athracht daughter of Sárán. *See* Athracht of Killaraght.

Athracht of Killaraght (Ceall Athrachta), barony of Coolavin, Co. Sligo. According to the corpus of saints' genealogies, Athracht daughter of Talán – whose name was also written as Adhrocht and anglicized as Attracta and Atty – belonged to the same branch of Dál nAraidhe of north Down and Antrim as did Comhghall of Bangor.[1] The same source states, however, that she was a sister of Caomhán of Ardcavan, who is reputed to have been instrumental in arranging for a bridge to be laid across Lough Gara on Sligo's border with Roscommon.[2] This is precisely the area in which Athracht's cult also took root, as is already shown by her mention in Tíreachán's Life of St Patrick.[3] While in the territory of the Greagraighe, which corresponded to the area around Lough Gara, Patrick is said to have left paten and chalice in Athracht's church, and also to have placed the nun's veil on her head. The mid-ninth-century vernacular Life of Patrick, the so-called *Vita Tripartita*, attached both Athracht and her brother Caomhán to the Greagraighe of Lough Gara.[4] This latter source also maintained that Athracht refused the gift of a chasuble that had fallen from heaven, preferring to give it to another.[5]

A fragmentary Life of the saint was edited by John Colgan, mainly from the codex known as *Insulensis*, but it now survives only in the Franciscan copy of that collection.[6] The fragment, which was probably written by a Cistercian monk in the abbey of Boyle, establishes several local associations, including encounters with her uterine brother, Conall of Druim – taken by Colgan to be the saint of Kilconnell in Galway, but also more plausibly identified as patron of Drum, the original parish church of Boyle – Dochonna of Assylin, likewise near Boyle, and a saint named Faolán whom she is said to have raised from the dead.[7] This text also emphasizes the connections of the saint with Luighne, a name (preserved in the Sligo barony of Leyny) that later became synonymous with the diocese of

Achonry.[8] Killaraght lay just within this diocese, which is again represented by the saint in the tale known as 'Four Saints'.[9] In this, Athracht daughter of Sárán, a description which corresponds to an alternative descent from the Uí Eachach Cobha of Down, joined with others in drawing up an agreement between the sons of Amhalghaidh and the people of Luighne.[10]

In the Sligo parish of Kilcolman, adjoining Killaraght, and also in the Mayo parishes of Attymas, Kilbeagh and Kilcolman, holy wells marked Athracht's memory.[11] To judge by three invocations of the saint in poems on the Magaurans (Méig Shamhradháin) of the Cavan barony of Tullyhaw, devotion to Athracht also extended into Bréifne.[12] Curiously, a poem attributed to Moling, which cites the names of many saintly protectors of Leinster, also invokes Athracht daughter of Talán 'from the centre of Magh Luirg' in Roscommon.[13] Though Colgan, quoting external authorities, included the saint among those commemorated on 9 February (the day also assigned to her, under the guise of Tarahta, in the *Catalogus* compiled by Henry Fitzsimon), her usual day was 11 August.[14] On this day – for which a special Latin office was compiled for the diocese of Achonry – her church attracted pilgrims from far and wide, and her relics, including a cross reputedly received from St Patrick, were put on display.[15] As daughter of Sárán, she was allegedly also commemorated on 6 January.[16]

1 *CGSH* §398.1; *GRSH* 98; *Lgen.* 733.6; *DIB* i, 195; *BiblSS* ii, 576–8. **2** *CGSH* §398.2. **3** *PTBA* 148 §31. **4** *BP* 1223–30; *VT* 108. **5** Ibid. **6** *ASH* 277–82; *MHH* 235 §210. **7** *ASH* 281 §11; OSL RN i, 243; *HOI* 64, 141. **8** *AU* iv, 4, 213; *HDGP* i, 14. **9** *IrT* iii, 5 §13. **10** Ibid.; cf. *CGSH* §354; *Lgen.* 732.9. **11** OSL SO 235; OSL MO i, 129; ii, 375, 378. **12** *BMag.* 2572, 3318, 4453. **13** *SG* i, 390. **14** *ASH* 277–82; *FEMN* 389; *Seanchas* 416; *MartT* 62 (Etracta); *MartG* 154; *MartD* 216. **15** *IER* (2nd ser.) 1, 39–40; *HOI* 58–69; *NotesEHDT* 354, 388. **16** *Lgen.* 732.9.

ATHRACHT of Kintale (Ceall tSáile), parish of Killygarvan, barony of Kilmacrenan, Co. Donegal. The corpus of saints' genealogies, followed by the lists of those commemorated on 11 August in the later martyrologies, places this saint in Críoch Chonaill.[1] As her feast coincides with that of her namesake at Killaraght in Sligo, the two virgins were doubtless identical.

1 *CGSH* §180; *MartG* 154; *MartD* 216; *HDGP* iv, 47.

ATTRACTA (ATTY). *See* Athracht.

AUSAILLE (AUXILIUS). *See* Usaille.

B

Bairre (Barra) of Cork. *See* Fionnbharr of Cork.

Bairre (Barra) of Newry. *See* Coilliodhan.

Bairrfhionn. Literally meaning 'fair-crowned' or 'fair-headed', this name is composed of *barr* 'top, crown' and *fionn*, 'fair'. In reverse order, these words also constitute the name Fionnbharr and, not surprisingly, there is some confusion between the two, with several saints becoming known by both forms. Finnian (alias Fionnbharr) of Movilla, was also known as Bairrfhionn, and Barra, the pet form of Fionnbharr (Finbarr) of Cork, derives from Bairrfhionn. There are strong grounds for believing that the same basic cult lies behind every mention of a saint named either Bairrfhionn or Fionnbharr.[1] Nevertheless, the saints so named are treated here in accordance with the written record, which regarded each bearer of the name as distinct. Most of those named Bairrfhionn receive little more than a bare mention, examples being the saints attached to the churches of Ceall Mhic Luighne, Ceann Tuirc and Ros Droichid, who figure only in the list of homonymous saints.[2] Though none of these churches has been positively identified, Ceall Mhic Luighne may be Killacloyne in the Cork parish of Caherlag, and the assertion of the list that Bairrfhionn was accompanied by Oilill would indicate that the saint commemorated on 1 July, together with a man of this name, was intended.[3] Ros Droichid is probably either Rosdrehid, parish of Cullenwaine in Offaly, or Rossdroit in the Wexford parish of the same name. Also known only from the list of homonymous saints is Bairrfhionn son of Cormac.[4]

1 *MakS* 1–29. **2** *CGSH* §707.56–8. **3** *HDGP* iv, 21; *MartT* 53; *MartG* 128; *MartD* 184. **4** *CGSH* §707.54.

Bairrfhionn of Aughkiletaun (Achadh Cailltéin), parish of Powerstown, barony of Gowran, Co. Kilkenny. This son of Aodh is among those included in the list of commemorations for 8 November, which also supplies the name of his church.[1] He was reputedly a brother of his namesake, Fionnbharr son of Aodh, of Little Island (Inis Doimhle), in the Waterford parish of Ballynakill, and this prompted John Colgan to remark: 'You might think he is the same as Fionnbharr because he has the same father and the same genealogy, but they are said to be brothers'.[2] Another pair of saintly brothers named Fionnbharr and Bairrfhionn, said to be descended through their father Aodh from the Uí Bhriain of Connacht, were assigned to the church of Aughrim (Eachdhruim Mac nAodha) in the barony and county of Roscommon.[3] It has been suggested that he was the same as Moroc (from *Mobharróc) of the Scottish church of Dunblane, whose feast also fell on 8 November.[4]

1 *MartO*² 233, 240; *MartG* 214; *MartD* 298. **2** *GRSH* 74 §4; *Lgen.* 718.6.7. **3** *Lgen.* 710.7. **4** *LegSS* 266–7, 399–400.

Bairrfhionn of Drumcullen (Druim Cuilinn), barony of Eglish, Co. Offaly. Occupying a church historically on the confines of the northern and southern halves of Ireland, this son of Muireadhach is the subject of two different statements of descent. Although usually attached to the Ceinéal Conaill of Donegal, the Midlands version of the Commentary on the Martyrology of Aonghas provides him with a descent from Fiacha son of Niall, eponymous ancestor of the Ceinéal Fiachach of Moycashel in Westmeath and the adjoining part of Offaly.[1] This descent approximately reflects the location of his church within Tír Cheall, but through his other pedigree he was made a kinsman (*comhbhráthair geinealaigh*) of Colum Cille, who is said to have miraculously recovered Bairrfhionn's staff from the sea near Assaroe in the Donegal parish of Kilbarron (Ceall Bhairrfionn).[2]

Bairrfhionn's association with the sea is thought to lie behind the *persona* of 'Barinthus', who is presented in the *Navigatio Brendani* at the head of a group of monks on a voyage to the 'Land of Promise', recently interpreted as an analogy of a journey from the earthly to the heavenly Jerusalem.[3] In this role he came to be known as Bairrfhionn Ua Néill, 'of the Uí Néill', and was provided with a *frater* named Mearnóg (alias Tearnóg), otherwise better known as Earnán, who was said to have occupied a church called Inis Caoin (*insula deliciosa*) at Slieve League in the Donegal parish of Glencolumbkille, possibly an oblique reference to the nearby Inis Caoil, now Inishkeel.[4] Bairrfhionn's church at Drumcullen is mentioned in the Life of Mochuda of Lismore as the first stop on this saint's journey southwards, following his expulsion from Rahan.[5]

Bairrfhionn's feast fell on 21 May which, perhaps significantly, in view of the strong possibility that both saints were ultimately identical, was also a feastday of his namesake, Fionnbharr of Cork.[6] His mother, Díodhnad daughter of Meachar, is otherwise unattested.[7]

1 *CGSH* §27; *GRSH* 38; *Lgen.* 697.10; *MartO*[2] 134; cf. *Lgen.* 172.7; *HDGP* iv, 123. **2** *BCC* 134. **3** *NSBA* 3 §1; *CeltT* 193–6. **4** *CGSH* §662.21; *NSBA* 4 §1; *BNÉ* i, 49 §§28–9. **5** *VSHP* i, 195 §61. **6** *MartT* 45; *MartO*[2] 125; *MartG* 100; *MartD* 134. **7** *CGSH* §722.82.

Bairrfhionn of Midíne, a place also reflected in the name Múscraighe Midíne, now approximately the equivalent of the baronies of Muskerry, north of the river Lee in Co. Cork. According to his pedigree, Bairrfhionn son of Muireadhach belonged to the Uí Eachach of Munster, who controlled an area approximately corresponding to the extent of the diocese of Cork.[1] It must seem likely, therefore, that this saint's descent was the south Munster version of the ancestry of his namesake, Fionnbharr (alias Barra or Bairrfhionn) of Cork. The latter is said to have been born in Ráith Raithleann, the chief place of the Uí Eachach, and the Connacht ancestry traditionally attached to him may be explained by reference to the succession about 1138 of Giolla Aodha, a native of Connacht, to the see of Cork.[2] Genealogies were regularly manipulated in this fashion and, as the branch of the Uí Eachach with which Bairrfhionn was associated had moved westwards into the area about Killarney by the mid-twelfth century, local resistance to the change would have been slight.[3] The cloth that covered the body of the saint reputedly formed part of Adhamhnán's reliquary.[4] An unpublished Office Life, compiled for the saint in his capacity as patron of the Waterford parish of Kilbarrymeaden, is preserved in a fourteenth-century manuscript in Corpus Christi College, Cambridge.[5] The saint's feast fell on 13 November.[6]

1 *CGSH* §356; *GRSH* 115. **2** *BBa*. 55–6; *MakS* 68–70. **3** Ibid. **4** *Celtica* 15, 36 §17. **5** *JCHAS* 58, 48; *MakS* 68n. **6** *MartG* 218.

Bairrfhionn Ua Néill. *See* Bairrfhionn of Drumcullen.

Balloin of Tisaxon (Teach Sagsan), parish of Monivea, barony of Tiaquin, Co. Galway.[1] According to his Life, Garailt of Mayo, one of the Anglo-Saxons that accompanied Colmán of Lindisfarne into exile in the west of Ireland after the synod of Whitby in 664, had a brother named 'Balanus'.[2] This man is doubtless identical with the 'fair and troopful' Balloin who was commemorated on 3 September at the church of Tisaxon.[3]

1 *ASH* 602 §5. **2** *VSHP* ii, 106 §2. **3** *MartG* 168; *MartD* 362; *GYHS* 806–7.

Banbhán of Oldleighlin (Leithghleann), barony of Idrone West, the seat of a diocese in Co. Carlow. Despite the attempt in one line of transmission to assign this bishop-saint through his father Donnghal(ach) to the Déise, Banbhán's pedigree – more in keeping with his patronage of Kilbannivane (from Ceall Bhanbháin) in the Kerry parish of Castleisland – usually attaches him to the Ciarraighe.[1] There are three feastdays associated with the name in the martyrologies, all of them probably referring to the same saint. At 1 and 9 May, one the octave of the other, he is commemorated as bishop and *sapiens*, and at 26 November, though glossed as bishop of Leighlin, he is said to have belonged to the Corca Dhuibhne of west and south Kerry.[2] The annals, which praise him as *uas cách sapiens*, 'wise above everyone', record his death in 686.[3] One set of annals states that he was also a *fear léighinn*, 'head of school', at Kildare.[4] His connection with south-west Munster is further underlined both by holy wells dedicated to him in the Limerick parishes of Killeedy and Monagay, and by the tradition that Inghean Bhaoith, patron of Killinaboy in Clare, was his mother.[5]

The saint is sometimes taken to have been the 'Banbanus / Banbhán' cited as an authority, both in a seventh-century Latin commentary on the so-called 'Catholic Epistles', and in an equally early Irish law tract called *Cáin Fhuithirbhe*.[6]

1 *CGH* 160b14; *CGSH* §322; *GRSH* 76; *Lgen*. 733.9; *MartD* 116. **2** *MartT* 38, 41; *MartO*[2] 237; *MartG* 88, 92, 226; *MartD* 116, 122, 318. **3** *AU s.a.* **4** ATig. *s.a.* **5** OSL LK ii, 24; *JRSAI* 85, 197; *IrT* iv, 93. **6** *Peritia* 2, 238; ibid. 5, 46; *SacE* 7, 78–80; *Éigse* 23, 16–26; *BK* 25.

Baodán. This name, which has many by-forms, including Baoide, Baoithín, Baoth, Dobhaodóg, and Buadán, derives from the word *baoth*, now meaning foolish, but historically also denoting innocent or guileless.

Baodán of Cloney (Cluain Annobhair), parish of Kilberry, barony of Narragh and Reban West, Co. Kildare. The church of Baodán (alias Baoithín / Mobhaoi) son of Sineall of the Maca Alla (alias Alltraighe) of north Kerry, lay beside the river Barrow on the modern boundary of Kildare with Laois, its strategic location being such that it was later chosen by Vikings as a suitable base.[1] Historically, this boundary separated Uí Mhuireadhaigh, within which Baodán's church lay, from

Uí Chriomhthannáin, whose most famous saint was Colum of Terryglass.[2] It is scarcely a coincidence, therefore, that both Baodán and Colum were commemorated on the same day (13 December). As Colum is usually taken to have been ultimately identical with Colum Cille, Baodán of Cloney probably originated as a localization of the Iona saint's first successor, Baoithín son of Bréanainn, whose feast likewise fell on the same day as that of his predecessor, viz. 9 June.[3] In a similar coincidence of anniversaries, Buithe (Buite) of Monasterboice allegedly died on the day that Colum Cille was born, which would suggest that he too was ultimately identical with his two namesakes, Baodán of Cloney and Baoithín of Iona.[4]

Baodán's name can also be written as Baoth or Baothanán (hypocoristic Mobhaoi, anglicized Boden or Booden), and one pedigree assigns him to the Conmhaicne, who had settlements in Connacht, among other places.[5] A list of Beinéan's pupils, cited in a Conmhaicne context, includes Baodán in reference either to the Cloney saint or to his namesake at Clonmacnoise.[6] Because of the similarity of names, he may have been the same as Mobhaoi Fada ('long') son of Seanach Fíorabairteach ('of true sayings') of the unidentified church of Aireadh Mobhaoi, which would provide him with a sister named Fraochnad.[7] The saint's mother, Síon daughter of Niall, was attached to an Alltraighe branch of the Corca Bhaiscinn from the district about Loop Head in Clare, and Baodán is said to have left this area for Leinster in the time of Faolán (†665) son of Colmán.[8]

Baodán's connections with the Dál gCais are stressed in at least one source, which simultaneously draws attention to a maternal relationship with Crónán of Roscrea, borne out by a passage in the latter's Life which states that Baodán (alias Mobhaoi) died while in Crónán's company at the Offaly church of Lusmagh.[9] He was mainly connected with Leinster and, as is shown by his mention in an early Irish litany, as well as by the presence of two holy wells named after him in the Wicklow parish of Boystown (near Derrylossary), his church may have had some association with Glendalough.[10] He may also have been patron of Grange in the Dublin parish of Holmpatrick.[11] The dates assigned to Baodán have been used to support the chronology of St Patrick, with the year of his death variously placed between 629 to 634.[12] The feast of the 'pious' saint of Cloney was celebrated on 13 December and perhaps also on 6 October.[13]

1 *AU s.a.* 845; *Peritia* 20, 274; *ISEVA* 163, 325. **2** *CeltL* 144. **3** *FEMN* 462n. **4** *AU s.a.* 519; cf. *MartT* 98. **5** *CGSH* §§128–9; *GRSH* 105; *Lgen*. 731.1, 733.2. **6** *AS*.Nov. iv, 179 §13. **7** *CGSH* §301; *HDGP* i, 44. **8** *CGSH* §722.22; *JKAHS* 3, 21–2. **9** *CGSH* §697.1; *VSHP* ii, 22 §2. **10** *IrL* 56; *CPPI* 126; *WWHS* 643–4; *JCKAS* 5, 203; *AH* 8, 39. **11** *IsPatrick* 54–5. **12** *PSP* 18–20; ATig. (= *AU s.a.* 629); *AI s.a.* 634. **13** *MartO²* 220, 251; *MartG* 190, 238; *MartD* 268, 334.

Baodán of Clonmacnoise (Cluain Mac Nóis), barony of Garrycastle, Co. Offaly. An annal entry for the year 664, which records the death of this bishop, describes him as 'abbot of Cluain', a short form of Cluain Mac Nóis.[1] This great church drew its abbots from a wide selection of ecclesiastical families and Baodán, ninth in succession to Ciarán, was attached to the Maca Cormaic (otherwise known as Dál gCormaic), a Leinster family associated with the eastern part of Laois.[2]

Among the saints of Dál gCormaic were Abán of Killabban and the two Sinchealls of Killeigh. Later annals, perhaps confusing him with his namesake at Cloney, assign Baodán to the Conmhaicne Mara who gave name to Connemara, thus establishing for him a connection with Connacht, from where many abbots of Clonmacnoise came.[3] A similar confusion may underlie the reference to Baodán in a list of Beinéan's pupils, cited in a Conmhaicne context.[4] Baodán's feast fell on 1 March.[5]

1 *AU s.a*; *DIB* i, 214. 2 *FEMN* 496; *SS* 260. 3 *AFM s.a.* 663. 4 *AS*.Nov. iv, 179 §13. 5 *MartT* 20; *MartG* 46; *MartD* 60.

Baodán of Dunleer (Lann Léire), barony of Ferrard, Co. Louth. This son of Maonán is usually featured together with his brother Furodhrán, also of Dunleer, and both saints are said to have descended from Fiachra Casán of the Oirghialla.[1] More particularly, the two appear to have belonged to a branch of that group known as Uí Chruinn whose pedigree is usually placed between those of Fir Rois and Uí Shéagháin, both from the Louth/Monaghan area.[2] A poem on the saints of Dunleer, preserved in the Book of Uí Mhaine, invokes the blessings of Finnian – who was associated with the neighbouring church of Drumcar – on Baodán, Furodhrán, and other Dunleer saints.[3] Fifty Britons are reputed to have been in Dunleer with the son(s) of Maonán.[4] Baodán's nephew, Teille son of Séighín (Séaghán), also attained sanctity in the Irish tradition, and he figures with Furodhrán in the well-known tale of *Buile Shuibhne* (Sweeney's frenzy).[5] The feast of Baodán and Furodhrán fell on 18 June, and the two saints were remembered together in the dedication of the church at Dunleer.[6]

1 *CGSH* §55; *GRSH* 70; *Lgen.* 714.15. 2 *BLec.* 79v^{ab}. 3 *CGSH* §737; *CSMA* i, 153. 4 *IrL* 66. 5 *IrT* iii, 55; *BS* §9. 6 *MartT* 51; *MartG* 118; *MartD* 172; *RNF* 249 (Brethanus et Frethanus).

Baodán of Killoscobe (Ceall Ua Scóba), barony of Tiaquin, Co. Galway. This saint was reputedly one of four (or six) children of Eoghan son of Murchadh of the Eoghanachta, two of whom (Beagán and Cúlán) remained in Munster whereas two others (Cormac and Diarmuid) are said to have gone to Connacht.[1] Baodán is alleged to have later followed his brothers to Connacht, settling among the Soghain of east Galway at a place variously called Ceall Bhaodáin and Ceall Ua Scóba, now Killoscobe.[2] Seventeenth-century sources speculate that he may have been the Baodán of 'Monu' commemorated on 23 March, at which date John Colgan also gave an account of him.[3] Baodán may have retained a connection with Munster through the church of Glenkeen in the Tipperary barony of Kilnamanagh Upper, which he surrendered, according to the Life of Fionnbharr, to the Cork saint.[4]

1 *IrT* iii, 1–8. 2 Ibid., 6 §18; cf. PNNI iv, 148–9. 3 *ASH* 728. 4 *BBa.* 68 §23; *MartD* 84; *GRSH* 115 (Buadan).

Baodán of Mostrim (Meathas Truim), barony of Ardagh, Co. Longford. An entry in the Martyrology of Tallaght for 24 January gives pride of place to Baodán of Mostrim, followed by Guasacht of Granard.[1] His feast is confirmed by the later martyrologies which render the saint's name as Buadán, and the name of his church, corruptly, as Eathas Cruim.[2] Nothing else is known of Baodán save that he remained patron of the parish of Mostrim, as can be seen from a reference to 'S. Vadanus' in an entry from the annates of Ardagh dating to 1410.[3]

1 *MartT* 11. 2 *MartG* 24; *MartD* 26 (but cf. ibid. 366, 368). 3 *AnnU* 175; *HDA* 730–1.

Baodán of Rubha Baodáin, now perhaps Bodenstown, barony of Naas North, Co. Kildare.[1] This saint is one of seven sons of Lughaidh son of Nathí, of a branch of the Laighin (Leinstermen) called Uí Chéithigh, who gave name to Ikeathy barony just north of Bodenstown.[2] The most famous of Baodán's brothers was Crónán (alias Mochua) of Clondalkin. Another brother, Baoithín, who bears essentially the same name as Baodán and was probably ultimately identical with him, was attached to the Kildare church of Gilltown (Inis Breisléin). Cainnear of Clonsilla was regarded as the mother of these saints.[3] As Bodenstown lies close to Naas, Baodán may be the saint of that name who found mention in a poem on Ceall Chearbáin, another name for Naas.[4] No feastday is recorded for either Baodán or his brother Baoithín, but a grange and chapel named after Baoithín (under the guise of 'Boyan') are mentioned in sixteenth-century documents.[5]

1 But cf. Logainm.ie 'Bodenstown'. 2 *CGH* 124a14; *CGSH* §243; *Lgen.* 727.13. 3 *CGSH* §722.77. 4 *MD* iv, 340; *Seanchas* 221. 5 *JCKAS* 2, 325; ibid. 3, 374.

Baodán Ab. *See* Éidchéan of Clonfad.

Baoghlach Oilithir, 'pilgrim'. This saint figures only in the corpus of genealogies, which assigns him through his father Faoldobhar to a branch of the Oirghialla known as Ceinéal Tuatáin.[1] Judging by the saint's pedigree, he was a younger contemporary of Cuana (Constans) of Eonish on Lough Erne who died in 778.[2] Some seventeenth-century commentators considered him to be identical with the Baothghalach commemorated on 5 October, unless – as seems more likely – this man was the brother (and successor) of Cormac of Trim.[3]

1 *CGSH* §59; *CGH* 141b51; *GRSH* 66; *Lgen.* 712.3. 2 *AU s.a.* 3 *GRSH* 66; *MartD* 266.

Baoithín. *See* Baodán.

Baoithín of Ennisboyne (Inis Baoithín), parish of Dunganstown, barony of Arklow, Co. Wicklow. This son of Fionna(ch) was provided with a descent from Lughaidh Laoighseach, progenitor of the Laoighse (whence Laois).[1] His mother Trea (alias Créadh) is described as a daughter of Rónán, king of Leinster, perhaps the ruler of that name who died in 624.[2] The saint's unconventional conception is set out in unsavoury detail in verse and prose, both of which describe the saint's father as a robber.[3] Baoithín is credited with four brothers, namely Baosach, Fiontan, Sligheire, and Cuimín, and among his cousins was Aona of Clonmacnoise.[4] He may be the Baoithín Bán, 'white', mentioned in a poem attributed to Moling, which calls upon him, with many other saints, to come to the assistance of the Leinstermen.[5] The church at Ennisboyne was also associated with Fiodhmhaine Ua Suanaigh, whose feast fell on 16 May, whereas that of

Baoithín fell a week later on 22 May.[6] A well visited on that day at Knockaneda in the Cork parish of Knocktemple was also dedicated to Baoithín.[7]

1 *CGSH* §156; *GRSH* 102; *Lgen.* 734.2, 749.3.6; *GT* 141 §30; *MartT* 98. 2 *CGSH* §722.65; *MartO*[2] 134; *AU s.a.* 3 *CGSH* §699; *MartO*[2] 134. 4 *CGSH* §722.65; *GRSH* 102; *GT* 141 §30. 5 *SG* i, 389. 6 *MartT* 45; *MartO*[2] 125; *MartG* 98, 102; *MartD* 130, 136. 7 *AICK* iv (pt ii), 466.

Baoithín of Gilltown. *See* Baodán of Rubha Baodáin.

Baoithín of Iona, Scotland. First coarb of Colum Cille, with whom he also shared a feastday (9 June), Baoithín son of Bréanainn was undoubtedly the most celebrated bearer of the name and, as the records of Baodán of Cloney and Buithe of Monasterboice show, he may also have been the original focus of the cults of many of the saints who shared his name in one or other of its possible forms. A close blood relation of Colum Cille, Baoithín figures prominently in the late seventh-century Life composed for his predecessor by Adhamhnán.[1] This describes him as Colum's *alumnus*, 'pupil', successor-designate, and constant companion, especially later in life. It also reveals that he was head of a monastery on the island of Hinba (perhaps Jura) in Argyll and prior of a church in Tiree. Baoithín's own Life, a short Latin text preserved in two collections, consists almost entirely of miracles attributed to the saint, whose activities are in the main confined to Iona and the surrounding districts.[2] Its comparison of Baoithín with John the Evangelist in his 'sincere innocence' and 'most prudent simplicity' may have been influenced by the derivation of the saint's name from *baoth*, 'guileless'.[3]

Other Lives that feature Baoithín – almost always in Colum Cille's company, or as his messenger – are those of Ruadhán of Lorrha, Cainneach of Aghaboe, Fiontan of Taghmon, and Molaise of Devenish.[4] The latter Life recounts Baoithín's vision (also recorded in notes added to martyrologies) of three shining but empty chairs in heaven which were interpreted for him by Colum Cille as seats awaiting Ciarán of Clonmacnoise, Molaise of Devenish and the founder of Iona himself.[5] The saint's own prophetic power may underlie a reference to Baoithín Oirthir ('of the east') who, according to a poem by Giolla Brighde Mac Con Midhe, foretold the birth of Aodh Ua Domhnaill, lord of the Ceinéal Conaill of Donegal.[6]

Despite his significant role on Iona, not many Scottish churches were associated with the saint, but he was venerated there under the guise of 'Bathan/ Bothan'.[7] Among the Irish churches linked to his cult are Taughboyne (Teach Baoithín), which gave name to a Donegal parish, close to Derry of Colum Cille, and Balrathboyne Glebe in the Meath parish of Balrathboyne, close to Kells, where a holy well also bears his name.[8] A late and otherwise unattested tradition asserts that he succeeded Colum as abbot of Derry.[9] As the feast of Buadán (alias Baodán) of Culdaff in the Donegal barony of Inishowen East, where the saint's bell is still kept, also fell on 9 June, it has been asserted, no doubt correctly, that he was identical with his namesake Baoithín.[10] Born, according to the Annals of Tighearnach in 536, Baoithín's obit is variously dated to 598 and 601 and, together with that of Colum Cille, his feast of 9 June was recorded in an early ninth-century calendar kept by an Irishman on the Reichenau in Lake Constance.[11]

1 *CGSH* §327; *GRSH* 38; *Lgen.* 697.5, 749.2.6; *VC*² 546; ibid. 11b–13b et passim; *IKD* 37; *GJ* 4, 228; cf. *MartT* 98; *DIB* i, 231. 2 *VSHH* 379–82; *MHH* 236; *Kenney* 443; *IKD* 37n. 3 *VSHH* 382 §13. 4 *VSHH* 167 §24, 188–9 §27, 200 §7, 249 §7; *VSHP* i, 159–60 §§21–2, ii, 139 §32, 228–9 §§5–7, 251–2 §29. 5 *VSHP* ii, 139 §32; *MartO*² 146; *MartD* 162–4. 6 *IrT* ii, 69 §7. 7 *CPNS* 151; *KSS* 276; *ACDS* 72–3; *Innes Review* 48, 50–1. 8 *MartD* 162; *OSL MH*, 43. 9 *GJ* 4, 228. 10 *DOH* 84; cf. OSL DL 32. 11 *AU/AI s.a.*; *IKD* 38–9; *AfL* 31, 52; *ATig. s.a.*

Baoithín of Taghboyne (Teach Baoithín), parish of Churchtown, barony of Rathconrath, Co. Westmeath. Baoithín (alias Mobhaoi) son of Cuana is attached by the genealogists to the Ceinéal Éanna, a branch of the Ceinéal Conaill in the area south of Inishowen in Donegal.[1] The Swillyburn river, which appears to have formed the southern boundary of Ceinéal Éanna, also served as a boundary of the Donegal parish of Taughboyne (Teach Baoithín).[2] This is one indication that the saint of the Westmeath Taghboyne and Baoithín of Iona, who reputedly gave name to the Donegal Taughboyne, were ultimately identical.[2] Another is the manner in which the late vernacular Life of Colum Cille brings the two together at the convention of Druim Ceat, among other places.[3] Many references to the saint occur in late verse concerning Colum Cille, attributed to Baoithín, one passage of which compares its subject's hospitality to that of Guaire and Cú Chulainn.[4] Another church associated with the saint, Ennisboyne (Inis Baoithín) in the Wicklow parish of Dunganstown, was more usually attached to Baoithín son of Fionna(ch).[5] Baoithín's mother Caomhnad is said to have belonged to the Dál mBuachalla of Down.[6] The saint's feastday fell on 19 February, and the notice in the Martyrology of Tallaght describes him as a bishop.[7] The notice in the Martyrology of Donegal states that he was also patron of Tibohine (Teach Baoithín) in the Roscommon barony of Frenchpark.[8] As such, he may also be the Baoithín remembered in the Mayo parish name of Crossboyne (Cros Bhaoithín), and perhaps also the saint of the name invoked in a poem by Donnchadh Mór Ó Dálaigh (†1244).[9]

1 *CGSH* §26; *GRSH* 58; *Lgen.* 708.1, 749.5.6; *CCDK* 120–31; cf. *MartT* 98. 2 *CCDK* 122. 3 *BCC* 74, 140, 362–4, 442–4, 448. 4 Ibid. 140; *ZCP* 7, 303–4. 5 *Rep. Nov.* 2.1, 51. 6 *CGSH* §722.55, p. 321. 7 *MartT* 18; *MartO*² 61; *MartG* 38; *MartD* 52. 8 *MartD* 52. 9 *DDé* 50; cf. *LME* vii, 251–4.

Baoithín of Taughboyne. *See* Baoithín of Iona.

Baoithín son of Alla. *See* Baodán of Cloney.

Baoithín son of Lughaidh. *See* Baodán of Rubha Baodáin.

Baoithín son of Sineall. *See* Baodán of Cloney.

Baoithín Oirthir, 'of the east'. *See* Baoithín of Iona.

Baothghalach of Trim (Áth Truim), baronies of Lower Moyfenrath and Upper Navan, Co. Meath. Three sons are said to have been born to Fuineacht daughter of Maol Fithrigh by Colmán grandson of Suibhne, namely Baothghalach, Cormac, and the celebrated poet Rumhan.[1] Although Baothghalach's brother Cormac has sometimes been taken to be an abbot of Armagh who died in 497, this assumption was probably influenced by the well-attested tradition that Trim was one of the first churches founded by Patrick.[2] The Cormac in question was an abbot of Trim who died in 746, ten years ahead of his brother and successor

Baothghalach (†756).[3] Some seventeenth-century sources assume, probably correctly, that Baothghalach was the saint of that name commemorated on 5 October.[4]

1 *CGSH* §§690.4, 722.74; *Lgen.* 753.53. 2 *MartG* 38; *MartD* 50; *NHI* ix, 238; *PTBA* 166–8; *BP* 697–712; *VT* 66–8. 3 *JEH* 1.2, 166–7; *AU s.a.* 4 *MartD* 266; *GRSH* 66.

Barrach. *See* Brígh of Barragh; Sárnad of Barragh.

Barrahane. *See* Bearchán.

Barry. *See* Bairre; Bairrfhionn; Bearach; Fionnbharr.

Basar. *See* Iobhar.

Beacon. *See* Beagán

Beag, 'little', is attached as a name to several saints, and there are many variants of it, e.g. Beagán, Mobheagóg, Bigeall and, in female guise, Beagnad, Bigseach.

Beag of Killerrig (Ceall Deirge Daimh), barony and county of Carlow. A son of Dubh Dúile, this saint (accompanied by Cuimín son of Fothlán) is listed among those subject to Brighid of Kildare.[1] His church is elsewhere remembered in a litany of mostly pilgrim saints as the home of seven saintly bishops.[2]

1 *CGSH* §670.48. 2 *IrL* 66.

Beag son of Dé Draoi, 'druid'. This saint is the subject of several different statements of his descent, one attaching him to the Oirghialla of south-east Ulster, another placing him among the Dál gCais of Thomond, and a third assigning him to Ceinéal Maine of Teathbha, a stretch of land comprising most of Longford and part of Westmeath.[1] The latter descent brings him closest to the setting of his best-known role, as chief *fáidh*, 'prophet', of Diarmuid son of Cearbhall, king of Tara. In this capacity, he was given the honour of foretelling, while in the company of Colum Cille, the future glory of the Columban church of Kells (Ceanannas), and also of identifying the circumstances of his royal patron's violent death.[2] One of his most characteristic roles was that of foretelling the births of other saints, including Bréanainn of Clonfert and Ciarán of Clonmacnoise.[3] Pseudepigraphical and doleful poems outlining portents of future disasters are regularly attributed to Beag, most notably in his so-called *baile*, 'mantic vision, frenzy'.[4]

Beag's unconventional conception through the medium of his father's cremated ashes is retold in the section of the Book of Uí Mhaine that contains the genealogies of the Dál gCais.[5] Other references to the saint include an encounter with Molaise of Devenish – then on a visit to the king at Tara – who proved wrong one of Beag's pronouncements, and a prophecy concerning a lake that moved at the command of Aodh of Rahugh.[6] According to the Martyrology of Donegal, his feastday fell on 12 October, but the other martyrologies refer on this day to a saint named Beag without further identification.[7] According to the annals, he died in 553 (or 558).[8]

1 *CGSH* §21.1–2; *CGH* 152a55; *GRSH* 69; *Lgen.* 714.9, 738.6; *BLCat.* ii, 311. 2 *LisL* 927–34; *IKD* 232 §38; *SG* i, 75. 3 *VSHP* ii, 98 §2; *LisL* 3341–6; 3971. 4 *ZCP* 9, 169–70; ibid. 10, 421–2; *Ériu* 18, 55–84. 5 UM 32va58. 6 *VSHP* ii, 138 §28; ibid. I, 40 §19. 7 *MartT* 79; *MartG* 194; *MartD* 272. 8 *AU s.a.*

Beag son of Maonán. This man is known only from a metrical list of those in service with Patrick, which describes him as the Armagh saint's *maor scuir*, 'horse-steward'.[1]

1 *CGSH* §672.19.

Beag Bile of Tullaghobegly (Tulacha Bheicbhile/Bheigile), barony of Kilmacrenan, Co. Donegal. The Ó Cléirigh collection of genealogies includes in its section of Ceinéal Conaill saints four sons of Tighearnach, named Beag Bile, Colmán, Cuán, and Connaidhil, alias Conán, who was remembered on 8 March at a place called 'Cnodair', near Assaroe, now possibly Knader in the Donegal parish of Kilbarron.[1] Curiously, the same set of brothers is elsewhere attached to a father named Síolán of the Clann Luighne, a branch of the Ciarraighe of north Kerry.[2] Little else is known of these brothers but a strong case has been made for identifying the northern Beag Bile with Bigeall (alias Beaglaoch), patron of Tullaghobegly, who was raised from the dead, according to Colum Cille's late vernacular Life.[3] A good deal of folklore has been preserved locally concerning Bigeall of Tulach, whose feast fell on 1 November, one of the principal days of the Celtic year.[4] On the other hand, a feast of 12 October, otherwise associated with Beag son of Dé, has been assigned to Beag Bile son of Tighearnach in seventeenth-century sources.[5] Locally known as 'Bee-Ella' the saint came to be regarded as a hermit who lived at 'Cnoc an Locha' in the Donegal parish of Clonca, subsequently a place of pilgrimage.[6] The cult appears also to have become established in north Connacht, at Kilbegly (Ceall Bheaglaoich) in the Roscommon parish of Moore, where a holy well was called after the saint, and perhaps also at an ecclesiastical site called 'Ceall Bheigile' in the Sligo parish of Templecrone.[7]

1 *GRSH* 38; *ASH* 563; *HDGP* v, 186. 2 *CGSH* §304; *CGH* 160b55. 3 *CCDK* 92–6; *KeltRh.* 135–8; *BCC* 102 §110. 4 *CCDK* 94–6; *MartG* 208; *MartD* 292. 5 *MartD* 274; *GRSH* 38. 6 *DOH* 83. 7 OSL RN i, 49.

Beagán of Churchtown (formerly Stagonil/Teach Conaill), Powerscourt townland and parish, barony of Rathdown, Co. Wicklow. Beagán son of Lughaidh is perhaps best known for his *tiughrann*, 'last verses', on Colum Cille. These verses, which, among many other praises, memorably exalt the Iona saint as *Columb Cille, Columb boíë, Columb biäss*, 'Columb of the church, Columb who was, Columb who will be', have been dated to the seventh century.[1] Beagán is credited with the authorship of another poem in praise of Colum Cille, arguably also composed in the seventh century.[2] His pedigree assigns him to the Ceinéal Eoghain, whose ancestor gave name to Tyrone and Inishowen.[3] The saint's name is sometimes confused with that of Breacán (alias Bracán) of Caw, and his feastday of 26 May is shared by his namesake, Beagán of Toureen.[4] His association with Colum Cille has encouraged the view that he was identical with Beagán *solitarius/eremita*, 'hermit', who received about 630 (together with Séighín, abbot of Iona) a letter from Cuimín concerning the Paschal question.[5] Beagán of Rum, allegedly a brother of Cuimín Fionn, abbot of Iona, is, however, a more likely recipient.

1 *Ériu* 26, 66–98; *Iona* 129–63. 2 *Ériu* 24, 1–34. 3 *CGSH* §32; *Lgen.* 701.12. 4 *GRSH* 44; *MartG* 104; *MartD* 139. 5 *ASH* 839; *MartD* 364; *LIS* 5, 568; cf. *IKD* 40–1; *CLCP* 7–15.

Beagán of Emlagh (Imleach Fiaich), barony of Lower Kells, Co. Meath. This son of Cúla is reported to have restored to life Breasal, a son of Diarmuid son of Cearbhall, king of Tara, and a quatrain in praise of the king is also attributed to him.[1] Having become remorseful after drowning his son in punishment for the theft of a cow belonging to a nun, Diarmuid had recourse to Beagán who finally responded to a plea for assistance from Colum Cille. Little else is known of the saint, but Cúla was his mother's name and, despite an attempt by Colgan to identify him with Beagán son of Murchadh, that of his father remains unknown.[2] He has been variously claimed for Síol Criomhthainn – another name for the Oirghialla of south-east Ulster – and Dál gCais of Thomond.[3] He is also said to have been one of Ireland's three *athlaoich*, a term used of laymen who went on to become monks, often in old age, and he is included in the version of the list of Ireland's twelve apostles preserved in the vernacular Life of Molaise of Devenish.[4] His feast fell on 5 April.[5]

1 *ZCP* 7, 305–7; *MartT* 102–4; *MartD* 94–6; *MartO²* 6. 2 *GRSH* 115. 3 *MartO²* 112; 4 Ibid.; *SG* i, 25, 34. 5 *MartT* 30; *MartO²* 104.

Beagán of Foithearbh Shinill, an unidentified place, perhaps in Co. Westmeath. This son of Colmán and his (otherwise unattested) brothers, Colán and Cogán, are mentioned in a miscellaneous section of the corpus of saints' pedigrees, mainly comprising saints associated with Brighid of Kildare.[1] Several churches in this section lay in the part of Westmeath now covered by the baronies of Fartullagh, Moycashel and Moyashel, all of which had strong Brigidine connections.[2] If Colmán son of Diarmuid, eponymous ancestor of the Clann Cholmáin, was Beagán's father, this would strengthen the case for a Westmeath location of his church, but only one son of this Colmán, namely Suibhne, is recorded in the genealogies.[3] The church of Kilbeggan in Moycashel may be named after the saint. Its patron's day was 24 July, the eve of the feast of St James.[4]

1 *CGSH* §663.13. 2 *BBr.* 6–10 §§17–29. 3 *CGH* 143bc52. 4 *PNW* 55.

Beagán of Ros Achaidh Liag. This *cruimhthear*, 'presbyter', is remembered in a miscellaneous section of the corpus of saints' pedigrees, which assigns to him two other presbyters as companions, Munna and Meachar.[1] He may be the same as the Beagán son of Bleidhín who figures as a penitent in the Life of Fiontan (alias Munna) of Taghmon, at a point shortly after an angel had told Fiontan that the place of his resurrection was to be Achadh Liag Eachdhroma, now perhaps a church site in the Wexford parish of Taghmon.[2]

1 *CGSH* §175. 2 *VSHH* 203–4 §§18, 22; *HDGP* i, 20.

Beagán of Rum, Scotland. Little is known of this saint who, according to the annals, died in 677.[1] In a note added to the Four Masters' genealogies of kings and saints (*Genealogiae Regum et Sanctorum Hiberniae*), apparently by John Colgan, Beagán is said to have been a brother of Cuimín Fionn, abbot of Iona.[2] A namesake, Beagán of Churchtown, has been taken to be identical with Beagán *solitarius/eremita*, 'hermit', who received about 630 (together with Séighín, abbot of Iona) a letter from a certain Cuimín concerning the Paschal question.[3] In view of his supposed relationship with Cuimín Fionn, Beagán of Rum may be regarded as a more likely recipient. He shared a feastday of 17 March with Patrick.[4]

1 *AU*/ATig. *s.a.* 2 *GRSH* 38. 3 *ASH* 839; *MartD* 364; *LIS* 5, 568; cf. *IKD* 40–1; *CLCP* 7–15. 4 *MartT* 24; *MartG* 56; *MartD* 80.

Beagán of Toureen (Tuairín Péacáin, earlier Cluain Aird Mobheagóg), parish of Killardry, barony of Clanwilliam, Co. Tipperary. Throughout Munster, the initial *b-* of this saint's name became *p-* (Péacán), as in Kilpeacon (Limerick) and Rathpeacon (Cork). The Tipperary saint, who through his father Murchadh (also named Anla son of Murchadh) is provided with an Eoghanacht pedigree, was the foremost southern representative of the cult.[1] The site of his church, with its remains of several stone crosses and inscribed stones, reflects this importance.[2] As a *Lughnasadh* site, it was the focus of a large annual assembly on 1 August, and both it and the saint receive mention in the Life of Abán, composed early in the thirteenth century, probably by Ailbhe Ua Maoil Mhuadh, bishop of Ferns.[3] The biographer credits Abán with founding the church, but acknowledges Beagán's presence there 'in three-day fasts, assiduous prayers, genuflections, wringings of hands, and nightly vigils'.[4] Beagán is also portrayed as a lover of vigils in the quatrain composed by Aonghas of Tallaght for his feast of 26 May.[5] In the later martyrologies, Beagán (alias Mobheagóg) is said to have been also associated with Teach Conaill in Uí Bhriúin of Cuala, later 'Stagonil', and now Churchtown in the Wicklow townland and parish of Powerscourt.[6] Further south, at Mullinavat in the Kilkenny parish of Kilbeacon, which is named after the saint, his feast was celebrated on 27 May.[7] Although the pattern was celebrated on 1 August at Toureen, devotions were also held on Good Friday.[8] The saint was possibly identical with Beagán son of Eoghan, son of Murchadh, one of several brothers, some of whom migrated to Connacht.[9] An obit of 690 is preserved for Beagán.[10] He may be the 'Mobheagóg Aird' listed among the guarantors of the Law of Adhamhnán.[11]

1 *CGSH* §199; *GRSH* 115; *Lgen.* 742.1.2. 2 *ECIM* 290–329. 3 *FL* 642–3; *PSICCSO* 159–70. 4 *VSHP* i, 17 §22; *BNÉ* i, 8 §25. 5 *MartO*² 126; cf. *MartT* 46. 6 *MartG* 104; *MartD* 138; *PNCW* 296–8; OSL WW 30. 7 *HADO* iv, 171–2. 8 OSL TY iii, 199; *FL* 642–2. 9 *IrT* iii, 1 §1. 10 *AU s.a.* 11 *CA* §28; but cf. *Peritia* 1, 189.

Beagán son of Eoghan. *See* Beagán of Toureen.

Beagán son of Sárán. *See* Breacán of Aughrim.

Beaglaoch. *See* Beag Bile.

Beagnad daughter of Cian. *See* Fíonán Cam.

Beagnad of Dalkey. *See* Beagnad of Kilbegnet.

Beagnad of Kilbeacanty (Ceall Bheaganta), barony of Kiltartan, Co. Galway. This saint is mentioned in one early source only, a poem listing the children of Inghean Bhaoith of Killinaboy which, while grouping Beagnad together with Greallán and Ceasán, places her on 'the edge of Aidhne', the name of a territory approximately equivalent to the later diocese of Kilmacduagh, to which the parish of Kilbeacanty belonged.[1] There is no basis to the belief that Féichín was patron of the parish.[2]

1 *IrT* iv, 93 §2 (read *Aidhne* for *aibhne*); *HDGP* i, 27. 2 *HADK* 431–3.

Beagnad of Kilbegnet (Ceall Bheagnadan), parish of Kilgorman, barony of Gorey, Co. Wexford, and of Tirhogar (Tír Chóigir), parish of Lea, barony of Portnahinch, Co. Laois. Beagnad daughter of Colmán is known from a list of saints belonging to the Dál Meisin Corb, whose principal saint was Caoimhghin of Glendalough.[1] In view of the close association of Dublin and Glendalough dioceses, she is probably identical with the patron of two Dublin parishes (Dalkey and Donnybrook) whose feast of 12 November is recorded in various post-Conquest calendars.[2] A litany-style prayer of invocation includes Beagnad among many other female saints.[3]

1 *CGSH* §182.14; *Lgen.* 725.9; *HDGP* iii, 131; *CPPI* 182; *TNW* 1071–2. 2 *JRSAI* 52, 14; *BOM* xlv; *Rep. Nov.* 2, 46, 48–9; ibid. 3, 173; *AAR* 247. 3 *MartT* 108; *IrL* 92.

Beagrall daughter of Eirnín. *See* Cearc of Aughlis.

Bean(n)án. *See* Beinéan.

Bean(us). *See* Beoán of Meenan.

Bearach of Kilbarry (Cluain Cairbthe / Ceall Bhearaigh), parish of Termonbarry, barony of Ballintober North, Co. Roscommon. Bearing a name also written Beireach (anglicized Barry), the saint belonged through a father variously named Aimhirghin and Neamhann (Neamhall) to the Uí Bhriain of Connacht and, more specifically, to Ceinéal Dobhtha, who held lands in Roscommon, on the east bank of the river Shannon.[1] The saint's mother, Fíonmhaith daughter of Carthach, is described as a sister of Fraoch of Cloone.[2]

The Latin version of the Life composed for Bearach survives only in the so-called *Insulensis* collection, made in two copies, shortly before and after 1400, at the priories of Saints' Island on Lough Ree and nearby Abbeyderg in Longford, the second of which contains a unique image of the saint.[3] The underlying collection may have been brought together by a member of the Mágraidhean family who had ancestral lands in the parish of Termonbarry.[4] Though rightly described as late and as 'concerned especially' with the dues that should be paid to the saint's church, the Life, which is also extant in a vernacular version, is nevertheless of great interest for the witness it bears to local secular and ecclesiastical concerns at the time of writing.[5] The close links between the local ruling family of Ceinéal Dobhtha, later Uí Ainlighe (O'Hanlys), and the patron of Termonbarry are clearly brought out in the Life – especially in its vernacular version – which begins by asserting that Patrick visited the home of Dobhtha, ancestor of that family and also of the saint, in order to foretell Bearach's birth sixty years later.[6] A miracle attributed to Patrick is said to have generated the local name Achadh Gréine, later 'Aughagrany' in the Leitrim parish of Cloone (Cluain Conmhaicne), named after the chief church of Fraoch, Bearach's maternal uncle.[7]

Following his birth at Cloone, Bearach was baptized by his uncle and given Fiontan as a baptismal name, his other name being explained as from *bir-ach*, because of the 'sharpness' of his miracles.[8] The saint's sister Midhabhair is also mentioned in connection with the church of Bumlin (Buimlinn), near Termonbarry.[9]

Among the many saints brought into contact with Bearach are Daigh son of Coireall who, according to the vernacular Life, was his first tutor, and Caoimhghin of Glendalough who is given this honour in the Latin Life, which also reveals some passages apparently drawn from the *vita* of the Glendalough saint.[10] Bishop Éidchéan of Clonfad, who is elsewhere said to have belonged to the same family as Caoimhghin, is given the honour of conferring orders on Bearach.[11]

An account of the founding of Bearach's church at Termonbarry is couched in traditional terms, with a wild animal assuring, as in many other Lives, the sacredness of the site, and this is followed by a prolonged dispute with a local poet concerning ownership of land, which is finally resolved at an assembly attended by numerous saints and kings, held in Lissardowlan (Lios Ard Abhla) in Longford, reputedly the exact centre of Ireland.[12] In the course of this dispute, recourse was had to a Scottish king who granted the saint the church of Aberfoyle (Eibearpuill), where the October market was later termed 'Féill Barachan' (Bearchán's feast).[13]

Other locations reputedly blessed by the saint, or offered to him, include a long list of places 'reddened' by his suddenly maddened oxen, as well as a site called Tuaim Achaidh, near Termonbarry, which is elsewhere said to have been granted in 1176 to Bearach's church by Ruaidhrí Ua Conchobhair, 'king of Ireland', thus providing an earliest possible date for the Life.[14] In the vernacular Life, Talmhach is accorded the distinction of giving Bearach the last rites.[15] Bearach's church at Kilbarry receives regular mention in the annals from 918, when the death of Daniel, its 'wonderful historian', was noted, until 1452, when a local chieftain, Giolla na Naomh Ua hAinlighe, then long retired from his chieftaincy, died and was buried there. Giolla na Naomh's predecessor Aodh was likewise buried there in 1405, in expectation 'of meeting Bearach'.[16]

The saint gave name to Kilberry (pronounced Kilbarry) in Meath, and apparently also to Kilbarrack in Dublin, and his cult may have travelled to west Connacht under the guise of Bearóg and Dobhearóg.[17] The Dublin connection led to the inclusion of his feast (15 February) under the guise of 'Berus' in some post-Conquest liturgical manuscripts.[18] The Seanbheireach, 'older Bearach', remembered on 10 June at Cooldrumman (Cúil Dreimhne), site of the celebrated battle in the Sligo parish of Drumcliff, may also represent the saint.[19] In addition to the usual Irish sources, the saint's feast is recorded in a Cologne martyrology compiled before 1500 by Grevenus.[20] In south Munster, the saint's day was traditionally known as *Lá 'le Beiriheart*, 'Beircheart's day'.[21] At Mostrim in Longford, where veneration of the saint was marked by 'Barry's Well', the pattern day fell on 15 August.[22] The saint's coarb was among the ecclesiastics entitled to be present at the inauguration of O'Connor as king of Connacht, and his crozier, popularly known as *Gearr Bearaigh*, and widely used in Roscommon to cure or swear upon, was kept by a member of the O'Hanly family before coming to the National Museum.[23] Bells associated with the saint, now all lost, are attested for Kilbarry and Glendalough in Ireland and Kilberry in Scotland.[24]

1 *CGSH* §25; *GRSH* 59; *Lgen.* 710.4; *HDGP* iv, 112–13; *DIB* i, 461. **2** *CGSH* §722.101. **3** *VSHP* i, xxxiii–xxxiv, 75–86; *MISL* (dust-jacket); *LDHS* 39–50. **4** Ibid. 43. **5** *Kenney* 403; *BNÉ* i, 23–43; *ILL* 365–6. **6** *BNÉ* i, 24 §5; *VSHP* i, 75 §3; cf. *CGSH* §§25, 722.101; *GRSH* 69; *Lgen.* 710.4. **7** *BNÉ* i, 24–6 §§7, 16; *VSHP* i, 76 §4. **8** *BNÉ* i, 26 §16. **9** Ibid. 26 §17. **10** *BNÉ* i, 26 §18; *VSHP* i, 77–9 §§6–10. **11** *BNÉ* i, 31 §42; *CGSH* §181.7. **12** *BNÉ* i, 32–7 §§46–66; *VSHP* i, 79–85 §§12–34. **13** *BNÉ* i, 35 §59; *KSS* 278–9; *CPNS* 225, 301; cf. *ACDS* 90. **14** *BNÉ* i, 39 §75; *AFM s.a.* **15** *BNÉ* i, 43 §90. **16** *AU s.a.* 918; *AFM s.a.* 1452; *ALC* 1405. **17** *CPL* 1, 356; *IER* (5th ser.) 1, 181; *Rep. Nov.* 2, 48; *LIS* 2, 544–6; OSL MO i, 98; ii, 8. **18** *Rep. Nov.* 2, 46, 48, *MartFC* 50–1. **19** *MartT* 49; *MartG* 114; *MartD* 166. **20** *MartT* 17; *MartO*^{2} 60; *MartG* 36; *MartD* 48; *AS*.Iun. vi, 105. **21** *LSUC* 358. **22** OSL LD 35. **23** *Éigse* 6, 138–9; *TKAS* 2, 340n; *ILSC* 75; *JRSAI* 2, 340; *MSPAG* 188. **24** *EMH* 482 §216; 488 §236; 494 §249.

Bearchán of Castlehaven (Gleann Bearcháin/'Glanbarryhane'), barony of Carbury West, Co. Cork. As Bearchán's church (St Barrahane's) lies within the former territory of the Corca Laoighdhe, it would appear that the saint was thought to belong to this family. The patronymic Maon, provided for him in the corpus of saints' pedigrees, does not agree, however, with the name Fiachra, given to his father in the genealogies of the Corca Laoighdhe.[1] Though the saint's well ('toberbarahane') was still frequented by pilgrims in the early nineteenth century, the day of the pattern has not been recorded.[2] Local tradition maintained that Bearchán came from Spain, but a member of the Uí Ghiolla Mhichíl branch of the Corca Laoighdhe was known as his *fear ionaid*, 'representative'.[3]

1 *CGSH* §265; *Lgen.* 747.2; GCL 46–8. **2** *CPR* i, lxx; *TDI* i, 298; *AICK* i, 282. **3** *SeanC* 84; *LGen.* 677.7.

Bearchán of Ceall Fhidhne, an unidentified church in Cluain Caoin of Dealbhna Eathra, approximately the present barony of Garrycastle in Offaly, on whose boundary lies a place called Clonkeen in the parish of Rahan.[1] Said to be a son of the Fidhne whose name became attached to the saint's church, Bearchán is otherwise unknown.

1 *CGSH* §268; *Lgen.* 749.9.

Bearchán of Clonsast (Cluain Sosda), barony of Coolestown, Co. Offaly. Variously described as a son of Muireadhach, Miocán, Macaomh, and Caoi, and known by the aliases Bearchán *Propheta*, 'prophet', and Bearchán *na Buile*, 'of the vision', the saint is usually assigned to the Cruithin or Dál Riada.[1] As this group had settlements in both Ireland and Scotland, Bearchán was considered to have borne the nickname of Fear Dhá Leithe, 'man of two parts', in token of his connection with both countries.[2] According to his pedigree, Bearchán's great-grandfather was Ainbhcheallach son of Fearchar, king of Dál Riada, who was taken into exile in Ireland in 698 and slain in battle with his brother in 718.[3] If genuine, this would give the saint a floruit in the late eighth century, but there is no record of his death in the annals. His mother, Fiamhain daughter of Diarmuid, is, however, presented as a grand-daughter of Laoghaire son of Niall, a contemporary of Patrick, which would date Bearchán, if he ever existed separately from his namesakes, to the sixth century.[4]

Largely because of the poems of prophecy attributed to him, Bearchán of Clonsast is the best-known bearer of the name. The most important of these poems, on the future kings of Ireland and Scotland, has been made the subject of two critical editions.[5] An extract from it, relating to the woes that would befall Ireland after the death of Brian Bóramha, is cited in the early twelfth-century text known as *Wars of the Gaedhil with the Gaill*.[6] In his *Expugnatio Hibernica*, completed by 1189, Gerald of Wales listed Bearchán (written *Braccanus*) among the four prophets of Ireland – the others being Moling, Patrick, and Colum Cille – when citing a prophecy on the discomfiture of the English.[7] A similar list, containing Bréanainn of Birr instead of Patrick, is cited in the entry on Bearchán's feast in the Martyrology of Donegal.[8] Bearchán's prophecies continued to be invoked in expectation of the birth of Ireland's saviour.[9] Bearchán's church of Clonsast is credited with possession of a book, named *Leabhar Bearcháin (na Cluana)* after the saint, which was still extant in the early sixteenth century, at which time it formed part of the library of the earl of Kildare.[10] A tub (*dabhach*) named after him was discovered in the early seventeenth century in the territory of Uí Bhearcháin, near Clonsast.[11] At Glenflesk (Gleann Fleisge) in the Kerry parish of Killaha, a folktale, which includes the mention of a large tub (*dabhach*), preserved the memory of a Bearchán whose prophecy concerning his death was fulfilled on the occasion of a visit to his house of three kings in the depth of winter.[12]

In the Clonsast area, the saint came to be remembered as Broghan (Brachan), as in 'St Broghan's Road' and 'Broghan's well', but devotion to him seems to have given way to another prophet, John the Baptist, on whose feast a great pattern used to be held at Clonsast.[13] Bearchán's own feast fell on 3/4 December.[14] The saint's cult is also attested in Scotland, where his fair in December was known as 'Barchan's Day'.[15] Bearchán, representing his church, is also among the saints said, tendentiously, to have owed tribute to Caillín of Fenagh.[16]

1 *CGSH* §§201, 473, 556, *GRSH* 80; *Lgen.* 721.4; *Éigse* 5, 86 §39; *LCAB* 137; *PR* 565–72; *BMisc.* 239 §3; *DIB* i, 462. **2** *MartO²* 249, 256. **3** *AU s.a.* **4** *CGSH* §722.63. **5** *ZCP* 18, 1–56; *ProphB.* **6** *CGG* 204. **7** *EH* 232. **8** *MartD* 326. **9** *IrT* ii, 69; ITS 51, 64; *Tdall* i, 40 §17, 65 §52; *AD* i, 108 §23; *BMisc.* 239 §3. **10** *ProphB* 113; RIA MS 23 P 16, 212; *IER* (5th ser.) 99, 105. **11** *MartD* xli. **12** *LSS* 63–5; ibid. app. i–iii. **13** *JRSAI* 75, 56–7; OSL OY i, 53; *AIOY* 117. **14** *MartO²* 256; *MartG* 232; *MartD* 326. **15** *CPNS* 194; *KSS* 279; *ACDS* 79. **16** *BFen.* 286.

Bearchán of Cluain Iomarchair. *See* Brocán.

Bearchán of Druim Dóithe, an unidentified church, probably near the town of Kildare. This son of Díoma, son of Aodh Crón, is attached by the genealogists to a branch of the Leinstermen called Uí Aodha Chróin, which held lands in the vicinity of Kildare.[1] His name may be preserved in the 'capella Insulae S. Berachani iuxta Dyrre-an-Mullyn', now perhaps Derrymullen in the parish of Kilmeage, which formed part of the deanery of Kildare.[2] He may also have been the saint named Bearchán credited with the composition of a quatrain on the baptismal stone of Fiontan of Clonenagh.[3] Finally, he may have given name to Clonfert (Cluain Fearta Bearcháin) in the Kildare parish of Balraheen.[4]

1 *CGSH* §§168.2, 261; *GRSH* 86; *Lgen.* 724.11; *CGH* 316a19–23. **2** *CDKL* 258; *Dinn.* 2, 31; but cf. ibid. 35. **3** *MartO²* 76, 403. **4** *CR* 10, 137; *HDGP* v, 121, 150.

Bearchán of Drumlohan (Druim Luacháin), parish of Stradbally, barony of Decies without Drum, Co. Waterford. The genealogists attached this son of Aodh to the Uí Bhrighde, a branch of the Waterford Déise, and it is probably no coincidence that a well dedicated to Brighid is also to be found in the parish of Stradbally.[1] Though all memory of Bearchán has disappeared locally, except for the place-name Carrickbarrahane (Carraig Bhearcháin, 'Bearchán's Rock'), the church assigned to him is well known for its Ogham cave.[2] Both John Colgan and Míchéal Ó Cléirigh took the saint to be the same as Bearchán son of Ultán of Cluain Caoi, now perhaps Kilbraghan in the Kilkenny parish of Kilmanagh, who was commemorated on 24 May, but this has been shown to be without foundation.[3] The saint is historically attested as 'Bercannus filius Aido' in a commentary on the seven epistles, possibly of Lismore origin, which is preserved in a Karlsruhe manuscript (Augiensis 233) formerly kept in the Reichenau on Lake Constance.[4]

1 *CGSH* §89; *Lgen.* 719.3; *WatLis.* 255. 2 *CIIC* i, 272–81. 3 *GRSH* 76; *Lgen.* 749.8; *MartD* 138; *SacE* 7, 77n; *CLTA* 61. 4 *SacE* 7, 76–8; *Peritia* 2, 238.

Bearchán of Glasnevin. *See* Mobhí.

Bearchán of Glenflesk. *See* Bearchán of Clonsast.

Bearchán of Kilbraghan. *See* Bearchán of Drumlohan.

Bearchán of Laragh (Ceall Láthraigh), parish of Kilcock, barony of Ikeathy and Oughterany, Co. Kildare. This son of Neamhnann (also written Neamhnall and Neamhan) is known only from an entry in the list of those subject to Brighid of Kildare which assigns him, together with his three sisters (Brígh, Coib and Lasair), two brothers (Brocán and Crónán), and others, to Ceall Láthraigh.[1] The saint's church is among the chapels assigned to the deanery of Clane in an early seventeenth-century list of Kildare churches prepared for John Colgan, which renders its name as *capella de Larhagh*.[2] A separate entry in the corpus of saints' pedigrees places the saint and his sisters in the unidentified church of Ceall Inghean Neamhnann.[3] Variant versions of the latter entry attach the family contrastingly to both the Dál Riada of north-east Ulster or Scotland and the Eoghanachta of Munster. Bearchán's sister Coib may be the saint so named in an early litany.[4]

1 *CGSH* §670.50; *Lgen.* 741.1; *HDGP* iv, 9. 2 *Dinn.* 2, 33, 38. 3 *CGSH* §239. 4 *MartT* 108; *IrL* 92; but cf. *MartT* 36 (Coib daughter of Cúrnán).

Bearchán of Rough Island on Lough Erne, parish of Belleek, barony of Lurg, Co. Fermanagh, which may now represent an earlier Inis Rocha.[1] Appropriately enough, in view of the possible location of his church on Lough Erne, the list containing eleven bearers of the name attaches Bearchán (son of Déaglán) to the Oirghialla, who held lands approximately equivalent to the present diocese of Clogher. His feast fell on 24 November.[2]

1 *CGSH* §264; *Lgen.* 716.2.3. 2 *MartG* 224; *MartD* 316.

Bearchán of Shankill (Seancheall), parish of Rathmichael, barony of Rathdown, Co. Dublin. This son of Déigeall is included in a list of eleven homonyms in the corpus of saints' pedigrees, which attaches him to the Dál Meisin Corb, thus making him a member of the family to which Caoimhghin of Glendalough also belonged.[1] The corpus of secular pedigrees likewise mentions the saint, placing him among the Uí Náir, to whom also belonged Fionnbharr of Killegar, Bearchán's near neighbour.[2] Though nothing else is known of Bearchán, he may be the same as Caoimhghin's monk 'Berchanus' who, while on a journey from Glendalough to the dwelling of Crónán (probably at Clondalkin), is said to have resisted the temptations of the flesh *fortiter*, 'strongly'.[3] If so, then devotion to him may also have spread to the Wicklow church and parish of Drumkay.[4] One source locates the saint (through confusion with a companion named Mosheanóg) at Ballaghmoon (Bealach Mughna) in Kildare.[5]

1 *CGSH* §263; *GRSH* 86. **2** *CGH* 120b37, 120b43. **3** *VSHP* i, 254–5 §43; *CPPI* 187. **4** *CPL* 9, 393; *CM* 156; *PNW* vii, 420; *AH* 2, 17. **5** TCD MS 1284, 131.

Bearchán son of Caoi. *See* Bearchán of Clonsast.

Bearchán son of Díoma, son of Feargna. The pedigree of this saint attaches him to the Uí Mháil, who held lands in the Glendalough area.[1] According to the secular genealogies, he was progenitor of a minor branch of that group, known as Uí Dhuibhthíre.[2] An aunt of his, Laise daughter of Feargna, is described as the seventh patron of Domhnach Sinchill, apparently an Uí Mháil church, with which Bearchán may also have been associated.[3]

1 *CGSH* §262; *GRSH* 86. **2** *CGH* 316 *m. i.*, 317c52. **3** *CGH* 316b 11–12; *CPPI* 132–3; *Lgen.* 724.12.

Bearchán son of Macaomh. *See* Bearchán of Clonsast.

Bearchán son of Miocán. *See* Bearchán of Clonsast.

Bearchán son of Ultán. *See* Bearchán of Drumlohan.

Bearóg of Aghadooey. *See* Aodh of Aghadooey.

Bearrán. Known from a list of *alumni* or students of Beinéan, this saint may be the same as the Bearrán commemorated without further description on 11 July.[1] It has been suggested that he was patron of Kilbarron (earlier form Kilbirrane) in the Tipperary barony of Lower Ormond, but this name has also been explained as a derivative of either Bairrfhionn or Barrán.[2]

1 *AS*.Nov. iv, 178; *MartT* 55; *MartG* 134; *MartD* 192. **2** *AS*.Iul. iii, 177B; *LIS* vii, 209; *BiblSS* iii, 86; *MakS* 22, 29; *CLTÁ* 56–8.

Béasgna. *See* Meascan.

Bebona daughter of Loarn. *See* Pompa daughter of Loarn.

Bee-Ella. *See* Beag Bile of Tullaghobegly.

Béibhil of Magheralin (Lann Rónáin Fhinn), barony of Iveagh Lower, Co. Down. This saint was a daughter of Séaghán (Séighín) and a sister of Teille of Tihelly. Two saintly uncles (also called *fratres*) of Béibhil – Baodán and Furodhrán

– were attached to the church of Dunleer (Lann Léire) in the Louth barony of Ferrard, which was also the area settled by Béibhil's family.[1] Her brother Teille figures, together with Furodhrán, in the well-known tale of *Buile Shuibhne* (Sweeney's Frenzy), as does Rónán Fionn, the eponym of Béibhil's church.[2] The saint's name, which may derive from *Bé+Fáil*, literally 'lady of Ireland', is also written as Béabhail (Béamhail), in relation to a grand-daughter of Blathmac son of Aodh, joint-king of Ireland, and several other famous women.[3]

1 *CGSH* §§55, 318; *BLec.* 79Vab. **2** *BS* §§2–11. **3** *BB* 79b21; *RC* 48, 185; *GPN* 30.

Beinéan, brother of Ceitheach. *See* Beinéan of Kilbennan.

Beinéan of Kilbennan (Ceall Bheinéin/Bheanáin), barony of Dunmore, Co. Galway. There were three (supposedly distinct) bearers of this name (Latin Benignus, Irish Beinéan, Bean(n)án, and Mionnán), all of them connected with Patrick and Connacht, and thus probably originally identical. One, a brother of Ceitheach of the Uí Oilealla (a name now reflected in the Sligo barony name of Tirerrill) is mentioned by Tíreachán in an account of those who accompanied Patrick to a place called Sealg in or near the Roscommon parish of Ogulla, and not far from Drumlish in the parish of Clooncraff, which is associated with Beinéan of Kilbennan.[1] Tíreachán went on to distinguish between this Beinéan, whom he assigned to a church named *cellola Benigni*, apparently nearby, and his namesake, the successor of Patrick at Armagh. He also provided Beinéan's brother Ceitheach, who was commemorated on 16 June, apparently at Oran in the Roscommon parish of the same name, with a mother belonging to the Saoirighe family who gave name to Domhnach Saoirighe, near the Meath church of Duleek.[2]

A second bearer of the name, Beinéan son of Luighne, is sometimes taken to be distinct from Patrick's successor at Armagh.[3] An inscription preserved in the Book of Armagh states that this Beinéan descended through his mother from Lughaidh son of Niada, who donated land on which to build a church later occupied by the saint.[4] This is the same Lughaidh as is mentioned in the Irish Life of Beinéan son of Seisgnéan, the third and best-known bearer of the name, in connection with the founding of the church of Kilbennan.[5] Clearly, therefore, the author of this text held the two saints to be identical.

A bishop, psalmist, and successor of Patrick, Beinéan son of Seisgnéan is introduced as both Benignus and Benineus in the two seventh-century Lives composed for Patrick, by Muirchú and Tíreachán. In the former text, he is described as Patrick's 'beloved and faithful holy boy', worthy to be his successor, and as miraculously untouched by fire during the stand-off with the druids at Tara.[6] In the latter, he is mentioned several times, once again with Patrick in his struggle with the druids, also as the brother of Mathona – of what seems to be Shankill in the Roscommon parish of the same name – who took the veil from Patrick, and finally as the Armagh saint's companion in north Connacht.[7] In addition to establishing for the saint associations with such churches as Drumlish in the Roscommon parish of Clooncraff, where he is reputed to have remained for twenty years, successive Lives emphasize Patrick's closeness to him, described by one scholar as a 'body-double' relationship.[8]

In addition to the short Anglo-Norman Life preserved in a thirteenth-century Glastonbury manuscript, a late Latin Life, interspersed with passages in Irish and bearing the title 'Life of Beinéan, disciple of Patrick', was composed for the saint.[9] Recycling miracles and other associations recounted in the Patrician literature, the text establishes for Beinéan connections with diverse parts of the country. These include both the Louth/Monaghan area, where he is said to have evangelized the Fir Rois, and Corca Mruadh in west Clare, where he was allegedly entitled to the revenues from 'Patrick's circuit'.[10] Mostly, however, the Life focuses on Beinéan's dealings with various rulers in the province of Connacht, including a meeting in Magh Seoil, now the Galway barony of Clare, which led to the foundation of Donaghpatrick (Domhnach Pádraig).[11] The Life also contains an account of the founding of Kilbennan, the saint's most important church, located near Donaghpatrick among the Conmhaicne of Connacht and, despite the separate tradition that this was the church of Beinéan son of Luighne, goes on to describe it as the son of Seisgnéan's principal church.[12] In the same passage, churches are assigned to Beinéan near Armagh, in the Glin district of Limerick, and in Britain.

The pedigree of Beinéan of Kilbennan attaches him variously to the Cianachta of Dungiven in Derry and Eoghanachta of Munster, and his mother Soidhealbh is said to have been a daughter of Cathaoir Mór, chief ancestral figure of the people of north Leinster.[13] His southern associations are also exemplified by the tradition that it was he who ordained the rents and stipends of Ireland, as laid out in the Book of Rights, a Munster compilation.[14] Beinéan of Kilbennan was also one of three bishops said to have assisted in drawing up the collection of early Irish law known as *Seanchas Mór*.[15]

In addition to the locations specified in the saint's Life, churches were named after Beinéan at a site near Killeany on Inishmore of the Aran Islands, and at Stabannan in the Louth barony of Ardee. Allegedly fourth in line of succession to Patrick at Armagh, and co-signatory with Patrick and others of the so-called Armagh canon, Beinéan is said to have died on 9 November (later his feastday) in 467.[16] Stations were also performed at his well in Kilbennan on Crom Dubh Sunday, which usually fell in late July or early August, and he may also be the 'Benatius' venerated, according to a catalogue of the churches of Elphin diocese, on 3 April at Kilcooley in Roscommon barony.[17] The saint's image adorns the so-called *Fiacail Phádraig*, a relic formerly kept at Cong.[18] A late tradition asserts that Beinéan founded Kilbennan at a spot where a stone from Croaghpatrick, placed in his pocket by Patrick as punishment for an unsuccessful act of deceit, fell out.[19] Also known in West Connacht as Mionnán, he gave name under this guise to a heap of stones (*leacht*) named Leac(ht) Mhionnáin in the parish of Oughaval, at the east base of Croaghpatrick, which allegedly represented his grave, and which traditionally marked the beginning of the *turas* to the Reek.[20] At his church in Glin he may also have been known as Mac Luighne, a name used for one of those called upon to assist Seanán of Scattery.[21]

1 *PTBA* 148; cf. *BP* 1215 (= *VT* 108), *Lgen.* iv, 479; *DIB* i, 448–9. **2** *PTBA* 146; *BP* 1185–91; *VT* 106; *MartT* 50; *MartG* 116; *MartD* 170. **3** *AB* 43, 255–6; *SaintPMN* 117. **4** *PTBA* 172.7; *AS*.Nov. iv, 178n. **5** Ibid. 178 §11. **6** *PTBA* 96, 100–2. **7** Ibid. 130, 140, 148; *BP* 1091–4; *VT 8; Ainm* 6, 26. **8** *BP* 1676–82; *VT* 144; *SS* 286–7. **9** *AB* 43, 258–60; *AS*.Nov. iv, 170. **10** Ibid. 172 §5, 174 §8; *SAM* 1, 31–44. **11** *AS*.Nov. iv 175 §10. **12** Ibid. 181 §15, 186 §21. **13** *CGSH* §§229, 448, 648; *GRSH* 122; *Lgen.* 661.6, 741.6; *AS*.Nov. iv, 171 §2. **14** *LC* 206–7. **15** *ZCP* 3, 15; *VT* 564; *Peritia* 5, 9; ibid. 8, 130 §§37–8; *Ériu* 45, 12 §8. **16** *MartG* 214; *MartD* 300; *IEKF* 58; *AS*.Nov. iv, 171 §1; *AU s.a.* **17** OSL GY i, 11–12; *TT* 177–8 (109). **18** *WLC* 96. **19** *Béaloideas* 16, 78. **20** OSL MO i, 434–5, 494; *Béaloideas* 16, 202; *FL* 80–1. **21** *ZCP* 10, 26 §22.

Beinéan son of Luighne. *See* Beinéan of Kilbennan.

Beireach. *See* Bearach.

Beircheart of Tullylease (Tulach Léis), barony of Duhallow, Co. Cork. Among the many remains within the ecclesiastical enclosure of Tullylease is a cross-slab bearing an inscription which invites a prayer for an ecclesiastic named Beireachtuine, an Irish version of the Anglo-Saxon *Beorhtwine*.[1] An annal entry (found only in the Annals of the Four Masters) notices this man's death on 6 December 839, a date that would suit the cross-slab.[2] The saint's name, which is also written Beirichtir and Beretchert, is duly found on this day in the later martyrologies.[3] Locally, however, and also at 'Berehert's Kyle' in the Tipperary parish of Solloghodbeg, the pattern, a large affair, was observed on 18 February which – despite the suggestion that this may have been because of an association with Colmán, bishop of Lindisfarne – would perhaps indicate that the cult had become entwined with that of Bearach of Termonbarry, whose feast was celebrated three days previously.[4] In west Kerry, Beircheart's feast actually fell on Bearach's day of 15 February.[5]

In north Cork, the saint's name was later anglicized as Benjamin or Ben, and this, together with a local tradition concerning an encounter between him and Patrick, led to confusion with Beinéan.[6] The O'Noonans (Uí Ionmhainéin) were hereditary wardens of Beircheart's church in Tullylease.[7] In the area about Cullen on the Cork/Kerry border, Beircheart was regarded as a brother of the three sisters named Latiaran, Lasair, and Inghean Bhaoith (Bhuidhe) and further east, near Mallow, he was taken to be a brother of Cránaid, albeit under the guise of Breanat.[8] There are townlands named Kilberrihert after him in the Cork parishes of Aghabulloge and Knocktemple, and in the Kerry parish of Ballincuslane, which mears with the Cork barony of Duhallow, and there are wells dedicated to him in the Cork parishes of Aghinagh and Macroom.[9] Elsewhere, he is named as a brother of the Saxon, Garailt of Mayo.[10]

1 *ECIM* 119–23; *CMCS* 24, 1–36, at 8–12; *JCHAS* 43, 106; ibid. 58, 12–13; *UJA* 6 (1st ser.), 267–75; *AICW* iv (pt ii), 451–3. **2** *ECIM* 119–23; *JCHAS* 43, 111–12; *AFM s.a.* **3** *MartG* 232; *MartD* 326. **4** *LIS* 2, 624–7; *CLTÁ* 64; *HTN* 263, 267. **5** *FSPP* 68; *LSUC* 358; *Béaloideas* 3, 239. **6** *CPR* i, lxviii; *UJA* 6 (1st ser.), 267–71. **7** *FNCC* 196–9; *AI s.a.* 1059; *UJA* 6 (1st ser.), 267–75. **8** *FL* 271; *HTN* 266; *PABD* 61. **9** *Béaloideas* 3, 214n; *AICK* iii, 328 (Sleveen). **10** *VSHP* ii, 107 §2.

Benjamin. *See* Beircheart.

Beoaidh/Beoán. *See* also Dobheóg.

Beoaidh *fo chochall*. *See* Beoaidh of Duncrun.

Beoaidh of Ardcarn (Ard Carna), barony of Boyle, Co. Roscommon. Although the saint's church (formerly a diocesan see) gained considerable importance, little is known of its patron, Beoaidh (anglicized Hugh) son of Olga (also written Olchú, alias Cochlán). The genealogists attached him to the Corca Laoighdhe of south Munster, and provided him with a sister named Ríoghnach, mother of Colmán of Templeshanbo.[1] The poem attributed to Cuimín of Connor singles out the 'house of guests' kept by Beoaidh and his generosity in giving presents.[2] The biographer of Caillín of Fenagh took advantage of this latter trait, by stating that Beoaidh not only entertained his subject, but also gave him land to the east of Ardcarn, as well as tribute.[3] He is probably identical with Beoaidh of Inishmagrath (Inis Mac Ratha, also known as Inch Island) on Lough Allen in the Leitrim parish of Drumreilly, who is included in a list prepared in the early seventeenth century for the Franciscan promoters of the Louvain scheme.[4] The list refers to a well named 'Tobar Beoaidh' which (now known as 'St Boey's well) is still frequented and, according to John Colgan, the saint's bell, known as *Ceolán Beoaidh*, was kept at the church of Ballinagleragh in the same Leitrim parish.[5] The feast of Beoaidh (Latin Bede) son of Olga fell on 8 March, and he is said to have died in the same year as Brighid of Kildare, i.e. in 524, and about the same time as Ailbhe of Emly, among others.[6] His coarb was among the ecclesiastics entitled to be present at the inauguration of O'Connor as king of Connacht.[7]

1 *CGSH* §§214, 722.105; *GRSH* 127; *Lgen.* 744.3; cf. *MartT* 116. **2** *ZCP* 1, 62; *MartD* 70. **3** *BFen.* 178, 188, 286, 296. **4** *Celtica* 1, 67; *Breifne* 4, 207. **5** OSL CN/LM 266; *HWI* 119; cf. *AILM* 188; *ASH* 563; *EMH* 478 §201. **6** *MartT* 21; *MartO*² 81, 92; *MartG* 50; *MartD* 70; *AU s.a.; LUM* 154Rb 29–30; *CPL* 9, 554. **7** *JRSAI* 2, 340; *MSPAG* 189.

Beoaidh of Duncrun (Dún Cruithne), parish of Magilligan, barony of Keenaght, Co. Derry. When Patrick left Magh Dhola, now represented by the parish of Clondermot on the east side of the river Foyle, he is said to have founded the church of Duncrun in 'Ard Eolairg', now apparently the hill of 'Canons Brae' in the parish of Magilligan.[1] There he placed Bishop Beoaidh – who may be identical with his namesake Beoaidh *fo chochall*, 'hooded', of Patrick's household – before going on to found seven *Domhnach*-churches in the area.[2] According to a 1607 suvey, Patrick was the patron of Duncrun, but the same source, and another early seventeenth-century account of the diocese of Derry, place Beoaidh (Beotis) in the Tyrone church of Termonamongan, where he appears to have also been known as 'Aibheóg' (Latin Davocus).[3]

1 *BP* 1855–9; *VT* 160; *GUH* 21–5; *HDGP* i, 85; *PNCL* 235. **2** *CGSH* §672.20. **3** *DYHS* 195–6; *Celtica* 1, 84; *UJA* (2nd ser.) 1, 251.

Beoaidh of Inis Dobheóg. *See* Dobheóg.

Beoaidh of Inishmagrath. *See* Beoaidh of Ardcarn.

Beoán of Feighcullen (Fiodh Cuilinn), barony of Offaly East, Co. Kildare. According to the genealogical tradition, Beoán was one of seven sons of Neasán who belonged to the powerful Uí Fhaoláin branch of the Uí Dhúnlainge of north Leinster.[1] Four of his siblings – Díocaill, Muireadhach (alias Crónán), Coireall, and

Flann – were located in a church named Eannga (possibly short for Tearmann Eannga, later Termoneeny in the Derry barony of Loughinsholin, whose patron, according to James Ware, was 'St McNessan') – while two others (Neise and Neaslugha) were patrons of the church on Ireland's Eye (Inis Mac Neasáin), off Howth in Dublin.[2] These are sometimes accompanied by their brother Díocaill in the record of their feast (15 March), whereas Beoán, whose status as bishop at Feighcullen is specified in an early seventeenth-century list of Kildare churches, was remembered on 8 August.[3]

1 *CGSH* §284.1; *GRSH* 86; *Lgen.* 727.26.27; *CGH* 118b21. 2 PNNI v, 213. 3 *MartT* 23, 61; *MartO²* 82, 98; *MartG* 54, 152; *MartD* 76, 212; *Dinn.* 2, 31.

Beoán of Meenan (Tamhlachta Meanainn), parish of Aghaderg, barony of Upper Iveagh, Co. Down. The early Life of Fursa, written between 650 and 730, names two of his associates, *Beanus* (Beoán) and *Meldanus* (Meallán), and according to the *Virtutes* compiled for the same saint about 850, the relics of these two were venerated with those of Patrick at Péronne in northern France.[1] Little else is known of either saint, but the entry for their feastday of 26 October attaches them to Tamhlachta Meanainn (generally taken to be Meenan, although this has recently been disputed) within Fursa's native *provincia*.[2] Some sources state that the two saints were *de Britonia*, 'from Britain', but on the evidence of their names this is unlikely.[3] Near Beoán's church, according to Giraldus Cambrensis, was a refuge for beasts and fowl, kept in honour of a saint who was noted for his protection not only of birds, but also of their eggs.[4] Local tradition accounted for the name of the parish (Achadh Dearg, misinterpreted as 'Bloody Ford') by reference to the killing there of several 'holy men'.[5] Beoán is thought to lie behind several commemorations in Scotland, albeit under the guise of Bean/Ma-Bean.[6]

1 *MGH.SRM* iv, 423–49; ibid., *Virtutes* §19; *CMCS* 17, 2–4. 2 *MartT* 84; *MartO²* 218; *MartG* 204; *MartD* 284; *MGH.SRM* iv, *Vita* §3; PNNI vi, 50. 3 *MartT* 84; *MartO²* 226. 4 *THEH* 124–5. 5 PNNI vi, 22. 6 *KSS* 277; *CPNS* 310–12; *LegSS* 250–1, 326–7.

Beoán of Ráith Osáin, an unidentified site near Trim, Co. Meath. This son of Athracht (Artrach) is known from the genealogical tradition, which attaches him to the descendants of Lughaidh son of Laoghaire, son of Niall, together with his brother Osán, eponym of the church to which both belonged.[1] Osán, who also figures with other members of the family in the *Additamenta* to Tíreachán's Life of Patrick, was remembered with several others of the clergy of Trim on 17 February, but Beoán's name is not in the list.[2] Early seventeenth-century sources, one of which erroneously names his father as Libhréan, speculate that his feast may have fallen on 3 December.[3]

1 *CGSH* §§662.45, 690.13; *GRSH* 49; *Lgen.* 705.9. 2 *PTBA* 170 §4; *MartT* 17; *MartG* 38; *MartD* 52. 3 *MartD* 324; *GRSH* 49.

Beoán of Teach Dobheóg, an unidentified church close to Bangor, barony of Castlereagh Lower, Co. Down. According to the death-tale of Eacha son of Mairidh, Beoán son of Innle was on his way to Rome to consult Pope Gregory – as he had been instructed by Comhghall of Bangor – when he was addressed from under his boat by Líobhan (Lí Bhan) daughter of Eacha, a survivor of the inundation that led to the formation of Lough Neagh.[1] At Líobhan's request, Beoán and his fellow-saints of Dál nAraidhe, including Comhghall, returned to the spot one year later, caught her in their nets and baptized her. Despite opposition from Comhghall, Beoán secured the privilege of her burial in his church. A poem on the saints whom Seanán of Scattery Island could call on for assistance probably refers to this saint, naming him Beóg 'from the great wave'.[2] John Colgan speculated that he might be the same as Dobheóg of Lough Derg.[3] He may also have been the patron of Ceall Bhiain (church of Bian), founded (probably near Downpatrick) by Fearghas son of Aonghas, in whose nets Líobhan was allegedly caught.

1 *LU* 3094–126. **2** *ZCP* 10, 24. **3** *GRSH* 82.

Beoán son of Earc. *See* Beoán of Feighcullen.

Beóg. *See* Beoán of Teach Dobheóg.

Beotis. *See* Beoaidh of Duncrun.

Berehert. *See* Beircheart.

Bia, patron and eponym of an unidentified church named Ceall Bhia. This man is known only from the list of saints said to have been subject to Brighid of Kildare.[1] His companion at the church, a man named Neamhan, is included by the Martyrology of Donegal in its list for 1 September.[2]

1 *CGSH* §670.40. **2** *MartD* 232.

Bian. *See* Beoán of Teach Dobheóg.

Bigeall of Imleach na Léagha (Leagha), an unidentified church possibly located in the parish of Lea (Léighe), barony of Portnahinch, Co. Laois. Together with his sister Bigseach, whose name also derives from *beag* 'small', this saint is among those said to have been subject to Brighid of Kildare.[1] The parish of Lea lies within the diocese of Kildare.

1 *CGSH* §670.22.

Bigeall of Tulach. *See* Beag Bile of Tullaghobegly.

Bigle Uiscidhe, 'watery', of Ráith Bhigleann, an unidentified church, possibly located in Co. Wicklow. Bigle is said to have belonged to the Dál Meisin Corb, whose best-known saint was Caoimhghin of Glendalough.[1] On the basis of his by-name *uiscidhe*, it has been suggested that the saint was possibly associated with the church that gave name to Killiskey in the Wicklow barony of Newcastle.[2]

1 *CGSH* §181.12. **2** *CPPI* 182.

Bigseach of Imleach na Léagha. *See* Bigeall of Imleach na Léagha.

Bigseach of Kilbixy (Ceall Bhigsighe), barony of Moygoish, Co. Westmeath. Bigseach is included in a list of saints and churches that appear to have had Brigidine connections.[1] According to early seventeenth-century sources, the saint belonged through her father Breasal to the Uí Fhiachrach of Connacht.[2] Her church, also known as Tristernagh, was chosen as the site of an Augustinian priory founded about 1200.[3] Bigseach's feast, which is shared by Cruimín of the neighbouring parish of Lackan, fell on 28 June and, at 4 October, a glossator of the Martyrology of Óengus identified her with an otherwise unattested Balbina.[4]

1 *CGSH* §663.10; *Lgen.* 751.20; *DIB* i, 523. 2 *MartD* 182; *GRSH* 61; *Lgen.* 711.3. 3 *MRHI* 197; *AnnU* 77; *CPL* 15, §833. 4 *MartT* 52; *MartG* 124; *MartD* 182; *PNW* 36, 299; *MartO* 220.

Bíthe daughter of Fiachna. *See* Brighid of Rathbride.

Bíthe of Inch (Inis Cúscraidh), barony of Lecale Lower, Co. Down. Though this name was used of both male and female saints, the best-known bearer was Bíthe (alias Dobhí, anglicized David) son of Comhghall of Inch, whose feast fell twice in late July (22, 29), first under the guise of Dobhí (Mobhíu), seven days later as Bít(h)e.[1] According to the genealogies, Bíthe (Dobhí) belonged to the Dál mBuain, a branch of the Ulaidh (Ulstermen), and this descent is in keeping with the juxtaposition of his church and the deanery of 'Dalboyn' in the early fourteenth-century taxation list of the diocese of Down.[2] The story of his miraculous birth may be preserved in the late vernacular Life of Mochua, who belonged through his mother to the Dál mBuain. On being beaten by his master, Comhghall of Bangor, Mochua is said to have burst into tears, only to have these enter the mouth of a barren woman who thereupon conceived and later gave birth to an infant named 'Dabhiu', a hypocoristic form of Bíthe.[3]

Bíthe is probably also the saint described as a *ceard*, 'craftsman, metal-worker', in the list of those 'in orders' with Patrick. The list groups him together with Tasach whose church of Raholp lay close to Inch.[4] A similar grouping is found in Patrick's Life, albeit at a different location, the later diocesan centre of Elphin, where the Armagh saint is said to have placed his 'copper-smith' Assicus (from Asach, a variant of Tasach), together with his nephew Bíthe and the latter's mother 'Cipia'.[5] The Tripartite Life later placed Bíthe of Elphin at Racoon Hill (Ráith Chonga) in the Donegal parish of Drumhome.[6] Finally, under the guise of Mobhíu, the saint was invoked as a guarantor of the Law of Adhamhnán.[7]

1 *MartT* 57–8; *MartO*² 164; *MartG* 140, 146; *MartD* 198, 204, 398. 2 *CGSH* §152; *GRSH* 96; *EA* 44; *CDI* v, 207. 3 *LisL* 4649–53. 4 *CGSH* §671.12; *Lgen.* 695.1; *BP* 2961–2, 3141; *VT* 250, 266. 5 *PTBA* 140 §21.2; *BP* 1073–4; *VT* 96. 6 *BP* 1730–3; *VT* 148. 7 *CA* §22.

Blán of Dunblane (Dún Bláin) and Kingarth (Ceann Garadh), both churches in Scotland. The Martyrology of Gorman, which states that Blán's chief church was at Dunblane, names his *oide*, 'mentor', as Cadán, a saint greatly honoured on the Isle of Bute, and the Martyrology of Donegal suggests that the latter may have been Cadán son of Madán of the north-east Ulster grouping of Dál nAraidhe.[1] An office Life of Blán, preserved in the Breviary of Aberdeen, describes Cadán not only as Blán's mentor, but also as his uncle.[2] It also states that, following his return home from an education in Ireland, Blán (anglicized Blane) was raised to the episcopate and travelled to Rome, before returning through England, where his church appears to have had some property.[3] In Ireland, he was venerated at

Greencastle in the Donegal parish of Moville and perhaps also at Kilbline (if this derives from Ceall Bhláin) in the Kilkenny parish of Tullaherin, and at Kilbolane (Ceall Bhláin) in the Cork parish of the same name.[4] According to a Life composed for Molaise of Leighlin, he was the latter's uncle.[5] 'Victorious Blán of the Britons' was remembered on 10 August.[6]

1 *MartG* 28, 154; *MartO²* 184; *MartD* 36; *KSS* 298; *CPNS* 273; *ACDS* 111–13. **2** *BrevA* pars aest. 77rv; *CPNS* 164–5, 273; *KSS* 280–1; *Innes Review* 32, 72; ibid. 52, 111–35; *LegSS* 180–91, 328–30. **3** Ibid. **4** *DOH* 83; *HADO* iii, 485; *HCK* 99; but cf. Logainm.ie 'kilbline'. **5** *VSHH* 341 §3. **6** *MartT* 62; *MartO²* 175; *MartG* 154; *MartD* 214.

Bláth. Among the numerous children assigned to Meadhbh daughter of Garbhán of the Uí Shaithghil of Ciarraighe Luachra (a tribal grouping associated with north Kerry) were Bláth and Bláthnad (little Bláth), both of whom were presumably one and the same.[1] Meadhbh's children were scattered all over the country, but there is no reason to suspect that Bláth (Bláthnad) was identical with the saint of that name commemorated on 18 January at the church of Cluain Greanaigh (Greancha), now possibly Clonygrange in the Meath parish of Killaconnigan.[2] A note added at 3 September to the Martyrology of Tallaght assigns Bláthnad – together with Ana who is also her companion at 18 January – to the church of Slanore (Snámh Luthair) in the Cavan parish of Kilmore.[3]

1 *CGSH* §722.99. **2** *JCS* 1, 196; *MartT* 9; *MartG* 18; *MartD* 20. **3** *MartT* 116.

Blathmhac of Iona, Scotland. Slain by heathens on Iona in 825, this son of Flann was one of the last saints to be included in the Martyrology of Tallaght, which was compiled about 830.[1] News of the saint's martyrdom reached the Continent, where Walahfrid Strabo (†849), later abbot of the Reichenau on Lake Constance, composed Blathmhac's Life in Latin hexameters.[2] According to the Life, which, though thin on names, may contain a kernel of genuine detail, Blathmhac, the son of a king, entered a monastery against the wishes of his family before later undertaking a pilgrimage to Iona. His refusal to reveal to his killers the whereabouts of Colum Cille's precious shrine is said by Walahfrid to have been the immediate cause of the saint's martyrdom. Little else is known of Blathmhac, but his attempt to perform the sacrifice of the Mass in a house in which a man had just died is held up as improper behaviour in the text of the *Monastery of Tallaght*.[3] Like that of his namesake, Blathmhac of Rath, this saint's feast fell on 24 July.[4]

1 *AU s.a.* 825; *FSHIM* 92; *DIB* i, 606–7. **2** *WSZL* 32–40; *IER* (2nd ser.) 9, 502–8. **3** *MT* §65. **4** *MartT* 57; *MartG* 142; *MartD* 200.

Blathmhac of Rath (Ráith Bhlathmhaic), barony of Inchiquin, Co. Clare. According to a genealogical tract on the Dál gCais of Thomond, Blathmhac (son of Eiltín son of Aodh) belonged to the same tribal grouping as the Uí Chiaróg of Rath, a hereditary family associated with the saint's church.[1] Among his relatives was Lasair daughter of Bréanainn Bán, allegedly also a saint but otherwise unknown. Elsewhere Blathmhac was thought to have been the father of Onchú who gave his name to Ceall Onchon, now Killonaghan in the Clare barony of Burren, and perhaps also to Killonahan in the Limerick parish of the same name.[2] Onchú was remembered on 9 or 14 July, whereas Blathmhac's feast was observed at Rath on 24 July, otherwise not only St Bartholomew's feast but also that of the martyr, Blathmhac of Iona, who was slain by heathens in 825.[3] In a late poem attributed to Seanán, Blathmhac is among the saints described as ready to respond to an appeal for assistance should Scattery Island suffer any wrong.[4] A separate poem lists him among the numerous offspring of Inghean Bhaoith of Killinaboy.[5] Together with Inghean Bhaoith, and numerous other Munster saints, he was called upon, in a poem in Classical Irish, to assist in releasing the churches of Leath Mogha (Ireland's southern half) from a bondage imposed by those of Leath Chuinn (northern half), championed by Finnian of Clonard.[6] He was given prominence in two Clare Lives of saints, as mentor of Flannán of Killaloe and as an associate of Mac Reithe of Kilmacrehy.[7] Blathmhac's crozier is now in the National Museum.[8]

1 *CoC* 13, 235; *LUM* 30Vb20. **2** *MartG* 132; *MartO²* 168; *MartD* 190; *ASH* 277; cf. *SATM* 43–4. **3** *ACoC* 56; *MartT* 54–5, 57; *MartG* 132, 136, 142; *MartD* 190, 194, 200. **4** *ZCP* 10, 28. **5** *IrT* iv, 93. **6** RIA MS 23L11, 263; *SAM* 24.1, 17, 20. **7** *VSHH* 282 §3; *MHH* 36–44 §§50–6, 61, 64. **8** *JRSAI* 24, 337–9.

Bláthnad. *See* Bláth.

Blidhreann. According to a metrical version of those 'in orders' with Patrick, this person, otherwise unknown in the Patrician tradition, was the saint's *cíormhaire*, 'comb-maker'.[1]

1 *CGSH* §672.26.

Blinne. *See* Moninne.

Blogdha grandson of Fodaidhe was, according to a metrical version of those 'in orders' with Patrick, head of the Armagh saint's school.[1] The form *Fodaidhe* may reflect *Potitus*, the name of Patrick's grandfather.[2]

1 *CGSH* §672.18. **2** Ibid. §1.

Blunny. *See* Maol Anfaidh.

Bóchra. *See* Acobhrán of Kilrush; Cainneach of Achadh Rathain; Feidhlimidh son of Iorlamhan.

Boden. *See* Baodán of Cloney; Buadán of Culdaff.

Boey. *See* Beoaidh of Ardcarn.

Bogha of Glenavy (Lann Abhaic), barony of Upper Massereene, Co. Down. Together with her two sisters, Laisre and Colmha, this daughter of Comhghall belonged to the Dál mBuain segment of the Ulaidh of north-east Ulster.[1] All three are associated with a church named Leitir in Dál nAraidhe, thought to be the same as Leitir Phádraig, where (according to a version of Patrick's Tripartite Life used by John Colgan) the church of Glenavy was founded.[2] A note added to the Commentary on the Martyrology of Aonghas speculates, however, that the three sisters may also have been venerated at Clonmore in the Carlow barony of

Rathvilly or, alternatively, at Camus in the Derry parish of Macosquin.[3] The feast of these sisters fell on 22 January.[4]

1 *CGSH* §151. 2 *TT* 147 §132; *EA* 236–7. 3 *MartO*[2] 50. 4 *MartT* 11; *MartO*[2] 37; *MartG* 20; *MartD* 24.

Boing daughter of Mac Reithe. *See* Líogh of Rosconnell.

Bolcán of Kilcooley (Ceall Chúile), barony and county of Roscommon. The name of this saint, also written Olcán, figures in all martyrological lists for 4 July.[1] In the later martyrologies, he is also found at 20 February in place of a saint named Olcán in the earlier record.[2] Although John Colgan brought the two names together, citing among other supports the presence in Dál Riada – where Bishop Olcán is said to have met Patrick – of a church named 'Kill Olcain' rather than 'Kill-Easpuic Bolcain', there would not appear to be sufficient grounds for their conflation.[3]

1 *MartG* 40, 130; *MartD* 54, 186; *HDGP* iii, 153. 2 *MartT* 18 (Olcán), 53. 3 *ASH* 375–8.

Booden. *See* Baodán of Cloney.

Borchill. *See* Meithean Chaol.

Bracán. *See* Breacán, Brocán.

Bran Beag, 'little', of Clane (Claonadh) in the barony of the same name, Co. Kildare. This saint is known only from the list of those commemorated on 18 May.[1]

1 *MartT* 44; *MartG* 98; *MartD* 132.

Brandubh. *See* Brannabh.

Branaid. *See* Breanat.

Brannabh of Lough Ramor (Loch Muinreamhair), near Virginia in the parish of Lurgan, barony of Castlerahan, Co. Cavan. This saint is known only from the record of his feast which fell on 6 February.[1] Some seventeenth-century sources proposed his identity with an otherwise unattested Brannabh of the Ulster descendants of Eachaidh son of Mairidh.[2]

1 *MartT* 15; *MartG* 30; *MartD* 40. 2 *MartD* 40; *GRSH* 95.

Brannabh of Rosbran (Ros Brannaibh), parish of St John's, barony of Narragh and Reban West, Co. Kildare. Although provided with two contrasting pedigrees – one otherwise untraceable, the other belonging to the Clann Bhruidhghe of Leinster – Brannabh son of Ceannfhada is probably the man of that name designated abbot of Kildare.[1] However, his name does not feature in the 'official' list of abbots of Kildare, drawn from the annals.[2] Two (otherwise unattested) brothers, named Cleithe and Coimre, are also assigned to Brannabh.[3]

1 *CGSH* §§164, 272.2; *GRSH* 86; *CGH* 124b27. 2 *NHI* 9, 260–1. 3 *CGSH* §164.

Brannabh of Tynagh (Teach nEachach), barony of Leitrim, Co. Galway. Brannabh's pedigree attaches him though his father Eacha (the apparent eponym of his church) to a branch of the Uí Mhaine of east Galway known as Uí Lomáin Ghaola.[1] These were settled in or near the townland of Finnure in the parish of Abbeygormacan, close to Tynagh.[2] A collateral of the same family named Bishop Maolán – allegedly the elder saint of the Uí Mhaine – is reputed to have brought together a large group of other saints of this area on the occasion of the battle of Cúil Dreimhne, but Brannabh was not one of them.[3]

1 *CGSH* §406; cf. *Lgen.* 327.3, 1137.10; *GYHS* 805; *Dinn.* 2, 25–6; *Ainm* 1, 23–40. 2 *Lgen.* iv, 454. 3 *IMN* 22, 5.

Brannabh son of Maonach. A brother of Fachtna of Ross Carbery, according to the genealogies, this saint was regarded as a bishop in his own right.[1] Along with Fachtna and six other brothers, Brannabh was attached to the Corca Laoighdhe, whose territory corresponded approximately to that of the diocese of Ross. Some seventeenth-century sources speculate that Brannabh may have been commemorated with Caoimhghin on 3 June under the guise of a grandson of Trianlugh, but this is otherwise unsupported.[2] He may be the bishop 'from the southern part of Leinster' who is said to have extracted from Fiontan of Clonenagh a promise that he would die shortly after him.[3] The three weeks this saint is supposed to have lived after Fiontan, who died on 17 February, would give an otherwise unrecorded feast in early March.

1 *CGSH* 298.2; *GRSH* 127–8; *AH* 1, 365. 2 *GRSH* 127; cf. *Celtica* 5, 50–1. 3 *VSHH* 150–1.

Breac (Breacán). As is shown by the list of homonymous saints, which features more than ten of the name, the word *breac*, 'speckled/trout', could be used of many holy men.[1] Some of those so named are attached to unidentified churches, and others (such as Breacán Cráibhdheach 'pious') are identified only by otherwise unattested epithets or comments. The name is frequently confused with Bearchán. In addition to Breacán, the word *breac* yielded the names Bricín and Mobhrioca.

1 *CGSH* §707.59–68.

Breac of Bealach Féile, a site probably near the river Burren, in either Urglin or Killerrig, now adjoining parishes in the barony and county of Carlow.[1] The pedigree of this son of Síolán, whose name is also rendered Mobhrioca and Breacán, attaches him to the Déise of Munster.[2] This affiliation has led to his identification with the authority named 'Brecanus' cited in the tract known as the Commentary on the Catholic Epistles.[3] His church was the scene of a battle between the men of Munster and Leinster in 735 and, while some annals state that the saint died in the same year, the Four Masters, who render his name as 'Mobrioccu', place both battle and death in their entry for 730.[4] Little else is known of him except that he shared a feast with Íde – who was also attached to the Déise – on 15 January.[5]

1 *HDGP* ii, 109; cf. *Dinn.* 3, 6–11. 2 *CGSH* §94; *GRSH* 76; *Lgen.* 719.4. 3 *SacE* 7, 80–4. 4 *AI*/ATig./ARos./*AFM s.a.* 5 *MartT* 8; *MartG* 16; *MartD* 16.

Breacán of Caw (Cath), parish of Clondermot, barony of Tirkeeran, Co. Derry. An entry in the Annals of Ulster for 1197 describes how the Foreigners of Ulster, having pillaged some churches in Keenaght (Cianachta), suffered defeat at the hands of a small force led by Ua Maoil Doraidh, king of Ceinéal Eoghain, assisted by the miracles of the three saints (Colum Cille, Cainneach and Breacán) who were patrons of the affected churches.[1] It has recently been argued that Breacán's church is likely to have been in Caw (Cath), which lies between Granshagh and Clooney, the sites of the churches associated respectively with Cainneach and Colum.[2] As these churches lay within the territory of Cianachta (now approximately the barony of Keenaght), the patron of Caw is likely to have been Breacán son of Earc, who is attached by the genealogists to the family that gave name to the barony.[3] As a variant genealogical tradition asserts that his father was named Ceannbharca, the saint is probably also identical with Breacán Cinn Bhairche of the list of homonymous saints.[4] An earlier form of Caw has been shown to have been Clonekey, which may be taken to reflect the Irish form Cluain Catha, attached to Breacán in later versions of the list of those commemorated on 16 July, and erroneously taken by Mícheál Ó Cléirigh to refer to Clonca in Inishowen.[5]

1 *AU s.a.* **2** *Ainm* 7, 86–7; cf. *PCV* 31; *PNCL* 90–2; *TT* 479.18. **3** *CGSH* §220; *GRSH* 122; *Lgen.* 742.15. **4** *CGSH* §§220, 707.61; *GRSH* 122. **5** *Ainm* 7, 87–8; *MartG* 138; *MartD* 194.

Breacán of Clonca (Cluain Catha). *See* Breacán of Caw.

Breacán of Clonkeen (Cluain Caoin), parish of Clonenagh and Clonagheen, barony of Maryborough West, Co. Laois. This saint is mentioned in a section of a genealogical tract which attaches him, together with Aona and Baoithín son of Fionna(ch), to the Laoighse of Cúil Bhuichle.[1] This *cúil* ('corner') has been plausibly identified as a place in Cluain Caoin, *i samhadh Fhiontain*, 'within the community of Fiontan [of Clonenagh]', later the manor of 'Sawfyntyn' and now Clonkeen near Portlaoise.[2] Not far away, in the parish of Offerlane, is the townland of Kilbrickan (Ceall Bhreacáin) which may be named after the saint.

1 *GT* 141. **2** *LSHS* 36–7.

Breacán of Dairinis, a place yet to be identified. This saint, whose name is also spelt as Bracán, is known from an entry in the tract on the mothers of the saints, which states that he was a son of Ríomh, daughter of Fiachna of the Cairbre Luachra branch of the Eoghanachta.[1] As such, he was a uterine brother not only of Cuimín Fada, but also of three noted lay-people – one a 'fool' (Comhdhán Dá Chearda), the two others kings (Guaire son of Colmán and Cuana son of Cailchín) – all of whom figured prominently among the *dramatis personae* of the so-called Guaire-cycle of tales.[3] Tantalizingly, despite the extensive literary records of his siblings, little beyond the saint's name and church has been preserved. Breacán, patron of both Inishmore on Aran and Kilbreckan in the Clare parish of Doora, is perhaps the most likely candidate.

1 *CGSH* §§652, 722.66; cf. *CGH* 151a1–5; *LL* 17381–2; *Ériu* 25, 92. **3** *Ériu* 25, 88–125.

Breacán of Eachdhruim Bhreacáin, possibly 'Cargan' in the parish of Dunaghy, barony of Kilconway, Co. Antrim.[1] Because of the location of his church, this Breacán is thought to be identical with the son of Sárán whose father fell foul of Patrick, according to the latter's Tripartite Life.[2] At Aughrim, which lay on the boundary between the kingdoms of Dál nAraidhe and Dál Riada, Breacán was accompanied by Ciarán (alias Ciaróg or Mochuaróg), who also shared his feastday. This fell on 7 May, within the octave of a similarly named bishop remembered on 1 May.[3] As another namesake, Breacán of Movilla in Newtownards, was commemorated two days previously, all three may have been originally identical.

1 *EA* 72, 335. **2** *BP* 1906–7; *EA* 378. **3** *CGSH* §707.65; *MartT* 40; *MartO*² 123; *MartG* 92; *MartD* 120; *Ainm* 7, 82–4.

Breacán of Inishmore (Inis Mór), barony of Aran, Co. Galway. Now patron of the imposing ecclesiastical site of Seven Churches, near the village of Eoghanacht on Inishmore, this son of Eacha Bailldearg, whose name might also be written as Bracán, and who was allegedly first called Breasal, was assigned by the genealogists to the main line of descent of the Dál gCais of Thomond.[1] Breacán's brother Conall Caomh (father of Molua *Lobhar* 'leper') is said to have been blessed by Ruadhán of Lorrha, patron of the Eoghanachta who vied with Dál gCais for hegemony over Munster.[2] Conall's son Aodh was reputedly the first king of Dál gCais to go to Cashel, near which he is said to have been blessed by Bréanainn of Clonfert.[3] Breacán's father Eacha Bailldearg, the first healthy child born to Caorthann following the latter's baptism by Patrick at Singland near Limerick, retained, according to the Tripartite Life, a red spot (*ball dearg*).[4]

A fourteenth- or fifteenth-century poem, which outlines Breacán's life and lists the churches claimed for him, states that he was a pupil of Pupa of Inishmore and founded his first church on the island at a place called Iobhar, whence his nickname Iobhrach.[5] Outside Aran, the centre of his cult was in Thomond, especially in the parish of Doora, near Ennis. The church of Kilbreckan in this parish was granted to the Augustinian abbey of Clare by Domhnall Mór Ua Briain in 1189, and it was probably a member of this community who composed the above-cited poem on the saint.[6]

Although of great interest as a record of the local churches and families associated with Breacán, the poem also makes some improbable assertions, including the right of the saint's successors to tribute from the 'king of Meath', on the basis that Breacán had founded Ardbraccan before relinquishing it to Ultán. Less improbable is the tale of his association with Flannán of Killaloe who is said to have sought advice from Breacán (Bracanus) before embarking on a journey to Rome.[7] The date of Breacán's feast is uncertain, but seventeenth-century sources place it on 1 May or 12 October.[8] On Inishmore, where a headstone inscribed *Capitis Brecani/cinn Bhreacáin*, 'of Breacán's head', allegedly stood, his feast appears to have fallen on 22 May.[9] A well dedicated to the saint gave name to a townland (Toberbrackan) in the Galway parish of Killeely. Elsewhere in Galway, at Kilbrickan in the parish of Kilcummin, a healing stone was named Leac Bhreacáin after him.[10] A well was dedicated to him at Toomullin in the Clare parish of Killilagh.[11]

1 *CGSH* §378; *GRSH* 119; *Lgen*. 738.5; *CoC* 13–14; *LM* 296; *SAL* 424–33. 2 *LM* 297. 3 Ibid. 4 *BP* 2415–21; *BMisc*. 460 §§4–19. 5 *Ériu* 15, 128–38; *LUM* 33ra11. 6 *Celtica* 15, 128–9; *HDK* 201. 7 *VSHH* 285–6 §§8, 11. 8 *GRSH* 119; *MartD* 116. 9 *ASH* 715 (12); OSL GY iii, 385; *IER* (3rd ser.) 7, 731. 10 *JGAHS* 64, 6. 11 *ACoC* 102.

Breacán of Movilla (Magh Bhile), parish of Newtownards, barony of Ards Lower, Co. Down. This saint is doubtless the same as Breacán, fosterling of Finnian (patron of Movilla), who is named in the list of homonymous saints.[1] As Breacán's feast fell on 29 April, eight days ahead of that of his namesake at Eachdhruim, the two saints may have been originally identical.[2] Described as abbot in the Martyrology of Tallaght, Breacán is styled bishop in the later martyrologies.

1 *CGSH* §707.68. 2 *MartT* 37; *MartG* 86; *MartD* 112.

Breacán of Tallow (Tulach Rátha/an Iarainn), barony of Coshmore and Coshbride, Co. Waterford. A sixteenth-century Roscommon manuscript, now Royal Irish Academy 23N10, which was in Cork by 1700, contains a calendar of saints.[1] While in Cork, the calendar received several local additions, among which was Breacán of 'Tula Reatha nó an Iaruinn', whose feast fell on 27 March.[2] Nothing else is known of this saint, but he may be the same as the man who gave name to 'Teampall Breacáin' in the townland of Ballybricken, parish of Barnahely, near Cork Harbour.[3] It has been plausibly suggested that the eponym of this church was probably one of the church founders placed about Cork Harbour by Mochuda of Lismore, which is a few miles only from Tallow.[4]

1 *RIA 23N10*, 143–60. 2 *JCHAS* 108, 133–7. 3 CorkD 92. 4 *JCHAS* 65, 19–20.

Breacán son of Sárán, son of Caolbhadh. Apart from his pedigree, which assigns him variously to the Dál nAraidhe and Dál bhFiatach, little is known of this saint.[1] Breacán's father Sárán, having laid a hand on Patrick, is said to have been deprived of heaven and earth, only to have the former restored by Bishop Olcán.[2] Breacán of Eachdhruim on the boundary of Dál nAraidhe and Dál Riada is sometimes thought to have been identical with the son of Sárán.[3]

1 *CGSH* §115.1.2; *GRSH* 69; *Lgen*. 732.3. 2 *BP* 1906–7, 1924. 3 *EA* 378.

Breacán son of Sárán, son of Colga. According to the genealogies, this man, whose name is variously rendered Breacán and Beagán, belonged to the Oirthir of an area now approximately coextensive with the present county of Armagh.[1] His mother Pompa (Babona), daughter of a Scottish king named Loarn, gave birth by Sárán to two other saintly sons, Cairneach and Rónán Fionn.[2] Seventeenth-century sources speculate that Breacán's feast may have fallen on 17 August.[3]

1 *CGSH* §§662.88, 722.29; *GRSH* 69. 2 *CGSH* §722.29. 3 *GRSH* 69; *MartD* 220.

Breacán son of Ubhán. *See* Breacán of Clonca.

Bréanainn This name, better known under its anglicized form, Brendan (Latin Brendanus), and sometimes rendered hypocoristically Mobhí, appears to have originated in the Welsh word *brenhin*, 'king'.[1] It was borne, according to the list of homonymous saints, by seventeen persons regarded as holy in the Irish tradition.[2] Most of these were probably localizations of the cults of the two main bearers of the name, the patrons of Birr and Clonfert, who head the list. The martyrologies also mention a number of otherwise unattested saints of the name.

1 *ZCP* 49–50, 878–88; *GPN* 34; cf. *AB* 78, 379–81; *CI* i, 103n. 2 *CGSH* §707.35–51.

Bréanainn of Birr (Biorra), barony of Ballybritt, Co. Offaly. The elder of the two saints named Bréanainn (whence his title of Brendinus Senior, alias Seanbhréanainn), although already attested in Adhamhnán's late seventh-century Life of Colum Cille, is poorly documented by comparison with his more celebrated namesake.[1] The saint's genealogy attached him through his father Neamhann to the descendants of Fearghas son of Róch, to whom the patron of Clonfert also belonged.[2] An early text presents him as the protector of all Ciarraighe, the tribal grouping with which Bréanainn of Clonfert is most closely associated, and a separate text maintains that he was owed a fee by the Uí Mhaine, whose territory later corresponded to the diocese of Clonfert.[3] From the beginning of his record, there are indications that Bréanainn and his namesake at Clonfert, which lies a little over ten miles from Birr, were originally identical. Adhamhnán, who demonstrably used oral tradition as a source, attributes to both saints of the name – each described as the founder of a monastery – a vision of Colum Cille accompanied by a column of light.[4] Furthermore, one of the Birr saint's two feastdays fell on 9 May, which would allow the main feast of the Clonfert saint (16 May) to be regarded as within its octave.[5]

It is clear from Adhamhnán's account that Bréanainn of Birr was held in high esteem by the community on Iona, which credited him with the intervention at an assembly in Tailte (now Teltown in Meath) that saved Colum Cille from excommunication.[6] Otherwise, however, the saint figures intermittently only in the traditions surrounding Colum Cille, being totally absent, for example, from Colum's late twelfth-century vernacular Life.[7] No Life survives for Bréanainn himself, although – if Henry Fitzsimon and James Ussher are to be believed – one still existed in the early seventeenth century.[8] The saint is featured in some Midland Lives, including that of Aodh of Rahugh which (like Adhamhnán's *Vita Columbae*) credits him with extra-sensory powers, and that of Ciarán of Seirkieran which enigmatically identifies Aghaboe as the boundary between Birr and Seir, and which groups him together with his namesake and the two Ciaráns in a *fraternitas*.[9] His association with Ciarán of Seir may be reflected in the dedication to Bréanainn at Aghaviller in the Kilkenny barony of Knocktopher.[10] Adhamhnán states that Colum Cille was miraculously made aware of Bréanainn's passing on 'his natal day', and he left the world, with his mother 'Mansenna', at Tallaght, according to the Life of Ciarán of Seirkieran.[11] Compared in manners to Bartholomew, Bréanainn was principally remembered on 29 November, and some annals state that he died in 565, others in 573.[12] His feast was recorded in an early ninth-century calendar kept by an Irishman on the Reichenau in Lake Constance.[13]

1 *VC*^{2} 468–70 (III.3), 486–8 (III.11) ; *DIB* i, 803. **2** *CGSH* §§124, 127; *Lgen*. 729.8; *CGH* 157, 30. **3** *ZCP* 8, 315; cf. *EIHM* 21n; *TEAB* 148 §§5–6. **4** *VC*^{2} 468–70 (III.3), 500 (III.17). **5** *MartT* 41, 43. **6** *VC*^{2} 468–70 (III.3); *AB* 55, 96–108. **7** *IKD* 180–202. **8** *WWRJU*, vi, 240; *MISL* 378. **9** *VSHH* 168, 353; *BNÉ* ii, 110. **10** *HADO* iv, 4. **11** *VC*^{2} 486–8 (III.11); *BNÉ* ii, 116–17 **12** *CGSH* §712.8; *CI* i, 106, 109. **13** *AfL* 31, 63.

Bréanainn of Clonfert (Cluain Fearta), barony of Longford, Co. Galway. The name of this saint – Latin Brendinus, Brendenus or Brendanus, anglicized Brendan – also appears in the hypocoristic form Mobhí. Through his father, Fionnlugh son of Alta (whence the Alltraighe of the area about Tralee in Kerry), Bréanainn acquired from the genealogists three brothers, Domhainghin of Toomyvara, Faithleach of Cloontuskert, and Faolán of Kiltullagh, none of whom is otherwise featured in the saint's record.[1] An opportunistic attempt was also made to establish consanguinity between him and Fursa, patron of Péronne in France and of Killursa (Ceall Fhursa) in Galway, close to Bréanainn's church at Annaghdown.[2] Curiously, though the circumstances of his birth are well documented, his mother, while named Cara in some versions of the saint's Life, otherwise remains nameless.[3] The saint is already attested about 700, albeit without any reference to a long voyage, in Adhamhnán's Life of Colum Cille. This features him under the guise of 'Brendenus mocu Alti' (Bréanainn of the Alltraighe) in two episodes, one involving an 'attendant' named Aodhán, the other as one of a number of 'holy founders of churches'.[4] Adhamhnán also attributes to him a vision similar to one accredited to his namesake, Bréanainn of Birr, one of several indications of the ultimate identity of the two saints.[5]

The saint's fame rests mainly on the *Navigatio Brendani*, 'the Brendan voyage', arguably the most influential of all medieval Irish texts, which appears to have been written by an Irish *peregrinus*, perhaps as early as the ninth century, possibly even earlier.[6] Inspired by the native vernacular tradition of *iomramha*, 'ocean-voyages', the text is preserved in more than 120 manuscripts of continental provenance, as well as in numerous medieval vernacular adaptations, beginning with an early twelfth-century French version, followed by German, Dutch, English, Italian, Occitan, Catalan and Norse re-tellings. The tale clearly captured the imagination of the medieval West, in the process creating a belief in the existence of a mythical St Brendan's Isle, featured in many medieval maps.[7] This was no small achievement for a text that may have been intended to do no more than paint a picture of the journey involved in the ideal monastic life, with its rules, prayers, devotions, and observance of the canonical hours.[8]

It is sometimes argued that the Life composed for the saint, which is preserved in five Latin and two vernacular versions (all of them contained in late manuscript collections), preceded and influenced the *Navigatio*.[9] The evidence for this is, however, extremely slight and, until such time as a critical edition is made of the saint's entire biographical dossier, final judgement on the question of date must be reserved. In the meantime, taking the Latin Lives as a guide, and setting aside the saint's so-called *vita secunda*, which is little more than an adaptation (possibly early twelfth-century) of the *Navigatio*, there are some obvious signs of lateness. These include the assertion in the first chapter that the saint belonged to the Ciarraighe (of whom he was one of the chief protectors) who only became the dominant dynasty in north Kerry after the decline of Bréanainn's more immediate family (Alltraighe), and the choice of Beag son of Dé as a prophet of the saint's greatness, which was probably influenced by the tenth-century rise to supremacy in Munster of the Dál gCais, to whom Beag was sometimes attached.[10]

The biography presents Bréanainn's wide-ranging activities against the background of at least four distinct geographical areas, each of which featured a church said to have been founded by him. His birth and early upbringing place him in the area just north of Tralee, historically settled by the Alltraighe, and important enough in the twelfth century to be chosen as the seat of the diocese of Kerry, located both at Ardfert – of which Bréanainn was patron – and Rattoo. In this section of the basic text, common to Latin and vernacular versions, contacts are established with various persons: the shadowy figure of Bishop Earc, likewise of the Alltraighe, who attended to his early education; Íde who is presented as Earc's foster-mother; Colmán son of Léinín, later patron of the diocese of Cloyne, whom Bréanainn is said to have converted to the religious life; Iarlaithe whom he directed to his place of resurrection at Tuam, later the archiepiscopal see in Connacht, with authority over Annaghdown and Clonfert, the two dioceses associated with Bréanainn; and finally, a king based in Magh Aoi, later – under the Uí Chonchubhair (O'Connors) – the centre of secular power in the western province, who offered the saint a place to build a church, a possible reference to Ogulla, whose patron was entitled to be present at O'Connor's inauguration.[11]

At this point a long account of the saint's voyage to the Land of Promise is interpolated, following which, on his return to Ireland, Bréanainn is brought to the Shannon estuary, where – on the island of Inis Dá Dhroma, now Inishdadroum in the parish of Killadysert – he founded a 'famous monastery'.[12] There can be little doubt that Inishdadroum here stands for the neighbouring – almost attached and much larger – Coney (formerly Canon) Island, so named from the canons regular of St Augustine, whose priory here was a dependency of Clare Abbey.[13] Another journey follows, this time to Britain, where the saint encounters the celebrated Gildas among others and, on his return to Ireland, he founds a church on the Lough Corrib island of Inchiquin (Inis Maca Cuinn) in the parish of Killursa, which was allegedly granted to him by Aodh son of Eacha, a direct ancestor of the Uí Chonchubhair kings of Connacht.[14] An account is then given of the founding of Clonfert (in 558, according to the annals), perhaps Bréanainn's most important church, where he remains until his death on a visit to his sister Brígh at Annaghdown (Eanach Dúin), and this is followed by the transfer of his remains to Clonfert.[15]

It bears noting that each of the four Irish centres of the saint's life-cycle, the cantred of Altry (from Alltraighe) in north Kerry, the Shannon estuary at the point where the river Fergus flowed into it, the eastern side of Lough Corrib and the Clonfert area, were to be chosen in the twelfth century as appropriate sites for the location of Augustinian priories, at Rattoo, Canon Island, Annaghdown and Clonfert, which would suggest that the Life, in the form in which it has survived, was informed by the mind of a canon regular and is unlikely to be an early composition.[16]

Bréanainn was among the Irish saints that attracted the attention of Giraldus Cambrensis, who refers to a written Life.[17] Elsewhere compared in manners to the Apostle Thomas, Bréanainn 'moccu Altae' was among those cited as sponsors of a certain type of vigil in the Old Irish Table of Penitential Commutations, and a Law named after him was proclaimed in Connacht in 744.[18] His cult travelled widely, not only within Ireland, where, among many other places, it reached Raheny near Dublin, Cannaway, Kilbrenan, parish of Moviddy, in the Cork barony of East Muskerry, and Kilmoe in the barony of West Carbery and Clonfert in the barony of Duhallow in the same county, but also in Britain – especially in Scotland – and on the Continent.[19] Its progress in the west of Ireland is exemplified by an early modern Irish tale describing how Bréanainn ensured the survival of the royal line of the Uí Mháille (O'Malleys) of Burrishoole in Mayo by bringing about a change of sex in an infant.[20] This is thought to have occurred at a well in the parish of Kilmeena, and just south of Burrishoole, in the townland of Lankill, parish of Aghagower, there is another well named after the saint, as was also the parish church in Breaghwy.[21] Also in Mayo, Inishglora (Inis Gluaire) 'of Brendan' in the parish of Kilmore, barony of Erris – a visit to which was part of a penance imposed on an Armagh cleric in 1541 – contained a well named after the saint, which no woman dare approach.[22] A well on Valencia Island, styled *tobar ola Bhréanainn*, 'St Brendan's anointing-well', is accompanied by a tradition that links the saint to seafaring, and a similar association underlies 'Fothair na Manach' – traditionally the saint's point of departure on his voyage – in the Corkaguiny parish of Kilquane, which also contains the saint's mountain resort of Cnoc Bréanainn, 'Brandon Hill'.[23] Elsewhere the saint is reputed to have baptized and blessed the progenitor of the Ceinéal Bréanainn of the Cavan barony of Tullyhaw, which points to devotion to him among the Magaurans.[24] Under the hypocoristic guise of Baoi, the saint was remembered at Toberboe (alias Killenny More) in the Laois parish of Aghmacart, of which, according to Bishop Phelan's list, 'Brandanus' was patron.[25] A poem allegedly made by Bréanainn on the sea is said to have formed part of Adhamhnán's reliquary, and a late medieval poem brings the saint to Greece and Rome, among other places.[26] Devotion to the saint was widespread on the Continent and, by the ninth century, a relic had arguably reached either Ferrières in France or the Rhineland.[27] The date assigned to the saint's death oscillates between 576 and 583.[28] Bréanainn's feast fell on 16 May.[29]

1 *CGSH* §§127, 384; *GRSH* 107; *Lgen.* 729.5.6.7; *DIB* i, 803–4. **2** *CMCS* 17, 1–14. **3** *VSHP* i, 98 §1; *VSHH* 324 §1. **4** *VC*[2] 260, 500 (= *VC*[1] I.26, III.17). **5** Ibid.; *TEAB* 732–3. **6** *NSBA*; *NSB*; *LOSB* 13–26; *Kenney* 406–12; *VSHP* i, xxxvi–xliii; *MISL* 390–1; *OV* 12–32; *SeaS* 127; *StH* 37, 9–26. **7** *LOSB* 13–26, 49–78, 285; *JKAHS* 17, 10–36. **8** *Kenney* 415; *SILH* 276–323; *MMTEIW*, 1–20; *CeltT* 193. **9** *MHH* 181, 237; *Kenney* 412–14; *LOSB* 3–12; *ZCP* 5, 124–41; *VSHP* i, 98–151; *VSHH* 56–78; 324–31; *AB* 48, 99–123; *BNÉ* i, 44–95; *LisL* 3304–914; *NSB*; *SeaS* 131–42; *ScriptOralia* 68, 313–57 (314). **10** *JKAHS* 2, 27–33; *VSHP* i, xlii; 98 §§1–2; ibid. ii, 270–92; *AB* 48, 103 §§1–2; *BNÉ* i, 44 §§3–4; *ZCP* 8, 315. **11** *VSHP* i, 98–103 §§3–11; *AB* 48, 104–9 §§3–11; *BNÉ* i, 45–8 §§6–24; *JRSAI* 2, 340. **12** *VSHP* i, 103–44 §§12–90; *AB* 48, 109–10 §12; *BNÉ* i, 48–80 §§27–157. **13** *MRHI* 162; *ACoC* 148–9. **14** *VSHP* i, 141–4 §§83–9; *AB* 48, 111–15 §§15–18; *BNÉ* i, 83–7 §§165–80. **15** *VSHP* i, 145–51 §§91–105; *AB* 48, 116–21 §§21–9; *BNÉ* i, 87–95

§§183–209; *AU s.a.* **16** *MRHI* 156–7, 162, 164–5, 191. **17** *THEH* 127–8. **18** *CGSH* §712.9; *Ériu* 19, 64 §23; *AU s.a.* **19** *CPR* i, lxix; *IER* (5th ser.) 21, 165; *NCHC* i, 64; *KSS* 284–7; *ACDS* 65–9; *CPNS* 274; *CarmG* ii, 232; *SIHI* 10–15; *AnH* 29, 8 §25. **20** *Éigse* 14, 3–12; *Béaloideas* 22, 169–82. **21** *HWI* 76; *CPL* 8, 87; OSL MO i, 490; *Béaloideas* 22, 156–7, 165–7. **22** *Anecd.* i, 34 §75; *JCLAS* 6, 152; *OnomG* 465; *UJA* (2nd ser.) 4, 90; *HWI* 145; *LIS* v, 456–7. **23** *Brendaniana* 278–80; *JKAHS* 22, 157; ibid. 30, 19; *UiR* 23; *TCCD* 132. **24** *BMag.* 2191–226. **25** *HADO* ii, 226–7; *CPL* 15, §691. **26** *Celtica* 15, 35 §14; *Éigse* 13, 92–8. **27** *SIHI* 10–15; *EIRD* 55–68; *RIW* 15–19. **28** *AU s.a.* **29** *MartT* 43; *MartO*[2] 124; *MartG* 98; *MartD* 130.

Bréanainn of Edercloon, parish of Mohill, barony and county of Leitrim, which may now represent an earlier Eadarchluain. This saint is known from two sources, the list of homonymous saints and the list of those commemorated on 13 December.[1] As this day is shared with Colum of Terryglass – an apparent localization of Colum Cille – the patron of Eadarcluain was probably identical with one of the two principal bearers of the name Bréanainn, both of whom figure prominently in the Life composed by Adhamhnán for the founder of Iona.[2]

1 *CGSH* §707.45; *MartG* 238; *MartD* 334. 2 *VC*[2] 260 (I 26), 468–70 (III 3)

Breanat (Branaid). *See* Beircheart; Cránaid.

Breeda. *See* Brighid.

Brendan. *See* Bréanainn.

Bricín of Tomregan (Tuaim Dreagain), an ecclesiastical site in the townland of Mullynagolman, parish of Tomregan, barony of Lower Loughtee, Co. Cavan, formerly in Bréifne of the Uí Raghallaigh (O'Reillys).[1] The saint's pedigree, which is preserved in later versions only of the corpus, attaches Bricín through his father Caol to an obscure branch of the Cianachta descended from an otherwise unattested Teimhéan (alias Corc), son of Tadhg son of Cian.[2] As the Cianachta were connected through their remote ancestor Oilill Ólum to the Eoghanacht of Cashel, it may have been the intention to provide the saint with a southern background similar to that credited to Náile of Kinawley whose Life gives prominence to Bricín, describing him as one of the chief saints of Bréifne, and invoking him as a guarantor of the inviolability of Náile's *tearmann*.[3] Together with Feidhlimidh, patron of the diocese of Kilmore, Bricín also found mention in the Life of Caillín of Fenagh, allegedly the saint's companion.[4] Bricín's *baile*, 'mantic vision', received by the saint at Eastertide, allowed an angel to reveal to him the disguised names of some future churchmen, as well as Patrick's role on the Day of Judgement.[5]

Bricín's main claim to fame is the year said to have been spent with him by Ceann Faoladh son of Oilill who lost his 'brain of forgetfulness' through a blow received at the celebrated battle of Moira (Magh Rath).[6] Brought to Tomregan by Seanach, coarb of Patrick, Ceann Faoladh took advantage of his wound by memorizing everything taught by Bricín in the three schools supposedly run by him, before going on to revise at Derryloran (Doire Lúráin) the tract on poets known as *Uraiceacht na nÉigeas*.[7] This legend is thought to have a bearing on the circumstances that led to the use of writing to transmit vernacular texts.[8] Two feastdays are accorded to Bricín, one of which (9 May) is in the Martyrology of

Tallaght under the guise of Dobhreacóg.[9] The other (more usual) day, although absent from the Martyrology of Tallaght, fell on 5 September.[10]

1 *MartD* 236. 2 *GRSH* 122; *Lgen.* 741.5; *DIB* i, 833. 3 *MHH* 108 §24; 122 §55. 4 *BFen.* 412. 5 *ZCP* 9, 449–57; *Éigse* 33, 49–56. 6 *CMR* 278–84. 7 Ibid.; *AurÉ* 2622–44. 8 *Studies* 11, 13–28, 435–46; *EILI* 84–6; *StC* 5, 62–6; *StH* 31, 55–8; *KLT* 64. 9 *MartT* 41; cf. *MartG* 92 (Bricín). 10 *MartO*[2] 192 (Brecc), 202; *MartG* 170; *MartD* 236; *Breifne* 7, 464–88.

Bride (Bridget). *See* Brighid.

Brígh. Large numbers of saints named Brígh are recorded in the hagiographical record, with eleven in the list of homonymous saints alone, many of whom are otherwise untraceable.[1] The basic meaning of the name, 'power, authority, virtue', is also present in the cognate Brighid (Brigit).[2] Several of those subject to Brighid of Kildare bear the name Brígh.[3]

1 *CGSH* §708.14–24. 2 *Lexique* B–87. 3 *CGSH* §670.4.35.50.52.73.78.

Brígh daughter of Aodh Damháin. *See* Luchtighearn of Tomfinlough.

Brígh daughter of Caomhlugh. Assigned by the genealogists to the men of Teathbha, a territory now comprising most of Longford and part of Westmeath, this saint figures in an episode in the Life of Brighid of Kildare.[1] Brighid, then on a visit to Teathbha, was invited by Brígh to her (unnamed) house, from which she banished a demon.

1 *BBr.* §31.

Brígh daughter of Cobhthach is said to have been the mother of several saints, including Séighín (probably of Rathvilly), Bishop Aodhán of Glendalough, and Bishop Éidchéan of Clonfad, along with one king, Aodh son of Ainmhire.[1] The *Bansheanchas* list of famous women also names her as mother of the king.[2] Her father Cobhthach is described as a son of Criomhthann son of Éanna Ceinsealach, progenitor of the Uí Cheinsealaigh, the ruling dynasty of south Leinster. A family named Ceinéal Cobhthaigh of Ard Ladhrann, now Ardamine in the Wexford barony of Ballaghkeen, descended from her father, and the townland of Kilbride is located in the neighbouring parish of Kiltennel.[3]

1 *CGSH* §§380.1, 722.64. 2 *RC* 47, 306, 331; ibid. 48, 181, 218. 3 *CGH* 316c60; *HDGP* i, 88.

Brígh daughter of Feargna. *See* Fíonán of Teach Oirthir.

Brígh daughter of Fiachra. *See* Brígh of Barragh.

Brígh daughter of Forannán. *See* Luchtighearn of Tomfinlough.

Brígh daughter of Neamhnann. *See* Bearchán of Ceall Láthraigh.

Brígh mother of Comhghall of Bangor. An entry in the tract on the mothers of the saints refers to Brígh mother of Comhghall 'the priest'.[1] That the Bangor saint is intended is made clear by Comhghall's Life, which gives the name of his mother as 'Briga'.[2] Prior to the birth of her famous son, while sitting in a chariot with her husband Séadna, Brígh is said to have caught the attention of Mac Nise of Connor who prophesied that she would bear a 'king who would rule over many'.[3] The birth happened, according to one tradition, at a place called 'Mourne', which may be reflected in the names Magheramorne and Lough Mourne in the Antrim parishes of Glynn and Carrickfergus.[4]

1 *CGSH* §722.41. 2 *VSHH* 332. 3 Ibid., 332, 406. 4 *VSHP* ii, 4; *EA* 269.

Brígh of Annaghdown (Eanach Dúin), barony of Clare, Co. Galway. This daughter of Fionnlugh, and sister of Bréanainn of Clonfert, figures twice in the Life of her much more celebrated sibling, first as a pupil of Bishop Earc, then as occupant of the Galway church of Annaghdown about the time that her brother is said to have died there.[1]

1 *VSHP* i, 99–100 §4; 149–50 §§102–3; *BNÉ* i, 46 §12; 93 §206.

Brígh of Barragh, barony of Forth, Co. Carlow, which may now represent an earlier Ceall Bhairnigh. This daughter of Greallán is known from the list of those subject to Brighid of Kildare, which assigns her, together with her sister Sárnad, and the three daughters of Fiachra of the Uí Dhúnlainge – variously named Brígh, Mughain, and Sárnad – to Ceall Bhairnigh, possibly a corrupt form of Beirreach (Barragh).[1] Associated with the group is the word *martar* which is sometimes used of a collection of relics of saints. Another Sárnad, described as a daughter of Eacha, is also attached to the church of Barragh, and it is worth noting that there is a townland of Kilbride (Ceall Bhrighde) in the parish named after the church.[2] By the early nineteenth century, local opinion considered the name of the parish to be derived from an otherwise unattested saint 'Barrach', a carpenter by trade.[3] A print on the base of a font outside the doorway of the medieval church of Barragh is now known as 'St Patrick's footprint'.[4]

1 *CGSH* §670.73; *HDGP* iii, 130. 2 *CGSH* §4. 3 OSL CW 391; *Carloviana* 55, 97; *Béaloideas* 4, 124–5. 4 *RIGI* 235.

Brígh of Kilmoney (Ceall Mhuine), parish of Rathangan, barony of Offaly East, Co. Kildare. An entry in the list of homonymous saints brings together Brígh daughter of Colga and a saint named Dúthracht.[1] Another list, this time of saints remembered on 12 November, likewise groups these together and – as is already assumed by early seventeenth-century sources – they are doubtless the same as the pair assigned by a third list (of saints subject to Brighid of Kildare) to the church of Kilmoney, together with a saint named Tighearn.[2] Kilmoney is located a few miles north-west of Kildare.

1 *CGSH* §708.21. 2 *MartG* 216; *MartD* 306; *CGSH* §670.52.

Brígh of Kilbride, parish of Abbeylara, barony of Granard, Co. Longford, which may now represent an earlier Ceall Bhríghe. The entry on Brígh daughter of Fearghas in the list of those subject to Brighid of Kildare is followed by entries relating to the churches of Abbeylara and Clonbroney, both in the same part of Longford.[1] The saints named for Abbeylara are said to have been daughters of Feargna son of Fearghas, which may mean that they were thought to be nieces of Brígh.[2] If so, the patron of Kilbride is also likely to have been the Brígh commemorated on 7 January in Cairbre, a people and territory located in the barony of Granard, unless her namesake and possible double, Brígh Chochlach of Carbury (Críoch Chairbre) in Sligo, is intended.[3] Remembered with Brígh on this day were the daughters of Feargna, doubtless the above-mentioned saints associated with Abbeylara.[4]

1 *CGSH* §670.4–6; *Lgen.* 752.12. 2 *CGSH* §708.19. 3 *MartT* 5; *MartG* 10; *MartD* 8. 4 *CGSH* §670.5.

Brígh of Teach Bríghe, an unidentified church, possibly near Kildare. Brígh figures both in the list of homonymous saints and in the list of those subject to Brighid of Kildare.[1] In the latter list, she is said to have performed two miracles, milking cows three times in one day and harvesting when the surrounding countryside was experiencing a rainstorm. Elsewhere these two miracles are attributed to Brighid herself, which suggests that Brígh was originally identical with the Kildare saint.[2]

1 *CGSH* §§670.78, 708.15; *Lgen.* 753.41. 2 *LH* i, 117; *LisL* 50, 197.

Brígh Chochlach, 'hooded', of Críoch Chairbre, now approximately the barony of Carbury, Co. Sligo. In the tract on the mothers of the saints, Brígh is numbered among the forty-seven children of Cuman daughter of Dallbhrónach of the Déise Breagh who gave name to the Meath baronies of Deece.[1] As Cuman was Brighid's maternal aunt, all forty-seven were thus closely related to the Kildare saint.[2] Several of Cuman's children were associated with Carbury and surrounding districts, so that Brígh's cult may reflect Brigidine influence in that area. These include Bishop Brón, patron of Killaspugbrone in Carbury who, according to Brighid's *vita prima*, returned home from a visit to Leinster with a chrismal belonging to the Kildare saint.[3] According to the same text, Brighid herself visited Magh Aoi in Roscommon, where the parish of Kilbride now bears her name.[4] The saint may have been a doublet of Brígh of Kilbride.

1 *CGSH* §722.10. 2 Ibid. §722.4–6. 3 *VP* §86. 4 *VP* §94.

Brígh Mhór of Seandomhnach in Fiodh Eoin. This place appears to have lain in Magh Thulach which, though now reflected in the name of the Westmeath barony of Fartullagh, may formerly have extended eastwards into neighbouring baronies. The saint and her church are known only from an entry in the corpus of saints' pedigrees, where she is accompanied by Crónán grandson of Eilmhín of Díseart Átha, now probably a site in the parish of Monasteroris, at Cushaling Bridge on the river Figile, which forms the Kildare/Offaly border.[1] Her own church has not been identified, but both Fiodh Eoin and Magh Thulach figure prominently in the Life of Brighid of Kildare, and the barony of Fartullagh contains a parish of Kilbride.[2]

1 *CGSH* §161; *Lgen.* 750.3; *HDGP* i, 142. 2 *BBr.* §§20–2.

Brighid. Like Brígh, Brighid's name, which is also commonly written Brigit, as in Old Irish, and anglicized as Bride, Breeda and Bridget, derives from a word meaning vigour or virtue. Although there are thirteen saints of the name in the list of homonymous saints, these and others so named are probably localizations of the same (originally pre-Christian) cult as is represented by Brighid of Kildare. Two of the three identified churches in the list – Oughterard (Uachtar Aird) in the barony of South Salt, and Rathbride (Ráith Bhrighde) in the parish of Tully, barony of Offaly East – are within the present county of Kildare, and the third – Bendinstown (Seanbhoth) in the parish of Ballyellin – is in the Carlow barony of Forth which takes its name from the Fothairt, Brighid's people.[1] One of those whose fathers are named in the list, Brighid daughter of Doma – sometimes styled Sean-Bhrighid, 'earlier/senior Brighid' – is otherwise included in the list of those commemorated on 7 February, and thus within the octave of the feast of the patron of Kildare.[2]

1 *CGSH* §708.7.10.12. **2** *MartT* 15; *MartG* 32; *MartD* 40; *ZCP* 19, 119 §11.

Brighid daughter of Aodh. According to the corpus of saints' pedigrees, this Brighid belonged to the Dál nAraidhe whose territory lay in north Down and south Antrim.[1] Within this area, close to the church and see of Connor, there were two places named Kilbride (Ceall Bhrighde), one in the parish of the same name, the other in the parish of Grange of Doagh. Brighid daughter of Aodh, whose name also figures in the list of homonymous saints, was probably patron of one, or both, of these.[2]

1 *CGSH* §111; *GRSH* 98; *Lgen.* 732.1. **2** *CGSH* §708.12; *EA* 64.

Brighid daughter of Léinín. *See* Aighleann of Killiney.

Brighid daughter of Muireadhach. *See* Brighid of Rathbride.

Brighid of Aharney (Achadh Togharta), barony of Galmoy, Co. Kilkenny. Formerly in the territory of Uí Dhuach, the church that gave name to Aharney is now known as Barony in the townland of Ballyconra.[1] An entry in the corpus of saints' pedigrees states that Brighid, along with Cuman daughter of Dallbhrónach and three other saints – all associated with the church of Aharney – were of the Fothairt, the people to whom Brighid of Kildare also belonged.[2] Brighid's associate Cuman is elsewhere said to have been a maternal aunt of the Kildare saint.[3] As the parish church of Aharney was dedicated to Brighid of Kildare, there can be little doubt that she and her local namesake were originally identical.[4]

1 *HDGP* i, 23. **2** *CGSH* §173. **3** *CGSH* §§2.1, 722.4. **4** *HADO* ii, 308.

Brighid of Coolcor (Cúil Chorra), parish and barony of Granard, Co. Longford. This saint is known from the list of those subject to Brighid of Kildare, which credits her with several associates, including a saint named Conlaodh, probably the first bishop of Kildare.[1] Also in the group is Bishop Mac Caorthainn who is doubtless the same as the man described by Tíreachán in his Life of Patrick as an uncle of Brighid of Kildare.[2] In the same passage, Tíreachán, who appears to have been concerned with claiming for Patrick churches associated with Brighid, specifies Coolcor. As her church lay in the parish of Granard, which Tíreachán also mentions in this passage, it bears noting that this is now located between the parishes of Abbeylara and Clonbroney, both of which – as is shown by the tradition of Brígh daughter of Feargna – also had associations with Brighid of Kildare. The townland of Kilbride in the parish of Abbeylara is close to the town of Granard.

1 *CGSH* §670.64; *Lgen*. 753.30. 2 *PTBA* 136.

Brighid of Feenish Island, parish of Kilconry, barony of Bunratty Lower, Co. Clare, which may now represent an earlier Cluain Infidhe. This daughter of Cú Chathrach is known only from an episode in the Life of Seanán of Scattery Island which, having assigned her to the otherwise unattested family of Uí Mhic Tháil, located the saint in Cluain Infidhe (perhaps Cluain Inse Fidhe) on the river Shannon.[1] The passage describes how Brighid commanded the waters of the river to take a basket containing a chasuble as a gift to Seanán. On the basis that her church was probably on Inis Fidhe (Fidhinis), which is mentioned in the Life of Mac Creiche, John Colgan conjectured that it lay near the mouth of the river Fergus.[1] This would now be Feenish Island off Kilconry which lacks, however, any trace of an ecclesiastical site.[2] That Colgan was probably nonetheless right is indicated by the presence on the neighbouring Coney Island of a well, Tobberbreedy, named after Brighid. In the immediately following section of the text, Seanán encountered Cainnear (Cainir) Chráibhtheach who may have given name to Kilconry.[3]

1 *LisL* 2399–415. 2 *ASH* 540. 2 *ACoC* 265. 3 *LisL* 2416–49; *PRIA* 6C (1900), 107; but cf. Logainm.ie 'Cill Chomhraí'.

Brighid of Kildare (Ceall Dara), barony of Offaly East, Co. Kildare. Historically the chief saint of the province of Leinster, Brighid daughter of Dubhthach was second in rank only to Patrick in the Irish tradition. On account of her feast of 1 February, one of the main days in the Celtic calendar, and the tradition of a perpetual fire at her church, as witnessed by Giraldus Cambrensis, the saint is thought to have had dubious origins, probably involving the pre-Christian cult of the Celtic divinity Brigantia.[1] Genealogically, Brighid was attached to a branch of the Fothairt known as Uí Bhreasail, a hereditary ecclesiastical family within the territory of Uí Fhailghe.[2] According to her Lives, the saint's *hereditas* lay in the present county of Offaly, in the baronies of Warrenstown, Coolestown and Lower Philipstown, all of which are still within the diocese of Kildare.[3] Her attachment to the Fothairt led to the opportunistic belief, fostered by the canons regular who had control of the site, and already attested in both the saint's Middle-Irish vernacular Life and in St Bernard's Life of Malachy, that she was born at Faughart (from Fochairt) in Louth, where, as at other places in that county, such as Dunleer, the story of her having gouged out an eye (or eyes) was also localized.[4]

Brighid's church at Kildare attained considerable early importance which, during the seventh century, allowed it to vie with Armagh for supremacy over the churches of the Irish.[5] As in Patrick's case, Kildare's quest for primacy led to the need for a Life of the saint, and though there has been much debate on the subject, this appears to have been first provided about 675, or slightly earlier, by Cogitosus who, conscious of the interests of the saint's church, claimed *paruchia* or jurisdiction for it 'from sea to sea'.[6] Seven more Lives, four Latin, three in the vernacular, and each with its own agenda, followed over the next thousand years, leaving the saint with a more extensive biographical dossier than any other Irish saint, except Patrick.[7]

While Cogitosus' focus was on Kildare and Leinster, the anonymous late eighth- or early ninth-century author of the saint's *vita prima*, who is sometimes held to have been earlier than Cogitosus, presented Brighid as an itinerant saint journeying mainly among the southern Uí Néill of Meath, Westmeath and Longford, but also connected nationwide, either through the *magus* served by her mother or by journeys that brought her to places in Connacht, Munster, Ulster and, of course, Leinster, including visits to such obvious centres of power as Magh Feimhin (Cashel) and Magh Aoi (Rathcroghan), where her coarb (in Ballintober) was later entitled to be present at O'Connor's inauguration.[8] By the late eighth century, Armagh's claim to primacy had apparently come to be accepted by the authorities at Kildare, as is shown both by Brighid's deference to Patrick in her dealings with him, and by the author's relegation of the Leinster bishop, Mac Caille of Croghan, who was given pride of place by Cogitosus, to the secondary role of disciple of two Uí Néill bishops, Meal and Mealchú – both allegedly British and disciples of Patrick – in the story of how Brighid received the veil.[9] The author's keen awareness of the usefulness of his genre as a means of emphasizing the high status of Brighid's successors at Kildare is also evident in the sub-text of the Life which presents the saint as an equal of bishops, providing sustenance for the churches of the Uí Néill at Eastertide, washing the bodies of the old and infirm – both episcopal functions – and being invited to accompany bishops on circuit.[10] No such sub-text was required in relation to this issue by the anonymous ninth-century author of Brighid's vernacular Life who cleverly manipulated the story of her consecration as a nun by stating that the officiating bishop mistakenly read out words of episcopal ordination.[11] His successor, the author of Brighid's eleventh- or twelfth-century vernacular Life, went even further, asserting that all of Kildare's abbesses enjoyed the same status, which was to remain the case until decreed otherwise at the synod of Kells in 1152.[12]

The saint's popularity outside Ireland is shown by the two external Lives composed for her; One, metrical in form, was written about 850 by Donatus, bishop of Fiesole in Italy (where the church of Santa Brigida was dedicated to Brighid), coincidentally a few years before a new church was built for her at Kildare. Another, Brighid's last pre-Conquest Life, was compiled by Laurence of Durham (†1154) in England, perhaps with the aid of a copy of the saint's Life supplied, or mediated, by Maol Maodhóg (Malachy) of Armagh.[13]

Brighid's cult spread well beyond Ireland to Britain and the Continent. In Ireland, the thirty-five townlands named Kilbride and the eight named Kilbreedy give an indication of the spread of her cult which, while centred in Leinster, including Dublin, where churches in the ancient town centre, in Killester and

Stillorgan preserved her memory, even reached the south coast, at Tower Street in Cork City, at Liscleary, near Carrigaline, where there stood an *ecclesia sancte Brigidae*, at Templebreedy near Crosshaven, at Myross, near Glandore, and at Templebreedy in the parish of Tullagh, near Baltimore.[14] For all her dubious origins, therefore, Brighid's record shows that she stood alone among the women saints of Ireland, a rival in importance to Patrick and Colum Cille, an abbess whom all other abbesses revered, a bishop in all but name, of such high status that she came to be regarded, possibly as early as the seventh century, as 'Mary of the Irish'.[15] The spread of Brighid's cult, both countrywide and beyond, led to the saint's localization in many areas, as in the case of Brígh of Teach Bríghe, who is said to have performed two miracles elsewhere attributed to the Kildare saint.[16]

Through her mother Broicseach, one of seven daughters of Dallbhrónach of the Déise Breagh (whence the Meath baronies of Deece), Brighid was associated with numerous other saints, including forty-seven nieces and nephews allegedly born to her aunt Cuman.[17] Among the important saints linked to her, or to her church, as evidenced by the saint's Lives, were: Aodh son of Breac of Rahugh who reputedly cured her headache; Bréanainn of Clonfert who is said to have visited her at Kildare; and Conlaodh, her craftsman and first bishop at Kildare.[18] A separate list details the numerous churches said to have been subject to her.[19]

Brighid is thought to have died in the same year (AD524) as Beoaidh of Ardcarn, and on the same night as Muircheartach son of Earc, king of Tara, and Colmán of Oughtmama.[20] Just as her alleged birth in Faughart is spurious, so also the tradition of her supposed burial in Downpatrick with Patrick and Colum Cille, which is traceable only to the late twelfth century.[21] This period also saw Giraldus Cambrensis take an interest in the saint's many miracles, especially those connected with fire, in the process drawing attention to a magnificent gospel-book – the product of 'angelic rather than human diligence' – then kept at Kildare.[22] The saint's 'hair-shirt' reputedly formed part of Adhamhnán's reliquary and bells associated with her are attested for Kildare, Croaghpatrick and Beckery, parish of Glastonbury, in Somerset, England.[23]

The feast of Brighid, 'the chaste head of Ireland's nuns', on 1 February has the distinction of being one of the first Irish feasts to be commemorated in external sources, including Willibrord's Calendar, the Echternach version of the Hieronymian Martyrology, and the martyrologies of Ado and Usuard.[24] A year of death in the 520s, at the age of seventy (elsewhere given as eighty-eight), allowed the computation of a year of birth in the 450s.[25] As the saint's cult is attested in many places throughout Ireland, Britain (especially in Scotland), and the Continent – where it often became confounded with that of Birgitta of Sweden – it was only appropriate that a thirteenth-century poet should address Brighid as *ógh na hEorpa*, 'virgin of Europe'.[26] Within Ireland, however, she remained first and foremost patron of the Leinstermen.[27] Holy wells dedicated to the saint, as at Liscannor, in the Clare parish of Kilmacrehy, and at Castlegar in the Galway parish of Ballynakill, sometimes also became the sites of *Lughnasadh* celebrations on or around 1 August.[28] A relic of the saint, accompanied by relics of her successor Darlughdhach and her bishop Conlaodh, had reached Saint-Maurice d'Agaune in the Swiss canton of Valais by 700, and by the mid-ninth century another relic is attested for the Rhineland.[29]

1 *EIHM* 38; *Ériu* 26, 19; *CeltM* 32–4; *IKHK* 155; *FMA* 27–31; *THEH* 120–1; *ÉtC* 24, 209–15; *KeltRh.* 319–27; *CICI* 151–6; *DIB* i, 837–40; *Ériu* 54, 82–92; *BiblSS* iii, 430–7; *SBK* 81–93; *Peritia* 21, 192–6. **2** *CGSH* §2, *CGH* 126a28; *GRSH* 74; *Lgen.* 718.1. **3** *BBr.* 44–6 (§6). **4** *TMIH* 56; *BCLMA* 100; *BCOC* 318; *TT* 547 §6; *MISL* 145; *LIS* ii, 25–33; OSL LH 113–14; *SAM* 2.1, 192–4; *JCLAS* 16, 113. **5** *CEIS* 84–5; *ECI* 428–9; *SBK* 111–221. **6** *ECI* 438; *TT* 518–26; *AS*.Feb. i, 135–41; *JRSAI* 117, 11–27; *SPW* 207–24; *Peritia* 1, 81–106, 107–45; *AIMA* 207–20; *StC* 35, 245–70; *PHCC* 14, 175–94; *DIB* i, 837–8. **7** *Kenney* 356–63; *MHH* 181–2; *BHL* i, 217–18. **8** *TT* 527–42; *AS*.Feb.. i, 119–35; *JRSAI* 119, 14–49; *Peritia* 1, 81–106, 107–45; ibid. 12, 1–23; ibid. 14, 268–78; *LCC* 15, 34–60; *JRSAI* 2, 340. **9** *TT* 529 §18; *PHCC* 14, 175. **10** *TT* 529 §§21–2; 530 §37; *ZCP* 19, 120 §13. **11** *BBr.* 174–85 §§18–19; *IrT* I, 2–18 §21; *IHS* 1, 121–34, 129–53. **12** *TMIH* 66; *LisL* 1345–50; *TIC* 72–3. **13** *PRIA* 77C, 57–192; *VSHH* 1–37; *CMCS* 35, 13–26; *FAI* 132. **14** *CGSH* §729.3; *HB* 12 §1; *SIHI* 16–45; *SCSW* 97–8; *JCHAS* 104, 77–96; ibid. 106, 87; *NCHC* i, 64; *CPR* i, lxx; *AICK* i, 280 (Ardra); *SBK* 168; *Keimelia* 519; *AH* 8, 15. **15** *MHDI* 32; *CGH* 125b19; *ZCP* 12, 293; cf. *Ériu* 12, 26 §32. **16** *LH* i, 117; *LisL* 50, 197. **17** *CGSH* §722.3–13. **18** *BBr.* 270–1; ibid. app. 25, 39. **19** *CGSH* §670.1–88. **20** *AU s.a.*; *Peritia* 14, 255–81; *IrT* iii, 84 §4; but cf. *LUM* 154rb 18, 21. **21** *TT* 258–63. **22** *THEH* 120–24. **23** *Celtica* 15, 34 §10; *EMH* 477 §197, 480 §207, 512 §292. **24** *AS*.Nov. ii.2, 71; HBS 55, 4; *MartA* 77; *MartU* 173; *MartT* 14; *MartO²* 58; *MartG* 28; *MartD* 34–6; cf. *MGH.SS* 15, 1, 506 §11; *CICI* 154–5. **25** *AU s.a.* 452, 456, 524, 526, 528; *JCHAS* 64, 73. **26** *TT* 623–6; *KSS* 287–91; *CPNS* 274–5; *ACDS* 116–31 *CarmG* i, 164–73; *SIHI* 16–45; *LIS* ii, 193–224; *Ériu* 54, 82–92; *CMCS* 16, 85–95; ibid. 35, 13–26; *StC* 8/9, 33–47; *Éigse* 7, 73 §10; *DIB* i, 839; *MSNAF* 139; *EIRD* 55–68. **27** *CGSH* §729.3; *LBran.* 2461–72. **28** *FL* 275–86; OSL GY i, 106; cf. *Celtica* 23, 231–60. **29** *RIW* 12–13, 15–19, 31.

Brighid of Magh Life, a name used of the plain about Kildare. Placed second after Brighid of Kildare in the list of homonymous saints, this daughter of Doma is otherwise included in the list of those commemorated on 7 February within the octave of the feast of her more celebrated namesake.[2] A second feast (9 March), again attaching her to the Liffey plain, is shared by Brighid of Móin Mhioláin – perhaps an ecclesiastical site in the Westmeath parish of Foyran – which is assigned (under the guise of Móin Mhaoláin) to three sons of Dáire in the list for 7 February.[2] It can scarcely be doubted that Brighid and her namesake at Kildare were originally identical.

1 *CGSH* §708.2; *MartT* 15; *MartG* 32; *MartD* 40. **2** *MartT* 21; *Ainm* 9, 26.

Brighid of Rathbride (Ráith/Rátha Brighde), parish of Tully, barony of Offaly East, Co. Kildare. This daughter of Fiachna is included among those subject to Brighid of Kildare, together with an otherwise unattested sister named Bíthe.[1] The church of the sisters is located near the Curragh in the territory of Uí Chormaic, a branch of the Fothairt closely related to the segment to which the patron of Kildare belonged.[2] As the churches of Rathbride and Kildare lie near one another, their homonymous patrons are likely to have been originally identical.[3] A separate list, this time of homonymous saints, provides Brighid of Rathbride with a father named Muireadhach and a companion – perhaps another sister – named Aodhamair.[4]

1 *CGSH* §670.79; *Lgen.* 753.42. **2** *CGH* 126a35–40. **3** *Dinn.* 2, 31. **4** *CGSH* §708.10.

Brighid of Shankill (Seancheall), barony of Gowran, Co. Kilkenny. In the corpus of saints' pedigrees, Brighid daughter of Mac Dara (Dáire) – also known as

Brighid Fhionn, 'fair' – is attached, along with her two sisters, Soghaois and Teamhair, and two uncles on her father's side, Iustán and Fiontan, to the Uí Bhairrche who were settled in various parts of Leinster, including Carlow (deanery of Obargy) and Wexford (barony of Bargy).[1] Nothing else appears to be known of these saints.

1 *CGSH* §260; *CGH* 121ba33–40; *GRSH* 86; *Lgen*. 463.6.

Brighid Mhór of Delgany. *See* Domhainghin of Delgany.

Briúinseach of Magh Treagha, a plain in Longford within the former territory of Teathbha (Teffia). This daughter of Criomhthann is known from the list of those subject to Brighid of Kildare who is said to have visited Teathbha on several occasions.[1] Her feast fell on 29 May.[2] A note added to Ó Cléirigh's index of the Martyrology of Donegal asks whether she is to be identified with Berriona/Buryan in Cornwall.[3]

1 *CGSH* §670.31; *BBr*. 270, 322–3; *DIB* i, 844–5. 2 *MartT* 46; *MartG* 106; *MartD* 140. 3 *MartD* 368; cf. *SCorn*. 78.

Broc/aidh/án. There is some confusion as to names containing the element *broc*, 'badger'. In some cases, especially in Munster, the modern form of the name Brocán shows lengthening of the first syllable, thus giving Brógán, as in Cluain Brógáin (Clonbrogan in Co. Tipperary) and Ceall Bhrógáin (Kilbrogan in Co. Cork).[1] The scant available metrical evidence shows, however, that the saint's name Brocán rimed with words or names containing a short initial syllable.[2] The position adopted here, therefore, as in the case of Beagán, whose initial syllable also appears to have undergone lengthening in Munster, is that *broc*, and not *bróg*, was the component that yielded such saints' names as Brocaidh and Brocán.

1 *ClLTÁ* iii, 70–2; *HDGP* iii, 136. 2 *MartG* 72 (Brocán/Colmán).

Brocaidh of Emlagh (Imleach Each/Brocadha) in the parish of Kilkeevin, barony of Castlereagh, Co. Roscommon.[1] An entry in the tract on the mothers of the saints lists the names of seventeen children of Dairearca, sister of Patrick, of whom Brocaidh was one.[2] A passage in Patrick's early Life likewise describes Brocaidh, whose father is given the name Gollaid, as the Armagh saint's nephew, assigning to him Emlagh and placing it in Ciarraighe of Connacht, another name for Ciarraighe of Magh Aoi which comprised the area between the towns of Roscommon and Elphin.[3] Here Brocaidh is said to have been visited by his brother Lomán of Trim, then at the point of death. Later, while among the Uí Bhriúin of Connacht in Magh Shealga – now approximately the parish of Ogulla in Roscommon – Patrick is said to have been accompanied by several bishops, including Brocaidh.[4] Further west, in the eastern part of the barony of Tireragh, there was also a church named after Brocaidh.[5] The saint was probably originally identical with his sibling, the like-named Brocán of Breaghey, and possibly also with Brocán of Mothel whose feast fell on the vigil of Brocaidh's day. The notice of Brocaidh's feast on 9 July refers to his church as Imleach Brocadha.[6]

1 *VT* 630; *JGAHS* 23, 73, 138–46; *Lgen.* Iv, 457. 2 *CGSH* §722.16. 3 *PTBA* 168; *BP* 715–16 (= *VT* 68); *Lgen.* Iv, 457; *HDGP* i, 58. 4 *PTBA* 147–8; *BP* 1213 (= *VT* 108). 5 *PHib.* I, 103. 6 *MartT* 54; *MartG* 132; *MartD* 190.

Brocán of Breaghey (Bréachmhagh), parish of Tynan, barony of Tiranny, Co. Armagh. An entry in the tract on the mothers of the saints lists the names of seventeen children of Dairearca, Patrick's sister, of whom Brocán was one.[1] A passage in Patrick's Life likewise describes Brocán as Dairearca's son, assigning to him the church of Breaghey in the territory of Uí Dhorthain in the present county of Armagh.[2] It must seem likely that this saint was identical both with his sibling, the like-named Brocaidh of Emlagh, and his namesake Brocán who, according to some versions of those in orders with Patrick, belonged to the Armagh saint's household.[3] As a scribe, Brocán figures prominently in the *Agallamh na Seanórach*, 'colloquy of the ancients'.[4]

1 *CGSH* §722.16. 2 *PTBA* 168; *BP* 715–16 (= *VT* 68); *CGH* 141a4–5; *HDGP* ii, 172. 3 *CGSH* §§671.15, 672.8.22. 4 *TEI* 20; *SG* i, 117.

Brocán of Cluain Iomarchair, an unidentified church in Ossory. This saint, whose name is also written Bracán and Bearchán, figures in the Life of Abán as the uncle of a thief who stole the latter's swine, only to be duly punished.[1] Abán and Brocán – who is otherwise known from an entry in the list of homonymous saints – went on to agree *fraternitas* 'until the end of the world'.[2] A note added to the notice of the saint's feast in the Martyrology of Aonghas states that Flannán of Killaloe – whose mentor is elsewhere said to have been 'Bracanus' – came sometimes to Brocán's church.[3] In some martyrologies, his feast falls on the same day (17 September) as that of his namesake at Ros Tuirc, likewise in Ossory, who has been taken to be identical with Brocán Claon, the author of a hymn in praise of Brighid of Kildare.[4] This may also be the Brogan who gave name to Clonbrogan (Cluain Brógáin/Brocáin) in the Tipperary parish of Magorban, where a holy well bears his name.[5] A note added to an entry on 'Broccanus episcopus' in the *Catalogus* of Ireland's principal saints states that Brocán was also commemorated at or near Ballyfarnoge in the Wexford parishes of Ballybrazil and Whitechurch, where the supposed marks of his feet were still to be seen.[6]

1 *VSHH* 269 §30 (Braccanus); *VSHP* i, 25 §37 (Bercanus). 2 Ibid.; *CGSH* §707.74. 3 *MartO²* 208; *VSHH* 285–6 §§8, 11. 4 *MartO²* 208; *MartD* 250. 5 OSL TY ii, 493; *ClLTÁ* iii, 70–2. 6 *Seanchas* 408 §41.

Brocán of Laragh. *See* Bearchán of Laragh.

Brocán of Mothel (Maothal Bhrocáin), barony of Upperthird, Co. Waterford. This saintly scribe figures in the martyrologies, which assign his feast to 8 July.[1] As this was the eve of the feast of Brocaidh of Emlagh, one may suspect that he and his namesakes at Mothel and Breaghey were originally identical. Brocán of Breaghey is presented as a scribe in one version of those in orders with Patrick of Armagh, and he figures prominently in this capacity in *Agallamh na Seanórach*, 'colloquy of the ancients'.[2] In Mothel, which later became the site of an Augustinian priory (*monasterium sancti Brogani*) dedicated to Brocán, the saint's feast was remembered on 6 July – more recently on the second Sunday of July – at a well named *Tobar Cuáin agus Brocáin* after the saint, together with Cuán of Airbhre who was locally taken to have been Brocán's first successor.[3] The scribe is probably also the same as the 'Brógán' who reputedly wrote *theas is thuaidh*, 'south and north', as if in reference to the patrons of both Breaghey in the North and Mothel in the South.[4]

1 *MartT* 54; *MartO*[2] 161; *MartG* 132; *MartD* 190. **2** *CGSH* §672.25; *TEI* 20; *SG* i, 117. **3** *WatLis*. 138; *AH* 12, 25 §31; *TKAS* 1, 497, 500; *Decies* 54, 57. **4** *InaF* i, 136 §10.

Brocán Claon, 'bent' of Ros Tuirc. The preface to a well-known hymn in praise of Brighid of Kildare, beginning *Ní char Brighid bhuadhach bith*, 'victorious Brighid loves not the world', describes the background to its composition in traditional style, as follows: 'The place of this hymn Slieve Bloom or Clonmore of Maodhóg; the person Brocán Claon; the time of Lughaidh son of Laoghaire, king of Ireland, and Oilill son of Dúnlaing, king of Leinster; the cause, namely that his mentor, Ultán of Ardbraccan, requested of him that he give account of Brighid's virtues in a brief passage of poetic harmony, for Ultán it was who brought together all of Brighid's miracles'.[1] With over 200 lines, the hymn can scarcely be described as brief. Despite the copious glosses later added to it, nothing further can be gleaned from the hymn concerning its author. This notwithstanding, John Colgan who gave the hymn first place among Brighid's Lives, identified Brocán with the abbot of Ros Tuirc in Magh Roighne of Ossory commemorated on 17 September.[2] Ros Tuirc has been tentatively identified as Kilbrickan (perhaps from an earlier Ceall Bhrocáin) in the Kilkenny parish of Earlstown.[3] A note added to the Martyrology of Aonghas links the saint to his namesake, Brocán of Cluain Iomarchair, an unidentified church in Ossory.[4] An ecclesiastical site named Kilbrickan – known in Irish as Cill Bhrocáin, 'Brocán's church' – in the Laois parish of Offerlane, which includes part of Slieve Bloom, is another possible Ossory dedication to the saint.[5] Under the guise of 'Brógán', the saint is cited as a prophet of prowess, together with Brighid, in a poem in praise of an east Leinster chieftain.[6]

1 *LH* i, 112; cf. ibid. 107; *DIB* i, 846–7. **2** *ASH* 609; *MartT* 72; *MartO*[2] 194; *MartG* 178; *MartD* 250. **3** *OLL* 3, 51–2. **4** *MartO*[2] 208. **5** *HADO* ii, 175–6. **6** *LBran*. 2473–88.

Brogan/Brógán. *See* Brocán; Brocán Claon.

Broghan. *See* Bearchán of Clonsast.

Broicseach daughter of Dallbhrónach. *See* Brighid daughter of Dubhthach.

Broineach daughter of Cláiríneach. Broineach (Bruineach) is mentioned in the genealogies of the Uí Laoghaire (O'Learys) of south Cork who, though originally settled in the Ross Carbery/Glandore area, were forced by the arrival of the Anglo-Normans to move inland to the mountainous area covered by the present Iveleary.[1] The saint was probably identical with the nun named Broineach, daughter of a Munster chief, who is said to have been abducted by a petty king from the church of Liadhain, mother of Ciarán of Seirkieran.[2] Ciarán was closely associated with the area now covered by the diocese of Ross.

1 *LM* 530. **2** *BNÉ* i, 104–5; *VSHP* i, 220–1; *VSHH* 348;

Broinnfhinn Bhreac daughter of Lughna. According to the tract on the mothers of the saints, Broinnfhinn was a sister of Bishop Iobhar, and a mother in her own right of Seanach Garbh, Miaca, Toimdheanach and Líthghin.[1] Her own mother (Basar) is said to have belonged to the Déise Breagh who gave name to the Meath baronies of Deece. Her saintly children are mainly associated with churches in the parishes of Clonsast (Offaly) and Monasterevin (Kildare).

1 *CGSH* §§721.2, 722.14.96.

Bromana. *See* Brónach of Kilbroney.

Brón of Killaspugbrone (Ceall Easpaig Bhróin), barony of Carbury, Co. Sligo. This son of Icne was one of the forty-seven children – mostly associated with churches in north Connacht – credited to Cuman daughter of Dallbhrónach, a sister of Brighid of Kildare.[1] Brón, whose name was sometimes written Rón, figures prominently in the Life of the Kildare saint, first in relation to an accusation by a woman of paternity of her child, shown by Brighid to be untrue, then in a passage which states that he returned home 'beside the sea' from a visit to his aunt with a chrismal received from her.[2] In the first of these episodes, Brón is said to have been a disciple of Patrick, and this is precisely how he figures in the dossier of the Armagh saint which not only gives the saint the rank of bishop, but also describes him as a servant and companion in Caiseal Iorra, another name for Killaspugbrone.[3] Brón died, according to the annals, in 512, and his feast fell on 8 June, otherwise the feastday of Patrick's biographer Muirchú.[4] Locally, there was no memory of the saint by the early nineteenth century.[5]

1 *CGSH* §722.7; *Anecd.* iii, 3 §5. 2 *VP* §§39; 85–6; *BBr.* §§40–1. 3 *PTBA* 138–40, 142, 146, 158; *BP* 1044–6, 1212, 1597–601, 1613, 1689–90 (= *VT* 94, 108, 138, 140, 146); *HDGP* iii, 16–17. 4 *MartT* 48; *MartG* 112; *MartD* 148; *AU s.a.* 5 OSL SO, 141.

Brónach daughter of Aodh. *See* Angais of Killart.

Brónach of Kilbroney (Ceall Bhróinche/Bhróncha), barony of Iveagh, Co. Down. Although a daughter of Míleac, 'with whom Patrick was in slavery', Brónach (also known as Inghean Mhíolchon and, in Latin, Bromana) is said to have been the mother of several noted saints, including Caolán of Nendrum, Damhnad of Tedavnet, and Fursa of Killursa.[1] Little else is known of the saint, but a poem attributed to Cormac son of Cuileannán refers to Patrick's rejection of the advances of the daughter of Míleac.[2] The authorities at Kildare may also have laid claim to her in the list of those said to have been subject to Brighid, which includes Brónach of Kilbroney.[3] Brónach's feast fell on 2 April, and the Down church now assigned to her was formerly also known as Gleann (Ceall) Seichis.[4] A traditional tale collected in Armagh attaches her to Baile na Cille, apparently now Ballykeel in the parish of Forkhill, and a *clog bán*, 'white bell', probably a relic of the saint, was discovered in the ruins of Kilbroney church near Rostrevor, where local lore, no doubt influenced by the career of her son Fursa, asserts that she came from France.[5] Her staff, now lost, was also venerated as a relic, and her image was believed to be the source of many miracles.[6]

1 *CGSH* §§702, 722.92; *EA* 115–16, 309. 2 *RC* 37, 351. 3 *CGSH* §670.36; *Lgen.* 753.4. 4 *MartT* 29; *MartG* 68; *MartD* 92; *EA* 114–16, 315. 5 *Béaloideas* 2, 57; *TDI* ii, 58. 6 *UJA* (1st ser.) 2, 48; PNNI i, 129, 134.

Brughach of Raymoghy, barony of Raphoe, Co. Donegal, or of Rateen, north of Lifford in the same county, both of which have been held to represent the modern forms of Ráith Maighe Eanaigh (Aonaigh).[1] Brughach son of Daigh, as he is commonly called in the literary tradition, is separated from Daigh by several generations in the genealogical tradition which, though attaching him to the Oirghialla and providing him with three saintly brothers, names his father as Éanna.[2] Both names are brought together in the Middle Irish Life of Colum Cille which speaks of a visit made at Christmas by Colum and his fosterer to Brughach son of Daigh at Ráith Maighe Eanaigh in Tír Éanna, south of Inishowen.[3] Normally designated bishop, Brughach is mentioned in at least three, possibly four, other literary sources. The Life of Patrick states that, having received orders from the Armagh saint, Brughach went on to confer them on Cairbre of Coleraine.[4] The *cáin* of Adhamhnán describes how the Iona saint's mother Rónad received a chain from Brughach before placing it around her son's neck.[5] Strangely, this text also includes Brughach in a list of 'kings' who rose to put Adhamhnán to the sword.[6] *Buile Shuibhne*, 'frenzy of Suibhne', refers to an erenagh of Brughach's church 'on the boundary of Tír Chonaill and Tír Boghaine'.[7] One recension of the tract known as *Catalogus Sanctorum Hiberniae*, includes *Mrugeus* (*Murgeus*), possibly in reference to Brughach, among its bishops.[8] The saint's feast fell variously on 1 or 3 November.[9]

1 *CCDK* 125, 249. 2 *CGSH* §108; *GRSH* 69; *Lgen.* 714.11. 3 *IKD* 226 §22. 4 *BP* 1944–6; *VT* 167. 5 *CA* §12. 6 Ibid. §17. 7 *BS* §20. 8 *AB* 73, 210, 313. 9 *MartG* 208, 210; *MartD* 290, 296.

Bruidiug of Coolcor (Cúil Chorra), parish and barony of Granard, Co. Longford. Despite his supposed association with Caoimhghin, of whom the bishop was statedly a fosterer, Bruidiug is included in the list of those said to have been subject to Brighid of Kildare.[1] Among several associates at Coolcor was a bishop named Mac Caorthainn who, though placed in a church allegedly founded by Patrick, is described by Tíreachán as Brighid's uncle.[2] In the same passage of Tíreachán's text, Patrick, having established a church in Corca Raoidhe (now the Westmeath barony of Corkaree) is said to have founded Cúil Chorra, before crossing the river Inny into what is now Longford. This has led to the suggestion that the 'obsolete name', Cúil Chorra, may be represented by Kilpatrick in the Westmeath parish of Leny, but Patrick was in Ardagh immediately after leaving Cúil Chorra, which would indicate that Coolcor near Granard, an area with strong Brigidine associations, was intended.[3]

1 *CGSH* §670.64; *Lgen.* 753.30; *CPPI* 183. 2 *PTBA* 136. 3 *PNW* 126.

Bruineach. *See* Broineach.

Buadán of Culdaff (Cúil Dabhcha), barony of Inishowen East, Co. Donegal. The fact that this saint's name derives from *baoth*, 'guileless', and that his feast may have fallen on 9 June would suggest that he was identical with Baoithín son of Bréanainn, constant companion and successor of Colum Cille whose feast was observed on the same day.[1] Locally, Buadán (English Boden, Latin Bodanus) was also remembered on 22 July, a day shared by Dobhaodóg of Clondavaddog in Fanad, another probable localization of Baoithín.[2] A stone in the river near his church, traditionally known as *dabhach Bhuadáin* (*Bhaodáin*), 'Buadán's vessel' – whence Cúil Dabhcha, 'recess of the vessel' – is reputed to have carried the saint from Scotland to Ireland.[3] It has been plausibly suggested that this journey is replicated in Adhamhnán's account of the ocean-voyage of a certain Baodán who was later buried in Derry.[4] Buadán's Bell, traditionally guarded by the 'Duffey or Dooey' family, is still kept in the parochial house at Bocan.[5]

1 *DOH* 84. **2** *Béaloideas* 6, 159; *DYHS* 163; *UJA* (2nd ser.) 1, 173; *AnH* 12, 85. **3** *Béaloideas* 6, 159. **4** *VC*[2] 248–50; *DLHS* 163. **5** *Béaloideas* 6, 160; *UJA* (2nd ser.) 4, 2; *DLHS* 109; *EMH* 392 §87.

Buadhmhaol. The Life of Beinéan places this saint among its subject's pupils.[1] As Beinéan, then among the Conmhaicne of Connacht, was accompanied by Patrick, Buadhmhaol may have been identical with the charioteer named for the Armagh saint in his Tripartite Life.[2] This man is said to have given his name to Ceall (Coill) Bhuadhmhaoil on the river Shannon, near the gateway to Connacht known as Snámh Dá Éan, which lay in the townland of Cloonburren in the Roscommon parish of Moore.[3]

1 *AS*.Nov. iv, 179. **2** *BP* 1029–31; *VT* 92. **3** Logainm.ie 'Snámh dá Éan'.

Buadhnad. *See* Osnad.

Buaidhbheo son of Lughaidh (Eacha). The corpus of saints' genealogies attaches Buaidhbheo to the Dál nAraidhe of north Down and south Antrim.[1] The saint also figures in the martyrologies which remember him, along with Dúileach of St Doolagh's near Dublin, on 17 November.[2] The manner of the saint's commemoration in the Martyrology of Gorman led to confusion with a juxtaposed saint named Aonghas.[3]

1 *CGSH* §100; *GRSH* 98; *Lgen*. 735.8.9; *MartO*[2] 242. **2** *MartO*[2] 235; *MartG* 220; *MartD* 312. **3** *MartD* 312; cf. *MartO*[2] 242.

Buithe of Monasterboice (Mainistir Bhuithe), barony of Ferrard, Co. Louth. This saint is perhaps best known for his association with Colum Cille whose twelfth-century vernacular Life credits its subject not only with laying out the boundaries of Buithe's church, as the latter had foretold, but also with being born on the day that Buithe died.[1] Despite the chronological difficulties, this anniversarial tradition points – as in the case of Baodán of Cloney – to Buithe's ultimate identity with Colum Cille's successor, Baoithín of Iona. The coincidence is also recorded in the annals for the year of Buithe's death (519, 523), and for the day of his feast (7 December) in some martyrologies.[2]

The Latin Life of Buithe – composed after Ireland's first Cistercian abbey had been founded in 1142 at Mellifont (perhaps named from 'Toberboice' in the townland of Mell, near Drogheda) – also records this tradition.[3] Preserved only in the Rawlinson or *Insulensis* collection, this short text of 31 chapters is composite, the first part ending at chapter 18 with Buithe's death and the second part given over to the saint's miracles.[4] In addition to a prophecy concerning the future greatness of Mellifont, the Life attributes to Buithe an education in monastic discipline and sacred scripture received abroad in *Ytalia*, probably an error for *Walia*, 'Wales', under a person named Tylianus / Tilianus, perhaps Teilo of Llandeilo who was likewise patron of a Cistercian abbey.[5]

The saint's return to Ireland via Scotland, where there are some dedications to him, and Dál Riada in Antrim, where he founded churches, finally brought Buithe to his 'paternal ground' of Cianachta, an area straddling the boundary between the present counties of Meath and Louth, to whose people he belonged, according to his 'official' pedigree.[6] There he founded the church named Mainistir Bhuithe (now Monasterboice) before going on to perform many miracles, several of which resulted in the endowment to his church of (named) local properties, an indication that the text may have served as a form of *libellus fundationis* for the monks of Mellifont.[7] According to the text, his death was preceded by a visit to heaven, Elias-like, during the month of May.[8] A separate tradition attributes a sea-voyage to the saint, accompanied by 150 pilgrims in three boats.[9]

That Buithe's church at Monasterboice attained high status in its own right can be seen in its possession of some of Ireland's finest High Crosses, one of them named after Muireadhach, whose obit in the annals for 924 describes him as both successor of Buithe son of Brónach and 'tanist-abbot of Armagh'.[10] Also indicative of the church's importance is its production (or possession) of books now lost, one named *Leabhar Mainistreach Buithe*, another *Leabhar Gearr*.[11] Buithe's name, which derives from *baoth*, 'innocent, guileless', was the source of two spurious associations: one with the Venerable Bede, who is compared to Buithe in a list of saints 'of like character'; the other with Latin *beatus* (among many other cognate words) in a gloss purporting to explain the name.[12]

Buithe's head was venerated as a relic, at least until the year 1521, when it was stolen from the church at Monasterboice, as was the stone pillow on which it rested, reputedly the petrified brain of Meas Geaghra which, having been originally used to slay the legendary king of Ulster, Conchubhar son of Neas, was subsequently revealed to the saint.[13] In the area about Monasterboice, where the saint continued to be invoked for assistance, his name came to be pronounced as Bween or Mween (sometimes written Maoin).[14] The 'bright feast of victorious Buithe from treasurous Monasterboice' fell on 7 December, the same day as the ordination of Ambrose of Milan, who was reportedly substituted for the saint as patron of the parish.[15]

1 *IKD* 233 §41. **2** *AU s.a.* 519, 523; *MartG* 234; *MartD* 328; cf. *LUM* 154rb 29–30. **3** *VSHP* i, xxxiv –vi, 87–97; at 92 §18; *StoryM* 13; *Peritia* 3, 324–5; *DIB* i, 977. **4** *VSHP* i, xxxiv. **5** Ibid. xxxv, 82–3 §§2, 4. **6** Ibid. 89 §6; *CPNS* 313–14; *KSS* 292; *CGSH* §231; *GRSH* 122; *Lgen*. 741.4. **7** *VSHP* i, 89–90, 93–4 §§8–9, 22–3. **8** Ibid. 92 §17. **9** *IrL* 62. **10** *AU s.a.* **11** *LisL* 3300; *LU* 2920–2. **12** *CGSH* §721.27; *MartO*[2] 256; *MartD* 328. **13** *JCLAS* 8, 187, 259, 273–4; *DTUH* 18–20; *CL* 74–86. **14** OSL LH 10, 20; *IOS* 87–8. **15** *MartO*[2] 250; *MartG* 234; *MartD* 328; OSL LH 37.

Buonia. *See* Mughain of Lyons.

C ☙

Cadán of Bute, Scotland. In a note to the Martyrology of Gorman at 1 February, Cadán is described as the *oide*, 'fosterer, mentor', of Blán of Dunblane.[1] He was greatly honoured on the Isle of Bute, and the Martyrology of Donegal speculatively proposed his identity with Cadán of Tamlaght-ard, a son of Madán of the north-east Ulster grouping of Dál nAraidhe.[2] According to Blán's Breviary Life, Cadán was his uncle as well as his mentor.[3] In Scotland, the saint was remembered on 17 May.[4]

1 *MartG* 28; *MartD* 36; *CPNS* 277; *KSS* 298–9; *ACDS* 109–11. **2** *MartD* 36. **3** *BrevA* pars aest. 77rv. **4** *KSS* 298.

Cadán of Tamlaght-ard (Tamhlachta Arda), alias Magilligan, barony of Keenaght, Co. Derry. As this son of Madán was attached to the Dál nAraidhe of north-east Ulster, he was probably identical with the servant whom some versions of the list of those in orders with Patrick assigned to Tamlaght-ard.[1] It appears that he was locally also remembered as Bishop 'Geadán' (Gedanus) or Ceathán.[2] The 1607 survey of Derry diocese used the same Latin form of the name (Cadanus) for Caoide of Donaghedy, which points to a possible connection between the two saints.[3] His tomb is thought to lie under the east gable of the ancient church in the townland of Tamlaght.[4] The Martyrology of Donegal speculatively proposed his identity with Cadán of Bute who was remembered on 1 February, but a local source gave preference to the Cadán included in the list for 12 December.[5] The surname Mac Giolla Chatáin, later anglicized as McIlhatton, may reflect devotion to the saint.[6]

1 *BP* 3134; *VT* 265, 574; *CGSH* §671.15; *Lgen.* 735.13. **2** *Celtica* 1, 84; *CGSH* §672.8. **3** *DYHS* 195–6; *UJA* (2nd ser.) 2, 152; *AnH* 12, 82, 108, 110. **4** *PNCL* 230; cf. *LIS* ii, 240. **5** *MartD* 36, 334; *LIS* ii, 240n; *MartG* 236. **6** PNNI viii, 27.

Caidín. *See* Caoide.

Cailchín of Kilculliheen (Ceall Chailchín), baronies of Gaultier and Waterford City, Co. Waterford. According to the genealogists, this saint was one of seven sons of Maonach son of Fachtna of the Corca Laoighdhe, a group whose territory was approximately equivalent to the diocese of Ross.[1] Among his better-known siblings were Fachtna, patron of this diocese, and Mainchín of Coolcashin (Cúil Chaisín).[2] As some members of the family were associated with churches in the diocese of Ossory, whose people were thought to have been closely connected with the Corca Laoighdhe, Cailchín is probably the saint after whom the church of Kilculliheen, near Waterford City, but within the diocese of Ossory, was named. This later became the site of a house of Augustinian canonesses, and here, according to Bishop Phelan's seventeenth-century list of Ossory patrons, Cailchín's feast was observed on 10 February.[3]

1 *CGSH* §298.2; *GRSH* 127; *Lgen.* 744.6.7. **2** *BBa.* 242. **3** *MRHI* 319; *HADO* iv, 205.

Caillín of Fenagh (Fiodhnacha Maighe Réin), barony and county of Leitrim. The pedigree of Caillín son of Niata attached him to the Conmhaicne whose settlements were mainly in south Leitrim, Longford and Galway.[1] The saint's mother is said to have been Deidhe daughter of Trian, a son of Dubhthach of the Maca Lughair who is traditionally regarded as the first man to have accepted Patrick's teachings.[2] As Caillín was patron of the powerful family of Uí Ruairc, his church attained considerable importance, and the saint himself (sometimes described as a bishop) was made the subject of a vernacular Life in prose and verse which survives in a copy reworked in 1516 for the saint's successor at Fenagh, allegedly from an 'old book' compiled – it has been suggested – between 1258 and 1281.[3] As one scholar has stated, however, the word 'Life' is something of a misnomer; the text, which is partly based on the Life of Bearach of Termonbarry, is rather a long list of the lands, privileges, and rights of sanctuary allegedly attached to Fenagh.[4]

Beginning with an account of the various *gabhála* (prehistoric invasions) of Ireland, the Life continues with lists of kings, both pre-historic, Christian, and future – some of them prophesied by Caillín – before treating extensively of the saint's conversion of Aodh Dubh son of Feargna, ancestor of the Uí Ruairc of Bréifne, and the tribute due to Fenagh from Aodh's family.[5] The remainder of the Life is taken up with accounts of Caillín's relationship with other important families, often mediated through their saints, and of the dues and privileges owed to his church by them, beginning with the Ceinéal Conaill and their patron Colum Cille, followed by his own people, the Conmhaicne, by the Ceinéal Eoghain, by numerous other families, and by long lists of saints, no doubt representative of their churches, including Patrick, Brighid, Ciarán, Finnian, and the more local Manchán of Mohill and Cruimhthear Fraoch of Cloone.[6] The remains of the saint were allegedly first buried in a place named Reilig Mochaomhóg before being disinterred and placed, together with relics brought from Rome, in the graveyard of the saint's church in Fenagh.[7] In sum, although of no value for the story of the saint, the text is an invaluable witness to the later ambitions of his church.

Miscellaneous additions to the Book of Fenagh include a vision attributed to Caillín and interpreted by Adhamhnán.[8] The vernacular Life of Maodhóg of Ferns, whom Caillín is said to have tutored and accompanied on a pilgrimage to Rome, is among other sources that speak of the saint.[9] It may be noted that one of Maodhóg's main churches, Drumlane in Cavan, lay close to Fenagh, and another of his churches, Rossinver in Leitrim, had a well dedicated to Caillín.[10] According to the Life of Beinéan, Caillín's father Niata granted property to Patrick, and the Fenagh saint is said to have been Beinéan's pupil, thus ranking him lower among the saints of the Conmhaicne.[11] Elsewhere, Caillín is assigned a prominent role in the story of the finding of the *Táin*, which includes the assertion that he was a uterine brother of Seanchán Torpéist, chief poet of Ireland.[12]

As the saint's name, sometimes written Cailléan, is a diminutive of Caille, a hypocoristic form of Colum, it is worth noting that his feast (13 November) is immediately preceded by that of Cuimín Fada son of Fiachna, whose name likewise derives from Colum.[13] Both saints may thus have originated as localizations of Colum Cille of Iona. In Connemara, which took name from Conmhaicne Mara, Caillín's day was celebrated annually by a large assembly of people at Ballyconneely in the parish of Ballindoon, where, despite his usual affiliation to the Conmhaicne, he was thought to have been the son of a Leinster king.[14] Among the seven relics of Caillín, as enumerated in a list compiled in the early seventeenth century, were his book, now known as the Book of Fenagh, and a *ceiharloghach*, presumably a gospel-book, now lost.[15] His shrine, possibly used for one of his book-relics, has been preserved, as has his so-called, lately burnt, bell.[16] His coarbs at Fenagh, the Uí Rodaighe, were reputedly granted the three virtues of hospitality, bravery and learning.[17] They were also among the ecclesiastics entitled to be present at the inauguration of O'Connor as king of Connacht.[18]

1 *CGSH* §146; *GRSH* 105; *Lgen*. 727.9; *BFen*. 4–6; ATig. ind; *DIB* ii, 245. **2** *CGSH* §722.2; *PTBA* 92; *BP* 531–6; *VT* 52. **3** *BFen*. 2–312; *DA* 38, 34; *ILL* 364. **4** BFen. (supp.) 14–18; *IML* 56; *PRIA* 1C4, 441–2; *IER* (5th ser.) 55, 517; *IML* 49–73. **5** *BFen*. 2–136. **6** Ibid. 136–74, 174–232, 232–312. **7** Ibid. 12, 310. **8** BFen. (supp.) 62–6. **9** *BNÉ* i, 200, §35, 257 §215. **10** *Celtica* i, 66. **11** *AS*.Nov. iv, 178; *SAM* 1, 34. **12** *TromG* 1240–1316. **13** *MartG* 216–18; *MartD* 304–6. **14** *IER* (3rd ser.) 10, 433–4; *AIGY* i, 124 (Keerhaunmore). **15** *Celtica* 1, 66; *EMH* 452–5 §150. **16** *JRSAI* 22, 151–3; *Seanchas* 331–40. **17** *ApalF* 165–6. **18** *JRSAI* 2, 340; *MSPAG* 189.

Caimín. This name originated as a hypocoristic form (*Caimme/Camma*), of Colum.[1] Like its cognates (Cuimín, Camán and Mochumma), Caimín served throughout Ireland as a convenient and affectionate way of referring to saints named Colum, the best-known of whom was Colum Cille.

1 *FG* 20–35.

Caimín of Inishcaltra (Inis Cealtra), alias Holy Island, on Lough Derg, barony of Leitrim, Co. Galway. Though it is common for saints to have two conflicting statements of descent, Caimín son of Díoma (or Colmán) is unusual in having three, all of which were brought together in the corpus of saints' pedigrees.[1] As all three cannot be correct, it may be assumed that his various supposed origins among the Uí Cheinsealaigh of south Leinster, Ciarraighe of south-west Munster, and Uí Bhriúin Rátha of the barony of Clare in south Connacht, reflect rival interests, over different periods, in the church, or churches, of the saint. The saint's mother is variously said to have been Cuman, maternal aunt of Brighid of Kildare, and Inghean Bhaoith of Killinaboy in Clare.[2]

An unpublished vernacular Life of the saint in metrical form is preserved in the Bibliothèque Royale in Brussels. Míchéal Ó Cléirigh, who transcribed the sole surviving copy in 1629 in deference to the instructions of his superiors – but against his own better judgement – formed an unfavourable opinion of it.[3] As most of the text is taken up with praise of the saint's church and burial ground on Inishcaltra, and the entitlements due from the peoples of Leinster and Munster, among others, John Colgan also made little use of it in his account of the saint.[4] He did, however, draw attention to Caimín's dealings with Guaire son of Colmán, king of the Uí Fhiachrach Aidhne who held lands in Connacht near the saint's church. Guaire – who figures prominently as a paragon of hospitality and generosity in both hagiography and secular literature – Caimín, and Cuimín Fada of Clonfert, are said to have been allowed a wish each, with the king choosing sufficient wealth to give away, Cuimín opting for enough books to fill his church, and Caimín wishing for as many diseases as would cover his body.[5]

A prophecy attributed to Bréanainn states that the relics of Colum of Terryglass would be taken to Inishcaltra, on which they remained for seven years, according to Colum's Life.[6] As this saint is regarded as a localization of Colum Cille, both Caimín and his near neighbour and ultimate namesake, Colmán of Clonrush, may also have originally represented the patron of Iona. Among other saints associated with Caimín was his uterine brother, Seanán of Scattery, who, besides invoking his aid, together with that of Colum of Terryglass, is featured with him in a poem of prophecy.[7] Similarly, according to a poem in Classical Irish, Caimín of Inis Cealtra, together with Inghean Bhaoith and numerous other saints, was called upon to help in releasing Ireland's southern half (Leath Mogha) from a bondage imposed on it by the northern half (Leath Chuinn), represented by Finnian of Clonard.[8] Listed, albeit under the guise of Mochamóg, among those cited in the Old Irish Table of Penitential Commutations as sponsors of a certain type of vigil, the saint is probably the same as Caimín 'the monk', who was thought to be similar in manners to Pastor 'the monk'.[9] The form Mochamóg is also used to describe him as one of Ireland's three noted *athlaoich* (former laymen).[10]

Patron of Kilcaimin in the parish of Ballinacourty, barony of Dunkellin in south Galway, and dedicatee of a burial ground at Ballykinvarga in the Clare parish of Kilfenora, Caimín may also have been patron of Kilcamin in the Offaly parish of Gallen, where a fragment of his bell was kept within the local burial ground, allegedly in the fork of a whitethorn bush.[11] The saint died in 651, according to the annals, and his feast of 24/25 March found its way into some external martyrologies, including Grevenus of Cologne's version of the Martyrology of Usuard and the martyrology of the Regensburg Schottenkloster.[12] In 1607, Pope Paul V granted a plenary indulgence to pilgrims to Inishcaltra, and two years later thousands are reported to have been on the island during the week before Easter, which presumably coincided with the saint's feastday.[13] The psalter said to have been written by Caimín, one of the treasures of the Franciscan Library, now in University College Dublin, in fact dates to the late eleventh or early twelfth century.[14]

1 *CGSH* §§290.1–3, 700.1–3; *CGH* 160a11; *GRSH* 87; *Lgen*. 727.20–22; *DIB* ii, 245. **2** *CGSH* §722.8; *IrT* iv, 93. **3** *MHH* 183; BBR 2324–40, 264r–273v; *ILL* 363; *ILL* 358, 363. **4** *ASH* 746–7. **5** Ibid.; *ZCP* 3, 207–8; *LisL* 304; *FFÉ* iii, 68–70. **6** *MartT* 118–19; *VSHH* 233 §30. **7** *ZCP* 10, 26; *IrT* iv, 69. **8** RIA MS 23L11, 263; *SAM* 24.1, 17, 20. **9** *Ériu* 19, 64 §23; *CGSH* §712.33. **10** *Anecd*. iii, 60. **11** *JRSAI* 2A, 59–60; *AIOY* §773. **12** *MartR* 48–9; *FSHIM* 236. **13** *AH* 3, 263; *PilgI* 54. **14** *NMAJ* 59, 13–29. check

11 ATig. *s.a.*; *MartT* 27; *MartG* 60; *MartD* 84; *AS*.Iun. vi, 171; *ASH* 746; *ACoC* 221–2n. **12** *FLK Cat*. 1–2; *InaF* i, 136 §13.

Caineach of Dál nAraidhe. *See* Rónán of Dromiskin.

Caineach Abadh daughter of Lughna. *See* Abán of Adamstown.

Cainne of Teach Cainne, an unidentified church in Déise Breagh, now approximately the baronies of Deece Upper and Lower, Co. Meath. A daughter of Brosán (Bearsán) son of Muireadhach, Cainne (alias Caoine and Caonna) is listed among the saints of Clann Lughdhach, another name for the Ceinéal Laoghaire who were mainly concentrated in the present county of Meath.[1] The coincidence of their names and locations allows for the possibility that, despite the difference in sex, she and Cainne son of Muireadhach were ultimately identical. One seventeenth-century source speculatively placed her feast on 5 November.[2]

1 *CGSH* §§662.51, 690.6; *Lgen.* 706.9. **2** *GRSH* 49 §7.

Cainne son of Muireadhach. *See* Aodh of Killeenmore; Cainne of Teach Cainne.

Cainneach. This name, also written Coinneach, derives from *Cainne*, a hypocoristic form of Colum, and is cognate with both *Coinne* (more commonly Mochoinne) and – with labialization of the double medial consonant – *Conna* (Mochonna).

Cainneach of Achadh Rathain, an unidentified church among the Uí Mhic Coille who gave name to the barony of Imokilly in Cork. This saint is one of three sons of Feidhlimidh remembered at Achadh Rathain on 28 November, the others being Acobhrán and Laidhgeann.[1] Their mother's name was Bóchra, and she is again found, together with her three sons, in the tract on the mothers of the saints.[2]

1 *MartO²* 237; *MartG* 228; *MartD* 320. **2** *CGSH* §722.36.

Cainneach of Aghaboe (Achadh Bó), barony of Clarmallagh, Co. Laois, and of Kilkenny City (Ceall Chainnigh), in the county of the same name, where he is remembered in a parish (St Canice's) and holy well (Kenny's Well). Both churches of the saint lay within the ancient territory of Osraighe, which gave name to the modern diocese of Ossory. The earliest witness to Cainneach (also written Coinneach and anglicized Canice and Kenny in Ireland, Kenneth in Scotland) is Adhamhnán's Life of Colum Cille, which mentions several journeys undertaken by the saint to Iona. Adhamhnán also attached Cainneach to the church of Aghaboe and, describing him as one of Ireland's 'holy founders', assigned him to a tribal group named Maca Dálann, 'descendants of Dála'.[1] Although a segment of the Ulaidh of north-east Ulster, this family – as is shown by the later Life composed for Cainneach himself – came to be associated with the Cianachta of Dungiven, who gave name to the Derry barony of Keenaght.[2]

Due to the high status of his churches within Ossory, Cainneach was made the subject of a Life that survives in three Latin versions, the earliest of which, in the *Codex Salmanticensis*, forms part of a group known as the O'Donohue Lives.[3] Principally on account of the agreement between the orthography of the onomastic element in these texts and Old Irish usage, some scholars have taken the view that the O'Donohue Lives date to as early as the period 750–850, or even earlier, while others have pointed to the presence in these texts of some late orthographic features, and also to the lack of a comparable collection from so early a period anywhere else in western Christendom.[4] Cainneach's Life, which is thought to possess 'more of the historical note' than other specimens of the genre, has recently been dated to *c.*766–80, not only on grounds of orthography, but also because of the background influences at work on its author.[5] Against this, however, the presence of several commonplaces in the Life, such as the saint's journey to Wales and his pilgrimage to Italy, both of which receive lengthy coverage, may be taken to indicate a much later date, in the late twelfth or early thirteenth century, when such external episodes became almost mandatory.

The Life brings the saint into the world in the Dungiven area, as a son of Laoidheach (Luightheach) Leiceard, 'the poet', and Mealla, whose name is recalled by the little parish of St Maul's in the city of Kilkenny. Reared at an unidentified site (Ceann Buighe) among the Uí Mhic Uais, the saint is then brought to Wales to be educated by St Docc in church law and the 'canons', a subject of study that first becomes a *topos* after Charlemagne (†814), and especially after Gratian's *Decretum* of *c.*1140.[6] Having received orders in Wales, a measure that – should the Life be late – would have been designed to impress the mainly Cambro-Norman adventurers responsible for the late twelfth-century invasion of Ireland, the saint undertook a pilgrimage to Rome, during which, having ill-advisedly promised a local king and his people that he would be buried among them, he was relieved by a fiery dragon of the toe of his right foot, locally preserved as a relic.[7]

Briefly back in Ireland, with miracles performed in profusion at the churches associated with him among his own people, the Cianachta of Derry, he again removed to Britain, to a place near 'Dorsum Britanniae', the ridge that divided Scotland, before returning to a site in Westmeath now known as Kilkenny West (Ceall Chainnigh) after the saint.[8] Visits to other foundations followed, mainly in the Midlands, including Aghaboe in Ossory and Monaincha in the parish of Corbally, near Roscrea in Tipperary, where he allegedly copied a gospel-book.[9] Before his death in Aghaboe, the saint is said by one version of his Life to have been attended by Fiontan Maoldubh.[10] Though yet to be made the subject of a critical edition, there are many traces in the text of the influence of Adhamhnán's Life of Colum Cille.[11]

Because of his status as diocesan patron, Cainneach figures prominently in the Lives of other saints, including the vernacular Life of Fionnbharr which, for opportunistic reasons, alleges that the Cork saint was the first occupant of Aghaboe.[12] He is often presented in the company of Colum Cille, with whom he is said to have exchanged poems of praise, and Comhghall of Bangor, and among other saints associated with him were Fiontan of Clonenagh, Fiontan of Taghmon, Aodh of Rahugh, Colmán of Lynally, Caoimhghin of Glendalough, Mochaomhóg of Leigh, and Seanán of Scattery Island.[13] Numbered among the twelve apostles of Ireland, he was said to be similar in manners to Philip the Apostle.[14]

Despite their treatment as separate saints, there are many features of Cainneach's dossier that point to the saint's ultimate identity with his namesake Colum Cille.[15] The place of Cainneach's birth in or near the Derry parish of Drumachose – of whose church, along with Balteagh and Faughanvale, he is now patron – was otherwise best known for its proximity to the location of the Convention of Druim Ceat at which Colum Cille famously attended.[16] Though Colum Cille is said to have secured the freedom of Scannlán son of Colmán, king of Osraighe, at this Convention and to have been promised in return tribute from the king's grateful people, the patron of the diocese of Ossory has always been Cainneach. Moreover, Cainneach's feastday fell on 11 October, the eve of the feast of Mobhí of Glasnevin who figures prominently in the story of Colum Cille, and immediately adjoining Glasnevin is the church of Finglas of which Cainneach was patron.[17]

Said to have been born in 516 or 527, and to have died in 599/600, Cainneach is among the few Irish saints to have had his feast (11 October) included by Usuard (†*c.* 975) of Saint-Germain-des-Prés near Paris in his martyrology, compiled on the orders of Charles the Bald, and the most popular text of its kind, until superseded in the late sixteenth century by the Roman martyrology of which it continues to form the basis.[18] His feast was also recorded in an early ninth-century calendar kept by an Irishman on the Reichenau in Lake Constance and a relic of his reached the Continent, arguably either at Ferrières in France or some church in the Rhineland.[19] Alas, by the early nineteenth century, the saint's day had been forgotten in the parish of Aghaboe, the site of his first foundation in Ossory.[20] Much earlier, in 1346, according to Friar Clyn, scant respect was shown in this parish for the 'bones and relics' of the saint which were burnt and completely destroyed by a local chieftain named Diarmuid Mac Giolla Phádraig.[21] Cainneach's head reputedly formed part of Adhamhnán's reliquary.[22] The attempt by the Martyrology of Donegal to identify the Cainneach commemorated on 31 January (the octave of another feast of Cainneach on 23 January) with the patron of Aghaboe, through his mother Mealla, is probably mistaken.[23] Finally, many churches in Scotland were dedicated to the saint and short office lessons in commemoration of him have been preserved in the Breviary of Aberdeen.[24]

1 *VC*² 16a, 63ab, 118a; cf. *CGSH* §§121.1–2, 707.333; *GRSH* 107; *Lgen.* 730.3–6; *DIB* ii, 246–7; *OLL* 1, 19–20. **2** *VSHH* 182 §§1–2; *VSHP* i, 152 §1; *Éigse* 14, 21 §11. **3** *VSHH* 182–98; *VSHP* i, xliii–xlv, 152–69. **4** *MISL* 297–339 at 329, 384; *CeltC* 182–9; *SS* 31–40; *LSLC* 34; *Speculum* 68, 261; *Ériu* 54, 99–100. **5** *VSHP* i, xlv; *Kenney* 395; *SS* 31–40 at 36. **6** *VSHH* 182–3 §§1–6; *VSHP* i, 152–3 §§1–5; *ODCC* 277–8; *HADO* iii, 193–4. **7** *VSHH* 183–4 §§6–9; *VSHP* i, 153–4 §§5–6. **8** *VSHH* 184–90 §§9–32; *VSHP* i, 155–62 §§7–27; *PNW* 10–11. **9** *VSHH* 191–6 §§33–52; *VSHP* i, 163–7 §§31–42; cf. *GJ* 14, 806–7; *IMN* 3, 76. **10** *VSHH* 198 §60; *VSHP* i, 169 §46. **11** *SS* 31–40. **12** *BBa.* 62 §15. **13** *ZCP* 9, 174; ibid. 10, 28; *VSHH* 147 §5, 149 §15, 168 §2, 208 §31, 214 §14, 364 §12; *VSHP* ii, 173 §18; *ACL* iii, 217–21; *ACL* iii, 217–21. **14** *VSHH* 82–3 §§2, 5, 101 §19; *CGSH* §712.7. **15** *FG* 20–35. **16** *Celtica* 1, 69, 82; *RC* 20/21; *DYHS* 195; *UJA* (2nd ser.) 2, 146, 148, 152; *Ainm* 7, 80; *AnH* 12, 82–3, 107–10. **17** *MartT* 78; *MartO*² 215; *MartG* 194; *MartD* 270–2; *IKD* 181, 278. **18** ATig./*AU s.a.*; *MartU* 320. **19** *AfL* 31, 60; *EIRD* 55–68. **20** OSL LS I, 26. **21** *AIFJC* 238–9. **22** *Celtica* 15, 35 §16. **23** *MartD* 32. **24** *KSS* 295–7; *ACDS* 61–3; *LegSS* 243–5, 369–70.

CAINNEACH of Ceall Tógh, perhaps an ecclesiastical site in the townland of Kilkenny (Ceall Chainnigh), parish of Breaghwy, barony of Carra, Co. Mayo.[1]

Tíreachán states that this saint's church, which he locates in Corca Teimhne (alias Teimhinrighe) in the barony of Carra (Ceara), was founded by Cainneach, Patrick's 'bishop and monk', before passing under the control of the community of Clonmacnoise.[2]

1 *HDGP* iv, 55. 2 *PTBA* 154 §39.8, 160 §47.4; *BP* 1390–403; *VT* 122.

Cainneach of Drumad, which may be short for Ceall Achaidh Dromada, now Killeigh, parish and barony of Geashill, Co. Offaly. This saint, who, together with his kinsman (and namesake), Mochuma of Maca Gaola, figures in the list of homonymous saints, is variously placed by the genealogists among the Gaolraighe of Uí Eachach in the Down barony of Iveagh, or among the (otherwise unknown) descendants of Feidhlimidh Gaol of Munster.[1] In the list, he is immediately preceded by Cainneach of the Maca Buachalla, a people whose *carn*, 'cairn', was located in Cuibh, whence Uí Eachach Cobha, the group that gave name to the baronies of Iveagh.[2] These saints can hardly be other than identical. The same early genealogical tract that mentions them or their families goes on, within a few lines, to refer to Cainneach of Maca Dálann, a name sometimes applied to Cainneach of Aghaboe whose Life brings him, among other places, to Killeigh.[3] This would indicate that these two saints were also one and the same.

1 *CGSH* §707.335.648; *Lgen.* 499.12; *CGH* 157, 16. 2 *CGSH* §707.334; cf. *CGH* 157, 25. 3 *CGH* 157, 30.

Cainneach of Magherintemple, parish of Drung, barony of Tullygarvey, Co. Cavan. Since this bearer of the name shared a dedication with 'Columba', he is likely to have been identical with Cainneach of Aghaboe.[1]

1 *Breifne* 4, 202; *CPL* 6, 153.

Cainnear of Ceall Chuilinn, an unidentified church in Cairbre, now the barony of Carbury, Co. Kildare. As Carbury lies a considerable distance from Kilcullen in the same county, this church is unlikely to be intended. Cainnear daughter of Cruithneachán is the first saint in the list of those said to have been subject to Brighid.[1] In second place is a namesake whose church, Cluain Coirinn, may now be Clooncurreen, parish of Moylough, in the Galway barony of Tiaquin. Cainnear's feast fell on 28 January, a few days ahead of Brighid's day.[2]

1 *CGSH* §670.1. 2 *MartT* 13; *MartG* 24; *MartD* 28.

Cainnear of Clonsilla (Cluain Dá Shaileach), barony of Castleknock, Co. Dublin. This saint was the mother of seven sons of Lughaidh son of Nathi, of a branch of the Laighin or Leinstermen called Uí Chéithigh, which gave name to Ikeathy barony in Kildare.[1] The best-known of her sons was Mochua (Crónán) of Clondalkin, and others of the family, including Baodán, Baoithín, Garbhán, and Seanchán, were also attached to churches in east Leinster. Clonsilla in Dublin is a few miles only from Clondalkin.

1 *CGSH* §§243; 722.77.

Cainnear of Clooncaura, parish of Kildimo, barony of Kenry, Co. Limerick, which may now represent an earlier Cluain Cláraidh. According to the Life of Molua of Kyle (Clonfertmulloe), his father Carthach of Uí Fhidhgheinte, now approximately the lands west of the river Maigue in Limerick, had a brother named Fiontan whose daughter Cainnear was born mute.[1] By rubbing her face against that of her cousin, she was subsequently cured and became attached to the church of Cluain Cláraidh.[2] Molua himself was venerated a little further west at Ardagh. Cainnear may also be identical with a namesake who, according to the Life of Mochaomhóg of Leigh, had her sight restored through Mochaomhóg's blessing.[3]

1 *VSHH* 133 §12; *GRSH* 98; *DIB* ii, 248. **2** But cf. *LnaÉ* 116. **3** *VSHP* 193 §34.

Cainnear of Clooncurreen. *See* Cainnear of Ceall Chuilinn.

Cainnear of Kilconry. *See* Cainnear Chráibhtheach.

Cainnear of Kirkinner. *See* Cainnear of Rinn Allaidh.

Cainnear of Lara (Leathráith), now Abbeylara, barony of Granard, Co. Longford. Cainnear was one of four daughters of Feargna son of Fearghas – the others being Dealbhnad, Deimhlir, and Fuinche (perhaps also Fainnear) – all of whom were attached to a church (Abbeylara) said to have been subject to Brighid of Kildare.[1] Within the parish bearing the name of their church is an old grave yard in the townland of Kilbride (Ceall Bhrighde), and the entry that follows in the list attaches its patron (Fainnear) to Clonbroney, close to Abbeylara.[2]

1 *CGSH* §670.5; *Lgen.* 752.13. **2** *CGSH* §670.6.

Cainnear of Rinn Allaidh, an unidentified church which, since it was also associated with Rónán of Dromiskin, probably lay in the eastern part of Meath or adjoining section of Louth. A daughter of Caolán (alias Faolán), Cainnear was attached by the genealogists to the Clann Éanna branch of the Ceinéal Laoghaire of Meath.[1] She was among those commemorated on 5 November which may have served as the octave of a second feast (29 October) assigned to the Cainnear who gave name to Kirkinner (*ecclesia sanctae Kenere*) in Galloway, Scotland.[2]

1 *CGSH* §§662.46, 690.8; *GRSH* 50; *Lgen.* 705.4 *CGH* 144g3–145a1. **2** *MartG* 212; *MartD* 298; *Lgen.* 706.8; *CPNS* 166; *KSS* 361; *LegSS* 252–4, 368–9.

Cainnear of Uí Dheagha. In the list of those said to have been subject to Brighid of Kildare, this saint is described as the *céadmhuintear*, 'chief wife', of Nainnidh son of Diarmuid who appears to be otherwise unknown.[1] Her own family attachment to Uí Dheagha points either to the later Wexford deanery of Oday or to the Kilkenny barony of Ida.

1 *CGSH* §670.36.

Cainnear Chráibhtheach, 'holy', of Bantry (Beanntraighe), parish of Kilmocomoge, barony of Bantry, Co. Cork. In what has been described as a 'truly beautiful legend, vulgarized by Thomas Moore', and preserved in the vernacular

Life of Seanán, Cainnear is said to have seen a vision in which a flame leading to heaven appeared above every church in Ireland, and none greater than that over Scattery Island.[1] On visiting Scattery, she was first refused permission to land on the island, which was barred to women, and directed to another island occupied by her sister, allegedly Seanán's mother. She persisted, however, died soon afterwards, and was given burial on the edge of Scattery. This episode has recently been interpreted in terms of gender hierarchies.[2] According to the tract on the mothers of the saints, Seanán's mother was Cuman, maternal aunt of Brighid of Kildare.[3] As the immediately preceding section of Seanán's Life concerns the area about Kilconry at the mouth of the river Fergus, it is tempting to regard Cainnear as eponym and patron of this church, despite the opinion that this role belonged either to an (otherwise unattested) saint named Conaire, or to a person or people named Comhraí.[4] In that case, Cainnear of Ceall Chainnire, a daughter of Cuman, would probably be identical with the saint.[5]

1 *LisL* 2416–46. **2** *Peritia* 15, 308–10. **3** *CGSH* §722.8. **4** *ACoC* 265; *CoC* 174; Logainm.ie 'Kilconry'. **5** *CGSH* §722.61; but cf. *HDGP* iii, 138.

Cairbre of Coleraine (Cúl Rathain), barony of Coleraine, Co. Derry. While among the Dál nAraidhe of north-east Ulster, Patrick is said to have received homage from a man named Nadh Sluaigh who surrendered to him Cúl Rathain (Coleraine) on the edge of the river Bann.[1] Here, it was then foretold, Bishop Cairbre son of Déigeall, a grandson – naturally of Nadh Sluaigh, but spiritually of Patrick – would have his church. Patrick's spiritual relationship is attributed to his having conferred orders on Brughach of Raymoghy, who in turn ordained Cairbre. The saint's descent from Nadh Sluaigh is otherwise well documented.[2] According to the Life of Eoghan of Ardstraw, Cairbre was among a group of people kidnapped by pirates and taken into captivity, first in Britain, where their freedom was obtained by Ninnian of Whithorn, then in Armorica, from which they eventually returned.[3] In the same text, Cairbre is said to have bestowed two horses on Eoghan who had generously given his own two in alms.[4]

Having regard to the area in which he was active, Cairbre may be identical with his namesake and co-bishop at Movilla in the Down parish of Newtown Ards whose feast fell on 3 May.[5] The bishop named Cairbre remembered on 1 November (a day shared with the above-mentioned Brughach) was tentatively assigned by the Martyrology of Donegal to Ceall Chairbre, later 'Kilcarbry' in the townland of Ardgillew, parish of Kilbarron.[6] Cairbre's feast at Coleraine fell ten days later, on 11 November.[7]

1 *BP* 1937–45; *VT* 166. **2** *CGSH* §104; *GRSH* 99; *Lgen.* 735.19. **3** *VSHH* 400. **4** Ibid. 402–3 §11 **5** *MartT* 39. **6** *MartG* 208; *MartD* 290; *DLHS* 174. **7** *MartO*^{2} 234; *MartG* 216; *MartD* 304.

Cairbre of Foithirbhe Mhór, an unidentified church, possibly in Kildare. This son of Feidhlimidh is known only from an entry in the corpus of saints' pedigrees which locates his church near three *Ros*-churches, including Rosbran in the Kildare parish of St John's.[1]

1 *CGSH* §164.

Cairbre of 'Kilcarbry' (Ceall Chairbre), the now obsolete name of a townland in the parish of Kilbarron, baony of Tirhugh, Co. Donegal.[1] This saint was remembered on 1 November, according to the Martyrology of Donegal, which placed the church named after him near Assaroe (Ballyshannon).[2] Traces of the church are still to be seen in the townland of Ardgillew.[3] Cairbre may be the same as the man mentioned in a poem attributed to Colum Cille which states that the founder of Iona brought with him westwards to 'Duibhghleann' – probably a kenning for Gleann Coluim Chille (Glencolumbkille) on Donegal's south-western tip, not far from Assaroe – twelve bishops of whom two only were named, Aodh 'from the mountain' – presumably Aodh of Rahugh – and Cairbre.[4] Aodh's local associations were with Slieve League, which lies within the parish of Glencolumbkille. On the other hand, the list for 1 November also includes Brughach, which gives some grounds for believing that this Cairbre was identical with his namesake at Coleraine.

1 *HDGP* iii, 138. 2 *MartD* 290. 3 *ASCD* 299. 4 *ZCP* 12, 394 §35.

Cairbre of Movilla. *See* Cairbre of Coleraine.

Cairbre son of Binneach. *See* Aodh of Inis Beoaidh.

Cairbre son of Colum (Colmán). *See* Díoma Dubh.

Cairbre son of Neamhan. This saint's mother, Fuinche daughter of Dallbhrónach, is said to have remained barren for a long time after marrying Neamhan, until her niece, Brighid of Kildare, blessed her womb.[1] Her first-born child was called Colmán and she gave birth to three more – Conall, Eoghan and Cairbre – all of whom were baptized from the well in which Bishop Iobhar of Begerin had been christened. Little else is known of the family, but the tract on the mothers of the saints omits Colmán from the list of Fuinche's children.[2] A separate text dealing with Iobhar states that Colmán was a king.[3] More recently, Colmán has been taken to be identical with Colum Ruadh son of Neamhan, which would mean that Bréanainn of Birr was a fourth brother, but this is nowhere else recorded.[4] According to an early seventeenth-century list detailing the churches within the diocese of Kildare, there were chapels dedicated to saints named Colmán and Conall at Clonyhurk and Ballintemple (parish of Geashill) in the deanery of Killeigh, who may represent two of Neamhan's children.[5] The saint may also have been the dedicatee of a church at Duleek in Meath.[6]

1 *CGSH* §728. 2 Ibid. §722.3 3 Ibid. §721.6. 4 *AB* 77, 432–3n. 5 *CDKL* 260; *Dinn*. 2, 32. 6 *PLPS* 71n.

Cairbre son of Rumhan. *See* Ceallach of Trim.

Cairbre Crom, 'bent' of Clonmacnoise (Cluain Mac Nóis), barony of Garrycastle, Co. Offaly. The saint named Cairbre Cronn, 'rounded', in the list for 6 March of the early ninth-century Martyrology of Tallaght was transmuted by later martyrologies into Cairbre Crom son of Fearadhach, bishop of Clonmacnoise, who was *ceann crábhaidh formhóir Éireann ina ré*, 'head of devotion of the greater part of Ireland in his time', at his death in 904.[1] This probable misidentification gave John Colgan support for the late date of *c*.900 which he assigned to the compilation of the Martyrology of Tallaght.[2] A moral tale relates how the Clonmacnoise prelate, by dint of his own prayer and that of his priests, attained release from Purgatory for the spirit of Maol Seachlainn son of Maol Ruanaidh, king of the Southern Uí Néill, after the king's death in 862.[3]

1 *MartT* 21; *MartG* 48; *MartD* 66. **2** *ASH* 4; *FSHIM* 112–13. **3** *MartD* 66; *ASH* 508–9; *TEAB* 465–73.

Cairbre Oilithir, 'pilgrim', of Kilcarbry (Ceall Chairbre) in the parish of Clonmore, barony of Bantry, Co. Wexford. This saint is known from an entry in the tract on the mothers of the saints which maintains that he and his nine brothers were sons of Díona, daughter of a king of the Saxons, by Brachan, king of the Britons (or Welsh), and eponym of Brycheiniog in south Wales.[1] Many of the saint's siblings, including Moghóróg of Delgany, Mochonóg of Kilmuckridge, Díoraidh of Edermine, and Eallóg of St Tulloge's, are associated with churches in east Leinster. This points to Kilcarbry, near Edermine, as the church most likely to have been associated with Cairbre.[2] Colgan erroneously took the saint, probably on the basis of the similarity of name, to have been the founder of Ceall Chairbre at Allt Fharannáin, now Alternan in the Sligo parish of Easky.[3]

1 *CGSH* §722.89. Cf. *EWGT* 14–16, 32–3. **2** *CECW* 206; *TNW* 1078. **3** *ASH* 312, 313 §14; *HDGP* i, 53.

Caireach. *See* Caoireach.

Caireall. *See* Coireall.

Cairinne of 'Chappelcaran' (which may represent an earlier Ceall Chairinne) in the townland of Bolabaun, parish of Killurin, barony of Shelmaliere West, Co. Wexford.[1] This saint is known from an entry in the tract on the mothers of the saints which maintains that he and his nine brothers were sons of Díona, daughter of a king of the Saxons, by Brachan, king of the Britons (or Welsh) and eponym of Brycheiniog in south Wales.[2] Perhaps because of the name ending in *–e*, Colgan took Cairinne to be a female.[3] Many of the saint's siblings – Moghóróg of Delgany, Mochonóg of Kilmuckridge, Díoraidh of Edermine, and Eallóg of St Tulloge's – are likewise associated with churches in east Leinster. A passage in the Latin Life of Finnian of Clonard brings its subject, then returning from Wales, to a place called *portus Kylle Caireni*, evidently at or near the Wexford coast.[4] Although located a few miles inland, Killurin lay close to the navigable river Slaney. The saint may also have given name to Saintkierans (St Kearns), in the Wexford parish of Tintern on the shore of Bannow Bay.[5] No feastday has been preserved for Cairinne.

1 *HDGP* iii, 138; *CECW* 130. **2** *CGSH* §722.89; *EWGT* 14–16, 32–3. **3** *ASH* 312, 313 §9. **4** *VSHH* 99 §11. **5** *HookP* 25.

Cairneach of Dulane (Tuiléan), barony of Upper Kells, Co. Meath. Citing Giolla Caomháin's version of the *Historia Brittonum*, the compiler of the corpus of saints' pedigrees stated that Cairneach son of Luitheach was so called because he belonged to the British of Cornwall, hence *Cairneach* from *Corn*.[1] The Irish version of the *Historia*, entitled *Leabhar Breathnach*, provides an extensive account of Cairneach's dealings with his supposed cousin, Muircheartach son of Earc, then said to have been in exile in Britain, of whom he foretold that he would be king of Ireland and Britain.[2] It also describes Cairneach, impossibly, as bishop of Tours in France which he supposedly left on pilgrimage, first to Cornwall, where he built an underground church, then to Ireland, where he became the first bishop of the Uí Néill about Tara. It states that Cairneach and two other saints, Bishop Dallán and Caomhlach, were born of a union between Babona (Pompa) daughter of Loarn, king of Scotland, and her brother-in-law Sárán, king of the Britons.[3] Although inconsistent with the descent noted above – which represents a conflated version of the two statements of ancestry of Cainneach of Aghaboe, probably borrowed because of the similarity of name – this variant tradition is also preserved in the corpus of saints' pedigrees, albeit in a form that assigns the saint to the Oirghialla of the area now corresponding to the diocese of Clogher.[4]

Cairneach figures prominently in the death-tale of his supposed nephew, Muircheartach son of Earc.[5] Described as entranced and engaging in battle with phantom battalions created by an Otherworld woman, Muircheartach is visited by Cairneach, accompanied by Masán, Casán, and Críodán, who temporarily restored his senses, only to have their work undone, and see the prophecy come true that the king would die by means of the so-called Threefold Death – drowning, wounding and burning. According to the death-tale, the king's body was brought for burial to Cairneach's church at Dulane, where he had already allegedly reburied Niall Naoighiallach, ancestral king of the Uí Néill, and a poem on the event is attributed to the saint.[6]

Since medieval times, Cairneach has been taken to be the Irish equivalent of Carannog of Llangrannog in south Wales, whose early twelfth-century Life credited him with a sojourn in Ireland that included the founding of churches in Leinster and a change of name to 'Cearnach', but this equivalence lacks linguistic support.[7] The name of the saint's church is attached to a lost manuscript named *Leabhar Gearr* ('short book') of Tuiléan (Dulane), and Cairneach is said to have contributed, with Patrick and Beinéan, to the compilation of the law tract known as *Seanchas Már*.[8] Situated close to Kells, Dulane may later have formed part of the Columban church's jurisdiction.[9] There were also churches associated with Cairneach and two companions (Masán and Casán) in Donegal, among them Drumleene in the parish of Clonleigh which the saint reputedly inherited from his mother's sister Earc.[10]

Cairneach's feast fell variously on 28 March and 16 May.[11] On the former day, he is accompanied, as in the death-tale of Muircheartach son of Earc, by a saint named Casán. Another companion in the death-tale, Críodán, is elsewhere stated to have been provided by Cairneach with a church named Ceall Earca, possibly in the Donegal parish of Burt.[12] Following a miracle involving the retention of water in a bottomless tub, which enabled the two saints to bathe together, Cairneach is said to have foretold that the body of Cianán of Duleek would remain incorrupt after death.[13] Cairneach's *míosach*, possibly a shrine containing a calendar, and allegedly one of the three battle-standards of the northern Uí Néill, is now in the

National Museum.[14] Finally, Cairneach was among the saints invoked as a guarantor of the Law of Adhamhnán, and, in addition to being named with Beinéan and Patrick among those chosen to arrange the *Seanchas Mór*, a *codach*, 'covenant', arranged by him between Muircheartach son of Earc and the Cianachta is also attested.[15]

1 *CGSH* §381; *Lgen.* 749.13; *DIB* ii, 249–50. **2** *LBr* §§24–5; *Lgen.* 112.5. **3** *LBr* §§24–5; *KeltRh.* 55. **4** *CGSH* §§123.1.2, 488, 722.29; *GRSH* 69;. **5** *AMME passim*; *BFen.* 336–8. **6** *LG* v, 360 §617; *MartO*[2] 246. **7** *VSBG* 142; *Seanchas* 408 §49; *CCH* 388; *IWMA* 138–47. **8** *ZCP* 3, 15; *Lgen.* 207.5; *VT* 564; *Peritia* 5, 9; ibid. 8, 130 §§37–8; *StC* 10/11, 15–28. **9** *AU s.a.* 969. **10** *DOH* 85; *JRSAI* 41, 96; *DLHS* 129–30; *LCAB* 13; *BFen.* 336–8; *SAM* 6, 14–15. **11** *MartT* 27, 43; *MartO*[2] 124; *MartG* 64, 98; *MartD* 88, 132. **12** *SGS* 6, 5–7; *Lgen.* 112.5. **13** *MartO*[2] 244; *BCC* 164–6 §158. **14** *AMME* §12; *DLHS* 126–31. **15** *CA* §22; *Ériu* 45, 12 §8, 25 §8.2; *IrT* iii, 5 §14.

Cairpre. *See* Cairbre.

Caiscéan son of Déigeall. Together with his brothers (Mearnóg and Meallal), Caiscéan (also written Caiscín, Caiséan and Caiscne) is said to have been a son of Cuman, sister of Colum Cille.[1] An early record of this relationship is set out in the appendix to Adhamhnán's Life of Colum which renders the parental names as Cuimne and Mac Déigill.[2] None of these appears to be attested elsewhere.

1 *CGSH* §§397, 722.24. **2** *VC*[1] 246; *VC*[2] 546.

Caisin of Drumadart. *See* Aghna.

Caisín son of Neamhan. *See* Casán son of Neamhan.

Caiseadhan of Kilcasheen, parish and barony of Moyarta, Co. Clare. This saint, also known by the Latin form Cassidus, is assigned by the genealogists to the Ciarraighe Cuirche who gave name to the Cork barony of Kerrycurrihy.[1] He figures in the Life of Seanán of Scattery Island who is reputed to have received instruction in the psalms and church discipline from Caiseadhan at the latter's church in Iorras (the Loop Head peninsula).[2] As he felt death approaching, Seanán is said by the same text to have prayed in the presence of Caiseadhan's relics. There appears to be no basis for Colgan's suggestion that this saint was identical with the Casán (Caisín) mentioned in the Life of Patrick.[3]

1 *JCHAS* 73, 60–70. **2** *LisL* 1954–7, 2472–85; *VSHH* 309. **3** *ASH* 174, 611 (*recte* 515).

Camán. *See* Comán.

Camulacus. *See* Caomhlach of Raithean.

Canice. *See* Cainneach.

Caoide of Churchtown (Baile an Teampaill), parish of Offerlane, barony of Upperwoods, Co. Laois. According to a list prepared in the late seventeenth century by Bishop Phelan of Ossory, a saintly bishop named either 'Cedus' or 'Edmundus', patron of Churchtown, was remembered on 20 November.[1] This day was the feast of Edmund, king of the East Angles and patron of Bury St Edmond's, who was martyred by Vikings in 869.[2] Cedus' identity is not so clear. It has been suggested that he was the same as Caoide of Donaghedy whose feast fell on 24/25 October, but given the inclusion of Churchtown among the possessions of the Cistercian abbey founded by the Anglo-Norman William Marshall the Elder shortly after 1200, he could just as well have been the Anglo-Saxon Chad (Ceadda), patron of Lichfield, among other places, whose tutor, Aidan of Lindisfarne, sent him to be educated in Ireland.[3] Chad's feast fell on 2 March.[4]

1 *HADO* ii, 174. 2 *ASE* 160–1; *ODS* 120–1. 3 *HADO* ii, 174; *ASE* 94; *ODS* 75. 4 *ASE* 94; *ODS* 75.

Caoide of Donaghedy (Domhnach Caoide), barony of Strabane Lower, Co. Tyrone. According to an early seventeenth-century manuscript fragment, the patron of Donaghedy was the abbot Cadinus (also rendered Gadinus in a contemporary document) whose feast fell in late October, four days before the feast of All Saints.[1] This accords with a statement by John Colgan who assigned Caoide's feast to 28 October, 'one of many days' of the saint.[2] Notes added to the Martyrology of Donegal place his feast on 24/25 October, and the index of the same text mentions relics of his, comprising bell and crozier.[3] A 1607 survey of the diocese of Derry used the same Latin form (Cadanus) for this saint as it did for Cadán of Tamlaght-ard, which points to a possible connection between the two.[4]

1 *Celtica* 1, 84; *MartD* xliii; *UJA* (2nd ser.) 1, 245. 2 *ASH* 162 (§2). 3 *MartD* 284–5; 372–4; *EMH* 484 §223. 4 *DYHS* 195–6.

Caoide of Kilkeedy, barony of Inchiquin, Co. Clare. By 1839 nothing was remembered locally of this saint except that his feast fell on 3 March, then known as *Lá Fhéil' Caoidhe*.[1] This feast is nowhere else recorded. John Colgan speculated that the man named 'Cutu/Ceta' in an account of the posthumous miracles of Seanán of Scattery might be the same as the patron of Kilkeedy.[2] The cult may also have spread to the like-named Limerick church (*ecclesia sancti Kidani* in a seventeenth-century document) of Kilkeedy.[3] Kedda was the anglicized form used by John O'Donovan.[4]

1 *ACoC* 38. 2 *ASH* 540 §31–4. 3 *CH* 2, 28. 4 *NMAJ* 2, 45.

Caoilbhe. *See* Pupa.

Caoiltighearn. *See* Caoimheall daughter of Caomhlugh.

Caoimheall daughter of Caomhlugh. An entry in the tract on the mothers of the saints, while attributing four children to Caoimheall (also rendered Caomhóg and Caoiltighearn) by a man named Colmaidh, describes her as a sister of Caoimhghin of Glendalough.[1] Among her children were at least three with Wicklow associations, viz. Daghán of Ennereilly, Méanóg of Glenealy, and Molioba of Ceall Molioba, near Glendalough.[2] The church named Ceall Chaoimhille after the saint was located in Uí Fhaoláin, now the northern part of Kildare.[3] Devotion to Caoimheall appears to have accompanied Caoimhghin to Ballybrennan in the Wexford barony of Forth, where a well called 'St Keevil's' was the scene of an annual pattern on 27 August.[4]

1 *CGSH* §722.19.72.102; *BNÉ* i, 125 §6. 2 *CPPI* 117–18. 3 *HDGP* iii, 140; *CGSH* p. 315. 4 OSL WX i, 281; *The Past* 2, 59; *CECW* 216.

Caoimheall of Ceall Chaoimhille. *See* Caoiltighearn; Caomhóg daughter of Ceinnfhionnán.

Caoimheall of Lusk, barony of Balrothery East, Co. Dublin, which may now represent an earlier Ceall Lusca. Like her namesake, Caoimheall daughter of Diarmuid, whose church of Díseart Brighde may have been located at or near Swords (perhaps earlier Ceall Shoird), this daughter of Aodh Barr is among those said to have been subject to Brighid of Kildare.[1] As Lusk and Swords are now adjoining parishes, the two saints were probably originally identical.

1 *CGSH* §670.26.29.

Caoimheall of Rathangan, barony of East Offaly, Co. Kildare, which may now represent an earlier Iomghán (Iomdhán).[1] Caoimheall is included among the saints of the Dál Meisin Corb, who were mainly connected with north-east Leinster, and particularly with the area about Glendalough in Wicklow.[2] Accompanying her in the list is the otherwise unattested Tréanán Draoi, 'druid'. Given her connection with the Glendalough area, she was probably the same as Caoimheall daughter of Caomhlugh.

1 *CPPI* 182. 2 *CGSH* §181.15.

Caoimheall of Swords. *See* Caoimheall of Lusk.

Caoimhghin of Glendalough (Gleann Dá Locha), parish of Derrylossary, barony of Ballinacor North, Co. Wicklow. 'A soldier of Christ … a high name (*ard n-ainm*) over the sea's wave', so wrote Aonghas of Tallaght about 830, when composing a metrical version of his laconic entry in the Martyrology of Tallaght at 3 June, the saint's feastday, which reads: Caoimhghin, 'abbot of Glendalough'.[1] In Aonghas' time, Glendalough was already a place of substance, capable of holding its own – 'with its 'cemetery of the western world' (*ruamh iarthair bheatha*) – among the churches of Ireland.[2] A fairly full list of its abbots is preserved, beginning with Caoimhghin who is said by the annalists to have died at the age of 120 years in 618 or 622.[3] Though there are variant versions of the date of his death, all sources agree that Caoimhghin son of Caomhlugh belonged to the Dál Meisin Corb, at one stage a dominant dynasty in the Wicklow area, and perhaps in north Leinster as a whole.[4] The composition of Caoimhghin's name (anglicized as Kevin) from *caomh*, 'fair', and *gein*, 'birth' – which is parallel to that of his father Caomhlugh (with the added divinity name Lugh), brothers Caomhán and Nadh Caoimhe, sister Caomhóg, and mother Caoimheall – would indicate remote pre-Christian origins.[5] There is, however, no overt trace of this in the five Lives composed for the saint, some Latin, others vernacular.[6]

Although all available in print, no critical edition and evaluation of the saint's Lives, one of which is preserved in the *Magnum Legendarium Austriacum* (Great Austrian Legendary), has yet been attempted.[7] Consequently, various opinions have been expressed regarding their date and value. On the one hand, it has been suggested that the Lives, though illustrating the development of extreme asceticism in the tenth and later centuries, have little historical value.[8] On the other hand, a great deal of historical information has been extracted from them, on the basis that they derive from an eighth-century original, edited over several centuries.[9] A dossier-style study may, however, yet reveal, as in the case of the Life of Fionnbharr of Cork, that the 'original' text was a much later composition, written perhaps in response to late twelfth-, or early thirteenth-century developments.[10] Episodes involving a claim to control over property in Dublin, or the existence of close relations between Glendalough and Armagh, whose saint is given the title of *archiepiscopus*, seem to be *prima facie* more at home in the twelfth than in any earlier century.[11]

The basic Life, as reflected by the Latin version in the Marsh's Library collection, is otherwise typical of its kind. It gives an account of the birth of the saint, his baptism by Crónán (Mochua) of Clondalkin, his education by three elders, Eoghan of Ardstraw, Lóchán and Éanna of Kilnamanagh (Ceall na Manach), his discovery and later founding of Glendalough, his encounters with various saints, and his many miracles, including the banishment of demons from the vicinity of his church and the inducement of a willow to bear apples, which, together with the story of a blackbird nesting in his outstretched hand (as recounted in Caoimhghin's vernacular Life), even reached the ears of Giraldus Cambrensis.[12]

The establishment of friendly relations with other saints, usually deputizing for their churches, is a feature of the Life. A friendship amounting to *confraternitas* is posited with Comhghall, Colum Cille, Cainneach, and Ciarán who was specially resuscitated to mark the occasion.[13] Without exception, the churches of these saints – Bangor, Durrow, Kells or Derry, Monaincha or Kilkenny, and Clonmacnoise – were to become, like Glendalough itself, locations of houses of canons regular of St Augustine in the period from the 1130s onwards, which may be another sign of the lateness of the Life.[14] The honour of rendering Caoimhghin the last rites is given to Moghóróg (Guaire) of Delgany who, perhaps significantly, in view of the predominantly Cambro-Norman character of the late twelfth-century conquest of Ireland, is described as a Briton.[15]

Not surprisingly, given the stature of his church, Caoimhghin figures in several other Lives, including that of Abán of Adamstown which counts him as one of 'three sons of eternal life' born of the Leinstermen, the other two being Abán himself and Moling of St Mullin's.[16] Bearach of Termonbarry is said to have studied under him, and Moninne of Killevy is seen to perform a miracle by banishing a demon from his side.[17] According to an early litany, forty saints were his associates in Glendalough, including a brother named Caomhán and the latter's uterine siblings, Muirdheabhair and Corcanadan.[18]

Though Caoimhghin's cult remained mainly confined to Ireland and Scotland, his feast is noticed in the English 'Martiloge' as well as in a Cologne version of the Martyrology of Usuard.[19] A miracle involving curative apples called after the saint is preserved in the Norse *Speculum Regale*.[20] According to the list of saints of similar manners, Caoimhghin was considered to be like Paul the Hermit, perhaps because of the tradition of his early eremitical life at Glendalough.[21] Said by the annalists to have died in 618/622, the saint was chiefly remembered on 3

June, but also on 11 May and 16 October.[22] His name is invoked in both Stowe Missal litanies, and he is among the handful of mainly Leinster saints commemorated both in the ninth-century calendar kept by an Irishman on the Reichenau and in the tenth-century metrical calendar of Hampson.[23] Annually, about the time of his main feast, Glendalough became a noted centre of pilgrimage, important enough to be regarded as one of four Irish equals of Rome.[24] The saint's church was rich enough to afford a well-equipped writing room, one of whose productions, the early twelfth-century Book of Glendalough (now Rawlinson B 502) is in the Bodleian Library, Oxford.[25] Among Caoimhghín's relics, which, presumably enshrined, were taken on tour in 790 together with those of Crónán of Clondalkin, was a bell named *Bobán* which was again used to bind an agreement between two twelfth-century kings.[26] Relics of the saint also found their way to the Continent, among other places to Sens and, arguably, either Ferrières in France or somewhere in the Rhineland.[27] The saint was patron of the secular families of Uí Thuathail (O'Tooles) and Uí Bhroin (Byrnes).[28]

1 *MartO²* 138; *MartT* 47. **2** *MartO²* 25. **3** *AU*/ATig. *s.a.*; *NHI* ix, 255–6; *CPPI* 111–43; *MartD* 142. **4** *CGSH* §§181.1, 250; *CGH* 120b26; *GRSH* 86; *Lgen.* 726.4; *VSHH* i, 234; *BNÉ* i, 125 §5; *AB* 46, 119; *CPPI* 17–18; *DIB* ii, 621–2. **5** *CGSH* §722.19; *SG* i, 148. **6** *MHH* 185, 239–40; *Kenney* 403–4; *ILL* 363–4. **7** *VSHP* i, 234–57; *VSHH* 361–5; *BNÉ* i, 125–67; *AB* 63, 122–9; ibid. 70, 313–15;*GCG* 145–64. **8** *Kenney* 404; cf. *BLCat.* i, 637–8. **9** *CPPI* 4–10; *WWHS* 140. **10** *BBa.*; *MakS*; *GCG* 137–44. **11** *VSHP* i, 245 §22, 249 §29. **12** *VSHP* i, 234–43 §§1–17; *BNÉ* i, 127–8 §20, 141 §9; *THEH* 113, 116. **13** *VSHP* i, 248–9 §§27–8. **14** *MRHI* 161–88. **15** *VSHP* i, 257 §48. **16** *VSHP* i, 3–4 §2. **17** *VSHP* i, 77 §6; *PRIA* 28C12, 214–15. **18** *IrL* 54–6; cf. ibid. 60. **19** HBS 3, 88; *KSS* 302; *AS*.Iun. vi, 315. **20** *Ériu* 4, 9. **21** *CGSH* §712.17. **22** *AU s.a.*; *MartT* 42, 80; *MartG* 94, 196; *MartD* 124, 278; *AU/ATig. s.a.* cf. *CI* i, 130n. **23** HBS 32, 14, 16; *AfL* 31, 52; *AB* 104, 99. **24** *BNÉ* i, 128 §23; 143 §10; 160–1 §§20–4. **25** *Éigse* 18, 161–76; *ZCP* 51, 130–47; *ZCP* 56, 71–88. **26** *AFM s.a.* 1144; *U s.a.*; *EMH* 488 §235; AClon. 1139. **27** *MSNAF* 138; *EIRD* 55–68; *RIW* 15–19. **28** *FFÉ* iii, 112.

Caoimhre daughter of Niall. *See* Crónán of Roscrea.

Caoireach Dheargáin, 'red or blush', of Cloonburren (Cluain Boireann), parish of Moore, barony of Moycarn, Co. Roscommon. The status of this saint's church within the territory of Uí Mhaine, now approximately coextensive with the diocese of Clonfert, can be gauged from the fact that seven garments, among other forms of tribute, were bestowed on it annually in honour of Caoireach.[1] Among other signs of the saint's stature are the competing statements of her descent. Through one tradition, which assigns her to the Ceinéal Laoghaire of Meath, she became a daughter of Bearach and brother of Rónán of Dromiskin.[2] A second tradition, which attaches her to Dál nAraidhe of north-east Ulster, treats her as a sister of Brughach of Raymoghy.[3] These two traditions are arguably brought together in the late twelfth-century tale *Buile Shuibhne*, 'frenzy of Suibhne', which, in addition to Caoireach's church, features both Rónán and Brughach.[4] A third tradition, which states that she belonged to the Oirghialla of the area now covered by the diocese of Clogher, transforms her into a sister of Éanna of Inishmore, an accusation against whom, it is said, caused her to blush, whence her by-name.[5] Finally, a fourth tradition states that she was the only 'good' descendant of Fearghas son of Eacha Muighmheadhón whose line, sometimes said to have become extinct, seems otherwise to have been represented by an erenagh family at Ceall Scíre, now probably Kilskeery in Tyrone.[6] Caoireach's reputation for great beauty is said to have induced Tiobraide son of Foramhain, king of Thomond, to seek her hand in marriage, only to be duped into accepting an equally beautiful disciple of the saint, named Ríceann of Kilreekill.[7] Caoireach's feastday fell on 9 February, and one set of annals places her death in 579.[8]

1 *TCHyM* 82. 2 *CGSH* §325.1.2; *GRSH* 50; *Lgen*. 706.6.7. 3 *CGSH* §110; *Lgen*. 714.12. 4 *Éigse* 15, 173–88. 5 *CGSH* §110 (Lb); *MartO*[2] 70–2; *GRSH* 70. 6 *SG* i, 327; *Lgen*. 108.2, 711.16. 7 *ACL* iii, 308–9. 8 *MartT* 15; *MartO*[2] 59; *MartG* 32; *MartD* 42; *CS s.a.*

Caol. A poem on those in orders with Patrick names Caol as his *giolla*, 'servant'.[1] As the previous line mentions *cruimhthear*, 'priest', the saint intended may be Cruimhthear Caol who was commemorated on 25 May at Ceall Mhór, now possibly Kilmore in the barony and county of Monaghan [2].

1 *CGSH* §672.10. 2 *MartT* 46; *MartG* 104; *MartD* 138.

Caol of Kilmainham (Ceall Mhaighneann), parish of St James, barony of Uppercross, Co. Dublin. Among those said to have been subject to Brighid were four daughters of Mac Iair, named Caol, Dearbhinill (replaced in some sources by Dairbhile alias Darbelinn), Dearinill and Coimhgheall.[1] These female saints are otherwise known from an entry in the martyrologies at 26 October, the earliest version of which locates them in Kilmainham.[2] Later sources place them variously in Killininny (Ceall na nInghean) near Tallaght, and at a house associated with Britons (Teach na mBreatan) within the sanctuary of Kells in Meath.[3]

1 *CGSH* §670.29. 2 *MartT* 84. 3 *MartG* 204; *MartO*[2] 228; *MartD* 284.

Caol, sister of Ruadhán. *See* Ruadhán of Lorrha.

Caolainn of Termon More (Tearmann Mór), parish of Kilkeevin, barony of Castlereagh, Co. Roscommon. The genealogists provide Caolainn daughter of Caol with a descent from the Ciarraighe, who gave name not only to the present county of Kerry, but also to settlements elsewhere, including north Roscommon.[1] A separate tradition assigns the saint to the Fir Mhaighe Féine of the Fermoy area in north Cork.[2] The connection with the Ciarraighe is reaffirmed in a section of the tract on the mothers of the saints 'bristling with difficulties' which attaches her mother, Meadhbh daughter of Ceartán, to the Uí Shaithghil branch of this family.[3] The saint figures in an account of the migration of the Ciarraighe to Connacht which, besides supplying Caolainn with the by-name *cráibhtheach*, 'pious', locates her church at Termon More, historically an area in which the Ciarraighe of Connacht had a settlement.[4] This is in the same parish as Clooncoose, where a male saint bearing the related name of Caolchú son of Caol was venerated. In at least one of her churches, at Cruach na Caoile (alias 'Cruagh Caolann') near St Macdara's island in the Galway parish of Moyrus, Caolainn apparently underwent a sex-change under the guise of Caolán 'Ó Doithe'.[5] Similarly, whereas an entry in the Martyrology of Tallaght at 19 June names Caolainn's church as Doire Caolainne (which is sometimes taken to be another name for Termon More), the later martyrologies assign this day to a male saint named Caolán.[6]

With her name anglicized as Keylan, the saint was remembered in the West as one of three maidens – the others being Deirbhileadh of Inishkea in Mayo, and (the otherwise unattested) Neimheadh – who never took offence and accepted no goods in compensation for outrage.[7] It was said of her that, like Brighid of Kildare, she gouged out her eyes to avoid being admired for them.[8] Elsewhere, she joined saints named Ciar and Cróine in a litany of virgins, and she is one of four female saints invoked in a poem by Donnchadh Mór Ó Dálaigh (†1244).[9] Despite her absence from the relevant list in the Martyrology of Tallaght, 3 February, traditionally the day of her commemoration in Connacht, is the likely feast of the saint.[10] In Connemara, red seaweed was gathered on this day.[11] The saint's monument was located at Ulaidh Caolainn in the Mayo barony of Carra.[12]

1 *CGSH* §296; *GRSH* 107; *Lgen.* 733.13. **2** *GRSH* 112; *MartD* 38. **3** *CGSH* §722.99; *JCS* 1, 193–8; *Celtica* 32, 115. **4** *AFM* iii, 238; *Speculum* 25, 184–9; *JCS* 1, 193. **5** OSL GY iii, 120; cf. *Béaloideas* 16, 203; *OFWC* 103–4. **6** *MartT* 51, 221; *JCS* 1, 194; *JCS* 1, 194–5; *MartG* 118; *MartD* 174. **7** *Ériu* 18, 66 §42. **8** OSL RN i, 182. **9** *MartT* 108; *IrL* 92; *DDé* 50. 10 *OFWC* 104. **10** *MartG* 28; *MartD* 38; *Béaloideas* 3, 485; OSL RN i, 182. **11** *Béaloideas* 3, 486. **12** *LGen.* 271.6.

Caolán. A derivative of *caol*, 'slender', this name was borne by several saints, eight of whom are included under the hypocoristic guise of Mochaoi in the list of homonymous saints.[1] The cult appears to have been particularly strong in east Ulster, most notably in the Down barony of Lecale (Leath Cathail).

1 *CGSH* §707.840–47.

Caolán of Annaghkeelaun (Eanach Caoláin), parish of Kilcummin, barony of Moycullen, Co. Galway. Arriving on the Lough Corrib island of Inishgarraun (Eachinis) in the parish of Kilcummin, Éanna of Inishmore was entertained by the priest Caolán who, lacking any food, was obliged to slay an ox used for ploughing which was subsequently miraculously restored.[1] According to Roderic O'Flaherty, this Caolán was worshipped on 25 April, but the martyrologies assign the saint's feast to 25 September, a day that enjoyed the same Roman notation as 25 April, which may have led to confusion.[2]

1 *VSHP* ii, 73 §30. **2** *OFWC* 23–4; *MartT* 74; *MartG* 184; *MartD* 258.

Caolán of Inishcaltra. *See* Caolán of Youghalarra.

Caolán of Kilclief. *See* Caolán of Nendrum.

Caolán of Nendrum (Aondruim), parish of Tullynakill, barony of Lower Castlereagh, Co. Down. While attaching Caolán (alias Mochaoi) to the Ulaidh of north-east Ulster, and presenting him as a close relative of two bishops, Mac Earca son of Fraochán and Lóchán son of Duachán, Caolán's pedigree variously names his father as Luachán, Uachán, and Duachán.[1] His mother, Brónach daughter of Míleac, 'with whom Patrick was in slavery', gave her name to Kilbroney (Ceall Bhróinche) in the Down barony of Upper Iveagh. She is said to have been the mother of several noted saints, including Damhnad of Tedavnet and Fursa of Killursa.[2]

Although patron of an important church, frequently mentioned in the annals, and reputedly containing a community of 450 monks, Caolán never became the subject of a Life.[3] He is known, however, from Lives of other saints, notably those of Colmán of Dromore and Finnian of Movilla, both of whom he is said to have tutored, as well as from the Tripartite Life which describes how Patrick discovered Caolán tending swine, preached to him, baptized and tonsured him, before going on to present him with various altar furnishings, and a famous crozier called *Eiteach*, 'winged'.[4] As it also mentions a yearly tribute promised by Caolán to Patrick, this passage was probably designed to underline Nendrum's affiliation to Armagh. Perhaps the most memorable tradition relating to Caolán is that of the heavenly bird that sang three strains for the saint while he was cutting wattles for his church in a wood. So beautiful was the singing that Caolán lost all sense of time, each strain lasting fifty years, with the result that when he returned to his church no one remembered him.[5] His long sleep (*codladh Mochaoi*) became proverbial.[6]

It has been suggested, probably correctly, that this saint was the same as his namesake at Kilclief (Ceall Chleithe), which is situated, like Nendrum, near Strangford Lough.[7] The latter saint is, however, given a separate descent through his father, Eachaidh son of Deargán, to a branch of the Eoghanachta of Munster, and he is described as a brother of Mac Táil of Kilcullen.[8] Kilmakee (Ceall Mochaoi) in the Antrim parish of Templepatrick takes its name from Caolán, and he was also venerated in Scotland.[9] The saint's name is sometimes confused, even locally, with that of Colmán.[10] Caolán's obit is assigned variously to 497 and 499, and his feast fell on 23 June.[11] The saint's head (*mullach*) may have formed part of the contents of Adhamhnán's reliquary.[12] Finally, a synchronistic poem on emperors and kings assigns Mochaoi to a church named Cluain Cha, possibly the same as Clonca in the Donegal barony of Inishowen, and also provides him with a descent from Lughaidh Lágha.[13]

1 *CGSH* §159; *GRSH* 82; cf. *MMN* 46–59; *DIV* vi, 537. **2** *CGSH* §§702.1–5, 722.92. **3** *HDGP* i, 67–8; *IrL* 66. **4** *BP* 321–7; *VT* 40; *VSHH* 357–8 §3; *EA* 189; *ASH* 438. **5** *AB* 47, 39–43; ibid. 49, 98. *MartD* 176; *CGSH* §732.1–2. **6** *ApalF* 179. **7** *EA* 217. **8** *CGSH* §238; *GRSH* 116. **9** *UJA* (3rd ser.) 27, 103–20. **10** *GRSH* 116. **11** *AU s.a.*; *MartT* 51; *MartO²* 142; *MartG* 122; *MartD* 176; cf. *CI* i, 144n. **12** *Celtica* 15, 35 §15. **13** *Peritia* 22–3, 116 §20.

Caolán of Youghalarra, barony of Owney and Arra, Co. Tipperary. While visiting Youghalarra in 1840, John O'Donovan discovered an inscribed stone in the local church which read: 'St COEA-NE-433'.[1] According to Samuel Lewis, who had been there a few years previously, the stone bore a head with the inscription 'St Coona, 434'.[2] The local saint, according to the same writers, was then named Cunnlan (Conlan) or Coolan (Coulan) and his feast fell on a day in late July, variously taken to have been 19/20, 25 or even 29 of the month. An entry in the early seventeenth-century *Genealogiae Regum et Sanctorum Hiberniae* refers to a saint named 'Cailin sive Cailanus' who was variously commemorated on 19 and 25 July.[3] This appears to refer to the Caolán remembered by the martyrologies on 25 July who, in turn, was probably identical both with the Youghalarra saint and with his namesake on Inishcaltra, commemorated on 29 July, who is credited with having written in verse Brighid of Kildare's sixth Life.[4] Local opinion attributed to Caolán the building not only of the church in Youghalarra, but also of the Franciscan abbey in Nenagh.[5] His crozier (*bachall*) was kept by descendants of the coarbs of his church, a family named Hogan (Uí Ógáin).[6] A note added to the original index of the Martyrology of Donegal erroneously identifies 'Conlán' of Youghalarra with a 'Conán' commemorated on 28 October.[7]

1 OSL TY iii, 51–2. 2 *TDI* ii, 730. 3 *GRSH* 96. 4 *MartT* 58; *MartG* 142, 146; *MartD* 202–4; *HDK* 140, 324; *ASH* 592, 596–8. 5 OSL TY iii, 300–01. 6 Ibid.; *HDK* 324. 7 *MartD* 388.

Caolchú of Clooncoose (Cluain Cuasa), parish of Kilkeevin, barony of Castlereagh, Co. Roscommon. The pedigree of Caolchú son of Caol attached him to the Ciarraighe of Aoi, the great plain between Roscommon and Elphin.[1] Ciúin is the name given to his mother, and Moingfhinn (from *mong* + *fionn*, 'fair mane / hair'), one of his two sisters – the other being Reabhradh – was associated with the church of Cloonkeen, likewise in the parish of Kilkeevin.[2] The only Caolchú noticed in the martyrologies is in the list for 24 September which locates him in Cluain (Laoi) Oirthir, now possibly Magheracloone in Monaghan.[3] Mícheál Ó Cléirigh's suggestion that this was the Caolchú numbered among the pupils of Fionnbharr of Cork has little to support it.[4] Also very unlikely is the suggestion that Caolchú may have been the Colga cited in the text of the *Monastery of Tallaght*.[5]

1 *CGSH* §335.1; *GRSH* 107; *Lgen.* 732.14. 2 *CGSH* §335.2. 3 *MartT* 74, 218; *MartG* 182; *MartD* 256. 4 *MartD* 256; *BBa.* 68, 250. 5 *MT* §§56, 65, 81; *GRSH* 107.

Caomhán. This derivative of *caomh*, 'fair', is very common among holy men, with twenty-one representatives in the list of homonymous saints, albeit under the hypocoristic guise of Mochaomhóg.[1] It is variously anglicized as Kavan and Keevaun.

1 *CGSH* §707.720–40.

Caomhán, associate of Patrick. Two saints named Caomhán are mentioned in the lists of those associated with Patrick. One is described as the saint's *macaomh*, 'lad', the other as his *saor*, 'craftsman'.[1] Of the latter it is said that he was the first in Ireland to build a stone church. The former is attached to the church of Kilrea (Ceall Riadha) in the Derry barony of Loughinsholin of which Patrick was patron.[2] A third associate of the name figures in a passage of the Tripartite Life that describes how Patrick, having founded many churches in Dál nAraidhe (now approximately south Antrim and north Down), left members of his household in them, including Caomhán in a place called Imleach Cluana in Seimhne, now probably Kilcoan (from Ceall Chaomháin) at Islandmagee (Seimhne) near Larne in Antrim.[3] Two other holy bearers of the name are provided with north-east Ulster pedigrees: Caomhán Breac is sometimes taken to be identical with Mac Nise of Connor; Caomhán son of Taca is presented as a close relative of Finnian of Clonard who is elsewhere shown to have had an equally close relationship with

Caomhán Santleathan of Ardcavan, likewise – according to yet another tradition – affiliated to the Dál nAraidhe.[4] The saint chosen to provide Colmán Eala, descendant of Eacha son of Mairidh, the eponym of Lough Neagh, with his initial instruction was also called Caomhán.[5] There are thus signs in the nominally distinct traditions of these east Ulster saints named Caomhán, some of them associates of Patrick, that point to their ultimate identity.

1 *CGSH* §§671.6, 672.6.14; *Lgen.* 695.1. 2 *DYHS* 195. 3 *BP* 1908–15; *VT* 164; *EA* 59. 4 *CGSH* §147; *GRSH* 114; *Lgen.* 733.6. 5 *VSHH* 209 §2.

Caomhán of Anatrim (Eanach Troim), parish of Offerlane, barony of Upperwoods, Co. Laois. This Caomhán (also known as Mochaomhóg, and locally anglicized as Kavan or Kaban) was assigned by the genealogists to the Dál Meisin Corb, a people closely associated with the area about Glendalough in Wicklow.[1] The list assigns two brothers to Caomhán – Muirdheabhair and Corconadan – and all three are again brought together in two other sources: among those commemorated on 3 November, and among the associates of Caoimhghin of Glendalough in an early litany.[2] While noting Caomhán's connection with Anatrim, the latter source locates his brothers at Díseart Muirdheabhra in Uí Chonaill Ghabhra, which gave name to Dysert in the Limerick parish of Robertstown, and at Doire Eidhneach, now Derrynaflan, near Horse and Jockey, in the Tipperary parish of Graystown. Other sources contend that Caomhán was a brother of Caoimhghin of Glendalough, thus equating him with his namesake, Caomhán Santleathan, who also had associations with the Laois area.[3]

The story of the founding of Caomhán's church is the subject of episodes in the Lives of other saints. In one, the main subject of the Life, Colum of Terryglass, is said to have had three disciples – Caomhán, Fiontan of Clonenagh, and Mochaoimhe of Terryglass – who set out together in quest of places in which to serve God, ending up at Anatrim.[4] In another, Mochaomhóg of Leigh, who has much in common with the saint, including his name, is said to have first settled in Anatrim before relinquishing it to Caomhán.[5] A well near Anatrim, variously called 'St Keevaun's' and 'St Kavan's', was the scene of an annual pattern in honour of the saint on 3 November, and the nearby church was named after him (Latin *Cawanus*).[6] On Inisheer of the Aran Islands, to which the saint's name became attached in the form Ára Chaomháin, he was reputed to be the most celebrated of all.[7] The grave claimed for him on the island was visited by sick people in the hope of recovering their health.[8] According to John Colgan, his feast was celebrated on Aran on 12 June, otherwise the day of Caomhán Santleathan.[9] From Aran the cult may have spread to the island of Inishglora, off the Mayo coast, on which an otherwise unattested Mochaomhóg is said to have befriended and subsequently baptized the celebrated 'Children of Lir'.[10]

1 *CGSH* §181.6; *Lgen.* 726.2; *AILS* 94. 2 *MartG* 210; *MartD* 296; *IrL* 54–6. 3 *GRSH* 86; *MartG* 210; *MartD* 296. 4 *VSHP* ii, 97 §3; *VSHH* 146 §3. 5 *VSHP* ii, 168–9 §11. 6 *HADO* ii, 146–50; *CPL* 16, §929. 7 *ASH* 715; *HDGP* i, 74; OSL GY iii, 429. 8 *OFWC* 88–90. 9 *ASH* 715. 10 *OCL* 31 §58, 72.

Caomhán of Kilrea. *See* Caomhán, associate of Patrick.

Caomhán son of Taca (Toca). *See* Caomhán, associate of Patrick.

Caomhán Breac of Russagh (Ros Each), alias Clonabraney, parish of Diamor, barony of Fore, Co. Meath. This son of Neas is provided with a Dál Riada genealogy which would place his origins in north-east Ulster.[1] The location of his church ties in, however, with an episode in the Life of Féichín of Fore which describes how a wright in service to Caomhán elected to remain with Féichín who had restored him to life.[2] Buried with Caomhán in Russagh was his uterine brother Mac Rustaing, on sight of whose grave, according to a note added to the Martyrology of Aonghas, women both farted and laughed.[3] Though Caomhán's regular feast fell on 14 September, the later martyrologists also identified him with Mac Nise of Connor who was remembered on 3 September.[4] The saint was considered important enough to have a date of birth (529) and obit (615) assigned to him by the annalists.[5] Devotion to the Holy Cross, the feast of which also fell on 14 September, was substituted for Caomhán in the parish of Diamor, but a well named after him continued to be remembered in the early nineteenth century.[6] At an earlier stage, Finnian of Movilla (whose feast fell on 10 September) may have been introduced as patron of Diamor, whose parish church was called *ecclesia sancti Finini*.[7]

1 *CGSH* §§206, 492; *GRSH* 81; *Lgen.* 722.6. **2** *VSHP* ii, 82 §15; *RC* 12, 344–6. **3** *MartO²* 206–8. **4** *MartT* 71; *MartO²* 194; *MartG* 168, 176; *MartD* 232, 248. **5** *AU s.a.*; cf. *LUM* 154 rb 31–2. **6** OSL MH 100; cf. *PNW* 38n. **7** *CPL* 20, §620.

Caomhán Breac, 'speckled', son of Lughna. According to the tract on the mothers of the saints, Caomhán Breac and several others, including Bishop Iobhar, were children of Basar of the Déise Breagh, a people who gave name to the Meath baronies of Deece.[1] His father's name was Lughna son of Corc of the Uí Eachach of Ulster who gave name to the Down baronies of Iveagh.[2] As Iobhar's church of Begerin near Wexford Harbour adjoined Ardcavan (from Airdne (Ard) Caomháin, 'high place of Caomhán'), it may be assumed that the eponym of the latter place (usually Caomhán Santleathan) and Caomhán Breac were one and the same.

1 *CGSH* §§721.2, 722.14.96. **2** Ibid. §96.

Caomhán Léith. *See* Mochaomhóg of Leigh.

Caomhán Oilithir, 'pilgrim', of Kilcavan (Ceall Chaomháin), parish of Castlebrack, barony of Tinnahinch, Co. Laois. This saint is known from an entry in the tract on the mothers of the saints which asserts that he and his nine brothers were sons of Díona, daughter of a king of the Saxons, by Brachan, king of the Britons (or Welsh) and eponym of Brycheiniog in south Wales.[1] Many of the saint's siblings, including Moghóróg of Delgany, Mochonóg of Kilmuckridge, Díoraidh of Edermine, and Eallóg of St Tulloge's, are associated with churches in east Leinster. Caomhán may also have been venerated in the Wexford area, albeit under the guise of Caomhán Santleathan of Ardcavan, and the abovementioned entry allows for this by adding *et in aliis locis*, 'and in other places', to his Laois church. Furthermore, Kilcavan is only twenty or so miles distant from Anatrim, which renders likely the ultimate identity of the two Laois saints named Caomhán. No local tradition of the Kilcavan saint appears to have been preserved, but the annual fair on 12 August may have stood in some relationship to the saint named Caomhán commemorated on 14 August.[2]

1 *CGSH* §722.89; *EWGT* 32–3. 2 *MartT* 63; *MartG* 156; *MartD* 218.

Caomhán Santleathan, perhaps 'wide saint', of Ardcavan (Airdne/Ard Caomháin), barony of Shelmaliere East, Co. Wexford. The mainline genealogy of this saint attaches him through his father Talán to the Corca Ólaim, a branch of the descendants of Fearghas son of Róch to which Bréanainn of Birr also belonged.[1] Other sources deviate, however, from this. According to one tradition, he was a brother of Athracht of Killaraght in Sligo who belonged to the Dál nAraidhe of north-east Ulster.[2] In this guise, he is credited with two actions relating to north Connacht, a bridge he arranged to have laid across Lough Gara on Sligo's border with Roscommon, and a curse he placed on the descendants of Ceannfhaoladh (†682) son of Colga, king of Connacht and ancestor of the Uí Fhlaithbheartaigh of west Connacht, depriving them of the kingship of the province.[3] Yet another tradition describes him as a brother of Cuach daughter of Caolbhadh of the Uí Bhairrche of Magh Ailbhe, the western part of a plain in north Carlow.[4] Through Cuach, he is said to have received three sites, all in the north-west corner of the county.[5]

Further wide-ranging associations are provided by his mother, Caoimheall daughter of Ceinnfhionnán, through whom he became a uterine brother of Caoimhghin of Glendalough and Nadh Caoimhe (Mochaoimhe) of Terryglass.[6] An association with Terryglass is also a feature of the cult of his namesake, Caomhán of Anatrim. In the Life of Finnian, the Clonard saint is said to have dallied with Caomhán, described as *senior*, 'elder', at Dairinis (another name for Ardcavan) on his way to and from St David's in south Wales.[7] The Irish version of the Life states that the saints made a union, and this raises the possibility that Clonard had an interest in Ardcavan.[8] Caomhán's feast fell on 12 June which was also the date of the local pattern at Ardcavan and at two other Wexford churches named Kilcavan after the saint and, according to John Colgan, on Aran.[9] In addition to the church of Drinagh in the Wexford barony of Forth, of which he was also patron, the saint was venerated at a site named Kilcavan in the Wicklow parish of Carnew, and he may have been patron of a chapel at Clonbulloge in the Offaly parish of Clonsast – mentioned in an early seventeenth-century list immediately after an unidentified place called *Cuasán Caoimhghin* – and also of Cloncreen in the same parish.[10]

1 *CGSH* §131; *GRSH* 111; *Lgen.* 733.5–6. 2 *CGSH* §398.2. 3 Ibid. 4 *CGSH* 165; *CGH* 316a35. 5 *Peritia* 4, 200. 6 *CGSH* §722.19; *BNÉ* i, 125 §6. 7 *VSHH* 97, 99. 8 *LisL* 2527–9. 9 *MartT* 49; *MartO*[2] 140; *MartG* 114; *MartD* 168; OSL WX i, 307; ibid. ii, 87; *CECW* 126–7, 203, 206; OSL WX i, 5; *ASH* 715; *TNW* 1079–83. 10 *The Past* 2, 59; OSL WW 101–2; *Dinn.* 2, 31, 34.

Caomhlach of Raithean. Among Patrick's bishops, as listed by Tíreachán, were Guasacht and Camelacus (alias Caomhlach) who are again brought together in a passage on the Armagh saint's foundations in Teathbha, now most of Longford and part of Westmeath.[1] There, Patrick pointed out to Caomhlach from the top of Granard hill a site named Raithean which the saint was to occupy. Sometimes implausibly taken to represent Rahan in Offaly, the site has yet to be definitely identified, though it has been suggested that it was at or near Abbeylara.[2] Caomhlach is elsewhere the subject of an early alphabet hymn preserved in the Antiphonary of Bangor, beginning *Audite bonum exemplum* which some scholars take to have been written by Colmán Eala.[3] The Irish version of *Leabhar Breathnach*, 'book of the Britons', names Caomhlach – together with Cairneach of Dulane and Bishop Dallán – among the children of a union between Babona, daughter of a king of Scotland, and her brother-in-law Sárán, king of Britain.[4] Caomhlach of Raithean was commemorated on 3 November.[5]

1 *UJA* 1, 174; *PTBA* 128 §6.2; 136 §16.7; *DIB* ii, 271. 2 *HDA* 60 3 *AntB* 44–6; *PSP* 41–5; *IIAM* 563–4. 4 *Lbret.* §24. 5 *MartG* 210; *MartD* 297.

Caomhnad. *See* Baoithín of Taghboyne.

Caomhóg daughter of Caomhlugh. *See* Caoiltighearn.

Caomhóg daughter of Ceinnfhionnán, mother of Caoimhghin of Glendalough. According to the Book of Leinster version of the secular genealogies, Caomhóg (alias Caoimheall) belonged to the Dál gCormaic Loisc of the area between Killeshin in Carlow and Killabban in Laois.[1] Because of the component *caomh*, 'fair', in her name, which is common among the close relatives of Caoimhghin, she has been rightly described as 'less credible' than other mothers of saints.[2] The names of the other children attributed to her – Caomhán Santleathan of Ardcavan, Nadh Caoimhe of Terryglass, and Caoimheall of Ceall Chaoimhille – all contain the same component.[3]

1 *CGH* 120a5. 2 *SS* 261. 3 *CGSH* §722.19; *BNÉ* i, 125 §6.

Carantód. This saint is known only from the tract on the mothers of the saints, where he is among fifteen bishops accounted as children of Dairearca, sister of Patrick.[1] The name seems Welsh in origin which would be in keeping with Patrick's own background and also with the declaration in his Tripartite Life that he was followed to Ireland by his sister, along with several other relatives.[2]

1 *CGSH* §722.16. 2 *BP* 895–8; *VT* 82.

Carthach. *See* Mochuda.

Carthach of Kilcar (Ceall Charthaigh), barony of Banagh, Co. Donegal. Variously described as nephew and son of Aonghas son of Nadh Fraoich, king of Cashel, Carthach figures prominently in the Life of his tutor, Ciarán of Seirkieran. Ciarán's biographer calls upon Carthach to intercede on behalf of an uncle and his servants, to become a pilgrim because of a sin of the flesh, and to return to Seir when Ciarán was in the company of Gearmán, also a pilgrim.[1] According to one tradition, Molua of Clonfertmulloe was begotten as a result of Carthach's sin.[2] There is little else recorded of the saint, but his feast fell on 5

March, a day shared with his tutor Ciarán.[3] In addition to Kilcar, where he was thought to have gone to do penance for his sin, two other churches are assigned to him in the martyrological record: one, an unidentified site at Druim Feardaimh (Feartáin) in the Kildare barony of Carbury; the other, at Church Island (Inis Uachtair) on Lough Sheelin between the counties of Cavan and Westmeath, which contains the ruins of his church.[4] There are wells in Kilcar – alternatively known as Ceall Chiaráin until the seventeenth century – named after both Carthach and Ciarán.[5] In one source, he is said to have been identical with Carthach of Kilcaragh, tutor of Mochuda of Lismore.[6] Finally, Carthach of Kilcar may have been the saint of the name who was invoked as a guarantor of the Law of Adhamhnán.[7]

1 *VSHP* i, 222–9 §§13, 15, 24, 29; *VSHH* 349, 351–2; *BNÉ* i, 109–10 §42, 116–23 §§27, 49, 63, 72; *AB* 59, 267–9. **2** *MartO*[2] 86. **3** *MartT* 20; *MartO*[2] 80; *MartG* 48; *MartD* 64. **4** *PNW* 49; *Béaloideas* 6, 146–8. **5** Ibid. 146; *DLHS* 176. **6** *MartO*[2] 86. **7** *CA* §22.

CARTHACH of Kilcaragh (Ceall Charthaigh), barony of Clanmaurice, Co. Kerry. This bishop is sometimes referred to as Sean-Charthach, 'elder/senior Carthach', to distinguish him from his pupil, Mochuda (alias Carthach) of Lismore, who allegedly remained 'under his discipline' until ordained by him.[1] Carthach is also said to have instructed Mochuda as to where he should erect his first church, at Kiltallagh (Ceall Tulach) in the Kerry barony of Trughanacmy.[2] In one source, he is said to be identical with Carthach of Kilcar, a son or nephew of Aonghas, king of Cashel.[3] He may be among those mentioned in a poem that lists the numerous children of Inghean Bhaoith, and he is probably the saint so named on whom, among many others, Seanán of Scattery Island could rely for assistance.[4] His memory had died out in Kilcaragh by the nineteenth century.[5]

1 *VSHP* i, 172 §10; *AB* 59, 268–9. **2** *VSHP* i, 174–5 §14. **3** *MartO*[2] 86. **4** *IrT* iv, 93 §7; *ZCP* 10, 28 §23. **5** *ACoK* 35.

CÁRTHANN. *See* Mac Caorthainn.

CAS of Bangor (Beannchar), barony of Ards Lower, Co. Down. In the Martyrology of Tallaght, the exemplar of which was kept for a time in Bangor, this saint heads the list of those commemorated on 26 April.[1] He is probably the same as the bishop named Cas Cobha, 'of Cuibh', a descendant of Fiodhbhadh son of Ros, son of Iomchadh, progenitor of the Uí Fhiodhbhadha of Dál nAraidhe who held lands just north of Bangor.[2]

1 *MartT* 36; *MartG* 84; *MartD* 110. **2** *BB* 168b3.

CAS of Míleac Fiaich. *See* Angán of Míleac Fiaich.

CASÁN, *cruimhthear*; see Casán son of Neamhan.

CASÁN son of Athracht. The list of saints of the Clann Lughdhach (another name for the Ceinéal Laoghaire of Meath) includes a group associated with Moylagh (Magh Lacha) in the Meath part of the barony of Fore.[1] One of the group, Ríceall by name, allegedly had a brother named Casán, and seventeenth-century sources speculatively identified this man with a namesake at Iomdhual, now possibly Imdel in the Down parish of Drumballyroney, who was commemorated on 28 March.[2]

1 *CGSH* §§662.45, 690.10; *GRSH* 50; *Lgen*. 705.9. 2 *GRSH* 50; *MartD* 88; cf. ibid. 146; PNNI vi, 165–7.

Casán son of Maonach. According to the genealogists, this saint, whose name (usually Casán) also took the forms Cuasán and Caisín, was one of seven sons of Maonach son of Fachtna of the Corca Laoighdhe, a family settled in the area now covered by the diocese of Ross.[1] His siblings included not only Fachtna of Ross, but also Mainchín whose church of Coolcashin (Cúil Chaisín) in Kilkenny may commemorate Casán, albeit under a variant form of his name.[2] Some of the seven brothers were associated with churches in the area later covered by the diocese of Ossory, the people of which were thought to have been closely connected with the Corca Laoighdhe.

1 *CGSH* §298.2; *GRSH* 127; *Lgen*. 744.6. 2 *BBa*. 242.

Casán son of Neamhan. While travelling through Leinster on a visit to Brighid of Kildare, Finnian of Clonard is reported to have come to an area called Fothairt Airbhreach, apparently near Croghanhill in the Offaly barony of Lower Philipstown.[1] Here he was welcomed by Casán (Caisín) son of Neamhan who complained that the king of the Fothairt was seeking payment of gold for his freedom, which Finnian miraculously provided. Assigned to the Dál mBuain of Ulster – the descendants of Eacha son of Mairidh, eponym of Lough Neagh – by some seventeenth-century sources, Casán is commemorated in the martyrologies at 1 March.[2] John Colgan took him to be the presbyter named Casán whom Tíreachán, Patrick's biographer, placed in the church named Domhnach Mór Maighe Eachnach, but his identification of the church as Donaghmore near Navan in Meath, close to Donaghpatrick, has been shown to be wrong.[3] When Patrick was baptizing the people of Luighne, whose territory appears to have lain towards Kells, he foretold of Casán that many would gain solace from his relics and that his miracles would be great.[4] This is probably also the saint named Casán who accompanied Cairneach, Masán, and Críodán, to the dwelling of Muircheartach son of Earc, king of Tara, when the latter was engaging in battle with shadowy Otherworld battalions.[5] The saints are said to have temporarily restored the king's senses, only to have their work undone, and the king die by means of the so-called Threefold Death. The Life of Colmán son of Luachán also refers to this saint, locating him in Domhnach Mór and describing him as *anmchara*, 'soulfriend', of Murchadh, king of Midhe.[6] The same text states that Casán was among those who bore eloquent testimony to the virtues of the recently deceased Colmán.[7]

1 *LisL* 2613–23. 2 *GRSH* 96; *MartT* 20; *MartG* 46; *MartD* 60. 3 *PTBA* 136 §16.2; *ASH* 779–82; *ILL* 82, 246; 267. 4 *BP* 805–31; *VT* 76–8. 5 *AMME* §§25–6, 43; cf. *BFen*. 338. 6 *BCML* §73. 7 Ibid. §104.

Cassidus. *See* Caiseadhan.

Cathal of Ballycahill, barony of Eliogarty, Co. Tipperary. A reinterpretation of the name Bealach Achaille (way of Achall) as Baile Cathail (Cathal's place) led to the mistaken assumption, already attested in the early seventeenth century, that the place was named after Cataldo, patron of Taranto in southern Italy, who was traditionally, but wrongly, regarded as an Irishman.[1] Cathal also came to be venerated in the Tipperary parish of Shanrahan, barony of Iffa and Offa West.[2]

1 *ASH* 544 §2; *PCNT* 315; *HDGP* ii, 100; *SacH* 355–63. **2** *ASH* 544–5; *SacH* 356.

Cathbhadh/(Cathubh). *See* Cobhthach.

Caurnán. *See* Cúrnán.

Causán. *See* Casán.

Cavan. *See* Cuán of Ahascragh.

Ceachtamair. *See* Aodhamair; Cinne.

Ceallach of Armagh (Ard Mhacha). The notice of Ceallach's death in 1129 describes him as Patrick's successor and archbishop of 'western Europe'.[1] The hyperbole was a natural one. Born in 1080, Ceallach (Latin Celsus) son of Aodh had succeeded to the abbacy of Armagh in 1105 on grounds of the hereditary rights of his family to the succession, had taken holy orders – which was a departure from all precedent in the secular family – and had been consecrated bishop and archbishop. During his tenure, a solid foundation was laid for the implementation of what is called the twelfth-century reform of the Irish church.[2] By engaging in several circuits of Ireland, north and south, in the years immediately after his consecration, he established good relations with the secular rulers of the day in the traditional manner, especially with those of Munster who were to the forefront of the movement towards ecclesiastical reform.[3] With the papal legate Gillebert, he presided over the synod of Rathbrassil in 1111, which established the diocesan framework for the reform, and subsequently (in 1121) brought Dublin on side by arranging with the Hiberno-Norse to have himself declared bishop of the see.[4] Then, by nominating Maol Maodhóg (Malachy) – whom he had consecrated as bishop of Connor – as his successor, he took all necessary steps to ensure that succession to the metropolitan see would no longer depend on hereditary right.[5] Having ordained 'many bishops and priests', and 'consecrated many churches', he died at the Patrician site of Ardpatrick (Ard Pádraig) in the Limerick barony of Coshlea on 1 April 1129.[6] His feast is recorded on this day in the martyrologies of Gorman and Donegal, but by the seventeenth century, to judge by a note added to the former text, and by an entry in the latter, it had come to be celebrated also on 6 April.[7] Ceallach's sanctity received recognition in the *Visio Tnugdali*, a text written at Regensburg in Germany in the middle of the twelfth century which placed him (under the guise of Celestinus) among four blessed bishops seen by Tnúthghal in Patrick's company in heaven.[8]

1 *AU s.a.* **2** *TCR* 19–39; *DIB* ii, 448–9. **3** *AU s.a.* 1106, 1108, 1110, 1116, 1120. **4** *AH* 3, 11–12; *AU s.a.* **5** *BCLMA* 43–4. **6** *AU s.a.*; *TIC* 42–4. **7** *MartG* 68, 70; *MartD* 92, 96. **8** *VisTnug*. 55.

Ceallach of Killala (Ceall Alaidh), barony of Tirawley, Co. Mayo. An entry in the martyrologies for 1 May commemorates Ceallán son of Eoghan Béal of the

Uí Fhiachrach, a people after whom the Sligo barony of Tireragh is named.[1] As Ceallán is a variant of Ceallach, there are grounds for identifying this saint as the hero of a Middle-Irish tale known as *Caithréim Cheallaigh*, 'the triumphal career of Ceallach'.[2] This outlines how Ceallach, then a pupil of Ciarán, was persuaded by his people to assume the kingship of Uí Fhiachrach, only to have his violent death foretold by his disappointed tutor at Clonmacnoise. On later relinquishing the kingship, Ceallach resumed his studies but, despite having made peace, Ciarán could not undo the terms of his previous prophecy. Ceallach was subsequently persuaded by his people to become bishop at Killala, and having also relinquished this post, he was eventually murdered by four of his companions who were later put to death by Ceallach's brother Muireadhach on Ardnaree in the parish of Kilmoremoy.[3] There is no other record of the saint, but he may be the eponym of Kilkelly (Ceall Cheallaigh) in the Mayo parish of Kilmovee. It is also likely that he was patron of Isertkelly (Díseart Ceallaigh) in the Galway barony of Loughrea, within the former territory of Aidhne, with which another branch of the Uí Fhiachrach was associated.[4] It has been suggested that this bearer of the name may have been the Ceallach son of Connmhach acclaimed in the poem attributed to Cuimín of Connor as a man who, though afflicted by blindness, deafness, and lameness, nonetheless loved devotion.[5] Ceallach son of Connmhach is also among those invoked in a poem calling on saints to assist Seanán of Scattery.[6]

1 *MartT* 38; *MartG* 88; *MartD* 116; *GRSH* 61; *Lgen.* 252.3; *DIB* ii, 446–7. **2** *CC*. **3** Ibid. 23 (ll. 750–4); *Dinn.* 1, 20. **4** *GYHS* 808–9. **5** *ZCP* 1, 66, 69. **6** *ZCP* 10, 26 §21.

Ceallach of Trim, baronies of Lower Moyfenrath and Upper Navan, Co. Meath. Ceallach was one of seven sons of Rumhan, a famous poet, regarded as the Irish equivalent of Homer and Virgil.[1] Two of Ceallach's brothers, Ceann Faoladh (possibly a bishop-abbot of the name who died at Trim in 821) and Suibhne (probably the abbot of Trim who died in 796) were given the title of bishop.[2] The four other brothers were named Cairbre, Conall, Muireadhach and Ruidhgheas. Ceallach's family appears to have been closely associated with the church of Trim, despite one seventeenth-century source which identified their father as Rumhan Duach of Osraighe, an area now approximately equivalent to the diocese of Ossory.[3]

1 *CGSH* §690.4; *Lgen.* 753.52. **2** *BB* 87d; *AU s.a.* **3** *GRSH* 93; *MartT* 17; *JEH* 1, 162–9.

Ceallach son of Dúnchadh. The feast of this saint, of whom little else is known, is recorded in the martyrologies at 18 July.[1] In the earliest of these texts the word *rex*, 'king', is appended to the name of the saint's father.[2]

1 *MartT* 56; *MartG* 138; *MartD* 196. **2** *MartT* 56.

Ceallachán of Clontibret (Cluain Tiobrad), barony of Cremorne, Co. Monaghan, and of Ballyoughtera, near Castlemartyr, barony of Imokilly, Co. Cork. Neither bearer of the name is well known. The former is the subject of an entry in the martyrologies at 24 September, but by 1835, when John O'Donovan visited the area, the name of the saint was no longer remembered.[1] He was probably identical with the Ceallachán (alias Ceallach) to whom, again according to O'Donovan, the Cavan parish of Mullagh was dedicated.[2] The latter's festival fell in Autumn which would suit the day assigned to the Clontibret bearer of the name. More recent opinion has sought to establish a connection between the Mullagh saint and Kilian of Würzburg in Germany, but there is no early evidence for this.[3] Ceallachán of Ballyoughtera, probably recorded corruptly as 'Martre Chalwallin', (Ceallachán's burial-place' in the Pipe Roll of Cloyne), was one of the patrons of the diocese of Cloyne, but no feastday has been recorded for him.[4]

1 *MartT* 74; *MartG* 182; *MartD* 256; OSL AH/MN 71. 2 OSL CN/LM 64–5. 3 *Breifne* 8, 1–19 at 3–5. 4 *CPR* i, lxix; *LIS* ix, 542–3; *PRC* 10, 169.

Ceallán of Ceall Daimhchinn, an unidentified church in Leinster, perhaps Kildavin in the parish of Barragh, barony of St Mullin's Upper, Co. Carlow.[1] This son of Libhréan is known from a poem attributed to Moling which states that he would assume an abbacy – probably that of St Mullin's – for twelve years.[2] He may also be intended in another poem attributed to Moling which invokes, among many other saintly protectors of Leinster, Ceallán 'of the church on the mountain', unless *cellán* of this text is to be understood as 'little church'.[3]

1 *HDGP* iii, 158. 2 *Anecd.* ii, 30 §10. 3 *SG* i, 390.

Ceallán of Fancroft (Fionnchoire/Fionnchoradh), parish of Seirkieran, barony of Ballybritt, Co. Offaly. Ceallán son of Neas (Mac Nise), accompanied by a number of other saints, including a brother (Díocaill), two sisters (Lasar and Colum) and another person named Conlaodh Cráibhtheach, 'pious', is the subject of an entry in the corpus of saints' genealogies.[1] The inclusion of Conlaodh, otherwise a bishop at Kildare, points to a Brigidine connection, and this is confirmed by an entry in the list of those subject to Brighid which assigns Mac Nise to Fancroft.[2] Connections such as these may later have encouraged the authorities at Kildare to seek jurisdiction over Seirkieran.[3]

1 *CGSH* §172. 2 *CGSH* §670.65. 3 *OLL* 3, 25–42.

Ceanannach of Ballynakill (Baile na Cille), barony of Ballynahinch, Co. Galway, and of Inishmaan (Inis Meáin) on Aran in the same county. In his account of West Connacht, Roderic O'Flaherty made mention of 'Kennanack', a son of the king of Leinster and patron of both Ballynakill and the 'midle island' of Aran, where the saint's church (Ceall Cheanannach) was described by John O'Donovan as one of the most perfect primitive churches he had seen in Ireland.[1] The saint's day, according to O'Flaherty, was 12 March, otherwise the feast of Pope Gregory the Great, and this coincidence, together with the fact that the memory of the Pope was also kept on the island, led to the assumption that the two saints were identical, and that Ceanannach's real name was Gregory.[2] An independent tradition, influenced no doubt by the belief that the saint's name derives from *ceann*, 'head', maintains that Ceanannach, one of the first preachers of Christianity in the West, was beheaded near the present village of Cleggan.[3] On Inishmaan, the saint's well was known as Tobar na Ceannainne (perhaps from *ceann fionn*, 'fair head') and nearby was another well called Tobar na Cinnirge (perhaps from *ceann dearg*, 'red head'), supposedly named after a daughter of the king of Leinster.[4] There was also a well named after the saint at Letterfrack.[5]

1 *OFWC* 86, 118–19. 2 Ibid. 80, 118–19n.; OSL GY iii, 289. 3 OSL GY iii, 10, 14, 106. 4 *OFWC* 86; *OÁr* 29; *Béaloideas* 4, 390–1. 5 *IER* (5th ser.) 27, 275.

Ceanannán son of Daol (Aol). The genealogists considered this saint to have been a brother of Aoidhghin of Bodoney who belonged to the Oirghialla, of the area now covered approximately by the diocese of Clogher.[1] Though his branch of the family established for him a relationship with the rulers of the Farney or Cremorne area in Monaghan, formerly within Oirghialla, Ceanannán may have been attached to the Patrician church of 'Domhnach Coinre' in Cothraighe, a territory that gave name to the Antrim barony of Cary.[2] John Colgan thought that this church was later represented by Ceall Domhnaigh (Domhnach), presumably now Kildowney in the parish of Ahoghill, but this is in the barony of Lower Toome, at some distance from Cary.[3] Ceanannán is also provided with a sister named Curcach whom early seventeenth-century sources identified as the saint of that name commemorated on 8 March [4] Ceanannán's name is also sometimes written as Ciarán, and the martyrologies commemorate only one saint of the name, at 26 March.[5]

1 *CGSH* §61.2. 2 *BP* 1896–7; *VT* 162. 3 *TT* 182 §201; cf. PNNI iv, 203–4. 4 *GRSH* 73. 5 Ibid.; *MartT* 27; *MartG* 62; *MartD* 88, 304.

Ceann Faoladh of Bangor (Beannchar), barony of Ards Lower, Co. Down. This abbot's name was added to the list of those commemorated on 8 April, probably while the copy of the Hieronymian martyrology that eventually reached Tallaght was still in Bangor.[1] From there, the name continued to appear in later martyrologies, including one compiled in Regensburg in Germany.[2] A signatory to the *cáin* or Law of Adhamhnán, Ceann Faoladh grandson of Aodh Breac died in 705.[3]

1 *FSHIM* 67; *MartT* 31. 2 *FSHIM* 236. 3 *CA* 16; *AU s.a.*; *MartD* 98.

Ceann Faoladh son of Rumhan. *See* Ceallach of Trim.

Ceara. *See* Ciar.

Cearbán. *See* Corbán.

Cearc of Aughlish (Achadh Lis), parish of Ballymore, barony of Orior Lower, Co. Armagh.[1] This daughter of Eirnín is known only from an entry in the corpus of saints' genealogies which states that both she and a saint named Beagrall, although belonging to the Déise of Munster, were sisters of Seanán of Aghacullion (Achadh Caol) in the Down parish of Kilcoo.[2] As has already been speculated in the early seventeenth century, Cearc may be the same as Earc (Earc Nasca), patron of Tullylish (Tulach Lis) which adjoins Ballymore.[3] Earc was commemorated on 12 May.[4]

1 *HDGP* i, 20. 2 Ibid. 13; *CGSH* §92.1–2; *GRSH* 77. 3 *GRSH* 77. 4 *MartT* 42; *MartO*[2] 124; *MartG* 94; *MartD* 124.

Cearc of Nutstown, parish of Ballymadun, barony of Balrothery West, Co. Dublin, which may now represent an earlier Cnoide (Noitte).[1] Cearc was one of three saintly 'virgins' of a once influential north Leinster family named Uí Luascáin, the other two being Taileach, mother of Finnian of Clonard, and Ríoghnach of Kilrainy (Ceall Ríoghnaighe) in the Kildare barony of Carbury.[2] As Finnian is said to have visited the area occupied by the Uí Luascáin during his travels in Leinster, the family's connection with Clonard must have been close.[3] Cú Chearca son of Faolán of the Osraighe is said to have received his name by committing himself to act as Cearc's watchdog for a year, his hounds having killed the saint's own dog.[4] No feastday has been recorded for Cearc.

1 *SS* 254, 264. 2 *CGSH* §166; *CGH* 121a17. 3 *LisL* 2613. 4 *Can.*[2] 58 §217.

Cearc of Tulach, an unidentified church, possibly in the barony of Cremorne, Co. Monaghan. An entry on Ninnidh Láimhiodhan, 'of the pure hand', in the corpus of saints' pedigrees states that Cearc (alias Searc) daughter of Eacha was his sister.[1] She was of the Ceinéal Laoghaire of Meath, and a tract on the saints of this family locates her variously at both Tulach and Teach na hEarfhoclaighe (later Teach Laoighe) in Mughdhorna, a territory mainly in Monaghan (Cremorne), but also extending into adjoining parts of Louth and north Meath.[2] One seventeenth-century source speculatively identifies Cearc with a saint named Cearclach, whose feast fell on 6 January.[3] The saint's name may be preserved in the townland name Ardkirk, parish of Donaghmoyne, on Monaghan's boundary with Louth.[4]

1 *CGSH* §22; *GRSH* 50; *Lgen.* 706.3. 2 *CGSH* §690.17; *BLec.* 62vd9–11. 3 *GRSH* 50. 4 *ClRec.* 20, 580.

Ceasán of Cloncasson (Cluain Ceasáin), parish of Clonsast, barony of Coolestown, Co. Offaly. This saint figures in two medieval tales, *Altram Tighe Dá Mheadhar* (fosterage of the house of two methers) and *Agallamh na Seanórach* (colloquy of the ancients), both of which describe him as a son of the king of Scotland and priest of the *mensa*, or *sagart méise*, 'mensal priest', of Patrick of Armagh.[1] He is said to have abandoned a church named Ceall Eithne at Newgrange in the parish of Monknewtown, by the river Boyne, and founded the church named after him at Cloncasson, where his coming was allegedly foretold by Fionn son of Cumhall.[2] He may be the same as Ceathán, a priest in the list of those in orders with Patrick.[3] The saint named Ceasán who figures among the many children of Inghean Bhaoith of Killinaboy in Clare is placed *ag altóir*, 'at an altar', a term for which *mias* (*mensa*) was also used.[4] It has also been suggested that he was identical with Ceasóg (Kessock), who was especially associated with Luss on Loch Lomond in Scotland.[5] The Office Life provided for this latter saint at 10 March in the Breviary of Aberdeen states that he was born into a royal family in Cashel of Munster, where he performed some miracles before moving to Scotland.[6]

1 *Ériu* 11, 203; *ZCP* 18, 226; AgS i, 41. 2 *AgS* i, 41–2. 3 *CGSH* §672.8. 4 *IrT* iv, 93. 5 *CPNS* 277–8; *KSS* 373–4; *ACDS* 136–8. 6 *BrevA* pars hiem. 66v–67; *LegSS* 76–9.

CEATHÁN, *cruimhthear*, 'presbyter'. *See* Ceasán.

CEDUS. *See* Caoide of Churchtown.

CÉILE CRÍOST of Kilteel (Ceall Chéile Chríost), barony of South Salt, Co. Kildare. The corpus of saints' genealogies attaches Céile Críost son of Eacha, along with a brother named Comhghall, to the Ceinéal Eoghain of mid-Ulster.[1] In keeping with this descent, Comhghall's church was located in the parish of Culdaff on the Inishowen (Inis Eoghain) peninsula in Donegal. Céile Críost's church in Uí Dhúnchadha of north Leinster – now mainly south Dublin and north Kildare – was probably the ecclesiastical site in the townland of Kilteel Upper.[2] Little else is known of Céile Críost, but a note added to the Franciscan copy of the Martyrology of Aonghas credits him with giving good advice to his companions on how to gain release from a temple in Rome.[3] According to the annals, Céile Críost died in 727, and he was remembered on 3 March, not only in native sources, but also, under the guise of Kelanus, in some post-Conquest liturgical manuscripts.[4]

1 *CGSH* §279; *Lgen.* 702.7.8. 2 *HDGP* iii, 141. 3 *FLK Cat.* MS A 7, 11v. 4 *MartT* 20; *MartO*[2] 80, 86, *MartG* 46; *MartD* 62; *AU*/ATig. *s.a.*; *Rep. Nov.* 2, 46, 48.

CEILLSEACH of Áth na gCeall, a site in the townland of Gortnagross, probably at or near Longfield's Bridge on the river Blackwater, in the parish of Ballyclogh, barony of Duhallow, Co. Cork.[1] Together with her six brothers, who included Laichtín of Freshford, and six sisters, among them Céirseach, Coircseach, Cróinseach and Soidhealbh, Ceillseach daughter of Tairbhín is said to have belonged to the people known as Múscraighe who gave name to the barony of Muskerry in Cork, among other places.[1] The saint's church lay on the bank of the river Blackwater, two miles or so west of Mallow, on the boundary of a people known as Tuath Ua bhFiannadhaigh, and close to the church of Cránaid of Kilcranathan.[2] Neither Ceillseach nor any of her siblings figures in the Life written for Cránaid.[3] However, her sister Soidhealbh may be the saint so named who, together with Laichtín and numerous other Munster saints, is called upon, in a poem in Classical Irish, to help in releasing Ireland's southern half (Leath Mogha) from a bondage imposed on it by the northern half (Leath Chuinn), represented by Finnian of Clonard.[4]

1 *CGSH* §666.1.2; *Lgen.* 752.2. 2 *CrC*[1] §8. 3 *MHH* 157–69. 4 RIA MS 23L11, 263.

CÉIRSEACH daughter of Tairbhín. *See* Ceillseach.

CEITHEACH of Oran. *See* Beinéan of Kilbennan.

CELSUS. *See* Ceallach of Armagh.

CHAD. *See* Caoide.

CHRISTIANUS. *See* Giolla Críost.

CIAN of Knockeyon (Cnoc Céin?), parish of Faughalstown, barony of Fore, Co. Westmeath. Situated on the hill of Knockeyon was an 'ancient chapel' dedicated, according to Sir Henry Piers in 1682, to a saint named 'Eyen or Keyen'.[1]

According to the same authority a pilgrimage was made to the site on the first Sunday in harvest, and this reference to the beginning of August is corroborated in other accounts.[2] As Cian was the father of Lugh, whence *Lughnasa* (*Lúnasa*), the Irish name for August, the saint so-named is probably intended by the form 'Keyen'. Also on this hill, near the pilgrimage site, was 'St Coragh's or Coiragh's Well', named after an abbot of Kells in Co. Kilkenny who, having sinned with a woman, retired to the hill as a hermit.[3] This man's name may reflect the Irish form *Cobhuir* (*Cobhrach*?). A saint of the name Cobhuir was remembered on 30 July, and again, under the diminutive guise of Cobhrán, on 2 August.[4]

1 *FL* 132; OSL WH ii, 289. **2** OSL WH ii, 294; *FL* 133. **3** *FL* 133. **4** *MartT* 59; *MartG* 146, 148; *MartD* 204, 208.

Cianán of Duleek (Daimhliag), barony of Lower Duleek, Co. Meath. In keeping with the location of his church, this bishop's pedigree attaches him to the Cianachta of Breagha, originally located in the area about Duleek, later also extending into Louth.[1] In the Tripartite Life, Patrick is said, however, to have met Cianán's father Séadna in Cianachta of Dungiven, now Keenaght in Derry, and blessed the child in the womb of his mother, who is named Eithne, niece of Eoghan, eponym of the Eoghanachta, in the office Life of the saint.[2] In a version of the Tripartite Life preserved in John Colgan's Latin translation, Patrick's escape route from captivity allegedly took him to the river Boyne, where a man named Cianán 'Senior' (alias Seanchianán) sold him to some merchants for a copper cauldron before repenting and converting.[3] That this was the Duleek saint under another guise is indicated not only by the name, but also by his attribute of a copper vessel which is a recurrent feature of the cult. In the Life of Ailbhe of Emly, which describes Cianán as one of the Emly saint's companions, the Duleek saint's *puer*, 'boy', is said to have misappropriated a copper vessel from the church of Sincheall Cam, only to be discovered by Ailbhe.[4]

In one of the best-known tales relating to Cianán, it is said that the remarkably preserved state of his body was because of his having bathed, together with Cairneach of Dulane, in a bottomless vessel.[5] Mochua of Timahoe, whose Life asserts that he consecrated the church at Duleek (newly built in stone as opposed to the timber structures that were fashionable up to then), is among others associated with Cianán.[6] The saint is also said to have presented a copy of the gospels to Patrick, and made a copy of his rule for the Armagh saint, who reciprocated.[7] After death, Cianán allegedly made a union with Colum Cille while the latter was standing at his tomb.[8] The saint was among those invoked as guarantors of the Law of Adhamhnán, and his name is also invoked in a poem attributed to Moling.[9] The 'riotous' rule at Duleek, and its effect on the surrounding area, are, however, lamented in a late medieval poem of prophecies.[10]

Though Cianán's main feast fell on 24 November, his name is also found in the lists for other days, including 19 November (Mochian), 29 November, and 25 February.[11] His feast of 24 November was recorded in an early ninth-century calendar kept by an Irishman on the Reichenau in Lake Constance.[12] According to the annals he died in 489 which would make him a contemporary of Patrick, and his body reputedly remained incorrupt over at least five hundred years after his death.[13] The correspondence between Cianán's name and that of his people (Cianachta), together with the persistence of his association with a marvellous vessel, indicate, however, that he originated as an ancestral deity. In one version of the descent of the Celtic god Lugh, who is likewise associated with a remarkable vessel, his father is named Cian, whence the diminutive Cianán.[14]

1 *CGSH* §195; *GRSH* 123; *Lgen.* 739.10; *HDGP* iv, 138; *DIB* ii, 512–13. **2** *BP* 1860–4; *VT* 160; *AB* 73, 363–71. **3** *VT* 22 (= *TT* 120); *LH* i, 98; *TLSP* 85. **4** *VSHH* 126 §33. **5** *MartO*[2] 244; *AB* 73, 368–9. **6** *VSHP* ii, 187–8; *AB* 73, 367–8. **7** *BCC* 166; *AU s.a.* 489. **8** *MartO*[2] 244; *BCC* 166. **9** *CA* §22. **10** *Ériu* 18, 60 §12; *Anecd.* ii, 28 §1. **11** *MartO*[2] 236; *MartG* 224; *MartD* 314. **12** *AfL* 31, 63. **13** *AU s.a.*; *WBP* 62 §15. **14** ITS 58, 34 §§6–7.

Ciar daughter of Ciarán. *See* Miodhan of Clonfad.

Ciar of Achadh Í, perhaps an ecclesiastical site in the parish of Fahy, barony of Longford, Co. Galway.[1] Ciar son of Aimrid is assigned to the Ciarraighe, the descendants of Ciar son of Fearghas, which would suggest that he originated as an ancestral deity.[2] Ciar's church lay close to Clonfert whose patron, the celebrated Bréanainn, also belonged to the Ciarraighe. According to another entry in the corpus of saints' pedigrees, Ciar shared Achadh Í with a saint named Mac Í (alias Colmán or Conna).[3] Some sources take him to have been identical with Mochiaróg – also known as both Mochuaróg and Ciarán – who was commemorated on 7 May, perhaps at Doire Eachdhroma in Magh Mhucramha, to the west of Athenry in Galway.[4]

1 *HDGP* i, 19. **2** *CGSH* 134; *GRSH* 107; *Lgen.* 732.13; *CGH* 160a40, 41. **3** *CGSH* §302. **4** *MartG* 92; *MartO*[2] 130; *MartD* 120; *CGSH* §707.347.

Ciar of Donaghmoyne. *See* Lasair of.

Ciar of Kilkeary (Ceall Chéire), barony of Upper Ormond, Co. Tipperary. Also known as Ciar Asgadh and Ceara, this saint was regarded as one of three holy virgins of the descendants of Conaire (otherwise the family group known as Múscraighe), the other two being Gobnaid and Sciath daughter of Meachar.[1] The Múscraighe were settled in various parts of Munster, including Upper Ormond, and Ciar's pedigree attaches her more particularly to a local family known as Uí Chainnigh.[2] Her father's name is variously given as Colla and Dubh Ré, and she is included as the latter's daughter among the saints subject to Brighid.[3] Dubh Ré is also the name given to her father in the entry on her two feastdays of 5 January and 16 October, the second of which may have been influenced by the presence of an African saint named Caera in the Roman list of the day.[4] A note added to the October feast in one source describes her as the mother of the children of Dubh in Magh Asgadh, where her church was located.[5] Under the guise of Ceara, she was wrongly taken by a Cork scribe to be the patron of Kilcrea (Ceall Chré) in the parish of Desertmore, near Ballincollig.[6] A passage in the Life of Munna of Taghmon credits Ciar with a prior foundation at Teach Teille, now Tihelly in the Offaly parish of Durrow.[7] The Life of Bréanainn of Clonfert describes how Ciar extinguished an infernal fire raging in Múscraighe Tíre, where her church lay.[8] A litany-style prayer of invocation includes Ciar among many other female saints.[9] Ciar died, according to the annals, in 681.[10]

1 *CGSH* §665.2.6; *DIB* ii, 513. 2 *CGSH* §403. 3 Ibid. §670.21; *Lgen.* 752.28. 4 *MartT* 5, 80; *MartO²* 44, 216; *MartG* 8, 196; *MartD* 6, 278; *Ainm* 3, 3. 5 *MartG* 196. 6 Maynooth MS M 84, 228. 7 *VSHH* 201 §13; *VSHP* ii, 230–1 §12. 8 *VSHP* i, 145. 9 *MartT* 108; *IrL* 92. 10 *ATig s.a.* 680.

Ciarán. The name Ciarán, from *ciar*, 'dark or tan', was borne, according to the list of homonymous Irish saints, by over twenty (reputedly distinct) saints, of whom only the first two – Ciarán son of Beoaidh, the *saor*, 'artisan', and Ciarán son of Luaighne (Laighne), patrons of the Offaly churches of Clonmacnoise and Seirkieran – attained prominence.[1] Some thirteen bearers of the name also figure in the martyrologies. As well as being used of the eponymous ancestor of the Ciarraighe tribal group (hence *Ciarraighe*, 'Kerry'), the name was also attached, albeit without the diminutive ending *-án*, to a number of female saints. As in most cases of homonymy, some if not all of those named Ciarán probably represented localizations of a single original cult but, where sufficient documentation has survived, the saints are treated here as distinct. Many are known only through their churches which, according to the previously mentioned lists, included: Tullyard (Ard Eo) in the Meath parish of Trim; Clonenagh (Cluain Eidhneach) in Laois; Annaghdown (Eanach Dúin) in Galway, near which, in the townland of Carrowbeg, parish of Killursa, there was a holy well dedicated to Ciarán of Clonmacnoise; Faithche, now either Faheeran in the Offaly parish of Kilcumreragh, or Fahy in Galway, where he may have been venerated under the guise of Mochiaróg; and various other unidentified locations such as Diorchaill, and Druim Iarainn.[2] Others in the list are known only by the names of their fathers, which include Cumascach, Fiontan, and Seanach. Ciarán is accompanied by Bréanainn at two of these sites, namely Tullyard and Annaghdown. Among the churches named in the martyrologies that have not been identified are Ros Cumhalcha, Teach Ua nGoirteach, and Uaimh. Because the later martyrologies sometimes assign saints, unattached in the earlier record, to churches named in the annals, the Ciarán located in Raymoghy (Ráith Maighe Aonaigh) in the list for 8 October may have been borrowed from an annal entry for 784.[3]

1 *CGSH* §707.339–59. 2 Ibid.; OSL GY i, 181. 3 *AU s.a.*

Ciarán of Castlekeeran (Bealach Dúin), barony of Upper Kells, Co. Meath. Apart from the preservation of his pedigree, which provides him (through his father Caorthann) with a descent from Fiacha Araidhe of north-east Ulster, little is known of Ciarán.[1] Yet he is said to have been an author who wrote about Patrick and also, supposedly, about Muircheartach son of Earc.[2] A 'laughable' tradition recorded in 1836 by John O'Donovan maintained that some of the High Crosses at Kells had been originally made for Castlekeeran before being carried away by Colum Cille under cover of night.[3] Local tradition held that the site was chosen as the last resting place of Féichín of Fore.[4] The notice of Ciarán's death in 775, a much later date than most saints in the Irish tradition, including Colum Cille (†595), describes him as *cráibhtheach*, 'pious'.[5] His feast was celebrated on 14 June, and two days earlier according to the Martyrology of Turin, which may reflect practice at the church of Templekeeran in the Meath barony of Skreen.[6] He may also have been patron of the adjoining parish of Munterconnaught in the Cavan barony of Castlerahan.[7] Finally, since the parish named after him is separated by one parish only from that of Teltown, he may well be the Ciarán named as one of three saintly guarantors of the famous assembly held in the latter parish.[8]

1 *CGSH* §466; *GRSH* 99. **2** *BP* 635–9; *VT* 60; *AMME* 991–2. **3** OSL MH 19–21. **4** *PNW* 65. **5** *AU s.a.* **6** *MartT* 50; *MartG* 116; *MartD* 170; *FIM* 128–9. **7** *Breifne* 4, 203. **8** *MD* iv, 158.

Ciarán of Clonmacnoise (Cluain Mac Nóis), barony of Garrycastle, Co. Offaly. The Clonmacnoise saint is more prominent in the hagiographical record than his namesake, Ciarán of Seirkieran, largely because of the outstanding role of his church as a centre of cultural and politico-ecclesiastical activity up to the end of the twelfth century.[1] Through his father Beoaidh (also Beodhán and Beonaidh), the saint is attached to the descendants of the Ulster hero, Fearghas son of Róch, and more specifically to the Latharna Molt who gave name to Larne in Antrim.[2] Variant versions of his descent have him belong either to the Corca Bhaiscinn or Corca Modhruadh of Clare.[3] His father Beoaidh, a *saor*, 'craftsman, artisan', whence Ciarán's frequent designation as Mac an tSaoir, is said to have spent some time in captivity in Wales before escaping back to Ireland, first to Ceinéal Conaill (Donegal), then to Ráith Chriomhthainn between Roscommon and Boyle (in the parish of Fuerty, according to local memory) close to the heartland of Connacht kingship, where Ciarán is said to have been born.[4] His mother Dairearca, while sometimes taken to have been Patrick's sister of that name, is in one instance traced through a father named Earcán to the Ciarraighe of Iorluachair, possibly because of devotion to Dairearca in south Kerry.[5] She is also said to have met Ciarán's father in 'Ceinéal Fiachrach', which may represent a slightly corrupt form of Ceinéal Fiachach (later 'Kenaliagh') of the Westmeath barony of Moycashel.[6] Ciarán is described as the third child of eight, but little is recorded of his siblings beyond their names.[7] The belief that the saint was born on the plain of Connacht in Roscommon probably reflects both the position of his main church on the boundary of Connacht and the power of the kings of that province during the second half of the twelfth century, when the tradition may have been first recorded.

Several (as yet unevaluated) Lives were written for the saint in Latin and Irish. The Latin text is preserved in three recensions, the Irish in one only.[8] It has been suggested that the 'primitive' or original Life was written not later than the ninth century, but this seems far too early for a text which, to judge by the longer recension in the Marsh's Library manuscript, is replete with associations that point to the twelfth century at the earliest.[9] Much prominence is given by the Life to Finnian of Clonard, whose church rivalled Clonmacnoise for primacy among the churches of the kingdom of Meath, each becoming a diocesan centre, and sharing between them jurisdiction over the lands of the kingdom. Ciarán is said to have attended the famous school run by Finnian, who foretold that his pupil's authority would extend over 'half of Ireland'.[10] Ciarán is also assigned a critical role in the story of a house of nuns at Clonard, which probably reflects the founding there of St Mary's, a house of Augustinian nuns, by Murchadh Ua Maoil Sheachlainn (†1153), king of Meath.[11] One of Murchadh's daughters (Agnes) became abbess of St Mary's, while another (Dearbhfhorgaill) rebuilt the Nuns' Church at Clonmacnoise in 1167.[12] In the absence of a full investigation of the Life, associations such as these may be taken as indicators of a (late) twelfth-century date.

It can scarcely be ignored that both Clonmacnoise and Clonard hosted houses of Augustinian canons.[13] There are at least three other likely traces of Augustinian involvement in the composition of the surviving fuller form of the Life: the choice of Ciarán's first teacher, Diarmuid of Inchcleraun in the Longford parish of Cashel, home to a priory of canons on Lough Ree; the saint's possession of (and sojourn in) Hareisland (Inis Aínghin) in the Westmeath parish of Bunown, likewise the site of a house of canons on Lough Ree; and the assertion that Ciarán returned from the dead to exchange vestments and establish a *fraternitas* with Caoimhghin of Glendalough, where the canons also had a priory.[14] Among other saints brought into contact with Ciarán were Seanán of Scattery Island, Ciarán of Seirkieran, Colum Cille, Bréanainn of Birr, and Aona of Laoighis, reputedly the saint's immediate successor at Clonmacnoise, and among the kings associated with him was Diarmuid son of Cearbhall.[15]

Such was its importance that Ciarán's church – founded, according to the annals, in 548 – finds mention in the earliest part of the hagiographical record. Adhamhnán's seventh-century Life of Colum Cille gives an account of how its subject, while dwelling in Durrow, paid a visit to Clonmacnoise, where he was given a welcome warm enough to suggest that there was then a close relationship between the two churches.[16] Clonmacnoise is also featured in the seventh-century Life of Patrick by Tíreachán, who maintained that it forcibly held several churches rightly belonging to Armagh, but the same author states that Ciarán was baptized by a disciple of Patrick named Iustus who had previously baptized the people of Uí Mhaine.[17] A legendary dun cow associated with Ciarán, named *Odhar Chiaráin*, is commemorated in the name of the earliest surviving vernacular manuscript, *Leabhar na hUidhre*, 'Book of the Dun Cow', compiled at Clonmacnoise in the late eleventh century.[18] Another relic, known as *adhart Chiaráin*, 'Ciarán's pillow', is featured in the story of how Cairbre Crom, a king of Connacht, was restored to life.[19]

In manners, the saint is said to have resembled John the Apostle, and such was the spread of devotion to him that other saints are said to have brought about his early death by fasting against him.[20] His age at death, which occurred, according to the annals, in 549, is put, Christ-like, at thirty-three, and his feast fell on 9 September, a day shared, coincidentally, with a saint bearing his mother's name, Dairearca, and which came to be regarded as the day of arrival in Ireland of the barnacle goose.[21] At Hareisland in the parish of Bunown, the saint's former patronage was replaced by that of the Blessed Virgin, but rounds continued to be performed on 8 September, not only the feast of Mary's birth, but also the vigil of Ciarán's day.[22] Together with Colum Cille, the saint was remembered as patron on Inchmore in the Longford parish of Abbeylara.[23] He was also patron of Clonbern (earlier Both Chiaráin) in the Galway barony of Ballymoe, of Kilkieran in the Galway parish of Moyrus, where the *turas* to his well is still made, and of Addergoole in the Mayo barony of Tirawley.[24] The Register of the diocesan see of Clogher ranked him among its bishops.[25] Perhaps because of Colum Cille's reputedly high regard for him, Ciarán was also widely venerated in Scotland.[26] Among the early sources to notice the saint's feast is the Martyrology of Usuard, compiled at Saint-Germain in Paris about 865, which otherwise contains few Irish saints, and an early ninth-century calendar kept by an Irishman on the Reichenau in Lake Constance.[27] Ciarán's church at Clonmacnoise was reputedly where the muster of the men of Ireland was to take place on the day of judgement.[28] The considerable extent of the church's possessions (or alleged possessions) is set out in a Registry which survived in a translation made in the seventeenth century.[29] Long after his lifetime, Ciarán's word was considered powerful enough to ensure that no chieftain of Leyny (Luighne) in Sligo died in bed, at least until 1151, when Conchubhar Ua hEaghra died under the protection of Ciarán's Law (*cáin*), which had previously been proclaimed in Connacht in 744, 788 and 814.[30] A relic of his, a gapped bell known as *Bearnán Ciaráin*, was rung on occasion to register the community's disapproval of the actions of lay rulers.[31] About the same time, several other relics of the saint, including his altar, his crozier (*Óireanach*), and what may have been his gospel-book (*Matha Mór*), were used to provide protection for an Ua Maoil Sheachlainn ruler of Midhe.[32] Relics of the saint also found their way to the Continent, among other places to Sens and, arguably, either Ferrières in France or the Rhineland.[33] Finally, his coarb at Aghkeran in the Roscommon parish of Fuerty was among those entitled to be present at the inauguration of the king of Connacht.[34]

1 *CSt* i, 47–9; *CCLC*; *DIB* ii, 513–14. **2** *CGSH* §125.1.2; *GRSH* 109; *Lgen*. 730.1–2. **3** *CGSH* §125.1. **4** Ibid. §125.2; OSL RN i, 127. **5** *CGSH* §722.16; *VSHH* 78; *MartD* 240; *LisL* 3989. **6** *LisL* 3989–4000. **7** *VSHP* i, 200. **8** *MHH* 183–4, 239; *Kenney* 378–80. **9** *Kenney* 379; *CCLC* 16–22; *VSHP* i, 200–16. **10** *VSHH* 80 §12; *VSHP* i, 205 §15, 206 §17. **11** *VSHP* i, 206 §16; *MRHI* 314–15. **12** *MRHI* 314–15. **13** *MRHI* 163–5. **14** *VSHP* i, 201 §4, 210–11 §§25–6, 28, 215 §32; *MRHI* 177–8; *AClon*. 82. **15** *VSHP* i, 208 §22, 210 §26, 212–13 §30, 215 §33; *Ériu* 6, 159–60; ibid. 19, 64 §25; *ApalF* 166–7. **16** *VC*[2] 14a–15b; cf. *LH* i, 157. **17** *PTBA* 142 §25.2; 146 §28.24. **18** *VSHP* i, 205 §15; *LU* ix–xiii; *Éigse* 15, 277–88; *TromG* 1282–4. **19** *ACL* iii, 224–5. **20** *CGSH* §712.6; *AB* 69, 104; *Éigse* 2, 183–6. **21** *AU s.a.*; *VSHP* i, 215 §32; *MartT* 69, 96; *MartO*[2] 193; *MartG* 172; *MartD* 240–2; *ÉtC* 17, 199 §5; cf. *JACAS* ii, 3–16; cf. *AU s.a.* 512. **22** *PNW* 4. **23** OSL LD 8. **24** OSL MO ii, 179; *GYHS* 812–13; *OFWC* 97. **25** *ClRec*. 7, 382. **26** *CPNS* 278; *KSS* 435–6; *ACDS* 86–8. **27** *MartU* 300; *AfL* 31, 58. **28** *SGS* 3, 75 §2. **29** *RClon*. (= *JRSAI* 1, 444–60); *CCLC*. **30** *AFM s.a.*; *AU s.a.* **31** ATig. *s.a.* 1043; *EMH* 481 §212. **32** *AFM s.a.* 1143. **33** *MNSAF* 138; *EIRD* 55–68; *RIW* 15–19. **34** *MSPAG* 189.

Ciarán of Clonsast. *See* Ciarán of Seirkieran; Coga.

Ciarán of Errigal (Aireagal Ciaróg), parish of Errigal Keerogue, barony of Clogher, Co. Tyrone. This saint, whose name was subject to various permutations, including the forms Ciaróg, Dochiaróg and Dosheanchiaróg, is known mainly from the list of homonymous saints.[1] Yet his church appears to have attained sufficient importance in the early ninth century to gain three mentions in the annals of the period.[2] One of these attributes to the saint a prophecy concerning an important battle fought in 825 at a place, apparently near the saint's church, called Leath Caim.[3] Later, the saint's *bachall*, 'staff', was among the relics captured by the 'Foreigners' under John de Courcy at Downpatrick in 1178.[4] The form 'Aghorogus', provided by Bishop Montgomery for the patron of Ballybogan in the Donegal parish of Clonleigh, may also represent Dochiaróg.[5]

1 *CGSH* §707.358; *HDGP* i, 44. **2** *AU s.a.* 810; *CS s.a.* 827; *AFM s.a.* 825, 837. **3** *AFM s.a.* 825; *JCHAS* 113, 134–6. **4** *MIA s.a.*; *MartD* xxxi. **5** *DYHS* 196.

Ciarán of Rostellan (Ros Gialláin), barony of Imokilly, Co. Cork. This saint is known from one source only, the early thirteenth-century Latin Life of Mochuda.[1] This relates how the founder of Lismore came into south Munster with a few companions, visiting while there Ciarán son of Fiontan (who is described as a bishop) at Rostellan, and asking him for advice on where to found his own church. Inspired by the spirit of prophecy, Ciarán replied that Mochuda should first journey into the lands of the Uí Néill before returning to south Munster, where he was destined to establish his major foundation. Declining the offer of Mochuda's homage, Ciarán is said to have surrendered his own church to the Lismore saint in perpetuity. This assertion, which is in line with the statement made elsewhere in the Life that Mochuda founded several churches in the vicinity of Cork Harbour, may relate to diocesan tensions between Lismore and Cork.[2]

1 *VSHP* i, 176 §16. **2** Ibid. 184 §29.

Ciarán of Seirkieran (Saighir), barony of Ballybritt, Co. Offaly. The genealogists attached Ciarán to the Osraighe (people of Ossory) through his father Luaighne (also written Laighne), reputedly the son of Rumhann Duach of this people's main line of descent.[1] His mother, Liadhain daughter of Maine Cearr, patron of Killyon (Ceall Liadhaine) in the parish of Drumcullen, near Seirkieran, and perhaps also of Killeane in the west Cork parish of Kilmoe, is said to have belonged to the Corca Laoighdhe of the area now covered by the diocese of Ross in south-west Cork.[2] In his person, therefore, Ciarán exemplified the close relationship thought, on none too clear grounds, to have existed between the Corca Laoighdhe and Osraighe, and this would also explain the presence of some of his churches within the diocese of Ross, at Kilkerranmore and on Clear-island.[3]

It has been stated that there was not among Irish diocesan patrons one whose dates could be fixed with less satisfaction than those of Ciarán.[4] This does not seem to have deterred his biographers who provided him with seven Latin and Irish versions of his Life, the latest of which, a vernacular version compiled probably in the seventeenth century, is preserved in numerous modern manuscripts.[5] Despite a recent attempt to date the original Life to as early as the mid-eighth century, it may have been written no earlier than the thirteenth, against the background of a church which, because it was physically separated from its diocese (Ossory), had become a bone of contention.[6] Arguably, there were two recensions of the Life, one written in the interests of the diocese of

Ossory, the other reflective of an apparent Kildare attempt to gain control of the saint's church.[7]

The saint was traditionally regarded not only as Ossory's 'first saint', but also as the first ordained bishop within Ireland as a whole, on the basis that he is said to have been consecrated by the Pope before Patrick – who allegedly gave instructions, which included the sound of a bell, up to then mute, as to where Ciarán should position his church at Seirkieran – ever reached Rome.[8] Ciarán's supposed pre-Patrician status has been shown, however, to belong in the realm of propaganda.[9] Seirkieran was the site of an Augustinian priory, and judging by many episodes in the Life of its saint, the author was a canon regular. Of three churches said to have formed *fraternitas* with Seirkieran, two (Clonmacnoise and Clonfert) had become seats of Augustinian houses by the middle of the twelfth century.[10] This also applied to Lorrha, whose patron Ruadhán was brought to visit Ciarán, and to Clonard, to whose saint (Finnian) Ciarán is said to have gone to school, although already an old man.[11] The oral version of Ciarán's Life recorded in the nineteenth century places the saint first in Fertagh in the parish of Johnstown, which, like Seirkieran, was the seat of a house of canons regular.[12] Although less well known than his Clonmacnoise namesake, Ciarán arguably exercised wider influence abroad through his (groundless) assimilation to the cult of Perran of Perranzabuloe in Cornwall, which led to the adaptation of one version of his Life for use as that of the Cornish saint.[13]

Ciarán was seen as something of a prophet, with a prophecy concerning the arrival of the Vikings in Ireland placed in his mouth.[14] A poem attributed to him extols the virtues of his church at Seirkieran, and an early litany speaks of what may have been a voyage undertaken by him, accompanied by fifteen men.[15] Given his south Clare connections, he may also be intended by the reference to Mac Luighne in a poem on the miracles of Seanán of Scattery.[16] Ciarán's feast of 5 March, kept locally until modern times, and historically observed in many other churches throughout Ossory, including Kilkieran, Rathkieran, Tullaherin and Stonecarthy, is shared by his pupil Carthach, patron, among other places, of the Donegal parish of Kilcar (Ceall Charthaigh), where Ciarán's well used to be the scene of an annual pattern.[17] Ciarán is also patron of Clonsast in the Kildare parish of Kilcock, where he was remembered on 30 April; the parochial church of Kilcock takes name from Coga, a hypocoristic form of Cóch, the name of Ciarán's foster-mother.[18] At the battle of Dún Bolg in 870, the Osraighe are said to have invoked Ciarán in the hope of gaining victory over the Leinstermen who placed their trust in Brighid.[19] A late fourteenth-century papal letter places the church of Ossory under the joint patronage of Ciarán as bishop and Cainneach as abbot and, according to John O'Donovan, in his time the saint was still venerated throughout the diocese of Ossory where people swore 'by his hand, *dar láimh Chiaráin*, and by his name, corrupted to *Parán*'.[20]

1 *CGSH* §288; *GRSH* 93; *Lgen.* 725.5–6; *CGH* 117f3; *DIB* ii, 514. **2** GCL 21–2; OCBG §2079; *VSHP* 217 §1. **3** *IKHK* 180; *CPL* 12, 809; *NCHC* i, 279; *MakS* 84–7; *Béaloideas* 58, 183. **4** *HADO* i, 5. **5** *MHH* 184, 239; *Kenney* 316–17; *OLL* 3, 41–2; *BNCS*; *SPW* 272–80. **6** *OYHS* 131–51; *OLL* 3, 25–42. **7** Ibid. 37–40. **8** *Celtica* 4, 129 §45; *VSHP* i, 218 §3; *BNÉ* i, 103 §4; *EMH* 480 §211. **9** *SSS* 376–99. **10** *VSHP* i, 230 §31;

MRHI 164–5, 194–5. **11** *VSHP* i, 231–2 §§33, 36; *MRHI* 163–4, 185. **12** *HADO* i, 8–9; *MRHI* 176; cf. OSL KK i, 133–4 (134). **13** *AB* 59, 217–71; CornS 29. **14** *Ériu* 18, 60 §8. **15** *ZCP* 13, 13; *IrL* 66. **16** *ZCP* 10, 26 §22. **17** *MartT* 20; *MartO*[2] 80; *MartG* 48; *MartD* 62–4; OSL OY i, 62; OSL KK passim; *Béaloideas* 6, 147. **18** *MartT* 38; *MartG* 86; *MartD* 114; *VSHP* i, 226–7 §§21–3. **19** *FAI* 140. **20** *CPL* 4, 508; *UL Camb. Add.* 622 (1, 2) 25.

Ciarán of Tubbrid (Tiobraid Mac nÉanna, alias Tiobraid Naoi), barony of Iffa and Offa West, Co. Tipperary. Though best known for its association with Geoffrey Keating (Seathrún Céitinn), author of *Foras Feasa ar Éirinn* (History of Ireland), Tubbrid was also the scene of active devotion to a saint named Ciarán son of Eachaidh, as is shown by the name used locally of the church, namely Cillín Ciaráin, 'Ciarán's little church'.[1] Keating mentions the patron of his native parish once only, proudly placing him third after the patrons of Clonmacnoise and Seirkieran in a selection from the many saints named Ciarán.[2] A passage in the Life of Déaglán (Declan) relates how the Ardmore saint insisted on baptizing the infant Ciarán, foretelling his future greatness, which was verified by many signs and miracles, including the founding of Tubbrid.[3] As Tubbrid lay within the diocese of Lismore, the Déise pedigree attached to the saint's namesake (Ciarán son of Brannabh) suggests that, despite the difference in paternal names, the two were originally identical.[4] To complicate matters further, the secular genealogies – which place the latter Ciarán in an unidentified location named Uaramar – state that Brannabh was otherwise known as Breasal.[5] Ciarán also figures in the Life of Tighearnach of Clones, whom he is said to have accompanied to Tours in France, shortly before the latter resuscitated a daughter of the king of Munster named Eithne, possibly the eponym of Temple-etney, near Tubbrid.[6] The list of homonymous saints also refers to Ciarán of Tubbrid, and the martyrologies, including one kept in the Regensburg *Schottenkloster*, commemorate him on 10 November.[7]

1 *WGK* 14–15. **2** *FFÉ* iii, 108. **3** ITS 16, 58. **4** *CGSH* §333. **5** *CGH* 143bc27. **6** *VSHH* 108–9 §§5–9; *VSHP* ii, 263–4 §§5–7. **7** *CGSH* §707.346; *MartG* 214; *MartD* 303; *FSHIM* 242; *MartR* 161.

Ciarán son of Brannabh. *See* Ciarán of Tubbrid.

Ciarán son of Tulchán. When receiving a visit from Cainneach of Kilkenny, Fiontan of Clonenagh allegedly discerned among a group of laymen involved in a killing an innocent voice whose bearer, as he foretold, would become one of his first monks.[1] This was Ciarán son of Tulchán, whose name is also featured in the list of homonymous saints.[2] As there is some evidence to suggest a close relationship between Fiontan and his namesake under hypocoristic guise, Munna son of Tulchán, the latter was probably thought to have had the same father as Ciarán.

1 *VSHH* 149 §14. **2** *CGSH* §707.339.

Cilléan of Aghacullion, parish of Kilcoo, barony of Upper Iveagh, Co. Down, which may now represent an earlier Achadh Caol.[1] Cilléan is known only from an entry in the tract on the mothers of the saints, duplicated in the corpus of saints' pedigrees.[2] This names his mother as Deirinill Cheathairchíochach, 'of the four nipples', and lists his uterine brothers, among whom was Domhanghart of Slieve

Donard. A second brother, Mura of Fahan, shared a feast of 12 March with a saint named Cilléan of Lullymore (Liolchach) in the Kildare barony of Offaly East, a possible double of the Aghacullion saint.[3]

1 *HDGP* i, 13. 2 *CGSH* §162, 722.27. 3 *MartG* 52; *MartD* 74.

Cilléan of Lullymore. *See* Cilléan of Aghacullion.

Cilléan son of Luibhnéan. A person bearing this name is included in the list of those commemorated on 14 April.[1] He is doubtless the abbot of the name who was among the signatories of the *cáin*, 'Law', of Adhamhnán in 697.[2] According to the text of the *cáin*, he was abbot of Birr in Offaly, but this has been disputed.[3]

1 *MartT* 32; *MartG* 76; *MartD* 102. 2 *CA* 16. 3 *Peritia* 1, 187.

Cilléan son of Tolodhrán. *See* Mocheallóg of Kilmallock.

Cillín of Iona, Scotland. Unusually for an early abbot of Iona, who would normally have belonged to the northern kindred of Colum Cille, Cillín's pedigree attaches him through his father Díocaill to the Ceinéal Conaill Chreamhthainne of Meath.[1] Styled anchorite of Iona in his annal obit of 752, and also known as Cilléan Droichteach (literally 'of bridges', but perhaps a translation of Latin *pontifex*, 'bishop, pontiff'), the saint appears to have succeeded to the abbacy of the island monastery after the death of a namesake in 726.[2] One of his first actions as abbot was to travel to Ireland to renew the *cáin* or law of Adhamhnán, allegedly with a view to making peace between the northern families of Ceinéal Conaill – who had a longstanding interest in the abbacy of Iona – and Ceinéal Eoghain.[3] Presumably as a means of strengthening his authority, he brought with him Adhamhnán's relics, and this act is commemorated in a much later poem which provides a detailed account of the relics.[3] Cillín's feast fell on 3 July.[4]

1 *CGSH* §344; *GRSH* 54.1; *AU s.a.* 726, 752. 2 *AU s.a.* 727; *Innes Review* 49, 77–8. 3 *CGSH* §714; *Celtica* 15, 25–41. 4 *MartT* 53; *MartG* 128; *MartD* 184.

Cillín of Tehallan (Teach Taláin), baronies of Cremourne and Monaghan, Co. Monaghan. On entering the territory of Uí Mhéith Thíre, now approximately the barony of Monaghan in the county of the same name, Patrick came to Teach Taláin, now Tehallan, where he left a bishop named Cillín and other followers.[1] 'St Cilian's church' (also known as St Sillian's) is now located in the townland of Templetate.[2] Moreover, Talán is probably the man named as doorman in the metrical list of those in orders with Patrick.[3] Though there is no record of Talán's feast, that of Cillín fell on 27 May.[4]

1 *BP* 2114–16; *VT* 180. 2 *AIMN* 87. 3 *CGSH* §672.10. 4 *MartT* 46; *MartG* 104; *MartD* 138.

Cillín of Uachtar Achaidh, an unidentified church. This son of Diarmuid is known from a list of the saints of Dál Meisin Corb who are generally associated with the area about Glendalough in Wicklow.[1] It has been suggested that he may have been the Cillín son of Diarmuid mentioned among the pedigrees of the Uí Liatháin of Munster, on the grounds that the church of Ceall Faoi, mentioned in the same passage, may refer to a place formerly called Kilfea in the townland of Ballymaghroe, parish of Killiskey, near Glendalough.[2]

1 *CGSH* §181.16. 2 *CGH* 151b26; *CPPI* 54, 188, 207; *PNW* 405–6.

Cinne of Druim Dubháin, now probably Drumgoan in the parish of Magheross, barony of Farney, Co. Monaghan. According to his Tripartite Life, Patrick, having preached for three days and nights in Leamhain, now perhaps Leons in the Monaghan parish of Magheracloone, which adjoins Magheross, raised from the dead Cinne's father, Eacha son of Criomhthann.[1] Eacha, whose son Cairbre Damhairgid died as king of Oirghialla, was persuaded by Patrick to forego his desire to have his daughter wed a man 'of good family', and to allow her instead to become a bride of Christ.[2] Patrick then entrusted Cinne (alias Cionna) as a pupil to Ceachtamair at Druim Dubháin, where both virgins were later buried. As Brighid is said to have fallen asleep during Patrick's marathon sermon at Leamhain, the Cinne venerated on the Kildare saint's feast of 1 February is likely to have been the virgin of Druim Dubháin.[3]

1 *BP* 2052–83; *VT* 176–8. 2 *AU s.a.* 514. 3 *MartT* 14; *MartG* 28; *MartD* 36.

Cionaodh of Killaconnigan, barony of Lune, Co. Meath, which may now represent an earlier Ceall Chonagáin. On a visit to this part of Meath in 1836, John O'Donovan was told that the local patron, 'Kineth, alias Cionnáth', was remembered on 16 November.[1] No such name is to be found on that day, or on any other, in the Irish martyrologies which do, however, commemorate a son of Fionnlugh named Mochonna, a hypocoristic derivative of Colum.[2] As this could also be rendered Conach or, in diminutive form, Conagán, the saint venerated at Killaconnigan could well have been a localized version of Colum Cille, Ireland's most important native saint.[3]

1 OSL MH 174. 2 *MartG* 220; *MartD* 310. 3 *FG* 20–35.

Ciúin. *See* Caolchú of Clooncoose.

Clavin of Kilclonfert. *See* Colmán of Templeshanbo.

Cleithe son of Ceannfhada. *See* Brannabh of Rosbran.

Cloithbheo daughter of Conchobhar. *See* Diarmuid of Castledermot.

Clothach of Díseart Mic Caille, an unidentified church. A group of miscellaneous entries attached to the corpus of saints' pedigrees places Clothach, along with Dairearca, in Díseart Mic Caille.[1] A namesake is included in the list of those commemorated on 3 May, otherwise also the feast of Conlaodh of Kildare.[2] This association, together with the naming of the saint's church after the bishop who placed the veil on Brighid, point to a connection with Kildare.

1 *CGSH* §663.6. 2 *MartT* 39; *MartG* 88; *MartD* 119.

Cneas daughter of Cochmhadh. *See* Neas daughter of Cochmhadh.

Cobhair (Cobhrán, Cobhrach?). *See* Cian of Knockeyen.

Cobhrán son of Éanán. *See* Breacán of Caw; Colmán of Kilmacrenan.

Cobhthach of Achadh Maic, an unidentified church in the Meath territory of Críoch Laoghaire. This saint is said by the genealogists to have been a son of Baodán (Baoth) and a brother of Diarmuid of Derrybrusk (Aireadh Seanaigh) at Lough Erne in Fermanagh.[1] One seventeenth-century source identifies him with the Cobhthach commemorated on 16 September.[2]

1 *CGSH* §§662.52, 690.18; *GRSH* 50; *Lgen.* 707.10; *HDGP* i, 21. 2 *GRSH* 50.

Cobhthach son of Fearghas. The history of the descendants of Íor of north-east Ulster mentions a bishop named Cobhthach, describing him as a son of Corbach, daughter of Maine of the Leinstermen, which would make him a uterine brother of the noted king, Diarmuid son of Cearbhall, and a close relative of Mac Cuilinn of Lusk.[1] This text also attributes to him a miracle involving the turning of a daughter into a son.[2] Since the late twelfth century, Cobhthach has been taken to be identical with the bishop so named in Achadh Cinn (now possibly an ecclesiastical site in the townland of Craigs in the Antrim parish of Ahoghill) who was commemorated on 6 April.[3] According to the annals, this bishop died in 555.[4] While in this part of Ulster, Patrick is said to have founded a church named 'Fótraid', leaving in it two of his people, Díomán the monk and Cobhthach the priest.[5] Colgan suggested that 'Fótraid' might now be represented by Racavan in the barony of Lower Antrim, not far from Craigs, but the other places mentioned in the passage (Armoy and Ramoan) lie much further north.[6] It may be, therefore, that Dunluce, which lies a little east of Armoy, and which contained a church allegedly named after Cuthbert (perhaps from Cathbhadh/ Cobhthach), was intended by Patrick's biographer.[7]

1 *ZCP* 13, 354. 2 Ibid. 359. 3 *MartG* 70; *MartD* 96; DQE 82; PNNI iv, 192–3. 4 *AU*/ATig. *s.a.* 5 *BP* 1892–5; *VT* 162. 6 *TT* 182 §195. 7 *EA* 76–7.

Cobhthach Caol, 'slender', of Drumbo (Druim Bó), barony of Castlereagh Upper, Co. Down. Described as a son of a king of Oirghialla, a group whose lands corresponded approximately to the area now covered by the diocese of Clogher, this saint is said to have occupied Drumbo, along with Mochuma (Cuimín) son of Aodhán.[1] The saint is probably identical with Cobhthach son of Aodh who, according to his pedigree, belonged to the Oirthir segment of the Oirghialla.[2] Among the latter Cobhthach's brothers, according to the same source, were Maighneann of Kilmainham – whose Life preserves the same tradition – Tua and Libhréan.[3] A note added to the pedigree in one seventeenth-century source locates the saint in Aird Uladh, now the Ards Peninsula in Down, and identifies him with the Cobhthach commemorated on 1 July.[4] Despite the preference in some sources for an otherwise unknown Cú Mhaighe, Cobhthach was doubtless also the same as the Cowey (sometimes anglicized Quintin) who gave name to Templecowey and Lough Cowey in the parish of Witter at the end of the Ards Peninsula.[5] Here, several traditions survived concerning the saint's ascetic habits.[6] On this day was also commemorated a saint named Cuimín who is assigned to Nendrum in the parish of Tullynakill, not far from Drumbo and close enough to the Ards Peninsula. Cobhthach's father Aodh is well known. As king of Oirthir and Oirghialla he is reputed to have offered land for a church to Mochta of Louth, only to have it refused on the grounds that the place would one day belong to Colum Cille.[7] Aodh died, according to the annals, in 610 'on pilgrimage at Clonmacnoise', which would place Cobhthach's floruit in the early seventh century.[8]

1 *CGSH* §141. 2 *CGSH* 54; *GRSH* 69; *Lgen.* 713.10. 3 *SG* i, 37. 4 *GRSH* 69. 5 *EA* 25; PNNI ii, 27–9, 37, 127–9, 139–40. 6 *HDC* i, 390–1; ibid. ii, 9–10. 7 *VSHH* 399 §16. 8 *AU s.a.*; *AFM s.a.* 606.

Cocca. *See* Coga.

Cóch. It has been suggested that this name, also written Cuach, was originally borne by an ancestral goddess of the Cauci, a tribe placed by Ptolemy in the Dublin/Wicklow area, and possibly later known as the Uí Chuaich of Uí Bhairrche, a group that had had settlements in Carlow and Wexford.[1] The tribal name is, however, treated as masculine. Among other forms derived from the name are Coga (Cocca) and Cognad (Coccnat).

1 *EIHM* 24–5.

Cóch of Kilcoe (Ceall Chóiche), barony of West Carbery, Co. Cork. An episode in the Life of Ciarán describes how the patron of Seirkieran was accustomed to spend Christmas at the church of his foster-mother Cóch (also written Coinche) which is said to have lain near the south coast.[1] Nearby in the sea was a rock named after Cóch, reputedly because she used to pray there. The name given to her church, Ros Beannchair, could now be represented by Rossmanagher in the Clare parish of Feenagh, but though this is near enough to the Shannon Estuary, it is far from the south coast.[2] It seems, therefore, that Cóch's Cork church may have been intended. This lay within the territory of the Corca Laoighdhe, a people with whom Ciarán had a close association. The saint may also have been patron of the Kildare parish of Kilcock, albeit under the guise of Coga (Cocca), a hypocoristic form of her name. Cóch's feast fell on 29 June.[3]

1 *VSHP* i, 226–7 §§21–3; *AB* 59, 270–1. 2 *VSHP* ii, 339. 3 *MartT* 52; *MartG* 126; *MartD* 182.

Cochmhas. *See* Coincheas.

Coga of Kilcock (Ceall Choga), barony of Ikeathy and Oughterany, Co. Kildare. A note added to the index prepared by Mícheál Ó Cléirigh for the Martyrology of Donegal refers to this saint's church, placing it in Midhe, a day's journey from Dublin.[1] Kilcock on the river Rye, which anciently divided the territory of Midhe (Meath) from Leinster, was doubtless intended. The note goes on to mention the saint's fair, holiday and church (*teampall*), but alas, apart from the inclusion of her name in the list of those commemorated on 6 June, little else is known of Coga.[2] It has been suggested that she was the same as Cóch, foster-mother of Ciarán of Seirkieran, and in support of this, within the parish of Kilcock is a place called Clonsast which may represent the Cluain Sosta assigned by the martyrologies at 30 April to a saint named Ciarán.[3] Kildare devotion to the saint is also attested at

Tobercocka in the parish of Lackagh (barony of Offaly West) and, further afield, she appears to have given name to Kilcoke in the Laois parish of Rathdowney, to Kilcoke in the Tipperary parish of Loughmoe East, and to Kilcock in the Roscommon parish of Kilmore, where her cult probably accompanied that of Brighid, patron of Kilbride in the same parish.[4]

1 *MartD* 378. 2 *MartT* 48; *MartG* 110; *MartD* 146. 3 *MartT* 38; *MartG* 86; *MartD* 114; *AB* 59, 270–1. 4 *JCKAS* 9, 258; OSL RN ii, 38; *CLTÁ* 95.

Cogán son of Colmán. *See* Beagán of Foithearbh Shinill.

Cognad of Urney (Earnaidhe), barony of Strabane Lower, Co. Tyrone. Having offered herself to God, Samhthann of Clonbroney, entered, according to her biographer, the church of Urney, then occupied by a virgin named Cognad, and also associated with Feime daughter of Coireall.[1] Although the church name is common enough, the Tyrone site is probably intended. Cognad is otherwise known from the list of those commemorated on 11 February.[2] Two days later, a namesake and probable double, Cuachnad, was commemorated at a place variously called Ros Fachtna and Ros Ráithe.[3] Cognad is invoked, along with Samhthann, in an early litany.[4]

1 *VSHP* ii, 254 §2. 2 *MartG* 34; *MartD* 46. 3 *MartT* 16; *MartG* 36; *MartD* 48. 4 *MartT* 108; *IrL* 92.

Coib daughter of Neamhnann. *See* Bearchán of Laragh.

Coibhdheanach of Ardstraw (Ard Sratha), barony of Strabane Lower, Co. Tyrone. A bishop of this name and church, who died in 707, is remembered in the martyrologies on 26 November.[1]

1 *AU s.a.; MartG* 226; *MartD* 318.

Coic daughter of Ochmhas. *See* Molua of Kyle.

Coilliodhan of Newry, barony of Lordship of Newry, Co. Down, which may now represent the Ceann Tráchta attached to the saint in the list of those said to have been subject to Brighid of Kildare.[1] Together with Coilliodhan in Ceann Tráchta were seven others – Bairre, Fíonán, Miodhnán, Manchán, and three daughters of Earcdhath – none of whom, much as Coilliodhan himself, appears to be known from other sources. A Brigidine connection with Newry is, however, confirmed by the Life of Dairearca (alias Moninne) whose silver vessel, received from Brighid, was carried by the waters of the river Liffey, first to the sea and then onwards to a lake-edge called *caput litoris* (Ceann Tráchta) four days distant from Kildare, where it was retrieved by a bishop variously named Rónán and Eirbhe (Herbe).[2]

1 *CGSH* §670.63; *Lgen*. 753.29. 2 *VSHH* 87; *PRIA* 28C12, 221.

Coimhgheall daughter of Earnach. *See* Seanán of Scattery Island.

Coimhgheall daughter of Mac Iair. *See* Caol of Kilmainham.

Coimre son of Ceannfhada. *See* Brannabh of Rosbran.

Coincheann daughter of Brónach. *See* Fachtna of Ros Mic Earca.

Coincheann daughter of Miodhghna. *See* Momhaodhóg of Fiddown.

Coincheann of Killagh Abbey (Ceall Achaidh Choinchinn), parish of Kilcolman, barony of Trughanacmy, Co. Kerry. This saint, one of seven descended from Mál son of Dobhtha of the Uí Bhriúin of Roscommon, gave name to the Kerry site.[1] Among Coincheann's relatives were Bearach of Termonbarry and Fionnchú of Brigown. The saint himself was commemorated with Crónán of Roscrea on 28 April and – should Caolachadh be a corrupt form of the name of his church – again on 20 August.[2] The saint's church at Killagh, which later became a house of the canons regular of St Augustine, is said to have been founded by Abán.[3] At some stage, however, it appears to have adopted as patron the saint who gave name to the local parish of Kilcolman.[4]

1 *Lgen.* 242.14, 715.4; *CGSH* §410.1; *HDGP* iii, 120. 2 *MartT* 37, 64; *MartG* 86, 160; *MartD* 224. 3 *VSHP* i, 17; *VSHH* 264; *MRHI* 182. 4 *JCHAS* 64, 41.

Coincheas daughter of Ochmhas. Although the name of Patrick's father Calpornius is well established from the saint's own writings, that of his mother was left to later biographers and genealogists. His earliest biographer (Muirchú) simply gave her the name Concessa, and the ninth-century author of the Tripartite Life, having copied this, added not only that she belonged to the Franks, but also that she was a sister of Martin, by whom the patron of Tours (whose real origins lay in Pannonia, now Hungary) was no doubt intended.[1] The genealogists gratefully accepted this doctrine, albeit with the exception of the author of the tract on the mothers of the saints who, while tracing her origins to the Britons, gave her the name Ondbaiun (alias Gombauin).[2] Despite the fact that Coincheas (alias Concessa, Cochmhas, Cosmos) is reasonably well attested, and despite some attempts to legitimize the tradition, the name is unlikely to have been borne by Patrick's mother.[3]

1 *PTBA* 66; *BP* 83–4; *VT* 8. 2 *CGSH* §§1.1, 722.1. 3 *SaintP* 90–1.

Coinead. *See* Connadh.

Coingealta. This saint is known only from an account of the famous battle of Cúil Dreimhne which relates how 'Coingealta' and other saints of Uí Mhaine, the area now covered by east Galway and south Roscommon, assembled under Bishop Maolán, the probable patron of Kilmoylan in the Galway barony of Clare.[1]

1 *IMN* 22, 5.

Coininghean. *See* Cuach.

Coinleán. *See* Mocheallóg of Inch.

Coircseach daughter of Tairbhín. *See* Ceillseach.

Coireall. This name, also written as Caireall and anglicized Kerrill, may derive from the root *car-*, 'love'. It is used variously of male and female saints, and it is not always possible to distinguish between them. Most are known only from lists that record little more than the bare name. These include the male Coireall Garbh, 'rough', son of Aodh, recorded only in a list of bishops of Ireland, and the female Coireall daughter of Áine, found, along with other female bearers of the name, in the list of homonymous saints.[1]

1 *CGSH* §§704.80, 708.25–31.

Coireall of Clonkeenkerrill (Cluain Caoin Choirill), parish of Clonkeen, barony of Tiaquin, Co. Galway. The saint's church was formerly one of the seven chief churches of the territory of Uí Mhaine, a status that entitled it to considerable tribute, as much as was due to the local churches of Patrick and Greallán.[1] Through his father, Cúrnán, Coireall is said to have belonged to the Soghain whose territory was located in east Galway.[2] Here, according to one late tradition, Coireall headed a community of 717 saints and, when visited by a lady named Cianóg, the wife of a successful nobleman, he foretold for her the birth of three daughters, one of whom (Osnaidh) would bear a daughter named Béibhionn who in turn would give birth to Brian Bóramha (†1014) and his six brothers.[3] This, needless to say, would give the saint a very late and unlikely date. The same tradition refers to Coireall as 'a second Patrick' in Connacht, and this implies that he may have been the saint of that name otherwise regarded as a disciple of Beinéan, Patrick's successor.[4] A separate tradition, already recorded by Tíreachán, refers to the ordination by Patrick's disciples of a bishop named Coireall at Tamhnach, apparently a place in Sligo, now possibly Tawnagh in the parish of Kilshalvy.[5] Since Beinéan is presented as Patrick's companion in this part of the text, the bishop is likely to have been ultimately identical with the patron of Clonkeenkerril, as may also have been the other representatives of the cult in the west of Ireland. These include Coireall of Aran in west Connacht who is among the saints said to have been invoked by Seanán of Scattery Island.[6] Nearer to Scattery, in the parish of Kilrush, the church of Kilcarroll (Ceall Choirill) was probably also named after him.[7] A poem on the numerous saints said to have been children of Inghean Bhaoith of Killinaboy includes Coireall 'noble, fair and just'.[8] A poem of prophecy beginning *Is olc atá Éire anocht*, 'wretched is Ireland tonight', is credited to Coireall son of Crónán, but this may be a forgery by Nicholas O'Kearney.[9] At Clonkeenkerrill, the saint was the subject of a vigorous cult and many tales concerning him survived in oral tradition.[10] His feast was kept locally on 13 June, but the commemoration was apparently held on 17 December at the not too distant church of Lackagh.[11]

1 *TCHyM* 78, 82. 2 *CGSH* §388; *GRSH* 99; *Lgen*. 737.1; *LLLSK* 33. 3 *ZCP* 7, 307–8; ibid. 13, 18–19. 4 *AS*.Nov. iv, 179 §13. 5 *PTBA* 142 §25n.; *BP* 1103–5; *VT* 98; *DEPPP* 343. 6 *ZCP* 10, 26. 7 *HTCC* 80. 8 *IrT* iv, 93 §4. 9 *SAM* 5.1, 130, 132. 10 *LLLSK* 49–64. 11 OSL GY i, 249; cf. *MartT* 50; *MartG* 116; *MartD* 168; OSL SO 251.

Coireall of Kilcurl (Ceall Choirill), parish and barony of Knocktopher, Co. Kilkenny. Bishop Phelan's early seventeenth-century list of patrons of churches in the diocese of Ossory includes 'Kirillus' of Kilcurl, who was remembered on 10 May.[1]

1 *HADO* iv, 29.

Coireall of Meithe. This saint is mentioned in the Life of Daigh of Inishkeen, which describes him as abbot of Meithe.[1] Following a miracle involving the manufacture of a golden altar dropped from heaven, Coireall is said to have become subject to Daigh. The saint is one of a number of bearers of the name, possibly all identical, associated with the Louth/Monaghan area. These include Coireall *oide*, 'tutor', who is mentioned in a poem recording the names of saints associated with Finnian of Dunleer.[2] Also belonging to this area is the female Coireall of an unidentified church named Ceall Aird in the territory of Críoch Rois, located on the bounds of Monaghan, Louth and Meath.[3] This latter saint is recorded in the list of homonymous female saints and, following her transmutation into a male, was taken speculatively in the early seventeenth century to have been a bishop who accompanied Colmán of Lynally.[4]

1 *VSHH* 392 §13. 2 *CGSH* §737.5. 3 *HDGP* iii, 124. 4 *CGSH* §708.29; *MartG* 116 (gloss), *MartD* 168; *BNÉ* i, 169 §8.

Coireall son of Neasan. *See* Beoán of Feighcullen.

Colán son of Colmán. *See* Beagán of Foithearbh Shinill.

Colga of Clonmacnoise (Cluain Mac Nóis), barony of Garrycastle, Co. Offaly. Most of the information on Colga of the Maca Duineachdha derives from what was known as the *Scuab Chrábhaidh*, 'besom of piety', a dolefully prophetic text which was attributed to him.[1] According to a note accompanying this text, Colga was visited by no less a personage than the apostle Paul who conversed with him, assisted him on his journey, and interceded for him at Clonmacnoise, where he was appointed *fear léighinn*, 'school director'. The annals date his death to 796, and the entry for his feast of 20 February in the Martyrology of Donegal implausibly suggests that he may have been identical with Colga of Kilcolgan.[2] He has also been identified with the Colga whose opinions are cited in the ninth-century text known as *The Monastery of Tallaght*.[3]

1 *IrL* xvii–xviii; *MartD* 54; *Kenney* 725–6; *DIB* ii, 661. 2 *AU s.a.*; *MartD* 54. 3 *MT* §56, 65, 81, p. 178.

Colga of Iona, Scotland. Information on this son of Ceallach derives almost entirely from Adhamhnán's Life of Colum Cille. According to this, he was one of the brethren on Iona, and served as a witness to several miracles performed by Colum. These included: a prophecy concerning the fate of an iniquitous layman in Colga's home district; the miraculous cure of his sister and mother by means of rock-salt; and a telepathic intervention that saved a member of the community in faraway Durrow from being injured through a fall from a roof.[1] Given the connection with Iona, the saint is likely to have been ultimately identical with his namesake at Kilcolgan.

1 *VC*² 278, 340, 494.

Colga of Kilcolgan (Ceall Cholgan), barony of Dunkellin, Co. Galway. Colga's genealogy attaches him through his father Aodh to the Uí Fhiachrach of Aidhne who held lands in south Galway and north Clare, approximately co-extensive with the diocese of Kilmacduagh.[1] Colga's church lay within this diocese, as did that of his sister, Faoileann of Killeely, which adjoins Kilcolgan. Patron of the diocese was Colmán (alias Mac Duach), many of whose associations point to his ultimate identity with his namesake, Colum Cille of Iona. Not least among these were Colum's connections with the area covered by the diocese, one of which relates to Colga, then on Iona, who was directed to return to Ireland and question his mother regarding a grave sin concealed by her, but miraculously revealed to Colum Cille.[2] On his return to Iona, Colga was informed about the circumstances of his own death which was to take place after many years as head of a church (Kilcolgan) within his own *patria* (native district). Later, while still on Iona, Colga is said to have been temporarily blinded by the heavenly light of a vision granted to Colum Cille which he witnessed.[3] The tract on the mothers of the saints names Cuilleann as Colga's mother, but it seems from an accompanying quatrain that Colga son of Fáilbhe, king of Cashel, was intended.[4] Some seventeenth-century sources implausibly suggest that the saint may have been identical with his namesake at Clonmacnoise, Colga of the Maca Duineachdha, who was remembered on 20 February.[5]

1 *CGSH* §90; *GRSH* 61; *Lgen.* 711.12. **2** *VC*[2] 240–2. **3** Ibid. 508. **4** *CGSH* §722.69. **5** *MartD* 54; *GRSH* 61.

Colla daughter of Díoma Meann. *See* Ultán of Ardbraccan.

Collán of Stackallan. *See* Colmán of Longfordpass.

Colmha daughter of Comhghall. *See* Bogha.

Colmán. The radical form of this name, i.e. Colum, was capable of generating an extraordinary number of diminutive and pet forms, including *Colla* (*Coille*), *Comma* (*Coimme*), *Conna* (*Coinne*), *Canna* (*Cainne*), *Camma* (*Caimme*, *Cumma*), all of which could be further extended by the use of prefixes (*mo-*, *do-*) or suffixes (*-óg*, *-ín*, *-án*), thus yielding such forms as Mocholla or Mochuille, Mochonna or Dochonna, Mochoinne or Dochoinne, Mochumma, Comán, Conán, and Caimín.[1] Colum Cille's cult spread to almost every corner of the country, and beyond, and as a consequence of the proliferation of by-forms of the name, combined with the strong localizing tendencies evident in the Irish tradition of the saints, many churches formerly associated with the founder of Iona are no longer immediately recognizable as such. What appear to be localized versions of Colum Cille are to be found at the important churches of Terryglass (Colum), Inishcaltra (Caimín), Roscommon (Comán), and Kilkenny (Cainneach), and many other bearers of the name, in one or other of its forms, are also to be regarded as local replications of the Iona cult. Where evidence for this exists, attention will be drawn to it here. For the most part, however, even where the names of the saints' churches are known, these are often now unlocatable. Of the nine churches of Colmán whose names begin with Cluain, for example, seven cannot now be located with any certainty. Given the number of saints involved, with almost 250 named either Colum or Colmán alone in the list of homonymous saints, only those sufficiently well attested are admitted here.[2]

1 *FG* 20–35; *SS* 237–49. **2** *CGSH* §707.75–321.

Colmán of Achadh Í, now perhaps a site in the parish of Fahy, barony of Longford, Co. Galway.[1] This son of Amhairghin is known only from the corpus of saints' pedigrees. Giving preference to an alternate name Mac Í, and providing him with the alias Conna, the genealogist attached Colmán to the Ciarraighe, who held lands not only in the present county of Kerry, but also in Connacht.[2] The saint's church lay within the diocese of Clonfert, whose patron (Bréanainn) also belonged to the Ciarraighe. Sharing with Colmán the occupancy of his church was a man named Ciar (alias Mochiaróg) son of Aimrid.[3]

1 *HDGP* i, 19. **2** *CGSH* §302; *HDGP* iv, 141. **3** *CGSH* §134.

Colmán of Ahamlish (Áth Iomghlaise), barony of Carbury, Co. Sligo. Known only from the later martyrologies which place his feast at 1 November, this son of Fíonán is likely to have been a localization of his namesake, Colum Cille.[1] A traditional connection between Colum and the area is established by the story of the battle of Cúil Dreimhne which maintains that, after the encounter, Colum went to confession to Molaise son of Déaglán, patron of Inishmurray in the parish of Ahamlish.[2] According to this tale, it was Molaise who imposed on Colum a penance of permanent exile.

1 *MartG* 208; *MartD* 290. **2** *BCC* 184 §§180–1; *VC*[1] 287; cf. *AB* 55, 97.

Colmán of Arboe. *See* Colmán of Moray.

Colmán of Ballynacorra. *See* Colmán of Cloyne.

Colmán of Clonard (Cluain Ioraird), barony of Upper Moyfenrath, Co. Meath. Colmán of the Maca Teallaibh is said to have succeeded Finnian as abbot of Clonard, and to have died in 654, the same year as saw the death of his own successor, Oisín Fada.[1] As in the case of Colum Cille and his immediate successor (Baoithín), Colmán shared a feastday (12 December) with his predecessor in addition to the abbot's chair.[2] The story of the expulsion of Mochuda from Rahan presents Colmán in an unfavourable light, as one of those who, having become jealous of Mochuda's success, assisted in expelling him.[3] When one of Mochuda's monks, afflicted by gout, desired to remain on, Colmán is said to have refused him permission, only to have the ailment transferred to his own foot.[4]

1 *AU s.a*; *DIB* ii, 689. **2** *MartG* 236; *MartD* 334. **3** *BNÉ* i, 301 §6. **4** Ibid. 306 §24.

Colmán of Clonee. *See* Colum of Terryglass.

Colmán of Clonkeen. *See* Colmán Cúile of.

Colmán of Clonpriest, barony of Imokilly, Co. Cork, which probably represents an earlier Cluain Bruchais (Bruchas). There are two early sources of information on this saint, the list of homonymous saints which gives his bare name and that of his church, and the notice of his feast of 12 July which he shared with Ultán of Cork, presumably the patron of Caherultan in the parish of Ballyoughtera, not far from Clonpriest.[1] Clonpriest's connection with Cork is separately attested in the Life of Fionnbharr which names Sineall of that church among its subject's pupils.[2] Sineall may be the same as a namesake belonging to the Uí Liatháin of east Cork, whose feast of 15 June was shared by yet another bearer of the name Colmán.[3] There would appear to be no foundation for the assertion in the Martyrology of Donegal that the saint was identical with Colmán son of Lughaidh, son of Aonghas, king of Cashel.[4]

1 *CGSH* §707.306; *MartT* 55; *MartG* 134; *MartD* 192; *RSTA* 200, 319. 2 *BBa.* 76 (l. 287); *MakS* 97–9. 3 *MartT* 50; *MartG* 116. 4 *MartD* 170.

Colmán of Clontibret (Cluain Tiobrad), barony of Cremorne, Co. Monaghan. An entry in the later martyrologies for 30 September marks the memory of Colmán of Clontibret.[1] According to the Martyrology of Tallaght, the same saint was commemorated on 13 June, albeit under the guise of a *cruimhthear*, 'presbyter', named Mochuma.[2] As this day fell within the octave of the feast of Colum Cille on 9 June, the likelihood must be that Colmán was a localization of the Iona saint. Nothing else is known of him, but papal letters refer to the saint as patron of the parish church in Clontibret.[3]

1 *MartG* 186; *MartD* 260. 2 *MartT* 50; cf. corruptly *MartG* 116; *MartD* 168. 3 *CPL* 9, 16 (Dacholmog); ibid. 16 §559.

Colmán of Clontivrin, parish of Clones, barony of Clankelly, Co. Fermanagh. Under the hypocoristic guise of Mocholm, Colmán is known from the list of homonymous saints, which also contains a reference to a namesake at Rosslea (Ros Laoigh) in the same parish as Clontivrin.[1] Colmán's feast fell on 9/10 March.[2]

1 *CGSH* §707.126.194; *Celtica* 1, 80. 2 *MartT* 21; *MartG* 52; *MartD* 72.

Colmán of Cloyne (Cluain Uamha), barony of Imokilly, Co. Cork. Colmán's church first attained more than local importance at the synod of Kells-Mellifont in 1152, when it became the seat of a bishopric.[1] Prior to this, it is scarcely noticed in the annals, three abbots only being recorded for the period before 1000, all of them belonging in the ninth century.[2] Yet, Cloyne's patron, Colmán son of Léinín, unusually for Irish saints, is thought to have left behind his own writings in the form of twenty lines of verse. Both their editor and most recent commentators believe these to have been genuinely composed by the saint.[3] The verse, which exemplifies *nua-chrotha*, 'new metrical forms', is not only religious, but also – curiously for a cleric connected with a southern church – concerned with kings of Tara, and should it date to 565–604, as has been suggested, it would mark the beginning of written literature in the vernacular.

As a noted *athlaoch* – one who abandoned a professional career for a life in religion, allegedly under the influence of Bréanainn of Clonfert – Colmán belonged to a group thought to have been instrumental in bringing writing to bear on orally transmitted native lore.[4] The saint's pedigree attaches him, together with his seven saintly sisters, including Aighleann, mother of Colmán of Myshall, to the descendants of Aonghas Catta, eponym of a rent-paying people called Catraighe.[5] The place-name Midíne, denoting a large area in Cork, including the baronies of Muskerry, is sometimes attached to his name, a distinction he shares with Fionnbharr of Cork.[6]

Despite the importance of his church as a diocesan see, Colmán never became the subject of a Life. He figures, however, in such other Lives as those of Bréanainn of Clonfert and, in one redaction only, Fionnbharr of Cork.[7] Both of these texts postdate the elevation of Cloyne to cathedral status, an event which receives positive mention in Bréanainn's Life. In Fionnbharr's Life, in line with the tendency of every redaction of the text to relegate churches of the diocese of Cloyne to dependent status, Colmán's church is presented as 'subject under the law' to Cork.

The saint's patronymic Léinín is often used to distinguish him – as Mac Léinín – from other bearers of the name Colmán, although, according to one tradition, his father's real name was Colga.[8] There is much about Colmán's career that remains puzzling, not least his involvement with poets, poetry and kings of Tara. A poem addressed to him by Gofraidh Fionn Ó Dálaigh (†1387), a professional poet of the MacCarthys of south Munster, asserts that, when renouncing poetry for orders in the church, Colmán bestowed his metrical skills on his foster-son Dalach, ancestor of the Ó'Daly (Uí Dhálaigh) poets.[9] As the editor points out, this is reminiscent of Colum Cille's championing of the poets, so that Colmán's resemblance to the Iona saint, possibly due to their ultimate identity, does not lie only in their common name. Through Cormac son of Díoma, a monk connected with Iona and Durrow, Colum Cille is said to have become entitled to tribute from the Uí Liatháin, whose territory formed a large part of the area now included in the diocese of Cloyne.[10]

Although not to the same extent as in Colum Cille's case, Colmán's fame as a poet lingered on, as is shown by Cuimín of Connor's tribute to him as a man 'who loved poetry'.[11] A late poem in vindication of the rights claimed in the Cork area for Seanán of Scattery Island, who is elsewhere said to have invoked the assistance of the Cloyne saint, is also attributed to Colmán, and a late (?) tract preserved in the *Leabhar Muimhneach* refers to tribute due to him and his church from every king of Cashel.[12] Local tradition preserved many reminders of the saint, including his wells, tower and rock, and he appears to have also been patron of the neighbouring church of 'Cor' that gave name to Ballynacorra and Middleton (Mainistear na Corann).[13] Colmán's day of birth is said to have been 15 October and his feast fell on 24 November.[14] Under the guise of Mochonóg (Colmán) Uamhach, 'of the cave', the saint was also remembered on 18 November.[15] Born, according to the Annals of Inisfallen, in 528, Colmán died, according to the same source, in 606.[16]

1 *NHI* ix, 293–4; *CCS*; *DIB* ii, 688–9; *HMDC* 5–8. **2** *AFM s.a.* 821, 857, 885. **3** *ZCP* 19, 193–209; *Ériu* 22, 63–5; *CCS* 41–3, 129–32. **4** *VSHP* i, 102, §8; *Anecd.* iii, 60; *LM* 90. **5** *CGSH* §215.1.2; *GRSH* 125; *Lgen.* 743.3. **6** *GRSH* 125. **7** *VSHP* i, 102; *BBa.* 115, 148. **8** *Anecd.* iii, 60. **9** *IBP* 70–2, 242–4; *Béaloideas* 58, 181–2. **10** *VC*[2] 440–6; *VC*[1] 270; *ZCP* 12, 390–2. **11** *ZCP* 1, 64. **12** *LisL* 2103; *ZCP* 10, 28 §23; *LM* 90; cf. *AB* 66, 202–4. **13** *JCHAS* 50, 81; *RSTA* 200; *CCS* 123–6. **14** *MartT* 80; *MartO*[2] 236; *MartG* 224; *MartD* 316. **15** *MartG* 220; *MartD* 312. **16** *AI s.a.*

Colmán of Colmanswell. *See* Colmán of Kilmacduagh.

Colmán of Connahy (Cluain Conachaidh), parish of Grangemaccomb, barony of Fassadinin, Co. Kilkenny. Within the parish of Grangemacomb (a grange of the Cistercian abbey of Jerpoint) is a place called Kilcolman, formerly 'Kilcolemanussin' (Ceall Cholmáin Uisean), and an old road in the area was known as *Bóthar an Chluainín*, 'road of the little Cluain', which may reflect the name of Colmán's church.[1] The saint was remembered on the same day (16 October) as such other bearers of the name as Colmán of Holdenstown (Bealach Buaidhghe) in the Kilkenny parish of Dunbell, and a namesake at Kilroot (near Carrickfergus in Antrim) who is said to have belonged to the family of Ailbhe of Emly.[2] Under the guise of Mochoime (a hypocoristic form of Colum or Colmán), the saint not only gave name to Grangemaccomb, but is also featured in the Life of Mochaomhóg which describes him as a 'disciple' of its subject.[3]

1 *HADO* ii, 192–4, 321. 2 *HADO* ii, 193, iii, 353, 356; *MartT* 80; *MartO²* 216; *MartG* 196; *MartD* 276; *VSHP* i, 54 §20; *VSHH* 124. 3 *VSHP* ii, 179 §29.

Colmán of Conry (Comhrar), barony of Rathconrath, Co. Westmeath. According to the tract on the mothers of the saints, Colmán was a son of Brónach, whose father Míleac is said to have held Patrick in captivity.[1] Colmán was one of three important bearers of the name attached to a triangle of churches in what are now Westmeath and the adjoining part of Offaly, the others being the patrons of Lynn (near Mullingar) and Lynally (near Tullamore).[2] When asked which holy man he would leave in his place, Colum Cille, then about to depart for Scotland, is said to have replied that all three Colmáns would act on his behalf and under his protection.[3] The three are again featured together in the Life of Colmán of Lynn, which gives an account of their visit to Éidchéan of Clonfad.[4] Though reserving his highest praise for the patron of Lynn, Éidchéan referred to Colmán of Conry as *An Conaillech cass*, 'the curly haired man from Conaille (north Louth)', who, he foretold, would be a deacon with the dignity of a priest. Colmán of Conry's' feast fell on 25 September, the vigil of the feast of his probable double, Colmán of Lynally.[5] Some early seventeenth-century sources maintain that the saint was descended from the Clanna Rudhraighe of north-east Ulster, and that he was identical with Colmán of Lynn.[6]

1 *CGSH* §§702.2, 722.92. 2 *MartO²* 136. 3 *BCC* 212 §219. 4 *BCML* §§31–4. 5 *MartT* 74; *MartG* 184; *MartD* 258. 6 *GRSH* 103; *MartD* 172.

Colmán of Coolkeeragh, parish of Clondermot, barony of Tirkeeran, Co. Derry, which may now represent the earlier Cúil Chaoireach attached to Colmán (alias Colmán Beag, 'small') in the list of homonymous saints.[1] Seven holy bishops are elsewhere said to have dwelt in his church.[2] Should Coolkeeragh be intended, then this Colmán, like his namesake at Cromkill in the same parish, would probably represent the cult of Colum Cille, patron of the neighbouring church of Enagh and also of Derry.[3]

1 *CGSH* §707.302. 2 *IrL* 70. 3 *PNCL* 93–4.

Colmán of Craobh. The preparations for the battle of Cúil Dreimhne included, according to one account, the sending by Colum Cille of emissaries to the Uí Mhaine of Connacht in quest of aid.[1] Among these was Colmán of the unidentified church of Craobh, who is described as Colum's kinsman (*fear muintire*). Colmán is said to have subsequently brought the Uí Mhaine to the district between the rivers Dubh and Drobhaois, now approximately the Leitrim parish of Rossinver, where the battle is supposed to have taken place. In fact, the site of the battle may have been at Cooldrumman in the Sligo parish of Drumcliff.

1 *IMN* 22, 6.

Colmán of Cranfield. *See* Tearnóg of Cranfield.

Colmán of Cromkill. *See* Colmán of Coolkeeragh.

Colmán of Derry. *See* Colum Cille.

Colmán of Díseart. *See* Colmán of Killelan.

Colmán of Donaghmore (Domhnach Feimhin), a parish straddling the baronies of Middlethird and Iffa and Offa East, Co. Tipperary. This bearer of the name is known from an entry in the corpus of saints' pedigrees, which attaches him to a tribal group known as Maca Miadhchon.[1] Also associated with the saint's church within the diocese of Lismore was Forannán of the Déise.[2] Adjoining the parish of Donaghmore is that of Colman (formerly Ceall Scéith) which may have taken its name from the saint.[3]

1 *CGSH* §663.2. **2** Ibid. §91.1. **3** *CLTÁ* 233–5.

Colmán of Dromore (Druim Mór), a parish and diocesan see in the barony of Upper Iveagh, Co. Down. The corpus of saints' pedigrees attaches Colmán (alias Mocholmóg) son of Conrathán (or Criomhthann) to the Dál nAraidhe who held lands in south Antrim and adjoining parts of Down.[1] The Life of Colmán likewise provides the saint with a descent from Dál nAraidhe, and this is reiterated in the entry on his feast of 7 June in some martyrologies which use the earlier tribal designation, 'Maccu Arti', i.e. Maca Araidhe.[2] The saint may also be the same as Colmán (alias Mochuma) of the Gaolraighe (Maca Gaoile/Guaile) who held lands in Iveagh.[3]

The saint's 'short and fabulous' Life, preserved only in the *Codex Salmanticensis*, a manuscript probably originally compiled at Clogher in Tyrone, declares in its first chapter that not only Patrick, who is said to have pre-ordained the location of his church, but also Colum Cille prophetically gave account of the saint's future greatness.[4] Caolán of Nendrum in the neighbouring diocese of Down is given the honour of teaching Colmán, and visits are arranged to Ailbhe, representing Munster's pre-eminent church of Emly, where he pursued his studies, and Mac Nise of the church and diocesan see of Connor who received him joyously, and counselled him on where to build his church on the river Lagan, as allegedly foreseen by Patrick.[5] Good relations with the authorities in south Leinster are also underlined by reference to Colmán's resuscitation, assisted by Aodh of Ferns, of a king of that area.[6] The saint is credited with three visits to Rome, on one of which, having been consecrated bishop by the Pope, Colmán is brought to Wales, where he is said to have prophesied the birth of the glorious bishop David.[7] In this way, the author of the Life provided the church of his subject with the best possible credentials, ecclesiastical and secular, thus no doubt improving its bargaining position in Ireland after the English Conquest, especially, perhaps, in its dealings with Cambro-Norman adventurers.[8]

Falling within two days of Colum Cille's day of 9 June, the date of Colmán's feast is an indication of the ultimate identity of the two saints. There are many others, among them the fact that the list for 7 June contains three other homonyms of the Iona saint – Colum *monachus*, 'monk', who is given precedence, Colum *gabha*, 'smith', and Mochoinne, a hypocoristic form of the name.[9] An entry in the list for the octave of Colmán's feast – 15 June – which locates the saint in Dartraighe Choininse, now the Monaghan barony of Dartree, uses the patronymic Corardan (Corodran), resembling the Conrathán of his official pedigree.[10] In the church of Drummully (Druim Ailche), which gave name to a parish partly in the barony of Dartree, but mainly in the Fermanagh barony of Coole, another namesake and probable double was remembered hypocoristically on 4 January under the guise of Mochumma (alias Comán).[11] Closer to Dromore, Colmán was also patron of the Down parish of Kilkeel.[12] The saint's cult is otherwise attested in Salterstown in Louth, where he was remembered on 7 June under the guise of 'Halamog', and this day (or its vigil) was also observed in some Scottish churches.[13] A full office Life of the saint, similar to that in the *Codex Salmanticensis*, is preserved in the Breviary of Aberdeen.[14] In Scotland, he was patron of the church of Inchmahome, Perthshire.[15]

1 *CGSH* §99; *GRSH* 101; *Lgen.* 735.6; *BB* 168bc51–3; *DIB* ii, 688; *SGS* 24, 253–65. **2** *VSHH* 357–60; *MartO²* 139; *MartG* 112; *MartD* 148. **3** *CGSH* §707.131.153.648; cf. PNNI vi, 104. **4** *Kenney* 466; *MirL* 91–100; *VSHH* 357 §1. **5** *VSHH* 357–8 §§3–6. **6** Ibid. 359 §10. **7** Ibid. 359 §§11–12. **8** *ScrV* 41–8. **9** *MartT* 48; *FG* 21–2. **10** *MartT* 50; *MartG* 116; *MartD* 170. **11** *MartT* 4; *MartG* 8; *MartD* 6. **12** *HDC* i, 15–16. **13** OSL LH 138; *CPNS* 279; *KSS* 304–5; PNNI iii, 15–17. **14** *LegSS* 124–9, 327–9. **15** *SGS* 24, 263.

COLMÁN of Drumirrin, parish of Inishkeel, barony of Banagh, Co. Donegal, which may now represent an earlier Druim Iairn. Although known only from the list of homonymous saints, the proximity of the saint's church, if correctly identified, to Glencolumbkille would suggest that Colmán was a double of his namesake Colum Cille.[1]

1 *CGSH* §707.162; cf. Logainm.ie 'Drumirrin'.

COLMÁN of Drumrat (Druim Ráithe), barony of Corran, Co. Sligo. According to his pedigree, Colmán son of Baoth (Baodán) belonged to the Corca Fhear Trí (people of the three male-divinities), alias Corca Thrí, who were located among the Luighne of Connacht, mainly in the Sligo barony of Leyny (Luighne).[1] He is doubtless the same as the Colmán son of Baoth remembered on 9 August with Nathí of Achonry, head of a diocese often named Luighne.[2] He may have shared the patronage of Drumrat with Féichín of Fore whose cult was strong in Sligo.[3] Kilcolman parish in the barony of Coolavin, not far from Drumrat and within the diocese of Achonry, possibly takes its name from him, but Athracht of the adjoining parish of Killaraght appears to have become its patron.

1 *CGSH* §411. **2** *MartT* 61; *MartD* 214. **3** OSL SO, 146.

Colmán of Dunboe (Dún Bó), barony of Coleraine, Co. Derry. This Colmán is known only from the list of homonymous saints.[1] The patron of the parish of Dunboe was Adhamhnán of Iona but, given the Columban influence in the Derry area, it seems likely that Colum Cille was also venerated locally, perhaps under the guise of Colmán.[2]

1 *CGSH* §707.193. 2 *Celtica* 1, 82.

Colmán of Dysart (Gleann Dealmhaic), parish of Pleberstown, barony of Gowran, Co. Kilkenny. The list of homonymous saints mentions this holy man, and the martyrologies, which place his church in Magh Raighne in Osraighe, now a large area in south Kilkenny, state that he was remembered on 5 November.[1] A note added to the feast in the *Leabhar Breac* names his church as Dysart (formerly Díseart Mocholmóg).[2] Adjoining the parish of Pleberstown is that of Columbkille, which leaves little doubt as to the ultimate identity of Colmán of Dysart.

1 *CGSH* §707.308; *MartO*[2] 232; *MartG* 212; *MartD* 298. 2 *MartO*[1] clxviii; *HADO* iv, 277; *OLL* 3, 52.

Colmán of Holdenstown (Bealach Buaidhghe), parish of Dunbell, barony of Gowran, Co. Kilkenny. This saint and his namesake of Clara (Clárach), adjoining Dunbell, were probably one and the same.[1] Colmán was remembered locally on 16 October, the same day as other namesakes and probable doubles, including the patron of a site formerly known as Kilcolman in the modern parish of Connahy in the same county, and the similarly named patron of Kilroot, near Carrickfergus.[2] The latter representative of the name is said to have belonged to the family of Ailbhe of Emly, who is credited with having miraculously produced the local stream that flows into Belfast Lough.[3] At Holdenstown, Colmán had two (otherwise unattested) companions, Guaire and Maol Dubh son of Ultán.[4] The former's memory may be preserved in the name Kilmogar (Ceall 'Mo-ghorra', perhaps 'church of my Guaire') in the parish of Clara.[5]

1 *HDGP* ii, 103; *CGSH* §§366, 707.259. 2 *HADO* ii, 193, iii, 353, 356; *MartT* 80; *MartO*[2] 216; *MartG* 196; *MartD* 276. 3 *VSHP* i, 54 §20; *VSHH* 124. 4 *CGSH* §366. 5 *HADO* iii, 359; but cf. Logainm.ie 'Kilmogar'.

Colmán of Inch (Inis Mocholmóg), barony of Gorey, Co. Wexford. Lying at the northern tip of Wexford, within the former territory of Uí Eineachghlais, Inch was one of the churches of the deanery of Wicklow. Initially granted to the diocese of Glendalough, 'with all appurtences', it later became a vicarage in the archdiocese of Dublin.[1] Little is known of Colmán, but his feast fell on 14 November.[2]

1 *CPPI* 239; *AH* 8, 54. 2 *MartO*[2] 234, 242; *MartG* 218; *MartD* 310.

Colmán of Inishbofin (Inis Bó Finne), barony of Murrisk, Co. Mayo. Most of the information on this historically attested saint derives from Bede's *Ecclesiastical History of the English People*.[1] According to Bede, Colmán had been sent from Ireland to succeed Fíonán, first head of the church of Lindisfarne in Northumbria after Aidan (Aodhán). He straightaway became involved in the so-called Easter controversy and represented, eloquently but unsuccesfully, the Irish party at the celebrated synod of Whitby in 664 which was followed by the adoption in Northumbria of the Roman method of dating Easter. Bede purports to recount the actual words of both Colmán and his chief protagonist, Wilfrid of Ripon, whose emphasis on the greater authority of St Peter of Rome over Colum Cille of Iona led to the rejection of the Irish viewpoint. Afterwards, Colmán left Northumbria for Iona and thence returned to Ireland, accompanied by both Irish and Saxon monks.

In Ireland, in 668, according to the annals, Colmán founded a church on Inishbofin, where his bell was later preserved, and following a dispute that arose between Irish and Saxon monks, established another at Mayo (Magh nEó) – later known as Mayo 'of the Saxons' – now the name of a parish in the county of the same name.[2] Famous as a centre of learning, Mayo continued to attract Saxons until at least the end of the eighth century, when Alcuin wrote to fellow-countrymen based there.[3] The most celebrated 'Saxon' associated with Mayo was Garailt whose *vita* presents Colmán quite unhistorically as abbot of Iona and archbishop of all England.[4] Colmán's name is included in the list of homonymous saints.[5] He died, supposedly in his eightieth year, in 676 and was remembered in Ireland on 8 August and, according to the Martyrology of Gorman, also on 13 November, unless this related to his namesake, Colmán Lobhar of Moynoe.[6] Among the more notable centres of his cult is the Mayo town of Claremorris in the parish of Kilcolman, named after the saint. An Office Life, preserved in the Breviary of Aberdeen, assigns his feast to 18 February, thus confusing him with Colmán of Moray.[7] His coarb at Mayo was among the ecclesiastics present at the inauguration of O'Connor as king of Connacht.[8]

1 *BEH* 296–308; *CSax.* 186–205; *DIB* ii, 690. 2 *BEH* 346–8; *MP* 72–5; OSL MO i, 218; *IER* (5th ser.) 27, 275; *Peritia* 15, 81–107; *AU s.a.* 3 *Kenney* 534–5. 4 *VSHP* ii, 107 §2. 5 *CGSH* §707.307. 6 *MartT* 61; *MartO*² 175; *MartG* 172, 218; *MartD* 212, 308; *AU s.a.* 7 *LegSS* 58–61, 336–7. 8 *JRSAI* 2, 340.

Colmán of Kilclonfert. *See* Colmán of Templeshanbo.

Colmán of Kilcolman, Co. Limerick. *See* Colmán of Kilmacduagh.

Colmán of Kilcolman, parish of Ardmore (Aird Mhór), barony of Decies-within-Drum, Co. Waterford. In addition to being included in the list of homonymous saints, this Colmán is probably the man said not only to have baptized Déaglán of Ardmore, but also to have prophesied his future greatness and foretold his mission among the southern Déise.[1] According to Déaglán's Life, there was to be *fraternitas* between him and Colmán, and this may reflect the location of Kilcolman (Colmán's church) within the parish of Ardmore. The saint's tree (*Crann Colmáin*), either an ash or a whitethorn, thought to have sprung from a dried stick, was highly venerated locally.[2]

1 *CGSH* §707.116 (add.); *VSHP* ii, 36–7 §5; ITS 16, 10–12, 161. 2 *JCHAS* 68, 37–8; *PND* 81.

Colmán of Kildare, barony of Offaly East, Co. Kildare. Two of those named Colmán in the list of homonymous saints are said to have been among the helpers of Brighid of Kildare, one her milker, the other her shepherd.[1] Only one saint of the name, Colmán Mór, 'great', son of Fearghas, is among the many said to have been subject to Brighid, but Ard Conaigh, the church to which he is assigned together with two companions (Conach, eponym of the site, and Luiceannán), has yet to be identified.[2]

1 *CGSH* §§707.300–1. 2 *CGSH* §670.81; *HDGP* i, 83.

Colmán of Killeenmore (Ceall/Cluain Iain Mhóir), parish of Whitechurch, barony of North Naas, Co. Kildare. Colmán's pedigree attaches him through his father Foirtchearn to the Déise, in keeping with the location of his church in the north-eastern corner of Kildare, close to the Meath baronies of Deece (Déise).[1] Elsewhere, the saintly bishop's line of descent from the Déise is placed among the genealogies of Síol Aodha Sláine, the dominant sept in the southern part of Meath.[2]

1 *CGSH* §87; *GRSH* 77; *Lgen.* 719.5. 2 *CGH* 144c11–25.

Colmán of Killelan, barony of Kilkea and Moone, Co. Kildare, which probably represents an earlier Ceall Ghialláin.[1] This Colmán is featured among many others in the list of homonymous saints.[2] His church, if accurately identified, was close to Moone which takes its name from Maon Coluim Chille, 'Moone of Colum Cille', thus making it probable that Colmán was another local version of the cult of the founder of Iona. Nearby was the church of Castledermot which could be the Díseart assigned to another Colmán in the list of homonymous saints.[3] The second litany of Irish saints states that Killelan was home to seven holy bishops.[4]

1 *HDGP* iv, 2. 2 *CGSH* §707.265. 3 Ibid. §707.135. 4 *IrL* 68.

Colmán of Killeroran, barony of Killian, Co. Galway. A miscellaneous item in the corpus of saints' pedigrees places Colmán son of Ainghin (Anghan), along with his two brothers, Cúrnán and Mac Reithe, in the church of Ceall Eadarghabhla in Fiodh Manach, now an ecclesiastical site in Killeroran.[1] His name figures in the list of saints commemorated on 14 July and, together with his brothers, he was remembered in a church named Ceall Mac nAinghin(e) in Fiodh Manach, now Ballynakill in the Galway barony of Ballymoe, which contains a townland named Kilcolumb.[2] The Killeroran saint may be the Colmán of Eadarghabhail found in the list of homonymous saints.[3]

1 *CGSH* §695; *HDGP* iii, 166. 2 *MartT* 55; *MartG* 136; *MartD* 194; *Lgen.* 237.7; *HDGP* iv, 11–12. 3 *CGSH* §707.109.

Colmán of Kilmacduagh (Ceall Mhic Dhuach), barony of Kiltartan, Co. Galway. Colmán's pedigree attaches him to the Uí Fhiachrach of Aidhne who held lands in Galway and north Clare approximately co-extensive with the diocese named Kilmacduagh after the saint's church.[1] How Colmán – who was also known as Colmán Mór and Mac Duach – came to have jurisdiction over what is now the diocese is explained in an attractive tale which tells how the saint, having fasted in the wilderness of the Burren for seven years and forty days, was rewarded about Eastertide by a sumptuous meal transported to his table from that of Guaire, king of Aidhne, celebrated for his generosity and later taken to be Colmán's brother.[2] Subsequently arriving at Colmán's house, Guaire, who was duly impressed by the length of the cleric's fast, offered his seed and race to him 'until doom'.

Saint and king are again brought together in the Life of Maodhóg of Ferns who, wishing to visit Cashel, is instead directed to Kilmacduagh, where Guaire lay ill. Having made the king well, and foretold the length of his reign, Maodhóg is said to have established a *fraternitas* between himself and Colmán, probably a veiled reference to the presence at Kilmacduagh – as at Ferns – of a priory of canons regular of St Augustine, known as 'Oheyne's monastery' after a family that traced its descent to Guaire.[3] This connection between the two saints also appears to underlie the tradition that the patron of Seanbhoth in Uí Cheinsealaigh of south Leinster, now Templeshanbo in the Wexford barony of Scarawalsh, close to Ferns, was Colmán of the Uí Fhiachrach, doubtless a double of Mac Duach. This man's feast fell on 27 October, a date that, according to a note by Mícheál Ó Cléirigh, was also more correctly the feast of Colmán of Kilmacduagh.[4]

Colmán of Kilmacduagh is listed, together with Ua Suanaigh of Rahan, among the numerous children said to have been born of Inghean Bhaoith of Killinaboy.[5] Elsewhere his mother is named as Ríoghnach, daughter of Cormac son of Fearghal, a great-grandson of Guaire Aidhne, which is at odds with other parts of the saint's story.[6] He is also invoked with Mochuille of Tulla in a poem attributed to Seanán of Scattery Island.[7] No Life was written for Colmán until the seventeenth century when Colgan pieced together various traditions concerning the saint, and these formed the basis of an Office Life composed a century or so later.[8]

There are varying traditions regarding Colmán's feast. Normally, this fell on 3 February, and its octave (10 February) was also marked by devotion to him – for example, in the Clare parish of Noughaval.[9] A pattern was held at Colmán's well in the parish of Carran on the last day of Summer, usually the last Sunday of July, which would suggest that it was a *Lughnasadh* site, whereas a pattern was held at the saint's well in the parish of Oughtmama on 15 November, and yet another at a well named after him in the Limerick parish of Darragh on 31 August.[10] As already pointed out, 27 (more correctly 29) October was also reckoned locally to be his feastday, and this is the official day of commemoration in the diocese.[11] A fragment of Colmán's crozier is still preserved in the National Museum, Dublin, but the saint's 'belt', suitable for wear by the chaste, and formerly kept by the local hereditary family of Uí Sheachnasaigh, has been lost.[12] Twigs of an ash-tree near the saint's church at Kilmacduagh, known as Mac Duach's *Cuaille*, were believed to be charms against accident.[13]

As noted under Colga of Kilcolgan, there are some indications that Colmán originally represented Colum Cille locally. Within the diocese, he himself may also have been the subject of localization, especially at Kinvarra in the Galway parish of Kinvarradoorus, whose saint, Camán (alias Seanchamán), a pet form of Colum, is featured in a tale known as *Iomramh Ua gCorra*, 'voyage tale of the Uí Chorra'. This describes how its 'heroes', when under orders from Finnian of Clonard to undo the harm they had previously done to churches in Connacht, finally arrived at Camán's church in Kinvarra, where, having built a boat, they subsequently took to the ocean on pilgrimage.[14] Camán's hearth in Kinvarra is elsewhere described as one of the three most prosperous in Ireland, vying only with Inishmurray and Kilmainham.[15] As if to confirm Camán's ultimate identity with Colmán, a holy well in the parish of Kinvarradoorus was dedicated to the latter saint.[16] Colmán, patron of Kilcolman (Ceall Cholmáin) in the parish of Kilmeedy, and of Colmanswell – both in the Limerick barony of Connello Upper – whose feast fell on 29 October, the same day as was observed in Kilmacduagh, may also have been a localization of the saint, and ultimately of Colum Cille.[17] Among the wells dedicated to the saint in the west of Ireland, usually under the guise of Mac Duach, was one at Kilmurvy on Inishmore of Aran.[18] The saint is reputed to have died about the same time as Ailbhe of Emly, among others.[19]

1 *CGSH* §376; *GRSH* 61; *Lgen.* 711.1; *BNÉ* i, 312. **2** *Ériu* 1, 44–6; *FSPP* 81; cf. *BLCat.* i, 638. **3** *VSHP* ii, 155–6 §37; *MRHI* 183; OCBG §1558. **4** *MartD* 38, 286. **5** *IrT* iv, 93. **6** *TCHyF* 60–2. **7** *ZCP* 10, 26. **8** *ASH* 244–8; *HADK* 102, 447–9. **9** *MartT* 14; *MartG* 28; *MartD* 38; *ACoC* 61. **10** *FL* 621; *ACoC* 30, 34; OSL LK ii, 88. **11** *HADK* 99–102. **12** Ibid. 69. **13** OSL GY ii, 169; *Béaloideas* 16, 200. **14** *Imm.* 100; *MCMHW* 90 §§19–20. **15** *SG* i, 42; cf. *DAMC* 15. **16** OSL GY ii, 171. **17** OSL LK i, 72, ii, 288; *JRSAI* 85, 197. **18** *AIGY* i, 126. **19** *LUM* 154rb 29–30.

Colmán of Kilmacrenan (Ceall Mac nÉanáin), a parish and barony in Co. Donegal. A series of four entries in the tract on the mothers of the saints is based on an addition to the Life composed by Adhamhnán for Colum Cille, relating to the latter's kindred.[1] One entry in both sources refers to Mionchloth (Mincholeth), mother of the sons of Éanán, one of whom was called Colmán. The author of the tract on the mothers, presumably recognizing that more than one son was involved, added a second, naming him Cobhrán, who may have been venerated, together with his maternal uncle Colum, at Clooney in the Derry parish of Clondermot.[2] Mionchloth's sons figure together in the name of the church of Ceall Mhac nÉanáin, now Kilmacrenan, in which, according to his late vernacular Life, Colum Cille was fostered, and in which was also kept a relic of his.[3] One seventeenth-century source suggests that Colmán's brother Cobhrán was the saint of that name commemorated on 19 July.[4] In view of his name and church, there can be little doubt that Colmán was originally the same as Colum Cille.

1 *CGSH* §§397, 722.23–6; *VC*[2] 546–8. **2** *TT* 479 (18); *PCV* 31n; *PNCL* 92; *MartG* 138; *MartD* 196. **3** *BCC* §§53, 93, 355 (h). **4** *GRSH* 39.

Colmán of Kilroot (Ceall Ruaidh), barony of Lower Belfast, Co. Antrim. This saint is said to have belonged to the family of Ailbhe of Emly, who is credited with miraculously producing an ever flowing river named Buanann, from *buan*, 'constant', at Kilroot, probably now the local stream that flows into Belfast Lough.[1] Alternatively, more in line with the location of his church, the saint is also found, together with Colmán of Dromore, among the Dál nAraidhe of south Antrim and north Down.[2] Interest in Colmán was not confined to the authorities at Emly; he is also among the saints introduced to the Life of his diocesan patron, Mac Nise of Connor, who is said to have saved him from danger, and instructed him in divine scripture.[3] In common with some other sources, this text also gives him the title of bishop.[4] The saint was remembered on 16 October, the same day as such other bearers of the name as Colmán of Kilcolman in the modern parish of Connahy in Kilkenny, and his namesake of both Holdenstown (Bealach Buaidhghe) and Clara – which adjoins Tiscoffin (*Teach Scoithín*), the house of Scoithín of the family of Ailbhe – in the same county.[5]

1 *VSHP* i, 54 §20; *VSHH* 124; *HDGP* ii, 216. **2** *BB* 168bc50–1. **3** *VSHH* 406 §9. **4** Ibid.; *MartG* 196; *MartD* 276. **5** *HADO* ii, 180, 193, iii, 353, 356; *MartT* 80; *MartO*[2] 216; *MartG* 196; *MartD* 276.

Colmán of Kinneigh (Ceann Eich), alias Castletownkinneigh, barony of East Carbery, Co. Cork. This saint, also known as Mocholmóg, is featured in the Life of Fionnbharr which, describing him as bishop, gives Colmán the dubious honour of attending school in Cork in the company of Colmán of Cloyne and Fachtna of Ross Carbery, among others, thus signalling the deference he and his successors at Kinneigh were required to show to Fionnbharr in perpetuity.[1] The relatively high status of his church is also reflected by the presence at Kinneigh of a round tower. Nothing much else is known of the saint but, in the lead-up to the battle of Clontarf, some servants of Cian son of Maol Muadh, who died in the year of the battle (AD1014), are reported to have drunk milk at his church without the saint's permission, as opposed to Domhnall son of Dubh Dá Bhoireann who paid homage to the saint and subsequently prospered.[2] He is probably the saint visited by an elderly couple, Cláirineach, king of a south Cork family, and his barren wife in the hope of issue, which, following a fast in Mocholmóg's company, was successfully brought about.[3]

1 *BBa.* 76 §34, 263; *MakS* 118–19. **2** *Ériu* 1, 93–4 §47. **3** *IrT* iv, §§54–7; *ApalF* 179.

Colmán of Lambay Island (Reachra), parish of Portraine, barony of Nethercross, Co. Dublin. Colmán son of Raoi (Roé) of Lambay was among the many saints said to have been born of Eithne daughter of Conchraidh.[1] As his feast fell on 16 June, the octave of Colum Cille's day, his cult is likely to have been a localized version of that of the patron of Iona.[2] The foundation of the church on the island is attributed to Colum Cille who reputedly left Colmán 'the deacon' in it.[3] Colmán's feast was shared by Athchaoin, one of his uterine siblings, whose church at Colp was near the mouth of the river Boyne.

1 *CGSH* §722.98. **2** *MartT* 50; *MartG* 116; *MartD* 170. **3** *IKD* 234; *BCC* §99; *EA* 292.

Colmán of Lindisfarne *see* **Colmán** of Inishboffin.

Colmán of Linns (Linn Duachaill), parish of Gernonstown, barony of Ardee, Co. Louth, near Annagassan in the parish of Drumcar [1]. This Colmán is known both from the list of homonymous saints and from the entry of his feast (30 March) in the martyrologies.[2] Colmán's church allegedly took its name from a demon that harmed many in the area before the saint consigned it to a nearby pool.[3]

John Colgan took the saint to be the same as Colmán of Lynn, but there is no mention of Annagassan in that man's Life.[4] The annals place Colmán's obit in the list for 699.[5]

1 *HK* 91; *MRHI* 397; *Ainm* 9, 24. 2 *CGSH* §707.319; *MartT* 28; *MartO*² 85; *MartG* 64; *MartD* 90. 3 *MartO*² 102. 4 *ASH* 792–3; *BCML*; *JCLAS* 28, 22–3. 5 ATig. / *AFM s.a.*

Colmán of Lismore (Lios Mór), barony of Coshmore and Coshbride, Co. Waterford. A bishop of this name is given prominence in the Life of Flannán of Killaloe, whose father Toirdhealbhach, in the tradition of what is termed *Geblütsheiligkeit*, 'lineage-holiness', reputedly fled from worldly affairs for a period in order to turn his mind to heavenly matters.[1] Proceeding without any companions to Lismore, Toirdhealbhach joined a large group gathered about Colmán whose fame was such that many heads of churches throughout Ireland, as well as secular leaders, had allegedly sought him out as a teacher. Various miracles followed, including three drops of blood that fell from above on a stone, which, when explained by Colmán as a sign that three sons of Toirdhealbhach had been slain, led to the latter's return to the world, but not before the saint, full of divine spirit, foretold that seven famous kings of his blood would rule over Ireland, four of whom are named.[2] Great may Colmán's fame have been, but little else is known of him. A well in the townland of Carrignagower, parish of Lismore, dedicated to Mocholmóg, was visited at Easter.[3] Otherwise, however, the nearest local dedication to a saint so named, at Ardmore, probably concerned the man reputed to have baptized Déaglán and prophesied his future greatness.[4] It may be that Flannán's biographer borrowed the name of Colmán (†703) son of Fionnbharr, abbot of Lismore, and a guarantor of the Law of Adhamhnán, as a suitable peg on which to hang his tale.[5]

1 *VSHH* 287–90 §§14–17. 2 Ibid. 289 §17. 3 *VSHP* ii, 36–7 §5; ITS 16, 10–12, 161. 4 *AIWD* 201. 5 *CA* §28; *Peritia* 1, 193; *AU s.a.*

Colmán of Longfordpass (Doire Mór), parish of Kilcooly, barony of Eliogarty, Co. Tipperary. Although better known by reference to his foster-mother (Daráine) – described as his true mother in the Life of Éanna of Inishmore – Colmán was usually considered to be a son of Aonghas, son of Nadh Fraoich, king of Cashel, and of Sant (perhaps from *sancta*), Daráine's sister, who is also said to have been the mother of Ailbhe of Emly.[1] According to the account of his birth, Colmán was given to Daráine to be reared because of the latter's barrenness.[2] The church named for the saint, Doire Mór on the borders of Munster and Leinster, or more particularly on Ely's border with Ossory, used to be taken to refer to a site in the parish of Kilcolman (named from the saint) in the Offaly barony of Ballybritt.[2] In one passage, however, the place is located in Magh Airbh, which gave name to the Cistercian foundation of Kilcooly (*Arvicampus*) in Eliogarty (from Éile Uí Fhógarta) on Tipperary's border with Kilkenny, and the abbot of Kilcooly is described in one charter as the coarb of Colmán.[3] This would leave the church close to Leigh (Liath Mochaomhóg), between which and Doire Mór there was little more than four miles, according to the Latin Life of

Mochaomhóg.[4] For this reason among others, more recent opinion favours the ecclesiastical site in the townland of Longfordpass North.[5]

As a supposed son of Aonghas son of Nadh Fraoich, whom Patrick is said to have baptized as first of the men of Munster, Colmán might be expected to have figured in the traditions surrounding the Armagh saint, but this is not the case. His absence from the Patrician record did not prevent local hagiographers from finding room for him. He figures in the Lives of Ailbhe of Emly (Munster's 'second Patrick') who is said to have met him in Rome, Mochaomhóg of Leigh, Ruadhán of Lorrha, Éanna of Inishmore who is cast as Colmán's maternal uncle, and Déaglán of Ardmore.[6] Colmán's feast is assigned variously to 20 May and 31 July.[7] The use of the designation, *Lá Colmáin ar na caiplibh*, 'Colmán's day on the horses', for the latter day would suggest that it was a *Lughnasadh* (1 August) celebration which often featured horse-racing or horse-bathing.[8] The feast of a namesake with Patrician connections, Colum son of Riaghal, supposedly the son of Dairearca (sister of Patrick), fell on 1 August, and this day was also the occasion of a pattern at Stackallan (Teach Colláin) in Meath, the name of whose patron (Collán alias Callán) derives hypocoristically from Colum, indicating that the same original cult underlay devotion to all of these saints.[9]

1 *CGSH* §§191, 722.59; *CGH* 148a52; *GRSH* 116; *Lgen.* 740.15; *ZCP* 8, 304; *VSHP* ii, 65–6 §12. **2** *VSHP* ii, 170; *MartO²* 172; *OnomG* 328. **3** *MartO²* 172; *MRHI* 137; *TIC* 133. **4** *VSHP* ii, 171. **5** *Peritia* 2, 273–4; *Peritia* 11, 359–69. **6** *VSHH* 122–4; *VSHP* i, 50–1; ii, 41, 65–6, 170, 250; *BNÉ* i, 327. **7** *MartT* 44, 59; *MartO²* 165; *MartG* 100, 146; *MartD* 134, 206. **8** *RIA 23N10*, 149; *FL* 143, 254. **9** *MartT* 59; *MartG* 148; *MartD* 208; *CGSH* §707.77; OSL MH 105.

Colmán of Lynally. *See* Colmán Eala.

Colmán of Lynn (Lann Mhic Luacháin), barony of Fartullagh, Co. Westmeath. The mainline statement of Colmán's descent, his *genealogia vera*, as the saint's Life describes it, attaches him through his father Luachán to the Clann Cholmáin who held sway in what is now the county of Westmeath.[1] Two divergent traditions, one of which is also recorded in the saint's Life, the other only in early seventeenth-century sources, respectively assign him to a more obscure branch of the descendants of Conall Creamhthainne of the southern Uí Néill, and to the Clanna Rudhraighe of north-east Ulster.[2]

On Spy Wednesday in the year 1122, the shrine containing Colmán's relics was discovered hidden in the ground at Lynn, having been allegedly buried for fear of Viking raids.[3] It is generally held that the saint's vernacular Life was composed soon after the elevation of the shrine.[4] There are, however, many features of the Life, including its excessive concern with grants of land and alliances, its tendency to confuse homonyms, its anachronisms, and what appears to be its use of the late twelfth-century Midlands version of the Martyrology of Aonghas as a source that point to a later date.[5]

The Life maintains that Colmán was born locally, near Lynn, his mother being Lasar of the Corca Raoidhe, the family that gave name to the Westmeath barony of Corkaree.[6] Lasar allegedly bore Luachán eleven children (seven daughters and four sons), all of whom are said to have gone on to occupy churches. Among the many saints with whom Colmán had contact were:

Éidchéan of Clonfad who baptized, taught, ordained and advised him; Finnian of Clonard; Colum Cille; Ciarán of Clonmacnoise; Mochuda of Rahan and Lismore; Maodhóg of Ferns; Fursa; and the saint's two namesakes at Conry and Lynally, with nearly all of whom he is said to have made 'unions'.[7] While staying in Lismore with Mochuda, he is described as having established a friendship with the king of the Fir Mhaighe of the Fermoy area, who gave him land on which to found the church of Kilworth (Ceall Uird).[8]

Along with the two other Colmáns (of Conry and Lynally), known collectively as 'the great Colmáns of Meath', the saint of Lynn is said to have made several journeys, including a visit to the Convention of Drumceat, where Colum Cille heaped praise on them, and a joint visit to Rome.[9] Elsewhere, when asked which holy man he would leave in his place, Colum Cille, then about to depart for Scotland, is said to have replied that all three Colmáns would act on his behalf and under his protection.[10] The Life, which throughout serves as a rich source of local name-lore, contains an account of the foundation of Lynn.[11] There are contradictory statements with regard to the saint's feast which is variously placed about Easter, in June, July and November.[12] The mainline martyrologies place it on 17 June, the octave (eight days) of the feast of Colum Cille of Iona, probably the original saint venerated at Lynn.[13]

1 *BCML* 4 §4. **2** *CGSH* §§12, 41; *BCML* 4 §3; *GRSH* 54, 103; *Lgen.* 704.1–2; *MartD* 172. **3** *AU s.a.*; *BCML* vi. **4** *BCML* vii; *Kenney* 454; *PNW* 186; *ZCP* 8, 568–9. **5** *BCML* viii, xi–xiii, §2; *FSHIM* 200–2; *OLL* 2, 5–6. **6** *BCML* 6–10 §§5–9. **7** Ibid. 10–102 §§10, 18, 20–3, 29, 31–5, 42, 52, 71–2, 79, 85, 97, 102. **8** Ibid. 18–26 §§19–26. **9** Ibid. 54 §52; 78–80 §§76–7. **10** *BLec.* 193rb; *BCC* 212 §219. **11** *BCML* 28 §29; *PNW* 189–93. **12** *BCML* 4 §2; *PNW* 188. **13** *MartT* 50; *MartG* 118; *MartD* 172.

Colmán of Mayo. *See* Colmán of Inishbofin.

Colmán of Míleac Fiaich. *See* Angán of Míleac Fiaich.

Colmán of Moray (Muiriabh), Scotland. The feast of this saint is noted by the Martyrology of Tallaght at 18 February, with the comment that he was from Moray 'north of Móna (Monadh)' which has been identified as the Grampians.[1] The twelfth-century scholiast of the Martyrology of Aonghas, although adding the same comment to his text's mention of Colmán, also stated that the saint was from Ard Bó in Ceinéal Eoghain, now Arboe in the Tyrone barony of Dungannon Upper, thus anticipating the feast of a nominally different saint of the name which fell, according to the other martyrologies, three days later on 21 February.[2] The earlier of the two feasts was observed in several Scottish churches, including Tarbat in Ross-shire, just north of Moray Firth.[3]

1 *MartT* 17; *CPNS* 279. **2** *MartO*[2] 76; *MartT* 18; *MartG* 40; *MartD* 54. **3** *CPNS* 278–9; *LegSS* 336–7.

Colmán of Moynoe. *See* Colmán Lobhar.

Colmán of Muckamore. *See* Colmán Eala.

Colmán of Myshall (Midhíseal), barony of Forth, Co. Carlow. This son of Eachaidh (Eacha) is assigned to two other churches in addition to Myshall, – Slanore (Snámh Luthair) in the Cavan parish of Kilmore, and Ros Glanna (rendered *rosc geal glanna*, 'bright, noble eye', in one manuscript) which is thought to have been Donaghmore in the Tyrone barony of Dungannon Middle.[1] The saint, whose name was also written Colum or Colum *Crosaire*, 'cross-bearer', is known from a number of sources, foremost of which is Adhamhnán's Life of Colum Cille.[2] This describes him as the founder of Slanore, and driver of a carriage bearing the Iona saint which, despite its lack of retaining bolts on the wheels, safely covered long distances. A later source places Colmán in a deputation of saints sent to Iona to appeal to Colum to return in preparation for the Convention of Drumceat.[3] Among other sources of information on the saint are entries in the corpus of saints' pedigrees which attach him, together with several siblings, to the Ceinéal Laoghaire of Meath.[4] His siblings were: Fiontan who was also attached to Slanore and Myshall; Lughaidh, patron of Teernacreeve; Nainnidh of Kiltoom; Muireadhach of Killala; and Comaigh daughter of Eacha. His mother is said to have been Aighleann daughter of Léinín, sister of Colmán of Cloyne.[5] Colmán's feast is variously assigned to 6 and 22 September, with the list for the latter providing him with an alternative father, named Cathbhadh.[6] Though the holy well at Myshall was named after Brighid, a pattern was held there on 14 September, halfway between Colmán's two feasts.[7] Finally, in the guise of Colum, alias Colum Crosaire, the saint is said to have been left in Donaghmore by Patrick, who reputedly founded the church.[8]

1 But cf. *DK* 27. **2** *VC*[2] 448; *SAM* 2.1, 168–70; *MartT* 68. **3** *Anecd.* iii, 2. **4** *CGSH* §§160, 349; *GRSH* 50–1. **5** *CGSH* §§160.1, 690.3, 722.31. **6** *MartT* 68, 73; *MartO*[2] 193; *MartG* 170, 182; *MartD* 238, 254; *SAM* 2.1, 169. **7** OSL CW 422. **8** *BP* 1980–2 (= *VT* 170); *HDGP* vii, 121–2.

Colmán of Oughaval (Tulach mac gComhghaill / Druim Togha), parish and barony of Stradbally, Co. Laois. The scribe of the corpus of saints' pedigrees in the Book of Leinster, Aodh Mac Criomhthainn, had connections with the church of Oughaval from which his book received its traditional name of *Leabhar na Nuachongbhála*, 'Book of Oughaval'.[1] It is unsurprising, therefore, that he should have paid particular attention to the two sons of Comhghall associated with the place, Colmán and Seanach, whose pedigree he twice recorded in slightly differing versions.[2] In neither case, however, is there any question concerning the tribal affiliations of the saints who belonged to a branch of the Laoighse settled in the area about Oughaval.[3] From his earliest mention onwards, Colmán was known by reference to this sept, as is shown by the Life of Colum Cille written by Adhamhnán. This asserts that Colum had a vision of angels carrying the soul of the holy bishop Colmán of the Maca Laoighse to heaven, and that travellers later confirmed that the bishop had died on the night in question.[4] The day on which Colmán's death or *natalis* was celebrated, 15 May, witnessed the passing of several namesakes, and since Colum Cille was also remembered on this day, all of these are likely to have originally represented localizations of the Iona saint.[5] Both patrons of Oughaval, Colmán (sometimes also called Colum) and Seanach – if the latter be the same as Seanach Garbh, 'rough' – are said to have succeeded Fiontan as abbot of Clonenagh, a church with which Aodh Mac Criomhthainn's family also had a close connection.[6]

1 *LL* xi–xvii. **2** *CGSH* §§145, 187; *Lgen.* 734.1.17; *AB* 69, 81–4. **3** *CGH* 127a14. **4** *VC*[2] 488–90. **5** *MartT* 43; *MartG* 96; *MartD* 128; *TT* 494.45. **6** *MartO*[1] lii; *CPCR* i, 210.

Colmán of Oughtmama (Ucht Máma), barony of Burren, Co. Clare. This saint, and two others named Colmán son of Lughaidh, each with a separate descent, one from Ceinéal Laoghaire of Meath, the other from the Eoghanachta of Munster, and the third from the Uí Bhriúin of Connacht, were said to have occupied the same church.[1] Described by John O'Donovan as one of the most beautiful of the early Irish churches he had seen, a pattern was held there in honour of Colmán on 15 November.[2] Although no such saint is to be found in the martyrologies, a note added to Colmán's pedigree by John Colgan places his feast on 13 November, the day of Caillín of Fenagh, whose name is a hypocoristic form of Colum (alias Colmán).[3] Located near the church of the three Colmáns was the well of Colmán son of Duach so that, as O'Donovan observed, the church of Oughtmama is likely to have been originally dedicated to the patron of the diocese (Kilmacduagh) on whose boundary it lay.[4] The patron of the neighbouring parish of Kilcorney was also named Colmán, with Báire as cognomen, and O'Donovan, who could find no historical reference to him, thought he might also be the saint of Oughtmama.[5] A poem attributed to Seanán of Scattery Island invokes a group of saints named Colmán, presumably referring to the patrons of Oughtmama.[6] Colmán is said to have died on the same night as Brighid of Kildare and Muircheartach, king of Tara, perhaps because the account of the latter's reign in the *Leabhar Gabhála* brings these two together with Colmán son of Duach.[7]

1 *CGSH* §331.1–3. *GRSH* 50, 59, 116; *IrT* iii, 86–7. **2** *ACoC* 29–30. **3** *GRSH* 59. **4** *ACoC* 30. **5** Ibid. 76–7. **6** *ZCP* 10, 26 §20. **7** *IrT* iii, 84 §4; *LG* v, 360 §617.

Colmán of Rosbran (Ros Brannaibh), parish of St John's (Athy), barony of Narragh and Reban West, Co. Kildare. The pedigree of this Colmán (also written Comán) attaches him through his father Ainmhire to the north Leinster family of Clann Bhruidhghe, which was powerful enough to provide an abbot of Kildare named Brannabh, the eponym of Colmán's church.[1] Nothing else is known of the saint, and there are no ecclesiastical remains in Rosbran.

1 *CGSH* §§272.1, 707.224.298; *GRSH* 87; *Lgen.* 726.16; *CGH* 124b27; *NHI* 9, 260–1.

Colmán of Rosslea. *See* Colmán of Clontivrin.

Colmán of Slanore. *See* Colmán of Myshall.

Colmán of Templeshanbo (Seanbhoth), barony of Scarawalsh, Co. Wexford. An entry in the tract on the mothers of the saints states that Ríoghnach daughter of Cochlán, the sister of Beoaidh of Ardcarn, had a son named Colmán and, in some manuscripts, Eacha is said to have been the saint's father.[1] As Beoaidh belonged to the Corca Laoighdhe of the area now covered by the diocese of Ross in Cork, it may be assumed that Ríoghnach also had southern connections. Elsewhere his mother – who is said to have had several other saintly children, including Aodhán (associated, like Colmán, with Templeshanbo) and the three Uí Shuanaigh – is named Fearamhla.[2] As patron of Templeshanbo under the guise of Colmán of the Uí Fhiachrach of (south) Connacht, the saint was probably identical with

Colmán of Kilmacduagh. According to the *baile*, 'mantic vision', attributed to Fíonnachta, an erstwhile king of Connacht who abandoned the kingship and settled near Templeshanbo, Colmán, having disturbed the king's dream, was left with the unhappy *fágbháil*, 'legacy', that he should always waken when most desirous of sleep.[3] A more fortunate endowment was the presence in his church pond of ducks which, however often they might be boiled by stealth in a pot, would remain unharmed, provided the water was from the pond.[4] The church at Templeshanbo was known as *ecclesia sancti Colmani*.[5] A connection of the saint with the Offaly church of Kilclonfert (earlier Cluain Fearta Mughaine) is indicated by the martyrologies, which commemorated Colmán son of Eacha of this church on 3 September.[6] According to a note added to the Martyrology of Tallaght, the Kilclonfert saint turned the water of his well into wine on three occasions, once for Colum Cille, then for Féichín of Fore, a third time for Ruadhán of Lorrha.[7] According to an early seventeenth-century list, the local church at Kilclonfert was named after Colmán, but by the early nineteenth century the name of his well had been corrupted to 'St Clavin's'.[8]

1 *CGSH* §722.105; cf. *MartT* 116. **2** *Lgen*. 253.1; *MartT* 116. **3** *ZCP* 13, 25–7. **4** *IVN* 216–18. **5** *AH* 18, 9 §29; *CH* 2, 31; *CPL* 10, 545. **6** *MartT* 116; *MartG* 168; *MartD* 232. **7** *MartT* 116; *MartO* 198. **8** *Dinn*. 2, 32, 37.

COLMÁN of Uí Fhiachrach. *See* Colmán of Kilmacduagh.

COLMÁN of Uí Liatháin. Given his affiliation to the Uí Liatháin, who held lands comprising a substantial part of the Cork diocese of Cloyne, this Colmán might well be regarded as a double of the patron of that church and diocese, especially since his feast fell on 25 July, the same day as Fionnbharr *sagart*, 'priest', who is likely to have been identical with the patron of Cork.[1] Some sources have taken the saint to be the same as Colmán 'nepos Líatán', a doctor of religion, who died in 731.[2] This latter Colmán could well be the person chosen by Maol Ruain to articulate, under the guise of Mocholmóg of Uí Liatháin, the view that mere intention, however continual, was insufficient to please God.[3] Colmán's name also figures in the list of homonymous saints.[3]

1 *MartT* 58; *MartG* 142; *MartD* 202. **2** *AU s.a.*; *MartG* 142; *MartD* 202. **3** *MT* §21. **4** *CGSH* §707.98.

COLMÁN son of Caol. *See* Aodh Fionn.

COLMÁN son of Cathbhadh. *See* Colmán of Myshall.

COLMÁN son of Corordán. *See* Colmán of Dromore.

COLMÁN son of Eacha. *See* Colmán of Templeshanbo.

COLMÁN son of Earc. *See* Colmán son of Iomras.

COLMÁN son of Eoghan. Like his namesake, Colmán Mucaidh, this saint is said to have belonged to the Ceinéal Mic Caorthainn branch of the Oirghialla.[1] Again like his namesake, he is sometimes presented as a layman with children.[2]

1 *CGSH* §60; *GRSH* 66; *Lgen*. 713.1. **2** *CGH* 141a44, 141b17, p. 416n.

COLMÁN son of Flannán. *See* Eiltín of Kinsale.

COLMÁN son of Iomras (Earc), *germanus* (brother/cousin) of Déaglán of Ardmore. Reference is made to this saint by way of an addendum to the entry on Déaglán in the corpus of saints' genealogies, which locates Colmán in the eastern part of Feimhean, a plain that lay approximately between Cashel and Clonmel in the county of Tipperary.[1] One set of manuscripts, containing the earliest recension of the tract, replaces Colmán with Conall, and a parish named after this saint, Kilconnell in the barony of Middlethird, a little east of Cashel, would suit the reference to the eastern part of Feimhean.[2] Colmán is probably identical with a namesake described in Déaglán's Life as one of two uterine brothers of the Ardmore saint – the other being Eacha or Eoghan – both of whom were allegedly sons of Aonghas, king of Cashel.[3] Also according to this text, Colmán, having received baptism and a monk's habit from Ailbhe of Emly, went on to become a saint. The supposed relationship with Aonghas suggests that Colmán was considered to be identical with Colmán son of Daráine of Longfordpass (Doire Mór), north of Cashel, whose main feast fell on 31 July, exactly seven days after that of Déaglán.[4]

1 *CGSH* §107.2, 662.112; *Lgen.* 715.6–7. 2 *CGSH* §107.2 (add.); *CLTÁ* 104–6. 3 *VSHP* ii, 41 §14; ITS 16, 22. 4 *MartT* 59; *MartO*² 165; *MartG* 146; *MartD* 200; cf. ITS 16, 165.

COLMÁN son of Lughaidh. *See* Colmán of Clonpriest.

COLMÁN son of Lughna. This saint is attached to the Dál mBuain (later Dalboyn, a cantred that included parishes in south Antrim and north Down) whose ancestor Buan was, according to tradition, the father of Míleac, Patrick's master in bondage.[1] A note added to one version of his pedigree speculated that Colmán may have been remembered on 2 February or 30 March, but there is no support elsewhere for this.[2]

1 *CGSH* §153; *GRSH* 96; *Lgen.* 728.9; *BP* 199; *VT* 16; *EA* 44, 234; *MedI* 234. 2 *GRSH* 96.

COLMÁN son of Neamhan. *See* Cairbre son of Neamhan.

COLMÁN son of Rónán. Little is known of this saint other than his pedigree which assigns him to the Ceinéal Fearghasa branch of the Ceinéal Eoghain of Tyrone and describes him as a bishop.[1] Glosses added to his name in some manuscripts locate him in unidentified churches, variously named 'Aill(e)' and Ceall Cholmáin. A seventeenth-century source speculates that his feast may have fallen on 1 January, but neither of the two Colmáns on this day appears to be a likely candidate for identification with him.[2]

1 *CGSH* §33; *GRSH* 45; *Lgen.* 701.13; *BLec.* 55va. 2 *GRSH* 45; *MartD* 2–4.

COLMÁN son of Síolán. *See* Cuán of Kilquane.

COLMÁN son of Ultán. *See* Colmán of Holdenstown.

COLMÁN BÁIRE. *See* Colmán of Oughtmama.

COLMÁN BÁN, 'white', of Kilcolmanbane (Ceall Cholmáin Bháin), barony of Maryborough East, Co. Laois. While this saint gave his name – which figures in the list of homonymous saints – to the parish of Kilcolmanbane, the adjoining parish of Kilcolmanbrack was probably named after the same saint under a slightly different guise.[1] His feast is placed by some martyrologies on 19 October, a day shared by Columbanus of Tours, whose name could easily have been misread as 'Colum Bán' by an Irish martyrologist.[2]

1 *CGSH* §707.101. 2 *MartT* 81; *MartD* 278; *AS*.Nov. ii, 562.

Colmán Beag. *See* Colmán of Coolkeeragh.

Colmán Briot of Gallen. *See* Mochonóg of Kilmuckridge.

Colmán Cearr, 'crooked', of Clonrush (Cluain Rois), barony of Leitrim, Co. Clare (formerly Co. Galway). This saint is known from the list of homonymous saints which locates his church – now probably in the townland of Meelick – on the edge of Lough Derg, and also from a seventeenth-century list of ecclesiastical appointments which names the church as *ecclesia sancti Colomani*.[1] His church lay close to that of Caimín of Inishcaltra, now Holy Island, and since both saints bore names ultimately derived from Colum, they were probably originally identical. There are grounds for believing that Caimín and his other namesake, Colum son of Criomhthann of Terryglass – who is regarded as a localization of Colum Cille of Iona – were also one and the same.[2] Colmán Cearr's feast fell on 13 January, and the entry for the day places him variously at Lough Derg (Deirgdhearc) and at an unidentified location named 'Sailbheach'.[3]

1 *CGSH* §707.119; *CH* 2, 56. 2 *FEMN* 462n. 3 *MartT* 7; *MartG* 14; *MartD* 14.

Colmán Cille, 'of the church'. Colmán's pedigree attaches him through his father Eoghan to the Oirghialla, and more specifically to the Oirthir (Orior) family of the Uí Nialláin who gave name to the baronies of Oneilland East and West in Armagh.[1] Colmán na nOirthear, 'of the Oirthir', cited as a suitable witness in a poem on the Oirghialla, may refer to the saint.[2] Some seventeenth-century sources speculated that the Colmán commemorated without further designation on 1 October may have been Colmán Cille.[3] The *Móire* attached to the name of his church in some texts may reflect a corruption.[4]

1 *CGSH* §66; *GRSH* 70; *Lgen*. 715.2; *CGH* 146f27. 2 *Ériu* 16, 184 §43; cf. *KLT* 138 §43, 223. 3 *MartD* 264; *GRSH* 70. 4 *CGSH* §66, p. 191; *Lgen*. 715.2.

Colmán Cráibhtheach (an Chrábhaidh), 'pious (of piety)'. The pedigree of this son of Seachnasach attaches him to the Ceinéal Fínghin branch of the Eoghanacht of Cashel, which produced several kings of Munster, including Feidhlimidh son of Criomhthann.[1] He has been taken to be identical with the abbot of Lorrha in the Tipperary barony of Lower Ormond who died in 710.[2] As such, he acted as a guarantor of the Law of Adhamhnán.[3] He is also said to have been, along with many other saints, a son of Inghean Bhaoith of Killinaboy.[4]

1 *CGSH* §324; *GRSH* 116; *Lgen*. 741.3; *CGH* 160b6–11; *IKHK* 292. 2 *AU s.a.*; *GRSH* 116. 3 *CA* §§22, 28; *Peritia* 1, 187. 4 *IrT* iv, 94 §9.

Colmán Cúile of Clonkeen (Cluain Caoin), parish of Clonenagh, barony of Maryborough West, Co. Laois. Also known as Colum Cúile, this son of Miodhghna was one of several saints said to have been descended from Criomhthann Án, ancestor of the Uí Chriomhthannáin (Uí Chriomhthainn Áin) of the Stradbally (perhaps earlier also Portlaoise) district in the county of Laois.[1] Although known by reference to the place named Cúil (now Coole in the parish of Clonenagh), Colmán was more specifically located in Clonkeen, 'in the congregation (*samhadh*)' of Fiontan of Clonenagh, whose coarbship later lay with the Uí Chriomhthannáin.[2] It was here, in the church founded by Colmán, that his namesake and probable double, Colum of Terryglass, was reared, according to the latter's Life.[3] His feastday fell on 18 August, five days after that of his brother, Momhaodhóg of Fiddown and he may also have been remembered on 6 October.[4]

1 *CGSH* §242.1.2; *Lgen.* 727.28; *LSHS* 37. 2 *CGH* 122bb12; *CGSH* §707.127. 3 *VSHH* 225 §4. 4 *MartT* 63–4; *MartG* 156–8; *MartD* 222; *MartO*[1] 154–5.

Colmán Eala of Lynally (Lann Eala), barony of Ballycowan, Co. Offaly. The two mentions of this saint in Adhamhnán's late seventh-century Life of Colum Cille involve sea passages between Iona and Ireland, one of which traversed the 'surging tides' of the whirlpool of Breacán, near Rathlin Island.[1] The saint's family attachment to the Maca Sailne (Seille), as stated by Adhamhnán, is elsewhere attested in some annal notices of his death in 611, allegedly at 55 years of age.[2] The family in question was probably a branch of the descendants of Eacha son of Mairidh of north-east Ulster, to whom the saint is more usually assigned through a father named Beoghain (Beoghna).[3] Among other saints belonging to this group was Mac Nise of Connor whose Life foretells the occupancy of Lynally by his relative Colmán.[4] That there was a close connection between the churches of Connor and Lynally is also apparent from the obit of a certain Cuinnidhéan who died at the northern church in 1038 as 'coarb of Mac Nise and Colmán Eala'.[5] This man's name may also have found mention in the opening chapter of the late vernacular version of Colmán's Life which refers to his 'followers' as Muintir Chuinneagáin, attaching them to the Uí Bhriúin of Connacht.[6]

Colmán's Latin Life, which, ignoring earlier indications of descent, opportunistically assigns the saint to the powerful Uí Néill, forms part of the so-called O'Donohue group in the *Codex Salmanticensis* whose texts have been dated to as early as the eighth century.[7] There are many features of these Lives that point, however, to the influence of the canons regular of St Augustine whose first foundation in Ireland dates to the 1130s.[8] This is perhaps no more than might be expected of a text relating to a church located within a few miles of Durrow whose Augustinian priory was founded in the 1140s by Murchadh Ua Maoil Sheachlainn, king of Meath, prior to his death there in 1153.[9] By arranging for Laisréan, 'servant of Colum Cille' and superior of Durrow, to accompany Colmán as he marked out the boundary of his church, the author of the saint's Life all but conceded that Lynally was subject to the Columban (later Augustinian) church.[10] The second church of which Colmán was patron, at Muckamore in Antrim – near Lough Neagh, a name derived from Eacha son of

Mairidh, primal ancestor of Colmán's family – was also to become the site of an Augustinian priory.[11]

In keeping with the saint's descent, the Salamancan Life locates the beginning of Colmán's career, his birth, upbringing, initial instruction, and early encounters with other saints in the north of Ireland, mostly in the area about Lough Neagh. Following his instruction by a saint named Caomhán, among others, he founded a little monastery (*monasteriolum*) with four monks, all of whom died of hunger.[12] Various miracles were then performed, including the resuscitation of a youth destined to become the saint known as Colmán Muilinn of Derrykeighan in north Antrim. Three important boundary rivers are featured in the text: the river Mion which separated Dál nAraidhe from Ceinéal Eoghain; the Bior, or Moyola, which served as a terminus of the diocese of Armagh; and the Dabhall, or Blackwater, which, like the Moyola, flows into Lough Neagh.[13] This section of the Life concludes with an account, based on Adhamhnán's work, of the saint's passage to Iona with the added assertion that Colum Cille gave Colmán the gift of a cruet (*ampulla*) which, on being left behind, later turned up near the altar of Daire Calach (perhaps for Calgach), now Derry, which was also to become the site of an Augustinian priory.[14]

The remainder of the Life is taken up with Colmán's activities in the Midlands, beginning with the above-mentioned story of the founding of Lynally which places the saint in Colum Cille's debt.[15] Like Colum Cille, Colmán is shown to have had the gift of second sight, illustrated here by his prior knowledge of the death of Pope Gregory, long before the news otherwise reached Ireland.[16] His contacts with various other saints, such as Mochuda of Rahan whose church lay close to Lynally, and Molua of Clonfertmulloe who is cast in a deferential role, receive attention in the Life, as do his visits to such churches as Ferns, Clonmacnoise, and Clonard, all of them later locations of houses of canons regular.[17] As if to emphasize the closeness of the perceived relationship with the church of Connor, Colmán foretells of its bishop, Díoma Dubh (†659), that he will provide succour and protection for all the churches of Ireland, a situation that arguably first became reality in the twelfth century in the person of Díoma's successor Maol Maodhóg (Malachy).[18] On the point of death, and surrounded by other saints, Colmán is said to have been allowed three petitions by the Lord, one of which requested that, if wisdom were ever to be lacking on the island, a wise man would still be found in Lynally.[19]

Colmán's vernacular Life, a verse and prose composition, is largely concerned with the fortunes of local families that clearly had an interest in the church of Lynally, including the above-mentioned Muintear Chuinneagáin, the Uí Mhaoil Mhuadh lords of the surrounding territory of Fir Cheall, and their close relatives, the Uí Dhuineachaidh.[20] At this point, relations with Durrow and Rahan appear to have soured, with monks of the former church being accused of stealing 'Roman' earth from the burial ground in Lynally, and Mochuda of Rahan cursing one of the local families, only to have his curse undone by Colmán.[21]

An early instructional tract entitled *Aibghitir Chrábhaidh* ('Alphabet of Piety') is attributed to Colmán in several manuscripts, but his authorship is the subject of much debate, as is his possible authorship of *Audite omnes amantes*, an early hymn in honour of St Patrick which is also attributed to Secundinus (Seachnall).[22] A tract on the Ceinéal Fiachach, progenitors of the Uí Mhaoil Mhuadh lords of Fir Cheall, places Colmán Eala first among their saints, naming the 'people of Tullamore', the Uí Eideagáin and their relatives, as the saint's local devotees, and delimiting his sphere of influence to the area 'south of the river Brosna'.[23] Colmán's connection with the district about Lough Neagh is elsewhere underlined by an encounter with Caoilte of the Fianna at 'Loch an Daimh Dheirg', near Moira in Down, and further north he was patron of the Antrim parish of Ahoghill.[24] There, in contrast to his more usual Columban associations, Colmán is said to have been one of Patrick's priests. Devotion to the saint also extended to churches in Scotland, including Colmonell in Ayrshire and Kilcolmonell in Kintyre.[25]

Colmán was one of three important bearers of the name attached to a small triangle of churches, the others being the patrons of Lynn near Mullingar (a place allegedly cursed by the saint), and Conry in the barony of Rathconrath.[26] All three were said to have acted on behalf of – or under the protection of – Colum Cille, with whom they were probably all ultimately identical.[27] They shared much in common besides their name. All three are again featured together in the Life of Colmán of Lynn, and Colmán of Conry's feast fell on 25 September, the vigil of the day of Colmán of Lynally.[28] His birth on 3 October was remembered in two early ninth-century martyrologies kept at Tallaght, and also in a calendar from the same period kept by an Irishman on the Reichenau in Lake Constance.[29] Colmán is said by the annals to have died in 611 at the age of 55, and his crozier was apparently still kept as a relic at Lynally in the early seventeenth century.[30] The saint's cross is elsewhere invoked as a protection against being thrown from a horse.[31] Within Leinster, Colmán was also venerated at Tullaghanbrogue in the Kilkenny baronies of Crannagh and Shillelogher.[32]

1 *VC*[2] 222, 356–8; *DIB* ii, 693. **2** ATig. (= *AU s.a.*), *CS*, *AFM*; *MartT* 74; cf. *OH* 1, 38–50. **3** *CGSH* §311; *GRSH* 95; *Lgen*. 728.4. **4** *VSHH* 406 §14. **5** *AU s.a.* **6** *BNÉ* i, 168 §1; *ILL* 362. **7** *VSHH* 209–24; *MISL* 297–339 at 329, 384; *CeltC* 182–9; *OH* 1, 38. **8** *MRHI* 146–52. **9** Ibid. 174–5. **10** *VSHH* 214 §14; cf. *VC*[2] 264. **11** *MRHI* 188–9; *EA* 98. **12** *VSHH* 209–11 §§1–4. **13** Ibid. 211–12 §§5–10. **14** Ibid. 213–14 §13; *MRHI* 168–9. **15** *VSHH* 214 §14. **16** *VSHH* 215–16 §20; *ZCP* 12, 373; *RC* 46, 249 §15. **17** *VSHH* 217–22 §§25–43. **18** Ibid. 217–18 §26. **19** Ibid. 224 §50. **20** *BNÉ* i, 168–9 §§1–10; OCBG §§882–9. **21** *BNÉ* i, 173 §§19–21, 180–2 §§36–9. **22** *ZCP* 3, 447–55; *Celtica* 8, 49–50; *ViewIL* 15; *IChr*. 203–15; *Ériu* 23, 115–16; *BK* 13; *CéliD* 140; *OH* 1, 42; *Iona* 195–207; *PSP* 40–6; *IIAM* 562–3. **23** *Lgen*. 172.2; *ZCP* 21, 5. **24** *SG* i, 158–9; PNNI iv, 158–61. **25** *KSS* 305; *CPNS* 187, 303; *CPL* 10, 493. **26** *MartO*[2] 136; *MartD* 384. **27** *BCC* 212 §219. **28** *BCML* §§31–4; *MartT* 74; *MartG* 184; *MartD* 258. **29** *MartT* 76; *MartO*[2] 214; *AfL* 31, 60. **30** *AU s.a.*; *MartD* xliv; *AU/ATig. s.a.* **31** *ZCP* 1, 455. **32** *HADO* iii, 385.

Colmán Fionn, 'fair'; see Cuman of Aireadh Bóinne.

Colmán Gaoile (Guaile). *See* Colmán of Dromore.

Colmán Iomramha, 'sea-voyage', of Fahan (Othain), barony of Inishowen West, Co. Donegal. According to the corpus of saints' pedigrees, Colmán son of Feargna (Fearghas) belonged variously to the Dál Riada and Fir Lí, both of which held lands in north-east Ulster, one in north Antrim, the other on the Derry side of the river Bann.[1] As Fahan lay within the diocese of Derry, which was closely associated with Colum Cille, the two saints were probably originally identical, in which case Colmán's sea-voyage would perhaps have been to Iona. The saint's feast fell on 8 July.[2]

1 *CGSH* §§237, 468. 2 *MartT* 54; *MartG* 132; *MartD* 190.

Colmán Iomramha of Inishmore of the Aran Islands (Ára), barony of Aran, Co. Galway. The saint intended by the reference to Colmán Iomramha of Ára in the list of homonymous saints is doubtless the same as Mocholmóg son of Colmán of Inishmore to whom the Uí Chorra are said to have told the story of their celebrated *iomramh* 'sea-voyage'.[1] In the notice of his feast (21 November), the saint's name is rendered Colmán son of Comán (a variant form of Colmán), and he is located in Inisheer (Ára Oirthir).[2] As this is also the feast of Columbanus of Bobbio in Italy, Colmán's sea-voyage may have been to the Continent. According to an Old Irish Table of Commutations, Mocholmóg son of Comán of Aran was one of the four chief sages of Ireland.[3] According to the Annals of Inisfallen, he died in 751.[4]

1 *CGSH* §707.148; *Imm.* 111. 2 *MartO*[2] 236, 244; *MartG* 222; *MartD* 314. 3 *Ériu* 19, 64 §23. 4 *AI s.a.*

Colmán of Kilclooney in the Armagh barony of Fews Lower. Of this saint very little is known. It has been shown, however, that he is found in early documents as Colmán of the Maca Coirtchidh and, as such, he figures in the martyrological lists for 18 October, which describe him as an abbot.[1] The lists of homonymous saints also include his name.[2]

1 *SAM* 2.1, 163–5; *MartT* 81; *MartG* 198; *MartD* 278. 2. *CGSH* 143 (§707.233).

Colmán Lobhar, 'leper'. In his seventeenth-century list of patrons of the churches of Ossory, Bishop Phelan assigned the feast of Colmán, patron of Ballygurrim in the barony of Ida, to 21 May, a day shared by Colmán Lobhar of Moynoe (Magh nEó) in the Clare barony of Tulla Upper.[1] When Moynoe was visited by John O'Donovan in 1839, there was no memory of the patron under this guise, but a holy well near the church was called after Mochonna, a hypocoristic form of Colmán which was also the name of the patron of the adjoining parish of Feakle.[2] As Moynoe also adjoins Inishcaltra, it is reasonable to suppose that Colmán and Caimín were representatives of the same original cult, more than likely that of Colum Cille. This supposition is supported by the presence in the list for 21 May of Bairrfhionn of Drumcullen, a representative of the cult of Fionnbharr (whose name also figures in the list), a close associate of Colum.[3] Colmán may also have been remembered on 13 November, unless Magh Eó in this case refers to Mayo.[4]

1 *HADO* iv, 89; *MartT* 45; *MartO*[2] 125; *MartG* 100; *MartD* 134. 2 *ACoC* 218. 3 *MakS* 19–23. 4 *MartG* 218; *MartD* 308.

Colmán Mór, 'great', son of Fearghas. *See* Colmán of Kildare.

Colmán Mucaidh, 'swineherd', of Arboe (Ard Bó), barony of Dungannon Upper, Co. Tyrone. Colmán's pedigree attaches him through his father Aodh Guaire (alias Guaire) to the descendants of Colla Uais of the Oirghialla, and more particularly to the Ceinéal Mic Caorthainn branch of that family.[1] His church lay on the edge of Lough Neagh, as is specified in several sources.[2] Here too there was apparently a branch of his family which, according to an episode in the Tripartite Life, gave Patrick a mixed reception.[3] Caorthann Mór, 'great', sought to expel the saint who then gave his blessing to Caorthann Beag, 'little', and prophesied that he would yet place the veil on the head of the child in the womb of Caorthann Beag's wife. This child was Trea, patron of Artrea (Aird Trea), a parish adjoining Arboe. Though Colmán is sometimes presented as a lay person with children, a poem by Fear Dorcha Ó Mealláin, possibly a native of Down, on the expulsion of the Irish to Connacht, when invoking the saint's protection, describes him as *ceann na gcliar*, 'head of the clergy'.[4] Colmán's feastday was celebrated on 21 February.[5] In Scotland, the saint's day fell three days earlier on 18 February.[6]

1 *CGSH* §49; *GRSH* 66; *Lgen.* 714.1.3; *CGH* 141a45–6. 2 *MartT* 18; *MartO*[2] 76; *GRSH* 66. 3 *BP* 1954–71; *VT* 168. 4 *CGH* 141b26; *ND* i, 36. 5 *MartT* 18; *MartG* 40; *MartD* 54. 6 *CPNS* 278–9.

Colmán Muilinn, 'of the mill', of Derrykeighan (Doire Caocháin), barony of Lower Dunluce, Co. Antrim. According to the corpus of saints' pedigrees, Colmán son of Conall and his uterine siblings – Caolán of Nendrum, Colmán of Conry, and Fursa of Péronne – belonged to the Ulaidh of north-east Ulster.[1] His mother was Brónach, whose father Míleac is said to have held Patrick in bondage.[2] Colmán himself is reputed to have been a member of a marauding group of laymen, before electing, despite the opposition of his leader, to follow Colmán Eala of Lynally, remaining with him for the rest of his life.[3] Colmán's cognomen, *Muileann/Molendarius*, is said to have been because of his practice of using the mill as a place in which to make obeisance to his brethren.[4] His association in the Great Book of Genealogies with the church of Domhnach Mór (Donaghmore in the Down barony of Upper Iveagh) derives from confusion with a neighbouring entry in other witnesses.[5] Colmán's feast fell on 1 January.[6]

1 *CGSH* §158; *GRSH* 103; *Lgen.* 734.16. 2 *CGSH* §722.92. 3 *VSHH* 211 §5. 4 *MartG* 6; *MartD* 2. 5 *Lgen.* 737.7; *CGSH* §159. 6 *MartT* 3; *MartG* 6; *MartD* 2.

Colmán Oilithir, 'pilgrim', of Ross, alias Ross Carbery (Ros Oilithir), barony of East Carbery, Co. Cork. In the main corpus of saints' pedigrees, Colmán son of Grillín (Greallán), whose name is also written Mocholmóg, follows immediately on Fachtna but, unlike the patron of the diocese of Ross who was assigned to the local family of Corca Laoighdhe, Colmán was attached to the Clann Cholmáin of Westmeath, a dominant dynasty in the Midlands from about the middle of the eighth century onwards.[1] Little else is recorded of the saint, but he figures, again together with Fachtna, in the list of those said to have attended Fionnbharr's famous school in Cork.[2] He was important enough to have given name to Ros Oilithir.[3] A stone lying in an enclosure named Ceall na gColmán (church of the

Colmáns) in the townland of Maumanorig, adjoining Kilcolman, parish of Marhin, near Ventry in Kerry, bears an inscription that reads: *Anm Colman Ailithir*, 'the name of Colmán Oilithir'.[4] The pattern day at this church in former times was 24 June.

1 *CGSH* §§222–3; *GRSH* 54; *Lgen.* 704.3. **2** *BBa.* 76, 263. **3** *CGSH* §223. **4** *CIIC* i, 186–8.

Colmán Stiallán, perhaps 'little strip' of Terryglass (Tír Dá Ghlas), barony of Lower Ormond, Co. Tipperary. An annal entry for 624 records the death of Colmán Stiallán (Stéallán).[1] He is doubtless identical with the Terryglass saint of this name commemorated on 26 May.[2] His name also figures in the list of homonymous saints.[3]

1 *AU s.a.* **2** *MartT* 46; *MartG* 104; *MartD* 138. **3** *CGSH* §707.209.

Colmán Uamhach, 'of the cave'. On the evidence of this saint's cognomen, it might be thought that replicated Colmán of Cluain Uamha, 'pasture of the cave', now Cloyne, but an annal entry noting the death in 725 of Colmán Uamhach, 'scribe of Armagh', suggests that there may have been two of the name.[1] Under the hypocoristic guise of Mochonóg Uamhach, the saint is included in the list of those commemorated on 18 November, seven days before that of the patron of Cloyne and thus suitable for consideration as an octave feast.[2] Míchéal Ó Cléirigh concluded that the patron of Cloyne must be the same as the Colmán Uamhach who is said to have written a Life of Patrick, but this surely refers to the scribe of Armagh.[3] The name also figures in the list of homonymous saints.[4]

1 *AU s.a.* **2** *MartG* 220; *MartD* 312. **3** *MartD* 316; *BP* 638; *VT* 60. **4** *CGSH* §707.149.

Colum. *See* also Colmán.

Colum daughter of Neas. *See* Ceallán of Fancroft.

Colum of Clonarney. *See* Colum Tuama.

Colum of Cluain Uail, an unidentified church in Leinster. A poem attributed to Moling calls upon this saint, along with many others, to come to the assistance of the Leinstermen.[1]

1 *SG* i, 390.

Colum of Culbrim, parish of Ballymoney, barony of Upper Dunluce, Co. Antrim, which may now represent an earlier Cúil Bhrióin. The list of homonymous saints refers to this son of Aodh Claon, who is otherwise accorded two feastdays, 8 November and 11 December.[1] On both days he is said to have been remembered at Cúil Bhrióin (alias Cúil Damháin). The same place is mentioned in a tract on the Dál bhFiatach of east Ulster, in connection with a man named Colum son of Crután (?) who was probably identical with the Culbrim saint.[3]

1 *CGSH* 707.90; *MartG* 214, 236; *MartD* 298, 332. **3** *BB* 168d28.

Colum of Donaghmore. *See* Colmán of Myshall.

Colum of Inishcaltra. *See* Colum of Terryglass.

Colum of Inishkeen (Inis Caoin) on Lough Melvin, parish of Rossinver, barony of Rosclogher, Co. Leitrim. An early seventeenth-century list of churches in the barony of Rosclogher twice refers to Inishkeen, attaching to it Siostán and Colum (Columba) and drawing attention to the presence on it of *Carcair Choinnigh*, 'Cainneach's [i.e. Colum's] prison', which shows that Colum had come to be known locally under two forms of his name.[1] The list assigns feasts of 17 July and 14 October respectively to Siostán and Colum, and these dates are confirmed by the martyrologies, which describe both as priests.[2] As the latter date fell a few days only after that of Cainneach of Kilkenny (11 October), it may be assumed that he and the patron of Inishkeen were originally identical. Colum's October day was shared by another namesake in hypocoristic guise, Cuimín of Kilcummin in the Galway barony of Moycullen, which would also indicate an original identity.[3] Curiously, however, Cuimín was commemorated locally on 13 July.[4] Colum of Inishkeen may also have been known hypocoristically as Mochamóg, the form used in the notice of a separate feast of 13 April, unless this be Mochomóg, brother of Fearghas of the like-named, but distinct, Inishkeen.[5]

1 *Celtica* 1, 66. 2 *MartT* 56, 79; *MartG* 138, 196; *MartD* 194, 276. 3 *OFWC* 54; *WLC* 168; *AIGY* i, 127. 4 OSL GY iii, 9. 5 *MartT* 32; *MartG* 76; *MartD* 100.

Colum of Killeigh, parish and barony of Geashill, Co. Offaly. This daughter of Aodh is placed in Drumad in Géisille (Geashill), which probably corresponds to the Drumad attached to the Irish form of Killeigh (Ceall Achaidh Drumada).[1] Colum's name figures in a list of miscellaneous items added to the Book of Leinster version of the corpus of saints' pedigrees.[2] She is also featured in the list of homonymous saints, under two guises, as daughter of Aodh and as patron of Drumad.[3]

1 *HDGP* iii, 120–1. 2 *CGSH* §663.5. 3 Ibid. §708.67.74.

Colum of Monaincha (Loch Cré), parish of Corbally, barony of Ikerrin, Co. Tipperary. The saint most closely connected with the church on the lake or island of Cré was Crónán, patron of the neighbouring church of Roscrea.[1] Colum is also associated with Monaincha, not only under his own name, as in the list of homonymous saints, but also under the guise of Cainneach who, desirous of fleeing from the world, is said to have spent the forty days of Lent there, writing a gospel-book known as *Glas Chainnigh*, 'Cainneach's blue-green [book]'.[2] Colum's feast, shared by various namesakes, including Cainneach, fell on 15 May.[3]

1 *VSHP* ii, 26 §16, 223 §52; *VSHH* 144 §67. 2 *VSHP* i, 167 §42; *VSHH* 195–6 §§48, 52. 3 *MartT* 43; *MartG* 96; *MartD* 128; *TT* 494 (45).

Colum of Terryglass (Tír Dá Ghlas), barony of Lower Ormond, Co. Tipperary. The pedigree of Colum son of Criomhthann traces his descent to the Uí Chriomhthannáin (or Uí Chriomhthainn Áin), a Leinster family that held lands near Stradbally on Laois' border with Kildare, and earlier also in the area about

Portlaoise [1]. His mother Mionchloth (alias Mionchlú) is said to have been a sister of Caoimheall (mother of Caoimhghin of Glendalough) whose people were the Dál gCormaic Loisc (otherwise the Uí Chormaic) of the area between Killeshin in Carlow and Killabban in Laois.[2] Colum's chief church, situated on the edge of Lough Derg, is said by Adhamhnán to have been visited by Colum Cille at a time when the keys of its door had been lost.[3] The door opened through the mediation of the Iona saint who was then revered by the whole community with honour. The detail of this passage has been taken to indicate that Colum of Terryglass was a localization of his namesake on Iona, and there is other evidence to support this view.[4]

His probable identity with the patron of Iona did not deter the community at Terryglass from regarding their patron as distinct and arranging to have a Life composed for him which is preserved in two recensions, one in the Salamancan codex, the other in the *Insulensis* collection.[5] Although sometimes thought to be an early composition, the Salamancan text, like almost all other Irish saints' Lives, contains evidence pointing to the period after the arrival of the external orders and, most likely, after the English conquest of Ireland.[6] According to the Life, Colum, having been baptized by Momhaodhóg of Fiddown, was reared at Cluain Caoin – now probably Clonkeen in the Laois parish of Clonenagh – by Colmán Cúile; both of these saints are said to have also belonged to the Uí Chriomhthannáin.[7] He then attended the famous school of Finnian at Clonard, with, among others, Colum Cille, before going first to Rome, where he received relics of Peter and Paul, and then to Tours in France which he left, after some miracles, with enshrined relics of St Martin. Arriving back in Ireland, he allegedly founded several churches in the area about Lough Derg before arriving at Inishcaltra (alias Holy Island), where his namesakes and probable doubles, Caimín and Colum, were venerated. Though most of the remainder of his life was spent on an island in the Shannon estuary, near Canon Island, the saint's remains were eventually brought to Terryglass and buried there.

Among the many saints brought into contact with Colum were Fiontan of Clonenagh, Neasán of Mungret, Ciarán of Seirkieran, and Aonghas of Clonmacnoise.[8] A special role was reserved for him by his teacher, Finnian of Clonard, who foretold that Colum would administer the last rites to him.[9] This he duly did, proceeding thereafter to Clonee (Cluain Í) in the Meath parish of Trim, some five miles from Clonard, where he spent one night, before dying there on the following day. Colum's relationship with Finnian reflects the arrangement of the martyrologies, which place the feasts of the two saints on successive days (12/13 December).[10] Like Finnian, Colum is said to have died – together with his namesake and probable double, Colum of Inishcaltra – of the 'great mortality' in 549, and to have lain buried for seven years in Clonee, where, according to the list of homonymous saints, his name, under its diminutive form Colmán, continued to be venerated.[11] Colum's remains were allegedly later brought by Odhrán Maighistir and Mochaomhóg to Caimín on Inishcaltra.[12] The fact that Colum's feast was shared by Baodán son of Sineall recalls the place of Baoithín, whose name is a variant of Baodán, in the list for the feastday of Colum Cille, another indication of the ultimate identity of the patrons of Terryglass and Iona. Described as a 'descendant of a true prince', and among those cited in the Old Irish Table of Penitential Commutations as sponsors of a certain type of vigil, Colum was regarded as one of the twelve apostles of Ireland, and was likened in manners to the apostle and evangelist Matthew.[13] The saint's 'hair-shirt' reputedly formed part of Adhamhnán's reliquary.[14] His original name is said to have been Cuinnidh, a derivative of *Cuinne/Coinne*, a pet form of Colum.[15]

1 *CGSH* §241; *GRSH* 87; *Lgen*. 724.9; *CGH* 122bb10–12, b26; *LSHS* 37. **2** *CGSH* §722.19.20; *MartO*[1] clxxxii. **3** *VC*[2] 410; *Ériu* 54, 68–72. **4** *FEMN* 462n; *Peritia* 1, 150–1. **5** *VSHH* 225–33; *AB* 72, 343–7. **6** *MISL* 297, 392; *Kenney* 385–6. **7** *VSHH* 225 §§3–4. **8** Ibid. 229–32 §§19, 24, 28–9. **9** Ibid. 102 §20, 231 §26. **10** *MartO*[2] 251; *MartG* 236–8; *MartD* 332–4. **11** *AU s.a.*; *MakS* 14–15; *CGSH* §707.210. **12** *MartT* 118–19; *MartO*[1] clxxxii; Cf. *VSHH* 232 §28. **13** *CGH* 122b26; *AB* 72, 346–7; *Ériu* 19, 64 §23; *VSHH* 83 §5; *CGSH* §712.11; *CGSH* §712.10. **14** *Celtica* 15, 35 §13. **15** *CGSH* §703.11.22.

Colum son of Fiachra, bishop. This man is twice mentioned in a tract on the Dál bhFiatach of east Ulster in connection with his father Fiachra, son of Cathbhadh son of Eachaidh Gunnad.[1] The editor of the tract thought that he might be the same as Colmán of Kilroot, but there is no supporting evidence.

1 *ZCP* 13, 350, 352.

Colum son of Flannán. *See* Eiltín of Kinsale.

Colum son of Riaghal. *See* Colmán of Longfordpass.

Colum Cille, 'of the church', of Iona, Scotland. According to both Adhamhnán and the wider genealogical tradition, Colum Cille, whose original name is said to have been Criomhthann, belonged to a branch of the Ceinéal Conaill of Donegal, closely related to the ruling line which ran through his first cousin Ainmhire.[1] His parents were named Feidhlimidh son of Fearghas and Eithne daughter of Mac Naoi (Latin *filius navis*), but though mentioning the latter's kindred, and locating it in Ireland, Adhamhnán gave it no name.[2] One later line of tradition assigned Eithne – also known as Deirbhfhinn Dualfhada/Bhéalfhada, 'long-tressed/wide mouth' – to the Laighin (Leinstermen), and more specifically to a family known as the Corbraighe which may have had connections with the Uí Bhairrche of Carlow and Wexford.[3] Another (more plausible) line of tradition attached Eithne to the Corbraighe of Fánaid, now Fanad in north Donegal.[4] Colum's four recorded siblings were a brother (Eoghan), of whom nothing else is known, and three sisters (Cuman, Mionchloth, Sineach) who gain mention in an attachment to Adhamhnán's Life of the saint.[5] One of these, Mionchloth, is credited with children of her own, the sons of Éanán who gave name to Ceall Mac nÉanáin, now Kilmacrenan in the Donegal barony of the same name, allegedly the church in which Colum was fostered by Cruithneachán.[6]

As Patrick was a Briton by birth, and as Brighid probably originated as a pagan divinity, Colum Cille (Latin Columba) son of Feidhlimidh may justly be regarded as the single most important native Irish saint. This is confirmed not only by his traditional place, at least as old as the twelfth century, in the group of three 'national' saints, but also by the posthumous spread of his cult to all parts of Ireland and Scotland, and well beyond. Yet, despite the fact that the record of his saintly activities began at a comparatively early date, with a Life composed shortly before 700 by Adhamhnán, Colum's eighth sucessor as abbot on Iona, much of the detail of this text must be treated with caution; as already stated by William Reeves, the supernatural incidents in Colum Cille's Life 'grew under successive biographers', Adhamhnán having 'a very great number'.[7] The dates framing what appears to have been a long life, for example, which credit Colum with a lifespan of seventy-seven (77), broken down into forty-three (4+3 = 7) years in Ireland and thirty-four (3+4 = 7) in Scotland, though still widely accepted as genuine, were designed to make as much use as possible of the numerologically 'perfect' digit seven.[8]

Although there is no denying Adhamhnán's wide learning and sophisticated style of writing, his purpose was to present the patron and founder of his church and *familia* as a complete saint, and to this end he used not only stratagems borrowed from previous hagiographers, such as Sulpicius Severus, author of the Life of Martin of Tours, but also oral tradition. As with all other works of this kind, his text was principally a commentary on the issues of his own time. The reprieve of a few months from death procured from heaven for Colum, who had allegedly expected to die in April, was surely designed to impress upon the brethren at Iona the need to preserve Eastertide, normally associated with April, as an occasion of joy rather than sorrow or strife, as it had become on Iona in Adhamhnán's own time because of the Easter controversy.[9]

Prior to the saint's birth, according to sources much later than Adhamhnán's Life, there were many prognostications of his future greatness. This is said to have been foretold by Patrick, Mochta of Louth, Eoghan of Ardstraw, Brighid of Kildare, and Buithe of Monasterboice, among others.[10] Adhamhnán asserted only that, through an angelic apparition, the saint's mother was given prior notice of her son's glorious destiny.[11] Colum's teacher, named Fionnbharr (also written Finnio and Vinniavus, and more popularly rendered Finnian), was probably the founder and patron of Movilla in the Down parish of Newtownards, near Bangor.[12] Although also remembered for his correspondence with Gildas, historian of Britain, which Columbanus of Bobbio cited, Fionnbharr's fame rested primarily on his role as Colum's tutor.[13] At Dromin in the county of Louth, for example, where the patron, Fiontan Fionn, was sometimes replaced by Finnéan (Finnian), the story of Colum's surreptitious copying of his teacher's gospel-book, and the celebrated Solomon-like judgement that ensued, were put forward as the main reason for the battle of Cúil Dreimhne and the saint's subsequent self-imposed exile.[14] What really induced Colum to leave Ireland for Iona – which he is reputed to have founded between about 558 and 574, when the grantor, a local king named Conall son of Comhghall, died – remains unclear.[15]

Whatever the reason for his exile, Colum has the distinction of being Ireland's earliest known founder of a church outside this island. According to Bede, who wrote his history of the English people about 730, the saint's mission was to the Picts whose king, Bruide, Colum is said to have converted.[16] Bede also asserts that it was the Picts who, following their conversion to the faith of Christ, granted the island of Iona to Colum. Though the extent of Iona's influence during the saint's lifetime must remain a matter for speculation, after his death in 597 it became, with Kildare and Armagh, one of the three most powerful ecclesiastical sites of the Gaelic world, and head of a widespread federation of churches, straddling both Ireland and Scotland.[17] Through its mission to Northumbria it reached out to the world beyond and became a conduit for external influences, as is shown, for example, by its mediatory role in the formation of an Irish martyrological tradition.[18]

One consequence of the need of the Columban *familia* to promote itself and to protect its interests was the production of several Lives of its founder saint, beginning with that written by Adhamhnán shortly before 700. In the early ninth century, following a decline in Iona's status, Kells in Meath became the focal point of the Columban *familia*, and this led to the production of a Life of Colum's biographer, Adhamhnán, in the mid-tenth century, again with a view to protecting and strengthening the influence of the community.[19] Later still, in the late twelfth century, when Derry had become the most important Columban church, its community arranged to have a vernacular Life written for the saint.[20] And in the early sixteenth century, in the county of Colum's birth, Donegal, where devotion to the saint retained more vigour than anywhere else, a local chieftain, Maghnas Ó Domhnaill, commissioned a new vernacular Life which brought together all that could then be found of Colum's hagiography.[21]

During the thousand or so years between the saint's death in 597 and the collapse of the native Irish polity in the early seventeenth century, scarcely a corner of the Gaelic world was unaffected by Colum's cult. John Colgan listed over sixty churches that claimed him, many of them baselessly, as founder, including Durrow, Raphoe, Drumcliff, Swords, Lambay, and even Kells, which was founded long after Colum's time.[22] In the diocese of Derry alone, he was patron of five churches, and in Scotland, after the decline of Iona, his cult became established in numerous other important centres, including Dunkeld, which exercised great influence, and Inchcolm, home to a house of Augustinian canons.[23] But these foundations represent a fraction only of the communities which, having heard his story, embraced his cult and adopted him as founder-patron. Because of cult-fragmentation, a feature of Irish devotion to the saints, many Columban churches are no longer regarded as such. The patron saints of Terryglass (Colum) and Kilkenny (Cainneach, a derivative of Colum), although originally identical with Colum Cille, came to be regarded as separate saints, as did many other bearers of the name, including Colmán of Dromore.[24]

The saint's reputation for book-learning and poetry manifests itself from the earliest part of his record. This is shown not only by Adhamhnán, but also by some early (possibly seventh-century) vernacular poems, including *Amhra Choluim Chille*, a semi-elegiac composition, thought by some to have been composed shortly after the saint's death in 597, but considered by others to be a ninth-century composition, and later credited with the power to avert evil.[25] The saint himself has been credited with the composition of many other poems, as well as a monastic rule, all of which date from much later than his lifetime. One manuscript alone, the *Saltair Choluim Chille*, 'Psalter of Colum Cille', contains 150 poems of his, and some Latin hymns, including an alphabet hymn beginning *Altus prosatur*, have also been attributed to him.[26] Books were also prominent among his relics. Adhamhnán speaks of books in the saint's own handwriting being used against drought affecting the island, and Colum's most famous surviving relic is a copy of the Psalter called the *Cathach*, now in the Royal Irish Academy, which was covered by a shrine now in the National Museum.[27] The Donegal custodians of this relic paraded with it in front of the powerful local family of the O'Donnells (Uí Dhomhnaill), before these went into battle.[28] The *duanaire*, 'poem-book', of the O'Donnells regularly invokes the name of the saint described as the saviour of the Ceinéal Conaill.[29] The fortunes of Colum's relics – including the Book of Kells, which came to be regarded as his gospel-book – and reliquaries find regular mention in the annals, and the saint's 'hair-shirt' reputedly formed part of the reliquary of his biographer Adhamhnán.[30] Among those cited in the Old Irish Table of Penitential Commutations as sponsors of a certain type of vigil, the saint was likened in manners to Andrew the apostle, co-patron of the Scots.[31] Like Maol Maodhóg and others, Colum Cille became a peg on which to hang prophecies, most notably, perhaps, in the account of the doleful portents of the *Scuab*, 'besom', out of Fanad and, similarly, in the poem addressed to Baoithín in which more portents of the end of the world are outlined.[32]

The saint's feast, still observed in many parts of Ireland and Scotland, fell on 9 June which, in Scotland, was sometimes taken to be the second Thursday in June, thus rendering all Thursdays 'propitious for man, beast and enterprise'.[33] It was shared by Baoithín, Colum's immediate successor as abbot of Iona, and more space is devoted to the commemoration of these two feasts in the Martyrology of Donegal than to any other.[34] The feast was also noticed from an early date in external martyrologies, calendars, and other sources, including the early eighth-century Echternach Calendar of St Willibrord, the ninth-century martyrologies of Ado and Usuard, and the tenth- or eleventh-century Life of Findan of Rheinau.[35] A late twelfth-century tradition asserts that Colum Cille's remains lie, together with those of Patrick and Brighid, in Downpatrick.[36] An even later tradition states that, while alive, Colum went to heaven every Thursday, whence the practice in Scotland of referring to this day as *Lá Choluim Chille*.[37] Many relics of the saint found their way to the Continent, among other places to Sens and, arguably, either to Ferrières in France or to some church in the Rhineland.[38] A relic of the saint, accompanied by relics of Adhamhnán and Finnian of Movilla, had also reached Saint-Maurice d'Agaune in the Swiss canton of Valais by the second half of the eighth century.[39]

1 *VC*^{2} 186; *AILC* 105; *CGSH* §§8, 397, 661, 703.1.22; *GRSH* 38; *Lgen.* 697.4; *CGH* 144e4. **2** *VC*^{2} 434; *VC*^{1} II.40; *AILC* 194. **3** *IKD* 226 §20; *CGH* 128b7; *RC* 20, 416 §143; *BCC* 10 §22; *CGSH* §397. **4** *CGSH* §§397, 661; *VC*^{2} 546–8. **5** *CGSH* §§397, 722.23. **6** *VC*^{2} 466–8; *VC*^{1} III.2; *AILC* 206; *BCC* 40–2 §§53–4. **7** *VC*^{1}, *VC*^{2}, *AILC*; *UJA* 6 (1st ser.), 24–5; *DIB* ii, 706–8. **8** *IKD* 27; *AB* 78, 381–90; *AILC* 9; *SCJ* 5, 7–18. **9** *VC*^{2} 516–18; *VC*^{1} III.23; *AILC* 225; *Peritia* 1, 160–77; ibid. 3, 50–70. **10** *IKD* 223–5 §§14–17. **11** *VC*^{2} 464–6; *VC*^{1} III.1; *AILC* 205. **12** *VC*^{2} 470–2; *VC*^{1} III.4; *AILC* 208; *IETÜ* 52–7; *FKHS* 407–14; *GNA* 207–14. **13** *SOC* 8 §7; *MakS* 28. **14** *BCC* 176–8 §168; *IMN* no. 22, 3–11. **15** *AU s.a.*; *IKD* 27–8. **16** *BEH* 220–4. **17** *IKD* 68–77, 88–97; *DIB* ii, 707. **18** *FSHIM* 57–74. **19** *BAd.* **20** *IKD* 209–89; *LisL* 652–1116; *TMIH* 90–124;

SGS 2, 111–71. **21** *BCC*; *DIB* ii, 707. **22** *TT* 493–5. **23** *Celtica* 1, 82; *ACDS* 40–2; *CR* 4, 97–103. **24** *FEMN* 462n; *FG* 20–35. **25** *RC* 20, 168, 254; *SSS* 67–75; *Ériu* 26, 66–98; *SnaS* 191–212; *Iona* 96–128; *ÉtC* 2, 274–5; *KeltRh.* 1–11; *AmraeCC* 77–157. **26** *Bod. Cat.* 88–101 (Laud. Misc. 615); *ZCP* 12, 385–96; ibid. 13, 7–10; *ACL* iii, 221–4; *LH* i, 62–89. **27** *VC*[2] 450–2; *Kenney* 629–30; *DLHS* 117–26. **28** *BCC* 182–4 §178; cf. *AMME* §12; *Kenney* 630; *Béaloideas* 16, 219–21. **29** *IrT* ii, 9–10, 20, 22, 69, 80, 87–91. **30** *AU s.a.* 788, 829, 831, 849, 1007, 1204, 1538; *Celtica* 15, 35 §14. **31** *Ériu* 19, 64 §23; *CGSH* §712.4. **32** *MartO*[2] 190; NLI G 10, 46b; *DIB* ii, 708; *TEAB* 690 §1; 697–704. **33** *MartT* 49; *MartO*[2] 139; *MartG* 112; *TT* 493–5; *VC*[1] 276–98; *CPNS* 279–81; *KSS* 306–7; *CarmG* ii, 241. **34** *MartD* 150–64. **35** HBS 55, 8; *MartA* 189; *MartU* 244; *MGH.SS* 15, 1, 505–6 §8; *PRIA* 98C1, 4–5. **36** *TT* 261. **37** *DD* 221 §11; *ApalF* 169–70. **38** *SIHI* 63–70; *MSNAF* 449; *EIRD* 55–68; *RIW* 15–19. **39** *RIW* 13, 32.

Colum Crom, 'bent', of Lorum (Leamhdhruim), barony of Idrone East, Co. Carlow. To judge by two entries added to the Book of Leinster version of the corpus of saints' pedigrees, the monastery of Terryglass in Tipperary had a proprietorial interest in the church of Lorum. One entry names several saints associated with that church, including Colum Crom, Darlughdhach, Mochuma, Rónán, Molaise – who was no doubt identical with the patron of the diocese of Leighlin, within which Lorum lay – and Colum of the Uí Chriomhthannáin, patron of Terryglass.[1] The other describes how the coarb of Colum of Terryglass obtained compensation for a wrong done to his priest in Idrone, which he then presented to the erenagh of Lorum.[2] Colum Crom of Lorum was probably a double of his namesake at Terryglass, as Mochuma (a pet form of the name Colum) also may have been.

1 *CGSH* §667. **2** Ibid. §668.

Colum Cúile, 'of Cúil/remote place'. *See* Colum Tuama; Rónán of Dromiskin.

Colum Tuama, 'of Tuaim/mound'. This saint is said to have belonged to the Clann Lughdhach, whose original patrimony allegedly extended from Lough Erne to Slieve Bloom.[1] His father was named Muireadhach, and his brother Colum Cúile (also regarded as a saint) is otherwise presented as an ancestor of both Rónán of Dromiskin and Scannlach daughter of Seachnasach.[2] The saint of Tuaim may have been identical with Colum of Clonarney (Cluain Earnáin) in Westmeath, where a relic of Patrick, known as *Bréifneach*, 'ringed', was kept.[3] Early seventeenth-century sources speculatively identified the two brothers with saints commemorated on 31 August and 29 September.[4]

1 *CGSH* §§662.90, 690.15; *Lgen.* 707.9; *BB* 87e[b]. **2** *CGSH* §325.1; *Lgen.* 706.6. **3** *PNW* 82n; *BP* 814–15; *VT* 74. **4** *GRSH* 50; *MartD* 262.

Columba. *See* Colum Cille.

Comadán of Kilcommadan (Ceall Chomadáin), parish of Aughrim, barony of Clonmacnowen, Co. Galway. The coarb of Comadán at Kilcommadan was one of the seven principal coarbs of the Uí Mhaine whose territory, mainly in east Galway, corresponded approximately to that of the diocese of Clonfert.[1] Though remembered locally at a well named after him in the townland of Doocreggaun, Comadán is nowhere else attested under that form of his name.[2] However, the fact that a fair was held locally on 14 October allows for the possibility that Comadán, whose name derives from *Comma*, a hypocoristic form of Colum, was identical with Colum of Inishkeen whose feast fell on this day.[3] The day was also shared by Cuimín of the west Galway parish of Kilcummin, whose name likewise derives from *Comma* (alias *Cuimme*).[4] Comadán's church is perhaps best known today for the tradition that a more modern 'saint', General St Ruth, leader of the Irish and French forces at the battle of Aughrim in 1691, was buried in its graveyard.

1 *TCHyM* 78. 2 OSL GY i, 566; *AIGY* ii, 343. 3 *TDI* i, 97; *MartT* 79; *MartG* 196; *MartD* 276. 4 *OFWC* 54; *WLC* 168; *AIGY* i, 127.

Comaigh of Slanore (Snámh Luthair), parish of Kilmore, barony of Loughtee Upper, Co. Cavan. Comaigh daughter of Eacha, like Colum Tuama, was one of the saints of the Clann Lughdhach.[1] She was a sister of Colmán son of Eachaidh who is said to have founded the church at Slanore. According to the Martyrology of Tallaght, Comaigh was remembered on 27 May, together with two others, Maolán and Cuint, but the latter (very unusual) name disappears, probably correctly, from the later record.[2]

1 *CGSH* §690.3; *GRSH* 49; *Lgen.* 706.5; *BB* 87e[b]. 2 *MartT* 40; *MartG* 104; *MartD* 138–40.

Comán. This name, and its alternative form Mochomóg, represent diminutives of a hypocoristic or pet name *Comma* – also written *Camma* (Camán), *Caimme* (Caimín), *Cumma* (Mochuma), and *Cuimme* (Cuimín). The radical non-hypocoristic name in all of these cases was Colum, which means that many of its bearers may have originated as localizations of the founder of Iona.

Comán of Drummully. *See* Colmán of Dromore.

Comán of Kinvarra. *See* Colmán of Kilmacduagh.

Comán of Maca Teimhne. While in the region of Teimheanraighe in Ceara (which gave name to the Mayo barony of Carra), Patrick is said by his biographer Tíreachán to have received a visit from a bishop of the local group named Corca Theimhne.[1] The bishop is unnamed, but the martyrologies for 27 February record the feast of Comán of the Maca (or Corca) Teimhne.[2] He may be the same as the saint who gave name to the parish of Kilcommon in the neighbouring barony of Kilmaine but, by the early nineteenth century, there was no local monument to mark this saint's memory.[3]

1 *PTBA* 160 §47.4. 2 *MartT* 19; *MartG* 44; *MartD* 58. 3 OSL MO ii, 215.

Comán of Roscommon (Ros Comáin) in the barony of Ballintober South, Co. Roscommon. The pedigree of Comán son of Faolchú attaches him to the Dál nAraidhe of north-east Ulster, and more particularly to a branch of that group named Soghain who also had settlements in Connacht.[1] The association with the Soghain endured; a late poem attributed to Seanán of Scattery Island invokes Comán, together with a hundred saints of the Soghain.[2] Another poem, allegedly composed by Comán himself, maintains that, were it not for Nuadha son of Feabhal, abbot of Armagh, the succession to the abbacy of Roscommon would always have been the prerogative of the Soghain.[3] The same poem states pretentiously that Comán and Muireadhach, ancestor of the powerful O'Connor (Uí Chonchobhair) dynasty, were born on the one night.

A brief Latin (office-style) Life of the saint, preserved among the collections of the Bollandists in Brussels, combines both provinces. It provides him with an Ulster origin and upbringing by parents corruptly named 'Kilcun' and 'Screabside'.[4] It then states that, having studied sacred scripture in Clonard under Finnian, Comán made his way to Connacht, where he founded his church in a beautiful valley named Ros.[5] The Ulster connection remained, as is shown by the Life composed for Mochua, patron of Balla in Mayo, which speaks of a visit made by its subject to his mother's people, Dál mBuain, in the present county of Down.[6] There Mochua encountered Comán, the *sagart méise*, 'table priest' of Fiachna son of Baodán, king of the Ulstermen, who did not take kindly to the visitor and, by complaining to Comhghall of Bangor, brought about his expulsion. Comán's Down church may have been Clonduff (Cluain Daimh) in the barony of Iveagh Upper, whose patron, Mochomóg (alias Comán) shared the feastday of 26 December with his Roscommon namesake and probable double.[7] Mochua's Life also places a prophecy of Comán's birth in its subject's mouth, at a point where he was among the Soghain of Uí Mhaine.[8]

A possible third focus of the saint's cult was Leithghleann, now Oldleighlin in the Carlow barony of Idrone West, where some sources place him.[9] He may also have been remembered under the guise of Comán son of Fionnbharr in the list for 29 July, where he is joined by a namesake, Cuimín son of Araidhe (perhaps of Dál nAraidhe).[10] The annals provide the saint with an obit in 747.[11] Posthumously, his Law was promulgated throughout Connacht on at least three occasions – 772, 780, and 793.[12] Comán's alleged remains were raised and enshrined at Roscommon in 1170.[13] His coarb was among the ecclesiastics entitled to be present at the inauguration of O'Connor as king of Connacht.[14]

1 *CGSH* §109; *GRSH* 99; *Lgen.* 736.3; *AB* 77, 174. **2** *ZCP* 10, 24 §19. **3** *ZCP* 13, 15. **4** *AB* 77, 183 §1. **5** Ibid. 184 §3. **6** *LisL* 139, 283. **7** *MartT* 1; *MartO*[2] 254, 262; *MartG* 246; *MartD* 348; *AB* 77, 172–7; PNNI iii, 69, 81–2. **8** *LisL* 4691–8. **9** *MartG* 246; *MartD* 348. **10** *MartT* 58; *MartG* 146; *MartD* 204. **11** *AU s.a.* **12** *AU s.a.* **13** *AFM s.a.* **14** *MSPAG* 189.

Comán son of Ainmhire. *See* Colmán of Rosbran.

Comán son of Dubhthan. This saint was one of seven sons of Dubhthan whose pedigree culminated in Briotan, eponymous ancestor of the Britons (Breatnaigh).[1] The other six were Comhrán, Dochonna, Feargna, Pilip, Lúirint (Lauirint), and Mainchín. Though little else is known of these, their sister Soibhean is said to have been the mother of Rodaighe (or Reodaighe) of Greallach, now Girley, near Kells in Meath.[2] Also worth noting is the place of a certain Feargna Briot, 'the Briton', among the abbots of Iona; he died in 623.[3]

1 *CGSH* §313.1; *Lgen.* 41.4; *GT* 51–2. **2** *CGSH* §722.84. **3** *MartG* 46; *MartD* 60; *IKD* 40n.

Comán son of Earnán. *See* Cuimín Fionn of Iona.

Comán son of Fionnbharr. *See* Comán of Roscommon.

Comhdhán. *See* Comhghán.

Comhghall. The list of homonymous saints records eleven bearers of this name, also written Coimhgheall, most of whom are otherwise unattested.[1] These include the patrons of such unidentified churches as Ceall Chíche, Cluain Creamha, and Ráith Shithbhe, the last named now possibly the Antrim church of Rashee (Ráith Shíthe), near Connor.[2] Also included is Comhghall, fosterling of Fionnbharr, who may have been the patron of Bangor. The main corpus of pedigrees also contains several saints of this name, whose provenance and location have yet to be discovered. One of these, Comhghall son of Coireall, is provided with an otherwise unattested pedigree.[3]

1 *CGSH* §707.322–32. **2** ATig. ind. 176. **3** *CGSH* §§382, 572.

Comhghall of Bangor (Beannchar), barony of Ards Lower, Co. Down. Adhamhnán, who emphasised the closeness of the relationship between the communities of Bangor and Iona, provides Comhghall son of Séadna with an affiliation to the 'mocu Aridi' (later Dál nAraidhe), who controlled the lands about Bangor.[1] This is in keeping with the wider genealogical tradition which invariably attaches the saint to this north-east Ulster family.[2] One of the earliest known texts from the Irish Church, the late seventh-century Antiphonary of Bangor, contains hymns in honour of Comhghall (also written Coimhgheall), as well as of the abbots, fourteen in number, who succeeded him, and of the *bona regula*, 'good rule', observed in his church.[3] In Adhamhnán's approximately contemporary work, Comhghall is singled out as one of Ireland's *sancti fundatores*, 'holy founders'.[4]

The two versions of the Life composed for Comhghall – one fragmentary and neither earlier than the late twelfth century – variously describe his father as belonging to a most noble branch of Dál nAraidhe and as a soldier (*miles*) in the employ of the local king.[5] According to these texts, Comhghall's greatness was foretold by several saints, including Mac Nise (alias Aonghas) of Connor and Patrick of Armagh. Prior to the birth of the saint, while sitting in a chariot with her husband Séadna, Comhghall's mother Brígh is said to have caught the attention of Mac Nise, who prophesied that she would bear a 'king who would rule over many'.[6] The occasion of his subject's visit to Tara was used by the author of Patrick's Tripartite Life as an opportunity to foretell the greatness of three saints – Colum Cille, Finnian, and Comhghall – each of whose fathers is said to have swallowed a tear caused by his cheek being touched by Patrick, and these three saints are again brought together in a fragment of Old Irish prose touching on the rule attributed to Comhghall.[7]

Comhghall was born, according to one version of his Life, at a place called '*in opido de Mourne*', which is thought to be preserved in the names Magheramorne and Lough Mourne in the neighbouring Antrim parishes of Glynn and Carrickfergus, on the northern side of Belfast Lough.[8] A man named Feidhlimidh, possibly the patron of the now obsolete Patrician foundation of 'Domhnach Mór' in Magheramorne, is said to have baptized Comhghall.[9] The saint reputedly travelled for his education, first to Fiontan of Clonenagh, then to the community of Ciarán of Clonmacnoise, before returning to his *patria*, where he was ordained priest by a bishop called Lughaidh, probably the man of that name connected with the church of Connor who died in 546/7.[10] Thereafter, according to the Life, he founded Bangor (which reputedly had 4,000 monks) and many other churches throughout Ireland, allegedly failing in an attempt to establish one on Rathlin Island (Reachrainn) whose tithes later belonged to Bangor.[11]

Much of the Life is taken up with establishing for the saint connections with important local churches, such as Movilla (of Finnian, alias Fionnbharr) and Nendrum (of Críodán).[12] Great emphasis is also placed on his encounters with Colum Cille, and on the spread of his influence outside north-east Ulster, especially among the Uí Bhairrche of Carlow who gave name to the later deanery of Obargy. This contained, among other parishes, that of Carlow whose church was dedicated to Comhghall.[13] Castledermot (Díseart Diarmada) in Kildare is also reputed to have been 'one of Comhghall's places', and the dynast who allegedly acted as his benefactor in Leinster, Cormac son of Diarmuid, belonged to a family from the Ferns area in Wexford, which, like Bangor, was the seat of an Augustinian priory.[14] The honour of rendering Comhghall the last rites was also given to a Leinster saint, Fiachra of Ullard (Oireard), a church near the river Barrow in the Carlow barony of Idrone (Uí Dhróna), and further north in Leinster, he was patron of Clontarf in the Dublin barony of Coolock, until replaced by John the Baptist.[15]

The saint was patron of three churches in the diocese of Derry: Camus in the parish of Macosquin; Tamlaght O Crilly; where his name was rendered Coulus in a 1607 list of patrons; and Desertmartin which local opinion later considered to have been built by Martin, 'uncle' of Patrick.[16] Among the saints of Ireland said to have studied in Comhghall's school at Bangor, which at one stage had Columbanus of Bobbio on its teaching staff, were Fiontan of Doon, Molua of Clonfertmulloe (alias Kyle), Fiontan of Taghmon, and Daigh of Inishkeen.[17] Comhghall was also associated with Seanán of Scattery Island and Mochaomhóg of Leigh.[18] A metrical rule attributed to the saint has also been preserved.[19] Comhghall was ranked among the apostles of Ireland, and was considered to be like James the Apostle in his manners.[20] The saint is said to have been born in 516 and his obit is placed at 601–2, with one set of annals claiming that he was ninety.[21] The entry for his feastday in the Martyrology of Tallaght, the exemplar of which was kept in Bangor before it reached Tallaght, credits Comhghall with ninety-one years, during fifty of which he held the abbacy.[22] The feast of 'triumphant' (*buadhach*) Comhghall fell on 10 May, but at Dunleer, where a well was dedicated to him, he may have been remembered at the end of June.[23] The saint's relics, subsequently taken for safety to Antrim, were removed violently from their shrine in Bangor in 824, and his staff was left to the 'Foreigners' after the battle of Downpatrick in 1178.[24] Relics of the saint also found their way to the Continent, among other places to the Rhineland, Sens and, arguably, Ferrières in France.[25] His name is invoked in both Stowe Missal litanies, and office lessons commemorating the saint are preserved in the Breviary of Aberdeen.[26]

1 *VC*[2] 500. **2** *CGSH* §97; *GRSH* 99; *Lgen.* 736.1; *ZCP* 14, 72; but cf. *PHCC* 5, 106–8. **3** HBS 4, x; *AntB* 81–2. **4** *VC*[2] 316, 490–2, 500. **5** *VSHH* 332 §1; *VSHP* ii, 3 §1; *AB* 62, 343–56. **6** *VSHH* 332 §1, 406 §12;

VSHP ii, 4 §5; *CGSH* §722.41. **7** *BP* 590–600; *VT* 58; *Ériu* 2, 222–4. **8** *VSHP* ii, 4 §5; *EA* 269. **9** *VSHH* 332 §2; *VSHP* ii, 5 §6; *BP* 1911; *VT* 164; *EA* 338; *MartD* 288. **10** *VSHP* ii, 6 §11; ATig. / *AFM s.a.* **11** *VSHP* ii, 7 §13; ibid. 18 §50; *IrL* 60; PNNI vii, 281. **12** *VSHP* ii, 9 §§18–19;13 §28. **13** Ibid. 16 §42; *JCKAS* 6, 377; *AAR* 26; *CM* 52. **14** *FAI* 152; *CGH* 122bb9; *HDGP* ii, 79 (Banna (2)), 109 (Bealach Foirceadail). **15** *VSHP* ii, 20–1 §§57–8; *SacH* 41 §48. **16** *Celtica* 1, 83; *DYHS* 195; OSL DY 225; *AnH* 12, 108, 111. **17** *VSHH* 114 §5, 134 §15, 199 §4, 390 §6; *SOC* xviii. **18** *ZCP* 10, 28; *IrT* iv, 68; *AB* 52, 355. **19** *Ériu* 1, 191–208. **20** *VSHH* 83 §4; *CGSH* §712.11. **21** *AU s.a.*; *AnH* 12, 108, 111. **22** *MartT* 41; *FSHIM* 62–9. **23** *MartT* 41; *MartO*[2] 123; *MartG* 94; *MartD* 123; *SAM* 2.1, 194–5; *JCLAS* 24, 355. **24** *MartD* xxxi; *MIA s.a.* **25** HBS 32, 14; *MSNAF* 59, 138; *EIRD* 55–68, *RIW* 16–19. **26** *LegSS* 120–3, 344–5.

Comhghall of Carrowmore (Both Chonais), parish of Culdaff, barony of Inishowen East, Co. Donegal.[1] This saint's pedigree attaches him through his father Eacha to the Ceinéal Eoghain, the descendants of an ancestor named Eoghan who also gave name to Tír Eoghain (Tyrone) and Inis Eoghain (Inishowen).[2] The saint's church, formerly known as Both Chonais, attained some fame, not least because of its association with Maol Íosa Ua Brolcháin (†1086), a man famous for his learning.[3] It never became a parochial church and the patronage of the parish of Culdaff was reserved for Buadán, a probable double of Baoithín of Iona.[4] Comhghall's brother, Céile Críost (†727), was patron of a church in Uí Dhúnchadha of Leinster, more precisely in the Kildare parish of Kilteel, bordering the county of Wicklow.[5] On the other side of the latter county, the church of Kilcoole (Ceall Chomhghaill) in the barony of Newcastle may have been named after Comhghall.[6] His feast fell on 4 September.[7]

1 *HDGP* ii, 164. **2** *CGSH* §279; *GRSH* 44; *Lgen.* 702.7–8. **3** *LCC* 16, 87–109; *DOH* 73; *AU s.a.* **4** *DOH* 84–5. **5** *HDGP* iii, 141. **6** *DOH* 87; *Mdub.* 18, 153. **7** *MartT* 68; *MartG* 170; *MartD* 236.

Comhghall of Galloon (Gabhal Liúin), barony of Coole, Co. Fermanagh. An entry in the list of homonymous saints describes Comhghall as a *dalta*, 'fosterling', of Tighearnach of Clones.[1] According to the Life composed for the Clones saint, Tighearnach founded Galloon at the head of Lough Erne, before subsequently placing it in the charge of Comhghall, his *dilectus*, 'beloved [pupil]'.[2] Known as one of the 'chief saints' of Lough Erne, Comhghall of Galloon in Dartraighe was remembered on 28 July.[3]

1 *CGSH* §707.329; *FHHS* 586–7. **2** *VSHP* ii, 267–8 §§14–18. **3** *MHH* 110 §29; *MartT* 58; *MartD* 204; *MartG* 144; *CPL* 8, 4.

Comhghall son of Dubhthach. This saint and his six brothers, Éigsín, Fear Corb, Trian, Gabhrán, Fachtna, and Eór (alias Eóil), though described as children of Dubhthach – reputedly the first man to believe in Christ following Patrick's visit to Tara – are otherwise little known.[1] Three of them, Fachtna of Kiltoom, Gabhrán and Eór, are also grouped together in the list of those commemorated on 14 November.[2] Although Dubhthach's connections were with Leinster, the pedigree of his children, which reveals many otherwise unattested combinations of father and son, attaches the family to the Connachta.[3]

1 *CGSH* §§305, 653; *BP* 532–6; *VT* 52. **2** *MartG* 218; *MartD* 310. **3** *BP* 2219–21; *VT* 188.

Comhghán of Cluain Connaidh, an unidentified church in Machaire Chuircne, now the barony of Kilkenny West, Co. Westmeath. A list of names prepared in the early seventeenth century assigns a feastday of 13 October to Comhghán.[1] This commemoration is confirmed by the martyrologies, the earliest of which describes the saint as a *céile Dé*, 'client of God'.[2] A second feast of 2 August is also credited to Comhghán *céile Dé*, who may be identical with the corruptly named 'Euanganus' of Ballingarry in the Limerick barony of Connello Upper.[3] Ballingarry lay close to Dysert, which took its Irish name (Díseart Aonghasa) from Aonghas *céile Dé*. In Scotland, where there were several churches named after him, Comhghán was regarded as a brother of Caointighearn, daughter of Ceallach of Cuala (the territory about Bray in Wicklow), and thus an uncle of Faolán of Strathfillan.[4] A Life written for him in the Breviary of Aberdeen, under the guise of Conganus, asserts that he was the son of a Leinster king and in line of succession to the kingship before leaving Ireland for Scotland.[5] A local tradition, preserved in northern Argyll, describes how Comhghán and his nephew Faolán, having fallen out with one another, left curses on their repective churches.[6]

1 *Celtica* 1, 78. 2 *MartT* 79; *MartO*[2] 216; *MartG* 196; *MartD* 276. 3 *MartT* 59; *MartG* 148; *MartD* 208; *SACCL* 409. 4 *CPNS* 281; *KSS* 310; *ACDS* 162–4. 5 *BrevA*. pars aest. 126–126v; *KSS* 310; *LegSS* 245–7, 345–6. 6 *CR* 4, 371–2.

Comhghán of Killeshin (Gleann Uisean), barony of Slievemargy, Co. Laois. The pedigree of Comhghán son of Diarmuid attaches him to the Dál gCais of Thomond through an otherwise unattested ancestor named Teimhne (Seimhne), supposedly the brother of Aonghas Tíreach of the main ruling line.[1] The ancestral name may have been borrowed from the tribal name 'Maca Teimhne' borne by Comán, Comhghán's companion on his feastday. Comhghán's record was prone to interference and corruption. His mother, Eithne daughter of Feidhlimidh, was, according to one implausible tradition, a sister of Colum Cille.[2] Elsewhere, either by mistaking *m*. (*mac*, 'son') for *i*. (*id est*), or through confusion of the saint with Modhíomóg (alias Diarmuid), likewise of Gleann Uisean, Comhghán received the alias Diarmuid.[4] The words of praise *cen dinnis*, 'without reproach', attached by Aonghas of Tallaght to the saint's name were similarly misinterpreted in one source as a place-name 'Ceann Innis', duly located in Thomond.[5] Comhghán's church, *ecclesia sancti Congani*, lay within the former territory of Uí Bhairrche, and attained some importance, not least through an early twelfth-century *fear léighinn*, 'chief teacher', named Duibhlitir Ua hUathghaile who wrote an Irish version of *Sex Aetates Mundi*, 'six ages of the world'.[6] A charter in the Book of Durrow mentions a property granted by the church to the Dál gCais, and this suggests that Comhghán's pedigree may have been fabricated to accommodate the interests of this powerful family.[7] A poem attributed to Moling calls upon Comhghán, along with many other saints, to come to the assistance of the Leinstermen.[8] He appears also to have been noted for prophecies.[9] The saint's feast fell on 27 February, and he is among the handful of mainly Leinster saints commemorated in the tenth-century metrical calendar of Hampson.[10] Comhghán of the Maca Teimhne died, according to the annals, in 664.[11]

1 *CGSH* §233; *GRSH* 119; *Lgen.* 738.17; *CoC* 12; *CMCS* 27, 33–7. 2 *CGSH* §722.91. 3 *MartO²* 78. 4 *GRSH* 119; *MartD* 58. 5 *FourIM* 165, 173;*HDGP* iv, 78; *OnomG* 226. 6 *SAM* 41–8; *JCKAS* 6, 377. 7 *Ériu* 10, 135–42; *SexAM* 42; *CMCS* 27, 33–41. 8 *SG* i, 389. 9 *Éigse* 5, 86 §39. 10 *MartT* 19; *MartO²* 63; *MartG* 44; *MartD* 58; *AB* 104, 93. 11 *AU s.a.*

Comhrán son of Dubhthan. *See* Comán son of Dubhthan.

Comnaid of Kilcomenty (Ceall Chomnada), barony of Owney and Arra, Co. Tipperary. When visiting Kilcomenty in 1840, John O'Donovan was told that 18 March was kept holy in the parish in honour of 'Cumenod' (also written Commaneth).[1] O'Donovan wrongly assumed that Cuimín Fada of Clonfert was intended, whereas the (otherwise unattested) female saint was in fact Comnaid.[2] The list of those commemorated on 18 March includes a saint named Comán, a masculine form of Comnaid.[3] Many reminders of the saint, including her well and bed, were pointed out locally.[4]

1 OSL TY ii, 21; *ACE* 264. 2 *CLTÁ* 102–4. 3 *MartG* 56; *MartD* 80. 4 *LIS* iii, 842–3; *AITY* 279.

Conach of Ard Conaigh, 'Conach's height', an unidentified church, somewhere in Leinster. Conach and his companions, Colmán Mór son of Fearghas, and Luiceannán, are among those said to have been subject to Brighid of Kildare.[1] Conach has been taken by one source to be a virgin named 'Conac', commemorated on 25 October.[2]

1 *CGSH* §670.81; *Lgen.* 753.44. 2 *MartD* 388.

Conall of Calry. *See* Conall of Drumcliff.

Conall of Clonallan (Cluain Dalláin), barony of Upper Iveagh, Co. Down. Conall's pedigree attaches him through his father Aodh to the Uí Eachach Cobha who gave name to the barony in which his church was located, near Carlingford Lough in the southern part of the county of Down.[1] It has been suggested that the saint was identical with Cairbre's successor at Coleraine, who is said to have provided Colum Cille with sustenance on his way back to Iona from the convention of Druim Ceat, but there is no documentary support for this.[2] Conall's feast fell on 2 April.[3]

1 *CGSH* §120; *GRSH* 99; *Lgen.* 732.8; *CGH* 161bd39–45; PNNI i, 49, 55. 2 *VC¹* 318–19; *EA* 114. 3 *MartT* 29; *MartG* 68; *MartD* 92.

Conall of Drum. *See* Conall of Drumcliff.

Conall of Drumcliff, barony of Islands, Co. Clare. A saint named Conall son of Domhnall is mentioned in a poem listing the children of Inghean Bhaoith of Killinaboy.[1] Grouped with him are three west Clare saints, Blathmhac of Rath (where there appears also to have been a well dedicated to Conall), Mac Reithe (Creiche) of Kilmacrehy, and Maol Dala of Corcomroe.[2] Together with Blathmhac and Maol Dala (Eala), and numerous other Munster saints, Conall son of Domhnall is called upon, in a poem in Classical Irish, to help in releasing Ireland's southern half (Leath Mogha) from a bondage imposed on it by the northern half (Leath Chuinn), represented by Finnian of Clonard.[3] Conall was probably patron of the church of Kilconnell in the parish of Kilmacrehy, as well as Drumcliff, the parish in which the town of Ennis is situated. A late eighteenth- or early nineteenth-century document refers to Drumcliff as *ecclesia sancti Conaldi*.[4] Further north, in the eastern part of Galway, he may have given name to the parish and barony of Kilconnell. Thought in this area to have been a contemporary of Patrick, as well as the object of a curse by both the Armagh saint and Íde, Conall is nonetheless credited with the 'building' of Aughrim priory in Kilconnell parish.[5] Colgan thought that Conall of Drum, who supposedly dissuaded his uterine sister, Athracht of Killaraght, from erecting a church too close to his own, might also be the Galway bearer of the name, but the Drum in question has been more plausibly identified as a place near Boyle.[6] Conall of Drumcliff may also be the man who gave name to a well in the Sligo parish of Calry (Callraighe) on the northern shore of Lough Gill – where his memory was celebrated on 2 June – and also to an island on the lake.[7] The Conall venerated at Tullagh in the Cork barony of West Carbery, whose birth was reputedly foretold by Ciarán of Seirkieran, may also belong here; it has been argued that the territory named 'Callary', formerly located in this general area, took its name from Callraighe.[8] A well ('Toberconnel') in the parish of Aghadown, adjoining that of Tullagh, was also dedicated to him.[9]

1 *IrT* iv, 93 §8. **2** *MHH* 36 §50; *Béaloideas* 67, 79. **3** RIA MS 23L11, 263; *SAM* 24.1, 20. **4** *HDK* 34. **5** OSL GY i, 565. **6** *ASH* 281 §11; *HOI* 62–4. **7** OSL SO 71; *HWI* 43–4; *LIS* vi, 26. **8** *CPL* 13, 768; *Lgen*. 676.3–4; *Éigse* 13, 225–6; but cf. *FNCC* 178. **9** *AICK* i, 284 (Glebe).

Conall of Inishkeel (Inis Caoil), barony of Boylagh, Co. Donegal. This son of Maine Caol (alias Caolmhaine) was attached to the Ceinéal Boghaine who, though also controlling the barony of Boylagh, gave name to the neighbouring barony of Banagh.[1] Dallán Forghaill, who received a promise of burial on Inishkeel, is credited with having composed a (no longer extant) eulogy of Conall (alias Conall Caol).[2] This Dallán may have given name to Clondallan (Cluain Dalláin) in the parish of Killygarvan, directly across Lough Swilly from Clonmany, which has a townland of Crosconnell (Cros Chonaill), possibly named after the saint.[3] Another cross named after him was located in Kilcashel townland in the parish of Inishkeel, and his 'healing stone' was kept at Bruckless in the parish of Killaghtee.[4] Conall's main claim to attention is the tradition that, while on a pilgrimage in Rome, he was responsible for writing with his own hand and bringing to Ireland the Law of Sunday (*Cáin Domhnaigh*) which had allegedly been sent from heaven to the altar of Peter.[5] Conall's reputation was such that several tales have been preserved concerning him in modern lore.[6] One of these states that he was first a married stone-mason until he committed patricide through jealousy, whereupon he did penance and grew into a saint. His *turas* was famous, and a relic of his, the *Bearnán Conaill*, 'Conall's gapped bell', now in the British Museum, was formerly in the custody of the local family of O'Breslen (Ua

Breisléin), to which Conall also belonged.[7] He may also have been venerated at Strabane in the Tyrone parish of Camus.[8] Conall's feast fell on 22 May, a day shared by Aghna, a possible patron of Drumadart in the neighbouring parish of Inver.[9] Other days credited to Conall by modern commentators are 29 January (otherwise Dallán's day), 12 and 20 May.[10]

1 *CGSH* §621; *GRSH* 38; *Lgen.* 158.7, 700.3; *ICF* 93–117; *HDGP* iv, 105–6; cf. OSL DL 202. **2** *RC* 20, 434–6. **3** *DLHS* 164. **4** *JRSAI* 68, 221–2; *JGAHS* 64, 5. **5** *Ériu* 2, 202–4 §§20–1, 212. **6** *Béaloideas* 1, 253–7; *DLHS* 165–6. **7** OSL DL 202; *Lgen.* 158.7; *JRSAI* 52, 5–9; ibid. 53, 160; *HWI* 151–2; *ICF* 73–9, 81–91; *EMH* 317–22 §8. **8** *DYHS* 195; *UJA* (2nd ser.) 1, 247; *AnH* 12, 81, 108, 110. **9** *MartT* 45; *MartG* 102; *MartD* 136; *ICF* 73. **10** *Ériu* 2, 212.

Conall of Kilconnell, Co. Galway. *See* Conall of Drumcliff.

Conall of Kilconnell, Co. Tipperary. *See* Colmán son of Iomras.

Conall of Tullagh. *See* Conall of Drumcliff.

Conall son of Neamhan. *See* Cairbre son of Neamhan.

Conall son of Rumhan. *See* Ceallach of Trim.

Conall Caol. *See* Conall of Inishkeel.

Conamhail of Iona, Scotland. This son of Fáilbhe is distinguished by the fact that he was among the early abbots of Iona not to belong to the Ceinéal Conaill of Donegal. His pedigree attaches him to the descendants of Colla Uais of the Oirghialla, a group that held lands later corresponding approximately to the diocese of Clogher.[1] He died in 710 and his name is featured in the list of those remembered on 11 September.[2]

1 *CGSH* §662.104; *GRSH* 39, 57. **2** *AU s.a.*; *MartT* 70; *MartG* 174; *MartD* 244.

Conán son of Tighearnach. *See* Beag Bile.

Conbhran of Míleac Fiaich. *See* Angán.

Connla. *See* Conlaodh.

Conlan. *See* Caolán of Youghalarra.

Conlaodh Cráibhtheach, 'pious', of Kildare (Ceall Dara), barony of Offaly East, Co. Kildare, and of Fancroft (Fionnchoire/Fionnchoradh), parish of Seirkieran, barony of Ballybritt, Co. Offaly. Conlaodh (alias Con(n)la, anglicized Conleth), bishop and close associate of Brighid at Kildare, was regarded, along with Tasach and Daigh, as one of the chief craftsmen (*cearda*) or artisans of Ireland.[1] His original name is sometimes said to have been Róincheann, 'seal-head', and his pedigree attached him to the Dál Meisin Corb of the area around Glendalough in Wicklow, a group that was otherwise mainly connected with Caoimhghin and his *familia*.[2] The saint figures prominently in Brighid's record. According to Cogitosus, who described Conlaodh as 'archbishop', Brighid once gave his vestments, which had come from overseas, to the poor, only to have them restored by Christ.[3] While in Brighid's company, Conlaodh is elsewhere given the honour of baptizing Tighearnach of Clones.[4] In the corpus of saints' pedigrees, the saint, together with a number of others, including Ceallán (alias

Mac Nise), is the subject of an entry which locates him in the Offaly church of Fancroft.[5] Here, too, the Brigidine connection is evident, as the list of those said to have been subject to Brighid includes Mac Nise of Fancroft.[6] Fancroft's location in the parish of Seirkieran may later have encouraged the authorities at Kildare to seek jurisdiction over the latter church.[7] According to tradition, Conlaodh had an unhappy end, being devoured by wild dogs at a place near Lyons (Liamhain) in the Kildare barony of South Salt, adjoining the Dublin barony of Newcastle.[8] The saint's feast fell on 3 May, and he appears also to have been remembered as Connla on 10 May, the octave of his main feast.[9] He is said to have died in 520 and his remains, located to the right of the altar in the great church of Kildare, according to Cogitosus, were placed in a gold and silver shrine in the year 800, one of the first such enshrinements to be noted in the annals.[10] A relic of the saint, accompanied by relics of Brighid and her successor Darlughdhach, had reached Saint-Maurice d'Agaune in the Swiss canton of Valais by 700.[11]

1 *CGSH* §82.2; *Ériu* 18, 64 §25. **2** *MartT* 39; *MartO*[1] lxxxiii; *BBr.* 18 §5; *CGSH* §§181.10; 252; *GRSH* 86; *CGH* 120b45 (add.). **3** *TT* 522 §29; *JRSAI* 117, 22 §28; *BBr.* 18 §5. **4** *VSHH* 108 §2; *VSHP* ii, 262 §2. **5** *CGSH* §172. **6** Ibid. §670.65. **7** *OLL* 3, 25–42. **8** *BBr.* 18 §5; *MartO*[1] lxxxiii; *TD* 74. **9** *MartT* 39; *MartO*[2] 122; *MartG* 88; *MartD* 118. **10** *TT* 523 §35; *JRSAI* 117, 25 §32; *AU s.a.*; *IEKF* 97; *AU s.a.* **11** *RIW* 12–13, 31.

Conmhac son of Criomhthann. *See* Aodh of Kilcrow.

Conna son of Amhairghin. *See* Colmán of Achadh Í.

Connadh daughter of Colmán. *See* Odhbha daughter of Colmán.

Connaidhil son of Síolán. *See* Cuán of Kilquane.

Connaidhil son of Tighearnach. *See* Beag Bile.

Constans of Eonish. *See* Cuana of Eonish.

Coran. *See* Cuarán.

Corbán of Naas (Ceall Chorbáin / Ceall Náis) in the Kildare barony of the same name.[1] Corbán (alias Cearbán) is said by a *dinnsheanchas*-style poem to have been attached with eight others, and as many kings, to Ceall Chorbáin, an early name for the church in Naas.[2] He is probably the same as the 'Corbanus' who brought Iobhar, then a youth, on a visit to Louth, where Mochta is said to have discovered the boy's talent for singing.[3] A namesake and probable double gave name to Kilcorban (Ceall Chorbáin) in the Galway parish of Tynagh.[4] An oratory near the cemetery at Duleek, dedicated to 'Karbani' or 'Carbani', may also refer to him, despite an editorial preference for Cairbre.[5]

1 *HDGP* iii, 149; *OnomG* 184. **2** *LL* 28009–24; *MD* iv, 340–2; *Seanchas* 221. **3** *VSHH* 398 §12. **4** *TribesI* 39n.; *HDGP* iii, 149. **5** *PLPS* 71n.

Corb daughter of Neamhnann. *See* Bearchán of Laragh.

Corc of Kilmore. *See* Corcán of Druim Cruinn.

Corcair Chaoin daughter of Eoghan. *See* Scíre of Kilskeer.

Corcán of Druim Cruinn. A list of the *forshloinnte*, 'additional families', of the Uí Eachach of the Down baronies of Iveagh includes a group named Corcraighe to which the priest (*cruimhthear*) Corcán belonged.[1] Although the name of his church (Druim Cruinn) appears to have fallen out of use, the saint may be the man commemorated in the name *Ecclesia Sancti Corcani*, 'church of St Corcán', in the *c.*1300 Taxation List for the diocese of Down.[2] The location of the *ecclesia* is not precisely known, but as the two names surrounding it in the list refer to places within the neighbouring parishes of Greyabbey and Inishargy in the Ards peninsula, the church is probably to be sought in that area. There was also a church dedicated to Corcán (alias Corc) in the diocese of Armagh, at a place variously called 'Keluion' and 'Kilmor' in papal documents, now probably Kilmore in the Armagh barony of Oneilland West.[3] The feast of Corcán (Corc) of Kilmore fell on 4 April.[4]

1 *ZCP* 8, 331; *Lgen*. 499.12. 2 *EA* 18–19; *PHib*. i, 127. 3 *AnnU* 12; *CPL* 18, §859; *HDGP* iv, 29–30. 4 *MartT* 29; *MartO*[1] lxxii; *MartG* 70; *MartD* 94.

Corcanadan of Derrynaflan (Doire Eidhneach, later Doire na bhFlann), townland of Lurgoe, parish of Graystown, barony of Slievardagh, Co. Tipperary. A person of this name is included in the list of saints of the Dál Meisin Corb of Co. Wicklow, which describes him as one of two brothers of Caomhán of Anatrim, the other being Muirdheabhair.[1] All three are brought together in two other lists of holy persons – those commemorated on 3 November and those associated, according to an early litany, with Caoimhghin of Glendalough.[2] The latter text locates Corcanadan at Derrynaflan. It has been suggested that the saint's name may have originated as a gentilic, i. e. Corca Nodain (Nudáin).[3]

1 *CGSH* §182.6; *Lgen*. 726.2. 2 *MartG* 210; *MartD* 296; *IrL* 54–6. 3 *CPPI* 178.

Cormac of Cashel (Caiseal), parish of St Patricksrock, barony of Middlethird, Co. Tipperary. Although holder of the kingship of Munster for seven years (902–8), the precise lineage of the king-bishop, Cormac son of Cuileannán, is uncertain, with two quite different Eoghanacht pedigrees assigned to him.[1] He did not belong to any of the main lines of Eoghanacht descent, and may have been a compromise appointee.[2] Cormac was part of a tradition of Munster ecclesiastical kingship, begun by his predecessor, Feidhlimidh son of Criomhthann. His clerical status did not, however, prevent him from being associated with the tragic figure of Gormlaith, daughter of Flann son of Maol Seachlainn, king of Midhe.[3]

A great deal of Cormac's fame rests on his literary associations. He is reputed to have arranged for the compilation of the lost miscellany known as the Psalter of Cashel (*Saltair Chaisil*), but this has been dated to a hundred years after his reign.[4] Many poems were also attributed to him, including one on the kings of Munster, another on the saints or churches that were to receive his relics (beginning with Emly, followed by Cork, and ending with Cashel which, appropriately enough, was to receive his psalter), and yet another poem on the causes of the battle of Magh Mhucramha.[5] A rule attributed to him has also been preserved.[6] Cormac's alleged authorship of the famous glossary named after him is still regarded as likely enough.[7]

Cormac is said to have been a foster-brother of Cearbhall son of Muireagán, king of Leinster, who lined out against him in 908 at Ballaghmoon (Bealach Mughna) in Kildare, an encounter that cost the saint-king his life.[8] He is among those prophesied in a poem attributed to Bearchán of Clonsast which memorably describes Cormac as *saoi, fáidh, file, easpag, ardbhile*, 'scholar, prophet, poet, bishop, noble man of distinction'.[9] His feast is variously placed on 14 and 15 September.[10]

1 *CGSH* §373; *Lgen.* 689.3; *CGH* 148a45, 150b28. 2 *IKHK* 214. 3 *Ériu* 16, 191–3; *MartD* 248; *IKHK* 164; *RC* 36, 285–8; *Ériu* 52, 16–17; cf. *FFÉ* iii, 198. 4 *Éigse* 23, 107–30. 5 *ZCP* 6, 270–1; *Celtica* 5, 207–17; ibid. 23, 307–10; *Ériu* 14, 154–65; *ZCP* 10, 45–7; *ACL* iii, 216. 6 *Ériu* 2, 62–8. 7 *CMCS* 15, 1–30. 8 *FAI* 150–62 §423. 9 *ZCP* 18 21. 10 *MartG* 176; *MartD* 248.

Cormac of Durrow (Dearmhagh), barony of Ballycowan, Co. Offaly. The pedigree of this son of Díoma attaches him to the Uí Liatháin of east Cork in south Munster, whence his common designation as Cormac Ua Liatháin.[1] Adhamhnán describes in his Life of Colum Cille how Cormac sought three times a 'desert' in the ocean.[2] A lengthy account of the saint's second and third voyages states that he reached the Orkney Islands, and that, through the intercession of Colum Cille and the prayers of the community on Iona, he was saved from many dangers.[3] An 'illustrious man' and a 'holy founder' of a monastery, Cormac is commonly associated, sometimes as abbot, with the Columban church of Durrow.[4] The saint's procurement of a relic for Durrow by cutting off Colum Cille's little finger allegedly led to an agreement that the Uí Liatháin would pay tribute to the Iona saint, and this may be reflected in the possible localization of Colum's cult at Cloyne, chief church of the Uí Liatháin, in the person of Colmán son of Léinín.[5] Another supposed result of the unsavoury procedure was a prophecy on Colum's part that Cormac would be eaten by wolves. A story describing how Cormac was torn to pieces by these animals, following a flight throughout the county of Offaly, survived locally until it was recorded in the course of the Ordnance Survey in 1838.[6] In addition to several wells in Offaly, Cormac gave name to the church of Ceall Chormaic, now Frankford, in the parish and barony of Ballyboy [7]. Also named after him are Tobercormick in the Westmeath parish of Ballymorin, and Kilcormick (*ecclesia sancti Cormaci*) in the Wexford barony of Ballaghkeen, where a pattern was held on 22 June, the morrow of the saint's feast.[8] Possible Scottish dedications to the saint have also been identified.[9] He is said to have formed a union (*aonta*) with Moling of St Mullins.[10]

1 *CGSH* §227; *GRSH* 115; *Lgen.* 740.6; *DIB* ii, 860. 2 *VC*[2] 222–4. 3 Ibid. 440–6. 4 Ibid. 501; *MartT* 51; *GRSH* 115. 5 *MartO*[2] 156; *ZCP* 12, 390–2; *VC*[1] 270. 6 OSL OY ii, 108. 7 *AIOY* 117. 8 *PNW* 24; OSL WX ii, 94; *HDF* 49; *CECW* 207; *MartT* 51; *MartO*[2] 141; *MartG* 120; *MartD* 174; *AH* 18, 13 §42; *CPL* 18, §783; *TNW* 1090–1. 9 *AITLP* 239–40; *ACDS* 90–2. 10 *Anecd.* ii, 28 §2.

Cormac of Killala (Ceall Alaidh), barony of Tirawley, Co. Mayo. This saint was one of four (or six) children of Eoghan son of Murchadh of the southern Eoghanachta, two of whom, Beagán and Cúlán, are said to have remained in Munster whereas the other two, Cormac and Diarmuid, left for Connacht.[1]

Arriving in north Connacht, Cormac was supposedly met at Magh nEó, now Mayo in the county of the same name, by Adhamhnán and Garailt of the Saxons, among others, before receiving from the Uí Amhalghaidh of Tirawley his choice of lands at Inbhear Muadha (now Killala Bay), near which, just south of the town of Killala, a ruined church (Ceall Chormaic) and well later marked his memory.[2] The impression is given that he had control of Killala and of all its lands and, while in north Connacht, he is said to have assisted in the birth of Aodhán son of Gabhrán (d. 606), king of Scotland, and to have foretold the births of Fiodhmhaine Ua Suanaigh, Nathí (Dathí) of Achonry, Féichín of Fore, and Mobhí of Glasnevin.[3] His involvement in the settlement of many dynastic disputes is given emphasis, and bathing in his *dabhach*, 'vessel', is said to have guaranteed survival in battle to members of the Clann Mhuireadhaigh, and ensured a choice of mate to women of the group, provided due payment was made to Cormac and his successors.[4] The spread of Cormac's cult included the Lough Mask area, where there was a church dedicated to him on Inishowen (Inis Eoghain), formerly an island in the lake.[5] He reportedly left great gifts, including the 'royal accoutrements' of the Uí Amhalghaidh, to the Uí Mhuireadhaigh of An Lagán, now the parish of Kilbride and part of Doonfeeny in the north of the barony of Tirawley.[6] Further south in the barony, in the parish of Kilbelfad, there was a church (Kilcormack) named after the saint.[7] Wells were named after Cormac in several places, including the Galway parish of Annaghdown, and perhaps also the Sligo parish of Toomour.[8] The feastday of the saint is unknown, but Colgan speculated that it may have been 13 December.[9]

1 *IrT* iii, 1–8; *GRSH* 116; *JCHAS* 92, 106–12. **2** *IrT* iii, 4 §9; *PHib.* i, 104; OSL MO ii, 227; *NotesEHDT* 337, 339. **3** *IrT* iii, 3 §8, 4 §9; 4–5 §11. **4** Ibid. 8 §22. **5** *WLC* 144; *JRSAI* 41, 229. **6** *Lgen.* 247.6; ibid. iv, p. 460. **7** *NotesEHDT* 349. **8** *WLC* 22; *IER* (5th ser.) 27, 275; *AISO* i, 441 (Cross). **9** *MartD* 336; *GRSH* 116.

Cormac of Trim (Áth Truim), north of river Boyne, barony of Upper Navan, Co. Meath. An entry on the saints of Trim assigns four sons to Fuineacht daughter of Maol Fithrigh by Colmán grandson of Suibhne, one of whom was Cormac, bishop and abbot.[1] Cormac's siblings were Baothghalach, Bishop Osán, and Rumhan, the latter a poet so celebrated that he became known as the Homer and Virgil of Ireland.[1] The same entry identifies Cormac further by reference to a couplet borrowed from the text of the Martyrology of Aonghas for 17 February.[2] A gloss on this entry speculates that Cormac may have been the first abbot of Armagh after Patrick, before dying in 497.[3] This speculation, no doubt influenced by the well-attested tradition that Trim was one of the first churches founded by Patrick, has been correctly rejected in favour of Cormac, abbot of Trim, who died in 746, ten years ahead of his brother and successor, Baothghalach.[4]

1 *CGSH* §§690.4, 722.74; *DIB* ii, 860. **2** *MartO*[2] 61. **3** Ibid. 74; *MartG* 38; *MartD* 50; *NHI* ix, 238. **4** *PTBA* 166–8; *BP* 697–712; *VT* 66–8; *JEH* 1, 166–7; *AU s.a.*

Cormac of Uí Liatháin. *See* Cormac of Durrow.

Cormac son of Eachaidh. This bishop-saint belonged to a branch of the Ceinéal Eoghain located on the eastern side of the Donegal barony of Inishowen (Inis

Eoghain), in an area known as the Bréadach.[1] Cormac had two brothers, Dochonna of Assylin and Lughaidh of Clonleigh, and apart from the seventeenth-century sources that placed his feast on 14 December, little else is known of him.[2] The list for the previous day includes a presbyter (*cruimhthear*) named Cormac who was venerated at Tulach Inneann, now possibly Tullynavinn in the Donegal parish of Moville Upper, within Inishowen.[3] Cormac's Well at Altamuskin in the Tyrone parish of Errigal Keerogue may also have taken its name from the saint.[4]

1 *CGSH* §35; *GRSH* 45; *Lgen*. 702.1; *HDGP* ii, 173. 2 *CGSH* §83; *MartD* 336; *GRSH* 45. 3 *MartG* 238; *MartD* 336. 4 *TEHS* 548.

Cormac Deochain. *See* Aodh of Kilcrow.

Coulan. *See* Caolán of Youghalarra.

Coulus. *See* Comhghall.

Cowey. *See* Cobhthach Caol.

Cránaid of Kilcranathan (Ceall Chránadan), parish of Ballyclogh, barony of Duhallow, Co. Cork. The site of Cránaid's church was later also the seat of a branch of the O'Callaghans (Uí Cheallacháin).[1] Although made the subject of what is grandly termed a Life – in fact it is no more than a short account in the vernacular of how the saint gouged out her eyes in order to avoid marriage – Cránaid (alias Craobhnad) daughter of Buicín is otherwise scarcely mentioned in the hagiographical record. The 'Life' is preserved in a number of manuscripts copied in the early seventeenth century, and also, albeit now largely illegible, in the mid-fifteenth-century Book of Fermoy, for which, given the location of devotion to her in the wider Fermoy area, it could well have been first compiled.[2] The saint's frustrated suitor, Cairbre Crom son of Criomhthann, was an important ancestral figure of the Eoghanacht of Glanworth, later represented by the Uí Chaoimh (O'Keeffes).[3]

Among places associated with the saint, according to the text, were Díseart Cránadan, now probably Hermitage near Doneraile, and Ardra (Ard Rátha) in the parish of Britway; the other patron of Ardra (if she was Brighid of Kildare rather than her namesake Brighid, sister of Colmán of Cloyne) is also said to have gouged out an eye to avoid marriage.[4] Cránaid was well remembered in local tradition, especially in the parishes of Clenor (at Killuragh) and Castletownroche (at Garranachole), between Mallow and Fermoy, where a legend similar to the contents of her above-mentioned Life, but describing the saint as having made a vow to Brighid to lead a religious life, was handed down until modern times.[5] Local tradition also credits her with two brothers, named 'Breanat' (probably Beircheart), patron of Wallstown in the barony of Fermoy, and Nicholas whose holy well was situated near a castle in the parish of Monamimy, both parishes being contiguous to Clenor.[6] Two trees in the parish of Clenor, one of which (at Annakisha North) is said to have sprung from the eye Cránaid gouged out, were highly venerated.[7] The saint was probably also remembered at Kilcronat in the east Cork parish of Mogeely, not far from Britway, and at Kilgrant (Ceall Chrónata) in the Tipperary barony of Iffa and Offa East.[8] Her feast of 9 March is among local additions to a sixteenth-century Connacht manuscript, later kept in the Fermoy area.[9]

1 *JCHAS* 92, 106. **2** *MHH* 157–69; *HMDC* 11–12. **3** *IKHK* 293; *Lgen.* 622.5; *Peritia* 15, 305–8. **4** *MHH* 160–1 §§1, 3; *BBr.* 5 §15; *CCS* 126. **5** *MHH* 158–9; *JCHAS* 2, 60–1; *MFCJ* 5, 128–30; *CPR* i, lxvii; *HTN* 303; *PABD* 10; *AICW* iv (pt ii), 463, 465, 471. **6** *PABD* 61; *MFCJ* 5, 128–30. **7** *JCHAS* 68, 38; *AICW* iv (pt ii), 471. **8** *CLTÁ* 107–9; *PHib.* i, 143. **9** RIA MS 23 N 10, 145; *JCHAS* 2, 61.

Craobh daughter of Mac Iair. This saint, one of three daughters of Mac Iair, the others being Lasair and Fionn, is known only from the tract on the genealogies of the saints, which attaches her to the Dál Meisin Corb.[1] Other daughters of Mac Iair are associated with Killiney, but their names differ.

1 *CGSH* §253; *GRSH* 87, 89, 90; *Lgen.* 457.20.

Craobhnad. *See* Cránaid.

Craobhnad of Kilcreevanty (Ceall Chraobhnada), parish of Kilbennan, barony of Dunmore, Co. Galway. Although her church is mentioned in the annals, nothing appears to have been recorded of the saint, other than her probable feast of 17 July.[1]

1 OSL GY i, 16; *ACoC* 1301.2; *MartG* 138; *MartD* 194.

Craoi of Kilkea (Ceall Chaoi) in the Kildare barony of the same name. Despite being in the company of Patrick's sister Ríceann, Craoi is said to have been subject to Brighid of Kildare. Nothing more is known of her.

1 *CGSH* §670.61.

Cravan. *See* Sceanbhán.

Créadh. An entry in the list of those subject to Brighid of Kildare refers to Créadh (alias Créidh), placing her, together with a companion named Croimseach, in three churches, Ráith Ghairne, Eadarghabhal and Fordruim, none of which has been satisfactorily identified.[1] It is worth noting that the Franciscan friary of Kilcrea (Ceall Chréidhe) in the Cork parish of Desertmore, which lay on the river Bride (Brighid), is said to have had Brighid as its patron, but Ciar (alias Ceara), who is commemorated on 16 October, has also been identified as the saint of this site.[2] 'Kilcreddy' in the Kilkenny parish of Derrynahinch, of which Brighid was believed to be patron, has also been taken to represent 'Crede's church'.[3]

1 *CGSH* §670.19. **2** *NCHC* i, 203n; *FranC* 39; Maynooth MS M 84, 228. **3** *HADO* iv, 18–19.

Créadhnad of Rathbride, parish of Tully, barony of Offaly East, Co. Kildare, a site that may formerly have been known as Ráith Scannlaighe. Créadhnad's mother Scannlach is alleged to have given possession of her *ráith*, 'fort', in the *tearmann*, 'sanctuary', of Brighid of Kildare to her daughter.[1] Rathbride was located in the territory of the Uí Chormaic, a family that may have been descended from Créadhnad's father Aodh Róin.[2] Aonghas son of Aodh Róin, who is included in a list of bishops of Ireland, appears to have been Créadhnad's brother.[3] The saint's grandfather is said to have been the saintly Crunnmhaol of Barragh.[4]

1 *CGSH* §698. **2** Ibid. §670.79; *CGH* 122bc44. **3** *CGSH* §704.125. **4** *GRSH* 87.

Criadha daughter of Earnán. *See* Cróine daughter of Earnán.

Críoda of Nurney (Earnaidhe), barony of Offaly West, Co. Kildare. Críoda (alias Críod) daughter of Baodán figures in the list of those said to have been subject to Brighid of Kildare.[1] Nothing else is known of her.

1 *CGSH* §670.57.

Críodán of Ceall Earca, an unidentified church, probably in the parish of Burt, barony of Inishowen West, Co. Donegal.[1] According to the death-tale of Muircheartach son of Earc, king of Tara, the dynast engaged in battle with shadowy battalions created by an Otherworld woman who had entranced him.[2] The king's senses were temporarily restored by Cairneach of Dulane, accompanied by three other saints, Masán, Casán, and Críodán, only to have their work undone, and the king die by means of the so-called Threefold Death. Críodán is elsewhere stated to have been provided by Cairneach with a church named after Muircheartach's mother Earc, who did penance while on her way from Tory Island (Torach) to a place called Críoch Rois Oiligh, possibly in north Donegal.[2] Críodán is probably the saint said to have foretold the birth of Féichín of Fore.[3]

1 *HDGP* iii, 167. **2** *AMME* 17 §§24–5. **2** *SGS* 6, 50–7; *Lgen.* 112.5. **3** *VSHP* ii, 76 §3.

Críodán of Kilcredaun (Ceall Chuireadáin / Chríodáin) in the parish and barony of Moyarta, Co. Clare. A holy well close to one of two ruined churches in the townland of Kilcredaun was ranked among the most popular in Ireland for the cure of all diseases, as Eugene O'Curry wrote in his account of the parish, but nothing was then remembered concerning its patron Críodán (alias Cuireadán or Crodán).[1] As his church was apparently affiliated to that of Seanán on Scattery Island, it may be assumed that the 'Critanus' invoked with Seanán in a twelfth-century litany compiled in the Regensburg *Schottenkloster* referred to the patron of Kilcredaun.[2] Local tradition maintained that he had two saintly siblings, Cuán and Cróine, respectively patrons of 'Ceall Chuáin' in the townland of Kiltrellig, parish of Kilballyowen, and of Kilcrone in the townland of Lisheencrony, parish of Moyarta.[3] The saint named Cuireadán, commemorated on 7 March, the vigil of the feast of Seanán, at an (unidentified) site named Druim Lára, may have been the patron of Kilcredaun.[4] There was a well dedicated to Críodán at Kilcredaun in the Clare parish of O'Briensbridge.[5]

1 *ACoC* 119–20. **2** *ZCP* 10, 16–18; UCC MS U.331; *CKV* 60. **3** *Dinn.* 4, 10. **4** *MartT* 21; *MartG* 50; *MartD* 68; *ACoC* 120. **5** *PRIA* 6C (1900), 107.

Críodán son of Dáire. *See* Maolán of Kilmoylan.

Críodán son of Iollann. The list of saints commemorated on 11 May twice refers to this saint, first placing him, apparently with a priest named Cormac, in the unidentified church of Achadh Finnigh, 'on the brink of the Dodder' in Uí Dhúnchadha, a name used of a territory that included south Dublin, and then locating him under the guise of Mochríodóg, but in the same company, on Aran.[1] In the latter place, he is said to have interrogated the devil as to how he should reach heaven, only to receive a reply in metrical form outlining the ideal clerical life.[2] No memory of Críodán appears to have survived on Aran but, as an abbot named Caoimhghin was also remembered on 11 May, the saint's Leinster church may have had some association with Glendalough.[3]

1 *MartT* 42; *MartG* 94; *MartD* 124. **2** *MartT* 110–12. **3** *CPPI* 187–8.

Críodán Ceartrannach, 'fair-sharing', of Bangor (Beannchar), barony of Ards Lower, Co. Down. This saint, whose mother, Eithne daughter of Sárán, was allegedly a sister of Rónán Fionn of Magheralin, was attached to the community of Comhghall at Bangor.[1] Críodán is featured in Comhghall's Life as an old man and anchorite who witnessed angels touching and blessing Comhghall while he celebrated Easter Mass.[2] The entry on his feastday of 16 September in the later martyrologies describes Críodán as Comhghall's *ceallóir*, 'cellarer', a man noted for his justice in disbursing the monastery's provisions.[3]

1 *CGSH* §722.103. **2** *VSHP* ii, 9. **3** *MartG* 178; *MartD* 250.

Cróchán/Crohane. *See* Cruachán.

Croimín. *See* Cruimín.

Croimseach. *See* Créadh.

Cróine. The list of homonymous saints includes seventeen bearers of this derivative of *crón*, 'tawny/tan-coloured', most of whom are otherwise unattested.[1] Of the ten churches named in the list, few can be identified, and the same applies to the seven saints provided with patronymics. One saint of the name, attached to the church of Ceall Chróine, is said to have been a sister of Patrick, otherwise unrecorded. She may be identical with the Cróine commemorated at a church variously named Inis Locha Chróine – now possibly Lough Croan in the Roscommon barony of Athlone – and Ceall Chróine.[2] One seventeenth-century source speculates that this bearer of the name was the same as Cróine of Ardnahue.[3]

1 *CGSH* §708.49–65. **2** *MartT* 12; *MartG* 24; *MartD* 28. **3** *MartD* 28.

Cróine daughter of Earnán. According to her pedigree, Cróine (alias Criadha) was one of three sisters, the others being Dairneasa and Sineach, all of whom were grandnieces of Bréanainn of Birr.[1] She was associated with a place called Margach which is probably to be identified with Sliabh Mairge, now the Laois barony of Slievemargy.[2] Her church may have been at Díseart Mairge, an unidentified site in the same area, likewise associated with a saint named Cróine.[3]

1 *CGSH* §124; *GRSH* 111; *Lgen.* 734.9. **2** *CGSH* §670.68. **3** Ibid. §708.60.

Cróine daughter of Séadna. *See* Cróine of Ardnehue.

Cróine of Ardnehue (Ceall Inghean nAodha), parish of Killerrig, barony and county of Carlow. Cróine daughter of Aodh and her two sisters, Cuman and Ríoghnach, were attached to the Ceinéal Maine of Teathbha, a stretch of land comprising most of Longford and part of Westmeath.[1] A second church, Domhnach Mór Sanct Brighde (now probably Donaghmore in the Kildare barony of North Salt), is assigned to this Cróine in the list of those subject to Brighid of Kildare.[2] Included in the same list is a namesake, and probable double, who gave name to Inis Cróine, now Incha Croan on Lough Ennell, near Mullingar in Westmeath.[3] Another possible double is Crón daughter of Séadna of Carlow who is invoked as one of the sainted protectors of Leinster in a poem attributed to Moling.[4] The saint's feastday fell, according to one seventeenth-century source, on 27 January.[5]

1 *CGSH* §§81, 708.54, 711.87; *Lgen.* 703.1–2. **2** *CGSH* §670.38; *Lgen.* 753.9. **3** *CGSH* §670.13; *PNW* 167. **4** *SG* i, 389. **5** *MartD* 28.

Cróine of Gallow, barony of Upper Deece, Co. Meath, a site that may now represent the former Galamh or Galamh Laighean. Among the Midland saints called upon to bemoan the fall of *Bile Tortan*, a famous tree located near Ardbraccan in Meath, was Cróine of Galamh who drew attention to the protection it gave until, in falling, it crushed many of the Conaille people.[1] Otherwise included in the list of homonymous female saints, Cróine was remembered on two days, 1 January and 4 September.[2] On the latter day, she was accompanied by her reputed brother, Ultán of Ardbraccan, who was also among those lamenting the fallen tree. As Cróine's feasts are recorded only in the Martyrology of Tallaght, her church may have been associated with the *céile Dé* movement.[3] A litany-style prayer of invocation possibly invokes this Cróine among many other female saints.[4]

1 *MD* iv, 240–46. **2** *CGSH* §708.51; *MartT* 3, 68. **3** Cf. *OnomG* 435. **4** *MartT* 108; *IrL* 92.

Cróine of Incha Croan. *See* Cróine of Ardnehue.

Cróine of Kilcrone. *See* Críodán of Kilcredaun.

Cróine of Templecrone (Teampall Cróine), barony of Boylagh, Co. Donegal. The pedigree of Cróine daughter of Diarmuid attached her to the Ceinéal Boghaine, who gave name to the barony of Banagh, adjoining Boylagh.[1] Cróine's uncle, Seachnasach (†605) by name, belonged to the leading branch of this family.[2] The saint was also known as Cróine Bheag, and her feast of 7 July came to be regarded as a suitable time for digging early potatoes.[3]

1 *CGSH* §38; *GRSH* 39; *Lgen.* 700.2. **2** *CGH* 144f48; *AU s.a.* **3** *MartT* 54; *MartG* 132; *MartD* 188; *IrT* iii, 44n; *FL* 45.

Cróinseach daughter of Tairbhín. *See* Ceillseach.

Crom of Toomour. *See* Lughach.

Crón. *See* Cróine.

Crónaid. *See* Cránaid.

Cronaghan. *See* Cruithneachán.

Crónán. A diminutive form of *crón*, 'tawny/tan-coloured', this was a common name, with almost twenty bearers listed in the martyrologies. Furthermore, under the hypocoristic guise of Mochua, almost sixty are included in the list of homonymous names.[1] Among those known by both forms of the name were the patrons of Clondalkin and Roscrea.

1 *CGSH* §707.484–543.

Crónán of Balla. *See* Mochua of Balla.

Crónán of Carran. *See* Colmán of Tomgraney.

Crónán of Clashmore (Glais Mhór), barony of Decies within Drum, Co. Waterford. The record of the patron of Clashmore is both meagre and confused. Locally remembered as Mochua, the saint's original name (Crónán) is the form adopted by all the martyrologists in the list for his feastday of 10 February which describes him as a son of Meallán, and this patronymic is repeated in the Life of Mochuda, which includes him among the twelve disciples of the Lismore saint.[1] Commemorated on the previous day was a saint named Cuarán *sapiens* 'the wise', likewise of the Déise, whose name also yields the hypocoristic form Mochua. Towards the end of his life, Mochaomhóg of Leigh is said to have resuscitated a monk named Cuan Cearr – likewise the basis of a hypocoristic Mochua – who then went on to found the church of Glais Mhór, presumably a reference to the present Clashmore.[2] Although sometimes applied to Clashmore, a note added to the Martyrology of Aonghas that accuses the Vikings of Inbhear Domhnann, perhaps Malahide, of slaying the whole community at Glais Mhór *in una nocte*, is unlikely to refer to the Waterford church.[3] Located south of Swords by one glossator, 'Glashmore Abbey' in the townland of Mooretown, parish of Swords, where there is a holy well dedicated to the saint, may be intended.[4] A king of the Déise of Breagha was slain here in 1034.[5] The vigil (9 February) of the saint's feast found its way, under the guise of 'Trouanus episcopus', into the copy of the Martyrology of Usuard prepared by Grevenus in Cologne in the late fifteenth century.[6]

1 *MartT* 16; *MartO*[2] 59; *MartD* 44; OSL WD 169; *PND* 89; *VSHP* I, 182 §34. **2** *VSHP* ii, 182 §33; *ASH* 589. **3** *MartO*[2] 72; *Wat.Lis.* 128; *Rep. Nov.* 2, 81; *AHWD* 12, 42. **4** *AMBR* 53; *AU s.a.* **5** *AS*.Iun. vii, 93.

Crónán of Clondalkin (Cluain Dolcáin), barony of Uppercross, Co. Dublin. This saint was the best-known of seven sons of Lughaidh son of Nathí of the Uí Chéithigh, a branch of the Laighin (Leinstermen) that gave name to the Kildare barony of Ikeathy.[1] The mother of these saints, Cainnear, was attached to the church of Cluain Dá Shaileach, now probably Clonsilla, a few miles from Clondalkin.[2] To judge by a joint *commotatio*, 'circuit', in 790 of his relics with those of Caoimhghin of Glendalough, a close association had developed between the two churches which is still reflected in the presence at Clondalkin of 'St Kevin's well'.[3] This connection is confirmed by two other sources, a litany of Irish saints which names Crónán, under the guise of Mochua, among the members of Caoimhghin's *familia*, 'community', and passages in the Life written for Caoimhghin that mention Crónán, in one case assigning to him the honour of baptizing the Glendalough saint.[4] A manuscript containing a calendar of saints of probable Glendalough origin, now in Karlsruhe, but formerly on the Reichenau, bears Crónán's name on its cover.[5] A poem attributed to Moling calls upon him, with many other saints, to come to the assistance of the Leinstermen, and he is featured in another poem among those lamenting the fall of the famous tree, *Bile Tortan*.[6] He may also have been patron of Kildrought (Ceall Droichid), later Celbridge, in the Kildare barony of North Salt, not far from Clondalkin.[7] Crónán's feast fell on 6 August.[8]

1 *CGSH* §243.1.2; *GRSH* 87; *Lgen*. 724.8; *CGH* 124a15; *DIB* vi, 538–9; *Seanchas* 182–4. **2** *CGSH* §722.77. **3** *AU s.a.* **4** *IrL* 54; *VSHP* i, 234 §1, 254–5 §43; *CPPI* 174–5; *JRSAI* 74, 195. **5** *Thes*. ii, 256; *AfL* 31, 36. **6** *SG* i, 389; *MD* iv, 240–6. **7** *JCKAS* 2, 324; *AH* 8, 46. **8** *MartT* 60; *MartO*[2] 176; *MartG* 150; *MartD* 212.

Crónán of Cloney. *See* Crónán of Roscrea.

Crónán of Díseart Átha Mac Lughna (Mughna), a place near the river Figile, which divides the Kildare parish of Rathangan from that of Monasteroris in Offaly.[1] As this site is at no great distance from Cloney in the parish of Kilberry, the local cult of Crónán probably reflects that of his better-known namesake at Roscrea, reputedly a first cousin of Cloney's patron, Baodán.[2]

1 *HDGP* i, 142. **2** *CGSH* §697.3; *VSHP* ii, 22 §2.

Crónán of Inchicronan/Killokennedy. *See* Colmán of Tomgraney.

Crónán of Roscrea (Ros Cré), barony of Ikerrin, Co. Tipperary. Crónán son of Odhrán is said to have belonged to the Cianachta, among whose representatives were the Uí Chearbhaill (O'Carrolls) and Uí Mheachair (Mahers) of Éile, secular lords of the area about Roscrea.[1] According to one tradition, the saint's mother was Caoimhre (Mochaomhra) of the Corca Bhaiscinn of south-west Clare, whereas another source assigns this role to Inghean Bhaoith of Killinaboy.[2] Possibly because of the importance of Crónán's church which briefly, between about 1150 and 1170, attained the status of a diocesan see, the saint was made the subject of a Life, now preserved in Latin only.[3] This text has been dated to the eleventh or early twelfth century (1000–1150), but no critical edition has yet been made.[4] Its reference to the obscure Ráith Bheagáin as a place, apparently in north Munster, worthy of a visit from the king of Cashel would indicate a later date because this name, then evidently well known, is otherwise found only in the Life composed for Abán of Killaban in the early thirteenth century.[5]

The Life shows great interest in the affairs of two locations, Roscrea itself and Monaincha in the parish of Corbally.[6] The foundation of Seanros, near Monaincha, is graphically described, as is the move from there to the 'public way' at Roscrea itself. Although both locations were long established, with each receiving mention in documents from the ninth century or even earlier, nowhere else are they brought together in relation to one person and the community that recognized him as head. It seems likely, therefore, that the union of interest between Roscrea and Monaincha, underlying their treatment in the Life, was the presence in both communities of canons regular of St Augustine, who arrived in the area about 1140.[7]

Otherwise, property interests in or near Éile, and the saint's sojourn at the Offaly church of Lusmagh (Lusmhagh), which is the focus of nine chapters, may relate to diocesan concerns; despite having Crónán, or his putative cousin Mochonna, as patron, Lusmagh is now the only parish east of the river Shannon to belong to the diocese of Clonfert.[8] Among the many miracles attributed to Crónán, while in Lusmagh, was one connected with the miraculous production of the Book of Díoma, now in the Library of Trinity College Dublin.[9] Other saints featured in the Life include Crónán's first cousin, Mobhaoi (alias Baodán) of Cloney, who allegedly accompanied the saint to Assaroe to read the scriptures there, and Mochaomhóg of Leigh, who is said to have received hospitality from him.[10] Crónán's association with Baodán is confirmed by an entry in the corpus of saints' genealogies.[11] Baodán is also provided with a brother named Crónán, possibly originally identical with the Roscrea saint, whose feast was celebrated twice, at Cloney on 30 August, and also, in the guise of a son of Sineall, on 11 November.[12] This Crónán was among those who allegedly died of the *Buidhe Chonaill* in 665.[13]

A visit by Molua of Clonfertmulloe to Crónán, then in Monaincha, to receive the last rites from him, is recorded in the Life of the former saint.[14] This honour may have been due to Molua's status as co-patron of the diocese of Killaloe, which had absorbed Roscrea. Following a failure on the part of Mochuda (Carthach) of Lismore to take up an offer of hospitality, allegedly because of the isolation of the saint's church, Crónán is said to have moved to the larger church in Roscrea, where, as a poem attributed to Cuana, king of the Fir Mhaighe in north Cork, states, 'he loved not niggardliness'.[15] Elsewhere, in a poem in Classical Irish, 'steadfast' Crónán, together with numerous other saints, may have been the bearer of the name called upon to help in releasing Ireland's southern half (Leath Mogha) from a bondage imposed on it by the northern half (Leath Chuinn), represented by Finnian of Clonard.[16] Crónán's feast fell on 28 April.[17] A week later, on 4 May, a saint named Crónán (alias Mochua) son of Cuimín, probably identical with the patron of Roscrea, was venerated in Sliabh Eibhlinne, now the Slieve Felim mountains on Limerick's border with Tipperary.[18] Crónán's coarb was entitled to a horse and garment from every chieftain of the Uí Mheachair of Éile, as well as a place of honour at the chieftain's inauguration.[19]

1 *CGSH* §225; *GRSH* 123; *Lgen.* 742.7; *VSHP* ii, 22; *VSHH* 274; *DIB* ii, 1022–3; *OCBG* §2046. **2** *VSHH* 274; *CGSH* §697.3; *IrT* iv, 94 §10. **3** *VSHP* ii, 21–31; *VSHH* 274–9; *MRHI* 59, 95–6, 192. **4** *Kenney* 460; *HDK* 63; *ANA* 44. **5** *VSHP* i, 18 §23; ii, 29 §24; *VSHH* 265 §18, 279 §21. **6** *VSHP* ii, 27 §17, 30 §26; *VSHH* 277 §14, 279 §21. **7** *MRHI* 187–8, 192. **8** *VSHP* ii, 22 §2, 24–6 §§7–16; *VSHH* 275–7 §§1, 7–13; OSL OY i, 199. **9** *VSHP* ii, 24 §9; *VSHH* 276 §8; TCD MS 59. **10** *VSHP* ii, 22 §2, 27–8 §19; *VSHH* 275 §1, 278 §17. **11** *CGSH* §697. **12** *MartT* 67; *MartG* 166, 216; *MartD* 228, 304. **13** *AU s.a.*; *IrT* iii, 85 §9. **14** *VSHP* ii, 223 §52; *VSHH* 144 §68. **15** *VSHP* i, 194 §61; *Ériu* 19, 78 §6. **16** RIA MS 23L11, 263. **17** *MartT* 37; *MartO²* 109; *MartG* 86; *MartD* 112. **18** *MartT* 39; *MartO²* 122; *MartG* 90; *MartD* 120. **19** *OCBG* §2046.

Crónán of Tomgraney (Tuaim Gréine), barony of Tulla Upper, Co. Clare. When visiting the parish of Tomgraney in late 1839, John O'Donovan could only lament the fact that nothing much of its saint had been discovered by 'investigators of Irish hagiology'.[1] O'Donovan could not even ascertain locally when the saint's feast was celebrated, opting instead for the evidence of the 'Irish Calendar' of the Four Masters, his name for the Martyrology of Donegal, which placed the feast on 19 October. A note added by John Colgan to the collection of genealogies made by the Four Masters speculates, not improbably, that this saint was Crónán son of Aonghas of the Uí Fhiachrach.[2] This family held lands in various parts of Connacht, including Tír Fhiachrach – now the Sligo barony of Tireragh – and Aidhne which was approximately equivalent to the diocese of Kilmacduagh. Although now in the diocese of Killaloe, Tomgraney lay close to the southern boundary of Kilmacduagh. There were other dedications to Crónán in the area, at Inchicronan west of Tomgraney, where the saint's feast reportedly fell 'in Harvest', at Killokennedy south of it, and probably also at Carran in the barony of Burren.[3] Though doubtless originally one and the same, the patrons of these three places were sometimes together called *na Crónáin* (the Crónáns).[4] A measure of the saint's importance to the Dál gCais ancestors of the Uí Bhriain of Thomond is the tradition that Inis Iobhthonn, apparently the island on which Limerick stood, was given to Crónán, as well as to Mainchín.[5] A trace of the donation may survive in the ruins of Kilquane, from Ceall Chuáin, 'little Cua's church', on the north bank of the Shannon, opposite Corbally; Cua was a pet form of Crónán.[6] The saint is again brought together with Mainchín of Limerick in a poem listing the progeny of Inghean Bhaoith of Killinaboy.[7] Similarly, unless Crónán of Roscrea is intended, the 'steadfast' Crónán called upon, together with numerous other saints, to help in releasing Ireland's southern half (Leath Mogha) from a bondage imposed on it by the northern half (Leath Chuinn), represented by Finnian of Clonard, may refer to the patron of Tomgraney.[8] Crónán's feast fell on 19 October.[9]

1 *ACoC* 214–16. **2** *GRSH* 62; cf. *CGSH* §24; *Lgen.* 711.4; *NL* 169–70. **3** *ACoC* 33, 181, 248–9; *CH* 2, 36. **4** *ZCP* 10, 26. **5** *CoC* 22; *NL* 168–70. **6** *CLuim.* i, 10–11; *BBL* 26, 28; *CGSH* §707.515. **7** *IrT* iv, 94 §10. **8** RIA MS 23L11, 263; *SAM* 24.1, 17, 19. **9** *MartT* 81; *MartG* 198; *MartD* 278.

Crónán son of Aonghas. *See* Crónán of Tomgraney.

Crónán son of Sineall (Silne). *See* Crónán of Roscrea.

Crónán Luachra. *See* Mochua Luachra.

Crónán Sapiens, 'the wise'. *See* Cuarán Sapiens.

Crotha daughter of Brión. *See* Aodh of Kilcrow.

Cruachán of Ceall Chruacháin, an unidentified church on the boundary of Laoighis (whence the present county of Laois) and Osraighe (now approximately the county of Kilkenny), a location that would suit Kilcronan in the parish of Dysartgallen, whose patron was, however, Mochua of Timahoe. This Cruachán (also written Cróchán) son of Tairbhín is said to have been one of seven brothers and sisters, mainly connected with the church of Áth na gCeall on the river

Blackwater in Munster, a site probably at Gortnagross a few miles west of Mallow in the parish of Ballyclogh.[1] The family belonged to the Múscraighe and Cruachán's siblings included Laichtín of the Kilkenny church of Freshford. Among churches named Kilcrohane after the saint in the south-west of Ireland was one in the Cork barony of West Carbery, where his feast was celebrated on 30 July, and another – in a parish containing Caherdaniel and Sneem – in the Kerry barony of Dunkerron South, where his feast fell either on the same day or a day later.[2] As already recorded in the eighteenth century by Charles Smith, near this latter church of Kilcrohane, in a 'cell hewn out of solid rock', locally known as Crohane's cave, Ciarán of Saighir is reputed to have composed his rule.[3] In former times, the feast of this *Lughnasadh* saint, who probably represents the pre-Christian Crom Cróich, fell on 1 August.[4] One tradition surrounding his feastday maintained that visions were afforded to devotees at the break of day, and completion of the saint's *turas*, 'rounds', was thought to relieve bad eyesight.[5] In the Kerry parish of Kilcrohane, the saint's name continued to be borne by males until modern times.

1 *CGSH* §666.1.2; *HDGP* i, 146. **2** *TDI* ii, 75; *ACoK* 154; *JKAHS* 22, 150; ibid. 30, 47–8; *Béaloideas* 15, 22–4. **3** *NCHK* 93; *ACoK* 152–3; *TH* ii, 18–19; *JCHAS* 64, 36; *Béaloideas* 15, 24. **4** *FL* 648–50. **5** *IrM* 1.3, 77–8; *Béaloideas* 15, 24; *IMN* 3, 77–8.

Cruaidh. A poem attributed to Moling calls upon this saint, among many others, to come to the assistance of the Leinstermen.[1] As suggested by Mícheál Ó Cléirigh, he was probably the saint variously named Cruadh and Cruaidh Cosfhada, 'long-legged', who was remembered on 26 October at the church of Ballon (Balana) in the Carlow barony of Forth.[2]

1 *SG* i, 389. **2** *MartG* 204; *MartD* 284; *HDGP* ii, 75.

Cruimín of Lackan (Leacain), barony of Corkaree, Co. Westmeath. The pedigree of Cruimín (Croimín) son of Cormac attaches him to the Cianachta, whose many branches included one located in Breagha, now most of Meath, and parts of Louth and Dublin.[1] He is already featured in Patrick's Tripartite Life which relates how the Armagh saint left 'venerable burial places' (*reilge sruithe*) in Lackan, along with some followers headed by Cruimín.[2] Another Patrician association is supplied by Cruimín's mother Dairearca, Patrick's sister, who is said to have had fifteen saintly children, many of them belonging to churches in the west Midlands.[3] Little else is known of the saint, but he reputedly attained the venerable age of nine score years 'without sadness' (*sine tristitia*).[4] Although his main feast was celebrated on 28 June – which was remembered locally as the 'day after [*recte* before] St Peter's' – the Martyrology of Tallaght credits him with a second feast of 29 December.[5]

1 *CGSH* §360; *GRSH* 123; *CGH* 145c14. **3** *CGSH* §722.16 **4** *MartO²* 158. **5** *MartT* 2, 52; *MartO²* 143; *MartG* 124; *MartD* 180; *PNW* 100, 126–7.

Cruimhthear Fraoch. *See* Fraoch.

Cruimhthiris of Kinnegoe (Ceann Gobha), parish of Loughgall, barony and county of Armagh. The author of the Tripartite Life asserts that Patrick was once visited at Armagh by nine daughters of the king of the Lombards, together with a daughter of the king of the Britons, but only one of the ten, a certain Cruimhthiris (Cruimhthir), is named.[1] Patrick sent the maidens to various sites in the vicinity of his church, with Cruimhthiris settling at Kinnegoe. The list of those in orders with Patrick describes her as one of his three embroideresses.[2]

1 *BP* 2746–59; *VT* 232. 2 *BP* 3142–3; *CGSH* §§671.13; 672.12.

Cruithneach, associate of Patrick. According to the metrical version of those in orders with Patrick, Cruithneach (meaning Pict) was one of his three stonemasons (*saoir*).[1] These are supposed to have been the first to build a stone church (*daimhliag*) in Ireland.

1 *CGSH* §672.14.

Cruithneachán of Kilcronaghan (Ceall Chruithneacháin), barony of Loughinsholin, Co. Derry. According to Adhamhnán, Cruithneachán (anglicized Cronaghan), when returning to his church one night, noticed a ball of fire above his sleeping foster-son, Colum Cille, which lit up the whole place.[1] Though Adhamhnán had no more to say of the saint, later biographers of the patron of Iona were more expansive. The saint's father was supplied with the name Ceallachán, and Cruithneachán is said to have also baptized Colum, giving him Criomhthann as a first name.[2] Colum's late vernacular Life creates the impression that the Donegal church of Kilmacrenan (Ceall Mhac nÉanáin) was where Colum was fostered, but the church named after his fosterer was Kilcronaghan in Derry.[3] The neighbouring Derry parish of Ballynascreen had Colum as its patron.[4] Cruithneachán's feast, arbitrarily placed by John Colgan on 7 March, is not noticed in any martyrology.[5] An early seventeenth-century description of the diocese of Derry renders his name as *Chronicanus*.[6]

1 *VC*[2] 466–8. 2 *IKD* 226 §21; *BCC* 40–8 (§§53–62). 3 *BCC* 40 (§53); *Celtica* 1, 83; *DYHS* 195. 4 *Celtica* 1, 82; PNNI v, 6–9. 5 *ASH* 600–1; *VC*[1] 191n; PNNI v, 114; *PNCL* 183.. 6 *AnH* 12, 108, 111.

Crunnmhaol of Barragh (Beirreach), barony of Forth, Co. Carlow. Crunnmhaol son of Rónán is known from a variety of sources. In one, he belongs to a group of saints located in Kilcrow (Ceall Chraoi) in the Kildare parish of Churchtown.[1] In another, he is assigned to the Uí Cheinsealaigh of south Leinster, provided with a son named Aodh Róin, and located in the church of Cluain Aird, now possibly Clonard, parish of St Peter's, in the Wexford barony of Forth.[2] The genealogical record also includes assertions that Crunnmhaol was an ancestor of two other saints, named Fíonnachta and Créadhnad.[3] The entry on his feastday of 22 June supplies Crunnmhaol with yet another location, at Barragh, which is presumably where he was thought to be buried.[4]

1 *CGSH* §367.2; *HDGP* iii, 150. 2 *CGSH* §273; *Lgen*. 727.24. 3 *CGSH* §275; *GRSH* 87. 4 *MartT* 51; *MartG* 120; *MartD* 174.

Cuach. *See* also Cóch.

Cuach daughter of Caolbhadh. *See* Caomhán Santleathan.

Cuach of 'Killynee' (Ceall Fhionnmhaighe), an ecclesiastical site in the townland of Bogland, parish and barony of Arklow, Co. Wicklow. Cuach (alias Coininghean) is known from the martyrologies, which commemorate her on 29 April.[1] A note added to the Martyrology of Aonghas asserts that she was suckled by a she-wolf and that Mac Táil of Kilcullen was reviled on account of her.[2] Her church was affiliated to Glendalough.[3]

1 *MartT* 37; *MartG* 86; *MartD* 112. **2** *MartO*[2] 120. **3** *CPPI* 193, 199.

Cuachnad of Ros Ráithe. *See* Cognad of Urney.

Cuán of Ahascragh (Áth Eascrach), barony of Kilconnell, Co. Galway. This saint is known from some entries in the corpus of saints' pedigrees which provide the name of his church, various forms of his own name (including Cuana, Mochua, Dochuailéan and Dochua Oiléin, 'of the Island'), a sobriquet *caoin*, 'pleasant', and a descent through his father Fearghas (or Tighearnach) from Conall Gulban son of Niall Naoighiallach, ancestor of the Ceinéal Conaill of Donegal.[1] His obit is assigned by one set of annals to the year 770, and he is otherwise known from the list of saints commemorated on 2 March.[2] The local day of commemoration at a well in the townland of Castlegar, apparently under the anglicized guise of 'Cavan', was 15 October.[3]

1 *CGSH* §§409, 657, 703.7, 707.501.532; *GRSH* 39. **2** ARos. *s.a.*; *MartT* 20; *MartG* 46; *MartD* 60. **3** OSL GY i, 116, 239.

Cuán of Airbhre, now probably the ecclesiastical site in the townland and parish of Kilcowan, barony of Bargy, Co. Wexford, and of Mothel (Maothail), barony of Upperthird, Co. Waterford.[1] The Life of Munna of Taghmon recounts how Ceallachán son of Díoma Camchos, 'crooked leg', king of the Fothairt (who gave name to the Wexford barony of Forth), was reared by Cuán, only to have Munna (who was rearing Ceallachán's saintly brother Cillín) prophesy that the Leinstermen would one day kill Ceallachán, which, it is said, duly took place.[2] Beyond an entry in the martyrologies for 10 July, and a reference in the list of homonymous saints, little else is known of Cuán.[3] A namesake and probable double of his, the patron of Kilcowanmore, likewise in Wexford, had a pattern day of 3 February, but this man's name has recently been identified as Comhghán.[4] At Mothel, the site of an Augustinian priory, where Cuán is thought to have succeeded Brocán, the saint is still remembered on 6 July at the well of *Tobar Chuáin agus Brocáin* in the townland of Ballynevin, the scene of 'stations' that used to attract a large concourse of people.[5] John O'Donovan suggested that he was also patron of Kilquane in the Kerry parish of Ballymacelligott, but this is more likely to have been Cuán son of Síolán of the Ciarraighe.[6]

1 *HDGP* i, 34; *PND* 402–3. **2** *VSHH* 204–5 §24. **3** *MartT* 55; *MartG* 134; *MartD* 192; *CGSH* §707.516. **4** OSL WX ii, 45; *CECW* 207; *TNW* 1094. **5** *WatLis.* 138; *TKAS* 1, 497, 500. **6** *ACoK* 65.

Cuán of Ceall Chuáin. *See* Críodán of Kilcredaun.

Cuán of Kilcoan (Ceall Chuáin), barony of Ida, Co. Kilkenny, and more specifically of an ecclesiastical site in the townland of Weatherstown, formerly known as Achadh Bearnchon (Bearchon) [1]. An entry in the corpus of saints' pedigrees locates Cuán son of Odhrán in Uí Bhearrchon, now reflected in the name Rosbercon, from Ros Ua mBearrchon (Ros of the Uí Bhearrchon), in the same barony.[2] The saint's pedigree attaches him, however, to the Uí Mhaine of Connacht who held lands later approximately coextensive with the diocese of Clonfert.[3] He may thus be identical with the patron of the parish of Kilquain, likewise from Ceall Chuáin, in the Galway barony of Longford, within the diocese of Clonfert. Although the saint's holy well still survives in Weatherstown, there is no record locally of his feast.[4] The saint's name was also written as Cuana and Mochua.

1 *HDGP* i, 11. **2** *CGSH* §§377, 601. **3** Cf. *CGH* 145e48–f14. **4** *HADO* iv, 91.

Cuán of Kilquane (Ceall Chuáin), barony of Corkaguiny, Co. Kerry. This son of Síolán is attached to the Clann Luighne, a branch of the Ciarraighe.[1] Little else is recorded of him in early sources beyond the fact that he had three brothers, named Colmán, Beag Bile, and Connaidhil.[2] Under the guise of Cobhán, he is reported to have banished a *piast*, 'water monster', from a lake (Loch Cráilí) in the adjoining parish of Kilmalkedar.[3] He may also be the patron of several other places named Kilquane in Kerry, including – despite John O'Donovan, who identified the saint with Cuán of Mothel – Kilquane in the parish of Ballymacelligott.[4]

1 *CGSH* §314; *CGH* 160b55. **2** Ibid. **3** *Béaloideas* 2, 217–18; ibid. 8, 62–3; ibid. 51, 100–1; *Éigse* 11, 105; *SeanM* 314; *TCCD* 124. **4** *ACoK* 65.

Cuán of Míleac Fiaich. *See* Angán.

Cuana of Eóinis, now either White Island or Davy's Island on Lough Erne, in the parish of Magheraculmoney, barony of Lurg, Co. Fermanagh.[1] According to his pedigree, Cuana (alias Constans) son of Fualascach belonged to Ceinéal Tuadáin, a branch of the Oirghialla of Clogher.[2] He led an anchoritic life on Eóinis and, by the time of his death in 778, he had built up a reputation for wisdom.[3] He may also be the man named Cuana who is invoked as a legal witness in a poem on the Oirghialla.[4] His feast fell on 14 November.[5] Long after his death, his remains were divided into three parts, one of which remained on the island, whereas, according to the Register of Clogher, the other parts were translated to Clogher – together with the relics of three Britons brought to Eonish by Cuana – and placed in Mac Caorthainn's reliquary.[6]

1 *Peritia* 16, 477–8; *FHHS* 576. **2** *CGSH* §51; *GRSH* 66; *Lgen.* 713.7; *CGH* 142a2; *Peritia* 16, 477–8. **3** *CGH* 142a2; *AU s.a.* **4** *Ériu* 16, 184 §43. **5** *MartG* 218; *MartD* 308. **6** *ClRec.* 1.1, 32; ibid. 7, 396.

Cuana of Kilcoona (Ceall Chuana), barony of Clare, Co. Galway. In his *Topographical Dictionary of Ireland*, Samuel Lewis devoted eight lines to the parish of Kilcoona – a sure measure of its lack of importance in his eyes – in the course of which he asserted that St 'Columb', presumably Colum Cille, was said to have founded the local abbey.[1] The saint who gave his name to the parish was, however, at one stage considered important enough to have a Latin Life written for him which survives in fragmentary form only, in a single collection known as *Salmanticensis*.[2] A note added to the Life states that it was translated from Irish into Latin, and almost all extant references to Cuana of Kilcoona derive from this text.[3] From its fragmentary remains, it is difficult to know what led to the production of this 'much padded Life of an obscure saint'.[4] Lying close to the parish of Claregalway, Kilcoona may have had some connection with the local Franciscan friary which was founded about 1250.[5] The house of canons regular at Annaghdown was also in close proximity and, in view of the probability that *Salmanticensis* was compiled in the house of canons at Clogher in the county of Tyrone, this represents a more likely provenance.[6] The attention paid by the saint's biographer to Fursa, patron of the church of Killursa (Ceall Fhursa) within the deanery of Annaghdown, likewise the location of a house of canons regular, also points to Augustinian influence.[7]

Two other saints are featured in the surviving fragment of the Life, Maighneann who exchanges his ailments with Fursa, and Inghean Bhaoith (alias Fíonmhaith) who is presented as Cuana's mother.[8] This would seem to be an attempt to identify the saint with Cuana Ógh (son of Miodharn) of Cloncowan in the Meath parish of Rathmolyon, who is separately included among Inghean Bhaoith's numerous children.[9] A connection with the west of Ireland is elsewhere implied for this latter saint – commemorated on 10 April – by his role as one of the 'fellows' of Forannán of Alternan in Sligo.[10] At Kilcoona, the saint came to be regarded as a brother of Fursa and Éanna, patrons of the neighbouring parishes of Killursa and Killeany.[11] The title given to Cuana's Life describes him as abbot of Lismore, and this shows that at some stage he was held to be the same as his 'pious and holy' namesake commemorated on 4 February, a view also taken by John Colgan in the early seventeenth century.[12] Through a possible confusion of his church in Clare barony with Clare county, Cuana may have given its modern name to the so-called Kilshanny bell, alias the bell of St Cuana, which was received before 1850 by T.L. Cooke of Birr from the parish priest of New Quay in Clare, and is now in the British Museum.[13]

1 *TDI* ii, 71 (Kilcooney). **2** *VSHH* 407–10. **3** Ibid. 410n; *HDGP* iii, 153. **4** *Kenney* 467. **5** *MRHI* 245. **6** Ibid. 156–7; *MirL* 91–100. **7** *VSHH* 409 §§9–10; cf. *MartO*[2] 44–6; *MRHI* 156–7. **8** *VSHH* 408–9 §§7, 10. **9** *IrT* iv, 93 §1. **10** *MartT* 31, 226; *MartO*[2] 105; *MartG* 74; *MartD* 98; *Anecd.* iii, 2. **11** OSL GY i, 186. **12** *MartT* 14; *MartO*[2] 58; *MartG* 30; *MartD* 38; *FourIM* 171; *ASH* 249–52. **13** *JRSAI* 2, 62; *CCSt.* 47–53; *Seanchas* 331–40; *EMH* 450–2 §149.

Cuana of Lismore. *See* Cuana of Kilcoona.

Cuana of Oirghialla. *See* Cuana of Eonish.

Cuana, Patrick's smith. This man is known only from a miscellaneous list of Patrick's achievements and associates which describes him as one of three smiths responsible for the saint's bells.[1] The other two were Mac Táil and Mac Céacht, the latter being the only one of the three retained in a separate list.[2]

1 *BP* 2959; *VT* 250. **2** *BP* 269; *VT* 266.

Cuana son of Miodharn. *See* Cuana of Kilcoona; Cuana Ógh.

Cuana son of Odhrán. *See* Cuán of Kilcoan.

Cuana Ógh, 'virgin', of Ros Eó in Magh Locha of Breagha, now probably Cloncowan (perhaps from Cluain Cuana) in the parish of Rathmolyon, barony of Lower Moyfenrath, Co. Meath. The list of those commemorated on 10 April includes this saint.[1] Described as royal, excellent, and noble in body and spirit, Cuana came to be regarded, from the fourteenth century on, if not earlier, as a son of Miodharn, who is attached by his pedigree to the Ceinéal Éanna.[2] The Life written for Forannán of Alternan in Sligo contains a list of its subject's *comhbhráithre naomh*, 'fellow-saints', headed by Cuana son of Miodharn.[3] Elsewhere he is preceded only by Seanán of Scattery Island in the long list of those said to have been children of Inghean Bhaoith, which would suggest that he was thought to be identical with Cuana of Kilcoona in Galway, whose mother is given the same name.[4] Cuana of Ros Eó died in 721.[5]

1 *MartT* 31, 226; *MartO²* 105; *MartG* 74; *ILL* 77–8. 2 *CGSH* §§351, 662.32; *GRSH* 58; *Lgen*. 708.3, *MartO²* 114; *MartD* 98. 3 *Anecd*. iii, 2. 4 *IrT* iv, 93 §1; *VSHH* 408 §7. 5 *AU s.a.*

Cuanán Glinne of Movilla (Magh Bhile), parish of Newtown Ards, barony of Ards Lower, Co. Down. An annal entry for the year 747 notes the death of Cuanán, abbot of Movilla.[1] Cuanán (alias Cuana) was remembered annually on 3 February.[2] Where the *gleann*, 'glen', was located has yet to be established, unless it be the site that gave name to the Antrim parish of Glynn. It is also worth noting that a saint named 'Cunanus' (perhaps from Cuanán) was remembered as patron of the church of Ballyrolly in the parish of Down.[3]

1 *AU s.a.* 2 *MartT* 14; *MartG* 28; *MartD* 38. 3 *CPL* 19, §328.

Cuarán Sapiens, 'the wise'. The word usually attached to this saint's name, Latin *sapiens*, Irish *eagnaoidh*, denoted a wise or learned man. Almost all mentions of Cuarán emphasize his scholarship. The earliest of these, a note added to an eighth-century gospel book kept in Würzburg, Germany, describes the saint as a pupil of Moshiona, scholar and abbot of Bangor, and allegedly the first of the Irish to learn the computus by heart from a certain learned Greek.[1] The pupil, it is said in the same note, was himself styled 'teacher of the whole world', not least perhaps because he is thought to have written down what he learned from his master. Cuarán belonged to the Maca Nadh Seamhan (otherwise Seimhne) of the Déise and, as his master died in 610, the saint may be assigned to the early seventh century.[2] The earliest record of his feastday (9 February), while confirming both his descent and his reputation for scholarship, gives him an alias Crónán.[3] Later notices locate him in the Déise of Munster, or alternatively at Timahoe (Teach Mochua) in Laois, thus drawing attention to the possibility that he was also known by the pet form Mochua.[4] One source provides him with the epithet *nóna*, 'of the none', supposedly because he was the first to divide up the celebration of none, or more likely of the Mass, which had previously gone on for an hour and a half.[5] Many churches are named Kilcoran (Ceall Chuaráin) after him, especially in Munster, with one located in Youghal, close to the modern Decies, and another in the Tipperary parish of Tubbrid, near Cahir, formerly within the Déise of Munster.[6] The saint was also remembered at a well in the townland of Cooraun (perhaps from Cuarán) in the Wexford parish of Edermine and, under the guise of Mochuaróg, he was possibly patron of 'Kilmuchorog', now the Limerick parish of Kilmurry.[7] Cuarán's memory appears to have endured long after his death and not only in the south of Ireland. An entry in the Annals of Ulster for 1121 dates the death in the monastery of Derry of Domhnall Mac Lochlainn, 'high-king' of Ireland, to the fourth (*recte* fifth) ides of February, 'the feast of Coran of the wisdom'.[8]

1 *Thes.* ii, 285; *AB* 64, 225; *DIB* vi, 539–40. 2 *AU s.a.*; *CGH* 140b25; ibid. 157, 50; *LL* 43690; *ZCP* 14, 52. 3 *MartT* 15; cf. *MartO*² 59. 4 *MartG* 32; *MartD* 42; *MartO*² 70. 5 *MartO*² 70; *AB* 64, 220–5, 244. 6 *CLTÁ* 110–11. 7 *HDF* 45; *CECW* 217; *SATM* 46, 205; *LnaÉ* i, 104. 8 *AU s.a.*

Cuculanus. *See* Cúlán.

Cuddy. *See* Mochuda.

Cuimín. This name is a diminutive of *Cuimmc* (also *Cumma*, *Caimme*), a hypocoristic or pet form of Colum. The name often served, therefore, as a means of providing local devotees of Colum Cille, founder of Iona, with an appropriately endearing form of his name.

Cuimín of Kilcummin. *See* Colum of Inishkeen; Cuimín Fada of Kilcummin.

Cuimín son of Díoma. *See* Cuimín Fada of Kilcummin.

Cuimín son of Fiachna. *See* Cuimín Fada of Clonfert.

Cuimín son of Fionnach. *See* Baoithín of Ennisboyne.

Cuimín son of Fothlán. *See* Beag of Killerrig.

Cuimín Cadhan, 'pious', of Annaduff (Eanach Dubh), barony and county of Leitrim. According to his pedigree, Cuimín son of Crunnchú belonged to the Dál gCais of Thomond.[1] A note adds that – despite the location of the saint's church in Connacht, far away from Thomond – a horse and trappings were due to Cuimín's successor from the king of Dál gCais, once the latter had taken the hostages of Cashel and had his hair cut.[2] Against this, a seventeenth-century source dealing with the churches of Leitrim states that the saint was the son of a king of Leinster and that a certain grass growing on an island in the nearby lake of Loch an Daimh was associated with the saint.[3] A poem preserved in the Book of Fenagh mentions Cuimín (under the guise of Dochuma) in conjunction with Patrick 'of Kiltubbrid', a site not far from Annaduff.[4] The two saints and their churches are again brought together in a late fifteenth-century list of annates, and also in a list of 'united' parishes from the same period which renders the saint's name as 'Cominus' and that of his church as 'Benachumbi', perhaps from Beann Dochuma.[5] The saint's feast is not known from early sources, but a seventeenth-century text speculates that it may have fallen on 1 June, which would bring Colum Cille's feast within its octave.[6] Elsewhere, a choice is offered between 1 June and 22 August.[7] The saint was locally remembered under the guise of 'Comin Ea'.[8]

1 *CGSH* §330. 2 *GRSH* 119; *Lgen.* 738.7–8. 3 *Celtica* 1, 67. 4 BFen. (supp.) 82; *Celtica* 1, 67, 75. 5 *AnnU* 165; *CPL* 13, 344. 6 *MartD* 142. 7 *GRSH* 119. 8 OSL CN/LM 180.

Cuimín Fada, 'long', of Clonfert (Cluain Fearta), barony of Longford, Co. Galway. Although Cuimín Fada (Latin Cumianus Longus) became the subject of a 'mass of legend', the genealogical tradition consistently attached him to the Eoghanachta of south Munster, hesitating, however, between the Cashel and Killarney (Loch Léin) branches of that family.[1] The legendary (and unseemly) story of his birth to his own sister Ríomh – or, as some sources suggest, to a lady named Mughain – as the result of an alcohol-induced, incestuous union with the saint's father Fiachna, became the stuff of a whole cycle of literature.[2] Ignoring Fiachna's order that the child be killed, his mother is said to have abandoned him, Moses-like, in a basket (Irish *cuimín*, whence, as is assumed inaccurately, the saint's name) at a church sometimes said to have been Killeedy (Ceall Íde) in Limerick, where he was raised.[3] Himself both son and grandson of his father, Cuimín was supposedly related through his mother's (and sister's) womb to such noted literary characters as the two kings, Guaire son of Colmán, famous for his hospitality, and Cuana son of Cailchín, king of the Fir Mhaighe of the Fermoy area, as well as the celebrated 'fool', Comhghán Mac Dá Chearda, 'son of two crafts', with whom the saint figures in a number of tales.[4] It has been suggested that Cuimín and Marbhán ('dead one') – likewise, according to a tale concerning the finding of the *Táin*, King Guaire's half-brother – were one and the same.[5]

A prophecy concerning Cuimín's own death, made while he was at school with Fionnbharr of Cork, foretold that he would die at a place called Corcach. Despite the saint's best efforts to avoid all places so named by means of constant travel, some of which is recounted in a text entitled *Imtheachta na nÓinmhideadh*, 'wanderings of the fools', the prophecy eventually came true in 662, in his seventy-second year, according to the annals, which date his birth, however, to 592.[6] An elegy attributed to Colmán of the Maca Cluasaigh, a quatrain of which is cited in the Annals of Ulster, extols him not only as bishop and king, but also as the one Irishman most worthy of occupying the papal see or, as here described, 'seat of Gregory'.[7]

Several Latin texts are attributed to Cuimín: a penitential which not only circulated widely on the Continent, but was also deemed worthy of mention in a similar text in Old Irish; a hymn in praise of the apostles beginning *Celebra Iuda*, the famous paschal letter attributed to Cummian, and some other works recently identified as his.[8] An extensive preface to the hymn in praise of the apostles, said to have been composed in Derry, relates the circumstances of Cuimín's birth and his role – as foretold by Colum Cille – as *anmchara*, 'soul-friend', of Domhnall son of Aodh, king of Tara. Probably through confusion with the Iona saint's successor, Cuimín Fionn son of Earnán, a Life of Colum Cille was also attributed to the saint.[9] Among the churches associated with Cuimín was Clonfert, where he is said to have been bishop.[10] A western connection may also underlie a reference to Cuimín Fada son of Mughain Mholbhthach among the Uí Amhalghaidh of north Connacht in a text known as 'Four Saints', unless this was because of confusion with Cuimín Fada son of Conaing of Kilcummin.[11]

The saint's principal area of activity was in south Munster, as is shown by the Life of Mochaomhóg, which describes how Cuimín's previous blessing of a king of the Déise of the Limerick area prevented his being cursed by the subject of the Life.[12] Born in 590 or 592, the saint died, according to the annals, in 662, and his feastday fell on 12 November (*Mí Gamh*, 'winter month'), the vigil of the feast of his namesake and probable double, Caillín of Fenagh, who also figures prominently, along with Cuimín's other possible double, Marbhán, in *Tromdhámh Ghuaire*.[13] A 'wise man, brilliant, and famous', and one of the four chief sages of Ireland, Cuimín was likened in manners to Pope Gregory of the *Moralia*.[14] Under the guise of Sean-Chuimín, he was invoked with Bréanainn in a poem by Donnchadh Mór Ó Dálaigh.[15] His remains were raised at Clonfert in 1162 and enshrined with those of Maoineann.[16]

1 *CGSH* §232; *GRSH* 116; *Lgen.* 738.10; *CGH* 151b15; *Hereditas* 198; *Béaloideas* 39–41, 198; *MartO*² 242; *Ériu* 25, 95–6; *Ériu* 28, 17; *LH* i, 16; *DIB* ii, 1084–5; *IIAM* 583–7. **2** *Hereditas* 198–9; *Béaloideas* 39–41, 198–9; ibid, 200; *Ériu* 25, 88–125; 28, 32–70; *KeltRh.* 51–4. **3** *Hereditas* 198–9; *Béaloideas* 39–41, 198–9; *MartO*² 242. **4** *CGSH* §722.66; *CGH* 151b15–18; *Hereditas* 200, 203n; *Béaloideas* 39–41, 200, 203n; *Ériu* 5, 18–44. **5** *Ériu* 28, 55; *TromG*. **6** RIA MS B iv 1, fos 149–78; *Hereditas* 199–201; *Béaloideas* 39–41, 199–201; *AU s.a.* **7** *FAI* 12 §19; *Bruchst.* 41–3 §96; *Ériu* 28, 17–31; ibid. 31, 111–22. **8** *IrP* 5–7, 108–35; *Ériu* 7, 144 §21; *LH* i, 16–21; *CLCP* 7–15; *Peritia* 5, 46; ibid. 10, 32–51; ibid. 13, 100; *DIB* ii, 1085; *CLCP* 7–25; *IIAM* 577. **9** *LH* i, 16–18; *BCC* 246 §243. **10** *MartG* 216. **11** *IrT* iii, 4 §9. **12** *VSHP* ii, 180 §30. **13** *MartO*² 234; *MartG* 216; *MartD* 304; *TromG* 1234–315; *Bruchst.* 41 §96.7; *AU s.a.* **15** *Dán Dé* 50. **14** *Ériu* 19, 64 §23; *CGSH* §712.24; *FAI* 12 §19. **15** *AFM s.a.*

Cuimín Fada, 'long', of Kilcummin (Ceall Chuimín), barony of Tirawley, Co. Mayo. Dubhaltach Mac Fhir Bhisigh was a native of Caoille Conaill in the north-east corner of Tirawley between Rathfran Bay and Lacken Bay, near which his family had maintained a hereditary school.[1] He wrote, therefore, in his Great Book of Genealogies with authority based on local knowledge of his own district which included Kilcummin. Here, according to Mac Fhir Bhisigh, using the Book of Lecan as his source, Cuimín son of Díoma and his seed after him, the Uí Chuimín, dwelt and, when the saint died, he was buried in a big cairn, still pointed out, under the feet of Ua Suanaigh, i.e. Fiodhmhaine Ua Suanaigh.[2] In a following note, Mac Fhir Bhisigh asserted, however, that 'it was not that Cuimín who first blessed the place, but Cuimín Fada son of Conaing (or Conall)'.[3] His statement concerning Cuimín son of Díoma was probably based on the first chapter of a short tract on the 'Sons of Ua Suanaigh' which asserts, however, that this bearer of the name was buried in the Offaly church of Rahan.[4]

Many local features at Kilcomin (Ceall Chuimín) in the Offaly barony of Clonlisk, including a well, field, seat, rock and trees, were named for the local version of the saint, and tradition held that Cuimín and Crónán of Roscrea had a row concerning a boundary that ended in violencee, which may also have involved the bringing to Kilcomin (alias Díseart Cuimín) of the relics of Peter and Paul from where they subsequently 'escaped' back to Roscrea.[5] His bell was also preserved locally.[6] Little else is known of either Cuimín, but the tract known as 'Four Saints', preserved in the Book of Lecan, asserts that Cormac of Killala – who blessed the seed of Eachaidh Breac, and foretold the birth of Ua Suanaigh – lived among the Clann Amhalghaidh, along with several other saints, including one named Cuimín Fada son of Mughain Mholbhthach.[7] Despite the reference to Mughain Mholbhthach, who sometimes replaces Ríomh as the mother of Cuimín

Fada son of Fiachna, the patron of Kilcummin is probably intended. His burial place was thought to lie near the well dedicated to him in Kilcummin.[8] At Kilcummin he was remembered as 'judge and arbitrator' in all disputes.[9]

1 *HDGP* iii, 50; *Lgen.* i, 2. 2 *Lgen.* 255.1.2; *BLec.* 71rd, 10–20; OSL MO i, 191; *JRSAI* 67, 268. 3 *Lgen.* 255.1.2; cf. ibid. 248.6. 4 *BNÉ* i, 312 §1. 5 OSL OY 183–4; *JCHAS* 68, 37; *MartO* 78. 6 *JRSAI* 2A, 57. 7 *IrT* iii, 4. 8 *LSS* 11. 9 *JGAHS* 64, 7.

Cuimín Fionn, 'fair', son of Earnán (Eirnín/Arnáine), abbot of Iona, Scotland. A list of pedigrees of the abbots of Iona, preserved in the Book of Glendalough version of the corpus of saints' pedigrees, includes Cuimín son of Arnáine of the Ceinéal Conaill of Donegal.[1] The seventh abbot after Colum Cille, Cuimín Fionn (Latin Albus) succeeded Suibhne in 657.[2] His term of office coincided with the holding of the synod of Whitby in 664, which led to the adoption of Roman practice with regard to the calculation of the date of Easter, and a subsequent decline in Irish influence in Northumbria. Cuimín, who visited Ireland in 661, returning to Iona by 664, is best known for his alleged authorship of a book on the miracles of Colum Cille, cited by Adhamhnán, and of a letter on the paschal question, sometimes attributed to him.[3] Sometimes confused with Cuimín Fada of Clonfert, he was also known as a son of Fiachna, as is shown by an entry in the Martyrology of Tallaght made – probably on Iona itself – on the day of his commemoration (24 February).[4] Cuimín, abbot of Iona, died in 669.[5] Under the guise of Comán son of Earnán, he was also commemorated on 18 March, according to the Martyrology of Donegal only.[6] Some Scottish sites, including Fort Augustus (earlier Ceall Chuimín), were dedicated to him.[7]

1 *CGSH* §338; *Lgen.* 698.1. 2 *IKD* 43–4; *Celtica* 21, 146–9; *DIB* ii, 1084. 3 *VC*[1] 375–6; *VC*[2] 474; *Peritia* 16, 40–67; ibid. 17–18, 183–98; *CLCP* 7–15. 4 *MartT* 18; *MartG* 42; *MartD* 56. 5 *CGSH* §662.18; *GRSH* 40; *AU s.a.* 6 *MartD* 80. 7 *KSS* 316–17; *CPNS* 303.

Cuinnidh. *See* Colum of Terryglass; Mac Cuilinn of Lusk.

Cuireadán. *See* Críodán.

Cuireadán of Ros Minn Bhaireann. Among the guarantors of the Law of Adhamhnán was a certain bishop named Cuireadán.[1] The same man, described as a holy bishop and abbot, is commemorated in the martyrologies at 16 March.[2] It has been suggested that he was identical with Cuireadán, alias Boniface/Queritinus, of Rosemarkie in Scotland, but the evidence for this is very slight.[3]

1 *CA* §22; *Peritia* 1, 191. 2 *MartT* 24; *MartG* 56; *MartD* 76. 3 *KSS* 281; *CPNS* 315; *Peritia* 1, 191; *CBR*; *GELB* 299–300.

Cúlán of Coolaun (originally Killcoolaun), near Glenkeen (Gleann Caoin) in the barony of Kilnamanagh Upper, Co. Tipperary. Of the four sons of Eoghan son of Murchadh of the Eoghanachta of Munster, only Cúlán (also written Cúiléan, as in Giolla Cúiléin of the Éile, or Cúilín and anglicized Coulane/Coolen) is said to have remained in the southern province.[1] Two others, Cormac and Diarmuid, travelled to Connacht and the third, Éimhín, settled in Leinster. A text in the Book of Lecan dealing with the four saints is mainly concerned with the activities of the pair that settled in the western province but, having placed Cúlán in Glenkeen, it also states that he blessed two local families, one named Clann Mhurchadha, the other Uí Luighdheach (whence 'Ileagh') who gave name to Borrisoleigh (Buirgheas Ua Luighdheach), near Glenkeen.[2] It also asserts that the saint foretold the decline of these families, should they ever become involved in a prey on the king of Cashel. Cúlán's main claim to attention is the celebrated relic associated with him, a twelfth-century bell known as 'Barnane Cuilawn' (*Bearnán Cúláin*), formerly kept at his church, then later found in the hollow of a tree and now in the British Museum.[3] Although nowhere recorded in Irish martyrologies, Cúlán's feast is assigned to 18 February in some sources, including a version of the Martyrology of Usuard made in Cologne shortly before 1500.[4] In the Catalogue of the principal Irish saints, Cúlán's name became Cuculanus.[5]

1 *IrT* iii, 2 §4; *CGH* 154a28. **2** Ibid. 3 §2; *CLTÁ* 117–18. **3** *JRSAI* 2A, 61–2; ibid. 52, 1–3; ibid. 53, 162; *TRIA* 14, 31–45; *LIS* ii, 621–3; *TIC* 221. **4** *GRSH* 116; *AS*.Iun. vi, 111; *Seanchas* 410 (§86). **5** *Seanchas* 410 §86; *FEMN* 355 (§153); cf. *HCIC* 49.

CUMAN. Probably a hypocoristic or pet form of Colum(b) in origin, this name was common among females, with seventeen included in the list of homonymous saints.[1] Though almost all of these are otherwise unattested, many bearers of the name are associated with Brighid of Kildare. These include Cuman (daughter of Colmán) of Cluain Caoin, now possibly Clonkeen in the Limerick barony of Clanwilliam, who, together with her sister Lasair, was among those said to have been subject to Brighid.[2] Similarly included among Brighid's subjects was Cuman daughter of Cuimín of Clonfad (Cluain Fada) in the Laois parish of Offerlane, who may have shared a church with Afraic daughter of Cumhlachtach, abbess of Kildare.[3]

1 *CGSH* §708.32–48. **2** *CGSH* p. 318; ibid. §670.83. **3** *CGSH* §670.47.

CUMAN of Aharney (Achadh Toghartha), an ecclesiastical site in the townland of Ballyconra, parish of Aharney, barony of Galmoy, Co. Kilkenny.[1] Cuman's main claim to fame was through her sister Broicseach, mother of Brighid of Kildare. Like Broicseach, and five other siblings – Caoimheall, Fuinche, Fionnbharr, Feidhealm, and Sanct Broc – she is said to have belonged through her father Dallbhrónach to the Dál gConchobhair of the Déise of Breagha who gave name to the Meath baronies of Deece.[2] It is further maintained that, when pregnant, Cuman was met and blessed by Patrick, the cross he made with his crozier remaining imprinted on her forehead.[3] On the same occasion, Patrick is said to have prophesied that Cuman would give birth to many saints, both male and female – forty-five, according to the tract on the mothers of the saints.[4] She is also said to have been the mother of two kings, one of whom, Tuathal Maolgharbh, held the kingship of Tara, according to the official king-lists.[5] Many of those named as her children, including her first-born, Bishop Maine of Aghanagh, were associated with churches in north Connacht, and these are brought together in an assembly with Colum Cille by the author of the Life of Forannán of Alternan.[6] Cuman's own church, which was dedicated to Brighid, lay among the Uí Dhuach in the part of the county of Kilkenny formerly known as Magh Airgeadrois.[7] There was confusion between Cuman and Inghean Bhaoith of Killinaboy who is said to have given birth to many of the same children.[8] There is no record of Cuman's feast.

1 *HDGP* i, 23. 2 *CGSH* §§2.1, 173, 722.4; *Lgen.* 7695.3. 3 *CGSH* §722.6. 4 Ibid. 5 Ibid.; *CAn.* 74 §286; *IKHK* 90–2. 6 *Anecd.* iii, 3. 7 *HADO* ii, 308–10. 8 *IrT* iv, 93–4.

Cuman of Aireadh Bóinne, now perhaps an ecclesiastical site on the line that divides the townlands of Kilnagalliagh and Monagalliagh, parish of Clonard, barony of Upper Moyfenrath, Co. Meath. This daughter of Maine is known from an entry in the corpus of saints' pedigrees which places her in Aireadh (Airear) Bóinne, together with her two sisters, Dearmhór and Eithne, a cleric named Colmán Fionn, and Dubhán the Priest.[1] The three females were daughters of Maine son of Cearbhall, possibly the king of Uisneach of that name, during whose reign Patrick is said to have died.[2] According to a hymn in praise of Brighid of Kildare, a miracle gave Cuman's harvesters a dry day when rain was all around her church.[3] Together with her sisters, Cuman was commemorated on 6 July.[4]

1 *CGSH* §179; *HDGP* i, 42. 2 *VT* 552. 3 *LH* i, 117. 4 *MartT* 54; *MartG* 130; *MartD* 188.

Cuman of Ardnehue (Ceall Inghean nAodha), parish of Killerrig, barony and county of Carlow. Cuman and her two sisters, Cróine and Ríoghnach, were attached through their father Aodh to the Ceinéal Maine of Teathbha, a stretch of land comprising most of Longford and part of Westmeath.[1] A second church, Domhnach Mór Sanct Brighde, now probably Donaghmore in the Kildare barony of North Salt, was assigned to her sister Cróine in the list of those subject to Brighid of Kildare.[2] Unless, therefore, the local cult was that of Cuman, daughter of Cairbre, of Naas, the saint may also have given her name to Stacumny (Teach Cuimne, 'Cuman's dwelling/church') in the barony of South Salt, not far from Donaghmore.[3]

1 *CGSH* §§81, 708.54, 711.87. 2 *CGSH* §670.38. 3 Ibid. §708.34.48 add.

Cuman of Ards (Aird Uladh), Co. Down. In keeping with the location of her church, Cuman's pedigree attaches her through her father Ailléan (Oilléan) to the Dál bhFiatach of east Ulster.[1] Her church, named Daire Inghine Ailléin, may now be Derry in the parish of Ballyphilip, barony of Ards Upper.[2] Her feastday was celebrated on 29 May.[3]

1 *CGSH* §196; *GRSH* 82; *Lgen.* 498.8. 2 *MartO*[2] 136; *EA* 23–4; PNNI ii, 47–8. 3 *MartT* 46; *MartO*[2] 126; *MartG* 106; *MartD* 140.

Cuman of Naas (Ceall Náis), barony of Naas North, Co. Kildare. According to the corpus of saints' pedigrees, Cuman daughter of Cairbre and her sister Soidhealbh, likewise of Naas, belonged to the Uí Dhúnlainge, one of the ruling dynasties of north Leinster.[1] Either this Cuman or her namesake, Cuman daughter of Aodh, may have given name to Teach Cuimne, 'Cuman's dwelling or church', now Stacumny in the barony of South Salt.[2] Two namesakes, and possible replicates of Cuman's sister Soidhealbh, one described as a daughter of Cuanán, the other as a daughter of Margán, are also included in the list of those subject to Brighid of Kildare.[3]

1 *CGSH* §248; *GRSH* 87, 91; *Lgen.* 726.12; *CGH* 316a47 add. 2 *CGSH* §708.34.38 add. 3 Ibid. §670.75.84; OSL KE i, 65–6.

Cummian. *See* Cuimín.

Cunnlan. *See* Caolán of Youghalarra.

Curcach daughter of Daol (Aol). Bearing a name probably derived from *corc*, 'red, crimson', this saint is known from an entry in the corpus of saints' pedigrees that traces her descent, together with that of her two brothers, Aoidhghin of Bodoney and the presbyter Ceanannán, to Colla Meann of the Oirghialla whose lands corresponded approximately to the extent of the later diocese of Clogher.[1] Curcach was speculatively identified in the early seventeenth century as the saint of that name commemorated either on 8 March or 8 August.[2] The saint remembered on the latter day, who was attached to the church of Cluain Lothair, now Cloonlogher in the Leitrim barony of Dromahaire, is more likely to have been the same as Curcach of Kilcorkey, sister of Caoireach Dheargáin.[3]

1 *CGSH* §61.2; *Lgen.* 715.5. 2 *GRSH* 73; *MartD* 212. 3 *MartT* 21; *MartG* 152; *MartD* 212.

Curcach daughter of Éanna. *See* Curcach of Kilcorkey.

Curcach of Kilcorkey (Ceall Churcaighe), barony of Castlereagh, Co. Roscommon. Assigned to the Greagraighe in the list of those commemorated on 16 November, this saint was doubtless the patron of Kilcorkey where the local feast was observed on 21 July.[1] This part of Roscommon and adjoining parts of Sligo were associated in the Greagraighe.[2] She may also be the same as Curcach daughter of Éanna of Cluain Lothair, now Cloonlogher in the Leitrim barony of Dromahaire, whose feast fell on 12 February.[3] She was thought to be a sister of Caoireach Dheargáin.[4] It has been suggested that the Curcach who gave name to Cork Abbey (Mainistear Churcaighe) near Bray was identical with the saint remembered on 21 July.[5] If a saint is intended by this place-name, however, Curcach of Kilcorkey in the county of Wexford is a more likely candidate.

1 *MartG* 220; *MartD* 198, 310. 2 *LSLC* 295–7; *JCS* 1, 196. 3 *Celtica* 1, 65, 79. 4 *CGSH* §110; *Lgen.* 714.12. 5 OSL DB 67.

Curcach of Kilcorkey, Graveyard, townland of Knockbrandon Upper, parish of Kilnahue, barony of Gorey, Co. Wexford, which may now represent an earlier Ceall Inghean Luain. Among the saints said to have been subject to Brighid of Kildare were two daughters of Luan, Curcach and Míoda, who gave name to the church of Ceall Inghean Luain.[1] A close companion in the same section of the list belonged to the Uí Dheagha who gave name to the deanery of Oday in the Wexford barony of Gorey. It may be, therefore, that Curcach gave name to Kilcorkey in the parish of Kilnahue.[2]

1 *CGSH* §670.36. 2 *HDGP* iv, 5–6; *TNW* 1090.

Cúrnán of Kilcornan (Ceall Chúrnáin), parish of Kilkerrin, barony of Tiaquin, Co. Galway. An entry in the corpus of saints' pedigrees refers to three sons of Ainghin, variously named Mac Reithe, Cúrnán, and Colmán, the last of whom is located in Ceall Eadarghabhla in Fiodh Manach, now the parish of Killeroran in the Galway barony of Killian.[1] The church of the three brothers, Ceall Mhac nAinghin, which elsewhere figures in an account of the battle of Tarbhgha, was in the Galway parish of Ballynakill, adjoining Kilkerrin, a few miles north of Killeroran.[2] The two other Galway sites named after Cúrnán, in the parishes of Monivea and Stradbally, probably also reflected veneration of this saint.

1 *CGSH* §695. **2** *Celtica* 11, 133–40; *Lgen*. 237.7; *HDGP* iv, 11–12.

Cúrnán son of Sineall. This saint, together with four siblings that included Mobhaoi (alias Baodán) of Cloney (Cluain Annobhair) and a paternal uncle, Dúileach of St Doolaghs in the Dublin parish of Balgriffin, was attached to the Conmhaicne of Connacht.[1] A saint of the name is also included among the supposed pupils of Beinean of Kilbennan near Tuam, who likewise belonged to the Conmhaicne.[2] There are several churches named Kilcornan (Ceall Chúrnáin) in Galway and north Clare, all of which probably represent the same original cult. One seventeenth-century source speculates that this saint may also have been identical with Cúrnán Beag.[3]

1 *CGSH* §§128–9; *Lgen*. 733.2. **2** *AS*.Nov. iv, 179. **3** *MartD* 8.

Cúrnán Beag, 'little', of Kilcornan (Ceall Chúrnáin), barony of Kenry, Co. Limerick. This man is said by Míchéal Ó Cléirigh to have been the saint of the name commemorated on 6 January.[1] No other martyrology specifies the name of his church, and no local information was available when John O'Donovan visited the area in 1840.[2]

1 *MartD* 8. **2** OSL LK 66.

D ☙

Da-. *See* Do-

Daghán of Áth Dagháin. *See* Daghán of Ennereilly.

Daghán of Ennereilly (Inbhear Daoile), barony of Arklow, Co. Wicklow. Bearing a name derived either from *daigh*, 'fire', or *daigh-*, 'good', the former being the more probable, Daghán (Latin Daganus) son of Colmaidh is said to have belonged to the Dál Meisin Corb, who were mainly associated with Wicklow, and especially with the area about Glendalough.[1] The saint's mother, variously named Caoiltighearn and Caomhóg, is described as a sister of Caoimhghin of Glendalough, and among Daghán's siblings was Méanóg of Glenealy, likewise in Wicklow.[2] Together with another brother, Molioba by name, Daghán was one of forty saints said to have been companions of Caoimhghin – probably another way of saying that their churches were subject to Glendalough – and the church assigned to him later lay within this diocese.[3] The saint's associations were, however, wider than this. Poems in the *bóramha* tract, attributed to Bran, king of Leinster, and the emblematic saint Moling, invoke assistance from, among others, *cúigear ceolach*, 'a musical quintet', of one household, four only of whom are named, viz. Daghán, Bishop Eoghan, Abán and Caoimhghin.[4] That his reputation extended to the western borders of Leinster is shown by the Lives of Molua of Clonfertmulloe and Mochaomhóg of Leigh. In the former text, Daghán of Áth Dagháin, possibly another name for Ennereilly, is given two roles: one describes how he brought a copy of Molua's rule to Rome, to be read by Pope Gregory whom it greatly impressed; the other credits him with a prophecy made at Molua's request that Laichtín would succeed to the abbacy of Clonfertmulloe (alias Kyle) in the Laois barony of Clandonagh.[5] The latter text explains how Mochaomhóg acted as Daghán's teacher and, having promised to render him the last rites, resuscitated the saint following his death at the hands of robbers.[6] The fact that a Welsh saint named Pedrawg is also alleged to have acted as Daghán's teacher shows that he was known outside Ireland.[7]

Within Ireland, there is much to be said for Daghán's ultimate identity with his namesake, Daigh of Inishkeen, not least the fact that the daughters (Ingheana) of Colum, who share Daghán's feastday of 13 September, are featured in Daigh's Life.[8] The coincidence of his feast and the day of the celebrated battle of Ballaghmoon in 908 is noted by the annals, which also give the year of Daghán's death as 641.[9] Although sometimes supposed to be identical with the 'Bishop Daghán' mentioned by Bede in connection with a letter bearing on the paschal controversy, this has been disputed.[10] Daghán is also known from Scottish sources which place his feast on 29 May.[11]

1 *Celtica* 9, 212 (but cf. *Ériu* 26, 17n); *CGSH* §256; *GRSH* 87; *Lgen.* 726.3.5. **2** *GRSH* §722.72.102. **3** *IrL* 55–6; *CPPI* xx–xxi, *et passim*. **4** *SG* i, 382, 389. **5** *VSHP* ii, 222 §§47, 50; *VSHH* 144; *HDGP* i, 15. **6** *VSHP* ii, 177–8 §§26–7. **7** *CPPI* 124–5. **8** *Dinn.* 6, 83–7; *MartT* 70–1; *MartG* 176; *MartD* 246–8.

9 *AU*/*AFM*/*CS s.a.*; *AU s.a.* 908/*ATig. s.a.* 640. **10** *VB* ii, 83; *BEH* 146; *AB* 64, 235; *Peritia* 19, 77–85; *UJA* (3rd ser.) 1, 34; *DIB* iii, 2–3. **11** *KSS* 320–1.

Dahalin. *See* Daithle.

Daigh of Inishkeen (Inis Céin), barony of Farney, Co. Monaghan. There is a measure of confusion concerning the tribal affiliations of this saint, styled a bishop in the Irish tradition. According to the main line of the genealogical record, Daigh son of Coireall belonged to a branch of the Ceinéal Eoghain that was settled in the Bréadach, on the east side of the Donegal peninsula of Inishowen.[1] A separate tradition provides Daigh with a descent from the Déise who gave name to the Meath baronies of Deece, among other places, and yet another source – the Latin Life compiled for the saint – states that he was born among the Cianachta of Breagha who held lands along the Louth/Meath border, mainly in the barony of Ferrard.[2] The name given to his mother likewise varies, between Deidhe daughter of Trian and Deithidhe daughter of Masán.[3] Daigh's sibling Feimc is also listed among Deidhe's children.

As might be expected, it is Daigh's Life that provides most information on the saint, or on the view taken of him in the church for which the text was written. Despite its own stature, sufficiently great to attract the regular attention of the annalists, Inishkeen is unlikely to have produced the Life, which, although dated to the ninth century in a recent study, shows many signs of an Augustinian provenance.[3a] Laisréan of Devenish, the seat of a priory of canons regular, is given the privilege of baptizing and educating Daigh.[4] Mochta, patron of the Augustinian priory of Louth, one of the richest of its kind, is shown in an extensive introductory section to have recognized Daigh's future sanctity, and to have foretold the affiliation of Inishkeen to Clonmacnoise.[5] This suggests that the text may have been written in the Augustinian priory at Clonmacnoise in the mid- to late twelfth century, perhaps about the time that the Life of Éanna of Inishmore was apparently also being compiled there. Among other patrons of Augustinian priories featured in the text are Comhghall of Bangor, Colum Cille of Durrow, Finnian of Clonard, and Ruadhán of Lorrha.[6] Daigh's reputation as one of Ireland's finest craftsmen, a distinction he shared with two other bishops, Tasach and Conlaodh, is also underlined. Especially associated in this regard with Ciarán of Clonmacnoise, he is said to have fashioned numerous bells, shrines, reliquaries, crosses, chalices, and 'sixty whole gospels'.[7]

Among places reputed to have been visited by Daigh were kingdoms in the northern part of Sligo, including Uí Oilealla (Tirerrill), Luighne (Leyny), and Cairbre (Carbury).[8] A link with north Connacht is also evident in the martyrological list for 19 February which features Baoithín of Tibohine and Nuadha of Estersnow, both churches in north Roscommon, together with Daigh (under the guise of Neamhnall's son).[9] Commemorated on the previous day, according to some sources, was another son of Neamhnall, Bearach of the Roscommon church of Termonbarry who, according to his Life, was Daigh's disciple.[10] Also commemorated on 18 February was Molioba of the Uí Eachach of Ulster, allegedly a brother of Daghán, one of many pointers to the ultimate identity of the patrons of Inishkeen and Ennereilly.[11] Among other saints said to have been associated with Daigh was Moling who is shown invoking his name.[12] Curiously, although regarded by the Register of Clogher as the fifth occupant of its see, this is nowhere mentioned in the saint's Life, nor is any connection established for him with Mac Caorthainn.[13] The saint is thought to have died on 18 August 587, but the bishop named Daigh, commemorated two days earlier (16 August) in the later martyrologies, probably also refers to him.[14] Interestingly, his successor as patron of the parish of Inishkeen was another famous craftsman, Joseph, husband of Mary.[15]

1 *CGSH* §19; *GRSH* 45; *Lgen.* 701.1; *BB* 73de; *DIB* iii, 3–4. **2** *CGSH* §469 (La); *VSHH* 389 §1. **3** *CGSH* §722.2; *VSHH* 389 §1. **3a** *CHSC* 154–7. **4** *VSHH* 389 §1. **5** *VSHH* 389–90 §§2–4; *MRHI* 165, 169, 185–6; cf. *ClRec.* 11, 325; *CCLC* 77–9. **6** *VSHH* 390–2 §§6, 8, 11. **7** Ibid. 389–90 §3; *CGSH* §82.2; *MartT* 126. **8** *VSHH* 393 §§18–21. **9** *MartT* 13; *MartG* 38; *MartD* 52; *Dinn.* 6, 83–7. **10** *KSS* 278; *LIS* ii, 629; *VSHH* 391–2 §10; *BNÉ* i, 26–7 §§18–24. **11** *Dinn.* 6, 83–7. **12** *Anecd.* ii, 28 §6. **13** *ClRec.* 7, 378. **14** *MartT* 64; *MartO*[2] 177; *MartG* 158; *MartD* 220–2; *AU s.a.* **15** *HCM* 388.

Daigh son of Neamhnall. *See* Daigh of Inishkeen.

Dair/Dar/Dear/Deir. Meaning daughter, and usually followed by a name in the genitive case, this prefix derives from the Indo-European root that gave *daughter* in English and *tochter* in German.[1]

1 *Celtica* 3, 178–9.

Dairbhile. *See* Dearbhinill, Deirbhileadh.

Daircheall. *See* Moling of St Mullin's.

Dairearca daughter of Earcán. *See* Ciarán of Clonmacnoise.

Dairearca daughter of Mochta. *See* Moninne of Killevy.

Dairearca, sister of Patrick. Though the earliest Patrician documents know nothing of a sister named Dairearca, her name occurs in the mid-ninth-century Tripartite Life, first as the mother of Meal of Ardagh and Ríóg of Inishbofin who are thought to have followed Patrick to Ireland, then as a nun making altar-cloths for her brother.[1] She is joined in this latter capacity by two other supposed sisters of Patrick, Tighris and Lubaid, and her name is again mentioned, albeit corruptly, as Earc daughter of Dáire in the guise of embroideress to her brother.[2] The relatively modest number of seven sons and two daughters credited to Dairearca in the Tripartite Life increases twofold in the tract on the mothers of the saints which lists fifteen (sometimes seventeen) sons, mainly bishops, and two daughters.[3] According to the preface to the hymn beginning *Audite omnes*, Dairearca co-authored it with the much more celebrated Seachnall of Dunshaughlin.[4] She is sometimes confused with her namesake, the mother of Ciarán of Clonmacnoise, and also with her sister Lubaid, mother of the Maca Baird. Her feastday fell within the octave of Patrick's, on 22 March.[5] Dairearca's cult spread to the south-west of Ireland, and a large pattern marked her feast on Valencia Island until discontinued about 1850.[6] The presence of her cult in Kerry may explain why an entry on Ciarán of Clonmacnoise, allegedly one of her many children, attaches Dairearca through an otherwise unattested pedigree to the Ciarraighe.[7]

1 *BP* 895–902, 2963–4; *VT* 82, 252; *DIB* iii, 53–4. 2 *BP* 3142; cf. *CGSH* §§671.13, 672.12; *Lgen.* 692.5. 3 *CGSH* §722.16; *MartO*[2] 68. 4 *LH* i, 3; *VT* 382. 5 *MartT* 26; *MartG* 60; *MartD* 84. 6 *JKAHS* 22, 157. 7 *MartD* 240.

Dairí. An entry in the Annals of Innisfallen for the year 810 reads: 'The law concerning cows [promulgated] in Munster by Dairí and by Adhuar son of Eichean'.[1] The female saint invoked here in the name of the law was Dairí (alias Soidhealbh) daughter of Cathaoir of the Uí Amhalghaidh of Tirawley (Tír Amhalghaidh) in north Mayo.[2] Here, the saint is said to have been met by Cormac son of Eoghan, originally from Munster, on his wanderings in north Connacht. Dissatisfied with the service given to him, Cormac foretold that Dairí's place would only ever produce the milk of a thin stripper-cow (*caolghamhnach*), whence, allegedly but erroneously, the local name Magh Ghamhnach, now Moygawnagh, a parish in the barony of Tirawley.[3] Dairí's church was located at Kildaree (from Ceall Dairí) in the adjoining parish of Crossmolina, where local tradition wrongly took her name to mean 'two kings' (*dhá rí*).[4] Other (similarly named) churches dedicated to her are to be found in the Galway parishes of Killursa and Templetogher. Why she came to be associated with an ecclesiastical law concerning the theft of cattle, one of Ireland's four chief laws, is not clear.[5] Plainly, however, she was highly regarded west of the Shannon. The feast of Dairí *Bóchána*, 'of the law on cows', fell on 2 November or, according to one source, a week before this, on 26 October.[6]

1 *AI s.a.* 2 *CGSH* §39; *GRSH* 62; *AB* 81, 60–9. 3 *IrT* iii, 2 §5. 4 *Celtica* 21, 564–5; OSL MO i, 98. 5 *ZCP* 21, 338. 6 *MartG* 210; *MartD* 294; *GRSH* 62.

Dairneasa daughter of Earnán. *See* Cróine daughter of Earnán.

Dairtinne of 'Killart' (Ceall Araidh/Aird) in the townland of Oldcourt, parish of Kilberry, barony of Narragh and Reban West, Co. Kildare. Among those said to have been subject to Brighid of Kildare at Killart were Aodh son of Eirnín and his three daughters, Angais, Dairtinne and Brónach.[1] Although neither Brónach nor Angais is known from any other source, Dairtinne is among those commemorated on 3 July by the martyrologies, which locate her church among the Uí Earcáin, a group closely related to Brighid's branch of the Fothairt.[2]

1 *CGSH* §670.70; *Lgen.* 753.35; *HDGP* iii, 124. 2 *MartT* 53; *MartG* 128; *MartD* 186.

Daithle (Dahalin). *See* Earc of Altraighe.

Dalann. *See* Libhréan of Inis Mór.

Dalbhach of Coole Abbey (Cúil Chollainge), parish of Coole, barony of Barrymore, Co. Cork. A poem enumerating twenty-four saints – along with the holy king of Cashel, Feidhlimidh son of Criomhthann – said to have been joined in union with Maol Ruain of Tallaght, includes the names of Dalbhach and his church.[1] This would suggest that both saint and church were associated with the anchoritic group known by the name of *céili Dé*, 'clients of God', that flourished approximately between 750 and 850.[2] Although probably founded in this period like many others connected with the movement, Dalbhach's church was first blessed by Abán, according to the latter's biographer.[3] Attached by his pedigree through a father variously named Brannabh and Brónach to the local family of Uí Liatháin, Dalbhach was remembered, according to Cuimín of Connor, for his 'austere repentance', an appropriate trait, perhaps, for one involved with the *céili Dé*.[4] The saint's obit is entered in the annals for 800, and his feast is assigned by the martyrologists to 23 October.[5] A notice of Dalbhach's feast was also added in Cologne to Grevenus' copy of the Martyrology of Usuard, albeit under the guise of 'Daluath'.[6]

1 *CGSH* §§713.8.14, 724.3; *GRSH* 117; *Lgen*. 738.9. **2** *CéliD*. **3** *VSHP* i, 17 §22; *BNÉ* i, 8 §25. **4** *CGSH* §240; *GRSH* 117; *ZCP* 1, 64 §69. **5** *AI s.a.*; *MartT* 83; *MartG* 202; *MartD* 280. **6** *AS*.Iun. vii, 625.

DALLÁN FORGHAILL, 'of witness', of Kildallan (Ceall Dalláin), barony of Tullyhunco, Co. Cavan. Called both Dallán son of Earc (Forghall) and Eachaidh (Eacha) son of Oilill, this man is best known for the eulogy (*amhra*) he reputedly composed in honour of Colum Cille.[1] The late preface added to the text relates how Dallán – chief poet of Ireland, and belonging to the Másraighe of Magh Shléacht in the Cavan barony of Tullyhaw – recited part of the poem to Colum who forbade him to continue until after his death, promising heaven to the poet and to everyone who would repeat the poem daily.[2] The poem was allegedly begun at Áth Féine in the Westmeath parish of Tyfarnham, and continued along the road of Asal as far as Portloman (Teach Lomáin), near Loch Owel in the same county. Dallán is also credited with eulogies in honour of Seanán of Scattery Island and Conall Caol of Inishkeel, the former text still extant, the latter no longer in existence.[3] He is said to have been killed by 'foreigners' on Inishkeel and – as a reward for his poem on Conall – also buried there. A dialogue between Dallán, Baoithín, and Colum Cille whom he supposedly welcomed to the Convention of Druim Ceat, includes a quatrain offering the patron of Iona a poem in exchange for a reward.[4] According to the Life of Maodhóg of Ferns, reputedly the saint's first cousin, Dallán's church was at Kildallan, and his feast is said to have been observed there on 14 September (perhaps *recte* December).[5] Some sources, including entries in the martyrologies for Dallán's other feast of 29 January, locate him in Maighean, now possibly Tullamaine in the Kilkenny barony of Shillelogher, adjoining which, at Burnchurch, Dallán was remembered on 31 July, but more probably a still unidentified Maighean in Magh Shléacht in the Cavan parish of Templeport, adjoining Kildallan.[6] The Irish version of *Leabhar Breatnach*, 'book of the Britons', names Bishop Dallán, together with Cairneach of Dulane and Caomhlach, among the children of a union between Babona, daughter of a king of Scotland, and her brother-in-law, Sárán, king of Britain.[7] Under the guise of 'Bishop Eachaidh (Eacha)' – the name also used in a poem on the Oirghialla which invokes him as a witness – the saint may have been chosen as the first tutor of Molaise of Devenish.[8] His close relationship with Conall of Inishkeel led to him being remembered in some Donegal place-names, including

Clondallon (Cluain Dalláin) in the parish of Killygarvan, directly across Lough Swilly from Conall's church.[9] He appears also to have been the original patron of the Down parish of Clonallan (Cluain Dalláin), later associated with Conall son of Aodh, while a gloss added to a pedigree in the Book of Lecan attaches him to the Dál bhFiadach of north Down.[10]

1 *MartT* 13; *CGSH* §633; *RC* 20, 30–183, 249–89, 401–37; *Lgen.* 712.5. 2 *RC* 20, 132–4. 3 *ZCP* 3, 220–5; *AB* 66, 215–21; *SSS* 7–31; *RC* 20, 434–6. 4 *Éigse* 12, 167 §4. 5 *BNÉ* i, 265 §229; cf. *CGSH* §§633, 662.105; *GRSH* 67; OSL KK ii, 31. 6 *MartT* 13; *MartG* 26; *MartD* 30; *GRSH* 67; *HADO* iii, 375; *MD* iii, 396; *IIAM* 568. 7 *LBret.* §24. 8 *VSHP* ii, 132 §5; *SG* i, 19; *Ériu* 16, 183 §42; cf. *KLT* 138 §42, 219. 9 *RC* 20, 434–6; *DLHS* 164. 10 *ASH* 205; PNNI i, 55–6; *UJA* (1st ser.) 2, 47; *CGH* 330b10; cf. *IIAM* 567.

Daluath. *See* Dalbhach.

Damhán of Feamore (Fiodh Mór, perhaps also Cluain Fada), parish of Oldleighlin, barony of Idrone West, Co. Carlow. Damhán son of Laighneach is said to have been one of two brothers of Abán of Adamstown – the other being Miaca (Miach) assigned to Feamore.[1] There can be little doubt but that the saint was also patron of Kildavin (Ceall Damháin) in the Wexford barony of Forth. Located near Forth Mountain, the only hill of any size in the south of the county, Damhán's Wexford church appears to have been a *Lughnasadh* site, with a tradition to the effect that the saint's feast fell on 1 August, locally called 'St Davin's Day'.[2]

1 *CGSH* §287.2; *GRSH* 88; *Lgen.* 727.9–11. 2 *FL* 648; OSL WX i, 366; *HDF* 174; *CECW* 207 but cf. *TNW* 1098–9.

Damhán son of Daimhín. This saint, also known as Damhán Scéine, is provided with a descent from Colla Dá Chríoch of the Oirghialla, who controlled a territory approximately corresponding to the present diocese of Clogher.[1] His grandfather, Cairbre Damhairgid, king of Oirghialla, is thought to have believed following a sermon given by Patrick at a place called Leamhain, near Clogher in the county of Tyrone.[2] Damhán's father Daimhín may have been the king of Oirghialla said by Colum Cille never to have refused or rebuked a cleric.[3] His father also figures, as a brave man of the Connachta, in the Life of Maodhóg of Ferns which asserts that, in gratitude for being resuscitated after drowning in Lough Erne, Daimhín promised perpetual allegiance to Maodhóg.[4] Of Damhán himself, little is recorded. A namesake of his who gave name to the (unidentified) Kildare church of Teach Damháin was assigned a feastday of 12 February, but only through confusion with a Roman saint named Damianus.[5] A seventeenth-century source, having located Damhán in the curiously named 'Inghean', placed his feast on 13 June, more properly the day of Damhnad of Tedavnet.[6] As the saint's name, a derivative of *damh*, 'ox', was common among the Oirghialla, it may be assumed – especially since archaeologists have discovered an image of an ox during excavations at Clogher – that Damhán originated as an ancestral divinity.[7]

1 *CGSH* §56; *GRSH* 70; *Lgen.* 714.5. 2 *BP* 2052–67; *VT* 176. 3 *LisL* p. 306–7. 4 *BNÉ* i, 197 §28. 5 *MartO²* 74; *MartD* 46; *CGSH* §287.2; *Ainm* 3, 3. 6 *GRSH* 70. 7 *BUPNS* (2nd ser.) 4, 27–31.

Damhnad of Caldavnet (Ceall Damhnadan), parish of Tedavnet (Teach Damhnadan) in the barony and county of Monaghan. Brónach daughter of Míleac (the man with whom Patrick was 'in slavery'), patron of Kilbroney (Ceall Bhróinche) in the Down barony of Upper Iveagh, is thought to have been the mother of several noted saints, including Caolán of Nendrum, Damhnad of Tedavnet, and Fursa of Killursa and Péronne.[1] Little is otherwise known of Damhnad from native sources, beyond the day of her commemoration (13 June), the (conflicting) assertion that she was one of seven saints yet to die, and an arbitrary attempt by the author of the Life of Lasair of Kilronan, who had a penchant for misappropriating saints, to transform her into a sister of his subject.[2] Her cult was, however, vigorous enough, as she was also patron of the parish of Kildalkey in Meath, perhaps in succession to Neamhnad who is otherwise known from the list of those said to have been subject to Brighid of Kildare.[3] At Kildalkey, and also in Gheel in Belgium, where she was wrongly taken to be identical with Dympna, she was remembered on 15 May.[4] On the other hand, at 'Eas Damhnada' in the Cavan townland and parish of Lavey, her stations were performed all Summer, but especially on St John's night (23 June).[5] A relic of the saint, called *bachall Dhamhnaid*, 'Damhnad's staff', was held in high regard in the Tedavnet area, at least until the early nineteenth century, in the belief that to swear falsely by it brought about a distortion of the face.[6] Acquired by George Petrie in 1835, it is now in the National Museum of Ireland. A second highly regarded relic, named *Ballach Damhnadan*, 'Damhnad's spotted one', possibly a book-shrine, survived until the early nineteenth century.[7]

1 *CGSH* §§702.1–5, 722.92. **2** *MartT* 50; *MartG* 116; *MartD* 168; *BL Cat.* ii, 471; *AB* 55, 287–95; *Ériu* 5, 74, 82; *GRSH* 45; *LSLC* 291–302; *Ériu* 54, 80–1. **3** *CGSH* §670.49; *Ériu* 54, 80–1; OSL MH 174; cf. OSL AH/MN 39–40; *JCLAS* 11, 243–51. **4** *Kenney* 510; OSL MH 174; *BiblSS* iv, 618–20; *DIB* iii, 35; *IER* I ser. 7, 71; *DDSC* 19–20. **5** OSL CN/LM 120, 122; *CPL* 5, 450. **6** OSL AH/MN 69–70; *IER* I ser. 7, 71. **7** *Peritia* 17–18, 503–5.

Damhradh daughter of Oilill Fionn. *See* Angán of Míleac Fiaich.

Daráine. *See* Colmán of Longfordpass.

Darchaorthainn daughter of Éanna. Although the pedigree of this saint attaches her to the descendants of Colla Uais of the Oirghialla, approximately the equivalent of the diocese of Clogher, her church is said to have been at Uachtar Aird, a site possibly in the present townland and parish of Oughterard, barony of Salt South in Kildare.[1] This location would, however, better suit the pedigree of Darchaorthainn daughter of Cormac of the Uí Dhúnlainge of north Leinster, patron of Tullowphelim in Carlow. Seventeenth-century sources identify the daughter of Éanna with the saint commemorated on 8 March.[2]

1 *CGSH* §62; *GRSH* 67; *Lgen.* 713.2. **2** *GRSH* 67; *MartG* 50; *MartD* 70.

Darchaorthainn of Tullowphelim (Tulach Ua bhFeilmeadha), barony of Rathvilly, Co. Carlow. This daughter of Cormac and her sister Eithne are known only from the corpus of saints' pedigrees and related texts, which assign them to the Uí Dhúnlainge, a powerful dynasty in north Leinster.[1] One text adds the information that their relics were preserved at Tullowphelim, which takes its name from the Uí Fheilmeadha, an important branch of the Uí Cheinsealaigh of south Leinster.[3] There may have been some confusion between this saint and her namesake (and likely double), Darchaorthainn daughter of Éanna.

1 *CGSH* §247; *GRSH* 87–8; *Lgen.* 467.11. 2 *CGH* 316a46 add. 3 Ibid. 317c1.

Darlughdhach of Kildare (Ceall Dara) in the county of the same name. The so-called *vita prima* of Brighid, which may be dated to the late eighth or early ninth century, speaks of a pupil named Darlughdhach who overcame strong carnal desire by placing burning coals in her sandals.[1] The same text states that as death was approaching, Brighid, having received a request from Darlughdhach that she be allowed to die on the same day, announced that she would be her successor for exactly one year before dying, like herself, on 1 February.[2] Little else is known of Darlughdhach, but her cult travelled with that of Brighid to Abernethy in Scotland, where she is thought to have lived in the time of Neachtan, third king of the Picts, and, curiously, also to Freising in Bavaria, where she was allegedly honoured.[3] Her feast of 1 February is recorded with that of Brighid in most martyrologies.[4] A second feast of 10 February, observed at an (unidentified) place named Leamhach, may also refer to her.[5] A relic of the saint, accompanied by relics of her predecessor Brighid and bishop Conlaodh of Kildare, had reached Saint-Maurice d'Agaune in the Swiss canton of Valais by 700.[6]

1 *ASH* 229; *TT* 539–40 §99; *SS* 278; *DIB* iii, 61. 2 *ASH* 230; *TT* 541–2 §132; *SS* 278–9. 3 *SIHI* 17, 43; *ASH* 230; *CPNS* 275; *KSS* 321; *LegSS* 391–2. 4 *MartT* 14; *MartG* 28; *MartD* 36. 5 *MartT* 16; *MartD* 44; cf. OSL CN/LM 71. 6 *RIW* 12–13, 31.

Darlughdhach of Lorum. *See* Colum Crom of Lorum.

Dathí. *See* Nathí.

Daughter(s). *See* Inghean(a)/Dair.

Daurthach. *See* Durthach.

David. *See* Bíthe of Inch.

Davin. *See* Damhán.

Déaglán of Ardmore (Aird Mhór), barony of Decies within Drum, Co. Waterford. As with many other saints, Déaglán (whose father is variously named Earnbhran, Earcbhran, Earc and Ros) is provided with several conflicting statements of descent. The oldest version of the corpus of saints' pedigrees assigns him, together with Brighid of Kildare and Fiontan of Clonenagh, to the Fothairt who gave name to the baronies of Forth in Carlow and Wexford.[1] A second line of descent attaches him to an obscure family named Dál Meicon.[2] In the Ardmore tradition, preserved mainly in the saint's Life, he was taken to belong to the dominant local dynasty of the Déise, of which he was later patron.[3] In a narrative entitled *Tugaid Ionnarbha na nDéise*, 'cause of the expulsion of the Déise', this dynasty traced its origins through various kings of Tara to Meath, where its name is still preserved in the local baronies of Deece.[4]

Déaglán's biographer, who was probably at work towards the end of the twelfth or early thirteenth century, was not slow to take advantage of associations such as these in order to present his subject in (historically speaking) the best available circles. The Tara tradition was used as an appropriate introduction to the saint's Life, which is preserved in one Latin recension, as well as in a vernacular version based on the Latin text and now represented by numerous (mostly eighteenth- and nineteenth-century) manuscripts.[5] Naming the saint's parents as Earc and Deithidhe, the Life places his birth near Lismore, thus giving him a birthright in the rival centre of ecclesiastical supremacy in south-east Munster.[6] Having been baptized by Colmán – possibly either the patron of Kilcolman, near Ardmore, or Colmán of Lismore – Déaglán is said to have been educated by Díoma, who has been variously located at Kildimo in Caonraighe (Kenry) in Limerick, within the ambit of the powerful Dál gCais (Uí Bhriain) dynasty, or at Connor in Antrim, which had attained high status through the early twelfth-century reformer Maol Maodhóg (Malachy).[7] A journey to Rome followed, to receive episcopal orders from no less an authority than the Pope himself, subsequent to which the saint is said to have met Patrick, then only on his way out to the Eternal city, thus establishing for Déaglán a spurious, so-called pre-Patrician, status.[8] He is also said to have brought back from Rome the celebrated *Duibhín Déagláin*, later highly regarded as a relic.[9]

At home, one of Déaglán's first actions was to visit Cashel, traditionally the centre of secular power in Munster and, by the late twelfth or early thirteenth century, when the Life was probably composed, also the seat of the southern archbishop. Here, the patron of the archdiocese, Ailbhe of Emly and Cashel, duly found mention, as did Déaglán's uterine brother, Conall (alias Colmán) son of Iomros, who was associated with the Tipperary church of Kilconnell within the diocese of Lismore.[10] A second visit to Cashel brought him together not only with Ailbhe, but also with Patrick, to whom Déaglán paid due homage, a reminder of which is the *magnus et lucidissimus fons*, 'large and most crystal-clear fountain', still known as Patrickswell in the parish of Inishlounaght, near Clonmel, again within the diocese of Lismore.[11]

The remainder of the Life is taken up with the saint's miracles, some local, others performed during travels to such places as his ancestral *patria*, 'homeland', near Tara in Meath, and Ossory, where he is said to have founded a church. He baptized and foretold the greatness of Ciarán son of Eachaidh who went on to found the Tipperary church of Tubbrid, near Cahir, within the diocese of Lismore.[12] The privilege of rendering Déaglán the last rites was given to a relatively minor saint named Mac Liag whose importance to the saint's biographer is likely to have derived from his patronage – later, alas, completely forgotten – of the church of Kilmacleague within the diocese of Waterford.[13] In this way, by establishing for his patron numerous appropriate associations, in Lismore, Ardmore, and Waterford, and by procuring for him the blessings of such powerful ecclesiastical patrons as Ailbhe and Patrick, not to mention the local secular authorities, Déaglán's biographer set out the case of his church for cathedral status at a time when it was actively seeking diocesan standing.[14] About the same time as the Life was compiled, the church of Ardmore was also being (re)built.[15]

Extolled by the martyrologist Aonghas as the 'head of hundred thousands', Déaglán remained the object of intense devotion down to modern times, with his feastday of 24 July attracting enormous crowds to the picturesque seaside location of his church and holy well at Ardmore.[16] A poem from the 1790s, composed by Tadhg Gaelach Ó Súilleabháin on the subject of the saint's annual pattern, attended by both *pobal geal Dé*, 'God's bright people', and *cléir na salm*, 'the psalm-singing clergy', addresses Déaglán as *órga, onóraigh, Easpaig*, 'golden, honoured, Bishop'.[17] Among the local relics was a highly venerated piece of marble known as *Duibhín Déagláin*, and the saint's tooth reputedly found its way into Adhamhnán's reliquary.[18]

1 *CGSH* §107.1 (add.); *GRSH* 74; *Lgen.* 715.6; *DIB* iii, 133–4. **2** *CGSH* §107.2 (add. Lb, La). **3** *VSHP* ii, 35; ITS 16, 6; *FFÉ* iii, 112. **4** *Cymmrod.* 14, 104–35; *Ériu* 3, 135–42; *FTorna* 209–23; *Anecd.* i, 15–24. **5** *VSHP* i, lx–lxii; ii, 32–59; ITS 16, 2–72; *SPW* 244–71; *ILL* 368. **6** *VSHP* ii, 35–7 §§3–6; ITS 16, 8–10 §§2–3, 161. **7** *VSHP* ii, 37–8 §7; ITS 16, 14 §5, *MartD* 6. **8** *SSS* 376–99. **9** ITS 16, 164. **10** *VSHP* ii, 41 §14; ITS 16, 22 §16; *CLTÁ* 104–6. **11** *VSHP* ii, 45–7 §§18–19; ITS 16, 34–40 §§22–4. **12** *VSHP* ii, 54 §31; ITS 16, 58 §37. **13** *VSHP* ii, 58 §§xxxviii–xxxix; ITS 16, 68–70 §§45–6, 176–7; OSL WD 22. **14** *MRHI* 62. **15** *AI s.a.* 1203. **16** *MartT* 57; *MartO*[2] 164; *MartG* 142; *MartD* 200; ITS 16, xvi–xxvi; *LSS* 88; *Decies* 54, 54. **17** *TG* 222–4. **18** ITS 16, 164; *AJ* 8, 8–11; *LSS* 91–4; *Celtica* 15, 34 §9; *EMH* 485 §225.

Dealbhnad daughter of Feargna. *See* Cainnear of Lara.

Dearbhfhraoich daughter of Eacha. The saint's pedigree not only attaches her to the ruling line of the territory of Oirghialla, approximately the equivalent of the diocese of Clogher, it also makes her a brother of Cairbre Damhairgid, a well-known king of that territory who died, according to the annals, in 514.[1] Dearbhfhraoich's main claim to fame is the tradition that she was the mother of Tighearnach of Clones. Tighearnach's Life states that Dearbhfhraoich, one of three 'most handsome' daughters of Eacha, fell in love with a man named Cairbre, a soldier of Leinster origin in her father's service, became pregnant and, having given birth, hid herself from the public eye.[2] Taken by his father to Brighid of Kildare, the child was baptized and named Tighearnach, 'lord(ly)', because of his descent from many kings. A quatrain invoking Dearbhfhraoich's aid has also been preserved.[3]

1 *CGSH* §47; *GRSH* 70; *Lgen.* 716.4; *AU s.a.* **2** *VSHP* ii, 262 §2; *VSHH* 107. **3** *MartO*[2] 110.

Dearmhór daughter of Maine. *See* Cuman of Aireadh Bóinne.

Deborah. *See* Gobnaid.

Declan. *See* Déaglán.

Deichtear daughter of Muireadhach Muindearg. *See* Santán of St Ann's Chapel.

Deidhe daughter of Trian. When Patrick went to Tara, where the men of Ireland were celebrating its feast, only two men allegedly rose to show him respect, Dubhthach of the Maca Lughair and Dubhthach's pupil, Fiac of Sleaty.[1] Patrick is said to have blessed Dubhthach, a poet by profession, and his progeny, and to have given him the honour of being the first man at (pagan) Tara to believe in the word of God. His progeny, which included Deidhe's father Trian, was numerous, amounting, according to the tract on the mothers of the saints, to thirty male and female saints throughout Ireland.[2] Some eight of these are said to have been children of Dubhthach's granddaughter Deidhe who is accorded second place after Patrick's mother in the same tract. Among the eight were Caillín of Fenagh, Daigh, Feime, Feidhlimidh of Kilmore, and Diarmuid of Inchcleraun.[3] Two (Caillín and Daigh) became the subjects of written Lives. That of Caillín names the saint's mother only in a marginal note, whereas that of Daigh renders it Deithidhe, 'care'.[4]

1 *BP* 523–36; *VT* 52. **2** *CGSH* §722.2. **3** Ibid. **4** *BFen.* 10n; *VSHH* 389 §1.

Deimhlir daughter of Feargna. *See* Cainnear of Lara.

Deineath of Donaghmore (Domhnach Mór), barony of Clandonagh, Co. Laois. Among those said to have been subject to Brighid of Kildare was this saint, located, together with Pól and Martan, at Donaghmore.[1] In the neighbouring parish of Bordwell are a townland called Kilbreedy, named after Brighid, and a graveyard called Kilmulfoyle (Ceall Mhaol-Phóil), a name indicative of local devotion to Pól, and a few miles away, in the parish of Kyle, is the townland of Kilmartin (Martan's church).[2] In a separate entry of the same list, Deineath is again assigned, together with Pól, to Inis Beoaidh, possibly the place known as Inis Beoáin in the Kildare parish of Feighcullen.[3] As both Pól, whose name also occurs in diminutive guise at the church of Stapolin (Teach Póilín) in the Dublin parish of Baldoyle, and Martan bear non-Irish names, that of Deineath may also be of external origin.

1 *CGSH* §670.37; *Lgen.* 753.8. **2** *HADO* ii, 57. **3** *CGSH* §670.39.

Deirbhileadh of Inishkea (Inis Ceithigh / Géidhe), parish of Kilmore, barony of Erris, Co. Mayo. This daughter of Cormac, whose name can also be written Dairbhile or Dirbhileadh, and anglicized Dervla, was among those said to have been descended from Fiachra son of Eacha Muighmheadhón who gave name to the Sligo barony of Tireragh (Tír Fhiachrach).[1] Her mother was Cuman daughter of Dallbhrónach whose womb is said to have been blessed by Patrick, and she figures, along with many siblings, among those whom the biographer of Forannán of Alternan brought together to meet Colum Cille.[2] There is little mention of Deirbhileadh in the hagiographical record, but she was remembered as one of three maidens, the others being Caolainn and Neimheadh, who, according to a poem of prophecies, never took offence and accepted no goods in compensation for outrage.[3] The island of Inishkea was often used as a convenient boundary, as in the tale of 'Four Saints' which states that Cormac son of Eoghan received his choice of site between the river Moy and the island.[4] The same text includes Deirbhileadh among the saints of Tír Amhalghaidh (whence the Mayo barony of Tirawley). The island of Inishkea, famous, according to one text for its heron, is also featured in the tragic story of the Children of Lir, as one of the remote places to which the unfortunate children came daily to feed.[5] Deirbhileadh's feast fell on 3 August, but the pattern was observed two days earlier on Inishkea.[6] A possible second commemoration on 26 October locates the saint in Achadh Cuilinn, which may be another name for her church in the parish of Kilmore.[7] A litany-style prayer of invocation includes Deirbhileadh among many other female saints, and she is the first of the female saints invoked in a poem by Donnchadh Mór Ó Dálaigh († 1244).[8] She was regarded as one of the chief saints of Erris, with a well and church (Ceall Deirbhileadh) dedicated to her at Fallmore, within the parish of Kilmore, and also a well at Doonfeeny in the adjoining barony of Tirawley.[9]

1 *CGSH* §662.78; *GRSH* 62; *Lgen.* 711.8; *DIB* iii, 40–1. **2** *CGSH* §722.6.10; *Anecd.* iii, 3 §5. **3** *Ériu* 18, 66 §42. **4** *IrT* iii, 4 §9; *AFM s.a.* 1248. **5** *OCL* 31 §58; *Anecd.* i, 38 §103. **6** *MartG* 148; *MartD* 210; OSL MO i, 214, 326. **7** *MartG* 204; *MartD* 284; *HDGP* i, 15; *Dinn.* 5, 87–8. **8** *MartT* 108; *IrL* 92; *DDé* 50. **9** OSL MO i, 214, 247, 501; *NotesEHDT* 312–13; *AbEMLS* 101–5.

Deirbhionn Dualfhada. *See* Colum Cille.

Deirbhinill/Deirinill daughter of Mac Iair. *See* Caol of Kilmainham.

Déirdre. *See* Íde.

Deirinill Cheathairchíochach, 'of four paps'. In accordance with her cognomen which suggests nursing, Deirinill is said to have been the mother of four (sometimes five or six) children whose associations were mainly with the area now covered by the county of Down.[1] These include Domhanghart son of Eacha who gave name to Slievedonard, Cilléan of Achadh Caol, now possibly Aghacullion in the parish of Kilcoo, Oilléan, and Aodhán, father of Mochuma of Drumbo.[2] At Drumbo, according to the Tripartite Life, Patrick cursed Deirinill's husband, Eacha son of Muireadhach, promising him a short life and the scattering of his descendants, but blessing the child still in his wife's womb, the 'famous and wonderful' Domhanghart.[3]

1 *CGSH* §§162, 722.27; *Lgen.* 750.4. **2** *HDGP* i, 13. **3** *BP* 2655–71; *VT* 224.

Dervla (Derrivla). *See* Deirbhileadh.

Diarmuid. This name is said to derive from *dí-formad*, 'lack of jealousy'.[1] Among the many familiar or hypocoristic forms of the name are Díoma (Díomán) and Modhíomóg. Ten persons of the name are included in a list of Irish bishops.[2]

1 *DIL* D 64. **2** *CGSH* §704.129–38.

Diarmuid of Aharney (Achadh Toghartha), more precisely Barony church in the townland of Ballyconra, parish of Aharney, barony of Galmoy, Co. Kilkenny. Barony church was dedicated to Brighid of Kildare.[1] Not surprisingly, therefore, it is in her company, together with her aunt Cuman and some other saints, that Diarmuid is assigned to the church.[2]

1 *HADO* ii, 308–12. **2** *CGSH* §173; *Lgen.* 751.4.

Diarmuid of Aireadh Seanaigh, an ecclesiastical site in the parish of Derrybrusk, barony of Tirkennedy, Co. Fermanagh.[1] Diarmuid son of Baodán (Baoth) and his brother Cobhthach are included among the saints of Clann Lughdhach whose associated places extended from the shores of Lough Erne in Fermanagh, where the church of the former lay, to Ceinéal Laoghaire in Meath, where the latter's church was located at an unidentified place named 'Achadh Maic'.[2] Seventeenth-century sources speculate that Diarmuid may have been the saint of the name commemorated on 12 October or 20 December.[3] He is more likely to be identical with the bishop named Diarmuid son of Eachaidh who was commemorated at 'Aireadh Ionnaigh' on 6 January.[4]

1 *HDGP* i, 43–4; *FHHS* 584. 2 *CGSH* §690.18; *Lgen.* 707.10. 3 *MartD* 274; *GRSH* 51. 4 *MartT* 5, 116; *MartG* 10; *MartD* 8.

Diarmuid of Castledermot (Díseart Diarmada), barony of Kilkea and Moone, Co. Kildare. This saint was attached to the Down family of Ceinéal Déamáin, and his grandfather Aodh Rón, king of the Ulaidh of east Ulster, was killed in what appears to have been an important battle against the northern Uí Néill at Muirtheimhne in 735.[1] His mother, Cloithbheo daughter of Conchobhar, is said to have belonged to the Dál gConchobhair, possibly the family of that name in the Ardbraccan area of Meath.[2] Diarmuid's royal lineage is worth noting because it is sometimes the name of his grandfather that is used in preference to that of his father Fearghal.[3] His own inclinations were, however, towards asceticism and he became involved in the anchoritic group of the so-called *céili Dé*, 'clients of God'.[4] He was included in the *aonta*, 'union', of clerics associated with Maol Ruain, founder of the church of Tallaght, one of the principal promoters of the anchoritic way of life.[5] A considerable number of new foundations appear to have been made about this time, and the fact that his name is attached to the church suggests that Diarmuid's *díseart*, 'hermitage', was also newly founded. It has been suggested that he was identical with the Diarmuid who glossed the psalms of the Milan manuscript, but beyond the identity of name, there is little support for this view.[6] The annalist, noting Diarmuid's death in 825, described him as 'teacher of religion for all Ireland'.[7] His was one of the last names to be included in the list of commemorations added to the martyrology drawn up at Tallaght between 828 and 833.[8] Diarmuid's feast fell on 21 June.[9]

1 *CGSH* §142; *GRSH* 82; *Lgen.* 723.1; *AU s.a.* 2 *CGSH* §722.93. 3 Ibid. §§142 (add.), 722.93. 4 *CéliD* 148, 161. 5 *CGSH* §713.10.15. 6 *CéliD* 161. 7 *AU s.a.* 8 *FSHIM* 90. 9 *MartT* 51; *MartG* 120; *MartD* 174.

Diarmuid of Inchcleraun (Inis Chlothrann), alias Quaker's Island, parish of Cashel, barony of Rathcline, on Lough Ree of the river Shannon, where it divides Roscommon from Longford. According to the corpus of saints' pedigrees, Diarmuid son of Lughna belonged to the Uí Fhiachrach of Tireragh (Tír Fhiachrach) in the county of Sligo.[1] This background may be reflected in the presence of a church named Kildermot (Ceall Diarmada) in the Mayo parish of Attymas which borders on Tireragh. The saint's mother is said to have been Deidhe daughter of Trian of Leinster, among whose children were some others with Connacht associations, including Caillín of Fenagh and Mainchín son of Collán of Corran.[2] Diarmuid is best known for his poem *Cealtair Díchill*, 'cloak of concealment', in which he invokes a litany of other saints, beginning with the apostles and ending with Aodh son of Breac of Rahugh *áitt a mbiam*, 'of the place in which I am wont to be', as a protection for himself.[3] The place in which Diarmuid used to be had no welcome for women, if the assertion of a *mirabilium* preserved in a Norse text that no female dare enter his churchyard is to be believed.[4] He is, however, credited with having shared the fruits of at least one miracle with Brighid daughter of Cú Chathrach by receiving with her some salt sent in a basket up the river Shannon by Seanán of Scattery Island.[5] When rung, the bell of the saint's *clogás*, 'bell-tower', on Inchcleraun was allegedly heard seven miles away in Roscommon.[6] Diarmuid was also patron of the Westmeath parish of Faughalstown, where he was apparently sometimes known as Germanus.[7] His feast fell on 10 January, a day shared by a namesake and possible double, Díomán of Inis Caoin.[8] This latter saint may be the Diarmuid son of Cathbhadh of Tirerrill who is said to have become a disciple of Daigh of Inishkeen.[9]

1 *CGSH* §328; *GRSH* 62; *Lgen*. 711.13; *DIB* iii, 257–8. **2** *CGSH* §722.2. **3** *LB* 262ab; *MartD* 12. **4** *Ériu* 4, 8; cf. *MartD* 400. **5** *LisL* 2399–415. **6** OSL RN ii, 194. **7** *PNW* 53n. **8** *MartT* 10; *MartO*[2] 35; *MartG* 12; *MartD* 12. **9** *VSHH* 399 4 §§19, 28.

Diarmuid of Killeshin (Gleann Uisean), barony of Slievemargy, Co. Laois. Diarmuid (alias Modhíomóg) son of Siabhar was attached by the genealogists to the Uí Bhairrche, who gave name to a deanery (Obargy) in Carlow and a barony (Bargy) in Wexford.[1] His mother is said to have belonged to a local Leinster family named Uí Mhic Caorthainn, and it seems that the saint's church was located on a boundary between the lands of his paternal and maternal families.[2] Despite the importance of his church, reflected by its reputation for learning and its well-known Romanesque doorway, surprisingly little has been recorded of Diarmuid, whose role as patron of Killeshin was later shared by Comhghán son of Diarmuid.[3] He and his church are mentioned in the *Notulae* added to the Book of Armagh, which shows that the authorities in Armagh had some interest in the place about the middle of the ninth century.[4] By referring to him lovingly as 'my little Diarmuid' (*mo Dhíomóg*), his foster-mother is said to have been the source of his alias.[5] The saint's feast fell on 8 July.[6]

1 *CGSH* §293; *GRSH* 88; *Lgen*. 727.15–16; *CGH* 121a42; *CMCS* 27, 33–7. **2** *CGH* 120a9; *CMCS* 27, 36. **3** *MartO*[2] 168; *CMCS* 27, 36–7. **4** *PTBA* 181. **5** *MartO*[2] 168. **6** *MartT* 54; *MartO*[2] 161; *MartG* 132; *MartD* 188.

Diarmuid son/grandson of Aodh Rón. *See* Diarmuid of Castledermot.

Diarmuid son of Cathbhadh. *See* Diarmuid of Inchcleraun.

Diarmuid son of Cuana. *See* Lúireach of Maghera.

Diarmuid son of Eoghan. *See* Modhíomóg of Glenkeen.

Diarmuid son of Muireadhach. *See* Aodh of Killeenmore.

Díchleithe of Dysert (Díseart Triallaigh), barony of Clanmaurice, Co. Kerry. This man, one of the saints of the Uí Eachach of the area about the river Moy in north Connacht, was reputedly a uterine brother of Aodhán and Colmán, both of the Wexford church of Templeshanbo. His own journey to Kerry is said to have been determined both by a desire to find the Lord and a wish to escape from his stepbrothers who bound him by placing an iron lock between his head and feet before casting the key into the sea. This was duly swallowed by a salmon which, having followed the saint's boat to Dysert, was caught by a fisherman, thus enabling Díchleithe's release from his fetters. Bearing a name thought to mean 'concealment', the saint was also known as Triallach because of the journey he undertook. All this is related in a passage of the Great Book of Genealogies compiled by Dubhaltach Mac Fhir Bhisigh, the sole source of information on Díchleithe.[1]

1 *Lgen.* 253.1–254.3; *TCHyF* 38; cf. *ACoK* 33–4.

Díghe daughter of Tulchán. *See* Munna of Taghmon.

Dílgheadach son of Cairbre. A poem attributed to Moling calls upon this saint, along with many others, to come to the assistance of the Leinstermen.[1] His name literally means 'forgiving'.

1 *SG* i, 389.

Díne daughter of Bracán. *See* Díona.

Díocaill of Ireland's Eye (Inis Mac Neasáin), parish of Howth, barony of Coolock, Co. Dublin. This saint, also known as Díocaill Dearg, 'red', was one of seven sons of Neasán of the Uí Dhúnlainge of north Leinster, others being Beoán of Feighcullen and Colmán Cráibhtheach.[1] The genealogists placed Díocaill with three of his brothers in a place called Eannga, possibly a shortened form of Ceall Eannga (later perhaps 'Killagone' in the Kildare parish of Cadamstown); according to others he shared with Neise and Neaslugha the patronage of Ireland's Eye.[2] Nothing more seems to be recorded of the three brothers, other than their feast which fell on 15 March.[3] Some sources mistakenly place the saints on Innisfallen (Inis Faithlinn) in the Kerry parish of Aghadoe.[4]

1 *CGSH* §284.1.2; *GRSH* 88. **2** *MartO*[2] 82, 98; *HDGP* iii, 167. **3** *MartT* 23; *MartO*[2] 82. **4** *MartG* 54; *MartD* 76.

Díocaill son of Cearnach. *See* Mac Liag of Drumglass.

Díocaill son of Neas. *See* Ceallán of Fancroft.

Díocha of Saul (Sabhall), barony of Lecale Lower, Co. Down. On returning to Ireland to begin his mission, Patrick was eager, according to his biographer Muirchú, to redeem himself from the slavery he had previously experienced.[1] Following a landing at Inbhear Sláine, perhaps the estuary of the river Quoile, Patrick and his companions are said to have been found a short distance inland by the swineherd of a 'good-by-nature' pagan, Díocha (also Modhíocha) son of Tricheamh, who lived near a 'barn' (Latin *horreum*, Irish *sabhall*) later called Sabhall Phádraig (literally 'Patrick's barn').[2] It was from here that faith in Christ traditionally began to spread in Ireland and, according to the later Tripartite Life of Patrick, Díocha was the first to be baptized and his home at Saul the first church to be founded in the country.[3] On the strength of his offer of a home to Patrick, Díocha was promised a heavenly abode, as well as a blessing on his offspring. Among those for whom descent from Díocha was claimed were Breacán son of Sárán, Dobheóg of Lough Derg, and Samhthann of Clonbroney.[4] He is also said to have had a brother named Oilill, the grandfather of Finnian of Movilla.[5] Díocha's feastday fell on 29 April.[6]

1 *PTBA* 78; cf. *TLSP* 94. 2 *PTBA* 78; *HADDC* i, 225–33. 3 *BP* 373–95; *VT* 36; *EA* 220–2. 4 *CGSH* §§115.2, 184, 185; *Lgen.* 723.10. 5 *CGSH* §136.1.2. 6 *MartG* 86; *MartD* 114.

Díodhnad daughter of Meachar. *See* Bairrfhionn of Drumcullen.

Díognad daughter of Gaibhrín. *See* Aonghas Láimhiodhan; Fiontan of Clonenagh.

Díoma. *See* also Diarmuid.

Díoma of Dorrha. *See* Modhíomóg of Glankeen.

Díoma of Killagone. *See* Díoma of Teach Díoma; Eannag of Ceall Eannga.

Díoma of Teach Díoma, an unidentified church, probably in Co. Kildare. This son of Seanach is featured in final position in the list of those said to have been subject to Brighid of Kildare which, while attaching him to the Fothairt (Brighid's family), places him in Teach Díoma, and proclaims him a bishop.[1] Two possible feastdays, 9 or 22 March, are named for him in one seventeenth-century source, and the first of these two days is shared by namesakes and likely doubles of Brighid.[2] A separate entry in the list of those subject to Brighid attaches a Bishop Díoma to a church named Ceall Eannga, later perhaps the now obsolete 'Killagone' in the Kildare parish of Cadamstown.[3]

1 *CGSH* §670.88; *Lgen.* 753.48. 2 *GRSH* 75; *MartT* 20; *MartG* 50; *MartD* 72. 3 *CGSH* §670.71; *HDGP* iii, 167.

Díoma Dubh, 'black', son of Aonghas. The genealogists attach this bearer of the name to a branch of the Dál gCais of Thomond known as Uí Chearnaigh.[1] As is shown by Kildeema in the Clare parish of Kilfearagh, and Kildimo in the Limerick barony of Kenry, there is local evidence of the cult of a saint named Díoma.[2] A saint of the name is also included, together with Mainchín of Limerick and Crónán (probably of Tomgraney), among the progeny of Inghean Bhaoith of Killinaboy.[3] According to the Life of Déaglán of Ardmore, its subject was sent *ad legendum*, 'to study', to a certain Díoma who is variously taken to have been the saint so named of Kildimo in Limerick, or of the Antrim see of Connor.[4] Together with Déaglán at Díoma's church was a youth named Cairbre son of Colum (Colmán) who, it is said, was later to be a venerable bishop and saint. In the Life of Colmán of Lynally mention is made of a *puer*, 'boy', named Díoma Dubh of whom future sanctity and the protection of the churches of Ireland was foretold.[5] This is more likely to be a reference to the bishop at Connor who died in 659 and was remembered, according to some sources, on 6 January.[6] The church of 'St Dermitius' in the Down parish of Slanes may also have been named after Díoma under the radical form of his name.[7] It has been argued that the cult of the saint named Díoma travelled countrywide in association with that of Beinéan, among whose disciples was Modhíomóg of Kildemock, close to Stabannan (Teach Beinéin) in the Louth barony of Ardee.[8] A well dedicated to

Díoma in the parish of Killeenadeema in south-east Galway was visited in Spring, at 'potato-sowing' time, which would suggest that one or other of the saints of the name remembered on 9 and 22 March was intended.[9] On the other hand, the Díoma commemorated on 12 May was a son of Cas which may indicate affiliation to Dál gCais.[10]

1 *CGSH* §226; *GRSH* 119; *Lgen.* 738.3; *CoC* 21. **2** *ACoC* 116. **3** *IrT* iv, 94 §10; *MartD* 402. **4** *VSHP* ii, 37–8 §7; ITS 16, 14 §5; *MartD* 6, 402. **5** *VSHP* i, 266 §19; *VSHH* 218 §26. **6** *VSHP* ii, 355; *AU s.a.*; *MartT* 5; *MartG* 10; *MartD* 6. **7** *CPL* 15, §553. **8** *JCLAS* 13, 225–51; *AS*.Nov. iv, 179. **9** OSL GY ii, 29; *MartD* 72, 84. **10** *MartT* 42; *MartG* 94; *MartD* 124.

DÍOMÁN of Clonkeen (Cluain Caoin) in the parish of the same name, barony of Clanwilliam, Co. Limerick. An entry in the annals for 811 states that a Munster anchorite named Díomán of Araidh – or more particularly of Kildromin (Ceall Dromann) in the parish of Kilteely, about six miles south of Clonkeen – 'ended his life happily'.[1] An entry in the martyrologies for 10 December records the feast of 'the good man' under the guise of Modhíomóg of Clonkeen.[2] The use of the hypocoristic form of the name is an example of a pattern not uncommon at this period, when the anchoritic lifestyle had become fashionable. Díomán's death, though peaceful according to the annals, is said to have been violent by the author of the *Wars of the Gaedhil with the Gaill* who was probably intent on putting the blame on the Norse.[3] The only other early source of information on Díomán is the list of those in union with Maol Ruain of Tallaght, which again indicates his association with anchorites and the so-called *céili Dé*.[4] Díomán appears to have been remembered under the guise of Modhíomóg at Clonkeen on 26 April, as well as on 10 December.[5] Under the same guise, sometimes anglicized Imoke or Sheemoge, he was remembered on 10 December at various churches in east Leinster, including Kilmademoge in the county of Kilkenny, possibly also the neighbouring parish of Kilmodum (from Cill Modhoma), and Coolhull in the Wexford parish of Bannow.[6]

1 *AU*/*AI s.a.* **2** *MartO*[2] 250; *MartG* 236; *MartD* 330. **3** *CGG* 4. **4** *CGSH* §§713.7, 714.2. **5** *MartT* 76; *MartG* 84; *MartD* 110. **6** *HADO* ii, 165; ibid. iii, 462; OSL WX ii, 88; *CECW* 205.

DÍONA daughter of the king of the Saxons. This person is known only from the tract on the mothers of the saints which attributes to her the motherhood of the ten sons of Brachan, king of the Britons, and eponym of Brycheiniog in south Wales.[1] As can be seen from the entries on Díoraidh, Eallóg, Mochonóg and Moghóróg, her sons included several saints associated with churches near the east coast of Leinster. She may also have been adopted by the Síol Maine of Longford/Westmeath who numbered among their four *cailleacha*, 'nuns', a certain Díne daughter of Bracán, the other three being Forbhaise daughter of Aodh, Lasair daughter of Rónán, and Sineach of the Longford church of Taghshinny (Teach Sinche).[2]

1 *CGSH* §722.89. **2** *Lgen.* 177.6.

DÍORAIDH of Edermine (Eadardhruim), barony of Ballaghkeen, Co. Wexford. This saint is known from an entry in the tract on the mothers of the saints which states that he and his nine brothers were sons of Díona, daughter of a king of the Saxons, by Brachan, king of the Britons (or Welsh), and eponym of Brycheiniog in south Wales.[1] Many of the saint's siblings, including Moghóróg of Delgany, Mochonóg of Kilmuckridge, and Eallóg of St Tulloge's, are also associated with churches in east Leinster. A person named Díoraidh (Dirath) died as a bishop at Ferns in 693, and it has been suggested that he was identical with the man named *Dirathi* who was remembered with the family of Munna of Taghmon on 21 October.[2] There are also saints of the name in the martyrological lists for 13 January and 27 July, and the second of these has been taken to be identical both with the bishop at Ferns and with Díoraidh son of Brachan.[3]

1 *CGSH* §722.89; *EWGT* 14–16, 32–3. 2 *AU s.a.* 3 *MartT* 7; *MartG* 14, 144; *MartD* 14, 204.

Dobhairre. *See* Fionnbharr.

Dobhaodóg of Clondavaddog (Cluain Dabhaodóg), now the name of both a civil parish and a townland (parish of Gartan) in the barony of Kilmacrenan, Co. Donegal. When visited by John O'Donovan in 1835, the parishioners could remember nothing of Dobhaodóg, except that he lived before Colum Cille and that he did not allow cuckoos and rats into his parish.[1] Little can be added here, other than the derivation of his name from *baoth*, 'guileless', and the probability that he and Buadán of Culdaff in Inishowen are localizations of Colum's constant companion and successor, Baoithín son of Bréanainn. Dobhaodóg's feast fell on 22 July, a day shared by Buadán of Culdaff.[2]

1 OSL DL 47–8. 2 *MartT* 57; *MartG* 140; *MartD* 198; *DLHS* 163; *Béaloideas* 6, 159.

Dobharchú son of Onchú. *See* Mac Onchon.

Dobhearóg of Kildavaroge. *See* Aodh of Aghadooey.

Dobheóg of Lough Derg (Gleann Geirg), parish of Templecarn, barony of Tirhugh, Co. Donegal. Although said by the genealogists to have belonged through a father named Luainín to the Dál bhFiatach of east Ulster, Dobheóg (also known as Mobheóg, Beoaidh, Latin Beot(i)us/Abeogus) was included among the ten sons of Díona, daughter of the king of the Saxons, by Brachan, king of the Britons.[1] If the author of the vernacular Life of Bréanainn of Clonfert is to be believed, Dobheóg was numbered among the 'chief saints' of Ireland.[2] Alas, despite being described as *venerabilis* by Philip O'Sullivan Beare, he was destined to be sidelined in the twelfth century, when the canons regular of Armagh, conscious of the attractiveness of Lough Derg as a place of pilgrimage, introduced Patrick and his purgatory to Station Island on the lake.[3] Although himself reputed to have indulged in ascetic practice, the saint's name has all but disappeared locally, with the island containing his church now known as Saints Island (earlier Oiléan Dobheóg), and the parish, formerly Tearmann Dobheóg, now Templecarn.[4] Another island named Inis Dobheóg, possibly on Lough Erne, retained its connection with the saint.[5] The saint's name is also present in the botanical name of a heather, *Daboecia cantabrica*, peculiar to the west of Ireland, which he allegedly brought from Italy.[6] Dobheóg was remembered on two days,

1 January and 24 July, and in its entry on the first of these, the 'local' Martyrology of Donegal gave the saint pride of place.[7] The July day may have been the octave of another feast because it has been shown that the name sometimes used in Donegal for Swithun's day (15 July), with its portents of rain, namely *lá Léabhóige*, probably derives from *lá fhéil Daibheóige*, 'the feast of Dobheóg'.[8] John Colgan speculated that he might be the same as Beoán son of Innle.[9] In death, Dobheóg was thought to remain powerful, taking revenge in 1070 and again in 1196, according to the annals, on pillagers of his church at Templecarn.[10]

1 *CGSH* §§184, 722.89; *GRSH* 82; *Lgen*. 723.5; *ClRec*. 7, 406. **2** *BNÉ* i, 88 §185. **3** *SZ* 7, 11; *MRHI* 193; *MPPP* 21–30; *SZ* 7. **4** *ZCP* i, 66; *FHHS* 588–9; *ClRec*. 7, 406. **5** *Celtica* 1, 65. **6** *Béaloideas* 17, 258–9. **7** *MartT* 3 (Aed Locha Geirg); *MartG* 6, 142; *MartD* 4, 200. **8** *StH* 6, 58–62. **9** *GRSH* 82. **10** *AU s.a.*; *Ainm* 7, 75–6.

Dobhí son of Comhghall. *See* Bíthe of Inch.

Dobhonna of Kilnamanagh (Ceall na Manach), barony of Frenchpark, Co. Roscommon. Dobhonna (also Dabhonna, Dobhoinne) is one of seven sons of Restitutus (Welsh Rhystud) of the Lombards (Maca Baird) by a sister of Patrick, usually named Lubaid, but sometimes also Dairearca.[1] By far the best-known of Dobhonna's siblings were Seachnall of Dunshaughlin and Usaille of Killashee. Dobhonna figures in his own right in Patrician literature in connection with a son of Éanna of Airteach (the area about Kilnamanagh) named Cormac.[2] Having been handed over in fosterage to four of Patrick's followers, Cormac is said to have spent some time with Dobhonna at Kilnamanagh. Later part of the possessions of the community of Clonmacnoise, the churches in this area were, it seems, regained for Armagh in the early ninth century by Nuadha of Estersnow (Díseart Nuadhad), a local successor of Patrick.[3]

1 *CGSH* §§664, 722.15; *Lgen*. 751.23; *BP* 895–902; *VT* 82. **2** *BP* 874–91; *VT* 80–2. **3** Ibid.; cf. *Ulidia* 39–46.

Dobhrígh of Cloonloughan (Cluain Lócháin), parish of Castleconor, barony of Tireragh, Co. Sligo. Cuman daughter of Dallbhrónach, an aunt of Brighid of Kildare, is said to have had her womb blessed by Patrick.[1] She was certainly considered fertile, being credited with forty-seven children, forty-five of whom, including Dobhrígh, were regarded as saints. Although Cuman herself was associated with a church in Leinster, many of those named as her children, including Dobhrígh, were attached to churches in north Connacht. Nothing more is known of the saint.

1 *CGSH* §722.10.

Dochaide of Aghincurk, parish of Ballymyre, barony of Fews Upper, Co. Armagh, which may now represent the Achadh Corcaighe attached to Dochaide in the list of those said to have been subject to Brighid of Kildare.[1]

1 *CGHS* §670.34; *Lgen*. 753.2.

Dochiaróg. *See* Ciaróg.

Dochonna son of Dubhthan. *See* Comán son of Dubhthan.

Dochonna of Assylin (Eas Mac nEirc; Eas Uí Fhlainn) in the townland of Mocmoyne, parish of Boyle, Co. Roscommon. Belonging, according to the genealogists, to a branch of the Ceinéal Eoghain located on the eastern side of Inishowen (Inis Eoghain), in an area called the Bréadach, Dochonna (alias Mochonna) was one of three sons of Eacha (alias Eachaidh), the others being Lughaidh of Clonleigh in the Donegal barony of Raphoe North and a bishop named Cormac.[1] Dochonna is given the distinction of being the first Ceinéal Eoghain representative mentioned in the metrical version of the genealogies of the saints.[2] Colum Cille, according to various versions of his Life, founded Dochonna's church while preaching in Connacht.[3] This agrees with a tradition preserved in the Tripartite Life which attributes to Patrick – none too pleased, it is said, because he had just fallen into the river Boyle – a prophecy that Colum Cille would one day found a church there.[4] As Dochonna is a hypocoristic form of Colum, there is every reason to believe that the two saints connected with the church were originally identical.[5] They also possibly share a feastday on 8 March, when Dochonna (alias Mochonna) was joined by Mochonna of Derry who died, according to the annals, in 706.[6] In the Assylin area, Dochonna's church attained considerable importance, to the extent that its coarb (named Ua Flainn, whence the later name of the place, Eas Uí Fhlainn) was ranked third, after the coarbs of Patrick and Brighid, among the distinguished ecclesiastics present at the inauguration on Carnfree of the O'Connor (Ua Conchobhair) kings of Connacht.[7]

1 *CGSH* §83; *GRSH* 45; *Lgen.* 702.1. 2 *CGSH* §662.33. 3 *IKD* 236 §48; *BCC* 156 §152. 4 *BP* 1655–62. 5 *FG* 25–6. 6 *MartT* 21; *MartG* 50; *MartD* 70; *AU s.a.* 7 *MSPAG* 188; *JRSAI* 2, 340.

Dochonna of St Patrick's Island. *See* Maol Finnian; Mochonóg of Kilmuckridge.

Dochua of Killoe (Ceall Eó) in the barony and county of Longford. Dochua (alias Caolán and Dochaoi) is one of several saints said to have descended from Branán son of Dobhtha, progenitor of the Ceinéal Dobhtha (later represented by the Uí Ainlighe, anglicized Hanleys) in Roscommon.[1] Although little else is known of Dochua, two members of his wider family, Fionnchú of Brigown and Bearach of Termonbarry, were important enough to become the subjects of vernacular Lives. Dochua finds mention, together with an apparent sibling, Fáilbhe Fionn, and several other local saints, in Bearach's Life, which describes an assembly held at Lissardowlan (reputedly the centre of Ireland) in the parish of Templemichael, adjoining Killoe.[2] Dochua and Fáilbhe are again brought together in the list of those remembered on 30 June.[3]

1 *CGSH* §410.1; *Lgen.* 242.14. 2 *BNÉ* i, 36 §62. 3 *MartT* 53; *MartG* 126; *MartD* 182.

Dochua son of Neamhan. *See* Mochua of Ticknevin.

Dochuailéan. *See* Cuán of Ahascragh.

Dochuailéan of Scrín Dochuailéin. The genealogists attached Dochuailéan through his father Guaire to Ceinéal Binnigh, a branch of Ceinéal Eoghain that held lands in Derry.[1] Little else is known of the saint, but he may be intended by the reference in one version of Colum Cille's Middle-Irish Life to 'Da Cuilen', allegedly a cleric of Colum's 'own fatherland' who was left as coarb in Derry.[2] Together with Colum Cille and other saints, he is featured in one manuscript among those said to have foretold the onslaught of the plague known as the *Scuab*, 'besom', out of Fanad.[3] Though probably somewhere in Derry (within Ceinéal Binnigh), the location of his *scrín*, 'shrine', and of the people associated with it, has not been established.[4] Dochuailéan's feastday fell on 12 March.[5]

1 *CGSH* §36; *GRSH* 45; *Lgen*. 702.2.9; *GUH* 14–20. 2 *SGS* 2, 142 §26. 3 NLI G 10, 46b; *TEAB* 690 §3. 4 *Lgen*. 144.1. 5 *MartT* 22; *MartG* 52; *MartD* 74.

Dodhrán of Doora (Dubhdhoire), barony of Bunratty Upper, Co. Clare. This saint is known from an account of a visit to the parish in 1839 by John O'Donovan who held him to be a fabrication from *dúr* (recte *dobhar*), 'water'.[1] As in many other cases, the name may indeed have been fabricated, most likely from the name of the parish, but as O'Donovan notes, the saint's memory was celebrated annually on 3 November. Interestingly, while there is no trace of Dodhrán in the list for that day in the native martyrologies, the feast was noticed in the martyrology kept in the Regensburg *Schottenkloster* and again, albeit under the guise of 'Dorani episcopi', in Grevenus of Cologne's version of the Martyrology of Usuard.[2] Furthermore, among those commemorated on the day was Bréanainn of Glaise Dá Cholptha, a probable double of Bréanainn of Clonfert whom a story preserved in the Book of Lismore brings to Doora in Thomond, where, it is stated, 'he served the Lord'.[3] Similarly, according to a poem in Classical Irish, both Dodhrán *ó Dh[ubhdh]aire*, 'from Doora', and Bréanainn were among the mainly Munster saints called upon to help in releasing Ireland's southern half (Leath Mogha) from a bondage imposed on it by the northern half (Leath Chuinn), represented by Finnian of Clonard [4]

1 *ACoC* 177; cf. *OC* 18, 46. 2 *AS*.Iun. vii, 647; *FSHIM* 242. 3 *MartG* 210; *MartD* 296; *MB* 32. 4 RIA MS 23L11, 263; *SAM* 24.1, 17, 19–20.

Doirbhéan Fada, 'tall', of Iona, Scotland. A manuscript copy of Adhamhnán's Life of Colum Cille of Iona, catalogued as Generalia 1 in the Stadtbibliothek of Schaffhausen, Switzerland, is followed by a colophon that states: 'Whoever may read these books of the miraculous powers of Columba, let him pray to God for me, Doirbhéan (Dorbbene), that I may possess after death eternal life'.[1] Doirbhéan (also Dorbhán, Dorbhaine) son of Ailtín was abbot of Iona for five months prior to his death in 713 and, like so many of his predecessors in that office, he was regarded as a descendant of Conall Gulban, progenitor of the Ceinéal Conaill of Donegal.[2] The Schaffhausen copy of his predecessor's Life is the oldest surviving manuscript of its kind. As can be seen from an entry for 28 October in the Martyrology of Tallaght, Doirbhéan's name, like those of many other abbots of Iona, found its way into the lists of those commemorated in the text underlying all Irish martyrologies.[3]

1 *VC*[2] 542–3; *DIB* iii, 414–15. 2 *AU s.a.*; *IKD* 59; *CGSH* §342; *GRSH* 40. 3 *MartT* 85; cf. *MartG* 204; *MartD* 286.

Domhainghin of Delgany (Sruthair Ghuaire), barony of Rathdown, Co. Wicklow. The list of those said to have been subject to Brighid includes a reference to two bishops, the brothers Domhainghin and Nathí, based in Delgany, whose function it was to confer orders on the nuns and clerics of Kildare.[1] The two, said to be from Munster, had a sister named Brighid Mhór. These assertions are nowhere else attested. Also with them in Delgany, according to the same source, were Bishops Seanach and Moghobóg of Leighlin. There are numerous dedications to Brighid of Kildare in the south Dublin/north Wicklow area, including one at Tully which is also in the barony of Rathdown.[2] The fact that the brothers are said to have come from Munster indicates a possible connection between this saint and Domhainghin of Toomyvara.

1 *CGSH* §670.86. **2** *CPPI* 133–4; *MartO*[2] 64.

Dolua. *See* Molua

Domhainghin of Toomyvara (Tuaim Mhúscraighe), parish of Aghnameadle, barony of Upper Ormond, Co. Tipperary. According to the genealogists, Domhainghin was one of four sons of Fionnlugh of the Kerry family of Ciarraighe Luachra, the others being Bréanainn of Clonfert, Faichleach of Cloontuskert, and Faolán of Kiltullagh.[1] Domhainghin is possibly the subject of an episode in the Life of Mochuda of Lismore, which describes how a bishop of this name ordained some of Mochuda's disciples at the Offaly church of Rahan, before these settled on Spike Island in Cork Harbour.[2] Domhainghin's feastday fell on 29 April.[3]

1 *CGSH* §384; *GRSH* 107; *Lgen.* 729.13. **2** *VSHP* 1, 184 §39. **3** *MartT* 37; *MartG* 86; *MartD* 112.

Domhanghart of Slieve Donard (Sliabh Domhanghairt), Co. Down. According to the genealogists, Domhanghart son of Eacha belonged to the Dál bhFiatach of the area now covered by the county of Down, where the mountain named for the saint was also located.[1] The saint's mother, Deirinnill Cheathairchíochach, 'four-papped', is said to have given birth to four other saints, two of whom, Cilléan of Aghacullion and Mochuma of Drumbo, were also associated with Down churches.[2] It was at Drumbo, according to the Tripartite Life, that Patrick cursed the saint's father Eacha, promising him a short life and the scattering of his descendants, but blessing the 'famous and wonderful' Domhanghart, then still in the womb of Eacha's wife.[3] Local tradition remembered the saint (variously called Donard, Donnart and Donnaght, and latinized by Gerald of Wales as *Dominicus*) as a fierce and warlike pagan chief who, greatly impressed by Patrick's miraculous restoration to life of a bull, became a meek and humble disciple.[4] In addition to Slieve Donard, Domhanghart was associated with Maghera (Ráith Mhurbhuilg) in the barony of Upper Iveagh, where relics of his, a bell known as *glúnán* and a shrine of the saint's 'shoe', was kept.[5] Here he was remembered on 24 March, but the pilgrimage to his church on Slieve Donard, a *Lughnasa* celebration attended by thousands, was held on 25 July.[6] A late tradition, possibly connected with the belief that he lived on the mountain for 400 years, states that he was one of seven 'undying' saints.[7] However, according to the annals he died either in 466 or 507.[8] A short office Life of the saint was published by John Colgan.[9]

1 *CGSH* §358; *GRSH* 83; *Lgen.* 723.7; *ZCP* 13, 336; *UJA* (1st ser.) 2, 49; PNNI iii, 154–7. 2 *CGSH* §§162, 722.27. 3 *BP* 2655–71; *VT* 224. 4 OSL DN 96–7; *THEH* 141. 5 *EA* 27, 207–8; *HDC* i, 47; *JRSAI* 53, 174; *ASH* 743; *EMH* 469 §181. 6 *MartT* 26; *MartG* 60; *MartD* 84; *FL* 84–96. 7 *BL Cat.* ii, 471; *MartO*[1] lxv; *AB* 55, 287–95; ibid. 61, 106–7; *HDC* i, 52. 8 *AU s.a.* 9 *ASH* 743.

Domhéanóg. *See* Éanna of Inishmore.

Domhnall Ua hÉanna, bishop of Killaloe, barony of Tulla Lower, Co. Clare. This son of Murchadh is one of the few persons dating to later than 800 who are admitted to the corpus of saints' genealogies. Domhnall's pedigree is preserved only in the so-called H (TCD MS 1298) version which may have been compiled at Killaloe in or around 1100, shortly after the archbishop's death in 1098.[1] His obituary notice in the Annals of Ulster describes him as a 'noble bishop of the west of Europe', eminent in both Roman and Irish law.[2] It goes on to state that he died on 22 November, but none of the later martyrologies find room for him on that day. He has been described as the 'most distinguished Irish cleric' of his time and, through his correspondence with Lanfranc and Anselm of Canterbury, he showed leadership in the promotion of reform in the Irish church.[3]

1 *CGSH* §407; ibid. p. xxxvii. 2 *AU s.a.* 3 *Ériu* 24, 57; *TIC* 115, 208–9.

Domhongóg Oilithir, 'pilgrim', of Tory Island (Torach) in the parish of Tullaghobegly, Co. Donegal. This saint was attached through his father Sárán to a branch of the Ceinéal Eoghain (whence Tyrone and Inishowen) known as Ceinéal Tighearnaigh.[1] Although not lying immediately adjacent to Inishowen, Tory Island was close enough to it, and it has been suggested that this part of Donegal was under Ceinéal Eoghain influence in the seventh and eighth centuries.[2] Domhongóg's affiliation to Ceinéal Eoghain is matched by that of his companion saint on Tory, Earnán son of Colmán.[3] He may have been a brother of Ceallach (†658), abbot of Fahan, which has led to the suggestion that Tory was a daughter house of Fahan.[4] So little is known of Domhongóg (alias Domhnóg) that he has been confused with Modhomhnóg Oilithir of Tibberaghney.[5]

1 *CGSH* §40; *GRSH* 45; *Lgen.* 701.6; *ZCP* 8, 296; *CGH* 146d31. 2 *CCDK* 89. 3 *CGSH* §16. 4 *AU s.a.*; *Peritia* 20, 332, 340. 5 *GRSH* 45; *MartD* 132.

Donnán of Eigg, an island off Argyll on the west coast of Scotland. Donnán's church is famous for one event, the martyrdom by burning on 17 April 617, the eve of Easter, of the saint and members of his community, sometimes numbered one hundred and fifty, at other times variously fifty-two and fifty-four.[1] Said to have been surprised by robbers intent on killing them, while singing psalms in their church, Donnán and his followers moved to the nearby refectory, so as to make the task easier for their assailants.[2] The saint and his companions were thus among the few martyrs to whom the Irish (or Scottish) church could lay claim, and the entry on their feast of 17 April in the Martyrology of Tallaght lists many of their names.[3] The knee-cap of the saint finds mention in a poem detailing the relics allegedly held by Adhamhnán.[4] Donnán gave name to several churches in Scotland and, by the ninth century, a relic of his had reached the Continent, arguably at Ferrières in France or at some church in the Rhineland.[5] The saint's martyrdom became the subject of a tale, now lost, and some sources place the event on a rock (or island) named 'Aldasain / insula Alasina', now Ailsa Craig in the Firth of Clyde.[6]

1 *AU*/*ATig*. *s.a.*; *CGSH* §717; *MartD* 104; *AB* 63, 121–2; *IrL* 66; *DIB* iii, 383–4. **2** *CGSH* §717; *AB* 51, 126–30; *MartO*[2] 114. **3** *MartT* 33. **4** *Celtica* 15, 35 §13. **5** *LegSS* 351; *EIRD* 55–68; *RIW* i 15–19. **6** *CPNS* 283; *KSS* 325; *ACDS* 153–6; *Peritia* 17–18, 265–9; *Anecd.* ii, 47 §8; *CGSH* §717; *MartO*[2] 114; *FSHIM* 236.

Donnán of Hareisland, parish of Bunown, barony of Kilkenny West, Co. Westmeath. According to the Latin Life of Ciarán of Clonmacnoise, Hareisland was first occupied by its subject, who subsequently relinquished it to Donnán of the Corca Bhaiscinn of south-west Clare.[1] The much later vernacular Life of Ciarán states that Donnán was both the son of a brother of Seanán of Scattery, named Liath in *Genealogiae Regum et Sanctorum Hiberniae*, and a uterine brother of Seanán himself.[2] However, Donnán is not among those listed as children of Seanán's mother, either in the tract on the mothers of the saints or in a poem on Fíonmhaith daughter of Baoth.[3] Donnán was remembered on Hareisland in Lough Ree on 7 January.[4]

1 *VSHP* i, 211 §28. **2** *LisL* 4361–2; *GRSH* 78. **3** *CGSH* §722.8; *IrT* iv, 93–4. **4** *MartT* 5; *MartG* 10; *MartD* 8.

Donnchadh of Clogher, barony of Ferrard, Co. Louth. This saint is known principally from a note added to the Martyrology of Donegal which, having assigned to Donnchadh (Latin Donatus, anglicized Donough or Denis) an otherwise unrecorded feast of 30 October, states that fine weather is guaranteed on this day.[1] According to the same note, not one man from Clogher was ever drowned. Local tradition in the townland of Bellcotton, parish of Termonfeckin – where a well at which he was accustomed to pray was named after him – placed the saint's feast variously on 25 September and 9 October.[2] A wind that blew about the time of his feast was known locally as 'St Denis' gale' and a well and stone named after the saint were located near his church in Clogher.[3] A rock near Clogherhead was known as 'St Denis' Boat'.[4] Dennis's well at Elm Park in the Dublin parish of Clontarf may also be called after him.[5]

1 *MartD* xlv–xlvi; cf. *Celtica* 1, 80. **2** *JCLAS* 1.4, 36–7; ibid. 4, 160; ibid. 7, 184. **3** Ibid. 7, 184; ibid. 24, 346. **4** *Béaloideas* 12, 186–7. **5** *AHWD* 12.

Donnart. *See* Domhanghart.

Doranus. *See* Dodhrán; Drónán.

Doríóg. *See* Moríóg.

Dorothy. *See* Íde.

Douglus. *See* Lughaidh of Clonleigh.

Dreamhan son of Caol. *See* Aodh Fionn.

Droine of Ceall Draighneach (Droineach), parish of Rossinver, barony of Rosclogher, Co. Leitrim. The sole source of information on this saint, whose name may derive from that of her church, states that her feast, unnoticed in the martyrologies, fell on 2 September and also that there was a miraculous local well dedicated to her.[1]

1 *Celtica* 1, 65.

Drónán of Cromwellstown (Ceall Easbaig Dhrónáin; 'Kildronan'), parish of Kilteel, barony of South Salt, Co. Kildare.[1] According to the genealogists, Drónán son of Fianghalach belonged to a branch of the Ceinéal Laoghaire of Meath named Uí Mhaoile Tibhre (Rubha).[2] Despite his status as bishop, Drónán found his way into a secular genealogy which provides him with a son named Giollagán.[3] He is probably identical with the bishop named 'Dron(n)án' commemorated on 12 December.[4] The saint has been confused with 'Doranus', patron of Kildrinagh in the Kilkenny parish of Tubbridbritain.[5]

1 *HDGP* iii, 165. 2 *CGSH* §84; *Lgen.* 707.4; *CGH* 145b23. 3 *BLec.* 62Vc (corruptly *Dronain m. Diangalaig*). 4 *MartG* 236; *MartD* 334. 5 *HADO* ii, 372.

Drugán son of Draighean. *See* Ainmhire of Kilroe.

Dothearnóg. *See* Earnán of Inis Caoin.

Drostán. *See* Troscán.

Druighean daughter of Léinín. *See* Aighleann of Killiney.

Dubh Dúin of Aghanloo (Áth Lunga), barony of Keenaght, Co. Derry. According to the genealogists, this saint belonged through his father Fearghas to the Cianachta, a claim that suits the location of his church in the barony named after this people.[1] Though nothing more is known of Dubh Dúin, his church is said to have been visited by Colum Cille, then in search of a relic for his shrine at neighbouring Tamlaght-ard (Magilligan).[2] The occupant of the church, whose thumb miraculously became available for the shrine, was named Tice (Tige?), alias Tuggins (Latin Tuggeus).[3]

1 *CGSH* §508. 2 *BCC* 149–50. 3 *DYHS* 195; *UJA* (2nd ser.) 2, 151; *AnH* 12, 82, 108, 110.

Dubhán, *cruimhthear*, 'presbyter'. *See* Cuman of Aireadh Bóinne.

Dubhán of Hook Point/Head (Rinn Dubháin Oilithir), and more specifically of Churchtown in the parish of Hook, barony of Shelburne, Co. Wexford. This saint is known from an entry in the tract on the mothers of the saints which states that he, along with his nine brothers, were sons of Díona, daughter of a king of the Saxons, by Brachan, king of the Britons (or Welsh), and eponym of Brycheiniog in south Wales.[1] Like Dubhán, many of the saint's siblings, including Moghóróg of Delgany, Mochonóg of Kilmuckridge, Díoraidh of Edermine, and Eallóg of St Tulloge's, are associated with churches in Leinster. Dubhán's cult spread along the coast into Waterford, as is shown by the dedication at Kilduane (Ceall Dubháin) in the parish of Monksland.[2] A seventeenth-century source speculates that the saint may have been the Dubhán *sagart*, 'priest', commemorated on 12 February, but local tradition places the feast in the second week of July.[3]

1 *CGSH* §722.89; *EWGT* 14–16, 32–3; *CECW* 129; *HookP* 25. 2 *WatLis*. 195; *PND* 165. 3 *MartD* 46.

Dubhán of Monasterevin (Ros Glaise), barony of Offaly West, Co. Kildare. This son of Laighneach was one of seven brothers of Abán of Killabban, all of whom were attached to the Uí Labhradha or Uí Chormaic of Leinster.[1] Three of Dubhán's brothers (Seanach, Líthghin, and Toimdheanach) are also assigned to Monasterevin, a church much better known for its association with Éimhín. Though nothing else is recorded for certain of Dubhán, he may be the saint of this name invoked as a potential assistant by Moling on his quest to have the *bóramha* tribute remitted.[2]

1 *CGSH* §287.1.2; *GRSH* 88; *Lgen*. 727.11; *MartO*² 74. 2 *SG* i, 382.

Dubhthach of Iona, Scotland. A son of Dubhán, and successor of Colum Cille, Dubhthach belonged, like many other abbots of the Columban *familia*, to the Ceinéal Conaill.[1] His predecessor in the abbacy, Maol Brighde son of Tornán, belonged to the same branch of this family. It has been suggested that the headship of the Columban *familia* was moved from Iona to Kells during Dubhthach's twelve-year tenure (927–38).[2] He died in 938 and, although seventeenth-century sources identify him with the Dubhthach commemorated on 5 February, it has also been suggested that his day was 7 October.[3] Some holy wells in Donegal recall the saint by name, one in Annagry, parish of Templecrone, another on an island (Inishdooey) between Inishbofin and Tory, in the parish of Tullaghobegly, where he is reputed to have built a church following his failure to reach Tory in a crozier-throwing contest with Colum Cille and others.[4] He was also remembered in northern Argyll in Scotland.[5]

1 *CGSH* §348. 2 *IKD* 79–80. 3 *AU s.a.*; *MartD* 40; *GRSH* 40; *VC*¹ 393. 4 *Béaloideas* 6, 152–3; *CCDK* 94–5; *UJA* 6 (1st ser.), 353. 5 *CR* 4, 371–2.

Dubhthach grandson (or son) of Lughar of the Maca Lughair of Leinster. When Patrick went to Tara, where the men of Ireland were celebrating its feast, only two arose, according to Muirchú, to show him respect, namely Dubhthach of the Maca Lughair and Dubhthach's pupil, Fiac of Sleaty.[1] Patrick thereupon blessed Dubhthach, a poet by profession, and his progeny, and gave him the honour of being the first man at (pagan) Tara to believe in the word of God.[2] The honour of being the first to build a wooden church (*dairtheach*) and stone cross was also claimed for Dubhthach.[3] The prologue to the *Seanchas Már* features Dubhthach as one of those chosen to arrange Irish laws in cooperation with Patrick and others, an event that is sometimes seen as a token of the mutual respect and tolerance between poet and cleric.[4] Dubhthach's saintly progeny was numerous, running – through his grand-daughter Deidhe – to thirty male and female saints throughout Ireland, according to the tract on the mothers of the saints.[5] Seven chidren, including Comhghall and Fachtna, are assigned to Dubhthach himself.[6] Dubhthach's whereabouts within Leinster are unclear, but a poem links him both to Criomhthann son of Éanna of the Uí Cheinsealaigh, and to Criomhthann's son Daithí, whose descendants appear to have been located in or about the parish of Kilbride in south Wicklow.[7] Given his associations with Leinster, Dubhthach is probably the saint of that name cited as a companion by Moling in pursuit of his quest for remission of the *bóramha* tribute.[8] This is also the view taken by the Martyrology of Donegal, which remembered Dubhthach on 7 October.[9]

1 *BP* 523–36; *VT* 52; *RC* 37, 336 §26. 2 *Peritia* 5, 25–6. 3 *RC* 37, 336 §27. 4 *Ériu* 45, 11–13, 19 §8; *VT* 564; *CMCS* 19, 1–18; *StC* 10/11, 15–28; *CICI* 16. 5 *CGSH* §722.2. 6 Ibid. §653. 7 *RC* 37, 336 §27–30; *CGH* 118b27, 316c38, 62. 8 *SG* i, 382. 9 *MartD* 269.

Dúileach of St Doolagh's (Clochar), parish of Balgriffin, barony of Coolock, Co. Dublin. An entry in the tract on the mothers of the saints assigns to Sín daughter of Niall of the Corca Bhaiscinn, a group settled in the area around Loop Head in Clare, four sons by Sineall of the Conmhaicne of Connacht, of whom one, Malach (alias Amhalghaidh), was Dúileach's father.[1] All four sons are again brought together in the corpus of saints' genealogies.[2] Despite a western parental background on both sides, Dúileach, like his uncle, Baodán son of Sineall of Cloney, became patron of a Leinster church. He figures hardly at all in the wider hagiographical literature, but his patronage extended to Grangegorman (formerly 'Kildulyc') within the borough of Dublin, which was the first grange of Christ Church cathedral.[3] This explains the presence of the saint's feastday of 17 November in the calendar used at Christ Church.[4] At St Doolagh's, where his 'bed' was held in high repute by women fearful of death in child-bed, his feast was reportedly also celebrated on 1 August.[5] The saint's *historia* was reputedly still extant at Malahide in the early seventeenth century.[6] Finally, Dúileach was among the saints invoked as guarantors of the Law of Adhamhnán.[7]

1 *CGSH* §722.22; *AH* 8, 20–1. 2 Ibid. §§128–9; *GRSH* 106; *Lgen*. 733.1. 3 *CCCD* 31–2; *JCHAS* 49, 54. 4 *MartO*[2] 234; *MartG* 220; *MartD* 312: *BOM* 71, 179. 5 *Rep. Nov.* 3, 123. 6 *Seanchas* 410 §98. 7 *CA* §22.

Dúileachán son of Iorlamhán. *See* Bóchra.[2]

Duinseach of Killinchy (Ceall Duinsighe), barony of Dufferin, Co. Down. The martyrologies, which commemorate this saint on 11 December, state that she was the patron of three churches in the area about Strangford Lough (Loch Cuan), but name Ceall Duinsighe only.[1] This and the other two churches have recently been plausibly located at Killinchy itself, at a place called Killinchy in the Woods and at Dunsy Island.[2]

1 *MartG* 236; *MartO*[2] 258; *MartD* 332. 2 *Celtica* 23, 113–24.

Duirtheach of Killadreenan (Ceall Achaidh Draighnighe), parish of Newcastle Lower, barony of Newcastle, Co. Wicklow. Styled a bishop, Duirtheach (Daurthech) and a companion named Feidhealm are among those said to have been subject to Brighid of Kildare.[1] Neither saint is known from any other source.

1 *CGSH* §670.69; *Lgen*. 753.34.

Duirtheach of Nendrum (Aondruim) on Mahee Island, parish of Tullynakill, barony of Castlereagh Lower, Strangford Lough, Co. Down. Duirtheach (Dúthracht) son of Tricheamh was one of seven brothers, two of whom, Díocha of Saul and Ros (Rus) of Downpatrick, are brought into contact with Patrick by the latter's biographers.[1] The others included Laoghaire of Downpatrick, Oilill of Movilla, and Eoghan of Kilclief. In the passage of the ninth-century Tripartite Life that mentions them, reference is also made to Caolán (Mochaoi), the more important patron of Nendrum.[1] Through his pedigree, which assigns him to the local Dál bhFiatach, Duirtheach is shown to have been related to Finnian of the church of Movilla, to which his brother Oilill (Finnian's grandfather) was also attached.[2] A feastday of 16 May has been assigned to him in some seventeenth-century sources.[3]

1 *CGSH* §136.2; *PTBA* 78; *BP* 373–427; *VT* 36–40. 2 *CGSH* §136.1.2; *GRSH* 82. 3 *MartG* 98 (add.); *MartD* 130; *GRSH* 82.

Duistric daughter of Trust. *See* Lonán of Trevet.

Dula of Uí Mhaine. *See* Maolán of Kilmoylan.

Dúnchadh of Clonmacnoise (Cluain Mac Nóis), barony of Garrycastle, Co. Offaly. A grandson of Braon, and successor of Ciarán of Clonmacnoise, Dúnchadh died 'on pilgrimage' in Armagh on 19 January 989. The notice of his death describes him as an excellent scribe and most religious man.[1] He is said to have spent thirteen years in Armagh, performing several miracles during his stay there, allegedly including the last raising from the dead in Ireland.[2] He is also identified as the *garbhoineach*, 'rough-faced one', who would maintain three *séise*, perhaps 'designs', associated with Iona, those of Adhamhnán, Colum Cille and Séighín.[3] Dúnchadh was included by the Four Masters among the saints of Ceinéal Maine of Teathbha, a stretch of land comprising most of Longford and part of Westmeath.[4] None of the martyrologies record Dúnchadh's feast of 19 January.

1 *AU s.a.* 2 *ZCP* 3, 35–6. 3 *ZCP* 13, 456 §51. 4 *GRSH* 57; cf. *MartD* 404.

Dúnchadh of Iona, Scotland. Like most other successors of Colum Cille, Dúnchadh son of Ceann Faoladh belonged to the Ceinéal Conaill, in his case to the same branch as his predecessor Adhamhnán.[1] His tenure of the abbacy, between 710 and 717, was marked by several important developments, including the adoption on Iona of the Roman method of calculating Easter, and the likely arrival there from Northumbria of a copy of the Hieronymian martyrology.[2] In both cases, Dúnchadh was probably influenced by Egbert, a Northumbrian who had previously spent many years in Ireland.[3] As the Easter question was contentious, rivals for the headship of the Columban *familia* appear also to have been a feature of Dúnchadh's period in office.[4] His name is first in the list of those commemorated on 25 May in the martyrology then kept on the island.[5]

1 *CGSH* §341; *GRSH* 40. 2 *VC*[1] 379–81; *IKD* 57–9; *AU s.a.* 3 *BEH* 554–5; *FSHIM* 48–9, 318. 4 *IKD* 57–9. 5 *MartT* 46; *MartO*[2] 126; *MartG* 104; *MartD* 138; *FSHIM* 57–61.

Dúrán. *See* Dodhrán.

Dúthracht. *See* also Duirtheach.

Dúthracht daughter of Éanna. *See* Dúthracht of Leamhchaill.

Dúthracht of Kilmoney (Ceall Mhuine), parish of Rathangan, barony of Offaly East, Co. Kildare. An entry in the list of homonymous saints brings together Brígh daughter of Colga and a saint named Dúthracht.[1] Another list – of saints remembered on 12 November – likewise groups the two together and, as early seventeenth-century sources also assumed, they are probably identical with the like-named pair assigned to the church of Kilmoney (along with a companion named Tighearn) in the list of those subject to Brighid of Kildare.[2] Dúthracht's church is located a few miles north-west of Kildare.

1 *CGSH* §708.21. 2 *MartG* 216; *MartD* 306; *CGSH* §670.52; *Lgen.* 753.23.

Dúthracht of Leamhchaill. A saint of this name and (unidentified) church was commemorated on 25 October.[1] Some seventeenth-century sources speculate that she may have been identical with Dúthracht daughter of Éanna, sister of Caoireach Dheargáin.[2]

1 *MartT* 84; *MartG* 202; *MartD* 282. 2 *GRSH* 70; *MartD* 282; cf. *CGSH* §110.

Dúthracht of Oghil, parish of Monasterevin, barony of Offaly West, Co. Kildare, which may now represent an earlier Domhnach Eochaille. Like her namesake and probable double at Kilmoney, Dúthracht belonged to a church said to have been subject to Brighid of Kildare, where she had two (otherwise unknown) companions, Peadrán and Teamhair.[1] This church is also mentioned in a litany of Irish saints as the home of seven holy bishops.[2]

1 *CGSH* §670.82. 2 *IrL* 66; *LisL* 1680.

E ☙

Eacha of Cluain Réadach, an unidentified church, probably in Co. Carlow. According to the corpus of saints' genealogies, Eacha son of Cathán and his brother, Maighistir of Ceall Mhaighistreach, a site in the townland of Pollerton Little, parish and barony of Carlow, belonged to the Uí Bhairrche, who gave name to the deanery of Obargy in the Carlow barony of Idrone, and also to the Wexford barony of Bargy.[1] Neither saint would appear to be otherwise attested.

1 *CGSH* §259; *GRSH* 88; *Lgen.* 727.31; *CGH* 121b11; *HDGP* iv, 14.

Eachaidh of Tallaght (Tamhlacht), barony of Uppercross, Co. Dublin. As second abbot of Tallaght in succession to Maol Ruain, Eachaidh (anchorite and bishop) was among those who belonged in an *aonta*, 'union', with his predecessor.[1] During his incumbency, the church of Tallaght showed that it was a force to be reckoned with, even in the Uí Néill jurisdiction, by preventing Aodh son of Niall, the overking, from holding the Fair of Tailte; the ostensible reason was a violation of sanctuary, for which handsome compensation was subsequently made.[2] Eachaidh died in 812 and his name was added to the house martyrology on 28 January.[3]

1 *CGSH* §§713.11.15, 724.2. 2 *AU s.a.* 811. 3 *AU s.a.*; *MartT* 13; *MartG* 24; *MartD* 28.

Eachaidh son of Colla. *See* Dallán Forghaill.

Éadamair. *See* Aodhamair.

Éadaoin of Tumna (Tuaim Nua), barony of Boyle, Co. Roscommon. On visiting Tumna in 1837, John O'Donovan was shown the grave of St Héidin (Eidin), or 'Edaoin in Irish', with curious stones over it called *deichneabhair*, 'decades', probably from the rosaries said there on pattern day.[1] O'Donovan had never heard of the woman before and was apparently told nothing else that he saw fit to record. The saint's pedigree, which attaches her through her father Lighean to the Uí Bhriúin of Connacht, is also preserved, as is the record of her feast on 5 July.[2] In the seventeenth century, her name began to be confused with the form 'Moduena' which was probably borrowed from a gloss on Moninne in the list of the following day.[3] In Scotland, where her name was given the Latin form Medana, the saint was remembered variously on 5 July and 19 November.[4] Finally, Éadaoin, representing her church, is among those said tendentiously to have owed tribute to Caillín of Fenagh.[5]

1 OSL RN i, 278; *HOI* 145. 2 *CGSH* §§401, 510; *GRSH* 59; *MartT* 53; *MartG* 130; *MartD* 186. 3 *GRSH* 59; *MartD* 186. 4 *CPNS* 163; *KSS* 238, 396. 5 *BFen.* 286.

Eagmhacht. *See* Iobhar.

Ealáir of Monaincha (Loch Cré), parish of Corbally, barony of Ikerrin, Co. Tipperary. The church of Ealáir (Latin Hilarius) was located in an area later controlled by the Éile family of Uí Chearbhaill, which probably explains the saint's spurious Cianachta pedigree, preserved uniquely in *Genealogiae Regum et Sanctorum Hiberniae*.[1] Described as an anchorite and scribe, the saint is also named as an authority on *céile Dé* practice in 'The Monastery of Tallaght', a ninth-century treatise on the teaching of Maol Ruain and his disciples.[2] His place in the body of the list for 7 September is an indication of his inclusion in the Martyrology of Tallaght from the very beginning.[3] Ealáir 'of the Island' died in 807, and his feast fell on 7 September.[4]

1 *GRSH* 123 §11. 2 *MT* 128, 135. 3 *MartT* 69. 4 *AU s.a.*; *MartT* 69; *MartG* 172; *MartD* 238.

Ealcha. *See* Pupa.

Eallóg of St Doologe's (Ceall Meallóg/St Tulloge's) in the town and county of Wexford. Bearer of a hypocoristic name (also written Meallóg or Teallóg) that probably derives from Oilill, this saint is known from an entry in the tract on the mothers of the saints which states that he, along with his nine brothers, were sons of Díona, daughter of a king of the Saxons, by Brachan, king of the Britons (or Welsh), and eponym of Brycheiniog in south Wales.[1] Many of the saint's siblings, including Moghóróg of Delgany, Díoraidh of Edermine, and Mochonóg of Kilmuckridge, are also associated with churches in east Leinster. Near Wexford town were two other places, Kerlogue (Ceall Eallóg), where Eallóg was later replaced by James the apostle, and Kilmallock (Ceall Meallóg), possibly named after the saint.[2] He was apparently also remembered at the church of Kilcloggan in the Wexford parish of Templetown and at Templeogue (from Teach Meallóg) in the Dublin parish of Tallaght.[3]

1 *CGSH* §722.89; *EWGT* 14–16, 32–3. 2 *CECW* 128–9, 206; *TNW* 1069–71. 3 Ibid.; *HookP* 25; Ibid.; *CECW* 128–9, 206; *HookP* 25; *AH* 8, 30.

Éanán/Éanna. These forms derive from *éan*, 'bird', the former a diminutive, the latter adjectival in the sense of 'bird-like'. A hypocoristic form is represented by Méanóg. The names were common enough to be included in the list of homonymous saints, with a total of thirteen representatives.[1]

1 *CGSH* §707.360–72.

Éanán of Drumraney (Druim Rátha/Ráithe), barony of Kilkenny West, Co. Westmeath. Writing of his visit to the parish of Drumraney in September 1837, John O'Donovan drew attention to a 'conspicuous hill' which he identified as Bruidhean Dá Choga, the scene of a legendary *toghail*, 'siege', that led to the death of Cormac son of Conchobhar, king of Ulster.[1] A man living at the foot of the hill declared to O'Donovan that a nearby stream had served as the boundary of the patrimonies of three ancient families of Westmeath. Perhaps not surprisingly, therefore, the local saint, Éanán son of Eirín (Eirnín), was himself made the subject of three conflicting pedigrees which attached him variously to Clann Cholmáin – the leading family of Midhe – Luighne (or Cianachta) and Fothairt.[2] Though there is no connection between this and his genealogies, he was also known by three separate forms of name; Éanóg, apparently the more usual local form of the name; Éanán, the name attached to his well and to the patronage of his church; and the hypocoristic Momhíonóg, under which he was entitled to tithes from an island on Loch Maighe Uath (or Luatha), the lake that gave name to the parish of Ballyloughloe.[3] Elsewhere, a poem lists Éanán among saints that appear formerly to have belonged to the *Fianna* of Fionn son of Cumhall.[4] Éanán's church may have been affiliated to the great monastery of Clonmacnoise which is known to have had property in the Drumraney area.[5] This would explain why the saint's feast is among the few local additions to the Irish version of the Martyrology of York which appears to have been compiled at Clonmacnoise.[6] The saint's inclusion, under the guise of both Éanóg and Éanán, in the Life of Aodh of Rahugh (who miraculously arranged to have food on the table at Drumraney) may also be noted.[7] Aodh's church of Killare lay close to Drumraney. Éanán is said to have died in 633, and he was remembered on two days, 19 August and (principally) 18 September.[8]

1 *PNW* 8–11; ITS 61. **2** *CGSH* §42; *GRSH* 75; *Lgen*. 739.2–3. **3** *BCML* 52 §50; *PNW* 5n; *CPL* 8, 145; *ILL* 269. **4** *ZCP* 5, 179–83. **5** ITS 61, 4–6. **6** *FourIM* 188, 194. **7** *VSHH* 180 §46; *VSHP* i, 42 §32. **8** *MartT* 64, 72; *MartO*² 177, 195; *MartG* 160, 178 (Éanna); *MartD* 224; *PNW* 9; *ATig*. *s.a.* 632.

Éanán of Glenealy and Rosminogue. *See* Méanóg.

Éanna. *See* also Éanán.

Éanna of Inishmore, barony of Aran (Árainn), Co. Galway. According to an early king-tale, Éanna (also Éinne, anglicized Enda) son of Conall, one of Ireland's three *athlaoich* (former laymen) of renown, belonged to the Cianachta, whose main settlements were in the southern part of Louth and in the Derry barony of Keenaght.[1] The wider (and later) hagiographical tradition mostly attaches Éanna, however, together with his supposed sister, Caoireach Dheargáin, by way of what has been described as a 'false pedigree', to the dominant line of the Oirghialla; these controlled lands approximately equivalent to the diocese of Clogher which the saint is said to have once governed as bishop.[2] The saint's maternal record also provides a link to the Cianachta by describing Éanna's mother, variously named Aoibhinn and Brígh, as the daughter of Ainmhire, king of the Fir Arda Cianachta who gave name to the Louth barony of Ferrard.[3] To compound the confusion surrounding Éanna's descent, a separate source describes the saint as a son of this same Ainmhire, belonging not to the men of Ferrard, but to the Creamhthainn, a people settled in the Meath barony of Slane.[4] There is also some confusion as to which of the Aran Islands first fell to Éanna. The above-cited king-tale states that he was given Inisheer by Aonghas son of Nadh Fraoich, king of Cashel, though the church named Ceall Éinne after him is located on the main Aran island of Inishmore, and this association is also indicated by the appellation Éanna Áirne.[5]

Éanna was undoubtedly the best-known of the many saints of those islands, justly called Árainn na Naomh, 'Aran of the saints', and his foundation was important enough to inspire the composition of a biography preserved in the *Insulensis* collection of saints' Lives.[6] Criticized as a 'late production', valuable mainly for its local topographical interest, the Life, despite its doublets and other imperfections, is a good example of how the canons regular of St Augustine produced texts designed to protect their properties.[7] The place of production seems not to have been Aran itself, but Clonmacnoise whose patron, Ciarán, is given greater prominence than any other in the list of Éanna's associates.[8] Said to have joined Éanna on Aran, where his memory survives in the form of a holy well and *teampall*, Ciarán is made the subject of a vision which showed Aran and Clonmacnoise united by the roots of a tree, and a *fraternitas* is also posited between the churches of the two saints.[9]

But if Éanna's church was appropriate to the house of canons in Clonmacnoise, as seems likely, the author of his Life also found room for other Augustinian foundations, or their patrons, some minor, others less so. On returning to Ireland from his monastery overseas – named Latium, probably in reference to Rome – Éanna is said to have landed, like Patrick before him, at Colptha (later Colp), near the mouth of the river Boyne, which became an Augustinian house in the late twelfth century.[10] Finnian, patron of Clonard, one of the earliest and most important of the country's Augustinian foundations, is given the key role of interpreting the previously mentioned vision that outlined the relationship between Éanna's church on Aran and Clonmacnoise.[11] Moninne (alias Dairearca), patron of Killevy, later a convent of Augustinian nuns, is featured in an episode involving a miraculous sharing of vessels with Éanna's sister Fuinche; she plays an important role in Éanna's development, as the instrument of his conversion from layman to man of the church and as the mentor who advised him, while on pilgrimage in Rome, to return to Ireland and settle on Aran.[12]

Several chapters of the Life are taken up with Éanna's sojourn in Rome, where one of his companions was Pupa, a name said to derive from *Papa*, 'Pope'; according to another source, Pupa abandoned the papacy to retire to Inishmore, where he was also known as Neamh, and where his name became attached to one of three 'angelic' burial places.[13] Éanna's other companion in Rome was no less a person than Ailbhe of Emly, patron of Munster's chief church and diocese. Although nowhere remembered on the island, Ailbhe's role reflects what seems to have been Aran's place within Munster rather than Connacht, a position also echoed by the tradition that Éanna, having requested the assistance of Ailbhe, sought the permission of the king of Cashel, Aonghas son of Nadh Fraoich, before settling in Aran.[14] Besides the time spent in Rome, Éanna is sent by his biographer to the monastery of Rosnat, later Whithorn (alias Candida Casa), likewise the seat of a house of (Premonstratensian) canons regular, to serve under its master, Ninnian (or Maucennus) by name.[15]

Placed on the edge of the western ocean, Éanna's church on Aran was ideally placed to attract visitors in quest of *terra repromissionis*, 'the land of promise'. These included Bréanainn of Clonfert and Annaghdown, both Augustinian houses, who is said to have received Éanna's blessing prior to his ocean-voyage.[16] The biographer of Ailbhe of Emly, who is also credited with an ocean-voyage, described Inishmore as a place in which no one knew how many saints were buried.[17] Similarly drawing attention to the innumerable host of saints on the island, the biographer of Ciarán credited his subject, then on Inishmore, with a vision of Clonmacnoise's future greatness.[18] Colum Cille's late vernacular biographer gave an account of how his patron, having identified the occupant of a tomb on Inishmore as an abbot of Jerusalem who had come as a pilgrim and died there, was refused any part of the island by Éanna, only to curse it with 'every want', especially of firewood; allegedly, the people of Aran then still made fire of dried cow-dung only.[19] Éanna was among those exalted 'in his hard, narrow prison of stone' in the poem attributed to Cuimín of Connor, and in a poem in Classical Irish, he was called upon, together with numerous other (mainly Munster) saints, to assist in delivering Leath Mogha (Ireland's southern half) from a bondage imposed on it by Leath Chuinn (the northern half), championed by Finnian of Clonard.[20]

On the mainland, the saint was patron of several churches, including Killeany (Ceall Éinne) in the Galway barony of Clare, where he came to be regarded as a brother of Cuana and Fursa, patrons of the neighbouring parishes of Kilcoona and Killursa.[21] He was also patron of Killeany in the Burren, of Spiddle in the Galway parish of Moycullen, and of Barna in the parish of Rahoon.[22] Various other members of his family, including sisters named Líobha (alias Lóichín) and Fuinche, and a nephew, Colmán son of Daráine – through whom he would have been regarded as a blood relation of Ailbhe of Emly and Aonghas of Cashel – are said to have attained sanctity.[23] In Munster, Éanna may have been remembered as Momhéanóg (alias Domhéanóg) in the Tipperary parish of Killavinoge and in the Cork parishes of Drinagh (Killaveenoge), Durrus (Killoveenoge), and Templemichael (Killaminoge).[24] Éanna's feast fell on 21 March, and his chasuble reputedly formed part of Adhamhnán's reliquary.[25]

1 *Anecd.* iii, 60; *HDGP* iv, 137. **2** *VSHP* i, lxiv; *CGSH* §67; *GRSH* 70; *VSHP* ii, 60 §1; *ClRec.* 7, 380; *DIB* iii, 627. **3** *CGSH* §722.85; *VSHP* ii, 60 §1. **4** *MartT* 25. **5** *HDGP* i, 72; *SAL* 47–60. **6** *VSHP* ii, 60–75. **7** *Kenney* 374. **8** *VSHP* ii, 71–4 §§25–8, 31–2. **9** Ibid. 72 §§26–7. **10** Ibid. 65 §11; *MRHI* 166 **11** *VSHP* ii, 74 §32. **12** Ibid. 60–5 §§2–11. **13** Ibid. 69 §21; *CGSH* §§379.3, 735. **14** *VSHP* i, 56 §25; ibid. ii, 65 §12; *VSHH* 125; *Éigse* 9, 18–29. **15** *VSHP* ii, 62–3 §§6–7. **16** Ibid. i, 107 §§14–15. **17** Ibid. i, 56 §25; *VSHH* 125. **18** *VSHP* i, 208 §21; *LisL* 4289–96. **19** *BCC* 158–60 §§155–6; *GJ* 4, 162; *Béaloideas* 2, 385. **20** *ZCP* 1, 64; RIA MS 23L11, 263; *SAM* 24.1, 17, 20. **21** OSL GY i, 186. **22** *ACoC* 72; *OFWC* 61; *Béaloideas* 48–9, 149–52; *AIGY* i, 117 (Barna). **23** *CGSH* §§67, 722.59.85; *GRSH* 71; *VSHP* ii, 65 §12. **24** *CLTÁ* 185–7. **25** *MartT* 25; *MartO*[2] 83; *MartG* 58; *MartD* 82; *Celtica* 15, 34 §12.

Éanna of Kilnamanagh (Ceall Mhanach Eascrach/Ceall na Manach), parish of Tallaght, barony of Uppercross, Co. Dublin. An early litany of Irish saints invokes a group gathered around Caoimhghin of Glendalough that has been styled *familia Coemgeni*.[1] Featured among those in the group were Éanna and Lóchán, both of whom are assigned to Kilnamanagh, and immediately following this invocation is another which places twenty-seven bishops at their church. This is not the only evidence of the affiliation of Kilnamanagh to Glendalough. Both Éanna and Lóchán are also said to have belonged, with Caoimhghin, to the Dál Meisin Corb, one of the dominant families in the south Dublin/Wicklow area.[2] What appears to have been the privileged position of their church within the Glendalough *familia* is reflected by the tradition that Caoimhghin was sent to there to receive his initial education.[3] A well named after Caoimhghin at Kilnamanagh still bears witness to the connection with Glendalough.[4] A companion saint (Eoghan) at Kilnamanagh, who was also assigned to the Dál Meisin Corb, was taken to be the like-named patron of the diocese of Ardstraw. The biographer of the Ardstraw saint asserts, without mentioning either Éanna or Lóchán, that, having founded Kilnamanagh, he spent fifteen years there, during which time he taught Caoimhghin.[5] A variant tradition provides Éanna's other companion Lóchán with a father named Cathal of the Uí Fhiachrach of Connacht.[6] It also attaches Lóchán to Ceall Mhic Cathail, now Kilmacahill in the Kilkenny barony of Gowran. Éanna and Lóchán were remembered together on 31 December, the same day as the feast of his namesake and probable double, Méanóg of the Wicklow church of Glenealy.[7]

1 *IrL* 54–6; *CPPI* 174–9. 2 *CGSH* §181.3; *Lgen*. 726.2. 3 *VSHH* 361 §2; *VSHP* i, 235 §4. 4 *CPPI* 176. 5 *CGSH* §181.2; *VSHH* 401 §3. 6 *CGSH* §15; *GRSH* 63; *MartO*² 263. 7 *MartT* 3; *MartO*² 255; *MartG* 250; *MartD* 350.

Eannag of Ceall Eannga, which may later have been represented by the now obsolete 'Killagone' in the parish of Cadamstown, barony of Carbury, Co. Kildare.[1] This son of Neamhnann, whose name possibly derives from Latin *innocens*, 'innocent', is known only from the list of those subject to Brighid of Kildare.[2] Accompanying him at the church named after him were Fiachra Caoch and Díoma. The fact that Fiachra was probably identical with a namesake bearing the cognomen Caol who was commemorated on 25 July at a church named Cluain Caoin (Caoichne), now perhaps Clonkeen in the parish and barony of Carbury, provides some support for the suggested identification of Ceall Eannga with 'Killagone'.[3]

1 *HDGP* iii, 167. 2 *CGSH* §670.71. 3 *MartT* 58; *MartG* 142; *MartD* 202.

Earalt. *See* Garailt.

Earc. This name, which had several possible meanings, including 'heaven, speckled, spotted or red-eared cow, bee', was used variously of men and women. Its best-known bearer was Earc of Slane.

Earc, bishop. *See* Libhréan son of Dall.

Earc daughter of Dáire. *See* Dairearca.

Earc of Alltraighe, later mainly the barony of Iraghticonnor, north Kerry.[1] Although ignored by the genealogists, this son of Oghamhain figured prominently in the traditions surrounding the birth of Bréanainn of Clonfert. Described as *anmchara*, 'soul-friend', of Fionnlugh, father of Bréanainn, Earc is said to have explained for Fionnlugh a vision granted to his wife, which showed her bosom full of gold and her breasts shining like snow, as signs of a glorious birth to be.[2] The privileges of baptizing Bréanainn and providing him with a basic education were also granted to Earc who is given the rank of bishop.

Two possibilities have been raised as to the location of Earc's church in north Kerry; one involves an otherwise unattested place called 'Termon-Eirc' in the townland of Lerrig, parish of Kilmoyly, near Ardfert; the other, an ecclesiastical site named 'Ceall Mhic an Deagha' in the townland of Glenderry, parish of Ballyheige.[3] Adjoining Kilmoyly, in the parish of Ardfert, and townland of Tubrid More, is the so-called Wethers' Well (Tobar na Molt), with which Earc was also connected.[4] At Glenderry, however, as already recorded in the eighteenth century by Charles Smith in his history of Kerry, there was a small chapel dedicated to 'Mac Ida', and an image of the saint, kept by a family named Corridon which claimed to have brought its tutelary saint there from Clare.[5] Part of a penance imposed on an Armagh cleric in 1541 was to visit a number of sites in Munster, including that associated with 'McEdeaga'.[6]

In the same parish of Ballyheige, in the townland of Glandahalin East, was a church named after its patron Daithle (Dahalin) who was regarded as Mac an Deagha's sister.[7] Since it derives from Daigh, the form Mac an Deagha provides a possible link to Earc of Slane, whose father was similarly named. The Slane saint is said to have belonged to the same group of descendants of Fearghas son of Róch as Bréanainn of Birr, namesake and probable double of the patron of Clonfert.[8] Besides tending to Bréanainn at birth, Bishop Earc is said to have provided the last rites to another noted Kerryman, Fiontan son of Bóchra, descendant of Noah, who was connected with a place in north Kerry, variously called Dún Tulcha and Tulach.[9]

1 *HDGP* i, 54–5. 2 *CGSH* §716.3.4; *VSHH* 324–5 §1; *VSHP* i, 98 §1; *BNÉ* i, 44–5 §3; *LisL* 3334–40. 3 *Brendaniana* 36–40. 4 *JRSAI* 88, 153. 5 *NCHK* 211; *ACoK* 46. 6 *JCLAS* 6, 152. 7 *ACoK* 46–7; *JKAHS* 17, 124. 8 *GRSH* 111. 9 *Ériu* 4, 160 §36.

Earc of Donaghmore (Domhnach Mór), barony of North Salt, Co. Kildare. Earc's pedigree attaches him through his father Feargna to the Osraighe of the territory approximately equivalent to that of the later diocese of Ossory.[1] His church, also known as Donaghmore of St Brighid, appears to have been affiliated to Kildare.[2] Since Earc's feastday fell on 27 October, he was probably ultimately the same as Earc of Slane whose feast was just six days later, on 2 November.[3]

1 *CGSH* §281; *GRSH* 93. 2 *CGSH* §670.38. 3 *MartT* 85; *MartO*[2] 219, 228; *MartG* 204; *MartD* 286.

Earc of Slane (Sláine), barony of Upper Slane, Co. Meath. According to his earliest biographers, Patrick, having lit the paschal fire on the hill of Slane, was summoned to Tara, where only one person, Earc (alias Earc Sláine) son of Daigh, rose before him to show respect.[1] Earc went on to become Patrick's *breitheamh*, 'judge', and his church at Slane reputedly became so important that Patrick's successor, after first receiving homage, was obliged to show respect to Earc's successor by raising his knee.[2] To show lack of respect to Earc, whose practice it was to spend the day immersed in the waters of the Boyne, was fraught with risk, as is recounted in the story entitled *Fleadh Dhúin na nGéadh*, 'feast of the fort of geese', which serves as a prelude to the battle of Moira (Magh Rath).[3] The theft of eggs laid by Earc's geese led to a curse on a feast arranged by the king of Tara that even the hastily summoned 'twelve Irish apostles', led by Finnian of Movilla, could not undo.[4]

Earc's feast of 2 November points to his having originated as a deity linked to the great feast of *Samhain*, 'November-eve', in the possible guise of Ealcmhar, lord of Brugh na Bóinne, now Newgrange in the parish of Monknewtown, adjoining Slane. There were several other commemorations of saints bearing the same or a related name about this time of the year.[5] These included his namesakes, Earc of Donaghmore (27 October), Earc of Míleac (24 October) and, in female guise, Earcnad (Latin Archanata / Ergnata) of Dál nAraidhe, who was associated with the Antrim parishes of Doagh Grange (29 October) and Duneane (8 January).[6] As *Samhain* was otherwise known as a pagan Easter, Earc's presence at various feasts of Tara would therefore have been most appropriate.[7] The connection with geese may be linked to Earc's pairing with Martin of Tours in the list of the Irish and external saints similar in manners.[8]

The genealogists traced the saint to a group of the descendants of Fearghas son of Róch to which Bréanainn of Birr is said also to have belonged.[9] This would suggest that he and his namesake, Earc of Alltraighe, mentor of Bréanainn of Clonfert, may also have been originally identical. According to the entry on his feastday of 2 November, Earc was also associated with the church of Lullymore (Loilgheach) in the barony of East Offaly.[10] The proximity of the latter church to Kildare would explain why Brighid's biographer saw fit to bring her together with Earc.[11] One strand of the descent of Eoghan of Ardstraw names Earc as his father and, according to an early text, he was Ireland's fourth *athlaoch*, 'former layman'.[12] According to the annals, the saint died in 513, during the reign of Muircheartach son of Muireadhach who is credited with having adopted his alternate paternal name, viz. Earc, because he was loved by the saint.[13] According to Tíreachán, Earc was buried in Carnes (Cearna), in the Meath parish of Duleek.[14] His relics, presumably enshrined, were taken on tour in 776, and his crozier was among valuables destroyed by 'foreigners' at Slane in 950.[15]

1 *PTBA* 88 (I 17.3), 132 §§12–13; *DIB* iii, 635. **2** *BP* 470–5, 3125; *VT* 44, 264; *MartT* 124. **3** *FDG* 138–65. **4** Ibid. 233–45. **5** *MartO*² 232; *MartG* 210; *MartD* 292. **6** *CPL* 20, §606; *MartT* 6; *MartO*² 34, 42; *MartG* 12; *MartD* 10; *ASH* 41–2; PNNI iv, 79. **7** *IT* iii, 198.24. **8** *CGSH* §712.16. **9** *CGSH* §130; *GRSH* 111; *Lgen*. 502.8.14; *ZCP* 8, 331–2; cf. *TLSP* 99. **10** *MartG* 210; *MartD* 292; *JCKAS* 9, 426–8. **11** *TMIH* 70. **12** *CGSH* §§130, 251; *MartO*¹ 132; *Anecd*. iii, 60. **13** *AU s.a.*; *LUM* 154r54; *LG* v, 362 §617. **14** *PTBA* 130 §8.1. **15** *AU s.a.*

Earc Nasca of Tullylish. *See* Cearc of Aughlish.

Earcnad of Dál nAraidhe. *See* Earc of Slane.

Earnain. No fewer than eleven female saints of this name, also spelt Earnan, are included in the list of homonymous saints, but none of them can be otherwise identified.[1] This may be due to confusion caused by the similarity of the name to its masculine counterparts, Earnán and Eirnín.

1 *CGSH* §708.96–106.

Earnán. Although this name and its variant Eirnín were taken to derive from *iarann*, 'iron' – already by the time of Adhamhnán who latinized it as *ferreolus* – the first syllable does not seem to have been long.[1] It rimes on at least two occasions with *deagh-*.[2] As most bearers of the name stood in some form of relationship to Colum Cille, these may represent localizations of an originally single cult.

1 *VC*² 532. 2 *MartG* 14; 158.

Earnán of Cloonrallagh (which may now represent an earlier Cluain (or Druim) Reilgeach), parish of Templemichael, barony and county of Longford, or of Clonrelick, parish of Ballyloughloe, barony of Clonlonan, Co. Westmeath. The Uí Chaocháin descendants of Fearghas Caochán, brother of Niall Naoighiallach, were associated with the Meath church of Kilskeer (Ceall Scíre), near Kells.[1] As Earnán son of Eoghan (or Eacha) belonged to this family, he is often grouped together with another of Fearghas' few saintly descendants, Scíre, eponym and patron of Kilskeer.[2] Little else is known of the saint, whose name was also written Eirnín and Eirne, but his feast fell on 5/6 August.[3]

1 *CGH* 139b47. 2 *CGSH* 37; *GRSH* 65. 3 *MartT* 60, *MartG* 150; *MartD* 212.

Earnán of Drumhome (Druim Thuama), barony of Tirhugh, Co. Donegal. Earnán's father (Eoghan) is said to have been Colum Cille's younger brother 'Iogen' who reputedly accompanied his sibling to Iona.[1] John Colgan took Earnán to be identical with Eirnín of Corkaree ('Corca Fhir Raoidhe') who is said by Adhamhnán to have seen the heavens lit up above Drumhome, of which he was patron, on the night of Colum Cille's death.[2] The saint was remembered on 1 January, not only in Donegal, but also at Kildellig in the Laois parish of Aghaboe, whose patron Cainneach was probably originally identical with Colum Cille.[3]

1 *GRSH* 38; *MartD* 4; *VC*² 546. 2 *ASH* 7–9; *VC*² 532–6; OSL DL 240. 3 *MartT* 3; *MartG* 6; *MartD* 4; *HADO* ii, 64; *FG* 20–35.

Earnán of Enniskeen. *See* Earnán of Inis Caoin.

Earnán of Inis Caoin. A well-known episode of the *Navigatio Brendani*, 'voyage of Bréanainn', attributes to a certain Bairrfhionn (probably of Drumcullen) a previous journey to the Land of Promise. When relating this to Bréanainn, Bairrfhionn spoke of his *frater*, 'brother/kinsman' – sometimes styled *mac*, 'son' – named Tearnóg (Mearnóg), a hypocoristic form of Earnán, who had abandoned him in order to dwell on an island called Inis Caoin (*insula deliciosa*), near Slieve League (*mons lapidum/Sliabh Liag*) in the county of Donegal, later the starting point of the voyage undertaken by Bairrfhionn and his kinsman.[1] He was probably the same saint as Dothearnóg – later Rabharnóg – who, according to the Life of Náile, was forced to relinquish his church at Kinawley (Ceall Náile) in Fermanagh in favour of the subject of the text, whom he had offended.[2] The cult was replicated at the Meath church and parish of Enniskeen (Inis Caoin), albeit without any surviving reference to Bairrfhionn or Bréanainn. Here, a well in the vicinity of the church marked his memory and a pattern was held on the eve of 13 July, the day on which, according to the martyrologies, Earnán of Inis Caoin was commemorated.[3] Given that Drumhome adjoins Kilbarron, which took its name from Bairrfhionn, the Earnán associated with the former church may be identical with the patron of Inis Caoin.

1 *NSBA* 4 §1; *VSHP* i, 104–5 §13; *BNÉ* i, 48–9 §§28–9; *Celtica* 11, 16–17. 2 *MHH* 105–9 §16–28; OSL FH 84. 3 *RM* 2.3, 35; ibid. 5.3, 7; *MartG* 136; *MartD* 194; *DK* 155.

Earnán of Tory Island (Torach), parish of Tullaghobegly, barony of Kilmacrenan, Co. Donegal. Although in a part of Donegal formerly known as Ceinéal Lughdhach after a branch of the Ceinéal Conaill, Tory's early associations may have been with Ceinéal Eoghain whose eponymous ancestor gave name to both Inishowen (Inis Eoghain) and Tyrone (Tír Eoghain).[1] The two saints associated with the island, Earnán (also Eirnín/Mearnóg) son of Colmán and Domhongóg, were assigned by the genealogists to the Ceinéal Eoghain, with the former belonging to the Ceinéal Maoin branch located in the Donegal barony of Raphoe, and later also in Tyrone.[2] By the late twelfth century, Earnán had come to be viewed as a local Donegal saint, to judge by Colum Cille's first vernacular biography. This attributes the founding of the church on Tory to Colum, whence the description of the island as *insula Columbina*, before leaving in it Earnán, a 'venerable man' of his people.[3] The Iona saint's later vernacular biography provides a much more elaborate, folklore-based, description of the church's foundation, adorning it with accounts of saintly contests and deceptions from all of which Colum Cille emerged triumphant.[4] One episode relates to the rejection by a woman from India of the grave occupied by her brothers, and a similar fastidiousness concerning the company one should keep in Tory's burial place is attested in the tenth-century Life of Adhamhnán, Colum's biographer and successor.[5] A poem attributed to Colum Cille on the attractions of the island credits Pope Gregory with some interventions, but neglects to mention Earnán.[6]

Earnán's feast fell on 17 August, according to the Martyrology of Donegal.[7] However, other martyrologies, while naming the saint on this day, do not identify his church.[8] As the following day was the feast of his namesake, Eirnín of Cluain Deochra, who, as a boy, was brought together with Colum Cille at Clonmacnoise, and went on to become famous 'among all the churches of Ireland', the saints may have been originally identical.[9] The 'Arnain' included among the apostles of Ireland by Molaise's vernacular biographer was possibly the patron of Tory.[10]

1 *CCDK* 89. 2 *CGSH* §§16, 40; *GRSH* 46; *Lgen*. 701.3. 3 *IKD* 236 §49; *LisL* 997–9; *HCIC* 9. 4 *BCC* 102–4 §111. 5 *BAd*. 54 §11, 76. 6 *ZCP* 10, 341–2. 7 *MartD* 222 (cf. *GRSH* 46). 8 *MartT* 64; *MartG* 158. 9 *VC*² 216–18. 10 *SG* i, 24, 35.

Earnán Miodhluachra. *See* Mearnóg of Kilmarnock.

Edan. *See* Aodh of Rahugh; Maodhóg of Ferns.

Eiche of Kilglass (Ceall Ghlaise), barony of Ardagh, Co. Longford. Among her many other saintly children, Patrick's sister Dairearca is reputed to have given birth to two virgins – Eiche and Lallóg – who together occupied, according to the tract on the mothers of the saints, the church of Kildalloge (Ceall Lallóg) in the Roscommon parish of Kiltrustan.[1] The author of the Tripartite Life of Patrick took a different view, placing Lallóg only in the church named after her at

Kildalloge and Eiche in the church of Kilglass, near Ardagh, which was also associated with her brother Meal (Mel).[2] Although all memory of Lallóg appears to have faded at Kildalloge, a pattern in honour of Eiche was held annually on 8 September at Kilglass, perhaps due to rival devotion to the Virgin Mary whose nativity was celebrated on this day.[3] The feastday assigned by the martyrologists to Eiche fell on 5/6 August.[4]

1 *CGSH* §722.16; *Dinn.* 5, 116. **2** *BP* 899–900; *VT* 82. **3** *TDI* ii, 98. **4** *MartT* 60; *MartG* 150; *MartD* 210.

Éidchéan of Clonfad (Cluain Fada Baodáin), parish of Killucan, barony of Farbill, Co. Westmeath, and of Teach Dochua Mhic Neamhain, now Ticknevin, parish of Kilpatrick, barony of Carbury, Co. Kildare. Although his main church was located at some distance from the county of Wicklow, Éidchéan son of Maine Éigeas, bishop and poet, was nevertheless regarded as one of the saints of Dál Meisin Corb whose chief representative was Caoimhghin of Glendalough.[1] A variant tradition assigns the saint to the Osraighe who gave name to Ossory.[2] When T. O'Connor visited Éidchéan's church in 1837, he was told that six bishops were buried there and a seventh nearby, and this accords with an entry in an early litany which speaks of seven holy bishops in Clonfad.[3] Another episcopal connection is provided by the statement that Colum Cille – the name of whose successor, Baoithín, may be present under the guise of Baodán in the full Irish name of Clonfad – came to Éidchéan to receive bishop's orders only to be ordained priest by mistake.[4] Though Colum then declared himself content with his priestly status, he proclaimed that no one else would ever receive orders in Clonfad. This is belied by another tradition which speaks of a visit to Clonfad by the three Colmáin, all probably ultimately identical with Colum Cille, whose future status – bishop, priest and deacon – was foretold by Éidchéan on the basis of the vat chosen by each for his bath.[5] One of the three, Colmán of Lynn, is said to have been prophesied, baptized, and educated by Éidchéan.[6]

That Clonfad was a church of substance is shown by the fact that several of its abbots are listed in the annals. According to a poem of prophecies, to lay siege to Éidchéan's church would bring death to any king.[7] The other foundation associated with the saint, at Ticknevin, which figures in a list of saints with largely Brigidine connections, places Éidchéan close to Brighid's church of Kildare.[8] His mother, Brígh daughter of Cobhthach, provided him with two notable siblings, Bishop Aodhán of Glendalough, and Aodh son of Ainmhire, high-king of Ireland.[9] To judge by the presence in its precincts of a cross named after Éidchéan, Clonmacnoise may also have gained influence over the saint's church at Clonfad.[10] The high regard in which the saint and his church were held is also shown by the vernacular Life of Bearach of Termonbarry, which gives Éidchéan the honour of conferring orders on its subject.[11] The saint was possibly identical with the 'Mac an Éigis' regarded as similar in manners to Ambrosius of Milan.[12] Éidchéan is said to have died in 578, or alternatively in 584, and his feast was celebrated on 11 February.[13]

1 *CGSH* §§181.7, 558; *GRSH* 88; *Lgen.* 725.3. **2** *CGSH* §641. **3** *PNW* 44–5; *IrL* 74. **4** *MartO*[2] 72; *BCC* 62–4 §76. **5** *BCML* 30–2 §33. **6** Ibid. 6 §7, 10 §10, 18 §18. **7** *Ériu* 18, 58 §2. **8** *CGSH* §663.3. **9** Ibid.

§722.64. **10** *AFM s.a.* 1070 (ii, 898–90). **11** *BNÉ* i, 31 §42. **12** *CGSH* §712.20. **13** *AU s.a.*; *MartT* 16; *MartO*² 60; *MartG* 34; *MartD* 44.

Eidin. *See* Éadaoin.

Éigneach of Desertegny (Díseart Éignigh), barony of Inishowen West, Co. Donegal. Bearing a name that is anglicized as Egney or Aigne (Latin Egnaghus), and corruptly rendered 'Lighne' of the order of canons regular in a list of patrons of the diocese of Derry, this saint is otherwise little known.[1] A local well, located at the Gap of Mamore and known as *Tobar a' Mhaidhm Móir*, commemorates the saint, who is thought to have meditated there.[2] The saint may also have been patron of the Wexford church of Killegney.[3]

1 *DYHS* 194; *UJA* (2nd ser.) 1, 177; *Celtica* 1, 83; *AnH* 12, 84. **2** *Béaloideas* 6, 157; *BOI* 98; *HWI* 65. **3** *TNW* 1112–13.

Éigsín son of Dubhthach. *See* Comhghall son of Dubhthach.

Eiltín of Clonduff, parish of Balraheen, barony of Ikeathy and Oughterany, Co. Kildare, which may now represent an earlier Cluain Dabhcha. A miscellaneous set of entries, preserved as an addendum to the corpus of saints' pedigrees, relates to churches spread across the counties of Kildare, Offaly and Westmeath, which seem to have been associated with the cult of Brighid.[1] Cluain Dabhcha, the church assigned to Eiltín, was shared by a companion named Ultán, and Clonduff now adjoins the parish of Taghadoe (Teach Tua), the name of whose patron served as a hypocoristic or pet form of Ultán.[2]

1 *CGSH* §663.1–13; *Lgen.* 751.20. **2** *MartT* 88.

Eiltín of Kinsale (Ceann Sáile) in the barony of the same name, Co. Cork. The imposing church raised in Kinsale in honour of Eiltín (alias Meilteóg, and now better known as Multose) has been described as a 'spacious and venerable cruciform structure'.[1] The saint's profile in the hagiographical literature, though modest enough, is anything but straightforward. One possible genealogy, which accords him two brothers, Colum (Colmán) and Mochonna, attaches him through his father Flannán to the Corca Laoighdhe of the area now approximately corresponding to the Cork diocese of Ross.[2] Despite the fact that both he and his brother Colum are said to have fathered children, seventeenth-century sources nonetheless regarded this Eiltín as patron of the church of Kinsale.[3] On the other hand, if intended by the author of the vernacular Life of Fionnbharr who – perhaps in error for Coibhdheanach, his grandfather according to the Corca Laoighdhe genealogy – named his father as Cobhthach, Eiltín son of Flannán may have been venerated at the church of Ceall na hInse, a site on Inchydoney Island, from where he is alleged to have attended the famous school of Cork.[4] An alternative descent for the Kinsale saint is provided by an entry on Maghna (sister of David of St David's in Wales) in the tract on the mothers of the saints, which states that Meilteóg's father was Eise (or Eisean) of the Artraighe of Cliú, a territory approximately corresponding to the diocese of Emly.[5] This entry also provides the saint with a brother named Moghoba, whence Kilgobbin in the parish of Ballinadee (Baile na Daibhche), near Kinsale. Ballinadee may in fact have had Eiltín as its main patron, if the corrupt '*Sanct. Eldridae de Dwaghe*' in a 1628 copy of a much earlier document represents his name.[6] Three churches named Killelton after the saint are located in south Munster, two in the Kerry parishes of Kilgobban and Aghavallen, and one in the Waterford parish of Stradbally. Eiltín's feast at Kinsale fell on 11 December, but he may also have been commemorated at the Inchydoney church, this time called Ceall Inse, on 1 November.[7] According to some writers, by the mid-eighteenth century the saint's devotees had come to regard him as a female named Multosia.[8]

1 *TDI* ii, 233; cf. *SHK* 10–12. **2** *CGSH* §323; *GRSH* 127; *Lgen*. 744.4; *CGH* 155b13; GCL 16; OCBG §2067. **3** GCL 16; *GRSH* 127; *MartD* 332. **4** *BBa*. 76 §34, 261–2; *HDGP* iv, 35. **5** *CGSH* §722.94. **6** *NCHC* i, 71. **7** *MartO*[2] 251; *MartG* 208, 236; *MartD* 290, 332. **8** *NCHC* i, 219; cf. *TDI* ii, 233.

EILTÍN of Seanchua. The list of those subject to Brighid of Kildare locates three saints in Seanchua, Eiltín grandson of Maolán, Lóichín son of Iollann, and Neas.[1] Of these, only Eiltín (alias Ailtín) appears to be otherwise known, by virtue of his feast which fell on 11 January.[2] Both Shancough in the Sligo barony of Tirerrill and the Kildare site of Kilshanchoe, parish of Dunfierth, barony of Carbury, not far from Kilbride in the adjoining parish of Cloncurry, have been suggested as possible locations of Seanchua.[3] According to Dubhaltach Mac Fhir Bhisigh, there was also a church named 'Cill Ailltin' after the saint at Inishcrone in the Sligo parish of Kilglass.[4]

1 *CGSH* §670.43. **2** *MartT* 7; *MartG* 14; *MartD* 12. **3** *MartT* 228; *CGSH* p. 332. **4** DQE 96.

EILTÍN son of Cobhthach. *See* Eiltín of Kinsale.

ÉIMHÍN of Donaghmore (Domhnach Mór Sanct Brighde), barony of North Salt, Co. Kildare. This son of Ailtín is known only from the list of those said to have been subject to Brighid of Kildare which provides him with a companion saint named Crón daughter of Aodh.[1] The affiliation of his church to Kildare is reflected in its name's reference to Brighid. Interestingly, the like-named Éimhín of Monasterevin also figures in an episode involving a person named Crón who is, however, described as a sister of Molua of Kyle.[2]

1 *CGSH* §670.38; *Lgen*. 753.9. **2** *VSHH* 141 §45.

ÉIMHEARÁN of Fenagh and Drumreilly, Co. Leitrim. Travelling in Co. Leitrim in 1836, John O'Donovan wrote that holy wells in the parishes of Fenagh and Drumreilly were dedicated to Éimhearán (anglicized Everaun and Everan), whom he thought to be the 'Mabhrán' left by Patrick at Domhnach Maighe Sléacht, now possibly a site at Kilnavert in the parish of Templeport, barony of Tullyhaw, Co. Cavan, which adjoins Drumreilly.[1] There is no record of this saint's feastday, but seven bishops of Drumreilly were remembered on 15 January.[2]

1 *DKil* 403; OSL CN/LM 206; *BP* 1019–25; *VT* 92; *FL* 604–5. **2** *MartT* 8; *MartG* 16; *MartD* 16.

ÉIMHÍN of Leatha. *See* Éimhín of Monasterevin.

ÉIMHÍN of Monasterevin, alias Rosglas (Ros Glas/Glaise), barony of West Offaly, Co. Kildare. There is a good deal of confusion in the traditions surrounding this saint. One states that he and his brothers – Cormac, Cúlán, Buadhán, Diarmuid – were sons of Eoghan son of Murchadh of the Eoghanachta of Munster, which would tie in with the name Ros Glaise na Muimhneach, 'of the Munstermen', sometimes attached to his church.[1] According to this tradition, the celebrated battle of Ballaghmoon (Bealach Mughna) in Kildare, which cost the king of Munster, Cormac son of Cuileannán, his life, was fought in defence of the saint's church, and a relic of his, the *Bearnán Éimhín*, 'gapped [bell] of Éimhín', was used to swear upon by the Munstermen. A second tradition which names his father as Iamhán and his mother as Iamhnad, while preserving the link with Munster, and more particularly with the Dál gCais of Thomond, provides him with an obscure tribal affiliation to a family named Uí Sheanaigh of the Corca Shoilginn of Cruach, now the townland and parish of Croagh in the Limerick barony of Connello Lower.[2] As both parental names, like that of Éimhín himself, derive from the same root – possibly *éimh*, 'prompt, ready' – the saint may represent an ancestral cult.[3] The account given of a visit of Molua, patron of Killaloe, to Éimhín, 'a man ready with miracles and born of the same nation', is probably to be understood against the saint's alleged Dál gCais background.[4]

The location of Éimhín's church in Leinster also led to more local traditions, not least the one associated with his *cáin*, 'Law', which has been interpreted as an attempt to set out a charter for Monasterevin, and which may have contributed to the saint's fame as an authority on monastic behaviour.[5] Faced by an imminent plague, the king of Leinster, Bran of the Uí Fhaoláin, and forty of his nobles are said to have sought counsel from Éimhín who decided that, God willing, he and fifty of his monks should die in exchange for the lives of an equal number of lay people. This duly occurred, but not before the saint had extracted from the king and his chieftains pledges on behalf of Monasterevin and its freedoms. According to one account, the manner of his death was tantamount to martyrdom.[5a]

A passage in the Life of Abán of Adamstown in Wexford asserts that Éimhín was buried in New Ross (Ros Mic Threóin), where there was a church named St Evin's.[6] Another Leinster tradition places a saint named Éimhín – together with Mac Táil of Kilcullen and Tighearnach of Clones – among the saints of the Uí Bhairrche, locating him in a place called Leatha.[7] The latter name is often used of Latium on the Continent, but here it may reflect *Latiniacum*, now Lagny near Paris, with which, according to Fursa's Life, a certain 'Eminianus' was also associated.[8] Two sobriquets are attested for Éimhín, one of which, *bán*, 'white', may also be taken to mean 'holy' or 'blessed', the other *án*, 'noble', though the association with *Áine* in a seventeenth-century poem may refer to Knockainy in the Limerick barony of Smallcounty.[9] A late tradition, apparently initiated by Jocelyn of Furness, states that Éimhín wrote a Life of Patrick.[10] The saint's feastday fell on 22 December, but a man named Éimhín was also commemorated on 7 January and 18 December.[11] The saint's staff was left to the 'Foreigners' after the battle of Downpatrick in 1178.[12]

1 *IrT* iii, 1–2 §3; *GRSH* 116–17. **2** *CGSH* §§697.2.4, 722.34; *MartT* 126; *SS* 261; *Ériu* 40, 93–7; cf. *Celtica* 17, 67 §24; *HDGP* vi, 120. **3** *Ériu* 37, 187–8; *GPN* 86. **4** *VSHP* ii, 219–20 §39. **5** *Anecd.* i, 40–5; *Ériu* 4, 39–46; *Celtica* 17, 63–9; ibid. 18, 35–52; ibid. 21, 588–92; *AB* 78, 390–95. **5a** *MartO* 260; *RC* 45, 166.

6 *VSHH* 267; *VSHP* i, 21 §28; *COD* i, 121, 349, 352; *CJRI* (1295–1303), 219; *PSICCSO* 163–4. 7 *CGSH* §387; *CGH* 121a39–42 8 *VSHH* 50 §30, 52 §6; *SS* 254, 261. 9 *VSHH* 141 §45; *MartT* 126; *FSPP* 80. 10 *TT* 106 (179), 217. 11 *MartT* 88; *MartO*² 253; *MartG* 214; *MartD* 344. 12 *MartD* xxxi; *MIA s.a.*

Eirnín. *See* also Earnán; Mearnóg; Tearnóg.

Eirnín of Cluain Deochra, sometimes thought to be either Cloondara or Ballynakill in the parish of Killashee, barony and county of Longford, but perhaps more likely to be the obsolete 'Clooneoghra' in the Longford barony of Moydow, now perhaps represented by Cloonagh in the parish of Kilglass.[1] Once, according to Adhamhnán, when Colum Cille was establishing the monastery of Durrow, he made a visit to Clonmacnoise, where he was made welcome by the community.[2] While there, a boy scorned by the community attempted to approach Colum from behind, only to be noticed by the saint who blessed him and prophesied that he would be a man of great eminence. This was Eirnín son of Craisín, also known as Eirnéan (Latin Erneneus) and Mearnóg, who went on to relate these events to Adhamhnán's predecessors, Séighín and Fáilbhe.[3] According to the Middle-Irish Life of Colum, Eirnín later became the patron of Cluain Deochra.[4] The notice of his feast, which fell on 18 August, attaches the saint, however, to both Rathnew (Ráith Naoi) in the county of Wicklow and Kildreenagh (Ceall Draighneach) in the Carlow parish of Dunleckny.[5] At Cluain Deochra, he is said to have been visited by Féichín of Fore, who went on to free a mill near the guesthouse from a troublesome rattle.[6] He appears also to have given name, under the guise of Mearnóg, to Portmarnock in Dublin, where his well was the scene of a pattern about 18 August.[7] His relics were later translated from Portmarnock to St Mary's Abbey in Dublin, where a chapel was erected in his memory.[8] Nearer to Clonmacnoise, he may also have given name to St Erneen's well in the East Galway parish of Leitrim.[9] Eirnín died, according to the annals, in 635.[10]

1 *ILL* 261; *JACAS* 2.8, 16–20; *ibid.* 2.9, 27–30. 2 *VC*² 214–18. 3 *CGSH* §707.766. 4 *IKD* 235 §47. 5 *MartT* 64; *MartO*² 177; *MartG* 158; *MartD* 222; *HDGP* iii, 164. 6 *ASH* 138. 7 *Rep. Nov.* 2, 375. 8 *CSMA* ii, xxiii–xxiv; *AH* 8, 22. 9 *OSL GY* ii, 9. 10 *AU s.a.*

Eirnín of Corkaree. *See* Earnán of Drumhome.

Eirnín of Cranfield. *See* Tearnóg of Cranfield.

Eise, Patrick's artisan. Those in orders with Patrick included three *cearda*, 'artisans', Eise (Easa), Bíthe and Tasach.[1] Though Bíthe and Tasach are known from other sources, Eise is otherwise allowed a cameo appearance only in the Patrician literature, together with his fellow artisans, as a maker of altar vessels.[2] He may be the same as Eise (Heise) of the unidentified church of Aireadh Fada who was commemorated on 24 February.[3]

1 *CGSH* §671.12; *BP* 3141; *VT* 266. 2 *BP* 2961–2; *VT* 250. 3 *MartG* 42; *MartD* 56.

Eistean daughter of Moiche. *See* Fáilbhe of Díseart Cinn Chláir; Muicín of Mayne.

Eithearn of Donaghmore, barony of Lower Navan, Co. Meath, which may now represent an earlier Domhnach Mór Mhic Laithbhe. Little is known of Bishop Eithearn son of Laithbhe who is said to have belonged to the Snobhraighe, an obscure branch of the Mughdhoirn of Ulster.[1] Among the churches founded by Patrick in Magh Breagh in Meath was a great *Domhnach* 'for the son of Laithbhe' which may have been Donaghmore.[2] Variously known as Mac Laithbhe and Eithearn, the saint was remembered on 20 May and again, within the octave of this feast, on 27 May.[3]

1 *CGSH* §133; *Lgen.* 732.12; *CGH* 142b42. 2 *PTBA* 130 §8.1. 3 *MartT* 44, 46; *MartG* 100, 104; *MartD* 134, 138.

Eithne is a popular name of females in the Irish tradition, with frequent attestations in the literature relating to both pre-Christian and Christian Ireland. It also figures prominently in hagiography, with nine of the name included in the list of homonymous saints, together with five others said to have been mothers of saints, including Eithne daughter of Díoma, mother of Colum Cille.[1] Of the homonymous saints named Eithne, the majority are otherwise unrecorded.

1 *CGSH* §§708.107–15; 722.23.46.91.98.103.

Eithne daughter of Baoth (Baoide). Together with her sister Soidhealbh, Eithne is given the distinction of having nursed Christ who, according to a note added to the entry on their feast of 29 March in the early martyrologies, came to the two saints in the form of an infant, preached to them and baptized them.[1] The genealogists attached the saints to the Uí Fhailghe who gave name to the Kildare baronies of Offaly, but whose territory also extended into neighbouring parts of the counties of Offaly and Laois.[2] Their church, named Teach Inghean mBaoide, is said to have been located either near Swords in Dublin (which has been taken as a pointer to Donabate) or in Uí Fhailghe.[3] As it is mentioned in connection with Clann Cholgan, whose lands were co-extensive with the barony of Lower Philipstown in the eastern part of Offaly, the latter location is the more likely of the two.[4] An early litany-style prayer possibly invokes Eithne's sister Soidhealbh.[5]

1 *MartT* 28; *MartO*[2] 102. 2 *CGSH* §257. 3 *MartG* 64; *MartO*[2] 102; *MartD* 88; *AH* 8; *AH* 8, 19. 4 *CGH* 123e42. 5 *MartT* 108; *IrL* 92.

Eithne daughter of Conchradh. *See* Athchaoin of Colp.

Eithne daughter of Cormac. *See* Darchaorthainn of Tullowphelim.

Eithne daughter of Díoma. *See* Colum Cille.

Eithne daughter of Feidhlimidh. *See* Comhghán of Killeshin.

Eithne daughter of Ian. *See* Aodh of Killeenmore.

Eithne daughter of Laoghaire. *See* Feidhealm Ruadh daughter of Laoghaire.

Eithne daughter of Maine. *See* Cuman of Aireadh Bóinne.

Eithne daughter of Oilill. *See* Mughain of Lyons.

Eithne daughter of Sárán. *See* Criodán Ceartrannach; Rónán of Dromiskin.

Eithne mother of Aodh. *See* Aodh of Rahugh.

Eithne of Ceall Eithne, at Newgrange, parish of Monknewtown, barony of Upper Slane, Co. Meath. The tale known as *Altram Tighe Dá Mheadhar*, 'fosterage of the house of two methers', is among many relating to Patrick's alleged dealings with the pre-Christian Otherworld.[1] It describes how Eithne of the Tuatha Dé Danann, having been left behind on the lawn in front of the *brugh*, 'mound', at Newgrange when her companions re-entered it, was discovered there by one of Patrick's clerics. Having converted to Christianity, she died and was buried nearby. The site named after her was then occupied by Ceasán who later moved to the church named after him at Cloncasson (Cluain Ceasáin) in the Offaly parish of Clonsast.[2] A *mairbhne*, 'elegy', attributed to her is sometimes also credited to Patrick.[3]

1 *Ériu* 11, 184–225; *ZCP* 13, 17; ibid. 18, 189–230; ibid. 43, 115–17. 2 *Ériu* 11, 203; *ZCP* 18, 226; *AgS* i, 41. 3 *Béaloideas* 4, 264–76.

Eithne of Kilrush. *See* Sineach of Kilrush.

Eithne of Temple-etney, barony of Iffa and Offa East, Co. Tipperary. Representatives of the Ordnance Survey were told in 1840 that Eithne was still remembered locally and that her pattern was formerly held 'with solemnity' on a day about 25 September.[1] This may be Eithne, daughter of a king of Munster, the unwilling prospective bride of a British king, supposedly resuscitated by Tighearnach of Clones.[2] Tighearnach, then on his way home from Tours, was accompanied by Ciarán of Tubbrid, a church located not far from Temple-etney.

1 OSL TY ii, 419. 2 *VSHH* 108–9 §§5–9; *VSHP* ii, 263–4 §§5–7.

Eliva. *See* Ailbhe of Shancough.

Elly. *See* Ailbhe of Emly.

Enda. *See* Éanna of Inishmore.

Eochaidh/Eocha. *See* Eachaidh/Eacha.

Eoghan. This derivative of *eo*, 'yew', combined with *gein*, 'birth', was borne not only by several saints, but also by some notable ancestral figures, including the eponym of Ceinéal Eoghain (still present in Tír Eoghain, alias Tyrone, and Inis Eoghain, alias Inishowen) and the ancestor who gave name to Eoghanachta, the tribal grouping that controlled the greater part of the southern province of Munster.

Eoghan, brother of Colum Cille. Appended to Adhamhnán's Life of Colum Cille is a list of his subject's close relatives which included his younger brother, 'Iogen' (later Eoghan), and three sisters, Cuman (Cuimne), Mionchloth and Sineach.[1] Much the same information is provided by an entry in the corpus of saints' genealogies but, whereas Colum's sisters are otherwise attested as mothers of saints, Eoghan is elsewhere recorded as the father of Earnán of Drumhome.[2] Moreover, when not tracing their descent to the family of St Virgilius (alias Feirghil of Aghaboe), the O'Friels (Uí Fhirghil) of Kilmacrenan considered themselves to be descended from Eoghan.[3]

1 *VC*[2] 546–8. 2 *CGSH* §§397, 661; *GRSH* 38; *MartD* 4. 3 *DPH* ii, 233; *Lgen.* 152.2.

Eoghan of Aharney. *See* Eoghan son of Neamhan.

Eoghan of Ardstraw (Ard Sratha), barony of Strabane Lower, Co. Tyrone. As the variant forms of his father's name (Bishop Earc and Coinneach) indicate, Eoghan was the subject of rival statements of descent. One assigned him, together with his father Earc, patron of Slane and reputedly Patrick's judge, to the descendants of Fearghas son of Róch.[1] The second (more usual) descent placed him within the *familia* of Caoimhghin of Glendalough, the saints of Dál Meisin Corb.[2] The latter descent carried most appeal for the author of Eoghan's short biography – improbably dated to the eighth or early ninth century – which is preserved in the Salamancan codex, now in the Bibliothèque Royale, Brussels.[3] Sometimes unfairly criticized for its lack of historical interest – all such texts are important and often unique witnesses to the times and concerns of their authors – Eoghan's Life, having designated Coinneach of Leinster as the saint's father, provided him with a mother named Muinneach of the group (Mughdhoirn) that gave name to the Monaghan barony of Cremorne (Críoch Mughdhorn).[4]

A connection is then immediately established between the saint and both Tighearnach of Clones and Cairbre of Coleraine in a manner possibly modelled on the account of how Patrick came to Ireland, except that here the journey is presented in reverse. Eoghan and Tighearnach are said to have been twice abducted as children, first by pirates operating out of Britain – with the result that they joined Cairbre as students of Ninnian (or Maucennus) at Whithorn (Rosnat/Candida Casa) – and then by similar brigands originating in Armorica, with all three eventually sent back to Whithorn.[5]

Returning to Ireland, Eoghan founded his first church in Leinster, at Kilnamanagh (Ceall na Manach) in the Dublin parish of Tallaght, where, as other sources allege, he had companions named Éanna and Lóchán, likewise of Dál Meisin Corb.[6] Ignoring these two, Eoghan's biographer states that his subject taught Caoimhghin, described as his brother's son, a statement for which there is no genealogical basis. Leaving the Dublin area for the north of Ireland, Eoghan founded Ardstraw, before again meeting Tighearnach, allegedly the founder, with Eoghan as assistant, of three northern churches, Clones (Cluain Eois), Galloon (Gabhail Liúin), on the boundary of the diocese of Clogher, and *Silva Humilis*, an enigmatic name possibly used to refer to a church in a wooded area called Killeter (*Coill Íochtair*) in the parish of Termonamongan, near Strabane.[7]

Much else in the Life awaits explanation, including the basis of the saint's relationship with Cairbre of Coleraine who, like Tighearnach, is again later brought into contact with Eoghan.[8] Cairbre's church lay within the diocese of Ardstraw, a little north of Maghera which, by the middle of the twelfth century, had superseded Ardstraw as diocesan centre.[9] Adjoining the parish of Coleraine was Killowen (Ceall Eoghain), named after the saint, which became the site of a Dominican friary in 1244.[10] Some episodes, such as those placed at Lackagh (Leacach) in the parish of Longfield West which adjoins Ardstraw, and at Creevy (Craoibheach) in the parish of Ardstraw, are local.[11] The saint is said to have cursed the descendants of Lughaidh son of Séadna (Secney) of the line of Conall son of Niall, ancestor of the powerful O'Donnells (Uí Dhomhnaill) of Donegal, leaving the lineage with the sole prospect of being royal counsellors of judges.[12] This may be connected with a thirteenth-century dispute with Raphoe concerning diocesan boundaries. Introducing this episode is a statement that Eoghan foretold the birth of Colum Cille, likewise descended from Conall son of Niall, and this is repeated in Columban hagiography.[13] Another name for Colum was Mochonna and, in the Iona saint's later vernacular Life, Eoghan's prophecy is attached to a bearer of this form of the name (also known as Macarius) who is treated as a separate person.[14]

Eoghan is otherwise featured, this time in the company of Colum Cille, in the Life of Cainneach of Kilkenny who had paternal connections with the Derry area.[15] The saint is probably also the bishop named Eoghan Fionn whose curse was invoked by the biographer of Náile on those neglectful of tribute due to the Kinawley saint.[16] Eoghan is now patron, under the anglicized guise of Eugene, of the diocese of Derry (formerly centred in Maghera and Ardstraw), and of various local churches, such as Bovevagh (shared with Adhamhnán), Cumber, Longfield and Cappagh.[17] Eoghan's feast fell on 23 August.[18]

1 *CGSH* §§130, 251; *MartO*[1] 132; cf. *TLSP* 99; *DIB* iii, 632–3. **2** *CGSH* §§181.2, 251; *GRSH* 88; *Lgen*. 733–4; *MartO*[1] 132. **3** *VSHH* 400–4; *ClRec*. 11, 319; *CHSC* 157–8. **4** *VSHH* 400 §1; *Kenney* 400. **5** *VSHH* 400–1 §§2–3. **6** *VSHH* 401 §3; *CGSH* §181.3; *CPPI* 174–9; *DIB* iii, 632. **7** *VSHH* 401 §5; *AH* 3, 7, 24; p.c. (Seosamh Ó Dufaigh); cf. *ClRec*. 11, 320n. **8** *VSHH* 402–3 §§11–12; cf. *ClRec*. 11, 308–9. **9** *MRHI* 62, 93. **10** Ibid. 223; *DOH* 104. **11** *VSHH* 402–3 §§10, 14. **12** Ibid. 403 §15. **13** *IKD* 224 §16; *BCC* 24 §40. **14** *BCC* 254, 258, §§250, 255–6. **15** *VSHH* 189 §27; *VSHP* i, 160–1 §22; *BCC* 216 §220. **16** *MHH* 121 §53. **17** *DYHS* 195–6; *AnH* 12, 83. **18** *MartT* 65; *MartO*[2] 178; *MartG* 162; *MartD* 226; *AnH* 12, 107, 109.

EOGHAN of Kilclief (Ceall Chleithe), barony of Lecale Lower, Co. Down. This man was one of seven sons of Tricheamh, two of whom, Díocha of Saul and Ros (Rus) of Downpatrick, are brought into contact with Patrick by the latter's biographers.[1] Through his pedigree, which assigns him to the local Dál bhFiatach, Eoghan is shown to have been related to Finnian of the church of Movilla in the parish of Newtown Ards, to which another brother, Oilill (Finnian's grandfather), was also attached.[2] Possibly, therefore, Eoghan, abbot of Movilla, remembered on 31 May, was identical with the saint.[3] Alternatively, he could be the same as Bishop Eoghan of Rashee (Ráth Sídhe), near Connor in Antrim, who died in 618, the same year as witnessed the death of Comhghall of Bangor.[4]

1 *CGSH* §136.2; *PTBA* 78; *BP* 373–427; *VT* 36–40. **2** *CGSH* §136.1.2; *GRSH* 83; *Lgen*. 723.10. **3** *MartT* 47n.; *MartG* 106; *MartD* 140. **4** ATig. *s.a.*; *EA* 68.

EOGHAN of Movilla. *See* Eoghan of Kilclief.

EOGHAN son of Neamhan. Eoghan's mother, Fuinche daughter of Dallbhrónach, is said to have remained barren for a long time after marrying Neamhan, until her niece, Brighid of Kildare, blessed her womb.[1] Her first-born was named Colmán, and she gave birth to three other children, Conall, Eoghan and Cairbre, all of whom were allegedly christened from water of the well in which Iobhar of Begerin had been baptized. The tract on the mothers of the saints, though excluding Colmán from the list of Fuinche's children, presents a similar picture.[2]

Given Fuinche's position as maternal aunt of Brighid, it may be that Eoghan was identical with the bishop of that name at Aharney (Achadh Toghartha) in the county of Kilkenny, now Barony church in the townland of Ballyconra.[3] An entry in the corpus of saints' pedigrees states that this Eoghan, together with four others of the Fothairt (to whom the patron of Kildare also belonged), including Brighid and Cuman daughter of Dallbhrónach (Fuinche's sister), were associated with Aharney.[4] As the parish church was dedicated to Brighid of Kildare, and as both Cuman and Fuinche were this saint's maternal aunts, there can be little doubt that Aharney was at some stage subject to Kildare.[5] A church named after Eoghan (Latin Eugenius) in what appears to be Clonkeen in the Laois parish of Abbeyleix may also have been dedicated to the saint.[6]

1 *CGSH* §728. 2 Ibid. §722.3. 3 *HDGP* i, 23. 4 *CGSH* §173. 5 *CGSH* §§2.1, 722.4; *HADO* ii, 308. 6 *CPL* 15, §691.

Eoghanán (Iogenán) son of Aonghas. One of seven 'beautiful' brothers said to have come to Ireland from Scotland, Eoghanán's pedigree attaches him to the tribal grouping of Dál Riada.[1] His church, like those of some of his brothers, may have lain in the Irish Midlands, among the Uí Fhailghe, possibly at Lackagh (Leacach/Ceann Leacaigh?) in the Kildare barony of West Offaly, in which case he would also have been possibly identical with the Pictish Eoghanán, a priest in Leinster mentioned by Adhamhnán in connection with a miraculously restored book of hymns in the hand of Colum Cille.[2] Another line of transmission identifies Ard Leacaigh in Magh Éine, now probably the old burial ground in the townland of Finner, in the Donegal parish of Inishmacsaint, as Eoghanán's church.[3] A separate tradition, found in *Agallamh na Seanórach*, 'colloquy of the ancients', locates the saint in Dál nAraidhe, approximately north Down and south Antrim, describing him as one of Patrick's presbyters.[4] Although many of his brothers are brought together on the same feastday (12 June), Eoghanán was remembered on 19 December.[5] The proximity of the June feast to that of Colum Cille recalls the fact that a poem on the brothers is attributed to the founder of Iona.[6]

1 *CGSH* §§209, 701.5; *GRSH* 80. 2 *CGSH* §701.2; *VC*[2] 342–4; *SBDeer* 383. 3 *MartT* 87; *MartD* 342; *HDGP* i, 89; *Éigse* 27, 40. 4 *SG* i, 158–61. 5 *MartT* 87; *MartG* 242; *MartD* 342. 6 *CGSH* §701; *Ériu* 32, 106–7.

Eóil (Eór) son of Dubhthach. *See* Comhghall son of Dubhthach.

Eothach son of Draighean. *See* Ainmhire of Kilroe.

Eolang of Aghabulloge (Achadh/Aithbhe Bolg), barony of East Muskerry, Co. Cork. The biographer of Fionnbharr, at work about 1200, set out to prove that the clergy of Cloyne and Ross – dioceses that had first been established at the synod of Kells-Mellifont in 1152 – in reality owed deference to the bishop of Cork.[1] He achieved his aim mainly by reference to the patron saints of churches within these two dioceses who were invariably introduced to the text in deferential roles. One of these was Eolang (also Eolangán) of Aghabulloge who was presented as Fionnbharr's father-confessor in succession to a saint named

Mac Cuirb.[2] By allowing Fionnbharr to visit Eolang, an action that normally betokened homage, the biographer set the scene for even greater deference on the part of Eolang who refused either to meet or to speak to the Cork saint until the latter returned to his own church. At their subsequent meeting, Eolang is said to have surrendered his church to Fionnbharr, and requested from him the privilege of burial within the same graveyard. The representative role given to Eolang in the Life stemmed from the importance of his own church within Múscraighe, later Muskerry, one of several petty kingdoms comprising the diocese of Cloyne.[3] Elsewhere, Eolang received special mention in a text which described him as one of three *seanóirí*, 'elders', of the Múscraighe group, and a poem of forty quatrains on God's anger is attributed to him in some manuscripts.[3] Little else is recorded of the saint, but that his feast fell on 5 September.[4] Scribal confusion, originating in the early martyrologies, led to the mistaken belief that the saint was attached to the Laois church of Aghaboe (Achadh Bó) rather than Aghabulloge (Achadh Bolg).[5] His name (anglicized as Olan) is still popular in the Aghabulloge area and local lore places him in the company of Laichtín, patron of the parish of Donaghmore and also a *seanóir* of the Múscraighe. A well dedicated to the saint lies near his church, and within the churchyard is an Ogham stone, known familiarly as 'St Olan's Cap', to which barren females, among others, were wont to have recourse.[6] There is another well in the parish of Mourneabbey. The Uí Chruimín (Cremins) were Eolang's coarbs at Aghabulloge.[7]

1 *MakS.* **2** *BBa.* 76–80 §§35–9. **3** *CKHS* 45–62; *CGSH* §665.1.5; *Lgen.* 720.5.9; *IrT* i, 36. **4** *MartT* 68; *MartO*² 192; *MartG* 170; *MartD* 236. **5** *CKHS* 45–62. **6** *NCHC* i, 177; *JCHAS* 52, 8–9; *Béaloideas* 10, 105–6; *CIIC* i, 104–5. **7** *BBa.* 34, 49; *BMisc.* 354 §1.

ETHERNANUS. *See* Iotharnaisc.

EUANGANUS. *See* Comhghán of Cluain Connaidh.

EUNAN. *See* Adhamhnán.

EVERAUN. *See* Éimhearán.

F

Fachtna. This name is attested from earliest times, as is shown by its use as a variant of the paternal name of Conchubhar son of Cathbhadh (or Fachtna), king of Ulster. It has been suggested that the name is either related to the word *facht*, 'hostility', or a derivative of the Indo-European root *vakt-*, 'say', which otherwise yields Latin *vox*, 'voice', *vocare*, 'call'.[1] The latter derivation would suit the notion of prophetic power and wise judgement, both of which are attributed to Conchubhar's father.

1 Cf. *UrS* 260.

Fachtna, associate of Patrick. The metrical list of those in Patrick's household includes Fachtna, 'of the mighty people of Tara', who appears to be otherwise unknown.[1]

1 *CGSH* §672.20.

Fachtna of Kilfenora. *See* Fachtna of Ross Carbery.

Fachtna of Kiltoom, parish of Faughalstown, barony of Fore, Co. Westmeath, or of Kiltoom, barony of Athlone, Co. Roscommon, both names deriving from Ceall Tuama. Dubhthach son of Lughar, reputedly the first man to have believed in God at Tara, is said to have had seven sons, three of whom, Fachtna (alias Fiachna), Gabhrán and Eóil, are also grouped together in the list of those commemorated on 14 November.[1] Although Dubhthach's connections were with Leinster, the pedigrees of his children – which reveal many otherwise unattested combinations of father and son – attach the saints to the Connachta.[2] It is generally assumed that their church was at Kiltoom in Westmeath – with John O'Donovan (wrongly) deriving Faughalstown from Fachtna – but it could just as well have been at Kiltoom in Roscommon.[3] Neither church later had Fachtna as its patron; the saint usually attached to the Westmeath church was Ninnidh (alias Nainnidh), whereas both Colum Cille and Patrick were remembered as patrons of the Roscommon church, albeit on 15 May, a day otherwise reserved for several namesakes of the Iona saint, such as Dochonna, Cainneach and Colum (alias Cainneach) of Monaincha.[4]

1 *CGSH* §§305, 653; *MartG* 218; *MartD* 310; *BP* 534–6; *VT* 52. **2** *BP* 2219–21; *VT* 188. **3** *PNW* 53n. **4** *MartT* 43; *MartG* 96; *MartD* 128; *TT* 494 (45); OSL RN i, 117.

Fachtna of Ros Mic Earca. The pedigree of this son of Brónach, who is given two sisters, Coincheann and Náire, places his church on the edge of either Lough Foyle or Lough Neagh.[1]

1 *CGSH* §139.1.2; *GRSH* 83; *Lgen.* 737.5.

Fachtna of Ross Carbery (Ros Oilithir), barony of East Carbery, Co. Cork. This saint was attached through his father Maonach (alias Mongach) to the Corca Laoighdhe of the area later approximately comprising the diocese of Ross.[1] Following the English conquest of Ireland, Fachtna's branch of the family – the Uí Laoghaire lords of the lands immediately about Ross Carbery – was forced to move northwards to a mountainous area in mid-Cork, later known as Iveleary (Uíbh Laoghaire). Despite his status as patron of the diocese of Ross, Fachtna was never made the subject of a written Life, but a place was found for him in two other such texts, compiled for Mochaomhóg of Leigh and, most notably, for Fionnbharr of Cork. In the former text, which refers to the large number of scholars at Ross Carbery, the miraculously induced breast-milk of Mochaomhóg's mother, then at Killeedy in Limerick, is said to have been used by Íde to restore Fachtna's failing eyesight.[2] Mochaomhóg's biographer, who had Cistercian interests at heart, was probably aware of the presence near Ross Carbery of the abbey *De fonte vivo*, otherwise Abbeymahon.[3] Alternatively, he may have been motivated by an awareness of the connection brought about after 1177 by the movement of the Uí Dhonnabháin (O'Donovans) from south Limerick into Carbery, or of the more ancient ties of obscure origin between Corca Laoighdhe and Osraighe, later corresponding to the dioceses of Ross and Ossory, because his second mention of Fachtna shows the saint protecting a king of Ossory.[4]

It was these perceived ties that helped to shape Fachtna's role in Fionnbharr's Life, which was composed about 1200, mainly with a view to arguing the case for a restoration of Cork's authority over the churches of Ross and Cloyne. Fionnbharr's biographer repeatedly called either upon Fachtna himself or on close associates – including his brothers, Caisín, Lóchán, and Mainchín – to defer to the Cork saint, thus establishing a time-honoured precedent for the respect due to Fionnbharr's successor from the clergy of Ross.[5] Fachtna's brothers are presented as having recognized ahead of all others the signs of Fionnbharr's budding sanctity, taking him with them to Ossory to ensure his proper education, and entreating him to consecrate their churches, in other words, treating him as if he were their bishop.[6] Among those said to have attended Fionnbharr's famous school in Cork were Fachtna himself and Colmán Oilithir, 'the pilgrim', also of Ross Carbery, their gratitude to their teacher being so great that they felt obliged to surrender their churches to him in perpetuity.[7]

What the clergy of Ross Carbery, a church otherwise noted for its expertise in Latin learning, may have thought of all of this is nowhere recorded.[8] Ciarán of Saighir, who exemplified above all others the link between Ross and Ossory, is said to have foretold Fachtna's birth, and a poem attributed to Cuimín of Connor singled out the saint as one generous to a fault who also loved teaching.[9] The saint's name is invoked in one of the Stowe Missal litanies.[10] Fachtna's feast of 14 August is said in some sources to have been remembered not only in Ross, but also at Molana Abbey near Youghal in east Cork.[11] It was also the day observed in the cathedral parish of Kilfenora in Clare, which would suggest that Fachtna (locally called Fechnan of Fechtnan, Latin *Ffynchia*) was also patron of this diocese.[12] The story of how Fachtna founded his *teampaillín*, 'little church', a mile east of Ross Carbery has been recorded from oral tradition, as has the tradition that he was born near Lough Hyne in the parish of Tullagh.[13] There is a well dedicated to the saint in the townland of Rossbrin, parish of Skull.

1 *CGSH* §222; *GRSH* 127; *Lgen*. 676.1, 744.2; *CGH* 155b7; GCL 46; *DIB* iii, 682. **2** *VSHP* ii, 165–6 §4. **3** *MRHI* 125. **4** *VSHP* ii, 179 §28; *FNCC* 124. **5** *CGSH* §298. **6** *BBa*. 58–62 §§7–14; *MakS* 76–90. **7** *BBa*. 76 §34. **8** *Triads* 2 §17. **9** *MartO*² 88; *ZCP* 1, 64; *Lgen*. 676.3–4. **10** HBS 32, 14. **11** *MartT* 63; *MartO*² 176; *MartG* 156; *MartD* 218; *GRSH* 127. **12** *ACoC* 81, 88; *CPL* 17, §651; *JNMArchS* 1, 104. **13** *SeanC* 361–3; *Béaloideas* 7, 114.

Fáilbhe of Díseart Cinn Chláir (Mic Con Locha). This son of Cú Locha (Conlugh?) is assigned by Dubhaltach Mac Fhirbhisigh to a branch of Ceinéal Conaill.[1] The tract on the mothers of the saints gives the name of his mother as Eistean daughter of Moiche, sister of Muicín of Mayne in the Kilkenny barony of Fassadinin.[2] Finally, the notice of his feast of 11 July places his church in Cuircne, a territory that lay within the Westmeath barony of Kilkenny West.[3]

1 *Lgen*. 698.2. **2** *CGSH* §722.95. **3** *MartT* 55; *MartG* 134; *MartD* 192.

Fáilbhe of Iona, Scotland. This son of Píobán is said to have belonged to a branch of the Ceinéal Conaill that provided several abbots to the church on Iona, among them Cuimín Fionn and Laisréan.[1] It has also been suggested that he and his consanguines belonged to a family known as Ceinéal Duach.[2] A brother of his, named Fíonán, reputedly the founder of the church of Ray (Ráith) in the Donegal parish of Raymunterdoney, was commemorated on 25 November.[3] Fáilbhe was twice cited by Adhamhnán as a source of information on matters relating to Colum Cille and, during his eleven-year tenure of the abbacy of Iona (669–79), he undertook a prolonged visit to Ireland.[4] The saintly abbot died in 679 and was commemorated on 22 March.[5]

1 *CGSH* §339; *GRSH* 41; *Lgen*. 697.13; *DIB* iii, 694. **2** *CCDK* 98–9. **3** *MartG* 226; *MartD* 318. **4** *VC*² 200–2, 218; *VC*¹ 376; *IKD* 45–6. **5** *MartT* 26; *MartO*² 83; *MartG* 60; *MartD* 84.

Fáilbhe of Killower (Ceall Fhobhair), barony of Clare, Co. Galway. When Patrick and Beinéan were travelling in Connacht, they came, according to the latter's Life, to the place called Killower, where the patron of Armagh founded a church for Bishop Fáilbhe.[1] Nothing else is known of the saint, but the parish of Killower is close to Beinéan's church of Kilbennan. John Colgan speculatively identified Fáilbhe with a namesake commemorated without a named church on 11 January, and again on 16 April.[2]

1 *AS*.Nov. iv, 176–7. **2** Ibid. 176n; *TT* 268; *MartD* 12, 104.

Fáilbhe of Rathvilly (Ráith Bhile(ach)), in the barony of the same name, Co. Carlow. This son of Eacha Cliothar (or Ceanannán) was accompanied at Rathvilly by Séighín Gabhail son of Seanach, both saints being attached by the genealogists to the Uí Cheinsealaigh of south Leinster.[1] The ancestor of this group, Criomhthann son of Éanna Ceinsealach, is said to have been converted to

Christianity through Patrick's teaching at Rathvilly.[2] Fáilbhe's companion Séighín may have been – together with some other notable persons, including Bishop Aodhán of Glendalough and Aodh son of Ainmhire, king of Tara – a son of this Criomhthann's granddaughter, Brígh daughter of Cobhthach.[3] He may also be the saint commemorated on 24 August with Faolán (possibly an error for Fáilbhe) and Abán.[4]

1 *CGSH* §274.1.2; *GRSH* 92; *Lgen.* 726.8–9. 2 *PTBA* 174 §12.6; *VT* 342. 3 *CGSH* §§380.1, 722.64. 4 *MartT* 65; *MartG* 162; *MartD* 226.

Fáilbhe Fionn of Killoe. *See* Dochua of Killoe.

Fainche. *See* Fuinche.

Fainnear. *See* Fuinche of Abbeylara.

Faircheallán/Faircheallach. *See* Foircheallán.

Faithleach of Cloontuskert (Cluain Tuaiscirt), barony of Ballintober South, Co. Roscommon. During a visit in 1837 to the remains of Cloontuskert, the site of a house of Augustinian canons, John O'Donovan was told that its saint 'Faileach' (locally pronounced Fawl-ye), patron of a well at 'Killaghy' (now Culliaghy) about a mile west of Lanesborough in Roscommon, was keenly remembered.[1] In his account of the parish, O'Donovan's contemporary, Samuel Lewis, rendered the saint's name as Faithleg.[2] The genealogists took the saint to be one of four sons of Fionnlugh, the others being Bréanainn of Clonfert, Faolán of Kiltullagh, and Domhainghin of Toomyvara.[3] Bréanainn is elsewhere said to have surrendered his *manchaine* – the service due to his monastery at Annaghdown – to Faithleach, which may mean that the canons of both places had made a new arrangement regarding revenues.[4] A legendary account of a battle fought at Tarbhgha in Connacht in 822 states that Faithleach fostered one of the protagonists, Diarmuid son of Tomaltach, ancestor of Uí Dhiarmada (later Uí Chon Cheanainn) of north-east Galway.[5] Despite local claims to his being well remembered, no feastday has been recorded.[6] His coarb was among the ecclesiastics entitled to be present at the inauguration of O'Connor as king of Connacht.[7]

1 OSL GY i, 641; OSL RN i, 113; *HOI* 271. 2 *TDI* i, 379. 3 *CGSH* §384; *Lgen.* 729.13. 4 *CGSH* §394.1.7. 5 *Celtica* 11, 135 §1; *AU s.a.* 6 OSL GY i, 641. 7 *JRSAI* 2, 340; *MSPAG* 188–9.

Faithleann of Innisfallen (Inis Faithlinn) on Lough Leane (Loch Léin), parish of Aghadoe, barony of Magunihy, Co. Kerry. In keeping with the location of his church, the deacon Faithleann was attached to a branch of the Eoghanachta named Cairbre Luachra that held lands in the Killarney area.[1] His father Aodh Damhán, king of Iarmhumha (West Munster) at his death in 633, was first punished and then rewarded in the Life of Mac Reithe of Kilmacrehy.[2] A sister of his, Brígh daughter of Aodh Damháin, is known from the tract on the mothers of the saints which states that she – or perhaps her namesake, Brígh daughter of Forannán – was mother of Luchtighearn of Tomfinlough in the Clare barony of Bunratty.[3] In transmuted form, and after undergoing a change of sex, Luchtighearn became known as Latiaran in the Cork parish of Cullen, not far from Killarney.[4] Apart from giving his name to Innisfallen, Faithleann is little known. At Innisfallen, moreover, his cult gave way to that of Fíonán Cam of Kinnitty. His feastday is recorded in two lists (4 June and 5 September).[5]

1 *CGSH* §235; *GRSH* 117; *Lgen.* 738.12; *CGH* 151a4. 2 *MHH* 20 §24, 21 §28; *AI s.a.*; *CGH* 151a4. 3 *CGSH* §722.104B. 4 *FL* 269–74. 5 *MartT* 48, 68; *MartG* 110, 170; *MartD* 146, 236.

Fanahan. *See* Fionnchú.

Faobharchú son of Muireadhach. *See* Aodh of Killeenmore.

Faoileann daughter of Aodh / Eoghan. *See* Faoileann of Killeely.

Faoileann of Killeely (Ceall Fhaoile), barony of Dunkellin, Co. Galway. This saint, also known as Aoileann and reputedly a sister of Colga of the adjoining parish of Kilcolgan, was attached by the genealogists through her father Aodh to the Uí Fhiachrach of Aidhne, a territory in south Galway and north Clare, approximately co-extensive with the diocese of Kilmacduagh.[1] Both her church and that of her brother lay within this diocese. Though the tract on the mothers of the saints names Cuilleann as the mother of both saints, it seems from an accompanying quatrain that Colga son of Fáilbhe, king of Cashel, was the son intended for her.[2] Faoileann became the subject of a rival local pedigree which made her a daughter of Eoghan Aidhne.[3] Under this guise, she was commemorated on 13 November, whereas, according to seventeenth-century sources, Faoileann daughter of Aodh was remembered on 3 March.[4] Not far from Killeely, at Isertkelly, where an image of the saint was kept, many miracles were reputedly performed at her well.[5] Faoileann's cult travelled extensively, especially in the Clare / Limerick area, where a well in the parish of Kilmurry, and supposedly also the parochial name Killeely, near the city of Limerick, recall the saint.[6] At Killeely, however, the earliest forms of the local church's name include a form 'Killelele' which could derive from *Ceall Oilealla*, 'Oilill's church'.[7] An otherwise unknown saint named Oilill is featured among an array of mainly south Clare and Limerick saints invoked in a recently discovered litany, compiled between 1175 and 1200 in the *Schottenkloster* at Regensburg in Germany.[8] The patron of Killeely, near Limerick city, became known in later times as Lelia, sister of Mainchín of St Munchin's, and she was commemorated on 11 August, with an octave on the 18th.[9] A saint Faoile(ann) also gave name to the Wexford parish of Killila.[10]

1 *CGSH* §90. 2 Ibid. §722.69. 3 Ibid. §386; *GRSH* 62. 4 *MartT* 20;*MartG* 46, 218; *MartD* 62, 308; *GRSH* 62. 5 *MartD* 414; *HDGP* ii, 38. 6 *ACoC* 237, 256. 7 *LLog.* i, 102; *BBL* 61. 8 UCC MS U.331; *CKV* 60. 9 *NMAJ* 1, 39; ibid. 3, 108; *IER* (4th ser.) 2, 370; *SATM* 42–3. 10 *TNW* 1120–1.

Faolán of Aachen, Germany. Visitors to Aachen will notice, almost within the shadow of its celebrated cathedral (*Dom*), a church dedicated to Foillan, the local version of Faolán (son of Fiontan) who accompanied his brother Fursa, first to the kingdom of the East Angles in England, where he was left in charge of a monastery at Burgh Castle, then to the Continent, where, with his other brother Ultán, he founded a church at Fosses in Belgium.[1] Land for the church was allegedly given by Itta of Nivelles, mother of St Gertrude, whose strong Irish associations included a feastday of 17 March, shared with Patrick.[2] One day, about the year 655, on his way to his brother in Fosses with three disciples, Faolán was waylaid by thieves in a wood near Nivelles and treacherously beheaded.[3] His remains were later discovered by Gertrude, with some divine assistance, and brought first to Nivelles and then to Fosses which became the centre of a widespread cult, with an abbey, named Saint-Feuillen du Roeulx, located on the supposed site of the saint's death.[4]

That news of the saint's martyrdom also reached Ireland is clear from his commemoration with Fursa on 16 January (the feast of the finding of his relics in both Fosses and Aachen) and also on 31 October in the earliest martyrologies.[5] Like his brother Fursa, Faolán may also have attracted devotees in Connacht. He gave name to 'Killilan' in the townland of Cahertinny and his feast was observed at 'Tobar Adhlain' (Tobar Fhaoláin?) in the townland of Doogarraun, in the Galway parish of Kilconickny, not far from Kiltullagh, whose patron Faolán may also have originally represented the saint.[6] Faolán's brother Ultán reputedly ended his days, about 686, as abbot of Fosses. John Colgan considered the latter to be identical with the Ultán son of Maol Sneachta commemorated on 1 May, but there is no supporting evidence.[7]

1 *BEH* 274; *DIB* iii, 1035–6. 2 *AB* 75, 379–93. 3 *ASH* 99–105; *AB* 75, 393–406. 4 *SIHI* 98–102. 5 *MartT* 8, 80; *MartO*² 219, 230; *MartG* 16, 206; *MartD* 18, 288. 6 OSL GY i, 473; *JGAHS* 6, 145. 7 *SIHI* 99; *MartD* 116n.

Faolán of Kiltullagh (Ceall Tulach), barony of Athenry, Co. Galway. The coarb or ecclesiastical successor of Faolán of Kiltullagh was one of the seven *príomhchomharbadha*, 'chief coarbs', of the Uí Mhaine, whose territory mainly comprised the eastern part of Galway.[1] According to the genealogists, Faolán was one of four sons of Fionnlugh of the Ciarraighe Luachra of north Kerry, the most famous of whom was Bréanainn of Clonfert.[2] The other two sons, Faithleach and Domhainghin, were respectively located in Cloontuskert in Roscommon, and Toomyvara in Tipperary. One account of the celebrated battle of Cúil Dreimhne relates how the saints of Uí Mhaine, including Faolán (adorned with the epithet *amhlobhar*, 'mute'), urged their people to support Colum Cille's allies.[3] This same epithet is applied to Faolán of Strathearn (Sraith/Ráith Éireann) in Scotland, who is also said to have been remembered on 20 June at Killelan (Ceall Fhaoláin) in the Kildare barony of Kilkea and Moone.[4] Faolán's day at Kiltullagh has not been recorded, but a pattern was held a few miles away, at 'Tobar Adhlain' (Tobar Fhaoláin?) in the townland of Doogarraun, parish of Kilconickny, on 31 October.[5] This was otherwise the feast of Faolán of Aachen, brother of the more celebrated Fursa, whose cult had also spread to Galway, at Killursa, near Lough Corrib.

1 *TCHyM* 76–8. 2 *CGSH* §384; *GRSH* 107; *Lgen.* 729.13. 3 *IrM* 22, 5. 4 *MartD* 174; *HDGP* iii, 170. 5 OSL GY i, 473.

Faolán of Murher (Magh Oirthir), barony of Iraghticonnor, Co. Kerry. All that is known of Faolán son of Gus is contained in the genealogies of the Alltraighe, which describe him as a bishop and place him in Murher, presumably a reference to the ecclesiastical site in the townland of Glebe.[1] A pattern was later held there on 8 September in honour of the Blessed Virgin.[2] The saint's cult may also have spread among the Corca Dhuibhne, to whom the Alltraighe were attached, with possible traces surviving in the names Killelane and Killelan, derived from Ceall Fhaoláin, in the parishes of Dingle (Corkaguiney) and Caher (Iveragh).

1 *JKAHS* 2, 29, 34. **2** *ACoK* 14–15. **3** *CorcaD* 142; *UíR* 17; *TCCD* 22.

Faolán of Strathearn (Sraith / Ráith Éireann), a district in Scotland between Tay and Forth, and supposedly also of Killelan (Ceall Fhaoláin), barony of Kilkea and Moone, Co. Kildare, and 'Kilwhelan' in the townland of Cashel, parish of Ballyroan, barony of Cullenagh, Co. Laois.[1] Faolán son of Aonghas – sometimes, like his namesake, Faolán of Kiltullagh, referred to as *amhlobhar*, 'mute' – is assigned by the genealogists, albeit the late authorities only, to the main line of the Eoghanacht kings of Cashel.[2] Moreover, whereas a note added to some versions of the Martyrology of Aonghas is the sole evidence for his connection with the Kildare and Laois churches, the principal other sources of his feast on 20 June specify only the saint's association with Scotland.[3] Despite the assertion that he was one of twenty-two disciples sent out by Ailbhe of Emly in quest of Ultimate Thule, little else is known of the saint, whose namesake, Faolán of Strathfillan, was regarded as one of Scotland's foremost saints.[4]

1 *CPNS* 227–8, 285; *HDGP* iii, 170. **2** *CGSH* §662.221; *GRSH* 117; *NSW* 187. **3** *MartO*[1] cvi (cf. *MartD* 174); *MartT* 51; *MartG* 120; *MartO*[2] 156; *PNB* 9–14, 39, 76; *LegSS* 22–6, 360; *NSW* 195–201. **4** *CPNS* 227, 285; *KSS* 341.

Faolán of Strathfillan, Scotland. According to the Irish martyrologies, a saint named Faolán son of Fearadhach was commemorated on two separate days, 9 January and 26 August, at the church of Cluain Maosgna in Fir Thulach (Fartullagh), an unidentifed ecclesiastical site, later known as 'Kylmisken' in the Westmeath parish of Lynn.[1] Despite his evident popularity, there is no other mention of Faolán in Irish sources. He also came to be regarded as patron of several churches in Scotland, including Strathfillan, where he enjoyed considerable prestige, not least because he was held to have contributed to the victory of Robert Bruce over the English at the battle of Bannockburn.[2] The Life pieced together for him in the Breviary of Aberdeen places his birth in Ireland as a son of Fearadhach (Feriach) and Caointighearn (Kentigerna).[3] Educated at the monastery of Munna, presumably Taghmon (Teach Munna) in Wexford, he is said to have later been elected abbot in succession to his teacher before leaving, apparently in the company of his mother and an uncle named Comhghán, to settle in Scotland, at Strathfillan in the upper part of Glendochart, where he remained until his death. A fair was held in his honour on 9 January at Killin, and the people of Killilan in Kintail in Scotland laid claim to possession of his remains.[4] His feast also found its way into the version of the Martyrology of Usuard compiled in the late fifteenth century by Greven in Cologne.[5]

1 *MartT* 6, 66; *MartO*[2] 34; *MartG* 12, 164; *MartD* 10, 228; *PNW* 193; *DIB* iii, 684. **2** *KSS* 345; but cf. *CPNS* 285. **3** *BrevA* pars hiem. 26v–27v; *CPNS* 284–5; *KSS* 341–6; *Peritia* 17–18, 269–70; *ACDS* 165–71; *Innes Review* 32, 63. **4** *CPNS* 284. **5** *AS*.Iun. vi, 22.

Faolán son of Draighean. *See* Ainmhire of Kilroe.

Faolán Amhlobhar. *See* Faolán of Kiltullagh; Faolán of Strathearn.

Faolchú of Iona, Scotland. Like most other successors of Colum Cille, Faolchú son of Dorbhán belonged to the Ceinéal Conaill, albeit in a different line to that of his predecessors.[1] He assumed the abbacy of Iona in 716 at the advanced age of seventy-four and, during the final two years of his tenure, before his death in 724, he may have been assisted as abbot by a man named Feidhlimidh.[2] During his time in office, Egbert, a Northumbrian who had spent many years in Ireland, was a member of the community on Iona, and this man's influence may have led to the reception on the island of the coronal tonsure.[3] He is taken to have been identical with Faolchú, a bishop remembered in the Irish martyrologies on 30 April.[4]

1 *CGSH* §343; *GRSH* 40; *Lgen.* 698.7. 2 *VC*[1] 381–2; *IKD* 60. 3 *BEH* 554–5; *FSHIM* 48–9, 318; ATig. *s.a.* 717. 4 *MartT* 39; *MartG* 86; *MartD* 114.

Faolchú son of Faolchar. *See* Pupa.

Farnan. *See* Mothoiréan of Tullow.

Farrell. *See* Feirghil.

Feadán of Kilfiddane. *See* Sceanbhán.

Feadhbhair of Boho (Both Roichnigh), barony of Clanawley, Co. Fermanagh. Like several other daughters of Dallbhrónach, including Cuman and Caoimheall, Feadhbhair (also written Fionnbharr and, perhaps, Fiadhabhair) had links to the cult of her niece, Brighid of Kildare.[1] She is said to have been subject to Brighid at her church in the townland of Toneel, parish of Boho, which she shared with her sister Sanct Bhróg.[2] Local tradition in the neighbouring parish of Devenish maintained that she had first intended to build her church in a place called 'Kildrum' (*recte* Fardrum?), where a holy well is named after her, only to have her work mysteriously undone.[3] A deer, laden with her books on its horns, is said to have then directed her to Monea in the parish of Devenish, where she built a church. She was remembered annually on 6 November, and perhaps also on 7 July (under the guise of Fiadhabhair) in the Leitrim parish of Oughteragh.[4]

1 *CGSH* §722.3.13. 2 Ibid. §670.8; *Lgen.* 752.15; *HDGP* ii, 166. 3 OSL FH 71–2. 4 *MartT* 54; *MartG* 132, 212; *MartO*[2] 240; *MartD* 188, 298.

Feadhbhar/Fearadhach sons of Caol. *See* Aodh Fionn.

Fear Corb son of Dubhthach. *See* Comhghall son of Dubhthach.

Fear Dá Chríoch. *See* Mac Caorthainn of Clogher.

Fearghal. *See* Feirghil.

Fearghas, bishop in Uí Mhaine. This saint is known from an account of the battle of Cúil Dreimhne which relates how Fearghas, together with other ecclesiastics of Uí Mhaine, an area approximately corresponding to that of the diocese of Clonfert, assembled under their elder, Bishop Maolán.[1] Fearghas is probably also the bishop of that name invoked in the company of Maoineann of

Clonfert and Mac Solaimh 'in the West' in a poem on the miracles of Seanán of Scattery Island.[2]

1 *IMN* 22, 5. 2 *ZCP* 10, 24 §19.

Fearghas of Downpatrick (Druim Leathghlaise), barony of Lecale Upper, Co. Down. An entry in the annals for 584, repeated at 590, notes the death at Downpatrick of Bishop Fearghas son of Aonghas, who, according to the annalist, founded a nearby church named Ceall Bhiain.[1] The pedigree of the bishop attaches him variously to the local family of Dál nAraidhe, whose territory lay in north Down and south Antrim, and to the Oirghialla, whose territory was approximately equivalent to that of the diocese of Clogher.[2] He was probably identical with Fearghas of Míleac, later 'Miloc', an ecclesiastical site in the Antrim parish of Camlin.[3] This adjoins Lough Neagh, whose origin tale states that Líobhan daughter of Eacha (eponym of the lake), having survived underwater until after the arrival of Christianity, was eventually caught in nets belonging to Fearghas.[4] The saint's feast fell on 15 February.[5]

1 *AU s.a.*; *HDGP* iii, 132. 2 *CGSH* §114; *GRSH* 100; *Lgen.* 712.8. 3 *EA* 3–4. 4 *LU* 3106–31. 5 *MartT* 17; *MartG* 36; *MartD* 50 (Aodh for Aonghas).

Fearghas of Inishkeen (Inis Caoin), parish of Cleenish, barony of Clanawley, Co. Fermanagh. This son of Éanna, and his three brothers, Brughach, Muireadhach, and Mochomóg, belonged, according to the genealogists, to the descendants of Colla Dá Chríoch, otherwise the Oirghialla, whose territory later corresponded to that of the diocese of Clogher.[1] Inishkeen on Lough Erne was situated within this diocese, and it was here that Fearghas rose to fame as patron of the local parish church and as one of the *ardnaoimh*, 'chief saints', of the area.[2] Here, too, he was remembered annually on his *natale* or feastday of 29 March, followed, little more than two weeks later (13 April), by his brother Mochomóg, unless the latter be Colum (under hypocoristic guise) of the like-named but distinct Inishkeen.[3]

1 *CGSH* §108; *GRSH* 71; *Lgen.* 714.11. 2 *MHH* 110 §29; *AnnU* 38; *CPL* 10, 636. 3 *MartG* 64, 76; *MartD* 88, 100, 414; *GRSH* 71.

Fearghas son of Colmán Beag. This bishop's uncle (Colmán Mór) was regarded as the eponymous ancestor of Clann Cholmáin, who governed the western section of the lands of the southern Uí Néill (now principally the county of Westmeath), and provided several claimants to the high-kingship of Ireland.[1] The descendants of Colmán Beag, on the other hand, were associated with a minor kingdom named Caoille Follamhain in or around the parish of Killallon in the Meath part of the barony of Fore.[2] Although several saints of the name are listed in the martyrologies, none can be identified with this Fearghas.

1 *CGSH* §395; *GRSH* 55; *Lgen.* 704.6; *CGH* 143bc53; *IKHK* 281. 2 *HDGP* iii, 51.

Feargna of Ceall Mhic an Fhile, an unidentified church, probably in Co. Mayo. Like his uncle Feilig, Feargna son of Fiontan was attached to a branch of the Conmhaicne associated with a place called Críoch Mhic Earca, another name for

Ceara, now the south Mayo barony of Carra.[1] His father was a poet,whence his own designation as Mac an Fhile, 'son of the poet', and his attachment to the church named after him.[2] Unfortunately, neither his church nor his feastday – despite some speculation surrounding 18 September and 11 October – has been identified, but this did not deter a scholiast of the Martyrology of Aonghas from identifying him with an abbot of Iona, named Feargna Briot, who died in 623 and was remembered on 2 March.[3]

1 *CGH* 161a38; *Lgen.* 537.4. *CGSH* §334; *GRSH* 106. 2 *CGSH* §334 (add.). 3 *GRSH* 106; *MartO*[2] 86.

Feargna son of Ainmhire. Little is known of this man who, according to the genealogists, belonged to the descendants of Colla Uais of Oirghialla, a territory later approximately equivalent to the diocese of Clogher.[1] He may be intended by a reference to 'Ferginminth' in the Register of Clogher which states that his remains were translated, along with those of Cuana, from Eonish to Clogher.[2] Some seventeenth-century sources thought him to be identical with a priest named Feargna remembered on 18 September.[3]

1 *CGSH* §353; *GRSH* 67; *Lgen.* 712.6. 2 *ClRec.* 7, 396, 398n. 3 *MartT* 72; *MartG* 178; *MartD* 252; *GRSH* 67.

Feargna son of Dubhthan. *See* Comán son of Dubhthan.

Feargna Briot of Iona, Scotland. Fourth abbot of Iona and successor of Laisréan (†605), Feargna was exceptional in that, unlike his predecessors and most of his successors – and despite the best efforts of seventeenth-century sources which provided him with a Ceinéal Conaill pedigree – he may have been, as his by-name suggests, a 'Briton'.[1] There is no trace of a Ceinéal Conaill pedigree in the early record and a scholiast of the Martyrology of Aonghas went as far as to identify him with Feargna 'son of the poet' of Ceall Mhic an Fhile.[2] A Briton named Feargna was known, however, to early genealogists who included him among the six brothers of Comán son of Dubhthan and, though no attempt is made to connect him with the abbacy of Iona, it may be noted that Adhamhnán, when describing Feargna (whose name is rendered Virgno) as a witness to an angelic light that descended on Colum Cille, cited an 'honourable priest' named Comán, Feargna's sister's son, as the source of his information.[3] Following a long tenure of the abbacy of Iona, Feargna died in 623.[4] His name is first in the list of those commemorated on 2 March, the 'fair feast' of Feargna of Iona.[5] This description led to the replacement of his name by *Finnius .i. candidus* in one late twelfth-century martyrology.[6] The feast is also among those noted by the compiler of the late eleventh-century martyrology of the *Schottenkloster* in Regensburg and, curiously, the sixteenth-century Antiphonary of Armagh, which showed little interest in Irish saints, found room for it.[7] The later martyrologies provide Feargna with the status of a bishop, but this has been contested.[8]

1 *IKD* 39–40; *VC*[1] 372–3; *GRSH* 41; *MartD* 60. 2 *MartO*[2] 86. 3 *CGSH* §313; *VC*[2] 504–8. 4 *AU s.a.* 5 *MartT* 20; *MartO*[2] 80; *MartG* 46; *MartD* 60. 6 *FourIM* 174. 7 *JCLAS* 11, 9. 8 *MartG* 46; *MartD* 60; *Innes Review* 51, 68–71.

Feathghna Fighleach, 'of vigils', of Armagh (Ard Mhacha). A gloss added by one source to the pedigree of this man – which attaches him through his father Neachtan to the Clann Eachdhach of Oirghialla – asserts that he was the coarb of Patrick (in other words the abbot of Armagh) who died in 874, and this is confirmed by the 'official' list of Patrick's successors, as preserved in the twelfth-century Book of Leinster.[1] Although designated *sanctus* only in the earliest martyrology, the Feathghna commemorated on 12 February also later came to be identified as Patrick's successor.[2] By describing this bearer of the name as *ceann creidmhe na nGaodhal* (head of religion of the Gaeil), however, the later martyrologies immediately reveal the annals as their source; the exactly corresponding Latin wording of the Annals of Ulster is *caput religionis totius Hiberniae*.[3] Adding to the questionable nature of the identification is the fact that the same annals assign the obit of Feathghna, abbot of Armagh, to *in pridias nonas Octimbris* (6 October).

1 *CGSH* §306; *LL* 6040; *DIB* iii, 766–7. **2** *MartT* 16; *MartG* 34; *MartD* 47. **3** *AU* *s.a.* 874; *FSHIM* 112.

Feber. *See* Feadhbhair.

Fechnan. *See* Fachtna of Ross Carbery.

Feeg. *See* Fiac.

Féichín of Fore (Fobhar), parish of St Feighins, barony of Fore, Co. Westmeath. Bearing a name derived from *fiach*, 'raven', Féichín son of Caolcharna, like many other saints, was made the subject of competing pedigrees. One of these provided him with an attachment to the Clann Cholmáin overlords of the area in which his church was located.[1] Another assigned him to the Fothairt, the family of Brighid of Kildare, who were mainly settled in Leinster.[2] Here, too, there was confusion because the author of his vernacular Life placed his origins among the Luighne of Sligo.[3] Yet another pedigree, which also names his three brothers (Muirchú, Diarmuid and Cú Aille), located Féichín among the Cianachta, a people who had settlements in various parts of the country.[4]

Féichín's extensive biographical dossier has yet to be studied closely. It consists of a relatively short Latin Life with attached hymns, and a long, apparently composite, vernacular Life.[5] Both now survive in single manuscripts, but John Colgan brought together at least three vernacular versions, two prose, one metrical, all now lost, to construct a composite Life.[6] Also lost is the copy kept in the library of the earl of Kildare in the early sixteenth century.[7] In the absence of a detailed study, it is not clear where these texts were composed and what interests they were designed to serve. Shortly after the English conquest, Fore became the seat of a powerful Benedictine abbey with scattered property interests, some of them well outside the community's immediate sphere of influence.[8] A list of its possessions in 1540–41, when the abbey had been suppressed, drew attention to 'divers other rectories' in Bréifne Uí Raghallaigh in Cavan 'where the king's writ does not run', and there were doubtless many others elsewhere.[9]

Féichín, locally anglicized as Festy, was considered founder-patron of some churches in Connacht, two of which – Ballysadare (Eas Dara) in Sligo, and Cong (Cunga) on Mayo's border with Galway – became seats of Augustinian canons.[10] As the canons were noted for their awareness of the value of hagiography, it may be assumed that their concerns are reflected in the substantial interest shown by Féichín's biographers in Connacht churches, including Ballysadare – which is specifically described as one of the saint's first foundations in his native area of Luighne – Drumrat, and 'his own monastery' of Cong.[11] A colophon attached to the first half of one version of the saint's vernacular Life states that it was translated from Latin by a son of the abbot of Cong, and a second version is said to have been drawn from a *codex Immaciensis*, a manuscript from Omey, one of Féichín's more important foundations in west Connacht, initially shown to him, it is said, by angels.[12] But, though his biographers place greatest emphasis on Féichín's activities in north and west Connacht and the Fore area, the peripatetic saint is also brought to many other districts, especially in the vernacular Lives. These bring him to Teathbha (Longford/Westmeath), Cairbre Gabhra (Longford), Fir Bhile (Farbill in Westmeath), Uí Fhiachrach Aidhne (south-west Galway), Críoch na gCéadach (the barony of Warrenstown in north Offaly), Naas in north Kildare, and Cashel in Munster, among other places.[13]

Numerous saints are said to have been associated with Féichín, including Colum Cille who allegedly foretold his birth, Nathí of Achonry who is given the privilege of educating the young saint, and Rónán son of Bearach, with whose assistance he combated a plague.[14] As in all such Lives, the choice of associated saints and rulers was usually made on a calculated basis. The prominence given by the saint's biographers to Rónán, for example, which is mirrored by incidents in Rónán's twelfth-century Latin Life, could be taken to reflect the importance attaching to Rónán's church at Dromiskin in Louth that clearly went back further than its emergence in the fourteenth century as a seat *inter Anglicos* of the archbishop of Armagh.[15] Féichín's vernacular Lives may have been late compositions, as is indicated by the apparent controversy surrounding the election of a Welshman to succeed the saint.[16] The Latin Life of the saint, which is part of a collection made on Saints' Island in Lough Ree shortly before 1400, may not have been a much earlier composition. It presents Englishmen in a negative manner, showing them to have been punished for deriding the saint and, unusually in saints' Lives, ends with hymns in his honour.[17]

Other saints' Lives also find room for the patron of Fore. These include the Life of Mochaomhóg of Leigh which uses two forms of the saint's name, 'Fecheanus' and 'Mofecta', and that of Garailt of Mayo which states that the plague was brought about by Féichín's prayers.[18] The Life of Mochua of Balla, the parish adjoining that of Mayo, brings Mochua to Fore, attributing to him a miracle at Lough Lene elsewhere said to have been performed by Féichín himself.[19] The saint's mill at Fore, which was not to be entered by women, attracted the attention of Giraldus Cambrensis, and some traditions concerning Féichín and his foundations survived both at Fore and at Termonfeckin – locally thought to be contemporaneous with the saint's chief church – into the nineteenth century.[20]

After the arrival of the Benedictines at Fore in the 1180s, Féichín shared patronage of the site with Taurin of Évreux in France.[21] The note added to the saint's name in the original index to the Martyrology of Donegal, to the effect that he was patron of Ceinéal Fhéichín in the south of the Galway barony of Leitrim appears, however, to be based partly on the coincidence of name, but there is a well dedicated to the saint at Lackan in the parish of Ballynakill.[22] Regarded as similar in manners to Anthony the monk, and austere in his devotion, Féichín is said to have fallen victim in 665/668 to the great plague known as *Buidhe Chonaill*, together with Ailearán the learned who is credited with having drawn up a list of Féichín's miracles.[23] Both saints are said to have previously fasted against the plague.[24] His feast was usually celebrated on 20 January, but at Termonfeckin it fell nine days later.[25] Tradition held that he was buried at Ciarán's church (Castlekeeran) on the river Blackwater, near Kells.[26] In the Wexford parish of Carn, the saint's name may have been anglicized as Vauk, and in Scotland, where the saint's name was anglicized Vigean (Latin Vigeanus), there are also some churches dedicated to him.[27] Traces of the saint's cult in Leinster are also found in the Ossory parishes of Sheffin, which takes its name from him, and Danesfort, where there was a site called 'Cill Fhéichín'.[28] Among the saint's relics was a bell, and his 'cursing stone' was preserved at Leac Fhéichín in the townland of Dooghta, parish of Cong.[29] Finally, Féichín was among the saints invoked as guarantors of the Law of Adhamhnán, and his name is also invoked in a poem attributed to Moling.[30]

1 *CGSH* §315; *GRSH* 54; *Lgen*. 739.1. **2** *GRSH* 75; *MartD* 22. **3** *RC* 12, 321 §§1–2; *CGH* 338h67. **4** *CGSH* §614. **5** *VSHP* ii, 76–86; *RC* 12, 318–53; *DIB* iii, 734–5. **6** *ASH* 130–44. **7** *IER* (5th ser.) 99, 105. **8** *MRHI* 106–7. **9** *EIMP* 273. **10** *AFM s.a.* 1261; OSL GY iii, 43; *MRHI* 160–1, 166. **11** *RC* 12, 338; *ASH* 134 §8; 135 §19; OSL SO 146. **12** *RC* 12, 329 §17; *ASH* 135 §22, 139 (*notae*). **13** *ASH* 133–8 §§14–16, 21, 30, 32, 42 **14** Ibid. 133–4 §§2, 7, 136 §29. **15** *RC* 12, 352 §47; *ASH* 136–7 §§29, 36; *AB* 17, 164–5 §§6–7; *LSLC* 299. **16** *ASH* 139 §48. **17** *VSHP* ii, 82–3 §§18–19; 84–6 §22; *CL* 47–9. **18** *VSHP* ii, 113 §12, 179 §29; *CGSH* §703.5. **19** *LisL* 4679–87; *RC* 12, 344 §39; *VSHP* 81–2 §14. **20** *THEH* 134; *PNW* 60–6; OSL LH 64, 75. **21** *MRHI* 106; *SAM* 4.1, 171–5; *AnnU* 59. **22** *MartD* 416; OSL GY 516. **23** *CGSH* §712.18; *ZCP* 1, 62; *BMisc*. 348 §17; *AU s.a.*; *VSHP* ii, 80 §12; *IrT* iii, 85 §9; *LUM* 154vb 18. **24** *LH* i, 25. **25** *MartT* 10; *MartO*[2] 37; *MartG* 20; *MartD* 22; OSL LH 77. **26** *PNW* 65. **27** *The Past* 2, 19–20; ibid. 26, 42–8; *CPNS* 321–2; *KSS* 456–8; *ACDS* 145–6; *Innes Review* 5, 105. **28** *HADO* ii, 326–7; iii, 389. **29** *AFM s.a.* 1144; *JGHAS* 64, 5; *EMH* 485 §227. **30** *CA* §22; *Anecd*. ii, 28 §1.

FÉICHÍN of Kilcrumper: Among the saints attached to the Leinster family of Dál gCormaic, alias Maca Cormaic, was a man named Mofhiacha, alias Fiacha, whose feast fell on 27 December.[1] The name *Féichín* is a diminutive of *Fiach(a)*, and it is scarcely a concidence that a namesake named Féichín Maca Luighbhe was remembered on the following day. The saint's attachment to the Maca Cormaic may explain the presence in the Cork parish of Kilcrumper of a now obsolete ecclesiastical site named Cill Fhéichín; the founding of Kilcrumper is attributed to Abán, the best-known of the saints assigned to the Maca Cormaic.[2]

1 *MartT* 1; *MartG* 248; *MartD* 348. **2** *CrC*[2] §4; *HDGP* iii, 171; *VSHH* 264 §17; *VSHP* i, 17 §22.

Feidhealm. The name appears to derive from *feidhil*, 'enduring, constant', which also yields the male name Feidhlimidh. Five females of the name are included in the list of homonymous saints.[1]

1 *CGSH* §708.128–32.

Feidhealm. *See* Mac Cuilinn of Lusk.

Feidhealm daughter of Oilill. *See* Mughain of Lyons.

Feidhealm daughter of Dallbhrónach. *See* Íde.

Feidhealm daughter of Maine. *See* Munna of Taghmon.

Feidhealm daughter of Rónán. Among the saints of the Dál gCais of Thomond were Feidhealm and her sister Rónaid.[1] They were attached to the Clann Ailghile branch of the family which appears to have been settled in the area about Corrofin.[2] Their nephew, Feardomhnach son of Díoma, is said to have granted Inis Iobhthann – apparently the island on which Limerick was built – to Mainchín.[3] It has been suggested that Feidhealm also had a church in the Municipal Borough of Limerick, at Killalee in the parish of St John's.[4] In some seventeenth-century sources, the sisters are given feasts on 11 January (Feidhealm) – which John Colgan chose to attach to Feidhealm Ruadh – and 5 August (Rónaid), more properly the day of Rathnad of Ceall Rathnaide.[5]

1 *CGSH* §204; *GRSH* 120–1; *Lgen.* 649.13. 2 *CoC* 61–3. 3 *CGH* 153a25–30. 4 *NMAJ* 1, 102–4; ibid. 3, 107–8; *LLog.* i, 99; *SATM* 38–40. 5 *GRSH* 120–1; *MartD* 212.

Feidhealm of Killadreenan. *See* Duirtheach.

Feidhealm Ruadh, 'red-haired', daughter of Laoghaire. This saint, and her sister, 'white-haired' Eithne, made a fleeting entry into the hagiographical record, courtesy of Patrick's biographer Tíreachán. Apparently a native of Connacht, Tíreachán brought the two daughters of Laoghaire, king of Tara, to a well near Cruachain (later Rathcroghan), seat of the kings of the western province, where they were met by Patrick.[1] An enquiry as to who was God led to a lengthy sermon and the conversion and baptism of the two sisters, whose desire to see the face of Christ could only be satisfied by their immediate deaths. Neither saint is commemorated in the martyrological record, but John Colgan chose to identify Feidhealm with the saint of that name remembered in the Martyrology of Tallaght only on 11 January, and Eithne with an (otherwise unattached) namesake on 26 February.[2]

1 *PTBA* 142–4 §26; *BP* 1106–52; *VT* 100–2. 2 *ASH* 24–6, 415–16; *MartT* 7, 18.

Feidhlimidh of Cashel, barony of Middlethird, Co. Tipperary. Although not many Irish kings attained the status of sanctity, Feidhlimidh son of Criomhthann, king of Cashel, was among those that did. The notice of his death in 847 describes him as the 'best of the Irish', king, scribe, and anchorite.[1] The kindness shown to him by the obituarists is not shared by modern historians who have given him the unenviable distinction of being the first great Irish king to introduce the practice of burning and plundering churches.[2] The churches plundered by him, including Kildare, Durrow, and Clonmacnoise, lay mainly in the Midlands, an area which any aspirant to the high-kingship from Munster, as Feidhlimidh was, would have needed to control. His misdeeds are said to have eventually brought on him the vengeance of Ciarán, patron of Clonmacnoise, who was imagined to have pursued the king and given him a thrust of his crozier, thus leading to an internal wound and death.[3] Yet, the calendar date of his death (28 August) quickly found its way into the Martyrology of Tallaght, thus allowing Feidhlimidh to become the only Irish person remembered on that day.[4] Without any known descendants of his own, Feidhlimidh, whose great-grandfather Colmán was also known for his piety, was attached to the Ceinéal Fínghin branch of the Eoghanacht of Cashel.[5] Together with twenty-four others, he was numbered among those 'in union' with Maol Ruain of Tallaght, and this earned for him a reputation as a friend of the *céili Dé*, 'clients of God'.[6] An awareness of this tradition may underlie the statement in Patrick's Tripartite Life that, since Feidhlimidh's time, there were to be twenty-four at the table of the king of Cashel.[7] Among others included in this list was Flannán of Killaloe and, despite chronological difficulties, his Life's reference to a saintly king of the name who ruled over all of Ireland, and who acted as Flannán's tutor, may refer to Feidhlimidh.[8] A poem attributed to Guile of Áth Lóich describes how Feidhlimidh obtained the hostages of all the Irish provinces.[9]

1 *AU s.a.* **2** *IKHK* 212. **3** *AFM s.a.* 844; *CCC* §2; *InaF* i, 86 §248. **4** *MartT* 66; *MartG* 166; *MartD* 228; *FSHIM* 111–12. **5** *CGSH* §312; *GRSH* 117; *CGH* 150b10–11. **6** *CGSH* §§713.9, 724.1.5. **7** *BP* 3144–6; *VT* 266. **8** *VSHH* 295–6 §28. **9** *BMisc.* 305.

Feidhlimidh of Kilmore (Ceall Mhór), barony of Upper Loughtee, Co. Cavan. Although patron of a church that became a diocesan see, Feidhlimidh is nowhere provided with a pedigree on the male side.[1] His mother is said, however, to have been Deidhe daughter of Trian, whose progeny also included Daigh of Inishkeen and Diarmuid of Inchcleraun.[2] The diocese governed from Feidhlimidh's church corresponded to the kingdom of Bréifne, ruled by the Uí Ruairc (O'Rourkes) and Uí Raghallaigh (O'Reillys).[3] The bells of Feidhlimidh, which were doubtless kept at Kilmore, were rung when the Uí Raghallaigh needed to be restrained, according to the Life of Maodhóg of Ferns.[4] In the early seventeenth century, when exiled into the hilly country of Sliabh Cairbre between Cavan and Leitrim, the Uí Raghallaigh continued to venerate Feidhlimidh, observing his feast and insisting on the cessation of servile work on the day.[5] Together with Bricín of Tomregan, and Feidhlimidh's uterine brother, Daigh of Inishkeen, the saint is also said to have been a companion of Caillín of Fenagh.[6] He was sometimes thought to have been a brother of Tighearnach of Clones and, according to the Register of Clogher, both he and Tighearnach occupied the see of Clogher and the same grave at Clones.[7] A well near Clogher was allegedly named after him, and another (Toberfelim) in the Longford parish of Granard probably also takes its name from him.[8] His feast fell on 3 August, with an octave on the ninth of the same month.[9] The latter day was shared by Nathí of Achonry and a number of companion saints. The saint's name was anglicized as both Phelim and Felix.[10]

1 *MRHI* 87–9. 2 *CGSH* §722.2. 3 *HDGP* ii, 189. 4 *BNÉ* i, 285 §272. 5 *AnH* 3, 205. 6 *BFen.* 412. 7 OSL CN/LM 84; *ClRec.* 7, 378. 8 *ClRec.* 7, 378; OSL LD/WH i, 25. 9 *MartT* 60–1; *MartG* 148, 152; *MartD* 208, 214; *AnH* 3, 205. 10 *Breifne* 4, 202.

Feidhlimidh of Magheramorne, parish of Glynn, barony of Lower Belfast, Co. Antrim, which may now represent an earlier Domhnach Mór. Possibly the patron of the now obsolete Patrician foundation of Domhnach Mór, Feidhlimidh is said to have baptized Comhghall of Bangor.[1] A saint of the name was remembered at a church named Domhnach on 30 October.[2]

1 *BP* 1911; *VT* 164; *EA* 51, 338; *MartD* 288. 2 *MartG* 206; *MartD* 288.

Feidhlimidh son of Iorlamhán. According to an entry in the tract on the mothers of the saints, Bóchra had three sons by Iorlamhán, named Dúileachán, Feidhlimidh and Liadhnán.[1] Apart from Feidhlimidh, who is mentioned with Muicín, Scoithín, and other saints, in a poem attributed to Moling of St Mullins, nothing else is known of Bóchra's three children.[2] In Moling's poem, which renders Feidhlimidh's name as 'Fidlin', the focus is on the Uí Dheagha of Ossory (whence the Kilkenny barony of Ida), and the Uí Dheagha of Leinster who gave name to the later Wexford deanery of Oday.[3]

1 *CGSH* §722.71. 2 *Anecd.* ii, 36 §22. 3 Ibid. 34 §1, 36 §23.

Feighen. *See* Féichín.

Feilig Fionn, 'fair', of Kilfelligy (Ceall Fheilge/Fhilge), parish of Killoscobe, barony of Tiaquin, Co. Galway. In their account of the people known as Conmhaicne, the genealogists maintained that Cúscraidh's son Fraoch was ancestor of a branch settled in Críoch Mhic Earca (approximately the equivalent of the present barony of Carra in Mayo), to which also belonged Feilig the deacon, son of Beochroidhe.[1] According to the early martyrologies, which record his feast of 16 April, Feilig's connections were with Uí Dhiarmada, the land of the Uí Chon Cheanainn (O'Concannons), first the east Galway parish of Moylough, later adjoining the approximate equivalent of the east Galway parish of Kilkerrin, north-east of Tuam.[2] One modern editor thought that the saint more properly commemorated on this day was Felix of Saragossa in Spain, which may explain why the later martyrologies ignored Feilig.[3] There can be little doubt, however, that the patron of Kilfelligy, traditionally regarded as the first church to have been built in the parish of Killoscobe, a few miles south of Kilkerrin, was intended.[4] Later, through confusion with Dúileach of St Doolaghs in the parish of Balgriffin, Dubhaltach Mac Fhir Bhisigh mistakenly asserted that Feilig's church was in Fine Gall, now Fingal in north Dublin, and that both Dúileach and he shared a feast of 17 November.[5]

1 *CGH* 161a38; *Lgen.* 537.4, 733.7; *CGSH* §137; *GRSH* 106; *Lgen.* iv, 437. 2 *MartT* 33; *MartO*[2] 107; *Celtica* 26, 66–88. 3 *MartO*[2] 421; *Ainm* 3, 3–4. 4 *LLLSK* 74. 5 *Lgen.* 733.7.

Feime of Urney (Urnaidhe/Earnaidhe), barony of Strabane Lower, Co. Tyrone. Bearing a name that possibly represents a hypocoristic or pet form of Feidhealm,

Feime daughter of Coireall was attached, together with her brother Daigh, to a branch of the Ceinéal Eoghain settled in the Bréadach, now on the east side of Inishowen in north Donegal; both Feime and Daigh were children of Deidhe daughter of Trian.[1] Feime's church at Urney, where she appears to have been also known as Fuime (Latin Euphemia), lay well south of Inishowen, however, on the Tyrone side of the river Finn.[2] Otherwise associated with virgins named Cognad and Samhthann, Urney nevertheless belonged, with the churches of Inishowen, to the diocese of Derry.[3] Little else is known of Feime, but her confusion with the virgin and martyr, Euphemia of Chalcedon, resulted in her being accorded a feast of 16/17 September.[4] Another confusion, this time lexicographical in origin, saw her name being extrapolated from the word *feidhm*, 'effort', in the text of the Martyrology of Aonghas for 21 January, thus leading to a second bogus feast.[5] A final confusion is marked by the rendering of the saint's name as *Fernae/Fenicus* in an early seventeenth-century document.[6]

1 *CGSH* §§18, 19, 722.2; *GRSH* 46; *Lgen.* 701.1. **2** *Celtica* 1, 84; *GRSH* 46; cf. *MartD* xliv §27; *CCDK* 131; *DYHS* 196. **3** *VSHP* ii, 254 §§2–4; *MartD* 46; *CCDK* 293–5. **4** *MartT* 71; *MartO²* 208; *MartG* 178; *MartD* 250. **5** *MartO²* 37, 50; *FourIM* 13, 32; *Ainm* 3, 4. **6** *UJA* (2nd ser.) 1, 249; *AnH* 12, 107, 109.

Feirghil of Aghaboe (Achadh Bó), barony of Clarmallagh, Co. Laois. An entry in the annals for 789 records the death of Feirghil, abbot of Aghaboe.[1] Mainly on the authority of the Four Masters, who doctored Feirghil's obit by switching it to 784 and adding that the abbot died in Germany in the thirtieth year of his episcopacy, it has been suggested that this man was identical with a celebrated Irish *peregrinus*, Virgilius (Virgil), bishop of Salzburg in Austria.[2] The temptation was there: Irish *Feirghil* represents a borrowing of Latin *Virgilius*, and the bishop of the name is known to have flourished in the mid-eighth century. As it happens, the name and chronology of Feirghil son of Maol Dúin of Clann Éanna, a leading branch of the Ceinéal Laoghaire of Meath, would also suit.[3] Feirghil's father (or grandfather) Maol Dúin was slain in 728, and a close relative, Aonghas son of Fearadhach, king of Laoghaire, died in 766.[4] But even if John Colgan had no doubt in the matter, adding a note to Feirghil's pedigree which identified him with the bishop of Salzburg, the equation, like that with the abbot of Aghaboe, remains speculative.[5] Among other places laying claim to the patron of Salzburg is the Cork parish of Killeagh near Youghal which, in a field belonging to the monastery of Mount Melleray, contains a well named after a certain Fearghal (Farrell), the focus of local devotion until the 1930s.[6] When not tracing their descent to Eoghan, brother of Colum Cille, the O'Friels (Uí Fhirghil) of Kilmacrenan allegedly considered themselves to be descended from Feirghil's family (*S. Virgilii familia*).[7]

1 *AU s.a.* **2** *AFM s.a.*; *Kenney* 523; *AB* 78, 100–9; *SAM* 11, 301–17; *OLL* 1, 21–2. **3** *CGSH* §85; *GRSH* 51; *Lgen.* 707.3; *CGH* 144g56. **4** *AU/AFM s.a.*; cf, *AB* 78, 110n. **5** *GRSH* 51; *AB* 78, 92–123. **6** *CPR* i, lxix; *DiocCl.* 69; *AICK* ii, 177 (Lagile). **7** *Lgen.* 152.2; *DPH* ii, 233.

Felix. *See* Feidhlimidh of Kilmore.

Festy. *See* Féichín.

Fiac of Sleaty (Sléibhte), barony of Slievemargy, Co. Laois, not far from Carlow town. Fiac, whose name (anglicized Feeg) probably represents a hypocoristic form of *fiach*, 'raven', is assigned by the genealogists through his father (variously Earcaidh and Mac Earca) to the Uí Bhairrche of the Carlow / Laois area, and a list of their saints places him second behind Tighearnach of Clones.[1] There was good reason to give him prominence. Arriving in Tara, Patrick was greeted respectfully by one man only, Dubhthach of the Maca Lughair, *poeta optimus*, 'an excellent poet', with whom, according to Muirchú – the Armagh saint's earliest biographer – there was a young poet named Fiac who went on to become a 'renowned' bishop at Sleaty, 'where his relics are worshipped'.[2]

Much of the saint's renown was because of Armagh interest in his church, which appears to have been part of the northern church's *paruchia*, with a later dedication to Patrick.[3] Among the last actions attributed to Patrick by Tíreachán, writing in the seventh century, was the consecration of Fiac at Sleaty.[4] Additional notes contained in the Book of Armagh, a ninth-century compilation, expand on this, stating that, while on a visit in Leinster, Patrick requested of Dubhthach that he nominate a person suited to become a bishop 'of good kin, one wife and one child', conditions that were fulfilled only by Fiac, then returning from Connacht.[5] The same passage describes how Patrick consecrated Fiac's church at Sleaty, and how Fiac's successor, Bishop Aodh, drew up a testament granting the church to Armagh. Although some of this no doubt reflects special pleading on behalf of Armagh, the close association between it and Sleaty must have continued over several centuries. Its expression through the founder-saints of both churches also assumed metrical form in a ninth-century hymn in praise of Patrick, beginning *Géanair Pádraig i Neamhthor*, 'Patrick was born in Neamhthor', which was anachronistically said to have been composed by Fiac, the Armagh saint's 'bard', and also through a prayerful invocation of Patrick, sometimes attributed to the patron of Sleaty.[6]

Fiac's feastday fell on 12 October, and commemorated with him on this day was his 'only son' Fiachra, who was also attached to Sleaty.[7] This feast has the distinction of being present in the earliest surviving copy of the Hieronymian Martyrology, written at Echternach in Luxembourg shortly after 700.[8] Its presence may be explained by reference to the fact that Willibrord, founder of Echtarnach, had spent twelve years at Clonmelsh in Carlow, not far from Sleaty, in advance of his mission to the Continent.[9] A note attached to the feast in one Irish manuscript relates how Patrick and Seachnall of Dunshaughlin arranged to have a chariot sent to Fiac to facilitate his Lenten practice of removing himself, with little sustenance, to a cave at Druim Gabhla, now possibly Drumgowla in the Leitrim parish of Kiltoghert, a place noted for its caves.[10] The saint was also patron of Killeagh (Ceall Fhiaigh) in the Meath part of the barony of Fore, but here the pattern day fell on 1 November.[11]

1 *CGSH* §286; *GRSH* 89; *Lgen*. 724.2; *CGH* 121a38–9; *DIB* iii, 766–7. **2** *PTBA* 92 (I 19.3); cf. *BP* 531–4; *VT* 52. **3** *JCKAS* 6, 377; *AAR* 26; *CM* 52. **4** *PTBA* 162 (51.4). **5** *PTBA* 176 §13. **6** *LH* i, 96–103; 105–6; *CGSH* §672.23. **7** *MartT* 79; *MartO*[2] 216; *MartG* 194; *MartD* 272. **8** *AS*.Nov. ii.2, 552–3. **9** *FSHIM* 8n. **10** *ZCP* 8, 106–7; *TDI* ii, 214. **11** OSL MH 89; Logainm.ie 'Ceall Fhiaigh'.

FIACHNA/FIACHRA. So confused are these two names, both of them derivatives of *fiach*, 'raven', and the histories of the saints that bore them that they are most easily treated together, beginning with Fiachra Goll, 'purblind', of Clonfert (Cluain Fearta) in the Galway barony of Longford. According to the genealogists, this Fiachra belonged through his father Dáire to the Uí Bhairrche of the Laois/Carlow area.[1] His name is found in some versions of the list of notable Uí Bhairrche saints in which, possibly because of a misunderstanding of *Goll* as *Gall*, 'Gaul', he is located in Leatha, either Armorica (now Brittany) or Latium, the area about Rome.[2] This may explain why, in a note added to this Fiachra's pedigree, John Colgan wondered whether he might be the hermit named Fiacre whose cult, centred on Meaux, spread widely in France.[3] The French feast of 30 August was first introduced to the Irish calendar in the late twelfth century by the compiler of the Martyrology of Gorman, who probably borrowed it from a copy of the Martyrology of Usuard of Winchester provenance.[4] However, it came to be observed, in the form of its vigil, at St Fiachna's well in the Kerry parish of Kilcaskan; nearby, in the townland of Gearhanagoul, was a celebrated bush associated with Fiachna.[5]

A saint variously named Fiachra or Fiachna was well known in the Carlow/Kilkenny area; the Uí Bhairrche also laid claim to Fiachra son of Fiac of Sleaty, and an abbot of the name was associated with the church of Ullard (Iorard or Earard) in the Carlow barony of St Mullin's Lower. To this man, variously rememembered on 8 February, 4 March, and 2 May, there came, according to the Life of Comhghall, an angel, to advise him of the great privilege he had been granted, of rendering last rites to the patron of Bangor who also had Uí Bhairrche connections.[6] Through a misreading of the Irish name of his church, this Fiachra was sometimes taken to be an abbot of Clonard (Cluain Ioraird) in Meath, a church with which he had no connection.[7] Local and diocesan historians came to regard him on tenuous evidence as identical with the hermit of Meaux who, having first lived at Kilferagh and Clontubbrid in the Kilkenny parish of Sheffin, where he was remembered on 8 February, supposedly then removed to France.[8]

The Fiachra (Fiachna) commemorated on 8 February is said to have been associated with Conwal (Congbháil) in the Donegal barony of Kilmacrenan.[9] This dedication is more likely, however, to have belonged to Bishop Fiachra (Fiachna), a son of Fearghas son of Eoghan, eponym of both Tír Eoghain (Tyrone) and Inis Eoghain (Inishowen).[10] Two possible feastdays are speculatively assigned to this saint in seventeenth-century sources, 30 March and 29 April, but yet another saint named Fiachna, a monk of Mochuda who gave name to Kilfeighny (Ceall Fhiachna) in the Kerry barony of Clanmaurice, is elsewhere credited with the second of these feasts.[11]

A saint named Fiachra (Fiachraich) son of Colmán was also known to the genealogists, who placed him among the Uí Mhéith, a branch of the Oirghialla spread over parts of Armagh, Monaghan and Louth (whence Omeath).[12] The list of Patrick's coarbs at Armagh, as preserved in the Book of Leinster, provides this Fiachra with a ten-year tenure of the abbacy as well as an unidentified church named Eanach Seanmháil.[13] Placed between Duach (†548) and Feidhlimidh

(†578), Fiachra was unknown to the annalists and accordingly finds no place in the 'official' list of Patrick's successors.[14] In his capacity as prelate, he was, however, known to the author of the tale of the 'Settling of the Manor of Tara'. Having described Fiachra's mother as a *druineach*, 'embroideress', this writer arranged to have him visited by messengers of Diarmuid son of Cearbhall, king of Tara, who was eager to take counsel on how the manor was to be divided.[15] Seventeenth-century sources credit him with a feastday of 25 July which earlier sources attach to Fiachra Caol, 'slender', of the unidentified church of Cluain Caoin (Caoichne).[16] This latter saint could well be identical with Fiachra Caoch son of Feidhlimidh, one of Brighid's subjects attached to the church of Ceall Eannga, later possibly 'Killagone' in the Kildare parish of Cadamstown.[17] Patrick is said to have left one of his disciples, Bishop Fiachra by name, in the Antrim church of Culfeightrin (Cúil Eachtrann).[18] Later recorded under the guise of 'Fechtany', this man was assigned a feast of 28 September by John Colgan in the knowledge that a bishop named Fiachra was commemorated on that day.[19] An otherwise unknown Fiachna, lauded by Cuimín of Connor as a man who never said a 'naughty word', was taken by Míchéal Ó Cléirigh to have been the saint honoured either on 30 March or 29 April.[20]

1 *CGSH* §292; *GRSH* 89; *Lgen*. 462.1, 724.4. **2** *CGH* 121a40 (add). **3** *GRSH* 89. **4** *MartG* 166; *MartD* 228; *FSHIM* 165–9. **5** *ACoK* 235; *Béaloideas* 10, 143; *AIKY* i, 543. **6** *MartT* 15; *MartO*² 59; *MartG* 88; *MartD* 118; *Carloviana* 55, 89; *Béaloideas* 4, 107. **7** *MartG* 32; *MartO*² 71; *JIA* 21, 139. **8** *HADO* ii, 327–30. **9** *MartG* 32; *MartD* 42. **10** *CGSH* §30; *GRSH* 46; *Lgen*. 701.11. **11** *MartD* 90, 114; *MartO*² 120; *VSHP* i, 182–3 §§34–5. **12** *CGSH* §64; *GRSH* 70; *Lgen*. 715.3. **13** *LL* 6002. **14** *NHI* ix, 237–41. **15** *Ériu* 4, 126 §§3–4. **16** *GRSH* 70; *MartD* 202; *MartT* 58; *MartG* 142. **17** *CGSH* §670.71. **18** *BP* 1891–8; *VT* 162. **19** *EA* 79; PNNI vii, 106; *MartT* 75; *MartG* 186; *MartD* 260. **20** *ZCP* 1, 66; *MartD* 90.

Fiacre. *See* Fiachna (Fiachra).

Fiadhabhair. *See* Feadbhair.

Fiamhain daughter of Diarmuid. *See* Bearchán of Clonsast.

Fiddaune. *See* Feadán.

Finbarr. *See* Fionnbharr.

Findelua/Finicula. *See* Inghean Bhaoith.

Fínghin. This name, which literally means 'wine-birth', is not common among saints. No saint of the name is recorded in the genealogies and one only, Fínghin son of Odhrán Feabhla, in the martyrologies (5 February).[1] Though the cognomen, Feabhail, 'Foyle', would suggest a northern saint in this case, most associations of the name are with southern churches, especially in Clare, where Fínghin was patron of Quin, Templemaley, and Kilraghtis.[2] This Fínghin is said to have been a son, among many others, of Inghean Bhaoith, patron of Killinaboy in the same county.[3] Along with Inghean Bhaoith and numerous other (mainly Munster) saints, Fínghin is called upon, in a poem in Classical Irish, to help in releasing Ireland's southern half (Leath Mogha) from a bondage imposed on it by the northern half (Leath Chuinn), represented by Finnian of Clonard.[4] The fifth of February was kept holy in the Kerry parish of Killaha, near Killarney, an area in which Fíonán (from Fínghin?) was particularly popular.[5] The 'Fingenus' remembered on 12 November in the martyrology of the Regensburg *Schottenkloster* may be the patron of Quin.[6]

1 *MartT* 14; *MartG* 30; *MartD* 38. 2 *ACoC* 172, 175, 182, 196. 3 *IrT* iv, 93 §5. 4 RIA MS 23L11, 263; *SAM* 24.1, 17, 19. 5 *ACoK* 179. 6 *FSHIM* 242; *MartR* 162.

Finlaggan. *See* Fionnlugh.

Finncheall of Kildrumsherdan (Díseart Finnchille), barony of Tullygarvey, Co. Cavan. This saint's church in the townland of Drumhurt – sometimes wrongly thought to be at Knockbride in the barony of Clankee – was dedicated to both Brighid of Kildare and Finncheall.[1] Little else is known of Finncheall, but she was remembered at Slieve Gorey (Sliabh Guaire) on 25 January, within seven days of Brighid's feast.[2] The name Finncheall is also included in the list of those remembered on 24 April which, like 25 January, enjoyed the Roman notation of eighth of the calends.[3] This would suggest that the same saint was intended. The later martyrologies assign the similarly named virgin Finnseach (possibly also remembered in Scotland as 'Findoca'), whose day fell on 13 October, to Slieve Gorey.[4]

1 *AnnU* 230, 234; *CPL* 5, 450; ibid. 15, §774; *DK* 125–6; *CínCC* 227–8. 2 *MartT* 12; *MartG* 22; *MartD* 26. 3 *MartT* 37; *MartG* 82; *MartD* 108. 4 *MartT* 79; *MartG* 196; *MartO*[2] 224; *MartD* 276; *CPNS* 286–7; *LegSS* 247, 362–3.

Finneach daughter of Díbheachán. *See* Fíonán of Teach Oirthir.

Finneach daughter of Seanach Fionn (Ciarán). *See* Miodhan of Clonfad.

Finneach of Dorn. *See* Sineach of Killinny.

Finnéan. *See* Finnian.

Finnéan of Dromin. *See* Fiontan Fionn of Dromin.

Finnian. This (now commonly used) version of the name is based on the Latin form Vinnianus/Finnianus.[1] The Latin form is in turn derived from Finnio, an Irish adaptation of a British hypocoristic or pet form ending in *–au/-aw*.[1] The full radical form of the name in Irish was Fionnbharr (or with back-formation Bairrfhionn), but a number of churches, and especially Movilla and Clonard, gave preference to the pet form.

1 *IETÜ* 52–7; *FKHS* 407–14.

Finnian of Clonard (Cluain Ioraird), barony of Upper Moyfenrath, Co. Meath. Clonard has been described as one of the 'most important' of the early churches of Ireland, worthy of mention in the same category of 'great houses' as Armagh and Clonmacnoise.[1] Its saint was ranked among Ireland's principals, bearing comparison in manners with no less a figure than St Paul, enjoying a reputation as tutor of the 'twelve apostles' of Ireland, and cast with Patrick in the role of judge of the Irish on Doomsday.[2] Despite the genealogists who provide connections for the saint through his father Fiontan (sometimes rendered Fionnlugh) to the descendants of the Ulster hero, Cealtchar son of Uitheachair, and through his mother Tealach to the Uí Luascáin of north Leinster, Finnian's probable affiliation to the cult of his namesake at Movilla is shown by a number of factors, beginning with his name, but also extending to his reputation as a teacher and his close association with Colum of Terryglass, a probable localization of Colum Cille.[3]

The question of the remote origins of the saint would have counted for little at Clonard, which was more concerned with projecting an image of its own importance through what appears to have been a productive scriptorium, at least from the twelfth century on. Not only has a full list of Finnian's successors as abbots survived, the saint himself was made the subject of several Lives in Latin and Irish.[4] Unfortunately, although one study has been made to date of the historical value of the Lives, they have yet to be brought together and edited in dossier fashion.[5] Despite the fact that none of the manuscript evidence for the Lives is earlier than the fourteenth century, it has been implausibly argued that the Irish Life – whose earliest surviving copy was made in the fifteenth century – is the most 'primitive' of the saint's biographies, dating from not later than the ninth or tenth century, largely on the evidence of a materialistic outlook thought to be reminiscent of the period after the arrival of the Danes.[6] Against this, however, it has also been suggested that the Irish Life represents an adaptation of a Latin Life, which itself shows no sign of being early.[7] The second opinion is the one favoured here.

The author of the vernacular adaptation, who was presumably at work in Clonard, all but conceded the lateness of his text by stating that the saint was born *ibhus*, 'here', in Leinster; Meath was probably not felt to be part of Leinster until after the arrival of the Normans in the late twelfth century.[8] Some changes made to the vernacular Life succeed only in making a nonsense of the text, as when Dairinis (now Ardcavan, near Wexford town) of the source is altered to read Tairinis (Tours in France) in relation to a visit made by Finnian to Caomhán of Ardcavan, or when 'Croíbe Mór', later Craobh Ghrealláin and now Creeve in the barony and county of Roscommon, is metamorphosed to read 'Cairbre Mhór', the Sligo barony of Carbury.[9]

Also indicative of a date of composition after the arrival in Ireland of the Anglo-Normans is the almost unholy haste with which Finnian is transported to south Wales, and shown to be on the best of terms with three of the principal saints of that area, David, Cadog and Gildas, a situation bound to impress the invading adventurers, most of whom had family links in that part of Britain.[10] On the other hand, a date before about 1220 may be inferred from the mention by the biographer of Abán of Adamstown, who was at work around that time, of Finnian's baptism at the hands of his subject.[11]

Several associations claimed for the saint by his biographers, though bringing him to places far removed from Clonard, would appear to have local resonances. The time he spent as a youth with Bishop Foirtchearn in Uí Dhróna, for example, founding, according to the vernacular Life, several churches – Aghowle, Rossacurra, Drumfea, and Kilmaglush – within a few miles of each other in an area now comprising the Wicklow parish of Aghowle, and the Carlow parishes of Myshall and Fennagh, may stem partly from the fact that the local dynasty of

Uí Fheilmheadha was closely linked genealogically to the Fir Thulach who gave name to the Westmeath barony of Fartullagh, just west of Clonard.[12]

If the original Life belongs in the period about 1200, then the location of a house of Augustinian canons named *Dunum* (later Down, alias Abbeydown, in the Wexford parish of Moyacomb), within five miles of the saint's Carlow/Wicklow foundations, may also have played a role because the Clonard house of canons – named St Mary's and founded in 1144 – was among the most important in the country.[13] Similarly, the presence near Clonard of an Augustinian convent of nuns founded by Murchadh Ua Maoil Sheachlainn (†1153) may explain the interest shown by the biographer in the affairs of Finnian's sister (Ríoghnach) and mother who, with the mother of Ciarán, presumably of Clonmacnoise, is said to have dwelt in a nearby *cella*.[14] What makes this link especially likely is the fact that Murchadh's daughter Agnes was abbess of the convent in Clonard in 1167, when her sister Dearbhfhorgaill was rebuilding the Nun's Church in Clonmacnoise, later (in 1195) confirmed to the nuns at Clonard.[15] The biographer's concern with Ruadhán above all other disciples assigned to Finnian is probably also because of the presence in Lorrha of an Augustinian house of canons, founded about the middle of the twelfth century.[16] A posthumous miracle attributed to Finnian involving Colmán Eala may have been influenced by the probable dependence of Colmán's church at Lynally on Durrow, which became the seat of an Augustinian priory in the 1140s, again founded by Murchadh Ua Maoil Sheachlainn.[17]

The saint's journey to north Connacht, where he is said to have founded many churches, including Achonry (subsequently relinquished to Nathí) probably owes something to the influence of the Uí Dhubhthaigh (O'Duffys), the leading ecclesiastical family in Connacht, whose church and home place at Lissonuffy (Lios Ua nDubhthaigh), likewise the site of an Augustinian priory, was within a few miles of Finnian's church at Clooncraff.[18] A cross made for Finnian's coarb at the latter church was kept at Cong, the main church of the Uí Dhubhthaigh, and also the location of an Augustinian priory.[19] Because of the tradition that he was tutor of some of the most prominent of the saints of Ireland, and first of the 'second order' of saints, Finnian received mention in numerous other Lives.[20]

His association with Colum son of Criomhthann, who is reputed to have rendered him the last rites, is dealt with much more extensively in the Life of the Terryglass saint. This asserts that Colum died on the day after Finnian at Clonee (Cluain Í) in the parish of Trim, close to Clonard, and lay buried there, according to some, for seven years.[21] The martyrologies record the feasts of the two saints on successive days (12, 13 December), and Finnian's sister's son and immediate successor, Mocholmóg (Colmán) of the Maca Teallaibh, was remembered on his predecessor's day, as well as on 9 February.[22] Finnian's feast of 12 December – traditionally regarded as bringing bad weather (*roinn ar an uair*) – was recorded in an early ninth-century calendar kept by an Irishman on the Reichenau in Lake Constance.[23] The saint's day also mysteriously found its way into a Visigothic manuscript of about the same period, compiled in Spain.[24] A feast of 23 February is also recorded.[25] The statement in the annals that Finnian was among those who died in the great plague of 549 may be discounted, first because of his probable identity with his namesake of Movilla, who died in 579, and second because of the suspect nature of the list containing his name.[26] Among many other churches claiming Finnian as patron, Nohovaldaly in the Cork barony of Duhallow, where his feast was celebrated on 13 December, may be the furthest south.[27] The saint's relics, presumably enshrined, were taken on tour in 776.[28] His coarb at the Roscommon church of Clooncraff was among the ecclesiastics entitled to be present at the inauguration of O'Connor as king of Connacht.[29]

1 *Kenney* 374; *CEIS* 217; *DIB* iii, 793–5. **2** *CGSH* §712.3; *VSHH* 83 §5. **3** *CGSH* §§122, 722.56; *GRSH* 114; *Lgen.* 732.10; *CGH* 130b4, 161b31 add; cf. *RM* 7.3, 29–36; *MakS* 1–12, 13–29. **4** *NHI* ix, 243–4; *Kenney* 375–6; *VSHH* 96–107; *LisL* 2503–786. **5** *EHR* 69, 353–72. **6** Ibid. 359–60; *IHS* 9, 13–14. **7** *Kenney* 375. **8** *LisL* 2747–8; *EHR* 69, 358. **9** *LisL* 2527, 2714. **10** *VSHH* 97–8 §§4–10; *LisL* 2527–66; *ScrV* 41–8. **11** *VSHP* i, 23 §22; *VSHH* 96 §2; *PSICCSO* 159–70. **12** *LisL* 2526; OCBG §1772; *PNW* 162; *BCML* 92 §90, 94 §92. **13** *MRHI* 163–4, 169. **14** *VSHH* 102 §21; *LisL* 2661–71. **15** *MRHI* 314–15; *JRSAI* 21, 197. **16** *MRHI* 185. **17** *VSHH* 107 §35, 224 §49; *MRHI* 174–5. **18** *LisL* 2696–718; *MRHI* 185. **19** *IARP* 108–9; *WLC* 100. **20** *VSHH* 82–3. **21** Ibid. 102 §20; *LisL* 2769–73. **22** *CGSH* §722.97; *MartT* 15; *MartO*[2] 251; *MartG* 32, 236–8; *MartD* 42, 332–4; cf. *BCML* 92 §90, 94 §92. **23** *AfL* 31, 64; *Béaloideas* 3, 130, 134; OSL LH 142. **24** *AB* 72, 347–52. **25** *MartD* 420; *FEMN* 363, 390. **26** *AU s.a.*; *MakS* 14–17. **27** *NCHC* 1, 294; *PABD* 340–1. **28** *AU s.a.* **29** *JRSAI* 2, 340; *MSPAG* 189.

Finnian of Dromin. *See* Fiontan Fionn.

Finnian of Movilla (Magh Bhile), parish of Newtownards, barony of Ards Lower, Co. Down. The earliest mention of this saint – under the guise of *Vennianus auctor*, 'Finnian the writer' – is contained in a letter written about AD600 to Pope Gregory the Great by Columbanus of Bobbio, who referred to the saint's correspondence with Gildas.[1] A penitential text by Columbanus also reveals the influence of a similar text attributed to Finnian.[2] Before leaving Ireland for the Continent about AD590, Columbanus had taught at Bangor, a few miles from Movilla which, by association, became the first of Finnian's churches to be mentioned in the written record.[3] The next earliest mention of the saint is in the Life composed by Adhamhnán shortly before AD700 for his illustrious predecessor, Colum Cille, which states that the founder of Iona, while 'acquiring knowledge of sacred scripture' from an elderly bishop named Finnian (alias Fionnbharr), performed his first miracle by changing water, Christ-like, into wine.[4] In this way, Adhamhnán established for Finnian two associations that were to become integral features of his cult, teaching and sacred scripture.

Although Adhamhnán, like Columbanus, failed to identify the church of the saint, it may reasonably be assumed that Colum, a native of Ceinéal Conaill (approximately co-extensive with the diocese of Raphoe), would have received his education principally in the north of Ireland, which points to Movilla. Adhamhnán's silence proved unsatisfactory to later writers who, probably due to confusion, named both Movilla and Clonard as schools attended by Colum.[5] Following this lead, modern scholars have also been divided, mostly either opting for Clonard over Movilla or reserving their judgement, but the fact that Clonard's Finnian is nowhere given the radical or full form of the name used by Adhamhnán, viz. Fionnbharr, would appear to rule out this church.[6] Besides Movilla and Clonard, there were numerous other churches throughout Ireland associated with a saint of this name, and by limiting the choice to two churches only, scholars have ignored the possibility that all saints of the name were originally one and the same.[7]

Regardless of where the saint's church was located – and Movilla must be regarded as the strongest contender – Finnian (alias Fionnbharr and Bairrfhionn) became the focus of a vigorous cult which quickly spread throughout Ireland and beyond, to parts of Britain and the Continent.[8] In spreading, the cult was unavoidably affected by the requirements of local devotion. The saint's name, for instance, can be shown to have alternated between full and familiar forms according to local preference, which is a feature of almost all Irish cults. With the passage of time, however, localization inexorably led to fragmentation, thus giving rise to the apparently groundless assumption that not one but many saints of the name had once been active in Ireland.

Mainly because of the British pet form of his name, viz. Vennianus (from Finnio, the equivalent of British Gwyniaw), the view has been taken by some that Finnian was British in origin, coming to Ireland as a missionary in much the same way as Patrick had done.[9] The onomastic evidence by no means unambiguously points to British origins. The British ending *–io* of the pet form of the name was used side by side with the much more common and fully Irish other forms of the saint's name, viz. Fionnbharr, Bairrfhionn and their derivatives. However, since there is independent early evidence to indicate that the saint was regarded as an outsider, he may have been a native of one of the Irish settlements in south-west Britain, where he could easily have acquired his pet name from British-speaking neighbours.[10] This would also explain his familiarity with Gildas who lived and worked on the edge of the area of Irish settlement in south Wales.[11] The community at Movilla evidently had little time for the saint's probable external origins, assimilating him instead to a branch of the local family of Dál bhFiatach to which several other saintly relatives, including a grandfather (Oilill) and some granduncles, were also affiliated, and providing him with an obviously Irish mother, named Lasair.[12]

Despite the prominence received by Movilla in the written record, which may have been largely due to its proximity to Bangor, the church appears never to have produced a written Life of its founder saint. This deficiency was later remedied at Lucca in Italy, where apologists for the local saint, Frediano (Latin Frigidianus), whose floruit is independently attested by a mention in the writings of Gregory the Great (†604), misappropriated some elements of the tradition surrounding Finnian in order to establish the identity of the two.[13] The Irish element in this Life, which may have reached Lucca by means of a network involving the house of canons regular at Movilla and Irishmen resident in (or on their way to) Rome, partly corresponds to the contents of the *praefatio* to the hymn of St Mugentius of Whithorn (*Candida Casa*). This relates how Finnian, having gone to Whithorn with two companions (Ríóg and Talmhach) to study under Mugentius, became involved in a subterfuge which resulted in his mentor receiving a blow on the head, thus setting the scene for the composition of the hymn beginning *Parce Domine*, 'spare, O Lord'.[14] On going to Ireland, Finnian is said to have taken the religious habit at Movilla and, after various miracles – one of them involving punishment inflicted on a man named Art, king of Oirghialla, a territory approximately corresponding to the extent of the diocese of Clogher – he left for Lucca in Tuscany where, the fame of his good deeds having spread, he was elected bishop, a position he held for twenty-eight years.[15]

Finnian's *alter ego* in Scotland, Wynnin of Kilwinning in Ayrshire attracted two Lives, one in the form of an office preserved in the Breviary of Aberdeen, which is thin on onomastic detail, the other in Capgrave's *Nova Legenda*.[16] The latter text provides a good deal of local Irish colour, naming the saint's parents as Cairbre and Lasair, alluding to a prophecy of his sanctity by Patrick, and stating that he was educated by both Colmán, presumably of Dromore, and Caolán of Nendrum.[17] It also attributes to him a pilgrimage to Rome and dealings with various Irish kings. The wider literature found room for Finnian in a number of contexts, some cursory, as when he was shown assisting Beag son of Dé in blessing a secular dynast of the Dál bhFiatach, some less so, as when he encouraged Tuán son of Coireall to recount the invasions of Ireland, or when he, together with Aodh of Rahugh, blessed Mughain, wife of Diarmuid son of Cearbhall, so as to ensure the birth of Aodh Sláine, the eponymous ancestor of a powerful Meath dynasty.[18] Among other texts containing mention of Finnian is the Life of Fiontan of Doon which, characteristically, speaks of the saint's *evangelium*, 'gospel-book'.[19] This particular association would suggest that Finnéan of Dromin (Druim Ing) in the Louth barony of Ardee, who, according to some sources, famously refused Colum Cille permission to copy his gospel-book, was another localization of the saint.[20]

Likened to James the Apostle in manners, Finnian was regarded as chief patron of the men of Ulster.[21] According to special pleading in Capgrave's text, Finnian's body was taken to Scotland after his death and buried in Kilwinning. He was also patron of the Donegal church of Moville (Magh Bhile), likewise a claimant to the saint's burial place.[22] The saint's obit is assigned to the year 579 and, although his main feastday was observed on 10 September, he was also remembered on 11 February and, if he be identical with Finnéan of Dromin, on 10 (sometimes 8) October.[23] A relic of his reached the Continent, where it was kept, arguably, at Ferrières in France or at a church in the Rhineland.[24] Another relic, accompanied by relics of Colum Cille and Adhamhnán, reached Saint-Maurice d'Agaune in the Swiss canton of Valais by the second half of the eighth century, and by the mid-ninth century another relic is attested for the Rhineland.[25]

1 *SCO* 8 §7. **2** *IrP* 5. **3** *IV* 158–60. **4** *VC*² 324–5. **5** *IKD* 227–8 §§25–6; *BCC* 54–6 §§69, 71; *UJA* 6 (1st ser.), 5–6. **6** *Kenney* 240; *ECI* 290–93; *IrP* 4; *VC*¹ lxii; *VC*² 68–9; *DIB* iii,795–6. **7** *JCHAS* 82, 63–82; *IETÜ* 52–7; *FKHS* 407–14. **8** *MakS* 13–29. **9** *ÉtC* 15, 607–17; *IEKF* 19–20, 52–72; *SaintP* 133–46; *GNA* 207–14; *DNHS* 71–84; *Innes Review* 52, 1–28. **10** *MartO*² 193; *LH* i, 22; *MakS* 9; *FPM* 187–202; *ECI* 291. **11** *IBVSH* 32–9. **12** *CGSH* §§136.1.2, 722.40; *GRSH* 83; *Lgen.* 723.3; *ZCP* 14, 56–8. **13** *ASH* 634–7. **14** *LH* i, 22. **15** *ASH* 635–7. **16** *NLA* i, 444–7; *BrevA* pars hiem. 38–9; *DNHS* 85–102; *Innes Review* 32, 64; cf. *KSS* 463–6; *ACDS* 81–4; *CGSH* §§136, 722.40; *BB* 116b40; *LegSS* 42–5, 422–3. **17** *NLA* i, 444–7; *KSS* 465; *ASH* 438; *EA* 189. **18** *CGSH* §§712.5, 729.1; *Ériu* 35, 101; *CAn.* 37–8 §134. **19** *VSHH* 114–15 §6. **20** *IMN* 22, 3; *LU* 548–51. **21** *CGSH* §§712.5; 729.1; *ZCP* 13, 350; *SG* i, 83–4. **22** *DYHS* 195; *UJA* (2nd ser.) 1,172; *BOI* 14–15; *AnH* 12, 85. **23** *AU s.a.*; *MakS* 14–17; *MartT* 16, 70; *MartO*² 193; *MartG* 34, 174; *MartD* 44, 242; *SAM* 2.1, 197. **24** *EIRD* 55–68; *RIW* 15–19. **25** *RIW* 13, 32.

Finnseach. *See* Finncheall.

Fintan. *See* Fiontan.

Fiodhairle/Fiodhghas sons of Fiodhbhadhach. *See* Fiodhmhaine.

Fiodhmhaine of Rahan (Rathan), barony of Ballycowan, Co. Offaly. Bearing names derived from *fiodh*, 'wood', compounded with *muine*, 'grove', *airle*, 'counsel', and *gus*, 'strength', the three sons of Fiodhbhadhach (also from *fiodh*, 'wood') were individually named Fiodhmhaine, Fiodhairle, and Fiodhghas. As a group, however, they were known as Uí Shuanaigh, and their descent was traced to the Uí Fhiachrach (whose ancestor gave name to Tír Fhiachrach, now Tireragh in Sligo), and more specifically to Eachaidh Breac whose seed, including Fiodhbhadhach, is said to have been blessed by Cormac of Killala.[1] Their mother, whose name is variously rendered Fearbhla and Fearamhla, is said to have belonged to another branch of Uí Fhiachrach.[2] She was considered to have been the mother of three other saints, Aodhán of Cloonoghil, Díchleithe of Dysert, and Colmán of Templeshanbo, a church with which Aodhán was also associated.[3]

Although the north Connacht background to the cult, exemplified by the ecclesiastical names Ceall Ua Suanaigh (corruptly written 'Collinusuanig') in the diocese of Killala, and Ardachadh Ua Suanaigh (now Ardagh in the Mayo barony of Tirawley), remained well known, three churches outside that province were principally associated with the Uí Shuanaigh.[4] These were Rahan in Offaly (Fiodhmhaine), Kinsale (Ceann Sáile) in Cork or, more probably, Kinsaley in Dublin (Fiodhairle), and Glascarrig (Glascharraig) in the Wexford parish of Donaghmore (Fiodhghas).[5] The association with Rahan receives most coverage in the literature, with one whole tract devoted to an account of Fiodhmhaine's stewardship after Mochuda had been expelled from the church.[6] One episode in this tract, also in the Life of Colmán of Lynn, involves a meeting between Colmán and Maol Tuile of Dysart (described as Fiodhmhaine's *bron-dalta*, 'bosom-foster-child'), and their cursing in verse of a local father and seven sons.[7] The main concern of the writer of the tract was, however, to show local chieftains and landowners that the saint's coarbs were to be treated respectfully, with most of the exemplary punishment meted out to twelfth-century representatives of the Uí Mhaoil Mhuadh (O'Molloys), which is precisely the period that has annalistic references to Fiodhmhaine's successors.[8] A separate tale describes how the Ceinéal Fiachach ancestors of the Uí Mhaoil Mhuadh, having murdered satirists under Uí Shuanaigh protection, were forced to forfeit two townlands in recompense.[9]

The annal entry noting Fiodhmhaine's death in 757 describes him as an anchorite; before this, in 744 and 748, what was presumably his Law (*lex nepotis Suanaigh*) had been twice proclaimed over the Northern Half of Ireland.[10] Despite his alleged association with Kinsale (or Kinsaley), Fiodhairle is styled abbot of Rahan in his 762 obit, as also in the notice of his feastday.[11] Also, while Fiodhmhaine and Fiodhairle are accorded separate feastdays, 16 May and 1 October, there is no trace of Fiodhghas in the martyrological record.[12] The later martyrologies name Ennisboyne (Inis Bhaoithín) in the Wicklow parish of Dunganstown as another of Fiodhmhaine's churches. A passage in the tract entitled 'Four saints' purports to explain the name *suanach* as 'sleepiness', a trait which, in accordance with a promise made by Cormac of Killala, would not attach to any member of the group.[13] References in two poems relating to Seanán of Scattery probably advert to the representative of the family at Termon (previously Tearmann Uí Shuanaigh) in the Galway parish of Kilmacduagh.[14] The same member of the family is called upon, in a poem in Classical Irish, along with numerous other saints, to help in releasing Ireland's southern half (Leath Mogha) from a bondage imposed on it by the northern half (Leath Chuinn), headed by Finnian of Clonard, whose church is elsewhere associated with 'Ua Suanaigh'.[15] A poem of prophecies also refers to one or other of the brothers, and 'Ó Suanigh' is among the mainly Connacht saints invoked in a poem by Donnchadh Mór Ó Dálaigh (†1244).[16]

1 *CGSH* §§383, 545; *IrT* iii, 4. **2** *BNÉ* i, 312 §2; *TCHyF* 36. **3** *Lgen.* 253.1; *TCHyF* 36. **4** *PHib.* i, 103–4; *HDGP* i, 103. **5** *IrT* iii, 3 §7; *Lgen.* 253.3; *TCHyF* 36. **6** *BNÉ* i, 312–16. **7** Ibid. 314–15 §§7–8; *BCML* 76–8 §75. **8** *AFM s.a.*1113, 1136, 1166; cf. *ZCP* 21, 5. **9** *TribesI* 17n.; *MIAS* 179–80. **10** *AU s.a.* **11** ATig. *s.a.* **12** *MartT* 43, 76; *MartO*² 124; *MartG* 98, 188; *MartD* 130, 264. **13** *IrT* iii, 3 §7. **14** *ZCP* 10, 26 §21; *IrT* iv, 93 §5. **15** RIA MS 21L11, 263; *BCML* 78 §75. **16** *Ériu* 18, 58 §4; *DDé* 51.

FÍONA daughter of Ceann Faoladh/Colmán. *See* Íde.

FÍONÁN. This name, which derives from *fíon*, 'wine', perhaps as a pet form of Fínghin, literally 'wine-birth', was a common appellation, with eleven bearers in the list of homonymous saints.[1] Among churches – many of them unidentified – mentioned in this list are Cluain Caichne, Eanach Luaighne, and Murbholg. Otherwise unattested paternal names include Colmán and Eoghan.

1 *CGSH* §707.441–51.

FÍONÁN of Ceann Tráchta. *See* Coilliodhan.

FÍONÁN of Cua. *See* Fíonán of Druim Abhradh.

FÍONÁN of Druim Abhradh, possibly another name for Ceann Abhradh, now Seefin in the Ballyhoura (Bealach Eabhradh) Hills, on the southern boundary of Co. Limerick.[1] The genealogists attached Fíonán son of Garbhán to the Uí Éanna branch of the Eoghanachta of Munster, who were settled in Áine, the area about Knockainy (Cnoc Áine) in Limerick.[2] The church that probably marked Fíonán's local memory, at Kilfinnane (from Ceall Fhíonáin) in the barony of Coshlea, was only a few miles south of Knockainy.[3] Seventeenth-century sources provide a choice of possible feastdays, varying between 13 February – also assigned to Fíonán of Drumnid – and 8 December, otherwise the feast of Fíonán of Cua (short for Sliabh gCua), now the Knockmealdown mountains between the counties of Waterford and Tipperary.[4] At Ardfinnan (Ard Fíonáin) on the Tipperary side of these mountains, yet another Fíonán, sometimes thought to have been the 'leprous' patron of Swords, was venerated.[5] Finally, one of the holy wells in the Clare parish of Kilshanny was dedicated to 'Mac Crabhain', which may represent Mac Garbháin, a possible local version of Fíonán son of Garbhán.[6]

1 ATig. ind. 116; *NMAJ* 1, 39. **2** *CGSH* §216; *GRSH* 117; *Lgen.* 740.9; *HDGP* i, 32–3. **3** *NMAJ* 1, 39; *Éigse* 29, 155n. **4** *GRSH* 117; *MartG* 234; *MartD* 330. **5** *MartD* 76. **6** *ACoC* 99; *JNMArchS* 1, 150.

Fíonán of Drumnid (Druim Neoid) in the parish and barony of Mohill, Co. Leitrim. The scribe of the Book of Lecan altered his exemplar's copy of the pedigree of the Munster saint, Fíonán son of Garbhán, to read Fíonán son of Aodh, providing him with a church in Leitrim, and tracing his descent to the Uí Bhriúin of Connacht.[1] As Lecan (Lacken) was also situated in north Connacht, he was no doubt moved to do this by local knowledge and loyalty. Although ignored by Dubhaltach Mac Fhir Bhisigh, the last of the great scholars of Lecan, at least one seventeenth-century version of the pedigrees of the saints gave prominence to Fíonán.[2] A note added to this version of the pedigree supplies a choice of two feasts, 13 February and 4 October, the first of which is also mentioned in relation to Fíonán of Druim Abhradh.[3] Although also speculatively attached to Fíonán of Drumnid in the Martyrology of Donegal, neither day is elsewhere attested.[4] A list of saints from the area, drawn up in the early seventeenth century, makes no mention of Fíonán, but he was probably also remembered at Cloonfinnan (Cluain Fíonáin?) in the parish of Mohill, not far from Drumnid.[5]

1 *CGSH* §216. **2** *GRSH* 59. **3** Ibid. 117. **4** *MartD* 48, 266. **5** *Celtica* 1, 66–7; but cf. Logainm.ie 'Cloonfinnan'.

Fíonán of Ray (Ráith), parish of Raymunterdoney, barony of Kilmacrenan, Co. Donegal. This son of Píobán is said to have belonged to a branch of the Ceinéal Conaill that provided several abbots of Iona, among them Fíonán's brother (Fáilbhe), Cuimín Fionn, and Laisréan.[1] It has also been suggested, however, that he and his consanguines belonged to a family known as Ceinéal Duach.[2] He was regarded as a fosterling of Colum Cille, and a great thirst that seized him is said to have led to a Moses-like miracle performed by Colum involving three blows to a rock in order to produce water at a place later called Eas Fíonáin.[3] Another miracle saw his church receiving a cross that had been promised by Colum Cille to whoever would find a book left by the wayside, and bring it back dry, which, with the help of a crow that spread its wings over the book, Fíonán duly did.[4] In addition to Ray, he was associated with a church named Ceall Fhíonáin among the Fir Cheara of the present Mayo barony of Carra, possibly Church Island in the parish of Ballintober.[5] Here he is reputed to have rejected the presence of the Munsterman, Cormac of Killala, thus leading to a curse on his church and its ultimate abandonment.[6] Though he was commemorated on 25 November, a *turas* used to be made on the first Sunday of May to the *eas*, 'cataract', named after him.[7] His well was in the townland of Errarooey More.[8]

1 *CGSH* §339; *GRSH* 41. **2** *CCDK* 98–9. **3** *BCC* 108 §114; OSL DL 74. **4** OSL DL 77–8; cf. *Béaloideas* 3, 53–4. **5** *IrT* iii, 2 §4; *HDGP* iii, 173; *NotesEHDT* 270, 278. **6** *IrT* iii, 2 §4. **7** *MartG* 226; *MartD* 318; OSL DL 79. **8** *ASCD* 303.

Fíonán of Teach Oirthir, an unidentified site in the barony of Narragh and Reban, Co. Kildare. Two Lives of saints (Patrick and Fiontan of Clonenagh) throw light on the tradition surrounding this saint. Coming into the area west of the river Liffey, Patrick is said to have been warned by Brígh daughter of Feargna of Uí Earcáin, Fíonán's sister, that a trap had been laid for him near Moone in

Kildare by the Laoighis, who gave name to the neighbouring county of Laois.[1] Though the Laoighis were cursed as a result of this, Brígh's family, including her father and brother, received Patrick's blessing. Brígh's (and Fíonán's) father was to receive even greater acclaim from Fiontan's biographer as a good and famous man who, despite having twelve sons and several daughters, relinquished worldly things and died in the aura of sanctity.[2] Although neither account mentions Fíonán by name, he was well known to the genealogists who attached him to the Uí Earcáin branch of the Fothairt.[3] As Brighid also belonged to the Fothairt, it is not surprising to find a Fíonán, along with two unnamed sisters and two (otherwise unattested) daughters of a man named Díbheachán – Finneach and Moinis – among the saints said to have been subject to Kildare.[4] In this capacity, he could also be represented by 'Moenóc' (perhaps from Mofhíonóg) of Glassely (Glais Éile) in the parish of Narraghmore, which adjoins Moone, and perhaps also by the Fiontan (*recte* Fíonán?) assigned to Tippeenan (Teach Fíonáin?) in the Kildare parish of Fontstown in an early sixteenth-century papal document.[5] In the list for 4 October, one of the days allotted speculatively to Fíonán son of Feargna by seventeenth-century sources, he is accompanied by Mofhíonóg.[6]

1 *BP* 2195–206; *VT* 186–8. 2 *VSHP* ii, 103–4 §18. 3 *CGSH* §7; *GRSH* 75; cf. *AB* 76, 389, 401. 4 *CGSH* §670.54; *Lgen.* 753.25. 5 *CGSH* §670.56; *CPL* 17, §934. 6 *GRSH* 75; *MartT* 77; *MartG* 190; *MartD* 266.

FÍONÁN son of Draighean. *See* Ainmhire of Kilroe.

FÍONÁN son of Oireannán. An entry in the annals for 676 notes the death of this saint, whose name also figures in the list of those commemorated on 12 February.[1] This day was marked annually by a visit to Fíonán's well in the Kerry parish of Kinard.[2]

1 *AU s.a.*; *MartT* 16; *MartG* 34; *MartD* 46. 2 *TCCD* 151.

FÍONÁN CAM, 'bent/squint-eyed', of Kinnity (Ceann Eitigh), barony of Ballybritt, Co. Offaly; of Innisfallen (Inis Faithlinn), parish of Aghadoe, barony of Magunihy, Co. Kerry; and of several other churches in the same county. The priest-poet, Seán Ó Conaill, a native of south Kerry, appealed for aid to three saints named Fíonán in his well-known *Tuireamh na hÉireann*, 'elegy of Ireland', assigning one to Clonard (Cluain Ioraird) in Meath, another to Innisfallen on Lower Lake, Killarney, and the third to Waterville Lake (Loch Luighdheach) in Iveragh.[1] The first is a mistake for Finnian of Clonard, but the second and third refer to a single saint who, although mainly commemorated in Kerry, is often associated in the literature with Kinnitty. The genealogists had no doubt on the question of Fíonán's origins; they attached him through his father Maonach to the descendants of Conaire (Síol Conaire) and, more immediately, to the Corca Dhuibhne whose name survives in the barony of Corkaguiny, but who also represented the people of the Iveragh peninsula.[2] Fíonán was regarded as one of the chief protectors of the Corca Dhuibhne and as one of three *coinnle*, 'candles', of the Múscraighe, the others being Laichtín and Seanán.[3] His mother, Beagnad daughter of Cian, is said to have been a virgin who conceived while bathing – in Killarney Lake, according to one version.[4] Although attached by early liturgical texts, such as the ninth-century Martyrology of Aonghas, primarily to the Midlands church of Kinnitty, from the twelfth century onwards accounts of the saint and his activities give equal or even more space to his *patria* in south Kerry, where there are numerous surviving dedications to him.[5] The late twelfth-century Martyrology of Gorman assigns him not only to Kinnitty, but also to Innisfallen, and this division of focus is upheld by his biographers.[6]

Fíonán was made the subject of several written Lives, the earliest being that of the Salamancan codex (*codex Salmanticensis*) which was probably compiled in a house of canons regular of St Augustine at Clogher in Tyrone in the early fourteenth century.[7] This version of the saint's Life was the source of two other Latin Lives, one in the Kilkenny codex (*codex Kilkenniensis*) now preserved in Marsh's Library, Dublin, the other in two manuscripts in the Bodleian Library, Oxford.[8] Fíonán was also made the subject of two vernacular Lives preserved in early seventeenth-century manuscripts.[9] The Salamancan text, which most closely represents the source of all versions of Fíonán's Life, has been dated by some scholars to the eighth century, but there are many aspects of it that point to a date, at the earliest, in the second half of the twelfth century.[10]

The author's main concern was with the saint's activities in south Kerry, in the areas about Lower Lake (Loch Léin), Killarney, and Waterville Lake (Loch Luighdheach). The saint is said to have been born of a noble family in Corca Dhuibhne, to have performed various miraculous cures as a child, and to have been educated by the pre-eminent Kerry saint, Bréanainn of Clonfert, whose own vernacular Life gives Fíonán the privilege of being the only one who could look at his face, because of its abundance of grace.[11] Bréanainn is said to have directed Fíonán to the place of his resurrection at Kinnitty, but almost immediately afterwards the saint was brought back to Kerry, where he arranged for the miraculous transfer of a boat from Killarney to Waterville.[12] Then, having returned to the Midlands for one episode, he was again in his 'own country' performing many miracles, including the relief of a threat posed by Neachtan, king of Uí Fhidhgheinte, an area corresponding to east Limerick.[13] Back in Kinnitty once more, Fíonán taught manners to a Munster king named Fáilbhe Flann, before blessing him, and almost immediately showed favour to a man named Carthach, providing him with a single shoe, a symbol associated with sovereignty.[14] In the remainder of the Life, the saint is shown to have had dealings with the Ciarraighe of north Kerry and the Eoghanacht of Raithleann in Cork, as well as associations with two persons in south Kerry, Mocheallóg, probably of Kilmakillogue (Ceall Muicheallóg) in the parish of Touosist, and an unnamed craftsman in Waterville.[15] The saint's death is then described, without any mention of where it occurred.

The fact that the saint's Life allows him to spend most of his time in Kerry scarcely favours a Midlands authorship. The text's focus on Killarney's Lower Lake and Waterville Lake reflects the positions of churches that formed part of the spread of devotion to Fíonán, who was patron of Innisfallen and of several places in the Waterville area, including the church of Killemlagh. These associations are first attested in documents dating from the late twelfth century, by which time Augustinian canons had established a priory on Innisfallen before proceeding to facilitate pilgrims to Skellig Michael by locating a house in the parish of Prior, near Waterville, of which Fíonán was also patron.[16] With its scriptorium dating at the latest to the middle of the twelfth century, Innisfallen would have been a likely place of composition for the Life.[17] An Augustinian connection would also explain the choice of Fíonán's mentor because Bréanainn was not only patron of the diocese of Kerry, but also of Clonfert, the seat of a house of canons, founded possibly as early as the 1140s, and located a mere fifteen miles or so from Kinnitty.[18]

The politics underlying the Life can be best explained in relation to the twelfth century, with three of the kings that received favours from the saint – Feidhlimidh, Fáilbhe Flann, and Carthach – appearing in the same order in the pedigree of the powerful Mac Carthaigh (MacCarthy) family which first came to prominence in south Munster about 1100.[19] During the 1120s, Cormac, a prominent member of this family, was involved with Toirdhealbhach Ua Conchobhair of Connacht in a prolonged struggle for supremacy which involved numerous other Munster families, including those of south Kerry. In 1124, Muircheartach Ua Muircheartaigh, king of the Eoghanacht of Lough Leane, was banished by Cormac to Connacht, returning in the following year to raid Corca Dhuibhne and the Killarney area with the aid of a fleet of boats.[20] This series of incidents may underlie the episode in Fíonán's Life that describes how the saint saved Corca Dhuibhne from invasion at the hands of a king of the Uí Fhidhgheinte named Neachtan, who is described in one source as an ancestor of Muircheartach Ua Muircheartaigh.[21]

On the basis of cumulative evidence, therefore, Fíonán's Life is likely to have been first written down in the mid- to late twelfth century. Later Lives of the saint pursued their own agenda. The latest of them, a vernacular Life surviving in at least eight manuscripts, may have been written at 'Killagh Abbey' in the Kerry parish of Kilcolman, near Milltown, which Abán, having foretold Fíonán's birth, is elsewhere said to have bestowed upon the saint.[22]

The saint's feastday is the subject of confusion. In south Kerry it falls on 16 March, the day assigned by the martyrologies to a namesake, Fíonán Lobhar, 'leprous one', of Swords.[23] However, in the later martyrologies, Innisfallen is named as one of this saint's churches.[24] The day assigned to Fíonán Cam was 7 April, when, it seems, he was remembered at Kinnity, but the later martyrologies again allude on this day to the fact that the saint belonged to the Corca Dhuibhne of south Kerry to whom he bequeathed that they should never be without a famous nun.[25] If patron of Killinane (Ceall Fhíonáin?), near Cahersiveen, he was also commemorated on 3 March.[26] Patterns were held at his well near Kenmare on 3 May and 14 September and he was remembered at Nohavaldaly on the Cork-Kerry border on 14 December.[27] The cult also spread out from Kinnity, for example, to Rearymore in Laois, where a holy well preserved his memory.[28] The saint's rib reputedly formed part of Adhamhnán's reliquary, and his grave (*Leacht Fhíonáin*) was reputedly located on a hill in the Kerry parish of Killinane.[29]

Finally, Seán Ó Conaill's above-mentioned appeal for aid to Fíonán was by no means unique. An unpublished poem in Classical Irish calls upon the saint, together with numerous others, including several of the 'seed of Conaire', to help in releasing the churches of Ireland's southern half (Leath Mogha) from a bondage imposed on them by the northern half (Leath Chuinn), represented, ironically, by Finnian of Clonard, one of Fíonán's companions in Ó Conaill's poem.[30]

1 *FSPP* 81. **2** *CGSH* §211; *GRSH* 78; *Lgen.* 720.7.11–12; *IrR* 1911, 603; *DIB* iii, 779. **3** *ZCP* 8, 315; *CGSH* §665.7. **4** *MartO*² 112; *VSHH* 153 §1, *VSHP* ii 87 §1. **5** *MartO*² 105; *HCI* 367; *JKAHS* ser.2. vol.7, 15–36. **6** *MartG* 56; *JCS* 5, 120–4. **7** *VSHH* 153–60; *MirL* 91–100. **8** *VSHP* i, lxvii–lxx; ibid. ii, 87–95. **9** *MHH* 188–9; *ZCP* 2, 545–64. **10** *MISL* 297–339; *CeltC* 182–9; *PMIS* 79–90; *JCS* 5, 115–26. **11** *VSHH* 153–4 §§1–8; 326 §4; *LisL* 3426–34. **12** *VSHH* 154–5 §§10–11. **13** Ibid. 155–7 §§12–21. **14** Ibid. 158 §§26–7. **15** Ibid. 159–60 §§30–5. **16** *MRHI* 180, 192; *JKAHS* 22, 148. **17** *AI* xxix–xxx; *Bod. Cat.* i, 202. **18** *MRHI* 164–5. **19** *FNCC* 49–50. **20** *AI s.a.* **21** *CGH* 327a39. **22** *ZCP* 2, 545–64; *BNÉ* i, 8 §24; cf. *SSS* 309. **23** *MartT* 24; *MartO*² 82; *MartG* 56; *MartD* 76; *NCHK* 100; *UíR* 26; *Béaloideas* 29, 126. **24** *MartG* 56; *MartD* 76. **25** *MartT* 30; *MartO*² 105; *MartG* 72; *MartD* 96; *ZCP* 19, 175; *PRIA* 55C4, 83. **26** *ACoK* 145; *UíR.* 49; *JKAHS* ser.2. vol.7, 27. **27** *ACoK* 233; *AIKY* i, 543–4; *AB* 53, 215. **28** OSL LS i, 204; *CDKL* 260; *Dinn.* 2, 32. **29** *Celtica* 15, 34 §11; *UíR* 51. **30** RIA MS 23L11, 263; *AM* 24.1, 17, 21.

Fíonán Lobhar, 'leprous one', of Swords (Sord), barony of Nethercross, Co. Dublin, and of Clonmore (Cluain Mór), barony of Rathvilly, Co. Carlow. According to his earliest vernacular Life, Colum Cille founded a church at Swords – whence the designation Sord Coluim Chille – in which he left Fíonán Lobhar, a 'venerable man of his community', together with a gospel written by his own hand.[1] Colum's later vernacular Life adds to this account the assertion that Cainneach (patron of the neighbouring church of Finglas) and Comhghall were also present.[2] As far as the genealogists were concerned, Fíonán (son of Conall) belonged to the Cianachta, a segment of which (Cianachta Breagh) occupied lands close to Swords, mainly in the Louth barony of Ferrard.[3] Fíonán's other church was often called Cluain Mór Maodhóg after Maodhóg of Clonmore.[4] Probably because of this extended form of the name of Fíonán's other church, the biographers of the patron of Ferns also took an interest in the saint, attributing to him a vision that showed Maodhóg and Brighid of Kildare arriving together in a chariot at Ferns on Maodhóg's feastday.[5] This occasion is said to have given Maodhóg the opportunity of forecasting Fíonán's death three days after his own, which would give him an otherwise unrecorded feastday of 2 February. His regular feast, which, by assigning him not only to Swords, but also to Innisfallen, displays some confusion with that of his namesake Fíonán Cam, fell on 16 March.[6] The saint was apparently also patron of the church in Malahide parish, adjoining Swords parish, and he was widely venerated in Scotland.[7]

1 *IKD* 234 §43. **2** *BCC* 98 §102. **3** *CGSH* §193; *GRSH* 123; *Lgen.* 742.3. **4** *MartO*² 70. **5** *VSHH* 247 §53; *VSHP* ii, 162 §57; *BNÉ* i, 274–5 §§253–5. **6** *MartT* 24; *MartO*² 82; *MartG* 56; *MartD* 76. **7** *CPNS* 285–6; *KSS* 347; *AH* 8, 22.

Fíonmhaith daughter of Baoth. *See* Inghean Bhaoith.

Fíonmhaith daughter of Carthach. *See* Bearach of Kilbarry; Fraoch.

Fíonmhaith daughter of Fionghaine. *See* Mochuda.

Fionn daughter of Mac Iair. *See* Craobh daughter of Mac Iair.

Fíonnachta of Fionnchoradh. *See* Fíonnachta of Limerick.

Fíonnachta of Limerick (Luimneach Fíonnachta), parish of Kilcavan, barony of Gorey, Co. Wexford. Dubhaltach Mac Fhir Bhisigh praised this son of Tomaltach highly, describing him as a 'singular saint' of the Síol Muireadhaigh – later the Uí Chonchobhair (O'Connors) – who left the kingship of Connacht for the love of God, and obtained heaven for his brothers.[1] An account of his desertion of the kingship is preserved in a tale entitled *Baile Fíonnachta*, 'Fíonnachta's mantic vision'.[2] His brother Muirghius allegedly attempted to restrain Fíonnachta, but the saint finally reached a place called Formaol in Uí Cheinsealaigh, later 'Formoyle', near Limerick in the Wexford parish of Kilcavan, where, having marked out the site of his church, he fell asleep and had a prophetic dream concerning the future kings of Connacht. When disturbed by Colmán of Templeshanbo, Fíonnachta angrily left him with the unhappy *fágbháil*, 'legacy', that he should always waken when most desirous of sleep.

There is good reason to believe that this tale of an erstwhile king of Connacht who settled in south Leinster had more local origins in the person of Fíonnachta son of Colga of the Uí Cheinsealaigh.[3] Likewise of royal parentage, this Fíonnachta's father, and brother Cairbre, were associated with Ard Ladhrann, now probably the moat of Ardamine, some six miles from Limerick.[4] Fíonnachta's family also provided kings of Uí Dheagha, later the deanery of Oday, which contained both Ardamine and Limerick, and he himself was attached to a church named Fionnchoradh which may have lain near Courtown Harbour in the same area.[5] Also noteworthy is the fact that some of the place-names in Fíonnachta's story are replicated in south-east Clare in the form of Formoyle in the parish of Killokennedy, a few miles east of Kilfinaghta (Ceall Fhíonnachta), just north of Limerick city.[6] The Limerick parish of Killeenoghty and 'Chapelfeenaghty' in the townland of Lattoon, in the Galway parish of Ahascragh, may also be named after the saint.[7] Fíonnachta's obit occurs in the annals for 848.[8] Moreover, while no feastday is recorded for the saint, the Fíonnachta remembered on 14 November, who was taken by the martyrologists to have been a king of Ireland of that name, may refer more correctly to Fíonnachta of Limerick.[8] Remembered on the same day were Mocholmóg of the parish of Inch which adjoins Kilcavan, and sons of Dubhthach of the Maca Lughair who appears to have been connected with the area now straddling Wexford's boundary with Wicklow.

1 *Lgen.* 709.1. **2** *ZCP* 13, 25–7. **3** *CGSH* §275; *GRSH* 89. **4** *LL* 390b12; *AU*^{2} 722.2; *HDGP* i, 88. **5** *CGH* 337a44; *MedI* 253n. **6** p.c. (Kevin Murray). **7** *AIGY* ii, 322. **8** *AU s.a.* **9** *MartG* 218; *MartD* 308.

Fíonnachta son of Colga. *See* Fíonnachta of Limerick.

Fionnad. *See* Fiodhnad.

Fionnbharr. Deriving from *fionn*, 'fair', and *barr*, 'top/crown', this name is common, with seven representatives in the list of homonymous saints, together with five under the hypocoristic guise of Finnio/Finnian, and another seven entered in the same list as Bairrfhionn (from *barr* + *fionn*), which often interchanges with Fionnbharr.[1] The hypocoristic forms Bairre/Barra and Dobhairre derive from Bairrfhionn, and both forms are among the earliest attestations of the saint's name.[2] The earliest surviving written example of the name, on an Ogham-stone in south Wales, preserves both forms as *Barrivendi filius Vendubari*.[3] All saints of the name probably originated as localizations of a single cult, centred on Finnian (Fionnbharr) of Movilla, as can be shown by reference to its principal representatives, including Finnian of Clonard and Fionnbharr of Cork. That this probably also applied to less well-attested bearers of the name can be seen by reference to Fionnbharr of Clonlisk (Cluain Loiscthe) in the Offaly parish of Kilcomin, who is known only from the list of eponymous saints.[4] Clonlisk's position within the parish of Kilcomin, literally the church of Cuimín, a name that derives from Colum, conforms to a regular pattern of locating dedications to Fionnbharr (Bairrfhionn) close to those of Colum (Cille).[5]

1 *CGSH* §707.52–8.373–84. 2 *MartT* 74; *MartO*² 176; *VSHP* ii, 234 §22. 3 *LHEB* 512, 645. 4 *CGSH* §707.381. 5 *MakS* 22–3.

Fionnbharr of Clonlisk. *See* Fionnbharr.

Fionnbharr of Cork (Corcach), in the county of the same name. Fionnbharr was thought to descend through his father, a smith named Aimhirghin, from the Uí Bhriúin of Connacht and, more specifically, from a branch of that group (Uí Bhriúin Rátha) that held lands in the Galway barony of Clare, east of Lough Corrib, in and about the parish of Annaghdown.[1] On the evidence of the same genealogy, Fionnbharr had a brother named Modhíocha (Díocha) who plays no part in the remainder of his record. There is scarcely a saint to rival Fionnbharr, whose name was also rendered Bairre (Barra) and anglicized as Fin(n)bar(r) or Barry, for the number of manuscript copies of his Life, some thirty in total, not counting twenty-one calligraphic copies of the vernacular Life made by Patrick Stanton in the 1890s.[2] All recensions of the Life, from the earliest in Latin to the latest in the vernacular, are available in modern editions, and ever since the original text was composed at the end of the twelfth century, it has been held that the saint was a native of Cork, albeit of Connacht ancestry, who, having received his education in Ossory, returned to found several churches in the Cork area, beginning with a church in or near Macroom, followed by a school at Gougane Barra in the parish of Inchigeelagh, and culminating in a church and school on the site of the present Church of Ireland cathedral of St Fin Barre.[3] Examination of the Life shows, however, that all its salient features can be explained by reference to southern ecclesiastical affairs at the end of the twelfth century, when the bishop of Cork was endeavouring to bring under his control the neighbouring sees of Cloyne and Ross, which had previously – until the synod of Kells-Mellifont in 1152 – formed part of his jurisdiction.[4]

Cork's first bishop, Giolla Aodha Ua Muighin – eponym of the present Gillabbey (Mainistir Ghiolla Aodha) – who was appointed about 1140, was a Connachtman. As it was deemed appropriate that a saint's successor should belong to his patron's wider family, the claim of a Connacht (Uí Bhriúin) ancestry for Fionnbharr – through his father Amhairghin, rather than his mother, an unnamed servant of a local Uí Eachach (later Uí Mhathghamhna) king – was probably put forward during Giolla Aodha's term of office and, despite competition from a local pedigree, generally accepted.[5]

As Ossory was thought on somewhat obscure grounds to be closely connected with the area corresponding to the diocese of Ross, the claim was put forward that Fionnbharr received his primary education there, with each of his teachers – all close relatives of Fachtna, patron of Ross – required to show due deference to his pupil.[6] On the other hand, the saint's own pupils, at his two famous schools of Gougane Barra and Cork, most of whom are traceable to churches in the two neighbouring dioceses, were required to show their teacher due respect.[7] Allegedly among the saint's pupils were Fachtna, who is said to have granted his church to Fionnbharr in perpetuity and, according to one version of the Life, Colmán, patron of Cloyne.[8] Furthermore, Fionnbharr's handpicked father-confessor, Eolang, was attached to Aghabullogе, one of the more important churches within the diocese of Cloyne, which is likewise said to have been surrendered to the Cork saint in perpetuity.[9]

Other late twelfth-century concerns of Fionnbharr's biographer included his church's relations with local political interests, and especially the Clann Charthaigh (MacCarthys), who, having controlled all three dioceses from their headquarters in Cork, found themselves, after the arrival of the English, pushed back to an area about six to ten miles west of the town. With a view to accommodating this powerful family, two minor churches in this area, Desertmore (Díseart Mór) and 'Kilnacloona(gh)' (Ceall na Cluaine) in Ballineadig townland, parish of Aglish, were accorded high status. One was chosen as a repository of episcopal relics and the other was given the distinction of being the location of the saint's death before the transfer of his remains to Cork.[10]

As the saint's Life can thus be explained plausibly as a response to late twelfth-century issues, there is little to contradict the view that Fionnbharr of Cork originated as a localization of the cult of his much earlier attested namesake, Fionnbharr, alias Finnian.[11] The original saint, whose localizations appear to have included many others, among them the celebrated Finnian of Clonard, was probably attached to the Down church of Movilla in the Ards peninsula. Author of the earliest known Irish penitential, this man is already cited under the guise of 'Vennianus' in a letter to Gregory the Great from Columbanus of Bobbio, written about 600.[12] Columbanus stated that the saint corresponded with Gildas, the celebrated historian of Britain, on a point of monastic discipline and, when composing his own penitential, the patron of Bobbio drew on the writings of both saints.[13] Another claim to attention was Fionnbharr's role as tutor of Colum Cille, to which Adhamhnán gave great emphasis.[14] Clearly, the reputation gained by this notable cleric – who may have been born in one of the Irish settlements in Wales, whence his 'British' pet name Uinniau (alias Vinnio and Finnio) – would have led to a wide diffusion of his cult.[15]

That it was Finnian's story that reached the southern church is indicated by several attributes held by the saints of Movilla and Cork in common, in addition to a shared name and a reputation for learning and teaching. The feastday of the Cork saint, for example, fell on 25 September, contiguous to a cluster of feasts commemorating Finnio (Finniavus), one of which (28 September) is shared by Gildas.[16] The saint named Fionnbharr venerated at Carrickmacross in the county of Monaghan, where a well was named 'Tober-Inver' after him, probably represented the patron of Movilla.[17] The church of Killeenavarra (Ceall Fhionnbhairr) in the Galway barony of Dunkellin may also represent a dedication to the saint and, under the guise of Barr, there were several commemorations of the saint in Scotland in late September, including the Hebridean isle of Barra (27 September) and Dornoch in Caithness, where the Breviary of Aberdeen version of his Office Life appears to have been compiled.[18] Of all localizations of the cult of Fionnbharr, none has flourished more than that of the patron of Cork, who is still revered in the southern city not only as patron of the diocese, but also as patron of a parish (St Finbar's) and of many sporting and other associations. The site of his supposed school at Gougane continued to attract huge numbers of pilgrims until well into the nineteenth century, and perhaps no other local saint has received more coverage in local journals and periodicals.[19] Fionnbharr's generosity towards the poor was acclaimed by Cuimín of Connor and, as well as being lauded for his virtue in the face of carnal temptation, he was thought to be similar in manners to Augustine of Canterbury.[20] The saint was reputedly surrounded in 'great Cork' by 717 bishops, and Fionnbharr's name and that of his companion Neasán were allegedly 'written in heaven'.[21] A relic of the saint, in the form of a gospel-book, proved of no avail as a protection, when the Munster king, Mathghamhain son of Cinnéidigh, was slain by Maol Muadh son of Bran in 976.[22]

1 *CGSH* §314; *GRSH* 59–60; *Lgen.* 710.1; *JCHAS* 110, 59–63. **2** *BBa.* 34–200; *MHH* 180, 235–6; *DIB* iii, 780. **3** *BBa. passim*; *VSHP* i, 65–74; *BNÉ* i, 11–22; *AB* 69, 324–47. **4** *MakS passim*. **5** Ibid. 58–61, 66–7; *JCHAS* 110, 59–63. **6** *MakS* 76–90. **7** Ibid. 87–9. **8** *BBa.* 148–50. **9** Ibid. 152–4; *MakS* 101–2. **10** *BBa.* 80, 88, 156–8; *MakS* 114–16. **11** *MakS* 1–29. **12** *SCO* 8, §7. **13** *IrP* 5. **14** *VC*[2] 324–6. **15** *FKHS* 411–12; *FPM* 187–202. **16** *MartT* 74; *MartO*[2] 196; *MartG* 184; *MartD* 258; *MakS* 13–29. **17** *SATDF* 171. **18** *GYHS* 797; *CPNS* 272–3; *KSS* 275–6; *ACDS* 141–2; *BBa.* 168–70; *LegSS* 234–7, 361–2. **19** *JCHAS* 40, 57–61; ibid. 41, 13–19, 85–91; ibid. 42, 16–24, 96–100; ibid. 48, 1–8; ibid. 67, 82–8; ibid. 68, 104–6; ibid. 70, 1–6; ibid. 82, 63–82; ibid. 90, 1–13; ibid. 96, 117–24; ibid. 110, 59–64. **20** *ZCP* 1, 64 §73; *CGSH* §712.35; *Seanchas* 235 §5. **21** *IrL* 54. **22** *CGG* 90.

Fionnbharr of Drumcolumb (Druim Coluim), barony of Tirerrill, Co. Sligo. One of the first churches said to have been founded by Colum Cille in Connacht was at a place formerly called Druim na Macraidhe, later Druim Coluim Chille, now Drumcolumb.[1] While there, having raised a cross and deposited a bell named *glasán*, 'little greyish one', Colum is said to have placed in charge a holy priest of his household named Fionnbharr. This is doubtless the same saint as was attached by the genealogists to the Luighne of Connacht – whence the name of the barony of Leyny – along whose boundary with Tirerrill the greater part of the parish of Drumcolumb now lies.[2] A feature of the *wanderkult* of Fionnbharr was the regular proximity of its dedications to those of Colum Cille, with both confined to a single site at Drumcolumb.[3]

The vernacular Life of another representative of the cult, Finnian of Clonard, likewise brought its subject to Drumcolumb, rendering its name 'Druim idir dhá Loch' in line with the church's location between Lough Arrow and Lough Gill.[4] Finnian allegedly found two previous occupants of the site, named Maoise and Ainmhire, who surrendered it to him. This shows how the community at Clonard also recognized – opportunistically, but nonetheless correctly – the identity of their saint with Fionnbharr of Drumcolumb.[5] Through his father Breasal, Fionnbharr of Drumcolumb became an uncle of Mobhí of Glasnevin, who is said to have been visited by Colum Cille immediately after he had spent some time with Finnian at Clonard.[6] Fionnbharr's feastday has not been recorded.

1 *BCC* 156 §154. 2 *CGSH* §412. 3 *MakS* 23. 4 *LisL* 2696–704. 5 *MakS* 23. 6 *CGSH* §§266, 317, 412; *IKD* 228 §29, 255.

FIONNBHARR of Killegar (Ceall Adhgair), parish of Powerscourt, barony of Rathdown, Co. Wicklow. This son of Aodh, son of Connas, is assigned by the genealogists to a branch of the Dál Meisin Corb of Wicklow known as Uí Chonnais.[1] It has been suggested that he was identical with the patron of Kilruddery in the parish of Bray, which is separated from Powerscourt by one parish only (Kilmacanoge).[2] His church would have fallen within the *paruchia* of Glendalough, whose patron, Caoimhghin, also belonged to the Dál Meisin Corb. Fionnbharr's feastday has not been recorded.

1 *CGSH* §255; *GRSH* 89; *Lgen.* 458.9; *CGH* 120b43. 2 *CPPI* 182.

FIONNBHARR of Kilruddery. *See* Fionnbharr of Killegar.

FIONNBHARR of Little Island, parish of Ballynakill, barony of Gaultiere, Co. Waterford, a site formerly known as Inis Doimhle on the boundary between Uí Cheinsealaigh and the Déise.[1] According to the genealogists, this son of Aodh son of Dallán belonged to the Fothairt who gave name to the Carlow and Wexford baronies of Forth.[2] Both he and his brother, Bairrfhionn of Aughkiletaun, whose name (from *barr* + *fionn*) is basically the same as his brother's, were associated with churches in south Leinster. Because of the similarity of name, Colgan was moved to remark of Bairrfhionn: 'You might think he is the same as Fionnbharr because he has the same father and the same genealogy, but they are said to be brothers'.[3] Supporting the probability of their ultimate identity is the fact that a saint named Bairrfhionn was also venerated at Little Island. His feast fell, however, on 30 January, as against that of Fionnbharr on 4 July.[4] Also connected with Little Island was Neasán, which would indicate that Fionnbharr and the patron of Cork, likewise associated with Neasán, belonged to the same *wanderkult*.[5]

1 *Ainm* 8, 60; cf. *Peritia* 16, 451–4. 2 *CGSH* §6; *GRSH* 74; *Lgen.* 718.6–7. 3 *GRSH* 74 §4. 4 *MartT* 13, 53; *MartO*[2] 160; *MartG* 26, 130; *MartD* 31, 186. 5 *MartO*[2] 249, 256; *MartG* 230; *MartD* 324; *MakS* 30–2.

FIONNCHADH of Killarga (Ceall Fhearga), barony of Drumahaire, Co. Leitrim. The saint's birth is said to have been prophesied by Molaise of Devenish, then travelling in Críoch Chairbre (the Sligo barony of Carbury).[1] Blessing the future bishop in his mother's womb, Molaise foretold that he would be one of five 'great saints' in the headship of what seems to have been the church at Ahamlish, the others being Molaise himself, Beoaidh, Maodhóg, and Fraoch. Ahamlish was otherwise associated with Molaise son of Déaglán, doubtless a double of the Devenish saint. Elsewhere Fionnchadh is described as a former member of the *Fianna* of Fionn son of Cumhall, and he is located in Drumcliff.[2] Fionnchadh's feast of 12 November was noticed, albeit under the guise of Fingenus, in the martyrology used in the Regensburg *Schottenkloster*.[3]

1 *Celtica* 1, 65; *SG* i, 23–4; *VSHP* ii, 135 §19. 2 *ZCP* 5, 180. 3 *MartG* 216; *MartD* 306; *FSHIM* 242.

FIONNCHÚ of Brigown (Brí Ghabhann), barony of Condons and Clangibbon, Co. Cork. The genealogists resolved their uncertainty as to which ancestry should be attached to Fionnchú (anglicized Fanahan) by providing him with two conflicting statements of his descent, one from Dobhtha, progenitor of Ceinéal Dobhtha who held lands in Roscommon, the other from Colla Meann, ancestor of the Mughdhorna who gave name to the Monaghan barony of Cremorne (Críoch Mhughdhorn).[1] A similar indecision is discernible in the opening lines of the vernacular Life composed for Fionnchú, probably in the fourteenth century, if not later, which combines both traditions by tracing Fionnchú's father (variously named Séadna and Fionnlugh) to the Ceinéal Dobhtha, while describing him as a *brughaidh*, 'hospitaller', of the Mughdhorna of Ulster.[2] Fionnchú's mother, his father's second wife, is said to have been Iodhnaid daughter of Flann of the Cianachta of Dungiven (Gleann Geimhin) in Derry and, during her pregnancy, an obscure saint named Maol Tuile son of Cuilche prophesied the birth of a wondrous child.[3] Following a journey through Connacht to Cashel in Munster, whose king gave the family some land at a place called Ráith Ua gCuile, the child was finally born and immediately taken to be baptized to Ailbhe of Emly.[4] The countrywide odyssey thus created by his biographer for the child continued with a period of schooling under Comhghall at Bangor, to whose office of abbot he is said, completely unhistorically, to have succeeded.[5] Returning southwards, Fionnchú is shown receiving a grant of land from the king of Munster which enabled him to found a church at Cúil Mhuilt – where, according to a separate source, Fionn son of Cumhall had once also foretold the saint's birth – renaming it Brí Ghabhann (Brigown) at the request of seven smiths (*gaibhne*) who gave him seven iron sickles for penitential purposes.[6]

Though one might expect Fionnchú's peregrinations to have ceased at that point, this was not the case. He was successively brought by his biographer to the area about Tara in Meath, to south Leinster, and to the district of Cruachain (Rathcroghan) in Connacht.[7] In all these places, some of them notable traditional centres of power, he assisted local dynasts and received rewards in land or taxes in perpetuity. Meanwhile, he mediated between the men of Ulster and Munster, ingratiated himself with the Dál gCais ancestors of the powerful Uí Bhriain (O'Briens), and devoted a good deal of time to the affairs of the Ciarraighe Cuirche, who gave name to the south Cork barony of Kerrycurrihy.[8] Closer to home, he inspired Cairbre Crom, king of Cashel, and ancestor of the Uí Chaoimh (O'Keeffes), who wielded great influence in north Cork, to victory over the Uí Néill.[9] Care was thus taken throughout the saint's Life to mention politically important centres, even if these had long since become no more than symbols of former glory, such as Tara, Dionn Ríogh in Leinster, Rathcroghan, Uí Chaisín of Clare whose lands included Magh Adhair, traditional place of inauguration of the Uí Bhriain, and of course, Cashel.[10]

Among the saints brought into contact with Fionnchú were Rónán Fionn, allegedly his mother's sister's son, usually associated with Magheralin (Ceall Lainne) in Down, and Fiontan of Clonenagh who is said to have been his *dalta*, 'fosterling'.[11] There is some evidence to suggest that the Life was written in the Cistercian abbey of Fermoy which may have had a claim to lands in north Cork associated with Fionnchú. The text survives in a copy statedly drawn from the Book of Monasterboice, near Mellifont, Ireland's first Cistercian foundation.[12] The fact that Tracton Abbey was located in the barony of Kinalea, where it adjoins Kerrycurrihy, may have had some bearing on the author's obvious interest in that area. Although no account is given of the saint's death, he is said to have visited Rome towards the end of his life in order to do penance for all the battles he had been involved in.

Fionnchú's penitential excesses were commemorated in a poem attributed to Cuimín of Connor, and the saint figures in two poems of mournful prophecy, one of which is said to have been composed by himself in conversation with a man named Séadna, possibly his father.[13] He is also invoked, with two other saints of Cloyne diocese, Colmán son of Léinín and Molaga, in a poem attributed to Seanán of Scattery Island.[14] Fionnchú's crozier, now lost, was used for swearing purposes, whereas a relic known as 'Fanahan's candlestick', now kept locally, in fact related to Molaga of Aghacross.[15] Fionnchú died, according to the annals, in 652, and his feast fell on 25 November, one day after that of his diocesan patron, Colmán of Cloyne.[16] The pattern at the saint's well in the townland of Ballynamona attracted numerous pilgrims.[17]

1 *CGSH* §§320.1.2, 410.1; *Lgen.* 710.5; *CGH* 142a19, b33; *DIB* iii, 781–2; *HMDC* 12–13. **2** *LisL* 2788–91. **3** Ibid. 2795–810. **4** Ibid. 2812–35. **5** Ibid. 2883–7. **6** Ibid. 2925–37; *MartO*[1] clxxii. **7** *LisL* 2965–3156. **8** Ibid. 3157–204. **9** Ibid. 3205–74; *Lgen.* 622.5. **10** *LisL* 2815, 2890, 2968, 3050, 3124, 3140. **11** Ibid. 2939–87, 3056–61. **12** Ibid. 3300–2; *MRHI* 139–40. **13** *ZCP* 1, 64; *Ériu* 18, 60 §13; *ZCP* 3, 31–2; cf. *BLCat.* i, 637. **14** *ZCP* 10, 28 §23. **15** *CrC*[1] 28–9; *NCHC* i, 316; *JRSAI* 53, 166. **16** ATig. *s.a.*; *MartO*[2] 236; *MartG* 226; *MartD* 316–18. **17** *Béaloideas* 14, 110–11; ibid. 15, 254; *AICW* iv (pt ii) 457.

FIONNLUGÁN of Tamlaght Finlagan. *See* Fionnlugh of Doon.

FIONNLUGH. This name derives from *fionn*, 'fair', and *lugh*, 'bright', both of which were used of the Celtic divinity, Lugh (alias Fionn), who was venerated throughout the territories once dominated by the Celts.[1] The extent of devotion to the divinity is shown by such toponyms as Lyon, Laon, Lizier, in France, Leiden in Holland, and Liegnitz in Silesia (now in Poland), all of which derive from **Lugu-dun-*, 'Lugh's dwelling', together with Wien in Austria and Vienne in France, both of which derive from **Uindo-bona*, 'Fionn's place'. In Ireland, the divinity was well known under both forms of his name, Fionn (most prominently in the guise of the son of Cumhall) and Lugh.[2] Following the arrival of Christianity, devotion to Lugh continued in the form of numerous saints' cults, including those of Laichtín, Molua, and Luchtighearn.[3] The saints named Fionnlugh doubtless also represented Christian versions of the pagan cult but, although numerous, with twenty-two in the list of homonymous saints, their written record is sparse.[4] No bearer of the name was made the subject of a Life, and only four are known from the martyrologies (3 January, 11 May, 7 June, 13 November). Among churches associated with saints named Fionnlugh were Teach Luim (Mic Luim), now perhaps Tigroney in the Wicklow parish of Castlemacadam, and Eanach Liag, now possibly Annaleck in the Kilkenny parish of Powerstown.[5]

1 *CeltM* 24–5. **2** ITS 43, lxx–lxxxv. **3** *ZCP* 36, 138–56. **4** *CGSH* §707.419–40. **5** *CGSH* §707.425.434.

Fionnlugh of Doon (An Dún, alias Dún Bleisce), barony of Coonagh, Co. Limerick. According to the Life composed for his brother Fiontan, Fionnlugh's association with east Limerick was short-lived. Having become angry with his brother, Fiontan allegedly foretold that Fionnlugh's resurrection would not be in Ireland, with the result that he went overseas to Scotland.[1] This may represent an attempt to identify Fionnlugh son of Píobán with his namesake Fionnlugán who, according to Adhamhnán, saved Colum Cille's life by coming between him and a spear-thrusting assailant on the island of Hinba (probably Jura) in Scotland.[2] Fionnlugán (anglicized Finlagan) is not widely commemorated in Scotland but, on returning to Ireland, the saint's cult became established in at least two places, at Tamlaght Finlagan in the Derry barony of Keenaght and, under the guise of Felicianus (also Finlicanus), at Bordwell in the Laois parish of Aghaboe.[3] That the cult had returned in Columban company is indicated by the fact that Cainneach, Colum Cille's double, was patron both of the neighbouring Derry church of Drumachose, and also of Aghaboe.[4] In most of his churches, including Doon, the saint's memory was celebrated on 3 January, but the previous day was preferred in Bordwell.[5] Seventeenth-century sources understood Fionnlugh and his brother Fiontan to have been sons of Díomán of the Dál bhFiatach in east Ulster.[6]

1 *VSHH* 116–17 §§13–14. **2** *VC*[1] 378–80; *CPNS* 82–3, 304; *SS* 284. **3** *CPNS* 304; *KSS* 348; *MartO*[2] 40; *Celtica* 1, 84; *DYHS* 195; *HADO* ii, 58–9; *CPL* 13, 773; *AnH* 12, 83, 107, 109. **4** *Celtica* 1, 82; *FG* 20–35. **5** *DOH* 88; *HADO* ii, 58–9; *MartT* 4; *MartO*[2] 33; *MartG* 8; *MartD* 6. **6** *GRSH* 83; *Lgen.* 723.2; *MartD* 6. cf. *CGSH* §370.

Fionnlugh son of Díomán. *See* Fionnlugh of Doon.

Fionnoll son of Caol. *See* Aodh Fionn.

Fiontan. There are two schools of thought as to the origins of this name, one deriving it from *fionn*, 'fair, white', compounded with *sean*, 'ancient', the other regarding it as a compound of *fionn* and *teine*, 'fire'.[1] It is among the most common of saints' names, with over fifty representatives in the list of homonymous saints.[2] Although little else is recorded of the vast majority of these, some of the minor churches associated with Fiontan may reflect the spread of the cult of the most important bearer of the name, the patron of the Laois church of

Clonenagh. His cult is thought to have been implanted in the south Dublin/north Wicklow area as a result of Uí Dhúnlainge expansionism.[3] Achadh Draighnighe, for example, may refer to Killadreenan (Ceall Achaidh Dhraighnighe) in the Wicklow parish of Newcastle, a church otherwise connected with Feidhealm and Bishop Duirtheach, both subjects of Brighid of Kildare, a close relative of the Clonenagh saint.[4] In that case, one might also tentatively identify the church in the list named Ceall Locha as Killough in the parish of Kilmacanoge, a little north of Killadreenan.[5] Cluain Laogh of the list of churches associated with Fiontan is likely to be Clonleigh in the Donegal barony of Raphoe North, and Meathas Mór is probably Mass More in the same parish.[6] Several saints of the name Fiontan are better known by the hypocoristic form Munna.

1 *EIHM* 318–19. 2 *CGSH* §707.385–416.439 add. 3 *CPPI* 79. 4 *VSHP* ii, 72 §28; *CGSH* §§670.69, 707.407. 5 *CGSH* §§705.27, 707.400.440 add. 6 Ibid. §§83, 705.26, 707.389.440.

FIONTAN of Clonenagh (Cluain Eidhneach), barony of Maryborough West, Co Laois. Hailed as the equivalent of Benedict of Nursia and head of the monks of the whole of Ireland, Fiontan son of Gaibhrín (Garbhán) has just claim to be regarded as the most noted bearer of the name.[1] As he was attached to the Ceinéal Eachdhach, another name for the Fothairt of north Leinster, Fiontan was related genealogically to Brighid of Kildare and followed in third place after her and Patrick in the layout of the corpus of saints' pedigrees in the Book of Leinster.[2] His mother was called Fionnad and a sister of his, named Díognad (also Díoghnad and Díogha), was regarded as mother of Aonghas Láimhiodhan (alias Muicín) of the Kilkenny church of Moyne.[3] The importance of Fiontan's church may be measured by the fact that the names of some sixteen of its higher clergy are recorded for the period from about 750 to 1000.[4] A book, now lost, named after the church was used to record decisions made at the Synod of Ráith Bhreasail in 1111, and it has recently been suggested that the Book of Leinster, otherwise linked to Terryglass and Kildare, may have been compiled at Clonenagh.[5]

Fiontan was made the subject of a Life which, though described as 'late and of no special distinction' by one scholar, in its earliest form is part of the so-called O'Donohue collection of Lives, which has been dated, mainly on the basis of its archaic system of spelling names, to as early as the eighth century.[6] This version of the Life, which spawned two later versions, and is now also available in translation, has been dated even more precisely to the 730s, on the evidence of a bloody battle said by the saint's biographer to have been fought in south Munster.[7] It should be stated, however, that other Lives in this collection, such as that of Fíonán Cam of Kinnitty, exhibit features that point to a date not earlier than the twelfth century. The Life composed for Fiontan likewise contains evidence that argues against an early dating, as, for example, the manner in which the link between Clonenagh and Terryglass, first attested in an annal entry for 845, permeates the text.

In the opening chapter, Criomhthann is substituted for Gaibhrín as the name of the saint's father, probably with Colum son of Criomhthann of Terryglass in mind, and subsequently the young saint is sent to Colum, who is given a leading role in determining the location of Fiontan's church at Clonenagh.[8] While engaged in this activity, Fiontan and Colum are said to have visited a site preordained for the use of Mobhaoi of the Maca Alla (another name for Baodán of Cloney), at a point where the lands of Colum's people, the Uí Chriomhthannáin, were divided by the river Barrow from those of the Uí Mhuireadhaigh. It is scarcely a coincidence that this Baodán's feast also falls together with that of Colum on 13 December. It would seem, therefore, that Fiontan's Life is to be studied in conjunction with that of Colum of Terryglass, which presents the story of the 'discovery' of Clonenagh in much the same terms as described above.[9] On the basis of his use of the form Mochaoimhe instead of Nadh Caoimhe for one of Fiontan's companions in this episode only, it has been argued that Colum's biographer is more likely to have been the borrower.[10] Against this, however, Colum's biographer correctly uses the form Fiontan Maca Eachdhach to refer to the Clonenagh saint whereas Fiontan's biographer erroneously applies it to one of the saint's companions who is then excised from the tale.

Another feature of the text indicating lateness is the manner in which representatives of locations associated with the canons regular of St Augustine, who founded their first house in Ireland in the late 1120s, are woven into Fiontan's itinerary.[11] The evidence is, of course, nowhere explicit and sometimes indirect, as when Baodán's preordained church at Cloney in the Kildare parish of Kilberry happens to be close to Kilrush, which was founded for the canons in the early thirteenth century.[12] An indirect allusion to Kilrush may also be implied by the episode involving the layman, Feargna son of Cobhthach, whom Fiontan persuaded to relinquish worldly goods for a life in religion.[13] Feargna belonged to the Uí Earcáin and two of his children, Brígh and Fíonán, were connected with churches in their father's area, including Kilrush.[14] When Fiontan was brought to the Carlow church of Agha (Achadh Arghlas), he found himself within a few miles of Leighlin, the site of a house of canons.[15] The implications of the names of Fiontan's two companions, Caomhán of Anatrim and Mochaoimhe of Terryglass, during his quest for a suitable place to found a church, are also indirect. Both companions were close relatives of Caoimhghin, whose church at Glendalough had hosted a house of canons since the mid-twelfth century.[16]

More direct links to houses of canons arguably underlie the introduction to the text of Colum Cille – who may be taken here to represent Durrow – Cainneach of Kilkenny, Sincheall of Killeigh, and Comhghall of Bangor, whose own Life accords Fiontan the role of mentor and master; each of the churches associated with these saints contained a house of canons regular.[17] The person chosen to minister to Fiontan on his deathbed, his like-named successor, Fiontan Maoldubh, was otherwise connected with the church of Durrow in Ossory, close by the Augustinian priory of Aghamacart.[18]

Together with other bearers of the name, such as Fiontan Maoldubh and Munna (alias Fiontan) of Taghmon, the saint probably represented a single original cult, subsequently localized at Durrow, Taghmon, Clonenagh, and other places. If the annals are to be believed, Fiontan died in 603, on a Thursday, according to a poem attributed to Colmán son of Fearghas, which had also been the day of his birth.[19] At Clonenagh, and also at Cromoge in the same parish, the memory of Fiontan 'the prayerful', a man renowned for his abstinence and diet of herbs, was celebrated on 17 February, and tales about the church he built at Clonenagh and his dealings with Brighid survived until the 1940s.[20] This day was also remembered in the Kerry parish of Kinard but, despite Thomas O'Connor who thought that Fiontan of Clonenagh was intended, the saint of the day, known locally as Fíonán, is otherwise attested as Fiontan son of Oireannán who died in 676.[21] Fiontan's namesake, and likely double, Fiontan of Clonkeen (Cluain Caoin) in the parish of Clonenagh, and possibly of the Dublin parish of Killo'grange (formerly Clonkeen), was commemorated nine days earlier, on 7 February, and three days later, on 21 February, fell the feast of another namesake, Fiontan Corach, likewise of Clonenagh. In the county of Wexford, Fiontan was remembered on 17 February at Glebe (parish of Mayglass) in the barony of Forth which takes its name from the Fothairt, the people to whom the saint belonged.[22] Judging by the number of mentions of his feast in post-Conquest liturgical manuscripts, devotion to the saint also flourished in the Dublin parish of Howth, where 'Fintan's well' in the townland of Sutton South continued to be visited until at least the 1950s.[23] Fiontan is also among the handful of mainly Leinster saints commemorated in the tenth-century metrical calendar of Hampson.[24] He was patron of the Uí Mhórdha of Laois.[25] Furthermore, his relics were allegedly translated to Leighlin in 1348, with a view to having him canonised.[26]

1 *CGSH* §712.34. **2** Ibid. §3; *GRSH* 75; *Lgen.* 718.2; *CGH* 126a28; *ZCP* 8, 301; *Ériu* 54, 92–4. **3** *CGSH* §182.2. **4** *AFM* ind. 32. **5** *FFÉ* i, 78, iii, 32; *LigeG* xi–xxi. **6** *Kenney* 386; *MISL* 297–339; *DIB* iii, 799. **7** *VSHH* 145–53; *VSHP* i, lxx–lxxi; ii, 96–106; *OLL* 1, 28–49 at 40. **8** *VSHH* 145 §§1–3; *VSHP* ii, 96–7 §§1–3. **9** *VSHH* 228–9 §§13–14. **10** *OLL* 1, 40. **11** *MRHI* 146–52. **12** Ibid. 184. **13** *VSHH* 152 §21; *VSHP* ii, 103–4 §18. **14** *CGSH* §7; *BP* 2202–6; *VT* 188; *CGH* 316a22. **15** *MRHI* 184; *VSHH* 150 §19; *VSHP* ii, 104 §19. **16** *MRHI* 176–7; *CGSH* §181.56. **17** *VSHH* 146–52 §§2, 5, 11–12, 20; *VSHP* ii, 3–6 §§3–4, 9–11; 96 §2, 98 §5, 100–01 §§11–12, 103 §17. **18** *VSHH* 153 §23; *VSHP* ii, 106 §22; *MartG* 200; *HADO* ii, 210–45. **19** *AU s.a.*; *FAI* 4 §6. **20** *MartT*; *MartO*[2] 61 (*MartO*[1] lii); *MartG* 38; *MartD* 50; *MartFC* 51; *IrL* 60; *Béaloideas* 9, 28; ibid. 11, 189. **21** *ACoK* 133; but cf. *JRSAI* 90, 69; *AU s.a.*; *TCCD* 151. **22** OSL WX i, 289; *CECW* 217; *AB* 69, 80–1; *The Past* 2, 58. **23** *Rep. Nov.* 2, 46, 48, 53, 77. **24** *AB* 104, 93. **25** *FFÉ* iii, 112. **26** *AB* 104, 93.

Fiontan of Doon (An Dún, alias Dún Bleisce), barony of Coonagh, Co. Limerick. Fiontan is among the fifty or so Irish saints who were made the subjects of biographies, albeit in his case in the form of a brief Latin Life preserved in a single manuscript, the *Codex Salmanticensis*, now in the Bibliothèque Royale, Brussels.[1] In this, the names of his otherwise unattested parents are revealed, namely Píobán son of Tuile from the southern part of a plain in east Limerick known as Cliú (Cliach) and Ailinne daughter of Artghal, a noble from the area about Pallas Grean (Latin *Solaris*).[2] The name of Fiontan's sister Finne, about whose burial mound (*tumulus*) many miracles were performed, is likewise confined to this text, unless her mention was intended to evoke the hill (*tumulus*) of Finninne near Donaghmore, a few miles east of Limerick city, from which Patrick is said to have blessed the people of Thomond.[3]

The concerns of the Life are predominantly local, the author's abiding aim being to validate lands or churches allegedly surrendered to Fiontan in perpetuity. Cases in point are Kilrush (Ceall Rois) in the Limerick city parish of St Munchin's, and Kilmacogue – which may now represent Ceall Mhac Toighe of the Life – in the parish of Doon, both of which are said to have been offered to the saint, with their appurtenances, on the strength of miracles.[4] Further afield, in west Limerick, a claim is made to possession of the hill of Gabhair, from which Conall Gabhra, ancestor of the Uí Chonaill Ghabhra of Connello, took his name.[5] The manner in which possession of Doon itself was gained is described in some detail, its previous occupant, Colmán son of Conchadh, receiving Fiontan hospitably and abandoning his church in favour of him.[6] This is also put forward as the occasion on which Fiontan took offence at an action of his brother Fionnlugh, and foretold that the place of the latter's resurrection would not be in Ireland. Colmán, for his part, having agreed a covenant (*fedus*) with Fiontan, was instructed to follow a stag until he encounter a fox emerging from a cave, at which site he was to build his church. The biographer would appear in this instance to be laying claim to one or other of the three Kilcolmans in the county of Limerick.

Among other saints brought into contact with Fiontan were Comhghall of Bangor, whose school he attended, and Finnian of Movilla, whose gospel-book he procured, despite difficulties put in his way by pirates.[7] The connection with east Ulster recalls the fact that saints named Fionnlugh and Fiontan, both sons of Díomán, of the east Ulster sept of Dál bhFiatach, were understood by some seventeenth-century sources to have been identical with the Doon saints.[8] Following a miracle located at Terryglass on Lough Derg, the text is brought to an abrupt end, allegedly in the interest of brevity, and no account is given of the saint's death.

Doon being a relatively minor church, as is shown, for example, by the fact that it was noticed once only in the annalistic record, the Life is unlikely to have been produced there.[9] A far more likely provenance is the Cistercian abbey of Abington (Mainistear Uaithne) in the parish adjoining Doon, which was founded about 1200.[10] Doon may have been one of Abington's rectories and in that case a Life of its saint would have been regarded as a suitable means of providing the abbey with written title to some of its possessions. This might also explain the biographer's assertion that Fiontan attended Comhghall's school in Bangor. The most noted twelfth-century abbot of Bangor, and successor of Comhghall, was no less a figure than Maol Maodhóg (Malachy) of Armagh, who was instrumental in bringing the Cistercians to Ireland.[11] That the Cistercians were eager to avail of traditions surrounding local saints in order to promote their own interests is evident from a number of other Lives, such as those of Buithe and Mochaomhóg.

The saint's feastday, on which he was joined by his brother Fionnlugh, fell on 3 January and, as this was removed by two days only from the feast of both Fiontan of Myshall and Fiontan son of Toictheach on 1 January, it may be inferred that all three saints represented the same original cult.[12]

1 *VSHH* 113–17. **2** Ibid. 113–14 §2. **3** *BP* 2411–14; *VT* 206. **4** *VSHH* 114 §4, 117 §15. **5** Ibid. 115–16 §11. **6** Ibid. 116 §12. **7** Ibid. 114–15 §§5–7. **8** *CGSH* §370; *GRSH* 83; *MartD* 6. **9** *AI s.a.* 774. **10** *MRHI* 126. **11** Ibid. 114–20. **12** *MartT* 4; *MartO*² 33; *MartG* 8; *MartD* 6.

Fiontan of Durrow. *See* Fiontan Maoldubh.

Fiontan of Killerr, parish of Drumatemple, barony of Ballymoe, Co. Roscommon, which may now represent an earlier Ceall Oirthir. This Fiontan, styled *cruimhthear*, 'priest', is known from three sources, the list of homonymous saints, the martyrologies for 13 July, and a mention in the Life of Mochta of Louth.[1] The latter source states that Fiontan, a disciple of Patrick, was present on Croaghpatrick during Lent, only to be cast down from the mountain and dismembered by the many adversarial demons surrounding his master. Subsequently revived and left without a scar by Patrick, Fiontan allegedly went on to become abbot of Killerr. Much nearer to Croaghpatrick, at Claggan in the parish of Kilcommon, barony of Erris, there was a church (Kilfintan) dedicated to Fiontan, which may relate to the same saint.[2]

1 *CGSH* §707.440 add; *MartG* 136; *MartD* 192; *VSHH* 398 §11. 2 *NotesEHDT* 347.

Fiontan of Lann Maoil Duibh. *See* Fiontan Fionn; Fiontan Maoldubh.

Fiontan of Myshall (Midhíseal), barony of Forth, Co. Carlow, and of Slanore (Snámh Luthair), parish of Kilmore, barony of Loughtee Upper, Co. Cavan. This son of Eachaidh is known from an entry in the corpus of saints' pedigrees which attaches him, together with several siblings, to the Ceinéal Laoghaire of Meath.[1] Among his siblings were Colmán (Colum), also attached to Slanore and Myshall, Lughaidh, patron of Teernacreeve, Nainnidh of Kiltoom, Muireadhach of Killala, and Comaigh daughter of Eacha, also of Slanore. His mother is said to have been Aighleann daughter of Léinín, a sister of Colmán of Cloyne.[2] Fiontan's feastday, which, according to one source, was celebrated at a place named Bealach, and which was shared by saints named Colmán son of Eachaidh (possibly the saint's brother) and Fiontan son of Toictheach (Taictheach), probably his double, fell on 1 January.[3] As this was removed by two days only from the feast of Fiontan of Doon, it may be inferred that all three saints of the name represented the same original cult.

1 *CGSH* §160; *GRSH* 50–1; *Lgen.* 707.12. 2 *CGSH* §§160.1, 690.3, 722.31. 3 *MartT* 3, 116; *MartG* 7; *MartD* 4; cf. *CGSH* §707.394.

Fiontan son of Fearghas. *See* Brighid of Shankill.

Fiontan son of Díomán. *See* Fiontan of Doon.

Fiontan son of Tál. *See* Fiontan Fionn.

Fiontan son of Toictheach. *See* Fiontan of Myshall.

Fiontan son of Tulchán. *See* Munna of Taghmon.

Fiontan Corach. *See* Fiontan of Clonenagh.

Fiontan Fionn, 'fair', abbot/priest at Dromin (Druim Ing/Fhinn), barony of Ardee, Co. Louth. The genealogists were undecided as to whether Fiontan son of Eoghan belonged to the Cianachta or, by way of a confused sequence of names, to the Eoghanachta of Munster.[1] A segment of the Cianachta, known as Cianachta Breagh, held lands mainly in the barony of Ferrard, which would suit the local pedigree.[2] Dromin itself is said to have lain among the Uí Shéagháin who controlled the abbacy of Dunleer (Lann Léire), close to Dromin, but within the barony of Ferrard.[3] A poem preserved in the late fourteenth-century Book of Uí Mhaine invokes the blessings of Finnian, who was sometimes associated with the church of Dromin under the guise of Finnéan, on Baodán, Furodhrán and other Dunleer saints.[4] Likewise under the guise of Finnian, the patron of Dromin famously refused Colum Cille permission to copy his gospel-book, thus leading to the crucial battle of Cúil Dreimhne.[5] This particular association would suggest that Finnéan was originally a localization of Finnian, Colum Cille's teacher, and the saint's feast (*Lá 'il Finnéin*) was celebrated at Corstown in the neighbouring parish of Drumcar towards the middle of December, which points to Finnian, patron of Clonard, whose day was 12 December.[6]

Fiontan's mother was known as Neamh of Luaighne, a name used of an area in the vicinity of Tara.[7] Not far from Tara, close to Rosnaree on the river Boyne, a church called Lann Maoil Duibh was also associated with a saint named Fiontan.[8] According to the martyrologies, Fiontan's memory was celebrated at Dromin on 10 October, but local custom required that the feast be observed two days earlier.[9] The saint named Fiontan son of Tál, commemorated, according to the martyrologies, on 9 October, was probably identical with the patron of Dromin. On this day, a saint named Mainne, an allowable variant form of Munna, which in turn was the hypocoristic or pet form of Fiontan, was remembered at the Meath church of Donore within the former territory of Cianachta.[10] Here, however, there may have been confusion with Moninne of Killevy, the vigil of whose feast (6 July) was also remembered as pattern day.

1 *CGSH* §213.1.2; *GRSH* 123; *Lgen.* 739.7–8; *DIB* iii, 798. **2** *HDGP* iv, 138. **3** *MartG* 194; *IKHK* 118. **4** *CGSH* §737. **5** *IMN* 22, 3; *LU* 548–51. **6** *JCLAS* 24, 350; *CSMA* i, 39. **7** *CGSH* §722.39. **8** Ibid. §86.2. **9** *MartT* 78; *MartO*² 215; *MartG* 194; *MartD* 270; OSL LH 192–3; *JCLAS* 24, 347–8; *SAM* 2.1, 197. **10** OSL MH 137.

Fiontan Maoldubh, 'cropped', of Durrow (Dearmhagh in Uí Dhuach), barony of Clarmallagh, Co. Laois. Considerable confusion surrounds the story of this son of Amhalghaidh. He was twice called upon by saints' biographers to administer the last rites to their subjects, one of whom was Fiontan of Clonenagh, the other Cainneach of Kilkenny.[1] In the former case, it is also stated that he was appointed abbot in succession to Fiontan, but the entry on his feast in the later martyrologies assigns him to the church of Durrow, where a holy well was dedicated to him, and a parish church named after him.[2] He is also said to have belonged to the Eoghanacht of Cashel, but this is corroborated neither by the genealogists nor by a scholiast of the Martyrology of Aonghas who, having noted the statement, provided an alternative genealogy, attaching him, under the guise of Maoldubh, and through his father Amhalghaidh, to the Uí Bhriúin of Connacht.[3]

Maoldubh son of Amhalghaidh, as he is otherwise consistently known, is speculatively provided with three feasts in a seventeenth-century source, none of which is confirmed elsewhere.[4] Fiontan Maoldubh was commemorated on 20 October, the vigil of the feast of Munna (alias Fiontan) son of Tulchán, who may

– like Fiontan of Clonenagh – have been ultimately identical with him.[5] In the note added by the above-mentioned scholiast, which attributes to the saint as little evil as could be carried by a fly, Fiontan is said also to have been a pupil of Féichín and cellarer of the congregation at Fore.[6] His feast was observed at Durrow on 16 November, a day otherwise assigned to his namesake at Loughill in the adjoining parish of Rosconnell.[7] An obit of 629 is assigned to Fiontan.[8]

1 *VSHH* 153 §23; 198 §60; *VSHP* i, 169 §46, ii, 106 §22. **2** *MartO*² 217; *MartG* 200; OSL LS i, 100; *CPL* 15, §691. **3** *MartO*² 224. **4** *CGSH* §662.83; *MartD* 278; *GRSH* 60. **5** *MartT* 81; *MartO*² 217; *MartG* 200; *MartD* 278. **6** Cf. *AB* 69, 77–81; ibid. 70, 312–13. **7** *HADO* ii, 210; *MartG* 220; *MartD* 310. **8** *ATIg.* *s.a.* 628; cf. *CI* i, 137n.

Fioth. *See* Ioth.

Flann. Meaning 'red', especially 'blood-red', this name is perhaps best known through the saints who gave name to Derrynaflan (Doire na bhFlann) in Tipperary. Otherwise, it is common enough as a saint's name, with some seven representatives. Its diminutive (Flannán) is also attested.

Flann of Derrynaflan (Doire na bhFlann), parish of Graystown, barony of Slievardagh, Co. Tipperary. Though associated, according to one set of annals, with three Munster churches (Lismore, Emly and Cork) that had all become involved with the *céile Dé* ascetics, Flann son of Foircheallach was also co-patron of Derrynaflan, along with Flann son of Dubh Tuinne (Conna). A beautifully fashioned set of altar vessels (chalice, paten, basin and strainer), probably assembled around the time of the two Flanns, was discovered at this site some years ago.[1] The place of the two saints among the *céili Dé* is also evident from their inclusion in the list of those 'in union' with Maol Ruain, and the asceticism practised by Flann son of Dubh Tuinne is elsewhere specified in the rule attributed to the patron of Tallaght.[2]

Otherwise known as Flann Fionn, 'the fair', the son of Foircheallach may have been identical with the saint of that name associated with Cullen (Cuilleann) in the Cork barony of Kinelea, who was commemorated on 14 January.[3] Flann allegedly belonged to the Ciarraighe who gave name, among other places, to the Cork barony of Kerrycurrihy (Ciarraighe Cuirche), near which Cullen now lies.[4] He is sometimes mentioned in the same context as a saint named Carthach – probably Mochuda (alias Carthach) of Lismore – and the two are among many saints said to have been children of Inghean Bhaoith.[5] According to a poem in Classical Irish, Flann (under the guise of 'the son of Aircheallach'), together with Inghean Bhaoith and numerous other saints, was called upon to help in releasing Ireland's southern half (Leath Mogha) from a bondage imposed on it by the northern half (Leath Chuinn), represented by Finnian of Clonard.[6] Flann was probably also patron of Kilflyn in north Kerry and, although nothing was remembered of him by the time John O'Donovan reached the parish in 1841, elsewhere in the county, at Murirrigane in the parish of Cloghane, rounds were made at his well and he was thought to be a brother of Bréanainn.[7] Flann died in 825 and was commemorated on 21 December.[8] Under the guise of *na Flainn*, as reflected in the Christian name Giolla na bhFlann, his cult flourished in conjunction with that of his namesake and co-patron, especially among the Uí Shúilleabháin (O'Sullivans) who, before moving to south-west Munster, had controlled an area near, and possibly including, Derrynaflan.[9]

1 *AI s.a.* 825; *TDH* 36–41; *IEKF* 135–48. **2** *CGSH* §§713.3.4.14, 724.5; *Celtica* 2, 300; *Herm.* 44 §8. **3** *MartT* 8; *MartG* 16; *MartD* 14. **4** *GRSH* 108; *MartD* 342. **5** *ZCP* 10, 28 §23; *IrT* iv, 93 §7. **6** RIA MS 23L11, 263; *SAM* 24.1, 17. **7** *ACoK* 36; *TCCD* 218; *JKAHS* 17, 122; ibid. 29, 64; *JRSAI* 90, 69. **8** *MartT* 87; *MartG* 242; *MartD* 342. **9** *LM* 493.

FLANN son of Dubh Tuinne (Conna). *See* Flann of Derrynaflan.

FLANN son of Maol Dúin, abbot of Iona, Scotland. Twenty-fourth in line of succession to Colum Cille, Flann belonged, like most other abbots of the island monastery, to a branch of the Ceinéal Conaill, in his case the Ceinéal Lughdhach, whose lands were co-extensive with the Donegal barony of Kilmacrenan.[1] Apart from the notice of his death in 891, little else is recorded of him, but in early seventeenth-century sources he was speculatively identified with the Flann commemorated on 20 April.[2]

1 *CGSH* §346; *GRSH* 40; *Lgen.* 698.6; *CCDK* 84–96. **2** *GRSH* 40; *MartD* 106.

FLANN son of Neasán. *See* Beoán of Feighcullen.

FLANN FEABHLA, 'of Feabhail', of Armagh (Ard Mhacha). Listed among the abbots of Armagh and successors of Patrick, Flann belonged to a branch of the Oirghialla known as Uí Mhéith.[1] One segment of Uí Mhéith gave name to Omeath in north Louth while another, Uí Mhéith of Macha, was associated with the area about Armagh. Flann's father, Scannlán son of Fínghin, died as king of Uí Mhéith in 674/5, and his family's circumstances would probably have contributed to the saint's advancement in the ecclesiastical sphere.[2] Flann succeeded Séighín in the abbacy of Armagh in 688, and enjoyed an unusually long tenure of twenty-seven years.[3] While Flann's predecessor was still abbot, Aodh of Sleaty brought his testament to Armagh, and Aodh's successor Conchadh later brought a copy to Flann with a grant of his church 'till doom'.[4] In 690, during Flann's term of office, Armagh was burned.[5] Also during his tenure, Adhamhnán's Law, designed to protect women and non-combatants, was proclaimed, with Flann's name heading the long list of dignitaries who are said to have endorsed it.[6] The well-known story of the problematic 'Settling of the Manor of Tara', set in the reign of Diarmuid (†565) son of Cearbhall, anachronistically names Flann as one of the first to be consulted on the question.[7] Flann died in 715 and, according to an otherwise unsubstantiated seventeenth-century note, was commemorated on 24 July.[8]

1 *CGSH* §65; *GRSH* 71; *Lgen.* 714.7. **2** *AU s.a.* **3** *NHI* ix, 238. **4** *PTBA* 178 §16.1. **5** *AU s.a.* **6** *CA* 16 §28; *Peritia* 1, 185. **7** *Ériu* 4, 126 §4, 152 §31. **8** *AU s.a.*; *GRSH* 71.

FLANN FIONN of Cullen. *See* Flann of Derrynaflan.

FLANNAID of Clondulane (Cluain Dalláin), barony of Condons & Clangibbon, Co. Cork. While travelling in Munster, Mochuda of Lismore is said to have arrived at Ballyhooly (Áth Ubhla), near the river Blackwater, in the Cork barony of Fermoy.[1] Discovering an apple in the water at the ford (whence Áth Ubhla), he used it to cure the lame arm of the daughter of a local king, Cuana son of Cailchín. Named Flannaid, the girl subsequently elected to become a bride of Christ and, following Mochuda's expulsion from Rahan, she founded a church at Clondulane, described as being within her mentor's *paruchia*. Nothing else is known of Flannaid.

1 *VSHP* i, 185 §40; ITS 16, 110; *HMDC* 13–14.

FLANNÁN of Killaloe (Ceall Dalua), barony of Tulla Lower, Co. Clare. In keeping with his patronage of the diocese of Killaloe, Flannán (alias Flannán Mór, 'great') son of Toirdhealbhach was thought by the genealogists to belong to the leading branch of the Dál gCais, which produced Brian Bóramha, among others.[1] Flannán's brother, according to the genealogists, was Aodhán, patron of the Kildare church of Kilmeage (Cluain Domhail), near the Hill of Allen, but he is nowhere else featured in Flannán's record. Moreover, the fact that Aodhán is said to have been alive at the time of the battle of Allen in 722 gives Flannán a notional floruit at odds with his presence in the list of those 'in union' with Maol Ruain of Tallaght who died in 792.[2]

The saint was made the subject of a Latin Life which survives in a number of manuscripts, including the *Codex Salmanticensis* and two Rawlinson codexes now in Oxford.[3] Dismissed as ' wholly valueless' by one commentator on account of its perceived lack of 'historical content', the Life has been worthily adjudged by another to be a document unique among the Lives of the early Irish saints because its form, style and subject matter would suggest continental rather than Irish composition.[4] A separate line of transmission in several manuscripts of the Great Austrian Legendary (*Magnum Legendarium Austriacum*) supplies an account of a miracle at Lismore, now absent from the insular manuscripts, which reveals firm evidence of a provenance for the Life in one of the Irish monasteries in Germany, the so-called *Schottenklöster*, most likely that in Regensburg whose abbot Gregorius is named as a witness to the miracle.[5] The saint's Life is also unique in that it can be dated securely on the basis of its mention of a recent event, the capture and destruction of Milan in 1162 by the Holy Roman emperor Fredericus.[6] A more local concern with the fortunes of the Uí Bhriain dynasty also provides dating evidence through a prophecy placed in the mouth of Colmán of Lismore eulogizing the family's kings as if they were Roman emperors (*Romani imperatores cesares*), and naming several who would govern all of Ireland, including Muircheartach (†1119).[7]

The list of saints chosen to educate Flannán reveals a local bias in keeping with the Life's probable origins in one of the *Schottenklöster*, whose communities were largely drawn from the southern province of Munster.[8] The saint was first sent briefly to Blathmhac whose church of Rath lay in the barony of Inchiquin near the western boundary of the diocese of Killaloe.[9] He was then brought to the heart of the diocese, the home of his parents at Killaloe, where, in disregard of all notional chronology, he subjected himself to the rule of Molua (Dalua), who is elsewhere treated as a contemporary of such luminaries of the so-called Age of Saints (approximately AD500–650) as Comhghall, Maodhóg, and Cainneach.[10]

Flannán's biographer used Molua, said to have been among the most glorious of Irish saints, with devotion to him extending as far as the Hebrides and Orkneys, to announce to an assembly of prelates in the presence of Flannán's father Toirdhealbhach the terms of a prophecy placed in the mouth of the ocean-voyager Bréanainn.[11] Allegedly told to others during the voyage – the tale of which would have been well known in Regensburg – Bréanainn's prophecy concerned a man born of royal blood on the banks of the Shannon who would put to flight the chieftains and rulers of darkness. Communicated to Molua in a dream, the prophecy gave him an excuse to relinquish his church at Killaloe (Ceall Dalua/Molua) to Flannán, insisting only that it retain his name, a strategem probably designed to explain why the name of the patron of the diocese differed from that of the saint commemorated in the name of its chief church.

To prepare himself for the duty of governance, Flannán planned to travel to Rome, but not before he sought advice from a certain 'Bracanus'.[12] Depending on which saint of the name was intended, the choice of this mentor could have been because of any one of a number of factors, or a combination of them. On the assumption that Breacán of Inishmore (Aran) and of Kilbreckan in the Clare parish of Doora was intended, he and Flannán were closely related, according to the genealogists, with Breacán's father Eacha Bailldearg and brother Conall figuring in Flannán's direct line of descent.[13] Breacán's grandfather Caorthann is said to have received baptism from Patrick, whose intervention led to the *ball dearg*, 'red spot', borne by his son Eacha Bailldearg, and the saint's nephew, Aodh by name, was traditionally regarded as the first Dál gCais king of Cashel.[14] The choice of this Breacán could also have been influenced by designs Killaloe may have had on the Aran Islands, the chief centre of Breacán's cult, or by Domhnall Mór Ua Briain's grant of the lands of Kilbreckan to the Augustinian house of Clare Abbey.[15] On the other hand, the saint intended could also have been Brocán of Cluain Iomarchair in Ossory, who is elsewhere said to have been visited by Flannán.[16] In that case, the biographer would possibly have been laying a marker for the eastern limit of the diocese of Killaloe, as he may already have done in the west by his mention of Blathmhac.

Returning from Rome with pilgrims who were granted an island named *Ferdinea* (*Fredinea*), possibly Friars' Island on the river Shannon near Killaloe, Flannán was warmly greeted by his father Toirdhealbhach who subsequently abandoned worldly affairs to adopt a monk's habit at Lismore under an obscure saint named Colmán.[17] The twelfth century witnessed several such desertions of the world for a monk's habit in Lismore by kings of Munster, mostly under duress. But whatever the precise reason for the choice of Lismore, which only came within the sphere of influence of the Dál gCais in the late eleventh or early twelfth century, Flannán's biographer was perhaps concerned with the sainting of a royal ancestor of the Uí Bhriain, in the process devoting nine sections to Toirdhealbhach's affairs, including an account of an occasion on which future kings of his line were named, beginning with Brian Bóramha.[18]

The remainder of the Life is taken up with Flannán's miraculous achievements at home in Munster and as far away as Scotland, where his journey to an island named 'Mananch' possibly reveals an awareness of the presence of his cult in a group of islands off Lewis in the Hebrides.[19] The lead-up to the saint's death provided his biographer with an opportunity of enunciating, in the spirit of the twelfth-century reform, the doctrine that ecclesiastical successors were to be chosen not on grounds of consanguinity or royal influence, but on the basis of their spiritual qualities.[20] Before dying, he arranged to have the bones of his father – again in the tradition of sainting of royal ancestors – raised and enshrined.[21] The author of Flannán's Life, and of that of another local saint named Mochuille, may have been Magister Marianus Scotus (†*c.*1180) of the *Schottenkloster* in Regensburg, who appears to have been a native of the district around Tulla in Clare.[22]

With little regard for traditional chronology, Flannán is elsewhere found in association with such saints as Abán, with whom he allegedly formed a *fraternitas*, and Seanán of Scattery Island, whose propagandist boldly claimed tribute from him.[23] In a poem in Classical Irish, Flannán son of Toirdhealbhach, together with numerous other saints, was called upon to help in releasing Ireland's southern half (Leath Mogha) from a bondage imposed on it by the northern half (Leath Chuinn), championed by Finnian of Clonard.[24] Among churches dedicated to the saint are Ceall Easpaig Fhlannáin (Lonáin), now Killaspuglonane, near Ennistimon, and Ballindoon in west Galway, where he gave name to 'Inisflannan' and 'Irrosflannan'.[25] Unless he was the same as his namesake at Killard (Ceall Aird) in the barony of Ibrickan on the south-west coast of Clare, who died in 778, the year of Flannán's death has not been recorded.[26] He was accorded first place in the earliest version of the list of saints commemorated on his feastday of 18 December.[27] Part of a penance imposed on an Armagh cleric in 1541 was to visit a number of sites in Munster, including that associated with Flannán, presumably at Killaloe.[28] After the saint's death, so great was the flow of pilgrims to his grave that papal permission was allegedly sought, and obtained, to raise and translate the remains, which were then enshrined.[29] The translation took place on 26 August, according to the martyrology of the Regensburg *Schottenkloster*.[30]

1 *CGSH* §230; *GRSH* 119; *Lgen.* 738.1; *CGH* 152b23; *DIB* iii, 1004. **2** *CathA* 3 §4; *CGSH* §§713.5, 724.5. **3** *VSHH* 280–301; *MHH* 245–6; *IEME* 213–31; *MirL* 52–7. **4** *HDK* 9; *Kenney* 405; *IEME* 215; *TIC* 92–6. **5** *IETC* 202–4. **6** *VSHH* 286 §10; *IEME* 216; *Kenney* 405. **7** *VSHH* 289 §17. **8** *IEKF* 390–1; *BGBR* 26, 18–21. **9** *VSHH* 282 §3. **10** *VSHP* ii, 206–25. **11** *VSHH* 284 §7. **12** Ibid. 284–5 §8. **13** *CoC* 12–14; *HDK* 201. **14** *BP* 2415–21; *VT* 206. **15** *IRC* 329. **16** *MartO*[2] 208; cf. *OLL* 3, 51–2. **17** *VSHH* 287–92 §§14–22. **18** Ibid. 289 §17. **19** *CPNS* 304; *KSS* 350; *ACDS* 92–3. **20** *VSHH* 298 §32. **21** Ibid. 299–300 §34. **22** *MirL* 55–8. **23** *VSHH* 270 §31; *VSHP* i, 25 §37; *ZCP* 10, 26 §21; *IrT* iv, 71 §4. **24** RIA MS 23L11, 263; *SAM* 24.1, 17, 19. **25** *ACL* 94n; *OFWC* 24, 112. **26** *AI s.a.*, p. 517. **27** *MartT* 80; *MartG* 240; *MartD* 340. **28** *JCLAS* 6, 152. **29** *VSHH* 299–300 §34. **30** *MartR* 123; *FSHIM* 240.

Foirceadal of Ceall Tidhil, now either Kilteale, barony of Maryborough East, Co. Laois, or, more likely, Kilteely, barony of Coonagh, Co. Limerick.[1] This saint is known only from the genealogies, of which one line attaches him to the Laoighis – which would suit the Laois location of his church – and the other – more in keeping with the Limerick site – to the Eoghanachta of Munster.[2]

1 *HDGP* iv, 54. **2** *CGSH* §234; *GRSH* 117; *Lgen.* 740.16.

Foircheallán. This saint – also named Foircheallach – is known only from the list of those subject to Brighid of Kildare, which locates him, along with a companion named Maolán, at Ceall Chonnala, an ecclesiastical site in the townland of Barrettstown in the Kildare parish of Oldconnell.[1] Only one saint of the name is recorded in the martyrologies (10 June), but he is assigned to Fobhar, now perhaps Fore in the Westmeath parish of St Feighins.[2]

1 *CGSH* §670.46; *Lgen.* 753.17; *HDGP* iii, 149. 2 *MartT* 49; *MartG* 114; *MartD* 164.

Foirdeoir of Emlagh (Imleach Foirdeorach), parish of Kilkeevin, barony of Castlereagh, Co. Roscommon. A battle fought in 822 between rival Connacht families, the Uí Bhriúin and Uí Mhaine, at a place called Tarbhgha later led to the composition of a tale in explanation of the background to the event.[1] One of the protagonists, Diarmuid (†833), king of Connacht, sought to have removed from office Ailghile, abbot of Clonmacnoise. The latter turned for assistance to his uterine sister, a nun named Foirdeoir who cursed Diarmuid and also, with the exception of a child still in the womb, his descendants, depriving them of kingship. The abbot, who was otherwise remembered in the name of a well called 'Thobural Gyly' (*Tobar Ailghile*) to the east of the river Suck, may have been pressed into service by the author of the tale from another annal entry which records the death in 751 of 'Aelghal', anchorite of Emlagh (of Foirdeoir) and of Clonmacnoise.[2] The close connection between the two churches is confirmed by yet another annal entry, dated 1025, which records the death of a successor of Ciarán (at Clonmacnoise) and of Comán (at Roscommon) 'of the family of Imleach Foirdeoireach'. A raid by the 'Foreigners' of Dublin on Connacht in 1177 led to the burning of Emlagh.[3]

1 *AU s.a.*; *Celtica* 11, 133–40; cf. ibid. 26, 67–9; *Lgen.* 234.7. 2 *AFM s.a.*; *COD* i, §258. 3 Ibid. *s.a.*

Foirtchearn of Ballyovey (Odhbha / Oideamh), barony of Carra, Co. Mayo. Foirtchearn, whose name derives from *for-tighearn*, 'overlord', was among the forty-seven children said to have been born to Cuman daughter of Dallbhrónach, maternal aunt of Brighid of Kildare.[1] The siblings grouped around him in the list of Cuman's offspring, including Greallán of Creeve and Lomán of Lough Gill, were mainly associated with east Connacht, and these are again brought together in the Life of Forannán of Alternan, allegedly as members of a group gathered to meet Colum Cille.[2] The fact that Foirtchearn's closest companion in the two texts is named Laobhán would suggest that these were two of the three smiths credited to Patrick, the third being Mac Céacht.[3] In the list of Patrick's associates, Foirtchearn's church is, however, given as Ráith Sheimhne (Aidhne), now possibly Islandmagee in the Antrim barony of Lower Belfast. By the early nineteenth century there was no memory of Foirtchearn in Ballyovey, and the 'original patron' was locally thought to have been Ciarán, presumably of Clonmacnoise.[4]

1 *CGSH* §722.9. 2 *Anecd.* iii, 3 §5. 3 *CGSH* §§671.11, 672.13; *BP* 3138–40; *VT* 266. 4 OSL MO ii, 65–73.

Foirtchearn of Island Magee. *See* Foirtchearn of Ballyovey.

Foirtchearn of Trim (Áth Truim), baronies of Lower Moyfenrath and Upper Navan, Co. Meath. In keeping with the location of his church, the genealogists assigned Foirtchearn son of Feidhlimidh to the Ceinéal Laoghaire of the southern part of Meath.[1] On arriving in Ireland, Patrick, according to a tradition dating to the seventh century, left a companion named Lomán at the mouth of the Boyne, instructing him to sail up-river.[2] Upon reaching what is now Trim, Lomán was discovered reading the gospel by Foirtchearn who immediately believed and was baptized. Foirtchearn's mother, allegedly a Briton, and his father Feidhlimidh (who is said to have been the son of a Briton, and capable of speaking British to Lomán) were likewise converted, and the whole family, with its lands and wealth, were offered to Patrick and Lomán 'till Doomsday'. This foundation-charter, the purpose of which would have been to validate Armagh's claim to authority over Trim, is the basis for almost everything that is known about Foirtchearn, who is said to have later briefly succeeded Lomán at Trim, where he was followed by a long line of family members, all of them bishops or abbots.[3] The same text formed the basis of entries in the martyrologies at 17 February and 11 October commemorating Foirtchearn, Lomán, and others associated with the church of Trim.[4]

A note to the latter feast states that Foirtchearn dwelt not only at Trim, but also at a church called Killoughternane (Ceall Fhoirtchirn) in the Carlow parish of Sliguff, where there is a holy well dedicated to him.[5] It was here that Finnian of Clonard received, according to his vernacular biographer, an early education from Bishop Foirtchearn, founding while in the area three churches, one of which, Drumfea (Druim Fiadh), is in the parish of Fennagh, and the other two, Rossacurra (Ros Cuire) and Kilmaglush (Magh Ghlas), in the parish of Myshall.[6] All three parishes, Sliguff, Fennagh and Myshall, are clustered together.

1 *CGSH* §45; *GRSH* 51; *Lgen.* 706.12. **2** *PTBA* 166–8 §1; *BP* 697–710; *VT* 66; *MedT* 34–47. **3** *MedT* 41. **4** *MartT* 17, 78; *MartO*² 215, 222; *MartG* 194; *MartD* 272; *JEH* 1, 162. **5** *LisL* 2524–6; *HDGP* iii, 174; *Béaloideas* 4, 108; OSL CW 275–7; *AICW* 76. **6** *LisL* 2524–6.

Foramhla. *See* Fearbhla.

Forannán. *See* also Mothoiréan; Torannán.

Forannán. The origins of this name are obscure. It is borne by a relatively small number of saints, almost all of whom are sparsely recorded. Among these are Forannán son of Cuanán who, with his brother Muirdheabhair, is known only from a genealogy attaching him to the Dál nAraidhe of north-east Down and south Antrim.[1] Another bearer of the name, known only from an entry in the martyrologies for 15 February, which describes him as 'son of Aodh', has been speculatively identified in seventeenth-century sources as Forannán of Alternan.[2]

1 *CGSH* §106; *GRSH* 100; *Lgen.* 735.5. **2** *MartT* 17; *MartG* 36; *MartD* 50; *GRSH* 46; *ASH* 336–40.

Forannán of Alternan (Allt Forannáin), parish of Easky, barony of Tireragh, Co. Sligo. Forannán's pedigree, preserved only in the late, perhaps sixteenth-century, vernacular Life written for him, attaches the saint through his father Conn to the Ceinéal Eoghain of Tyrone, albeit by means of an otherwise unattested son of

Eoghan named Fionnbharr.[1] The clearly doctored pedigree may have been designed to provide the saint, and more especially his successors – from whose book the only extant copy of Forannán's Life was made – with favourable connections at a time when the Uí Néill of Tyrone were among the most powerful families in the country.[2] The saint's successors, Muintear Mhaonaigh, who are reputed to have ousted a previous family of coarbs 'through treachery', traced their own descent to the dominant local family of Uí Dhubhda.[3] One of their ancestors, Tiobraide son of Maol Duibh (Dúin), is said to have presented Forannán's church to Colum Cille, together with Skreen (Scrín Adhamhnáin), not far from Alternan in the barony of Tireragh, and Ceall Chuanna on the river Easky, now probably the ecclesiastical site in the Sligo village of Easky.[4] The saint's church at Alternan appears later to have formed part of the possessions of the Cistercian house of Abbeyknockmoy (founded in 1190) before passing back to the mother house of Boyle.[5]

A substantial part of Forannán's Life is given over to the activities of Colum Cille (accompanied by a large group of mainly north Connacht saints) in Tireragh, first at Skreen, and then at Alternan, where Forannán was left to pursue his ascetic practices. These are said to have involved spending the first part of each night up to his armpits in a vat of cold water, the second part lying on a stone pillow, and the third listening to the sounds of the sea and its wildlife.[6] Particular emphasis is laid on the saint's vat and its curative powers, and also on a miraculous banner which appears to have been carried around. Cures, it is stated, were closely linked to the alms that accrued to the saint's successor, and a solemn curse was laid on those who failed to pay the tax due to him. In this way, an advertisement was put in writing, already possibly in the sixteenth century, for a pilgrimage that continued to attract large numbers until well into the twentieth century.[7] The pilgrims came on the last Sunday of July and, in typical Garland Sunday fashion, having performed their rounds, engaged in dancing and other amusements.[8] In seventeenth-century sources, the saint is taken to be the same as Forannán son of Aodh who was commemorated on 15 February.[9] He may also have been identical with Torannán, abbot of Banchory, near Aberdeen in Scotland, who, in the guise of Mothoiréan, was associated with Drumcliff, across Sligo Bay from Easky. The association of his church at Alternan with Boyle would suggest that he is the 'Arannán' invoked in a poem by Donnchadh Mór Ó Dálaigh (†1244), who died in the abbey of Boyle.[10]

1 *Anecd.* iii, 1 §1; *GRSH* 46; *ILL* 366. **2** *Anecd.* iii, 7; cf. *LSLC* 298–301. **3** *Anecd.* iii, 7 §10. **4** Ibid.; cf. *HDGP* iii, 153. **5** *CBC* 12; *NotesEHDT* 289; *MRHI* 124. **6** *Anecd.* iii, 4–5 §§6–7. **7** Ibid. 5–6 §9. **8** *FL* 609; *TDI* i, 594. **9** *MartD* 50; *GRSH* 46; *ASH* 336–40. **10** *DDé* 50; *ACon.* 1244.7.

Forannán of Donaghmore (Domhnach Mór Maighe Feimhin), barony of Iffa and Offa East, Co. Tipperary. In keeping with the location of his church, Forannán son of Rónán was attached by the genealogists to the Déise who gave name to the Waterford baronies of Decies, within and without Drum, but whose sphere of influence also extended into south Tipperary.[1] Locally he was known as Marannán (from Mo Fhorannán), as is shown by the name of his well in the townland of Ballynaraha in the Tipperary parish of Kilsheelan.[2] His father Rónán may also be commemorated locally at Rathronan (Ráith Rónáin), the name of a Tipperary parish close to Donaghmore. Great-aunts of his, Ingheana Cainnigh (Daughters of Cainneach), were associated with the church of Molough (Magh Locha), some ten miles away, where they were commemorated on 24 September.[3] Molough lay near the river Suir at a point where Déaglán, patron of the Déise, reputedly cast his crozier to save a nearby castle from burning.[4] Forannán's feastday has not been recorded, despite early seventeenth-century opinion which, speculatively but impossibly, held him to be identical with both Forannán (†852), abbot of Armagh, and Forannán (fl. 950), abbot of Waulsort in Belgium, who was commemorated on 30 April.[5] ±He may be the Forannán brought together with Déaglán in the 1528 litany of the Benedictines of Abingdon in England.[6]

1 *CGSH* §91.1; *GRSH* 77; *Lgen.* 719.6; cf. *CGH* 327h10. 2 *Wat.Lis.* 209. 3 *MartT* 74; *MartG* 182; *MartD* 256. 4 ITS 16, 62 §41. 5 *MartD* 114; *GRSH* 77. 6 *HBS* 119, 48.

Forbhaise daughter of Aodh. *See* Díona.

Fothadh na Canóine, 'of the canon', of Fahan (Othain), barony of Inishowen West, Co. Donegal. The genealogists attached Fothadh to the Ceinéal Binnigh, a segment of Ceinéal Eoghain located chiefly in the Derry baronies of Coleraine and Loughinsholin.[1] According to the late twelfth-century preface of the Martyrology of Aonghas, Fothadh was the first to be shown the text, an honour that may have been inspired by Armagh politics of the period.[2] The occasion was allegedly a synod held in 804 at Rathcore (Dún Cuair), near Trim, under the presidency of Connmhach, abbot of Armagh, which appears to have coincided with a hosting to Leinster by Aodh Oirdnidhe, overking of the Uí Néill. It was on that occasion that Fothadh procured from Aodh exemption from military service for all inmates of the churches of Ireland, an achievement celebrated in a poem attributed to the cleric, beginning *Eaglais Dé bhí*, 'church of living God'.[3] Coincidentally, the obits of Aodh Oirdnidhe and Fothadh are also brought together in entries for the year 819.[4]

1 *BB* 70a47–b1; *HDGP* iv, 104–5. 2 *MartO*[2] 10; *FSHIM* 196–7. 3 Ibid.; *AU s.a.* 804; *Kenney* 473; *VC*[1] 255. 4 *AU s.a.*

Fraoch of Cloone (Cluain Chonmhaicne), barony of Mohill, Co. Leitrim. Since a collateral ancestor, also named Fraoch, was the first of five sons of Cúscraidh, chief ancestral figure of the Conmhaicne, the origins of the presbyter (*cruimhthear*) Fraoch son of Carthach are likely to have lain in pre-Christian devotion.[1] The location of the saint's church at the *cluain*, 'pasture, meadow', of the Conmhaicne, presumably the family's traditional place of assembly, would tend to support this inference. The branch of the family to which the saint belonged was known as Conmhaicne Réin, and its territory lay in the western part of Bréifne, corresponding approximately to the county of Leitrim, later the lands of the Uí Ruairc.[2] Cruimhthear Fraoch's successor was one of twelve coarbs entitled to participate in the inauguration of the king of Bréifne, and a relic of the Uí Ruairc known as the *míosach* (monthly one, probably calendar) was kept at Cloone.[3] Fraoch's sister Fíonmhaith is said to have been the mother of two saints,

Bearach of Termonbarry and Miodhabhair of Bumlin, both of whom were associated with Roscommon churches situated not far from Cloone.[4] A prophecy concerning Bearach's birth, put in the mouth of Patrick, is said to have given rise to the now obsolete place-name 'Aughagrany' in the parish of Cloone.[5] Bearach is also thought to have been born near Cloone at a spot later marked by a cross and stone and, having baptized the infant, Fraoch bestowed three blessings on him, previously received from Colum Cille.[6] Fraoch is also given the honour of building and consecrating Bearach's church at Termonbarry, with the assistance of Daigh son of Coireall.[7]

A note added to the name of the saint's grandfather Néidhe (Néithe) in the Book of Ballymote states that he bestowed Caillín on Fraoch 'in perpetuity' (*tré bhithe beathadh*).[8] Caillín's church at Fenagh, which gave name to the parish adjoining Cloone, is presumably intended, but the Book of Fenagh presents the relationship between the churches of the two saints in a different light. Mindful of the revenue that came from burials, Caillín is said to have promised hell to those who might choose to be buried anywhere but at Fenagh, and specifically 'with Cruimhthear Fraoch'.[9] Moreover, although he was allowed to have possession of Fenagh after Caillín's death, Fraoch was to hand over every third penny he earned, and he too was to have the privilege of being buried at Fenagh.[10] As Caillín appears to have been originally a localization of Colum Cille, it is fitting that Fraoch should also have figured in the traditions surrounding the latter saint. Colum's late Irish Life relates how he was received hospitably by Fraoch in the wake of the battle of Cúil Dreimhne, and how the saints made between them a colloquy (*iomagallamh*).[11]

An unbroken road, built 'by many saints', is said to have formerly led from Fraoch's church to the chief seat of the diocese at Kilmore, a distance of ten miles.[12] Locally, Cruimhthear Fraoch's name was pronounced as 'Cruher Ree' (Croichearach/Croichar Riogh), and a Latin form 'Fregida' is also attested.[13] He was known by the diminutive form Fraochán, for example at the ancient church site of 'Cross' near Cong, which suggests that he was also intended by the reference to the saint of this name – the son of Cuman (alias Cneas) daughter of Cóchmhaidhe – at Druim Gamhna (now perhaps Drumgownagh in the parish of Cloone).[14] The vernacular biographer of Molaise of Devenish clearly held Fraoch in high regard, naming him as one of Ireland's twelve apostles, and he is elsewhere described as one of the *ardnaoimh*, 'chief saints', of the Conmhaicne.[15] The saint's feastday, which found its way into a late fifteenth-century Cologne copy of the Martyrology of Usuard, fell on 19/20 December.[16]

1 *CGH* 161a37; *CGSH* §149; *GRSH* 105; *Lgen*. 729.11. **2** *CGH* 161a39; *HDGP* ii, 189. **3** *BNÉ* i, 203 §46; *Celtica* 1, 66, 79. **4** *CGSH* §722.101; cf. *MartT* 116 (Midabair). **5** *BNÉ* i, 24; *HDGP* ii, 252. **6** *BNÉ* i, 26 §§16–17. **7** Ibid. 33 §50. **8** *BB* 161 marg. **9** *BFen*. 190–2. **10** Ibid. 288, 290; cf. BFen. (supp.) 74. **11** *BCC* 186–8 §182. **12** *Celtica* 1, 66, 79. **13** *CGSH* §149 (b); *Celtica* 1, 66; *BFen*. 192n; *CPL* 13, 344. **14** *WLC* 74–5. *CGSH* §§443 (La), 722.78; **15** *SG* i, 24, 35; BFen. (supp.) 68, 88. **16** *MartT* 87; *MartG* 242; *MartD* 342; *AS*.Iun. vii, 756; OSL RN ii, 131.

FRAOCHÁN of Boghlone (Bóchluain) in the parish of Clonenagh and Clonagheen, barony of Maryborough West, Co. Laois. This man is known only from an entry in the later martyrologies which places his feastday on 20 November.[1] A note to the Martyrology of Aonghas alleges that he was known as *easconn*, 'impure', because of his failure to receive baptism until his thirtieth year, and another version of this text assigns him to an unidentified place named Druim Dághanna in Dál nAraidhe in north-east Ulster.[2] The saint's day is noted in at least one Scottish calendar, and it has been suggested that he was patron, under the guise of Asston (Irish *easconn*), of the church of Kyrke Asston on the Isle of Man.[3] Fraochán had been forgotten at Boghlone by the early nineteenth century.[4]

1 *MartG* 222; *MartO*[2] 242; *MartD* 314. **2** *MartO*[2] 244; *MartO*[1] 169; *HDGP* viii, 19. **3** *KSS* 351; *PIM* 597–8. **4** OSL LS i, 79–80.

FRAOCHNAD daughter of Dúnán Dearg. *See* Martan.

FRAOCHNAD daughter of Seanach. *See* Baodán of Cloney.

FREGIDA. *See* Fraoch.

FUINEACHT daughter of Lóichín. *See* Mochua of Timahoe.

FUINEACHT daughter of Maol Fithrigh. *See* Cormac of Trim.

FUIREAMHAIN. *See* Aoidhghin of Teach Deireascain.

FUINCHE. This name, also written Fainche, derives from a word which has two possible meanings, 'scald-crow' and 'black fox'. It is common enough in the wider literature, sometimes in association with ancestral figures, and is well represented in hagiography, with twelve of the name – most of them otherwise unidentifiable – included in the list of homonymous saints.[1]

1 ITS 59, 118 §180; *CGSH* §708.116–27.

FUINCHE daughter of Aonghas. *See* Fuinche daughter of Bleidhín.

FUINCHE daughter of Bleidhín. The genealogists attach this saint to the Dál nAraidhe of north Down and south Antrim, to whom a namesake and probable double, Fuinche daughter of Aonghas, likewise belonged.[1] Fuinche daughter of Bleidhín may have been a sister of Ceallach son of Bleidhín, king of Latharna, now Larne in Antrim.[2] Her feastday is not recorded.

1 *CGSH* §§112, 113, 708.125 (add.); *GRSH* 100; *Lgen*. 732.2. **2** *CGH* 143b3.

FUINCHE daughter of Conall Dearg. *See* Éanna of Inishmore; Moninne.

FUINCHE daughter of Dallbhrónach. Having married Neamhan, this saint is said to have remained barren for a long time, until her niece, Brighid of Kildare, blessed her womb.[1] Colmán was the name of her first-born, but she also gave birth to three more children, named Conall, Eoghan and Cairbre, all of whom were christened from the waters of the well in which Bishop Iobhar of Begerin had been baptized.[2] The tract on the mothers of the saints refers to Colmán's three brothers only.[3] No feast is recorded.

1 *CGSH* §728; *Lgen*. 695.3. **2** *CGSH* §728. **3** Ibid. §722.3.

Fuinche daughter of Rónán. This saint was among the several children credited to Rónán, patron and eponym of Kilronan, near Boyle, the best-known of whom was Lasair of Aghavea.[1] As the relationship with Rónán was in most cases spurious, it may be assumed that Fuinche represented some other bearer of the name, possibly Fuinche Gharbh of Rossory.[2] The two feasts (1, 21 January) assigned to Fuinche in an early seventeenth-century source are also baseless.[3]

1 *Ériu* 5, 74, 82. 2 *LSLC* 291–302. 3 *GRSH* 46.

Fuinche of Abbeylara (Leathráith), barony of Granard, Co. Longford. Feargna son of Fearghas is said to have had four daughters, Dealbhnad, Deimhlir, Cainnear, and 'Fuin' (probably an abbreviation for Fuinche).[1] All four were attached to Abbeylara, where they were subject to Brighid of Kildare whose name is preserved locally in Kilbride, a townland in the parish. Moreover, the entry that follows in the list of saints subject to Brighid attaches its saint, named Fainnear *Cúigir*, 'of five' – a possible variant of Fuinche – to Clonbroney (Cluain Brónaigh), adjoining Abbeylara.[2] Elsewhere, Clonbroney, possibly one of the churches later granted to the Cistercian abbey at Abbeylara, is said to have been founded by Fuinche.[3] The saint was remembered at Clonbroney on 11 December.[4] She may also have given name to Clonfinfy (Cluain Fuinche) in the Longford parish of Killashee.

1 *CGSH* §670.5. 2 Ibid. §670.6. 3 *VSHP* ii, 254 §5. 4 *MartG* 236; *MartD* 332.

Fuinche Gharbh, 'rough', of Rossory (Ros Oirthir), barony of Magheraboy, Co. Fermanagh. The tract on the saints of Clann Lughdhach – whose patrimony is said to have once stretched from Lough Erne to Slieve Bloom – places Fuinche daughter of Criomhthann second after her uncle, Aodh son of Guaire.[1] Aodh's church adjoined that of Fuinche (which was reportedly founded at Rossory in 1084) at Lisgoole in the same parish, near Lough Erne, later the site of a Franciscan friary.[2] A second location is attested for Fuinche in the heartland of Ceinéal Laoghaire – now mainly the Meath baronies of Upper and Lower Navan – at a church named Díseart Fuinche, possibly the same as 'Chell Fonche' which belonged to the Augustinian abbey at Trim.[3] Further south, among the Eoghanacht of Cashel, Fuinche was attached, according to the martyrological lists for 21 January, to the unidentified church of Cluain Chaoi.[4] The record for the saint's more usual day of 1 January was the subject of some confusion, with the oldest martyrology assigning Fuinche (written Findche) to Loch Rí, now Lough Ree on the river Shannon.[5] Some seventeenth-century sources attach her to the Ceinéal Eoghain, thus identifying her with a namesake, the daughter of Coireall.[6] The saint's nickname is said to have originated when, in order to escape being wed, she sprang into Lough Erne and passed under water until she arrived, covered in shells and sea-slime, whence her roughness, at Diarmuid's church of Inchcleraun on Lough Ree.[7] Her bells used to be rung against offenders, with those of her neighbours, Maodhóg, Molaise, and Náile.[8]

1 *CGSH* §690.2; *Lgen.* 706.4; *DIB* iii, 695. 2 *AU s.a.*; *MRHI* 254. 3 *BB* 87d14–20; *HDGP* iii, 175. 4 *MartT* 10; *MartO*[2] 37; *MartG* 20; *MartD* 24; *ClLTÁ* 83–4. 5 *MartT* 3; *MartG* 6; *MartD* 2; *ClRec.* 8, 291. 6 *MartD* 2; *GRSH* 46. 7 *MartO*[2] 50. 8 *BNÉ* i, 285 §272; *MHH* 121, 124 §§53, 58.

Fuinche Gharbh daughter of Coireall. *See* previous entry.

Fulartach of Dysart, parish of Dunfierth, barony of Carbury, Co. Kildare, which may now represent an earlier Díseart Fulartaigh.[1] Coming into Dál nAraidhe of north Down and south Antrim, Patrick is said to have been humbly welcomed by Conla son of Caolbhadh who received the saint's blessing and a promise that his line would produce 'kings and chiefs'.[2] There is no mention of saints but, according to the genealogies, Fulartach (also written Fualartach) son of Breac was also in direct line of descent from Conla.[3] The saint's associations were with southern churches: Díseart Fulartaigh was allegedly located in Uí Fhailghe, whence the Kildare baronies of Offaly which, while contiguous to Carbury, were at some distance from Dunfierth; Clonard, of which he is said to have been a bishop, lay in Meath.[4] Against this latter connection, his namesake at Clonard is recorded as having died in 779, whereas the anchorite, Fulartach son of Breac, allegedly died twenty years earlier, in 759/760.[5] Having, like many other saints, two feastdays, 29 March and 21 December, the day of Fulartach's death remains uncertain, but John Colgan thought that one of these days might apply more properly to a bishop named 'Felartus' who, along with two unnamed sisters, accompanied Patrick while he was in Magh Seilge, now approximately the area about Rathcroghan in Roscommon.[6]

1 DQE 106n. **2** *BP* 1908–9; *VT* 164. **3** *CGSH* §103; *GRSH* 100; *Lgen.* 735.14. **4** *MartG* 64; **5** *AU s.a.* 779; ATig. *s.a.* 759; ARos. §§192, 209. **6** *MartT* 28, 87; *MartG* 64, 242; *MartD* 88, 342; *ASH* 787; *BP* 1205–19; *VT* 106–8.

Furodhrán of Dunleer (Lann Léire), barony of Ferrard, Co. Louth. This saint is usually accompanied by his brother Baodán, also of Dunleer, and both are said to have descended through their father Maonán from Fiachra Casán of the Oirghialla or, more particularly, of a branch of that group known as Uí Chruinn, whose pedigree is placed between those of Fir Rois and Uí Shéagháin, both from the Louth area.[1] A poem on the saints of Dunleer invokes the blessings of Finnian – who was associated with the neighbouring church of Dromin – on Baodán, Furodhrán and other Dunleer saints.[2] There were reputedly fifty Britons with Furodhrán at Dunleer.[3] The saint's nephew, Teille son of Séighín, also attained sanctity in the Irish tradition, figuring, along with Furodhrán, in the well-known tale of *Buile Shuibhne* (Sweeney's frenzy).[4] The feast of Baodán and Furodhrán was observed in Dunleer on 18 June, which also appears to have been the patron day in the neighbouring parish of Mosstown.[5]

1 *CGSH* §55; *GRSH* 70; *Lgen.* 714.15; *BLec.* 79v[ab]. **2** *CGSH* §737. **3** *IrL* 66. **4** *IrT* iii, 55; *BS* §9. **5** *MartT* 51; *MartG* 118; *MartD* 172; OSL LH 208.

Furodhrán son of Cairbre Crom. Despite being attached by the genealogists to a leading branch of the Eoghanachta – located at Glanworth (Gleannamhain), near Fermoy, in Cork – which produced a series of kings of Munster in the period between about 580, when Furodhrán's father died, and 820, this saint is otherwise practically unknown.[1] Both the saint's father and brother (Aodh Flann Cathrach) were regarded as kings of the southern province and Cairbre Crom is said to have given the important church of Cloyne (Cluain Uamha), later a diocesan see, to God and to Colmán son of Léinín.[2]

1 *CGSH* §414. **2** *LM* 143–4; *Anecd.* iii, 61.

Fursa of Killursa (Ceall Fhursa), barony of Clare, Co. Galway, and of several other churches in Ireland and abroad, including Haggardstown in Louth, Péronne in Picardy, and Lagny near Paris. The saint's name, sometimes rendered Fursa Cráibhtheach, 'pious', and anglicized as Fursy or even Purce, is thought to derive either from Latin *virtus*, 'miracle', or Indo-European *vort*, 'turn, twist', but in view of its palatalized form Fuirse, it may in fact represent a pet form of the name Furodhrán.[1] The saint is well attested historically and, drawing on an early Life written in Latin sometime after 649/650, Bede, the early eighth-century historian of the English, already provided an extensive account of Fursa's career.[2]

Having left Ireland sometime after 630 with several companions, including his brothers Ultán and Faolán, Fursa first founded a church in East Anglia, before moving to Gaul, where he established the monastery of Lagny. On his death in 649 or 650, the saint's body was taken to Péronne which was to become the centre of his cult on the Continent and, under the guise of *Peronna Scotorum*, 'Péronne of the Irish', the focal point of the so-called Irish *paruchia* in northern Gaul. In 880, Péronne was destroyed by the Norse and, though it continued to attract Irish pilgrims, Lagny probably reasserted thereafter its position as the main focus of the saint's cult.

By naming two of his associates as 'Beanus' and 'Meldanus', the author of the saint's early Life provided a clue to Fursa's Irish background because these, under the guise of Beoán and Meallán, are otherwise attached to a church named Meenan (Tamhlachta Meanann) in the Down parish of Aghaderg.[3] This is near Donaghmore whose patron (Mac Earca) is placed, along with Fursa, among the offspring of Brónach daughter of Míleac, patron of the church of Kilbroney (Ceall Bhrónaighe), near Rostrevor, in the same general area.[4] A few miles away, in the former territory of the Conaille, now mainly the northern part of the county of Louth, lay Haggardstown whose patron was also Fursa, locally named Purce.[5]

The east Ulster focus of Fursa's early tradition, which saw him assigned variously to Dál nAraidhe and Conaille, was marked by strong Patrician associations, replicated at Péronne, but these are all but absent from the later version of his legend, first recorded in the Latin Life written for the saint about 1100 at Lagny.[6] In this text, which contains extensive coverage of Fursa's birth, youth and early manhood, replete with onomastic and genealogical details, the focus is largely on west Connacht. In keeping with an alternative pedigree, which attached the saint to the Eoghanachta, Fursa's father Fiontan is treated as a son of a king of Munster who fell in love with Geilghéis daughter of Aodh Fionn.[7] Sometimes described as a daughter of the king of Connacht, Geilghéis is here presented, perhaps by way of acknowledgment of the south-east Ulster tradition, as a niece of Bréanainn, king of Magh Mhuirtheimhne, the plain of Louth.[8] Having married without permission, the couple was sent into exile by Geilghéis' irate father who allegedly first tried to burn them at the stake.[9] Fiontan thereupon took Geilghéis to his 'uncle' (*patruus*), Bréanainn, patron among other churches of Annaghdown near Lough Corrib, and after nine months the child Fursa was born.[10] Having been baptized by Bréanainn, the saint's first miracle involved the resuscitation of the children of his maternal granduncle, Bréanainn, king of Magh Mhuirtheimhne.[11] Later, before leaving Ireland, he is said to have built a monastery at what is now Killursa, near Annaghdown, and was properly reconciled with his father-in-law, Aodh Fionn, who did penance.[12]

In arranging to have Fursa's Life brought up to date, Arnulf, abbot of Lagny, secured, no doubt unwittingly, a 'continental edition' and wide dissemination for what amounted to a complete travesty of the saint's earlier Irish history. Not only were Fursa's south-east Ulster origins almost totally obscured, his genealogical record was also blatantly manipulated with a view to creating a clever piece of propaganda on behalf of the prominent Connacht ecclesiastical family of Uí Dhubhthaigh (O'Duffys), whose genealogy traced their descent to a grandson of the saint's maternal granduncle, Bréanainn.[13] In addition to forging a genealogical link between Fursa and the Uí Dhubhthaigh, the text also established, with little regard for contradictory evidence elsewhere, a close relationship between Fursa and Bréanainn, patron of Annaghdown. In this way the Life provided a genealogical basis for Uí Dhubhthaigh title to churches in Connacht, dedicated to either Bréanainn or Fursa, and especially to the later diocesan centre at Annaghdown and the neighbouring church of Killursa. The precise circumstances surrounding the transition of Fursa's infancy tale from its original Connacht context to the scriptorium of the monastery of Lagny in France remains a matter for speculation. The survival of the text shows, however, that there must have been frequent cultural exchanges between the west of Ireland and the Continent around the beginning of the twelfth century.

Despite the vigorous nature of his continental cult, Fursa remained popular in Ireland, as is shown among other ways by the translation of his early Life into the vernacular.[14] Native hagiographers also found room for him in the records of several other saints. These included: Fionnbharr, at whose grave in Cork he is said to have witnessed a ladder of gold leading to heaven; Crónán, whose decision to found Roscrea is described as having met with 'Bishop' Fursa's approval; Mochaomhóg of Leigh, who secured with Fursa (again treated as a bishop) the release from captivity of a king's son named Scannlán; Colmán son of Luachán, who is said to have formed a *fraternitas* with the saint, granting to him part of the burial ground at Lynn and, three years after his own death, allowing Fursa, then on a journey around Ireland 'from church to church', to elevate his remains; and Molaise, at the grave of whose grievously wronged sister, located in unconsecrated marshy ground outside Leighlin, Fursa, whose words of advice were included by Maol Ruain in his teaching of the daughter of a king 'in the eastern countries', and who guaranteed Molaga, the freedom of his *tearmann*, is alleged to have witnessed a company of angels leading to heaven.[15] Acknowledging that Fursa would need to 'come from afar', a poem promising woe on those who would trespass over the boundary of Seanán's church at Scattery Island invoked the saint, and a prophecy of more general woe was elsewhere put into Fursa's mouth.[16] Also attributed to Fursa is the driving into a lake in the Galtee mountains of a ferocious dragon which, again according to prophecy, would rise at the end of the world and afflict the country in vengeance for John the Baptist, sentiments that are elsewhere echoed in the text known as the *Scuab*, 'besom', out of Fanad.[17] A poem attributed to Cuimín of Connor states that Fursa loved nothing better than a cold well in which to recite his psalms.[18] In a poem in Classical Irish, the saint, together with Éanna and numerous others, was called upon to help in releasing Ireland's southern half (Leath Mogha) from a bondage imposed on it by the northern half (Leath Chuinn), championed by Finnian of Clonard.[19] At Killursa, he came to be regarded as a brother of both Éanna and Cuana, patrons of the neighbouring parishes of Killeany and Kilcoona, and he was also remembered in the neighbouring parish of Kilkilvery.[20] Fursa was also patron of the Cork parish of Clonmeen, where his well is still frequented.[21] A well was also dedicated to him at Killurly in the Kerry parish of Killinane.[22] Fursa died, according to the annals in 648/9, and his feast of 16 January is recorded in both continental and insular calendars and martyrologies.[23] A second feast, possibly that of the translation of his remains, fell on 9 February.[24] The vision attributed to him in his early Latin Life is dated by the Annals of Ulster to 627.[25]

1 *ASH* 76 §viii; *RC* 25, 386; *CMCS* 17, 1–14; *DIB* iii, 1131–2. **2** *BEH* 268–76; *TBF*; *MGH.SRM* iv, 423–49; *VFBA* 1–21. **3** *CMCS* 17, 2; *FIO* 1–15. **4** *CGSH* §§702.1, 722.92. **5** OSL LH, 296–7. **6** *CGSH* §157.1; *GRSH* 104; *Lgen*. 737.11–12; ARos. §124; *Ériu* 5, 110–11; *ASH* 75–82; *CMCS* 17, 1–14. **7** *ASH* 75 §1. **8** Ibid.; *CGSH* §§157.2; 722.33; ARos. §124. **9** *ASH* 75 §§4–5. **10** Ibid. 76 §§7–8. **11** Ibid. 76–7 §9. **12** Ibid. 77 §§11–12, 89 §14. **13** *CMCS* 17, 1–14; *BNÉ* i, 192 §9. **14** *SIHI* 108–13; *RC* 25, 385–404. **15** *VSHP* i, 74 §15, ii, 26–7 §17, 180–1 §31; *VSHH* 277 §15; *BBa*. 86 §24; *BCML* §§42, 97–9; *ZCP* 9, 241 §6. **16** *ZCP* 10, 26 §21; ibid. 9, 168. **17** RD §47; NLI G 10, 46b; *TEAB* 690 §5. **18** *ZCP* 1, 64. **19** RIA MS 23L11, 263; *SAM* 24.1, 17, 22. **20** OSL GY i, 186, 276. **21** *CPR* i, lxviii; *PABD* 108–10. **22** *UiR* 55. **23** *AS*.Nov. ii, 42; *MartA* 61; *MartU* 162; *MartT* 8; *MartO*[2] 36; *MartG* 16; *MartD* 18; *AU s.a.* **24** *ASH* 282–300; *BiblSS* v, 1321; *DIB* iii, 1131–2. **25** *MGH.SRM* iv, 435; *AU s.a.*

G

Gabhrán son of Aonghas. *See* Garbhán son of Aonghas.

Gabhrán son of Dubhthach. *See* Fachtna of Kiltoom.

Gall Cráibhtheach, 'pious', of Lullymore (Liolchach), barony of Offaly East, Co. Kildare. After the defeat of the forces of the northern Uí Néill at the Hill of Allen in 722, Aodh Alláin, the son of the slain overking, Fearghal son of Maol Dúin, reportedly fled to Lullymore, where, dressed as a cleric, he helped to dig the embankment surrounding the church for its holy men, Modhíocha son of Amhairghin and the Gall Cráibhtheach, thus not only saving his own life, but also leaving a covenant of his people in the church.[1] The pious Gall may also have had a church named after him in Kilcock, and he was among those invoked as a saintly protector of the Leinstermen in a poem attributed to Moling.[2] By way of contrast, in his other apparent role as patron of the church of Inchagoill in the Galway parish of Cong, he was called upon for assistance in a poem said to have been uttered by Seanán of Scattery Island in Munster.[3] His cognomen, *cráibhtheach*, is sometimes replaced by the Latin form *prudens* and one version of the notice of the saint's feast (2 November) erroneously separates *prudens* (written *prudein*) from Gallus, as if they were distinct names.[4] By way of further confusion in this list, Earc of Slane is also assigned to the church of Lullymore.[5] The saint died in 730, and by the early seventeenth century, Lullymore's patron was Patrick.[6] A slab on Inchagoill was thought to mark the Gall's grave.[7]

1 *CathA* 9–10 §14. **2** *CDKL* 261; *Dinn.* 2, 33; *SG* i, 382. **3** *ZCP* 10, 26 §21. **4** *MartG* 210. **5** Ibid.; *MartD* 292. **6** OSL GY iii, 6; *AU s.a.* **7** *Dinn.* 2, 31.

Garailt of Mayo (Maigh Eó), townland of Mayo Parks, parish of Mayo, barony of Clanmorris, Co. Mayo. Famous for its connection with Saxons, whence Magh Eó na Sagsan, the church of Mayo was founded by Colmán of Inishbofin, who had been expelled from Northumbria after the synod of Whitby in 664.[1] Renowned as a centre of learning, Mayo maintained its connection with Englishmen at least until the end of the eighth century, when Alcuin wrote letters to fellow-countrymen there.[2] Mention of Garailt (also Gearalt, Latin Geraldus) is rare in early sources, but, according to an early litany, he was surrounded at the church in Mayo (later called *ecclesia sancti Geraldi*) by no fewer than 3,300 saints, together with fifty saints of Luighne (Leyny) in Sligo.[3]

Garailt's fame was no doubt partly because of the Life composed for him in Latin, probably after 1370, when what was previously a collegiate church became a house of canons regular.[4] Extant only in the *Insulensis* collection, put together about 1385 in a house of canons on Lough Ree, Garailt's Life has been described as 'extremely fabulous', but this only holds when the text is considered against historical fact and chronology, which it blatantly disregards.[5] Colmán, for instance, is presented as abbot of Iona and archbishop of all England, positions never held by him, and the name of Garailt's supposedly royal father Cusperius is otherwise unattested.[6] The saint's biographer cleverly creates the image of a genuinely English saint by providing him with brothers, otherwise also associated with England or with Saxon foundations in Ireland, such as Balanus (alias Balloin) of Tisaxon, Berikertus (alias Beircheart) of Tullylease, and Hucbritannus, who probably represents Echbrichtus (Egbert), a noted English member of the community on Iona, remembered on 24 April, along with Wilfrid of Ripon, Colmán's chief protagonist at the synod of Whitby.[7]

Having thus established Garailt's credentials, the remainder of the Life is concerned with the saint's activities in Ireland, mainly in Mayo, with due reference to ultimately beneficial encounters with some important west of Ireland dynasts. These included Oilill of the Uí Dhubhda (O'Dowds), the most powerful local family, whose son, Cathal by name, Garailt is shown as raising from the dead, an act that earned for him the lands on which to found his first church, enigmatically named Eilithir.[8] The much more important church of Mayo was allegedly also founded by Garailt – rather than its real founder Colmán – on lands granted to the saint by Raghallach, progenitor of one of the leading lines of the Uí Chonchobhair (O'Connor) kings of Connacht.[9]

The saint is said to have divided his community into three groups whose separate duties were: to seek alms in 'English parts'; to engage in building work on the monastery; and to celebrate the divine offices.[10] One can well imagine this to have been true of the preparations that attended the arrival of the canons regular in Mayo in the late fourteenth century, when *Anglicanae partes* would probably have denoted the parts of Ireland then controlled by the English. Another indication of a possible concern with the affairs of the canons regular is the manner in which Féichín was singled out for election, with Garailt, at a convention held in Tara in order to decide how the Irish people should react to the prospect of the great plague known as *Buidhe Chonaill*.[11] Besides being associated with Fore in Westmeath, Féichín, a victim of the plague, according to the annals, was patron of Ballysadare in the Sligo barony of Leyny, the site of a house of canons.[12] Returning to Connacht, Garailt is portrayed as the saviour of the king (Etranus) and people of Corann, now the Sligo barony of Corran and adjoining parts, who took shelter under his cloak.[13] The saint is then said to have spent the rest of his life in Mayo and, impossibly, to have been succeeded by Adhamhnán of Iona who, while on a circuit of Ireland, allegedly visited Garailt before his death in order to join him in a confraternity.[14]

Much the same detail forms a background to the tale of 'Four Saints' preserved in the Book of Lecan, which describes how Adhamhnán, Cormac son of Eoghan, Dairí daughter of Cathaoir, and the Saxons (Garailt and his 100 saints) joined in a union.[15] Interestingly, both Adhamhnán and Dairí are elsewhere associated with famous *cána*, 'ecclesiastical laws'.[16] The number of Garailt's companion saints varies, with 300 cited in a story of how he cursed the wife of Ó Caomháin who had turned him away from her husband's fort.[17] The saints of Luighne also accompany Garailt, under the guise of 'Eralt', in a poem enumerating those who would come to the aid of Seanán of Scattery.[18] Alas, despite his local high status as abbot and bishop, all memory of Garailt and his companions had faded by the early nineteenth century.[19] According to the annals, the saint died in 732.[20] His feast, which found its way into a copy of the Martyrology of Usuard compiled in Cologne in the late fifteenth century, fell on varying days between 10 and 13 March.[21] A saint named Gearóid, patron of the Monaghan parish of Donagh, may be identical with Garailt, but there is no record of this man's feastday.[22] The form Gearóid was also used in a dedication in the townland of Temple, in the Galway parish of Clonkeenkerrill.[23]

1 *BEH* 296–312; *CSax*. 200–5; *AIRV* 411–26; *DIB* iv, 52. **2** *Kenney* 534–5. **3** *IrL* 56; *MP* 72; *Peritia* 15, 90–2. **4** *MRHI* 186. **5** *VSHP* i, lxxi–lxxii; ii, 107–15; *ASH* 599–606. **6** *VSHP* ii, 107 §2. **7** Ibid.; *MartT* 36; *MartG* 82; *ASI* 10. **8** *VSHP* ii, 108–10 §§4–6; *Lgen*. 270.1–2; *CGH* 338f60; OCBG §1545. **9** *VSHP* ii, 111 §8; *CGH* 145e38; *IKHK* 300. **10** *VSHP* ii, 112 §10. **11** Ibid. 112–13 §12. **12** *AU s.a.* 665; *MRHI* 160. **13** *VSHP* ii, 113–14 §13. **14** Ibid. 114–15 §§14–15; *CSax*. 200–5. **15** *IrT* iii, 2 §5. **16** *CA*; *Celtica* 21, 561–6. **17** *Lgen*. 270.1. **18** *ZCP* 10, 26 §20. **19** OSL MO ii, 445. **20** *AU s.a.*; *ASH* 604. **21** *MartT* 22; *MartG* 54; *MartD* 74; *ASH* 604; *AS*.Iun. vi, 153. **22** OSL AH/MN 40; but cf. *TDI* i, 464. **23** *JGAHS* 60, 12.

Garbhán of Ceall Neise (Nise), which may now be represented by an ecclesiastical site in the townland of Grange Upper, parish of Grangesilvia, barony of Gowran, Co. Kilkenny.[1] Together with Neas and Mac Caorthainn, Garbhán son of Oireannach is among those said to have been subject to Brighid of Kildare at the church of Ceall Neise.[2] Though nothing else is known for certain of these saints, their names crop up elsewhere in similar, probably related, groupings. Garbhán, for example, and his brother Ceallán, both sons of Neas, were associated with the church of Fancroft (Fionnchoire) in the Offaly parish of Seirkieran, where their companion was Conlaodh Cráibhtheach, Brighid's bishop.[3] Similarly, Mac Nise of Fancroft, Mac Caorthainn, and Conlaodh were elsewhere grouped together with a female saint named Brighid, doubtless the patron of Kildare, at the church of Coolcor (Cúil Chorra) in the Longford parish of Granard, a few miles from Kilbride (Ceall Bhrighde) in the neighbouring parish of Abbeylara.[4]

1 *HDGP* iv, 39. **2** *CGSH* §670.41; *Lgen*. 753.11. **3** *CGSH* §172. **4** Ibid. §670.64.

Garbhán of Clonshanbo (Cluain Seanbhó), barony of Ikeathy and Oughterany, Co. Kildare. This saint was one of seven sons of Lughaidh son of Nathí of a branch of the Laighin or Leinstermen named Uí Chéithigh, whence Ikeathy.[1] The most famous of his brothers was Crónán (alias Mochua) of Clondalkin in Dublin, and all seven were born to Cainnear of Clonsilla.[2] The Life of Caoimhghin speaks of a Garbhán who surrendered his church 'near the town and bay of Dublin' to the patron of Glendalough.[3] Though this saint is likely to have been Garbhán of Kinsaley (Ceann Sáile) in the barony of Coolock, who was commemorated on 9 July, the coincidence of name and the Dublin associations held in common point to his identity with the patron of Clonshanbo.[4] It has also been argued, however, that Garbhán, patron of the Donegal church of Killygarvan (Ceall Gharbháin), one of whose townlands was named Ceall Sáile (Kintale), was intended in the list of those remembered on 9 July.[5] A commemorative date of 15 January has been recorded for Garbhán of Clonshanbo, whose name is rendered 'Germanus' in an early seventeenth-century list of Kildare churches.[6]

1 *CGH* 124a14; *CGSH* §243; *Lgen.* 727.13. 2 *CGSH* §722.77. 3 *VSHP* i, 256 §45. 4 *CPPI* 187; *MartT* 54; *MartG* 132; *MartD* 190. 5 *DLHS* 173. 6 OSL KE i, 72; *CDKL* 261; *Dinn.* 2, 33.

Garbhán of Killygarvan. *See* Garbhán of Clonshanbo.

Garbhán of Kilmagarvoge, parish of Tullowphelim, barony of Rathvilly, Co. Carlow, probably earlier known as Ceall Gharbháin.[1] Together with Fiontan of an unidentified church named Fochailleach and Mocholmóg of Clonard, Garbhán was reputedly one of three saintly children of Ríoghnach, sister of Finnian of Clonard.[2] Finnian himself is said to have spent sixteen years in the nearby Wicklow church of Aghowle, where, as an angel informed him, he would join his monks on the Day of Judgement.[3] Garbhán was commemorated on 26 March.[4]

1 *HDGP* iv, 1. 2 *CGSH* §722.97. 3 *LisL* 2599–603. 4 *MartT* 27; *MartG* 62; *MartD* 86.

Garbhán of Kinsaley. *See* Garbhán of Clonshanbo.

Garbhán son of Aonghas, bishop. The tract on the saints of Clann Lughdhach, otherwise Ceinéal Laoghaire – whose patrimony is said to have stretched from Lough Erne to Slieve Bloom – has a single reference to a saint belonging to the descendants of Laoghaire's brother, Conall Creamhthainne, who was also known as Conall Earr Bhreagh.[1] This man, Garbhán (Gabhrán) by name, also figures independently in the corpus of saints' pedigrees, and in the late vernacular Life written for Forannán of Alternan.[2] The reason for his inclusion in the Clann Lughdhach list is unclear because his associations were with the western part of the kingdom of Midhe, now mainly the county of Westmeath. A tract on the Cuircne of the Westmeath barony of Kilkenny West names him as one of seven sons of Aonghas, two others being Bishop Seanach and Bishop 'Treaslaice'.[3] Kilgarvan Glebe in the parish of Kilcleagh and barony of Clonlonan, which adjoins Kilkenny West, now probably represents the church of this Garbhán.

1 *CGSH* §690; *Lgen.* 704.5; *CGH* p. 555. 2 *CGSH* §§690.16; 539, 573; *GRSH* 55; *Anecd.* iii, 2 §3. 3 *BB* 80a1–3.

Garbhán son of Fionnbharr. According to the vernacular Life of Fionnbharr of Cork, a man of this name was one of the saint's students at the school of Gougane.[1] Various attempts have been made to identify the saint and the church to which he is likely to have been attached. Kilgarvan in the parish of Templerobin on Great Island, Kilgarvan in the Kerry barony of Glanarought, Ballygarvan in Carrigaline parish, and most recently, the now obsolete Dungarvan in St Anne's-shandon parish in Cork city, have been proposed.[2] As parts of Dungarvan in Cork had passed into the possession of the Abbey of St Thomas in Dublin shortly before Fionnbharr's Life was written, the saint's biographer, whose aim was to restore, consolidate and increase the authority of the bishop of Cork, is likely to have had this local place in mind.[3]

1 *BBa.* 66 §21. 2 *JRSAI* 22, 249; *HDCK* 27; *JCHAS* 90, 91–103. 3 *RSTA* 202, 205, 215; *JCHAS* 90, 91–103.

Garbhán son of Neas. *See* Garbhán of Ceall Nise.

Geamán. According to Adhamhnán, Colum Cille, while studying 'in the region of the Laighin', i.e. Leinster, with an aged man named Geamán (Latin Gemmanus) – in later versions of the Life renamed Gearmán – pronounced a curse on a cruel man who had just slain a young girl.[1] The editors of the Life thought Geamán's church might not be far from Clonard, but Colum Cille's connection with that church is deeply suspect.[2] On the other hand, according to the Life of Finnian of Clonard, Geamán 'the master' composed a poem for which he sought no other reward than the removal from his land of its barrenness.[3] A man named Geamán of Domhnach Mór, which could be any one of a number of churches in Leinster or elsewhere, is included in a list of bishops.[4]

1 *VC*[1] 382; *IKD* 227 §25. 2 *VC*[1] 70; *MakS* 2–6. 3 *LisL* 2672–7. 4 *CGSH* §704.185.

Gearalt/Gearóid. *See* Garailt.

Gearmán. *See* Diarmuid of Inchcleraun; Geamán.

Geilghéis daughter of Aodh Fionn. *See* Fursa.

Geintéan of Aghanagh (Eachaineach), barony of Tirerrill, Co. Sligo. While in Magh Luirg, now part of the Roscommon barony of Boyle, Patrick was persuaded by Bishop Maine of the Uí Oilealla – a people whose name became attached to the neighbouring Sligo barony of Tirerrill (Tír Oilealla) – to soften a curse he had imposed on the local family of Ceinéal Mac nEirc.[1] The cause of the curse, allegedly the forcible retention of Patrick's horses, is much more likely to have been Armagh's resentment of the presence in the lands of this family, at Eas Mac nEirc (now Assylin near Boyle), of a Columban foundation.[2] Bishop Maine, described as a priest (*cruimhthear*) of Patrick's household, was attached to Aghanagh, together with Geintéan. This is probably the same person, albeit under the guise of Geintín, as is assigned by the list of those subject to Brighid of Kildare to an unidentified place, possibly also in Tirerrill, named Tír Ghuaire, where his companion was Séighín.[3] Following him in this list was a saint named Eiltín of Shancough (Seanchua) in the same barony.[4] A connection with the patron of Kildare is also exemplified by Bishop Maine, one of many children credited to Cuman, Brighid's maternal aunt.[5] Geintéan's feastday fell, along with that of Maine, on 2 September.[6]

1 *BP* 1664–75; *VT* 144. 2 *IKD* 236 §48. 3 *CGSH* §670.42. 4 Ibid. §670.43; *Lgen.* 753.12. 5 *CGSH* §722.7. 6 *MartG* 168; *MartD* 232.

Gelasius. *See* Giolla Mic Liag.

Geraldus. *See* Garailt.

Germanus. *See* Diarmuid of Inchcleraun.

Giallán of Killelan, barony of Kilkea and Moone, Co. Kildare, which probably represents an earlier Ceall Ghialláin.[1] A marginal note added to the list in the Martyrology of Tallaght for 2 October describes how Oinmhe, son of a king of Leinster, then a hostage with Brighid of Kildare, was renamed Giallán (from *giall*, 'hostage').[1] From this Giallán, according to the note, Ceall Ghialláin in Uí Mhuireadhaigh of south Kildare took its name. Giallán (alias Oinmhe) was commemorated on 2 October, and the same name figures in the list for 6 September in the Martyrology of Tallaght only.[2] According to a litany, there were seven holy bishops at Ceall Ghialláin.[3] Giallán may have been identical with 'Togiallóg grandson of Luan', described as an *eagnaidh*, 'learned person', who is said to have endorsed the Law of Adhamhnán.[4]

1 *MartT* 116; *MartO*[2] 220. 2 *MartT* 68, 76; *MartG*; *MartD* 264. 3 *IrL* 68. 4 *CA* §28; *Peritia* 1, 193.

Giolla Aodha Ua Muighin, bishop of Cork. Bernard of Clairvaux, our only source of information for what transpired in 1140 after the death of Ua Sealbhaigh, successor of Fionnbharr, recounts in his Life of Maol Maodhóg (Malachy) how 'not one of the nobles of the country but rather a poor man ... and he happened to be an outsider' was elected bishop of Cork.[1] The 'poor man' left nameless by Bernard was Giolla Aodha, a Connachtman, hence his description as an 'outsider', who had formerly been a monk at Errew on Lough Conn in Co. Mayo.[2] As an intruder had never before come from so far away to assume the highest ecclesiastical office in Cork, it would seem that his accession was designed to serve principally as an instrument of church reform. Also, while still little more than a fledgling monastery, through Giolla Aodha's appointment the house of canons regular founded in 1137 had now thrust upon it the task of supervising Cork's ecclesiastical affairs for almost the whole of the remainder of the twelfth century.[3] Giolla Aodha was destined to give his name to the priory, later known as Gill Abbey (Mainistear Ghiolla Aodha) and, perhaps more importantly, his Connacht background arguably led to the adoption of a west of Ireland pedigree for his patron Fionnbharr.[4] Giolla Aodha also found himself obliged to oversee a radical reorganisation of the area under his jurisdiction. At the synod of Rathbrassil in 1111 Cork had been given control over a very large area extending roughly from the river Blackwater to the sea. At Kells-Mellifont in 1152, on the other hand, Cork was forced to cede considerable territory to the new dioceses of Cloyne and Ross. There is no evidence to show that Giolla Aodha resisted these sweeping changes; indeed, his presence at Kells-Mellifont among the signatories of the synodal decrees indicates that he acquiesced in them. Giolla Aodha died in 1172, but there is no record of the day of his death.[5] He is, however, included among mainly Connacht saints in a poem written by Donnchadh Mór Ó Dálaigh.[6]

1 *BCLM* 92. 2 *AFM* 1172. 3 *MRHI* 167–8. 4 *MakS* 66–7, 70–3. 5 *AFM s.a.* 6 *DDé* 51.

Giolla Críost Ua Morgair, bishop of Clogher, Co. Tyrone. Giolla Críost (Latin Christianus), a brother of the noted reformer Maol Maodhóg, was elected bishop of Clogher in 1135, probably on the death of its first incumbent, Cionaodh Ua Baoighill.[1] On Giolla Críost's death in 1138 (or 1139), followed by his burial in the Augustinian priory of Peter and Paul in Armagh, he was described by Bernard of Clairvaux as Maol Maodhóg's equal 'in holiness of life and zeal for righteousness'.[2] Little else is known of Giolla Críost, but the author of the *Visio*

Tnugdali, a text written at Regensburg in Germany a few years after the saint's death, placed him and his brother among four blessed bishops seen by Tnúthghal in Patrick's company in heaven.[3] Giolla Críost (alias Criostán), 'who shunned ease for sake of lasting life', was remembered on 12 June.[4]

1 *NHI* ix, 273; *BCLMA* 66n. 2 *BCLMA* 66; *BCOC* 266; *AFM s.a.* 1138. 3 *VisTnug.* 55. 4 *MartG* 114; *MartD* 168.

Giolla Mic Liag of Derry and Armagh. According to its preface, the Martyrology of Gorman was written when Ruaidhrí Ua Conchobhair was king of Ireland, and Giolla Mic Liag (Latin Gelasius), son of Diarmuid 'the poet', was archbishop of Armagh, thus giving the text a date between 1166, when Ruaidhrí began to reign, and 1173–4, when Giolla Mic Liag died.[1] That the martyrology was written towards the end of this period is indicated by the fact that the archbishop's name was added to it at 27 March, under its Latin form Gelasius, with the description *geam amhra, ceann Banba,* 'a notable gem, Ireland's head'.[2] New martyrologies were the products of ecclesiastical reform and, during Giolla Mic Liag's long tenure of the coarbship of Patrick at Armagh (1148–74), two reforming synods had stamped their authority on the Irish church. The first was that of Kells-Mellifont in 1152, which oversaw the reorganization of the Irish diocesan system; the second, perhaps the least well known of the pre-Norman reforming synods, was held in 1162 at Clane in Kildare.[3] Presided over by Giolla Mic Liag, and attended by twenty-six bishops and many abbots, the main concerns of this synod were the enforcement of *riaghail agus soibhéas* (regulation and good conduct), the reaffirmation of the archiepiscopal status of Patrick's successor, and the granting to the primatial church of Armagh of regulative control over the teaching practiced in all other Irish schools.[4]

Then seventy-five, Giolla Mic Liag had twelve years left in which to oversee the implementation of the decisions taken at Clane. These led not only to the production of the Martyrology of Gorman but also to the preparation of a new edition of the early ninth-century Martyrology of Aonghas, with added preface and an extensive commentary, and possibly also to the compilation of the Martyrology of Drummond.[5] Prevented by old age and infirmity, according to Giraldus Cambrensis, from attending the synod of Cashel in 1172, Giolla Mic Liag subsequently confirmed its statutes in Dublin.[6] Again according to Giraldus, the 'common people' thought of Giolla Mic Liag (who by then allegedly depended on a white cow for sustenance) as a saint.[7] By the time of his death on the Wednesday after Easter (27 March) in 1174, he had spent thirty-seven years in the see of Armagh (to which he was appointed by Maol Maodhóg), preceded by sixteen in the 'abbacy of Colum Cille' in Derry [8]. A possible trace of the emphasis on the primacy of Armagh, reaffirmed at Clane, is the reference in Giolla Mic Liag's death notice not only to his status as archbishop but also as *primaith* (primate), a word not used of any of his predecessors.[9]

1 *MartG* 4; *LL* 6063; *PRIA* 35C9, 331. 2 *MartG.* 62; *MartD* 88. 3 *AU s.a.* 4 ATig./*AU s.a.* 1162. 5 *FSHIM* 173–204; *FourIM* 7–9. 6 *EH* 100. 7 Ibid. 8 *BCLMA* 62; *IKD* 109–23; *DIB* iv, 91–3. 9 *AU s.a.* 1174.

Giolla Mochaidhbheo of Armagh. The annals for 1174 notice not only the death of Giolla Mic Liag, archbishop of Armagh, but also that of Giolla Mochaidhbheo, abbot of the Augustinian priory of St Peter and Paul in Armagh, at the advanced age of seventy.[1] The Annals of Ulster, followed by the Four Masters, describe him as a 'diligent, steadfast servant of the Lord' who died on 31 March.[2] The Martyrology of Gorman, whose author would probably have known Giolla Mochaidhbheo, followed by that of Donegal, goes even further; having given his name the Latin form Maccabeus, it portrays him as 'the tower of piety and firmness, wisdom and knowledge, labour and prudence of his time'.[3] Sadly, despite his evident achievement, Giolla Mochaidhbheo is nowhere else noticed in the surviving record. Mochaidhbheo, the saint to whom he was devoted, was remembered on 11 October.[4] Moreover, in his capacity as one of seven saints said to have been 'yet to die', Mochaidhbheo was attached to 'Sliabh Br[eagh]', a hilly area on the borders of the counties of Louth and Meath.[5]

1 *AU*/ATig./*AFM s.a.* 2 Ibid. 3 *MartG* 66; *MartD* 90. 4 *MartG* 194; *MartD* 272. 5 *BL Cat.* ii, 471; *AB* 55, 288–9.

Glúnshalach son of Costamhail. Attached by the genealogists to the Dál nAraidhe of north Down and south Antrim, Glúnshalach is reputed to have been a noted outlaw on Sliabh Fuaid, now the Fews of south Armagh, before his conversion to the faith.[1] The story of his conversion is retold in the Life composed by Conchobhrán for Moninne of Killevy, which describes Glúnshalach (written *Glunelath*) as a tyrant active in a district near Killevy, more precisely named as Magh Mhuirtheimhne (*campus Macdathevene*), a plain in the present county of Louth.[2] On being persuaded to lay his head in Moninne's lap, Glúnshalach was granted a vision of heaven which showed him the place reserved for Caoimhghin of Glendalough. Since nothing less than this place would satisfy him, Glúnshalach, together with his sister's son, Aifín, converted and joined Moninne at Killevy. Advised of the danger of losing the place reserved for him, Caoimhghin also made his way to Killevy, only to be reassured by Moninne. Background to this 'somewhat ridiculous' episode may have been provided by the list of saints commemorated on 3 June, which includes not only Caoimhghin, but also Glúnshalach, Aifín and, in some sources, Moninne.[3]

1 *CGSH* §119; *GRSH* 100; *Lgen.* 734.21; *MartD* 144. 2 *PRIA* 28C 212–14 §§10–11. 3 *MartT* 47; *MartG* 128; *MartD* 144–6; *Celtica* 5, 48–9.

Gobán. This name derives from *Gob(ba)*, a hypocoristic or pet form based on *gabha/gobha*, 'smith', with masculine suffix *–án* (Gobán) and feminine suffix -*nait/-naid* (Gobnaid). A number of saints' names, including not only Gobán (Gobbán) and Gobnaid, but also Moghobóg, reflect this hypocorism, as does the name of the legendary craftsman, the Gobán Saor. In a non-hypocoristic form, the name was borne by Goibhne, smith of the Tuatha Dé Danann, an Irish version of the Celtic smith-god, known in Wales as Govannon. Among places associated with saints named Gobán (alias Moghobóg or Moghoba) are Kinsale (Ceann Sáile) in Cork, close to Kilgobbin (Ceall Ghobáin) in the parish of

Ballinadee. This latter saint, allegedly a cook and also, together with Eiltín of Kinsale, a son of Maghna, sister of David of Wales, is said to have accompanied two disciples of Ailbhe of Emly to Rome.[1] A bishop named Gobán son of Nascann (Nasc) was numbered, with his brothers Srafán and Laisréan, among twelve disciples of Mochuda of Rahan, later placed in charge of the church of Spike Island (Inis Pich) in Cork Harbour.[2] This Gobán was remembered with Neasán of Cork on 17 March, while the feastday of his namesake and probable double, Gobán of Ardcavan (Airdne Dairinse), near the town of Wexford, fell nine days (26 March) later.[3] A week later (1 April), a saint of the name Gobán was given pride of place in the Martyrology of Tallaght, which may have led to John O'Hanlon giving the church of Kilgobbin in the Dublin barony of Rathdown, not far from Tallaght, more prominence than any other in his entry for this day [4] Another Cork church associated with the cult, this time in the guise of Gobán Corr, 'stooped', was Fanlobbus (Fán Lóbaist) in the barony of East Carbery. Its saint was reputed to have received from Fionnbharr of Cork a silver altar vessel and golden altar cross in exchange for his church.[5]

1 *VSHH* 128 §45; *VSHP* i, 60 §38; *CGSH* §722.94. **2** *VSHP* i, 182 §34, 184 §39; *CGSH* §707.818. **3** *MartT* 24, 27; *MartG* 56, 62; *MartD* 80, 86; *HDGP* i, 42. **4** *MartT* 29; *MartG*; *MartD*; *LIS* iv, 9; *Rep. Nov.* 1, 30. **5** *BBa.* 70 §24; cf. *NCHC* i, 68.

Gobán son of Cormac. *See* Aodh of Kilcrow.

Gobán Corr. *See* Gobán.

Gobán Fionn, 'fair'. According to the genealogists, Gobán Fionn son of Lughaidh belonged to the Uí Liatháin of the area now comprising part of east Cork.[1] As such, one would expect devotion to him to have centred on a southern church. This was also the view taken by Míchéal Ó Cléirigh in a note added to his entry on Gobán Fionn of Killamery (Ceall Lámhraighe), near Callan in the county of Kilkenny.[2] In the same note, though drawing on other martyrologists, Ó Cléirigh allowed for the possibility that Gobán Fionn's church was either at Seagoe (Teach Dá Ghabha) in the Armagh barony of Oneilland East, or at Clonenagh (Cluain Eidhneach) in Laois, where his relics were reputedly kept, possibly in a church named 'ecclesia sancti Gauueni' after him.[3] A more local concern was expressed by the scribe copying the genealogies of the saints at Lackan (alias Lecan) in the Sligo parish of Kilglass; he attached Gobán to the church of Kilgobban (Ceall Ghabhann) in the neighbouring Mayo parish of Killala, where later tradition took the saint to be the Gobán Saor.[4] Also known as Moghobóg, the patron of Killamery was attached to a family named Lámhraighe (Maca Láimhe) after which the church was named, and under that guise he was linked to two other churches, Leighlin (Leithghleann) and Delgany (Sruthair Ghuaire).[5] His association with Leighlin lasted until he relinquished the site to its present patron Molaise, electing, according to the latter's biographer, to settle elsewhere, but not before the two saints had agreed a *fraternitas*.[6] At Killamery, the saint's feast fell on 6 December, also the feast of St Nicholas, to whom a well in the churchyard was dedicated.[7] He died, according to the annals, in 661.[8]

1 *CGSH* §236; *GRSH* 117–18; *Lgen.* 740.7; *CGH* 151b26; *DIB* iv, 113–14. 2 *MartD* 326–8. 3 *MartG* 232; *MartO*² 256; *EA* 117–18; *MartD* 424; *CM* 52. 4 *CGSH* §326 (*BLec.*); OSL MO i, 244. 5 *CGSH* §670.86, 707.810. 6 *VSHH* 342 §8. 7 OSL KK ii, 96. 8 *ATig. s.a.* 660.

Gobnaid (Gobnad) of Ballyvourney (Boirnech/Búirnech/Baile Bhúirne), barony of West Muskerry, Co. Cork. Although best known for her connection with Ballyvourney, Gobnaid was patron of many other churches or holy wells. These included Kilgobnet (Ceall Ghobnaid/Ghobnadan) in the Cork parishes of Clondrohid, Kilshannig and Magourney, Knockane in Kerry, and Ballynahinch in the Limerick parish of Knocklong, and Castletown in the Limerick parish of Corcomohide. Churches or wells were also named for her in Banteer in the Cork parish of Clonmeen, Kilgobnet in Waterford, Dunquin (Dún Chaoin) in Kerry, and Inisheer (Inis Oírr) of the Aran Islands. Her legend, which survived only in oral tradition, traces her origins to Inisheer, whence she journeyed via several of the churches named after her to Ballyvourney, there to find the nine white deer foretold for the site of her future church.[1] Over centuries, the custodians of her cult and *airchinnigh* of her church in Ballyvourney were the O'Herlihys (Muintear Iarlaithe), and these were also keepers of her image, one of the few surviving Irish medieval statues in wood, still kept locally and thought to have miraculous powers.[2] Gobnaid's church lay on the boundary between the territories of Uí Eachach Mhumhan and the descendants of Conaire known as Múscraighe Midíne, to whom she was genealogically attached, as opposed to the claim by Charles Smith that she was a daughter of O'Connor Sligo.[3] That Gobnaid herself was originally a patron of ironworkers is indicated by the implications of her name, which is based on the hypocoristic *Gobba*, from *gabha*, 'smith'. Excavation at her church in Ballyvourney yielded considerable evidence of ironworking on the site.[4] Her feastday of 11/12 February – sometimes held on the tenth, as at Knockane in Kerry – places her in contiguity to Brighid, whose pagan precursor and namesake was also regarded as a patron of ironworking.[5] At one time patron of the Múscraighe Mhic Dhiarmada, Gobnaid remains the subject of a vigorous local cult, with rounds being done at her church in Ballyvourney on almost every Sunday of the year, but especially at Whit.[6] The saint is credited with having kept bees and this motif figures prominently in the modern statue at Ballyvourney, carved by the noted sculptor, Séamus Murphy. Gobnaid 'of visible glory' is said to have had Ireland as her *fairche*, 'diocese', and the saint's feast was widely celebrated, especially throughout Munster, and even in places unconnected by name with the saint, as at Kilgarrylander (adjoining Kilgobban, from Gobán, the male equivalent of Gobnaid) in Kerry.[7] An early eighteenth-century account by John Richardson gives a detailed description of the *turas* at Ballyvourney, which was reputedly granted a papal indulgence.[8] The saint was noted for her curative powers of 'every strange disease', including smallpox, and some poems invoking her assistance have survived, as has the bell associated with her.[9] Gobnaid's name has been variously anglicized as Deborah and Abigail (pet form Abby).

1 *JCHAS* 57, 51–5; *DIB* iv, 114. 2 *JCHAS* 57, 49–50; *Éigse* 6, 327; *JRSAI* 76, 164–7; *Béaloideas* 58, 184–5. 3 *CGSH* §665.2.6; *Lgen.* 720.6.10; *NCHC* i, 185. 4 *JCHAS* 57, 32–5. 5 *MartT* 16; *MartO*² 60; *MartG* 34; *MartD* 46; *Anecd.* iv, 15 §150; *JRSAI* 69, 177–8; *MCMHW* 202–3; cf. *NCHC* i, 185 (14 Feb.); *TH* i, 63–5.

6 *ASH* 315 §6; *FFÉ* iii, 112–13; *JCHAS* 57, 59–61. 7 *ZCP* 13, 19; *ACoK* 72. 8 *Éigse* 6, 327; *JRSAI* 76, 164–7; *NCHC* 185–7. 9 *Éigse* 6, 326–32; *Béaloideas* 58, 185–7; *EMH* 458 §156.

Gormán of Kilgorman (Ceall Ghormáin), barony of Gorey, Co. Wexford. According to the later martyrologies, this saint was remembered 'in East Leinster' on 25 October.[1] The author of one such text, compiled in verse by Maolmhuire Ua Gormáin, used the term *aiste*, 'of the metres', to describe Gormán, which allows for the possibility that he may have felt an ancestral affinity towards the saint.[2] Nothing else is known of Gormán, but his church may have had an association with Glendalough, to whose diocese it later belonged.[3] By the early nineteenth century, the saint's feast had been forgotten.[4]

1 *MartG* 202; *MartD* 284. 2 *MartG* 202. 3 *CPPI* 199, 239; *CECW* 181. 4 OSL WX i, 2.

Greall. A derivation from *greall* (Latin *gryllus*, 'cricket or grasshopper') has been proposed for this name, among whose possible forms were Grealla, Greallán, and Greallóg.[1]

1 *MartG* 369.

Grealla. *See* Manchán son of Siollán.

Greallán Craoibheach of Creeve (Craobh [Ghreallláin]), barony and county of Roscommon. Although patron of the important tribal grouping of Uí Mhaine, later most prominently represented by the Uí Cheallaigh (O'Kellys) of the eastern part of Galway, Greallán's pedigree is nowhere to be found in the corpus of saints' pedigrees. The tract on the mothers of the saints names him, however, among the forty-five holy persons said to have been born of Cuman daughter of Dallbhrónach, maternal aunt of Brighid of Kildare.[1] Many of these, including Greallán (anglicized Grellan), had associations with east Connacht, and they are again featured in the Life of Forannán of Alternan as a group brought together to meet Colum Cille.[2]

In common with other east Connacht saints, such as Forannán, Beinéan, and Caillín, Greallán was made the subject of a vernacular Life, composed possibly as late as the second half of the fifteenth or early sixteenth century.[3] As with other Lives of its kind, that of Greallán is largely concerned with setting down in writing the various dues owed to the saint's church, with special emphasis on those of the Uí Mhaine, on whose behalf, the saint – then at his church of Kilcloony (Ceall Chluaine) in east Galway – is said to have intervened, thus allowing them to take possession of their territory.[4] This clearly tendentious text is the only source of information on the paternal background of the saint, who is alleged to have been the son of otherwise unattested parents, Cuillín son of Cairbre Cluaisdearg of Leinster and – in contradiction of the statement in the above tract – a lady named Eithne.[5]

As soon as the child was capable of travel (*ionaistir*), Patrick, who is said to have foretold his birth, took him under his wing, bringing him first to Dublin, as would have been considered appropriate when the Life was written, and subsequently to Connacht.[6] There he was given the privilege of upstaging his mentor by resuscitating Eoghan Sriabh, 'striped', son of Duach Galach, ancestor of the Uí Chonchubhair (O'Connors) of Roscommon, while Patrick was still at prayer for the same purpose. The mark of Greallán's nails on Eoghan are used to explain the origin of the latter's cognomen, and the miracle is cited as a basis for the land and tribute due to the saint from the O'Connors at the spot where the miracle occurred, previously known as Achadh Fionnabhrach, but from then on as Craobh Ghrealláin – interpreted here as Greallán's branch of land – now Creeve, where his coarb later enjoyed the privilege of being present at the inauguration of the O'Connor kings of Connacht.[7] According to the Life of Finnian, this church was in fact founded by the Clonard saint, who later relinquished it to his 'disciple' Greallán.[8]

The remainder of the Life is concerned with the saint's interventions on behalf of the Uí Mhaine and the tribute owed to his church at Kilcloony, not only from these, but also from his father's people, the men of Leinster. Probably in the knowledge that Greallán was remembered in the name of a church in east Cork, now Kilgrellane in the parish of Cloyne, the sons of Oilill of Munster (possibly the Uí Liatháin, descendants of Oilill Flann Beag), who otherwise had no part in the saint's activities, were also required to pay tribute.[9] Greallán is said to have left to the Uí Mhaine (O'Kellys) his crozier which, if borne into battle, would always ensure victory. The crozier survived locally until the nineteenth century in the care of its hereditary custodians, the Uí Chrónghaile (Cronellys).[10] A possible association with the Westmeath barony of Corkaree is evinced by the tradition that a priest named Greallán taught Fiontan of Taghmon, and the Registry of Clonmacnoise assigns to him an unidentified church in Leinster named 'the monastery of Gryllan'.[11] Together with Colum Cille, Fursa, and other saints, Greallán is featured among those said to have foretold the onslaught of the plague known as the *Scuab* ('besom') out of Fanad, and he is elsewhere among the Connacht saints invoked, again with Fursa, in a poem on Seanán of Scattery Island.[12] The saint's feast fell on 10 November, but he was also honoured on 17/18 and 29 September, among other places at Killooaun in the Galway parish of Ballymacward.[13] According to Dubhaltach Mac Fhir Bhisigh, there were two churches named Ceall Ghrealláin in Tír Fhiachrach (whence Tireragh in Sligo), but these have not been located.[14]

1 *CGSH* §722.9; cf. *IrT* iv, 93 §2. **2** *Anecd.* iii, 3 §5. **3** *AS*.Nov. iv, 483–95; *ILL* 366. **4** Ibid. 492–3; *TCHyM* 8–14. **5** *AS*.Nov. iv, 489 §1. **6** Ibid. 488–90 §§1–3. **7** Ibid. 490 §3; *MSPAG* 189. **8** *VSHH* 105 §31. **9** *AS*.Nov. iv, 494 (B); *CGH* 151a47; *JCHAS* 45, 25; cf. *BBa*. 250. **10** *AS*.Nov. iv, 487; *TCHyM* 81n; OSL GY i, 119. **11** *VSHH* 198–9 §3; *RClon*. 458. **12** NLI G 10, 46b; *ZCP* 10, 26 §21; *TEAB* 690 §4. **13** *MartT* 72; *MartG* 178, 214; *MartD* 250–2, 302; *CE* ii, 262; OSL GY i, 511–12. **14** DQE 96; *HDGP* iv, 3.

Gregory. *See* Grioghóir.

Greillseach. *See* Manchán son of Siollán.

Grellan. *See* Greallán.

Grioghóir Béalóir, 'golden-mouthed', son of Gormaltach (Maonach), Pope. Possibly because of the occurrence of the place-name Castle Gregory (Caisléan

Griaghaire) in the parish of Killiney, on the Dingle Peninsula in west Kerry, a pedigree was fabricated for Pope Gregory the Great, tracing his descent to the Corca Dhuibhne who gave name to the present barony of Corkaguiny.[1] He is said to have visited Ireland during his lifetime, staying on Aran, before returning to Rome.[2] Also, a note added to the entry on the Pope's feast in the Martyrology of Aonghas states that Gregory's remains, having been committed to the river Tiber with an ounce of gold on top, ended up on a beach in Aran, whence the name Gregory's Sound off that group of islands.[3] By way of contrast, the Life of Colmán son of Luachán, one of many Lives of Irish saints to mention Gregory, merely alleges that several loads of the soil of the pontiff's grave in Rome were carried back to Ireland.[4] Ceanannach (Kennannack, Kenach), the patron of Ballynakill in west Galway and of Inishmaan (Inis Meáin) on Aran, whose feast, like that of the Pope, fell on 12 March, was thought by some to be identical with Gregory.[5] A poem in Irish on the Gregorian chant, which describes the Pope as 'Grioghóir, abbot of Rome from Ireland', provides him with the patronymic Tuileagnaidh.[6] Finally, Colmán Eala of Lynally is said to have received news of Gregory's death long before it otherwise reached Ireland, and a late poem asserts that Gregory granted Colum Cille abbatial authority over Ireland and Scotland.[7]

1 *CGSH* §553; *Lgen.* 721.6; *ZCP* 3, 39 §§14–15; ibid. 8, 115 §§24–5; ibid. 12, 373; *BLec.* 107rd27–37; *GRSH* 78; *ZCP* 3, 39 §§13–15; *DLTC* 276–82, 295 §§23–5; *RC* 46, 231; *RC* 49, 184–5. **2** *RC* 46, 247–9 §14. **3** *MartO*[2] 96; cf. *IrT* iii, 85 §8; *ZCP* 12, 374; *RC* 46, 247–9 §14. **4** *BCML* 80 §76. **5** *OFWC* 80, 118–19. **6** *ZCP* 8, 115 §§23–4. **7** *VSHH* 215–16; *RC* 46, 249§15; *ZCP* 12, 373, 394 §24.

Guaire of Holdenstown. *See* Colmán of Holdenstown.

Guaire of Palmerston. *See* Moghóróg.

Guaire Beag, 'small', of Aghadowey (Achadh Dubhthaigh), barony of Coleraine, Co. Derry. Guaire Beag son of Laisre (Laisrín) was attached by the genealogists – together with his like-named cousin and co-patron of Aghadowey, Guaire Mór, 'big', son of Colmán – to the Uí Thuirtre branch of the Oirghialla.[1] Their kingdom originally lay west of the river Bann – mainly in the barony of Loughinsholin, immediately to the south of the barony of Coleraine – before they moved north-eastwards across the river into Antrim.[2] Guaire Beag is also credited with the founding of Agivey, just north of Aghadowey.[3] Seygorry (from Suidhe Ghuaire, 'Guaire's seat') in the parish of Aghadowey no doubt takes its name from one or other of these saints, but little else is recorded of them, beyond their feastdays which fell on 8/9 and 22 January.[4] An early seventeenth-century account of the diocese of Derry corruptly renders the saint's name as Gormus/Gromus.[5]

1 *CGSH* §§52–3; *GRSH* 67; *Lgen.* 713.8–9 **2** *GUH* 16; *MedI* 224, 232. **3** *DOH* 88; *PNCL* 5. **4** *MartT* 6, 11; *MartG* 12, 20; *MartD* 10, 24; *Celtica* 1, 83. **5** *UJA* (2nd ser.) 2, 153; *AnH* 12, 81, 108, 110.

Guaire Mór, 'big', of Aghadowey. *See* Guaire Beag.

Guasacht of Granard (Gránard) in the parish and barony of the same name, Co. Longford. Among Patrick's bishops, as listed by Tíreachán, were Guasacht and Camelacus (alias Caomhlach) who are again brought together in a passage on the Armagh saint's foundations in Teathbha, now most of Longford and part of Westmeath.[1] There, Patrick pointed out to Caomhlach from the top of Granard Hill the site of his future church, a place called Raithean. According to the Tripartite Life, Patrick left Guasacht (described as a son of his former master, Míleac) behind at Granard, together with two sisters, both called Éimhear, who were the first to occupy the adjoining church of Clonbroney.[2] According to the same passage, Guasacht's erenagh at Granard held the privilege of placing the veil on the heads of the nuns at Clonbroney. Alas, later erenaghs, the Sheridan family, induced the wrath of the poet, Aonghas na nAor Ó Dálaigh, who described the family of the *gainnchill*, 'church of scarcity', of Granard 'as a people without clemency, without truth, a thirsty tribe, without butter'.[3] The feast of Bishop Guasacht son of Míleac fell on 24 January.[4]

1 *UJA* 1, 174; *PTBA* 128 §6.2; 136 §16.7; cf. *CGSH* §704.109. **2** *BP* 995–1003, 1950–53; *VT* 90, 168. **3** *TribesI* 48–9. **4** *MartT* 11; *MartG* 22; *MartD* 26.

H ☙

I ☙

Ia No saint of this name is known from the Irish lists of the saints but a person named Ia is thought to have given name to the Cornish church of St Ives, following the arrival of the saint's cult from the Breton church of Plouyé.[1] According to the extensive record that grew up about the cult in Cornwall, the saint was a disciple of Finbarr and this tradition, as well as the saint's name has given rise to the belief that she was patron of Killeagh, from *Ceall Ia* in the Cork barony of Imokilly.[2] Regrettably, however, no evidence has survived in the Irish record to show that *Ia* was ever used either as a personal name or as a lexical item.[3]

1 *SCorn.* 144–5 **2** *HMDC* 9–10; *Celtica* 29, 307. **3** *HDGP* iv, 3–4.

Iamhnad daughter of Sineall. *See* Éimhín of Monasterevin.

Iarlaithe of Clonfeakle (Cluain Fiacla), barony of Dungannon Middle, Co. Tyrone. Travelling along the road known as Slighe Mhiodhluachra into the land of the Ulstermen, Patrick is said to have met some badly treated slaves of the local king, Trian son of Fiac.[1] Having gone to Trian's house, and fasted against the king without gaining any satisfaction, Patrick foretold his early death and lack of successors but, following an appeal from the king's wife, he blessed her womb which contained twin saints to be, Séadna and Iarlaithe. The latter, Patrick stated, would become his successor at Armagh. Though little else is known of Séadna beyond his status as a bishop and his feast of 16 June, Iarlaithe's name figures among the early abbots of Armagh in succession to Beinéan to whom, according to the latter's Life, he rendered the last rites.[2] One version of the list of Patrick's coarbs locates the saint in Clonfeakle, where the parish church was later dedicated to him.[3] Iarlaithe's pedigree, which attached him to the Dál bhFiatach of Down, was sometimes conflated with that of his namesake in Tuam.[4] The annals contend, no doubt retrospectively, that he died in 481, and John Colgan took him to be the Iarlaithe commemorated on 11 February.[5]

1 *BP* 2586–611; *VT* 220–2. **2** *MartT* 50; *MartG* 116; *MartD* 170; *NHI* ix, 238; *AS*.Nov. iv, 186. **3** *LL* 5995; *AnnU* 7. **4** *CGSH* §15; *GRSH* 83; *Lgen.* 724.1; *BNÉ* i, 47–8 §21. **5** *AU s.a.*; *MartT* 16; *MartG* 34; *ASH* 307–8.

Iarlaithe of Tuam (Tuaim Dá Ghualann), baronies of Clare and Dunmore, Co. Galway. In keeping with the location of his church, Iarlaithe son of Lugh was attached by the genealogists to the Conmhaicne of Connacht.[1] His mother, Moingfhinn daughter of Cíordhubhán, is said to have belonged to a family named Ceinéal Cineann (Cíorann), a separate branch of the Conmhaicne associated with Críoch Mhic Eirce, a name used for the lands of Fir Cheara, now represented by the Mayo barony of Carra.[2] Despite the fact that he was bishop-patron of the only archdiocese in the west of Ireland, Iarlaithe (anglicized Jarlath) was never made the subject of a Life. He is featured, however, in some other Lives, including that of Bréanainn of Clonfert. Bréanainn's biographer indulged in special pleading on behalf of his subject, who was also patron of the fledgling diocesan see of Annaghdown, later united to Tuam, by recounting how the youthful Bréanainn, having gone to study under Iarlaithe, not only foretold the place of his mentor's resurrection, namely Tuam, but also received from him a request that they change places, the master becoming the pupil.[3] Similarly subservient status, this time within the Conmhaicne group, is attributed to Iarlaithe in the Life of Beinéan who allegedly not only taught Iarlaithe, but also ordained him and consecrated his church.[4] More respect is shown to Iarlaithe in the Life of Éanna which casts him as a member of a delegation sent to Rome to take papal advice on who should be declared chief saint of Aran.[5] Two poems of prophecy invoke his name, one of them with reference to a place named Lann, the other citing a man named Maol Corghais who also figures in a prophecy ascribed to Iarlaithe himself.[6] A poem attributed to Cuimín of Connor extolled Iarlaithe as a man who did not practise niggardliness, and elsewhere he is described as one of the *ardnaoimh*, 'chief saints', of the Conmhaicne.[7] He is said to have died on the same night as Oilill Molt, king of Ireland, and he is credited with three feastdays, 11 February, 26 December, and 6 June, the latter day being observed only in his own church at Tuam.[8] A relic of his was known as *bachall bhuidhe*, 'yellow crozier'.[9]

1 *CGSH* §297; *GRSH* 106; *Lgen*. 734.12; *DIB* iv, 892. **2** *CGSH* §722.88; *CGH* 161a38, b2. **3** *VSHP* i, 102–3 §§9–10; *GYHS* 802–4. **4** *SAM* 1, 34 §§11–12; *AS*.Nov. iv, 178. **5** *VSHP* ii, 70–1 §23. **6** *Ériu* 18, 62 §17; *ZCP* 10, 24 §19; *MartD* 348; *ACL* ii, 142. **7** *ZCP* 1, 66; BFen. (supp.) 68, 88. **8** *IrT* iii, 84 §2; *MartT* 16; *MartG* 34; *MartD* 348; *ASH* 308–9; *GRSH* 106; OSL GY i, 46. **9** *AFM s.a.* 1136.

Iast son of Brachan. This saint is known from an entry in the tract on the mothers of the saints which states that he, together with his nine brothers, were sons of Díona, daughter of a king of the Saxons, by Brachan, king of the Britons (or Welsh), and eponym of Brycheiniog in south Wales.[1] Many of the saint's siblings, including Moghóróg of Delgany, Mochonóg of Kilmuckridge, Díoraidh of Edermine, and Eallóg of St Tulloge's, were associated with churches in east Leinster, but Iast was attached to an unidentified place, presumably in Britain, called Sleamhnacha Alban.

1 *CGSH* §722.89; *EWGT* 14–16, 32–3.

Íde of Killeedy (Cluain Creadhail / Ceall Íde), barony of Glenquin, Co. Limerick. After Brighid of Kildare, Íde was perhaps the best-known of all Irish female saints. Her fame extended well beyond Ireland, with a mention in a poem by Alcuin (†804) which refers to her, together with Brighid, as *clara per urbes*, 'famous throughout the world', and *fidelis*, 'faithful', as well as in litanies preserved in two ninth-century manuscripts, now kept in Orléans in France and Basel in Switzerland.[1] In Ireland, she was attached to 'the most noble race' of the Déise, who held lands in three places: Meath, where they gave name to the baronies of Deece; Waterford, whence the present baronies of Decies; and the district known as Déis Deiscirt, about Ardpatrick in south Limerick.[2] A variant version of the saint's pedigree attached her to the Uí Chonaill Ghabhra lords of most of west Limerick, where their name is still preserved in the baronies of Connello.[3] Killeedy is located to the west of Connello, but a second church named Kilmeedy (Ceall Míde) after the saint, under the guise of Míde (M'íde, 'my Íde'), lies within the barony. The fact that the dominant local dynasty bore the name Ua Cinn Fhaoladh over a long period in the twelfth century would have proved no hindrance to the local cult of Íde daughter of Ceann Faoladh.[4] The saint's mother, named Feidhealm daughter of Dallbhrónach in one entry, thus establishing for her a maternal link with Brighid of Kildare, was called Neacht in another, and Íde's sister Fíona was reputedly the mother of the Northumbrian king, Flann Fíona son of Ossa.[5]

Curiously, neither parent is named in Íde's Life despite the fact that, in order to give the text more verisimilitude, a son of one of its characters is said by the saint's biographer to have been alive at the time of writing.[6] The Life, which has yet to be examined closely, was twice edited in the seventeenth century, by John Colgan and the Bollandists, and is also available in a modern edition.[7] It survives in three redactions, two of which were made in Ireland, the third – as part of the Great Austrian Legendary – on the Continent, probably in Regensburg. Beginning with a series of angelic visitations that foreshadowed an initially reluctant acceptance by Íde's father that she should take the veil, the saint is brought away from her native place to the territory of the Uí Chonaill Ghabhra, where, again with angelic guidance, she is directed to the site of the church that was to be hers.[8] The prophecy, again by an angel, that she would be the mother-figure (*matrona*) of the Uí Chonaill is then confirmed with acclaim by both king and people, accompanied by offers of property.

The scene is thus set for a series of mostly miraculous interventions by the saint, involving several male and female saints. These were: Bréanainn of Clonfert to whom she revealed the three qualities most pleasing and most displeasing to God; Aona (Aonghas) of Clonmacnoise, her associate in death as in life, who, when gravely ill, sent messengers seeking water blessed by Íde; Comhghán, the Dál gCais patron of Killeshin, who summoned her to be at his side as he died; Mochaomhóg of Leigh (Leamakevoge), her sister's son, who, following the miraculous resuscitation of his father, was conceived and born at Killeedy; Caoireach Dheargáin of Cloonburren, and the virgin Ríceann who, though usually associated with Kilreekill in Galway, is here placed in Magh Life in Kildare, possibly because there was a local dedication to Íde at Kilmead (Ceall Míde) in the parish of Narraghmore.[9] These latter saints are again brought together in a tale set in east Galway which describes Ríceann as Caoireach's disciple.[10]

No firm date has been established for the Life, but its presence in the Great Austrian Legendary means that it had already been written by the final quarter of the twelfth century.[11] In its surviving form, the Life has some late features, which means that it is unlikely to have been composed much earlier than 1175.[12] As to provenance, the vested interests served by saints' Lives were usually either those of a bishop, keen to confirm claims to jurisdiction over disputed churches on the edges of his diocese, or of a recent monastic foundation, eager to establish for itself an 'ancient history' rooted in the locality that also validated in writing some of the possessions previously granted to it. In Íde's case, there is little to suggest that diocesan interests were being served. Neither the diocesan see at Limerick nor any of its emblematic saints, such as its patron Mainchín, is featured in the text. The only local diocesan patron mentioned is Seanán of Scattery Island to whom, in conjunction with Íde, and according to an angelic utterance, the territory of Uí Chonaill was to be subject.[13] During the period 1152 to 1188, when the Life appears to have been written, Seanán's church was endeavouring to establish itself as a cathedral church and, though he made no obvious effort to sustain his concern with Scattery, Íde's biographer may have been in sympathy with this development.[14]

Only one monastic foundation is known from the wider district about Killeedy in the period before 1200, the Cistercian abbey of Abbeyfeale whose foundation is dated to 1188, but could have been earlier.[15] As Abbeyfeale and Killeedy, which now form neighbouring parishes, are separated by little more than five miles, Cistercian influence is possible, and this might also underlie the assertion that Mochaomhóg (allegedly Íde's nephew) was born, and spent his youth, at Killeedy. Cistercian concerns are clearly discernible in Mochaomhóg's own Life which casts its subject in a deferential pose towards Bishop Colmán of Doire Mór in Magh Airbh – whence the Cistercian monastery of Kilcooly, alias *Arvicampus*, in Tipperary – and allows him to perform a miracle at Inis Leamhnachta (Inislounaght), the site of the Cistercian monastery *De Surio*.[16] There are, however, also several indications of possible Augustinian influence on Íde's Life, which, if genuine, would presuppose a much earlier date of foundation, either for the house of canons in Rathkeale or for the convent of canonesses at Shanagolden than presently thought. Her connections with Bréanainn and Aona, who are featured more often than any other saint in the Life, may reflect the fact that both of the principal churches of these saints, Clonfert and Clonmacnoise, were seats of houses of canons or canonesses.[17] In the Life of Bréanainn himself, Íde is not only given the important role of acting as the saint's foster-mother, she is also mentioned in a chapter where the subject of the Life founds a monastery in the Shannon Estuary, on Inishdadroum (Inis Dá Dhroma), next to Canon Island, a dependency of the Augustinian house of Clare Abbey.[18]

In addition to three early litanies, including two of continental provenance, which invoke her name together with that of Brighid, Íde finds mention in several Lives, including that of Mochaomhóg which gives extensive coverage to the circumstances of his miraculous birth at Killeedy.[19] She is cast in a prophetic role in relation to Mochuda of Lismore, and is said to have received a visit from Maodhóg of Ferns.[20] Perhaps the best-known of her roles is the manner in which, having been deprived of the company of a stag-beetle which had been sucking away part of her body, she blackmailed God into sending the Infant Christ to be fostered by her.[21] Hardly memorable for its unsavoury details, the story is redeemed by an accompanying poem of six quatrains, beginning *Íosagán oiltear liom im dhiseartán*, 'Jesukin who is nursed by me in my little hermitage', one of the most celebrated poems in the entire corpus of Irish literature. Cuimín of Connor held Íde up as an example of 'great fostering' and humility, and Aonghas of Tallaght extolled her as a lover of severe fastings and a succourer of many diseases.[22] A poem chiding the saint for lack of attention was composed by Gearóid Iarla.[23] The annals, which attribute efficacy to her prayers during a battle fought in 552, state that she died in 570, the same year as saw the death of her associate, Aona of Clonmacnoise.[24] Her feast fell on 15 January and she continues to be venerated in the area about Killeedy, with four holy wells dedicated to her in south-west Limerick.[25] Proper lessons, a prayer and hymn, for recital on the feastday, were approved by the Vatican in 1868.[26] Her name has been anglicized as both Ita and Ida, and a tradition preserved outside the Life of the saint states that her first name was Déirdre (Dorothea/Dorothy).[27]

1 *MGH.PL* i, 342; *SIHI* 43, 189 (B) (C), 191; cf. *LH* I, 14; *DIB* iv, 927. **2** *CGSH* §93; *GRSH* 77; *Lgen.* 720.1–2; *BP* 2433; *VT* 208. **3** *CGSH* §93 (La). **4** *AI s.a.* 1029.5, 1049.4, 1050.8. **5** *CGSH* §§722.12.52–3; *Lgen.* 720.2. **6** *VSHP* ii, 126 §28. **7** *ASH* 66–74; *AS*.Ian. i, 1062–8; *VSHP* i, lxxii–lxxiv, ii, 116–30; *FLLSP* 233; *Peritia* 14, 421–8. **8** *VSHP* ii, 118 §8–9; *Peritia* 14, 425–7. **9** *VSHP* ii, 120–5 §§13, 18, 20, 22, 24, 35. **10** *ACL* iii, 308–9. **11** *FLLSP* 233; *AB* 17, 97–122. **12** *VSHP* i, lxxiii. **13** Ibid. 118 §8. **14** *MRHI* 96–7. **15** Ibid. 190–1, 323. **16** *VSHP* ii, 170 §15, 181 §32. **17** *MRHI* 164–5. **18** *VSHH* 329 §13; *MRHI* 162. **19** HBS 32, 14; *VSHP* ii, 164–7 §§1–8; *SIHI* 189–90. **20** Ibid. i, 181 §30; ii, 159 §49; *VSHH* 245 §45. **21** *MartO*² 44; *EIL* 26–9; *MIL* 64–7; *CMCS* 1, 39–52. **22** *ZCP* 1, 62 §41; *MartO*² 36. **23** *StH* 3, 15–16. **24** *AU s.a.* **25** *MartT* 8; *MartO*² 36; *MartG* 16; *MartD* 16; OSL LK i, 77; *JRSAI* 85, 197. **26** *IER* (2nd ser.) 4, 364–6. **27** *MartD* 16; *FourIM* 170; HBS 3, 10; *ASH* 73.

Imoke. *See* Díomán of Clonkeen.

Imor. *See* Aodhamair.

Inghean/Ingheana, 'daughter/daughters'. Many saints, both female (*inghean*) and male (*mac*), are known by reference to their fathers. In the case of males, this method is sometimes used to identify single saints, as is shown by the titles *Aoinmhic Éireann*, 'Ireland's singular sons', applied to a list containing 82 entries.[1] With some exceptions, most notably Inghean Bhaoith of Killinaboy, no such category has survived for females, whose presentation is normally in groups, as exemplified by the title *Ingheanradha naomh Éireann*, 'Ireland's saints, designated daughters', attached to a list containing 108 entries.[2] Sons are also grouped together in this way, as is shown by the title *Macradh Naomh Éireann*, 'Ireland's saints, designated sons', which accounts for no fewer than 210 entries.[3] The vast majority of the saints in these lists, male and female, are otherwise unattested.

1 *CGSH* §710. **2** Ibid. §711. **3** Ibid. §709.

Inghean Bhaoith of Killinaboy (Ceall Inghine Baoith), barony of Inchiquin, Co. Clare. When Eugene O'Curry visited Killinaboy in 1839, the vigour of the saint's cult was waning, but 'Innerwee' (Inghean Bhaoith) had been a 'favourite name' of females in the parish until shortly before.[1] He was unable to ascertain the saint's own 'particular' name, but this is recorded as Fíonmhaith (elsewhere garbled as *Findelua* or *Finicula*) in a poem which attributes to her fifty-six offspring, mostly associated with churches in Clare and adjoining parts of Limerick and Galway, and beginning with Seanán of Scattery Island who is otherwise said to have been her brother.[2] Most of those mentioned, including Seanán, are also independently provided with different mothers.[3] As if to reconcile conflicting traditions, however, in the final quatrain of the poem it is said that Fíonmhaith was also known as Cuman daughter of Dallbhrónach, an aunt of Brighid of Kildare, and this is precisely the name attached to the mother of Seanán, and others in the list, in the 'official' tract on the mothers of the saints.[4] A story has been preserved in explanation of the double name, which asserts that Fíonmhaith, daughter of a king of Corca Dhuibhne and mother of Seanán, went to Monasterboice and was reared there by Cuman's father Dallbhrónach who used the term *cumain* (understood as *comaoin*, 'favour') when addressing her.[5] Elsewhere, in a poem in Classical Irish, Inghean Bhaoith, together with numerous other saints, was called upon to help in releasing Ireland's southern half (Leath Mogha) from a bondage imposed on it by the northern half (Leath Chuinn), championed by Finnian of Clonard; in fact, Inghean Bhaoith may have been called upon twice by the poet, as Fíonaith (perhaps for Fíonmhaith) is also mentioned.[6]

Although the saint's name is nowhere to be found in the martyrologies, O'Curry supplied a pattern day of 29 December, and noted other instances of devotion to her in Clare.[7] Her cult spread southwards, to 'Killinewee' in Glenmore townland in the Limerick parish of Killeedy, and to Dromtarriff in the Cork barony of Duhallow, where her feast was celebrated on 5 or 6 May.[8] This feast may have been borrowed, however, from her neighbour Lasair, patron of Killasseragh in the parish of Kilmeen, whose name is included in the list of those remembered by the martyrologies on 7 May.[9] Among the many variant forms or corruptions of the saint's name – including Inghean Bhaodáin and Inghean Bhuidhe (anglicized Innewee) – and that of her church are Naomhaidhe (alias Iothbhuidhe) and Cillín Naomhaidhe.[10] Her name may have been anglicized as Winifrid, alias Winnie, a very common name among females in the parish of Killinaboy.

1 *ACoC* 12. **2** *IrT* iv, 93–4; *Celtica* 1, 76; *CH* 2, 29; *OC* 24, 12–17; *CPL* 9, 520. **3** *LisL* 1797. **4** *CGSH* §722.7–10. **5** *GT* 180–1 §169. **6** RIA MS 23L11, 263; *SAM* 24.1, 17, 21. **7** *ACoC* 13, 41, 77; *OC* 16, 30; ibid. 24, 14–15; *JNMArchS* 48, 30. **8** OSL LK i, 79–80; *OC* 24, 13; *FL* 270; *JCHAS* 2, 319; *SACCL* 405; *PABD* 167. **9** *MartT* 40; *MartG* 92; *MartD* 120. **10** *Celtica* 1, 76.

Inghean Mhíolchon. *See* Brónach of Kilbroney.

Ingheana Aodha. *See* Angais.

Ingheana Baoith. *See* Eithne daughter of Baoth.

Ingheana Cainnigh. *See* Forannán of Donaghmore.

Ingheana Caocháin. *See* Ingheana Cathbhadh.

Ingheana Cathbhadh of Kilcolagh (Ceall Chomhlach), barony of Frenchpark, Co. Roscommon. This group of seven daughters is one of two such families of saints listed among the forty-five children of Cuman daughter of Dallbhrónach, the maternal aunt of Brighid of Kildare.[1] The other group is Ingheana Caocháin of Uí Fhiachrach of Aidhne, a territory approximately equivalent to the diocese of Kilmacduagh. Many of these, including both groups of daughters, had associations with east Connacht, and each is again featured among the saints said by the biographer of Forannán of the Sligo church of Alternan to have been brought together with the purpose of meeting Colum Cille.[2] The maternal connection with Brighid suggests that the group may also have been known as the daughters of Cobhthach at Cloonsellan (Cluain Salainn) in the Roscommon parish of Kilteevan, where, together with Teamhair daughter of Eirnín, they were subject to Brighid, patron of the adjoining parish of Kilbride.[3] The daughters of Cathbhadh were commemorated by the martyrologists on 2 July, albeit in connection with an unidentified church named Aireadh Fada.[4]

1 *CGSH* §722.9. 2 *Anecd.* iii, 3. 3 *CGSH* §670.68. 4 *MartT* 53; *MartG* 128; *MartD* 184; *HDGP* i, 43.

Ingheana Ceadáin of Cluain Each. This group of daughters is known only from the list of those subject to Brighid of Kildare.[1] As Brighid was patron of Kilbride in Roscommon, the church assigned to the group may now be represented by a no longer identifiable ecclesiastical site in the townland of Clooneigh, parish of Kilteevan, which adjoins Kilbride.

1 *CGSH* §670.24.

Ingheana Cobhthaigh. *See* Ingheana Cathbhadh.

Ingheana Coluim of Teach Inghean gColuim. One of the many miracles attributed to Daigh son of Coireall of Inishkeen in the Monaghan barony of Farney was the resuscitation of three daughters of Colum, for whom, having taught them letters, he subsequently founded a monastery named *Domus Filiarum Columbe*.[1] An entry in the Martyrology of Tallaght for 14 September, the day after the feast of Daigh's namesake and probable double, Daghán of Ennereilly, commemorates the daughters of Colum *i Creamhthannaibh*, 'in Creamhthainn/ Creamhthanna', a territory that lay, like Daigh's own church, close to the present border of Monaghan with Louth.[2] The later martyrologies bring the two commemorations together in the list for 13 September.[3] The fact that there was a dedication to Brighid at Kilbride in the parish of Louth, which adjoins Inishkeen, would suggest that these daughters were the same as the daughters of Colum of the church of Ceall Chalaidh (equally unidentified) who are said to have been subject to the Kildare saint.[4]

1 *VSHH* 392 §15. 2 *MartT* 71; *Dinn.* 6, 83–7. 3 *MartG* 176; *MartD* 248. 4 *CGSH* §670.9; *HDGP* iii, 139.

Ingheana Conaill of Kenny (Ceanna Each), parish of Mullingar, barony of Moyashel and Magheradernan, Co. Westmeath. A list of saints and churches with probable links to the spread of the cult of Brighid of Kildare includes the daughters of Conall.[1] A chapel of Mullingar in medieval times, Kenny lies seven to eight miles north west of Kilbride (Ceall Bhrighde) in the same county.[2]

1 *CGSH* §663.7. 2 *PNW* 224.

Ingheana Dallbhrónaigh. *See* Cuman daughter of Dallbhrónach.

Ingheana Earcdhaith. *See* Coilliodhan.

Ingheana Fearghais. The later martyrologies commemorate the seven daughters of Fearghas on 24 May, locating them in an unidentified church named Teach Inghean bhFearghais after the saints.[1] The earliest of the martyrologies places them, however, in Inishcaltra, now Holy Island, in Lough Derg on the river Shannon.[2] Since others in the list are attached to churches in the area about Lough Derg, this may also apply to the (unidentified) church of the daughters of Fearghas.

1 *MartG* 102; *MartD* 138. **2** *MartT* 45.

Ingheana Feargna. *See* Brígh of Kilbride.

Ingheana Luain. *See* Curcach of Kilcorkey.

Ingheana Maine. *See* Cuman of Aireadh Bóinne.

Ingheana Mic Iair. *See* Caol of Kilmainham.

Ingheana Léinín. *See* Aighleann.

Ingheana Oilealla. *See* Mughain of Lyons.

Ingheana Treana. *See* Líogh.

Inne Bheag, 'small', daughter of Breacán. Among the first to be included in the list of those subject to Brighid, Inne Bheag and her sister Inne Mhór also find mention in the ninth-century Irish Life of the Kildare saint who, while apparently in Teathbha (most of Longford and part of Westmeath), was asked to consecrate their church.[1] Named Ceall Dá Inneann (Daindein/Daninde) after the sisters, the church has not been identified.[2]

1 *CGSH* §670.3; *Lgen.* 752.11; *BBr.* 12 §35; *LH* i, 120. **2** *HDGP* iii, 157.

Inne Mhór. *See* Inne Bheag.

Iobhar of Begerin Island (Beigéire), parish of St Margaret's, barony of Shelmaliere East, Co. Wexford. Bearing a name meaning 'yew', Iobhar became the subject of much pseudo-etymological speculation, including the amusing assertion that, on eating an onion during pregnancy, his mother's face assumed the colour of a yew.[1] Speculation also surrounds his genealogical affiliations, as is shown by two consecutive entries in the corpus of saints' pedigrees, one attaching him through his father Lughna to the Uí Eachach – whence the Down baronies of Iveagh – the other assigning him to Dál nAraidhe whose territory lay immediately north of Uí Eachach.[2] Elsewhere, he is attached to the Sordraighe, a branch of the Mughdhoirn in a territory called Creamhthainn (Creamhthanna) on the borders of Monaghan, Louth and Meath.[3] The text recounting the circumstances of Iobhar's birth declares that he descended from a branch of the Ulstermen named Artraighe, of the area where north Louth now mears with Meath.[4] Alleging that his mother – variously named Basar, Lasair, and Sas – belonged to a branch of the Déise that gave name to the Meath baronies of Deece, the text, possibly influenced by the Roman tradition of *tria nomina*, also declares that Iobhar was his *cognomen*, with Neannán as *nomen*, and Éagmhacht as *agnomen*.[5]

In addition to Iobhar, Basar is said to have provided Lughna with seven other children, including Caineach Abadh, otherwise thought to have been the mother of Abán of Killabban.[6] This would explain why the early thirteenth-century Life composed for Abán portrays his maternal uncle Iobhar – described as originally from Ulster, but subsequently 'granted' to the men of Leinster – as his teacher on Begerin Island, later also Iobhar's resting place.[7] Despite the view that the man named Iobhar visited by Brighid in Geashill (Magh Ghéisille) in Offaly was a quite different saint, he was possibly identical with the patron of Begerin who would then also qualify for consideration as the person said to have baptized the twelve sons of Barr son of Caorthann, ancestral figure of the Laoighse, all of whose descendants were to serve Iobhar.[8]

Although mainly located in Leinster, Iobhar's ecclesiastical connections also extended to parts of the country closer to his parental home, as is shown by an incomplete Latin Life preserved among the collections of the Bollandists in Brussels.[9] This names Mochta of Louth as the saint's mentor, and establishes for Iobhar an association with the church of Kilbrew (Ceall Fhoibhrigh, alias Foibhreach) in the Meath barony of Ratoath.[10] The miracle attributed to Iobhar while staying with Mochta is retold in the latter saint's Life, and a poem on Patrick's Purgatory addresses Iobhar together with Mochta and other saints.[11] A link with the Aran Islands in the west of Ireland is suggested by an episode in the Life of Moninne (Dairearca) of Killevy, which describes a visit made to Iobhar there by Moninne, subsequent to which he moved to Begerin.[12] Although there now seems to be no direct trace of the saint in Aran's ecclesiastical nomenclature, there was a temple in the parish of Killeany on Inishmore dedicated to Mac Lughna (Luinge).[13] This could have been interpreted either as Iobhar himself, by reference to his father Lughna, or as a brother of his, specifically named Mac Lughna.[14] In Leinster, a well (St Iver's) was named after him in the townland of Bigrock in the Wicklow parish of Arklow, and he may also have been patron of Killary parish in the Meath barony of Lower Slane.[15]

The saint is commonly thought to have been identical with the so-called pre-Patrician saint named Iobhar who, along with Ailbhe, Ciarán of Seirkieran, and Déaglán, is said to have first brought Christianity to Ireland, and to have been engaged in conflict with Patrick before finally making peace.[16] The list of saints of similar manners, which compares him to another precursor, John the Baptist, places him ahead of Patrick.[17] The vernacular Life of Molaise of Devenish accords him the high status of one of Ireland's apostles, and a document prepared in the early seventeenth century describes him as the second bishop of Kildare.[18] He has also the distinction of being one of the saints selected for mention by Giraldus Cambrensis who attributed to him the banishment of rats from 'Ferneginan' (probably *Fearann na gCeinéal*) in Wexford.[19] The annals propose dates varying between 500 and 504 for the death of the saint, allegedly at the age of 333, at about the same time as Brighid, according to an unpublished poem, and the martyrologies assign his feast to 23 April.[20]

1 *CGSH* §721.9; *AB* 77, 439, 442; *DIB* iv, 892–3. 2 *CGSH* §96.1.2; *MartO²* 118; cf. *GRSH* 100; *Lgen.* 735.15. 3 *CGH* 142b37–40; cf. *CGSH* §496; *MartO²* 100. 4 *CGSH* §721.9; *AB* 77, 439, 442. 5 *CGSH* §721.3; *AB* 77, 448; *CGSH* §§415, 722.14; *MartO²* 100. 6 *CGSH* §722.14.79. 7 *VSHP* i, 8 §9; *VSHH* 258–9 §5. 8 *SSS* 386–7; *CGH* 127a20–5; *Lgen.* 557.5; cf. *IrL* 60. 9 *AB* 77, 439–41. 10 Ibid. 441 §9; cf. *CGH* 142b40; *HDGP* iii, 174. 11 *VSHH* 398 §12; *TEAB* 522. 12 Ibid. 84 §§3–4; *PRIA* 28C210 §5. 13 *OÁr* 39. 14 *CGSH* §722.14. 15 OSL WW 423; *RM* 5.3, 6. 16 *VSHP* i, 220 §7, ii, 45 §18; *MartO²* 118; *SSS* 376–99. 17 *CGSH* §712.1. 18 *SG* i, 25, 34; *Dinn.* 2, 30. 19 *THEH* 120; *OnomG* 410. 20 *AU s.a.*; *LUM* 156rb 18; *MartT* 35; *MartO²* 108; *MartG* 82; *MartD* 108; *FLK Cat.* MS A 7, 16r.

Iobhar of Emly (Imleach Iobhair), barony of Clanwilliam, Co. Tipperary. When Patrick was in Cullen (Uachtar Cuilleann) in Uí Chuanach, on the borders of the later Limerick barony of Coonagh, an infant is said to have been eaten there by pigs.[1] Having failed to persuade a *céile Dé* in his company to bring the child back to life, Patrick ordered Bishop Iobhar and Ailbhe to do so. Iobhar and Ailbhe are again brought together in the Life written for the patron of Emly which uses a visit to Patrick in Cashel as an excuse to accord precedence to Ailbhe.[2] A poem of prophecies elsewhere forecasts that an attack on the two saints will cause lamentation.[3] Despite these mentions, Bishop Iobhar may have originated as an extrapolation from the name of the church to which he and Ailbhe were attached, viz. Imleach Iobhair, 'Emly of the Yew'.

1 *BP* 2319–33; *VT* 198. 2 *VSHH* 125 §31; *VSHP* i, 55 §24. 3 *Ériu* 18, 60 §13.

Iollann of Rathlihen (Ráith Liphidean), parish of Killoughy, barony of Ballyboy, Co. Offaly. The first taste of ecclesiastical life experienced by Aodh of Rahugh was, according to his Life, at the church of Bishop Iollann.[1] The church is not named, but as Iollann son of Eacha was attached by the genealogists, like Aodh, to the descendants of Niall Naoighiallach, it may be that Rathlihen was intended.[2] Iollann also gave name to Castledillon (Díseart Iolladhan) in the county of Kildare.[3] Little else is known of him, but that his feast fell on 10 June.[4]

1 *VSHH* 168–9 §3; *VSHP* i, 35 §3. 2 *CGSH* §690.12; *GRSH* 51. 3 *JCKAS* 9, 246. 4 *MartT* 49; *MartG* 114; *MartD* 164.

Íomhar Ua hAodhagáin of Armagh. According to Bernard of Clairvaux, Íomhar was a *vir sanctissimae vitae*, 'a man of the holiest life', serving God with fastings and prayers day and night.[1] He taught Maol Maodhóg, still a young man, the rule of life and obedience, and commanded him to found a church in Bangor.[2] He himself was responsible for the erection of the church of SS Peter and Paul in Armagh which was consecrated by Ceallach, bishop of Armagh, in 1126.[3] This was one of the first priories of canons regular of St Augustine in Ireland.[4] Íomhar died in Rome in 1134, while on pilgrimage.[5] His feast, which fell on 13 August, was noticed by Grevenus of Cologne on 12 November in his late fifteenth-century version of the Martyrology of Usuard.[6]

1 *BCLMA* 11. 2 Ibid. 11, 13, 31. 3 *AU/AFM s.a.* 4 *MRHI* 157. 5 *AFM s.a.* 6 *MartG* 156; *MartD* 218; *AS*.Iun. vii, 671.

Iomráiteach of Imleach. This son of Dúnchadh, whose name signifies 'famous', was one of the saints of Uí Fhiachrach of the Sligo barony of Tireragh

(Tír Fhiachrach).[1] His church may be represented by Imleach Íseal in this barony, now Castletown in the parish of Easky, which was associated with a family named Uí Mhaoil Dúin. The eponym (Maol Dúin) of this family figures in Iomráiteach's pedigree.[2]

1 *CGSH* §392; *Lgen.* 711.15. 2 *Lgen.* 275.5.

IOTH of Aghade (Áth Fadhad/Fiodhad), barony of Forth, Co. Carlow. Among the so-called *Additamenta* in the ninth-century Book of Armagh is an account of how Patrick, having converted Criomhthann son of Éanna Ceinsealach, progenitor of the Uí Cheinsealaigh of south Leinster, besought the king to allow Iserninus, his former co-pupil at Auxerre, and others, apparently including Bishop Ioth (Fioth), to return from exile.[1] Subsequently, Patrick is said to have given Iserninus' (unnamed) church to Ioth and founded with him Aghade, whose name appears, despite the *dinnsheanchas* tradition to the contrary, to have been taken by the Armagh scribe to reflect that of the bishop.[2] Little else is known of the saint, but a poem attributed to Moling calls upon him, among many others, to come to the assistance of the Leinstermen.[3] The saint's church later became the site of a cell of Augustinian nuns.[4] Ioth's feast fell on 14 July.[5]

1 *PTBA* 174 §12.6. 2 Ibid. 176 §12 (7); RD §36. 3 *LL* 39312–13; *SG* i, 389. 4 *MRHI* 312. 5 *MartG* 136; *MartD* 194.

IOTHARNAISC of Clane (Claonadh), in the Kildare barony of the same name. This saint was one of seven sons of Aonghas said to have come to Ireland from Scotland and, in keeping with this tradition, his pedigree attached him to the tribal grouping of Dál Riada which had settlements in both countries.[1] The churches assigned to the brothers, including that of Iotharnaisc, were mainly located in the Irish Midlands. In Scotland, Iotharnaisc (alias Ethernanus or Ethernascus) was remembered – albeit on both 2 and 22 December – at Lathrisk in Fife, and he was considered important enough to merit a collect in the Breviary of Aberdeen.[2] While four of the saint's brothers – Aghadán, Torannán, Mochuille, and Troscán – were brought together by the Martyrology of Donegal on 12 June, Iotharnaisc's feast of 22 December was shared with Tua (Ultán), patron of Taghadoe (Teach Tua), near Clane.[3] Iotharnaisc's name, which was possibly Pictish in origin, found its way under the guise of Ethernasius (probably from the Breviary of Aberdeen) into a Cologne version of Usuard's martyrology, compiled in the late fifteenth century by Grevenus.[4] A poem on the brothers, attributed to Colum Cille, has also been preserved.[5]

1 *CGSH* §§209, 701.1; *GRSH* 80; *Lgen.* 721.8; *Ériu* 32, 106. 2 *BrevA* pars hiem. 6v–7v; *CPNS* 321; *KSS* 333–4; *ACDS* 139–41; *Innes Review* 32, 61–2; *LegSS* 3–5, 11, 357–8; *SBDeer* 375–7. 3 *MartD* 166–8; *MartT* 88; *MartO²* 253; *MartG* 244; *MartD* 342. 4 *AS*.Iun. vii, 760; *Innes Review* 32, 61–2. 5 *CGSH* §701.

ISERNINUS. *See* Ioth; Usaille.

ÍTE. *See* Íde.

IUSTÁN son of Fearghas. *See* Brighid of Shankill.

IVER. *See* Iobhar of Begerin.

J ☙

Jarlath. *See* Iarlaithe.

Jenny. *See* Sineach of Kilshine.

K

Kavan. *See* Caomhán of Anatrim.

Kealyn. *See* Caolainn.

Kedda. *See* Caoide of Kilkeedy.

Keeril. *See* Coireall.

Keevaun. *See* Caomhán of Anatrim.

Keevil. *See* Caoimheall daughter of Caomhlugh.

Kennannack. *See* Ceanannach.

Kenneth/Kenny. *See* Cainneach.

Kerrill. *See* Coireall.

Kessock. *See* Ceasán.

Keverne. *See* Acobhrán.

Kevin. *See* Caoimhghin.

Kidanus. *See* Caoide of Kilkeedy.

Kieran. *See* Ciarán.

Kilian. *See* Ceallachán; Mocheallóg of Inch.

L ☙

Labhrás. *See* Lorcán.

Laichtín of Freshford (Achadh Úr), barony of Crannagh, Co. Kilkenny, and of Ballyhoura (Bealach Eabhradh) on Limerick's southern boundary with Cork. Bearing a name (also written Lachtnán, Laichtnín, Molachtóg) that derives ultimately from Lugh, this son of Tairbhín is one of a number of Irish saints who can be regarded as christianized versions of the celebrated Celtic divinity.[1] Within the genealogical tradition, he was attached to the Múscraighe, a vassal grouping with lands mainly in Munster.[2] Together with Seanán of Scattery Island and Fíonán Cam of Kinnitty, Laichtín was a '[shining] candle' of this group.[3]

Although never made the subject of a Life in his own right, he figures in those of others. Mochuda's biographer, playing on the (mistaken) belief that the saint's name derives from *lacht*, 'liquid', made use of a visit by Laichtín to Rahan to explain how his subject broke a rule of not accepting cattle as a gift.[4] The biographer of Mochaomhóg of Leigh (Liath Mochaomhóg, later Lemakevoge) placed Laichtín among a group of saints – including Mochaomhóg, Molua, Fionnbharr, and Luchtighearn – sent by their master, Comhghall of Bangor, to found churches throughout Ireland.[5] Only Laichtín's church is identified, and its name (Achadh Úr, 'fresh field') is explained by reference to the humidity caused by the streams that ran through it. A more southern focus of the cult is implied by references to the saint in other Lives, including the metrical Life of Seanán, likewise of the Múscraighe, which refers to a visit made by Laichtín to Scattery Island, and the Life of Déaglán which names the saint among seven gathered at a place named Magh Sciath, near Lismore, to witness a sign in the heavens at Déaglán's birth.[6] The Life composed for Molua of Kyle includes a prophecy that Laichtín would succeed him.[7] Associations with Seanán are also attested outside the Lives, in two poems of prophecy, one listing those invoked by the Scattery saint in his time of need, the other attributed jointly to Seanán, Laichtín, and Comhghall of Bangor.[8]

Most of the surviving dedications to Laichtín are located in Munster, most notably at Donaghmore in Cork, where the enshrined (early twelfth-century) relic of his arm, known as *Lámh Laichtín*, 'Laichtín's arm' (now in the National Museum) was kept, but also at Grenagh, Kilnamartery, Ballyhay, and Imphrick in the same county, at Killaghteen and Knocknagranshy in the Limerick parishes of Ardagh and Monasternenagh, at Lislaughtin in the Kerry parish of Aghavallen, where, in John O'Donovan's time, people were in the habit of swearing by his arm (*dar láimh Laichtín*), at various holy wells in Clare, including those in Kilfarboy and Kilnamona, and at Donaskeagh in the Tipperary parish of Rathlynin.[9] The holy well dedicated to him in the parish of Imphrick was located in the townland of Ballyhoura (Bealach Eabhradh), a place associated with Laichtín in an early poem on Múscraighe saints.[10] Probably because of his patronage of Kilfarboy, his name was also included among a group of mainly Clare saints in a recently discovered litany, compiled in the Regensburg *Schottenkloster*.[11] In a poem in Classical Irish, Laichtín, together with numerous other saints, was called upon to help in releasing Ireland's southern half (Leath Mogha) from a bondage imposed on it by the northern half (Leath Chuinn), championed by Finnian of Clonard.[12] Similarly, in a poem attributed to Cuimín of Connor, he is remembered as Munster's protector, and an early genealogical text more specifically assigns to him, under the guise of Molachtóg, the protection of the Múscraighe.[13] In this capacity, he was also associated with a lake named 'Siadus' (possibly now Loughmuskry in the parish of Clonbeg), which was surrounded by steep rocks on the summit of Sliabh gCrot (Galteemore) in Múscraighe Breoghain.[14] The honey of bees, brought by the saint out of Connacht, allegedly liquefied under the Summer sun and flowed from hives on the rocks into the lake. The date of his obit in the annals varies between 622 and 626–7.[15] The day of his feast, which also found its way into Cologne versions of the Martyrology of Usuard, was 19 March.[16] The fact that this coincided with the feast of St Joseph sometimes led to Joseph's substitution for Laichtín, as at Kilnamona in Co. Clare.[17]

1 *ZCP* 36, 146, 156. **2** *CGSH* §§202, 665.3.7.8; 666.1; *GRSH* 78; *Lgen*. 720.7.11. **3** *CGSH* §665.7. **4** *VSHP* i, 188 §47. **5** *VSHP* ii, 168 §10 **6** *VSHH* 318; *VSHP* ii, 38 §10, 40 §13; ITS 16, 22 §15. **7** *VSHH* 144 §68. **8** *ZCP* 10, 28 §23; *IrT* iv, 68–70. **9** *CPL* 9, 74; *NCHC* i, 176; *ACoC* 60, 107; *JCHAS* 4, 17; *AH* 24, 2–3 §7; *Béaloideas* 67, 77; ibid. 69, 83–106; *CPR* i, lxviii–lxix; *Éigse* 29, 169; *UL Camb.* Add. 622 (1, 2) 39; *ACE* 195. **10** *AICW* iv (pt ii), 456. **11** UCC MS U.331; cf. HBS 32, 14; *CKV* 60. **12** RIA MS 23L11, 263; *SAM* 24.1, 17, 20. **13** *ZCP* 1, 66; ibid. 8, 315. **14** *SZ* 3–4. **15** *AFM*/ATig./*AI s.a.* **16** *MartT* 25; *MartO²* 83; *MartG* 58; *MartD* 80; *AS*.Iun. vi, 163. **17** *JCHAS* 51, 163.

Laidhgeann of Kyle (Cluain Fearta Molua/Clonfertmulloe), barony of Clandonagh, Co. Laois. An annal entry for 661, which records the demise of Laidhgeann son of Baoth (alias Baoth Bannach), describes the saint as *sapiens*, 'wise, learned'.[1] He is commonly taken to be identical with the like-named author of an abridgement of one of Pope Gregory's most popular works, *Egloga de moralibus Job*, and was the reputed composer of one of the earliest Irish *loricae*, recently dated to 659, which is sometimes also attributed to Gildas.[2] Elsewhere, he is cited as an authority in the seventh-century Latin commentary on the Catholic Epistles, and it has been suggested that he was the successor of Molua (Lughaidh) of Kyle mentioned in Cummian's letter on the Easter question.[3] Little else is known of the saint, whose name (apparently derived from *ladhg*, 'snow') is also written as Laidcenn (Latchen) and, in hypocoristic guise, Mo Laige (Mo Luggae), but his writings probably emanated from the scriptorium at Clonmacnoise, where his teacher 'Bicgu' is said to have officiated as head of the elders.[4] The record of his feastday (12 January) includes, in the later martyrologies, an attachment to the church of Kyle.[5]

1 *AU s.a.* **2** *Kenney* 270–2, 278–9; *SacE* 7, 92–6; *Peritia* 10, 68–9; *Ériu* 24, 35–51; *DIB* v, 329–30. **3** *Peritia* 2, 238; *IIAM* 589–91. **4** Ibid. 12, 200; *Ériu* 13, 143. **5** *MartT* 7; *MartO²* 35, 42; *MartG* 14; *MartD* 14.

Laidhgeann son of Feidhlimidh. *See* Cainneach of Achadh Rathain.

Laighneach of Killinagh (Ceall Laighneach), barony of Tullyhaw, Co. Cavan. This man was thought locally to have been the unwelcome Leinster suitor who caused Brighid to gouge out her eyes, before becoming a saint himself and building with her the church at Killinagh.[1] A nearby well is called after Brighid.[2] While the saint's name may have been extrapolated from that of the church, it is worth noting that Laighneach of the unidentified church of Ceall Fheirbe is said to have been subject to Brighid.[3]

1 OSL CN/LM 18; *DK* 109; *Breifne* 4, 204. 2 *UJA* (3rd ser.) 2, 102. 3 *CGSH* §670.77; *Lgen.* 753.40.

Laisre. This name, which is used commonly of both male (Laisréan/Molaise) and female saints (Laisre/Lasar), derives from the word *lasar*, 'flame, fire'.[1] Most popular in the hypocoristic form Molaise, no fewer than forty-three bearers of the name are included in the list of homonymous saints.[2]

1 *Ériu* 54, 66–8. 2 *CGSH* §707.580–623.

Laisre daughter of Comhghall. *See* Bogha.

Laisre son of Colum. *See* Laisréan son of Colmán.

Laisréan. *See* also Molaise.

Laisréan of Durrow (Dearmhagh), barony of Ballycowan, Co. Offaly, and of Iona in Scotland. Laisréan son of Fearadhach was attached to the same branch of Ceinéal Conaill as his illustrious predecessor and close relative, Colum Cille.[1] He followed Colum's immediate successor (Baoithín) as abbot of Iona and held the office for five years (600–5).[2] Prior to this he appears to have spent some time at Durrow, where he was also abbot. Here, as Adhamhnán states, his harassment of monks constructing a large building changed to an order to cease work and take food, following an extra-sensory intervention by Colum, then on Iona.[3] While still in Ireland, Laisréan is said in a much later text to have assisted Colmán in marking out the site of his church at Lynally, thus indicating that the latter church was subject to its neighbour Durrow, by then probably the site of a house of canons regular of St Augustine.[4] Laisréan died in 605 and was remembered annually on 16 September, together with his namesake and probable double, Laisréan (Lasrán, Molaise) of Mondrehid (Mion) in the Laois parish of Offerlane.[5] Though this latter saint was made the subject of a more local (Leinster) pedigree, he shared a feastday with the abbot of Iona, and served as patron of a church lying within a parish whose chief patron (Cainneach) appears to have been ultimately identical with Colum Cille.[6] A late poem attributed to Colum Cille details some of the entitlements of Laisréan's church at Durrow.[7]

1 *CGSH* §336; *GRSH* 41; *Lgen.* 697.11. 2 *VC*[1] 372; *IKD* 39. 3 *VC*[2] 264–6. 4 *VSHH* 214 §14. 5 *AU s.a.*; *MartT* 71; *MartO*[2] 194, 208; *MartG* 178; *MartD* 248–50. 6 *CGSH* §243.1; *GRSH* 90; *FG* 20–35. 7 *ZCP* 10, 339.

Laisréan of Holywood (Ard Mic Nasca), barony of Lower Castlereagh, Co. Down. Laisréan son of Nasc is known from two sources, the Life of Mochuda of Lismore and the martyrologies. Mochuda's Life brings the saint southwards, together with two brothers named Gobán and Srafán, to the sea-girt church at Spike Island in the Cork Harbour parish of Templerobin, whereas the martyrologies place his commemoration on 25 October at Holywood.[1] Remembered with him in the lists for that day, and no doubt identical with him, was Laisre son of Colum (a variant form of the name Laisréan son of Colmán) who, according to the genealogists, belonged to the Dál nAraidhe of north Down and south Antrim.[2] A passage in the Life of Íde brings this Laisréan on a visit, allegedly from far away, to Killeedy in Limerick in the company of Luchtighearn, who is said to have been much better known to the local community.[3] Laisréan's companion was probably the same Luchtighearn as was sent, according to the Life of Mochaomhóg of Leigh, by Comhghall of Bangor to found a church elsewhere [4] In view of these associations, and despite the disparity in patronymics, Laisréan son of Colmán was probably identical with his namesake (the son of Nasc) at Holywood.

1 *VSHP* ii, 182, 184 §§34, 39; *MartT* 84; *MartO*[2] 218, 226; *MartG* 202; *MartD* 282; *EA* 272–3; *HDGP* i, 93. 2 *CGSH* §374. 3 *VSHP* ii, 127 §31. 4 Ibid. 168 §10.

Laisréan of Mundrehid. *See* Laisréan of Durrow.

Laisréan son of Colmán/Nasc(ann). *See* Laisréan of Holywood.

Lallóg of Kildalloge (Ceall Lallóg/Seanlios), parish of Kiltrustan, Co. Roscommon. Dairearca, sister of Patrick, is reputed to have given birth to fifteen bishops and two virgins (Eiche and Lallóg), both of whom occupied, according to the tract on the mothers of the saints, the church of Seanlios, now Kildalloge.[1] The author of the Tripartite Life of Patrick took a different view, placing Lallóg only in the church named after her at Kildalloge, and Eiche, together with her brother Meal, in the church of Kilglass (Ceall Ghlaise), south of Ardagh in Longford.[2] Memory of Lallóg appears to have faded at Kildalloge, and Patrick was the later patron of the parish in which her church lay.[3]

1 *CGSH* §722.16; *Dinn.* 5, 116. 2 *BP* 899–900; *VT* 82; *HDGP* iv, 2. 3 OSL RN ii, 79–80.

Lann daughter of Béac. *See* Lúireach of Maghera.

Lanus. *See* Laobhán.

Laobhán of Ballyovey (Odhbha/Oidheamh), barony of Carra, Co. Mayo, and of Inchmore on Lough Ree, parish of Bunown, barony of Kilkenny West, Co. Westmeath. Bearing a name that may derive from *laobh*, 'crooked', Laobhán was one of forty-seven children said to have been born to Cuman daughter of Dallbhrónach, maternal aunt of Brighid of Kildare, whose womb had allegedly been blessed by Patrick.[1] The siblings grouped around him in the list of Cuman's offspring, who were mainly associated with east Connacht, are again brought together in the Life of Forannán of Alternan in order to meet Colum Cille.[2] Laobhán's closest companion in the two lists, Foirtchearn, shared with him the church of Ballyovey, and the two saints are also featured among the three smiths named in the list of those in orders with Patrick, the third being Mac Céacht.[3] Though credited with having made Patrick's celebrated sweet-sounding bell, the

Fionn Faoidheach, Laobhán is assigned to a place named Domhnach Laobháin, now probably Killaan in the Galway barony of Kilconnell.[4] Elsewhere, under the guise of 'Líobhún', he is placed by the author of a poem in praise of the river Shannon in the church on Inchmore, allegedly founded by him in the fifth century, and the same form of his name became attached to a holy well in the Sligo townland and parish of Toomour.[5] In view of his links to churches in east Connacht, he is probably identical with the saint commemorated – according to the Martyrology of Donegal – along with Nathí of Achonry on 9 August.[6] This was close to Garland Sunday, on which day 'Láán' (Laobhán) was remembered at Killaan.[7] Another saint of the name was remembered on 1 June at a place called Áth Éigis, possibly an old name for Killeevan (Ceall Laobháin) in the Monaghan barony of Dartree, and if the same name is intended, 'Lanus', patron, according to a 1607 survey of the diocese of Derry, of Coolaghy in the Tyrone parish of Ardstraw, may also represent this saint.[8] At Killeevan, the saint's name was anglicized as Laban.

1 *CGSH* §722.9. **2** *Anecd.* iii, 3 §5. **3** *CGSH* §§671.11, 672.13; *BP* 3138–40; *VT* 266. **4** *HDGP* iv, 9. **5** *PÉ* §129; OSL SO 153. **6** *MartD* 214. **7** OSL GY i, 606. **8** *MartT* 47; *MartG* 108; *MartD* 142; *HDGP* i, 130; OSL AH/MN 139; *DYHS* 196; *LIS* vi, 12–13.

Laoighseach. *See* Aghna.

Laoghaire son of Tricheamh. *See* Duirtheach of Nendrum.

Lapán. Bearers of a name that probably represents a hypocoristic form of *Labhraidh*, 'he [who] speaks', the various saints named Lapán are otherwise little known. These included: the so-called *cruimhthear* ('priest') Lapán of Clonmethan (Cluain Meadhóin), barony of Balrothery West, Co. Dublin; the patron of Ceall Molapóg, a burial ground in the townland of Donore, parish of Lorum in Carlow, the scene of a defeat suffered by the men of south Leinster in 1041; the patron of Killappoge in the Roscommon parish of Killummod; and the bishop who gave name to St Lappan's burial ground, previously Ceall Easpaig Lapáin, on Little Island near Cork city.[1] Two saints of the name are commemorated in the martyrologies – Lapán son of Ciarán (11 February) and Lapán of Cluain Aithghin, now possibly Clonatin in the Wexford parish of Kilmakilloge, on 3 November, which may also have been the pattern day at Donore.[2]

1 *CGSH* §669.2; *AFM s.a.* 1041n.; CorkD 91, §36; *CPL* 9, 197; *Béaloideas* 4, 108. **2** *MartT* 16; *MartG* 34, 210; *MartD* 46, 296; *Carloviana* 55, 90.

Lasair. *See* Laisre.

Lasair. *See* Colmán of Lynn; Finnian of Movilla; Iobhar of Begerin.

Lasair daughter of Bréanainn Bán. *See* Blathmhac of Rath.

Lasair daughter of Colmán. *See* Cuman.

Lasair daughter of Fearghas. *See* Aodh Beag.

Lasair daughter of Mac Iair. *See* Craobh daughter of Mac Iair.

Lasair daughter of Neamhnann. *See* Bearchán of Laragh.

Lasair daughter of Neas. *See* Ceallán of Fancroft.

Lasair of Aghavea. *See* Lasair of Kilronan.

Lasair of Ceall Archalgach. *See* Aodh Beag.

Lasair of Delgany (Deirgne), barony of Rathdown, Co. Wicklow. The list of those said to have been subject to Brighid of Kildare places this saint in Delgany, along with two others, Mosceallóg and Lóchán.[1] Nothing else is recorded of the three, but the main saint of Delgany, Moghóróg (Guaire), belonged to the *familia* of Caoimhghin of Glendalough, as did Lóchán of Kilnamanagh in the parish of Tallaght.[2] As Kilnamanagh is just north of Kilbride (Ceall Bhrighde) in the parish of Bray, there may have been local Brigidine influence.[3]

1 *CGSH* §670.85. **2** *CGSH* §181.3. **3** *CPPI* 176–7, 187.

Lasair of Donaghmoyne (Maighean), barony of Farney, Co. Monaghan. According to a note added to the Martyrology of Donegal, the church of Donaghmoyne had two patrons, Ciar and Lasair, the latter a daughter of Eagán (Eoghan).[1] Bearing names that respectively mean 'dark or tan' and 'flame', neither saint is otherwise well known, but Lasair's day was kept on 18 April, when local people used to resort to a well called 'Tubber Lasair' in the townland of Aghavilla.[2] As this day was shared by Molaise (from *laisre/lasair*, 'flame'), patron of the diocese of Leighlin, both saints are likely to have originally represented the same cult. Ciar, whose name is sometimes wrongly written 'Clera', was regarded as the spiritual sister of Mac Caorthainn and Tighearnach, bishops of Clogher, the second of whom allegedly consecrated another of her churches at Killanny (Ceall Eanaigh) in the Louth barony of Ardee.[3] Ciar is also thought to have been the patron and eponym of Killahear graveyard in the townland of Corlat and parish of Aghnamullen, which adjoins Donaghmoyne.[4] Finally, although there is no supporting evidence, she is taken to have been commemorated under the guise of Ceara on 9 September, otherwise the feast of Ciarán of Clonmacnoise.[5]

1 *MartD* xlv, 376; cf. OSL AH/MN 118; cf. *ROLN* §490. **2** *MartT* 34; *MartG* 78; *MartD* 106; *SATDF* 162; *HCM* 358. **3** *SATDF* 162; *ClRec.* 1.1, 34; ibid. 7, 404. **4** *LIS* ix, 242–4. **5** Ibid.; *MartT* 69; *MartG* 172.

Lasair of Killasseragh (Ceall Lasra), parish of Kilmeen, barony of Duhallow, Co. Cork. This saint was one of three sisters – the others being Latiaran of Cullen and Inghean Bhaoith (Bhuidhe) of Dromtarriff – who were patrons of three adjoining parishes in the barony of Duhallow.[1] Stories about the sisters lived on in the folklore of the district until modern times, including the belief that angels made a road from one parish to the other to enable them to communicate more easily.[2] The site of Lasair's well, a much discussed matter, has been identified, with that of her church, in the townland of Knockmanagh, very close to Killasseragh.[3] Her name is in the list of those commemorated by the martyrologies on 7 May, the day after the local feast of Inghean Bhaoith.[4]

1 *FL* 270. **2** Ibid. 578. **3** *PABD* 243. **4** *MartT* 40; *MartG* 92; *MartD* 120; *FL* 270.

Lasair of Killossery (Ceall Lasra), barony of Nethercross, Co. Dublin. One of the many miracles attributed to the intercession of Brighid of Kildare was the repair of a loom-beam accidentally burnt by a widow when cooking an only calf as sustenance for the saint.[1] A hymn in praise of Brighid, said to have been composed by Brocán Claon, locates this miracle in Magh Caol, which is identified in a note as the fort of a king of Breagha in Fine Gall, now Fingal in Dublin.[2] Allusion is made to this same miracle in the list of those considered to be subject to Brighid which places it more narrowly at Killossery in Uí Bhreasail, in an area of Fingal formerly known as 'Obrassil', now the townland of Brazil.[3] Though Lasair, who gave name to this church, is not credited with the miracle, the early vernacular Life of Brighid recounts how the saint, having killed her only ewe in order to put food on the table for her visitor from Kildare – to whom, the biographer adds, she also gave her church – went on to provide sustenance on the same occasion for a second unexpected visitor, Patrick of Armagh.[4]

1 *LisL* 1665–7. 2 *LH* i, 124. 3 *CGSH* §670.11; *Lgen.* 752.18; *Nomina* 7, 23–30. 4 *BBr*, 16 §44.

Lasair of Kilronan (Ceall Rónáin), barony of Boyle, Co. Roscommon, of Aghavea (Achadh Beithe), barony of Magherastephana, Co. Fermanagh, and of Killesher (Ceall Laisre) in the same county. Some time after the foundation about 1215 of the Premonstratensian monastery of Holy Trinity on Loughkey by Clarus Mac Maoilín, archdeacon of Elphin, the church of Kilronan was granted to it.[1] The management of the church (rebuilt in 1339) and of its lands on behalf of the monastery was entrusted to the hereditary erenagh family of Uí Dhuibhgeannáin (O'Duignans), who may also have had charge of her miracle-working bell.[2] Excepting the neighbouring church of Kilmactranny, which also belonged to Holy Trinity, Kilronan is the only O'Duignan church to be noticed in the Connacht annals. It is also the only one to have produced, probably about the time that the church was rebuilt, a saint's Life which, somewhat misleadingly, has been attached to Lasair in her role as patron of Aghavea.[3] An entry in the Annals of Clonmacnoise for 1398, which describes David O'Duignan of Kilronan as 'Cowarb of the virgin St Lassar', shows that Lasair was in fact principally co-patron of Kilronan (also known as Killinginironan, 'church of daughter of Rónán'), whose eponymous saint (Rónán) is presented as her father.[4] By attaching Lasair of Kilronan to Aghavea, the O'Duignan author of the text would probably have intended to curry favour with the Maguires, then newly established lords of Fermanagh, or (as has been recently argued) to support Maguire designs on Clones, which lay within the sphere of influence of the MacMahons.[5] The presentation in the text of Damhnad of Tedavnet in Monaghan as Lasair's sister – despite the lack of any other genealogical support – may reflect the same intent.

Lasair's biographer was prepared to go so far as to present her father Rónán, again despite the conflict with all previous tradition, as the like-named patron of Dromiskin in Louth, doubtless because this place had become by the fourteenth century a manor from which the archbishop of Armagh periodically administered his archdiocese.[6] As for the genealogical affiliations of Lasair and her father, they were attached to no less a family than 'Muintear Néill', the O'Neills of Tyrone, the most powerful of all Irish noble families in the period between about 1350 and 1600.[7] In the political circumstances of the time, the O'Duignans could not have pitched any higher their own aspirations to be well connected genealogically through their saints.

Described by her biographer as a pupil of Molaise of Devenish, Lasair is said to have spent five years in Aghavea, performing various miracles, before she set off for Killesher (Ceall Laisre) at the head of Lough Macnean.[8] Subsequently, she is supposed to have founded two other churches named Ceall Lasrach, one, unidentified, in the Galway barony of Tiaquin, the other at Killasser in the Mayo barony of Gallen.[9] All of this is by way of preamble to the story of the founding of her main church at Kilronan, at which point emphasis is given to the tax due to her from the area between Tirerrill and the river Shannon.[10] No account is given of the saint's death.

In her guise as patron of Aghavea, Lasair was called upon by the biographer of Náile, who was allegedly her teacher, to punish those who neglected to pay the Kinawley saint's tribute.[11] The saint may also have been adopted by the Síol Maine of Longford/Westmeath, among whose *cailleacha*, 'nuns', was a Lasair daughter of Rónán.[12] The feastday of the saint fell on 13 November, at least at Aghavea, the only church mentioned by the martyrologists on that day.[13] She may also have been commemorated on 19 April, under the guise of Laise, at Clonmin (Cluain Minn?) in the Fermanagh parish of Galloon.[14] At Killesher, a holy well was named for the saint, near her church on the edge of Lough Macnean.[15] At Kilronan, Lasair's well was the scene of an annual pilgrimage.[16]

1 *CBC* 129, 154. **2** *ACoC s.a.*; *EMH* 481–2 §214. **3** *MHH* 191; *Ériu* 5, 74–103; *ClRec.* 18, 299–318; *ILL* 365. **4** *Ériu* 5, 74; *LSLC* 298–300. **5** *Ériu* 5, 78; *ClRec.* 18, 299–318 at 315–17. **6** *Ériu* 5, 78; *LSLC* 299; *MPA* 74. **7** OSL RN 281; *HOI* 158; *Ériu* 5, 90, 92. **8** *Ériu* 5, 78–82; ibid. 54, 66–8; OSL FH 78–9. **9** *Ériu* 5, 88–92. **10** Ibid. 94–102. **11** *MHH* 121 §53; *BLCat.* ii, 571. **12** *Lgen.* 177.6. **13** *MartG* 218; *MartD* 308. **14** *MartT* 34; *MartG* 80; *MartD* 106. **15** OSL FH 78–9. **16** *HWI* 24–5.

Latiaran of Cullen (Cuileann), barony of Duhallow, Co. Cork. This saint was regarded as one of three sisters – the others being Lasair of Killasseragh and Inghean Bhaoith (Bhuidhe) of Dromtarriff – each of whom was patron of an adjoining parish in the barony of Duhallow.[1] Stories concerning the three lived on in the folklore of the district until modern times, including the assertion that angels made a road from one parish to the other to enable the saints to communicate more easily.[2] Of the three, Latiaran was by far the best-remembered. Bearing a name that probably derives from Luchtighearn, a compound of the name of the Celtic divininty named *Lugh* and *tighearn*, 'lord', the saint was closely associated with the celebration of the Celtic feast of *Lughnasadh*, 'Lugh's feast', which fell on or about 1 August. Latiaran's day was 25 July or (more recently) the nearest Sunday, when people gathered at the saint's well beside the ruins of an old church and graveyard in the village of Cullen.[3] Many of the practices typical of the *Lughnasadh* festival were observed, including rounds at the well, consumption of berries, dancing, carousing at stalls set up in the village, and faction-fighting.

The main story related of Latiaran involved a daily visit to the local forge to borrow an ember which she carried back in her apron. On one occasion, having heard the smith speak of the beauty of her feet, Latiaran looked down at them in a moment of vanity, only to have her apron catch fire. Her cursing of the smith followed, together with a prophecy that Cullen would never again hear a smith's anvil. The association of the saint with a smith and his embers has been taken to reflect the possible identity of Latiaran with Brighid and Gobnaid.[4] The three sisters of Duhallow are said to have had two saintly brothers, John of Mushera, a local variant of John the Apostle whose feast fell on 24 June, and Beircheart of Tullylease.[5] While the saint was usually remembered in late July, a second feast of 10 November has also been recorded.[6] Local tradition maintains that she is buried under Cloch na gCúrsa (stone of the rounds) at the entrance to the burial ground in Cullen (townland of Mullaghroe North).[7] A well dedicated to her was located in the townland of Claragh More, parish of Drishane, which adjoins the parish of Cullen.[8] Pilgrimage to Cullen is already attested in the early eighteenth century.[9]

1 *FL* 270; *PABD* 130; *SD* 1986, 31–5. **2** *FL* 578. **3** Ibid. 268–75. **4** *MCMHW* 202–3. **5** Ibid. 271; *PABD* 130. **6** Maynooth MS M 84, 229. **7** *PABD* 131–2. **8** *AICW* iv (pt ii), 458. **9** *PnaB* 3811–13.

Lauirint. *See* Lúirint.

Leannán, *cruimhthear*, 'priest'. A poem on the saints said to have been in orders with Patrick refers to his bell-ringer Leannán (alias Lionnán the priest).[1] Although nothing else is recorded of this man in Patrician literature, the name again figures, with those of Fursa and Greallán, among a group of Connacht saints invoked in a poem on Seanán of Scattery Island.[2] A Connacht connection may also underlie a colophon in a late fourteenth-century manuscript compiled at Ballymote in Sligo, which invokes God, the Trinity, and 'saingte Lindeann (perhaps from Linnéan)', because 'they were on one day'.[3] Assuming that Trinity Sunday – either the first Sunday after Pentecost or the fiftieth day after Easter – was intended, the saint's feast would have fallen sometime between mid-May and mid-June.

1 *CGSH* §672.11. **2** *ZCP* 10, 26 §21. **3** *BB* 36r; CMIS 3n.

Leathnán son of Cantón. *See* Santán.

Leevan. *See* Laobhán.

Lelia of Killeely. *See* Faoileann; Liadhain daughter of Eacha.

Liadhain daughter of Diarmuid. According to the Dál gCais genealogies, Liadhain belonged to the family of Uí Chonghaile, which gave name to the present Clare parish of Ogonnelloe, on the edge of Lough Derg.[1] No trace can now be found of the saint in this area, but John Colgan stated that there was a church named after her in the diocese of Killaloe, in the region of Uí Chaisín which corresponds to part of the territory of the McNamaras, formerly known as the barony of Dangan.[2] Among the castles of this area was Rossmanagher in the parish of Feenagh, and this place may be again featured, under the guise of Ros Beannchair, in the Life of Ciarán of Seirkieran, albeit in relation to Ciarán's foster-mother Cóch.[3] A seventeenth-century source placed Liadhain's feast on 11

August and it has been suggested that she was patron of the Limerick parish of Killeely.[4]

1 *CGSH* §198; *GRSH* 120; *Lgen.* 738.2; *CoC* 27. 2 *GRSH* 120; *CoC* 96, 102. 3 *ACoC* 297–8; *VSHP* i, 226–7 §§21–2. 4 *GRSH* 120; *NMAJ* 3, 108.

Liadhain daughter of Eacha. Attaching her to the descendants of Laoghaire son of Niall, the genealogists gave Liadhain a sister Cearc and a brother Iolladhan.[1] The latter association may be significant, as Iolladhan's church lay in Killoughy, a few miles north of Killyon (Ceall Liadhaine) in the Offaly parish of Drumcullen which took its name from the mother of Ciarán of Seirkieran. There is also a parish of Killyon in Meath, between Trim and Clonard, which would suit the pedigree of the saint, but this is taken to derive from Ceall Liatháin.[2] A few miles further south, at Kilkeeran in the parish of Castlejordan, was a dedication to Ciarán.[3] Sometimes taken to have been identical with Lelia of Killeely near Limerick, whose name may in fact derive from Oilill, Liadhain is said by seventeenth-century sources to have been remembered on 11 August.[4]

1 *CGSH* §662.59; *GRSH* 51; *Lgen.* 707.8; *DIB* v, 500. 2 OSL MH 215–16. 3 Logainm.ie 'Kilkeeran'. 4 *NMAJ* 1, 39; ibid. 3, 108; *SATM* 42–3; *LLog.* i, 102; *MartD* 216; *GRSH* 51; cf. *DiocL* 122.

Liadhain mother of Ciarán. *See* Ciarán of Seirkieran; Liadhain daughter of Diarmuid; Liadhain daughter of Eacha.

Liadhnán son of Iorlamhán. *See* Bóchra.[2]

Liamhain daughter of Calpruinn. *See* Neachtan of Fennor.

Liathán. While among the seven saints thought to be still alive, Liathán would appear to be otherwise unattested.[1] He may have been the deacon commemorated in the name Ceall Deochain Liatháin, now Killagholehane in the Limerick barony of Glenquin.[2] Alternatively, the site named Killane in the Antrim parish of Ahoghill may derive from Ceall Liatháin.[3]

1 *BL Cat.* ii, 471; *AB* 55, 290 2 *HDGP* iii, 163. 3 PNNI iv, 182.

Libhear. Although sometimes thought to derive from Latin *liber*, 'free', this name, with its hypocoristic forms (Lioba, Molioba, Dolioba) and diminutives (Liobhrán, Libhréan) is much more likely to be native in origin.[1] It was borne by numerous saints, fifteen of whom are in the list of homonymous saints.[2] It was also a common secular name.[3] Of the almost twenty locations assigned in lists and martyrologies to saints of the name, or variants thereof, only a few are now identifiable.

1 *GPN* 122. 2 *CGSH* §707.463–77. 3 *CGH* p. 672 (ind.).

Libhear of Aghaboe (Achadh Bó), barony of Clarmallagh, Co. Laois. While based in north-east Ulster, in the company of Comhghall and Colum Cille, Cainneach of Aghaboe is said to have resuscitated a young, impious man named Libhear son of Araidhe, disobedient to his mother, who, on repenting, had his legs bound together by fetters the key of which was thrown into the sea.[1] Seven years after accompanying Cainneach to Britain, Libhear was directed by his mentor to return to Ireland, to a place near the river Liffey, where he recovered the key in a fish caught by local fishermen, and subsequently remained in a place named Leathdhumha (Leatuimhe) of Cainneach. Although this place has yet to be identified, Libhear is probably the man of this name who succeeded Cainneach as abbot of Aghaboe, dying, according to the annals and later martyrologies, on 8 March 619.[2]

The saint's connection with east Ulster, where he was first met by Cainneach, would suggest that he may also be associated with a number of churches in that part of the country. In Dál nAraidhe (north Down / south Antrim), Patrick is said to have left a priest named Libhear in the church of Ceall Ghlas, probably in (or east of) the Down parish of Donaghmore.[3] At Eanach Ealta in Uí Eachach, now Annahilt on the edge of the barony of Lower Iveagh, a saint named Molioba, a hypocoristic form of Libhear, was remembered on two days, 18 February and 26 December.[4] Nearby, at Gortgrib (Gort Cirb) in the parish of Knockbreda, a few miles north of Annahilt, a namesake was remembered on 5 August, according to the later martyrologies.[5] From the same general area, the list of homonymous saints includes two others of the name, Libhear of Clochar, now possibly Clogher in the parish of Drumbo, between Annahilt and Gortgrib, and his namesake of Larne (Inbhear Latharna) in Antrim.[6]

In Leinster, the cult appears also to have put down roots in hypocoristic guise, possibly as Liobán at Newtownstalaban (Teach Liobáin) in the Louth parish of Tullyallen, and as Molioba, designated son of Araidhe in the section of an early litany given over to the forty saints gathered about Caoimhghin of Glendalough.[7] Sometimes described as a son of Colmaidh, this repesentative of the cult is more firmly attached to Glendalough by the statement that his mother was Caoimhghin's sister, variously named Caoiltighearn and Caomhóg.[8] These traditions probably reflect the presence within the *paruchia* of Glendalough of a church near Wicklow named Ceall Molioba after the saint.[9] At Glendalough, the saint was remembered, sometimes as bishop, on 8 January.[10] Mention of Libhear of Tamhlachta in this list may echo the association of the name Libhréan with that of Tallaght, near Dublin, in the preface to the Martyrology of Aonghas.[11]

1 *VSHH* 186–7 §19; *VSHP* i, 157–8 §15; *CGSH* §707.463; *DIB* v, 501. 2 *AU s.a.*; *MartG* 50; *MartD* 70. 3 *BP* 1900–3; *VT* 162–4; *HDGP* iv, 2. 4 *MartT* 17; *MartO*[2] 61; *MartG* 38, 246; *MartD* 52, 348. 5 *MartG* 150; *MartD* 212; *EA* 11, 379. 6 *CGSH* §707.464.473. 7 *IrL* 56; *CPPI* 116–17. 8 *CGSH* §722.72.102. 9 *CPPI* 116, 238. 10 *MartT* 6; *MartG* 12; *MartD* 10. 11 *CGSH* §707.474; *MartO*[2] 6.

Libhréan of Clonfad (Cluain Fada Libhréin), barony of Fartullagh, Co. Westmeath. This saint was probably the eponymous founder of the church named after him.[1] His father, Aodh son of Colga, king of Oirthir, a segment of Oirghialla that gave name to Orior in Armagh, died, according to the annals, in 610 as a pilgrim in Clonmacnoise.[2] Aodh is the subject of mention in the Life of Mochta of Louth which states that its saint refused an offer of land from the king, allegedly because he knew that it was destined for the use of Colum Cille.[3] Libhréan's three siblings were Cobhthach – probably identical with Cobhthach

Caol son of a king of Oirghialla – Maighneann of Kilmainham, and Tua. The patron of Clonfad was commemorated on 11 March, not only in native sources, but also, under the guise of 'Liberus', in some post-Conquest liturgical manuscripts, which would suggest that his church had become impropriate to some Dublin abbey.[4]

1 *PNW* 173–4. 2 *CGSH* §54; *GRSH* 71; *Lgen.* 713.10; *AU s.a.*; *AFM s.a.*606. 3 *VSHH* 399 §16. 4 *MartT* 22; *MartO²* 81; *MartG* 52; *MartD* 72; *Rep. Nov.* 2, 46, 48, 53.

LIBHRÉAN of Inis Mór. According to the Life of Seanán of Scattery Island, one of the first places visited by its subject on returning to west Clare was the (unidentified) island of Inis Mór in Iorras Deiscirt, an area thought to have corresponded to the parishes of Kilballyowen, Kilfearagh and Moyarta on the Loop Head peninsula.[1] Having ensured the restoration to its mother of a child that fell from a cliff, Seanán is said to have left several of his company on the island, including three (otherwise unattested) bishops – Dalann, Séadna, Earc – and Libhréan son of Dall, after whom was named a well on the island. Although there is nothing to connect the two beyond a coincidence of names (saint and church), Seanán's disciple may have been the same as the Libhear son of Luiséan commemorated on 1 August, with his brothers Fáilbhe and Ailbhe, at a place called Inis Mór.[3]

1 *CoC* 78. 2 *LisL* 2155–93. 3 *MartT* 59; *MartG* 148; *MartD* 208.

LIBHRÉAN son of Luiséan. *See* Libhréan of Inis Mór.

LÍOBHA daughter of Conall. *See* Éanna of Inishmore.

LÍOBHAN daughter of Eacha. The origin tale of Lough Neagh (Loch nEachach, 'Eacha's Lake'), named after the saint's father, relates how Líobhan (also known as Fuinche and Muirghin), having survived under water until after the arrival of Christianity, was eventually caught in nets belonging to Fearghas of Downpatrick who, according to the annals, died in 584 or 590.[1] Fearghas is said to have also founded the unidentified Ceall Bhiain (named after Bian, a possible variant of Beoán), and this may tie in with the tradition that Líobhan was baptized and buried at the church of Beoán son of Innle.[2] Through her alias Muirghin, 'born of the sea', the saint became confused with Muirghin, abbot of Killeshin, whose feast of 27 January was accorded to her.[3] A saint named Líobhan is also included in the list of those commemorated on 18 December.[4]

1 *CGSH* §300; *GRSH* 97; *LU* 3106–31; *AU s.a.* 2 *HDGP* iii, 132; *LU* 3125–6. 3 *MartT* 12; *MartO²* 38, 52; *MartG* 24; *MartD* 28. 4 *MartT* 86; *MartG* 240; *MartD* 340.

LIOBHRÁN of Martairtheach. Assigned to Martairtheach in the list of homonymous saints, Liobhrán no doubt corresponds to the man named Libhear of the same church in the list of those commemorated on 2 November.[1] Where this saint's church lay is a different matter. While on his way into Munster, Patrick left behind, according to the Tripartite Life, relics and some disciples at Martairtheach in Magh Roighne, a plain in the mid-west of Kilkenny which appears to have no local trace of Libhear.[2] Another possibility is Martry (Martairtheach?) in the Meath barony of Navan Lower, where an ecclesiastic named Fiachra died in 755.[3] This was the scene of a battle in 1055 between the communities of Armagh and Clonard, possibly brought about by Martry's proximity to Teltown, the scene of annual *Lughnasadh* celebrations.[4] There is, however, no trace of Libhear in this area either. The list of bishops of Clogher in John Lynch's *De praesulibus Hiberniae* places a man named 'Liberius' in second place after Mac Caorthainn, adding that he was remembered, like his namesake at Martairtheach, on 2 November.[5]

1 *CGSH* §707.477; *MartG* 210; *MartD* 294. 2 *BP* 2277–9; *VT* 194. 3 *AU s.a.*; *OnomG* 536, but cf. Logainm.ie 'Martry'. 4 *AU s.a.*; OSL MH [31]. 5 *DPH* i, 178.

Líobhún. *See* Laobhán.

Líogh of Rosconnell (Ros Conaill), barony of Clarmallagh, Co. Laois. This daughter of Mac Reithe, whose name was also written as Doing, is known only from the list of those said to have been subject to Brighid of Kildare.[1] With her at Rosconnell were her (otherwise unattested) sister Tighearn, and a group called Ingheana Treana (daughters of Trian).

1 *CGSH* §670.87.

Líoghach Bhreaghmhaineach. *See* Muireadhach of Killala; Ninnidh Láimhiodhan.

Líthghin of Clonmore (Cluain Mór Líthghin), parish and barony of Geashill, Co. Offaly, and of Monasterevin (Ros Glaise), barony of West Offaly, Co. Kildare. This saint was one of seven brothers of Abán of Killabban, who belonged through their father Laighneach to the Uí Labhradha (or Uí Chormaic) of Leinster.[1] Three of Líthghin's brothers, Dubhán, Seanach, and Toimdheanach, are also assigned to Monasterevin, a church much better known for its association with Éimhín. Although little else is known of Líthghin, his mother, allegedly a sister of Bishop Iobhar, was named Broinnfhinn Bhreac.[2] The church named after him at Clonmore later became known as 'Balleenlawn church', while a nearby well gave name to the adjoining townland of Toberleheen.[3] Líthghin's feast fell on 16 January.[4] He is possibly the saint named 'Líthéin' whose curse was invoked, with that of Brighid, in a poem written in classical metre.[5]

1 *CGSH* §287.1.2; *MartO²* 74; *GRSH* 90; *Lgen.* 727.11. 2 *CGSH* §722.96. 3 *AIOY* §§642, 759. 4 *MartT* 8; *MartG* 16; *MartD* 18. 5 *Éigse* 10, 314.

Lobhrán of Uaithne, an area whose name is preserved in those of two adjoining baronies, Owneybeg in Limerick and Owney and Arra in Tipperary. Twenty-four saints are said to have belonged to a union (*aonta*) led by Feidhlimidh son of Criomhthann, among them many connected, like Lobhrán, with mid-Munster.[1] All were associated with the *céile Dé* group of churches which came to the fore within the Irish church in the second half of the eighth century and remained vigorous until about the middle of the ninth. Though there is no other record of Lobhrán, he is probably the saint who founded and gave name to Díseart Lobhráin, now Inch St Lawence in the barony of Clanwilliam, west of Owneybeg. As the modern form shows, Lawrence was later substituted for Lobhrán, and the feast of the Roman martyr (10 August) was also adopted.[2]

1 *CGSH* §§713, 724. **2** Dinns. 6, 153–4; *NMAJ* 3, 153–4; *SATM* 46–7.

LÓCHÁN. Representing a diminutive of Lóch, from *lóch*, 'bright, radiant', and probably cognate with the divinity name Lugh, Lóchán (alias Luachán and Lóichín) was borne by a number of holy men, six of whom are included in the list of homonymous saints.[1] Perhaps because of the regular association of their likely pre-Christian predecessor with high places, five of the six are linked to names containing the element *druim*, 'ridge'. Though all five have yet to be identified, Lóchán's most famous *druim* is now Drumlohan in the Waterford parish of Stradbally, whose *cillín*, 'church site', contains ten ogham stones.[2] No memory of the saint associated with the site has, however, survived.

1 *ZCP* 36 (1977), 138–56; *CGSH* §707.478–82. **2** *CIIC* i, 267–77.

LÓCHÁN of Kilmacahill (Ceall Mhic Cathail), barony of Gowran, Co. Kilkenny. The saint's church, the first of two Leinster churches mentioned in the Life of Fionnbharr of Cork, lay at the pass of Bealach Gabhráin, easily the best-known of the ancient routes into Ossory.[1] The background of the saint associated with the local church is unclear. On no apparent authority, the early seventeenth-century Martyrology of Donegal identified him with Lóchán son of Cathal of the Uí Fhiachrach of Connacht.[2] Although retaining the Connacht identification, John Colgan also allowed for the possibility that Lóchán might have belonged through his father Maonach to the Corca Laoighdhe of south-west Cork.[3] No authority is given, but Fionnbharr's Life, which identifies Lóchán of Kilmacahill as one of the three Munster clerics charged with the Cork saint's basic education, could have been cited in support.

This is not to say that any more weight should be given to the word of the late twelfth-century Cork writer than to that of the Martyrology of Donegal. Of the two, the Cork authority had most to gain from the identification, his purpose being to create the impression that the Kilmacahill saint was none other than Lóchán of the Uí Eachach who, according to the corpus of saints' genealogies, was one of seven brothers of Fachtna, patron of Ross.[4] Lóchán's surrender to Fionnbharr of the right to consecrate the newly constructed church of Kilmacahill, as is asserted in the Life, would then have taken on an ulterior meaning. As Canon Law reserved the consecration of a church for a bishop or his deputy, Lóchán would thus have acknowledged Fionnbharr, patron of Cork, as his bishop, and the diocese of Ross, of which Lóchán's brother Fachtna was patron, would have been regarded as subject to the jurisdiction of the bishop of Cork.[5] The same strategy was arguably employed by Fionnbharr's biographer at Coolcashin in the Kilkenny barony of Galmoy, whose patron Mainchín was another of Fachtna's brothers.[6] Coolcashin adjoins the parish of Rathlogan –

probably a derivative of Ráith Lócháin, 'Lóchán's dwelling' – where a well, still frequented in modern times, was dedicated to a saint 'Ullacawn/Eelakun', a possible reflex of Lóchán.[6]

1 *BBa.* 60 §11. 2 *MartD* 350. 3 *ASH* 248 §2. 4 *CGSH* §248.2. 5 *MakS* 86–7. 6 *BBa.* 62 §14; *HADO* ii, 299.

Lóchán son of Cathal. *See* Éanna of Kilnamanagh; Lóchán of Kilmacahill.

Lóchán son of Duachán. *See* Caolán of Nendrum; Mac Earca.

Lóichín daughter of Conall Dearg. *See* Éanna of Inishmore.

Lóichín son of Dubh Dlighidh. *See* Molaga of Aghacross.

Lóichín son of Iollann. *See* Eiltín of Seanchua.

Lomán. Although sometimes thought to derive from *lom*, 'bare', the name may in fact represent the diminutive of a pet form *lomma*, perhaps from Labhraidh, which is attested in a dedication at Kilmalum (Ceall Moloma) in the Kildare parish of Tipperkevin.[1]

1 *GPN* 124; *PNCW* iv, 250–3; *Rep. Nov.* 2, 124.

Lomán of Lough Gill (Loch Gile), Cos Sligo/Leitrim, and of Trim (Áth Truim), baronies of Lower Moyfenrath and Upper Navan, Co. Meath. According to the mainline genealogies, Lomán son of Dallán belonged to the descendants of Colla Dá Chríoch of Orior (Oirthir) in Armagh.[1] Both Tíreachán's *Additamenta* and the author of the Tripartite Life (who depended on Tíreachán) disagreed, identifying Lomán of Áth Truim as of British descent, and as one of several nephews of Patrick who attained episcopal status.[2] The tract on the mothers of the saints expanded this tradition further, describing Lomán as one of fifteen bishop-sons of Dairearca, sister of Patrick.[3] The same text distinguished between Lomán of Trim and his namesake at Calry on Lough Gill, whom it included among the more numerous children of Cuman, aunt of Brighid of Kildare.[4]

Apparently because of their connections with north-east Connacht, many of Cuman's children, including Lomán, were brought together in the Life of Forannán of Alternan in order to meet Colum Cille.[5] Lomán's cult can thus be seen to have had ramifications involving all three national saints, but this member of the 'third order' of Irish saints was probably best known as Patrick's *hostiarius*, 'pyx-bearer', and was remembered as such on 11 October.[6] The Martyrology of Tallaght also lists him among the Trim saints commemorated on 17 February, a month that held two other feastdays of a saint named Lomán, on the fourth day (sometimes mistakenly said to have been at Lough Gill) and on the seventh at Lough Owel.[7] He may also be the saint who gave name to Kilmalum (Ceall Moloma), formerly Domhnach Imleach, in the Kildare parish of Tipperkevin.[8] Moloma is attached to Domhnach Imleach in the Leinster section of the *Notulae* in the Book of Armagh, which describes him as an exorcist, and also in the martyrologies, which remember him on 19 or 20 June.[9] The saint was commemorated under the guise of 'Loma' on 29 June in a fifteenth-century post-

Conquest Dublin antiphonary, probably because Tipperkevin had by then become a prebend of the diocese of Dublin.[10]

1 *CGSH* §§350, 694; *GRSH* 71; *Lgen.* 714.8. **2** *PTBA* 166–8; *BP* 711–13; *VT* 68; *JEH* 1, 162–5; *MedT* 34–47. **3** *CGSH* §722.16. **4** Ibid. §722.9. **5** *Anecd.* iii, 3 §5. **6** *VSHH* 82 §3; *MartT* 17, 78; *MartO*[2] 215; *MartG* 194; *MartD* 272. **7** *MartT* 14–15, 17; *MartG* 32; *MartD* 38–40. **8** *PNCW* iv, 250–3; *Rep. Nov.* 2, 124; *DEPPP* 338; *AH* 8, 38. **9** *PTBA* 181 §40; *MartT* 51; *MartG* 120; *MartD* 174; *AB* 46, 409–10. **10** *Rep. Nov.* 2, 46, 124.

Lomán of Lough Owel (Loch Uair) in Westmeath. Attached by the genealogists to the Ceinéal Conaill of the area now covered approximately by the Donegal barony of Raphoe, Lomán son of Oireannán was associated with two churches in the vicinity of Lough Owel, one on Church Island (Inis Mór), the other at Portloman (Teach/Port Lomáin), which may also have been known as Teach Mic Luim.[1] In the former place, Lomán is said to have lived on 'Alexandric herbs'.[2] In the latter, he was allegedly visited by Bishop Éidchéan of Clonfad on the night that Colmán son of Luachán of Lynn was born, when marvellous kinds of music were heard about the church.[3] The saint is said to have later made a covenant with Colmán, and this may represent a claim by Lynn to authority over Portloman.[4]

Lomán's church lay on the roadway of Slighe Asail, along which was sung – as far as the cross at Portloman, according to tradition – the celebrated *Amhra*, 'sacred song', of Colum Cille, begun at Áth Féine in the neighbouring parish of Tyfarnham.[5] This cross is no longer standing, but a stone called *leac Lomáin*, associated with the saint, marked the beginning of the station formerly performed at his church.[6] His crozier and chain, used by women in childbirth, were still extant in the early seventeenth century.[7] A tradition then also survived to the effect that he had been carried through the air in a boat from Lough Owel to Trim which, when taken together with the statement that he was a nephew of Patrick, would suggest that he had come to be identified with Lomán son of Dallán.[8] To judge by a visit allegedly made to a friend there by Maighneann of Kilmainham, Lomán's church on Lough Owel may have later been associated with the Knights Hospitallers.[9] A poem lists Lomán among saints that appear formerly to have belonged to the *Fianna* of Fionn son of Cumhall.[10] Lomán's feastday normally fell on 7 February, though it is said in one source to have fallen on the third of that month at Portloman.[11]

1 *CGSH* §10; *GRSH* 41; *Lgen.* 697.9; *MartO*[2] 68; *CGSH* §707.434.482. **2** *MartD* xlii. **3** *BCML* §10. **4** Ibid. §42. **5** *RC* 20, 134; *HDGP* i, 132. **6** *PNW* 30–1. **7** *MartD* xli–xlii, 434. **8** Ibid. **9** *SG* i, 37. **10** *ZCP* 5, 179–83. **11** *MartT* 17; *MartO*[2] 59; *MartG* 32; *MartD* xli, 40.

Lon Garadh of Kilgory (Ceall Ghabhra), parish of Killabban, barony of Slievemargy, Co. Laois, and of Cashel, formerly 'Cashelgarwe/Castlegarrow' (Díseart Garadh), parish of Offerlane, barony of Upperwoods, in the same county.[1] For a man whose death is said to have been marked by the fall from their shelves of Ireland's book-satchels, gospel-books, and books of learning, and the general demise of knowledge, precious little else has been recorded of Lon, beyond the fact that he was also considered worthy of comparison with Augustine of Hippo, a likening which has led to the suggestion that he may have been the Augustinus who wrote *De mirabilibus sacrae scripturae*.[2] His death is said to have been supernaturally revealed to Colum Cille who, having been denied access to Lon's books, had previously left a curse on them.[3] Although his feastday fell on 24 June, pilgrimages are said to have been also made to 'Longory's well' in Kilgory during the month of May.[4]

1 *HADO* ii, 177–80. 2 *CGSH* §§712.19, 720; *MartO*[1] cxli–cxlii; *IIAM* 595. 3 *Bod. Cat.* i, 98; *MartO*[1] cxli–cxlii. 4 *MartT* 52; *MartG* 122; *MartD* 178; *OKR* 7, 44; *AILS* 96.

Lonán of Killulagh (Coill Uailleach), barony of Delvin, Co. Westmeath. When Patrick was baptizing the people of Luighne (whence the Meath barony of Lune) at Donaghmore (Domhnach Mór), he is said to have foretold that no person having recourse to the relics of Casán – who was yet to be buried there – would be disappointed.[1] A woman named Rígheall then begged of Patrick that he bless her son, one Lonán son of Seanach (reputedly a former member of the *Fianna* of Fionn son of Cumhall) who, having gone on to read the psalms with Casán, is said to have taken possession of Killulagh.[2] When visited by John O'Donovan in 1837, Lonán's patronage of the parish was still vividly remembered, albeit without reference to a pattern day.[3] His church appears also to have had some interest in the area about Drumcree in the neighbouring parish of Kilcumny which, according to an eleventh-century poem attributed to Cuán son of Lothchán, was given by God to Féichín and Lonán *ón lind*, 'from (across?) the sea'.[4] However, a late seventeenth-century visitation list, prepared for the diocese of Meath, names 'Cumny' as patron of Drumcree.[5] The saint's feastday fell on 12 November.[6]

1 *BP* 827–40; *VT* 76. 2 *ZCP* 5, 180. 3 *PNW* 80. 4 *LL* 19680–3. 5 *RM* 5.4, 112. 6 *MartG* 216; *MartD* 306.

Lonán of Trevet (Treóid), barony of Skreen, Co. Meath. Although attached to its church in the medieval record, Lonán is no longer remembered in the townland of Trevet, where the ruins of his abode adjoined a well dedicated to Patrick, patron of the parish.[1] The entertaining circumstances that gave rise to Lonán's conception are recorded in the preface to a hymn attributed to Mugintius of Whithorn.[2] Having fallen in love with Ríóg of Inchbofin in Westmeath, who accompanied Finnian to Mugintius' school at Whithorn, Drustic daughter of Drust, king of the Britons, was duped into believing that she had slept with the object of her love, when Talmhach, another of Finnian's companions, had been sent in his place. Lonán of Trevet was the issue of this liaison, as is also affirmed by a quatrain in the tract on the mothers of the saints, supplemented by another in the Martyrology of Aonghas.[3] The name of the saint's church was imaginatively thought to derive from the *tré-fóid*, 'three sods', marking the burial place of Art son of Conn.[4] Lonán's feast fell on 1 November.[5]

1 OSL MH 165. 2 *LH* i, 22. 3 *CGSH* §722.100; *MartO*[2] 238. 4 *LU* 9847–8; *MartD* 290. 5 *MartO*[2] 232; *MartG* 208; *MartD* 290.

Lonán son of Dáire. *See* Maolán of Kilmoylan.

Lonán son of Dubhthach, of Dionn Fhlatha in Ceinéal Lughair, in or near the parish of Kilbride in north Wexford.[1] Lonán was among eleven bearers of the name in the list of homonymous saints.[1] With two other sons of Dubhthach, Nainnín (alias Moninne) and Molaise, and a relative named Mochomóg of the Maca Lughair, Lonán belonged to a group attached to Dionn Fhlatha in the list of those subject to Brighid of Kildare.[2] None of these is, however, among the seven sons elsewhere credited to Dubhthach.[3]

1 *CGSH*§670.45.72. **2** Ibid. §707.452–63; *BP* 531–6; *VT* 52. **3** *CGSH* §670.72; *Lgen*. 753.37.

Lorcán (Laurence) of Christ Church, Dublin, and Glendalough. The Book of Glendalough, also known as Rawlinson B 502, gave due prominence to the Uí Mhuireadhaigh (later Uí Thuathail), historically one of north Leinster's chief families which by the 1120s, when the book was compiled, held the lordship of a large part of the present county of Kildare and parts of Wicklow, including the powerful church of Glendalough.[1] At this time also, the family controlled the kingship of Uí Mhuireadhaigh and the headship of Glendalough, the latter receiving precedence from the scribe, who placed Giolla Comhghaill, coarb of Caoimhghin, in first place. Giolla Comhghaill was murdered by a rival family in 1127, but his son, Muircheartach Ua Tuathail, held the lordship of Uí Mhuireadhaigh until 1164. About this time, the Book of Leinster was being compiled and its scribe, having written out Muircheartach's pedigree, grandly describing its subject as king of Leinster, added a note on his children, first of whom was Lorcán *ardeasbog Laighean*, 'archbishop of Leinster', followed by Giolla Comhghaill, king of Uí Mhuireadhaigh, and Mór, wife of Diarmuid na nGall, also described as king of Leinster.[2] By then, Lorcán had already left Glendalough, where he had held the abbacy until 1162, and was now head of the community in Christ Church, and archbishop of Dublin. Moreover, at that point he had ceased to attract the attention of the native chroniclers and, for this reason, the record of his career depends almost entirely on an account of his life and miracles compiled at Eu in Normandy in the period between his death in 1180 and canonization in 1225.[3] As the text was drawn up in part from testimony provided by Irish informants, and as its treatment of Irish names of persons and places is generally accurate, its witness to Lorcán's career is considered to be reliable.[4]

Born about 1128, Lorcán spent some time as a boy in hostageship at the house of Diarmuid, king of Leinster, as a means of ensuring his father's loyalty.[5] Harshly treated at first, he was sent to the monastery of Glendalough about 1140, where he remained until elected abbot about 1153, probably with Diarmuid's support, at the young age of twenty-five.[6] At Glendalough, which, we are told, was famous for the many miracles performed there by Caoimhghin, Lorcán led an exemplary life, protecting those in danger, and adopting the name of the levite and martyr Laurentius (Irish Labhrás).[7] His elevation to the rank of archbishop of Dublin in 1162 was again probably largely due to Diarmuid's support.[8] One of his first acts was to introduce the rule of the canons regular of St Augustine to the community at Christ Church, Dublin's cathedral, much as he appears also to have previously done at Glendalough, where the Augustinian priory of St

Saviour's is thought to have been founded by him.[9] During Lent, he is said to have been in the habit of returning to Glendalough, where he followed the example of Caoimhghin by retiring to a cave.[10]

The remainder of Lorcán's relatively short life was spent in the shadow of the English conquest of Ireland, which began in 1169. For the next eleven years, until his death in 1180, the archbishop was primararily engaged in diplomacy which involved regular visits to England and, further afield, to Normandy, in the hope of securing favourable terms for the Irish church from a reluctant Henry II.[11] A visit to the Pope in Rome during this time saw him appointed papal legate, a position which, it was thought, would strengthen his hand in the negotiations.[12] On occasion, Henry sought to avoid meeting Lorcán and, in 1180, while on a mission to the court to negotiate on behalf of the 'high-king', Ruaidhrí Ua Conchobhair of Connacht, Lorcán found himself obliged to follow the king to Normandy, where he subsequently fell ill at the priory of Eu.[13] Here, he died 'in the fullness of his days' – although only about 52 – on the 18th calend of December (14 November).[14]

Apart from the Annals of the Four Masters, which erroneously attributes martyrdom to Lorcán, and the Annals of Clonmacnoise, both probably retrospectively, and both placing the death in England, none of the Irish annals records Lorcán's death.[15] Nor is there any record in these sources of any action undertaken by him during his lifetime, other than his presence at the synod of Clonfert in 1179, which is noted (under the wrong year) in the Annals of Clonmacnoise.[16] He receives a bare mention from Geoffrey Keating, who renders his name Labhrás, in connection with the negotiations that accompanied Earl Strongbow's siege of Dublin.[17]

The saint was buried where he died, at Eu and, following the elevation of his remains five years later and their reburial in a crypt by the altar of St Leger, moves were set in train to have Lorcán canonized.[18] He was canonized by Pope Honorius III on 11 December 1225, and his remains were translated on 10 May of the following year to their present position in front of the main altar of the church. Notices of the saint's death and translation were entered in the calendar and martyrology of the Book of Obits of Christ Church, which survives in a copy made about 1253, and also in several post-Conquest Dublin calendars.[19] The Christ Church martyrology also lays claim to possession of some relics of Lorcán.[20] Otherwise, however, if the seventeenth-century Martyrology of Donegal and some late calendars are set aside, no vernacular text of this kind notices Lorcán's feast.[21]

1 *CGH* 117c1; *CínCC* 316–33; *DIB* ix, 604–7. **2** *LL* 44938–51 (337d); *CGH* 117c26. **3** *AB* 33, 121–82. **4** *Rep. Nov.* 1, 54–9. **5** *AB* 33, 129 §2. **6** Ibid. 130–1 §4, 182. **7** Ibid. 132–5 §5. **8** Ibid. 136–7 §7. **9** *MRHI* 170–1, 177. **10** *AB* 33, 141–2 §10. **11** Ibid. 141–6 §§12–15. **12** Ibid. 146–7 §16. **13** Ibid. 152–5 §§25–6. **14** Ibid. **15** *AFM s.a* 1180; *AClon.* 214. **16** *AClon.* 213. **17** *FFÉ* iii, 336. **18** *AB* 33, 156, 158–63 §§27, 29–31; *PPPMI* 327–8. **19** *BOM* 65, 71, 114, 178; *MartFC* 88, 198; *Rep. Nov.* 1, 313; ibid. 2, 45, 48–9, 63. **20** *BOM* 4, 141; *MartFC* 131. **21** *MartD* 308; *Celtica* 4, 168 §268).

LORN of Aghamore. *See* Lorn of Kilcoony.

Lorn of Kilcoony (Ceall Chunna), parish of Ballyclog, barony of Dungannon Upper, Co. Tyrone. Lorn (also Loarn) was among the fifteen bishops and two virgins said to have been born of Dairearca, sister of Patrick.[1] Within the list, he is placed immediately after Lúrán of Derryloran (Doire Lúráin), not far from Kilcoony in the same barony. Bishop Lorn is also associated with the church of Bright (Breachtan) in the Down barony of Lecale Upper, where he is said to have censured Patrick for driving away a boy playing nearby.[2] The later martyrologies provided Lorn with a feast of 11 September.[3] Twelve days before, on 30 August, fell the feastday of a namesake and probable double, Lorn of Aghamore (Achadh Mór) in the Mayo barony of Costello, who was counted among Patrick's bishops.[4]

1 *CGSH* §722.16. 2 *BP* 416–20; *VT* 38–40. 3 *MartG* 174; *MartD* 244 4 *MartT* 67; *MartG* 166; *MartD* 228; *HDGP* i, 21; *PTBA* 170 §6.

Luach. *See* Lughaidh of Clonleigh.

Luachán. *See* Lóchán.

Luaithrinn of Killoran (Ceall Luaithrinn), barony of Leyny, Co. Sligo. Usually attached by the genealogists to the Cianachta, this daughter of Colmán was sometimes assigned to the Luighne who gave name to the barony of Leyny.[1] Formerly, as is shown by several references, this part of Leyny may have lain within the territory of Corann, whence the name to the adjoining barony of Corran.[2] It was among the saints of the Luighne that Luaithrinn was numbered, as is shown by the text entitled 'Four Saints' which attributes to Cormac of Killala a prophecy concerning her and other local patrons, including Nathí (Dathí) and Mobhí.[3] It was allegedly through Luaithrinn's intercession that the daughter of a king of Cianachta, hitherto barren, became pregnant with Niall Frasach (†778), later overking of Tara.[4] A litany-style prayer of invocation includes Luaithrinn among many other female saints.[5] The saint's feast fell on 8 June and she may also have been remembered on that day in Springlawn (*Cluain Luaithrinne*) in the Galway parish of Ballynakill, barony of Killian.[6]

1 *CGSH* §197; *GRSH* 123; *Lgen*. 742.5. 2 *MartD* 148. 3 *IrT* iii, 4–5 §11. 4 *FAI* 66 (§177). 5 *MartT* 108; *IrL* 92. 6 *MartT* 48; *MartG* 112; *MartD* 148; Logainm.ie 'Springlawn'.

Lubaid, sister of Patrick. Among Patrick's sisters, who are first mentioned in the ninth-century Tripartite Life, Lubaid (Lupait) appears to have been accorded seniority. She figures more often than any other, initially as the subject of one of the first miracles attributed to Patrick, who revived her as a child close to death, then as a captive with her brother in Ireland and, having been discovered in the 'sin of lust', as the object of the saint's wrath, resulting in her death.[1] The issue of her illicit liaison, Aodhán of Inis Lothair, does not figure among the children of the Maca Baird (An Bard/Restitutus/Reistitiúid), credited to her in the tract on the mothers of the saints.[2] With Patrick's other sisters, Tighris and Dairearca (with whom she is sometimes confused), and mother Cochmhas, Lubaid is elsewhere in the Tripartite Life described as a nun responsible for providing altar linen, and as an embroidress.[3]

1 *BP* 134–44, 195–200, 2774–87; *VT* 12, 16, 234. 2 *CGSH* §722.15. 3 *BP* 2963–4, 3142–3; *VT* 252, 266.

Luchair of Ceall Ealgraighe, now possibly an ecclesiastical site in the townland of Calliaghstown, parish of Kells, Co. Meath. Luchair allegedly possessed a cow at Ceall Ealgraighe which was forcibly taken from her by Breasal, son of Diarmuid, king of Tara, who, having been put to death by his father, was restored to life by Beagán of Emlagh.[2] Nothing else is known of Luchair, but her feast fell on 23 December.[3]

1 *HDGP* iii, 166. 2 *ZCP* 7, 305–7; *MartT* 102–4; *MartD* 94–6. 3 *MartT* 88; *MartG* 244; *MartD* 346.

Lucherinus. *See* Luchtighearn.

Luchraidh, Patrick's *saor*, 'artificer'. Patrick is reputed to have had three artificers, of whom Luchraidh was one.[1] Nothing else is known of him.

1 *CGSH* §672.14.

Luchtighearn of Tomfinlough (Tuaim Fionnlocha), barony of Bunratty Lower, Co. Clare. When visited in 1839 by Eugene O'Curry, there was no patron saint remembered in the parish of Tomfinlough, despite the presence of a holy well near the church, but a visit to the church now will show that memory of the local saint has been revived.[1] Luchtighearn son of Lughaidh is said to have belonged to the Tradraighe whose lands were almost co-extensive with the barony of Bunratty, and his mother Brígh, whose womb was allegedly blessed by Colum of Terryglass, was variously associated paternally with Aodh Damháin (†633), king of west Munster, and with Forannán, of a branch of the Oirghialla whose terrritory later corresponded approximately to that of the diocese of Clogher.[2]

Among other mentions of the saint is one in a passage in the Life of Mac Reithe of Kilmacrehy. This describes how Mac Reithe, accompanied by Mainchín, patron of Kilmanaheen (the parish adjoining Kilmacrehy), visited Luchtighearn at Tomfinlough on the way home from Emly, Munster's primatial church, to request that he assist in seeking a delay in the payment of cattle-tribute by the people of Thomond to a Connacht king.[3] Similarly, in a poem in Classical Irish, Luchtighearn, together with numerous other saints, was called upon to help in releasing Ireland's southern half (Leath Mogha) from a bondage imposed on it by the northern half (Leath Chuinn), championed by Finnian of Clonard.[4] The biographer of Mochaomhóg of Leigh (Lemakevoge) placed Luchtighearn among a group of saints, including Molua, Fionnbharr, and Laichtín, sent by their master, Comhghall of Bangor, to found churches throughout Ireland, whereas the biographer of Colum of Terryglass described Luchtighearn as Colum's disciple.[5] According to the Life of Íde of Killeedy, Luchtighearn was a frequent visitor to her church, once arriving there in the company of Laisréan of Holywood.[6] The saint is included, together with Sceanbhán and Blathmhac, among those on whom Seanán of Scattery could rely and also, grouped together with the same saints, among the numerous children of Inghean Bhaoith of Killinaboy.[7]

Because of a modern misunderstanding of a note by John Colgan that refers to Tomfinlough as 'Inis Tomensis', Luchtighearn has also come to be regarded as patron of Ennistimon.[8] As patron of Kilkeasy in the Kilkenny barony of Knocktopher, where his mill is said neither to have ground on a Sunday, nor to have worked with anything that was stolen, he was remembered variously as 'Luthernus' and 'Lucherinus'.[9] Though the saint's regular feast fell on 28 April – mistakenly placed by Bishop Phelan of Ossory on 28 May – at Cullen in the Cork barony of Duhallow, where Luchtighearn was transmuted into a female named Latiaran, the main day was 25 July or, as the calendar in Maynooth manuscript M 84 asserts, 10 November.[10] There, too, in keeping with the origin of the name, from *Lugh-tighearn*, 'lord Lugh', the saint was patron of the local *Lughnasadh* festival.[11]

1 *ACoC* 200. 2 *CGSH* §722.104B; *CGH* 141b40–54, 151a4; *AI s.a.* 633; *VSSH* 230 §22. 3 *MHH* 23 §§34–5. 4 RIA MS 23L11, 263; *SAM* 24.1, 17, 20. 5 *VSHP* ii, 168 §10; *VSSH* 230 §22, 231 §27. 6 Ibid. 127 §31. 7 *ZCP* 10, 28 §22; *IrT* iv, 93 §7. 8 *ASH* 72 (26); *LIS* iv, 530; *MRHI* 383. 9 *THEH* 133; *IVN* 216–17; *HADO* iv, 5–6. 10 *MartT* 37; *MartG* 86; *MartD* 112; *HADO* iv, 5; Maynooth MS M 84, 229. 11 *FL* 268–74.

Lughach of Coolbanagher (Cúil Bheannchair), barony of Portnahinch, Co. Laois, and of Banagher (Cúil Bheannchair), parish of Devenish, barony of Magheraboy, Co. Fermanagh. Two other churches were also assigned to Lughach son of Lughaidh (alias Luchta), at Rattoo in the Kerry barony of Clanmaurice, and at Toomour in the Sligo barony of Corran. The Kerry church is best suited to the saint's pedigree, which attaches him to the Ciarraighe, and echoes his maternal descent from Meadhbh daughter of Garbhán of another branch of the same family.[1] At Toomour, his memory appears to have given way to an otherwise unattested Crom whose day fell on 9 July, eight days after the feast of Lughaidh son of Luighe (perhaps from Lugh).[2] Despite the number of his churches, possibly based on a list compiled to serve several saints of the name, little else is recorded of Lughach.[3] His feastday fell on 6 October.[4]

1 *CGSH* §§295, 722.99; *GRSH* 108; *Lgen*. 733.12. 2 OSL SO 149; *MartT* 53; *MartG* 128; *MartD* 184. 3 *JCS* 1, 196–8. 4 *MartT* 77; *MartO*[2] 215; *MartG* 190; *MartD* 266.

Lughaidh of Ceanna Droma, now probably Kilbarry in the parish of Castlelyons, barony of Condons and Clangibbon, Co. Cork.[1] This son of Fiontan is known from two sources only, the list of homonymous saints, under the guise of Molua, and the early vernacular Life of Fionnbharr, according to which he received a gift of an altar vessel of white bronze, on surrendering his church to the patron of Cork.[2]

1 *HDGP* iv, 87. 2 *CGSH* §707.562; *BBa*. 68 §23.

Lughaidh of Clonleigh (Cluain Laogh), barony of Raphoe North, Co. Donegal. According to the genealogists, this son of Eacha belonged to a branch of the Ceinéal Eoghain located in an area called the Bréadach on the eastern side of Inishowen (Inis Eoghain).[1] His two brothers, also saints, were Dochonna of Eas Mac nEirc, now Assylin in the Roscommon barony of Boyle, and Bishop Cormac who was possibly identical with a priest so named at Tulach Inneann, now perhaps Tullynavinn in the parish of Moville Upper, barony of Inishowen.[2]

Despite the importance that was allegedly once attached to his church, little is known of Lughaidh (alias Luach), beyond his feastday which fell on 24 March.[3] Apparently misled by John Colgan, John O'Donovan considered Cairneach of Dulane to have been patron of the parish of Clonleigh.[4] Documents dating to the early seventeenth century used the corrupt (Latin) forms *Cluoghus*, *Douglus* and *Doughus* to refer to the saint.[5]

1 *CGSH* §83; *HDGP* ii, 173. 2 *MartG* 238; *MartD* 336. 3 *MartT* 26; *MartG* 60; *MartD* 86; *Celtica* 1, 79, 84. 4 OSL DL 157. 5 *DYHS* 196; *UJA* (2nd ser.) 1, 248; *AnH* 12, 109.

Lughaidh of Cluain Fionnchoill. Although given the privilege by Adhamhnán of being one of the Irish saints to whom Colum Cille's death was revealed in a vision, the 'just and wise' Lughaidh son of Tulchán is otherwise unknown.[1] He may have been related to Munna son of Tulchán of Taghmon to whom Adhamhnán gave the same privilege. Despite the best efforts of Adhamhnán's editors, Lughaidh's church has not been satisfactorily identified.[2]

1 *VC*[1] 530–2. 2 *ASH* 453; *TT* 386; *VC*[1] 235–6.

Lughaidh of Kilpatrick (formerly 'Dromiskelle'/Druim Ionasclainn), barony of Fore, Co. Westmeath.[1] According to the genealogists, Lughaidh was a son of Aonghas son of Nadh Fraoich, ancestor of all the main lines of descent of the Eoghanacht dynasties of Munster, and well known as Patrick's protagonist on the latter's first visit to Cashel, as retold in the saint's Tripartite Life.[2] Curiously, in an earlier passage of the same text, Lughaidh is introduced as a member of Patrick's *familia* or household and provided with the alias 'Dolua Craoibhighe', under which guise he has been shown to be patron and eponym of the Westmeath parish of Killua.[3] In other respects, Lughaidh was obscure by comparison with his brother, Colmán son of Daráine, who is featured in several Lives of saints. Lughaidh's feast fell on 2 November, a day shared with Earc Sláine, Patrick's judge.[4]

1 *ILL* 118–19. 2 *CGSH* §321; *GRSH* 118; *Lgen.* 740.4; *CGH* 148a53. 3 *BP* 841–2; *VT* 76; *PNW* 46–7; *ILL* 117–19. 4 *MartG* 210; *MartD* 294.

Lughaidh of Kilroosk, which may now represent an earlier Cúil Rúscach, parish of Killasnet, Co. Leitrim.[1] A list of churches in the diocese of Kilmore, compiled in the early seventeenth century, includes a reference to Lughaidh of Cúil Rúscach, accompanied by the calendar date of 12 February.[2] The list of those commemorated on this day likewise includes Lughaidh, of whom, however, nothing else is known.[3]

1 *Celtica* 1, 65; *Census 1659*, 568. 2 *Celtica* 1, 65. 3 *MartT* 16; *MartG* 34; *MartD* 46.

Lughaidh of Teernacreeve (Tír Dhá Chraobh), parish of Castletownkindalen, barony of Moycashel, Co. Westmeath. Lughaidh (alias Lugh) son of Eachaidh is known from an entry in the corpus of saints' pedigrees which attaches him, together with several siblings, to the Ceinéal Laoghaire of Meath.[1] Among his brothers and sisters were Colmán (Colum) of Slanore, Nainnidh of Kiltoom, Muireadhach of Killala, and Comaigh, also of Slanore. His mother is said to have been Aighleann daughter of Léinín, a sister of Colmán of Cloyne.[2] Little else about the saint is on record, but that his feast fell on 31 January.[3]

1 *CGSH* §160; *Lgen.* 707.12. 2 *CGSH* §722.31. 3 *MartT* 13; *MartG* 26; *MartD* 32.

Lughaidh of Uí Mhaine. *See* Maolán of Kilmoylan.

Lughaidh son of Luchta. *See* Lughach of Coolbanagher.

Lughaidh son of Ocha (Oiche?). *See* Molua of Kyle.

Lughaidh Oilithir, 'pilgrim', of 'Ceall an Oilithir' on Garumna Island, parish of Killannin, barony of Moycullen, Co. Galway, and of Clongesh (Cluain Géise), barony and county of Longford. A note added to the entries for 12 May in the Martyrology of Tallaght states that the *Oilithir* remembered on that day was a brother of Muadhán Oilithir of Ceall Mhuadháin, now perhaps 'Grave Yard' in the townland of Kilmahon and parish of Killoe, which adjoins Clongesh.[1] Little else is known of either saint, but Muadhán's feast fell on 6 March.[2] A note added by Míchéal Ó Cléirigh to his entry on Muadhán speculates (erroneously) that he may have been the saint of the name mentioned in the Life of Fionnbharr, and it has also been suggested that he was the Muadhán who treated Colum Cille inhospitably, when the latter was on his way to visit Cruimhthear Fraoch at Cloone after the battle of Cúil Dreimhne.[3] Yet another Muadhán, who was remembered on 30 August, gave name to Aireagal Muadháin, a church that is taken to be Errigal Trough in the Monaghan barony of Trough.[4] Muadhán may also have given name to Tymon in the Dublin parish of Tallaght.[5]

1 *MartT* 112; *HDGP* iv, 30; cf. *JACAS* 2, 24–7. 2 *MartT* 21; *MartG* 48; *JACAS* ii, 27. 3 *MartD* 64; *HDA* 620–23. 4 *MartT* 67; *MartG* 166; *MartD* 228. 5 Logainm.ie 'Tymon'.

Lughna of Aonach Finn, an unidentified church in Slieve Aughty (Eachtgha) on the borders of Galway and Clare. Lughna is known from two poems, one enumerating the saints ready to come to the assistance of Seanán of Scattery, the other listing the numerous progeny of Inghean Bhaoith of Killinaboy.[1]

1 *ZCP* 10, 26 §20; *IrT* iv, 93 §3; *HDGP* i, 64.

Lughna of Kiltrasna (Ceall Trasna), parish of Killeany, barony of Clare, Co. Galway, This *cruimhthear*, 'priest', one of seven sons of Restitutus (An Bard/Reistitiúid), was regarded both as Patrick's disciple and as his sister's son.[1] His mother's name was Lubaid (Lupait) and among his siblings was the much better-known Usaille, patron of Killashee.[2] Lughna's other claim to fame was his role as Patrick's *luamhaire*, 'steersman'.[3] Lying not far north of Kiltrasna, a holy well at 'Toberloona' (Tobar Lughna) in the townland of Cornfield, parish of Robeen, may also have been dedicated to him and, representing his church, he is among the saints said, tendentiously, to have owed tribute to Caillín of Fenagh.[4] Nearby, on Lough Mask, was a site named Fearta Tíre Féic, at which Brighid was fostered.[5] He was remembered on 20 January.[6]

1 *CGSH* §177; *Lgen.* 751.8. 2 *CGSH* §722.15. 3 Ibid. §672.25. 4 *Lgen.* 272.3.4, 279.8; *BFen.* 286. 5 *CGSH* §178; *Lgen.* 751.8. 6 *MartT* 10; *MartG* 20; *MartD* 22.

Lughna of Letterluna (Leitir Lughna), barony of Ballybritt, Co. Offaly. Lughna's church was located in the townland of Letter, and nearby was a well, 'Tober Lugna', said to have been frequented annually on 27 April.[1] However, when visited in 1837 by Thomas O'Conor, the saint's day was not remembered.[2] The martyrologists placed Lughna's feast two days earlier, on 25 April, a day shared by Mac Caille of Croghan.[3]

1 *AIOY* 118–19. **2** OSL OY ii, 205. **3** *MartT* 36; *MartG* 84; *MartD* 110.

Lughna of Tobberloona. *See* Lughna of Kiltrasna.

Lughna son of Maonach. A brother of seven other saints, including Fachtna of Ross, Lughna was attached to the Corca Laoighdhe, whose territory corresponded approximately to that of the diocese of Ross.[1] One seventeenth-century source speculatively suggested that he was identical with Lughna the deacon who was commemorated on 31 December.[2]

1 *CGSH* §§298.1, 730; *Lgen.* 744.5. **2** *GRSH* 128.

Luiceall daughter of Léinín. *See* Aighleann of Killiney.

Luiceannán. *See* Conach.

Luidhean daughter of Léinín. *See* Aighleann daughter of Léinín.

Luighbhe of Drumbo. *See* Molua son of Sineall.

Luigsech. *See* Laoighseach.

Lúireach of Maghera (Ráith Lúirigh), barony of Loughinsholin, Co. Derry. Attached to the Uí Mhic Uais, Lúireach (Lúrach) was one of four sons of Cuana son of Dáire.[1] A brother of his, Béag, attained the headship of his people and ultimately also the kingship of the kingdom of Oirghialla, later approximately the equivalent of the diocese of Clogher, before dying at the side of his overlord and claimant to the high-kingship, Aodh son of Ainmhire, in the battle of Dún Bolg in Wicklow in 598.[2] A second brother, Diarmuid, was attached to the church of Ceall Mhaoláin Maighe na Sealga, now possibly Kilwullaun in the Galway parish of Donaghpatrick.[3] The church named after Lúireach lay within the territory of the Uí Thuirtre who, having crossed the Bann, gave name to the deanery of Turtery in Antrim.[4] A saintly sister named Lann is also attested.[5]

Lúireach's main claim to fame was his choice as the bishop brought 'from afar' to baptize Cainneach of Kilkenny, a native, according to the latter's Life, of the area about Dungiven in the county of Derry.[6] Under the guise of Lúrán (Luarán/Lúrach), patron of the Tyrone church of Derryloran (Doire Lúráin), a little south of Maghera, he was associated with a *duanaire*, 'poem book', and his church was reputedly the location of a revision undergone by *Uraiceacht na nÉigeas*, 'the primer of the poets'.[7] Despite the chronological difficulties raised by his apparent floruit of *c.*600, he came to be regarded as a son of Patrick's sister Dairearca.[8] What appears to have been Lúireach's main feast fell on 17 February, but he was also remembered at Derryloran on 29 October.[9] When opened, his grave at Maghera reputedly revealed a silver crucifix.[10] The saint shares his name with the patron of Killury in the Kerry barony of Clanmaurice, but, though rounds used to be made at this saint's well, the day has not been recorded.[11] In an early seventeenth-century description of the diocese of Derry his name is written *Lourachus*.[12]

1 *CGSH* §79; *GRSH* 67; *Lgen.* 713.4; PNNI v, 168. **2** *CGH* 333c43; *AU s.a.* **3** *HDGP* iv, 18. **4** *CGH* 333c47–51; *MedI* 232; *SacH* 230–46. **5** *CGSH* §307. **6** *VSHH* 182 §§1–2; *VSHP* i, 152 §1. **7** *CGSH* §722.16; *AurÉ* 2622–44; *Peritia* 8, 133 §60. **8** *CGSH* §722.16. **9** *MartT* 17, 85; *MartG* 38, 206; *MartD* 52, 286. **10** *PNCL* 220. **11** *ACoK* 43; *JKAHS* 17, 124; *JRSAI* 88, 155. **12** *AnH* 12, 108, 110.

Lúirint son of Dubhthan. *See* Comán son of Dubhthan.

Lunny. *See* Maol Anfaidh.

Lupait. *See* Lubaid.

Lúrán. *See* Lúireach.

Luthernus. *See* Luchtighearn.

M

Mac (Mic), 'son (sons)'. Many saints, both male (*mac*) and female (*inghean*), are known by reference to their fathers. In the cases of both males and (much less frequently) females this method is sometimes used to identify single saints, as is shown by the title *Aoinmhic Éireann*, 'Ireland's singular sons', applied to a list containing 82 entries.[1] More commonly, however, the sons were more than one, as is shown by the title *Macradh Naomh Éireann*, 'Ireland's saints, designated sons', which accounts for 210 entries.[2] The presentation of women in groups of this kind is exemplified by the title *Ingheanradha naomh Éireann*, 'Ireland's saints, designated daughters', attached to a list containing 108 entries.[3] The vast majority of the saints in these lists, male and female, are otherwise unattested. On occasion, *mac* appears to have diminutive force, as in Mac Laisre for Laisréan (Molaise) and Mac Luim for Lomán.

1 *CGSH* §710. 2 Ibid. §709. 3 Ibid. §711.

Mac Alprainn. *See* Patrick.

Mac an Deagha. *See* Earc of Altraighe.

Mac an Éigis. *See* Éidchéan; Onchú.

Mac an Fhile. *See* Feargna of Ceall Mhic an Fhile.

Mac an tSaoir. *See* Ciarán of Clonmacnoise.

Macartan. *See* Mac Caorthainn.

Mac Aoibhléin. *See* Aonghas of Tallaght; Maonach of Dunleer; Mocheallóg of Inch.

Mac Bric. *See* Aodh of Rahugh.

Maccabeus. *See* Giolla Mochaidhbheo.

Mac Caille of Croghanhill (Cruacha of Brí Éile), straddling the parishes of Croghan and Ballyburly, barony of Lower Philipstown, Co. Offaly. While in the territory of the Uí Néill, Patrick is said by his seventh-century biographer Tíreachán to have founded a large number of churches, including one in Magh Thulach – later represented by the Westmeath barony of Fartullagh – in which Brighid 'received the veil from the hands of Mac Caille'.[1] Tíreachán's source was probably the seventh-century Life of Brighid, compiled by Cogitosus, which also attributes this action to Mac Caille, albeit without reference to a place.[2] Later versions of Brighid's veiling, though still making reference to Magh Thulach, present Mac Caille in a subordinate role, as assistant to Meal, patron of Ardagh.[3] These sources place the saint at Croghanhill in a part of Offaly that later belonged to the diocese of Kildare.[4] Mac Caille again figures, together with Meal, in the list of fifteen bishops born, according to the tract on the mothers of the saints, to Dairearca, sister of Patrick.[5] Patrician propagandists went as far as to describe Mac

Caille as 'Patrick's bishop', and a well on Croghanhill is dedicated to Patrick.[6] His obit is entered in the annals for 490 and his feastday was 25 April.[7]

1 *PTBA* 136 §16.3; *DIB* v, 755; *CI* i, 79n. **2** *TT* 519 §3. **3** *BBr.* 6 §§17–18. **4** *LH* i, 114; *MartO²* 66, 118. **5** *CGSH* §722.16. **6** Ibid. §672.5; *CDKL* 260; *Dinn.* 2, 32; *AIOY* 115. **7** *MartT* 36; *MartO²* 108; *MartG* 84; *MartD* 110; *AU s.a.*

Mac Caorthainn of Clogher (Clochar), barony of Clogher, Co. Tyrone. Patron of a see that was later often known by the population name Oirghialla, Mac Caorthainn (anglicized Macartan) was attached by the genealogists through his father Cainneach to the Dál nAraidhe of north Down and south Antrim.[1] Although this would provide a suitable explanation for the form Fear Dá Chríoch, 'man of two territories', which is said, perhaps spuriously, to have been the saint's first name, it is nowhere cited as such.[2] This is but one of the many disharmonies in the saint's record. Another, the belief that he was among the seventeen children born of Dairearca, Patrick's sister, is affirmed only by a note added to the Martyrology of Aonghas.[3] The saint's Patrician links were otherwise strong enough to have him regarded as Patrick's *tréinfhear*, 'strong man, champion', whose duties included carrying his master over rough ground, and a poem on Patrick's Purgatory addresses him and other saints.[4] Later, when old and infirm, and with all his companions already established in churches, he is said to have petitioned Patrick finally to grant him also a church, whereupon he was left in Clogher, and with him, allegedly, the famous (still extant) reliquary 'sent from heaven' and known as *Domhnach Airgid*.[5] Much earlier, in the seventh-century Life composed by Muirchú, Clogher was given the considerable honour of being the starting point of the journey that carried Patrick's remains to Downpatrick.[6]

Mac Caorthainn's own Life, a late composition that survives in acephalous form in two sources, the Salamancan codex and, in a slightly revised version, the Register of Clogher, likewise finds room for Patrick in the story of the founding of Clogher. It allows Patrick to instruct Mac Caorthainn as to where he should build the church – on level ground in front of the royal seat of Oirghialla – and enumerates the relics that the church was to hold, including a crozier and shrine containing, among other items, hairs of the Blessed Virgin and a fragment of the Holy Cross.[7] Sometimes implausibly taken to reflect Clogher concerns from as early as the eighth century, the Life in its present form dates to after the synod of Rathbrassil in 1111, when the see, which is mentioned in the Life, was first established.[8]

A mere fragment by comparison with other such texts, Mac Caorthainn's Life was probably compiled in the house of canons regular in Clogher, where the Salamancan codex also appears to have been kept.[9] Its principal aim was to demonstrate the efficacy of spiritual power, especially when faced with the obduracy of temporal authority. Representative of the latter authority, and the only other local name to figure in the surviving fragment, was Eachaidh, king of Oirghialla, who appears as maternal grandfather of that saint in Tighearnach of Clones' Life.[10] Wishing to install his grandson in the episcopal see, Eachaidh proposed to expel Mac Caorthainn, only to have his plan thwarted by

Tighearnach's humility. Together with Tighearnach, Mac Caorthainn is included in the list of Ireland's apostles, as preserved in the vernacular Life of Molaise of Devenish, and Náile's biographer invoked his assistance, under the guise of Bishop Cárthann, against those neglectful of the Kinawley saint's tribute.[11] According to the Register of Clogher, Mac Caorthainn ceded primacy in the occupancy of his see to Mochta of Louth.[12] Although his main feast fell on 24 March, Mac Caorthainn was also remembered as Fear Dá Chríoch on 15 August.[13] He died, according to the annals, in 506 and his relics, including a bell and a head-bone, were kept at Clogher.[14]

1 *CGSH* §95; *GRSH* 95; *Lgen.* 728.7; *AU* ind. (Airgialla, Dalaraide)); *DIB* v, 756–7. **2** *CGSH* §703.13; *MartO²* 186. **3** *MartO²* 68. **4** *CGSH* §§671.4, 672.5; *BP* 2041–51; *MartD* 220; *TEAB* 522 §ff. **5** *BP* 2041–51; *TRIA* 18.1, 18; *Kenney* 638–9. **6** *PTBA* 120 §11.9. **7** *VSHH* 343–6 at 344 §1; *ClRec.* 7, 424–30; ibid. 20, 43–69. **8** Ibid. 11, 305–25; *VSHH* 346 §7. **9** *ClRec.* 14.2, 71. **10** *VSHH* 111 §14, 344 §2. **11** *SG* i, 24, 35; *MHH* 121 §53. **12** *ClRec.* 7, 376–8. **13** *MartT* 26, 63; *MartO²* 176, 186; *MartG* 60, 156; *MartD* 218–20. **14** *AU s.a.*; *ClRec.* 7, 375; *EMH* 484–5 §224.

MAC CAORTHAINN of Coolcor (Cúil Chorra), parish and barony of Granard, Co. Longford. To judge by the sixteenth chapter of his Life of Patrick, which is concerned with the saint's activities among the southern Uí Néill, Tíreachán was acutely aware of the presence locally of prior interests, and especially those of Kildare whose patron Brighid is twice explicitly mentioned.[1] One mention relates to Mac Caille, who is said to have veiled Brighid. The other, while attributing to Patrick a church at the *fossa* (Irish *ráith*, 'fort') of Dallbhrónach (incidentally the name of the Kildare saint's grandfather), states that it was held by Brighid's uncle, Mac Caorthainn. As it happens, Mac Caorthainn is not among the many uncles claimed for Brighid in the tract on the mothers of the saints.[2] Tíreachán went on to attribute to Patrick the founding of Coolcor, which is almost certainly the church otherwise associated with Mac Caorthainn – together with several companions, including Conlaodh – in the list of those said to have been subject to Brighid of Kildare.[3] Kilbride (Ceall Bhrighde) in the parish of Abbeylara lies close to the town of Granard, a few miles only from Coolcor.

1 *PTBA* 136 §§16.1, 16.3. **2** *CGSH* §722.3–13. **3** *PTBA* 136 §16.5; *CGSH* §670.

MAC CÉACHT, Patrick's smith. Known only from the various versions of the list of the twenty-four 'in orders' with Patrick, Mac Céacht's duty was to provide his patron with bells.[1]

1 *CGSH* §§671 (11), 672.13, 710.50; *BP* 2959–60, 3138–40; *VT* 250, 266.

MAC CÉILE. In a poem on the two branches of the Uí Dheagha – of Ossory and of Leinster – placed in the mouth of Moling of St Mullin's, five saints are named as witnesses, the first two of whom, Muicín (alias Aonghas Láimhiodhan) and Scoithín, were associated with churches in north Kilkenny (Moyne) and south Laois (Slievemargy).[1] Mac Céile is third in the list, which is completed by a Bishop Colmán, possibly of Connahy in the parish of Grangemacomb, not far from Moyne, and the obscure Feidhlimidh son of Iorlamhán. Although otherwise unattested, Mac Céile's church is probably also to be sought in north Kilkenny.

1 *Anecd.* ii, 36 §22.

Mac Coinne of Áth Dá Lárag, near Kells, barony of Upper Kells, Co. Meath. Since *mac* appears occasionally to have had diminutive force, Mac Coinne may represent Cainneach, a hypocoristic or pet form of Colum, patron of the nearby church of Kells. Mac Coinne (also Cainne), the 'great bishop', was remembered on 1 December.[1] Another (or the same) bishop of the name was attached through his father Fionnbharr to the descendants of Conall Cearnach, among whose branches were the seven Soghain, of whom Mac Coinne was declared to be the head.[2]

1 *MartO*[2] 257; *MartG* 230; *MartD* 324; *Ainm* 7, 85. **2** *BB* 164a44–6.

Mac Creiche. *See* Mac Reithe.

Mac Cuilinn of Lusk (Lusca), barony of Balrothery East, Co. Dublin. Said to have been originally known as both Cuinnidh – a variant hypocoristic form of Colum – and Luachán (Lóchán), Mac Cuilinn son of Cathmhogh was attached by the genealogists to the Cianachta, among whose branches was one located in Breagha, in the area immediately north of Lusk in Fingal (Fine Gall).[1] His mother, variously named Feidhealm and Tuilelaith, daughter of Maine of the Leinstermen, was related to both Cobhthach son of Fearghas, a bishop, and Diarmuid son of Cearbhall, king of the southern Uí Néill.[2] The lessons of the Life written for Mac Cuilinn in the Breviary of Lusk, which were borrowed almost completely from the Office Life composed about 1300 for Fionnbharr of Cork, have been rightly described as an 'impudent fraud'.[3] With little to go by, other than the fact that Fionnbharr was allegedly first known as Lóchán, the audacious author contented himself by and large with substituting Mac Cuilinn's name for that of the Cork saint.[4]

Outside this forgery, little is recorded of the saint. His name is invoked in the company of Colum Cille, Cainneach and Comhghall in a poem in praise of the patron of Iona, and he is said to have been sent as a messenger, along with Odhrán of Latteragh, to explain to Ciarán why the saints of Ireland were fasting against him, namely with the aim of shortening the Clonmacnoise saint's life and preventing his assumption of authority over all the churches of the country.[5] He and Odhrán are again brought together in the entry recording the latter's death in 548 but, according to most annals, Mac Cuilinn had already died in 496/498.[6] His feast fell on 6/7 September and holy wells were dedicated to him at Lusk and Grallagh in north Dublin.[7] Finally, his name is invoked in a poem attributed to Moling and, also, in a poem which locates him on Rathlin Island in Co. Antrim, together with three other saints, Colum Cille, Cainneach and Comhghall.[8]

1 *CGSH* §§319, 703.3; *GRSH* 124; *Lgen.* 739.9; *MartO*[2] 202; *DIB* v, 890. **2** *CGSH* §722.49; *ZCP* 13, 354. **3** *AB* 69, 328–30, 338–43; *BBa.* 163, 287–92. **4** *AB* 69, 328; *BBa.* 163. **5** *ZCP* 10, 53 §6; *AB* 69, 104. **6** *AU s.a.* 496/498; *AI* 496; ATig. *s.a.* 548. **7** *MartT* 68–9; *MartO*[2] 193; *MartG* 170; *MartD* 236; *Rep.Nov.* 2, 75; *AHWD* 12. **8** *Anecd.* ii, 28 §1; ZCP 10, 53 §6.

Mac Cuill of the Isle of Man (Mana). Perhaps because Armagh had some claim to jurisdiction over the Isle of Man, a great deal of space is devoted to Mac Cuill (alias Machalus, Maughold) in the Patrician record from Muirchú onwards.[1] Attaching him to the Maca Greaga (Greagraighe), a family whose settlements were scattered around Ireland, Muirchú described how the 'fierce and wicked' Mac Cuill first planned to kill Patrick, as he had previously killed many wayfarers, before converting in the face of a powerful miracle which saw one of his followers, feigning death, become fully dead. Ordered by Patrick to leave Ireland in fetters in an oarless and rudderless boat, Mac Cuill landed on the Isle of Man (Evonia), where he was met and succoured by two (otherwise unattested) holy bishops, named Conindrus and Rumilus, whom he later succeeded as bishop of Man. His affiliation to the Greagraighe was not entirely undisputed. Later genealogists numbered him among the saints of Uí Bhairrche, a people who gave name to both the Carlow deanery of Obargy and the Wexford barony of Bargy.[2] Little else is known of Mac Cuill, but confusion with Mac Caille led to his feast being assigned to 25 April.[3] At Kirk Maughold on Man the annual fair was held on 25 October.[4] Finally, an anonymous poem in Welsh on St Mechyll of Llanfechell in Anglesey identifies its subject, opportunistically, as Mac Cuill of Man.[5]

1 *PTBA* 102–6; *BP* 2612–46; *VT* 220–3; *PIM* 273–5; *DIB* v, 890–1. 2 *CGSH* §387; *Lgen*. 724.2; *CGH* 121a40; *MedI* 128, 250. 3 *ASH* 60 §7; *TT* 34 §71; *ODS* 254; *KSS* 380. 4 *ZCP* 13, 362–4. 5 *MWPSS* 70–2, 132–9.

Mac Cuirb of Aglishcormick (Eaglais Chormaic), a church in the barony of Clanwilliam, on Limerick's border with Tipperary , which takes its name from Cormac (*Corb –mac*), the equivalent through back-formation of Mac Cuirb. The saint belonged to the Dál Modula, an ecclesiastical family associated with the area about Emly on the Tipperary side of the border. He is otherwise known only from the various versions of the Life of Fionnbharr of Cork, which accord him particular honour. First, having himself allegedly been a pupil of Pope Gregory in Rome, and thus eminently qualified, he is given the task of instructing Fionnbharr in the scriptures and ecclesiastical rules, effectively higher learning.[1] Second, he is accorded the privilege of being the first to be interred in the sacred ground of Fionnbharr's newly founded church in Cork.[2] Mac Cuirb was chosen by Fionnbharr's discerning biographer probably because he was associated through a common ancestor with Ailbhe, patron of the primatial Munster church of Emly.[3] In this way, the Cork saint could be viewed as having vicariously received the blessing of Munster's highest ecclesiastic.

1 *BBa*. 66 §20, 140 §10. 2 Ibid. 76 §35. 3 *MakS* 108–11.

Mac Dara of St Macdara's Island (Cruach Mhic Dara / Oileán Mic Dara), off the southern coast of Connemara, in the parish of Moyrus, barony of Ballinahinch, Co. Galway. Few Irish saints have continued to attract as much devotion as Mac Dara, alias Sionach (Seanach), whose pattern is still observed annually on 16 July.[1] Many stories were told of the saint and of the misfortune that attended those sailors or fishermen who neglected to show due respect to Mac Dara when passing his island, with its remarkable early church, described as a 'petrified wooden construction'.[2] The saint's alias, still reflected in *Leac Sionach*, the name traditionally used of his altar-stone, derives from *sean*, 'old'. This is the form used in the martyrologies which, in contrast to the date of the saint's annual pattern, assign the festival of Sionach of Mac Dara's Island to 28 September.[3]

1 *CCT* 94–100; *PilgI* 96–9; *OFWC* 97–9, 102. 2 OSL GY iii, 116–19; *EarlyCI* 59; *Béaloideas* 3, 486. 3 *MartG* 186; *MartD* 260.

Mac Duach. *See* Colmán of Kilmacduagh.

Mac Eara of Kilmacar, barony of Fassadinin, Co. Kilkenny. Allegedly because he was in fear of the *Gaill*, 'foreigners / vikings', Moling of St Mullin's divided his books in three, taking one part to Aonghas Láimhiodhan of Moyne who carelessly placed them in the cave of Dearc Fearna (now probably Dunmore Cave in the neighbouring Kilkenny parish of Muckalee), thereby causing them to be damaged by floodwater.[1] A second batch was sent to Mac Eara who passed them on for repair to Ruadhán, doubtless at Tullaroan (Tulach Ruadháin) in the barony of Crannagh. As Mac Eara's 'house' is described as lying north of St Mullin's, there can be little doubt but that Kilmacar was intended, especially since Aonghas' church at Moyne lay close by.[2] Mac Eara, whose name has been speculatively rendered Mocheara or Mochara, is nowhere else attested and patronage of the parish later fell to Peter and Paul.[3]

1 *Anecd.* ii, 36–8. 2 Ibid. 38 §§18–20. 3 OSL KK i, 27; *HCK* 46.

Mac Earca of Donaghmore (Domhnach Mór Maighe Cobha), barony of Upper Iveagh, Co. Down. The genealogists attached Mac Earca son of Fraochán to the Ulaidh of north-east Ulster, and presented him as a close relative of Caolán of Nendrum and of Bishop Lóchán son of Duachán.[1] His mother, Brónach daughter of Míleac – the man 'with whom Patrick was in slavery' – gave name to Kilbroney (Ceall Bhróinche) in the Down barony of Iveagh Upper.[2] She is said to have been the mother of several noted saints, including Caolán, Damhnad of Tedavnet, and Fursa of Killursa.[3] Little more is known of Mac Earca, but he may have been identical with the bishop consecrated, according to Tíreachán, by Patrick at Ardstraw, shortly before the latter crossed the river Bann and entered the territory of the Ulaidh at Coleraine.[4] The church at Donaghmore was dedicated to him under the (Latin) guise of 'Archanus'.[5] Mac Earca's feastday fell on 17 September.[6]

1 *CGSH* §159; *GRSH* 104; *Lgen.* 737.8; PNNI i, 85. 2 *CGSH* §722.92. 3 Ibid. 4 *PTBA* 160 §48.2. 5 *RNF* 84. 6 *MartT* 73; *MartG* 178; *MartD* 250.

Mac Earca son of Draighean. *See* Ainmhire of Kilroe.

Mac Eirc A saint of this name was associated with Teltown in Co. Meath, one of Ireland's three most famous places of assembly.[1] Together with Patrick and Ciarán of 'Carn', possibly the patron of Castlekieran, some ten miles west of Teltown, Mac Eirc reputably acted as a guarantor of the assembly.[2] According to the Annals of Ulster, relics of his were also brought to Teltown in 784.[3] Only one saint of the name is commemorated in the martyrologies, which assign him to 18 November and, in one case, place him in an unidentified church named Ceall Achaidh.[4]

1 *Triads* 35; *SG* 73. 2 *MD* iv, 152. 3 *AU*[2] 784.9. 4 *MartG* 220; *MartD* 312.

Mac Í son of Amhairghin. *See* Colmán of Achadh Í.

Mac Ida. *See* Mac an Deagha.

Mac Laisre of Kilmaclasser (Ceall Mhic Laisre), barony of Burrishoole, Co. Mayo. During his visit to this relatively small parish in 1838, John O'Donovan was told how the local patron, corruptly called Mac Glaise, was deceived by Miodhna, patron of the larger neighbouring parish of Kilmeena, during a race to determine the boundary between their two jurisdictions.[1] It has recently been suggested that the story was invented to account for an early conflict in diocesan ownership.[2] As *mac* sometimes has diminutive force, Mac Laisre may represent Laisréan (alias Molaise of Devenish) whose cult spread into north Connacht, among other places to Inishmurray off the Sligo coast.[3]

1 OSL MO i, 491; *CnM* 20, 129. 2 p.c. (F. Mac Gabhann). 3 *IMPAL* 30.

Mac Laisre son of Conall Eachluath. Although attached by the genealogists to the Dál gCais of Thomond, either through its main line as a brother of the eponym Cas, or through a minor son named Cainneach (of the thirteen assigned to Cas), Mac Laisre is otherwise little known.[1] The saint of the name included in the list of those commemorated on 12 September is taken by some seventeenth-century sources to have been Mac Laisre of Thomond, but despite the alternative tradition that this man was the abbot of Armagh who died in 623, he is more likely to have been a doublet of Molaise of Devenish whose feast also fell on this day.[2] The same sources separately speculate that the Armagh prelate may have been Mac Laisre son of Lughaidh (Ubán) of the Ceinéal Eoghain.[3]

1 *CGSH* §203; *GRSH* 120; *Lgen*. 740.11; *CGH* 152a54. 2 *MartT* 70; *MartG* 174; *MartD* 246; *GRSH* 120; *NHI* ix, 238. 3 *MartD* 246; *GRSH* 47; *CGSH* §352.

Mac Laisre son of Lughaidh. *See* previous entry.

Mac Laisre son of Muireadhach. *See* Aodh of Killeenmore.

Mac Laisréin. *See* Molaise of Kilmolash.

Mac Laithbhe. *See* Eithearn of Donaghmore.

Mac Léinín. *See* Colmán of Cloyne.

Mac Liag of Drumglass (Druim Glas), barony of Dungannon Middle, Co. Tyrone. One of two sons of Cearnach – the other being Modhíocha – Mac Liag's pedigree attached him to the descendants of Colla Uais of the Oirghialla, and more specifically to the Ceinéal Mic Caorthainn branch of that family.[1] His church at Drumglass lay within a few miles of that of his uncle (Colmán Mucaidh) at Arboe.[2] According to an episode in the Tripartite Life, Mac Liag's family gave Patrick a mixed reception.[3] Caorthann Mór, 'great', sought to expel the saint, who then gave his blessing to Caorthann Beag, 'little', and prophesied that he himself would later place the veil on the head of the child in the womb of Caorthann Beag's wife. This child was Trea, patron of Artrea (Aird Trea), now the name of a parish in the barony of Dungannon Upper, adjoining Arboe and within a few miles of Drumglass. Speculative seventeenth-century sources identified Mac Liag with a similarly named bishop, commemorated at a place called Liathdhruim on 8 February.[4] Druim Lighean (now Drumleene in the Donegal parish of Clonleigh) may be intended; the name Giolla Mhic Liag Ua Donnghaile, chieftain of the Fir Dhroma Lighean, implies devotion to the saint.[5] A rector of the name Ua Donnghaile is, however, also recorded at Drumglass.[6]

1 *CGSH* §310; *GRSH* 67; *Lgen.* 361.5, 712.4. **2** *CGSH* §49; *GRSH* 66. **3** *BP* 1954–71; *VT* 168. **4** *MartT* 15; *MartG* 32; *MartD* 42; *GRSH* 67. **5** OCBG 540; *Lgen.* 133.7; *SAM* 6, 13. **6** *AnnU* 15.

Mac Liamhna. *See* Neachtan.

Mac Lughna, bishop. Lughna of the Artraighe of Ulster is said to have had eight children, four sons and four daughters, by Basar of the Déise Breagh, the people who gave name to the baronies of Deece in Meath.[1] Of the four boys, Mac Lughna (alias Mac Luinge/Lunga) was reputedly the best-loved of his father, whence his naming after him.[2] Alas, Mac Lughna, with no other record but this, was also perhaps the least-attested of Lughna's male children, the others being Iobhar, Caomhán Breac, and Mobheóg.[3]

1 *CGSH* §§721.1–14; 722.14. **2** Ibid. §721.12. **3** *AB* 77, 447, 449.

Mac Luighne. *See* Ciarán of Seirkieran.

Mac Nise of Kilrush. *See* Sineach of Kilrush.

Mac Nise of Clonmacnoise (Cluain Mhac Nóis), barony of Garrycastle, Co. Offaly. Mac Nise was reputedly among the eight present with Ciarán on the 'eighth of the calends of February' (25 January), when the latter saint founded Clonmacnoise.[1] Also among the eight was Aona (alias Aonghas), Ciarán's successor and Mac Nise's immediate predecessor as abbot. As Aona lay dying, Mac Nise is reported to have sought water blessed by Íde of Killeedy, only to learn that the latter was already dead when his messengers arrived.[2] After many years in office – put at sixteen in some sources – Mac Nise, 'an Ulsterman', and third abbot of Clonmacnoise, died in a year that oscillates between 585 and 591.[3] The feast of the'chaste of Cluain', which is given precedence in the earliest list, fell on 13 June.[4]

1 *LisL* 4375; *MartO²* 148. **2** *VSHP* ii, 129–30 §35. **3** *MartG* 116; *AU s.a.* 585, 591; *AClon. s.a.* 587; *FEMN* 493–4. **4** *MartT* 50; *MartO²* 140; *MartG* 116; *MartD* 168.

Mac Nise of Connor (Coinnire), barony of Lower Antrim, Co. Antrim, historically the seat of a diocese. Although sometimes referred to as Aonghas, this son of Faibhreach was more popularly known as Mac Nise, from his mother Neas (alias Cneas).[1] There is confusion with regard to the saint's descent. One would expect him to be attached to the Ulaidh of north-east Ulster and this is the case in later sources.[2] The earlier genealogies place him, however, among the Laoighse, either by error or due to confusion with his namesake Aona (alias Aonghas).[3]

The saint's name entered the record early, in the *Notulae* of the ninth-century Book of Armagh, which served as rough notes for Patrick's Tripartite Life.[4] There, Mac Nise is said to have been taught the psalms by Patrick, who was then in Dál nAraidhe.[5] Because of an apparent misdemeanour involving Patrick's sister, Mac Nise was, however, cursed by his teacher, losing his hand in the process, whence the local name Carn Lámha, 'cairn of the hand', at or near Connor.[6] Elsewhere in the Tripartite Life, Mac Nise is presented as having benefitted from Patrick's anger towards Bishop Olcán of Armoy (Oirthear Maighe), whose *fearann*, 'lands, jurisdiction' was destined to fall to him, though then a young boy of the Armagh saint's household.[7]

The late, office-style, Life composed for Mac Nise likewise establishes many associations for him with Patrick, who foretells his greatness and the future subservience to him of his tutor Olcán, a name here written as Bolcán.[8] Patrick is also given the task of consecrating Mac Nise bishop. Among other saints brought into Mac Nise's Life are Colmán of Kilroot, and the like-named Colmán of Lynally who is said to have belonged to the same family (*parentala*) as Mac Nise.[9] The saint is also given the honour of foretelling the birth of Comhghall, founder of Bangor and patron of the neighbouring diocese of Down.[10] Some sources state that Mac Nise was identical with Caomhán Breac, whose mother was also called Neas.[11] He died, according to the annals in 507, and his feastday fell on 3 September.[12]

1 *VSHH* 404; *CGSH* §722.58. **2** *GRSH* 97; *Lgen.* 728.3; *DIB* vi, 168–9. **3** *CGSH* §357. **4** *PTBA* 180 §10. **5** *BP* 1880–3; *VT* i, 162, 163n. **6** *HDGP* iii, 76. **7** *BP* 1932–4. **8** *VSHH* 404–5 §§1–5. **9** Ibid. 406 §§9, 14; cf. *GRSH* 95, 97. **10** *VSHH* 406 §12. **11** *MartO*^{2} 198; *MartD* 232; cf. *CGSH* §§206, 722.48. **12** *MartO*^{2} 192, 198; *MartG* 168; *MartD* 232; *AU s.a.*

Mac Nise of Fancroft. *See* Ceallán of Fancroft.

Mac Oíbhléin. *See* Mac Aoibhléin.

Mac Onchon. Variously known as Mac Onchon and Dobharchú son of Onchú, this saint was attached to an unidentified church named Ráith Scothbhan in the list of those subject to Brighid of Kildare.[1] His church may have lain somewhere along the Barrow valley among the Uí Bhairrche, the population group to which, according to the genealogists, the saint belonged but, because of the connection with Brighid, it is tempting to regard Mac Onchon as the *scriba*, 'scribe', of Kildare who died in 730.[2] There is independent evidence to show that he was known as a *saoi*, 'learned person'.[3]

1 *CGSH* §670.36; *Lgen.* 753.7. **2** *CGSH* §192; *Lgen.* 762.1; *CGH* 121bb23; *AU s.a.* **3** *CGH* 121ac53; *CGSH* §670.36.

Mac Reithe son of Ainghin (Anghan). *See* Colmán of Killeroran; Mac Reithe of Kilmacrehy.

Mac Reithe of Kilmacrehy (Ceall Mhic Reithe), barony of Corcomroe, Co. Clare. Reporting for the 1839 Ordnance Survey of the parish of Kilmacrehy, Eugene O'Curry could provide no account of its patron 'Mac Crithe', other than to assert, mistakenly, that he might be Mochta of Louth.[1] Some years later, having in the meantime become aware of the existence of a Life of the saint in the collection of Irish manuscripts of the Bibliothèque Royale, Brussels – which had been copied in the Franciscan friary in Ennis in 1634, and recopied a year later in the Donegal friary by Míchéal Ó Cléirigh from a manuscript written for Mac Reithe's coarb in 1524 – O'Curry described it accurately as a 'document of great importance in the investigation of the genealogies and topography' of west Clare, the Aran Islands, Kerry and Tipperary.[2]

Since edited and translated, this prose and verse text has been less favourably received by modern commentators, as a 'piece of extravagant folklore padded with miracles collected to create a title to revenues' and as 'utterly unhistorical'.[3] Even when viewed simply as a title to revenues, a saint's Life can be an important historical document which, though almost useless as a source of genuine information on the saint, usually has a great deal to say about the affairs of his or her church at the time when the text was written, as a rule several centuries after its subject had allegedly lived. In Mac Reithe's case, so seductively 'authentic' are some of the materials used by the biographer, that a recent study of its contents could find in them a 'consistent grasp of personalities and political relationships' in the saint's area of operations, i.e. south-western Ireland, from as early as about the middle of the sixth century.[4]

As with most texts of this kind, however deceptive its appearances, Mac Reithe's Life is to be read as a commentary on the perspective from the saint's church at some point after the arrival of the Normans – when it first became necessary to set out in writing claims to title and property that might previously have been set forth orally. It is not to be assumed automatically that the Life was designed to promote the particular interests of Mac Reithe's church at Kilmacrehy. Nearby, in the parish of Kilshanny, was a house of canons regular of St Augustine which would have been well equipped to undertake the compilation of a text of this kind, and a little further away was the cathedral church of Kilfenora. Noteworthy, for example, is the statement that the lands of Mac Reithe's first benefactor, Béigeadhán by name, were the location 'today' of Ceall tSeanbhotha, which the editor of the Life, tentatively but probably correctly, identified as Kilshanny.[5]

At the time of writing, and perhaps at the wish of his biographer, the saint's name, historically Mac Reithe, 'ram's son', became fixed as Mac Creiche, 'son of plunder', which gave scope for literary creativity in the form of numerous encounters with reavers.[6] Another appellation, Mac Croidhe Ailbhe, 'son of Ailbhe's heart', conjured up as the saint's original name, cleverly created the impression that Mac Reithe and the church represented by him deserved special treatment from the ecclesiastical authorities in Munster, traditionally represented by Ailbhe's church in Emly.[7] The saint's pedigree, likewise a forgery, attached him through his father Peaslán, and via an ancestor named 'Erce', to the Corcamruadh

Nionais.[8] This name was formerly used of the territory now represented by the baronies of Corcomroe and Burren, together with the Aran Islands, which was approximately the equivalent of the diocese of Kilfenora.[8]

The impression that Mac Reithe's Life had a much wider perspective than would have been warranted by the sole concerns of Kilmacrehy is maintained by the gradually expanding range of the actions attributed to the saint. First, he is described as teacher and father-confessor of Mainchín, patron – although now scarcely remembered locally – of the neighbouring church of Kilmanaheen. Mainchín was the saint's regular companion, accompanying him to Rome, allegedly to procure the 'fair-voiced' *Fionn Faoidheach* (otherwise Patrick's bell), and also by his side during a journey with Ailbhe to the site on Aran from which the latter was to set out for the Land of Promise.[9] There followed a summons to save Mac Reithe's maternal people, the Ciarraighe, from the effects of a vicious plague and, again accompanied by Mainchín, to assist them in recovering a prey of cattle and people taken from the Altraighe of north Kerry by the Eoghanacht of Loch Léin (Killarney), in the process acquiring for himself, and for his heirs, enormous amounts of tribute.[10] As has been shown by a study of this part of the Life, the saint's biographer was drawing on reliable genealogical sources.[11]

Subsequently, Mac Reithe is shown interceding on behalf of his paternal relatives, the Corcamruadh, with Aodh son of Eacha, direct ancestor of the later Uí Chonchobhair (O'Connor) kings of Connacht, with a view to persuading Aodh to rescind a tribute owed to him, and simultaneously achieving for himself and his successors the payment of various dues.[12] The final substantial episode in the text, in which Mac Reithe rids Thomond of the attentions of an unpleasant lake monster called Broicseach, by throwing at it his skull cap, lasted longest in local folk memory.[13] Its purpose in the Life was to stress the efficacy of Mac Reithe's powers over those of other local saints, among them Blathmhac of Rath, and to set out a long list of the dues that were owed to him by grateful local families.

Remarkable about all these events is the presentation of the saint throughout as a man of advanced age, from 140 at Loch Léin to 180 at death.[14] The saint's alleged maternal connections with the Ciarraighe are possibly mirrored paternally in a miscellaneous item preserved in the corpus of saints' pedigrees.[15] This locates Mac Reithe son of Ainghin (Anghan) son of Reathach – names attested only or mainly among the Ciarraighe – and his two brothers, Cúrnán and Colmán, in the church of Ceall Eadarghabhla in Fiodh Manach, now Killeroran in the Galway barony of Killian.[16] Together with his brothers, this Mac Reithe was also remembered in a church in east Galway named Ceall Mac nAinghin(e), now Ballynakill in the Galway barony of Ballymoe.[17] Here, according to a later tale, he fostered a daughter of Criomhthann son of Lughaidh, king of Uí Mhaine, named Riceann (Ricín), who later gave birth to Dúnghal, ancestor of the Clann Mhic Con Mara (McNamaras) of Thomond, before becoming a saint in her own right, and patron of the parish of Clooney in the barony of Bunratty Upper.[18]

Mac Reithe also figures in other Lives, usually in a shadowy role. In that of his mentor Ailbhe, for example, he is located in a place named *Civitas Ultani*, where the saints together miraculously discover a lost calf.[19] In the Life of Éanna of Inishmore, he is sent as a messenger to Rome with Finnian and Iarlaithe, and in that of Colum of Terryglass, he follows the instructions of an angel by relinquishing Inishcaltra (Holy Island) on Lough Derg on the river Shannon and moving elsewhere.[20] A trace of this abandonment is also present in the unpublished metrical Life of Caimín of Inishcaltra, which states that Mac Reithe went north (perhaps to one of the Galway churches associated with him), leaving his blessing on the island church.[21]

Miscellaneous other texts also find room for the saint. The list of children attributed to Inghean Bhaoith places him in a group that includes such neighbours as Blathmhac of Rath, Conall of Kilconnell in the parish of Kilmacrehy, and Maol Eala (Dala?) who also figures in Mac Reithe's Life.[22] Curiously, while all three companion saints and Inghean Bhaoith are called upon in a poem in Classical Irish, together with Mainchín, possibly of Kilmanaheen, and numerous other saints, to help in releasing Ireland's southern half (Leath Mogha) from a bondage imposed on it by the northern half (Leath Chuinn), championed by Finnian of Clonard, Mac Reithe is not included.[23] In contrast to Mac Reithe's tribute-grasping presentation by his biographer, he is said by Cuimín of Connor to have loved 'a prison hard and pure' from Shrove to Easter, eating only bread and cress.[24] His reputation was, however, rarely far removed from tribute, as is shown by the final quatrain of an (unpublished) poem, which speaks of Mac Reithe receiving cattle from the men of Munster (Clanna Cuirc).[25]

Through confusion with a cook named 'Mac Rith', who reputedly served Mochta of Louth, combined with the use of *Mac Ochta*, 'bosom-son', to describe Mac Reithe, the saint's feastday is sometimes assigned to 11 August.[26] In Kilmacrehy, however, in keeping with the dubious origins of the saint, Mac Reithe's feast was observed on 2 August, where it appears to have merged with the pre-Christian *Lughnasadh* celebrations centred on St Brigid's Well, a mile or so from the saint's church.[27] He and his companion saint, Mainchín of Kilmanaheen, are thought to have been buried on either side of the altar in the church of Kilmacrehy.[28]

1 *ACoC* 92. **2** *MHH* 51 §72; *MM* 630. **3** *MHH* 8; *FEMN* 461n. **4** *Ériu* 30, 95; cf. *FG* 46–56. **5** *MHH* 14 §7, 94; *HDGP* iv, 49–50. **6** *MHH* 8, 15 §10; *Ériu* 30, 105–7; cf. *OC* 17, 24. **7** *MHH* 15 §10. **8** *CoC* 82–7. **9** *MHH* 16–18 §12–19; *ACoC* 105; *BP* 3139; *VT* 266; *EMH* 466 §172. **10** *MHH* 18–23 §19–33. **11** *FG* 46–56. **12** *MHH* 23–6 §§34–40; *IKHK* 299–301. **13** *MHH* 36–45 §§49–67; *FL* 283. **14** *Ériu* 30, 96–7. **15** *CGSH* §695. **16** Ibid. p. 315. **17** *Lgen.* 237.7. **18** *AIL* iii, 308–9; OCBG §2001; *ACoC* 182, 208. **19** *VSHH* 127 §37; *VSHP* i, 58 §32. **20** *VSHH* 229 §15. **21** BBR MS 2324–40, 264–73 at 270v. **22** *IrT* iv, 93 §8; *MHH* 36 §50, 39 §55, 42 §61. **23** RIA MS 23L11, 263. **24** *ZCP* 1, 64. **25** *LUM* 214r[a] 20. **26** *LUM* 155r[a] 20–2; *MHH* 10n; *Ériu* 30, 115. **27** *FL* 282–6. **28** *JRSAI* 41, 16.

Mac Rímhe, bishop. While travelling in the coastal part of the lands of Uí Fhiachrach (Tireragh) in north Sligo, Patrick arrived at a place called Muireasc, now represented by the parishes of Easky and Templeboy. There he blessed his 'son' Mac Rímhe who, according to Tíreachán, wrote an alphabet for him.[1] The later Tripartite Life account of the journey added to Mac Rímhe's name the church of Ceall Chorca Raoidhe, located evidently among the Corca Raoidhe of An Corann, now the barony of Corran in the same county.[2]

1 *PTBA* 158 §45. **2** *BP* 1601–2; *VT* 138; *HDGP* iii, 149–50.

Mac Rustaing. *See* Caomhán Breac son of Neas.

Mac Táil of Oldkilcullen (Ceall Chuilinn), parish and barony of Kilcullen, Co. Kildare. As Tíreachán was completing his account of Patrick, he found a few loose ends to tie up. In the final chapter, he brought his subject to Leinster, and more particularly to the territories of Uí Bhairrche (mainly in north Carlow) and Magh Life in Kildare.[1] There Patrick is said to have ordained Usaille of Killashee, one of the Armagh saint's disciples, and a regular companion named Iserninus, placing the latter with Mac Táil son of Eachaidh in Kilcullen. The author of the Tripartite Life, who contented himself with rendering much the same account, elsewhere named Mac Táil (literally 'son of adze') as one of Patrick's three smiths, the others being Mac Céacht and Cuana.[2] Curiously, Mac Táil's name nowhere figures in the lists of those 'in orders' with Patrick, perhaps because he was also thought to be Brighid's *anmchara*, 'soul-friend'.[3]

The genealogists found room for Mac Táil, along with Tighearnach of Clones, Fiac of Sleaty, and others, in their list of Uí Bhairrche saints, and he is invoked in the *bóramha* tract as one of many saintly protectors of Leinster.[4] His affiliation to the Uí Bhairrche was not undisputed. The corpus of saints' genealogies attached him to an otherwise unattested line of descent from Aonghas son of Nadh Fraoich, ancestor of the Eoghanachta of Munster, thus making him a brother of Caolán of the Down church of Kilclief, namesake and probable double of Caolán of Nendrum in the same county.[5] This descent may be connected with the belief that the saint's original name was Eoghan, although a variant tradition made this the name of his father, allegedly a *saor*, 'wright', and yet another authority substituted Aonghas for Eoghan.[6] Mac Táil is among the saints cited in a poem forecasting doleful times.[7] An obit of 549 (also 551), the year of the great plague known as *Buidhe Chonaill*, is recorded for the saint, and his feast, which fell on 11 June, is among the handful of mainly Leinster feasts remembered in the tenth-century metrical calendar of Hampson.[8] It has been suggested that he was patron of the church of St Michells, on the river Poddle in the most ancient part of Dublin.[9] A relic of the saint reached the Continent, where it was kept, arguably, either at Ferrières in France or at some church in the Rhineland.[10]

1 *PTBA* 162 §51.2–4. **2** *BP* 2192–4, 2959–60; *VT* 186, 250. **3** *ZCP* 19, 120 §13. **4** *CGSH* §§671–2; *CGH* 121a39–40; *SG* i, 389. **5** *CGSH* §238; *GRSH* 118; *Lgen*. 740.8. **6** *MartT* 49; *MartO*[2] 148; *GRSH* 118; *MartD* 166. **7** *Ériu* 18, 60 §10. **8** *AU*/ATig. *s.a.*; *MartT* 49; *MartO*[2] 140; *MartG* 114; *MartD* 166; *AB* 104, 99. **9** *AH* 8, 14. **10** *EIRD* 55–68; *RIW* 15–19.

Mac Treana of Kilmactranny, barony of Tirerrill, Co. Sligo. When visiting Kilmactranny in 1836, the representatives of the Ordnance Survey were told that 10 September was 'Mac an Treanaigh's' day.[1] This was in fact Ailbhe of Emly's day and its adoption in the parish may be explained by reference to the presence in Derrysallagh townland of a well dedicated to Ailbhe, under the guise of 'Eilibh', supposedly the sister of Lasair of Kilronan.[2] Despite the change of sex, the juxtaposition of dedications to Ailbhe and Mac Treana was a natural one. Both saints are elsewhere brought together in the pedigrees of the ecclesiastical families associated with Emly.[3] These pedigrees show that Mac Treana has been substituted locally for Colmán son of Trian, no doubt to distinguish him from the many other saints named Colmán. Apart from a minor role in the Life of Lasair of Kilronan, where the release of one of Mac Treana's clerics is brought about by Lasair's intercession, little else is known of the saint.[4]

1 OSL SO 237. **2** Ibid. 239; *LSLC* 291–5. **3** *CGH* 326h6–16. **4** *Ériu* 5, 90–2.

Mac Uíbhléin. *See* Mac Aoibhléin.

Machain daughter of Léinín. *See* Aighleann of Killiney.

Machutus. *See* Mochta of Louth.

Madoc. *See* Maodhóg of Ferns.

Madóg Oilithir. *See* Santán.

Maghna sister of David. *See* Séadna of Clonbeg.

Maighistir of Ceall Mhaighistreach, a site probably in the townland of Pollerton Lower, parish, barony and county of Carlow.[1] According to the corpus of saints' genealogies, Maighistir son of Cathán and his brother Eacha of Cluain Réadach, an unidentified church, probably also in Carlow, belonged to the Uí Bhairrche, whence the name of the deanery of Obargy in the barony of Idrone.[2] Neither saint would appear to be otherwise attested.

1 *HDGP* iv, 14. **2** *CGSH* §259; *GRSH* 88; *Lgen.* 727.31; *CGH* 121b11.

Maighneann of Kilmainham (Ceall Mhaighneann), parish of St James, barony of Uppercross, near Dublin. Maighneann was one of four sons of Aodh son of Colga, a king of Oirthir – whence the barony of Orior in Armagh – who died in Clonmacnoise in 610 'as a pilgrim'.[1] The Life of Mochta of Louth states that its subject refused an offer of land from this Aodh, allegedly because he knew that it was destined for the use of Colum Cille.[2] Aodh's three other sons – Maighneann's siblings – were Cobhthach (probably Cobhthach Caol son of the king of Oirghialla), Libhréan (probably of Clonfad), and Tua. The name given to the saint's mother was Sineall – a daughter of Ceinnfhionnán and sister of Seinshincheall of Killeigh – who belonged to Uí Labhradha, a Leinster family that also numbered Abán of Killabban among its saints.[3]

The site named after Maighneann on Meath's border with Cavan, likewise Kilmainham, figures little in the surviving record of the saint which is mainly concerned with his church near Dublin. Following the foundation by Strongbow of the Knights Hospitallers' priory of St John the Baptist at Kilmainham in the 1170s, this became the chief house of the order, with extensive landholdings throughout Ireland.[4] Despite the fact that it was an Anglo-Norman foundation, located within a few miles of the centre of English administration in Ireland, the Life produced for its patron was in the vernacular. The text, unfortunately incomplete, survives in a manuscript written in the late fifteenth century by Uilliam Mac An Leagha, and although available in published form, it has yet to be edited critically.[5]

Described as 'late and fabulous', the text begins with a copy of the saint's pedigree, before immediately bringing him to the Lough Owel district in Westmeath where he meets Lomán of Portloman and preaches a sermon on the Last Judgement, a recurrent theme of the Life.[6] There follows a series of encounters with other saints, such as Finnian of Movilla, Molaise of Leighlin, Fionnchú of Brigown, Moling of St Mullin's, and Mochuda of Rahan, who mainly act as foils for the expression of Maighneann's views on such matters as discipline, chastity, pilgrimage and eschatology. In almost all cases, the saint is presented as a visitor to his fellow- saints, but he and Fionnchú are brought to Inishmore on Aran, where they agree a union with Éanna and other saints.[7] Dublin is represented among the saint's companions by Maol Ruain of Tallaght, who hears Maighneann's confession, chiding him for his failure to undertake manual labour, and a *céile Dé* based in Kilmainham is shown reciting Maighneann's virtues.[8]

As there would appear to be no other obvious connecting thread either between the various saints encountered by Maighneann or the places mentioned, the Life may have been compiled in the spirit of *devotio moderna*, a movement which, having begun in the Netherlands in the late fourteenth century, spread widely, affecting many of the religious orders of the period.[9] Although no place was found for Fursa of Killursa in the Life, this saint is elsewhere recorded as having made a union with Maighneann, exchanging with him his 'troubles', including headache, piles and a ravenous reptile.[10] Among other churches dedicated to Maighneann is Kilmactalway in the Dublin barony of Newcastle.[11] The saint's feast fell on 18 December.[12]

1 *CGSH* §54; *GRSH* 71; *Lgen*. 713.10; *AU s.a.*; *AFM s.a.*606. **2** *VSHH* 399 §16. **3** *CGSH* §§282, 287, 722.90. **4** *MRHI* 334–5. **5** *BL Cat*. ii, 446–7; *SG* i, 37–49. **6** *Kenney* 466; *SG* i, 37–8. **7** *SG* i, 40. **8** Ibid. 40–2, 44–5. **9** *ODCC* 475. **10** *MartO*² 44–6. **11** *AH* 8, 28; *PRIA* 97C 269. **12** *MartT* 86; *MartO*² 252; *MartG* 240; *MartD* 338.

MAINCHÍN. *See* also Manchán.

MAINCHÍN of Coolcashin (Cúil Chaisín), barony of Galmoy, Co. Kilkenny. When leaving Ossory for Munster, Fionnbharr of Cork came, according to his biographer, to Coolcashin, where he marked out the boundary of a church which was then granted to him in perpetuity.[1] No saint is named for the church, but Mainchín would have been in the mind of the Cork saint's biographer because, according to the genealogists, he was one of seven sons of Maonach, others being Fachtna, patron of the church and diocese of Ross, and Lóchán, patron and eponym of the parish of Rathlogan (Ráith Lócháin), now adjoining Coolcashin; Lóchán's church at Kilmacahill had also been consecrated by Fionnbharr.[2] The biographer's aim was to show that Fachtna's closest relatives were deferential towards the patron and first bishop of Cork, whose successor at the time of writing (about 1200) had designs on the diocese of Ross.[3] According to Bishop Phelan's list, Mainchín shared a feast of 2 January with other representatives of the name.[4]

1 *BBa*. 62 §14. **2** *CGSH* §298.2; *GRSH* 128; *Lgen*. 744.7; *BBa*. 60 §11, 62 §13. **3** *MakS* 66, 87. **4** *HADO* ii, 307, 334.

Mainchín of Kilmanaheen. *See* Mac Reithe of Kilmacrehy; Mainchín of St Munchin's.

Mainchín of St Munchin's, barony of North Liberties, Co. Limerick. A large number of supposedly distinct saints named Mainchín (Manchán) are recorded. One of these, Manchianus (*Manchéne sapiens/doctor noster*), an authority cited in a seventh-century commentary on sacred scripture, is possibly identical with the wise Mainchín remembered, like Mainchín of Limerick, on 2 January, which, despite the reservations of some scholars, may mean that the two saints were ultimately one and the same.[1] Otherwise, little is recorded of the Limerick saint, but that he was granted King's Island (Inis Iobhthann/Siobhthann) by the progenitor of the Uí Eachthighirn, a branch of Dál gCais that owned extensive lands just north of the city in the later medieval period.[2] The present Church of Ireland edifice of St Munchin's is located on King's Island, at a place overlooking the river Shannon, just within the ancient town wall.

Mainchín's pedigree assigns him through his father Séadna to a leading branch of the Dál gCais, with one (unreliable) source naming his mother as Inghean Bhaoith, patron of Killinaboy in Clare.[3] Perhaps because the saint's successors had to contend with the rival interests of the community at Mungret, head church of the powerful Uí Fhidhgheinte, located a few miles south-west of the town, St Munchin's appears never to have attained much importance.[4] It is entirely ignored by the annalists, and neither Mainchín nor his church find mention in Patrick's ninth-century Tripartite Life which brought its subject to the area immediately about Limerick.[5]

The Norse settlement on King's Island may have contributed to the lack of interest in Mainchín's church and, with the foundation of the cathedral church of St Mary's in the late twelfth century, it became a prebend.[6] The author of a poem on the last testament of Cormac son of Cuilleannán, king of Cashel, stipulated that the king's ring, amice, and shirt, 'a triad about which Munstermen would fall', were to be brought to Mainchín of Limerick.[7] Local tradition identified two (fictitious) patrons of churches in Limerick, Rose of Kilrush, in the parish of St Munchin's, and Lelia of Killeely, as sisters of the saint.[8] He was probably ultimately identical with Mainchín of Kilmanaheen, near Lahinch in Clare, who figured prominently in the Life of Mac Reithe, but of whom little was remembered locally.[9] Either as patron of Kilmanaheen or of St Munchin's, Mainchín also figures in a poem in Classical Irish which calls on numerous saints, including Neasán and Inghean Bhaoith, to help in releasing Ireland's southern half (Leath Mogha) from a bondage imposed on it by the northern half (Leath Chuinn), championed by Finnian of Clonard [10] Poems relating to Seanán feature Mainchín, both as respondent to the Scattery saint, and as one of his many helpers in time of need.[11] A well is dedicated to the saint at Bruree in south Limerick.[12] Though, as already stated, Mainchín's feast fell on 2 January, the Martyrology of Donegal suggests, probably correctly, that he was (also) commemorated three days earlier on 29 December.[13] Locally, his name was anglicized as Munchin and Mannix.

1 *SacE* 7, 90–2; *Kenney* 276; *MartT* 4; *MartO*[2] 33; *MartG* 6; *MartD* 4; *LIS* i, 33; *DIB* vi, 305; *NL* 169–70. **2** *CGH* 153a29; *SATM* 40–1; *SACCL* 357–8. **3** *CGSH* §202; *GRSH* 120; *Lgen.* 740.10; *CGH* 152a49; *BLec.* 230Ra43; *IrT* iv, 94 §10. **4** *MRHI* 94. **5** *BP* 2379–429. **6** *BBL* xxii. **7** *RC* 37, 352 §8. **8** *LIS* i, 31. **9** *ACoC* 105. **10** RIA MS 23L11, 263; *SAM* 24.1, 17, 21. **11** *IrT* iv, 95–7; *ZCP* 10, 26 §20. **12** *JRSAI* 85, 198; *DiocL* 95; *SACCL* 422. **13** *MartD* 350.

Mainchín son of Caol(bhadh). Although treated separately, Mainchín (Manchán) enjoyed the same paternal descent as the seven 'sons of Caolbhadh' of the Uí Oilealla, a family whose lands in Connacht corresponded approximately to the present Sligo barony of Tirerrill.[1] As a group, the sons of Caolbhadh occupied two churches, Cloonard (Cluain Aird) in the Roscommon parish of Tibohine, and Imleach Gaileang in Luighne, now perhaps Emlaghfad in the Sligo barony of Corran, adjoining Leyny. Mainchín is probably identical with his namesake, the son of Collán, who is placed *isin Chorunn*, 'in the Corann', now the Sligo barony of Corran, but formerly a much larger area.[2] This Mainchín's mother was Deidhe, daughter of Trian and granddaughter of the noted Dubhthach of Maca Lughair.[3] Although Mainchín son of Caolbhadh's seven brothers were commemorated together on 24 April, the feast of Mainchín son of Collán fell on 13 January.[4]

1 *CGSH* §§391, 393.1–8; *GRSH* 64; *Lgen.* 712.2. **2** *CGSH* §722.2. **3** Ibid. **4** *MartT* 7; *MartG* 14; *MartD* 14.

Mainchín son of Collán. *See* Mainchín son of Caol(bhadh).

Mainchín son of Dubhthan. *See* Comán son of Dubhthan.

Mainchín son of Muireadhach. *See* Aodh of Killeenmore.

Maine of Aghanagh (Eachanach), barony of Tirerrill, Co. Sligo. While in Magh Luirg, now part of the Roscommon barony of Boyle, Patrick is said to have been persuaded by Bishop Maine son of Caochán of the Uí Oilealla (a family whose name became attached to the neighbouring Sligo barony of Tirerrill) to soften a curse he had imposed on a local family named Ceinéal Mac nEirc.[1] The cause of the curse, allegedly the forcible retention of Patrick's horses, is more likely to have been Armagh's resentment of the presence among this group, at Assylin (Eas Mac nEirc), near Boyle, of a Columban foundation.[2] Bishop Maine, described as a member of Patrick's household, was attached to the church at Aghanagh, together with a man named Geintéan (Geintín). Despite the connection with Armagh, which goes back at least to the middle of the ninth century, when the so-called *Notulae* were added to the Book of Armagh, Bishop Maine and his church also had both Brigidine and Columban associations. The former is exemplified by the saint's place among the many children of Cuman, Brighid's maternal aunt.[3] This tradition also found room for Patrick, who blessed Cuman's womb with the sign of the cross, whence the nickname *crosach*, 'crossed', that became attached to the saint.[4] Elsewhere, among many others of Cuman's children, especially those with north-east Connacht connections, Maine is said to have joined in an assembly at which Colum Cille was also to attend.[5] A well named after Maine and the imprint of the saint's knees were pointed out at Aghanagh, and a bell associated with the saint was preserved locally until the nineteenth century.[6] Maine's feastday fell, with that of Geintéan, on 2 September.[7]

1 *BP* 1664–75; *VT* 144. 2 *IKD* 236 §48. 3 *PTBA* 180 3 *CGSH* §722.6.7. 4 Ibid. 5 *Anecd.* iii, 3. 6 *AISO* i, 434; *EMH* 482–3 §217. 7 *MartG* 168; *MartD* 232.

MAINE son of Eichean, bishop. The attributes of *claoine* (crookedness) and *costadhaighe* (constancy), allegedly proclaimed by Patrick for the descendants of Bishop Maine's father, Eichean, were at least even-handed.[1] The family in question, a minor branch of the powerful Ceinéal Eoghain, appears to have held lands on the east side of Inishowen (Inis Eoghain), in a place known as the Bréadach.[2] One branch of the family, Uí Chomhaltáin, was based in Armagh, and Maine's nephew, according to the genealogies, was Aodhán, patron of Kilmore in the county of Monaghan.[3] The Maine son of Eoghan commemorated on 24 November has been taken to be identical with the son of Eichean.[4]

1 *BLec.* 58Vab. 2 *CGSH* §28; *GRSH* 47; *Lgen.* 149.7, 701.9; *HDGP* ii, 173. 3 *BLec.* 58Vab; *Lgen.* 149.7. 4 *MartG* 224; *MartD* 316; *GRSH* 47.

MAINE son of Eoghan. *See* Maine son of Eichean.

MAINE son of Niall. *See* Rónán of Dromiskin.

MAINE son of Sineall. According to the genealogists, Maine was one of five sons of Sineall son of Nadh Fraoich of the Conmhaicne, a family whose settlements were located mainly in Connacht.[1] His better-known siblings included Baodán of Cloney and Malach, father of Dúileach of St Doolagh's, near Dublin. Although omitted from the official list, he was probably also regarded as a son of Síon daughter of Niall of the Corca Bhaiscinn of south-west Clare.[2]

1 *CGSH* §129; *GRSH* 106, 113; *Lgen.* 733.2. 2 *CGSH* §722.22.

MAITHGHEIM daughter of Aodhán. *See* Molaise of Leighlin.

MALACH (MALÁN) son of Sineall. *See* Dúileach of St Doolagh's.

MALACHY. *See* Maol Maodhóg.

MANACH. One of twenty-four 'in orders' with Patrick, Manach the priest (*cruimhthear*) is described as his firewood-provider.[1] Nothing else is known of him.

1 *CGSH* §§671.16; 672.26; *BP* 3136; *VT* 266.

MANAGHAN. *See* Manchán of Mohill.

MANCHÁN. *See* also Mainchín.

MANCHÁN. Sometimes thought to be a diminutive of *manach*, 'monk, Manchán is more likely to derive from a native name.[1] The list of homonymous saints includes eight bearers of the name, many of them otherwise unattested.[2]

1 *GPN* 134. 2 *CGSH* §707.785–92.

MANCHÁN of Ceann Tráchta. *See* Coilliodhan.

MANCHÁN of Lemanaghan (Liath Mancháin), barony of Garrycastle, Co. Offaly. According to one version of his descent, Manchán son of Siollán (otherwise Sineall or Ionnach) belonged, with Fursa of Killursa, Colmán of Lynn and others, to the Ulaidh of north-east Ulster; another version placed him among the Eoghanachta of Munster; a third, confounding him with his namesake, Manchán son of Fáilbhe, assigned him to the Ceinéal Conaill; and a fourth declared that he was a Welshman.[1] The identity of his mother varied accordingly. On the one hand, she was said to be Brónach daughter of Míleac, among whose other children were Fursa and Colmán; on the other, she was named Mealla – also mother of the saint's two sisters, Grealla and Greillseach, of whom nothing else is recorded.[2] A shared Ulster background was used by the author of the Life of Colmán of Lynally to project a close relationship between his subject and Manchán.[3]

The parishes of Lynally and Lemanaghan are separated only by that of Rahan. The story of the expulsion of Rahan's patron Mochuda found room for a man named Manchán, described as sub-erenagh of Clonmacnoise, who acted as a messenger between Rahan and saints envious of Mochuda's success.[4] His reward was hunger for himself and his successors, but modern visitors, marvelling, like Michéal Ó Cléirigh before them, at the splendour of his (probably early twelfth-century) shrine, will surely ponder on the wealth that his church must have attracted at some stage of its history.[5]

In manners, the saint is said to have been similar to Jerome and, despite the many inconsistencies this would entail, it has been suggested that he was identical with the 'Manchianus, *doctor noster*', cited as an authority in a commentary on sacred scripture, formerly preserved in the Reichenau on Lake Constance.[6] Manchán (Mainchín) *sapiens*, 'the wise', was associated with Laois churches, at one of which – Mondrehid (Muin Droichid) in the parish of Offerlane – he is said to have died in 652.[7] He is thought to have previously had an eye ailment which was cured by contact with the laid-out corpse of Molua of the neighbouring parish of Kyle.[8] Against this, Manchán of Lemanaghan is said to have died, with many other saints, in 665, the year of the *mortalitas magna*, 'great plague'.[9] The saint is credited with the authorship of a number of pious poems, including an *anmchairdeas*, 'soul-friendship'.[10] Whereas Manchán of Lemanaghan was remembered on 24 January or, as at Kilcleagh, on 29 September, Manchán *sapiens* was remembered on 2 January.[11] Adjoining Lemanaghan is the parish of Kilmanaghan which also took name from the saint, and next to this is the parish of Kilcleagh in Westmeath whose saint was known as Moynaghan, doubtless an anglicized form of Manchán.[12] At Lemanaghan itself, the 'cell' of his mother Mealla lies close to Manchán's well.[13]

1 *CGSH* §§188, 577; *GRSH* 104; *Lgen*. 737.3–4; *AClon*. p. 107; *CCDK* 242; *DIB* vi, 337. **2** *CGSH* §722.80 (92). **3** *BNÉ* i, 168 §4. **4** Ibid. 301 §7. **5** *MartD* 26; *IARP* 74–77–8, 111; *InsT* 269–74. **6** *CGSH* §712.22; *SacE* 7, 84–92; *Peritia* 2, 200–14, 238; ibid. 3, 205; *PHCC* 1, 3. **7** *AU s.a.* **8** *VSHH* 145 §68. **9** *AU s.a.* **10** *ZCP* 7, 310–12; *Ériu* 1, 38–42; *EIL* 28–30. **11** *MartT* 4, 11; *MartO*^{2} 33; *MartG* 6, 22; *MartD* 4, 26; *PNW* 12; cf. *MartO*^{2} 52. **12** *PNW* 12. **13** *AIOY* 118.

Manchán of Mohill (Maothail) in the barony of the same name, Co. Leitrim. Apparently known locally as Managhan, Monahan and Morris, Manchán is one of those included in the list of homonymous saints.[1] He is chiefly remembered for his role in the Life of Caillín of Fenagh who, sensing that he was soon to die, instructed Manchán to bury him in a place called Reilig Mochaomhóg and, after twelve years, to disinter his remains, placing them in a shrine with important relics he himself had previously brought from Rome.[2] Caillín is also said to have uttered on his deathbed a doleful prophecy to Manchán, who rendered him the last rites, and succeeded him as abbot of Fenagh for seven years before being succeeded in turn by Cruimhthear Fraoch.[3] This supposed succession was no doubt influenced by the fact that all three saints were patrons of adjoining parishes within the barony of Mohill in south Leitrim. Fraoch and Manchán were also brought together by the biographer of Bearach of Termonbarry – a church located close by Mohill – at an assembly of kings and saints held at Lissardowlan in the Longford parish of Templemichael.[4] Although Manchán's pedigree has not been preserved, he may be identical with his namesake, the son of Fáilbhe, who was attached to the Ceinéal Boghaine (whence the Donegal barony of Banagh).[5] Manchán's feast, celebrated on 14 February, the eve of the feast of Bearach of Termonbarry, was the occasion of a local fair called after him.[6] The saint's shrine was covered with a gold layer in 1166 on the instructions of Ruaidhrí Ua Conchobhair, king of Connacht.[7] In 1430, possibly on the day of the saint's feast, the local Mac Raghnaill family killed a son of the powerful Ua Ruairc of Bréifne, whose companions subsequently took refuge in Manchán's church.[8]

1 *BFen.* 12–13n; *TDI* ii, 376; *CGSH* §707.786. 2 *BFen.* 12, 108, 290. 3 Ibid. 284, 308–10. 4 *Celtica* 1, 66–7; *BNÉ* i, 36 §62. 5 *CGSH* §§13, 524; *GRSH* 41; *Lgen.* 700.4. 6 *MartT* 17; *MartG* 36; *MartD* 48; *BFen.* 12n; *JACAS* 1.3, 65. 7 *AFM s.a.* 8 *AU s.a.*

Manchán of 'Teampall Mancháin' in the townland of Ballymorereagh (Baile Mór Riach), parish of Dingle, barony of Corkaguiny, Co. Kerry. Located about three miles from Dingle, Manchán's church, also known as *Teampall Geal* because of the whiteness of its stones, is a fine example of early Christian stonework. In front of the church is an ogham stone. Little is known of its patron, but, according to local tradition, he was one of three brothers, the other two being Fiontan of Kilfountain in the parish of Kildrum, and Faolán of Killelane in the parish of Dingle.[1] His well was frequented on Sundays, and especially on Easter Sunday.[2]

1 *TCCD* 45. 2 *ACoK* 115–17; *CIIC* i, §170; *TCCD* 31.

Manchán son of Fáilbhe. *See* Manchán of Mohill; Manchán of Lemanaghan.

Manchán Sapiens. *See* Manchán of Lemanaghan.

Mannix. *See* Mainchín of St Munchin's.

Mantán of Wicklow (Ceall Mhantáin), baronies of Arklow and Newcastle, Co. Wicklow. Despite the importance of his church, later the site of a Franciscan friary, Mantán is rarely mentioned in the sources.[1] A namesake, described as a deacon and as a disciple of Patrick, incurred the Armagh saint's wrath in the Limerick territory of Uí Fhidhgheinte, when he refused to share food he was preparing for the local king with jugglers.[2] Patrick said of Mantán that his church on earth would not be lofty, a description that the Wicklow site, should it be intended, scarcely deserves. In Wicklow, local tradition, relying on the Irish word *manntach*, 'gapped', explained the saint's name by reference to his loss of some of his front teeth.[3] The saint's feast is unknown, but John Colgan tentatively identified Mantán with a namesake who, according to one source, was venerated on 2 March at 'Blarus', now perhaps Blaris in the Down barony of Castlereagh Upper.[4]

1 *MRHI* 261. 2 *BP* 2379–400; *VT* 202–4. 3 OSL CN/LM 114; OSL WW 289. 4 *ASH* 451n; *FLK Cat.* MS A 7, 11v; *EA* 377–8; *LIS* iii, 81.

Maodhóg of Clonmore (Cluain Mór), barony of Rathvilly, Co. Carlow. A poem attributed to Moling by the author of the *bóramha* tract invokes the protection of the 'golden vessel', Aodh (alias Maodhóg) son of Eoghan of Clonmore, among many other Leinster saints.[1] In his commemoration of Maodhóg, Aonghas *céile Dé*, 'client of God', likewise placed the saint in the front rank of Leinster saints, describing him as a 'martial kinsman' of Dúnlaing, eponymous ancestor of the Uí Dhúnlainge kings of north Leinster.[2] According to the genealogists, Maodhóg belonged to a branch of this family called Clann Bhruidhghe, powerful enough to provide an abbot of Kildare named Brannabh.[3] A poem of doleful prophecy also establishes a connection with Brighid's church by proclaiming woe for the plunderer of Kildare who would seek Maodhóg's protection.[4]

Despite his evident stature, Maodhóg never became the subject of a Life. Nor did he figure often in Lives of other saints, except that of Comhghall of Bangor, who is said to have cured him of a leprous disease acquired while he was studying the 'twelve minor prophets' at the church of a certain Sineall.[5] Since Comhghall was patron of some churches in the Carlow area, this was a natural association. Despite a statement to the contrary by Míchéal Ó Cléirigh, who appears to have confused Maodhóg with his namesake, Aodhán son of Maine, the saint was not regarded as a uterine brother of Aodh son of Ainmhire, overking of the northern half of Ireland.[6] Like Aodhán, he figured among the cast of the *bóramha* tale, which nominally deals with the struggle of the Leinstermen to avoid paying a cattle-tribute to successive so-called 'high-kings' of Ireland.

Maodhóg's attendance upon his own overking, Brannabh son of Eacha of the Uí Fheilmeadha, arguably later became part of the traditions surrounding the career of his better-known namesake at Ferns.[7] A pattern at the well of St Mogue's in the townland of Glebe, near Clonmore was held on 31 January, the 'last day of winter', otherwise the feast of Maodhóg of Ferns.[8] The saint's regular feast of 11 April was shared by another namesake and likely double, Aodh of Eachdhruim, now perhaps Aughrim in the Wicklow parish of Ballykine, not far from Clonmore, and at nearby Preban, where there is a well dedicated to him under the name of Aidan.[9] Maodhóg's church appears to have become a noted centre of pilgrimage, with its five thousand graves and *martra*, 'relics', of the saints of Ireland, according to a poet named Brocán Cráibhtheach, 'pious'.[10] Included among the relics was the saint's little finger (*lúidín*), which was allegedly cut off while Maodhóg was still alive at the request of Onchú 'grandson of the poet', a noted collector of relics, but only on condition that Onchú's collection remain in Clonmore.[11] In Scotland, Maodhóg was remembered on 11 April on the Isle of Bute under the guise of Mahew (Latin Maccaeus).[12]

1 *SG* i, 389. 2 *MartO*[2] 106. 3 *CGSH* §285; *GRSH* 85; *Lgen*. 727.25; *CGH* 124b25–30; *DIB* vi, 221. 4 *Ériu* 18, 58 §6. 5 *VSHP* ii, 19 §54. 6 *MartD* 100. 7 *LL* 38330–77; *VSHP* ii, 149 §24, 161 §55. 8 OSL CW 335, 373, 382; *Carloviana* 55, 92; *Béaloideas* 4, 113–14. 9 *MartT* 32; *MartO*[2] 106; *MartG* 74; *MartD* 100. 10 *ZCP* 24, 142 §§55–7. 11 *MartO*[2] 70. 12 *Innes Review* 17, 9–10.

Maodhóg of Ferns (Fearna), barony of Scarawalsh, Co. Wexford. Patron of a church located close to the east coast of south Leinster, Maodhóg, or Aidan, as he is now better known, was perhaps the saint most frequently mentioned, after Patrick, in records relating to Irish activity in southern Britain, especially in Wales. Yet the genealogists were at one in assigning him to an obscure branch of the Oirghialla, descended from Colla Uais, and associated, according to some sources, with the Fir Luirg, whose name survives in that of the Fermanagh barony of Lurg.[1] Within this barony lies the parish of Magheraculmoney (Cúil Mhaine), whose patron, Deochain Aodh son of Maine, was probably ultimately identical with Maodhóg. The saint's mother, Eithne, 'descendant of Amhalghaidh', is variously described as belonging either to the Uí Mhic Uais or to a branch of the more important Connacht family that gave its name to Tír Amhalghadha, now Tirawley in Mayo.[2] All sources agree that Maodhóg's place of birth was Inis Breachmhaighe, an island on Brackley Lough in the Cavan parish of Templeport, a few miles north-east of Saint Mogue's Island on Templeport Lake and close to Drumlane, one of the main centres of the saint's cult in south-west Ulster.[3]

Several versions of the saint's Life have been preserved, beginning with a Latin text in a collection of Lives of Welsh saints, brought together about 1200, possibly at Brecon Priory, and now in the British Library.[4] This text is similar to that used by the editor of the earliest version preserved in Ireland, in the so-called Kilkenny collection, which in turn was adapted to provide two abbreviated Latin Lives and two vernacular *beathadha*, one of which was hugely expanded to accommodate the interests of the saint's churches in south-west Ulster.[5] All these redactions, to which may be added the recently discovered version of the abbreviated Latin text sent by Philip O'Sullivan Beare to Iohannes Bollandus in 1635, have been rightly described as interesting sources for the social and intellectual conditions of the times in which they were written.[6] In the continuing absence of a critical edition of the entire biographical dossier, dates for the individual versions of the saint's Life have yet to be determined reliably.

It has been suggested that the earliest Latin Life may have been translated from the vernacular about 1100, but the supporting evidence is slight.[7] The fact that there are many indications of Augustinian prejudice at work on the text would argue against a date earlier than the mid- to late twelfth century, when Drumlane, whose saints are summoned in the first chapter to pray for an end to the previous sterility of the saint's mother, became the seat of an Augustinian priory.[8] A few chapters later, Maodhóg's *collactaneus* (fellow-pupil) at Drumlane is introduced as Molaise of Devenish, and having gone together on pilgrimage, the young saints are miraculously directed towards their future foundations, Devenish in the north and Ferns in the south, both of them seats of Augustinian priories.[9] Later in the text, following a visit to Cashel in Munster, Maodhóg is directed to Kilmacduagh west of the Shannon, where he cures the gravely ill King Guaire.[10]

This place was also the seat of an Augustinian priory and, according to the Latin text of the Kilkenny collection, its patron, Colmán son of Duach, and Maodhóg together 'made prayer and *fraternitas* (brotherhood)'.[11] As noted by the editor of the text, this version of the Life, which stands at the head of the entire Irish dossier of the saint, actually makes use of the word *canonicus*, 'canon', in place of the *clericus* used by the text preserved in the Welsh collection.[12]

Among other signs of a late twelfth-century date for the 'original Life' is the emphasis placed on the saint's sojourn with St David in Wales, which accounts for eight chapters.[13] This example of opportunistic hagiography, arguably based on a model devised in the late eleventh century in Wales, and common in Irish Lives of this period, was probably designed to show that Maodhóg's churches, and especially Ferns, were on excellent terms with the Welsh Church, whose clerics would have been respected, at least in theory, by the mainly Cambro-Norman adventurers involved in the late twelfth-century conquest of Ireland.[14] Relative lateness is also indicated by the apparent influence of the *bóramha* tale, whose earliest surviving version is contained in the late twelfth-century Book of Leinster.[15] Seemingly aware of the fact that the *bóramha* tract had in mind Maodhóg of Clonmore, the author of the Life simply brought the Ferns saint to Clonmore, before showing him to have intervened successfully on behalf of the Leinstermen against the forces of the high-king, Aodh son of Ainmhire.[16]

Much of the saint's Life is taken up with the local affairs of Ferns, including the story of its foundation which, misogynistically, involved the expulsion of women washing in the nearby stream.[17] The donor of the site is named as Beag son of Eoghan, who belonged to the Uí Fheilmeadha branch of the south Leinster dynasty of Uí Cheinsealaigh, otherwise connected genealogically with Ferns through a certain Drúth Fearna.[18] Several other secular figures of note are featured in the Life, including two representatives of important dynasties in south-west Ulster, [Cairbre] Damhairgid son of Eacha, ancestor of the Maguires of Fermanagh, among other families, and Aodh Fionn (Albus), ancestor of the Uí Ruairc of Bréifne.[19] Most prominently featured is Brannabh son of Eacha, a seventh-century king of south Leinster, belonging like Beag son of Eoghan, to the Uí Fheilmeadha.[20]

The saint's travels within Ireland included visits to two places in the Déise of Waterford, Fennor (Fionnabhair) in the parish of Islandikane, close to Waterford Harbour, and Churchtown in the parish of Dysert (Díseart Nairbhre) in the parish of Ardmore, of which Maodhóg was later patron .[21] His memory was also kept alive at Cloncagh in the Limerick barony of Connello, an area he is said to have visited on two occasions, one of them involving a meeting with Íde.[22] Among other saints featured in the Life are his 'soul-friend', Molua, patron of Killaloe and Clonfertmulloe, Munna of Taghmon, and Mochua Luachra who was designated the saint's successor.[23] No account is given of the circumstances surrounding the saint's death, but some posthumous miracles are noted, including one that names Moling as his successor at Ferns.[24]

The expanded second vernacular Life of the saint, which freely intersperses verse, pays as much attention to his northern churches, at Rossinver (Ros Inbhir) in Leitrim, and especially at Drumlane in Cavan, as it does to Ferns.[25] Arranging to have his birth and subsequent greatness foretold not only by Patrick at Drumlane, but also by the mythical pre-Christian hero, Fionn son of Cumhall, at Ferns, the text (possibly as late as the sixteenth century) provided a member of the powerful ecclesiastical dynasty of Uí Dhubhthaigh (O'Duffys), who are numbered among Maodhóg's coarbs, with the privilege of fostering the saint.[26] Unlike the earlier Latin Life, which allowed him to go as far as Britain only, this text brings him to Rome, accompanied not only by some northern saints, but also by ancestors of coarbial families associated with his main churches.[27] From this pilgrimage, he is said to have returned with two relics, the famous *Breac Maodhóg*, formerly kept at Drumlane, now in the National Museum, and the *Bachall Bhrannaibh*, 'staff of Brannabh'.[28] Much attention is paid in the Life to the affairs of the kings of Bréifne, with interesting commentary on the manner in which these were inaugurated, and detailed accounts in prose and verse of their indebtedness to Maodhóg and his successors, who are duly named.[29]

At this point Maodhóg is brought from Drumlane to Ferns, where a substantial section of the Life is given over to a fresh account, albeit more in keeping with late medieval style, of the events narrated in the saint's earlier Lives, interrupted only by an interlude involving a return to Drumlane and a description of the circumstances surrounding the founding of Rossinver.[30] The final part of the Life again finds the saint mainly in Drumlane, where his seven relics and their powers are cited, especially in ensuring payment of dues, not only from the Uí Ruairc and Uí Raghallaigh families of Bréifne, but also further afield from the great families of Fermanagh. These dues, which are set out in great detail in prose and verse attributed to Giolla Mochuda Ua Caiside, the author of a long poem on the saint's life, were allegedly to be divided between Maodhóg's three main churches, north and south.[31] Dallán, patron of the parish (Kildallan) adjoining Drumlane and, according to the genealogists, a first cousin of the saint, is also featured as a willing listener to a detailed listing of Maodhóg's entitlements.[32] The Life ends, as did the Latin text, with a description of some of the miracles performed after the saint's death.[33]

Doubtless because of the importance of his Leinster church, and its strategic location near one of the main points of departure from Ireland to Britain, Maodhóg's name found its way into several other saints' Lives, including that of his *amicus anime*, 'soul-friend', Molua, in an episode similar to that recounted in Maodhóg's own Life.[34] Molua's church at Clonfertmulloe figured in a journey said to have been made by Colmán of Lynally to Ferns to assist Maodhóg in resuscitating his royal friend Brannabh son of Eacha, so that he might receive the last rites.[35] A similar episode is found not only in Maodhóg's own Life, but also, in abbreviated form, in the Life of Colmán of Dromore.[36] The Life of Maodhóg's *collactaneus* Molaise attributes to the two a sharing of the relics brought back from Rome by the Devenish saint.[37] An echo of the assertion that Maodhóg was succeeded at Ferns by Moling of St Mullin's is also found in the latter's Life.[38] That the privilege of succession to the see of Ferns had evidently become something of a *topos* is indicated by the assertion in Seanán's Life that he not only made a union with Maodhóg, but also followed him in the abbacy.[39] In his capacity as patron of Bréifne churches, the saint received great prominence in the Life of Náile of Kinawley, whom he is said to have favoured in various ways.[40] Within Bréifne he was no doubt also patron – albeit in the guise of Aodh – of Drumkerril (Druim Coirill) in the parish of Drumlane and, similarly disguised, of Drumshinny (Druim Seanaigh) in the Cavan parish of Killashandra.[41] Although treated positively by the author of Maodhóg's Life, Munna of Taghmon was elsewhere made the subject of a satire, attributed variously to the Ferns saint and to Colum Cille.[42]

Regarded as patron of the Uí Cheinsealaigh, Maodhóg was said, for no obvious reason, to have resembled the third-century Pope Cornelius in manners.[43] The saint is also among those cited in the Old Irish Table of Penitential Commutations as sponsors of a certain type of vigil.[44] Maodhóg died, according to the annals, in 620, 625, or even 660, and his feast fell on 31 January, which became the occasion of a cattle fair in the Wexford parish of Fethard.[45] However, the pattern at 'St Edan's' well in the parish of Clongeen in the same county was held on 15 May, and *lá 'le Maodhóg*, 'Maodhóg's day', fell on Mary's Day (15 August) at Kilnahue.[46] While Vogue / Mogue were anglicized forms of Maodhóg, it has been argued that Vauk, whose very popular pattern in the Wexford parish of Carn was held variously on 20 January or 20 June, was a local version of Féichín of Fore.[47] According to one early seventeenth-century source, Maodhóg's feast at Rossinver fell on 3 (*recte* 31?) January, and in Wales the saint was remembered on 28 February.[48] Although well remembered at Drumlane, where attention used to be drawn to the impression of his knee on a rock at Gloonmogue (*Glúin Maodhóg*), he gave way to Laurence the deacon as patron of the parish.[49] The saint's feast is arguably also mentioned in the Life composed at Rheinau on the borders of Germany and Switzerland for the local patron Findan, a native of Leinster.[50] Maodhóg is also among the handful of mainly Leinster saints commemorated in the tenth-century metrical calendar of Hampson.[51] In Leinster, Maodhóg also became patron of two Ossory parishes, Dunkitt and Dysartmoon.[52]

1 *CGSH* §63; *GRSH* 67; *Lgen*. 714.2; *VSHP* ii, 141n.; *MartO*² 54; *Breifne* 1, 118–33; *DIB* vi, 220–1. **2** *VSHP* ii, 295 §1; *BNÉ* i, 190 §1; cf. *CGSH* §722.46.60. **3** *VSHP* ii, 141 §3, 295 §2; *BNÉ* i, 190 §4; *Kenney* 449; OSL CN / LM 19–20; *Breifne* 1, 127–9; cf. *AnnU* 237; *CPL* 10, 637. **4** *VSBG* viii–xi; *VSHP* ii, 295–311. **5** *VSHP* i, lxxv–lxxviii; ibid. ii, 141–63, 295–311; *VSHH* 234–47; *BNÉ* i, xxxiii–xxxvii, 183–90; *MISL* 223–7; *Peritia* 1, 322. **6** *MS Bollandien* 452; *Kenney* 449. **7** *MISL* 395; *Peritia* 1, 322. **8** *VSHP* ii, 141 §1, 295 §1; *MRHI* 170. **9** *VSHP* ii, 143 §8, 296 §8; *MRHI* 169, 175–6. **10** *VSHP* ii, 306 §37. **11** Ibid.; *MRHI* 183. **12** *VSHP* i, lxxv (n.). **13** Ibid. ii, 144–7 §§11–18, 297–300 §11–18. **14** *ScrV* 41–8. **15** *LL* 37639–39321. **16** *VSHP* ii, 149 §24, 161 §55, 301 §24, 309 §54; *LL* 38330–77. **17** *VSHP* ii, 151 §27, 302 §27. **18** *CGH* 317c4, 15, 20n. **19** *VSHP* ii, 143–4 §§10–11, 297 §10–11. **20** Ibid. 149 §24, 153 §33, 157 §43, 161 §55, 301 §24, 303 §29, 309 §54; *CGH* 317cb20, 30. **21** *VSHP* ii, 148 §§21–2, 300–1 §§21–2; *OnomG* 347. **22** OSL LK i, 170, 180; *SACCL* 336, 413; *VSHP* ii, 154 §35, 159 §49, 305, §35, 308–9 §48. **23** Ibid. 148 §20, 152 §29, 154 §34, 300 §20, 302 §28, 305 §34. **24** Ibid. 162 §58, 310 §57. **25** *BNÉ* i, 190–290. **26** Ibid. 192–4 §§8–16; *Breifne* 10, 147–54. **27** *BNÉ* i, 200 §§35–6, 203 §46. **28** Ibid. 201 §38; *TIC* 221; *MDub*. 7, 94. **29** *BNÉ* i, 201–7 §§40–53. **30** Ibid. 207–44 §57–193, 233–7 §§149–60. **31** Ibid. 257 §215, 260 §221. **32** Ibid. 265–73 §§229–46. **33** Ibid. 279–89 §§264–77. **34** *VSHH* 140 §43; *VSHP* ii, 148 §20, 219 §38. **35** *VSHH* 221 §§39–40; cf. *MT* §18. **36** *VSHP* ii 157–8 §43; *VSHH* 359 §10. **37** *VSHP* ii, 135–7 §§20, 24. **38** Ibid. 193 §8. **39** *LisL* 2044–8. **40** *MHH* 105, 108–9, 121–2 §§16–17, 24, 27–8, 53–4.

41 *CGSH* §707.20.29. **42** *Anecd.* iv, 74 §878; *MartO*² 226. **43** *CGSH* §712.29; *ASH* 315 §6; *FFÉ* iii, 112–13. **44** *Ériu* 19, 64 §23. **45** ATig./*AU s.a.*; *MartT* 13; *MartO*² 39; *MartG* 26; *MartD* 32; *CECW* 205, 211; *TDI* i, 628; *ATig. s.a.* 620, 659/*AU s.a.* 625; *MartT* 13. **46** OSL WX i, 297; *CECW* 213. **47** *The Past* 2, 19–20; ibid. 26, 42–8. **48** *Celtica* 1, 65; *LWS* 173n. **49** OSL CN/LM 7, 11. **50** *MGH.SS* 15, 506 §9. **51** *AB* 104, 92. **52** *HADO* iv, 137, 185.

Maoin. *See* Buithe.

Maoineann of Clonfert, barony of Longford, Co. Galway. An attractive tale, preserved in the late twelfth-century Book of Leinster, relates how Maoineann (also Maona or Maoine) asked Bréanainn whether death was to be feared, only to have recited for him a list of the negative aspects of the condition, followed by a eulogy on the heavenly realm – which was to be sought after – as compared to that of earthly kings which led only to various types of misfortune.[1] Maoineann is thought to have accompanied Bréanainn as a psalmist from Britain to Ireland, where they first settled in Inchiquin (Inis Maca Cuinn), an island on Lough Corrib in the Galway parish of Killursa.[2] He is also said to have been with Bréanainn shortly after the founding of Clonfert, when he was asked to place the latter's staff over the body of a dead boy, thus bringing him back to life, and the two saints are again together in a tale that relates how Bréanainn prevented demons from taking his mother's corpse, over which Maoineann was holding vigil.[3] The saint's western connections appear to underlie the reference to him in a poem attributed to Seanán of Scattery, which invokes his assistance.[4] His obit in the annals for 572 describes him as bishop of Clonfert, and the day of his commemoration (1 March), also observed at some churches in Scotland, was shared with a much better-known Briton, David of Wales.[5] A namesake and probable double was remembered at the Kildare church of Cloncurry (Cluain Conaire), whose patron, according to an early seventeenth-century list, was Brendan, presumably of Clonfert.[6] It has been suggested that he was ultimately identical with Ninian of Whithorn in Scotland, but the evidence is slight.[7] The saint's feast fell on 16 September, and his remains were raised at Clonfert in 1162 and enshrined with those of Cuimín Fada.[8] In Scotland, Maoineann possibly came to be known as Monan — of St Monan's in Fife — and as such became the subject of an Office Life, as found in the Breviary of Aberdeen, and of an entry in Hermann Greven's martyrology.[9]

1 *CGSH* §715; *TEAB* 445–51. **2** *VSHP* i, 143 §88n. **3** Ibid. 145 §91; *RC* 31, 309–11. **4** *ZCP* 10, 24 §19. **5** *AU s.a.*; *MartT* 20; *MartO*² 80; *MartG* 46; *MartD* 60; *EIM* §58; *CPNS* 294–5; *KSS* 412–13; *Innes Review* 32, 66. **6** *Dinn.* 2, 31. **7** *CPNS* 295; *KSS* 387; *Innes Review* 19, 57–74. **8** *MartT* 71; *MartO*² 194; *MartG* 178; *MartD* 248; *AU s.a.*. **9** *LegSS* 62–4, 398–9; *AS. Iunii* vi, 121.

Maoise. *See* Fionnbharr of Drumcolumb.

Maol Anfaidh of Molana Abbey (Ceall Mhaoil Anfaidh, alias Dairinis), parish of Templemichael, barony of Coshmore and Coshbride, Co. Waterford. Assigned by the genealogists to the Osraighe (whence the later diocese of Ossory), Maol Anfaidh son of Anbhfhothach came to be associated with the church on a little island (*Insula sancti Molanfid*) near the mouth of the river Blackwater, which, from the twelfth century, was the location of a house of canons regular of St

Augustine.[1] Little is known of him, but the inclusion of his name among those 'in union' with Maol Ruain of Tallaght would indicate a floruit in the late eighth or early ninth century.[2] A twelfth-century tradition states that, having witnessed a little bird wailing, he received news from an angel of the death of Molua of Kyle.[3] The saint may also have been venerated under the guise of 'Mullana' (Blunny / Lunny) in the Limerick parish of Tullabracky (in the former territory of Déis Bheag), the church of which he is reputed to have founded.[4] The saint shared his feast of 31 January with Maodhóg of Ferns.[5]

1 *CGSH* §183; *GRSH* 94; *Lgen.* 727.4–5; *CGH* 129b40; *MRHI* 187; *AH* 12, 34 §50. 2 *CGSH* §713.2.14. 3 *AB* 69, 88–9; *MartO*[2] 56. 4 OSL LK ii, 94; *DiocL* 116; *SACCL* 433. 5 *MartT* 13; *MartO*[2] 39; *MartG* 26; *MartD* 32.

Maol Brighde of Armagh (Ard Mhacha) and of Iona in Scotland. Maol Brighde son of Tornán belonged to the same branch of the Ceinéal Conaill as his successor on Iona, Dubhthach son of Dubhán.[1] Like his successor, who held Raphoe as well as Iona, Maol Brighde enjoyed a dual abbacy, according to the custom of the period, being elected to Armagh in 883 and to Iona in 891.[2] As coarb of Adhamhnán, he may also have held Raphoe. His prior tenure of the abbacy of Armagh, a position that he appears to have retained until his death in 927, has been taken to mean that he was based in Ireland throughout, and that Iona lost at this time its long-held position as abbatial seat of the coarb of Colum Cille.[3] While coarb of both saints, he is reputed to have raised treasure from the men of Munster, to be used as ransom for captives taken by Britons.[4]

The gospel book of Mac Durnan (Mac Tornáin), apparently compiled in Armagh in the tenth century, is named after the saint. Its title and present location in Lambeth Palace, London, are explained by a note on one of its folios to the effect that the English king Athelstan (†939) gave the gospels of 'Maeilbrithus mac Durnan' as a gift to the church of Canterbury.[5] His fame abroad is reflected by his death notice in one of the annals which describes him as 'head of the piety of all Ireland and of the greater part of Europe'.[6] He may also be the Maol Brighde mentioned in the *baile*, 'mantic vision', attributed to Bricín of Tomregan.[7] The name of Maol Brighde's mother, Saorlaith daughter of Cuileabhaoth, has also been preserved.[8] According to the later martyrologies, the saintly abbot's feast fell on 22 February.[9]

1 *CGSH* §347; *GRSH* 42; *Lgen.* 698.9; *DIB* vi, 221–2. 2 *NHI* ix, 239, 257; *VC*[1] 392–3. 3 *IKD* 74–6. 4 *FAI* 178 §449. 5 *Kenney* 645. 6 *AFM s.a.* 7 *ZCP* 9, 450 §4. 8 *CGSH* §722.87. 9 *MartG* 40; *MartD* 54.

Maol Céadair of Kilmalkedar (Ceall Mhaoil Chéadair), barony of Corkaguiny, Co. Kerry. The length of Ireland, according to an old saying, was from Tigh Móire at Dún Chaoin (Dunquin) on the tip of the Dingle peninsula to Donaghadee in the north-east corner of the county of Down. Maol Céadair son of Rónán may be said to have personified this measure of Ireland through his genealogical affiliation to the Dál bhFiatach of east Ulster and the location of the church named after him at Kilmalkedar, west of Mount Brandon on the Dingle peninsula.[1] Beyond recording the local tradition that the church had been erected by Bréanainn and 'Maol Cealtair', John O'Donovan had little to say of the saint in his lengthy account of the parish.[2] Judging by the notice of his feastday of 14 May, which he shared with Mochuda of Lismore, he was traditionally regarded as a son of an (otherwise unrecorded) Ulster king.[3] It has been suggested that the saint's name derives from *céadar*, an Irish borrowing of Latin *cedrus*, 'cedar', in this case signifying the principal timber from which the Holy Cross was made.[4] The local *turas*, 'pattern', from Kilmalkedar to the summit of Mount Brandon was held on 29 June.[5]

1 *CGSH* §140; *GRSH* 84; *Lgen*. 722.8. 2 *ACoK* 95–110; cf. *TCCD* 116. 3 *MartT* 42; *MartG* 96; *MartD* 126. 4 *SAM* 14, 58–67; *ZCP* 8, 107. 5 *TCCD* 125.

Maol Corghais of Aran (Ára) in the barony of the same name, Co. Galway. Among the numerous saints said to have been born of Inghean Bhaoith of Killinaboy was a certain Maol Corghais, described as *teine teann chóigidh Chonnacht*, 'stiff fire of the province of Connacht'.[1] This is doubtless the man of the name included in the list of homonymous saints, where he is assigned to Aran.[2] A further reference to him is found in the poem listing those who might be called to assist Seanán of Scattery Island.[3] There are no means of knowing whether he was the saint of the name commemorated on 12 March, a day otherwise observed on Aran because of its association with Pope Gregory.[4]

1 *IrT* iv, 93 §4. 2 *CGSH* §707.859. 3 *ZCP* 10, 24 §19. 4 *MartT* 22; *MartG* 52; *MartD* 74; *OFWC* 118n.

Maol Dala (Eala). This saint is remembered in a poem detailing the children of Inghean Bhaoith of Killinaboy in Co. Clare.[1] Grouped with him are three Clare saints, Blathmhac of Rath, Mac Reithe (Creiche) of Kilmacrehy, and Conall of Kilconnell. Maol Dala (Eala) is again featured in Mac Reithe's Life, together with Mac Aoibhlín and Blathmhac. This describes him as one of the local patrons who joined with Mac Reithe in expelling from the locality a fearsome water-monster.[2] He is also among those called upon, in a poem in Classical Irish – again together with Blathmhac and Conall, and numerous other saints – to help in releasing Ireland's southern half (Leath Mogha) from a bondage imposed on it by the northern half (Leath Chuinn), championed by Finnian of Clonard.[3] There is no record of either Maol Dala's church or his feast.

1 *IrT* iv, 93 §8. 2 *MHH* 36 §50, 39 §55, 42 §61, 45 §68. 3 RIA MS 23L11, 263; *SAM* 24.1, 17, 20.

Maol Díthreibh of Terryglass (Tír Dá Ghlas), barony of Lower Ormond, Co. Tipperary. Maol Díthreibh was one of several saints said to have been 'in union' with Maol Ruain of Tallaght.[1] He was thus involved, like many other anchorites, with the group that went under the name of *céili Dé*, 'clients of God'. How deep his involvement was is shown by his part in the 'Monastery of Tallaght', one of the principal texts associated with the group.[2] This sets out the teachings of both Maol Ruain and his interlocutor Maol Díthreibh, who appears to have been known personally by the author of the tract.[3] Maol Díthreibh died in 840, too late to have his name added to the Tallaght martyrologies which were compiled about 830, and thus also absent from later lists of feasts.[4]

1 *CGSH* §§713.6.14, 724.5; *DIB* vi, 222. 2 *PRIA* 29C5 (1911) 115–79; *CéliD* 101–14. 3 *CéliD* 101. 4 *AFM s.a.*

MAOL DÓID of Muckno (Mucnamh), barony of Cremorne, Co. Monaghan. When drawing up an (extensive) list of additions to his copy of the Martyrology of Usuard, Hermann Greven (†1480) of Cologne came across in one of his sources the entry: *In Hibernia, Maldod confessoris*, which he duly copied.[1] Although no doubt well aware of Ireland's reputation as an *Insula Sanctorum*, the Cologne Carthusian can have had little knowledge of the circumstances that led to the presence in his source of the name of a relatively obscure Irish saint. His information has recently been shown to have come from another Cologne martyrology, drawn up in the early eleventh century for the use of the Benedictine monks of either Gross St Martin or St Pantaleon, both of which were governed by an Irish abbot named Elias (Oilill) between 1019 and 1042.[2] On hearing of Elias' death in 1042, an Irish annalist recorded it as follows: 'Oilill of Muckno, head of the Irish monks in Cologne, rested'; it was doubtless this connection that led to the inclusion of Maol Dóid's name in the Cologne source used by Greven.[3]

The Irish record of the saint is more straightforward. The genealogists attached him through his father Fínghin to the Uí Mhéith, whose name survives in the part of Louth known as Omeath, but whose lands also extended into Monaghan.[4] An uncle of his, Scannlán (†673) son of Fínghin, was the first king of Uí Mhéith to be recorded in the annals, and this man's son, Flann Feabhla (†715), abbot of Armagh, figures prominently in the story of the 'Settling of the Manor of Tara'.[5] The name of a later member of the family, Ionnrachtach, was adopted in the surname Ua hIonnrachtaigh (O'Hanratty), and remarkably, when John O'Donovan visited the area in 1835, he was told that 'Maol Dóighidh' – locally taken to mean 'Myles of the Burning' because of the saint's miraculous escape from a conflagration agreed between Patrick and a local chieftain as proof of the truth of the Christian faith – was one of the Hanrattys.[6] By then an origin legend had gained currency which described how Muckno was founded at a place identified for the saint by a (heavenly) pig that had swum across the nearby lake. Although the swim was based on the erroneous belief that Muckno derived from *muc-snámh*, 'pig-swim', the presence of an animal, usually wild, often formed an integral part of foundation-stories. The list of aliases of the saints states that Maol Dóid's original name was Aodh.[7] He is said to have been one of the many who died of the plague known as the *Buidhe Chonaill*, and his feast, though assigned by one source to 24 March, was usually observed on 13 May.[8] The parish church of Muckno was named after the saint under the guise of 'Meldocius'.[9]

1 *AS*.Iun. vi, app. 274; *ClRec*. 20, 473–90. 2 *FSHIM* 119–46 at 138–9. 3 Ibid.; *AU s.a.* 4 *CGSH* §50; *GRSH* 71; *Lgen*. 715.1. 5 *AU s.a.*; *NHI* ix, 238; *Ériu* 4, 126 §3. 6 OCBG §1672; OSL AH/MN 77–80, 87, 93–7, 101; *ClRec*. 6, 137–8, 151; *ClRec*. 20, 488–9. 7 *CGSH* §703.14. 8 *IrT* iii, 85 §9; *FourIM* 49; *MartT* 42; *MartG* 96; *MartD* 126. 9 *CPL* 8, 435; *ClRec*. 7, 406.

MAOLDUBH of Cloncurry (Cluain Conaire Mhaolduibh), barony of East Offaly, Co. Kildare. This man was among those said to have been subject to Brighid of

Kildare, which no doubt applies to the church named after him.[1] Close by was the church of Kilmoney (Ceall Mhuine) in the parish of Rathangan, which also figures in the list, immediately after Cloncurry.[2] Possibly with Maoldubh were two companions named for him in the list, Moghreallóg and Mocheallóg. Maoldubh's name is included among those commemorated on 18 December.[3]

1 *CGSH* §670.51; *Lgen.* 753.22. 2 *CGSH* §670.52. 3 *MartT* 86; *MartG* 240; *MartD* 340.

Maoldubh of Cluain Mór Léith. If his pedigree were true, Maoldubh would have basked in the reflected glory of his father Aodh Finnliath (†879), claimant to the so-called 'high-kingship', and his brother Niall Glúndubh (†919), eponymous ancestor of the powerful family of Ua Néill of Tyrone.[1] The mainline genealogists assign to Aodh Finnliath two sons only, however, Niall Glúndubh and Domhnall, king of Oileach, the likely progenitor of the Ua (Mac) Lochlainn line of kings.[2] Maoldubh elsewhere attracted the attention of an anonymous poet who extolled his asceticism and flawlessness.[3] A seventeenth-century source speculatively suggested that he was commemorated either on 18 or 23 December.[4]

1 *CGSH* §86.1; *GRSH* 47; *Lgen.* 702.5. 2 *CGH* 140a28; *IKHK* 284. 3 *CGSH* §86.1. 4 *GRSH* 47.

Maoldubh of Fore (Fobhar), parish of St Feighins, barony of Fore, Co. Westmeath. Although assigned through his father Amhalgaidh to the Uí Bhriúin of Connacht, Maoldubh's supposed ancestor, Conall son of Brian (Brión), is nowhere else attested.[1] In notes added to the feast of Fiontan Maoldubh on 20 October, scholiasts of the Martyrology of Aonghas made much of his pedigree, not least by maintaining that the saint's seed, Muintear Mhaolduibh, were based at Fore, where Maoldubh had been a cellarer (*ceallóir*).[2] This is followed by several quatrains, variously attributed to Féichín of Fore and Míchéal, extolling Maoldubh's virtues. The first and last quatrains are elsewhere quoted in relation to Maoldubh of Cluain Mór Léith.[3] The saint has possibly been confused with Maoldubh Beag, 'little', who was commemorated as abbot of Fore on 2 October.[4]

1 *CGSH* §662.83; *GRSH* 60; *Lgen.* 710.10; *AB* 69, 86–8. 2 *MartO*[1] clviii–clix; *MartO*[2] 224. 3 *CGSH* §86.1. 4 *MartG* 188; *MartD* 264.

Maoldubh of Lann Mhaolduibh, near Rossnaree, parish of Knockcommon, barony of Lower Duleek, Co. Meath. The site of Maoldubh's church became famous as the place near the river Boyne designated for a tragic tryst between the lovers Baile son of Buan and Oileann daughter of Lughaidh, which resulted in the death of each and their union beyond the grave [1] Otherwise, little is known either of the church or of its saint. The single entry in the corpus of saints' pedigrees that refers to him, together with a companion named Fiontan, immediately follows the pedigree of Maoldubh of Cluain Mór Léith.[2]

1 *MM* 472. 2 *CGSH* §86.1.2; cf. *Lgen.* 702.5.

Maoldubh son of Ultán. *See* Colmán of Holdenstown.

Maol Finniain of St Patrick's Island (Inis Phádraig), off Skerries, parish of Holmpatrick, barony of Balrothery East, Co. Dublin. The martyrologist, Maol Muire Ua Gormáin, brought his list of names for 6 February to an end with a couplet commemorating 'Finnian', whose name is glossed 'Maol Finniain, abbot of Inis Phádraig'.[1] There appears to be no other direct reference to this man, but the obit of Maol Finniain son of Flannagán, king of Breagha (now Meath with parts of Dublin and Louth), who died in 903, extols its subject as a 'religious layman'.[2] This has led to the suggestion that the king and abbot may have been one and the same.[3] The island is otherwise known for a raid on it in 798 by Vikings, who broke the shrine of Dochonna.[4]

1 *MartG* 30; cf. *MartD* 40. 2 *AU s.a.* 3 *IsPatrick* 125–39; *FSHIM* 160. 4 *AU s.a.*

Maol Fithrigh. *See* Maol Geimhridh.

Maol Geimhridh. Kilmaleery in the barony of Bunratty Lower was the last of the parishes of the county of Clare, which had cost him 'so much labour, toil and pain', visited by John O'Donovan.[1] He stated that the name was known locally as 'Cill Mailiaraidh', and that a holy well dedicated to the saint was much frequented.[1] As there is no such name as Maol Iaraidh, it has been suggested that it stood for either Maol Uidhre or Maol Fithrigh.[2] There is no other evidence of the existence of a saint named Maol Uidhre, and as Maol Fithrigh is known only from an addition to the Martyrology of Donegal at 8 October, Maol Geimhridh, who is independently attested as a saint associated with Aran, may be the saint commemorated in the name of the parish of Kilmaleery.[3]

1 *ACoC* 266. 2 *CoC* 52; Logainm.ie. 3 *MartD* 270; *CGSH* §707.858.

Maol Íosa Ua Brolcháin. One branch of the genealogy of Ceinéal Fearadhaigh of the Tyrone barony of Clogher culminated in Maol Íosa, whose ancestor, five times removed, was named Brolchán.[1] Elsewhere, Maol Íosa, who is described as a cleric, is said to have had three brothers, as well as an aunt named Mór, the mother of Maol Muire, abbot of Armagh, who died in 1020.[2] This would suit Maol Íosa's own floruit, since he died, according to the Annals of Ulster, in 1086, 'eminent in wisdom and piety and in poetry in both languages'.[3] The reference to his command of both languages – Irish and Latin – is borne out by his most famous composition, *Deus meus adiuva me*, which is still sung today.[4] Seven other poems are ascribed to Maol Íosa, all of them religious and one, on the eight vices, extending to sixty-six quatrains.[5] There is nothing in the poems that sheds any light on Maol Íosa's career, but his proven reputation has led to the attribution to him by modern scholars of four other poems, including the well-known *A Chrínóc*, supposedly written in celebration of an old psalm-book.[6] He has also been put forward as the possible author of the *Passions and Homilies* preserved in the *Leabhar Breac*.[7]

According to John Colgan, Maol Íosa spent his youth in Both Chonais, a site at Carrowmore in the Donegal parish of Culdaff, whose founding is attributed to Comhghall of Bangor.[8] This would suit the assertion that Díocha, grandfather of Brolchán (eponymous ancestor of Maol Íosa's family), was blessed by Maol

Rubha of Applecross, Comhghall's supposed successor at Bangor.[9] Little else is known of Maol Íosa's life, but that he died as a member of the community at Armagh, apparently while on pilgrimage in Lismore.[10] His feast, first recorded in the late twelfth-century Martyrology of Gorman, was celebrated on 16 January.[11]

1 *CGH* 146d14–30; *HDGP* iv, 119–20. **2** OCBG §§604–7. **3** *AU s.a.* **4** *EIL* 52–4; *MÍOB* 52; cf. *LH* i, 159. **5** *MÍOB* 42–77. **6** *OldI* 154–60; *MIL* 74–8; *MÍOB* 80–2. **7** *PIBA* 1, 67–8. **8** *ASH* 108; *CGSH* §662.34. **9** OCBG §603. **10** *AI s.a.* 1086. **11** *MartG* 16; *MartD* 18; *AU s.a.* 1086.

Maol Maodhóg of Bangor and Armagh. About the time that Maol Maodhóg, now better known as Malachy, was born, approximately 1094–5, Anselm of Canterbury was penning his first letter to the bishops of Ireland, addressing it to *seniori Domnaldo*.[1] This was not Domhnall son of Amhalghaidh, abbot of Armagh, the last unordained representative of the Clann tSíonaigh (the ecclesiastical family later denounced by St Bernard as *generatio mala et adultera*), who was then completing his circuit of Munster, from which he 'brought away his full tribute'.[2] The 'senior' written to by Anselm was Domhnall Ua hÉanna (†1098), bishop of Killaloe, one of the few prelates of the period to share with Maol Maodhóg (whose descent was traced to the Ceinéal Conaill of Donegal) the privilege of being elevated to the rank of a saint.[3]

Another to share in this distinction was, however, Domhnall son of Amhalghaidh's successor at Armagh, Ceallach (Latin Celsus) son of Aodh, who, although gaining the abbacy in 1105 on the basis of the hereditary rights of his family, went on to take holy orders and allow himself to be consecrated bishop and archbishop.[4] During Ceallach's tenure, a solid foundation was laid for the implementation of what is called the twelfth-century reform of the Irish church, including the establishment of dioceses, hitherto little known in Ireland, at the synod of Rathbrassil in 1111. Maol Maodhóg, whose father Mugh Róin was head of the school at Armagh, did not belong to the Clann tSíonaigh. Moreover, by nominating him, first to the see of Connor and then, as his own successor, to the see of Armagh, Ceallach ensured that the metropolitan see would never again be a hereditary birthright.[5]

Following his succession to Ceallach, Maol Maodhóg gave further (equally influential) impetus to reform, by presiding over the arrival and consolidation in Ireland of some continental orders, most notably Cistercians and canons regular of St Augustine, both of which may have established their first houses in the mid- to late 1120s.[6] At Bangor and at Armagh, where his mentor, the reform-minded Íomhar Ua hAodhagáin, founded the stone church of St Peter and Paul in 1126, Maol Maodhóg may have been personally instrumental in introducing the Augustinian rule.[7]

As a young man, the saint spent some years in Lismore, where his tutor Malchus (Maol Íosa ua hAinmhire), a former bishop of Waterford and archbishop of Cashel, had received his training in Winchester.[8] At Lismore, he met and became friendly with Cormac Mac Carthaigh, king of Cashel, then removed from the kingship by his brother. Possibly under Maol Maodhóg's influence, Cormac went on to found several well-known religious houses in Munster, including the chapel named after him in Cashel, 'twelve churches' at Lismore, and the

Augustinian priory of Gill Abbey in Cork, a city in whose election of a bishop, the prelate took a personal interest and part.[9] This was a prelude only to Maol Maodhóg's subsequent career, as archbishop of Armagh and, following his resignation from this see in 1136, as bishop of Down.[10]

It was in the latter capacity that Maol Maodhóg decided to make the first of two pilgrimages to Rome, in quest of the *pallia* that were needed for the holders of Ireland's two archiepiscopal sees, at Armagh and Cashel. The long journey to Rome was made via the court of King David in Scotland, and York in northern England. There, he may have been instrumental in procuring for Laurence of Durham (†1154) a copy of Brighid's *vita prima*, which Laurence reworked, and perhaps also in purveying the (erroneous) view that Cuthbert of Durham and Lindisfarne was of Irish origin, which Eugenius, bishop of Lismore, may later (1184–5) have 'confirmed'.[11]

On the Continent, Maol Maodhóg visited Clairvaux, where St Bernard first met him, before going on to spend a month in Rome. There, although refused his request for the *pallia*, he was appointed apostolic legate to Ireland. On the return journey, he again visited Clairvaux before going on to Arrouaise, the centre of continuing reform of the Augustinian canons and, on the final leg of his journey, he once more spent some time at the court of the king of Scotland.[12] While in Clairvaux, he was arguably responsible for providing the church authorities of Taranto in southern Italy with the detail needed – much of it connected with the Lismore area – to underpin the belief that their patron Cataldo was of Irish origin.[13]

Back in Ireland, Maol Maodhóg travelled countrywide in the exercise of his apostolic and pastoral duties, performing many healing miracles, bringing peace to warring factions, and arranging for the introduction of continental monastic rules in the Cistercian abbey at Mellifont and in the Augustinian priory of Louth.[14] He also convened a synod held at Inis Phádraig (St Patrick's Island) near Dublin in 1148, following which, apparently presentient of his imminent death, Maol Maodhóg again set out to meet the Pope, then in France, to request of him the granting of *pallia* for the four archiepiscopal sees, Dublin and Tuam having now been added to Armagh and Cashel.[15] He failed to meet the Pope, who had returned to Rome, but managed to reach Clairvaux, where he died *vivens mortuus*, 'appearing more like one alive', on the feast of All Souls, the fourth of the Nones of November.[16]

So impressed was St Bernard by this holy man that he felt compelled 'to tell that which of necessity he saw', compiling, at the request of 'Conganus', abbot of Inishlounaght, and no doubt with the assistance of Irish informants, a Life so full of local detail that it serves as arguably the most important witness to the history of the twelfth-century reform.[17] Bernard also wrote a letter of consolation to Maol Maodhóg's Irish brethren and delivered two sermons on the virtues of the saint.[18] The feast of Maol Maodhóg, 'sage of synods', originally celebrated on 2 November, was moved shortly afterwards to the following day.[19] Maol Maodhóg's sanctity received almost immediate recognition in the *Visio Tnugdali*, a text written at Regensburg in Germany a few years after the saint's death, which placed him and his brother Giolla Críost among four blessed bishops seen by Tnúthghal in Patrick's company in heaven.[20] The necrology begun in the Regensburg *Schottenkloster* about the same time likewise drew attention to the saint, entering his name in the form 'Maelmorhorgius episcopus Hiberniae' among those commemorated on 1 November.[21] His sanctity received papal sanction in 1190 at the hands of Clement III.[22] The prophecies for which Malachy was later mainly remembered, concerning succession to the papal throne, English domination of Ireland, and the kings of Castile in Spain, have been shown to be fabrications.[23]

1 *Kenney* 761; *DIB* vi, 308–11. **2** *BCLMA* 45; *BCOC* 234; *AU s.a.* 1094. **3** *CGSH* §§407, 662.29–30; *PHCC* 5, 111. **4** *TCR* 19–39. **5** *BCLMA* 43–4; *IER* (5th ser.) 70, 961–78; ibid. 71, 134–8, 317–31; *DIB* vi, 309. **6** *MRHI* 114–20, 146–52; but cf. *TIC* 137; *DIB* vi, 310. **7** *MRHI* 157, 161; *RM* 3.2, 124–31; but cf. *TIC* 136. **8** *BCLMA* 18–24; *BCOC* 31, 202–10. **9** *MIA s.a.* 1138; *BCLMA* 36–42, 92–4; *BCOC* 230–2, 306–8; *JCHAS* 54, 41–60. **10** *BCLMA* 43–64; *BCOC* 246–64; *Peritia* 10, 197–99. **11** *BCLMA* 67–70; *BCOC* 267–72; *Kenney* 362; *RSC* 144–54; *Peritia* 2, 137–9; *RM* 3, 155–7; *TIC* 121. **12** *BCLMA* 70–9; *BCOC* 272–84. **13** *CasaIt.* 108–12. **14** *BCLMA* 80–116; *BCOC* 282–354; *MRHI* 139–40; 185–6; *SAM* 22.2, 8–24. **15** *Kenney* 767; *HIC* ii.1, 54. **16** *BCLMA* 117–30; *BCOC* 354–76; *DIB* vi, 310. **17** *BCLMA* 4; *BCOC* 180; *Kenney* 767; *SAM* 3.2, 318–32; *TIC* 101–8. **18** *BCLMA* 137–60; *BCOC* 380–424. **19** *MartG* 210; *MartD* 294–6; *MartFC* 190. **20** *BGBR* 26, 75; *VisTnug.* 55. **21** *BGBR* 26, 27n., 75; *IEKF* 396–7. **22** *BiblSS* viii, 581. **23** *Kenney* 767; *AB* 51, 318–24; *ProphSS* 108–37; *AH* 5, 20–38.

Maol Muire Ua Gormáin of Knock Abbey, parish and county of Louth. Partly in response to a decree of the synod held at Clane in 1162 which enjoined 'rule and good order' on the Irish Church, and partly because of the need to emphasize the healthy state of the Irish liturgy after the arrival of the Normans in 1169, a series of new martyrologies was produced at the end of the twelfth century.[1] The first of these, the metrical and vernacular Martyrology of Gorman – which survives in a unique copy made by Míchéal Ó Cléirigh in 1630, now in the Bibliothèque Royale, Brussels (MS 5100–4) – was composed in *Rinnard Mór* metre by an Augustinian canon, Maol Muire Ua Gormáin, at Knock Abbey (Cnoc na nApstal), near Louth, between 1168 and 1170.[2] The date proposed for the martyrology depends partly on information provided by the author – who stated that he was writing in the time of Ruaidhrí Ua Conchobhair (†1173/4), king of Ireland, Giolla Mic Liag (†1174), archbishop of Armagh, and Aodh Ua Caollaidhe (†1182), bishop of Clogher – and partly on an entry in an antiphonary formerly belonging to the church of Armagh which mentions the completion of the 'chief books of the order of the year' at Knock Abbey during the reign of Donnchadh Ua Cearbhaill (†1168–9).

Little is known of Maol Muire beyond his status as abbot of Knock Abbey. He appears to have belonged to the same distinguished ecclesiastical family as Flann Ua Gormáin (†1174) who, on his return to Ireland from his studies abroad, became head of the school of Armagh, and possibly, Fionn Ua Gormáin, bishop of Kildare.[3] The text of Maol Muire's martyrology provides some evidence of his personal interests. For example, his devotion to St Augustine is made clear by the inclusion in the text of three feastdays of the saint, at 28 August, 4 September, and 11 October. His reference to the 'black monks' of Derry at 9 June would suggest that Augustinian canons had a foundation there long before the traditional date of their arrival in the early thirteenth century.[4] Other than the use of *truagh* (8 August) and *truaghán* (6 March), a term reminiscent of Latin *pauper*, to describe his monkish status, Maol Muire does not refer directly to himself. Among the sources used by him were copies of the Martyrology of Tallaght – his, almost exclusive, source of Irish saints – and the Martyrology of Usuard. His is the earliest Irish martyrology to reveal the presence in Ireland of a copy of Usuard's popular text. The year of his death may have been 1181 and, according to an entry in the seventeenth-century Martyrology of Donegal, he was commemorated on 3 July.[5]

1 *FSHIM* 147–224. **2** Ibid. 147–71; *MartG* xviii–xxi. **3** *FSHIM* 149–50; but cf. *Ogma* 105–11. **4** *MRHI* 168–9. **5** *FSHIM* 154; *MartD* 186.

Maol Odhráin of Kilmoleran (Ceall Mhaoil Odhráin), barony of Upperthird, Co. Waterford. A holy well dedicated to Maol Odhráin (anglicized Molleran), who gave name to this parish, is in the townland of Carrickbeg.[1] Now also regarded as the patron saint of the nearby Tipperary town of Carrick-on-Suir, Maol Odhráin – not Mo Ailearán, as sometimes thought – is nowhere else attested.[2] Despite the presence of several saints of this name in the martyrologies, none can now be identified with the patron of Kilmoleran.

1 *WatLis.* 115. **2** Ibid. 111; *PND* 400.

Maol Ruain of Tallaght (Tamhlacht), barony of Uppercross, Co. Dublin. Having founded the monastery of Tallaght – in 774, according to one set of annals – Maol Ruain son of Colmán came to be regarded as one of the leading Irish churchmen of his day.[1] The saint's church became known as one of the 'two eyes of Ireland' (the other being Finglas), possibly because of the many external influences that flowed through it.[2] He was greatly involved with the anchoritic group that went under the name of *céili Dé* (Culdees, clients of God) which, though mainly associated with Tallaght, led to the foundation of many new churches throughout the country.[3]

The early ninth century saw the literary flowering of the *céili Dé*, and among other works produced at this time were two martyrologies, the first in prose, the second metrical, both of which commemorate Maol Ruain (†792).[4] The metrical text, which extols Maol Ruain as 'the splendid sun of the island of the Gaeil', also mentions the saint in both prologue and epilogue.[5] In the prologue, where he is described in solar terms as 'the sun of Midhe's south plain', his grave is presented as a place of pilgrimage and healing. In the epilogue, the author (Aonghas of Tallaght) refers to Maol Ruain as his tutor, as does the preface added to the martyrology in the late twelfth century.[6] In this preface, Aonghas is said to have sought out Maol Ruain as his *anmchara*, 'soul-friend', and to have been recognized by the Tallaght saint as the 'prophesied one'. In other texts of this period, such as the 'Monastery of Tallaght', the teachings of Maol Ruain were set out in detail.[7] Elsewhere the saint is presented as a model teacher of good moral behaviour.[8] Maol Ruain is also commemorated in the Stowe Missal, the earliest surviving Irish text of its kind, and likewise a product of the anchoritic reform, which capitalizes the letters of his name and accords it first place in a section of a litany.[9]

Many contemporaries were gathered around the saint or followed his teachings in a union of mostly Munster saints that included the two Flanns of Derrynaflan, Flannán of Killaloe, Maol Anfaidh of Molana Abbey, and Feidhlimidh son of Criomhthann, king of Munster.[10] No Life survives for Maol Ruain, and Lives of other saints fail to mention him so that, despite the many references to him in texts associated with Tallaght – some of which purport to be his writings – little is known of the saint's background. He is, however, associated with Sliabh Mairge (which gave name to the Laois barony of Slievemargy) in a short extract from the Book of Leinster, and he is among those called upon by the author of a poem attributed to Moling to come to the assistance of the Leinstermen.[11] His genealogy assigned him to a line of descent of the Ulaidh of north-east Ulster to which Colmán Eala and Seanán of Laraghbryan also belonged, and his mother was named Broicseach.[12]

Maol Ruain's feast, which fell on 7 July, continued to be observed up to the late nineteenth century, by which time the saint, now designated Mollroone (Mollroony), had come to be regarded as a female, whose loaf and griddle – the base of a high cross and hollowed out stone – were pointed out in Tallaght graveyard.[13] Birds, it is said, cease to sing in the area about Tallaght on the saint's day, which is among the handful of mainly Leinster feasts remembered in the tenth-century metrical calendar of Hampson.[14] The saint's cult spread southwards to the parish of Artramon in Wexford, where an image, found near the well named after him in the townland of Ballynaleck, was honoured annually on 7 July, until stolen in 1980.[15] A little further north-east, in the parish of Skreen (Scrín Mhaoil Ruain), a church was dedicated to the saint at Ballymore.[16]

1 *AFM s.a.* 769. **2** *Triads* 2 §8. **3** *CéliD* passim; *DIB* vi, 226. **4** *MartT* 54; *MartO*² 161. **5** *MartO*² 26, 266–7. **6** Ibid. 12. **7** *PRIA* 29C5 (1911) 115–79; *CéliD* 101–14. **8** *IrT* i, 34–5. **9** *WWRJU* 16. **10** *CGSH* §713. **11** *IrT* i, 34–5; *SG* i, 389. **12** *CGSH* §§316, 722.38; *GRSH* 97; *Lgen.* 728.5–6. **13** *MartT* 54; *MartO*² 161; *MartG* 132; *MartD* 188; OSL DB 57, 59; *JCKAS* 5, 18. **14** *ÉtC* 17, 199 §4; *MartT* 94; *AB* 104, 101. **15** *JRSAI* 76, 162–4; *AIWX* 149 (St Edmond's). **16** *JRSAI* 76, 162–4; *CECW* 213.

Maol Rubha of Applecross (Abor Crossan), Scotland. Maol Rubha's birth-year of 641/2 can be determined by reference to the notice of his death in 722, which gives his age as eighty.[1] His father Ealganach belonged to a branch of the Ceinéal Binnigh segment of Ceinéal Eoghain, whose lands lay along the west side of the river Bann, mainly in the Derry barony of Coleraine.[2] His mother, variously named Suaibhseach and Subhthan, is said to have been a niece of Comhghall of Bangor.[3] This would explain Maol Rubha's earliest known ecclesiastical associations with Bangor, where, according to mainly martyrological sources, he succeeded his maternal granduncle as abbot.[4] This is confirmed, however, neither by the list of abbots in the Antiphonary of Bangor nor by the early annals.[5] The only intervention attributed to the saint while coarb of Comhghall was his blessing of Díocha, ancestor of the powerful northern ecclesiastical family of Muintear Bhrolcháin, to which Maol Íosa belonged.[6] Maol Rubha left Bangor for

Scotland in 671 and, two years later, founded the church of Applecross, both events proving notable enough to merit entries in the annals.[7] Regarded as the most famous Irish saint in Scotland, next to Colum Cille, Maol Rubha enjoyed over fifty years in the abbacy of Applecross, until his death in 722, the cause of which is anachronistically attributed by the Breviary of Aberdeen to his wounding by Norsemen.[8] The saint's cult spread widely, especially in the west of Scotland, where numerous churches are named after him.[9] Maol Rubha's name underwent many mutations in Scotland, where, apparently because of confusion with St Rufus of Capua, he was remembered on 27 August, as opposed to his usual day of 21 April in the Irish record.[10]

1 *AU s.a.* 2 *CGSH* §17; *GRSH* 47; *Lgen.* 701.7; *BLec.* 55Ra5; *GUH* 38–53; *DIB* vi, 227. 3 *CGSH* §722.50.86. 4 *MartT* 35; *MartG* 80; *MartD* 106. 5 *Thes.* ii, 282; *NHI* ix, 241–2. 6 *ZCP* 8, 300. 7 *AU s.a.* 8 *CPNS* 287–9; *KSS* 383; *ACDS* 172–7; *LegSS* 196–9, 382–4; *SBDeer* 387–9. 9 Ibid. 10 *MartT* 35; *MartO²* 107; *MartG* 80; *MartD* 106; *CPNS* 287.

Maol Tuile son of Cuilche. *See* Fionnchú of Brigown.

Maol Tuile of Dysart (Díseart Maoile Tuile), barony of Moyashel and Magheradernon, Co. Westmeath. Said by some sources to have belonged to the Ceinéal Laoghaire of Meath, Maol Tuile son of Nóchaire is otherwise known for his affiliation to the union of saints gathered about Maol Ruain of Tallaght.[1] His connections with the *céili Dé*, 'clients of God', whose newly founded churches often took the form of hermitages (*dísirt*), suggest that he was not only the patron, but also the likely founder of Dysart of Maol Tuile.[2] His place in the list of those associated with Maol Ruain indicates that his floruit was in the late eighth or early ninth century, with his death occurring before 830 when the Tallaght martyrologies, which commemorate him, were compiled.[3] The Life composed for the children of Ua Suanaigh of Rahan mentions Maol Tuile in connection with a visit to Colmán of Lynn, a church located close to Dysart on Lough Ennell, where he is described as Ua Suanaigh's 'bosom-fosterchild'.[4] The martyrologies place the saint's feast on 30 July, but the name also figures in the list for 29 May, when the saint was remembered as 'Meltilly' at Dysart, according to a local tradition.[5] He may also be the Maol Tuile intended in the note added to the Martyrology of Donegal which speaks of his wonder-working staff, well, yellow bell, and statue.[6] The 'Meltolinus' remembered on 8 November in the martyrology of the Regensburg *Schottenkloster* has not been identified.[7]

1 *CGSH* §§662.59, 690.14; *BB* 88d; *GRSH* 52; *Lgen.* 706.11. 2 *PNW* 203–4; cf. *RM* 6.1, 11 (Mulbilius). 3 *FSHIM* 75–98. 4 *BNÉ* i, 314 §7. 5 *MartT* 46, 59; *MartG* 106, 146; *MartD* 140, 205; *PNW* 43n. 6 *MartD* 444; *EMH* 485 §226. 7 *FSHIM* 242; *MartR* 160.

Maolán of Annagh (Eanach), barony of Lower Loughtee, Co. Cavan. An entry in the martyrologies for 4 January records the feast of Maolán of Eanach.[1] That Annagh was intended is made clear by entries in a fifteenth-century Armagh register, and also in a papal letter dated 1501, which refer to the church of 'Molanus/Maylanus' of 'Ea(n)ga', now Annagh, in the diocese of Kilmore.[2]

1 *MartT* 4; *MartG* 8; *MartD* 6. 2 *RIM* 112; *CPL* 17, §821; *DK* 21; cf. *AnnU* 251; *Breifne* 4, 205–6.

Maolán of Killaspugmoylan in the parish of Kilconickny, Co. Galway. This son of Dáire, a bishop and elder, is listed, together with several other bishops and ecclesiastics, among the saints of the Uí Mhaine who, at the request of Colum Cille, joined forces against Diarmuid son of Cearbhall, king of Tara, in the lead-up to the battle of Cúil Dreimhne.[1] Nothing much else is known of those named in the list, which includes other bishops (Aodh son of Seanach, Dula, Luchta, Lulach, Lughaidh), a priest named Ruadhán, and sundry ecclesiastics (Coinghealta, Aodhamair, Faolán Amhlobhar). Maolán's pedigree attaches him to a branch of the Uí Mhaine, known as Uí Lomáin Ghaola, which held lands in or near the townland of Finnure in the parish of Abbeygormacan, a little east of Killaspugmoylan.[2] A collateral member of the same family, Brannabh son of Eacha, was attached to a church named Teach Eachach, now Tynagh, adjoining Abbeygormacan.[3] Given his association with the Uí Mhaine patrons of Clonmacnoise, Maolán may have been intended by the author of *Eachtra Léithín*, 'Léithín's adventures', when he spoke of Maolán son of Naoi, describing him as one of Ciarán's clerics and a man capable of many miracles.[4] Despite John O'Donovan, who thought Meallán of Lough Corrib might be intended, he was probably also patron of Kilmoylan in the Galway barony of Clare.[5] The notice of what may be Maolán's feast of 7 February provides him with two brothers, Críodán and Lonán, and a church named Móin Mhaoláin.[6]

1 *IMN* 22 (1926) 5. **2** *CGSH* §405; cf. *Lgen*. 327.3, 1137.10; ibid. iv, 454. **3** *CGSH* §406. **4** *CR* 10, 132; *LSS* 40–55. **5** OSL GY i, 285–6. **6** *MartT* 15; *MartG* 32; *MartD* 40; but cf. *Ainm* 9, 26.

Maolán of Slanore. *See* Comaigh.

Maolán of Tullaghmelan (Tulach Mhealláin), barony of Iffa & Offa West, Co. Tipperary. Both this church and Kilmelan in the parish of Moycarky take their name from a saint named Maolán.[1] When visited by representatives of the Ordnance Survey in 1840, attention was drawn to a limestone inscription in the church, which was taken to read: 'Maolán eapscop, 25 Dec.'.[2] A bishop of this name, 'void of weakness', was remembered on 25 December, but nothing else is known of him.[3]

1 *CLTÁ* 163. **2** OSL TY i, 63. **3** *MartT* 1, *MartG* 246; *MartD* 348.

Maolán son of Naoi. *See* Maolán of Kilmoylan.

Maona. *See* Maoineann.

Maonach of Dunleer (Lann Léire), barony of Ferrard, Co. Louth. The Annals of Ulster note the passing of Maonach, abbot of Dunleer, under the year 721.[1] At least since the twelfth century, this abbot has been taken to be the Maonach commemorated on 17 October, and his paternal name has been filled in as Cláirín (Láirín).[2] A poem on the families of south Munster, attributed to Cathán Ua Duinnín, and its prose commentary speak of Maonach as having left Dunleer for south Munster (Deasmhumha) in the company of a youth named Mac Airtniadh, ancestor of the Desmonds (Uí Dheasmhumha).[3] Devotion to Maonach is well attested in the south, as is shown by the poem listing those whom Seanán of

Scattery might call on in his hour of need; 'great' Maonach son of Láirín is presented in this poem in the immediate company of Flann son of Foircheallach and Mochuda, both of whom had links to the Ciarraighe of north Kerry.[4] This would suggest that Maonach may also have been regarded as patron of Kilmeany in the parish of Knockanure, unless this name derives from Coill Mhaonaigh, 'Maonach's wood' [5]. In that case, confusion with his namesake, Maonach son of Aoibhléan (Aoibhlín), who figures in the Life of Mac Reithe as Mac Aoibhléin, and who, with many others, including Seanán, was said to have been a son of Inghean Bhaoith of Killinaboy, is also possible.[6] 'Maoineach of Aghadoe', one of the saints invoked by Seán Ó Conaill in his *Tuireamh na hÉireann*, may also represent the cult.[7] Maonach's name found its way with those of other Irish saints into a martyrology written in the fifteenth century in Cologne, in which, on 17 October, it is rendered *Monachus*, and also into the martyrology of the Regensburg *Schottenkloster*, where the spelling is *Maenachi*.[8]

1 *AU s.a.* **2** *MartT* 80; *MartG* 198; *MartD* 278. **3** *LM* 183, 531. **4** *ZCP* 10, 28 §23. **5** Cf. Logainm.ie 'Coill Mhaonaigh'. **6** *MHH* 36 §50; *IrT* iv, 94 §9. **7** *FSPP* 80. **8** *AS*.Iun. vii, 610; *FSHIM* 241; *MartR* 150.

MAONACH son of Aoibhléan. *See* Maonach of Dunleer.

MAONAGÁN of Athleague (Áth Liag), barony of Athlone, Co. Roscommon. This saint is provided with an incomplete pedigree in the main corpus of saints.[1] Judging, however, by the name and descent of his grandfather, Seanach son of Séadna, he may have belonged to a branch of the Dál gCais genealogically close to the Dealbhna, a segment of which was settled on the lands about the saint's church at Athleague.[2] Revenue that came to Maonagán's church from the family of Diarmuid Fionn (†833) son of Tomaltach, king of Connacht, was due, according to a tract preserved among the genealogies of Diarmuid's descendants, to an intervention by the saint that enabled Sadhbh daughter of Maol Ruanaidh, previously barren, to give birth to Mothlán, ancestor of the Uí Mhothláin, apparently of the area about Kilbride in the Galway parish of Abbeygormacan.[3] Maonagán's bell allegedly provided baptismal water for the child, and the saint's feast, which, together with the saint himself, had been locally forgotten by the early nineteenth century, was celebrated on 7 February.[4]

1 *CGSH* §408. **2** *Lgen.* 653.12, 654.1; *TCHyM* 82. **3** *AU s.a.*; *Lgen.* 234.4–6. **4** OSL RN i, 103; *MartT* 15; *MartG* 32; *MartD* 40; *EMH* 482 §115.

MARANNÁN. *See* Forannán of Donaghmore.

MARCÁN of Burrishoole, in the barony of the same name, Co. Mayo. According to local legend, Marcán was cursed by Brighid, patron of nearby Kilbride, because of a quarrel between the saints, with the effect that his church, until then on dry ground, was covered by the overflow of a lake.[1] Despite this, the church continued to be the focus of local pilgrimage at the beginning of August.[2]

1 OSL MO ii, 5; *JRSAI* 49, 90–1. **2** *LF* 3, 103–10.

MAROGH. *See* Mura.

Martan of Donaghmore (Domhnach Mór i bhFeibhe), barony of Clandonagh, Co. Laois. Among those said to have been subject to Brighid of Kildare at Donaghmore was this saint, together with Pól and Deineath.[1] In the neighbouring parish of Bordwell is a townland called Kilbreedy, named after Brighid's church, and a few miles away in the parish of Kyle is a townland of Kilmartin (Martan's church). This man was possibly the same as Bishop Martan son of Dúnán Dearg of Cúil Bhreacáin, an unidentified church placed in Tuath Dá Mhaighe of Uí Fhailghe. This area, later known as Tethmoy, now corresponds to the Offaly baronies of Warrenstown and Coolestown, both of which belong to the diocese of Kildare.[2] More pertinently, this area is also said to have been the *hereditas* of Brighid's father Dubhthach.[3] The genealogists attached Bishop Martan to the Dál gCais of Thomond whose former influence in this locality is still reflected in the place of the parish of Kyle (alias Clonfertmulloe), and its townland of Kilmartin, within the diocese of Killaloe.[4] Martan may also have been patron of Killermogh, which adjoins Bordwell. Its pattern day, known as *lá 'il Muirthín* (*Muiltín*, *Muitín*, *Muibhín*), may stand for Martan's day.[5]

1 *CGSH* §670.37; *Lgen.* 753.8. **2** *OnomG* 650–1. **3** *BBr.* 2 §6. **4** *CGSH* §190; *GRSH* 120. **5** OSL LS i, 105.

Masán of Kilmessan. *See* Cairneach.

Mathona of Shankill. *See* Beinéan of Kilbennan.

Maughold. *See* Mac Cuill.

Maurchaoil. *See* Meithean Chaol.

Meachar of Ros Achaidh Liag. *See* Beagán of Ros Achaidh Liag.

Meachar son of Draighean. *See* Ainmhire of Kilroe.

Meadhbh daughter of Ceartán/Garbhán. *See* Caolainn; Lughach.

Meadhrán son of Mac Raith. *See* Odhrán of Latteragh.

Meal of Ardagh (Ardachadh) in the barony of the same name, Co. Longford. Although never made the subject of a Life in his own right, Meal (now anglicized Mel) was of sufficient status, through his church, to attract the attention of biographers of many other saints, including the two pre-eminent national saints, Brighid and Patrick. The latter's biographers appear to have been first in the field, with Tíreachán including Meal among the bishops consecrated by Patrick, and locating him in the 'two Teathbha', a territory that corresponded to most of Longford and part of Westmeath.[1] Expanding on Tíreachán's brief reference, the author of the Tripartite Life noted the tradition, also alluded to in the tract on the mothers of the saints, that Meal and Ríóg of Inchbofin were of British origin – *ut dicunt muintear a gceall*, 'as is maintained by the communities of their churches' – and related through a sister named Dairearca to Patrick himself.[2] He also states that Patrick founded Ardagh, leaving Meal there with a brother named Mealchú, and separating Meal from his sister – he east, she west of Brí Léith (a hill near Ardagh) – because of a (false) accusation that they had sinned together.[3]

The first Kildare biographer to notice Meal was the author of the so-called *vita prima*, who gave him, together with his brother Mealchú, the privilege of placing the veil on Brighid's head in his own church at Ardagh, relegating Mac Caille of Croghanhill, who had been accorded the honour by Cogitosus, to the role of acolyte.[4] The occasion was marked by the ash beam supporting the altar of the church in Ardagh becoming a hard wood known as acacia, which can neither grow old nor be consumed by fire, a miracle that found its way into the universal commemoration of Brighid's feast, beginning with a mid-ninth-century martyrology compiled in Lyon in France.[5] So important had Meal evidently become for Kildare's hagiographers that they also accorded him and his brother Mealchú the honour of foretelling Brighid's birth.[6] Meal's death is recorded for the year 487, but the close association with Brighid remained, with the saint's feast falling on 6 February, well within the octave of Brighid's day.[7] Brighid's day (1 February) went on to become a patron day in the parish of Ardagh.[8] The entry for 6 February in Whytford's 'Martyrologe' added to Meal's name those of his brothers, Mealchú, Muinis (patron of Forgney), and Ríóg.[9]

1 *PTBA* 128 §6.3; 136 §16.6; *DIB* vi, 474. **2** *BP* 895–99; *CGSH* §722.16; *MartO*[2] 68. **3** *BP* 947.94. **4** *TT* 529 §18; *BBr*. 48 (174–5). **5** *MartA* 77. **6** *LisL* 1175–81. **7** *AU s.a.*; *MartT* 15; *MartO*[2] 59; *MartG* 30; *MartD* 40. **8** OSL LD 39, 76. **9** HBS 3, 23; *RM* 6.1, 11.

Mealchú. *See* Meal.

Meall Chráibhtheach, 'pious', of Derryvella (Doire Mheille), parish of Kilcooly, barony of Slievardagh, Co. Tipperary, and of Bealach Gabhráin, the road between Leighlinbridge in Carlow and Gowran in Kilkenny. Meall (mistakenly spelt Ineall in some sources) was among the many children credited to Cuman, paternal aunt of Brighid of Kildare.[1] As such, she is also featured, together with many siblings, in the vernacular Life of Forannán of Alternan.[2] She may be the Meall Mhuimhneach, 'of Munster', invoked as a guarantor, with Patrick and Brighid, by Dubhthach of the Maca Lughair.[3] Another possible reference – in the tract on the mothers of the saints – names Mealla as mother of both Cainneach of Kilkenny and Tighearnach of Derryvella.[4] Cainneach's Life attaches the saint's mother, however, to the Uí Mhic Uais of the northern part of Ireland.[5] According to the Martyrology of Tallaght – the only source to record it – Meall's feast fell on 31 March.[6]

1 *CGSH* §722.10. **2** *Anecd*. iii, 3 §5. **3** *RC* 36, 264 §30; ibid. 37, 336 §30. **4** *CGSH* §722.18. **5** *VSHH* 182 §1; *VSHP* i, 152 §1. **6** *MartT* 28.

Mealla, sister of Caoimhghin. *See* Abán.

Mealla, mother of Cainneach. *See* Cainneach of Aghaboe; Meall Chráibhtheach.

Meallal son of Déigeall. *See* Caiscéan.

Meallán of Meenan (Tamhlachta Umhaill/Meanainn), parish of Aghaderg, barony of Upper Iveagh, Co. Down. According to the early Life of Fursa, written between 650 and 730, two of his associates were named *Beanus* (Beoán) and *Meldanus* (Meallán) and, according to the *Virtutes* compiled for the same saint about 850, the relics of these two were venerated, along with those of Patrick, at Péronne in northern France.[1] Little else is known of Beoán and Meallán, but the entry for their feastday of 26 October assigns them to Meenan, within Fursa's native *provincia* of south-east Ulster.[2] Although some sources maintain that the two saints were *de Britonia*, 'from Britain', this is unlikely on the evidence of their Irish names.[3] Devotion to Meallán spread to the Monaghan church of Errigal Trough, of which he was patron, and further west, to a church on Inis Maca Cuinn, an island on Lough Corrib in Galway, now known as Inchiquin.[4] At this latter church, which appropriately lay within the parish of Killursa (from Ceall Fhursa), the saint was commemorated on 7 February.[5] Even further west, at Lettermullan (Leitir Mheallláin) in the Connemara parish of Kilcummin, there may also have been devotion to the saint. A dedication to 'Bishop Meallán' in the Cork parish of Killaspugmullane may also recall this saint.[6]

1 *MGH.SRM* 4, 425; *CMCS* 17, 2–4. **2** *MartT* 84; *MartO²* 218; *MartG* 204; *MartD* 284; *EA* 112–13. **3** *MartT* 84; *MartO²* 226; *AnnU* 45. **4** *MartO²* 44; OSL AH/MN 34, 49; *AnnU* 45. **5** *MartT* 15; *MartO²* 59; *MartG* 32; *MartD* 40; OSL GY i, 276. **6** CorkD 91.

Meangán. Among those said to have been subject to Brighid of Kildare were two saints of the Dál Meisin Corb of the Glendalough area, a sister and brother named Scoth and Meangán.[1] Two churches were assigned to these saints, one of them unidentifed, the other, Cluain Maosgna, perhaps the now obselete 'Kilmysken' in the Westmeath parish of Lynn.[2] Patron of this parish was Colmán son of Luachán, but neither Meangán nor his sister finds mention in Colmán's vernacular Life.[3] A Brigidine connection is elsewhere recorded in a note to the *Liber Hymnorum* which states that the Kildare saint cured a virgin (probably Scoth) affected by dropsy in this church.[4] Though Meangán is nowhere else attested, his sister was remembered at Cluain Maosgna on 16 July.[5]

1 *CGSH* §670.33. **2** *PNW* 193. **3** *BCML*. **4** *LH* i, 119n. **5** *MartT* 56; *MartG* 138; *MartD* 194.

Méanóg of Glassely. *See* Fíonán of Teach Oirthir.

Méanóg of Glenealy (Gleann Faidhle), barony of Newcastle, Co. Wicklow, and of Rosminogue (Ros Mór Méanóg), barony of Gorey, Co. Wexford. This son of Colmaidh bears a name (also written Momhéanóg) that derives, in hypocoristic guise, from *éan*, 'bird'. There are two versions of Méanóg's maternal descent, both of which establish for him a close relationship with Caoimhghin of Glendalough. One names his mother as Caoiltighearn, sister of Caoimhghin; the other gives this honour to another sister of the Glendalough saint named Caomhóg.[1] Both traditions concur in the names of Méanóg's siblings, Daghán of Ennereilly, Molioba of Ceall Molioba, and Mobhaoi (perhaps a doublet of Baodán of Cloney). Méanóg also figures among the forty saints invoked with Caoimhghin in the first litany of Irish saints.[2] He was remembered at Glenealy on 29 December, a day shared with his namesake and probable double, Éanna of Kilnamanagh in the Dublin parish of Tallaght, and a month later, on 30 January, he was remembered at Rosminogue.[3] He was also possibly the man invoked as Méanóg of Ros Muchnaigh (perhaps another name for Rosminogue) in a poem attributed to Moling of St Mullin's that lists a host of Leinster saints.[4] By the early nineteenth century, and probably much earlier, local devotion in Glenealy had switched to the Virgin Mary.[5]

1 *CGSH* §722.72.102. 2 *IrL* 55–6; *CPPI* 175. 3 *MartT* 2, 13: *MartG* 26; 248; *MartD* 30, 350. 4 *SG* i, 390. 5 OSL WW 367–8.

Mearnóg. A hypocoristic form derived from Eirnín (Earnán), the name Mearnóg figures prominently in the list of homonymous saints, which records twenty bearers.[1] Martyrologies and genealogical tracts as a rule show preference for other forms of the name, including the radical forms (Eirnín / Earnán), and such hypocoristic variants as Tearnóg.

1 *CGSH* §707.763–84.

Mearnóg of Aberchirder in Banffshire, Scotland. This is perhaps the best-known bearer of the name, especially in Scotland, where lessons concerning the saint were written into the Breviary of Aberdeen.[1] Anglicized as Marnan (from Mearnán) or Marnoch (Marnock), the saint was highly regarded as a bishop whose place of burial at Aberchirder later became an important centre of pilgrimage. Mearnóg's cult spread widely and he was commemorated each year on 1 March. On the previous day (28 February), the Irish martyrologies remembered a saint named Tearnóg, a variant form of Mearnóg.[2] It has been suggested that the Scottish saint may also be identical with Eirnín son of Craisín, a disciple of Colum Cille, but the latter's feast fell on 18 August.[3]

1 *BrevA* pars hiem. 60–1. 2 *MartT* 19; *MartG* 44; *MartD* 58. 3 *KSS* 392–3; *LegSS* 64–7.

Mearnóg of Cranfield. *See* Tearnóg.

Mearnóg of Kilmarnock, Scotland. Unlike his namesake at Aberchirder, the patron of Kilmarnock (Ceall Mhearnóg / Cill Mhearnáig) was not made the subject of lessons in the Breviary of Aberdeen. Reeves mentioned him in his discussion of Eirnín son of Craisín but, as the latter's feast fell on 18 August, there is unlikely to have been any immediate connection between the two.[1] At Kilmarnock, Mearnóg was remembered on 25 October, and this would suggest that he was identical with the Earnán Miodhluachra commemorated in the Irish martyrologies on the following day.[2] As Miodhluachair appears to have been located in south Armagh, the reference is probably to Téarnóg son of Ciarán who, according to an inscription, consecrated the ecclesiastical site at Kilnasaggart (Ceall na Sagart) in the Armagh parish of Forkhill.[3] Tearnóg son of Ciarán died in 715.[4]

1 *VC*[1] 26n; cf. *LegSS* 250, 390–1. 2 *MartG* 204; *MartD* 284; *ACDS* 74–6; *CPNS* 187–8, 291–2; *UJA* 1, 223–4; cf. *AS*.Iun. vii, 628 (Marnoci). 3 *AHHS* 305, 327; *UJA* 1, 221–5. 4 ATig. *s.a.*

Mearnóg of Portmarnock. *See* Eirnín of Cluain Deochra.

Mearnóg son of Déigeall. *See* Caiscéan.

Meascan, *cruimhthear*, 'presbyter', of Domhnach Meascan, an unidentified church, apparently on or near the river Faughan in Co. Derry. This man was among those said to have been in orders with Patrick.[1] Appropriately enough, given the meaning of his name, a derivative of *measc*, 'mix, muddle, intoxicate', the role attributed to Meascan was that of *círbhshire*, 'brewer'. Patrick is said to have founded several churches named Domhnach along the river Faughan, including Domhnach Dola, where Meascan's immediate companion and possible double, Cruimhthear Béasgna (Beasgna?), was placed, but few of these have been identified.[2] A place named Donnybrewer in the parish of Faughanvale has been suggested as a possible location for Domhnach Meascan, but mainly on the basis of the saint's role as brewer.[3]

1 *CGSH* §§671.9; 672.7; *Lgen.* 695.1; *BP* 3131. 2 *BP* 1806–9; *VT* 154. 3 *PNCL* 173.

Meena. *See* Miodhna.

Meilteóg. *See* Eiltín

Meithean Chaol, 'slender', of Dysart (Díseart Meithle Caoile), barony of Ferrard, Co. Louth This daughter of Cana is one of several saints descended from Branán son of Dobhtha, progenitor of the Ceinéal Dobhtha, later represented by the Uí Ainlighe (Hanleys) of Roscommon.[1] Though little else is known of her, an aunt bearing the same name, Meithean Fhionn, 'fair', daughter of Branán, follows her in the list.[2] Two members of the same family – Fionnchú, patron of the church of Brigown, and Bearach of Termonbarry – were important enough to become the subjects of vernacular Lives. A few miles from Brigown (near Mitchelstown), the name Kilbeheny, if derived from *Cill* rather than *Coill Bheithne* (or *Mheithne*), may recall Meithean.[3] The martyrologists attached Meithean Chaol to Dysart, where she was remembered on 12 November.[4] The local church was called 'Tea'pall Maurchaoil', now St Borchill's, after the saint and a holy well was dedicated to her.[5] It has also been suggested that she was patron of Kilmeane in the Roscommon barony of Athlone, but this name derives from Ceall Mhiadháin.[6]

1 *CGSH* §410.2; *Lgen.* 242.14. 2 *CGSH* §410.3. 3 *LLog.* i, 135; cf. *HDGP* iv, 19. 4 *MartG* 216; *MartD* 306. 5 OSL LH 122–3; *JCLAS* 24, 355. 6 OSL RN ii, 205; *HDGP* iv, 19.

Meithean Fhionn. *See* Meithean Chaol.

Mel. *See* Meal.

Meldocius. *See* Maol Dóid.

Miaca of Feamore (Fiodh Mór, alias Cluain Fada?), parish of Oldleighlin, barony of Idrone West, Co. Carlow. Miaca (alias Miach) son of Laighneach is said to have been one of two brothers of Abán of Adamstown, the other being Damhán, patron of Kildavin in the Wexford barony of Forth.[1] Miaca may have been the same as a namesake – one of four children of Broinnfhinn Bhreac, sister of Iobhar of Begerin – assigned to Monasterevin (Ros Glaise) in Kildare.[2]

1 *CGSH* §287.2; *Lgen.* 727.11. 2 *CGSH* §722.96.

Miadhaine of Rahara (Ráith Aradh), barony of Athlone, Co. Roscommon. Miadhaine was one of forty-seven children, many of them associated with churches in east Connacht, credited to Cuman, aunt of Brighid of Kildare.[1] Like many others in the group, Miadhaine (written 'Maghaine') also figures in the list of the saints said by the author of the Life of Forannán of Alternan to have attended on Colum Cille during his *saorchuaird*, 'noble visit', in Connacht.[2] The saint was probably originally identical with the like-named Miodhan (Miodhnad), patron of the Roscommon church of Killukin.

1 *CGSH* §722.10. **2** *Anecd.* iii, 3 §5.

Mianach son of Fáilbhe. Like his three brothers – Manchán, Riaghán, and Rodaighe – Mianach belonged to the Ceinéal Boghaine branch of Ceinéal Conaill (whence the name of the Donegal barony of Banagh).[1] His brother Riaghán is remembered in the name of the church of Kilrean in the parish of Killybegs Lower.[2] Although little else is known of him, Mianach's feast is recorded in the list for 18 July.[3]

1 *CGSH* §525; *GRSH* 41. **2** *CCDK* 235. **3** *MartT* 56; *MartG* 138; *MartD* 196.

Michean of St Michan's (Ceall Mhichean), Dublin. The earliest mentions of the saint who gave name to St Michan's are in late twelfth-century martyrologies. The martyrology compiled in verse by Maol Muire Ua Gormáin about 1170 places the saint's feastday on 25 August.[1] In adopting this date, however, Maol Muire may have drawn on a copy of the martyrology kept, since about 1030, at Christ Church in Dublin, which he is known to have used.[2] In both texts, Michean is grouped together with four Roman martyrs.[3] The saint's origins are obscure. In the late sixteenth century, Meredith Hanmer, then attached to St Michan's, suggested that the saint was a Dane, and this view continues to have adherents.[3] In the seventeenth century, a Life was pieced together by Henry Fitzsimon which declared the saint to have been a son of a Canaanite king who travelled across Europe from the Holy Land, eventually arriving in Dublin.[4] The same author included Michanus, 'whose basilica is in Dublin', in his list of the chief Irish saints.[5] More recent opinion allows for the possibility of an Irish origin for the saint's name, perhaps as a reflex of Cainneach, through such hypocoristic forms as Mochaineóg or Mochainne.[6]

1 *MartG* 164; *MartD* 226. **2** *FSHIM* 167–8; *MartFC* 143–4; *DMW* 126. **3** *DMW* 123. **4** Ibid. 125–6. **5** *FEMN* 378 §545; *Seanchas* 415 §200. **6** *DMW* 119–40 at 127–31; *IsPatrick* 147.

Míde. *See* Íde.

Míoda daughter of Luan. *See* Curcach of Kilcorkey (WX).

Miodha Miodhbhrise of Sligo (Sligeach). Miodha son of Fachtna was among the forty-seven children said to have been born to Cuman daughter of Dallbhrónach, maternal aunt of Brighid of Kildare, whose womb had allegedly been blessed by Patrick.[1] The sibling nearest to him in the list of Cuman's offspring, Lomán of Lough Gill, and many others, were likewise associated with east Connacht, and together with these, Miodha (written *Mifrisi* in line with the saint's cognomen) figures in the Life of Forannán of Alternan among those brought together to attend on Colum Cille.[2] Miodha was commemorated in Sligo on 17 February, otherwise the feast of Fiontan of Clonenagh, a close relative of Brighid.[3]

1 *CGSH* §722.9. 2 *Anecd.* iii, 3 §5. 3 *MartT* 17; *MartG* 38; *MartD* 52.

Miodhabhair. *See* Fraoch of Cloone.

Miodhan of Clonfad (Cluain Fada), parish and barony of Offerlane, Co. Laois. This daughter of Ciarán is mentioned twice in the list of those said to have been subject to Brighid, each time in relation to a different church.[1] One is the unidentified Ros Iarnghlais; the other is Clonfad. In both cases, the churches are said to have hosted several other saints, including Miodhan's sister Ciar and a companion named Finneach, variously described either as a third sister or as a daughter of Seanach Fionn. All three are said to have belonged to an obscure family named Ceinéal Cormaic. Miodhan (alias Miodha) is probably identical with the like-named Miodhnad (diminutive of Miodhan) of Killucan (Ceall Lúcainne) in the Westmeath barony of Farbill, north of Offerlane and adjoining the Pass of Kilbride, a name that provides evidence of Brigidine influence in the area. The patron's name is rendered 'Migneta' in a late fifteenth-century papal letter, and 'Minad' in a late seventeenth-century visitation list.[2] When visiting Killucan in 1837, T. O'Conor was shown, 'within ten perches' of the churchyard gate, a dried out holy well called *Tobar Miodhnad*, 'Miodhnad's well', which was thought to have reappeared in the neighbouring townland of Rathnarrow.[3] The saint's day locally was 18 November. She was considered to have belonged to the Hanley family (Uí Ainlighe), and to have come to Killucan from Slieve Baun in the Roscommon parish of Cloonfinlogh, adjoining another parish named Killukin. There is nothing in the genealogies of the Uí Ainlighe to confirm this descent, but the martyrologies also commemorate Miodhnad on 18 November.[4] In one of these commemorations, the phrase *bile as mbághaid*, 'a sacred tree which ye proclaim', is used of the saint, perhaps in recognition of the position of her church within Fir Bhile (Farbill). An early litany-style prayer of invocation includes Miodhnad among many other female saints.[5] The saint was probably identical with the like-named Miadhaine of Rahara, and possibly also with 'Medan/ Medana' of Kirkmaiden in Wigtonshire, Scotland, whose day fell on 19 November.[6] The Miadhán (*recte* Miodhán, a diminutive of Miodha?) contained in the name of the Rocommon parish of Kilmeane, which adjoins Rahara, may also represent the saint, albeit in the guise of a male.[7]

1 *CGSH* 670.32.47; *Lgen.* 752.40. 2 *CPL* 15, §687; *RM* 5.3, 10; cf. *ROLN* §297; *ILL* 248. 3 *PNW* 44. 4 *MartG* 220; *MartD* 312. 5 *MartT* 108; *IrL* 92. 6 *KSS* 396; *ACDS* 133; *Innes Review* 32, 78. 7 *HDGP* iv, 19.

Miodhna of Kilmeena (Ceall Mhiodhna?), barony of Burrishoole, Co. Mayo. During his visit to the relatively small parish of Kilmaclasser in 1838, John O'Donovan was told how the local patron, wrongly called Mac Glaise (*recte* Mac Laisre), was deceived by Miodhna (anglicized Meena), patron of the larger parish of Kilmeena, during a race to determine the boundary between their two jurisdictions.[1] It has recently been suggested that the race may have been invented to account for a conflict in diocesan ownership.[2] Little else is known of Miodhna, but he may be identical with the saint of this name in the list of children credited to Dairearca, sister of Patrick.[3] Some others of these, including Brocaidh and Lallóg, had connections with churches west of the Shannon.

1 OSL MO i, 491; *CnM* 20, 129. 2 p.c. (F. Mac Gabhann). 3 *CGSH* §722.16.

Miodhnad of Killucan/Killukin. *See* Miodhan.

Miodhnán. *See* Coilliodhan.

Míolla. *See* Abán.

Mionchloth. *See* Colmán of Kilmacrenan; Colum of Terryglass.

Mion(n)án. *See* Beinéan.

Moagra. *See* Moshagra.

Mobhaoi. Eleven of this name, a derivative of *baoth*, 'innocent, guileless', are included in the list of homonymous saints.[1] Many of these are equally well known under other forms of the name, for example Mobhaoi (alias Baodán/Baoithín) of the Maca Alla, or Mobhaoi (alias Baodán) son of Sineall.[1]

1 *CGSH* §707.793–803.

Mobhaoi son of Colmaidh. *See* Méanóg of Glenealy.

Mobhaoi Fada. *See* Baodán of Cloney.

Mobheagóg of Míleac Fiaich. *See* Angán of Míleac Fiaich.

Mobheagóg of Toureen. *See* Beagán of Toureen.

Mobheóg (Dobheóg). This hypocoristic form of Beoán (from *beo*, 'living, spirited') figures prominently enough in the hagiographical record, with ten bearers in the list of homonymous saints.[1] Most of these are otherwise either unattested or better known under a variant form of the name, for example Mobheóg (alias Beoán) son of Neasán. The best-known bearer of the name, the patron of Lough Derg in Donegal, is more often referred to as Dobheóg.

1 *CGSH* §707.637–46.

Mobheóg of Artraighe of Ulster. Eight children, four sons and four daughters, are credited to the saint's father Lughna, his mother being Basar of the Déise Breagh, a people who gave name to the Meath baronies of Deece.[1] Mobheóg, the second born of the four sons, allegedly received his name because of his mother's habit of affectionately calling him *mo mhac beoga óg*, 'my young lively son'.[2] It has been suggested that he was identical with the saint of the name commemorated at Ardcanrisk (Ard Caoinrois), near Wexford town, on 16 December and, in view of the saint's maternal connection with the Déise, he could well be the patron named 'Mabiog', who is assigned to the church of Fews in the Waterford barony of Decies-without-Drum in a sixteenth-century unpublished, and unnumbered, copy of a Papal Bull preserved in the Archives of the Marques of Waterford at Curraghmore House, Co. Waterford.[3]

1 *CGSH* §§721.1–14; 722.14. 2 Ibid. §721.10. 3 *AB* 77, 446; *MartG* 240; *MartD* 336; *HDGP* i, 82; *AMW*.

Mobhí. *See* Bíthe.

Mobhí Bearchán. *See* Mobhí Cláirineach.

Mobhí Cláirineach, 'flat-faced', of Glasnevin (Glas Naoidhean), barony of Coolock, Co. Dublin. What appears to be the earliest mention of this saint, in Adhamhnán's Life of Colum Cille, explains the condition of his face as a mark of his disobedience towards his teacher on Iona, on whom he spied through a keyhole.[1] The latter part of the name given to the saint by Adhamhnán, 'Berchanus cognomentus Mesloen', is otherwise unattested. Mobhí figures prominently in the later Lives composed for the founder of Iona which present him as Colum Cille's teacher rather than pupil, and link him to the founding of Derry.[2] According to an Old Irish Table of Commutations, Mobhí and Colum Cille, with the advice of the Archangel Michael, decreed a penitential commutation.[3] The genealogical tradition assigns Mobhí through his father Beoaodh (Beonaid/Beoán) variously to the Corca Thrí of Luighne, now represented by the Sligo barony of Leyny, and to the Fothairt of Leinster, and also provides him with a mother named Uaininn (Uaine) daughter of Fionnbharr, together with a saintly paternal uncle in the form of Fionnbharr of Drumcolumb.[4] He is said to have been born in Kilmacteige (Ceall Mhic Thaidhg) in the barony of Leyny.[5] As this parish adjoins the eastern boundary of the Mayo barony of Gallen (from *Gaileanga*) and the Mayo parish of Kilmovee, it is probably no coincidence that Mobhí's principal church of Glasnevin formerly lay within an area known as Gaileanga Beaga.[6] The saint's link with Colum Cille is reinforced by the date of Mobhí's feast of 12 October, the day after that of Cainneach of Aghaboe, whose name and tradition point to his having been identical with the founder of Iona before his cult underwent localization and separation.[7] Two weeks earlier, on 30 Sepember, Mobhí Cláirineach (misread as *cailleach*, 'nun', in the later martyrologies) was remembered at Donnybrook on the other side of the river Liffey.[8] Mobhí is also among those said to have been disciples of Finnian of Clonard.[9] The name 'Berchanus Caecus', 'blind', attached to the 'senior' saint of the name, whom Caoimhghin is said to have visited, is probably another version of Mobhí (alias Bearchán) *na Fáistine*, 'of the prophecy', and, despite some reservations, this may also apply to Mobhí Bearchán of the Wicklow parish of Delgany (Sruthair Ghuaire).[10] The saint is said to have received the greater part of the prophecies attributed to him – some of which have been preserved – from Colum Cille, with whom he also appears to have intervened on behalf of poets.[11] The annalists state that Mobhí died of the bubonic plague in 545.[12] His *crios*, 'belt', was noted as a guarantor of truth, and the saint himself was invoked as a guarantor of the Law of Adhamhnán.[13] A well dedicated to the saint was located in the townland of Grange in the Dublin parish of Holmpatrick.[14]

1 *VC*[2] 510–12 (= *VC*[1] III 21); *DIB* vi, 536–7. **2** *IKD* 228–30, 278; *BCC* 60–6. **3** *Ériu* 19, 64 §24. **4** *CGSH* §§266, 317, 412; *GRSH* 74; *Lgen.* 718.5; *MartO*[2] 222–4; *LH* i, 184. **5** *MartO*[2] 222–4. **6** *TP* xiii (57). **7** *MartT* 78–9; *MartO*[2] 215–16; *MartG* 194; *MartD* 270–4; *FG* 20–35. **8** *MartT* 75; *MartG* 186; *MartD* 262. **9** *VSHH* 83, 101. **10** *VSHP* i, 249–50, ii, 348; *CPPI* 187; *FFÉ* iii, 52, 172. **11** *MD* iv, 276, 449; *DD* 221 §13. **12** *AU s.a.* **13** *IKD* 230 §32, 279; *CA* §22. **14** *Rep. Nov.* 2, 73.

Mobhrioca son of Síolán. *See* Breac of Bealach Féile.

Mochab. *See* Mochob.

Mochaidhbheo of Sliabh Breagh, a hilly area on the borders of the counties of Louth and Meath. This saint is known from two sources, a late list of seven saints said never to have died and, contradictorily, the later martyrologies which assign him a feastday (i.e. a date of death) of 11 October.[1] The fact that his name is the last in the martyrological list indicates a floruit possibly later than the so-called Age of Saints. A devotee of his, Giolla Mochaidhbheo, died as abbot of the Armagh priory of St Peter and Paul on 31 March 1174.[2]

1 *AB* 55, 285–95; *BL Cat.* ii, 470; *MartG* 194; *MartD* 272. 2 *AU s.a.*

Mochamóg. *See* Caimín of Inishcaltra; Mochomóg.

Mochaoi. *See* Caolán.

Mochaoimhe of Terryglass (Tír Dá Ghlas), barony of Lower Ormond, Co. Tipperary. This saint is known from a list of the saints of the Dál Meisin Corb, a people closely associated with the area about Glendalough.[1] Under the guise of Nadh Caoimhe, he is included, along with Caoimhghin of Glendalough, among the children of Caoimheall daughter of Ceinnfhionnán.[2] The saint also figures in the Life of Fiontan of Clonenagh, who is said to have dwelt at Terryglass, together with Mochaoimhe and his namesake Caomhán, before setting out in their company in quest of a place in which to serve God, ending up in the county of Laois.[3] The same tradition is preserved in the Life of Colum of Terryglass which, while referring to the saint as Nadh Caoimhe, and describing him as a disciple, states that he brought his master's remains to be buried in Terryglass.[4] His name became attached to a burial ground at Terryglass, known as Tulach Mochaoimhe, the last resting place of the poet, Flann son of Lonán, and he may also have been patron of Ballyogan in the south Dublin parish of Tully.[5] The saint died, according to the annals, in 588, and his feast fell on 1 May.[6]

1 *CGSH* §181.5; *Lgen.* 726.2. 2 *CGSH* §722.19. 3 *VSHP* ii, 97 §3; *VSHH* 146 §3, 228 §13. 4 *VSHH* 229–30 §19; 233 §31. 5 *IrT* i, 24; *BL Cat.* ii, 480; *Keimelia* 518. 6 *MartT* 38; *MartO*² 122; *MartG* 88; *MartD* 116; *AFM s.a.* 584.

Mochaomhóg. According to the list of homonymous saints, this name, a pet form derived from *caomh*, 'comely, beautiful', was borne by twenty-one saints, many of whom were better known by reference to the diminutive form Caomhán.[1]

1 *CGSH* §707.720–40.

Mochaomhóg of Leigh (Liath Mochaomhóg/'Leamakevoge'), parish of Twomileborris, barony of Eliogarty, Co. Tipperary. Mochaomhóg (Latin Pulcherius) belonged – through his father Beoán, reputedly a *saor*, 'craftsman' – to the Conmhaicne, whose settlements were mainly in Connacht.[1] His mother Neas is said to have been a sister of Íde of Killeedy.[2] The saint was deemed important enough to be made the subject of a Life preserved in both a Latin version and an apparent Irish translation.[3] Perhaps because of the relatively unimportant status of the saint's church at Leigh, Mochaomhóg's Life has attracted little attention, with one commentator dismissing it as 'evidently late and largely fictitious', a judgment that could be applied to the vast majority of Irish saints' Lives, without diminishing their importance as historical documents.[4] In Mochaomhóg's case, although the Life awaits a critical edition, there are many pointers to a provenance other than in his own church of Leigh. Chief among these is the manner in which the saint is cast in a deferential pose towards Bishop Colmán, whose church at Longfordpass (Doire Mór) was located in Magh Airbh (*Arvicampus*), otherwise the name of the Cistercian foundation of Kilcooly.[5] Between Leigh (Liath Mochaomhóg) and Longfordpass, within the parish of Kilcooly, there was, according to the Life, little more than four miles.[6]

A Cistercian provenance for Mochaomhóg's Life is also indicated by several other associations established by the saint's biographer, which include his resuscitation of a dead man at Inishlounaght (Inis Leamhnachta), near Clonmel, the site of the Cistercian house *de Surio*, already founded by 1148.[7] The saint is also brought on a visit to his 'disciple', Mochoime (Mochuma), patron of the church and parish of Grangemacomb in the barony of Fassadinin, part of the property of the Cistercian house of Jerpoint.[8] Although itself an earlier foundation, Kilcooly became a daughter-house of Jerpoint in 1184.[9] Accompanying Mochaomhóg on the visit to Mochoime was Féichín, otherwise best known as patron of the Benedictine abbey at Fore.

Despite the saint's paternal link with Connacht, his biographer describes how he was born to Neas at her sister's church of Killeedy in Limerick, where his father was then exercising his craft.[10] This gave the biographer the opportunity of attributing, incongruously, a cure of the blindness affecting Fachtna of Ross Carbery to the miraculous application of Mochaomhóg's mother's milk, although the infant was yet unborn.[11] Ross Carbery was the seat of a Benedictine house and nearby was the Cistercian house of Abbeymahon.[12]

Following his education by Comhghall of Bangor, Mochaomhóg is said to have returned to Ossory, appropriating on the way the church of Anatrim (Eanach Troim) in the Laois parish of Offerlane, before relinquishing it to his namesake and probable double, Caomhán.[13] Among other saints introduced into the Life were Molua, patron of Killaloe and Kyle (Clonfertmulloe), Daghán, Fionnbharr, Luchtighearn, Fursa, and Laichtín, the story of whose foundation at Freshford (Achadh Úr) is also told.[14] Towards the end of the Life, the founder of Clashmore (Glais Mhór), near Lismore, is featured under the guise of Cuan Cearr, a form which, like Crónán (traditionally the name of the patron of the church and parish), yields a hypocoristic Mochua.[15]

Supposedly born about the same time as Molua of Kyle (554), albeit under the guise of Caomhán Léith, and provided by the annalists with an obit of 656, Mochaomhóg is nonetheless credited with having attained a biblical age of over 400.[16] As an indication of his continuing popularity, his genealogy was added to a manuscript written in the early fifteenth century for James Butler, known as the White Earl, and his name also figures among those mentioned as guardians in the so-called *lorica* of Colum Cille.[17] Together with Iarlaithe, Cruimhthear Fraoch, and Caillín, he was hailed as an *ardnaomh*, 'chief saint', of the Conmhaicne of Connacht who allegedly owed him tribute.[18] A site named Cros Mochaomhóg in the Mayo parish of Cong may have recalled the saint and the Kilkenny parish of Kilmakevoge was named after him.[19] Mochaomhóg's feastday of 13 March, which was twice used as a point of reference by the compiler of the Annals of Ulster, found its way under the guise of both Mochomogus and Kevoca into Greven's version of the Martyrology of Usuard, compiled in Cologne in the late fifteenth century.[20] The form Kevoga, with feminine ending, was borrowed from the Breviary of Aberdeen which had transformed the saint into a fictitious female.[21] Mochaomhóg's feast was also recalled on 13 March at Kilnamanagh in the Cork barony of Bear.[22] Were Mochaomhóg's feast to fall during Lent, which it would have done on a regular basis, a 'year of storms' was sure to follow.[23] The saint's head reputedly formed part of Adhamhnán's reliquary.[24]

1 *CGSH* §362; *GRSH* 106; *VSHP* ii, 168 §1; *DIB* vi, 537–8. **2** *CGSH* §722.48; *VSHP* ii, 168 §1. **3** *VSHP* i, lxxix; ibid. ii, 164–83; *ILL* 364. **4** *Kenney* 455. **5** *MRHI* 137–8; *VSHP* ii, 170 §15. **6** *VSHP* ii, 170 §15; *Peritia* 2, 273–4; ibid. 11, 359–69. **7** *VSHP* ii, 181 §32; *MRHI* 135. **8** *VSHP* ii, 179 §29; *HADO* ii, 321. **9** *MRHI* 136. **10** *VSHP* ii, 164 §1. **11** Ibid. 165–6 §4. **12** *MRHI* 107, 125. **13** *VSHP* ii, 168–9 §11; *AB* 52, 355–6. **14** *VSHP* ii, 168 §10, 178 §27, 180–1 §31. **15** Ibid. 182 §33; *WatLis*. 128; *MartT* 16; *MartO²* 59; *MartD* 44; OSL WD 169; *AFM* i, 267n; *HADO* iv, 92. **16** *LUM* 154rb 50; *AU s.a.*; *MartT* 98 **17** *Celtica* 5, 71; *ZCP* 10, 347 §24. **18** BFen. (supp.) 68, 88. **19** *CPL* 10, 581; *ASH* 589. **20** *AU s.a.* 1109, 1119; *MartT* 23; *MartO²* 82; *MartG* 54; *MartD* 75; *AS*.Iun. vi, 153. **21** *CPNS* 189; *KSS* 374–7; *ACDS* 134; *BrevA* pars hiem. 68; *LegSS* 80–3, 376. **22** *Dinn*. 6, 13. **23** *AFM s.a.* 917; (ii, 598). **24** *Celtica* 15, 35 §15.

Mochaomhóg of Inishglora. *See* Caomhán of Anatrim.

Mochaomhóg of 'Killadda' (Ceall Fhada) in the townland of Lag, parish of Caherduggan, barony of Fermoy, Co. Cork. This son of Congharbh is reputed to have 'blessed' – in other words founded – the church of 'Killadda', then the burial church of the *tuath* of Magh Finne, the 'noblest' of the western *tuatha* in the area north-east of Mallow.[1] Although otherwise unattested as such, he may also have been venerated by reference to his father at the Limerick church of Killeenagarriff (Ceall Mhic Con Gairbh).[2]

1 *CrC²* §9; *CrC¹* §6. **2** *HDGP* iv, 20; *LnaÉ* i, 103.

Mochaomhra daughter of Niall. *See* Crónán of Roscrea.

Mocheallóg. This is a hypocoristic or pet form of Ceallach or Ceallán. Although sometimes thought to derive from *ceall/cill*, 'church', a derivative of Latin *cella*, this name (also found in Cillín, alias Cilléan, anglicized Kilian) is almost certainly of native origin.[1] Six bearers of the name are included in the list of homonymous saints.[2]

1 *GPN* 48. **2** *CGSH* §707.804–9.

Mocheallóg of Cloncurry. *See* Maoldubh of Cloncurry.

Mocheallóg of Inch (Inis Labhrainne), parish of Ballinvoher, barony of Corkaguiny, Co. Kerry. Although listed among the saints of Síol Conaire (the descendants of Conaire), Mocheallóg son of Aoibhléan (Aoibhlín) belonged more specifically to the Corca Dhuibhne who gave name to the barony of Corkaguiny.[1] Here also were three sites associated with the saint, Inch, Inishvickillane (Inis Mhic Aoibhléin) in the parish of Dunquin, and a site at Ballinrannig on the boundary of the parishes of Dunurlin and Marhin, recently identified as *An Teampall Bán*.[2] Mocheallóg is featured in the Life written for his kinsman, Fíonán Cam of Kinnitty, who was brought on a visit to the saint to tame a wolf, probably at Kilmakilloge – literally the church of Mocheallóg – in the parish of Tuosist, later a popular centre of pilgrimage in south Kerry.[3] The saint is described as Mocheallóg *Senis*, 'old', which would suggest that the biographer was distinguishing between two of the name. He may also be the Aoibhléan (Oiblan) said to have requested of Moling of Luachair that he allow him to glimpse the infant Jesus, who was supposedly in the habit of visiting the latter saint.[4] The Mocheallóg who gave name to Kilmallock in Limerick is sometimes identified with the Kerry bearer of the name.[5] In the case of Kilmallock, however, the notice of the saint's feast of 26 March describes him as a son of Tolodhrán.[6] At Kilmakilloge, where the saint was also known as Coinleán (Cuínleán / Quinlan), the pattern day of 8 July gave rise to a link with the cult of the martyred Kilian of Würzburg in Germany who was remembered on the same day.[7] Near Kilmakilloge was a lake on which three green sods full of rushes allegedly used to float.[8] There may have been some connection between Mocheallóg and his namesake, Mac Aoibhléin (Aoibhlín), who figures among the saints of Clare in the Life of Mac Reithe, and who, along with many others, including Seanán, was said to have been a son of Inghean Bhaoith of Killinaboy.[9] In a poem in Classical Irish, Mac Aoibhléin, together with numerous other saints, including Inghean Bhaoith, was called upon to help in releasing Ireland's southern half (Leath Mogha) from a bondage imposed on it by the northern half (Leath Chuinn), championed by Finnian of Clonard.[10] The name Giolla Mic Aoibhléin borne by a successor of Bréanainn of Clonfert and Ardfert, who died in 1166, reflects later Corca Dhuibhne devotion to the saint.[11]

1 *CGSH* §554; *GRSH* 78; *Lgen.* 721.7. **2** *CGSH* §662.127; *Herm.* 48, 213–14; *Dinn.* 1.2, 25–6; *Feasta* Nov. 1979, 13; *CínCC* 259–61. **3** *VSHH* 159 §32; *VSHP* ii, 93–4 §24; *JKAHS* 2, 103–4. **4** *CínCC* 266. **5** *ASH* 749. **6** *MartT* 27; *MartG* 62; *MartD* 88. **7** *ACoK* 231; *MartT* 54; *MartG* 132; *MartD* 190; *TH* iii, 17–18; *FL* 45; *JKAHS* 2, 103–4; ibid. 22, 5–34,156; ibid. 23, 69–90; *CínCC* 302–8. **8** *SZ* 11. **9** *MHH* 36 §50; *IrT* iv, 94 §9; but cf. *CínCC* 266. **10** RIA MS 23L11, 263; *SAM* 24.1, 17, 21. **11** *AFM s.a.*

Mocheallóg of Kilmallock (Ceall Mocheallóg), in the barony of the same name, Co. Limerick. The saint who gave name to Kilmallock is sometimes identified with Mocheallóg of Inch.[1] The notice of his feast of 26 March describes him, however, under the guise of Cilléan, as a son of Tolodhrán.[2] This day is shared by a namesake, Cillíne (also Kilian or Chillianus), at Aubigny in France.[3] A French connection is likewise possibly implied by an entry in the Martyrology of Aonghas which asserts that Mocheallóg died 'in Leatha', a name sometimes used in the broad sense of the Continent, but more particularly of Brittany (Letavia) or Rome (Latium).[4] A note added to this entry, though acknowledging the use of Leatha in reference to Rome, insists on the separate use of the name for a 'great wood' in Uí Chairbre of Munster, the part of Limerick in which Kilmallock lay.[5]

Little else is known of the patron of Kilmallock, but his cult seems also to have travelled to Leinster, to the Kilkenny parish of Derrynahinch, where, under the guise of 'Killocus' (Ceallach) and 'Muculvelinus' (Mac Aoibhléin?), he was likewise remembered on 26 March.[6] Although corruptly written Motalogus, his name also found its way, via a martyrology published by the Jesuit Petrus Canisius at Dillingen in Germany in 1562, into the *Catalogus* of Ireland's chief saints, drawn up by Henry Fitzsimon.[7]

1 *ASH* 749. 2 *MartT* 27; *MartO*[2] 84; *MartG* 62; *MartD* 88. 3 *SIHI* 124. 4 *MartO*[2] 84; *DIL* L 135. 5 *MartO*[2] 100. 6 *HADO* iv, 17. 7 *FEMN* 344n., 377 §508; *Seanchas* 414 §215.

Mochob of Kilmore (MH). *See* Athchaoin of Colp.

Mochobha of Lismore (Leas Mór), barony of Coshmore and Coshbride, Co. Waterford. This saint was one of seven brothers and seven sisters, mainly connected with the church of Áth na gCeall on the river Blackwater, probably at Longfield's bridge in Gortnagross a few miles west of Mallow, in the Cork parish of Ballyclogh.[1] The family belonged to the Múscraighe, and among Mochobha's siblings were Laichtín of Freshford, and Cruachán of Ceall Chruacháin. Mochobha may have been assigned to Lismore because of the similarity of his name to that of Mochuda.

1 *CGSH* §666.1; *HDGP* i, 146.

Mochoime of Grangemaccomb. *See* Mochaomhóg of Leigh.

Mochoinne. *See* Mochonna.

Mocholla. *See* Mochuille.

Mocholmóg of Aran/son of Colmán. *See* Colmán Iomramha of Inishmore.

Mocholmóg of Clonard. *See* Finnian of Clonard.

Mocholmóg of Dromore. *See* Colmán of Dromore.

Mocholmóg of Uí Liatháin. *See* Colmán of.

Mochomóg. One of many possible hypocoristic or pet forms of Colum, the name Mochomóg is based on *Comma*, which also yielded the diminutive Comán.

Mochomóg of Clonduff/Roscommon. *See* Comán of Roscommon.

Mochomóg of Dionn Fhlatha. *See* Lonán.

Mochomóg of Inishkeen (Inis Caoin) on Lough Erne, parish of Enniskillen, barony of Tirkennedy, Co. Fermanagh. Of the four sons of Éanna attached to a branch of the Oirghialla, whose territory now corresponds approximately to that of the diocese of Clogher, Mochomóg (alias Mochaomhóg) was probably the least well known.[1] One of his siblings, Brughach, was associated with a Donegal church, but Mochomóg came to be identified, at least in one seventeenth-century source, with a namesake (Mochamóg) remembered at Inishkeen on 13 April, unless this be Colum (alias Mochomóg) of Inishkeen in the Leitrim parish of Rossinver.[2] Two weeks earlier (29 March), another brother, Fearghas by name, was remembered on this same island.[3]

1 *CGSH* §108; *GRSH* 71; *Lgen.* 714.11. 2 *MartT* 32; *MartG* 76; *MartD* 101; *GRSH* 71. 3 *MartG* 64; *MartD* 88, 414.

MOCHONNA. One of many possible hypocoristic or pet forms of Colum, the name Mochonna is based on *Conna* (*Coinne*), which was otherwise represented among the saints by Conna, Dochonna, and Mochonóg or, with palatalization of the medial consonants, Coinne, Dochoinne, Mochoinne. As one would expect of a form derived from Colum – by far the most important holy name in early Christian Ireland – Mochonna was a popular appellation, with twenty-eight examples in the list of homonymous saints.[1] Mochonna (Conna) is often equated with – or substitutes for – the radical form Colum, or a diminutive thereof, as in the case of Colmán son of Amhairghin. Ten of the homonymous saints named Mochonna have exact equivalents among those named Colmán, and at least three such pairs are formed by saints called Mochonóg.[2] Most notably, as is shown by the dossier of Dochonna of Assylin, Mochonna came to be used of the *fons et origo* of the cult, Colum Cille himself.[3]

1 *FG* 20–35; *CGSH* §707.679–706. 2 *FG* 25–6. 3 Cf. *CGSH* §§707.679, 724.4.

MOCHONNA of Assylin. *See* Dochonna.

MOCHONNA of Feakle (Fiacail), barony of Tulla Upper, Co. Clare. On visiting Feakle in 1839, John O'Donovan was told that the parish took its name from a tooth (*fiacail*) lost there by its patron Mochonna, whose name was preserved, along with those of Mochuille of Tulla, Fínghin of Quin, and Rícín of Cloney in a rime in Irish 'in every one's mouth'.[1] All four patron saints, but 'most of all' Mochonna, are again brought together in a poem in Classical Irish which calls upon mainly Munster saints to assist in freeing the churches of Leath Mogha from a bondage imposed by Leath Chuinn, under the headship of Finnian of Clonard.[2] The saint's feastday has not been recorded, but Colmán Lobhar of the neighbouring parish of Moynoe, who was remembered on 21 May, was also known by the pet form Mochonna, to judge by a holy well near his church.[3] The saint appears to have also been venerated by the Clann Chon Mara (McNamaras) of Clare, albeit under the guise of Mochoinne.[4]

1 *ACoC* 182. 2 RIA MS 23L11, 263; *SAM* 24.1, 17, 20. 3 *ACoC* 217. 4 *CoC* 40; *CT* i, 101.

MOCHONNA of Lusmagh. *See* Crónán of Roscrea.

MOCHONNA of Monkstown, barony of Rathdown, Dublin. An Elizabethan fiant links the name Mochonna to the sub-townland of Carrickbrennan in the Dublin parish of Monkstown.[1] It is thought that this was the saint remembered on 13 January in the martyrologies, which assign him variously to Inchpatrick in the Dublin parish of Holmpatrick and a place called Leamhchoill, now possibly Longhill in the Wicklow parish of Kilmaconoge.[2]

1 *CPPI* 201. 2 *MartT* 7; *MartG* 14; *MartD* 14; cf. *Keimelia* 520.

MOCHONÓG of Kilmuckridge (Ceall Mhucraise), barony of Ballaghkeen, Co. Wexford, and more particularly of a church in the townland of Killincooly Beg in that parish.[1] Mochonóg is known from an entry in the tract on the mothers of the saints which states that he, along with his nine brothers, were sons of Díona, daughter of a king of the Saxons, by Brachan, king of the Britons (or Welsh), and eponym of Brycheiniog in south Wales.[2] Many of the saint's siblings, including Moghóróg of Delgany, Díoraidh of Edermine, and Eallóg of St Tulloge's, are associated with churches in east Leinster. Mochonóg's other church at Gallen (Gailinne) in the Offaly barony of Garrycastle was also associated with a man named Colmán Briot, 'Briton', and as the two saints shared both a name (Colmán alias Mochonóg) and a British origin, there can be little doubt but that they were identical.[3] It has also been suggested that Colmán Briot and Dochonna of St Patrick's Island were one and the same.[4] Now featuring the remains of several early graveslabs and an ornamented cross fragment, the location of Gallen 'of the Britons' within the kingdom of Dealbhna Eathra – which also contained the renowned and acquisitive monastic settlement of Clonmacnoise – left it vulnerable to attack, most notably by the 'saint'-king of Cashel, Feidlimidh son of Criomhthann, who destroyed it in 823.[5] An act of treachery in the doorway of the church of Gallen in the year 1003 was immediately met by the wrath of God and Mochonóg, resulting in the death of the perpetrator.[6] The saint may also have been patron of Timahoe in the Kildare parish of Clane, and the suggestion that Mochonóg's church may have been in Scotland has little to support it.[7] No feast has been recorded for the saint.

1 *CECW* 209; *DIB* vi, 538. 2 *CGSH* §§707.626, 722.89; *Lgen.* 750.11; *EWGT* 14–16, 32–3. 3 *CGSH* §707.257; *FG* 26; *RM* 6.1, 13. 4 *IsPatrick* 138. 5 *AU s.a.* 6 *AFM s.a.* 7 *CPNS* 282; *CDKL* 241.

Mochonóg Uamhach. *See* Colmán Uamhach.

Mochríodóg. A pet form of Críodán, Mochríodóg is attested mainly in the list of homonymous saints, which records fifteen bearers of the name.[1]

1 *CGSH* §707.825–39.

Mochta of Inishmot. *See* Mochta of Louth.

Mochta of Louth (Lughmhadh), an ecclesiastical site and former diocesan see that gave name to the present parish, barony and county of Louth. The earliest mention of Mochta (Latin Maucteus) is in the Life of Colum Cille compiled by Adhamhnán shortly before 700. Adhamhnán attributed to Mochta – described as 'a certain British stranger … and disciple of the holy bishop Patricius' – a prophecy to the effect that in the 'last days of the world' a boy named Columba would be born, whose monastery would be separated from his own by one 'small hedge'.[1] Such prophecies are commonplace, but whereas later biographers allow others, such as Patrick and Brighid, also to foretell Colum Cille's birth, Adhamhnán gave the honour to Mochta alone.[2] The saint's status as a disciple of Patrick is corroborated in an annal entry, possibly also written on Iona, recording his death in 535, which quotes from an autograph letter the words 'Mochta, sinner, priest, and disciple of saint Patrick'.[3] The date of his obit, which has loomed large in the debate surrounding Patrick's mission, has most recently been explained in line with Columban rather than Patrician chronology.[4]

Mochta's connection with Louth is almost unwavering and, while no mention is made of this church in early sources, its location near the east coast would have made a suitable dwelling for a man whose origins statedly lay in Britain, possibly, as in the case of Finnian of Movilla, among the Irish settled there. The alleged proximity of his church to that of Colum Cille, which has greatly puzzled scholars, may have turned on the lands held by a people named Dál or Maca Runtair who figure both in Adhamhnán's text and in an episode involving Mochta and Patrick in the ninth-century Tripartite Life. In Adhamhnán's text, a man named Mothrianóg (Trenanus) of the Maca Runtair is presented as an emissary sent by Colum Cille from Iona to Ireland.[5] In the Tripartite Life, Patrick is brought to a place named Ardpatrick (Ard Pádraig), contiguous to Louth, but apparently among the Dál Runtair, where, wishing to found a church, he is said to have met Mochta daily, before leaving the place for Armagh, on angelic advice dispensed in the form of a written letter.[6] As there is no trace of Mochta in the seventh-century Patrician Lives, it may be that Colum Cille's association with the area about Louth, which is implied by the presence of Mothrianóg of the Maca Runtair on Iona, was subsequently replaced by Patrician interests, perpetuated in the local name Ardpatrick. Though Adhamhnán might well have felt that his subject's interests – the abiding focus of his text – would have gained from a connection with Mochta, he may unwittingly have given the author of the Tripartite Life an excuse to bring his subject to Louth, in the process ousting Colum Cille in a manner that clearly carried sufficient local appeal to ensure that the change would forever be commemorated topographically.

Except for a brief period in the late twelfth century, when it replaced Clogher as a diocesan see, thus giving rise to the tradition that Mochta was Clogher's 'first bishop', Louth and its hinterland have formed part of the diocese of Armagh.[7] The church remained sufficiently important to attract the canons regular of St Augustine who established a priory there in the 1140s.[8] Well known for their interest in local saints, the canons were no doubt responsible for Mochta's Latin Life, preserved in the so-called Salamancan codex.[9] The author of the Life was aware of Mochta's earlier associations with both Patrick and Colum Cille, embellishing each episode with additions no doubt felt by him to be important. With the probable aim of enhancing the status of Louth within the archdiocese of Armagh, Mochta is said to have briefly succeeded Patrick.[10] Mochta's relinquishment of a site in favour of Colum Cille , then yet to be born, is said to have followed an offer of the place by Aodh (†610) son of Colga, king of a segment of Orior based in the area about Armagh.[11] Having thus accommodated two of Ireland's chief saints, Mochta's biographer also brought Brighid of Kildare into the narrative, at least obliquely, by allowing the saint to give directions as to the location of her future church.[12] A concern with Leinster affairs is also evident in an episode which brings Corbán – probably representing Ceall Chorbáin, an earlier name for the Kildare church of Naas – accompanied by a young Iobhar of Begerin, on a visit to Mochta, who is said to have recognized the young boy's singing talents.[13] The association with Iobhar is echoed in a text preserved in the late twelfth-century Book of Leinster, which attributes to Mochta a prophecy concerning the future greatness of the Begerin saint.[14]

Among other saints introduced into the Life are two also associated with Mochta elsewhere. One is Daigh of Inishkeen in the Monaghan barony of Farney, whose own Life features Mochta prominently, but who is here given the honour of rendering the Louth saint the last rites.[15] The other is Triananus, who is probably to be identifed with the previously mentioned Trenanus (alias Mothrianóg) of the Maca Runtair.[16] Influenced perhaps by the saint's alternative appellation, Seanmhochta – literally 'old Mochta', but ordinarily the earlier of two saints so named – both Mochta's biographer and a poem added in the margins of his feastday attributed to him a grand old age of 300 years.[17] A poem attributed to Cuimín of Connor, which gives Mochta pride of place after the three national saints, asserts that he lived frugally for a hundred years, while a separate quatrain lauds his generosity.[18]

Among other places associated with the saint were Clonsilla in the Dublin barony of Castleknock, under the guise of 'Machutus', and Kilmore in the Longford parish of Columbkille, if this latter place is intended by the reference to *ecclesia S. Moctha de Kilmor* in the annates of the diocese of Ardagh.[19] The Uí Raghallaigh (O'Reillys) of Bréifne were wont to swear by Mochta's cloak (*dar bhrat Mochta*).[20] Inishmot (Inis Mochta) in the Meath barony of Lower Slane is called after a namesake, Mochta *na hInse* son of Cearnachán, a priest of Armagh who died in 922 and was remembered on 26 March.[21] Mochta of Louth's feast fell on 19 August, the day after that of Daigh of Inishkeen and the vigil of the feast of Mothrianóg, and he was also remembered on 24 March, the octave of the feast of Patrick who became patron of the parish of Louth.[22] Alone of the martyrologies, that of Tallaght records the name of his mother Cuman.[23] After death, Mochta was thought to have remained powerful, as is shown by the vengeance he took on Annadh Ua Ruairc, who plundered Louth in 1043.[24]

1 *VC*[2] 182. **2** *VSHH* 366; *IKD* 223 §13; *BCC* 11 §24; *DIB* vi, 436–7. **3** *AU s.a.* **4** *PSP* 14–17; *StH* 2, 72; *BLH* 85–93; *AILC* 244–5. **5** *VC*[1] 242–4. **6** *BP* 2680–96; *VT* 226. **7** *MRHI* 92–3; *ClRec.* 7, 376. **8** *MRHI* 185–6. **9** *VSHH* 394–400; cf. *CHSC* 157. **10** Ibid. 396–7 §7. **11** Ibid. 399 §16; *AU s.a.* **12** *VSHH* 397–8 §9. **13** Ibid. 398 §12. **14** *CGSH* §721.13–14. **15** *VSHH* 389–90 §§2, 4, 400 §§20–1. **16** Ibid. 399 §18. **17** *VSHH* 400 §19; *MartT* 114; *MartO*[2] 188; *MartD* 224. **18** *ZCP* 5, 62; cf. *MartT* 100, 114. **19** *MRHI* 105; *AIH* ii, 82; *AnnU* 169; *CPL* 15, §226. **20** *Seanchas* 414 §210. **21** *AFM s.a.*; *MartG* 62; *MartD* 88; *JCLAS* 1.1, 130; ibid. 10, 342–5. **22** *MartT* 26, 64; *MartO*[2] 84, 177; *MartG* 60, 160; *MartD* 222; OSL LH 236. **23** *MartT* 64. **24** ATig. *s.a.*

Mochua. This hypocoristic form, which was used for more than one name, became so popular that it accounts for almost sixty entries in the list of homonymous saints.[1] Though the majority of these saints are otherwise unattested, some are to be found elsewhere under the radical forms of their names, for example Cuán and Crónán. Of those best known as Mochua or Dochua full pedigrees survive for two only, the saints of Timahoe (Teach Mochua) in Laois and of Balla in Mayo, both of whom also attracted the attention of biographers.

1 *CGSH* §707.484–542.

Mochua of Balla, barony of Clanmorris, Co. Mayo. Mochua's pedigree, which survives in few versions of the corpus, attached him through his father Beagán to the Corca Dálann, a segment of the Ulaidh of north-east Ulster, to which, as the genealogy noted, Cainneach of Aghaboe also belonged.[1] In confirming his descent from the Ulaidh, the author of the saint's late vernacular Life provided him with a mother named Cuman (Cuimne), allegedly of the Dál mBuain (whence the deanery of 'Dalboyn' in the diocese of Down), and three (otherwise unattested) sisters named Briúinseach, Lugaid (Lucait) and Toidheall (Tuideall).[2] The saint's Ulster background is also recognized in the story of his early youth and upbringing which saw him attend Comhghall's school in Bangor. On being chastized by his master, his tears are said to have entered the mouth of a barren woman who thereupon conceived and gave birth to 'Dabhiu', a form of name by which Bíthe of Inch is probably intended.[3]

The saint's Life in the form of a homily, crudely put together in a mix of prose and verse, as one commentator described it, is datable to the fourteenth or fifteenth century.[4] It is incomplete in that it lacks an account of the saint's death. The text's main interest lies in the manner in which favour is curried with notable Connacht families of the time, including the Uí Eaghra (O'Haras) of Leyny and the Uí Fhlaithbheartaigh (O'Flahertys) of Iarchonnacht, both of whose ancestors, Taithleach son of Ceann Faoladh and Ceann Faoladh son of Colga, are placed in the saint's debt.[5]

Mochua's journey from Bangor to Balla follows a circuitous route along the east coast to an unidentified site in Fir Rois (in the Louth/Monaghan area), then inland to Fore, and on to Tihelly near Durrow, before crossing the Shannon into Soghain of Uí Mhaine, now approximately the Galway barony of Tiaquin, where the saint is said to have foretold the birth of Comán of Roscommon.[6] He is then brought to Lough Hackett (Loch Cime) in the Galway barony of Clare, where he encounters Ceallach son of Raghallach, ancestor of the Síol Aodha of Annaghdown in the same barony, who also shows deference to the saint.[7] The final part of his journey brings him to Balla (formerly Ros Dairbhreach) in Carra – on whose boundary the saint's church now lies – arriving there at the age of thirty-five and spending another twenty-one or (more likely) thirty-one years there, which would have left him with a round, and thus perfect, age of sixty-six at death, which occurred, according to the annals, either in 638 or 694.[8] At Balla, he was met and, after initial hostility, made welcome by representatives of the Uí Fhiachrach, one of whose chief strongholds was named Inishcoe (Inis Mochua) in the Mayo parish of Crossmolina.[9]

Many of the places visited by the saint on his long journey from Bangor to Balla had connections with the canons regular of St Augustine. Bangor itself was the seat of a priory, as were Durrow (within whose parish lies Tihelly), Roscommon whose patron he prophesied, and Annaghdown whose associated family was placed in his debt.[10] Balla, which gave name to a parish adjoining that of Mayo, was probably affiliated to the Augustinian priory at the latter location. When laying out the limits of Balla's property entitlements, the biographer twice mentioned Tráigh Eothaile, now Ballysadare, likewise the location of an

Augustinian priory, allegedly founded by Féichín, which would explain Mochua's visit to this saint's church at Fore.[11] Elsewhere, Mochua is twice numbered among those likely to come to the assistance of Seanán of Scattery Island.[12] By the early nineteenth century, memory of the saint and his feast of 30 March had faded in Balla.[13] A second feast, on 1 January, is noted in a calendar compiled by John Carpenter, archbishop of Dublin, and in an edition the same cleric prepared of Butler's *Lives of the Saints*.[14]

1 *CGSH* §372; *Lgen.* 731.3; *DIB* vi, 539. 2 *LisL* 4636–9. 3 Ibid. 4649–53. 4 *Kenney* 461. 5 *LisL* 4790–97, 4843–4; OCBG §§1360, 2040. 6 *LisL* 4654–708. 7 Ibid. 4709–21. 8 Ibid. 4722–50; *AU s.a.*; *ATig. s.a.* 637. 9 Ibid. 4751–86; *Lgen.* 276.10; *LisL* 4751–86; *LGen.* 276.10. 10 *MRHI* 161, 174, 191–2. 11 *LisL* 4778, 4784; *MRHI* 160. 12 *ZCP* 10, 26–8 §§21, 23. 13 OSL MO ii, 414; *MartT* 28; *MartO*² 85; *MartG* 64; *MartD* 90. 14 *RIA MS* 23 A 8, ii; LIS i, 24.

Mochua of Clondalkin. *See* Crónán of Clondalkin.

Mochua of Darragh (Darach Mochua), barony of Coshlea, Co. Limerick. This bearer of the name Mochua was remembered at a holy well in the townland of Darraghmore on 3 August.[1] The martyrologies note Mochua of Cruachán on this day.[2] The location of the saint's church on a diocesan boundary lent it importance, as is shown by its mention in the Life of Molaga of Aghacross.[3] Further west, under the guise of Mochua, the saint was patron of Kilmacow in the parish of Ballingarry, where the local church was corruptly named *ecclesia sancti Cuiniani* in a seventeenth-century document.[4]

1 *UCA* 106; *SACCL* 427; *JRSAI* 85,198. 2 *MartT* 60; *MartG* 148; *MartD* 210. 3 *IrT* iii, 17 §9. 4 *SACCL* 410; *UCA* 29, 106; *CH* 2, 30.

Mochua of Ticknevin (Teach Dochua mhic Neamhain), parish of Kilpatrick, barony of Carbury, Co. Kildare. Éidchéan of Clonfad is attached to Ticknevin in a miscellaneous list of what appear to be Brigidine churches, but both he and Mochua (alias Dochua) son of Neamhan are brought together in the Life of Colmán of Lynn, which states that the three churches of the saints made a union, to become 'one church', with Lynn in the west, Clonfad in the centre and 'Teach Mochua' in the east.[2] Together with two neighbouring churches, Lullymore (Liolchach) and Derrybrennan (Doire Branáin) in the parish of Kilpatrick, Ticknevin is said to have hosted not only a saint, but also a *fuath*, 'spectre'.[3] The church of Timahoe (Teach Mochua) in the parish of the same name, adjoining Kilpatrick, was probably also named after the saint, and a church dedicated to him is recorded at Barreen in the Kildare parish of Balraheen.[4] Given his patronymic, Mochua may have been patron of the parish of Kilmacnevan (from Ceall Mhic Neamhain?) in the Westmeath barony of Moygoish which John O'Donovan visited in November 1837, to find that the patron was St Matthew but that an old well bore the name of Brighid of Kildare.[5] Concerning 'Mac Naomháin', as O'Donovan wrote the name, local tradition could not provide the 'dimmest light'.[6]

1 *CGSH* §663.3, p. 333; *OnomG* 623. 2 *BCML* 34 §35. 3 *BLis.* 198va21. 4 *CDKL* 261; Logainm.ie 'Barreen'. 5 *PNW* 98. 6 Ibid. 303.

Mochua of Timahoe (Teach Mochua) or Fossy, barony of Cullenagh, Co. Laois. Arriving at Ushnagh Hill (Uisneach) in Westmeath, where the men of Ireland were gathered, Caoilte is said to have been greeted by Mochua son of Lonán, an *athlaoch*, 'ex-layman', of Patrick's followers who rose before him.[1] On being asked by Patrick to say something about Mochua, Caoilte recited the saint's pedigree, name by name, attaching him to the Ceinéal Muireadhaigh, a segment of the Ceinéal Eoghain of Tyrone. More commonly, however, Mochua is attached to the Fothairt, and thus shares a line of descent with Brighid of Kildare which led to his receiving a place of honour among the first five pedigrees of saints recorded by the scribe of the Book of Leinster.[2] His mother, Finneacht daughter of Léinín, belonged, according to the same book, to the Uí Mhic Caorthainn of an unidentified church named Ceall Chonaigh.[3]

As in the case of Mobhí, there was also a perceived connection with north-east Connacht, which the author of the saint's late (probably fourteenth-century) office-style Life, had no compunction in describing as 'an origin among the Luighne of Connacht'.[4] These gave name to the present Sligo barony of Leyny, and the fact that Ballysadare, the seat of an Augustininian priory mentioned twice in the Life of Mochua's namesake at Balla, is located in this barony may have some bearing on the tradition that Mochua originated there.[5] The same writer, though maintaining that the saint founded thirty churches throughout Ireland and Scotland, named only one other – 'Dayrinnys' in a *locus montanus* in Oirghialla. Placed in Sliabh Fuaid, now the Fews of Armagh, by a scholiast of the Martyrology of Aonghas, this place has been identified as Derrynoose in Armagh, where a well and cursing stone named after the saint were frequented until the beginning of the twentieth century.[6]

The office Life is mainly concerned with the saint's relationships with other saints, beginning with Colmán Eala. Located in the church of Killeshin (Gleann Uisean), instead of the more usual Lynally, Colmán is said to have visited Mochua in search of knowledge which, after he had failed to interpret a verse sung by a heavenly bird that descended on the saints, he went on to acquire through the expulsion of an 'unclean spirit' dwelling in him.[7] Munna, presumably of Taghmon in Westmeath, another associate, endured leprosy for seven years in order to overcome his pride, only to have it cured after that time by Mochua.[8] Cianán of Duleek is then brought into the Life at a point where, as he was beginning to build his stone church – supposedly the first ever to have been built in Ireland – he set out to seek assistance from his fellow-saints in the form of prayers for good weather.[9] Reaching Timahoe, Cianán found that his wish had been granted in response to the prayers of Mochua, who asked to be told when the church was ready so that he could consecrate it, which he duly did.

As in most Lives, traces of Augustinian influence are also evident in the text, most prominently in the episode involving Cianán of Duleek, whose church was the seat of two houses of canons regular.[10] In the case of Mochua's church, such concerns were to be expected, as it was one of the rectories impropriate at its dissolution to the Augustinian priory of Greatconnell in Kildare.[11] Said by the annals to have died in 658, the saint was remembered on 24 December at

Timahoe as both Mochua and Crónán (also eponym of Kilcronan in the neighbouring parish of Dysartgallen).[12] A brutal slaying at Timahoe in 1069 was reputedly avenged soon after 'in honour of Mochua, Fiontan and Colmán'.[13]

1 AcS 2354–7; *SG* i, 146. **2** *CGSH* §5; *GRSH* 75; *Lgen*. 718.4; *DIB* vi, 539. **3** *CGSH* §722.67; *CGH* 120a8. **4** *VSHP* ii, 184 §1; *LSHS* 69–70. **5** *MRHI* 160–1. **6** *VSHP* ii, 189 §§11–12; *MartO*² 262; *BUPNS* (1st ser.) 2, 34–6. **7** *VSHP* ii, 184–5 §§2–4. **8** Ibid. 185–7 §§5–7; *LSHS* 72–3, 82–5. **9** *VSHP* ii, 187–8 §§8–10. **10** *MRHI* 173–4; *LSHS* 74. **11** *EIMP* 161–2. **12** *MartT* 89; *MartO*² 254; *MartG* 246; *MartD* 346; *ATig. s.a.* 657. **13** *AFM s.a.*

Mochua son of Lughaidh. *See* Crónán of Clondalkin.

Mochua Luachra of Ferns (Fearna), barony of Scarawalsh, Co. Wexford. Approaching a ford at a place called Áth Iomdháin, Maodhóg of Ferns is said to have been questioned by his charioteer about his successor.[1] The unexpected reply was that it would be the person who opened the gate of the ford ahead of them, and this turned out to be a young man, part of a group of 'wanton, restless' scholars. Introducing himself as Crónán of the people of Luachair, and beseeching Maodhóg that he be allowed to spend the remainder of his life with him, the youth was renamed Mochua (the same name in hypocoristic guise) and later consecrated bishop. The vernacular version of Maodhóg's Life, perhaps influenced by the reference to Luachair, changed the form Mochua to Moling and supplied the saint with a pedigree more properly that of the patron of St Mullin's.[2] As it happens, Moling is also said to have occupied Maodhóg's see of Ferns, but the closeness of the connection between him and Mochua does not end there.[3] It is also exemplified by the calendar, which assigns to Mochua a feast (22 June) within the octave of Moling's day of 17 June.[4] Mochua was also remembered on that day at Killagowan in the Wexford parish of Meelnagh.[5] The saint died, according to the annals, in 654.[6]

1 *VSHP* ii, 154 §34, 305 §34. **2** *BNÉ* i, 243–4 §§191–3. **3** *VSHP* ii, 197 §17. **4** *MartT* 50–1; *MartG* 118, 120;*MartD* 170, 174. **5** OSL WX ii, 92; *CECW* 208. **6** *AU s.a.*

Mochuaróg. *See* Ciar of Achadh Í; Cuarán.

Mochuda of Lismore (Lios Mór), barony of Coshmore and Coshbride, Co. Waterford, and of Rahan (Rathan), barony of Ballycowan, Co. Offaly. According to the genealogists, Mochuda (a pet form of Carthach) belonged through his father (variously named Fionoll and Fínghin) to the Uí Fhirb (Fhearba), a branch of the Ciarraighe of north Kerry.[1] His mother, Fíonmhaith (also written Meadh) daughter of Fínghin, was attached to the Uí Mhic Coinne, a branch of the Corca Dhuibhne of south Kerry.[2] As with several other saints originating in Kerry, including Bréanainn of Clonfert, Fíonán of Kinnitty, and the closely related Lughaidh of Coolbanagher, Mochuda became associated with a Midlands church, in this case Rahan, lying close to the line traditionally thought to have divided Ireland into two halves. Unlike his confrères, however, whose southern churches, Ardfert, Innisfallen, and Rattoo, all in Kerry, came to be regarded as secondary, Mochuda's church at Lismore was to become his principal foundation, as well as one of the most important churches in the south of Ireland.

Not surprisingly, given the prestige of his church, abbots of which are recorded in the annals from about 700 onwards, the saint eventually attracted a biographer, whose Life of Mochuda now survives in several Latin and vernacular versions.[3] The Latin recension preserved in the Marsh's Library and Trinity College collections is closest to the original, which appears to date to the early thirteenth century, and this version also survives in a late vernacular translation.[4] Somewhat abbreviated Latin and Irish recensions are also extant, and an account is independently preserved of the circumstances thought to have surrounded the saint's expulsion from Rahan in 636, where, reputedly surrounded by 700 monks, he is said to have spent most of his life.[5] A critical study of the saint's entire biographical dossier has been recently completed in the form of a doctoral thesis.[6]

Although allowing Mochuda only a brief residence of eighteen months in Lismore, the Life nonetheless shows many signs of having been compiled there, not least in the number of local churches and saints named in the text.[7] Having been foretold by both Comhghall of Bangor, later to be the saint's mentor, and Bréanainn, with whom he was to divide the north Kerry region, Mochuda is said to have been born on the banks of the river Maine, which flows through the parish that took its name from his first foundation at Ceall Tulach, now Kiltallagh near Castlemaine.[8] Allegedly on excellent terms with the local king, Maol Tuile, ancestor of the powerful Uí Chonchobhair (O'Connors) of north Kerry, Mochuda is described as having chosen an elder or senior (*sean*) namesake, Carthach of Kiltomey (Tuaim) in the parish of Kilcaragh (Ceall Charthaigh), as his first teacher.[9] On the day of his ordination, he prophesied that a local chieftain, whose son he baptized, would hold the hostages of Uí Thorna, a name preserved locally in Abbeydorney (Mainistir Ua dTorna), home of a Cistercian abbey, and its surrounding parish, O'Dorney.[10] Following this, after a brief sojourn in Bangor and subsequent return to Kerry, the bishopric of which he duly accepted, the saint is brought by his biographer on a journey that led, via east Munster – where he witnessed angels arising and descending from the location of his later church at Lismore – to Clonfertmulloe (alias Kyle) and Lynally, and then on to Rahan, the site of his Midlands church, which he supposedly built with materials left by Colum Cille, a previous occupant of the site.[11]

The body of the Life is taken up with miracles performed in or near Rahan, interspersed with frequent return journeys to south Munster. Many episodes based in Rahan foreshadow events that concerned Lismore or the properties later impropriate to it. The list of the saint's twelve disciples at Rahan, for example, mainly comprises patrons of churches in the area influenced by Lismore, and their mention is followed by a series of encounters with Munster kings, one of which led to the founding of several churches in or near Cork Harbour, in the territory of Ciarraighe Cuirche, including Spike Island (Inis Pich) and a church at 'Ros Beag', now Ballybricken in the parish of Barnahely.[12] It has been suggested that Mochuda's prophecy concerning the ridicule due to Britons in his *civitas* – brought about following an attempt by two of their race to murder him – may relate to an early thirteenth-century struggle between the sees of Lismore and

Waterford, then occupied by a prelate of Welsh origin who was murdered by the king of the Déise.[13]

The lengthy account of the saint's expulsion from Rahan, also the subject of a separate text, provides the biographer with what seems to have been a welcome opportunity to condemn the monasteries of Clonard and Durrow, both of which became locations of important Augustinian houses in the course of the twelfth century, on the basis that they had connived with the secular power against Mochuda.[14] The saint's journey southwards was mainly marked by visits to sites of other Augustinian houses, at Seirkieran, Roscrea – as echoed, perhaps, by Kilmacuddy in the parishes of Bourney and Killea, near Roscrea – and Athassel.[15] Finally reaching Lismore, Mochuda was granted the site by Maol Ochtraigh son of Cobhthach, king of the Déise, and the brief account of his stay there gave the biographer an opportunity of extolling the monastery's virtues, including its success in attracting students from all over Ireland, England and Wales.[16] There are some signs, including an obvious concern with churches in west Kerry, and the stipulation that all successors of the saint were to belong to the Ciarraighe, that the first abbot of the Cistercian house at Mellifont, and subsequent papal legate and bishop of Lismore, Christian Ua Conairche, who died at Abbeydorney in 1186, may have influenced the contents of the Life.[17] The main concern of the biographer appears to have been, however, with the affairs of the see of Lismore, under threat of amalgamation with the see of Waterford in the late twelfth and early thirteenth century.[18]

Despite the ancient tradition that Mochuda (Mo Chatu Rathin) was also expelled from Lismore by a local Fermoy (Fir Mhaighe) chieftain, the vernacular text dealing with the saint's expulsion from Rahan shows little interest in Munster affairs. On the contrary, it reveals a detailed knowledge of the area about Rahan, which would suggest that it was inspired by concerns similar to those that caused the production of a tract on the Uí Shuanaigh family, Mochuda's local successors.[19] In contrast to this latter tract, however, which endeavours to teach manners to local chieftains, the 'Expulsion' targets monastic centres, such as Clonard, Durrow, Clonmacnoise, and Killeigh, all of which were sites of Augustinian priories.[20]

Other Lives that feature Mochuda are those of Colmán of Lynally and Déaglán of Ardmore. Déaglán's biographer states that his subject founded a church on the plain of Magh Sciath, south-west of Cappoquin, in the townland of Drumroe and parish of Lismore.[21] The fame of Mochuda's church as a centre of reform was such that it found mention under the guise of 'Lismor Muchutu' in the Life composed about 1090–1100 by Lifris for Cadog of Llancarfan in Wales, who is said to have been named after Mochuda (from *Cuda*).[22] The saint's connections with north Kerry, whose people (Ciarraighe) he had the duty of protecting together with Bréanainn of Clonfert, also ensured a place for him in the records of Clare saints.[23] He is among those considered ready to come to the assistance of Seanán of Scattery, and joins many others improbably said to have been children of Inghean Bhaoith of Killinaboy.[24] According to the last testament composed for Cormac son of Cuileannán, king of Munster, Mochuda, no doubt representing his church, was to receive precious vessels of gold and silver, and the saint's head reputedly formed part of Adhamhnán's reliquary.[25] A Middle Irish rule attributed to him has survived in verse, and a late poem ascribed to him extols the ecclesiastical life.[26] 'The booke of St Mochuda of Rathin and Lismore' is cited as a source both in a large miscellany of prose and verse and in an early seventeenth-century poem.[27] Likened in manners to Ciprian of Carthage (chosen probably because of the similarity of the name of the city to Mochuda's original name of Carthach), the saint is said to have died in 637.[28] His feastday fell on 14 May, and his name is invoked under the guise of Carthach in one of the Stowe Missal litanies.[29] Local tradition in the Killarney area, where he was known as Cuddy, maintained that the saint first slept for 500 years, and on awaking, left the imprint of his knees on a stone in the locality, before dying a few hours later.[30] At Burrow in the Dublin parish of Portraine, where a holy well was dedicated to him, he was also known as Cuddy.[31] The saint gave name to Kilmacot in the Wexford parish of Ballyvaldon.[32]

1 *CGSH* §§126, 703.4; *GRSH* 107; *Lgen.* 729.1–3; *BNÉ* i, 301 §1; *DIB* ii, 396. **2** *CGSH* §722.62; *Lgen.* 729.4; *BNÉ* i, 291 §1; *VSHP* i, 170 §1. **3** *NHI* ix, 262–3; *SS* 318. **4** *VSHP* i, xlv–xlviii, 170–99; ITS 26–31, 74–147; *SS* 324, 329–30. **5** *VSHH* 334–40; *BNÉ* i, xxxvii–xxxviii, 291–99; ibid. xxxviii–xxxix, 300–11; *IrL* 60. **6** UCC DP 2002 Thor.; cf. *SS* 317–36. **7** *VSHP* i, xlviii, 198 §68. **8** Ibid. 170–1 §§1–5, 174–5 §§14–15; *JKAHS* 22, 124. **9** *VSHP* i, 172–3 §9–11. **10** Ibid. 173–4 §12; *MRHI* 123. **11** *VSHP* i, 175–8 §15–20. **12** Ibid. 182–5 §§39–47. **13** Ibid. 187–8 §45; *NHI* ix, 308–9. **14** *VSHP* i, 190–4 §§53–60; *AU s.a.* **15** Ibid. 194 §§61–2. **16** Ibid. 197 §65; *JCHAS* 65, 18–23; ibid. 73, 65–6. **17** *MRHI* 123; UCC DP 2002 Thor. **18** *MRHI* 91–2. **19** *Peritia* 12, 194; *BNÉ* i, 300–16. **20** *BNÉ* i, 301–4 §§6–14. **21** *VSHP* i, 273 §36; ibid. ii, 37 §6; *VSHH* 217 §25, 218 §28, 224 §50; ITS 16, 12, 161 §30. **22** *VSBG* 48 §10. **23** *ZCP* 8, 315. **24** *ZCP* 10, 26 §22. **25** *RC* 37, 352 §4; *CGSH* §714.11; *Celtica* 15, 35 §15. **26** *ACL* iii, 312–21; *ZCP* 10, 13–14; *IER* (2nd ser.) 1, 112–18. **27** *ZCP* 8, 181; *Bod. Cat.* i, 68; *InaF* i, 136 §11. **28** *CGSH* §712.25; *AU s.a.* **29** *MartT* 42; *MartO*² 124; *MartG* 96; *MartD* 126; HBS 32, 14. **30** *ReisIrl.* 139. **31** *Rep. Nov.* 2, 80; *AHWD* 12, 20. **32** *TNW* 1137.

Mochuidbhriocht of Kilmahuddrick (Ceall Mochuidbhriocht), barony of Newcastle, Co. Dublin. The annals of St Mary's Abbey in Dublin, which have been dated to the thirteenth century, state that Cuthbert, bishop of Lindisfarne, was born in Kilmahuddrick.[1] Although entirely unhistorical, an Irish origin for Cuthbert is also recorded in a late twelfth-century Latin version of the saint's origins, entitled *Liber de Ortu Sancti Cuthberti*, which was plagiarized from traditions surrounding Moluóg of Lismore in Scotland.[2] Whether his cult was really introduced at Kilmahuddrick, or merely adopted opportunistically, is uncertain. Non-Irish names of saints are usually transmitted without any trace of the affection implied by the prefix *mo-*, 'my', present in the form *Mochuidbhriocht*.

1 *CSMA* ii, 287; *AnH* 16, 318. **2** *BHL* i, 305; *RSC* 144–54; cf. *ASH* 679.

Mochuille. This name, like its variants, Mocholla and Mochaille, derives from *Colla* (*Caille/Cuille*), a hypocoristic or pet form of Colum.[1] As with many other bearers of the name, therefore, saints named Mochuille are likely to have been localizations of the cult of Colum Cille of Iona.

1 *FG* 20–35.

Mochuille of Dreasnaidh. This man was one of seven sons of Aonghas said to have come to Ireland from Scotland and, in keeping with this tradition, was attached to the tribal grouping of Dál Riada which had settlements in both countries.[1] The church assigned to Mochuille, also written Dreasna or Innsnad, and located in Fothairt Fea, now the Carlow barony of Forth, has yet to be identified.[2] It may have lain near the (equally unidentified) Áth Slabach, the site of a battle between a branch of the Uí Dhúnlainge of north Leinster and their southern neighbours, the Uí Cheinsealaigh, following which Mochuille is said to have cursed the victorious Ceallach son of Maol Otraigh for a violation, presumably of his church.[3] There was a well ('Tobermathulla') named after Mochuille at Glencommaun in the Kilkenny parish of Tullahought.[4] The saint's feast of 12 June is recorded only in the Martyrology of Donegal, where he joins three of his brothers, Aghadán, Torannán, and Troscán.[5]

1 *CGSH* §§209; *GRSH* 81; *Lgen.* 721.8. **2** *CGSH* §701.5. **3** *CGH* 124b39–42; *Ériu* 32, 107. **4** *HADO* iv, 328. **5** *MartD* 166–8.

Mochuille of Tulla (Tulach na nEaspag), barony of Tulla Upper, Co. Clare. When the saint's parish was visited by the Ordnance Surveyors in late 1839, all memory of the patron's day had been lost, despite the presence locally of several holy wells named for him and, over fifty years later, when visited by T.J. Westropp, even Mochuille's name had been forgotten.[1] Yet the saint is well enough known from the literary record. His pedigree attaches him through his father Díocaill to the Fir Mhaighe Féine of north-east Cork, where the church of Kilmaculla (Ceall Mochuille) in the parish of Kildorrery is named after him.[2]

A Life was compiled for Mochuille in the German city of Regensburg, where an Irish monastery (*Schottenkloster*) was established in the late eleventh century.[3] The author of the Life, which probably dates to the third quarter of the twelfth century, asserts that, while still a young man in quest of scholarship in 'sweet towns' of Gaul, he was present when the relics of St Lambert were triumphantly used to recover the castle of Bouillon for the bishop of Liège, an event dated to 1141.[4] Judging by his eloquent and flowing, if slightly inflated, style, the author – probably a Clareman who may also have composed the Life of Flannán of Killaloe – imbibed assiduously from the teachings of his French masters.[5] His text – which survives in several manuscripts of the so-called *Magnum Legendarium Austriacum* (Great Austrian Legendary), and also, albeit in fragmentary form, in the *Codex Salmanticensis* – while available in print, still lacks a critical edition.[6] Accused of larding his narrative with so many miracles that it tends more to stupify than to edify, the author nevertheless provides an absorbing insight into how local devotion from the homeland could be used to promote the interests of his community in distant exile. The Great Austrian Legendary is thought to have been compiled by a group of monasteries in Regensburg, acting in concert, and Mochuille's Life, in common with several others, may have been written to satisfy the perceived need for *Schottenkloster* participation in the project.[7]

The fact that he sent Mochuille to Ailbhe, patron of the archdiocese of Cashel and Emly, to receive his early education allowed the author to introduce an episode concerning a successful venture into viniculture somewhere near Limerick by Ailbhe, using vines brought back from a visit to Rome.[8] Recognizing the signs of his pupil's budding sanctity, Ailbhe instructed a somewhat reluctant Mochuille to seek out a hermitage of his own, and this led to a journey northwards towards mountains separating the north of Ireland from the south, apparently the Slieveaughty district, where, hungry and thirsty, the saint's prayers miraculously induced the emergence of three wells that soon formed a lake.[9] Still locally remembered by a holy well in the townland of Flagmount and parish of Feakle, Mochuille then retraced his steps southwards, to a place where he discovered, as in so many other foundation legends, a wild animal, in this case a hind, which he soon tamed. At this site, then named *Dorsum Riascorum* (perhaps for Druim Riasg), subsequently known as *Collis Episcoporum* (Irish Tulach na nEaspag, anglicized Tulla), the saint established his main church.[10]

The remainder of the Life is taken up with accounts of miracles performed, either in favour of, or despite, local dynasts. One of these was Rónghal, eponymous ancestor of the Uí Rónghailc, lords of an area corresponding to the parishes of Kilnoe and Killuran, just east of Tulla; another was Forannán, possibly the son of Bréanainn in the genealogy of Uí Chaisín, who were overlords of the whole barony of Tulla Upper.[11] Forannán's wife, a 'most impious' lady who suffered the same dire fate as her husband, was allegedly the daughter of King Guaire to whom the saint now also taught manners over several chapters of the Life, before leading the king to the status of a paragon of generosity for which he is now mostly remembered.[12] Guaire's family, Uí Fhiachrach Aidhne, lorded over an area approximately coextensive with the diocese of Kilmacduagh.

By means of posthumous miracles, exercised through his relics, Mochuille is shown to have remained a powerful patron. A dispute relating to more recent times and involving two representatives of the the Uí Bhriain line dominant throughout north Munster, Theodoricus (Toirdhealbhach, †1086) and his son Tatheus (Tadhg, †1086), and an unnamed local noble who, having taken refuge in Tulla church, was laid under siege by the other two, is resolved when a sweet-smelling well miraculously emerges near the church.[13] Having thus manifested the saint's posthumous power, Mochuille's biographer devoted the final chapter to an equally persuasive demonstration by reference to the above-mentioned recapture of Bouillon in 1141 by the bishop of Liège, with the aid of the relics of Lambert.[14]

By such means, and drawing on two recent occurrences, one probably heard from locals before he left Ireland, the other witnessed by his own eyes, the author of the Life provided a text designed to appeal to two potential audiences. The authorities at home in Ireland on whom the *pauperes* in the *Schottenkloster* congregation depended for occasional benefactions were again reminded of the role that could be played by the Regensburg scriptorium in promoting their interests. At the same time, readers of the Great Legendary were provided with further evidence, if such were needed, of the efficacy, even long after death, of such saints as Mochuille and the better-known Lambert, whose cult, as is known from other sources, was then receiving special attention in Regensburg.[15]

In the Irish record, the saint figures among the numerous children of Inghean Bhaoith of Killinaboy, and is counted among those ready to come to the assistance of Seanán of Scattery.[16] Similarly, according to a poem in Classical Irish, Mochuille, together with Inghean Bhaoith and numerous other saints, was called upon to help in releasing Ireland's southern half (Leath Mogha) from a bondage imposed on it by the northern half (Leath Chuinn), represented by Finnian of Clonard.[17] There are holy wells – up to thirteen, according to Westropp – named for the saint in several Clare parishes.[18] Locally, he was regarded as a brother of Seanán Liath, patron of Kiltenanlea.[19] The martyrologies record the feast of a saint named Mocholla (a variant of Mochuille) at 23 March, without, however, assigning him to any church.[20] His Life was inserted in the Austrian Legendary at a point corresponding to 11 January, and his name was invoked in a Regensburg litany.[21] A book called after the saint was apparently still extant in Tulla in the mid-seventeenth century.[22]

1 *ACoC* 225–7; *JRSAI* 41, 5–19. **2** *CGSH* §218; *GRSH* 112; *Lgen.* 731.5; *IrT* iii, 13 §1, 15 §6; *CrC*[1] 47 §3, 85–6. **3** *IEME* 213–31; *MirL* 56–7; *SIB* 83–95; *TIC* 93n. **4** *MGH.SS* XX, 512–14; *Kenney* 467n. **5** *MirL* 55–8; *IEME* 213–31. **6** *AB* 17, 135–54; *MGH.SS* XX, 512–14; *VSHH* 410–13. **7** *BGBR* 26, 36–7. **8** *AB* 17, 138 §1. **9** Ibid. 140 §4; *ACoC* 182. **10** *AB* 17, 141 §5. **11** Ibid. 142–3 §§6, 8; *CoC* 38–9, 49–50. **12** *AB* 17, 144–9 §9–18. **13** Ibid. 149–54 §§15–21. **14** *MGH.SS* XX, 512–14. **15** UCC MS U.331. **16** *IrT* iv, 87 §3, 93 §3; *ZCP* 10, 26 §22. **17** RIA MS 23L11, 263; *SAM* 24.1, 17, 19. **18** *HTCC* 153, 180, 187, 194; *JRSAI* 41, 7; *ACoC* 182, 226, 229, 233, 238. **19** Ibid. 250. **20** *MartG* 60; *MartD* 84; cf. *JRSAI* 41, 8. **21** *FLLSP* 233; *AB* 17, 97–122; *CKV* 60. **22** *HTCC* 288.

Mochuma. The name Mochuma (from *Cumma*, alias *Cuimme*, *Camma/Caimme*, *Comma/Coimme*), a hypocoristic or pet form of Colum with prefix *mo*, 'my', accounts for thirty-two homonymous saints, most of whom are either otherwise unrecorded or known under other forms of the name, such as Mochuma (alias Cuimín) Fada or Mochuma of the Gaolraighe, alias Colmán of Dromore.[1] Together with such variants as *Conna* or *Colla*, the form *Cumma* was frequently used as a means of providing local devotees of Colum Cille, founder of Iona, with an appropriately endearing form of name.

1 *CGSH* §707.647–78. **2** *FG* 20–35.

Mochuma of Drummully. *See* Colmán of Dromore.

Mochuma of Drumbo (Druim Bó), barony of Upper Castlereagh, Co. Down. In keeping with the location of his church, Mochuma (alias Dochuma, Cuimín) was attached by the genealogists to the Dál bhFiatach of east Ulster.[1] The tract on the mothers of the saints, and a corresponding entry in the corpus of saints' pedigrees, provide him – or his father Aodhán – with several close relatives among the saints.[2] Through his mother, Deirinill Cheathairchíochach, 'of the four nipples', he became a brother (or nephew) of Domhanghart of Slievedonard and Cilléan of Aghacullion, both of whose churches were also located in the Down area. A third brother (or uncle) was Mura of Fahan. At Drumbo, according to the Tripartite Life, Patrick cursed Deirinill's husband, Eacha son of Muireadhach, promising him a short life and the scattering of his descendants, but blessed the child still in his wife's womb, the 'famous and wonderful' Domhanghart.[3] The feast of Mochuma's companion at Drumbo, Cobhthach son of the king of Oirghialla, fell on 1 July, which was also the day of Mochuma's namesake, and probable double, Cuimín (†659) of Nendrum.[4] Mochuma's own feast was celebrated on 10 August.[5]

1 *CGSH* §141; *GRSH* 83. 2 *CGSH* §§162, 722.27. 3 *BP* 2655–71; *VT* 224. 4 *CGSH* §141; *MartG* 52; *MartD* 74; *AU s.a.* 5 *MartT* 62; *MartG* 154; *MartD* 214.

Mochuma of Lorum. *See* Colum Crom.

Modhíocha. This name, a hypocoristic or pet form of Díocaill, was borne by six holy men in the Irish tradition, according to the list of homonymous saints.[1] The best-known of these was Díocha of Saul, whose feast of 29 April is mistakenly attached to Modhíocha of Lullymore in some seventeenth-century sources.[2] Although a brother, according to the genealogists, of the well-documented Fionnbharr of Cork, the latter Modhíocha is otherwise unattested.[3]

1 *CGSH* §707.819–24. 2 *GRSH* 60; *MartD* 114. 3 *CGSH* §314; *GRSH* 60; *MakS* 71.

Modhíomóg. Ultimately a hypocoristic derivative of Diarmuid, and also attested as Díoma and Díomán, this name was borne by a small number of saints.

Modhíomóg of Araidh/Clonkeen. *See* Díomán of Clonkeen.

Modhíomóg of Kildemock. *See* Díoma Dubh.

Modhíomóg of Killeshin. *See* Diarmuid of Killeshin.

Modhíomóg of Glenkeen (Gleann Caoin), barony of Kilnamanagh Upper, Co. Tipperary. This son of Eoghan is known from two main sources, the Life of Fionnbharr of Cork and the tract entitled 'Four Saints'. The former text states that he and his brother Baodán, both of them pupils of the Cork saint at Gougane Barra, surrendered to their master in perpetuity the church at Glenkeen.[1] This claim may reflect, obliquely, the presence within the diocese of Ross of Kilmackowen (Ceall Mhac nEoghain) in the parish of Kilcatherine, barony of Bear, a part of west Cork that was influenced by a movement of population from south Tipperary in the twelfth century.[2] The 'Four Saints' tract brings Modhíomóg, under the guise of Diarmuid, to a place called Ros Réidheadh in Connacht, which appears to have been another name for the church of Kilmacowen (Ceall Mhac nEoghain) in the Sligo barony of Carbury.[3] The same passage outlines the lands with which the church was endowed. A separate list of the saints said to have been disciples of Beinéan includes Modhíomóg and Baodán, who – given the Connacht background to the text – were probably the two sons of Eoghan.[4] The saint's 'holy stone' stood on a hilltop at Graigue in the Tipperary parish of Dorrha, where he was known by the pet form of Díoma.[5] Devotion to Modhíomóg (alias Diarmuid) may also be reflected by the name Kildermot (Ceall Diarmada) in the Mayo parish of Attymas. Despite the Martyrology of Donegal at 3 March, the saint's feastday has not been preserved.[6] Without the support of any other source, the Four Masters assigned Modhíomóg and his brothers to 15 January.[7]

1 *BBa.* 68 §23; 255. **2** CorkD 97. **3** *IrT* iii, 1, §1; *DEPPP* 338. **4** *AS.*Nov. iv, 179 §13. **5** *AITY* §1926. **6** *MartD* 62. **7** *GRSH* 117 §9a.

Modhiúid of Killamude. Neither the townlands of Killamude, which took their name from the saint, nor the parish in which they are located, namely Ballymacward in the barony of Tiaquin, have received much attention in the documentary record, a few lines only being devoted to the parish in the Ordnance Survey letters from Galway.[1] However, as *diúid* of the saint's name means 'simple', a West of Ireland glossator of the Martyrology of Aonghas took the opportunity of identifying the saint with a bishop named Simplex, remembered on 12 February in the Martyrology of Jerome.[2] The equation of the two was, however, correctly denied in another copy of the martyrology.[3]

1 OSL 'Galway', 62. *DIL* 'díuit'; *HDGP* iv, 24. **2** *MartO* 72. **3** *MartO* 72.

Modhoma of Kilmodum. *See* Díomán of Clonkeen.

Modhomhnóg Oilithir, 'pilgrim', of Tibberaghney (Tiobraid Fhachtna), barony of Iverk, Co. Kilkenny. Arriving back in Ireland from a visit to David in Wales, Molaga of Aghacross is said to have first gone to Dublin, where he received both tribute and possession of Lann Bheachaire in Fine Gall (apparently at or near Bremore in the parish of Balrothery, near Balbriggan), before going on to restrain bees that Modhomhnóg had brought to Ireland and failed to control.[1] This story was no doubt influenced by the Irish name Lann Bheachaire, literally 'the beekeeper's clearing', but the connection with Modhomhnóg and David of Wales is otherwise borne out by the latter's Life which describes in great detail how the patron of Tibberaghny brought the first bees to Ireland from St David's, despite his best efforts to leave them behind and, albeit with David's blessing, in the process depriving the Welsh church of its swarm and its descendants.[2] David's Life dates to no earlier than about 1090, but the connection of the saint with bees is already confirmed by the Martyrology of Aonghas, composed about 830.[3]

Bearing an Irish form of name, the radical version of which may have been Domhainghin, Modhomhnóg figures in the corpus of saints' pedigrees in borrowed clothing only, as a son of Sárán son of Tighearnán, more properly father and grandfather of Domhongóg of Tory.[4] A pedigree has, however, been preserved for his Welsh equivalent, Dyfnog ap Medrod, who shared a feast (13 February) with Modhomhnóg.[5] Bizarrely, through his place in the Catalogue of the principal Irish saints, albeit under the Latin form Dominicus, or because of his mention under the same guise by Giraldus Cambrensis, the saint came to be regarded as evidence that the founder of the Order of Preachers (Dominicans) at some stage came to Ireland.[6]

Modhomhnóg's main feast of 13 February had been transferred from Tibberaghny to Pilltown in the parish of Fiddown by the beginning of the nineteenth century.[7] The saint was also remembered about this day at Ennisnag in the Kilkenny barony of Shillelogher, under the guise of Mogue.[8] A second feast of the 'triumphant diadem' Modhomhnóg was celebrated on 18 May, and his commemoration was moved to 13 November at Banchory-Devenick near Aberdeen in Scotland.[9]

1 *IrT* iii, 21 §19; *AnH* 10, 195; *DIB* vi, 540. 2 *VSBG* 162 §43; *RSLD* 41–2. 3 *MartO*[2] 60; *Bech*. 40. 4 *MartT* 16; *MartG* 36; *CGSH* §40; *GRSH* 45; *Lgen*. 192.5; *BB* 88e. 5 *EWGT* 63 §51; *CPNS* 316. 6 *FEMN* 358 (§227); *THEH* 29; *MIDS* 14. 7 *MartT* 16; *MartO*[2] 60; *MartG* 36; *MartD* 48; OSL KK ii, 224. 8 *HADO* iii, 374. 9 *MartT* 44; *MartO*; *MartG* 98; *MartD* 132; *CPNS* 316; *KSS* 323–4.

Moeaca. *See* Féichín.

Moearnóg. *See* Mearnóg.

Moeilteóg. *See* Eiltín.

Moganus/Moginus. *See* Aonghas Láimhiodhan.

Mogheanóg of Killegland (Ceall Dumha Ghluinn), barony of Ratoath, Co. Meath.[1] After describing how Trim had been granted to its patron Lomán, twenty-five years before Armagh was founded, the author of the Tripartite Life stated that Lomán was a son of Patrick's sister, before going on to name his brothers, all of whom occupied Patrician churches, including Mogheanóg of Killegland 'in the southern part of Breagha'.[2] The sister in question was Dairearca (sometimes named Lubaid) and the list of her seventeen children, most of them bishops, also refers to Mogheanóg, who may be the same as Mogheanóg of Ceall Chumhaile, a disciple of Finnian of Clonard.[3] By the late seventeenth century, the saint's name had been replaced by 'Eglan' and, by 1836, no memory of him was preserved locally.[4] The patron of Kilmaganny (possibly from Ceall Mogheana) in the Kilkenny barony of Kells, may represent the same cult but, according to Bishop Phelan's seventeenth-century list of patrons in Ossory, which refers to the saint as 'Moganus', his feast fell locally on 23 August, whereas that of Mogheanóg was 26 December.[5]

1 *HDGP* iii, 165–6. 2 *BP* 711–20; *VT* 68. 3 *CGSH* §722.16; *MartD* 348; *VSHH* 83 §5, 101 §19. 4 OSL MH 269. 5 *HADO* iv, 71; *MartT* 1; *MartG* 246; *MartD* 348.

Moghoba. *See* Gobán Fionn.

Moghobóg. Nine saints of this hypocoristic name, originally based on *gabha*, 'smith', are included in the list of homonymous saints, of whom at least three are also known by the variant form Gobán.[1] Even where an identifiable church (Kilmainham) or tribal name (Maca Céin/Cianachta) is attached to the saint, little else is known of him. Moghobóg of Ráith Lámhraighe, who is given first place in the Martyrology of Tallaght's list for 11 February, is also remembered on that day in the martyrology of the Regensburg *Schottenkloster*.[2]

1 *CGSH* §707.810–18 (810–11, 818). 2 *FSHIM* 234. *MartR* 29.

Moghornán son of Restitutus (Reistitiúid) of the Maca Baird (Lombards). This is one of seven sons of Restitutus (Welsh Rhystud) of the Lombards by a sister of Patrick, usually named Lubaid, but sometimes also Dairearca.[1] Of Moghornán's siblings, the best-known were Seachnall of Dunshaughlin and Usaille of Killashee. Moghornán does not figure in any other part of the Patrician literature.

1 *CGSH* §§664, 722.15; *BP* 895–902; *VT* 82.

Moghóróg of Delgany (Deirgne), barony of Rathdown, Co. Wicklow. This saint, whose name derives from Guaire, is known from an entry in the tract on the mothers of the saints which states that he and his nine brothers were sons of Díona, daughter of a king of the Saxons, by Brachan, king of the Britons (or Welsh), and eponym of Brycheiniog in south Wales.[1] Many of the saint's siblings, including Mochonóg of Kilmuckridge, Eallóg of St Tulloge's, and Díoraidh of Edermine, are also associated with churches in east Leinster. That Moghóróg's church at Delgany was affiliated to Glendalough is indicated by the Life of that church's patron, which accords the saint the distinction of rendering the last rites to Caoimhghin.[2] Given the equivalence of their names, Moghóróg may be identical with Guaire Caecus, 'blind', alias Guaire son of Dall, 'blind one', patron of 'Dergory' (Doire Guaire), who also figures both in the Life of Caoimhghin and in the section of a litany given over to Glendalough saints.[3] A well dedicated to the saint, under the guise of Guaire, was located in the townland of Monatore in the Wicklow parish of Ballynure.[4] He may also have given name, under the same guise, to Palmerston (formerly 'Staghgori', probably from Teach Guaire) in the Dublin barony of Uppercross.[5] Moghóróg's feast fell on 23 December.[6]

1 *CGSH* §722.89; *EWGT* 14–16, 32–3. 2 *VSHP* i, 257 §48. 3 Ibid. 254 §42; *IrL* 56; *CPPI* 200. 4 OSL WW 99. 5 *AnH* 10, 189. 6 *MartT* 88; *MartG* 244; *MartD* 346.

Moghreallóg of Cloncurry. *See* Maoldubh of Cloncurry.

Mogue. *See* Maodhóg of Ferns; Modhomhnóg Oilithir.

Moingfhinn daughter of Cíordhubhán. *See* Iarlaithe of Tuam.

Moingfhinn of Cloonkeen. *See* Caolchú of Clooncoose.

Moinis daughter of Díbheachán. *See* Fíonán of Teach Oirthir.

Molaga of Aghacross (Áth Cros Molaga), barony of Condons and Clangibbon, Co. Cork, and of Labbamolaga, parish of Templemolaga, in the same barony and county. In keeping with the situation of his church at Labbamolaga (Molaga's *leabaidh*, 'bed'), which adjoins a pre-Christian site containing four orthostats, later taken to be petrified robbers, Molaga's origins lie in the cult of the great Celtic god Lugh, from whose name both Lóichín, diminutive of Lóch and variant of Lugh, and its hypocoristic form *Laga* (whence Molaga/Molaige) derive.[1] A trace of the divinity is also present in the saint's pedigree, which attaches him to a branch of the Uí Chúscraidh of Fir Mhaighe Féine, known as the *clann* or family of Luchta (from *Lugh*).[2]

In common with other saints local to the area, such as Fionnchú of Brigown and Cránaid of Kilcranathan, Molaga was made the subject of a vernacular Life, now preserved in three manuscripts, including the fifteenth-century Book of Fermoy.[3] A Latin translation of the text was published by John Colgan in 1645.[4] Together with Mochuille of Tulla and the local dynast, Cuana son of Cailchín, the saint is said to have been one of the 'honoured' members of the Uí Chúscraidh whose lands corresponded approximately to the area about Kildorrery, Aghacross, and Templemolaga.[5] Molaga's miraculous birth to parents of advanced years, Dubh Dlighidh and Mionchollaid, was foretold by Cuimín

Fada of Clonfert (accompanied by the 'fool', Comhdhán Dá Chearda) who also arrogated to himself the distinction of baptizing the saint.[6] A separate tradition maintains that Cuimín, Comhdhán, and the two kings, Guaire son of Colmán and Cuana son of Cailchín, both of whom also figure in the Life of Molaga, were uterine brothers.[7]

An important feature of the Life is its list of the boundaries of Molaga's *tearmann* which are laid down precisely, with several named guarantors, including the successor of Ailbhe, patron of the archdiocese of Cashel and Emly.[8] Having suffered the indignity of seeing his church burnt to the ground through the ineffectiveness of the local king, Cuana son of Cailchín, Molaga is said to have abandoned the area, travelling first to Connor in Ulster, near which he left his bell, thus giving rise to the name *Tearmann an Chloig*, 'sanctuary of the bell', possibly a reference to the see-lands at Ballyclug, near Connor.[9] This was followed by a journey to Scotland and Wales, where, having made a union with David, he allegedly adopted, in a manner reminiscent of Cadog's naming after Mochuda at Lismore, the hypocoristic form Molaga.[10]

On his return to Ireland, Molaga placed a king at Dublin Castle (Dún Duibhlinne) in his debt – defined as 'a penny for every Dublin nose every three years' and the grant of the church of Lann Bheachaire, apparently at or near the church of Bremore in the parish of Balrothery, where 'Mologa' was later venerated as patron – by curing a growth on the king's cheek.[11] On that occasion, he also restrained bees originally brought from Wales by Modhomhnóg Oilithir of Tibberaghny. He then continued on to Clonmacnoise before yielding to the entreaties of his contrite Fir Mhaighe kinsmen, and blandishments in the form of generous annual dues, to return to his church in north Cork.[12]

Often considered to be both jumbled and incomplete in its surviving form, the text of Molaga's Life has been taken to contain a 'coherent piece of advocacy' set in the context of instability that prevailed in south Munster in the period 1114–19, prior to the death of Muircheartach Ua Briain.[13] Although clearly the product of 'turbulent times', a later date of composition, possibly in the period about 1261, when the bishop of Cloyne was obliged to bring a series of actions to recover his episcopal lands, would seem more appropriate.[14] Mention of Dublin Castle, which was commissioned and built in the early thirteenth century, and the saint's journey to the Welsh homeland of the Cambro-Norman adventurers who subjugated Ireland, point to a post-Conquest author intent on endearing himself to those in authority in his own time.[15] The precise indications of the extent of Molaga's *tearmann* lands presuppose a threat to these of the kind that provoked the bishop's legal actions.

Although it has been stated that Cloyne and its concerns are absent from the text, its patron Colmán arguably figures in the guise of Mocholmóg in an episode designed to demonstrate the good relations enjoyed by the saints, or the communities of their churches, with the Eoghanacht Ghleannamhnach ancestors of the Uí Chaoimh (O'Keeffes), hereditary kings of the Fir Mhaighe Féine lands.[16] Though there is no overt reference to matters episcopal, there is an emphasis on such diocesan sees as Cashel and Emly (Ailbhe), Cork (Fionnbharr's coarb),

Clonfert (Cuimín Fada), Connor, Dublin, and Clonmacnoise (whose bishop may have had some hereditary rights in Kildorrery, near Aghacross).[17]

A recently discovered Regensburg litany containing numerous Irish saints also commemorates Molaga.[18] But, as most of the saints in this text are connected with Clare, Molaga's inclusion probably stemmed from an unidentified site named Carn Síodha in Corca Bhaiscinn, now south-west Clare, to which his biographer brought him.[19] He was also one of those considered likely to come to the assistance of Seanán of Scattery, unless this refers to his namesake and probable double at Singland.[20] Under the guise of Molaga Meann, the saint is among those cited in the Old Irish Table of Penitential Commutations as sponsors of a certain type of vigil.[21] A book, now lost, called *Leabhar Dubh Molaga*, was named after the saint.[22] In addition to his churches in north Cork, Molaga was patron of Timoleague (Teach Molaga) in south Cork, later the site of a Franciscan monastery, and probably also of a site in the townland of Crookhaven, parish of Kilmoe, formerly known as Ceall Molaige.[23] He had various feastdays, including two in the first half of Lugh's month of August, but the best-known of his feasts was 20 January, when a fair used to be held at the church of Aghacross.[24] A relic preserved locally, and known as 'Fanahan's candlestick', was found in one of Molaga's churches.[25]

1 *ZCP* 36, 143–5. **2** *CGSH* §217; *GRSH* 112; *Lgen.* 731.2; *IrT* iii, 12 §1; *DIB* vi, 545–6. **3** *IrT* iii, 11–22; *HMDC* 14–17. **4** *ASH* 145–51. **5** *CrC*[1] 83. **6** *IrT* iii, 13–16 §§2–6. **7** Ibid. 18–19 §13; *CGSH* §§652, 722.66. **8** *IrT* iii, 17 §9. **9** Ibid. 20–1 §16; *HADDC* iii, 419–20; *EMH* 463–4 §162. **10** *IrT* iii, 21 §18. **11** Ibid. 21 §19; *AnH* 10, 195. **12** *IrT* iii, 22 §20. **13** *CínCC* 127–40. **14** *PRC* 186. **15** *ICCH* 53–5; *ScrV* 41–8. **16** *CínCC* 136, 138. **17** *RClon.* 458. **18** UCC MS U.331; *CKV* 60, 64.83. **19** *IrT* iii, 18 §12. **20** *ZCP* 10, 28 §23. **21** *Ériu* 19, 64 §23. **22** *BL Cat.* iii, 188; *FFÉ* iii, 32, 88; *AB* 48, 122. **23** CorkD 96. **24** *MartT* 10; *MartO*[2] 37; *MartG* 20; *MartD* 22; *HTN* 244, 248. **25** *CrC*[1] 28–9.

Molaga of Singland (Saingeal), parish of St Patrick's, barony of Clanwilliam, Co. Limerick. On the death of Seanán, his body was brought to a 'house of prayer' on Scattery Island, to await the arrival of the saints of Limerick, including Molaga Cráibhtheach, 'pious', of Inis Tiobrad, and Morónóg of Inis Luaidhe.[1] As the editor of the text pointed out, these are now the neighbouring islands of Inishtubbrid and Inishloe, both on the river Shannon in the Clare parish of Killadysert, near Canon Island, the site of an Augustinian priory founded circa 1180.[2] Although somewhat removed from the town of Limerick, it may have been the intention of the writer to establish a connection with Molaga (alias Molanga) son of Fíonán of Singland. Well enough known from the genealogical record, which assigned him to the Clann Mhathghamhna branch of Dál gCais that lorded over Corca Bhaiscinn, this saint otherwise appears to have attracted little attention.[3] This may be because of the visit allegedly made by Patrick to Singland during the circuit of Munster invented for the saint by the mid-ninth-century author of the Tripartite Life; this may have led to Molaga's local sidelining in favour of Patrick who is still patron of the parish.[4] The inclusion of the name Molaga among the mainly Clare and Limerick saints commemorated in the recently discovered Regensburg litany may refer to the Singland saint, or to his namesake and probable double at Aghacross.[5] A well was dedicated to the saint at Tobermalug (Tobar Molaga) in the parish of Caherconlish.[6] Despite his mention in the Martyrology of Donegal at 13 August, the saint's feastday has not been preserved.[7]

1 *AB* 66, 209. 2 Ibid. 213–14; *MRHI* 162. 3 *CGSH* §205; *GRSH* 120; *CGH* 153a21. 4 *BP* 2415–21; *VT* 206. 5 UCC MS U.331; *CKV* 60, 64.83. 6 OSL LK ii, 415; *SATM* 38; *JNMArchS* 2, 23. 7 *MartD* 218.

Molaga Meann. *See* Molaga of Aghacross.

Molaise. Ultimately a derivative of *lasar*, 'flame', which generated the hypocoristic or pet form *laisse*, this version of the name proved to be popular, with over forty representatives in the list of homonymous saints.[1] Though most of these are otherwise unknown, some can be identified by reference to other parts of the hagiographical record. This applies to those provided with the patronymics Colmán, Fearadhach and Lughaidh, all of whom are better known under the guise of Laisréan (Lasrán). Many others were doubtless localizations of the patrons of Leighlin and Devenish, both of whom were made the subjects of substantial dossiers.

1 *CGSH* §707.580–623.

Molaise of Aughris (Eachros) in the parish of Templeboy, of Kilglass in the barony of Tireragh, and of Inishmurray (Inis Muireadhaigh) in the parish of Ahamlish, all in the county of Sligo. Attached by the genealogists to the Corca Raoidhe who gave name to the Westmeath barony of Corkaree, the two main churches of Molaise son of Déaglán were located on – and just off – the coast of Sligo.[1] The attachment to Corkaree, still exemplified by the presence of a church named Kilmalish (Ceall Molaise) in the Westmeath parish of Tyfarnham, is also in keeping with the saint's many associations with Colum Cille, on whose death another member of the Corca Raoidhe, Earnán (Eirnéan) by name, was granted a vision.[2]

The traditions surrounding the battle of Cúil Dreimhne impute to Molaise of Ahamlish, who had allegedly been sought out by Colum in the wake of the battle, the imposition of the heavy, and much-resented, sentence of permanent exile.[3] In keeping with other records, Colum's late vernacular biographer thought that the confessor was identical with Molaise of Devenish. The vernacular Life of the Devenish saint cites a prophecy made while he was travelling in Críoch Chairbre, now the Sligo barony of Carbury; according to this, Molaise, having blessed the future bishop Fionnchadh in his mother's womb, foretold that he would be one of five 'great saints' in the headship of his own local church which can only have been Ahamlish.[4] This may also explain why one version of the pedigree of Molaise of Devenish assigns him to Inishmurray.[5]

The somewhat tense relationship between Molaise and Colum Cille is highlighted by a local tradition which asserts that the two saints, one mild, the other impetuous, cooperated in the building of the church on Inishmurray only to have Colum subsequently leave for the mainland.[6] Molaise's other church of Aughris was the site of an Augustinian priory, as was Devenish, and this may explain why the two like-named patrons are frequently brought together.[7]

Representing the saint's first foundation, at least according to local tradition, Aughris was the scene of an annual *Lughnasadh* gathering held on the last Sunday in July, which brought people together from all over the baronies of Tireragh and Leyny.[8] That Molaise was a *Lughnasadh* saint is also indicated by his feastday of 12 August, a day shared with Muireadhach of Killala, the probable eponym of Inishmurray.[9] On Inishmurray, the day of pilgrimage was moved to the feast of the Assumption (15 August). A much-venerated wooden image of the saint, now in the National Museum, and locally known as 'Father Molash', was kept on the altar of the saint's church in Inishmurray.[10] At Kilglass, there was no memory of the saint's day by the early nineteenth century.[11]

1 *CGSH* §359; *Lgen.* 720.3. **2** *PNW* 34; *VC*[2] 534–6. **3** *BCC* 184 §§180–1; *VC*[1] 287; cf. *ClRec.* 13, 87. **4** *SG* i, 23–4; *VSHP* ii, 135 §19. **5** *CGSH* §§117 (add.), 707.580 (add.). **6** *HSCT* 152; *IMPAL* 32–3. **7** *MRHI* 158, 169. **8** *FL* 112–13. **9** *MartT* 62; *MartG* 154; *MartD* 216. **10** OSL SO 21; *IMPAL* 72, 77. **11** OSL SO, 290.

Molaise of Devenish (Daimhinis) on Lough Erne, barony of Magheraboy, Co. Fermanagh. In line with the conflicting assertions that are so often a feature of the Irish hagiographical record, there is little unanimity concerning the places and families connected with Molaise son of Nadh Fraoich. What is taken to be his earliest tribal affiliation, to the Maca Neachta, does not appear to be locatable.[1] Otherwise, however, the genealogists contrived to provide him with two churches, Devenish and Inishmurray (Inis Muireadhaigh), as well as two conflicting statements of his descent, one attaching him to Dál nAraidhe of north Down and Antrim, the other to the branch of the Eoghanachta in Munster that also produced Cormac son of Cuileannán.[2] The patron of Inishmurray, Molaise of Aughris, was very probably his double. The name of Molaise's mother, although absent from the tract on the mothers of the saints, is variously said to have been 'Mugnea' and Monua daughter of Miodhlugh of the Corca Raoidhe, the family to which Molaise of Aughris and Inishmurray was also attached.[3]

The importance of Molaise's chief church at Devenish may be measured not only by the round tower that still dominates the site, but also by the decision of the Augustinian canons to erect a priory there, probably in the mid-twelfth century.[4] Well known for their use of the records of the Irish saints as a means of promoting their own interests, the canons often arranged to have Lives composed for their patrons, and those of Devenish were no exception. Molaise's Life survives in two forms, a relatively short Latin version – sometimes unnecessarily taken to be based on a lost longer text – designed for reading on the saint's feastday, and a much later, and greatly expanded, vernacular version, combining prose and verse, recently dated to shortly after 1500.[5]

Though the vernacular version gives prominence to Molaise's southern ancestry, stressing the ties with both Tara and Cashel, the Latin Life, having drawn attention to a prophecy conerning the saint's birth made by Patrick sixty years previously, names his mother (Mugnea) only, attributing to her a vision, and describing how she followed the advice of a *magus* by delaying Molaise's birth for one day.[6] Both versions are in agreement on the name of Molaise's first tutor,

Bishop Eacha (or Eachaidh), who probably represents Dallán Forghaill (alias Eachaidh son of Oilill), the saint-poet best known for the eulogy he composed in memory of Colum Cille.[7] Further study is said to have taken place under Finnian of Clonard who assisted, according to the vernacular text, in the consecration of Molaise's church at Devenish.[8]

Among the various miracles credited to the saint are the artificial lengthening of daylight or, alternatively, the procurement of a pen from a bird's mouth so as to enable the completion of a gospel-book – possibly the famous *Soiscéal Molaise*, whose early eleventh-century shrine has been preserved. Both episodes confirm an interest in books that again appears in the form of a youthful book-carrier whose thirst precipitated a prophecy concerning Fionnchadh of Killarga.[9] A journey to Rome, via Tours, in search of relics to be shared with Molaise's confidant, Maodhóg of Ferns, also includes the miraculous appearance of a gospel-book. In this section, there are also references to various relics, apostolic and otherwise, allegedly held on Devenish, with specific mention in the vernacular Life of the *Breac Maodhóg*, apparently kept at the church of Drumlane.[10]

Among other churches or saints drawn into the Latin Life are: Bangor, where the saint is said to have preached; Colum Cille, who allegedly owed his penance of permanent exile to Molaise; Colum's first successor, Baoithín, who received a vision of three chairs, of gold, silver, and glass, the second of which was designed for Molaise; and Bréanainn, whose well-known voyage was preceded by a visit to Devenish.[11] To be noted is the fact that the churches of all of these saints, at Bangor, Kells, Derry or Durrow, Clonmacnoise and Clonfert, had become Augustinian priories.[12] In the vernacular Life, the much expanded list of Ireland's apostles mainly comprises patrons of Augustinian foundations, including Ruadhán of Lorrha, Maodhóg of Ferns, Tighearnach of Clones, Mochta of Louth, and Mac Caorthainn of Clogher, whose see the saint is elsewhere said to have occupied.[13]

Political affairs are introduced by reference both to Tara, where Molaise outsmarts the king's prophet, Beag son of Dé, and – more locally – to Conall *Rubeus* (Dearg) son of Daimhín, whose descendants are said to have been deprived of kingship, despite an hereditary entitlement spread over four generations.[14] Both versions of the Life end abruptly, the Latin text moving swiftly from the saint's normal activity to a notice of the lead-up to his death, and the vernacular text departing entirely from the script with an account of the expulsion of the Dartraighe of Munster to the area about Lough Erne, an event that can probably be explained by reference to dues later paid by this family to Molaise's successors.[15]

The dossier of the saint and his church, which is quite extensive by the standards of Irish churches, has yet to be edited critically. Several (mostly unpublished) metrical compositions appended to Molaise's vernacular Life not only set out *in extenso* the rights and dues of his successors, but also throw further light on his affiliations to the Corca Raoidhe (Corkaree) and Dartraighe.[16] The saint's maternal connection with the Corca Raoidhe may also lie behind the presence of a church named 'Killmalish' (now corruptly Kilmaglish) in the Westmeath parish of Tyfarnham, unless this is entirely due to the affiliation of Molaise's namesake at Aughris to the same group.[17] Eulogized as a 'chosen athlete of God' and as 'the light of all Ireland' in an alphabet hymn preserved in the twelfth-century *Liber Hymnorum*, and described elsewhere as similar in manners to Simon the Apostle, Molaise the bishop, 'hospitaller of the men of Ireland' and example of chastity, is said to have died either in 564 or 571.[18] A stone coffin on Devenish, known locally as 'Molush's grave', may be echoed in the statement attributed to Cuimín of Connor that the saint loved to be in a 'hard prison of stone'.[19] His immediate successor was Náile of Kinawley, at least according to the latter's Life.[20] Molaise's feast fell on 12 September, but was also celebrated locally on 15/16 of the same month.[21] Relics of his, including shrine and crozier, are mentioned in an early prose-tale.[22]

1 *CGSH* §707.597; *Kenney* 387; *PRIA* 29C4, 81; *DIB* vi, 546. **2** *CGSH* §117; *GRSH* 100; *Lgen*. 736.2; *SG* i, 17; *CGH* 148a45. **3** *VSHP* ii, 131 §3; *SG* i, 17. **4** *MRHI* 169. **5** *VSHP* i, lxxiv, ii, 131–40; *SG* i, 17–37; *Kenney* 388; *Breifne* 11, 541; *GILSL* 97–106. **6** *VSHP* ii, 131–2 §§1–4; *SG* i, 17–18. **7** *VSHP* ii, 132 §5; *SG* i, 19; cf. *BL Cat*. ii, 464–5 §10. **8** *VSHP* ii, 132 §6; *SG* i, 24–5. **9** *VSHP* ii, 133 §11, 135 §§18–19; *SG* i, 21, 23; *ClRec*. 13, 51–63. **10** *VSHP* ii, 135–7 §§20–4; *SG* i, 30–3; *TIC* 221; *IARP* 117–18. **11** *VSHP* ii, 137–9 §§26, 31–3; cf. *CGSH* §734. **12** *MRHI* 153–4. **13** *SG* i, 25, 34; *ClRec*. 7, 380. **14** *VSHP* ii, 134–5 §§14–17; *SG* i, 25–7. **15** *VSHP* ii, 139–40 §34; *SG* i, 35–6 **16** *BL Cat*. ii, 463–5 §§2–10; *ClRec*. 15, 7–24; *Peritia* 24–5, 230–40. **17** *PNW* 35n., 159. **18** *LH* i, 158; *CGSH* §712.12; *ZCP* 1, 62; *RC* 37, 351 §9; *AU s.a.*; *FC* 233–5. **19** OSL FH 72; *ZCP* 1, 62. **20** *MHH* 103–5 §§12–15. **21** *MartT* 70; *MartO²* 194; *MartG* 174; *MartD* 244–6. **22** *Ériu* 35, 76 §12.

Molaise of Kilmolash (Ceall Molaise) in the parish of Inishlounaght, barony of Iffa and Offa East, Co. Tipperary. While in the south of Magh Feimhin, a location that would accord with the position of Kilmolash, Déaglán of Ardmore is said to have converted a heathen who bestowed lands on him to which a saintly concourse, including Mochobha (of Lismore) and Mac Laisréin, came to give honour to God.[1] As Mac Laisre (of which Mac Laisréin is an extended diminutive form) is elsewhere attested as an alternative form of Molaise, we may take this to be probably also the case here, as has indeed been suggested by others.[2] Molaise of Kilmolash was venerated in the Déise of Munster on 17 January, not only in the barony of Iffa and Offa, but also in the Waterford parish of Kilmolash (barony of Decies without Drum), and perhaps also a little further west in the Cork parishes of Fermoy and Carrigtohill.[3] As the feastday was separated by two days only from the feast of Molaise Maca Neachta (alias Molaise of Devenish), we may assume, with John O'Donovan, that the two saints were originally identical.[4]

1 ITS 16, 48–52 §30. **2** Ibid. 174; *CLTÁ* 183–4. **3** *MartT* 9; *MartG* 18; *MartD* 20; *CPR* i, lxviii. **4** *CGSH* §707.597; *Kenney* 387; *PRIA* 29C4, 81; OSL WD 133.

Molaise of Leighlin, alias Oldleighlin (Leithghleann), barony of Idrone West, Co. Carlow. Variously attached to an obscure tribal group named Maca Iomdha and to a leading branch of the Ulaidh of Down, Molaise, 'flame of fire', is said to have been a son of Coireall Cruaidh, 'the hard', by Maithgheam (Geamma), daughter of Aodhán son of Gabhrán, king of Scotland, and thus a brother of Baodán who occupied the kingship of the Ulaidh until his death in 581.[1] Molaise's church was chosen at the synod of Rathbreasail in 1111 as one of the Leinster sees, probably because of the good relations that then prevailed between the Uí Riain kings of Uí Dhróna (Idrone), and Muircheartach Ua Briain who summoned the synod; one of the Uí Riain kings lost his life in 1103 on an expedition to Ulster in support of Muircheartach.[2]

Leighlin's diocesan status led to the founding there of a house of canons regular of St Augustine and, ultimately, to the composition of the Life of Molaise preserved in fragmentary form in the Salamancan codex.[3] Pretentiously awarding the saint the title of 'legate of the apostolic see', his biographer claimed miraculous power for him already at birth before asserting that he spent his first seven years in his mother's homeland of Scotland, where the principal centre of devotion to him is on Holy Island in the bay of Lamlash, off Arran.[4] While there, he is shown to have impressed Bishop Blán of Dunblane who is described as the saint's maternal uncle.[5] Returning to Ireland, the saint is sent to be educated to Munna, presumably at Taghmon, where he performed various miracles.[6] To escape worldly honours, he then went to an island between Scotland (*Scotia*) and Wales (*Britannia*), perhaps the Isle of Man, to pursue an eremitical life before travelling on to Pope Gregory in Rome who, having taught Molaise about the Bible and ecclesiastical institutions, ordained him, consecrated him bishop, and sent him back to Ireland to preach.[7]

Arriving in Ireland, Molaise is directed by an angel to Leighlin, where a previous occupant named Gobán – elsewhere taken to have been the patron of Killamery – made a union (*fraternitas*) with him before leaving the site.[8] Such was Molaise's fame that he is said to have been head of up to 1500 monks, thus fulfilling prophecies placed in the mouths of Patrick and Cainneach.[9] He is also thought to have made a pact with a bishop named Barrus, presumably Fionnbharr of Cork, who was intent on visiting Rome and, just as the text of the Life breaks off, Molaise is said to have acceded to a request by Ciarán, presumably of Seirkieran, and others to journey to Rome.[10] The emphasis on Molaise's adherence to Roman precepts, so characteristic of the Life, elsewhere took the form of an intervention on his part at a synod concerning the Easter question held on Magh Ailbhe, a plain straddling the south of Kildare and north of Carlow, with his teacher Munna representing the Irish side of the argument.[11] The saint's strictness towards his sister who, having become pregnant while preparing to be a nun, was refused burial in hallowed ground, provided the saint's biographer with an opportunity of underlining the power of singing psalms, especially the first psalm, which eventually gained her admittance to a consecrated burial ground.[12] A similar strictness towards his sister is imputed to Molaise of Devenish.[13]

Regarded as one of the twelve apostles of Ireland, and sometimes considered to have been similar in manners to Pope Bonifatius, Molaise, 'the victorious flame', is said to have died in 639, allegedly from the deadly effects of seeing the eyebrow of Moshiona of Emlagh.[14] The saint's feastday fell on 18 April, and a pattern continued to be held on that day at Oldleighlin until 1812, when it was discontinued on the orders of the local parish priest.[15] The day was also observed at the well named after the saint near the Carlow church of Lorum (Leamhdhruim), which was associated with Colum of Terryglass, among others.[16] The water of his well at Leighlin, familiarly called 'Melashee' after the saint, was reputed to have the miraculous virtue of finding truth.[17]

1 *AU s.a.* 639; *CGSH* §§143, 722.35; *GRSH* 84; *Lgen.* 722.7; *Molaise* 1–3; *DIB* v, 270–1. **2** *AU s.a.* **3** *MRHI* 184; *VSHH* 340–3. **4** *VSHH* 340 §§1–2; *KSS* 407–8; *CPNS* 305–7; *ACDS* 113–15; *Molaise* 21–33; *Carloviana* 44, 14–15. **5** *VSHH* 341 §3. **6** Ibid. 341 §§4–6. **7** Ibid. 341–2 §§7–8. **8** Ibid. 342 §8; *CGSH* §670.86. **9** *VSHH* 342 §9; *IrL* 74. **10** *VSHH* 342–3 §§10–13. **11** Ibid. 207 §§29–30, 254 §§25–6. **12** *ZCP* 9, 239–41; *MKM* 207–15. **13** *MT* §60. **14** *MartO²* 206; *VSHH* 82 §2; *AU s.a.*; *MartD* 106 (cf. *CGSH* §712.31) **15** *MartT* 34; *MartO²* 107; *MartG* 78; *MartD* 104–6; OSL CW 218–19; *Béaloideas* 4, 14–16; *Molaise* 75–8. **16** OSL CW 312; *Béaloideas* 4, 16–17; *CGSH* §667. **17** *Carloviana* 47, 31; *Molaise* 75.

MOLAISE of Lorum. *See* Molaise of Leighlin.

MOLAISE son of Dubhthach. *See* Lonán son of Dubhthach.

MOLANGA. *See* Molaga.

MOLASH. *See* Molaise.

MOLIOBA. This name, which is a hypocoristic form of Libhear, is borne by several saints, six of whom are listed in the martyrologies.

MOLIOBA of Annahilt/Gortgrib/son of Araidhe/Colmaidh. *See* Libhear of Aghaboe.

MOLING LUACHRA, 'of Luachair', of St Mullin's (Teach Moling), mainly in the barony of St Mullin's Lower, Co. Carlow, partly in the barony of Bantry, Co. Wexford. Most versions of Moling's pedigree assign the saint through his father Faolán to Uí Dheagha, a branch of the Uí Cheinsealaigh of south Leinster that gave name to the deanery of Oday in the Wexford barony of Gorey.[1] Another branch of the family gave name to the Kilkenny barony of Ida (Uí Dheagha Osraighe) which, though lying on the opposite side of the river Barrow to Moling's church of St Mullin's, had many associations with the saint. Perhaps because of his cognomen 'Luachra' (from Luachair, an area on the bounds between Cork, Kerry and Limerick), Moling was also provided with a Munster descent from the Ciarraighe of that area.[2] Statements of his maternal descent uniformly speak of an origin among the Ciarraighe Luachra, in one case taken to refer to a family named Ceinéal Séadna, possibly the same as Clann Shéadna, who were apparently based about Brosna in the barony of Trughanacmy, a focus of devotion to Moling in later times.[3]

The Carlow church of the saint became a noted centre of pilgrimage whose popularity endured down to modern times. The pilgrimage was normally held towards the end of July, thus indicating that Moling may have been a *Lughnasadh* saint.[4] Despite its traditional derivation from Moling's three famous leaps (Irish *lingidh*, 'leaps'), the saint's name may ultimately derive (through *lu-n-g-/li-n-g-*) from the divinity name Lugh, a christianized version of whom, Lúgadán by name, was patron of the Wexford parish of Templeludigan, adjoining St Mullin's and containing a townland named Monamolin (Muine Moling).[5] As a centre of pilgrimage, St Mullin's attracted the attention of the Augustinian canons, whose priory at Ferns received the church as an endowment from Diarmuid Mac

Murchadha before about 1160.[6] This probably led to Moling becoming the subject of a Latin Life – written at Ferns by a biographer eager to consolidate in writing the union of the two churches – that survives in two recensions, one a much shorter and highly condensed version of the other.[7] The biographer states that the saint, having been invited to accept the succession to Maodhóg, was elected archbishop, performed several miracles at Ferns, and left shortly before his death and burial at St Mullin's.[8]

The Latin Life consistently ignores Moling's connections with west Munster, emphasizing his affiliation to the Uí Dheagha, and arranging to have him found his church at a young age.[9] Proximity to the river Barrow is stressed, as is the saint's control over water on which he is shown walking.[10] The swiftness with which the site became a focus of pilgrimage, 'the greatest now in Ireland', also receives emphasis, as does his empathy with the people of Osraighe on the other side of the river Barrow, on whose behalf he intervenes with the Leinstermen.[11] There are some traces in the Latin Life of the influence of (independently extant) vernacular texts dating to the twelfth century, including *Baile Moling*, 'Moling's vision', which sets out future kings of Leinster, the *bóramha* tract, which details the saint's efforts to obtain remission of a tribute allegedly levied on Leinster by the Uí Néill, and *Agallamh na Seanórach*, 'colloquy of the ancients', which, besides stating that a namesake of the *Fianna*, Moling Luath, 'swift', previously lived there, devotes much space to St Mullin's and its topographical features.[12] There are curiously few other saints mentioned in the Latin text, and the *vir pius* named Aoibhléan (Oiblan), who is said to have provoked the miracle that showed Christ in Moling's lap, is otherwise unknown.[13]

As pointed out by several commentators, Moling's vernacular Life appears to bear little relationship to the Latin text.[14] It dwells at length on a number of episodes, one devoted to the circumstances of the saint's birth to his father's sister-in-law in the west (meaning Kerry), another describing how he was brought up under the tutelage of a man named Collanach, appointed by Bréanainn who had foretold the saint's birth thirty years previously, and who, according to a poem placed in the mouth of Fionn son of Cumhall, had preceded Moling in his occupation of Ros Broic (later St Mullin's).[15] An account follows of how the saint's name was changed from Taircheall to Moling after an encounter with fierce spectres, escape from whom necessitated three mighty leaps, and how, on leaving Kerry, he was directed eastwards, first to Clonkeen (Cluain Caoin Modhíomóg) in east Limerick, where Maodhóg of Ferns and he made a union, then to Cashel, where he sought a space for a church from a king named Fínghin, before proceeding on the advice of an angel to the site of St Mullin's.[16]

There follows a series of episodes relating to St Mullin's and Leinster, one involving the roofing of his church by the celebrated Gobán, another telling how a protagonist named Grág was sent to an untimely threefold death by the saint, and how the king of the Uí Néill was outsmarted by the saint's use of a device known as *lá an Luain*, 'Monday, i.e Doomsday', to bring about remission of the onerous *bóramha* tribute.[17] The Life then ends abruptly with a statement that Moling died in his eighty-second year, preceded by a half-hearted mention of his relationship with the madman, Suibhne son of Colmán, hero of the well-known tale, *Buile Shuibhne*, in which Moling and his church figure prominently.[18]

The patchwork vernacular Life succeeds in drawing attention to the important role played by the saint in the wider literature, which includes not only tales about the *bóramha* tribute and the madness of Suibhne, but also a collection of twenty-four poems ascribed to Moling.[19] These cover topics also dealt with in the saint's Lives, such as his relationship with Suibhne and Grág, his love of water, his favourite haunt, known as *An Taoidhean*, 'watercourse', allegedly constructed by himself and later a focus of pilgrimage, and his gift of prophecy.[20] Also provided is a metrical statement of his descent and his blessing of maternal relatives, the Ciarraighe.[21] Extensive notes on the saint were also added to the entry on his feast (and other entries) in the Martyrology of Aonghas, one of which echoes his love of the *Taoidhean* and local streams about St Mullin's, another his role in the *bóramha* tale, a third his relationship with Maodhóg, a fourth a visit made to him by the devil, a fifth underlining his adaptability in company, which has led to his description both as a 'man for all seasons' and 'all things to all men', and a sixth forecasting the onslaught of the plague known as *Scuab*, 'besom', out of Fanad on the feast of St John.[22]

An obit of 697 adds substance to the statement that Moling was among the signatories of the *cáin*, 'ecclesiastical tax', of Adhamhnán.[23] Many stories of Moling survived into modern folk tradition, not only in St Mullin's, but also across the river Barrow in or near the Kilkenny barony of Ida, in connection with such sites as his holy well in Listerlin, or cave at Coolnahau in the adjoining parish of Jerpoint West.[24] A gospel book named after the saint, later kept by the Kavanaghs of Borris Idrone of whom he was patron, is now in Trinity College Dublin.[25] Another book, now lost, called *Leabhar Buidhe Moling*, is cited as a source.[26] The feast of Moling, 'splendid sun over peoples', fell on 17 June, and a pattern was held locally on this day, among other places at Monamolin in Wexford, and also on 25 July, otherwise the feast of St James.[27] It was popularly believed that Moling, one of Leinster's chief saints, joined the trio of national saints in being buried at Downpatrick.[28] In the months of September and October, 1348, many thousands assembled at St Mullin's to 'wade in the water', from fear of the plague that had then begun to affect Ireland.[29] A holy well at Corbally in the Dublin parish of Tallaght is also dedicated to Moling, as was the church that gave name to Kilmalin, formerly Stamelyn, in the neighbouring Wicklow parish of Powerscourt.[30]

1 *CGSH* §249; *GRSH* 90; *Lgen*. 724.3; *AB* 46, 119; *MedI* 254; *DIB* vi, 552–3. **2** *CGSH* §249 (add.). **3** Ibid. §§249 (add.), 722.51; *Anecd*. ii, 31–2 §14.1.5; *BLM* 6 §5; *Gadelica* i, 107; *CGH* 161a1; *JKAHS* 22, 118; ibid. 29, 62–3; *SeánR* 197. **4** *FL* 263–8. **5** *BLM* 16 §22; *MartO²* 150; *ZCP* 36, 138–55; *TNW* 1294, 1624–5. **6** *MRHI* 175, 200; *IRC* 286–7. **7** *VSHP* ii, 190–205; *VSHH* 353–6; *StMull*. **8** *VSHP* ii, 193, 197, 202–3 §§8, 17, 27–8. **9** Ibid. 190–1 §§1–2. **10** Ibid. 191–2 §§4–5. **11** Ibid. 193–4, 196–7 §§9, 16. **12** Ibid. 192, 197–9 §§6, 19; *MM* 420–1, 628–9; *SG* i, 152–3, 364, 367, 381–90. **13** *VSHP* ii, 203–4 §29. **14** *VSHP* i, lxxxi; *Kenney* 462; *SML* 158–214. **15** *BLM* 1–16 §§1–22; *SG* i, 363–4, 366–7. **16** *BLM* 16–22 §23–33. **17** Ibid. 24–45 §§34–70. **18** Ibid. 46–8 §§71–7; *BS* §§74–86. **19** *Anecd*. ii, 20–41; *SML* 217–47. **20** *Anecd*. ii, 21–2 §1.6.17; 22–4 §§2.3 passim; 26–8 §5 passim; 40–1 §24; cf. *ZCP* 18, 90–9. **21** *Anecd*. ii, 31–2 §13; 34–6 §20. **22** *MartO²* 150–6, 190; NLI G 10, 46b; *StC* 2, 108–18; *EIL* 33; cf. *RC* 14, 188–94; *TEAB* 710. **23** *AU s.a.*; *CA* 16 §28; *Peritia* 1, 189–90. **24** *FL* 263–8; *StMull*.; *HADO* iv, 190–1. **25** *Kenney*

632; *ASH* 315 §6; *FFÉ* iii, 112–13. **26** *FFÉ* iii, 32; RIA MS 23 C 23, 201; *Lgen.* 481.1. **27** *MartT* 50; *MartO*[2] 141; *MartG* 118; *MartD* 170–2; OSL CW 442–3; *Carloviana* 55, 92; *Béaloideas* 4, 114–16. **28** OSL CW 443; *ZCP* 8, 110. **29** *AIFJC* 246–7. **30** *Rep. Nov.* 2, 85; *AHWD* 12; *Mdub.* xiii, 87.

MOLOMA of Kilmalum. *See* Lomán of Lough Gill.

MOLUA of Kyle (Cluain Fearta Molua / Clonfertmulloe), barony of Clandonagh, Co. Laois, of Killaloe (Ceall Dolua / Dalua), Co. Clare, and of Drumsnat (Druim Sneachta), Co. Monaghan. A good deal of confusion surrounds the remote ancestry of this son of Carthach. His people, the Corca Oiche, were placed among the descendants of Ír son of Míl, ancestor of the Ulaidh (whose lands were located in north-east Ulster), and an origin legend was invented to explain their presence in Munster. Entitled *De Causis Toirche Corco Che* [*Oiche*], 'of the reasons for the migration of the Corca Oiche', this legend forms an adjunct to the story of the emergence of Lough Neagh.[1] It relates how one branch of the family migrated to Cashel, whose king, Oilill Flann Beag, first granted to it lands named Magh Tailine, from where it moved west to Iorluachair, now the area in which the counties of Kerry, Limerick and Cork meet. There, it seems, the family was allowed possession of a place named Cluain Baird Mheic Úghaine which some sources locate in Corca Oiche.[2] Through no less a personality than Fionn son of Cumhall, the Corca Oiche (alias Corca Ché) were associated with the territory of Uí Fhidhgheinte, now approximately the lands comprising the diocese of Limerick, within which there was a dedication to Molua (alias Lughaidh) at Ardagh.[3]

The saint's mother Sochla, sometimes also called Coic or Cochmhas, is said to have belonged to the Dál mBirn, another name for Osraighe (people of Ossory), and he is reputed to have had two brothers, Lughar and Ioain, one sister, Cróine, and a first cousin, Cainnear of Clooncaura.[4] A separate (less well-attested) line of tradition asserted that Molua's father was none other than Carthach (disciple of Ciarán at Seirkieran) who, to expiate his sin of the flesh, was obliged to undertake a pilgrimage to Rome.[5]

The saint's chief church at Kyle, otherwise perhaps best known for its association with Laidhgeann, can by no means be described as of major importance, with few of its abbots mentioned in the early annals. Despite this, Molua was made the subject of a Latin Life that survives in three recensions, all of which derive from a common original.[6] A date in the twelfth century has been suggested for the original of the surviving Lives.[7] The earliest version, as preserved in the Salamancan Codex, forms part, however, of a group known collectively as the O'Donohue Lives, for whose texts early dates have been proposed, in some cases well before 800.[8] A final decision on date must await a full critical edition of the text but, as in other Lives of this group, for example those of Ailbhe and Fíonán Cam, there are indications that a date in the twelfth century at the earliest would also be more appropriate for Molua's Life.

Following a brief account of the saint's birth and family, the biography immediately attributes to him a series of miracles that ultimately prompted his father to seek out seven priests, known as sons of Caolbhadh, who discerned in him the odour of sanctity.[9] When subsequently also noticed by Comhghall, who asked that he be allowed to take the youth to Bangor, Molua had already performed many more miracles, including resuscitation, and the curing of the deafness of his first cousin, Cainnear of Cluain Cláraidh, now possibly Clooncaura in the Limerick parish of Kildimo.[10] Following a long sojourn at Bangor, where he acquired the enigmatic nickname, *Giolla na dTrí Naonbhar*, 'servant of the three nines', Molua spent much time at the Monaghan church of Drumsnat – a place best known for its association with a famous, no longer extant *cín*, 'book' – rejecting there an offer conveyed by an angel of authority over the lands between Lough Erne and Lough Neagh, approximately the archdiocese of Armagh, because of his aversion to the company of women.[11] Having first travelled southwards via Clonard, Molua, on being advised by a local dynast in Uí Fhidhgheinte that he would not be honoured in his own country – perhaps an oblique reference to his displacement at Killaloe by Flannán – once more proceeded north-eastwards to the Slieve Bloom area. There he was granted the site of a church at Kyle, on the confines of Munster and Leinster – but still within the eastern boundary of the diocese of Killaloe – by Bearach, king of the Laoighis and ancestor of the Uí Mhórdha (O'Moores).[12]

The remainder of the Life is devoted to Molua's actions as head of the church at Kyle, which, though mainly miraculous, also give to the saint what has been described as something of 'an individual personality', unusual in Irish hagiography.[13] There is insistence in the text on the value of regular confession, uncommon in church circles until the twelfth century, Sunday observance, and *stabilitas* or steadfast adherence to one's own community.[14] Running through the text is an apparently leading interest in sites later – i.e. from the mid-twelfth-century onwards – associated with houses of the canons regular of St Augustine. In addition to the previously mentioned churches of Bangor and Clonard, these included Seirkieran, Ferns, and both Monaincha and Roscrea.[15] Either Monaincha or Roscrea, which were within ten miles of Kyle, would be a more likely setting for an active scriptorium than Molua's own (relatively modest) foundation. The signal honour of being the saint's first place of repose after death is given to a site named Tuaim Domhnaigh, probably the present Toomyvara (alias 'Templedowney'), likewise the location of a house of canons dependent on Monaincha, and previously the scene of the saint's above-mentioned insistence on the value of regular confession.[16] A close examination of the saint's dossier will no doubt reveal further dating evidence, but the scarcely coincidental concern with sites favoured by the canons regular, who first reached Ireland in the 1130s, points to a date in the mid- to late twelfth century at the earliest.

The external element of the Life is not pronounced, but Maodhóg of Ferns is said to have been about to leave for St David's in Wales when met by Molua, and Pope Gregory is given the task of extolling the saint's virtues on the basis of a copy of his rule that had allegedly been brought to the pontiff by Bishop Daghán (Deganus).[17] In addition to the latter saint, four others are mentioned in the penultimate chapter of Molua's Life: Laichtín who was to succeed him; Crónán to whom he left his church, possibly an indication that the Life was written in Roscrea; Sceallán who administered the last rites; and Mainchín *Sapiens* whose portruding eyes were miraculously cured by proximity to the saint's corpse.[18] The concluding chapter of the Life mentions two – Fiontan son of Tulchán and Pope Gregory – of several saints said to have borne witness to the joy of the heavenly choirs welcoming Molua, others being Maol Anfaidh of Molana, likewise a house of canons regular, and Íde of Killeedy.[19]

An early genealogical text bears witness to Molua's duty of protecting his paternal people, the Corca Oiche (Ché).[20] Given his maternal connections with the Osraighe, the presence of Molua's cult at the Kilkenny church of Killaloe, where a wooden image of the saint was preserved and a pattern held in early August in his honour until the nineteenth century, is no surprise.[21] Furthermore, the traditional Osraighe connection with the Corca Laoighdhe of Ross diocese in Cork may explain why the saint is said to have assisted a disciple (and namesake), 'Cruimhthear Lughaidh', to found a church in the locality.[22] A poem added to the entry on Molua's feast in the Martyrology of Tallaght describes him as an *anmchara*, 'soul-friend', of no fewer than four other saints, David of St David's, Maodhóg of Ferns, Mochaomhóg of Leigh, and Comhghall of Bangor, and a note added to the Martyrology of Aonghas gives a fanciful explanation of how he acquired his name.[23]

Born according to the annals in 554, Molua is said to have died in 609, and his feast fell on 4 August, close to the festival of his namesake and probable original, the pre-Christian divinity Lugh.[24] The same day was observed in honour of the saint at the Monaghan church of Magheracloone, but the saint's holy wells at Ardagh and Emlygrennan in the county of Limerick were resorted to on the eve of the feast .[25] There were also holy wells dedicated to Molua in the Limerick parish of Doondonnell and in the Offaly parish of Roscomroe.[26] The saint's bell, *mionn Molua*, which was used in the Kyle area for swearing upon, may be intended by the reference to the 'little bell of the Island of Molua' in the list of items in Adhamhnán's reliquary.[27]

1 *ZCP* 8, 307–8. **2** *LG* v, 272 §554, 466 §cix.4. **3** *Lgen.* 435.5; *JNMArchS* 48, 29; OSL LK i, 70. **4** *CGSH* §§116.3, 722.47; *VSHH* 131 §1; *ZCP* 14, 103; *GRSH* 98–100; *Lgen.* 732.5. **5** *MartO*² 86. **6** *VSHH* 131–45, 382–8; *VSHP* i, lxxxiii–lxxxiv; ibid. ii, 206–25 **7** *Kenney* 398–9. **8** *MISL* 297–339; *CeltC* 182–9; *PMIS* 79–90; *Peritia* 24–5, 90–107. **9** *VSHH* 131–2 §§1–5; *VSHP* ii, 206–8 §§1–7; but cf. *LnaÉ* 116. **10** *VSHH* 132–4 §§6–15; *VSHP* ii, 208–10 §§8–15. **11** *VSHH* 134–6 §§16–28; *VSHP* ii, 210–14 §§16–25; *KLT* 63; *MRHI* 47–57; *ClRec.* 6, 79–80, 89–93; *IB* 421–71. **12** *VSHH* 137–8 §§29–33; *VSHP* ii, 214–16 §§26–8. **13** *Kenney* 399. **14** *VSHH* 138–9, 142–3, §§37, 51, 62; *VSHP* ii, 216–17, 223 §§30, 51; *ODCC* 1250–1. **15** *VSHH* 139–40, 144–5 §§40, 43, 67–8; *VSHP* ii, 218–19, 223 §§35, 38, 52. **16** *VSHH* 144–5 §68; *VSHP* ii, 223–4 §52; *MRHI* 195; *HDK* 87, 214–15. **17** *VSHH* 140, 144 §§43, 64; *VSHP* ii, 219, 222 §§38, 47. **18** *VSHH* 144–5 §68; *VSHP* ii, 223–4 §53. **19** *AB* 69, 88–9; *MartO*² 56, 182. **20** *ZCP* 8, 315. **21** *HADO* iii, 436–41; OSL KK ii, 53; *JRSAI* 76, 161–2. **22** *VSHH* 140–1 §44. **23** *MartT* 112; *MartO*² 180–2. **24** *AU s.a.*; *MartT* 60; *MartO*² 174; *MartG* 150; *MartD* 210; *ZCP* 36, 138–56. **25** OSL LK i, 70, 208; *UCA* 30; *SATDF* 174; *DiocL* 92–3; *JCHAS* 37, 90–2; *JRSAI* 77, 159–60; ibid. 85, 197; *SACCL* 402; *ClRec.* 6, 372–3; *CPL* 15, §773. **26** *SACCL* 400; *AIOY* 109, 119. **27** *JRSAI* 2A, 47–51; *HADO* ii, 138; *Celtica* 15, 34 §11; *EMH* 329–30 §21.

Molua son of Maonach. This saint was attached, with Fachtna of Ross and five other brothers, to the Corca Laoighdhe, whose territory corresponded approximately to that of the diocese of Ross.[1] He may have been identical with Molua of Kyle, who is reputed to have assisted a certain namesake (Lughaidh, *cruimhthear*, 'presbyter') to found a church at a place among the Corca Laoighdhe named Uachtar Arda (possibly now Ardagh in the parish of Ross), and he probably gave name to 'Island-Molloe', now Horse Island in the parish of Castlehaven.[2] One seventeenth-century source speculatively assigned to him a choice of two feasts (15 October/21 December).[3]

1 *CGSH* §§298.2, 730; *Lgen*. 744.6. 2 *VSHH* 140–1 §44; *FNCC* 154; Logainm.ie 'Horse Island'. 3 *GRSH* 128.

Molua son of Sineall. This man belonged to the family of Uí Dhearca Chéin which, despite its reputed descent from Brión son of Eacha Muighmheadhón, eponym of the Uí Bhriúin of Connacht, was associated with the area about the parish of Knockbreda in the Down baronies of Castlereagh.[1] Patrick was among those brought to this district to found an (unidentified) church at Ráith Easpaig Fhinnigh.[2] The district was also associated with Colum Cille, whence 'Knock-collumkill', now Knock in the parish of Knockbreda.[3] In view of Colum's association with Knockbreda and the inclusion of Brión in Molua's pedigree, the saint is likely to have been identical with the *frater* on Iona named 'Molua nepos Briuni' whose dagger, once blessed by his master, could wound no flesh.[4] A namesake (Luighbhe) and probable double of Molua was associated with the church of Drumbo, near Knockbreda. According to seventeenth-century sources, Molua's feast fell on 4 June.[5]

1 *CGSH* §77; *GRSH* 60; *Lgen*. 710.8–9; *CGH* 336a4–23; *EA* 339. 2 *BP* 1915; *VT* 164. 3 *EA* 12, 179. 4 *VC*[2] 390–2 (II 29). 5 *MartD* 146; *GRSH* 60.

Molua Craoibhighe. *See* Lughaidh of Kilpatrick

Molua Lobhar, 'leper', son of Conall Caomh. Almost all that is known of this man is contained in a passage in the genealogies of the Dál gCais which states that his father (Conall Caomh) was blessed by Ruadhán of Lorrha, that Breacán of Aran was an uncle of his, and that Aodh – reputedly the first king of Dál gCais to go to Cashel – was his brother.[1] The passage also asserts that he was a disciple of Mochuda, and this would suggest that he was considered to be identical with the Molua twice mentioned in the Life of the Lismore saint.[2] Outside this text, Molua is known only from the list of homonymous saints.[3] His feast has not been recorded, unless he was identical with the Lughair Lobhar remembered on 11 May.[4]

1 *CoC* 13–14; *LM* 296–7. 2 *VSHP* i, 182 §34, 196 §64n; *Lgen*. 638.5. 3 *CGSH* §707.563. 4 *MartT* 42; *MartG* 94; *MartD* 124.

Moluóg of Lismore (Lios Mór), Scotland. When extolling the virtues of the church founded by Comhghall at Bangor, Bernard of Clairvaux drew attention to 'one of the sons of that community', Luanus (.i.e. Lua/Molua) by name, who was said to be the founder of no fewer than one hundred monasteries.[1] This is usually taken to refer to the patron of Lismore, who is also thought to be the subject of a pedigree attaching him to the Dál nAraidhe of north-east Ulster.[2] The prominence thus given to Moluóg has been interpreted as an awareness on

Bernard's part of the saint's status as patron of Rushen on the Isle of Man, which was incorporated into the Cistercian order in 1148.[3] Little is recorded of the son of Luchta in Irish sources, but the compiler of the Breviary of Aberdeen prepared some biographical notices, according to which Moluóg was educated by Bréanainn, presumably at Clonfert, before proceeding to the north of Ireland and thence, courtesy of a floating stone, to Scotland, where, after initial difficulties, he founded Lismore and many other churches.[4] An earlier version of Moluóg's Life was borrowed in order to demonstrate the (spurious) Irish origins of Cuthbert of Durham.[5] In Ireland, the saint was thought to be associated with the Meath church of Kildalkey, and he may have given name to 'Kilmeloge' (Ceall Moluóg) in the Down parish of Kilkeel.[6] According to the annals, Moluóg died in 592.[7] The feast of 'the sun of Lismore of Alba', recorded, under the guise of Lugudus (Lughaidh) and Moluacus, as far away as Metz in Lorraine and Regensburg in Bavaria, fell on 25 June.[8] The saint's staff was highly venerated as a relic at Lismore.[9]

1 *BCLMA* 28; *SourcesC* 367, 216. **2** *CGSH* §121; *GRSH* 101; *Lgen.* 735.1–2. **3** *GELB* 299; *PIM* 87–8, 115. **4** *CPNS* 292–3; *KSS* 409–11; *ACDS* 157–61; *Innes Review* 32, 70; *GELB* 299–310; *LegSS* 148–58, 395–8; *SBDeer* 387–9. **5** *RSC* 144–54. **6** *MartO*[2] 158; PNNI iii, 60. **7** *AU*/ATig. *s.a.* **8** *MartT* 52; *MartO*[2] 142; *MartG* 122; *MartD* 178; *FSHIM* 138, 238. **9** *CR* 5, 363–4; *ACDS* 158.

Momhaodhóg of Fiddown (Fiodh Dúin), barony of Iverk, Co. Kilkenny. The Book of Glendalough's account of the Uí Chriomhthannáin of the Stradbally district in Laois begins with a reference to the family's two most celebrated sons, Miodhnua (alias Momhaodhóg) son of Miodhghna and Colum of Terryglass.[1] Belonging to the same family was Aodh Mac Criomhthainn, principal scribe of the Book of Leinster, who, doubtless because of a sense of loyalty, placed Colum and Momhaodhóg in first and second place among the saints of Leinster.[2] Despite the prominence thus accorded him, little else is known of the patron of Fiddown, other than the names of his brother, Colmán Cúile of Clonkeen 'in the congregation (*samhadh*)' of Fiontan of Clonenagh, and a sister named Coincheann whose church is not specified.[3] He is, however, listed among the guarantors of the Law of Adhamhnán.[4] Momhaodhóg's feast was celebrated at Fiddown on 13 August, the day assigned to him in most martyrologies, but inexplicably omitted from the Martyrology of Donegal.[5] This day was shared by Radegund, foundress of a famous abbey at Poitiers in France and, through a note added to the entry on the feast in the Martyrology of Cashel, Momhaodhóg acquired the distinction of being regarded as the French saint's son.[6] Another feast of the saint (23 March) is accompanied in the Martyrology of Aonghas by the description of Momhaodhóg as *mionn Alban*, 'diadem of Alba', and this has led to the assumption that he was also active in Scotland.[7]

1 *CGH* 122bb12. **2** *CGSH* §§241–2.1.2; **3** Ibid.; *GRSH* 91; *Lgen.* 727.28; *CGH* 122bb10. **4** *CA* §22. **5** *HADO* iv, 214; *MartT* 63; *MartO*[2] 176; *MartG* 156. **6** *FourIM* 180. **7** *MartT* 26; *MartO*[2] 83; *MartG* 60; *MartD* 84; *HADO* iv, 214; *KSS* 411–12.

Momhéanóg. *See* Éanna of Inishmore; Méanóg.

Monahan. *See* Manchán of Mohill.

Monan. *See* Maoineann.

Moneasóg. *See* Neasán.

Moninne of Killevy (Ceall Shléibhe), barony of Orior Upper, Co. Armagh. One of Ireland's chief female saints, Moninne (a form traditionally, if wrongly, thought to be based on the first words uttered by the poet Ninnín after she had cured his dumbness) was also known as Dairearca and Sáirbhile, and later as Blinne (Bline).[1] Though usually assigned by the genealogists, through her father Mochta, to the Uí Eachach Cobha of Down or their close relatives, the Conaille of Muirtheimhne in north Louth, one version of the pedigree assigned the saint through a father named Liolach to the Ceinéal Eoghain of Tyrone.[2] Moninne's mother is said to have been Cuman daughter of Dallbhrónach – an aunt of Brighid of Kildare – whose original barrenness had been removed by Patrick's blessing, thus allowing her to give birth to forty-seven children.[3]

Moninne's chief church, located in the townland of Ballintemple, near Slieve Gullion in Armagh, was later chosen as the site of a convent of Augustinian nuns, probably soon after the introduction of that order to Ireland in the 1130s.[4] This early date is suggested by the presence in England by the 1140s at the latest of a Latin Life written for her by a certain 'Conchubranus' (Conchobhrán), which was used by Geoffrey, abbot of Burton-upon-Trent between 1114 and 1151, as a model for his Life of St Modwenna, patron of his abbey and commonly supposed to have been identical with Moninne, originally perhaps for no more reason that the similarity of name and Ireland's reputation as a breeding ground of saints.[5] This version of Moninne's Life has been twice printed, latterly with a translation into English and some suggestions as to origins, but has yet to be made the subject of a full critical edition.[6] Accompanied by two poems, possibly also written by Conchobhrán, the Life is replete with onomastic matter, much of it corrupted in the course of transcription, and it claims for its subject several foundations in England, including Burton-upon-Trent.[7]

Much less rich in onomastic detail is the second of Moninne's Lives, preserved in the early fourteenth-century *Codex Salmanticensis*.[8] How this version of the saint's Life relates to Conchobhrán's is a vexed question that can best be solved by a critical edition. Despite the recent suggestion that it was partly based on the Salamancan Life, or on one like it, compiled in the late eighth or early ninth century, the view taken here is that Conchobhrán's text (which was probably commissioned by Geoffrey) is at the base of the much abridged version in the Salamancan codex.[9]

Both versions agree in providing the saint with a background in south-east Ulster, an early encounter with Patrick, and baptism at a local pool named Briu (Briughas) which has yet to be identified.[10] Her early ecclesiastical connections were with north Louth, specifically Faughart (Fochard) and Rúscach in the Cooley area.[11] She was then brought to Bishop Iobhar – first on the Aran Islands, then at Begerin, near Wexford town – before visiting Brighid (who was also patron of Faughart) and receiving from her the gift of a vessel that miraculously found its way to a place named 'Caput Litoris', probably Newry (Ceann Tráchta), adjoining Killevy, where it was found by a certain Rónán (according to

Conchobhrán) or Eirbhe (Salamancan Life), allegedly Moninne's brother.[12] An adaptation of this incident, describing how a vessel thrown into the sea by Fuinche daughter of Conall Dearg found its way to Moninne at Killevy, is contained in the Life of Éanna of Inishmore.[13]

In between, Conchobhrán's version of the Life gives an account of the conversion of the tyrant Glúnshalach who went on to be a saint. Persuaded to lay his head in Moninne's lap, Glúnshalach was granted a vision of heaven which showed him the place reserved for Caoimhghin of Glendalough. As nothing less would satisfy him, Glúnshalach, together with his sister's son, Aifín, converted and joined Moninne at Killevy. Advised of the danger of losing his place in heaven, Caoimhghin also made his way to Killevy, only to be reassured by Moninne.[14] Background to this incident may have been provided by the list of saints commemorated on 3 June which includes not only Caoimhghin, but also Glúnshalach, Aifín and, in some sources, Moninne herself.[15]

Having founded Killevy, Moninne is brought by Conchobhrán to England, to establish various churches, and to Rome, to meet no less a Pope than the Celestine who sent Patrick to Ireland, both episodes being again absent from the Salamancan Life.[16] Among the churches she is said to have founded in Ireland itself, besides Faughart and Killevy, was one in Swords in Dublin and another at Armagh.[17] As death approached in the year 517, reputedly at the advanced age of nine score, king and people implored her through an emissary variously named Rónán and Eirbhe to stay for another year, but too late because the apostles Peter and Paul had already been sent to receive her.[18] With Moninne's feastday falling on 6 July, the octave of the feast of Peter and Paul, the influence of the festal calendar is probable at this point.[19] According to Conchobhrán, Moninne died in Scotland, where there are some dedications to the saint under the guise of Medena, whereas, according to the Salamancan Life, her death took place in Ireland.[20]

Probably because of her association with Iobhar of Begerin, Moninne appears also to have been remembered on 6 July at Kilmannan (perhaps from Ceall Moninne) in Wexford, where a pattern was held, and perhaps also at a well named *Tobar Moninne* in the Kilkenny parish of Tullahought.[21] As the patron of Kilmannan is now taken to have been an otherwise unattested Mannán, whose bell, sent from heaven to replace a broken pitcher, was kept locally until the early nineteenth century, Moninne may have been transmuted into a male.[22] At the Meath church of Donore, where a pattern was held either on 5 July or 9 October, the name was remembered as Mainne.[23] However, this may have been a local hypocoristic version of the name Munna, which would point to an original saint called Fiontan.[23] In Omeath, *lá 'le Blinne*, 'Moninne's feastday', if wet, was a portent of forty days of rain.[24] A poem on the saint preserved in the late twelfth-century Book of Leinster contains a quatrain, later borrowed by the author of the well-known poem attributed to Cuimín of Connor, which alleges that, once she became a nun, Moninne never again ate her fill.[25] A litany-style prayer of invocation includes Moninne among many other female saints.[26] The saint's age at death is reputed to have been 180.[27]

1 *CGSH* §718.1–8; *MartO*[2] 166; *Béaloideas* 2, 57; *Dinn.* 4, 26. **2** *CGSH* §98.1.2; *GRSH* 101; *Lgen.* 735.17–18; *CGH* 162b13–c20. **3** *CGSH* §722.6–11. **4** *MRHI* 321. **5** *Kenney* 366–70; *GBLMM*. **6** *PRIA* 28C12, 201–51; *SAM* 9–10, 250–73, 117–41, 426–54; *AHHS* 63–98. **7** *SAM* 9, 250; 10, 432–4; *Peritia* 19, 1–19. **8** *VSHH* 83–95. **9** *Kenney* 368–9; *MISL* 396–7; *AHHS* 63–6; *Peritia* 9, 210–11; *GBLMM* xiv–xx; *CeltC* 171–2; *CI* i, 88n. **10** *VSHH* 83 §1; *SAM* 9, 252–6 §§1–3; *HDGP* ii, 200; cf. *CGSH* §718.6. **11** *VSHH* 83–4 §§2; *SAM* 9, 256 §3. **12** *VSHH* 84–7 §§3–13; *SAM* 9, 256–8 §§5–6; 10, 118–28 §§1–7. **13** *VSHP* ii, 63–4 §9. **14** *SAM* 9, 264–8 §§10–12. **15** *MartT* 47; *MartG* 128; *MartD* 144–6. **16** *SAM* 9, 270–2 §15; 10, 128–30 §8, 432–3 §3. **17** *SAM* 10, 433 §3. **18** *CGSH* §718.5; *MartO*[2] 166; *AU s.a.*; cf. *LUM* 154rb 23–4; *VSHH* 93, §§29–30; *SAM* 440–2 §9; *Peritia* 17–18, 270–1. **19** *MartT* 54; *MartO*[2] 161; *MartG* 130; *MartD* 186–8. **20** *VSHH* 93, §§29–30; *SAM* 440–2 §9; *Peritia* 17–18, 270–1. **21** *CECW* 209–10; *TNW* 1141–2. **22** OSL WX ii, 75; *EMH* 487 §232. **23** OSL MH 137. **24** *StH* 6, 63. **25** *CGSH* §718.4; *ZCP* 1, 62; *MartD* 188. **26** *MartT* 108; *IrL* 92. **27** *MartD* 185; *Ériu* 13, 66 §63.

Moresius. *See* Muireadhach of Banagher.

Moriallagh. *See* Muirdheabhair.

Moríóg of Inchbofin (Inis Bó Finne), parish of Noughaval, barony of Kilkenny West, Co. Westmeath. According to tradition, Moríóg (alias Doríóg or Ríóg) was one of seven sons of Restitutus (Welsh Rhystud) of the Maca Baird (Lombards) by a sister of Patrick, sometimes named Lubaid, at other times Dairearca.[1] A separate tradition assigns him to the Maca Laoighdhe, alias Corca Laoighdhe, of the area later comprising the Cork diocese of Ross, and attributes to him a sea-voyage.[2] By far the best-known of Moríóg's alleged siblings were Seachnall of Dunshaughlin and Usaille of Killashee. Moríóg is mentioned, together with another brother, Meal of Ardagh, in a passage of the Tripartite Life which locates him in Inchbofin.[3] Besides the Patrician connection, his church may have had an affiliation to Glendalough because he is included, with many others, in a list of saints invoked under the aegis of Caoimhghin.[4] The list of homonymous saints also attaches Moríóg to Glendalough.[5] Another interest in the saint's church may be reflected in the Lenten visit credited to Aodh of Rahugh, who miraculously changed Moríóg's meat to bread, fish, and honey.[6] The circumstances that gave rise to the conception of Lonán son of Talmhach – as recorded in the preface to the hymn attributed to Mugintius of Whithorn – involved Drustic daughter of Drust, king of the Britons, falling in love with Moríóg, only to be deceived into believing that she had slept with him, when Talmhach, another of Finnian's companions, had been sent in his place.[7] The saint's memory was also celebrated at a well named *Tobar Ríóg* in the parish of Kilmeane, on the Roscommon side of Lough Ree.[8] Moríóg's feast fell on 1 August.[9]

1 *CGSH* §§664, 672.21, 722.15.16; *BP* 895–902; *VT* 82; *MartT* 100. **2** *IrL* 66. **3** *BP* 895–902; *VT* 82. **4** *IrL* 54–6; *CPPI* 115, 174, 191. **5** *CGHS* §707.888. **6** *VSHH* 180; *VSHP* i, 43 §31. **7** *LH* i, 22. **8** OSL RN i, 89; *Éigse* 6, 211. **9** *MartT* 59; *MartG* 148; *MartD* 208.

Morónóg of Inishloe (Inis Luaidhe), parish of Killadysert, barony of Clonderalaw, Co. Clare. On the death of Seanán, his body is said to have been brought to a 'house of prayer' on Scattery Island, to await the arrival of the saints of Limerick, including Molaga of Inishtubbrid (Inis Tiobrad) and Morónóg of Inishloe, now neighbouring islands on the river Shannon, near Canon Island, the site of an Augustinian priory founded circa 1180.[1] Nothing else is recorded of Morónóg, other than his presence at the court of Guaire son of Colmán at

Dungory in the Clare parish of Kinvarradoorus together with Cuimín Fada of Clonfert, but among the holy wells of the parish was one dedicated to Ruadhán, whose name may have generated the hypocoristic or pet form Morónóg (perhaps from Moruadhnóg).[2] He may be identical with the 'Ronoge' (alias Renogue) venerated at a well in Ballinrea, near Carrigaline in Cork, whose pattern on St John's Eve (23 June), or on the following day, was reportedly attended by many thousands, until suppressed in the middle of the nineteenth century.[3] Elsewhere in Cork, at Kilbronoge in the parish of Skull, the name of the local church was written 'Kilmoronoge' in the 1659 census.[4]

1 *AB* 66, 209, 213; *MRHI* 162. **2** *ACoC* 148; *Ériu* 5, 28. **3** *TDI* i, 279; *The Fold* 18.7, 32–5; *JKAHS* 29, 58. **4** CorkD §75.

Morónóg of Kirk Marown (Keeill Marooney), Isle of Man. Taken to have been bishop of Man after Mac Cuill, and patron of the parish named after him, this saint's patronal fair was held on 2 February, and this has led to the suggestion that he was identical with Bishop Rónán of Lismore in Scotland whose feast fell seven days later (9 February).[1] Though nothing else is known of the Lismore bishop, the pedigree assigned to him in one source is that of Rónán Fionn, whose cult is much more likely to have spread to the Isle of Man.[2] It has also been suggested that the bishop may have been identical with Rónán of Kingarth (Ceann Garadh) in Scotland who died in 737.[3] He was known locally as Marooney or Marown.

1 *PIM* 151–2; *MartT* 15; *MartO²* 59; *MartG* 32; *MartD* 42. **2** *MartO²* 72. **3** *ZCP* 9, 364; ibid. 13, 365; *KSS* 441; *CPNS* 309; *AU s.a.*

Morris. *See* Manchán of Mohill.

Moshamhóg of Bohammer (Both Chomair), parish of Balgriffin, barony of Coolock, Co. Dublin. The list of homonymous saints contains three entries relating to the name Moshamhóg (perhaps from *samh*, 'Summer'), one with the epithet *Gall*, 'foreigner', another attaching the saint to Dublin (Duibhlinn), and the third assigning him to Bohammer.[1] All three probably refer to the same saint who, in addition to his church at Bohammer, gave name to Ceall Moshamhóg, later 'Kilmehauoc', near Islandbridge in Dublin.[2] According to one set of annals, a decisive battle between Norse and Irish was fought at Islandbridge in 919 (otherwise 917) in which the 'high-king', Niall Glúndubh, and many others of the northern nobility were slain.[3] Nothing else is known of Moshamhóg.

1 *CGSH* §707.623–5. **2** *HDGP* iv, 30; *OnomG* 204. **3** *AFM s.a.* 917 (ii, 592); *CGG* xci.

Moshagra of Saggart, barony of Newcastle, Co. Dublin. One of many saints of the Dál Meisin Corb, Moshagra (alias Moagra, Momhagra or Tagra) son of Seanán was patron of a church that appears to have been affiliated to Glendalough.[1] He was commemorated at Saggart on 3 March, two days after a namesake (Bishop Sárán) who was probably identical with him.[2] The later martyrologies add the names of two other churches associated with him, Clonenagh (Cluain Eidhneach) in Laois, and Fionnmhagh in Fothairt (possibly the same as Ceall Fhionnmhaighe in Fothairt of Leinster) which again belonged to

Glendalough, and has been identified as 'Killynee' in the townland of Bogland, parish and barony of Arklow.[3] The saint was also patron of Tomhaggard (Teach Moshagra?) in the Wexford barony of Bargy, where 'St Haggard's' pattern was held on 3 March.[4] The saint's chief claim to fame was his inclusion under the guise of Moagra and Moshagra among the signatories of the *cáin*, 'church tax', of Adhamhnán.[5] His name also figures (under the guise of 'Magrus') in some post-Conquest Dublin liturgical manuscripts.[6]

1 *CGSH* §181.9; *Lgen.* 458.2; *CPPI* 182. 2 *MartT* 20; *MartO²* 80, 86; *MartG* 46; *MartD* 62. 3 *CPPI* 193, 238; *HDGP* iii, 174. 4 OSL WX ii, 200; *CECW* 214; *TNW* 1677–8. 5 *CA* 16–18 §28; *Peritia* 1, 189. 6 *Rep. Nov.* 2, 46, 48, 53; *BOM* 63.

MOSHEANÓG. No fewer than twenty-two of this name (which ultimately derives from *sean*, 'old, senior') are included in the list of homonymous saints.[1] Most of these are either otherwise unattested or better known under another form of the name, such as Seanán, Seanach, or Moshiona. The patrons of Laraghbryan and Scattery Island, both of whom normally went under the name Seanán, are included in the list.[2] The latter saint probably also lurks in the list under other forms, such as Mosheanóg Beitheach, 'of the birch', whose feast was kept on 11 March, well within the octave of the main feast on Scattery Island, or Mosheanóg of Inis Dáchaorach, possibly the same as Inis Caorach, now Mutton Island off the Clare coast, which is said to have been visited by Seanán.[3] A disciple of Bréanainn named Mosheanóg figures both in the list of homonymous saints and also in Bréanainn's Life, under the guise of Seanán (alias Mochaomhóg, *sic recte* Mosheanóg) *puer*, 'boy', who, having been brought from Britain in the company of Maoineann, was raised from the dead.[4]

1 *CGSH* §707.741–62. 2 Ibid. §707.746.758. 3 Ibid. §707.742.748; *MartT* 22; *MartO²* 81; *MartG* 52; *MartD* 74; *LisL.* 2190–1. 4 *VSHP* 1, 145 §91; *BNÉ* i, 87–8 §§179, 184.

MOSHEANÓG of Ballaghmoon (Mughna / Bealach Mughna), adjoining Dunmanoge (Dún Mosheanóg), barony of Kilkea and Moone, Co. Kildare. According to the genealogists, Mosheanóg son of Seanchán belonged to the Dál Meisin Corb, a group mainly connected with east Leinster, and particularly with the area about Glendalough.[1] In keeping with his descent, Mosheanóg figured among the forty saints said to have been with Caoimhghin in Glendalough.[2] His church belonged to the *paruchia* (and later the diocese) of Glendalough.[3] Apart from the presence of a remarkable tree near his church at Ballaghmoon, little else is known of the saint but, in view of his east Leinster connections, he may also have been patron of Kilmannock in the Wexford parish of Kilmokea.[4] His feast, which he shared with Seanchán, a namesake and probable double, fell on 11 December.[5]

1 *CGSH* §§181.4, 291; *GRSH* 90; *Lgen.* 726.2; *CGH* 120b28. 2 *IrL* 54–6; *CPPI* 175. 3 *CPPI* 196. 4 *AF* 4–5 §3; *MartO²* 258; *TNW* 1143. 5 *MartO²* 251; *MartG* 236; *MartD* 330–2; OSL MH 43.

MOSHIOLÓG of Clonatin (Cluain Aithghin), parish of Kilmakilloge (Ceall Moshiológ), barony of Gorey, Co. Wexford. A poem attributed to Moling presents 'Bishop' Moshiológ as one of his *manaigh*, describing him as from Ulster and asserting that his *seinfhiacail*, 'old tooth', was to be feared by *ógáin*, 'young warriors'.[1] This was probably the same man *don ríoghraidh*, 'of the kingfolk', as was remembered on 13 July at Clonatin in 'Uí Dheagha of Uí Cheinsealaigh', later the barony of Gorey and the adjoining part of Ballaghkeen.[2] Moling's concern with the saint, as well as his description as a *manach*, indicates that either St Mullin's or Ferns had a proprietorial interest in Clonatin. He was again remembered on 25 July, where he is described as Moling's pupil.[3]

1 *Anecd.* ii, 30 §3. 2 *MartT* 55; *MartO²* 162, 168; *MartG* 136; *MartD* 192; *HDF* 151; *CECW* 209; OSL WX i, 10. 3 *MartT* 58; *MartG* 142; *MartD* 202.

Moshiona. The hypocoristic form Moshiona may stand for either Siollán or, less frequently, Seanán. The list of homonymous saints records five of the name, beginning with Moshiona of the Maca Lughair, followed by Moshiona of the Maca Minn (Muinn), both of whom are also included in the list of saints named Mosheanóg.[1] The latter is probably identical with the best-known bearer of the name, Siollán (alias Moshiona) of Bangor.

1 *CGSH* §707.743.761.889–93.

Moshiona of Ballyman (Gleann Munaire/'Glenmunder'), parish of Oldconnaught, barony of Rathdown, Co. Dublin. This saint is featured in both the list of homonymous saints and the litany headed by Caoimhghin of Glendalough.[1] He may be identical with the bishop named Silléan, patron of the church of Ceall Easpaig Shilléin, which was apparently located in north Wicklow, perhaps in the parish of Delgany, a little south of Oldconnaught.[2]

1 *CGSH* §707.892; *IrL* 54–6; *CPPI* 175; *Keimelia* 520. 2 *CPPI* 195; *HDGP* iii, 169.

Moshiona of Emlagh (Imleach Casáin), parish, barony and county of Louth. This saint, also known as Siollán, was remembered for a remarkable hair in his eyebrow which, if seen in the morning, would cause death to the viewer.[1] It is said to have brought about the death of Molaise of Leighlin.[2] Moshiona's name is among those included in the list of homonymous saints and, according to the martyrologies, he was commemorated on 11 September.[3]

1 *MartO²* 206. 2 Ibid. 3 *CGSH* §707.891; *MartT* 70; *MartO²* 193; *MartG* 174; *MartD* 244.

Moshionóg of Cluain Caoichne. *See* Sincheall.

Motheimhneóg son of Corbán. Attached by the genealogists to an obscure Munster family named Ceardraighe of Tulach Gosa, Motheimhneóg (alias Teimhnéan) is otherwise known for his role as cook to Molua of Kyle.[1] His feast fell on 23 or 24 December.[2]

1 *CGSH* §§116 (3), 224; *Lgen.* 743.2; *CGH* 150b54. 2 *MartT* 88–9; *MartO²* 253; *MartG* 246; *MartD* 344–6.

Mothoiréan of Drumcliff. *See* Mothoiréan of Tullow.

Mothoiréan of Tullow (Tulach Fhoirtchirn), parish of Tullowphelim, barony of Rathvilly, Co. Carlow. One of seven 'beautiful' sons of Aonghas, said to have come to Ireland from Scotland, Mothoiréan was attached to the tribal grouping of Dál Riada which had settlements in both countries.[1] Although various churches in the Irish Midlands are assigned to the saint's brothers, that of Mothoiréan at Tullow was located within the powerful Leinster kingdom of Uí Fheilmeadha.[2] Placed among a group of Carlow saints in a poem on the *bóramha* tribute, attributed to Moling, he is also one of the mainly Midland saints called upon to lament the fall of the sacred tree of Torta (*Bile Tortan*).[3] Perhaps because of his Scottish connections, re-emphasized by the attribution to Colum Cille of a poem on him and his brothers, the saint has been taken to be identical with Mothoiréan (Mothoria) of Drumcliff in Sligo and Torannán of Banchory (Beannchor), near Aberdeen in Scotland, whose feasts fell respectively on 9 and 12 June, in the first instance coincident with the feast of the patron of Iona.[4] Again perhaps because of the Scottish connection, he was also held to be the same as the pre-Patrician saint Palladius.[5] Mothoiréan was remembered, albeit under the guise of Forannán (Farannán, anglicized Farnan), on 12 June in the Kildare parish of Downings, where a well is named after him.[6] Mothoiréan's feast (12 June) found its way into a copy of the Martyrology of Usuard made by Grevenus of Cologne in the late fifteenth century, which grandly describes him as Ternanus, an archbishop in Ireland.[7] A short office Life of the saint is preserved in the Breviary of Aberdeen.[8]

1 *CGSH* §209; *GRSH* 81; *Lgen.* 721.8; *Ériu* 32, 105–6. **2** *CGSH* §209. **3** *SG* i, 389; *MD* iv, 240–46. **4** *CGSH* §701; *MartT* 49; *MartO²* 140, 148; *MartG* 112–14; *MartD* 164–6; *GRSH* 81; *IKD* 236 §48, 283; *BCC* 88 §94. **5** *MartO²* 148; *ACDS* 108–9. **6** OSL KE i, 115; *CDKL* 260; *Dinn.* 2, 33. **7** *AS*.Iun. vi, 333; *KSS* 450–1; *CPNS* 298–300; *Innes Review* 51, 84–5. **8** *LegSS* 141–3, 418–20.

Mothrianóg of Rúscach. One of seven sons of Aonghas – others being Aghadán, Eoghanán and Mothoiréan – said to have come to Ireland from Scotland, Mothrianóg's pedigree suitably attaches him to the tribal grouping of Dál Riada which had settlements in both countries.[1] Churches in the Irish Midlands are usually assigned to these brothers, and Mothrianóg's church of Rúscach(a) has been located among the Uí Fhailghe at a place named 'Roskaghbegg' in the State Papers for 1606.[2] However, there was also a place named Rúscach, near Carlingford in the Cooley area of Louth, associated with a certain Trenanus (Triananus/Mothrianóg) of the Maca Runtair who figures in the Life of Colum Cille.[3] Colum was the reputed author of a poem on the seven brothers.[4] Mothrianóg's feast fell on 20 August, the day after that of Mochta of Louth.[5]

1 *CGSH* §§209, 701.2; *GRSH* 81; *Lgen.* 721.8. **2** *CSPI* 1606–8, 61; *Ériu* 32, 106. **3** *VSHH* 84 §2; *VC¹* 242–4. **4** *CGSH* §701. **5** *MartT* 64; *MartG* 160; *MartD* 222–4.

Movee. *See* Mobhí.

Moynaghan. *See* Manchán of Lemanaghan.

Mua of Kilmoe. *See* Ultán of Ardbraccan.

Muadhán Oilithir of Aireagal/Ceall Mhuadháin. *See* Lughaidh Oilithir.

Muadhnad. *See* Osnad.

Mughain of Clogher (Clochar mac nDaimhín) in the barony of the same name, Co. Tyrone. This daughter of Daimhín is known only from an episode in the Life compiled by Adhamhnán for Colum Cille which recounts how, having fallen and broken her hip, Mughain invoked the name of the founder of Iona.[1] On becoming aware of her appeal to him, Colum sent an emissary bearing both a cure and a promise of twenty-three more years of good works.

1 *VC*[2] 336–8 (II 5).

Mughain of Kilmoon. *See* Mughain of Lyons.

Mughain of Lyons, barony of South Salt, Co. Kildare. The list of homonymous saints brings together three daughters of Oilill, named Feidhealm, Mughain, and Eithne.[1] Though Eithne appears to be otherwise unnoticed, Feidhealm and Mughain, are again brought together both by the genealogists and, with the poetic description of 'the two suns of the east of Liffey', by the martyrologists in their lists for 9 December.[2] Both sources identify the pair as daughters of Oilill son of Dúnlaing, king of Leinster, and locate their church in Ceall Inghean nOilealla, a site in the townland and parish of Lyons.[3] During his visit to Leinster, Patrick is said to have baptized Mughain and Feidhealm, together with their father and uncle, at a well north of Naas.[4] This is reminiscent of Patrick's baptism of Feidhealm and Eithne, daughters of Laoghaire, at a well near Cruachain (Rathcroghan) in Roscommon during his visit to Connacht.[5] The connection with Patrick, whose sister Dairearca was also venerated locally, suggests that the enigmatic 'Buain' of Killabuonia and *Tobar Buaine*, 'Buain's well' in the Kerry parish of Killemlagh, may represent the saint, by way of back-formation of the name from Mughain to Mhughain, whence the delenited form Bughain (modern Buain, alias Buonia).[6] She may also be the patron of Kilmoon on Sherkin Island in the Cork parish of Tullagh, whom the genealogists attached to the same branch of the Corca Laoighdhe (Corkalee) as Liadhain, mother of Ciarán of Seirkieran and Cape Clear island.[7] A note added to the Ormond recension of the genealogies of the saints asserts that Mughain daughter of Oilill gave name to Kilmoon in the Clare barony of Burren.[8] Moreover, along with Inghean Bhaoith of Killinaboy, this Mughain is featured in a poem in Classical Irish that calls upon numerous Munster saints to assist in releasing the churches of Leath Mogha (Ireland's southern half) from a bondage imposed by those of Leath Chuinn (northern half), championed by Finnian of Clonard.[9] Rounds continued to be made at the holy well in Kilmoon in the early nineteenth century, but no day was remembered for the saint.[10] While Mughain's main feast fell on 9 December, she was also remembered on the octave of this feast, viz. 15 December, at Cluain Boireann, now possibly Cloonburren in the Roscommon parish of Moore.[11]

1 *CGSH* §708.132. 2 Ibid. §246; *MartO*[2] 250, 258; *MartG* 234; *MartD* 330. 3 *CGSH* §246; *GRSH* 90; *Lgen*. 726.10; *HDGP* iv, 6. 4 *PTBA* 182.44; *BP* 2165–70; *VT* 184. 5 *PTBA* 142–4 §26; *BP* 1106–52; *VT* 100–2. 6 *Brendaniana* 280–4; *JKAHS* 30, 21; *UíR* 12, 29. 7 GCL 18–20; *JCHAS* 1 ser., 2, 38; CorkD 96. 8 *CGSH* §246; cf. ibid. §593. 9 RIA MS 23L11, 263; *SAM* 24.1, 17, 21. 10 *ACoC* 70. 11 *MartG* 238; *MartD* 336.

Muicín son of Moiche. *See* Aonghas Láimhiodhan.

Muinis of Forgney. *See* Meal.

Muirchú of Maca Mochtaine. Both of Patrick's seventh-century biographers, Muirchú (also written Murchú) and Tíreachán, came to be regarded as a saints. Muirchú is included in the list of those commemorated on 8 June, with first place being accorded to him in the Martyrology of Tallaght, the earliest text of its kind, whereas the name Tíreachán is entered at 3 July in the Martyrology of Gorman, presumably in reference to the biographer, and added from there to the Martyrology of Donegal.[1] Despite the assertions made by scholiasts of the Martyrology of Aonghas that he was eponym of Kilmorgan (Ceall Mhurchon) in the Sligo barony of Corran, or attached to a church among the Uí Fhaoláin of Kildare, Muirchú's affiliation to the Maca Mochtaine would indicate a provenance in the area about Armagh, unlike Tíreachán who appears to have been a native of Tirawley in north Connacht.[2] Judging by his inclusion in the list of signatories of the *cáin*, 'ecclesiastical law', of Adhamhnán, Muirchú may have lived until after 697.[3] The further statement in the later martyrologies that he had a brother named Meadhrán, commemorated on the same day, is unlikely, not least because the man so named was probably Medardus of Soissons in France whose feast also fell on that day.[4] No year of death is recorded for Tíreachán, who claims to have been a fosterling and pupil of Ultán, presumably of Ardbraccan.[5]

1 *MartT* 8; *MartO*[2] 139; *MartG* 112, 128; *MartD* 148, 184; *DIB* vi, 736–7; ix, 378–9; *BiblSS* ix, 666–8; xii, 499. 2 *MartO*[2] 144; *MartO*[1] 99; *ASH* 465.31–2; *Kenney* 332; *CeltT* 87–9. 3 *CA* 18 §28; *Peritia* 1, 196. 4 *MartU* 243. 5 *PTBA* 124.

Muirdheabhair of Dysert (Díseart Muirdheabhra), parish of Robertstown, barony of Shanid, Co. Limerick. The list of saints of the Dál Meisin Corb, a people closely associated with the area about Glendalough in Wicklow, assigns to Muirdheabhair two brothers, named Caomhán (of Anatrim) and Corconadan.[1] All three are again brought together in two other lists, one comprising the saints commemorated on 3 November, the other a section of an early litany consisting of associates of Caoimhghin of Glendalough.[2] Having noted Muirdheabhair's church at Dysert, the latter list locates his brothers respectively at Anatrim in the Laois parish of Offerlane, and at Derrynaflan (Doire Eidhneach, alias Doire na bhFlann), near Horse and Jockey in Tipperary. The saint is sometimes taken to have been identical with his namesake Muirdheabhair (alias Muirdhealach) son of Cuanán, whom the genealogists attached to the Dál nAraidhe of north-east Ulster.[3] According to an Old Irish Table of Commutations, Muirdheabhair was one of the four chief sages of Ireland.[4] His well at Dysert remained much frequented, at least until the early twentieth century.[5] In the Scottish parish of Tarves, where, according to a note added to some versions of the Martyrology of Aonghas, Muirdheabhair was also venerated, he was later replaced by a fictitious 'Englacius (Tanglan)', a name possibly drawn from that of a local stream.[6]

1 *CGSH* §181.6; *Lgen*. 726.2. 2 *MartG* 210; *MartD* 296; *IrL* 54–6; *StH* 20, 119n. 3 *CPPI* 180; *CGSH* §106; *GRSH* 101; *MartD* 296. 4 *Ériu* 19, 64 §23. 5 *DiocL* 111. 6 *MartO*[2] 240; *CPNS* 318–19; *LegSS* 262–3, 356.

Muirdheabhair son of Cuanán is attached by the genealogists (who also provide him with an otherwise unattested brother named Forannán) to the Dál nAraidhe of north-east Ulster.[1] He is sometimes confused with Muirdheabhair, brother of Caomhán of Anatrim, and both appear to have been remembered on the same day (3 November).[2] Under the guise of Muirdhealach (Muirghealach) he was venerated at a place called 'Gorman church' or 'Droim na Cille' at Malin Head, townland of Ballygorman, parish of Clonca, on the tip of the Inishowen peninsula, and patterns were traditionally held there on St John's Eve (23 June) and the feast of the Assumption (15 August).[3] Under the guise of Muirdhealach, he was also considered to be the same as Mura of Fahan (Fathain/Othain), likewise in Inishowen.[4]

1 *CGSH* §106; *GRSH* 101; *Lgen.* 735.5. **2** *DOH* 90; OSL DL 32. **3** *AnnU* 215; *BOI* 100; *Béaloideas* 6, 160–1; *DYHS* 195. **4** *Celtica* 1, 83.

Muireadhach of Banagher (Beannchor), barony of Keenaght, Co. Derry. This son of Éanna and his three brothers, Brughach, Fearghas and Mochomóg, belonged, according to the genealogists, either to the descendants of Colla Dá Chríoch (otherwise the Oirghialla), whose territory later corresponded to that of the diocese of Clogher, or to the Dál nAraidhe of north Down and south Antrim.[1] Little else is known of the saint, but he may be identical with his namesake, the patron of Killelagh (Ceall an Locha), likewise in Derry, who was commemorated on 2 January.[2] At Banagher, the saint also went under the slightly different guise of 'Murani sive Muiredhuih' [read Muireadhach], Latin Moresius, English Maurice, and at Killelagh the name was rendered 'Cromurmorius' (Cruimhthear Muireadhach) in two seventeenth-century documents [3]. Tradition asserts that the stones of his first church in the townland of Templemoyle underwent nocturnal transfer to the townland of Magheramore, where the presence of a stag marked a more appropriate location.[4] Here, too, the saint is supposed to be buried.[5] A well named Tobar Muiris (St Maurice's), located at Ardagh, parish of Clonmany, on the Inishowen peninsula, was dedicated to the saint.[6] Of the Irish saints named Muireadhach, he is the one most likely to have been also venerated in Scotland.[7]

1 *CGSH* §108; *GRSH* 71; *Lgen.* 714.11. **2** *Celtica* 1, 83; *DYHS* 195. **3** *DYHS* 195; *UJA* (2nd ser.) 2, 150; *BOI* 99. *Celtica* 1, 84; PNNI v, 140; *AnH* 12, 83, 108, 110. **4** *PNCL* 72. **5** Ibid. **6** *BOI* 99; *Béaloideas* 6, 158. **7** *KSS* 416–17; *CPNS* 293.

Muireadhach of Killala (Ceall Alaidh), barony of Tirawley, Co. Mayo. This son of Eachaidh is known from an entry in the corpus of saints' pedigrees which assigns him, together with several siblings, to the Ceinéal Laoghaire of Meath.[1] Among his siblings were Colmán (Colum), who was attached to Slanore and Myshall, Lughaidh, patron of Teernacreeve, Nainnidh of Kiltoom, and Comaigh daughter of Eacha, also of Slanore. He and his siblings (Colmán, Comaigh and Lughaidh) are said to have been children of Aighleann of Killiney, a sister of Colmán of Cloyne.[2] A rival tradition places him, together with Bishop Rón of Killasbugrone in Sligo, among the numerous progeny of Cuman daughter of Dallbhrónach.[3] Despite these divergent affiliations, and the later status of his church as a diocesan see, little else is recorded of Muireadhach (alias Murchadh).

As Bishop Muireadhach, he receives a bare mention in a section of the so-called 'Four Saints' tract that deals with Tirawley.[4] His feastday of 12 August was shared by Molaise of Inishmurray (Inis Muireadhaigh) off the coast of Sligo, which may have taken its name from him.[5]

1 *CGSH* §160; *GRSH* 50–1; *Lgen.* 707.12. 2 *CGSH* §§160.1, 690.3, 722.31. 3 Ibid. §722.7. 4 *IrT* iii, 4 §9. 5 *MartT* 62; *MartG* 154; *MartD* 216; *IMPAL* 30.

Muireadhach son of Neasán. *See* Beoán of Feighcullen.

Muireadhach son of Rumhan. *See* Ceallach of Trim.

Mullana. *See* Maol Anfaidh.

Multose. *See* Eiltín.

Munchin. *See* Mainchín of St Munchin's.

Munna (Munnu). This name, derived from *mo-fhionna*, served as a hypocoristic form of Fiontan.

Munna of Ros Achaidh Liag. *See* Munna of Taghmon.

Munna of Taghmon (Teach Munna), barony of Shelmaliere West, Co. Wexford, and of Taghmon, barony of Corkaree, Co. Westmeath. Munna son of Tulchán, undoubtedly the most important bearer of the name, and held, according to Adhamhnán, 'in high repute among all the churches of the Irish', was claimed as a member of various families, including the Ceinéal Conaill of Donegal, the Corca Raoidhe of Westmeath, and the Corca Oiche of Limerick.[1] Whatever may be the explanation for his adoption by the Corca Oiche, the Westmeath barony of Corkaree figured prominently in the traditions surrounding him.[2] His mother Feidhealm is said to have been a daughter of either Maine son of Niall Naoighiallach, ancestor of the peoples of Teffia (Teathbha), adjoining Corkaree, or of Maine's son Bracán.[3] While but a 'day's journey' from Derry, Munna is said to have been one of the first in Ireland to hear news of the death of Colum Cille, and he was also the subject of a prophecy previously made by the founder of Iona relating to the construction of a monastery 'in the coastal territories of the Laighin', probably a reference to the Wexford church of Taghmon.[4]

The Latin Life composed for Munna, of which there are four redactions, including a version labelled 'prior' in the Salamancan Codex (from which all others appear to derive), has yet to be made the subject of a comprehensive study.[5] Thought to be one of the 'most interesting and valuable' of Irish Lives, the Salamancan version forms part of the so-called O'Donohue group whose texts are considered by some scholars to date to as early as the eighth century.[6] As with many of these Lives, there are aspects of Munna's biography that point to a considerably later date, not earlier than the middle of the twelfth century. An immediate sign of lateness is the manner in which the saint is assigned to a lineage of substance, the Ceinéal Conaill branch of the Uí Néill, rather than to the obscure family of 'Moccu Moie' which represents the earliest statement of his descent.[7]

Despite the impression given by Adhamhnán that the saint never met Colum Cille during the latter's lifetime, Munna's biographer twice brings Colum into contact with the young saint, first at his home place, then at a school in Kilmore (Ceall Mhór Dhíthribh) in the Cavan barony of Upper Loughtee, before bringing him to Iona.[8] In the meantime, Munna had attended school under a priest named Greallán (presumably of Creeve), had been discovered by Comhghall of Bangor, whose rule he went on to learn, and had studied over a long period at Devenish with the 'wisest' man in the whole of Ireland and Britain, unnamed in the Salamancan Codex but called Sineall in other versions.[9] The saint's first settlements in Ireland were in the Midlands, at such places as Tihelly (Teach Teille) in the parish of Durrow, which he is said to have relinquished after five years to Ciar of Kilkeary.[10] While there, he is said to have performed a miracle at Ceall Bhigsighe, now Kilbixy in the Westmeath barony of Moygoish. Moving to south Leinster, Munna eventually founded his church at Taghmon after several encounters with other saints – one of whom was Comhghall of Bangor – and the remainder of the text deals mainly with Munna's interaction with local Fothairt kings.[11]

Further encounters with other saints become rare until towards the end of the Life when much attention is paid to an assembly relating to the Easter controversy held in Magh Ailbhe – a plain in the area straddling south Kildare and north Carlow – that involved Molaise of Leighlin as spokesman of the new, so-called Roman, system and Munna as advocate of the old order, the outcome being an agreement to differ.[12] An account of Munna's stay in *terra repromissionis*, 'land of promise', in the company of Colum Cille, Cainneach, and Bréanainn, includes instructions to a British anchorite on how to get there by navigating from Slieve League in Donegal in a cow-skin boat.[13] The choice of Munna's companions in this instance, each of them patron of a church that was to become the seat of a priory of canons regular of St Augustine, is one of several indications that the Life is unlikely to have been written earlier than about the middle of the twelfth century, when houses of this order had begun to be founded countrywide. The saint's visits to Devenish and Kilbixy (alias Tristernagh), likewise the locations of Augustinian priories, can be taken as yet another indication of lateness, as can his meetings with Comhghall and Molaise, both of whom were patrons of churches later associated with the canons regular.[14]

In keeping with the reputation gained through Adhamhnán's Life of Colum Cille of being an appropriate recipient of news of holy death, Munna is said to have been among the first to hear of the demise of Molua of Kyle, only to be afflicted seven days later with leprosy; Mochua of Timahoe is said to have cured him of this after seven years.[15] The influence of Adhamhnán's work is again discernible in the manner in which Cainneach's Life states that it was the saint's father (Tulchán) who brought him, though still a small child, to Iona, only to be held up as an example of how love of God was to take precedence over the love of one's own child.[16] Lives of other Leinster saints also find room for Munna: Maodhóg's Life twice mentions the saint; Abán's Life asserts that he and Munna joined in a *fraternitas*; Caoimhghin's Life reports the arrival of messengers from Munna, with news of a conversation of demons; Molaise of Leighlin's Life presents its subject as Munna's pupil.[18] To judge by a satirical quatrain on Munna, variously attributed to Colum Cille and Maodhóg, his church may not always have seen eye to eye with those of the other saints.[19]

Described as a *sagart*, 'priest', Munna – who is also provided with an otherwise unattested sister named Díghe – is probably the same as Cruimhthear Munna of a place named Ros Achaidh Liag, now perhaps a church site in the townland of Ardenagh and parish of Taghmon.[20] Fiontan Maoldubh, whose feast fell a day before that of Munna, and Fiontan son of Gaibhrín, to whose church of Clonenagh the saint is assigned by the later martyrologies, probably represented the same original cult. Under the guise of Fiontan, the saint was patron of Street in the Westmeath barony of Moygoish, and perhaps also of Shanbogh in the Kilkenny barony of Ida, where a pattern used to be held on the second Sunday of October.[21] He was thought to be similar in manners to the prophet Job.[22] Said to have died in 635, Munna was commemorated, with over two hundred of his community, on 21 October.[23] A pattern was also held on this day at Tacumshin in the Wexford barony of Forth, where the parish church was named after the saint, as was also a church in the parish of Carn in the same barony.[24] The saint was venerated widely in Scotland, and some lessons are devoted to him in the Breviary of Aberdeen.[25] Finally, Munna was among the saints invoked as a guarantor of the Law of Adhamhnán.[26]

1 *CGSH* §§116 (3), 155; *GRSH* 42; *Lgen.* 720.4; *VSHH* 198 §1; *MartT* 122; OCBG §831; *DIB* iii, 799–800. **2** *PNW* 151–4. **3** Ibid.; *CGSH* §722.37; *Lgen.* 177.6. **4** *VC*[1] 206–14 (I 2). **5** *VSHH* 198–209, 247–56; *VSHP* i, lxxxiv–lxxxvi; ibid. ii, 226–39; *MISL* 394. **6** *Kenney* 450; *MISL* 297–339. **7** *VSHH* 198 §1; *VSHP* ii, 226 §1; *VC*[1] 212 (I 2). **8** *VSHH* 198–200 §§2, 5–7; *VSHP* ii, 226–9 §§2, 5–7. **9** *VSHH* 198–9 §§3–4, 6; *VSHP* ii, 226–8 §§3–4, 6. **10** *VSHH* 200–1 §§11–13; *VSHP* ii, 229–31 §§9–12. **11** *VSHH* 201–3 §§14–20; *VSHP* ii, 231–3 §§13–18. **12** *VSHH* 207 §§29–30; *VSHP* ii, 236–7 §§36–7. **13** *VSHH* 207–8 §31; *VSHP* ii, 237–8 §28; *TEAB* 640 §251. **14** *MRHI* 146–200. **15** *VSHH* 145 §69, 206–7 §29; *VSHP* ii, 185–6 §§5–6, 224–5 §53, 235–6 §25. **16** *VSHH* 188 §26; *VSHP* i, 159–60 §21. **17** *VSHH* 240 §25, 246 §48, 270 §31, 341 §4; *VSHP* i, 25 §37, 244–5 §21, ii, 152 §29, 160 §52. **18** *VSHH* 341 §4. **19** *Anecd.* iv, 74 §878; 226. **20** *CGSH* §§155, 175, 705.21; *HDGP* i, 20; *HADO* iv, 194. **21** *PNW* 40. **22** *CGSH* §712.21. **23** *MartT* 82, 120–2; *MartO*[2] 217; *MartG* 200; *MartD* 280; *IrL* 62; OSL WX ii, 51–2; *AU s.a.* **24** *CECW* 214; *CH* 2, 25–6; *CPCR* i, 402; *The Past* 2, 21, 60; ibid. 26, 44. **25** *CPNS* 307; *KSS* 415–16; *ACDS* 71–2; *BrevA* pars aest. 131v–132; *LegSS* 248–50, 400–1. **26** *CA* §22.

Mura of Fahan (Othain Mhór), barony of Inishowen West, Co. Donegal. Allegedly first known as Díoma, and bearing the alias Gnia, Mura son of Fearadhach is attached by the genealogists variously to the Ceinéal Eoghain and Dál bhFiatach of east Ulster.[1] The Ulster connection is maintained through his mother, Deirinnill Cheathairchíochach, 'four-papped', who is said to have given birth to five saints, of whom three others – Cilléan of Achadh Caol, Mochuma of Drumbo, and Domhanghart of Slieve Donard – were associated with churches in the Down area.[2] Mura's main claim to attention was the affiliation of his church at Fahan – a place of some importance, mentioned several times in the pre-Conquest annals – to the *paruchia* of Colum Cille, an account of whom he is said to have written in metrical form.[3] A visit to his church by Aodh Uairiodhnach (†611), who allegedly showed extraordinary deference by drinking water from a stream used by Mura as a privy, led to a prophecy that Aodh would become king of Ireland.[4] According to one version of the celebrated satire, *Aisling Mhic Con*

Ghlinne (the vision of Mac Conglinne), the itinerant 'hero', a member of Mura's community at Fahan, was visited in his sleep by the saint who, having recounted to him a vision, instructed him both to memorize it and to retell it to Cathal son of Finghuine, king of Munster.[5] Mura appears also to have been known as Muirdhealach within the diocese of Derry (which included Inishowen), and this may mean that he was ultimately identical with Muirdheabhair son of Cuanán.[6] A diminutive form of his name may be preserved in the dedication of Ceall Mhuragáin (from Muragán), now perhaps the townland of Killymorgan in the Tyrone parish of Errigal Keerogue.[7] The O'Hogans (Uí Ógáin) of Tullaghoge (Tulach Óg) in the Tyrone parish of Desertcreat appear also to have held Mura in high regard, and, according to an 1609 inquisition, which gives his name as 'Marogh', the church at Stuaghan in the neighbouring parish of Tullyniskan was also dedicated to him.[8] The bell and staff of the saint, supposedly left to the 'Foreigners' after a battle at Downpatrick, now form part respectively of the Wallace Collection in London and the collection of the National Museum in Dublin, although some doubt has recently been cast on the attribution of the staff to Mura.[9] John Colgan, who claimed to have seen a copy of the saint's *acta*, now lost, spoke highly of Mura's staff or crozier, by which the O'Neills were wont to swear.[10] The saint's feastday fell on 12 March.[11]

1 *CGSH* §§20, 557, 703.6; *GRSH* 47; *Lgen.* 701.8; *Peritia* 20, 331–2; *DIB* vi, 779. **2** *CGSH* §§162, 722.27. **3** *AU s.a.* 725, 774, 1074, 1098, 1101; *BCC* 36–42, 168 §§50–4, 159; *VC*[1] vii, lxviii. **4** *FAI* 4–6. **5** *AMC* 114–16. **6** *Celtica* 1, 83. **7** *HDGP* iv, 32. **8** *AFM s.a.* 1024; *SAM* 6, 7–8, 10; *Cal.PR* Jas. I, 376: inq. Ult. app. II (Tyrone). **9** *MIA s.a.* 1178; *MartD* xxxi; *JRSAI* 52, 4–5. **10** *ASH* 587; *Seanchas* 415 §241; *UJA* 1, 271–3; *DLHS* 109, 113–16. **11** *MartG* 52; *MartD* 74; *DOH* 90–1.

Murchú. *See* Muirchú.

Murgalla. *See* Muirdheabhair.

N ɞ

Nadál. *See* Náile; Seanán of Scattery.

Nadán. *See* Náile.

Nadh Caoimhe of Terryglass. *See* Mochaoimhe of Terryglass.

Nadh Fraoich. The list of those subject to Brighid of Kildare included her charioteer, a priest named Nadh Fraoich, who is said to have dwelt at a church called Ceall Chúile Dumha, now perhaps Coole in the Laois parish of Offerlane.[1] Nadh Fraoich became a priest when Patrick enjoined upon Brighid, reputedly at an assembly held at Teltown (Tailte) in Meath, that neither she nor her successors should ever be without an ordained person in her company.[2] Nadh Fraoich is said to have been a learned man (*fear léighinn*) who occasionally preached the word of God – mainly to Brighid, after she had taken a vow never to eat without first hearing a sermon.[3] The learned charioteer is said to have belonged to the Fir Thuirbhe whose name may be preserved in the townland of Turvey, now spread between the adjacent parishes of Lusk and Donabate in north Dublin.[4] Sometimes also given the rank of bishop, Nadh Fraoich was remembered on 11 December.[5]

1 *CGSH* §670.74; *LSHS* 36–7; *HDGP* iii, 154. 2 *LisL* 1460–5. 3 *LH* i, 120–1; *MartD* 330. 4 *MartD* 330. 5 *MartG* 236; *MartD* 330; *CGSH* §704.64.

Náile of Kinawley (Ceall Náile), barony of Clanawley, Co. Fermanagh, of Killenaule (Ceall Danáil / Danáile), barony of Slievardagh, Co. Tipperary, and of Inver Glebe (Inbhear Náile), parish of Inver, barony of Banagh, Co. Donegal.[1] The saint's pedigree took cognisance of his supposed southern background, attaching him to the main line of the Eoghanacht of Cashel, and providing him through his celebrated father, Aonghas son of Nadh Fraoich, king of Munster, with such saintly brothers as Colmán son of Daráine, Faolán Amhlobhar, and Lughaidh of Dromiskin.[2] His uterine brother, Eachaidh son of Aonghas, was regarded as ancestor of the Eoghanacht of Oirthear Cliach who controlled the area about Emly, historically Munster's chief church.[3]

The saint's northern connections led to the composition of a Life written in the vernacular and preserved in an early seventeenth-century copy made in the Franciscan friary at Drowes from a manuscript apparently then kept in the Donegal barony of Banagh.[4] Accurately described as 'very late' and 'very poor', and containing a mixture of prose and verse typical of the vernacular Lives composed – possibly as late as the early to mid-sixteenth century – for patrons of south-west Ulster churches, Náile's Life focuses to a large degree on the taxes and tributes due to the saint and, through him, to his church.[5] Beginning with a statement of Náile's southern origins, including a prophecy allegedly made by Patrick to the saint's father at Cashel, the Life quickly brings him, on the instructions of an angel, to Colum Cille at Inver Glebe, where he is said to have founded a church.[6] His alleged succession to Molaise at Devenish – where, it has been suggested, the Life may have been written – is followed by an account of how the saint displaced Dothearnóg (Earnán) – later known as Rabharnóg – at the site that was to be named after him at Kinawley (Ceall Náile); at this point Náile forecast that his church would rival those of Bricín (Tomregan) and Maodhóg (Drumlane) among the chief churches of Bréifne, a name that was often used to refer to the diocese of Kilmore.[7]

The biographer's main focus was on the churches of Lough Erne and their saints, including Molaise, Sineall of Cleenish, and Seanach of Derrybrusk, and above all, on the various local branches of the Méguidhir (Maguire) family, whose ancestor Lughán (Luan) is shown seeking and receiving baptism from Náile.[8] There follows an account of how a piece of metal cast by Seanach into the jaws of a sea-monster molesting Colum Cille – and later recovered – was used to fashion a bell that first belonged to Tighearnach of Clones, another of the chief saints of Bréifne, then to Molaise of Devenish, and finally to Náile, who is said to have used it to great effect, mainly in the course of tax-gathering for his church.[9]

The remainder of the text is given over to a listing, in a metrical form reminiscent of the equally late Life of Caillín of Fenagh, of the various taxes due to the saint, especially from the Maguires, as well as the punishments to be meted out to those foolhardy enough to ignore or 'break' the saint's *cáin*, 'tribute-law'.[10] Some of those, including Maol Dúin, ancestor of the Síol Maoile Dúin, and Murchadh, brother of Lughán, are cursed together with their descendants. The Life, which has yet to be explored thoroughly for the influences at work on its author, ends abruptly, with no account of the saint's death.

The text was one of the sources used in the vernacular Life composed for Colum Cille by Maghnas Ó Domhnaill in 1532, which finds room both for Colum's encounter with Náile at Inver Glebe and for the dispatch by Seanach of the sea monster.[11] When John O'Donovan visited Kinawley in 1834, he noted that the saint's bell was still in the custody of its local keepers, and that Náile had been preceded in the place by Rabharnóg, apparently the local form of Dothearnóg (Earnán).[12] Although Náile's feast fell on 27 January, his well at Kinawley and the hill above it were also the scene of a *Lughnasadh* celebration on the last Sunday of July, known locally as 'Donagh Sunday'.[13] This may be because of his ultimate identity with the saint named Nadál (Natalis) of the Kilkenny church of Kilmanagh (Ceall na Manach) whose feast fell on 31 July.[14] Credited by Giraldus Cambrensis with having transmuted an Ossory couple into wolves, and remembered locally as Nadán, Nadál was chosen to act as one of the early mentors of Seanán of Scattery.[15]

1 *CLTÁ* 194–7; *MHH* 102–3 §§7, 11; 105 §16, 109 §26. **2** *CGSH* §§646, 662.220; *GRSH* 116–18; *Lgen.* 740.3. **3** *MHH* 100 §1; *IKHK* 293. **4** *MHH* 97–155; ibid. 125 §64; *ILL* 365; *Breifne* 11, 547. **5** *Kenney* 466. **6** *MHH* 100–3 §§1–11; OSL FH 84. **7** *MHH* 105–9 §§16–28; *ClRec.* 13, 88. **8** *MHH* 110–14 §§29–40; *MGF* 23 §1. **9** Ibid. 110–18 §§41–7; *EMH* 473–4 §187. **10** Ibid. 115–24 §§44–63. **11** *BCC* 142–4 §141, 344 §321. **12** OSL FH 83–4; *FL* 118. **13** *MartT* 12; *MartG* 24; *MartD* 28. **14** *FL* 118; *MartG* 146; *MartO*[2] 172; *MartD* 206; *CPL* 15, §256; cf. *IrL* 60. **15** *THEH* 101–2; *CMCS* 44–48–51; *HADO* iii, 427–30; *VSHH* 309–10 §§9–10; *LisL* 1959–67.

Nainnidh. *See* Ninnidh.

Nainnín son of Dubhthach. *See* Lonán son of Dubhthach.

Náire daughter of Brónach. *See* Fachtna of Ros Mic Earca.

Naomhuidhe. *See* Inghean Bhaoith.

Natalis. *See* Náile.

Nathanus/Nathalanus. *See* Neachtan of Dungiven.

Nathí of Achonry (Achadh Conaire), barony of Leyny, Co. Sligo. In keeping with the location of his church, Nathí son of Conamhail (alias Caomhlugh) was attached by the genealogists to the Luighne who gave name to Leyny.[1] Although patron of a diocese, albeit a relatively small one, he was never made the subject of a written Life, but he and his church were important enough to be featured in the Lives of some other saints. The story of Achonry's founding is told in the Life of Finnian, whose own church at Clonard seems to have had property interests in the area.[2] Instructed by an angel to found a church at a place deemed *amoenus* (Irish *caoin*), whence the alternative name of Achadh Caoin, 'pleasant field', Finnian duly did so, receiving the land from a repentant king, and leaving in charge the priest named Nathí.[3]

Another saint with connections both in Meath and locally in Leyny, Féichín of Fore and Ballysadare, is said to have been the beneficiary of land from a guilt-laden king while studying with Nathí at Achonry, which he generously handed over to his teacher.[4] Nathí reciprocated by predicting that Féichín's resurrection would take place at Fore. It is perhaps worth noting that in both cases Nathí was dealing with patrons of churches that became sites of Augustinian priories, at Ballysadare and Clonard.[5] Nathí and Féichín are again brought together in the tract known as 'Four Saints', which attributes to Cormac son of Eoghan a prophecy of both of their births, made in the presence of Nathí's father (or grandfather) Conamhail.[6]

A short tale in the Book of Lismore comments on how Nathí treated guests who arrived after mealtime, in this case Comhghall, Colum Cille and Cainneach, by keeping them without food until the early morning (normally fasting time) and then assessing their reactions.[7] The feastday of Nathí, the 'pious presbyter' (*cruimhthear*), now locally known as Nathy, was celebrated at Achonry on 9 August, otherwise the octave of the feast (1 August) of his namesake and probable double, Nathí of Taney.[8]

1 *CGSH* § 148; *GRSH* 124; cf. *Lgen.* 739.6. **2** *VSHH* 104 §28; *LisL* 2705–13. **3** *HDGP* i, 14. **4** *RC* 12, 324 §8; cf. *VSHP* ii, 77 §§4–5. **5** *MRHI* 160, 163. **6** *IrT* iii, 4–5 §11. **7** *IrT* i, 42–3. **8** *MartT* 59, 61; *MartO*[2] 175; *MartG* 148, 152; *MartD* 208, 214.

Nathí of Taney (Teach Nathí), formerly Sacoyle (Cúil Fhoithirbhe/Shachaille), baronies of Dublin/Rathdown, Co. Dublin.[1] This son of Seanach is known almost exclusively from the genealogies which attach him to the Dál Meisin Corb of the Glendalough area, and the martyrologies which accord him a feast of 1 August, eight days ahead of that of his namesake and probable double, Nathí of Achonry.[2] The bishop named Nathí associated with the Wicklow church of Delgany (Sruthair Ghuaire), who is said to have been responsible for the conferring of orders on Brighid's priests and nuns, was probably also ultimately identical with the patron of Taney.[3] *Tobernea* (Nathí's well) is still pointed out in Taney, and the saint's church was in the townland of Dundrum.[4]

1 *CPPI* 181; *StH* 15, 13; *DIB* vi, 863–4. **2** *CGSH* §§181.8, 254; *GRSH* 91; *Lgen.* 726.2; *MartT* 59, 61; *MartO*² 175; *MartG* 148, 152; *MartD* 208, 214; *Rep. Nov.* 1, 33–5. **3** *CGSH* §670.86. **4** *AH* 8, 28–9; *AbEMLS* 171–86.

NATHY. *See* Nathí.

NAOMHAIDHE sister of Seanán. *See* Inghean Bhaoith.

NEACHTAN of Dungiven (Dún Geimhin), barony of Keenaght, Co. Derry. An entry in the annals for 679 records the death of Neachtan, accompanied by the soubriquet *Neir*.[1] The same soubriquet is found in the (unfortunately lacunose) list of commemorations for 8 January in the Martyrology of Tallaght and also in some copies of the corresponding list in the Martyrology of Aonghas; in other copies, it is written *nár* (riming with *án*), taken by the editor to mean 'noble'.[2] In Aonghas' text, Neachtan is said to have come from *Alba* which, at this stage, could have meant either Britain as a whole or Scotland.[3] The later martyrologies, while omitting the saint's soubriquet, locate Neachtan in Dungiven, where, unless his namesake at Fennor is intended, he may have served as a mentor of Cianán of Duleek.[4] Although no memory of the saint has survived in the Dungiven area, there are several Scottish dedications, especially around the river Dee, and a Life, preserved in the Breviary of Aberdeen, was composed for the saint under the guise of Nathalanus.[5] This places his birth at Tullich in the diocese of Aberdeen, where there was a later dedication to the saint.[6]

1 *AU s.a.*; *ESSH* i, 185. **2** *MartT* 6; *MartO*² 34. **3** *MartO*² 34; cf. *ÉtC* 32, 175–87. **4** *MartG* 12; *MartO*² 42; *MartD* 10; *AB* 73, 365 (Nathanus); *LegSS* 20–3, 401–2. **5** *KSS* 417–19; *CPNS* 308, 329–31; *BrevA*. pars hiem. 25v–26v; cf. *SBDeer* 368–72. **6** Ibid.; *KSS* 419.

NEACHTAN of Fennor (Fionnabhair Abha), barony of Lower Duleek, Co. Meath. Bearing a name which has been taken to mean 'descendant of the waters', and which corresponds to that of *Neptunus*, the Roman god of the sea, Neachtan may have originated as a water- or river-deity, associated in particular with the river Boyne.[1] In the Ulster Cycle, Cú Chulainn is said to have made his inaugural foray to the borders of Ulster, where he found and killed the sons of Neachtan Scéine, custodians, it appears, of the source of the Boyne, which is overlooked by the *síodh* of Neachtan.[2] It is scarcely a coincidence, therefore, that Neachtan should have been regarded as patron of Fennor on the banks of the Boyne.[3] This was near Slane, whose patron, Earc Sláine, may have been a christianized version of the divinity Ealcmhar (otherwise also called Neachtan), lord of Newgrange.[4]

In Christian times, Neachtan came to be regarded as a disciple and nephew of no less a saint than the patron of Armagh, and was thus also known as Mac Liamhna – son of Liamhain, Patrick's sister – patron not only of Fennor, but also of Ceall Uinche in Conaille, a much discussed, but as yet unidentified, site in north Louth.[5] Patrick's other sister Lubaid, wife of the Lombard Restitutus, is sometimes substituted for Liamhain, and Neachtan's connections with Patrick may have led to his nomination, under the guise of Nathanus, as teacher of Cianán of Duleek.[6] Neachtan's cult may have wandered as far south as the parish of Kilnaughtin, at the side of the Shannon estuary in north Kerry but, when visited by John O'Donovan in 1841, nothing could be gathered concerning this saint.[7] Neachtan's feastday fell on 2 May, appropriately enough the day after the great pre-Christian feast of Bealtaine.[8] Ten days earlier, on 22 April, the saint was also commemorated.[9]

1 *EIHM* 368; *GPN* 144. **2** *TBC* 608–757; RD §19. **3** *MartG* 88; *MartO*[2] 128; *MartD* 118. **4** *EIHM* 516. **5** *CGSH* §722.1.75; *VT* 414, 432; *JCLAS* 1–2; *HDGP* iv, 62. **6** *CGSH* §§664, 722.15; cf. *Lgen.* 751.23; *AB* 73, 365. **7** *ACoK* 13. **8** *MartT* 38; *MartO*[2] 122; *MartG* 88; *MartD* 118. **9** *MartT* 35; *MartG* 82; *MartD* 108.

Neamh of Drumtullagh, barony of Cary, Co. Antrim, which may now represent an earlier Tulach Cheinéil Aonghasa. According to the Tripartite Life, Patrick placed a large number of bishops in churches founded by him in Dál Riada, including Neamh at Tulach which, if correctly identified, adjoins Ramoan (Ráith Mhuadháin), another of the churches mentioned in the Life.[1] A genealogical tract relating to Dál nAraidhe attaches the saint to an obscure family called Uí Bhrunnchon.[2] The same tract establishes for him family connections with Colmán of Kilroot, Colmán of Dromore, and Cas Cobha, probably of Bangor. Neamh died, according to the Annals of Tighearnach, in 540.[3]

1 *BP* 1895–6; *VT* 162; *EA* 251; pace *TT* 182 §199; PNNI vii, 211–13. **2** *BB* 168d1–5. **3** *ATig. s.a.*

Neamh of Maca Birn. *See* Pupa.

Neamhan. Assigned to an unidentified church named Ceall Bhia, Neamhan is known from two sources, the catalogue of saints said to have been subject to Brighid of Kildare, and the list of those commemorated, according to the Martyrology of Donegal, on 1 September.[2] His companion Bia gave name to the church.

1 *CGSH* §670.40; *Lgen.* 753.11. **2** *MartD* 232.

Neamhán. An entry in the martyrologies for 8 March commemorates a bishop named Neamhán at a place called Dairinis.[1] There were several places so named, but John Colgan speculatively located this one in south Leinster, presumably in reference to Dairinis Chaomháin, now Ardcavan, near Wexford town.[2] The same authority considered Neamhán (alias Naomhán) to be identical with the companion who went with Féichín of Fore to request of the joint kings of Tara, Blathmac and Diarmuid, that they release a prisoner named Aodh.[3]

1 *MartT* 21; *MartG* 50; *MartD* 70. **2** *ASH* 568. **3** Ibid.

Neamhainn, na seacht, 'the seven'. *See* Athchaoin.

Neamhnad of Cluain Mór Lughnadh, now possibly Clonmore in parish of Kildalkey, barony of Lune, Co. Meath. Neamhnad is known only from the list of those said to have been subject to Brighid of Kildare.[1] She may have been absorbed into the cult of Damhnad of Tedavnet, the present patron of the parish of Kildalkey.[2] The latter's normal feast was 13 June, but at Kildalkey, and also in Gheel in Belgium where she was taken to be identical with Dympna, she was remembered on 15 May.[3]

1 *CGSH* §670.49; *Lgen.* 753.20. 2 OSL MH 174; OSL LS i, 109. 3 OSL MH 174; *BiblSS* iv, 618–20.

Neamhnad Chiarraigheach, 'of Kerry'. *See* Moling.

Neannán. *See* Iobhar.

Neas daughter of Cochmhadh (Comhchadh). The tract on the mothers of the saints states that Neas (alias Cneas) of Dál gCeithirn, a segment of the Ulaidh of north-east Ulster, was the name of the mother of Bishop Mac Nise of Connor , and some annal notices of Mac Nise's death agree with this.[1] Another entry in the same tract provides a certain Fraochán of Druim Gamhna, now perhaps Drumgownagh in the Leitrim parish of Cloone, with a mother named Cuimhne (alias Cneas) daughter of Cochmhadh who must be the same person.[2] The office-style Life preserved for Mac Nise (son of Neas) names his mother simply as Neas.[3]

1 *CGSH* §722.58; ATig. p. 86. 2 *CGSH* §722.78. 3 *VSHH* 404.

Neas of Seanchua. *See* Eiltín of Seanchua.

Neas Urnaightheach, 'prayerful', daughter of Éanna. This saint was one of four saintly siblings attached to the Oirthir (Orior) branch of the Oirghialla, the others being Curcach, Caoireach Dheargáin and Dúthracht.[1] Neas Urnaightheach is invoked in an early litany.[2] A seventeenth-century source speculatively identified this saint with Neas of an unidentified church named Earnaidhe, who was remembered on 4 September.[3]

1 *CGSH* §110; *GRSH* 72; *Lgen.* 714.12. 2 *MartT* 108; *IrL* 92. 3 *GRSH* 72; cf. *IrL* 256.

Neasán of Cork. *See* Neasán of Mungret.

Neasán of Mungret (Mungairit), barony of Pubblebrien, Co. Limerick. The New Testament meaning of deacon, 'bishop's assistant', is especially appropriate in Neasán's case, in view of the failure of the saint's church of Mungret, historically the chief church of the area now covered by the diocese of Limerick, to attain cathedral status at the beginning of the twelfth century. Although abbots of Mungret continue to be recorded in the annals up to the end of the eleventh century, little is known of the church's affairs from then on. Furthermore, despite James Ussher, who maintained that he was quoting from a *Vita Nessani*, neither the saint's Life nor even his pedigree has survived.[1] Yet, Neasán frequently found mention in the records of other churches. One of the earliest and most notable mentions is in the ninth-century Tripartite Life of Patrick, where, following a favour rendered to him by Neasán, then still a child, the primatial saint is said to have foretold the greatness of the young boy's people, before baptizing him and founding for him his church of Mungret.[2] Although this was a piece of Armagh propaganda, it nonetheless underlines the importance of Mungret at that time. The late twelfth-century biographer of Ailbhe of Emly – historically Munster's chief church – assigned to Neasán the appropriately subservient role of visitor to his patron's church in quest of counsel on a moral issue, and the biographer of Colum of Terryglass gave his subject the privilege of acting as intermediary between Neasán and God.[3]

Neasán was among the saints who shared Patrick's day of 17 March, ostensibly in his guise as a Cork saint.[4] There are several pointers to the ultimate identity of the two bearers of the name, one of Mungret, the other of Cork, where a church was named after him.[5] The Limerick saint's main feastday of 25 July was shared by Fionnbharr, a coincidence used by the author of the shorter version of the vision of Mac Conglinne to set the scene for the arrival of his resourceful scholar-hero in Cork 'on the feast of Bairre and Neasán'.[6] Two early ninth-century litanies likewise invoked the two saints, one immediately after the other, and they are brought together, as teacher and pupil, in the school said to have been founded by Fionnbharr at Gougane Barra.[7] There are grounds for believing that the Mungret and Cork versions of the cult originated, like that of Fionnbharr, in Ulster – whence the appellation *Uladh*, 'of the Ulstermen', sometimes attached to Neasán – before travelling together to Munster.[8] An Ulster background would also suit Neasán's name which corresponds to that borne by the mother of Conchubhar son of Neas, legendary king of Eamhain Mhacha.

Devotion to the saint in Mungret led to his inclusion among the progeny of Inghean Bhaoith, and to his close association with Seanán of Scattery, who is said to have addressed a poem to Neasán and to have invoked his assistance 'over the brine', together with that of many others.[9] Under the guise of Moneasóg, the saint is said to have shared with Fíonán Cam the duty of protecting the Corca Dhuibhne of west and south Kerry.[10] Similarly, according to a poem in Classical Irish, Neasán, again together with Fíonán and numerous other saints, was called upon to help in releasing Ireland's southern half (Leath Mogha) from a bondage imposed on it by the northern half (Leath Chuinn), represented by Finnian of Clonard.[11] His name was also among the mostly Limerick and south Clare saints named in a litany written at Regensburg in the third quarter of the twelfth century.[12] Another list, this time of saints 'sleeping in union', although miscellaneous in its choice, includes his name.[13] Thought to be similar in manners to his fellow-deacon, Laurence the martyr, and remembered as a man who never uttered a falsehood, the saint was commemorated, as already remarked, on 25 July.[14] According to some annals, Neasán died in 556/7.[15]

1 *WWRJU* vi, 531; *SATM* 26–34; *SACCL* 367–8; *DIB* vi, 881. **2** *BP* 2379–406; *VT* 202–4. **3** *VSHH* 129–30 §50; *ibid.* 230–1 §24; *VSHP* i, 61–2 §42. **4** *MartT* 16; *MartG* 56; *MartD* (see *ASH* 630 §5); *CGSH* §705.13. **5** CorkD 87. **6** *MartT* 58; *MartG* 142; *MartD* 202; *AMC* 114. **7** *IrL* 54–5; *WWRJU* i, 14; *BBh.* 66 §21, 248. **8** *MartO*[2] 249; *MakS* 30–1. **9** *IrT* iv, 87, 94 §9; *ZCP* 10, 26 §19. **10** *ZCP* 8, 315. **11** RIA MS 23L11, 263; *SAM* 24.1, 17, 21. **12** UCC MS U.331; *CKV* 60. **13** *CGSH* §731.2. **14** Ibid. §712.26; *ZCP* 1, 64. **15** *AI, ATig. s.a.*; *AFM s.a.* 551.

NEASLUGHA/NEISE son of Neasán. *See* Beoán of Feighcullen.

NEIMHEADH. This saint was remembered as one of three maidens, the others being Caolainn and Deirbhileadh who, according to a poem of prophecies, never took offence and accepted no goods in compensation for outrage, rare attributes among Irish saints.[1] She may have been patron of the unidentified church named Ceall Neimheadha in Magh Aoi, now the plain of Roscommon, where a synod attended by Brighid of Kildare is reputed to have taken place.[2]

1 *Ériu* 18, 66 §42. 2 *IrT* iii, 4 §9.

Nessan. *See* Neasán.

Nia son of Coll. This man is known only from the metrical list of those in orders with Patrick, which describes him as the saint's foster-brother.[1]

1 *CGSH* §672.27.

Niall son of Tricheamh. *See* Díocha of Saul.

Ninnidh Láimhdhearg, 'of the red hand', of Inishmacsaint (Inis Samh / Maighe Samh) on Lough Erne, barony of Magheraboy, Co. Fermanagh. Bearer of the alternative cognomen *saobhroisc*, 'of the crooked eye', and often confused with his namesake and probable double, Ninnidh Láimhiodhan, the saint could lay claim not only to the exalted status of bishop, but also to inclusion among the 'twelve apostles' of Ireland.[1] Descended through his father Fearghas from the Ceinéal Éanna branch of Ceinéal Conaill of Donegal, he became patron of Inishmacsaint, where a bell thought to be his was preserved.[2] While studying with Finnian of Clonard, Ninnidh is said to have received a copy of Matthew's gospel from his fellow-pupil, Ciarán of Clonmacnoise, before the latter had time to finish reading it, whence the saying in Rome: *Non legam Marcum quo usque compleveram Mattheum*, 'I shall not read Mark until I'll have finished reading Matthew'.[3] Ciarán is also reputed to have spent some time with Ninnidh on Inishmacsaint before leaving to visit Éanna of Inishmore.[4] Little else is known of the saint, but he was remembered at Inishmacsaint either on 16 or 18 January.[5]

1 *LisL* 4142; *MartD* 20; *CGSH* §§23, 402; *VSHH* 83, 101. 2 *CGSH* §23; *GRSH* 58; *Lgen*. 708.2; OSL FH 53, 66; *EMH* 400–1 §93. 3 *LisL* 4142–60. 4 *VSHP* i, 207n. 5 *MartT* 9; *MartO*[2] 46; *MartG* 16; *MartD* 20; *CPL* 15, §495.

Ninnidh Láimhiodhan, 'of the pure hand', of Kiltoom (Ceall Tóma / Tuama), parish of Faughalstown, barony of Fore, Co. Westmeath. Travelling in Westmeath in 1837, John O'Donovan reported that there was neither well nor stone nor other monument at Kiltoom to mark the memory of Ninnidh, formerly patron of the church, but now displaced by Diarmuid son of Lughna.[1] Yet Ninnidh, whose pedigree attaches him through his father Eachaidh to the Ceinéal Laoghaire of Meath, had reason to be remembered.[2] Colum Cille himself is reputed to have heard out of the mouth of a 'certain man' in the graveyard of Kiltoom that its saint was Ninnidh of the Ceinéal Laoghaire, who gave communion to Brighid of Kildare and, according to one tradition, composed in her praise the hymn beginning *Christus in nostra insola*, 'Christ in our island', usually attributed to Ultán of Ardbraccan.[3] Four brothers, comprising Fiontan and Colum of Slanore, Lughaidh of Teernacreeve, and Muireadhach of Killala, and one sister named Cearc, are attributed to Ninnidh, and of these, Muireadhach and he were uterine brothers, born of Líoghach of Breaghmhaine, now Brawny barony in Westmeath.[4] Ninnidh is often confused with his namesake and probable double, Ninnidh Láimhdhearg, especially with regard to his feastday, and he is sometimes provided with two conflicting lines of descent within Ceinéal Laoghaire.[5] His feast appears to have fallen on 13 November.[6]

1 *PNW* 53. 2 *CGSH* §22; *GRSH* 52; *Lgen.* 705.3. 3 *MartO*[2] 46–8; *ZCP* 9, 174 §27; *LH* i, 14; *LisL* 1759–63. 4 *CGSH* §§22, 160.1.2, 722.32; *HDGP* ii, 180. 5 *MartO*[2] 46–8; *MartD* 20, 308; *GRSH* 52. 6 *MartG* 218; *MartD* 308.

Noone. *See* Nuadha.

Nuadha of Armagh (Ard Mhacha) and of Estersnow (Díseart Nuadhad) in the barony of Boyle, Co. Roscommon. While head of the church of Armagh, Nuadha (anglicized Noone) son of Feabhal undertook a journey to Connacht 'with Patrick's Law' in 810. In so doing, he was returning to his native district of Loch Uamha in the heart of Connacht. Despite Colgan, who placed Loch Uamha in Bréifne Uí Ruairc, and thus misled O'Donovan into identifying it as 'Loughnahoo' in Leitrim, Nuadha's native church was at Estersnow (from Díseart Nuadhad, 'Nuadha's hermitage').[2] The naming of the church after him indicates that this was a new foundation, which in turn implies that Nuadha was associated with the *céili Dé* reformers of his time in office.[3] His assumption of the abbacy of Armagh finds mention in Patrick's Tripartite Life. Having brought his subject to the district of Magh Luirg, now the plain of Boyle, the writer of the Life imputed to Patrick the assertion that 'a great part of that country' would belong to him afterwards 'as has been fulfilled in Nuadha of Estersnow (Loch Uamha)'.[4] A poem allegedly composed by Comán of Roscommon states that were it not for Nuadha son of Feabhal, abbot of Armagh, the succession to the abbacy of Roscommon would always have been the prerogative of the Soghain.[5] Nuadha died in 812 and he was remembered on 19 February, and perhaps also on 3 October, albeit under the guise of Nuadha 'the anchorite'.[6] A market used to be held every Saturday at his church.[7]

1 *AU s.a.* 810. 2 *ASH* 373; *AFM* ii, 1193; *Ulidia* 39–46. 3 *CéliD*. 4 *BP* 1672–4; *VT* 144. 5 *ZCP* 13, 15. 6 *AU s.a.*; *MartT* 18; *MartG* 38, 188; *MartD* 52, 266. 7 *CPCR* ii, 267.

O

ODA. *See* Odhbha.

ODHBHA daughter of Colmán. This saint is listed, together with her sister Connadh (Coinead), among those attached to the Ceinéal Laoghaire of the present county of Meath.[1] A note added by John Colgan to her pedigree located her in 'Rodium' of Brabant in Belgium, and supplied her with a feast of 27 November.[2] Colgan doubtless had in mind the unrelated Oda of Rolduc, now Oedenrode (Sint-Oedenrode), who was thought to have been the daughter of an Irish king, and whose feast fell on that day.[3] There is otherwise no trace of the saint in Irish sources.

1 *CGSH* §§631, 690.10. **2** *GRSH* 52; cf. *MartD* 458. **3** *BiblSS* 9, 1093–6; *FEMN* 381.567.

ODHRÁN. The name derives from *odhar*, 'dun-coloured', which, as is shown by the famous *odhar* of Ciarán of Clonmacnoise, was often used substantivally in the sense of a cow of this colour. The name was borne in diminutive form by many saints, with no fewer than fifteen in the list of homonymous saints.[1]

1 *CGSH* §707.896–911.

ODHRÁN, charioteer of Patrick. Once, while on a journey in or near Géisill in Uí Fhailghe, now Geashill in the Offaly parish and barony of the same name, Patrick is said to have changed places with his charioteer, only to have Odhrán pierced by a javelin thrown by a local dynast, bent on slaying the Armagh saint.[1] Other than his inclusion in the lists of those in orders with Patrick, little else is recorded of Odhrán.[2] His church at Díseart Odhráin in Uí Fhailghe is likely to have been located in or near Geashill. A well in the townland of Clonmore in the Meath parish of Castlejordan, which mears with the counties of Offaly and Kildare, was named after the saint.[3]

1 *BP* 2574–85; *VT* 218. **2** *BP* 3135; *VT* 266; *CGSH* §§671.14, 672.12; 707.897; *Lgen.* 695.1. **3** OSL MH 216.

ODHRÁN of Iona (Í), Scotland. Described in some late sources as abbot of Iona, Odhrán son of Ainghin is said to have belonged to the same branch of the Ceinéal Conaill as his later colleague Doirbhéan.[1] In reality he was a priest on Iona and, probably because the local cemetery (Reilig Odhráin) was named after him, he became the subject of a story suggesting that, with a view to consecrating the island, he had volunteered to become the first person interred on it.[2] His feastday of 27 October also belonged to his namesakes at Latteragh (Tipperary) and Killotteran (Waterford) and, through confusion with the saint named Oireannán commemorated on the same day, he later became attached to the church of Teach Oireannáin, sometimes taken to be the Westmeath church of Tyfarnham.[3] A cemetery dedicated to Odhrán on Inishmurray may also be his.[4]

1 *CGSH* §662.28; *GRSH* 43; *MartG* 204; *MartD* 286. 2 *IKD* 237 §52, 284; *VC*[1] 203; *ZCP* 12, 393; *CPNS* 309; *ACDS* 144–5. 3 *MartT* 85, 229; *MartG* 204, 325; *MartD* 286. 4 *Dinn.* 4, 64.

Odhrán of Íseal Ciaráin, at Bryanmore Upper (Bruidhean Dá Choga), parish of Drumraney, barony of Kilkenny West, Co. Westmeath.[1] Said to have been an older brother of Ciarán of Clonmacnoise, Odhrán son of Beoaidh is known mainly from Ciarán's record which assigns to him the priorship of Íseal Ciaráin.[2] Ciarán is described as having stayed with Odhrán for some time before founding his own first church. The Martyrology of Donegal speculates that he may have been the priest named Odhrán commemorated on 16 May.[3]

1 ITS 61, 5. 2 *VSHP* i, 200, 209–10 §§1, 23, 25; *LisL* 3994–8; *CGSH* §707.909. 3 *MartD* 132.

Odhrán of Killotteran. *See* Odhrán of Iona; Odhrán Maighistir.

Odhrán Maighistir, 'master', of Latteragh (Leitreacha Odhráin), barony of Upper Ormond, Co. Tipperary. Easily the best-known of the saints of this name, Odhrán (anglicized Oran and Otteran) son of Mac Raith was attached to the Uí Dhaighre of Múscraighe Tíre, whose lands straddled the two baronies of Ormond.[1] Seanán of Scattery also belonged to the Múscraighe, and this may explain why a member of his household named Odhrán is said to have been among those who buried him, before also succeeding him as abbot.[2] Together with his brother Meadhrán, Odhrán Maighistir is supposed to have visited Ciarán at Seirkieran with a view to making a pilgrimage, only to be told that, though his brother should remain, he was fated to return to his place of resurrection at Latteragh.[3] In the same passage, mention is made both of an otherwise unattested Life of the saint and of his part in the translation of the remains of Colum of Terryglass to Inishcaltra, elsewhere commemorated in quatrains attributed to Bréanainn.[4]

Odhrán is said to have acted with Mac Cuilinn of Lusk as an emissary to Ciarán of Clonmacnoise, to let the latter know that the saints of Ireland were fasting with the aim of accelerating Ciarán's death, lest the whole of Ireland come under his authority.[5] He is also reputed to have placed a curse on Cormac son of Coichean of the Dál gCais at a place called Rinn Arda Odhráin on Lough Derg because of the dynast's refusal to grant his people, the Múscraighe, a three-day truce.[6] Odhrán's church at Latteragh later became part of the property of the Augustinian priory at Toomyvara.[7] Given that he was one of Múscraighe's three *seanóirí*, the saint is likely to be intended in the dedication of a holy well to Oran at Ahaveheen in the Limerick parish of Cloncrew, just outside the later cantred of Muscridonegan.[8] Odhrán was remembered on two days, 2 and 26/27 October, the later of which – observed at Latteragh – was shared with namesakes on Iona and at Killotteran in Waterford.[9]

1 *CGSH* §§200, 665.1.5; *GRSH* 79; *Lgen.* 721.1–2. 2 *LisL* 2497; *AB* 66, 209–10. 3 *VSHP* i, 227–8 §25; *BNÉ* i, 121 §§54–5; *SG* i, 11; *MartT* 118. 4 *MartT* 118; cf. *MartO*[1] clxxxii; *VSHH* 232 §28. 5 *AB* 69, 104. 6 *BLec.* 229rc31. 7 *HDK* 473. 8 *JRSAI* 85, 198; *MedI* 156–7. 9 *MartT* 76, 85; *MartO*[2] 219; *MartG* 188, 204; *MartD* 264, 284; OSL TY i, 526.

Óengus/Óenu. *See* Aonghas/Aona.

Oíbinn. *See* Aoibhinn.

Óigshincheall. *See* Sincheall.

Oilearán Sapiens, 'of wisdom'. Known only by his first name (sometimes written Oirearán) and cognomen, Oilearán's reputation for wisdom derived from his authorship of a work interpreting the names in the genealogy of Christ as given in the Gospel of Matthew, and also of a poem on the canon of the gospels.[1] Elsewhere he is credited with having written about Patrick's miracles and, on the strength of this, and mainly by process of elimination of others, John Colgan attributed to him the so-called fourth Life (*quarta vita*) of the saint.[2] An account of Brighid's miracles has also been credited to Oilearán, and the authorship of her *vita prima* has recently been laid at his door, mainly on stylistic grounds.[3] The fact that he shared a reputation for wisdom with the like-named Oireannán of Tallaght has been a source of confusion. Having first included Oireannán (†803) among 'the most modern saints' commemorated in the Martyrology of Aonghas, its editor subsequently suggested that the much earlier Oilearán of the Wisdom might really have been intended.[4] This has led to the saint's association with such sites as Tyfarnham in Westmeath.[5] A more likely church is Clonard in Meath, of which, according to the later martyrologies, he was *fear léighinn*, 'chief teacher'.[6] Oilearán is among the saints said to have spoken in advance of the 'plague' known as the *Scuab*, 'besom', out of Fanad, and, perhaps not coincidentally, he is reputed to have fallen victim in 665/668 to the great plague known as *Buidhe Chonaill*, together with Féichín of Fore whose miracles he allegedly recorded.[7] His feastday fell on 29 December.[8]

1 *Kenney* 279–80; *Peritia* 10, 6–20; ibid. 15, 22–6; *AilIM*; *DIB* i, 59–60; *BiblSS* i, 644–5. **2** *BP* 637; *VT* 60; *TT* 35, 44; *DIB* i, 60. **3** *Peritia* 12, 1–23, 269; ibid. 13, 101; ibid. 433–68. **4** *MartO²* xxxviii; *Peritia* 17–18, 435–6. **5** *Kenney* 279. **6** *MartG* 248; *MartO²* 262; *MartD* 350; *Peritia* 10, 6–7. **7** *MartO²* 190; NLI G 10, 46b; *VSHP* ii, 80 §12; *IrT* iii, 85 §9; *LH* i, 25; *TEAB* 690 §2. **8** *MartT* 2; *MartO²* 255; *MartG* 248; *MartD* 350.

Oilléan. Oilléan is known only from an entry in the tract on the mothers of the saints, duplicated in the corpus of saints' pedigrees.[1] This names his mother as Deirinill Cheathairchíochach, 'of the four nipples', and provides a list of his uterine brothers, among them Mochuma of Drumbo. The saint is probably identical with the Oilleóg commemorated at an unidentified place called Cluain Eitchéin on 24 July.[2] This day was shared by Luighbhe who, like Oilléan's uterine brother, was attached to Drumbo.[2]

1 *CGSH* §162, 722.27. **2** *MartT* 57.

Oilill. Meaning a fairy or phantom, and productive of the hypocoristic form Oilléan (Ailléan), this name was borne by several euhemerized pre-Christian divinities, such as Oilill (Ailill), spouse of Meadhbh of Cruachain in Connacht and, in hypocoristic guise, Oilléan of Síodh Fionnachaidh in Armagh, harbinger of the annual destruction of Tara on November Eve. While borne by few enough saints, it generated such other pet forms as Eallóg, Oilleóg and Teille.

Oilill of Movilla (Magh Bhile), parish of Newtown Ards, barony of Ards Lower, Co. Down. This man was one of seven sons of Tricheamh, two of whom, Díocha of Saul and Ros (Rus) of Downpatrick, were brought into contact with Patrick by the latter's biographers.[1] Through his pedigree, which assigns him to the local Dál bhFiatach, Oilill is shown to have been the grandfather of Finnian of Movilla.[2] A speculative note added to the entry on the saint in *Genealogiae Regum et Sanctorum Hiberniae* identified him as the Bishop Oilill who died in 526 (or 536) and was commemorated on 12 (*recte* 13) January.[3]

1 *CGSH* §136.2; *PTBA* 78; *BP* 373–427; *VT* 36–40. 2 *CGSH* §136.1.2; *Lgen*. 723.3. 3 *GRSH* 84; *MartT* 7; *MartG* 14; *MartD* 14; *AU s.a.*

Oireannán of Tallaght (Tamhlachta), barony of Uppercross, Co. Dublin. The fact that he shared a reputation for wisdom with the like-named Oilearán has been a source of confusion. Having first included Oireannán (Aireannán), who died in 803, among 'the most modern saints' commemorated in the Martyrology of Aonghas, its editor subsequently suggested that the much earlier Oilearán of the Wisdom might really have been intended, only to be followed in this by others.[1] Having regard to its initial position and to its agreement in case (genitive) and language (Latin) with *sapientis* 'of wisdom', it is extremely unlikely that the corresponding reference in the Martyrology of Tallaght to Oireannán's position as abbot of Tallaght after its founder (Maol Ruain) represents a later addition.[2] Sometimes thought to have also given his name to the Westmeath church of Tyfarnham, Oireannán died in 803 and was remembered both on 11 August (apparently his main feast) and also, according to one martyrology, on 10 February.[3]

1 *MartO*[2] xxxviii; *Kenney* 279; *BiblSS* i, 643–4. 2 *MartT* 62. 3 *AU s.a.*; *MartT* 16, 62, 229; *MartO*[2] 175, 395; *MartG* 154, 325; *MartD* 216.

Oisín of Clonmore (Cluain Mór), barony of Ferrard, Co. Louth. In the course of his visit to Breagha, now Meath and adjoining districts in Louth and Dublin, Colum Cille is said to have founded many churches, including Clonmore among the Fir Arda (whence Ferrard), where he left Oisín son of Ceallach in charge.[1] Excepting the record of his feast of 1 January, Oisín is otherwise unattested.[2] Colum Cille remained patron of the local church and his feast was celebrated there annually on 9 June.[3]

1 *IKD* 233 §41; *BCC* §99. 2 *MartT* 3; *MartG* 6; *MartD* 2. 3 *VC*[1] 280–1; *TDI* i, 373.

Olan. *See* Eolang.

Olcán of Armoy (Oirthear Maighe), barony of Cary, Co. Antrim. According to the author of the Tripartite Life, Patrick's anger, when directed at Bishop Olcán of Armoy, resulted in the bishop's *fearann*, 'lands, jurisdiction' being transferred to a young boy of his household, namely Mac Nise.[1] Olcán is also found at 20 February in the Martyrology of Tallaght, with Bolgán replacing him in the later martyrologies [2] John Colgan brought the two names together, citing among other supports the presence in Dál Riada, where Bishop Olcán is said to have met Patrick, of a church named '*non Kill Olcain, sed Kill-Easpuic Bolcain*'.[3] There would not appear to be sufficient grounds, however, for the conflation of the two. At Cranfield, on the edge of Lough Neagh, where Olcán appears to have been patron, an altar was called after him, and the local feast was 29 June.[4]

1 *BP* 1932–4. 2 *MartT* 18; *MartG* 40; *MartD* 54. 3 *ASH* 375–8; cf. *Lgen*. 418.3. 4 *TEHS* 728; PNNI iv, 10; *UJA* (2nd ser.) 49.

Olcán of Kilcooley. *See* Bolcán.

Olga Cráibhtheach. *See* Ailbhe of Emly.

Onbha. *See* Séighín of Iona.

Onchú grandson/son of the Poet (Ua/Mac an Éigis). This man was clearly held in high regard in the early ninth century in the church of Tallaght, whose martyrologies referred to him in their lists for 8 February as 'one who gathered together the relics of the saints' and as one whose 'speech was concerning Christ'.[1] The later martyrologies identified the Carlow church of Clonmore (Cluain Mór Maodhóg), whose founder was allegedly persuaded to add his own little finger, as the repository of the saint's collection of relics.[2] It has been suggested that Onchú was the poet's son likened in manners to Ambrose of Milan, but this could also have been Éidchéan son of Maine Éigeas.[3]

1 *MartT* 15; *MartO*² 59. 2 *MartG* 32; *MartO*² 70; *MartD* 42; *IrL* 56. 3 *CGSH* §712.20; *MartD* 42.

Onchú of Killonaghan/Killonahan. *See* Blathmhac of Rath.

Ondbhauin. *See* Patrick.

Oran. *See* Odhrán Maighistir.

Osán of Ráith Osáin, near Trim, baronies of Lower Moyfenrath and Upper Navan, Co. Meath. This saint is known from the genealogical tradition, which supplies two statements of his descent. One asserts that he was a son of Athracht, and brother of Beoán who shared his church, the other that he was a uterine brother (through Fuineacht daughter of Maol Fithrigh) of Bishop Cormac of Trim.[1] Osán (alias Asán) also figures with members of his family in the *Additamenta* of Tíreachán's Life of Patrick.[2] He was remembered with several others of the clergy of Trim, including Cormac, on 17 February.[3] A holy well named 'St Assan's' at Raheny in the Dublin parish of the same name may also be dedicated to him.[4]

1 *CGSH* §§662.45, 690.13, 722.74; *GRSH* 49. 2 *PTBA* 170 §4. 3 *MartT* 17; *MartG* 38; *MartD* 52. 4 *Rep. Nov.* 2, 78; *AHWD* 12, 73; *LIS* iv, 512–13.

Osnad of Killasnet (Ceall Osnada), barony of Rosclogher, Co. Leitrim. Placed at Crícheadh in Gleann Dalláin, now Glencar Lough on the bounds of counties Sligo and Leitrim, Osnad was among the many children said to have been born to Cuman, paternal aunt of Brighid of Kildare.[1] Many of these, including Osnad, are also featured in the vernacular Life of Forannán of Alternan.[2] As the parish of

Killasnet directly adjoins Rossinver, it may also be assumed that Osnad was one of the three sisters assigned to Molaise, patron of Rossinver, in an entry in the martyrologies for 6 January.[3] The other sisters were Muadhnad (Buadhnad) of Caoille an Chosnamha (alias Ceall Bhuadhnadan), now probably Kealty in the Sligo parish of Drumcliff, and Talulla who was thought to be an abbess of Kildare.[4] There can be little doubt but that the saint and her namesake, Osnad daughter of Rónán of the Ceinéal Eoghain, were also identical.[5] Thought by later sources to be the Osnad commemorated on 10 November, the daughter of Rónán had a sister named Lasair whose Life states that she was educated by Molaise at Devenish.[6] Locally, the name of the saint's church at Killasnet, whose patron was Patrick, was thought to derive from Ceall Astair, 'church of the journey', in the belief that it had moved from its previous location in the townland of Castletown.[7] The yew at her church was regarded as one of Ireland's outstanding trees.[8]

1 *CGSH* §722.10. **2** *Anecd.* iii, 3. **3** *MartG* 10; *MartD* 8. **4** *Celtica* i, 66; *HDGP* iii, 49, *JGAHS* 21, 56–62. **5** *GRSH* 44. **6** Ibid.; *MartD* 302; *Ériu* 5, 75, 82. **7** OSL CN/LM 256. **8** *Éigse* 36, 13 §§2, 5, 16 §20; *ZCP* 5, 21–3.

Otteran. *See* Odhrán Maighistir.

P

Palladius. The entry for 431 in the Annals of Ulster states that Palladius, having been consecrated by Celestine, bishop of the city of Rome, was sent as first bishop to the Irish 'that they might believe in Christ'.[1] Both late seventh-century biographers of Patrick reveal familiarity with this tradition which ultimately derives from a slightly differently worded entry for the same year in the Chronicle of Prosper of Aquitaine.[2] One (Muirchú) embellished it by stating that Palladius, not wishing to spend a long time in a foreign and unreceptive country, decided to return home, dying on his way through Britain; the other (Tíreachán) had a note added to his *Collectanea* to the effect that Palladius was also known as Patrick, and that he suffered martyrdom at the hands of the Irish, a claim that is nowhere corroborated.[3] Later Lives of Patrick further augmented Palladius' history. The mid-ninth-century Tripartite Life maintained that, having landed at Inbhear Dé (perhaps at Wicklow) in Leinster, Palladius was expelled by Nathí son of Garrchú, eponym of the family of Uí Gharrchon, whose lands were by then largely confined to east Wicklow.[4] Moreover, according to the same source, prior to his expulsion, Palladius founded three churches, at one of which, Ceall Fhine, now perhaps an ecclesiastical site in the townland and parish of Kilpoole, he left books, a writing tablet, and relics of Peter and Paul.[5] On the basis of the relics allegedly left by Palladius, it has been suggested that the locations of the other two churches, Teach na Rómhán and Domhnach Airde, may be reflected in the later existence of two east Wicklow sites named Kilpedder, one in the parish of Kilcoole, the other, now obsolete, in the townland of Ballyrogan, parish of Redcross.[6] Leaving Ireland, Palladius is said by the author of the Tripartite Life to have died of a disease in the 'lands of the Picts', and this tradition is further elaborated in Patrick's *Vita Secunda* which asserts that the saint died at a place called 'Forddun' in the plain of 'Girgin', later Fordoun in the Mearns of Aberdeenshire.[7]

All the foregoing references to Palladius, either depend for their detail on the entry in Prosper's Chronicle, or expand on it for reasons that probably relate to the evolution of the story of St Patrick, of which it formed an integral part. The brevity and relative insignificance of the Palladian mission, as presented in these sources, arguably reflect deliberate seventh-century attempts to portray Patrick as apostle of all Ireland.[8] Moreover, if an eleventh- or twelfth-century note to Fiac's Hymn, which agrees almost entirely with the text of the Tripartite Life, is set aside, there are few other references to Palladius in Irish sources.[9] A passage in the Salamancan Life of Ailbhe of Emly places him anachronistically in the time of Conchubhar son of Neas, king of the Ulstermen, and brings him implausibly to Munster, where he baptizes the patron of Emly, then still a boy, teaching him the Christian truths and giving him the name Ailbhe.[10] (Other versions of Ailbhe's Life preserve some of this detail, while suppressing Palladius' name [11]). A note added to some versions of the Martyrology of Aonghas identifies Palladius with Torannán (alias Mothoiréan), patron, among other churches, of Banchory in Aberdeenshire (not far from Fordoun), who is elsewhere said to have been Palladius' disciple.[12]

Otherwise, Palladius is subsequently remembered principally in Scottish sources, including a biographical notice in the Breviary of Aberdeen which provides him with an Egyptian origin.[13] Having been sent to the *Scoti* (meaning the Scots) by Pope Celestine, he is said in this text to have preached throughout Scotland before arriving in Culross, where he ordained Searbh, for whom an Egyptian origin has also been claimed.[14] Palladius' death, after a long mission in Scotland, allegedly took place at Longforgan in the Carse of Gowrie, but this is probably in error for Fordoun, where his memory under the guise of Pade (alias Paldy) is usually (but not universally) taken to have been celebrated in a church, holy well and annual fair, held on 6 July.[15]

Although assigned to 27 January by Henry Fitzsimon, who normally drew on continental sources, no feast has otherwise been recorded for Palladius in Irish sources.[16] Moreover, despite an attempt to link his name to that of Cruimhthear Collaid, who is credited with having brought together an account of Patrick's miracles, no traces of a cult of Palladius survived in Ireland.[17] The scarcity of the Irish and Scottish sources relating to Palladius has been no obstacle to scholarly discussion of his history and identity. The century-old debate sparked by the claim in a note added to Tíreachán's Life that Patrick was an alias of Palladius reached a wide audience and generated a great deal of (sometimes heated) discussion.[18] More recent debate has centred mainly on the continental evidence for Palladius, his portrayal in Prosper's two texts, the Chronicle and *Contra Collatorem*, his Gaulish origins, his relationship to Germanus of Auxerre, and the possibility of his identity with the Palladius mentioned in a poem (*De reditu suo*) composed by Claudius Rutilius Namatianus.[19]

1 *AU s.a.*; cf. *AI* §389. **2** *CI* i, 63. **3** *PTBA* 72, 164–6; *Studies* 32, 323–6; *DIB* vii, 1044–5. **4** *BP* 288–99; *VT* 30; *TLSP* 87–8. **5** Ibid.; *Peritia* 3, 547–8; *HDGP* iii, 172. **6** *Peritia* 3, 548; cf. *TLSP* 88. **7** *BP* 298–9; *VT* 30; *FLLSP* 76–7; *TLSP* 36–7, 89–90. **8** *Peritia* 14, 208–10; *ECI* 237; *IsPatrick* 24–37; *DIB* vii, 1044–5. **9** *LH* i, 99; cf. *TLSP* 90. **10** *VSHH* 118–19 §3. **11** *VSHP* i, 46–7 §2; *SSS* 391. **12** *MartO*[2] 148; *KSS* 133, 428; *ACDS* 106–7; *SBDeer* 387. **13** *BrevA* pars aest. 24v–25v; *KSS* 428; *LegSS* 168–71, 406–7. **14** *BrevA* pars aest. 15–16v. **15** *KSS* 133, 156, 205, 427; *ACDS* 106; *Innes Review* 32, 71. **16** *FEMN* 382. **17** *JGAHS* 22, 34–42; *BP* 639; *VT* 60. **18** *CCBI* 35– 41; *TPat.*; *Studies* 32, 323–6; *PSP* 49–52; *AB* 63–76–80; ibid. 70, 317–26; *StH* 2, 133–48. **19** *StH* 33, 7–27; *SPOC* 192–6; *Celtica* 8, 112–25; *BiblSS* 10, 60–4; *Peritia* 14, 205–37; *ECI* 202–14; *IP* 157–90.

PÁN of Kilfane (Ceall Pháin), barony of Gowran, Co. Kilkenny. This saint is known from an entry in the tract on the mothers of the saints which states that he and his nine brothers were sons of Díona, daughter of a king of the Saxons, by Brachan, king of the Britons (or Welsh), and eponym of Brycheiniog, a territory in south Wales.[1] Many of the saint's siblings – including Moghóróg of Delgany, Mochonóg of Kilmuckridge, Díoraidh of Edermine, and Eallóg of St Tulloge's – were associated with churches in east Leinster, but Pán's church lay a little further west, in Ossory, where his memory was preserved only in the name of his church. His patronage of the parish gave way to that of the Blessed Virgin and no memory of his feastday has survived.[2]

1 *CGSH* §722.89; *EWGT* 14–16, 32–3. **2** *HADO* iii, 482–3.

Papán of Poppintree, parish of Finglas, barony of Coolock, Co. Dublin. An entry in the Martyrology of Tallaght for 31 July commemorates 'Papán in Seantreabh', now Santry, the name of a parish adjoining Finglas, where a well named 'St Pappin's' was located near the church.[1] A note in Latin added to the entry in the later Martyrology of Gorman states that 'Papanus' was a son of Aonghas, king of Cashel, but this was probably intended only for Colmán and Nadál, who are also mentioned.[2] Little else is known of the saint, but his 'sacred' tree is recalled by the name of a townland in the parish of Finglas, where his pattern was held annually.[3] The early seventeenth-century writer, Meredith Hanmer, mentions the saint's 'yeerely remembrance' at Santry, before wrongly identifying him with St Poppon of Stavelot in Belgium.[4]

1 *MartT* 59; *Rep. Nov.* 2, 78. **2** *MartG* 146. **3** *JCHAS* 68, 36; *AH* 8, 20. **4** *AIH* 185–6.

Pappin. *See* Papán.

Patrick (Pádraig/Patricius) of Armagh (Ard Mhacha). Uniquely among the saints of Ireland, Patrick's descent is vouched for in a document written by himself, the so-called *Confessio*, which names his father (Calpornius) and grandfather (Potitus) and locates his family in the village of '*Bannavem Taberniae/Taburniae*', a place sometimes thought to have been in Britain, but more likely to have been in the area about Boulogne-sur-Mer in north-western France.[1] As his father and grandfather were respectively described as a deacon and presbyter, Patrick clearly belonged to an ecclesiastical family. The saint's seventh-century biographer Muirchú, probably drawing on a copy of the *Confessio*, provided much the same descent, adding only that his mother's name was Concessa.[2] By the mid- to late ninth century, when the saint's Tripartite Life and a hymn anachronistically attributed to Fiac of Sleaty were compiled, more additions had been made to Patrick's 'earthly genealogy'. He was now attached to the Britons of Dumbarton in Scotland; was a nephew of St Martin of Tours through his mother who belonged to the Franks; and had been born and raised at a place called Neamhthor.[3] By now also, Patrick had two sisters (Lubaid and Tig(h)ris), both of whom were sold into captivity with him.[4] This treatment of the saint's background has been described as the final triumph of legend over history, but it was merely another chapter in the fabrication of a story that continued to attract accretions.[5] By the twelfth century, some ten (otherwise unattested) names, culminating in Britus (alias Britinus, son of Fearghas Leithdhearg son of Neimheadh), eponym of all the British according to the redactors of the early eleventh-century *Leabhar Gabhála*, had been added to the saint's pedigree and, with a view to establishing for Patrick a direct link with the origins of Christianity, his branch of the Britons had now been transformed into a group of Israelites who reached Britain following the dispersal of their race under Titus and Vespasian.[6] The number of his sisters had also increased, as had the number of their progeny, thus enabling many churches to assert an association with Armagh on a uterine basis.

The manipulation undergone by Patrick's genealogical background was matched by that of his biographical record. His own writings, *Confessio* and *Epistola*, reveal something of the character of a man deeply conscious of the importance of his mission and, despite his unworthiness as a *peccator* – both *rusticissimus* and *indoctus* – of his own central role in carrying it through.[7] Beyond the bare outline of his background, captivity, escape, recall to Ireland by way of dreams, and subsequent preparation for his mission, these texts are notably thin on onomastic detail. Only one local place-name, *silva Focluti*, located either in the Mayo barony of Tirawley or, more likely, in the area about Slemish in Co. Antrim, finds mention and, apart from Patrick's immediate forebears, only one contemporary person is named, the British chieftain Coroticus who, 'allied to the Scots and apostate Picts', had slain or taken captive many of the saint's converts.[8]

The Irish annals do little to compensate for the saint's restraint in naming names. Written retrospectively and drawing ultimately on Prosper's Chronicle, these record the mission to the Irish believing in Christ of the saint's predecessor Palladius, sent by Pope Celestine in the year 431, followed a year later – the first year of the reign of Sixtus – by Patrick's arrival in Ireland.[9] Subsequent entries relating to the saint's mission refer to: Seachnall (Secundinus), Usaille (Auxilius), and Iserninus, sent in 439 to assist Patrick; the foundation of Armagh in 444; and, under the guise of *Senis Patricius*, the saint's death, which is variously dated to 457 and 461.[10] Under the year 493, a lengthy entry records the death of Patrick, 'arch-apostle' of the Irish, who was apparently thought to be distinct from *Senis Patricius*.[11]

The lack of explicitness and evident confusion in these records, when combined with a natural interest in the genuine history of Ireland's apostle, has engendered a modern literature of enormous proportions.[12] A similarly motivated interest led to the fabrication of a medieval history of the saint – modified and augmented over several centuries – that began in the late seventh century with Muirchú and Tíreachán, the saint's earliest biographers.[13] Muirchú, who was apparently associated with the church of Armagh and therefore probably had access to the saint's own writings, augmented them considerably, using Sulpicius' Life of Martin of Tours as a model, with a view to establishing for his patron the best possible credentials, including a visit to the apostolic see in Rome.[14] This gave Patrick the opportunity of meeting the celebrated Germanus in Auxerre, whose predecessor Amathorex was given the honour of consecrating him bishop on the same day as he ordained Auxilius and Iserninus.[15] Though the saint's supposed sojourn in Gaul found an echo – already by about 700 – in verse attributed to Ceallán of Péronne, Muirchú's initial focus in Ireland was on two centres, Tara, the symbolic seat of northern overlordship, and south-east Ulster, supposedly the scene of Patrick's term as a slave, and also the location of the first foundation credited to him, at Saul (Sabhall), the barn of a man named Díocha, later regarded as a saint.[16] The saint's visit to Tara, perhaps the best-known of all the episodes invented by Muirchú, accounts for several chapters of the Life, with considerable emphasis on the coincidence with Eastertide, the lighting of the paschal fire, and the victorious outcome of Patrick's contest with the druids.[17] There followed a series of miracles, mainly concerned with Britons (Monesan, Coroticus) or Britain (Mac Cuill on the Isle of Man), but culminating in a lengthy account of the founding of Armagh.[18] The final part of Muirchú's cleverly structured text brought Patrick back to the scene of his slavery among the Ulaidh (Ulstermen), with the honour of giving the saint the last rites falling to Tasach, patron of Raholp in the parish of Ballyculter.[19] Evidently aware of rival claims to the saint's place of burial, Muirchú availed of a *topos* that left the final choice to oxen drawing a cart containing the saint's remains, which brought Patrick to Downpatrick (Dún Dá Leathghlaise).[20] As this coincidence may bear on Muirchú's own background, it should be noted that the parishes of Saul (the site of Patrick's first Irish church and previous captivity), Ballyculter and Down (alias Downpatrick) are contiguous.

Tíreachán's concerns were of a different order. Apparently a native of north Connacht, he devoted his opening remarks to Patrician churches 'beyond the Shannon'.[21] Then, having presented Patrick's background in summary form, he linked the founding of the saint's first western church to a man named Seisgnéan before identifying a youth called 'Benignus', who was allegedly inseparable from the saint, as his successor in the church of Armagh.[22] Beinéan son of Seisgnéan, as Benignus was later known, was closely associated with churches in Connacht, the most important of which was Kilbennan near Tuam. Tíreachán's concern with western matters is again discernible in the sequel to Patrick's visit to Tara, where members of the Uí Amhalghaidh dynasty of north Connacht reminded the saint of *silva Focluti*, the only local place-name mentioned in his *Confessio*, notionally identical with *Caille Fochladh* in north Mayo.[23] Having briefly adverted to some churches founded by Patrick in Meath and adjoining areas, Tíreachán then introduced his 'second book', on the deeds performed by the saint in Connacht.[24] This accounts for twenty-seven of the remaining thirty-two chapters of the Life, with the final five reserved for the saint's return to Meath, in completion of his 'circuit', taking in the north of Ireland en route. A few sentences only are accorded to Patrick's deeds in Leinster and Munster, no doubt because Armagh's authority in these regions was minimal in Tíreachán's time.[25]

By the early ninth century, Armagh's influence had extended almost countrywide, as can be gleaned from contemporary comments on the saint. Writing about 830, the Tallaght martyrologist Aonghas could hardly be restrained when he came to Patrick's feast of 17 March: 'The flame of a splendid sun, the apostle of the whole of Ireland, let Patrick, with his many thousands, be the protection of our misery'.[26] Earlier, in the prologue to his text, the same author had contrasted the increase in Patrick's fame with the quenching of the pride of his pagan protagonist Laoghaire, and had given the saint's church of Armagh a place of honour among the churches of Ireland, comparing its flourishing state with the utter decline of the king's once 'mighty burgh' of Tara.[27] The annals of the early ninth century record that Patrick's Law was proclaimed in 799 over

Connacht, to be followed by its promulgation among the Northern Uí Néill in 806, and again over Connacht in 811.[28]

In the meantime – sometime before 809 – the authorities in Armagh had begun to bring together in one volume the *libri Patricii* (writings of Patrick, along with the Lives composed for him in the seventh century), and the abbot of Armagh had presided over a meeting 'of the synods' of the Uí Néill held at Rathcore on the boundary of the northern and southern halves of Ireland.[29] The scene was clearly set for an even greater widening of Armagh's influence and, in 823, after he assumed the kingship of Munster, Feidhlimidh son of Criomhthann joined the bishop-abbot of Armagh, Artrí son of Conchobhar, in imposing the Law of Patrick on the southern province with the result that abbots of Armagh began to make regular visits to Leinster and Munster before Feidhlimidh died in 847.[30] With this increase in its authority came the need to protect once more the northern church's interests in writing. The *Additamenta* and *Notulae* of the Book of Armagh reflect this necessity, with the latter text serving as a blueprint for a new Life of the saint, the so-called Tripartite Life, which brought Patrick to all four provinces, including Munster, hitherto the subject of a bare mention in the record of the saint.[31] Previously confined to the provinces of Ulster and Connacht and the northern Midlands, the scope of Patrick's activities had now been widened to embrace almost the whole of Ireland, albeit in a manner which has been described as devoid of any historical validity.[32] Yet, though somewhat incomplete in their coverage of the country, the itineraries constructed for Patrick in the Tripartite Life undoubtedly have some historical resonance, most probably in respect of the journeys made by his successors at Armagh during the first half of the ninth century.

Although sometimes considered earlier in date, the poem attributed to Fiac of Sleaty, which gives an abbreviated account of the saint's life, shows signs of dependence on the Tripartite Life, beginning with the assertion that the saint was born in Neamhthor and ending with the claim that the men of Ireland watching over the body of the saint were lulled into sleep by heavenly music.[33]

Later abbreviated Lives of the saint, dating to the eleventh or twelfth century, some Latin, others vernacular, clearly drew on a text similar to the Tripartite Life. Sometimes implausibly thought to be even earlier in date than the Lives of Muirchú and Tíreachán, the ultimate source of the Latin abbreviations, known as *secunda*, *quarta* and, most popularly, *tertia*, which are preserved exclusively in non-Irish manuscripts, may have been a Latin adaptation of the Tripartite Life, specially prepared for use on the Continent.[34] Yet to be studied in its own right, the abbreviated vernacular version of the saint's Life likewise appears to depend on an adaptation made directly from the Tripartite Life, which is subject to varying emphases in the surviving manuscripts.[35] In the Book of Lismore, for instance, much more space is given to the saint's sojourn in Munster than in other versions.[36]

Comprehensive as its coverage had been, the Tripartite Life had left many notable gaps, waiting to be filled. Dobheóg had not yet been dislodged from his remote island in the lake of Loch Geirg, now better known as Lough Derg in south-east Donegal, to make way for Patrick, at the instigation of the Augustinian canons who established on it a dependency of St Peter and Paul's in Armagh about 1140.[37] The scene was then set for the emergence of Patrick's Purgatory, possibly the most widely known Irish ecclesiastical site throughout the late Middle Ages and even today an integral part of the fabric of Irish pilgrimage.

Also yet to unfold were the circumstances surrounding Patrick's visit to Dublin which is now recalled by his wells and cathedral church there. The details of this visit were first set down in twelfth-century texts, one vernacular and secular – *Leabhar na gCeart*, 'the Book of Rights' – the other Latin and hagiographical – Jocelin's *Vita Patricii*, commissioned about 1185 by Archbishop Tomaltach of Armagh, Bishop Malachy of Down, and the Norman adventurer, John de Courcy, the new ruler of the ancient kingdom of Ulaidh.[38] Though Jocelin's text appears also to be based on a source similar to the Tripartite Life, the author occasionally used his materials in a higgledy-piggledy fashion, with little regard for topography, locating, for example, an episode dealing with two brothers of the Ciarraighe of Airteach in north Roscommon among the Ciarraighe of Munster.[39] Jocelin's concerns were contemporary, as when he took the opportunity of a mention of Comhghall of Bangor to refer to such later luminaries of that church as Columbanus and Malachy.[40] He also devoted several chapters to Patrick's sojourn in Dublin whose inhabitants are taken, with no regard for chronology, to have been Norwegians.[41] His account, while otherwise unattested in the saint's biographical record, reflects the increasing influence of Dublin in both secular and ecclesiastical matters, which began in the late tenth century and came to a head after 1074 when bishops of Dublin, now consecrated at Canterbury, began to challenge Armagh's claims to primacy.

In Munster, the ninth-century Tripartite Life had also left loose ends, one of which, the conspicuous absence from the text of Déaglán of Ardmore, a supposed pre-Patrician saint and later patron of the diocese of Waterford and Lismore, was filled only in the late twelfth century, when the Life composed for the southern saint arranged two meetings with Patrick, one on the road to Rome, another at home in Munster; the latter meeting gave rise to a grant of lands – the usual source of revenue – to the primatial saint, now marked by the spectacular St Patrick's Well near Clonmel.[42] Besides being the subject of a modern vernacular Life which has only lately begun to attract attention, Patrick is also featured in the Lives of many other saints, often as a prophet of notable saints' births, and sometimes in the context of the hymn *Audite omnes*, allegedly composed for him by Secundinus, the singing of which was regarded as highly efficacious.[43] In addition to numerous pieces of poetry and prose, in Latin and Irish, ascribed to the saint, an early vernacular rule attributed to him has also been preserved.[44] The saint's *cáin*, 'ecclesiastical law', which his church in Armagh sought to have proclaimed throughout the country, especially in the period 725–850, was deemed to be one of the four laws of Ireland, and he is said to have assisted in drawing up the collection of early Irish law known as *Seanchas Mór*.[45]

The death of the saint, who was regarded as similar in manners to the apostle Peter, is dated by the annals to both 461 (*Senis Patricius*) and 493 (*Patricius*

Archiapostolus Scotorum), a dissonance in Patrick's record that has engendered not only considerable debate, but also the notion of more than one saint of the name.[46] By contrast, the day of the saint's death (17 March) has been fixed since earliest times, both in the Irish martyrologies and also in the universal martyrological record, beginning with the Calendar of Willibrord, which was compiled about 700.[47] Not all remembrance of the saint has been positive; his British origins led to the occasional accusation that he sided with the Foreigners against the Irish.[48] But these are facets only of an area of study so enormous in its proportions, especially when centennial anniversaries of the saint's life were to hand, that it came to be known as Patriciology. Today, memory of Patrick is centred annually on three main events; the observance of his feast which is now celebrated all over the English-speaking world and beyond; the pilgrimage to Croagh Patrick which attracts many thousands of devotees on the last Sunday in July, and which originated as a Christianization of the early August feast of the pagan divinity Lugh; and the pilgrimage in the saint's name to Lough Derg, the origins of which, as already stated, are traceable only to the twelfth century.[49] Patrick's reputed use of the shamrock to explain the mystery of the Holy Trinity, and his banishment of the snakes from the island of Ireland are late traditions.

1 *LSP* 235 §1; *AB* 63, 65–72; *BLSP* 52–3; *TLSP* 68–73; *DIB* vii, 1116; *IP* 54–74. **2** *PTBA* 66 §1.1.1. **3** *BP* 81–4; *VT* 8; *LH* i, 97. **4** *BP* 196; *VT* 16. **5** *StH* 2, 69; cf. *IEME* 166–7. **6** *CGSH* §1.1.2; *Lgen.* 696.2; *Ériu* 6, 117–20; *LG* iii, 126 §245; *TLSP* 66. **7** *LSP*; *BLSP*; *CMCS* 1, 21–38; *DisSP* 141–83; *DIB* vii, 1117–20; *TEP*. **8** *LSP* 242 §23; *BLSP* 66–7; *IHS* 3, 351–64; *DIB* vii, 1120; *IP* 130–2. **9** *AU s.a.* **10** *AU s.a.* **11** *AU s.a.* **12** *SPOC* 230–5; *SaintP* 289–316; *Thought* 5, 22–41; *IHS* 6, 247–60; ibid. 9, 1–12; ibid. 10, 131–55, 16, 119–37, 395–416; *AB* 62, 42–73; *SAM* 1961–2, passim; 193–204; ibid. 5.1, 200–04; *IER* (5th ser.) 97 *passim*; *CMCS* 4, 33–59; *StC* 14/15, 344–79; *ClavP*; *DIB* vii, 1115–25. **13** *PTBA*; *DisSP* 192–229; *MedAE* 43.3, 2219–33. **14** Ibid. 70, §1.4 (2); *Peritia* 4, 71–2; *DisSP* 112–30. **15** *PTBA* 70–4 §§1.6.1; 1.9.1, 2; *AB* 63, 73–93; *AB* 75, 160–74. **16** *ZCP* 20, 385; *PTBA* 76–8 §1.11. **17** Ibid. 84–98 §§1.15–22. **18** Ibid. 108–12 §1.24. **19** Ibid. 118 §2.9. **20** Ibid. 120 §2.11. **21** *PTBA* 122–4 §§II.1–3; *IKHK* 232; *ITS SS* 23, 117–53. **22** Ibid. 126 §5.1–5. **23** Ibid. 134–6 §§14–15. **24** Ibid. 138 §17. **25** Ibid. §51.2–4; cf. *Ériu* 45, 53–82. **26** *MartO²* 82. **27** Ibid. 24. **28** *AU s.a.* **29** *AB* 62, 42–73; *Scriptorium* 36, 3–28; *AU s.a.* 804; *DIB* vii, 1121. **30** *AU s.a.* 823, 836, 845–6. **31** *PTBA* 166–83; *BP* 2286–573; *VT* 194–216. **32** *Ériu* 11, 9. **33** *LH* i, 97, 103; *BP* 85, 3005–11. **34** *FLLSP* 1–39; *TLSP*. **35** *TMIH* 2–49; *LisL* 1–651; *Anecd.* iii, 29–42. **36** *LisL* 447–543. **37** *MRHI* 193; *MPPP*; *Lia Fáil* i, 1–48; *SZ* 7–10; *ClRec.* 16, 7–36; *HCIC* 18–31. **38** *TT* 64–116; *LC* 116; *TT* 90–1; *HDA* 19–50; *SLJF* 1–57, 141–70; *Rep. Nov.* 2.1, 6–16; cf. *MDub.* 18, 148–9. **39** *TT* 82 §76. **40** Ibid. 88 §98. **41** Ibid. 80–1 §§69–72; *SLJF* 153–9. **42** *VSHP* ii, 47 §19. **43** *CínCC* 1–43; *VSHH* 78 §1, 195 §48, 219 §33, 230 §24, 303, 332 §2, 342 §9, 357 §1, 363 §9, 366 §1, 404 §1. **44** *Ériu* 1, 216–24. **45** *Celtica* 21, 561; *Ériu* 2, 190; *Ériu* 45, 5–13. **46** *CGSH* §712.2; *StH* 2, 7–173; *NHI* i, 301–30; *AHHS* 43–5; *SaintP* 29–33. **47** *MartT* 24; *MartO²* 82; *MartG* 56; *MartD* 78; *FSHIM* 8, 13; HBS 55, 5; cf. *AS.*Nov. ii, 148. **48** *Celtica* 15, 67–8. **49** *AB* 50, 346–57; *FL* 71–84; *SIHI* 143–4, 181–2; *SAM* 1961–2, 68–75; ibid. 16.2; *HCIC* 18–31.

Peadrán of 'Killenny' (Ceall Lainne), an ecclesiastical site in the townland of Barrowmount, parish of Grangesilvia, Co. Kilkenny. According to a litany of Irish saints, Peadrán of Killenny was a member of Caoimhghin's *familia*, and this is borne out by an entry in the genealogical corpus which lists the saint among the Dál Meisin Corb of the area about Glendalough.[1] Thought to be identical with a Briton named Pedrawg of Padstow in Cornwall, whose Life represents him as a fellow-student of Caoimhghin, Peadrán is otherwise placed in the 'third order' of Irish saints.[2] If correctly identified, his church at Killenny later became the seat of a Cistercian abbey.[3] A namesake, attached with two companions (Dúthracht and Teamhair) to the church of Oghil (Domhnach Eochaille) in the Kildare parish of Monasterevin, is said to have been subject to Brighid of Kildare.[4] The latter church is also mentioned in a litany of Irish saints – together with Tully in Dublin (Tulach na nEaspag), likewise a Brigidine foundation – as the home of seven holy bishops.[5] Peadrán died, according to the annals, in 616 at the church of Lusk near Dublin.[6]

1 *IrL* 56; *CGSH* §181.11. **2** *CPPI* 124–5; *VSHH* 82 §3. **3** *MRHI* 138. **4** *CGSH* §670.82. **5** *IrL* 66; *LisL* 1680. **6** *AB* 73, 133; *AU s.a.*

Peadrán of Oghil. *See* Dúthracht; Peadrán of Killenny.

Pilip son of Dubhthan. *See* Comán son of Dubhthan.

Phelim. *See* Feidhlimidh.

Pól. *See* Deineath.

Pompa daughter of Loarn. *See* Cairneach of Dulane; Rónán of Dromiskin.

Poppin. *See* Papán.

Pupa of Inishmore, barony of Aran, Co. Galway. Several chapters of the Life of Éanna are taken up with a sojourn in Rome, where one of the saint's companions was Pupa (Pupu), a name said to derive from *Papa*, 'Pope', and also thought to reflect the name later given to Irish hermits in Iceland.[1] According to another source, this man abandoned the papacy to retire to Inishmore, where he was also known as Neamh, and where his name became attached to one of three 'angelic' burial places.[2] He went on, according to yet another source, to succeed Éanna on Aran.[3] This same source, which describes him as a *bráthair*, 'brother, kinsman', of Ciarán of Seirkieran, explains his various names as follows: Neamh was the name given to him by his parents; Pupa was because of his quest for the Chair of Peter; Caoilbhe was derived from *caol-bheo*, 'slender-alive', because of his 'thinness' during life.[4] The passage also places in Seanán's mouth an alliterative Latin quatrain in praise of Pupa, beginning *abbas almus amabilis*, which is elsewhere accompanied by a similar Irish quatrain.[5] The saint's association with Aran allowed the biographer of Bréanainn to include Pupa among a group bidding the Clonfert saint farewell at the beginning of his celebrated sea-voyage.[6] His connection with the Maca Birn (otherwise the Osraighe who gave name to Ossory) may underlie the invocation by Moling of a certain 'Elcho' (*recte* Aolchú?) – thus echoing another of his several names – among the Leinster saints who should assist in gaining remission of the *bóramha* tribute.[7] Pupa's feast of 14 June is shared by the translation of the remains of Benedict of Nursia and, according to one version of Usuard's martyrology, by the feastday of Bréanainn the voyager.[8] The saint died, according to the annals, in 655.[9]

1 *VSHP* ii, 69 §21; *AB* 47, 181–2. **2** *CGSH* §§379.3, 735; *Lgen*. 750.1. **3** *MartO*[2] 150. **4** Ibid. **5** Ibid.; cf. *CGSH* §735. **6** *BNÉ* i, 53 §48; *VSHP* i, 136. **7** *SG* i, 389. **8** *MartT* 50; *MartO*[2] 140; *MartG* 116; *MartD* 170; *AS*.Iun. vi, 337. **9** *AU s.a.*

Q ☙

Quinlan. *See* Mocheallóg of Inch.
Quintin. *See* Cobhthach Caol.

R ☙

Rabharnóg. *See* Earnán of Inis Caoin; Náile of Kinawley.

Raoire of 'Teampall Raoileann' (Tuaim Sruthra), townland of Ashford, parish of Creagh, barony of Moycarn, Co. Roscommon. Raoire (alias Raoile / Raoileann) is one of several saints said to have descended from Branán son of Dobhtha, progenitor of the Ceinéal Dobhtha, later the Uí Ainlighe (Hanleys).[1] Now taken locally to have been a male, little else is known of the saint, but Raoire's church, which formed part of the properties of Clonmacnoise, was located near a *longphort* belonging to a branch of the Uí Cheallaigh (O'Kellys) known as Sliocht Siocais.[2]

1 *CGSH* §410.1; *Lgen*.242.14. 2 *ParB* 12, 14; *JGAHS* 20, 145–50; *RClon*. 455; *TCHyM* 165.

Rathnad. *See* Feidhealm daughter of Rónán.

Reabhradh. *See* Caolchú of Clooncoose.

Reachtghas. *See* Reachtghniadh.

Reachtghniadh. Twenty-four (mainly Munster) saints, including Reachtghniadh and (an otherwise unattested) Reachtghas, are said to have belonged to a union (*aonta*) led by Feidhlimidh son of Criomhthann.[1] As all the saints in the list were associated with the *céile Dé* group of ascetics which flourished within the Irish church in the second half of the eighth century, and remained vigorous until about the middle of the ninth, Reachtghniadh (alias Reachtniadh) is likely to have been the abbot of Clonmacnoise of that name who died in 784.[2]

1 *CGSH* §§713, 724. 2 *AU s.a.*; *FEMN* 505 §27.

Renogue. *See* Morónóg of Inishloe.

Reodaighe of Girley (Greallach Maighe Tlachtgha), barony of Upper Kells, Co. Meath. The pedigree of Reodaighe (Ródaighe) son of Fáilbhe attaches him to a branch of the Ceinéal Conaill to which two tenth-century successors of Colum Cille, Maol Brighde (†927) and Dubhthach (†938), also belonged.[1] As both of these resided in Kells, the pedigree may have been foisted on the saint with a view to consolidating the Columban church's assertion of authority over Girley, otherwise confirmed by the inclusion of the saint and his crozier among the sureties of a charter preserved in the Book of Kells.[2] The saint's mother is said to have been Soibhean daughter of Dubhthan of the Derry church of Dunboe, of which Adhamhnán was patron.[3] Later known locally as Raod, the saint was remembered at Girley on 16 December.[4]

1 *CGSH* §13; *GRSH* 43; *Lgen*. 700.1. 2 IC 156–7 §3; cf. OSL MH 42. 3 *Celtica* 1, 82; *DYHS* 195. 4 *MartG* 240; *MartD* 339; *Rep. Nov.* 2, 51; OSL MH 41.

Riaghail of Illaunmore (Muicinis), an island on Lough Derg in the parish of Kilbarron, barony of Leitrim, Co. Galway.[1] Together with other saints of Dál gCais, including Caimín of Inishcaltra (also on Lough Derg), Riaghail was placed among the numerous progeny of Cuman daughter of Dallbhrónach, maternal aunt of Brighid of Kildare.[2] Either he or his namesake in the Down parish of Tyrella (Teach Riaghla) was also among the saints selected to be prophets of the notorious plague known as *Scuab*, 'besom', out of Fanad, due on the feast of St John.[3] Although little else is known of the saint, he has the distinction of having two days (17 September and 16 October) assigned to him in the Tallaght martyrologies, which may mean that his church was involved with the *céile Dé* ascetics.[4] The later martyrologies give the first of these days to his namesake at Tyrella.[5] The Tyrella saint may also be intended by the reference in the martytrologies to the Riaghail son of Buachaill commemorated on 13 April.[6] The Martyrology of Gorman reads 'Maca Buachalla', a family (otherwise known as Dál mBuachalla) which had Down connections.[7] The Tyrella saint was possibly also the author of a poem on the death in 704 of Aldfrith of Northumbria, which is attributed to Riaghail of Bangor.[8]

1 ATig. ind. 2, 170; *INP* i, 478. **2** *CGSH* §722.8. **3** *MartO*[2] 190; NLI G 10, 46b; *HDC* i, 126; *TEAB* 690 §6. **4** *MartT* 72, 80; *MartO*[2] 194, 216. **5** *MartG* 178, 196; *MartD* 250, 276. **6** *MartT* 32; *MartD* 100. **7** *MartG* 76; *CGSH* p. 321. **8** *FAI* §165.

Riaghail of Tyrella. *See* Riaghail of Illaunmore.

Ríceall/Ríceann. There is a good deal of confusion between the saints bearing these (perhaps ultimately identical) names which probably derive from the word *rí*, 'king'. One bearer, a daughter of Athracht of the Clann Lughdhach or Ceinéal Laoghaire of Meath, figures, along with her brother Casán, in a group of closely related persons, at least one of whom (Rónaid daughter of Fiachna) was associated with Moylagh (Magh Locha) in the Meath part of the barony of Fore.[1] Devotion to the saint appears to have been otherwise centred on both east Galway – where she gave her name to Kilreekill in the barony of Leitrim – and south Kildare, where – in the guise of Ríceann (alias Ríceall) sister of Patrick – she was included among those subject to Brighid at Kilkea.[2] When visiting Kilreekill in 1838, John O'Donovan could discover no memory of her festival, but he drew attention to John Colgan's suggestion that she might be a sister of Patrick.[3]

The east Galway saint named Ríceann (Ricín) is said to have been a daughter of Criomhthann, king of Uí Mhaine, allegedly the first man in Ireland to have killed a woman 'after the Faith', for which he surrendered his daughter to the church.[4] Reared by Caoireach Dheargáin at Cloonburren in the Roscommon parish of Moore, Ríceann allegedly went on to give birth to Dúnghal, ancestor of Clann Mhic Con Mara (McNamaras) of Thomond, before becoming a saint in her own right, as well as patron (under the guise of Ricín) of the parish of Clooney in the Clare barony of Bunratty Upper.[5] In this capacity, Ríceall (spelt Richill) was called upon, according to a poem in Classical Irish, together with numerous other saints, many of whom were from Thomond, to help in releasing Ireland's southern half (Leath Mogha) from a bondage imposed on it by the northern half (Leath Chuinn), represented by Finnian of Clonard.[6] The cult may also have travelled northwards in Connacht, to Leyny (Luighne) in Sligo, where Ríc(h)eall is said to have reverently received a visit from Daigh son of Coireall.[7]

The Kildare version of the cult is also attested in the Life composed for Íde of Killeedy. This provided her with a Columban disciple named Bishop Colmán whom she accompanied on a journey from the plain of the Liffey (shorthand for Kildare) to Killeedy in Limerick.[8] In this manner, Ríceann (Ríc(h)eall) can be said to have been associated with all three 'national' saints, Patrick, Brighid and Colum Cille. A possible association with Finnian of Clonard is also implied by the assertion in the latter's vernacular Life that he had a sister named Ríc(h)eann.[9] Only one saint of the name, this time in the form Ríc(h)eall, is to be found in the martyrologies, which noticed her feast on 19 May.[10]

1 *CGSH* §690.10; *Lgen*. 705.7.9. 2 *CGSH* §§670.61, 722; *VT* 432; *MartO*[2] 68. 3 OSL GY 483; cf. *TT* 229 §13. 4 *ACL* iii, 308–9; *OC* 37, 37. 5 Ibid.; OCBG 152 §2001; *ACoC* 182, 208. 6 RIA MS 23L11, 263; *SAM* 24.1, 17, 22. 7 *VSHH* 393 §18. 8 *VSHP* ii, 122–4 §§20, 24. 9 *LisL* 2661; cf. *GRSH* 114. 10 *MartT* 44; *MartG* 100; *MartD* 134.

Rícín. *See* Ríceann.

Rímhtheach daughter of Léinín. *See* Aighleann of Killiney.

Ríóg. *See* Moríóg.

Ríoghán of Kilrean (Ceall Ríogháin), parish of Killybegs Lower, barony of Boylagh, Co. Donegal. Like his brothers, Manchán, Mianach, and Rodaighe, the *cruimhthear* (presbyter) Ríoghán son of Fáilbhe belonged to the Ceinéal Boghaine branch of Ceinéal Conaill which gave name to the Donegal barony of Banagh.[1] Although little else is known of the saint, whose name derives from *rí*, 'king', his church had the distinction of being selected as a place to be visited by Suibhne Gealt after the battle of Moira (Magh Rath) in 636.[2] At Kilrean, from his perch in a tree, Suibhne was spoken to by the 'high-king', Domhnall son of Aodh, who had emerged victorious from the battle. The feast of the 'royal presbyter' Ríoghán fell on 9 August.[3]

1 *CGSH* §525; *GRSH* 41; *CCDK* 235. 2 *BS* §§15–17; *BCC* 380 §354. 3 *MartT* 61; *MartG* 152; *MartD* 214.

Ríoghnach. This name, a derivative of *ríoghain* 'queen' sometimes translated as *regina*, was borne by several holy women, six of whom are listed among the homonymous saints.[1] All of these were probably originally representative of the same east Leinster cult.[2]

1 *CGSH* §708.133–8; *MartD* 462. 2 *Ériu* 54, 94–5.

Ríoghnach daughter of Cochlán. *See* Beoaidh of Ardcarn; Colmán of Templeshanbo.

Ríoghnach daughter of Fearadhach. *See* Ríoghnach of Kilrainy.

Ríoghnach of Kilrainy (Ceall Ríoghnaighe), barony of Carbury, Co. Kildare, and of Templerainy (Ceall Ríoghnaighe), parish of Kilbride, barony of Arklow, Co. Wicklow. The two like-named churches of the daughter of Aodh were respectively located in the territories of Fothairt Oirbhreach and Uí Eineachghlais.

Along with her two sisters, Cuman and Crón, who were based at Ardnahue (Ceall Inghean nAodha) in the Carlow parish of Killerrig, Ríoghnach was attached to the Ceinéal Maine of Teathbha, a stretch of land comprising most of Longford and part of Westmeath.[1] Given the locations of her churches and other connections, the saint was almost certainly identical with her namesake Ríoghnach, sister of Finnian of Clonard.[2] In this capacity, the saint is said to have had several sons who attained sanctity, including Mocholmóg, Finnian's successor at Clonard, and Garbhán of Kilmagarvoke in the Carlow parish of Tullowphelim.[3] She also figures in the Life of her more famous brother, which states that Ríoghnach, together with her own mother and the mother of Ciarán (presumably of Clonmacnoise), dwelt in a *cella* near Clonard, probably an allusion to the later presence there of a house of Augustinian canonesses.[4] As Finnian's cult is elsewhere attested under the guise of Bairrfhionn, it may be assumed that Ríoghnach of Drumcullen, an Offaly church not far from the parish of Reynagh (Ceall Ríoghnaighe), was identical with the saint.[5] The parish of Reynagh includes the town of Banagher. The only feast (18 December) attested for Ríoghnach – albeit under the guise of a daughter of Fearadhach – was within the octave of the feast of Finnian of Clonard which fell on 12 December.[6] An early litany-style prayer of invocation includes possibly this Ríoghnach (albeit described as the daughter of Cochlán) among many other female saints.[7]

1 *CGSH* §§81, 708.135; *GRSH* 57; *Lgen.* 703.1; *ZCP* 10, 77; *HDGP* iv, 43, 130. 2 *CGSH* §722.97. 3 Ibid. 4 *VSHH* 102 §21; *LisL* 2661–71. 5 *CGSH* §708.137. 6 *MartT* 80; *MartG* 240; *MartD* 340. 7 *MartT* 116.

RÍOGHNACH sister of Finnian. *See* Ríoghnach of Kilrainy.

RÍOMH daughter of Fiachna. *See* Breacán of Dairinis; Cuimín Fada of Clonfert.

ROC of Salrock, parish of Ballynakill, barony of Ballynahinch, Co. Galway. This saint, thought to be the 'most miraculous' in the West, and famous for a struggle with the devil that led to the formation of the pass of Salrock, was probably extrapolated from the local name.[1] He is nowhere else attested, and the 'cursing stone' at Salrock is named after the seven daughters of the king of Britain.[2]

1 OSL GY iii, 30; *CLPD* 6, 18. 2 *JGAHS* 65, 6.

RÓDÁN. Among Patrick's Franks, according to Tíreachán, were two named 'Roddanus', one of whom founded the 'Old Church' (*senis ecclesia*) of Uí Oilealla.[1] Tíreachán has more to say of this foundation later in the text, where he describes how Patrick went from Elphin to the mound of Uí Oilealla, founding there a church 'still known' as Seincheall Dumhaighe, now Shankill, and leaving there, among others, the priest Ródán, whom the Tripartite Life elevated to the status of bishop.[2] The Tripartite Life also states that Ródán – described as herdsman among those in orders with Patrick – was left in a place in Muireasc called Ceall Easpaig Ródáin after the bishop.[3] Although this church has not been identified, within the parish of Tibohine, not far from Shankill, and just east of the barony of Tirerrill, is a townland of Kilroddan which may contain the saint's name. Saints of the name are commemorated on various days, including 18 January and 30 September.[4]

1 *PTBA* 128 §7.1. 2 Ibid. 140 §23; *BP* 1212–15; *VT* 108. 3 *CGSH* §§671.17; 672.12; *Lgen.* 695.1; *BP* 3136–7. 4 *MartT* 9, 75; *MartG* 18, 186; *MartD* 20, 262.

Roisín of Spike. *See* Ros.

Rón. *See* Brón.

Rónaid daughter of Rónán. *See* Feidhealm daughter of Rónán.

Rónaid daughter of Séighín. *See* Adhamhnán of Iona.

Rónán. This name, a derivative of *rón*, 'seal', was borne by many men thought to be holy in the Irish tradition, including nine in the list of homonymous saints.[1]

1 *CGSH* §707.912–20.

Rónán of Aghalurcher (Achadh Lurchaire), barony of Magherastephana, Co. Fermanagh. At least two (ostensibly distinct) bishops named Rónán son of Aodh are recorded. One, associated with Ráith Rónáin, a site in the Dublin parish of Tallaght, is said to have been an ancestor of the Uí Cheallaigh of Cuala branch of the Uí Mháil, despite his high ecclesiastical status.[1] This was an important dynasty which provided some kings of north Leinster in the late seventh and early eighth century.[2] Moreover, Rónán is accused of having slain his own brother.[3] The other Bishop Rónán was remembered on 23 December at Achadh Farcha, which usually denotes Agheragh in the Meath parish of Moybolgue, but in this case was mistakenly inserted for Achadh Lurchaire (Aghalurcher), whose saint (Rónán son of Aodh) is included in the catalogue of bishops preserved in the Register of the diocese of Clogher.[4] There is now a site named Kilronan within this parish, and in the mistaken belief that the correct Irish form of the parochial name was Achadh Urchair, 'field of the shot', a legend gained currency locally to the effect that the church was built where a shot from a sling came to earth.[5]

Aghalurcher adjoins Aghavea (Achadh Bheithe), the church associated with Lasair daughter of Rónán son of Ninnidh, eponym of the Roscommon church of Kilronan, near Boyle, which would suggest that the patrons of Aghavea and Kilronan were thought to be identical.[6] Together with several other saints of the Fermanagh area, including Tighearnach, Sineall and Seanach, Rónán son of Aodh was given a prominent place in the Life of Náile, whose church at Kinawley adjoins Aghalurcher.[7] The saint may also have been patron of Taghmaconnell in south Roscommon, where his memory was celebrated at a well in Sraduff on St John's Eve (23 June).[8]

1 *CGSH* §276; *GRSH* 91; *Lgen.* 461.1. 2 *IKHK* 288. 3 *CGH* 125a10–15. 4 *MartT* 88; *MartG* 244; *MartD* 344; *DPH* 1, 179; *ClRec.* 7, 380; PNNI v, 4, 8, 132–4. 5 OSL FH 107; *ClRec.* 19, 185–200. 6 *ClRec.* 18, 305; *Ériu* 5, 74. 7 *MHH* 110, 114, 118, 124 §§29, 40, 48, 60. 8 OSL RN i, 54.

Rónán of Ceall Rónáin. *See* Rónán of Dromiskin.

Rónán of Dromiskin (Druim Ionasclainn), barony and county of Louth. The genealogists attached Rónán son of Bearach to the Ceinéal Laoghaire (alias Clann Lughdhach) whose saints, though mainly concentrated in Meath, were associated with churches extending from Lough Erne to Trim.[1] Among Rónán's ancestors were a grandfather (Colum Cúile) and granduncle (Colum Tuama) who were also thought to be saints, and in one line of tradition Caoireach Dheargáin was taken to be his sister.[2] Rónán was sometimes given the epithet Fionn, 'fair', and under this guise he figures prominently in the literature, becoming hopelessly confused with his namesake, Rónán Fionn son of Sárán.[3] The confusion, probably deliberate in origin because of Dromiskin's status as a manor of the archbishop of Armagh, is most obvious in the well-known tale of Suibhne Gealt, 'the madman', where Rónán Fionn son of Bearach is given the role of pronouncing a curse on the eponymous hero of the tale. This is said to have occurred at Moira, the scene of a battle near a church called Lann Rónáin Fhinn (alias Ceall Lainne or Magh Lainne), now Magheralin in the Down barony of Lower Iveagh, which is normally associated with Rónán Fionn son of Sárán.[4] Despite the fact that the author of this tale traced Rónán's descent to the Ceinéal Laoghaire, there are compelling grounds for believing that he also had the more northern bearer of the name in mind because the latter's descent from Colla Dá Chríoch attached him to the Oirthir (whence Orior) whose saints are otherwise featured prominently in the story of Suibhne.[5]

This intermingling of the traditions surrounding the two saints is evident also on the topographical level. A separate account of Rónán's cursing of Suibhne, for example, locates the event at Dún na nGéadh, near Tara.[6] The Life of Fionnchú of Brigown presents Rónán Fionn of Magheralin, allegedly a first cousin of Fionnchú, as 'the senior saint' of Breagha, an area now comprising Meath and parts of Louth and Dublin, and thus more appropriate to the patron of Dromiskin, who belonged to the Ceinéal Laoghaire of Breagha.[7] Furthermore, whereas a sister, Eithne daughter of Sárán, is said to have been the mother of Críodán Ceartrannach of Bangor, through his own mother (Pompa daughter of Loarn) Rónán of Magheralin was provided with a uterine brother based in Breagha, namely Cairneach of Dulane.[8]

Of the two, only the patron of Dromiskin became the subject of a biography, preserved, oddly enough, in one collection only, the *Magnum Legendarium Austriacum*, 'Great Austrian Legendary', whose Irish Lives were supplied, mostly towards the end of the twelfth century, by the community of the *Schottenkloster* in Regensburg.[9] Regrettably surviving in incomplete form only, Rónán's Life provides a good deal of local (mainly Louth-Meath) detail. The saint's father is assigned to the Conaille, his mother (Caineach) to Dál nAraidhe – thus again bringing together the areas within which Dromiskin and Magheralin lay – and his birthplace is located at 'Rossinse', near 'Rossave'.[10] Among the saints brought into contact with him are Ultán of Ardbraccan and Mac Neasáin (presumably extrapolated from Inis Mac Neasáin, alias Ireland's Eye), and the local secular rulers with whom he had dealings included the Uí Aodha Shláine of Breagha and Dícuill son of Oisín of the main line of Conaille Muirtheimhne.[11] The Life was probably commissioned from one of the two Augustinian priories in Conaille (Louth and Knock) with a view to having it included in the Great Austrian Legendary. Under the guise of Rónán Fionn son of Bearach, the saint is also featured in the story of the Wanderings of Colum Cille's Clerics (*Mearughadh Cléireach Choluim Chille*), which shows the Fir Rois of the Louth/Monaghan area placing themselves under his protection, as well as that of Maine son of Niall, for they were the 'high saints' (*ardnaoimh*) of Ireland.[12]

Confusion with the Louth saint was not confined to the patron of Magheralin; an attempt was also made to portray Rónán son of Ninnidh, eponym of Kilronan, near Boyle, as the saint associated with Dromiskin (where his bell was allegedly then kept) probably because this church was a manor of the archbishop of Armagh, and later an administrative centre for his diocese *inter Anglicos*, which would have lent it great prestige.[13] Its high status from an early stage is indicated by the fact that the relics of its patron were enshrined in a 'gold and silver' casket in 801.[14] Magheralin was likewise not without importance. Following its plundering in 1178, it was described as an *ardneimheadh*, 'high church', and the saint's *bachall*, 'crozier', was caught up in the affray, together with that of Finnian of Movilla.[15]

Through his genealogical relationship with Caoireach Dheargáin who, in another guise, was supposedly a sister of Éanna, Rónán son of Bearach came to be known and venerated on Aran, whence Kilronan (Ceall Rónáin) on Inishmore, from where he is said to have accompanied Éanna and Pupa to view Bréanainn's boat as the latter set out on his sea-voyage.[16] The same Rónán was considered important enough, doubtless again because of his association with Dromiskin, to capture the attention of the biographer of Féichín, who brought him to Fore, together with Ultán of Ardbraccan.[17] The pedigree of Rónán Fionn son of Sárán became attached (erroneously) to a namesake at Lismore, remembered on 9 February, and under the guise of Morónóg (Marown), the saint was possibly also associated with Kirk Marown on the Isle of Man.[18] Though almost inseparable in the literary tradition, the two saints were parted in death. Rónán son of Bearach, remembered at Dromiskin on 18 and 30 November, is said to have died in the famous plague known as the *Buidhe Chonaill*, whereas the feast of his namesake at Magheralin fell on 22 May.[19] On the latter day, penitents visiting the saint's church were expected to give alms towards its repair.[20] After death, Rónán son of Bearach was thought to have remained powerful, as is shown by the vengeance he took on Annadh Ua Ruairc who plundered Dromiskin in 1043.[21] A note added to the entry for 19 November in a twelfth-century version of the Martyrology of Usuard, kept in Canterbury, states that Rónán's arm was kept as a relic there.[22]

1 *CGSH* §§325.1, 690.5; *GRSH* 52; *MartO*^{2} 242. **2** *CGSH* §690.7.15; *GRSH* 50; *Lgen*. 706.6. **3** *CGSH* §315 (1); *Lgen*. 714.13. **4** *BS* §§2–10; *CGSH* §§ (58), 318.2; PNNI vi, 216–17. **5** *BS* §2; *Éigse* 15, 173–88. **6** *FDG* 355–69. **7** *LisL* 2938–43. **8** *CGSH* §722.29. **9** *AB* 17, 161–6 §§1–9. **10** Ibid. §1. **11** Ibid. §§4–9. **12** *Ériu* 5, 78; *LSLC* 299; *MKM* 313; *BCC* 382 §355; *RC* 26, 134 §4. **13** *MKM* 313; *BCC* 382 §355; *RC* 26, 134 §4; *Ériu* 5, 78; *LSLC* 299. **14** *AU s.a.* **15** *MIA s.a.*; *MartD* xxxi. **16** *BNÉ* i, 53 §48. **17** *ASH* 136–7. **18** *PIM* 151–2; *MartO*^{2} 72. **19** *IrT* iii, 85 §9; *MartT* 45; *MartO*^{2} 125, 235; *MartG* 102, 220; *MartD* 136, 312; OSL LH 156. **20** *CPL* 7, 250. **21** ATig. *s.a.* **22** *VSHP* ii, 240n; *Propug.CV* 981.

Rónán of Kilronan. *See* Lasair of Kilronan; Rónán of Aghalurcher.

Rónán of Liathros, an unidentified site in Conaille Mhuirtheimhne, now approximately the northern part of Louth. This man, possibly a double of his namesake, Rónán son of Bearach at Dromiskin, a little further south, is known from two sources, the list of homonymous saints and the martyrologies, which remember him on 30 April.[1]

1 *CGSH* §707.920; *MartT* 38; *MartO²* 109; *MartG* 86; *MartD* 114.

Rónán of Lismore. *See* Morónóg.

Rónán of Lorum. *See* Colum Crom.

Rónán of Lough Erne. *See* Rónán son of Aodh.

Rónán Fionn of Magheralin. *See* Rónán of Dromiskin.

Ronoge. *See* Morónóg of Inishloe.

Rórán of Killeroran. *See* Rose of Kilrush.

Ros of Downpatrick, parish of Down, barony of Lecale Upper, Co. Down. This man was one of seven sons of Tricheamh of whom two, Ros and Díocha of Saul, were brought into contact with Patrick by his biographers.[1] Ros is shown by his pedigree to have had a brother, Oilill, whose grandson Finnian was the renowned founder of Movilla.[2] Little else is known of him, but some seventeenth-century sources speculatively identified him with Roisín of Spike Island, an early abbot of Cork, commemorated on 7 April, whose community was destined, according to Fursa of Killursa, to fall victim to the plague known as the *Scuab*, 'besom', out of Fanad.[3]

1 *CGSH* §136.2; *PTBA* 78; *BP* 373–427; *VT* 36–40. **2** *CGSH* §136.1.2; *GRSH* 84; *Lgen*. 723.10. **3** *GRSH* 84; *MartD* 96; NLI G 10, 46b; cf. *MakS* 32–3; *TEAB* 690 §5.

Rose of Kilrush (Ceall Rois), parish of St Munchin's, on the outskirts of Limerick. Like many other spurious saints, such as Solan of Killosolan who was said to have built his church in one night, and Rórán of Killeroran who was thought to be a brother of Cuán of Ahascragh, both in east Galway, Rose of Kilrush, supposedly a sister of Mainchín of St Munchin's, took her name from that of her church in Limerick.[1]

1 OSL GY i, 110, 238–9; *SACCL* 363.

Ruadhán of Lorrha (Lothra), barony of Lower Ormond, Co. Tipperary. Usually attached by the genealogists to the Eoghanacht of Cashel, the main branch of a dynasty that dominated Munster over many centuries, Ruadhán son of Fearghas Bearn was sometimes thought to have belonged more particularly to an obscure branch of the Uí Dhuach called Dubhraighe.[1] As the Uí Dhuach were mainly settled in the Kilkenny baronies of Fassadinin and Crannagh, there may be some connection between this descent and Bearn, the cognomen of Ruadhán's father, which is also found in Dál mBirn, an early name for Osraighe (now Ossory). Moreover, Tullaroan (Tulach Ruadháin) in the barony of Crannagh, which takes its name from the saint, is the probable location of an episode in Ruadhán's Life. The reference to Caol, mother of 'Ruadhán the priest', in the tract on the mothers of the saints may refer to Ruadhán's mother but, according to separate traditions, one of which relates to the death of Diarmuid son of Cearbhall, king of Tara, the saint's two sisters, were named Caol and Ruadhnad, and his mother was Inghean Bhaoith of Killinaboy.[2]

As Lorrha – the main focus of the saint's cult – was an important church, a biography was composed for Ruadhán, which has survived in Latin and Irish versions.[3] One Latin version, in the Salamancan codex, forms part of the O'Donohue group whose constituent texts are sometimes taken to date to as early as the period 750–850.[4] A critical edition of the entire biographical dossier of the saint has yet to be undertaken but, as in other Lives belonging to this group, such as that of Fíonán of Kinnitty, there are many indications of a much later date in the Life of Ruadhán.

Following his birth among the Uí Dhuach, Ruadhán is brought for his education to Bishop Finnian of Clonard, after which he founded his first church in Múscraighe in north Tipperary – doubtless at Kilruane (Ceall Ruadháin) in Lower Ormond – subsequently moving on angelic advice from there to where his *civitas*, now Lorrha, was located.[5] Interestingly, his arrival at Lorrha supposedly disturbed Bréanainn, who moved to the site of his own principal church at Clonfert. Ruadhán's wider wanderings then began, first to Ulster, where he settled at Slanore (Snámh Luthair) in the Cavan parish of Kilmore, among other places.[6] From Ulster, Ruadhán arrived in Connacht – among the Uí Oilealla who gave name to the Sligo barony of Tirerrill – to visit an otherwise unrecorded 'sister', Dairí by name, founding there the church of Shancough (Seanchua).[7] Close by, in the Roscommon parish of Tibohine, is Kilrooan (Ceall Ruadháin) which probably takes its name from the saint.

Returning to Munster, Ruadhán is shown performing various strategically well-placed acts, most of them miraculous. These included: the blessing of the hands of a youth in Araidh Chliach, the area about Emly, historically Munster's chief church; the restoration to health of the wife of the king of Cuala, near Dublin; the raising, at the request of Bréanainn, from the bottom of the Shannon Estuary of a sunken boat and its valuable passenger, the son of the king of the Britons, whom he protected from drowning; and the deference shown by him to Finnian of Clonard, in acceding to the latter's request that the community at Lorrha desist from receiving all the sustenance they needed from the sap of a miraculous tree.[8] There follows the 'Cursing of Tara' episode, the only one in the Life to have attracted much attention, where the king of Tara, having offended Ruadhán by taking prisoner a fugitive under the saint's protection, engaged with the holy man in a long litany of curses, including the prediction (often cited by later poets) that Tara would become desolate.[9] Various other miracles are then performed, including one while the saint was residing at Derrynaflan (Doire Eidhneach), and another involving the restoration to life of a number of kings at Tullaroan.[10] The concluding chapters present the saint overcoming, together with Colum Cille, a host of demons at Rahugh near Durrow, the church of Aodh son of Breac, before going on to list Ruadhán's many virtues.[11]

The itinerary thus drawn up for the saint took him, literally, all over the country, often to places named after him. But throughout his journey Ruadhán is seldom allowed to stray far from a priory connected with the canons regular of St Augustine, who had established themselves at Lorrha about the middle of the twelfth century.[12] Finnian, Ruadhán's tutor, to whom he showed great deference, was patron of Clonard, one of the earliest and most important of the Augustinian houses in Ireland.[13] The fact that Clonard became the seat of a bishopric in the twelfth century probably led to Finnian being twice described as a bishop. Like Finnian, Bréanainn was patron of a church (Clonfert) that became about the same time as Lorrha the site of a house of Augustinian canons, and the fact that Ruadhán is shown intervening on this saint's behalf in the Shannon Estuary by saving from drowning a son of the king of the Britons would have been sure to impress, especially after the English conquest of Ireland. Furthermore, it is scarcely a coincidence that Bréanainn's (only) foundation in this area, at Canon Island, took its name from the Augustinian canons.[14]

Closely related to the canons regular were the Premonstratensian canons whose priory on Lough Key not only included Shancough – the church allegedly founded by Ruadhán – among its possessions, but also acted as mother-house of the priory of Lough Oughter in Cavan, within a few hundred yards of the church of Slanore, supposedly visited by the Lorrha saint.[15] And finally, Pollrone (Poll Ruadháin), the location of the celebrated 'Cursing of Tara' episode, formed part of the possessions of the neighbouring convent of Kilculliheen, a house of Augustinian canonesses founded by Diarmuid Mac Murrough in 1151.[16] Clearly, a substantial part of the Life of Ruadhán can be explained by reference to Lorrha's position within the countrywide network of houses of Augustinian canons, thus pointing to an earliest possible date for the text in the second quarter of the twelfth century, when these priories began to be founded.

A saint of high status, one of Ireland's twelve apostles, and a close associate of the kings of Cashel – who are shown seeking and receiving his counsel, and displaying largesse to his church in a manner thought to reflect a desire of independence for his province – Ruadhán is elsewhere featured in the Lives of Finnian and Daigh son of Coireall, the second of which presents him as being in Clonard.[17] He also figures in the Life of Fionnbharr in relation to the church of 'Kilnacloona' – the location a few miles west of Ballincollig of the Cork saint's death – which is said to have been occupied by Ruadhán's disciples.[18] He was patron of the nearby church of Aghinagh, and several traces of his cult are elsewhere preserved in south Munster – among other places at Templeroan near Doneraile, Kilruane near Glanmire, Kilroan near Kinsale, and Kilruane near Ross Carbery – and in north Connacht, where he is reputed to have founded the Mayo church of Kilgarvan.[19] Among the dedications to him in Leinster was the Wexford church of Kilrane.[20] The saint's connections with Thomond are also strong, with one source opportunistically asserting that, despite being the traditional patron of the Eoghanacht of Cashel, Ruadhán also blessed Conall son of Eacha Bailldearg of the leading line of the rival Dál gCais, and another listing him among those who came to the assistance of Seanán of Scattery Island.[21] Similarly, according to a poem in Classical Irish, Ruadhán, together with numerous other saints, was called upon to help in releasing Ireland's southern half (Leath Mogha) from a bondage imposed on it by the northern half (Leath Chuinn), represented by Finnian of Clonard.[22] The vision attributed to Tnúthghal of Cashel, an account of which was written in Regensburg in the mid-twelfth century, also found a place for Ruadhán, as Tnúthghal's patron.[23] Ruadhán was said to have been similar in manners to the apostle Matthias.[24] He died, according to the annals, in 584 and was remembered as the 'lamp of Lothra' on 15 April, when, it is said, the cuckoo began to call.[24] His name is invoked in one of the Stowe Missal litanies.[25] Ruadhán was patron of the Uí Chinnéidigh (O'Kennedys) and among his relics was a bell, now in the British Museum.[26] A note attached to the *Kilkenniensis* version of Ruadhán's Life states that his arm was kept as a relic in Canterbury, but this is more likely to have been the arm of Rónán of Dromiskin.[27] The shrine of the Stowe Missal, now in the National Museum but formerly kept at Lorrha, may also have come to be regarded as a relic of the saint.[28]

1 *CGSH* §208; *GRSH* 118; *Lgen.* 738.14–15; *VSHH* 160 §1; *DIB* viii, 641–2. **2** *CGSH* §722.44; *VSHH* 164; *SG* i, 76; *IrT* iv, 93 §5. **3** *VSHH* 160–7; *VSHP* i, lxxxvi–lxxxvii, ii, 240–52; *BNÉ* i, xl, 317–29. **4** *MISL* 297–339. **5** *VSHH* 160–1 §§1–2; *VSHP* ii, 240–1 §§1–3. **6** *VSHH* 161 §§3–6; *VSHP* ii, 241–2 §§4–8. **7** *VSHH* 162 §7; *VSHP* ii, 242 §9. **8** *VSHH* 162–3 §§8–11; *VSHP* ii, 242–5 §§10–14. **9** *VSHH* 163–5 §12; *VSHP* ii, 245–9 §§15–18; *IKHK* 34, 53, 95, 97, 192, 211; *IEME* 172–5; cf. *MISL* 24; *DMU* 26–40. **10** *VSHH* 166 §§16–22; *VSHP* ii, 249–50 §§19–28. **11** *VSHH* 167 §§23–5; *VSHP* ii, 251–2 §§29–30. **12** *MRHI* 185. **13** Ibid. 163–4. **14** Ibid. 162. **15** Ibid. 205; *DK* 250. **16** *MRHI* 319; *HADO* iv, 149, 205. **17** *VSHH* 83 §5; 101 §19, 103–4 §§24–6; 392 §11; *Ériu* 9, 45 §§6–7; *RC* 37, 352 §9; *IEME* 175. **18** *BBa.* 70–2 §26–7. **19** *CPR* i, lxvii–lxviii; OSL MO i, 109. **20** *CPL* 11, 206; *CECW* 211. **21** *CoC* 14; *ZCP* 10, 28 §23. **22** RIA MS 23L11, 263; *SAM* 24.1, 17, 20. **23** *VisTnug.* 54–5. **24** *CGSH* §712.14; ATig. *s.a.*; *MartT* 33, 94; *MartO²* 106; *MartG* 76; *MartD* 102; *ÉtC* 17, 199 §3. **25** HBS 32, 14. **26** *FFÉ* iii, 112. **27** *VSHP* ii, 240n; *Propug.CV* 981. **28** *PRIA* 91C10, 285–95.

Ruadhán of Ráith. Associated with a church that has yet to be identified, this saint is said to have been one of seven sons of Lughaidh son of Nathí, who belonged to a branch of the Leinstermen named Uí Chéithigh, whence the Kildare barony of Ikeathy.[1] The most famous of his brothers was Crónán (alias Mochua) of Clondalkin. His mother was Cainnear of Cluain Dá Shaileach, probably now Clonsilla, a few miles from Clondalkin.[2] It may be assumed that Ruadhán was also associated with a church in the Dublin/Kildare area.

1 *CGH* 124a14; *CGSH* §243; *Lgen.* 727.13. **2** *CGSH* §722.77.

Ruadhnad sister of Ruadhán. *See* Ruadhán of Lorrha.

Ruanach of Inishmore (Inis Mór), parish of Aghalurcher, barony of Magherastephana, Co. Fermanagh. The genealogists attached Ruanach (alias Rúnach) son of Muireadhach (alias Maon) to a segment of the Ceinéal Eoghain of Tyrone known as Ceinéal Maoin.[1] His only claim to fame is a mention, albeit corrupt, in the preface to the Martyrology of Aonghas which attributes to him a quatrain on Diarmuid son of Cearbhall, king of Tara.[2] Little else is known of the saint, other than his feastday of 23 July.[3]

1 *CGSH* §§11, 31; *GRSH* §48; *Lgen.* 701.5; *CGH* 140a8. **2** *MartO²* 6, 442. **3** *MartT* 57; *MartG* 142; *MartD* 198.

Ruanus. *See* Tuán.

Rumhan of Trim. *See* Cormac of Trim.

Rus. *See* Ros.

S ☙

Saicheall. *See* Soicheall.

Sailmín son of Beoghain. This person is known from a single text, entitled *Eachtra Léithín*, 'the adventures of Léithín', which describes him as a saintly member of the community of Ciarán of Clonmacnoise, and as one of seven sons of Beoghain of Boireann (Burren), who gave name as a group to two sites called Cros na Macaomh, 'cross of the youths', one on the river Shannon, the other on the road to Cluain.[1] Together with a companion named Maolán son of Naoi, Sailmín is said to have overheard at Cloniff (Cluain Daimh) on the Shannon – a place apparently otherwise associated with seven holy bishops – a conversation between an eagle named Léithín and one of his brood.[2]

1 *CR* 10, 132. **2** Ibid. 133–43; *IrL* 72.

Sáirbhile. *See* Moninne.

Samhthann of Clonbroney (Cluain Brónaigh), barony of Granard, Co. Longford. Despite the location of her church in Cairbre of Teathbha, now the Granard area, Samhthann daughter of Diamrán (Diamarán / Diarán) was attached by the genealogists to the Dál bhFiatach of east Ulster.[1] She was part of a tradition that Patrick is said to have initiated, when, according to the Tripartite Life, he left behind at Granard two sisters, both called Éimhear, who were the first to occupy Clonbroney.[2]

Mentioned several times in the pre-Conquest annals, Samhthann's church appears to have enjoyed high status of a kind that later led to the composition of a Latin Life, now preserved in the Rawlinson (earlier *Insulensis* or Saints' Island) collection.[3] Described as 'late and brief', Samhthann's Life, having named her father (Dyamranus) and mother (Columba), brought her to the king of Cairbre (Críodán) with a view to having her married off under his sponsorship, a fate from which she is shown to have miraculously escaped, choosing God as her spouse, and serving initially under Cognaid at a place called Earnaidhe – now apparently Urney, near Strabane in Tyrone, which is also associated with Feime daughter of Coireall.[4] Following some precocious signs of sanctity, including a St Martin-like rending in two of her cloak, the saint was summoned to Clonbroney, allegedly in the wake of a dream had by its founder Fuinche.[5]

Although Clonbroney was to remain the centre of Samhthann's activity, contacts were also established for her with several kings, mostly of early eighth-century backgrounds, as well as with other churches. Included are two high-kings and several local dynasts: Cionaodh son of Íorghalach (†728) whose captive Follamhain, eponym of Caoille Follamhain in or near the barony of Fore in Meath, was miraculously released; Niall Frasach son of Fearghal (†778) who, perhaps as a hint to a more recent successor, is shown commissioning a gold and silver cover for the saint's crozier; Flann son of Connla whose father died as king of Teathbha in 741; and Inreachtach son of Reachtabhra of the Uí Thuirtre (later the Uí Fhlainn), of the area about Toome in the county of Antrim, who was born through the saint's intervention to a previously barren mother, mention of all of whom has led to the implausible suggestion that the Life itself was compiled in the late eighth century.[6]

Among other churches mentioned in the text are: Devenish (Daimhinis) on Lough Erne whose saint (Molaise alias Laisréan) also figures, albeit anachronistically, as a witness to the signs that followed Samhthann's death; Granard, not far from Clonbroney, which the saint visits; a *monasterium* of Cainneach, a 'famous' abbot said to have been born of a nun and reared by Samhthann; and the community of 'Iova insula', now Iona, who are depicted running into a storm, miraculously calmed, on the way to a landing near the Boyne estuary.[7] The Life, which was skilfully written with a view to presenting Samhthann (†739) as far as possible against a background of persons recorded in the annals of her period, is devoid of overt references to donations of property. There are some indications of a local provenance in the abbey of Abbeylara, a Cistercian house founded in the early thirteenth century.[8] The site at Abbeylara was previously associated with Fuinche, who is here declared to have founded Clonbroney.[9] The site of the Cistercian abbey, which is shown receiving Samhthann as a visitor, also went under the name of Granard.[10]

Outside her Life, Samhthann rarely figures in the hagiographical record, but she is anachronistically presented as one of the judges of a dispute between Bearach of Termonbarry and a druid-poet, and she, representing her church, is among the saints said, tendentiously, to have owed tribute to Caillín of Fenagh.[11] Elsewhere she is found among a group of female saints invoked for protection, while her praises, mainly as an ascetic, are sung in a poem attributed to yet another high-king, Aodh Allán son of Fearghal (†743).[12] A tale preserved in the *Monastery of Tallaght*, which comments negatively on soul-friendship with women, treats Samhthann as a contemporary of the late eighth-century saint, Maol Ruain of Tallaght.[13] The saint's feast fell on 19 December.[14]

1 *CGSH* §185; *GRSH* 84; *Lgen.* 723.11; *DIB* viii, 759–60. **2** *BP* 995–1003, 1950–53; *VT* 90, 168. **3** *VSHP* i, lxxxvii–lxxxviii, ii, 252–61. **4** *Kenney* 465; *VSHP* ii, 253–4 §§1–2; *StC* 20–1, 79. **5** Ibid. 254 §§3–5. **6** Ibid. 255 §7, 258 §17, 256–7 §§12–13, 259 §21; *MHA* 101. **7** *VSHP* ii. 255 §10, 260–1 §26, 259 §19, 258 §18, 259–60 §23. **8** *MRHI* 124. **9** *CGSH* §670.5. **10** *MRHI* 124. **11** *VSHP* i, 82–3 §19; *BNÉ* i, 36 §62; *BFen.* 286. **12** HBS 32, 14; *MartT* 108, 124; *ZCP* 13, 144; *DDé* 50. **13** *MT* §61. **14** *MartO*[2] 252; *MartG* 242; *MartD* 340.

SANCT BHRÓG daughter of Dallbhrónach. *See* Feadhbhair of Boho.

SANTÁN of St Ann's Chapel (Ceall Easpaig Shantáin), townland of Glassamucky Brakes, parish of Tallaght, barony of Uppercross, Co. Dublin, and of Killalish (Ceall Dá Lis), parish of Kilranelagh, barony of Upper Talbotstown, Co. Wicklow.[1] One of three sons of Cantón, king of the Britons, the others being Sanctán (no doubt a doublet of Santán) and Leathnán, the saint's name derives from *sanct* (*sant*), an Irish borrowing of Welsh *sant*, itself borrowed from Latin *sanctus*, 'saint'.[2] The saint is doubtless the same as his namesake, Santán son of Samuel Ceannísеal, 'head-bent' (whose name crops up as Sawyl Benisel in Welsh genealogies), brother of the pilgrim Madóg (from Welsh *Madawg*).[3] This Santán's mother was Deichtir daughter of Muireadhach Muindearg, king of Ulster.[4] On the basis of his name, Welsh background, and the location of one of his churches close to Dublin, it has been argued that Santán may represent Samson of Dol in Brittany, a saint of Welsh origin who is said to have founded a church near *Arx Etri*, now Howth north of Dublin.[5] The preface to an Old Irish hymn beginning *Ateoch ríg n-amra n-aingel*, 'I implore the wonderful king of angels', attributed to Santán, imagines him going west from Clonard to Inis Madóg, an unidentified church named after the saint's brother who allegedly came first of the two to Ireland.[6] Another church named Ceall Santáin after the saint was located at Fishloughan in the Derry parish of Kildollagh, near Mount Sandel (which may have taken name from it) in the adjoining parish of Coleraine, and a note added to the entry on the saint's feastday in May attaches him to Drumline in the Clare barony of Bunratty Lower.[7] Across the Irish Sea, in the Isle of Man, a parish was named Kirk Santan after the saint who, as in Ireland, was later confused with St Ann.[8] The feast of the saintly 'sage, soldier' and bishop fell on 9 May, and again on 10 June.[9]

1 *HDGP* iii, 157, 168. **2** *CGSH* §669.3; *Lgen.* 752.7. **3** *CGSH* §722.76. **4** Ibid. **5** *Peritia* 3, 320–3; *DIB* viii, 761. **6** *LH* i, 129. **7** *AU*[1] *s.a.* 1197; *DUPN* 111; MartO[1] 85. **8** *PIM* 133–4. **9** *LH* i, 131; *MartT* 41, 49; *MartO*[2] 121; *MartG* 92, 114; *MartD* 122, 166.

Santleathan. *See* Caomhán Santleathan.

Saorghas Doithneannach. This man is said to have blessed Bearach son of Meisceall of the leading Laoighis dynasty, whence the nickname Bearach *na Beannachtan*, 'of the blessing'.[1] Saorghas may be identical with a namesake commemorated on 30 May at an unidentified site named Druim, the only saint of the name to be remembered in the martyrologies.[2]

1 *CGH* 127a45. **2** *MartT* 47; *MartG* 106; *MartD* 140.

Saorlaith daughter of Cuileabhaoth. *See* Maol Brighde son of Tornán.

Sárán of Inis Mór in Imokilly (Uí Mhic Coille), now probably Great Island, of which Cóbh is the main town. This son of Aireachar is known only from the martyrologies, which remember him on 15 May.[1]

1 *MartT* 45; *MartO*[2] 124; *MartG* 96; *MartD* 128.

Sárán of Lissan (Liosán/Leasán) in the Tyrone barony of Dungannon Upper. This son of Tighearnán (alias Tighearnach) son of Maonach was commemorated at Lissan (in Slieve Gallion) on 21 October, and also at a place named Cluain Doacra after the saint in the district known as the Ceachair, on the borders of Longford and Leitrim.[1] Doacra (alias Moacra) is a hypocoristic form of Sárán. The location of the church in the Ceachair may point to Cluain Deochra, later the obsolete 'Clooneoghra' in the Longford barony of Moydow, now perhaps represented by Ballynakill in the Longford parish of Kilashee.[2]

1 *MartT* 73 marg.; *MartG* 180; *MartD* 252; *HDGP* iii, 118. **2** *ILL* 261; *JACAS* 2.8, 16–20.

SÁRÁN of Tisaran (Teach Sáráin), barony of Garrycastle, Co. Offaly. According to his pedigree, Sárán son of Brógán belonged to a branch of the Dál gCais of Thomond.[1] The segment to which Sárán belonged held the territory of Dealbhna Beathra, later the barony of Garrycastle, among whose churches was Clonmacnoise, now adjoining Tisaran.[2] Sárán, who was clearly not taken to be celibate, forms part of the pedigree assigned by the Four Masters to their patron, Toirdhealbhach Mac Cochláin, chief of that district.[3] Despite the proximity of Ciarán's church to that of Sárán, the saint finds no mention in the various Lives composed for the patron of Clonmacnoise, but he is mentioned in the *Registry of Clonmacnoise*, which devotes several lines to the 'holy cleark' named Sárán who built the church called *Teach Sáráin*, now Tisaran. Moreover, while his name was still remembered at Tisaran in the late seventeenth century, the patron of the local 'abbey' was later thought to have been 'Trena', possibly an echo of the local ancestral figure 'Treón/Tréan'.[4] The saint was taken by Míchéal Ó Cléirigh to be identical with the Sárán commemorated on 20 January.[5] Sárán's church and holy well at Tisaran were located in the townland of Moystown Demesne.[6]

1 *GRSH* 121. **2** *Lgen.* 659.10. **3** *GRSH* 5. **4** *RM* 6.1, 13; *TDI* ii, 621; *Lgen.* 659.8; *JRSAI* 4, 449; *CCLC* 311. **5** *MartT* 10; *MartG* 20; *MartD* 23. **6** *AIOY* 119; OSL OY 159.

SÁRÁN son of Brónach. Although well enough attested in martyrologies and place-names, the name Sárán is infrequently found in a context that allows identification of family affiliation. An exception is the *cruimhthear* (presbyter), Sárán son of Brónach, who was attached to the Luighne, whence the name of the Sligo barony of Leyny.[1] Although otherwise unknown at local level, it may be worth noting that Fionnbharr of Cork is credited with having received from a certain Sárán the gift of a church named Druim Eidhneach, now apparently Drom in the Tipperary parish of the same name.[2] A neighbouring saint, Diarmuid of Glankeen, who likewise allegedly surrendered his church to the Cork saint, was remembered at or near the Sligo church of Kilmacowen, on the edge of the present barony of Leyny.[3]

1 *CGSH* §413. **2** *BBa.* 68 §23, 255. **3** Ibid.; *IrT* iii, 1 §1.

SÁRNAD daughter of Aodh Gabhalfhada. This saint was attached to a branch of the Uí Fhiachrach of north Connacht named Ceinéal Cinn Ghamhna, later Uí Dhuibhghiolla.[1] Arriving among this group, Cormac of Killala was met by the descendants of Aodh Gabhalfhada, father of Sárnad.[2] Although nowhere else specified, Sárnad's church was probably the unidentified Dairinis Chéadna, mentioned with her in the list of those commemorated on 15 April.[3] Remembered on the same day were the sons of Draighean of Kilroe (Ceall Ró) in the parish of Killala and barony of Tirawley, who were also met by Cormac in this part of Connacht.[4] Alternatively, despite the phonological difficulty of the lenited final *-d*, it is tempting to assume, with John O'Donovan, that Sárnad was later represented among the southern Uí Fhiachrach, whose lands corresponded approximately to the diocese of Kilmacduagh, by Sórnach (anglicized Sourney) of Drumacoo in the barony of Dunkellin.[5] Regarded as feminine and normally accompanied by the definite article (*an*/the), the name of this saint was attached in Drumacoo to a bed (*leabaidh*), bush (*sceach*) and holy well (*tobar*).[6] She is probably the same as the saint highly venerated on Inishmore by the Aran islanders, who named a church (Teampall Asúrnaidhe) and also a bed and well after her.[7] The commemoration on 9 November of Sárnad daughter of Aodh in 'Tír Mhaine' – possibly a reference to the lands of Uí Mhaine in east Galway – may also refer to her.[8] Finally, Sárnad, along with many other saints, several of whom had connections with south Galway and north Clare, was called upon, according to a poem in Classical Irish, to help in releasing Ireland's southern half (Leath Mogha) from a bondage imposed on it by the northern half (Leath Chuinn), represented by Finnian of Clonard.[9]

1 *CGSH* §385; *Lgen*. 257.2, 711.9; *TCHyF* 54. **2** *IrT* iii, 4 §8. **3** *MartT* 33; *MartG* 76; *MartD* 102. **4** *IrT* iii, 6 §16. **5** OSL GY i, 301. **6** Ibid. iii, 370: *HADK* 32–4. **7** *ASH* 715 (but cf. ibid. 715); *SAL* 193–5. **8** *MartG* 214; *MartD* 300. **9** RIA MS 23L11, 263; *SAM* 24.1, 17, 21.

Sárnad of Barragh (Beirreach), now Barragh, barony of Forth, Co. Carlow. In keeping with the location of her church, Sárnad daughter of Eacha was attached by the genealogists to the Fothairt who gave name to the barony of Forth.[1] She belonged to a line that produced Muireann, abbess of Kildare, among others [2]. Not surprisingly, therefore, she figures – although disguised as the daughter of Fiachra of the Uí Dhúnlainge, the leading dynasty in north Leinster – among the saints said to have been subject to Brighid at a church named Ceall Bhairnigh, perhaps a corrupt form of Beirreach.[3] The connection with Kildare is still marked by the presence of a townland named Kilbride (Ceall Bhrighde) in the parish of Barragh. Seventeenth-century sources held her to be the Sárnad commemorated at an unidentified Dairinis Chéadna on 15 April.[4] An early litany-style prayer of invocation possibly includes this Sárnad.[5] By the early nineteenth century, local opinion considered the name of her parish to be derived from an otherwise unattested 'Barrach', a carpenter by trade.[6]

1 *CGSH* §4; *GRSH* 75; *Lgen*. 718.3. **2** *CGH* 126a53. **3** *CGSH* §670.73; *HDGP* iii, 130. **4** *MartT* 33; *MartG* 76; *MartD* 102; *GRSH* 75. **5** *MartT* 108; *IrL* 92. **6** OSL CW 391.

Scannlach daughter of Seachnasach, of Ard Scannlaighe, an unidentified site in Ceinéal Ardghail, in the south-west corner of Co. Meath.[1] The saint is said to have belonged to the Clann Lughdhach whose original patrimony allegedly extended far beyond Ceinéal Ardghail, from Lough Erne to Slieve Bloom.[1] Scannlach's grandfather (Colum Cúile) was also regarded as a saint and, according to one pedigree, Rónán of Dromiskin was a direct descendant of her brother Uiréan.[2] Little else is known of the saint, but she was remembered by the martyrologists on 10 December.[3]

1 *HDGP* i, 100. **2** *CGSH* §325.1; *Lgen*. 706.10. **3** *MartG* 326; *MartD* 330.

Scannlach wife of Aodh Rón. *See* Créadhnad of Rathbride.

Sceallán. According to his Life, Molua of Kyle, then at the point of death and subject to visions of the men of heaven communing with those of earth, asked of his *minister*, 'priest', Sceallán that he give him the last rites.[1] A *minister* named Sceallán also figures in the Life of Cainneach of Aghaboe, which adjoins Kyle, albeit in the context of a miraculous catch of fish that occurred at Assaroe in Donegal.[2] This may refer to the patron of a church named 'Kilmoshkillogue' in the townland of Charlestown, in the Kilkenny parish of Dunkitt, within Cainneach's diocese of Ossory.[3] This parish was dedicated to Maodhóg of Ferns, whose namesake of Clonmore enjoyed the same feast (11 April) as Sceallán.[4] A second feast attributed to Sceallán fell on 1 September.[5]

1 *VSHH* 144–5 §68; *VSHP* ii, 223 §52. 2 *VSHH* 186 §17; *VSHP* i, 157 §13. 3 *HADO* iv, 139. 4 *MartT* 32; *MartG* 74; *MartD* 100; *HADO* iv, 137. 5 *MartG* 168; *MartD* 232.

Sceanbhán of Clondagad (Cluain Dá Ghad), barony of Islands, Co. Clare. Visiting the parish of Clondagad in November 1839, Eugene O'Curry was told how a certain saint called 'Sgreavaun', patron of the local church, overcame another holy man named 'Feadaun', eponym of the neighbouring church of Kilfiddane, in a miracle-trial involving two withes (*gad*, whence Cluain Dá Ghad), one of which (Sgreavaun's) flowed upstream.[1] The phonetic change of *n* to *r*, common in western dialects, seems to have combined with metathesis to produce the local form Screabhán (alias Cravan) from an earlier Sceanbhán.[2] Under the latter guise, the saint is included, along with Luchtighearn and Blathmhac – also patrons of Clare churches – among those on whom Seanán of Scattery could rely for assistance, and Sceanbhán also figures, together with the same saints, among the numerous 'children' of Fíonmhaith (alias Inghean Bhaoith) of Killinaboy.[3] Nothing else appears to be known of Sceanbhán, but O'Curry recorded a pattern held on 10 September at a well dedicated to him in the parish of Kilmaley.[4] Another well (St Cravan's) was dedicated to him at Ballymacravan in the Clare parish of Kilshanny.[5] The well at Toberscanavan (Tobar Sceanbháin) in the Sligo parish of Ballysadare may also be named after him.

1 *ACoC* 163. 2 *HWI* 71. 3 *ZCP* 10, 28 §22; *IrT* iv, 93 §7. 4 *ACoC* 164–5. 5 *OC* 21, 54.

Sciath of Ardskeagh (Feart Scéithe), barony of Fermoy, Co. Cork. Sciath daughter of Meachar was one of three virgins of the descendants of Conaire, otherwise the family known as Múscraighe, the other two being Gobnaid and Ciar Asgadh.[1] Through her mother, Eithne daughter of Conchradh, she enjoyed a uterine relationship with several northern saints, including Athchaoin of Colp, Colmán of Lambay Island, and Earnán of Tory Island.[2] Sciath's church in the district known as Múscraighe Trí Maighe – later 'Muscridonegan', and now mainly the barony of Orrery and Kilmore and adjoining parts of the barony of Fermoy – was important enough to attract the attention of the biographer of Ailbhe, whose church at Emly may have had some proprietorial claim to it. Ailbhe is twice shown to have come to Sciath's assistance, sending her two deer to perform ploughing duties over many years, and likewise sending her a scribe to assist in the preparation of a gospel-book.[3] A much earlier notice of the importance of the saint and her church, which may have had some involvement with the *céile Dé* ascetics, is to be found in the Martyrology of Tallaght; having added Sciath's name to the list of those remembered on 6 September, one of her two feasts, the martyrologist recorded the arrival in Tallaght of the saint's relics.[4] Moreover, her memory was invoked in a litany preserved in the so-called Stowe Missal, which appears to have been compiled in the early ninth century.[5] Sciath's second feast fell on 1 January.[6] The saint is thought to have also been the patron and eponym of St Skay's chapel in the Scottish parish of Craig in Forfarshire.[7]

1 *CGSH* §665.2.6; *GRSH* 79; *Lgen.* 720.6. 2 *CGSH* §722.98. 3 *VSHH* 127 §§38–9; *VSHP* i, 58–9 §33. 4 *MartT* 68; *MartO*[2] 193; *MartG* 170; *MartD* 238; *CéliD* 135. 5 HBS 32, 14; *CéliD* 135. 6 *MartT* 3; *MartG* 6; *MartD* 4. 7 *CPNS* 332.

Scíre of Kilskeer (Ceall Scíre), barony of Upper Kells, Co. Meath. Along with her brother, Earnán son of Eoghan of Cluain (Druim) Reilgeach in Midhe (now possibly either Cloonrallagh in the Longford parish of Templemichael, or Clonrelick in the Westmeath parish of Ballyloughloe), Scíre was attached by the genealogists to the Uí Chaocháin – the descendants of Fearghas Caochán, brother of Niall Naoighiallach – who were associated with her church at Kilskeer.[1] She is said to have been one of two daughters of Cuman daughter of Dallbhrónach by Eoghan of the Uí Chaocháin, the other being Corcair Chaoin.[2] Like many of Cuman's progeny, Scíre is featured among the saints who, according to the biographer of Forannán of Alternan, came together to meet Colum Cille in north Connacht.[3] Her church appears to have formed part of the extensive properties of Colum Cille's church at Kells, its erenagh and her crozier being listed among the guarantors of a charter in the Book of Kells.[4] A second church named after her, at Kilskeery Glebe in Tyrone, formerly lay within the territory of Fir Mhanach.[5] Scíre was locally remembered at Kilskeer on 28 September, but the martyrologies agree in placing her feast on 24 March.[6] An early litany-style prayer invokes Scíre along with many other female saints.[7]

1 *CGH* 139b47; *CGSH* §37; *GRSH* 65; *Lgen.* 711.11.16. 2 *CGSH* §722.9; *GRSH* 65; *CGH* 139b47. 3 *Anecd.* iii, 3 §5. 4 IC 157; cf. OSL MH 47. 5 *MartD* 86. 6 OSL MH 45; *MartT* 26; *MartO*[2] 84; *MartG* 60; *MartD* 86. 7 *MartT* 108; *IrL* 92.

Scoithín of Tiscoffin (Teach Scoithín), barony of Gowran, Co. Kilkenny. The genealogists attached Scoithín son of Séadna to the ecclesiastical family of Dál Modhula (otherwise known as Dulraighe or Corca Dhula), a branch of the Araidh of East Limerick that was closely associated with Emly, the chief church of Munster over many centuries.[1] Also attached to this family was Ailbhe, Emly's patron and Patrick's rival for authority over the southern part of Ireland, and it has been suggested that this relationship led to other associations in the traditions surrounding Scoithín, including the proximity of his church to Clara, whose patron was identical with Colmán of Kilroot, the first church to be founded by Ailbhe in Ireland.[2] A common ancestor, Olga Cráibhtheach, 'pious', is reputed to have been in a place called Díseart Scoithín before his saintly progeny spread 'on pilgrimage' to the places of their resurrection.[3] Scoithín's place of resurrection was at Tiscoffin, but the saint had strong links with several other places in both Leinster and Munster. The Life of David of St David's (Menevia), perhaps influenced by the presence of a church named *sancti Scothini* in the local deanery of Elfel, presents him, variously under the guise of Scutinus and Scolanus, as a disciple of Maodhóg of Ferns.[4] Scoithín is also among the names invoked in a poem on the Uí Dheagha of Ossory, attributed to Moling.[5] Fionnbharr of Cork, the parish of whose associated church at Kilmacahill adjoined Tiscoffin, was allegedly instrumental in providing Scoithín with his name, having discovered him walking on the sea as if it were a plain of clover (*magh scoithsheamrach*).[6] A church near Liscannor in Clare – 'in the sea at the edge of the lands of Fir Arda, where one still sees the wave rising over the gable of the church building' – was named after Scoithín, and it has been remarked that this gave the saint something of the character of a sea-dweller.[7] Indeed, while there were allegedly two Clare churches called 'Kilstuiffeen / Kilstiffin' (Ceall Scoithín / Stuifinn), both of them located on the coastline and visible only at certain times, in at least one tale the saint was transformed into one of three warrior descendants of the legendary Fir Bholg, and his church off Liscannor became a repository for the booty of the three warriors.[8] Celebrated, among others by the writer George Moore, for having kept his virginity (to the astonishment of Bréanainn) among 'damsels beautiful, white-bosomed', Scoithín of 'the sweet stories' was apparently also noted for his curse.[9] Local tradition at Tiscoffin remembered him, not as a virgin, but as the father of numerous children who turned to sanctity only when he repented after being discovered planning to drown some of them.[10] The feast of Scoithín, the 'diadem of Slievemargy', fell on 2 January.[11] Finally, Scoithín was among the saints invoked as a guarantor of the Law of Adhamhnán.[12]

1 *CGSH* §189; *GRSH* 110; *Lgen.* 731.7. **2** *CGSH* §135; *GRSH* 110; *CGH* 326h6–25; *StH* 31, 30–1; *VSHH* 123 §22; *HADO* iii, 353. **3** *CGH* 326h25–52. **4** *VSBG* 160 §37. **5** *JCS* 1, 229; *Anecd.* ii, 36 §22. **6** *MartO²* 40. **7** *MartO¹* xxxii; *StH* 31, 30–2. **8** *BMG* 106, 112, 118; *ACoC* 97. **9** *ICT* 42–3; *ZCP* 1, 64; *RC* 36, 287; 37, 351 §7; *MartO²* 40; *Ériu* 18, 58; *Seanchas* 235 §7. **10** OSL KK i, 223–7; *HADO* iii, 360–1. **11** *MartT* 4; *MartO²* 33; *MartG* 6; *MartD* 4. **12** *CA* §22.

Scoth. *See* Meangán.

Screabhán. *See* Sceanbhán.

Seachlain. *See* Seachnall.

Seachnall of Dunshaughlin (Domhnach Seachnaill), barony of Ratoath, Co. Meath. This man was the first of seven sons of Restitutus (Welsh Rhystud) of the Lombards by a sister of Patrick, usually named Lubaid, but sometimes also Dairearca and Liamhain.[1] The saint is best known for his place among the signatories of the so-called Armagh canon, and for a Latin alphabet hymn (beginning *Audite omnes*) attributed to him, probably spuriously, in praise of Patrick, allegedly the first ever hymn composed in Ireland.[2] There is no mention of the hymn in the ninth-century Book of Armagh, the earliest surviving manuscript of the Patrician dossier but, writing at Tallaght about 830, the martyrologist Aonghas reveals an awareness of it.[3] A passage in the *Additamenta* of the Book of Armagh that shows Seachnall (alias Secundinus) protesting to Patrick about a chariot supplied the author of the Tripartite Life with a preamble to the story of how the hymn came about, which is summarized in *Liber Hymnorum*.[4] Knowing that his constant companion Seachnall had not long to live,

Patrick is said to have reluctantly agreed to the composition of the hymn, granting many favours as a reward to those who recited it. The place of composition is said to have been Dunshaughlin.

These and other details, largely based on episodes in Patrick's Tripartite Life, are included in the Life pieced together for Seachnall, possibly by Henry Fitzsimon, whose copy then came into the hands of the Bollandists.[5] Variously described as the Armagh saint's bishop and poet, the 'very learned and holy' Seachnall is also presented as Patrick's disciple and companion in the Life of Déaglán of Ardmore.[6] Reputedly the first bishop to rest in the soil of Ireland, and thought to have been similar in manners to another *sapiens*, Hilary of Poitiers, Seachnall is said to have died in 447 at the age of 75, nine years after he and his brother Auxilius are thought to have arrived in the country.[7] Despite his external origins, the Uí Fhiachrach of Connacht later declared him to be one of their own.[8] A cross in his memory was erected at Armagh, and his feastday was celebrated on 27 November.[9] Locally known in Dunshaughlin as 'Seachlain', his festival was later thought to fall 'just a month before Christmas'.[10]

1 *CGSH* §§664, 722.15; *Lgen.* 695.1; *LH* i, 3; *MartT* 100; *BP* 895–902; *VT* 82; *MartO*[1] clxxiii; *MartG* 226; *MartD* 318; *Ériu* 4, 74–90; *FSPP* 69; *DIB* viii, 822–3. **2** *IEKF* 58–9; *LH* i, 3–13; *IHS* 2, 129–53; *DisSP* 186–91. **3** *MartO*[2] 237. **4** *PTBA* 179 §15.1; *BP* 2848–68; *VT* 240–2; *LH* i, 4–6. **5** *AB* 60, 26–34. **6** *CGSH* §§671.1, 672.23; *VSHP* ii, 47 §20. **7** *CGSH* §712.28; *BP* 2867–8; *VSHP* ii, 47 §20; *AU s.a.* 439, 447. **8** *Lgen.* 247.1. **9** *AU s.a.* 1166; *MartO*[2] 237; *MartG* 226; *MartD* 318–20. **10** OSL MH 263.

SEACHNASACH son of Fíonán. Although thought to have been in descent from Lughaidh son of Laoghaire, progenitor of the Clann Lughdhach of Meath, Seachnasach is not included in the special section of the genealogical corpus devoted to the saints of this group.[1] Nor is he known from the early martyrological record. The later record identifies him with Seachnasach of a place named Ceann Locha who was commemorated on 30 July.[2] This latter saint was probably identical with the anchorite and bishop named Seachnasach who died at Loch Ceinin (perhaps for Ceann) in 823.[3] The anchorite was possibly the *céile Dé* of Ceall Ghuilbin, now probably Kilgulbin in the Kerry parish of O'Dorney, whom Maol Ruain of Tallaght instructed on a matter relating to carnal desire.[4]

1 *CGSH* §§75, 690; *GRSH* 53. **2** *MartG* 146; *MartD* 204; *GRSH* 53. **3** *AU s.a.* **4** *MT* §46; *HDGP* iv, 3.

SÉADNA, associate of Patrick. Possibly derived from the word *séad*, 'way, road', hence 'wayfarer', the name Séadna was borne, according to the list of homonymous saints, by thirteen persons, many of whom are otherwise unrecorded.[1] At least two of these had obvious Patrician connections. One, Séadna son of Trian, is said by the author of the Tripartite Life to have been blessed by Patrick – together with his twin, Iarlaithe of Clonfeakle – while still in his mother's womb, and baptized at birth by Seachnall.[2] Although his brother is said to have succeeded Patrick at Armagh, little else is known of this Séadna, other than his status of bishop, his affiliation to the Dál bhFiatach of east Ulster, and a feastday of 16 June.[3] The author of the Tripartite Life distinguished him from Séadna son of Dallán of Druim Maca Blaoi (possibly now Feegavla in the Monaghan parish of Donaghmoyne, adjoining Inishkeen), the recipient of wheat dropped from heaven, some of which he passed on to Patrick.[4] As this man's feast (9 March) coincided with that of Séadna of Ceall Áine, a church possibly located in the townland of Rathbranchurch in the Meath parish of Killary, both bearers of the name are likely to have represented a northern cult of the saint.[5] This may be also represented by the Séadna thought fit, with others, to act as guarantor in an early poem on the Oirghialla, a people of the area now covered by the diocese of Clogher, whose Register ranks a bishop of this name among the occupants of its see.[6] The Patrician connection is again exemplified by Séadna son of Corcrán, keeper of Patrick's books, who is known only from the metrical version of the list of those in orders with the Armagh saint.[7]

1 *CGSH* §707.921–32. 2 *BP* 2603–4; *VT* 220. 3 *GRSH* 84; *MartT* 50; *MartG* 116; *MartD* 170. 4 *BP* 2840–45; *VT* 240; *JCLAS* 3, 282–3; but cf. *Ainm* 9, 18. 5 *MartT* 21; *MartG* 50; *MartD* 72; *HDGP* iii, 123. 6 *Ériu* 16, 188 §43 (cf. *KLT* 221); *ClRec.* 7, 380. 7 *CGSH* §672.16.

Séadna, bishop. *See* Libhréan of Inis Mór.

Séadna of Clonbeg (Cluain Beag), barony of Clanwilliam, Co. Tipperary. Every great segment of the nobles of Ireland had, according to Geoffrey Keating, an attendant guardian saint, in testimony of which Keating listed, among others, Séadna (Séanna) of the Clann Bhriain Eatharlaigh (alias Mic Bhriain) of Eatharla, now Aherlow on the northern side of the Galtee Mountains, where the counties of Tipperary and Limerick meet.[1] Séadna son of Eise (Seise) of this area (earlier known as Artraighe of Cliú) is said by the tract on the mothers of the saints to have been a son of Maghna, sister of David of Menevia.[2] The same text considers him to have been a brother of Eiltín (Multose) of Kinsale in Cork.

1 *FFÉ* iii, 112–13; *ASH* 315 §6. 2 *CGSH* §722.94; *HDGP* i, 106.

Séadna son of Trian. *See* Iarlaithe of Clonfeakle; Séadna, associate of Patrick.

Seanach of Aghagower (Achadh Fobhair), barony of Burrishoole, Co. Mayo. Patrick is reputed to have left with this saint in Aghagower a tooth called *fear á*, an event – otherwise associated with Brón of Killaspugbrone – commemorated in three quatrains.[1] The 'holy bishop' Seanach of the Uí Oilealla, a sept that gave name to the Sligo barony of Tirerrill, but which also controlled some lands in Corca Thrí, in the adjoining baronies of Leyny and Corran, may be intended.[2] Bishop Seanach son of Conaire of the Araidh of Munster may represent the same cult, since two close collaterals of his, according to the genealogies, Ailbhe and Mac Treana, were respectively patrons of Shancough and Kilmactranny in the barony of Tirerrill.[3] Little is known of the saint, but an origin legend of the Uí Mháille (O'Malleys) of Burrishoole describes how he christened the head of the family.[4] The Seanach invoked in a poem by Donnchadh Mór Ó Dálaigh may also refer to him.[5]

1 *CGSH* §1.3; *BP* 1613–33; *ÉtC* 3, 95–104; *CnM* 8, 19–22; *PTBA* 150 §37.2–3. 2 *BLec.* 102vd5–6. 3 *CGH* 326h6–18; *LSLC* 291–303. 4 *Éigse* 14, 1–12. 5 *DDé* 50.

Seanach of Clonfad. *See* Seanach son of Aonghas.

Seanach of Coolcor (Cúil Chorra), parish and barony of Granard, Co. Longford. Though this son of Eichín is included in the list of those subject to Brighid of Kildare, his church is among those said by Tíreachán to have been founded by Patrick during his travels in the north Midlands, and more specifically in the Longford/Westmeath area.[1] However, in his account of this part of Patrick's journey, Tíreachán also had occasion to mention some of Brighid's associates in the area, including her uncle, Mac Caorthainn, and her mentor, Mac Caille.[2] It may be suspected, therefore, that Coolcor was originally a Brigidine church associated with Seanach, especially since the parish of Abbeylara (adjoining Granard) has a townland named Kilbride.

1 *CGSH* §670.64; *PTBA* 136 §16.5. **2** *PTBA* 136 §16.1, 3.

Seanach of Delgany. *See* Domhainghin of Delgany.

Seanach of Monasterevin (Ros Glaise), barony of Offaly West, Co. Kildare. This son of Laighneach was one of seven brothers of Abán of Killabban, all of whom were attached to the Uí Labhradha (or Uí Chormaic) of Leinster.[1] Three of Seanach's brothers (Dubhán, Líthghin, and Toimdheanach) were also placed in Monasterevin, a church much better known for its association with Éimhín, whence its Irish name, Mainistear Éimhín. Seanach's mother, Broinnfhinn Bhreac ('speckled') daughter of Lughna, is said to have been a sister of the Bishop Iobhar who figures prominently in the Life written for Seanach's sibling Abán.[2] In the entry relating to his mother, Seanach is given the epithet *Garbh*, 'rough', and assigned to a church named Ceall Mhór, but it is difficult to know which of the many places now known as Kilmore was intended. Among the successors of Patrick was, however, a *gabha*, 'smith', named Seanach Garbh, from Cluain Maca Greige, an unidentified church in Uí Nialláin.[3] This territory gave name to the two Armagh baronies of Oneilland, one of which contains a parish named Kilmore. On the other hand, an abbot of Clonfert named Seanach Garbh died in 621, and yet another of this name and epithet, this time described as the son of Buidhe, was commemorated on 10 September.[4]

1 *CGSH* §287.1.2; *GRSH* 91; *Lgen.* 727.11. **2** *CGSH* §722.96. **3** VT 542. **4** *AU s.a.*; *MartT* 70; *MartG* 174; *MartD* 242; cf. *MartO*[2] 78.

Seanach son of Aonghas, bishop. Said to have been a son of Aonghas son of Ardghal, Seanach was one of seven brothers, of whom one (Caolán) gave name to Kilkeelan (Cúil Chaoláin) in the Meath parish of Athboy, the site of a battle fought in 635.[1] Among Seanach's other brothers were two bishops, Garbhán (Gabhrán) and Treaslaice. As Athboy is not far from Clonard, Seanach may be the bishop who died at that church in 588, and was commemorated on 21 August.[2] According to the later martyrologies, this man was also connected with Clonfad (Cluain Fada Fine) in the Westmeath barony of Fartullagh.[3] A late seventeenth-century visitation list, prepared for the diocese of Meath, renders his name as 'Sinan'.[4]

1 *Lgen.* 166.4; *BB* 80a1–3; *AU s.a.*; ITS 58, 42 §§36, 38, 172. **2** *MartT* 65; *MartO*[2] 177. **3** *MartG* 160; *MartD* 226. **4** *RM* 5.4, 100.

Seanach son of Caol. *See* Aodh Fionn.

Seanach son of Coireall. This saint, allegedly a bishop, was one of nine to receive special mention in a text which described him, together with Eolang and Odhrán, as a *seanóir*, 'elder', of the Múscraighe group.[1] In Seanach's case, the Múscraighe of Ormond in north Tipperary were probably intended, to judge from a passage in the death-tale of Diarmuid son of Cearbhall, king of Tara, which describes how the fugitive Aodh Guaire first sought protection 'in the lands of the Múscraighe' from Seanach who then brought him to Ruadhán of Lorrha.[2] The same passage states that Seanach and Ruadhán had been at school together. Though his church of Cealla Ua Maigheach has yet to be identified, he is known to have been patron of Kilshannig in the Cork parish of Rathcormack, and perhaps also of the parish of Kilshannig in the barony of Duhallow, where, according to local tradition, the saint was buried.[3] The Duhallow parish contained a well dedicated to Gobnaid, one of Múscraighe's three famous nuns, and some sources take Seanach to be identical with the priest-saint of this name commemorated together with Gobnaid on 11 February.[4]

1 *CGSH* §665.1.5; *Lgen.* 720.5. **2** *SG* i, 76; *BNÉ* i, 322 §§28–9; *VSHP* ii, 246 §15. **3** *CPR* i, lxviii; *MFCJ* 2, 56. **4** *PABD* 268, 272–4; *MartT* 16; *MartG* 34; *MartD* 46.

Seanach son of Comhghall (Lughna). *See* Colmán of Oughaval.

Seanach Garbh. *See* Seanach of Monasterevin.

Seanach Maca Maoile. *See* Seanach Seanghabha.

Seanach Seanghabha, 'senior smith', of Derrybrusk (Doire Brusca) on Lough Erne, barony of Tirkennedy, Co. Fermanagh. One of Lough Erne's *ardnaoimh*, 'chief saints', and reputedly a uterine brother of Colum Cille, Seanach son of Éidchéan is said to have protected his sibling, in danger from a marine monster, by casting a lump of metal in the direction of the sea between Ireland and Scotland, which lodged in the monster's mouth.[1] Subsequently, when extracted from the monster's mouth and returned to the saint, this metal was used by Seanach to fashion three halidoms, one for himself and two for Náile of Kinawley. Given the location of his church, he is likely to have been the saint invoked as 'Seanach Maca Maoile' in an early poem on the Oirghialla whose territory included the area about Lough Erne.[2] Little else is known of Seanach whose cognomen might also be rendered simply as *gabha*, 'smith', but his feast fell on 11 May, a day coincidentally marked by the burning of Armagh in 1166.[3]

1 *MHH* 110 §29; 115–17 §§42–6. **2** *Ériu* 16, 183 42; cf. *KLT* 138 §42, 220. **3** *AU s.a.*; *MartG* 94; *MartD* 124; *JCLAS* 10, 176.

Seanán. No fewer than twenty-two of this name, disguised as Mosheanóg, are included in the list of homonymous saints.[1] Most of these are either otherwise unattested or better known under variant forms of the name, cases in point being the patrons of Laraghbryan and Scattery Island, both of whom were normally referred to as Seanán. The name derives from *sean*, 'old'.

1 *CGSH* §707.741–63.

Seanán of Aghacullion (Achadh Caol), parish of Kilcoo, barony of Upper Iveagh, Co. Down.[1] This son of Eirnín is known from an entry in the corpus of saints' genealogies which attaches him and his two sisters, Beagrall and Cearc, to the Déise of Munster.[2] The centres of their cults were, however, in east Ulster, with Cearc, for example, being probably identical with Earc, patron of the Down parish of Tullylish (Tulach Lis).

1 *HDGP* i, 20. 2 *CGSH* §92.1–2; *GRSH* 77; *Lgen.* 719.7.

Seanán of Laraghbryan (Láthrach Briúin), barony of North Salt, Co. Kildare. Attached by the genealogists to the same branch of the descendants of Eacha son of Mairidh – otherwise the Ulaidh of north-east Ulster – as Maol Ruain of Tallaght and Colmán of Lynally, Seanán son of Fiontan was likewise associated with a church in north Leinster.[1] Both versions of his maternal descent similarly relate to Leinster, one placing him among the numerous children of Deidhe daughter of Trian (whose father was Dubhthach grandson of Lughar), the other including him, together with his namesake of Scattery Island, among the even more numerous progeny of Cuman daughter of Dallbhrónach, the aunt of Brighid of Kildare.[2] Though his church was among the possessions of Glendalough, little else is recorded of the saint himself beyond the celebration of his feast on 2 September.[3] Although possibly selected through confusion with a Nicomedian saint named Zeno, this was close enough to commemorations of Seanán on 8 September in a post-Conquest antiphonary connected with the church of Saggart in Dublin, and devotions at a holy well in the Kilkenny parish of Kilmacow – which adjoins the parish of Rossinan (Ros Seanáin) – on 22 August, to suggest that all three like-named saints represented the same original cult.[4]

1 *CGSH* §299; *GRSH* 97; *Lgen.* 102.2, 728.1–2. 2 *CGSH* §722.2.8. 3 *CPPI* 195; *MartO*[2] 192; *MartG* 168; *MartD* 232. 4 *Rep. Nov.* 2, 48, 83; *HADO* iv, 134, 177; *Ainm* 3, 6–7.

Seanán of Scattery Island (Inis Cathaigh), parish of Kilrush, barony of Moyarta, Co. Clare, and of Inishcarra (Inis Cara), barony of East Muskerry, Co. Cork. In keeping with the location of his main church, the saint's pedigree attached him through his father Geirrgeann to the Corca Bhaiscinn of south-west Clare.[1] There are various versions of his maternal descent, one placing him among the numerous progeny of Cuman daughter of Dallbhrónach, aunt of Brighid of Kildare, another replacing Cuman with Inghean Bhaoith, patron of Killinaboy.[2] Yet another, the official Scattery version, names his mother as Coimhgheall daughter of Earnach of the Alltraighe, a people settled in the area about Kerry Head.[3] The early importance of the saint's church is made evident by the mid-ninth century Tripartite Life of Patrick which, having brought its subject to Uí Fhidhgheinte, approximately the area later represented by the diocese of Limerick, credited him with a prophecy concerning Seanán and his church on the island 'in the mouth of the sea'.[4]

The saint's church at Scattery later had pretensions to diocesan status which, following confirmation at the synod of Kells-Mellifont in 1152, continued to be recalled throughout the period 1200–1600, despite incorporation into the diocese of Killaloe.[5] Unsurprisingly, therefore, a Life was compiled for Seanán which survives in a number of versions, three Latin, one vernacular.[6] Two of the Latin texts, one in metrical form and preserved in the fourteenth-century *Codex Salmanticensis* and the fifteenth-century *Kilkennienis*, the other a nine-lesson breviary text used in Brittany and likewise dating to the fourteenth or early fifteenth century, are closely related, the breviary text deriving from the metrical Life.[7] A much earlier Latin prose Life is preserved in manuscripts of the Great Austrian Legendary (*Magnum Legendarium Austriacum*), which was compiled towards the end of the twelfth century, probably in Regensburg.[8] Hitherto unnoticed by commentators on the saint, this text is verbally close to the metrical Life of which it, or a related text, must have been the source.

The saint's vernacular Life has been preserved in five manuscripts, including the mid-fifteenth-century Book of Lismore, and a seventeenth-century French text prepared by Albert le Grand has also survived.[9] Both this latter text and the breviary Life were written in the interests of devotees of the man thought to be the Irish saint's Breton equivalent, Sané of Plou Sané.[10] As no attempt has yet been made to study critically the saint's entire dossier, conclusions relating to the Life must be regarded as preliminary. Despite this, it bears noting that all versions of the text reveal the same essential structure, which is indicative of the fact that a single text, probably in Latin and dating in all likelihood to the second half of the twelfth century, lies at the base of the entire biographical tradition. The vernacular Life in particular, though corresponding to Latin prose and metrical texts, contains some added episodes, as well as a considerable amount of added onomastic detail, typical of compositions of this kind.

The basic Life begins with an account of Patrick's prophecy of the saint's birth, drawn from the Tripartite Life, but located by the Latin Life among the Uí Chonaill, a segment of Uí Fhidhgheinte which gave name to the Limerick baronies of Connello.[11] In line with the Tripartite Life, the author of the vernacular Life also placed the event among the Uí Fhidhgheinte, adding that these would be subject to Seanán and locating the prophecy more specifically at Donaghmore (Domhnach Mór) in the east Limerick barony of Clanwilliam. Both Latin and vernacular texts advert to the miracle of dead wood coming to life that marked Seanán's birth at a place called Magh Lagha, now Moylough in the parish of Kilrush.[12] Having evinced signs of budding sanctity, Seanán went to Caiseadhan, patron of Kilcasheen (Ceall Chaiseadhain) in the parish of Moyarta, to receive a basic training, and thence to Nadál (Natalis) whom the vernacular Life located at faraway Kilmanagh (Ceall Mhanach Droichid) in the county of Kilkenny, possibly because this adjoins a parish named Killaloe (Ceall Dolua) whose patron was Molua of the diocese of Killaloe.[13]

Various miracles follow before the saint is sent to Kilmore (Ceall Mhór Aradh Tíre) – corruptly rendered Ceall Arat, or variants thereof in the Latin text – a few miles south of Nenagh in Tipperary.[14] At this point (marked by a lacuna in the metrical Life), the Latin prose and vernacular texts describe how Seanán sets out for Rome, visiting, according to the vernacular Life, Enniscorthy in the Wexford parish of Templeshannon (Teampall Seanáin) – where a church and well were named after the saint – and Maodhóg of Ferns on the way out; on the way back, Seanán takes in Tours, where he is presented with a gospel-book written by Martin, before proceeding to St David's in Wales.[15]

Arriving back in Ireland, somewhere in Leinster, according to the Latin text, but at Great Island in Cork Harbour, according to the vernacular Life – which adds an account of a long sojourn at Inishcarra of which the saint is still patron – Seanán slowly made his way to south-west Clare.[16] Then, as the metrical Life resumes, the saint, having taken possession of several islands off the coast, expelled a monster from Scattery, consigning it to a lake called Dubhloch (*lacus nigrus*), near Boolynagreana in the Clare parish of Inagh, and founded on Scattery what was to be his main church.[17] Here the saint spent the remainder of his Life, contesting his rights with various local dynasts, receiving respectful visits from Bréanainn, Ciarán, Féichín and Laichtín, trading gifts with Diarmuid of Inchcleraun, insisting to Cainnear Chráibhtheach that his island was off limits to females, and finally preparing for death at Caiseadhan's grave, ironically among women, according to the vernacular Life, in nearby Ceall na gCailleach, 'church of the nuns', now Kilnagalliagh in the parish of Kilfearagh.[18] Depending on which Life is followed, Martin of Tours rendered Seanán the last rites, or news of David's death was brought to Seanán as he lay dying, and the Latin text devotes much space to whether the day of his death (1 March), likewise David's day, or its octave (8 March) was to be the saint's feastday.[19]

Where and when the various versions of the saint's Life were written has yet to be established. Setting aside the texts from Brittany, which served the local Breton cult, a possible scenario, as in the case of Caoimhghin of Glendalough, is that the need for Lives in the Regensburg *Schottenkloster*, to provide suitable material for the Great Austrian Legendary, gave rise in the late twelfth century – and not the sixth as was proposed by John Colgan – to the original composition.[20] This could possibly have come to Regensburg from a house of canons regular in south Clare, probably Clareabbey, which may have been granted possession of Scattery in 1189.[21] In that case, a copy of the original Life would have remained in Ireland and become available at a much later stage, possibly as late as the fourteenth or early fifteenth century, for edition in the form of the vernacular Life.[22] This latter text may have been designed to promote the cause of the community on Scattery Island in its occasional pursuit of episcopal status, which is attested at various dates between 1350 and 1450.[23] Added impetus was no doubt given to this pursuit by the foundation of a secular college on the island, consisting of a prior and twenty-four canons, which is attested from the late fourteenth century onwards, and possibly earlier.[24]

An environment of this kind also provides a likely provenance for the considerable body of vernacular texts relating to the saint – originally kept perhaps in the volume styled *Leabhar Comharba Sheanáin*, 'Book of Seanán's Coarb' – that can be dated to about this time.[25] These texts consist of an account of his posthumous miracles, providing a long list of the saints who might be invoked should his church need assistance.[26] There are also several miscellaneous poems on the saint, including prophecies attributed to him and to such other saints as Bréanainn and Inghean Bhaoith of Killinaboy, whose numerous progeny, borrowed in part from that of Cuman daughter of Dallbhrónach, is said here to have included Seanán.[27] An earlier eulogy of the saint, styled *Amhra Sheanáin*, and credited both to Dallán – the same author as is said to have composed the better-known *Amhra Choluim Chille* – and Cormac son of Cuileannán, has been dated to about 900.[28] Although a poem on Pupa of Aran, attributed to Seanán, has been preserved on the margins of the twelfth-century Book of Leinster, the saint figures only rarely in the Lives of others, an exception being that of Ciarán.[29] This text speaks of a visit made by the patron of Clonmacnoise to the 'most holy' Seanán and, echoing an incident in the latter's Life, tells how a chasuble, having been consigned by Ciarán to the waters of the river Shannon, arrived safe and dry in Scattery.[30] Together with several other saints associated with churches in south Clare, Seanán is invoked in the recently discovered Regensburg litany.[31] He was also among the saints invoked as a guarantor of the Law of Adhamhnán.[32]

The saint's feast, which, as already mentioned, was a matter of concern to his biographers, is variously assigned to 1 and 8 March.[33] The latter day was celebrated in the Kerry churches of Kilshenane (Ceall Seanáin) and Lixnaw, among many other places, and a well dedicated to the saint near Castleconnell in the Limerick parish of Stradbally attracted numerous pilgrims.[34] Several churches in Scotland were also dedicated to him.[35] Possession of a stone from his grave on Scattery was thought to protect from shipwreck.[36]

1 *CGSH* §228; *GRSH* 79; *Lgen.* 722.1; *DIB* viii, 829–30. **2** *CGSH* §722.8; *IrT* iv, 93 §1. **3** *LisL* 1797–8. **4** *BP* 2379–429; *VT* 202–6. **5** *MRHI* 96–7; *Dinn.* 5, 52; *AFM s.a.*1188. **6** *MHH* 197, 254; *Kenney* 364–5. **7** *VSHH* 301–24; *AB* 66, 222–30; *AB* 66, 199–204. **8** *FLLSP* 233–4. **9** *LisL* 54–74; *VSB* 79–84, *SS* 116–18; *ASH* 602–11. **10** CornS 15, 25–30; *SS* 106–7. **11** *VSHH* 301–2 §§1–2; *LisL* 1792–9. **12** *VSHH* 303 §3; *LisL* 1887–9; *LisL* 1887–9, 1895. **13** *VSHH* 309–10 §§9–10; *LisL* 1954–67. **14** *VSHH* 312–14 §13; *LisL* 2013–30; *CGH* 152a4–9. **15** *LisL* 2044–58; OSL WX ii, 229, 252–3; *HDF* 11–12; *Dinn.* 3, 89–90. **16** *LisL* 2059–147; *JCHAS* 63–32–4; *Dinn.* 1, 53–4. **17** *VSHH* 314 §14; *LisL* 2194–236. **18** *VSHH* 314–24 §§14–26; *LisL* 2237–502; *Dinn.* 4, 123. **19** *VSHH* 323 §26 (ll. 846–52); *AB* 66, 207–8. **20** *ASH* 539, n. 15; *AB* 66, 202–3. **21** *HDK* 203; *Dinn.* 4, 114. **22** Cf. *AB* 66, 199. **23** *MRHI* 96–7; cf. *Dinn.* 4, 116. **24** *MRHI* 361; *Dinn.* 4, 115. **25** *AB* 66, 206. **26** *ZCP* 10, 1–35. **27** *IrT* iv, 68–98. **28** *ZCP* 3, 220–5; *AB* 66, 215–21; *SSS* 7–31. **29** *CGSH* §735. **30** *VSHP* i, 208–9, 212 §§22–3, 29. **31** UCC MS U.331; *CKV* 64.78. **32** *CA* §22. **33** *MartT* 20–1; *MartO*^{2} 80–1; *MartG* 46, 50; *MartD* 60, 68–70. **34** *ACoK* 39; *JKAHS* 17, 114; *JRSAI* 88, 153; *Béaloideas* 15, 254. **35** *KSS* 444. **36** *HCIC* 15; *SZ* 13.

SEANÁN LIATH, 'grey', of Kiltenanlea (Ceall tSeanáin Léith), alias Doonass, barony of Tulla Lower, Co. Clare. This son of Tairbhín is said to have been one of seven brothers and seven sisters (mainly) connected with the Cork church of Áth na gCeall, a site on the river Blackwater, in the townland of Gortnagross and parish of Ballyclogh, near Mallow.[1] The family belonged to the Múscraighe and among Seanán's siblings were Laichtín of Freshford and Cruachán of Kilcrohane. Locally thought to have been a brother of Mochuille of Tulla, and distinct from his namesake on Scattery Island, Seanán Liath shared with the latter the feast of 8 March, which suggests that they were ultimately identical.[2] At Doonass, the feast of the Assumption (15 August) has now replaced Seanán's day. A dedication to the saint is also attested in the west Limerick parish of Croagh.[3]

1 *CGSH* §666.1.2; *Lgen.* 752.1; *HDGP* i, 146. **2** *ACoC* 250; *MartT* 21 (7 Mar.); *MartO*^{2} 81; *MartG* 50; *MartD* 68–70. **3** *PRIA* 25 C 411 §200; 412 §206.

SEANBHRÉANAINN. *See* Bréanainn of Birr.

SEANCHÁN of Dowth (Dubhadh), barony of Upper Slane, Co. Meath. This saint, one of seven sons credited to Lughaidh, belonged to a branch of the Laighin or Leinstermen named Uí Chéithigh which gave name to the Kildare barony of Ikeathy.[1] The most famous of Seanchán's brothers was Crónán (alias Mochua) of Clondalkin. Cainnear of Clonsilla is said to have been the mother of these saints, most of whom were associated with churches in the Dublin/Kildare area.[2] Though little else is recorded of Seanchán, his memory lived on at Dowth whose missal, according to James Ussher, was known as 'St Schenghan's Book sive S. Sinani'.[3] A late seventeenth-century list of Meath churches gives his name as 'Sinnac', and Tobar Seancháin, a well near Dowth, continued to preserve his memory until at least the 1830s, when his feast was celebrated 'eight days before Christmas'.[4] Saints named Seanchaidh and Seanán – either of which forms is ultimately identical with Seanchán 'sive Sinanus' – were commemorated on 17/18 December, and the ninth-century Martyology of Tallaght identifies Seanchaidh as *ó Dubad*, 'from Dowth'.[5] It has been suggested that the saint was also patron of Shanaghan (formerly Teampall Seancháin) in the Donegal parish of Inishkeel.[6]

1 *CGSH* §243.1; *GRSH* 91; *Lgen*. 727.13. 2 *CGSH* §722.77. 3 TCD MS 786, 23v. 4 *RM* 5.3, 5; OSL MH 108. 5 *MartT* 86; *MartG* 240; *MartD* 338–40. 6 *ALC* ii, 320; *ICF* 263–4; *AFM* v, 1456*n*.

SEANCHUIMÍN. *See* Cuimín Fada of Clonfert.

SEANPHÁDRAIG. *See* Patrick.

SEANSHINCHEALL. *See* Sincheall.

SEARBH of Culross (Cuilleannros) between Mount Ochel and the Firth of Forth in Fife, Scotland.[1] The final entry in the tract on the mothers of the saints names the mother of Searbh (English Serf) son of Proc as Almha, daughter of a Pictish king, before going on to describe his father as king of the descendants of Canaan in Egypt.[2] Much the same tradition is preserved in the Latin Life written for Searbh (Latin Servanus) which, in addition to naming his father as Obeth son of Eliud, attributes to the saint a variety of improbable roles, including three years in Constantinople and seven years as Pope in Rome, in preparation for his arrival and subsequent mission in Fife, where Adhamhnán was among the first to meet him.[3] Another Life preserved in the Breviary of Aberdeen turns the saint into a Scot who was appointed suffragan by Palladius.[4] He is reputed to have witnessed wondrous signs at the birth of St Kentigern.[5] His festival, which is not noticed in the Irish martyrologies, was kept both on 1 July and 4 June.[6] The octave of the latter day, 11 June, was, however, the occasion of a pattern at Kilsharvan (Ceall Shearbháin) in Meath, which would suggest that its patron Searbhán was identical with Searbh.[7]

1 *CPNS* 209, 332–3. 2 *CGSH* §722.106. 3 *PLSS* ii, 119–24 §§1–5; *KSS* 445–7; *Innes Review* 44, 122–52; ibid. 50, 80–2; cf. ibid. 32, 70–1; *AITLP* 116–17. 4 *PLSS* i, xxxix; *BrevA* pars aest. 15–16v. *KSS* 445–6; *LegSS* 158–62, 414–16. 5 *ESSH* i, 129; *Innes Review* 21, 37–45. 6 *KSS* 447. 7 OSL MH 131.

SEARBHÁN of Kilsharvan. *See* Searbh.

Searc daughter of Eacha. *See* Cearc daughter of Eacha.

Searc of Rosserk (Ros Seirce / Eirc), parish of Ballysakeery, barony of Tirawley, Co. Mayo. A note on the name of the saint's church, located near the estuary of the river Moy, identifies Searc daughter of Cairbre as the 'miracle-worker' who blessed it.[1] Nothing else is known of the saint, but a friary of the Franciscan Third Order Regular was founded at Rosserk in the early fifteenth century.[2]

1 *Lgen.* 256.3; *BLec.* 71rd 37–44. 2 *MRHI* 274.

Séighín of Iona, Scotland. Belonging to the Ceinéal Conaill, and a close relative of Colum Cille, Séighín son of Fiachna assumed the abbacy of Iona on the death of Feargna Briot in 623.[1] An advocate of the Irish system of calculating the date of Easter, Séighín was involved in correspondence on the subject that included a letter received in 632/3 from Cummian, and another in 640 from Pope John IV.[2] Séighín deemed none of the Pope's arguments to be persuasive. Mentioned by Adhamhnán on a number of occasions as a source of stories relating to Colum Cille, Séighín's chief claim to fame was the mission sent by him to Northumbria on the invitation of King Oswald, which led to the founding in 632 of Lindisfarne by Aodhán (Aidan).[3] Although not named in the relevant annal entry, he is also credited with the founding of the church on Lambay Island in 635.[4] After thirty years in the abbacy of Iona, 'famous' Séighín died on 12 August 652.[5]

1 *CGSH* §337; *GRSH* 43; *Lgen.* 697.12. 2 *CLCP*; *IKD* 40–3; *Kenney* 220–1; *LSC* 37; *VC*[1] 373; *Peritia* 8, 1–17. 3 *VC*[1] 16 (I.1), 26 (I.3), 111 (II.4); *BEH* 218–20; *AU s.a.* 4 *AU s.a.*; *VC*[1] 374; *ECI* 250. 5 *AU s.a.*; *MartT* 62; *MartO*[2] 176; *MartG* 154; *MartD* 216.

Séighín Gabhail son of Seanach. *See* Fáilbhe of Rathvilly.

Shaughlin. *See* Seachnall.

Sheelin. *See* Síolán.

Sheemoge. *See* Díomán of Clonkeen.

Sillian. *See* Cillín.

Sinche. *See* Sineach.

Sincheall of Killeigh (Ceall Aichidh), parish and barony of Geashill, Co. Offaly. There were allegedly two saints of this name at Killeigh – distinguished variously as Seanshincheall, Doshincheall, Óigshincheall, and Sineall – one being a son of Ceanannán, the other a son of Corcán, and both attached by the genealogists to the same Leinster family of Uí Labhradha (Uí Chormaic).[1] It is only proper, therefore, that their records, doubtless much confused, be treated together.

Despite the fact that Killeigh achieved some prominence, with ten of its abbots recorded in the annals for the period before 900, and with the later presence on site of a house of canons regular of St Augustine and a Franciscan friary, no Lives have been preserved for the saints, nor do they figure in the Lives of others.[2] A tract, now lost, entitled *Mirabilia duorum Sincellorum*, 'the miracles of the two Sinchealls', is , however, mentioned in connection with a church named Cluain Caoichne which is said to have been surrendered to them.[3] Their church at Killeigh is featured in the Life of Cainnech of Aghaboe as the scene of a miraculous resuscitation of a *magister doctus*, 'learned master', and albeit negatively, as one of the churches conspiring against Mochuda in the tale of the latter's expulsion from Rahan.[4] A certain Caomhán of a church named Cluain Mic Threóin is said to have attended the younger Sincheall's school at Killeigh, leaving behind in writing a list of the school's 'rules and customs', including such misogynistic precepts as 'greatly avoiding women' and 'great hatred of their talk'.[5] The church is also mentioned, along with its 150 bishops and twelve pilgrims gathered about the two Sinchealls, in a litany.[6]

A poem of dire prophecy foresees the older Sincheall in the house of the king of Leinster.[7] He was among those who succumbed in 549 to the 'great mortality', supposedly at the advanced age of 330.[8] The younger saint is said to have been similar in manners to the apostle Thaddeus.[9] The feastdays of the saints fell on 26 March and 25 June, both days being the seventh of the kalends.[10] A marginal poem added to the March feast in the Martyrology of Tallaght compares the death of Sincheall to the day of doom.[11] On the feastday of Doshincheall in the year 1433, a 'general invitation' was issued by Mairghréag, wife of Calbhach Ua Conchobhair, 'king' of Uí Fhailghe, to the poets, musicians and chroniclers, to attend a banquet at Killeigh, where 'both meat and monies' were bestowed.[12] Five days ahead of the June feast, a possible double of the Killeigh saints, Sincheall (alias Sineall) of the Uí Liatháin of east Cork, was commemorated.[13] The Uí Liatháin saint may be the same as the patron of 'Ceall tSinchill' in the townland of Kilshinahan, parish of Kilbrittain in south Cork.[14] Finally, the above-mentioned church of Cluain Caoichne was dedicated to a Moshionóg (probably a hypocoristic of Sincheall) remembered on 10 May.[15]

1 *CGSH* §§282–3; *GRSH* 91; *Lgen.* 725.9; *CGH* 120a6; *DIB* viii, 958. **2** *AU* iv, 53; *MRHI* 182–3, 253. **3** RD §36. **4** *VSHH* 192 §39; *VSHP* i, 164 §32; *BNÉ* i, 304 §15. **5** *HibM* 41–2. **6** *IrL* 56. **7** *Ériu* 18, 60 §10. **8** *AU s.a.*; *MartO²* 100; *MartD* 86. **9** *CGSH* §712.13. **10** *MartT* 27, 52; *MartO²* 84, 142; *MartG* 62, 122; *MartD* 86, 178. **11** *MartT* 102. **12** *AU s.a.* **13** *MartG* 120; *MartD* 175. **14** CorkD 94. **15** *MartT* 41; *MartG* 94; *MartD* 124.

SINEACH. Probably derived from *sean*, 'old', this name, also written as Sinche, was popular enough to be included in the list of homonymous saints, which contains twelve (otherwise mainly unattested) representatives of the cult.[1]

1 *CGSH* §708.139–50.

SINEACH daughter of Earnán. According to her pedigree, Sineach was one of three sisters, the others being Dairneasa and Cróine (Crón), all of whom were grandnieces of Bréanainn of Birr.[1] Sineach is nowhere else recorded, but she may be identical with her namesake at Ardcrony (Aird Chróine) in the Tipperary barony of Lower Ormond, one of the bearers of the name in the list of homonymous saints.[2] A seventeenth-century source mentions her in association with the Sineach commemorated on 4 December.[3]

1 *CGSH* §124; *GRSH* 111; *Lgen.* 734.9. **2** *CGSH* §708.146. **3** *MartD* 326.

SINEACH of Crohane (Cruachán Maighe Abhna), adjoining Mowney (Magh Abhna), barony of Slievardagh, Co. Tipperary. This daughter of Feargna is known from a number of sources, including a late pedigree assigning her to the Eoghanacht of Cashel and the list of homonymous saints.[1] She is probably the Sineach invoked, along with Samhthann of Clonbroney, both in a litany preserved in the Stowe Missal and in a litany-like list of saints added to the text of the Martyrology of Tallaght.[2] The martyrologies remembered Sineach on 5 October.[3]

1 *GRSH* 118; *CGSH* §708.139. 2 HBS 32, 14; *MartT* 108. 3 *MartT* 77; *MartO*[2] 214; *MartG* 190; *MartD* 206.

Sineach of Killinny (Ceall Fhinnche, formerly Ceall na gCailleach), parish and barony of Kells, Co. Kilkenny. A raid on the southern part of Magh Raighne in 906 resulted in the destruction of Killinny and the 'lamentable' death of the king of Uí Dhróna (Idrone) who was responsible for the incursion.[1] The *cailleacha* (nuns) who gave name to the church are cited as Sineach (Sinche) and Reichtín. The latter may be the 'devout' virgin so named in the list of those commemorated on 27 October.[2] Sineach, on the other hand, is probably identical with a like-named daughter of Annudh, attached by the genealogists to the Osraighe, and remembered, according to the later martyrologies, on 22 August.[3] In placing the saint in Coolbanagher (Cúil Bheannchair) in the Laois barony of Portnahinch, the later martyrologists mistakenly borrowed the name of the church from the pedigree of Bishop Lughach, which follows immediately on that of Sineach in the corpus of genealogies.[4] Alternatively, she has been confused with Finneach of Dorn, who gave name to Killinny, and who was remembered on 2 February.[5]

1 *FAI* §431; *AFM s.a.* 2 *MartT* 85; *MartG* 204; *MartD* 286. 3 *CGSH* §294; *GRSH* 94; *MartG* 162; *MartD* 226. 4 *CGSH* §§294–5. 4 *HDGP* iii, 172; *MartT* 14; *MartO* 58.

Sineach of Kilrush (Ceall Rois), barony of West Offaly, Co. Kildare. This saint and her two companions at Kilrush (Eithne and Mac Nise) are known from the list of those said to have been subject to Brighid of Kildare.[1] Neither Eithne nor Mac Nise appears to be attested elsewhere, but Kilrush was chief place of a branch of the Uí Earcáin, apparently an ecclesiastical family with Brigidine connections.[2] Here, on the eve of the feast of Sineach, which, according to a note added to a copy of the Martyrology of Aonghas, fell on 9 November, the family's chieftain was slain and its wealth taken by a man named Maol Umha son of Colmán.[3] Sineach is doubtless the same as her namesake of Earnaidhe (Nurney in the parish of Kilrush) who figures in the list of homonymous saints.[4]

1 *CGSH* §670.53; *Lgen.* 753.24. 2 *CGH* 126a24. 3 Ibid. 316a20–3; *MartO*[2] 240. 4 *CGSH* §708.142.

Sineach of Kilshine (Ceall Shinche), barony of Morgallion, Co. Meath. On a visit to his *sodales*, 'companions', Abán is said to have sought out the virgin 'Seghnith' in one of his churches, named Ceall Ailbhe.[1] The church in question has been identified as an ecclesiastical site in the townland of Knightstown and parish of Kilshine.[2] 'Seghnith', who is said to have 'nourished' holy virgins under Abán's direction, has been taken, probably correctly, to be a corruption of Sineach, patron of the parish of Kilshine, approximately in the area occupied by the Uí Mhic Uais of Breagha, where, according to an entry in the Book of Ballymote,

Sineach daughter of Fionnbharr of the descendants of Conall Cearnach had a church named after her.[3] At Ceall Íochtair Thíre, an ecclesiastical site in the townland of Killeighter in the Kildare parish of Cloncurry, a saint named Sineach was also venerated.[4] Her church was reputedly close to the celebrated tree named *Bile Tortan* whose fall she, with other saints, lamented in verse.[5] The feast of this holy virgin, later known locally as Jenny or Jane, has not been recorded.[6]

1 *VSHP* i, 23 §32. 2 *HDGP* iii, 123. 3 *BB* 164a47–51. 4 RD §160. 5 *MD* iv, 240–46. 6 OSL MH 69; *RM* 5.3, 4.

Sineach of Taghshinny. *See* Díona.

Sineall, associate of Patrick. According to the list of those in orders with Patrick, Sineall of Ceall Airis was his bell-ringer.[1] Unfortunately, though the saint's feast of 12 January is recorded, the location of his church has not been established with any certainty.[2]

1 *CGSH* §§671.7; 672.6; *Lgen.* 695.1 *BP* 1329; *VT* 264. 2 *MartT* 7; *MartG* 14; *MartD* 14; *HDGP* iii, 124.

Sineall daughter of Ceanannán. *See* Maighneann.

Sineall of Cleenish (Claoininis) on Lough Erne, barony of Clanawley, Co. Fermanagh. This son of Maonach (Mianach), whose name is also recorded as Sileall or Sincheall, was regarded as one of Ireland's twelve apostles, all of whom are said to have received their training from Finnian at Clonard.[1] Sineall is also assumed to have been the 'Sinilis', versed in scriptural knowledge, who was selected as the first teacher of Columbanus of Bobbio, before the latter proceeded to Bangor.[2] Such was his reputation as a scriptural scholar that other saints were also brought to him for study, Munna of Taghmon being a case in point.[3] Regarded as the senior saint of Lough Erne, and third in line of succession to the see of Clogher, Sineall is said to have received a reward of land for having resuscitated the daughter of a king of Oirghialla.[4] He was also called upon by the biographer of Náile of Kinawley to act as guarantor – along with other *ardnaoimh*, 'chief saints', of the area – of the tribute due to Náile's church, and a poem on Patrick's Purgatory addresses him and other saints.[5] No pedigree has been preserved for Sineall, but his feast fell on 12 November.[6] His church on Cleenish appears to have been rebuilt in 1100.[7]

1 *VSHH* 83 §5, 101 §19. 2 *VCol.* 69 §3; *SCO* xviii. 3 *VSHH* 249 §6; *VSHP* ii, 228 §6. 4 *ClRec.* 7, 378. 5 *MHH* 110–14 §§29, 33, 40; *EBMEI* 522 §ff. 6 *MartG* 216; *MartD* 306. 7 *AU s.a.*

Sineall of Clonpriest (Cluain Bhruchais/Phruicheas), barony of Imokilly, Co. Cork. The Life of Fionnbharr names Sineall of Clonpriest among the saint's pupils at his famous Cork school.[3] Sineall may be the same as his namesake of the Uí Liatháin of east Cork, whose feast of 15 June was shared by a saint named Colmán, possibly his companion at Clonpriest.[4] Sineall (alias Sincheall) of the Uí Liatháin was also patron of two Leinster churches named Kiltennell (Ceall tSinill), in the Wexford barony of Ballaghkeen and in the Carlow barony of Idrone East, where the pattern used to be held on the Sunday before 24 June.[5] The proximity of Sineall's feast to that of one of the two Sinchealls of Killeigh on 25 June would suggest that all these saints represented the same original cult.

1 *CGSH* §707.306. 2 *MartT* 55; *MartG* 134; *MartD* 192. 3 *BBa.* 76 (l. 287); *MakS* 97–9. 4 *MartT* 50; *MartG* 116; *MartD* 170. 5 *HDF* 70; *CECW* 211; *Béaloideas* 4, 118–19; *TNW* 1161–2.

Síolán of Áth na gCeall, a site in the townland of Gortnagross, probably at or near Longfield's Bridge on the river Blackwater, in the parish of Ballyclogh, barony of Duhallow, Co. Cork.[1] This son of Tairbhín is named as the first of seven brothers and seven sisters, mainly connected with the church at Longfield's Bridge on the river Blackwater.[2] The family belonged to the Múscraighe and among Síolán's siblings was Laichtín of Freshford. The name was popular in south Munster, as is shown by Síolán son of Fáilbhe, a bishop attached to a branch of the Corca Laoighdhe settled in the area about Glandore, and by the church name Ceall tSíoláin, now Kilsheelan near the Tipperary-Waterford border.[3] Síolán (anglicized Sheelin) may also be the saint remembered – allegedly on 4 May – at Kiltillane in the Tipperary parish of Templemore.[4]

1 *HDGP* i, 146; *PRC* 28. 2 *CGSH* §666.1; *Lgen.* 752.1. 3 *CGSH* §221; *CGH* 155a20n; *GRSH* 128; *CLTÁ* 239–42. 4 *ACE* 280; *Ainm* 3, 7.

Síolán son of Fáilbhe. *See* Síolán of Áth na gCeall.

Siollán of Bangor, barony of Ards Lower, Co. Down. The list of homonymous saints records five bearers of the hypocoristic name Moshiona – which may stand for either Siollán or Seanán – beginning with Moshiona of the Maca Lughair, followed by Moshiona of the Maca Minn (Muinn), both of whom are also included in the list of saints named Mosheanóg (from Seanán).[1] Moshiona of the Maca Minn is probably identical with the best-known bearer of the name, Siollán (alias Moshiona), abbot of Bangor, a noted computistical scholar.[2] A measure of his renown is reflected in the oft-quoted contents of a note added to an eighth-century gospel-book, now in Würzburg, which describes him as scribe and abbot of Bangor, and the 'first of the Irish to have learned by rote the computus'.[3] In the same note, a pupil of his, Cuarán (Mochuaróg) of the Maca Neithsheamhóin of the Déise of Munster, is described as 'doctor of the whole world', and it has been suggested that Siollán's people, the Maca Minn or Meanraighe, may also have been settled in the southern province.[4] Under the guise of 'Sinlanus', the saint is included in a poem on the abbots of Bangor, preserved in that church's antiphonary.[5] Siollán died in 610 and was remembered on 28 February.[6]

1 *CGSH* §707.743.761.889–93. 2 *Thes.* ii, 285; *Kenney* 218; *DIB* vi, 718–19. 3 *Peritia* 1, 283–4. 4 Ibid. 286. 5 *AntB* 83. 6 *AU s.a.*; *MartT* 19; *MartO*² 63; *MartG* 44; *MartD* 58.

Síon daughter of Niall. *See* Baodán of Cloney.

Siostán of Inishkeen. *See* Colum of Inishkeen.

Sléibhín of Iona, Scotland. This son of Conghal has the distinction of being the last in a long line of Ceinéal Conaill abbots to have succeeded Colum Cille.[1] He assumed the abbacy in 752 on the death of Cillín and travelled to Ireland, probably almost immediately, to be present at the proclamation in 753 of the *Lex*

Columbae, 'Law of Colum Cille', an ecclesiastical law usually supported by a powerful provincial king – in this case Domhnall of the Midland kingdom of Midhe – and designed, among other aims, to raise revenue for the saint's *familia*. He was in Ireland in 754 and Colum's Law was renewed in 757.[2] He died in 767 and is taken to be the Mantan or Montan (*montanus* = *sléibhín*) commemorated, with another abbot of Iona named Feargna Briot, on 2 March.[3] The saint was also commemorated at Kilslevan in Islay.[4]

1 *CGSH* §345; *GRSH* 43; *DIB* viii, 997–8. 2 *AU s.a.* 752–3, 757; *VC*[1] 385–6; *IKD* 62, 66. 3 *AU s.a.*; *MartT* 20; *MartG* 46; *MartD* 60. 4 *CPNS* 309.

Sochla. *See* Molua of Kyle.

Soghaois daughter of Mac Dara. *See* Brighid of Shankill.

Soibhean daughter of Dubhthan. *See* Reodaighe of Girley.

Soicheall of Baslick (Baisleac Mhór), barony of Castlereagh, Co. Roscommon. Arriving among the Uí Bhriúin of Connacht, Patrick is said to have been surrounded by bishops, including Soicheall (alias Sachall, Latin Sachellus) who, according to an earlier passage in Tíreachán's text, earned a reprimand when he began to ordain bishops and priests without taking counsel with his mentor.[1] Duach Teangadh Umha ('brass-tongued'), a son of Brión (eponym of the Uí Bhriúin), is elsewhere reported to have incurred Soichell's wrath and solemn curse, dressed out in verse.[2] A tract bearing mainly on families in east Connacht brings Soicheall and Patrick together once more, as patrons of a group named Síol Fothaidh.[3] Mention is also made of Soicheall in *Agallamh na Seanórach*, 'colloquy of the ancients', in the role of Patrick's *príomhrannaire*, 'principal dispenser of food', and it has been suggested that his reception of relics from Patrick was an attempt to strengthen Armagh's ties with Baslick.[4] His relations with other saints were apparently not always cordial. A certain Diarmuid Éigeas of the local Ciarraighe, having sought with his family to obstruct Bearach of Termonbarry's designs on his homestead at a place named Rathan, is shown receiving short shrift from his protagonist and a prophecy of death at year's end, which duly came to pass, despite his having taken refuge within Soicheall's church at Baslick.[5] Soicheall's feast (1 August) was also celebrated at Taney (Cúil Shoichille), near Dundrum in Dublin, among other places.[6] Soicheall's coarb was among the ecclesiastics present at the inauguration of O'Connor as king of Connacht.[7]

1 *PTBA* 122 §2.6, 146–8 §§30.2, 32.5; *BP* 1205–19. 2 TCD H.2.7, 48d7. 3 *CGSH* §394.4; cf. *Lgen.* 240.18. 4 *SG* i, 171; *Peritia* 3, 310. 5 *BNÉ* i, 37–8 §§69–70. 6 *MartT* 59, 221; *MartG* 148; *MartD* 208. 7 *JRSAI* 2, 340; *MSPAG* 189.

Soidhealbh. *See* Teille.

Soidhealbh daughter of Baoth. *See* Eithne daughter of Baoth.

Soidhealbh daughter of Cairbre. *See* Cuman of Naas.

Soidhealbh daughter of Cathaoir Mór. *See* Beinéan.

Soidhealbh daughter of Tairbhín. *See* Ceillseach of Áth na gCeall.

Solan of Killosolan. *See* Rose of Kilrush.

Sorbhlaith daughter of Cuileabhaoth. *See* Maol Brighde of Armagh.

Sórnach/Sourney. *See* Sárnad daughter of Aodh.

Srafán of Coolcor (Cúil Chorra), parish and barony of Granard, Co. Longford. This saint is said to have been subject, along with many others, to Brighid of Kildare.[1] The church assigned to him appears also to have been claimed by Armagh as early as the seventh century, to judge by Tíreachán, who attributed to Patrick the founding of several churches in the Longford/Westmeath area, including one at Coolcor.[2] Tíreachán also had occasion to mention some of Brighid's associates in this area, including her uncle, Mac Caorthainn, and her mentor, Mac Caille.[3] Srafán may have been patron of a church much closer to Brighid, at Straffan (Teach Srafáin, 'Srafán's church') in north Kildare, and in this capacity he found mention in a poem on the church of Ceall Chorbáin, another name for the church of Naas.[4] The saint is probably the same as the Srafán who is said to have brought his sister's son *a Laighnibh*, 'out of Leinster', to the Cork church of Dromdaleague (Drimoleague), where he married locally and became a *ceann cinidh*, 'ancestor of a family'.[5] A holy well and road were named after him at Dromdaleague, according to local tradition.[6] A saint of the name was also commemorated at a church named Cluain Mór on 23 May.[7]

1 *CGSH* §670.64; *Lgen.* 753.30. 2 *PTBA* 136 §16.5. 3 *PTBA* 136 §16.1, 3. 4 *MD* iv, 340; *Seanchas* 221. 5 *LM* 176, 184, 530–1. 6 *JCHAS* 25, 100–1; *AICK* i, 282–3. 7 *MartT* 45; *MartG* 102; *MartD* 136.

Suaibhseach. *See* Maol Rubha of Applecross.

Subhach of Corann, now approximately the barony of Corran, Co. Sligo. A poem listing the saints willing to come to the assistance of Seanán of Scattery, should he need them, includes the 'noble sage' Subhach.[1] As Bearach of Termonbarry directly precedes him, this saint is likely to have been the Subhach commemorated in Corran on 1 August, and again on 21 November.[2]

1 *ZCP* 10, 24 §18. 2 *MartG* 148, 222; *MartD* 208, 314.

Subhalach of 'Kiltolagh' (Ceall tSubhalaigh), in the townland of Carrowkeel More, parish of Inchicronan, barony of Bunratty Upper, Co. Clare.[1] The fourteenth-century text known as *Caithréim Thoirdhealbhaigh*, 'the triumphant career of Toirdhealbhach', refers to *Ceall Shubhalaigh*, later 'Kiltoola/Kiltolagh'.[2] Moreover, a saint named 'Subhalaid[h]' is called upon in a poem in Classical Irish, along with Inghean Bhaoith of Killinaboy, Mughain of Kilmoon, and numerous other saints, to assist in releasing the churches of Leath Mogha (Ireland's southern half) from a bondage imposed by those of Leath Chuinn (northern half), championed by Finnian of Clonard.[3] While nothing else is known of the saint for certain, he may be identical with the anchorite Sodhalach, commemorated on 7 November.[4]

1 *HDGP* iv, 52. 2 *CT* i, 51, 82, 140; *CoC* 46. 3 RIA MS 23L11, 263; *SAM* 24.1, 17, 21–2. 4 *MartG* 212; *MartD* 298.

Sugaid/Succait. *See* Patrick.

Suibhne son of Rumhan. *See* Ceallach of Trim.

T

TAGÁN of Curraclone, barony of Stradbally, Co. Laois. When Patrick had consecrated Fiac as Leinster's first bishop, according to the Tripartite Life, he left with him seven of his followers, including one named Teagán.[1] This man is taken, probably correctly, to be the same as the pilgrim Tagán called upon, together with many others, to come to the assistance of the Leinstermen in a poem attributed to Moling.[2] Located by the poet 'in the land of Uí Chriomhthannáin', Tagán's church lay more particularly in a townland formerly called 'Kiltighan/Kiltigan' in the parish of Curraclone.[3] He was probably also identical with the like-named Teagán son of Bearach whose family, allegedly of Oirghialla origin, is said to have settled in Ogenty (Tír Ua nGeintigh), a cantred in Ossory, now essentially the area about Thomastown in Kilkenny.[4] Here also his church was located, at a site named Teampall Teagáin, earlier 'Kiltakan', in the townland of Grenan.[5] The saint's church later became part of the possessions of the Augustinian priory of Inistioge. Tagán may also have been the patron of other churches in Leinster, for example the Wicklow church of Kiltegan (Ceall Tagáin?). A saint of the same name was patron of the Tipperary church of Kiltegan.[6] Tagán is sometimes taken to have been identical with the Teige (Tecce) commemorated, according to the later martyrologies, on 9 September.[7]

1 *BP* 2234–8; *VT* 190. 2 *SG* i, 389 3 *HADO* ii, 224. 4 *CGSH* §69; *GRSH* 72; *Lgen*. 714.6; *CGH* 130a30–5; *JRSAI* 101, 127–8. 5 *HADO* iv, 265–6. 6 *CLTÁ* 242–4. 7 *LIS* 9, 250–1; *Carloviana* 55, 99; *Béaloideas* 4, 129 *MartG* 172; *MartD* 242.

TAILEACH. *See* Finnian of Clonard.

TÁILGEANN, AN. *See* Patrick.

TAIRCHEALL. *See* Moling.

TAIRCHEALL son of Muireadhach. *See* Aodh of Killeenmore.

TAIREALL, Patrick's craftsman. Along with Tamhán, the saint's harper, Taireall is known only from the metrical list of those in orders with Patrick.[1]

1 *CGSH* §672.13.23.

TALÁN, Patrick's doorman. *See* Cillín of Tehallan.

TALMHACH. A man named Talmhach was among those said to have attended Fionnbharr's celebrated school at Gougane Barra, which, given the evident concern of the Cork saint's biographer with proving that Ross and Cloyne owed deference to his patron, would suggest that Talmhach's church was located in one or other of these dioceses.[1] An apparently distinct saint of the name was given the honour of rendering the last rites to Bearach of the Roscommon church of Termonbarry, and of being selected to succeed this saint as head of his church.[2] The account of the conception of Lonán of Trevet, as presented in the preface to a hymn attributed to Mugintius of Whithorn, describes how Drustic daughter of Drust, king of the Britons, was duped into believing that she had slept with the object of her love, when a certain Talmhach, a companion of Finnian of Clonard, had been sent in his place.[3] Two saints of the name are remembered in the martyrologies, at 26 February and 14 March.[4] As the latter feast was followed by that of some sons of Neasán, who gave name to the island of Ireland's Eye, alias Inis Mac Neasáin, the 'S. Talmani' inscribed on a silver tongue (*lingula*) attached, according to James Ussher, to the Garland of Howth manuscript may refer to the Talmhach remembered on 14 March.[5]

1 *BBa*. 66 §21. **2** *BNÉ* i, 43 §90. **3** *LH* i, 22. **4** *MartT* 23; *MartG* 44, 54; *MartD* 58, 76. **5** *WWRJU* vi, 531.

Tamhán. *See* Taireall.

Talulla, abbess of Kildare. *See* Osnad.

Taobhóg of Kilteevoge (Ceall Taobhóg), barony of Raphoe, Co. Donegal. Locally regarded as a woman of the Diviny (Uí Dhuibheannaigh) family, the saint has recently been shown to represent the cult of Maodhóg (Taodhóg/Aodh) of Ferns in this part of Donegal.[1] The same saint may have given name to Tattevagh (Teach Taobhóige) in the Fermanagh parish of Aghalurcher.[2]

1 OSL DL 174; *DLHS* 177–8. **2** PNNI viii, 170–1.

Taoide of Church Island (Inis Taoide) on Lough Beg, parish of Ballyscullion, barony of Loughinsholin, Co. Derry. Church Island, the scene of a murderous attack by the Ulaidh in 1129, appears to have been a relatively important site within the former territory of the Uí Thuirtre. Otherwise, little is known of it or of its saint, but that his name might also be written Toit(e) or Tida.[1] The basin of a holy stone on the island was thought to contain curative water.[2] Speaking of an old church named Templemoyle in Muintear Fheodacháin, now a part of the Fermanagh barony of Clanawley, and more specifically of Cleenish parish, John O'Donovan gave the name of its founder or dedicatee as 'Thady', which might also represent Taoide.[3] A similar tradition is preserved in an early eighteenth-century 'History of Fermanagh', which states that Thady's well had the power to cure yellow jaundice.[4] Taoide's feast fell on 7 September.[5]

1 *AI*/*AU s.a.*; PNNI v, 59, 65; *AnH* 12, 108, 111. **2** *PNCL* 59; *DYHS* 195. **3** OSL FH 115; *MGF* 129, 131. **4** *ClRec*. 1.3, 136. **5** *MartT* 69; *MartG* 172; *MartD* 238.

Tasach of Raholp (Ráith Cholptha), parish of Ballyculter, barony of Lecale Lower, Co. Down. The list of those in orders with Patrick groups together his two craftsmen, Bíthe and Tasach, whose churches were located in close proximity to one another in Lecale barony, at Inch (Inis Cúscraidh) and Raholp.[1] A similar grouping is found in Patrick's Life, albeit at the later diocesan centre of Elphin, where the Armagh saint is said to have placed his 'copper-smith' Assicus (Asach) – whence the pet form Tasach – together with his nephew Bíthe and the latter's mother 'Cipia'.[2] The Tripartite Life subsequently placed Bíthe at Racoon Hill (Ráith Chonga), near Assaroe in Donegal, to which Tasach (Assicus) is also said to have retired before being buried there alongside Aodh of Rahugh, according to a late tradition.[3] The 'royal bishop' Tasach, who was given the signal honour of rendering Patrick the last rites, continues to be regarded as diocesan patron of Elphin, where his feast is celebrated on 27 April, two weeks on from his day in the martyrologies (14 April).[4] The later date appears to have been due to confusion with an otherwise unattested Usandus/Assanus, commemorated in the Hieronymian martyrology on that day, who was transformed into an Irish saint in the later martyrologies.[5] A relic of Patrick, known as *buacach Phádraig*, was kept at Elphin.[6]

1 *CGSH* §671.12; *Lgen.* 695.1; *BP* 2961–2, 3141; *VT* 250, 266; *DIB* i, 183–4. **2** *PTBA* 140 §21.2 (= *BP* 1073–4; *VT* 96). **3** *BP* 1730–3; *VT* 148; *DEPPP* 26; *ClRec.* 13, 86–7; *Béaloideas* 6, 149. **4** *DEPPP* 26; *PTBA* 118 §2.9; *MartT* 32; *MartO²* 106; *MartG* 76; *MartD* 102. **5** *MartG* 84; *MartD* 112. **6** *AFM s.a.* 1406.

Tathchomharc. *See* Tochomhracht.

Teagán of Grenan. *See* Tagán of Curraclone.

Teamhair daughter of Eirnín. *See* Ingheana Cathbhadh.

Teamhair daughter of Mac Dara. *See* Brighid of Shankill.

Teamhair of Oghil. *See* Dúthracht of Oghil.

Tearnóg of Cranfield (Creamhchoill), barony of Upper Toome, Co. Antrim. The grandfather of Tearnóg son of Ciarán was, according to the genealogists, Sárán son of Caolbhadh, king of the Ulaidh, who, having laid hands on Patrick, was deprived of heaven and earth, only to have the former restored to him by Bishop Olcán.[1] Among those named Mearnóg (a variant of Tearnóg) in the list of homonymous saints is one assigned to Cranfield.[2] Also located in this parish was Aughrim, the church of Tearnóg's uncle, Breacán son of Sárán. At Cranfield, Tearnóg was remembered under the guise of Eirnín on 31 May.[3] A saint named Colmán, whose well was frequented on May Eve and again on 29/30 June, was also attached to Cranfield.[4]

1 *CGSH* §101; *GRSH* 101; *Lgen.* 735.10–11; *BP* 1906–7, 1924; *VT* 164. **2** *CGSH* §707.782. **3** *MartG* 106; *MartD* 140. **4** PNNI iv, 7–10; *EA* 88; *ASH* 378 (16); *UJA* (2nd ser.) 49.

Teille of Tihelly (Teach Teille), parish of Durrow, barony of Ballycowan, Co. Offaly. Despite the traditional etymology proposed for the name – from Latin *tellus*, 'earth' – Teille (from *Do-Eille*) derives from Oilill, of which it was a pet form. The saint was attached by the genealogists through his father Séighín to the same branch of the Oirghialla as his uncles, Baodán and Furodhrán (both sons of Maonán) of Dunleer, and cousin Tua (alias Ultán) of Taghadoe (Teach Tua).[1] Teille and Furodhrán are together featured in the well-known tale of *Buile Shuibhne* (Sweeney's Frenzy), where Teille is shown receiving a blessing from another cousin, Rónán Fionn.[2] A sister named Béibhil is said to have dwelt in Rónán's church at Magheralin (Lann Rónáin Fhinn) in the county of Down, whereas Teille's mother Soidhealbh is thought to have shared the saint's church at Tihelly.[3] Little else is known of the saint, but Munna of Taghmon is reputed to have founded Tihelly before Teille (whom he foretold) arrived there from a place named 'Ager Miodhluachra', probably in the Louth area.[4] The saint's name is included under both guises, Teille and Oilill, in the list of those commemorated on 25 June.[5]

1 *CGSH* §318.1–5; *GRSH* 72; *Lgen.* 714.17. 2 *BS* §9. 3 *CGSH* §318.2–3. 4 *VSHH* 200–1 §§11, 13; *VSHP* ii, 231 §12. 5 *MartT* 52; *MartO*[2] 142; *MartG* 122; *MartD* 178.

Teimhnéan. *See* Motheimhneóg.

Thady. *See* Taoide.

Tice. *See* Dubh Dúin.

Tida. *See* Taoide.

Tiernaun. *See* Tighearnach / Tighearnán.

Tighearn daughter of Mac Reithe. *See* Líogh.

Tighearn of Kilmoney. *See* Brígh of Kilmoney.

Tighearnach. Seven saints bearing this name, which derives from *tighearn*, 'lord', are included in the list of homonymous saints, but all are otherwise unattested, except Tighearnach of Clones (Cluain Eois), who heads the list, and his namesake at Derryvella (Doire Mheille).[1]

1 *CGSH* §707.937–42.

Tighearnach of Clones (Cluain Eois), barony of Dartree, Co. Monaghan. The saint's paternal descent attached him through his father Cairbre to an obscure branch of the Uí Bhairrche of Leinster.[1] Although placed first in the list of Uí Bhairrche saints, he was the only representative of the family to have his chief church lie outside Leinster.[2] A number of brothers and other close relatives are said, however, to have been in a church named Shankill (Seanchill) in the Kilkenny barony of Gowran.[3] His mother Dearbhfhraoich, also noted for her sanctity, is said to have been a daughter of Eacha son of Criomhthann, king of Oirghialla, a territory which was to be the saint's main sphere of activity.[4]

The importance of Tighearnach's church at Clones, allegedly founded on the lands of a swineherd, can be gauged from the relatively large number of entries relating to it in the pre-Conquest annals.[5] Another measure of its high status is the fact that it was selected, probably before 1150, as the site of a house of canons regular of St Augustine, perhaps because it had some pretensions to diocesan status.[6] This may also be inferred from the office-style Latin Life composed for Tighearnach which attributes to him an episcopal status as well as the offer of a see, said to have been refused.[7] The liturgical origins of the Life are emphasized by two hymns (for vespers and matins) that follow it. Although sometimes taken to reflect quite early issues, the text may not be much earlier that the earliest of its two manuscript copies, the fourteenth-century Salamancan codex, the Lives of which were probably brought together at Clogher whose see, according to its Register, was occupied by Tighearnach.[8] Incomplete in this collection, Tighearnach's Life has been more fully preserved in the Rawlinson collection, now in Oxford.

The saint's biographer, having alleged that the child was born illegitimately in the king's palace near Clogher, brought him to Kildare, where Brighid asked Bishop Conlaodh to baptize him in the name Tighearnach because of his royal descent, an event that has been taken to reflect an early affiliation of Clones to the *paruchia* of Kildare.[9] Pirates are said to have then taken him (together with Eoghan of Ardstraw, according to another source) to the king of the Britons who, impressed by signs of his holiness, sent him to 'Monennus' (Maoineann) at the monastery of Rosnat – later Whithorn (Latin *Candida Casa*) – where great things were again foretold, including his founding of Clones.[10] There follow accounts of a journey to Rome, the procurement of relics of Peter and Paul, a visit to Martin at Tours in the company of Ciarán of Tubbrid, and a further encounter with a king of the Britons, this time in connection with the resuscitation of Eithne, daughter of the king of Munster, and probable eponym of Temple-etney (Teampall Eithne), near Ciarán's church of Tubbrid in south Tipperary.[11] Although the author's obvious interest in this area may reflect the presence at Cahir of a house of canons regular, the saint's later role as dedicatee of the priory of Aghmacart in the Laois barony of Clarmallagh is more likely to have been because of his genealogical connections with Leinster.[12]

The saint is then brought to his father's district (*patria*), where he requests and receives a site for his church and, following another visit to Kildare, he is found to be worthy of episcopal status and possession of a see at the expense of the incumbent, Mac Caorthainn of Clogher (corruptly rendered Maenchatinus), an offer which is politely declined. Not long afterwards, his worthiness is again exemplified by his raising from the dead of 'Doachus' (Dubhthach?), archbishop of Armagh.[13] Much of the remainder of the Life, preserved only in the Oxford collection, is taken up with his activity in the Lough Erne area, where he founded a church at 'Gaballensis' (Gabhal Liúin), now Galloon in Fermanagh – helped, according to another source, by Eoghan of Ardstraw – and where he was also patron of the church of Derryvullan (Doire Mhaoláin).[14] At Galloon, having placed a prominent ancestor of the powerful local family of Méguidhir (Maguire) in his debt, he left his beloved disciple Comhghall, before returning to Clones to die.[15]

The text reveals throughout an acute awareness of the issues of its own time, and especially the need to be on the correct side of the secular and ecclesiastical authorities, represented by the British (i.e. English) king, local chieftains, including Méguidhir of Fermanagh whose family-church at Aghalurcher had Tighearnach as co-patron, and the archbishop of Armagh.[16] The saint's alleged possession of the relics of Peter and Paul points to a concern with the affairs of the canons regular whose house in Clones was dedicated to the two chief apostles.[17]

In his capacity as patron of Galloon, Tighearnach figures prominently in the Life of Náile of Kinawley as one of the *ardnaoimh*, 'chief saints', of Lough Erne.[18] This text also refers to the saint's bell, the *glasán Tighearnaigh* which was probably kept at Galloon, whereas another apparent bell, described as *ceolán*, 'musical one', was later left to the 'Foreigners' after the battle of Downpatrick.[19] Tighearnach is provided with an obit of 549/50 and his feastday was celebrated on 4 April.[20] His paternal association with the Uí Bhairrche may be reflected in the pattern day of the church of Glebe, parish of Kilturk, barony of Bargy (from Uí Bhairrche) in Wexford, which fell on 4 April.[21] A stone cross in his memory stood at Donaghmoyne, the church of Lasair and Ciar, and he was also remembered at some churches in Scotland.[22]

1 *CGSH* §244; *GRSH* 92; *Lgen.* 724.2.7; *DIB* ix, 370; *TC* 67–80. **2** *CGH* 121a39; *MartO²* 110. **3** *CGH* 121ba33–52. **4** *CGSH* §722.42; *MartO²* 110. **5** *MartT* 102; *AU* iv, 75. **6** *MRHI* 164. **7** *VSHH* 111 §14; *VSHP* ii, 266 §12; *TC* 87–91. **8** *VSHH* 111 §14; *VSHP* ii, 266 §12; *ClRec.* 7, 376–8; ibid. 11, 305–25. **9** *VSHH* 107–8 §§1–2; *VSHP* ii, 262 §§1–2; *MartO²* 110; *ClRec.* 11, 321. **10** *VSHH* 108 §3, 400 §2; *VSHP* ii, 262–3 §§3–4. **11** *VSHH* 108–9 §§5–9; *VSHP* ii, 263–4 §§5–7; *TC* 55–6. **12** *MRHI* 156, 162; *HADO* ii, 235; *CPL* 15, §688. **13** *VSHH* 110–11 §§11–15; *VSHP* ii, 265–7 §§9–13. **14** *VSHP* ii, 267 §14; *VSHH* 401 §5; *AnnU* 28, 42; *CPL* 15, §848. **15** *VSHP* ii, 267–9 §§15–18. **16** *AU s.a.* 1447 (iii, 160); *ClRec.* 18, 305; ibid. 19, 189. **17** *MRHI* 164. **18** *MHH* 110 §29, 114 §40. **19** Ibid. 115–24 §§43–58; *MartD* xxxi; *MIA s.a.*; *EMH* 480 §210. **20** *AU s.a.*; *MartT* 29; *MartO²* 104; *MartG* 70; *MartD* 94. **21** OSL WX ii, 194; *CECW* 211. **22** *KSS* 452; *CLRec.* 7, 404.

Tighearnach of Derryvella (Doire Mheille), parish of Kilcooly, barony of Slievardagh, Co. Tipperary. This saint is known from a number of sources. The tract on the mothers of the saints describes him as a son of Mealla who, in the guise of Meall Chráibhtheach, was eponym of the church to which Tighearnach was first attached.[1] The annals, which record his death in 810, indicate that, though he was founder of Derryvella, he also became abbot of the more important Killeigh (Ceall Aichidh) in the Offaly parish of Geashill, both of which were apparently associated with the *céile Dé* ascetics of the period 750–850.[2] Placing his feast on 4 November, the martyrologies describe him as a 'jewel'.[3]

1 *CGSH* §722.18. **2** *AU s.a.*; *FSHIM* 84. **3** *MartG* 212; *MartD* 296.

Tighearnach Boircheach of Movilla (Magh Bhile), parish of Newtownards, barony of Ards Lower, Co. Down. Bearing a cognomen derived from Boirche, now Mourne, this saint is described in the annal notices of his death in 1061 as successor to Finnian of Movilla and 'chief confessor' of Ireland.[1] He was no celibate, however, as is clear from the fact that he was succeeded at Movilla by a son named Flaithbheartach.[2] Yet, the notice of his feast of 13 May – which may have found its way, albeit on 16 May, into a martyrology kept in Cologne – describes him not only as a confessor, but also as an anchorite.[3]

1 *AU s.a.* 1061. **2** Ibid. *s.a.* 1096. **3** *FSHIM* 138–9, 160–1; *FourIM* 62–3.

Tighearnán of Errew (Aireadh Locha Chon), parish of Crossmolina, barony of Tirawley, Co. Mayo. The genealogists attached this saint (also known as Tighearnach, anglicized Tiernaun) through his father Ninnidh variously to the descendants of Colla Uais of Oirghialla and – more in keeping with the location of his church – to the Uí Fhiachrach of north Connacht.[1] The Oirghialla descent brings the saint close to his namesake at Clones, with whom he was probably ultimately identical. Although little is recorded of Tighearnán, he is numbered, together with his neighbour, Mochua of Balla, among the saints whom Seanán of Scattery might invoke in time of need, and he is also included, along with

Seanán, among the progeny of Inghean Bhaoith of Killinaboy.[2] An entry in the Annals of Connacht for 1413 states that Tighearnán's appearance in nightly visions led to the release of a chieftain of the Barretts without ransom, followed by a handsome grant of land to the saint's church at Errew which, scarcely coincidentally, was about to become the seat of an Augustinian priory.[3] By the early nineteenth century, memory of the saint had faded at Errew, but a relic named *Mias Tighearnáin*, 'Tighearnán's plate', was still kept locally.[4] His feastday was celebrated on 8 April, within the octave of the feast of Tighearnach of Clones.[5]

1 *CGSH* §§80, 118; *GRSH* 68; *Lgen.* 713.5. **2** *ZCP* 10, 26 §21; *IrT* iv, 93 §4. **3** *ACon. s.a.*; *MRHI* 175. **4** OSL MO i, 359; *JCHAS* 49, 55; *JRSAI* 53, 175. **5** *MartT* 31; *MartG* 72; *MartD* 98.

Tighris. *See* Dairearca; Lubaid.

Tíreachán. *See* Muirchú.

Tiú of 'Row' (Rubha) in the townland of Echlinville, parish of Ballyhalberd, barony of Ards Upper, Co. Down.[1] This son of Fíonán was attached by the genealogists to the Dál mBuain, a branch of the Ulaidh of east Ulster.[2] Described as 'gracious', Tiú is assigned to 'Row' in the notice of his feast of 24 June. In former times, his chapel was impropriate to Movilla.[3]

1 *EA* 21; PNNI ii, 94. **2** *CGSH* §154; *GRSH* 97; PNNI ii, 94–5. **3** *MartG* 122; *MartD* 178; *EA* 21, 379; *CPL* 15, §308 (*Sancte Sciw*).

Tnuán. *See* Angán.

Tochomhracht of Kiltoghert (Ceall Tochomhracht), barony and county of Leitrim. Among the Leitrim churches in the diocese of Ardagh, according to a late fifteenth-century list of annates, was the rectory of 'Sancte Tachmurce de Cilltachmurc'.[1] A list of churches in the barony of 'Muintear Eolais', now Leitrim, drawn up in the late fifteenth century, includes 'Tachmurca of Cilltachmure', and a similar list, compiled in the early seventeenth century, refers to 'Tacmarc', patron of Kiltoghert, whose bejewelled bell gave succour to expectant mothers.[2] Also near the church, according to this list, was a large 'miraculous' well whose surrounding wall had the imprint of Patrick's knee. Two hundred years later, all that could be recorded of the saint was that she was the original founder of the church named after her.[3] Her name and lineage, Tochomhracht of the Conmhaicne (a family with lands mainly in Connacht), are featured in the list of those remembered on 11 June, but her church was also the scene of celebrations on Garland Sunday in late July.[4] The Leitrim church was among the possessions claimed by Clonmacnoise in Connacht, and the saint's cult travelled as far as Corcomroe in Clare, where a parish (Kiltoraght) is named after her.[5]

1 *AnnU* 164–5. **2** *CPL* 13, 344; *Celtica* 1, 67, 75; *EMH* 478 §200. **3** OSL CN/LM 215. **4** *MartT* 49; *MartG* 114; *MartD* 166; *FL* 606–7. **5** *CCLC* 242.

Toimdheanach son of Laighneach. *See* Dubhán of Monasterevin.

Toit. *See* Taoide.

Tola Cráibhtheach, 'pious', of Dysert, alias Dysert O Dea (Díseart Tola), in the barony of Inchiquin, Co. Clare. Although Tola son of Dúnchadh was variously attached by the genealogists to the Cianachta and Déise, his church, whose ruins are among the most impressive in the whole county, lay within the lands of the powerful Dál gCais dynasty.[1] When visiting the church in 1839, Eugene O'Curry was told that the saint's feastday (30 March) was still held holy, but little else is recorded of him.[2] A second *díseart* named after him was located in Dealbhna Mhór, which gave name to the Westmeath barony of Delvin.[3] This site is now represented by Dysert in the parish of Killulagh, a mere ten miles or so from Clonard, and this might explain why the notice of the saint's death in 738 describes him as abbot of the latter church.[3] An annal entry for 1013 records the death at Dysert of Dálach, coarb of Tola and Féichín – presumably of Fore, which adjoins Dysert.[4] His feast of 30 March is recorded in most martyrologies.[5] Tola's relics, presumably enshrined, were taken on tour in 793, and his crozier is now in the National Museum.[6]

1 *CGSH* §207; *GRSH* 124; *Lgen*. 742.4; *DIB* ix, 396. **2** *ACoC* 48. **3** *MartO*[2] 102. **4** *AU s.a.* **5** *MartT* 28; *MartO*[2] 85; *MartG* 64; *MartD* 90. **6** *JRSAI* 24, 339–40; *AU s.a.*

Torannán. *See* Mothoiréan.

Trea of Artrea (Aird Trea), barony of Dungannon Upper, Co. Tyrone. Leaving the territory of Dál nAraidhe (approximately north Down and south Antrim) for Uí Thuirtre, a kingdom originally lying mainly in the Derry barony of Loughinsholin, Patrick was brought by his mid-ninth-century biographer to a spot between Lough Neagh and Slieve Gallion, where he was met by the local king, Caorthann Mór, 'great', who threatened to expel him.[1] The saint duly punished Caorthann by depriving his family of the kingship, baptizing instead the family of his brother, Caorthann Beag, 'little', and blessing the unborn child in the womb of this man's wife, Moghan daughter of Fearghas Mór of Dál Riada in north Antrim. Thus was heralded the birth of Trea daughter of Caorthann of the Uí Thuirtre, on whose head Patrick is said to have later placed a veil brought from heaven through which only she was to see for the rest of her life.[2] Little else is known of either Trea or her church which is mentioned once only in the annals, in connection with its *airchinneach*, 'head', a man named Maol Brighde, 'devotee of Brighid', who died in 1127.[3] Already then, Brighid had probably joined Trea in the dedication of the local church.[4] Trea's feast was twice celebrated, first on 8 July and again on 3 August, about which time (on the last Sunday of July or first Sunday of August) the festival of *Lughnasadh*, locally known as Blaeberry Sunday, was celebrated on the slopes of Slieve Gallion.[5]

1 *BP* 1954–71; *VT* 168; *DIB* ix, 457–8. **2** *BP* 1954–71; *VT* 168; *CGSH* §76; *GRSH* 68; *Lgen*. 712.9. **3** *AU s.a.* **4** *AnnU* 7–8; *CPL* 9, 542. **5** *MartT* 54, 60; *MartG* 132, 148; *MartD* 190, 210; *FL* 150–2.

Trea daughter of Rónán. *See* Baoithín of Ennisboyne.

Tréan. *See* Tréidhe.

Tréidhe of Clongawny (Cluain Gamhna), parish of Mullingar, barony of Moyashel and Magheradernon, Co. Westmeath. This saint is known from two sources which offer differing versions of her name. A miscellaneous entry in the corpus of saints' genealogies, while placing her at Clongawny, writes her name as Tréan daughter of Mac Laodh.[1] The Life of Colmán son of Luachán, son of Laodh (Leadha) – doubtless the same as the Laodh of the previous source – presents the saint as Colmán's sister.[2] This source also states that she was the eldest of seven daughters, two others of whom (Broigheal and Buidhneach) are said to have joined Tréidhe – whose name was incorrectly taken to derive from *treadhan*, 'abstinence' – at Clongawny. Colmán's church of Lynn, close to Clongawny, probably had a proprietorial interest in the place.

1 *CGSH* §663.8. **2** *BCML* 8 §§8–9.

Tréanán of Maca Runtair. *See* Mothrianóg of Rúscach.

Tréanán Draoi, 'druid', of Iomghán (Iomdhán?), now possibly Rathangan in the barony of East Offaly, Co. Kildare.[1] Tréanán is included among the saints of the Dál Meisin Corb, who were mainly connected with north-east Leinster and particularly with the area about Glendalough.[2] Accompanying him in the list is an otherwise unknown saint named Caoimheall.

1 *CPPI* 182. **2** *CGSH* §181.15; *Lgen.* 725.11.

Treaslaice son of Aonghas. *See* Seanach son of Aonghas.

Trena. *See* Trian of Donaghmore.

Triallach. *See* Aodhán of Templeshanbo.

Trian of Brosna. *See* Trian of Donaghmore.

Trian of Donaghmore (Domhnach Mór), barony of East Muskerry, Co. Cork. This son of Tairbhín is included among seven brothers and seven sisters, mainly connected with a church at Áth na gCeall, a site in the townland of Gortnagross, probably at or near Longfield's Bridge by the river Blackwater, in the Cork parish of Ballyclogh.[1] The family belonged to the Múscraighe and among Trian's siblings was Laichtín of Freshford, who was also associated with Donaghmore. Trian of Donaghmore is among those named as having attended Fionnbharr's famous school in Cork, whose pupils were mainly drawn, tendentiously, from churches within the dioceses of Cloyne and Ross.[2] It has been suggested that the church of Templetrine, near Bandon, also took its name from this Trian (anglicized Trena).[3] As Patrick was leaving Munster, immediately after he had dealt with the ruling family of Múscraighe Tíre, he was entertained, according to the Tripartite Life, by Trian, a pilgrim *de Romanis*, 'of the Romans', at 'Craobhacha' near 'Brosnacha'.[4] The association with Múscraighe suggests that Trian of Donaghmore is intended and the site in question may now be Brosna in the Offaly parish of Kilmurryely.[5]

1 *CGSH* §666.1; *Lgen.* 752.1. **2** *BBh.* 76 §34; *MakS* 87–9. **3** *BHJ* 1, 55; Logainm.ie 'Templetrine'. **4** *BP* 2545–55; *VT* 216. **5** *HDGP* ii, 202–3.

Trian son of Deadh. Witness is borne to this saint both by genealogists who place him among the Dál nAraidhe of north Down/south Antrim, and by martyrologists who, in noting his feast of 22 March, locate him in Ceall Ealga, a corrupt rendering of Ceall Deilge, now either Kildalkey in the Meath barony of Lune, or Kildellig in the Laois barony of Clarmallagh.[1] The saint's northern background may be reflected by the use of 'St Espintriaym' (from Easbog Trian?) as an alias for the prebend of Dromara in the Down baronies of Lower and Upper Iveagh.[2] Trian's relics were brought on circuit in 743, when the *bolgach* disease was rampant, and again in 794.[3]

1 *CGSH* §105; *GRSH* 101; *Lgen*. 735.4; *MartT* 26; *MartG* 60; *MartD* 84; *HDGP* iii, 162–3. 2 *CPL* 18, §243. 3 *AU s.a.*

TRIAN son of Dubhthach. *See* Comhghall son of Dubhthach.

TRIANÁN. *See* Mothrianóg.

TROSCÁN of Ardbraccan (Ard Breacáin), barony of Lower Navan, Co. Meath. One of seven 'beautiful' sons of Aonghas, said to have come to Ireland from Scotland, Troscán's pedigree attaches him to the tribal grouping of Dál Riada.[1] Like those of most of his brothers, Troscán's church lay in the middle part of Ireland. Some of the brothers were remembered on 12 June, and Troscán's name is added to the list in the seventeenth-century Martyrology of Donegal.[2] The proximity of the June feast to that of Colum Cille recalls the fact that a poem on the brothers is attributed to the founder of Iona.[3] It has been suggested that Drostán of Deirtheach, who died at Ardbraccan in 719, was identical with Troscán.[4]

1 *CGSH* §§209, 701.4; *GRSH* 81. 2 *MartD* 168. 3 *CGSH* §701; *TMD* 35–8. 4 *AU s.a.*; *SBDeer* 382–4; *LegSS* 353.

TROSTÁN son of Fidhghin. *See* Aoidhghin of Teach Deireascain.

TUA. This hypocoristic or pet form of Ultán was popular enough to be included in the list of homonymous saints, with three representatives, in addition to the six entries in the same list that use the radical form of the name.[1]

1 *CGSH* §707.933–5.943–8.

TUA of Taghadoe (Teach Tua), barony of North Salt, Co. Kildare. Tua (alias Ultán) was one of four sons of Aodh son of Colga, king of Oirthir – whence Orior in Armagh – who died, according to the annals, in 610 'as a pilgrim' in Clonmacnoise.[1] The Life of Mochta of Louth states that its subject refused an offer from this Aodh of land, allegedly because he knew that it was destined for the use of Colum Cille.[2] Aodh's three other sons – Tua's siblings – were Maighneann of Kilmainham, Cobhthach (probably Cobhthach Caol son of the king of Oirghialla), and Libhréan (probably of Clonfad). The name given to the saint's mother was Sineall daughter of Ceinnfhionnán, a sister of Seinshincheall of Killeigh in Offaly who belonged to Uí Labhradha, a Leinster family that also numbered among its saints Abán of Killabban in Laois.[3] Teille of Tihelly near Durrow in Offaly was Tua's cousin on his father's side.

An addendum to the corpus of saints' pedigrees, relating apparently to Brigidine churches spread across the counties of Kildare, Offaly and Westmeath, locates Tua (Ultán) at Cluain Dabhcha in Fiodh Eóin which may now be represented by Clonduff in the Kildare parish of Balraheen, adjoining Taghadoe.[4] A *dinnsheanchas* poem composed in lamentation of the fall of the famous tree, *Bile Tortan*, features Tua among other Midland saints.[5] The saint's feast fell on 22 December, and the entry in the Martyrology of Tallaght explains, erroneously but attractively, the *Tua* version of the saint's name as being due to his habit of holding a stone in his mouth every Lent, which rendered him silent (Irish *taoi, tua*).[6] The later martyrologies place Tua (alias Ultán) in Clane (Claonadh), near Taghadoe in north Kildare.[7]

1 *CGSH* §54; *GRSH* 72; *Lgen*. 713.10; *AU s.a.*; *AFM s.a.*606. 2 *VSHH* 399 §16. 3 *CGSH* §§282, 287, 722.90. 4 *CGSH* §663.1–13. 5 *MD* iv, 240–6. 6 *MartT* 88; *MartO*² 253, 260. 7 *MartG* 244; *MartD* 342.

Tuán of Tamhlachta, an ecclesiastical site in the townland of Lisnacree, parish of Kilkeel, barony of Mourne, Co. Down.[1] With the encouragement of Finnian of Movilla, Tuán son of Coireall – allegedly because of his previous existence in the guise of Tuán son of Starn, son of Scara, Parthalón's brother's son – had his own *scéal* to relate concerning the various invasions of Ireland.[2] The two saints are said to have met at a *díseart* in the territory of the Ulaidh, which would suit the location of the church to which Tuán was attached. It has been argued that the story is based on earlier tales relating to inquiry about the hidden past.[3] So famous did Tuán become that Giraldus Cambrensis devoted some paragraphs to him, albeit under the corrupt form of 'Ruanus', attributing to the saint baptism by Patrick and the attainment of an 'incredible' age of 1500 years.[4] Not inappropriately, Tuán's feast fell on 1 April.[5]

1 *EA* 207; *HDC* 1, 9; PNNI iii, 64–5. 2 *LU* 1209–305; *LG* iii, 22 §222; v, 22–4 §385, 224 §511; *Ériu* 35, 93–111; cf. *ZCP* 3, 15, 31. 3 *Éigse* 20, 93–105. 4 *THEH* 142. 5 *MartT* 29; *MartG* 68; *MartD* 92.

Tuggins. *See* Dubh Dúin.

Tulloge. *See* Eallóg.

U ☙

Ua Suanaigh. *See* Fiodhmhaine.

Uaininn daughter of Fionnbharr. *See* Mobhí Cláirineach.

Uidhre son of Cuán, bishop. Bearing a name that may derive from *odhar*, 'dun-coloured', Uidhre was attached by the genealogists to a branch of the Corca Bhaiscinn of south-west Clare said to have been blessed by Patrick.[1] Notes added to the genealogy locate the saint variously in Ceall Róin (perhaps for Rónáin) and Achadh Fionn, now possibly represented by Aghafin in the Roscommon parish of Kilronan.[2] A saint named Odhrán, likewise a derivative of *odhar*, was commemorated on 8 May, and in some late sources a certain Uuiro (Wiro), alias Bearaidh, reputedly an archbishop of Dublin, but more correctly the patron of Roermond in Holland, whose ninth-century Life held him to be of Irish origin, was confused with Uidhre on this day.[3] A diminutive form of the saint's name, Uidhrín, may be preserved in the townland name Derryiron in the Offaly parish of Ballyburly.[4]

1 *CGSH* §210; *GRSH* 79; *Lgen*. 396.3; *CGH* 324g50–55. **2** *CGH* 324g54 (v.l); *HDGP* i, 18. **3** *MartD* 120–2, 478; *GRSH* 79; *BiblSS* xii, 1414–15; *TMD* 1–17, 175–8. **4** *ILL* 265–6.

Ultán. Apparently a derivative of *Ulaidh*, 'Ulstermen', used in the sense of 'little, i.e. beloved Ulsterman', Ultán and its hypocoristic form Tua account for nine entries in the list of homonymous saints.[1]

1 *CGSH* §707.933–5.943–8.

Ultán brother of Fursa. *See* Faolán of Aachen.

Ultán maca Cunga. *See* Ultán of Ardbraccan.

Ultán of Ardbraccan (Ard Breacáin), barony of Lower Navan, Co. Meath. During his visit to Meath in 1839, John O'Donovan discovered three wells named after Ultán son of Crónán (Rónán), locally called Hoult, one in Burry parish, another in Rathcore, and a third, of which he had least to say, in Ardbraccan.[1] The natives, according to O'Donovan, had been driven out of Ardbraccan and with them the record of the area's history in which Ultán would doubtless have figured prominently. Ironically, the earliest record of the saint presents him as an historian in his own right, as 'Ultanus episcopus Conchuburnensium', out of whose 'book or mouth', both Muirchú and Tíreachán drew for their seventh-century accounts of Patrick.[2] His reputation as an authority, thus established in relation to Patrick, could scarcely be ignored by the promoters of Brighid, who fathered on him two hymns in praise of the patron of Kildare – the Latin hymn *Christus in nostra insola*, and the beautiful vernacular hymn, beginning *Brighid bé bhithmhaith*, 'Brighid, ever-good woman' – and who attributed to his influence, for 'it was he who brought together all of Brighid's miracles', the composition by Brocán Claon of the equally attractive hymn, beginning *Ní char Brighid bhuadhach bith*, 'virtuous

Brighid loves not the world'.[3] Some modern scholars go as far as to credit him with the authorship of the so-called 'primitive' Life (*vita primitiva*) thought to lie behind Brighid's two early Lives, that of Cogitosus and the *vita prima*.[4] Brighid's mother belonged to the Dál gConchobhair among whom Ultán dwelt and, while his paternal descent attached him to the northern family of Dál nAraidhe, his mother, Colla daughter of Díoma Meann, is said to have belonged to the Gaileanga who gave name to the Meath barony of Morgallion, just north of Ardbraccan.[5]

Considered to have lived at a time when the worst effects of the great plague known as *Buidhe Chonaill* had taken hold, Ultán – whose namesake, Ultán of the Maca Cunga, allegedly died in the plague – is said to have taken into his care numerous orphaned children, thus giving rise from an early period to a high regard for him as protector of the young.[6] Among other saints linked to Ultán are Mochta of Louth, whom he is supposed to have succeeded as abbot, and Moninne of Killevy, the author, according to the same source, of a quatrain in his praise.[7] The biographer of Bearach presented Ultán, together with Finnian of Clonard, as an arbiter of disputes, and Maodhóg's biographer included him among his subject's closest companions, united with him 'in heaven and on earth' and – no doubt more in keeping with the writer's agenda – as the author of a list of dues owed to Maodhóg.[8] Noted for prophecies, he was also among those featured in a poem lamenting the fall of the famous tree, *Bile Tortan*, near Ardbraccan.[9]

The saint's cult, which reached Killanny on the Louth-Monaghan border, where he was taken to be a special friend of Mac Caorthainn, and indeed occupant, like his friend, of the see of Clogher.[10] It also reached Drumgoolan in the parish of Louth, Killinkere in Cavan, and perhaps also the parishes of Lusk and Donabate in north Dublin, where an Ultán son of Bruidhghe is attested among the 'Tuath Tuirbhe', now Turvey.[11] A member of the 'third order' of Irish saints, and noted for cold baths, according to Cuimín of Connor, Ultán is said to have died in 657 (or 663).[12] Despite the tradition that he died on the same night as Colum Cille, whose feast fell in June, Ultán was remembered on 4 September.[13] Closer to June, however, is a feast of 13 July, credited in the later martyrologies to Ultán 'son of Araidhe', presumably a reference to Maca Araidhe, another form of Dál nAraidhe, the people to whom the saint belonged according to his paternal descent.[14] The list of those commemorated on the previous day includes Ultán of Cork, who was thus probably also identical with the patron of Ardbraccan. The Cork Ultán may also have been the original patron of Kilmoe (Ceall Mua) in the barony of West Carbery, if Mua, the eponym of this church, acts, like Tua, as a hypocoristic form of the saint's name; the later patron was Bréanainn of Clonfert.[15] The Tyrone church of Clogher laid claim, no doubt tendentiously, to Ultán's bodily remains.[16] The saint's relics, presumably enshrined, were taken on tour in 785.[17]

1 OSL MH 25–6, 212–13, 161. **2** *PTBA* 62.6, 125 [III 1], 138 §18 (1); *BP* 636–7; *VT* 60. **3** *LH* i, 14–15, 107–28. **4** *Peritia* 12, 79–86, 269; *DIB* ix, 612. **5** *CGSH* §§363, 722.4.30; *GRSH* 101; *Lgen*. 733.14–15, 734.3–5. **6** *IrT* iii, 85 §9; *MartO*[2] 192, 198–200; *ZCP* 1, 66; cf. *RM* 14, 230–41. **7** *MartO*[2] 200. **8** *VSHP* i, 82 §19; *BNÉ* i, 200, 251 §§35, 207. **9** *Éigse* 5, 86 §39; *SAM* 5.1, 129; *ProphSS* 84–92; *MD* iv, 240–46; *DERMB* 216 §27; *BMisc.* 141 §35–9. **10** *ClRec.* 7, 378, 406; *CPL* 15, §773. **11** OSL AH/MN 93; OSL CN/LM 64; OSL LH 253; *ClRec.* 1.1, 34; *SATDF* 177; *CGSH* §194; *GRSH* 124; *BLec.* 22va. **12** *VSHH* 82 §3; *ZCP* 1, 66; *AU s.a.* **13** *IrT* iii, 85 §8; *MartT* 68; *MartO*[2] 192; *MartG* 170; *MartD* 234–6. **14** *MartG* 136; *MartD* 194. **15** *NCHC* i, 69; *JCHAS* 15, 127, 129. **16** *ClRec.* 1.1, 34; ibid. 7, 406. **17** *AU s.a.*

ULTÁN of Cork. *See* Colmán of Clonpriest; Ultán of Ardbraccan.

ULTÁN of Taghadoe. *See* Tua.

ULTÁN son of Bruidhghe. *See* Ultán of Ardbraccan.

ULTÁN son of Maol Sneachta. *See* Faolán of Aachen.

USAILLE of Killashee (Ceall Usaille), barony of North Naas, Co. Kildare. This son of Restitutus is first mentioned in Muirchú's seventh-century Life of Patrick which describes how Usaille (alias Auxilius, Auxilinus and Ausaille) and Iserninus were ordained on the same day as Patrick himself was consecrated bishop.[1] Muirchú's contemporary Tíreachán also brings the saint – whom he describes as an exorcist – and Iserninus together in his account of how Patrick established churches for his two companions in the Liffey plain.[2] Whereas Usaille was attached to the church named after him at Killashee, Iserninus was assigned, along with Mac Táil, to Oldkilcullen (Ceall Chuilinn). Both Usaille and Iserninus are invoked, together with Patrick and other bishops, in a litany preserved in the Stowe Missal, and these three are also named in the preamble to the 'First Synod of St Patrick', a piece of church legislation that dates to about 700, or even earlier.[3] Strangely, however, neither saint is included among the twenty-four said to have been 'in orders' with Patrick.[4] Usaille is thought to have been a son of Patrick's sister Lubaid and in one instance he is described as the Armagh saint's designated successor.[5] He also found a place, with Patrick, among the signatories of the so-called Armagh canon, which was the source of much controversy.[6]

Usaille of the 'sweet-sounding bell' is among the saints called upon by Moling to come to the assistance of the Leinstermen.[7] His church is mentioned by the author of the later version of *Agallamh na Seanórach* (colloquy of the ancients) who, like Tíreachán, credits Patrick with its founding.[8] The saint's feast normally fell close to that of Patrick on 19 March, but he was also commemorated on such other days as 27 August, 16 September and, exceptionally, 19 October.[9] A note on the name in the Ó Cléirigh index to the Martyrology of Donegal identifies Usaille *gan amhras*, 'without a doubt', as patron of Killymard (Ceall Ua mBaird) in the Donegal barony of Banagh.[10] Usaille died, according to the annals, in 459.[11]

1 *PTBA* 74; *DIB* i, 200. **2** *PTBA* 162. **3** HBS 32, 15; 238–53; *CSGMA* 1–17; *StH* 8, 49–59; *Peritia* 12, 238–53. **4** *CGSH* §671. **5** Ibid. §722.15; *MartT* 100. **6** *IEKF* 58–9. **7** *SG* i, 389. **8** *AgS* ii, 42. **9** *MartT* 25, 66, 71; *MartG* 58, 164, 178; *MartD* 228; *BOM* 168. **10** *MartD* 476; *CCDK* 75. **11** *AU s.a.*

V ☙

Vauk. *See* Féichín.

Virgilius. *See* Feirghil.

Vogue. *See* Maodhóg.

W ☙

Winifrid/Winnie. *See* Inghean Bhaoith.

INDEX OF PARISHES

(Civil parishes only are listed. Headwords are not duplicated in references to entries)

INDEX OF OTHER PLACES

INDEX OF ALTERNATE (MAINLY ANGLICIZED) NAMES

(These names are also found in their appropriate places in the main dictionary).

Abban *see* Abán.
Abigail *see* Gobnaid.
Adomnán *see* Adhamhnán.
Africa *see* Afraic.
Aghorogus *see* Ciarán of Errigal.
Aidan *see* Aodhán / Maodhóg.
Aigne *see* Éigneach.
Albert *see* Ailbhe.
Araght *see* Athracht of Killaraght.
Arannán *see* Forannán of Alternan
Attracta (**Atty**) *see* Athracht of Killaraght.

Barrahane *see* Bearchán of Castlehaven.
Barry (**Barra**) of Cork *see* Fionnbharr.
Barry of Termonbarry *see* Bearach.
Beacon *see* Beagán
Beanan *see* Beinéan.
Bearaidh *see* Uidhre.
Bee-Ella *see* Beag Bile.
Beotis *see* Beoaidh of Duncrun.
Berehert/Benjamin/ *see* Beircheart.
Blane *see* Blán.
Blunny *see* Maol Anfaidh.
Boden *see* Buadán of Culdaff.
Boey *see* Beoaidh of Ardcarn.
Booden *see* Baodán of Cloney.
Borchill *see* Meithean Chaol.
Breanat *see* Beircheart.
Breeda *see* Brighid.
Brendan *see* Bréanainn.
Bride *see* Brighid.
Bridget *see* Brighid.
Broghan *see* Bearchán son of Muireadhach.
Bromona *see* Brónach of Kilbroney.
Buonia *see* Mughain of Lyons.
Bween *see* Buithe.

Cadinus *see* Caoide of Donaghedy.
Camulacus *see* Caomhlach of Raithean.
Canice *see* Cainneach of Aghaboe.
Cassidus *see* Caiseadhan.
Cavan *see* Cuán of Ahascragh.
Cedus *see* Caoide of Churchtown.
Celsus *see* Ceallach.
Christianus *see* Giolla Críost.
Clavin *see* Colmán of Templeshanbo.
Colpa *see* Athchaoin.
Commaneth (**Cumenod**) *see* Comnaid.
Conleth *see* Conlaodh.
Coolen *see* Cúlán.
Coran *see* Cuarán.
Coulan *see* Caolán of Youghalarra.
Coulane *see* Cúlán.
Coulus *see* Comhghall.
Coragh (**Coiragh**) *see* Cobhair.
Cowey *see* Cobhthach Caol.
Cranat *see* Cránaid.
Cravan *see* Sceanbhán.
Crohane *see* Cruachán.
Cronaghan *see* Cruithneachán.
Cruher Ree *see* Fraoch of Cloone.
Cuculanus *see* Cúlán.
Cuddy *see* Mochuda.
Cummian *see* Cuimín.
Cunnlan *see* Caolán of Youghalarra.

Dahalin *see* Daithle.
Daluath *see* Dalbhach
David *see* Bíthe of Inch.
Davin *see* Damhán
Deborah *see* Gobnaid.

INDEX OF SUBJECTS

INDEX OF FEASTDAYS

January

1. Aodhán of Templeshanbo; Colmán son of Rónán; Colmán Muilinn; Dobheóg of Lough Derg; Earnán of Drumhome; Fiontan of Myshall; Fuinche Gharbh; Oisín; Sciath.
2. Fionnlugh of Doon; Mainchín of Coolcashin / St Munchin's; Muireadhach of Banagher; Scoithín.
3. Fionnlugh of Doon; Fiontan of Doon.
4. Mochuma of Drummully.
5. Ciar of Kilkeary.
6. Athracht of Killaraght; Cearc of Tulach; Cúrnán son of Sineall; Cúrnán Beag; Diarmuid of Aireadh Seanaigh; Díoma Dubh; Osnad.
7. Brígh of Kilbride; Éimhín of Monasterevin; Donnán of Hareisland
8. Ailbhe of Emly; Libhear of Aghaboe.
9. Faolán of Strathfillan.
10. Diarmuid of Inchcleraun.
11. Anfadhán; Eiltín of Seanchua; Fáilbhe of Killower; Feidhealm daughter of Rónán; Feidhealm Ruadh; Mochuille of Tulla.
12. Laidhgeann of Kyle; Sineall, associate of Patrick.
13. Colmán Cearr; Díoraidh; Mainchín son of Collán.
14. Flann of Derrynaflan.
15. Aithche; Breac of Bealach Féile; Éimhearán; Modhíomóg of Glenkeen; Garbhán of Clonshanbo; Íde.
16. Faolán of Aachen; Fursa; Líthghin; Maol Íosa Ua Brolcháin.
17. Molaise of Kilmolash.
18. Aithneann; Aodhamair; Bláth; Ninnidh Láimhdhearg; Ródán.
19. Dúnchadh.
20. Aona of Clonmacnoise; Féichín; Lughna of Kiltrasna; Maodhóg of Ferns; Molaga of Aghacross; Sárán of Tisaran.
21. Feime; Fuinche daughter of Rónán; Fuinche Gharbh.
22. Bogha; Guaire Beag.
23. Cainneach of Aghaboe.
24. Baodán of Mostrim; Manchán of Lemanaghan.
25. Aodh of Lisgoole; Finncheall.
26.
27. Cróine of Ardnahue; Líobhan; Náile.
28. Acobhrán; Cainnear of Ceall Chuilinn; Eachaidh of Tallaght.
29. Conall of Inishkeel; Dallán Forghaill; Féichín.
30. Ailbhe of Shancough; Éanán of Rosminogue; Fionnbharr of Little Island.
31. Aodh of Aghadooey; Cainneach of Aghaboe; Lughaidh of Teernacreeve; Maodhóg of Ferns; Maol Anfaidh.

February

1. Brighid of Kildare; Cadán of Bute; Cinne; Darlughdhach of Kildare.
2. Aithmhead; Colmán son of Lughna; Finneach of Dorn; Fíonán Lobhar; Morónóg.

29. Breacán of Movilla; Cuach of Killynee; Díocha; Domhainghin of Toomyvara; Fiachna / Fiachra.
30. Ciarán of Seirkieran; Faolchú of Iona; Forannán of Donaghmore; Rónán of Liathros.

May

1. Aoidhghin of Fore; Breacán of Aughrim; Breacán of Inishmore; Ceallach of Killala; Ultán son of Maol Sneachta; Mochaoimhe.
2. Fiachna / Fiachra; Neachtan.
3. Aoidhghin of Bodoney; Cairbre of Movilla; Clothach; Conlaodh Cráibhtheach; Fíonán Cam; Rónaid daughter of Séighín. Síolán of Áth na gCeall
4. Aodh of Rahugh.
5. Inghean Bhaoith.
6. Inghean Bhaoith.
7. Breacán of Aughrim; Ciar of Achadh Í, Lasair of Killasseragh.
8. Uidhre.
9. Banbhán; Bréanainn of Birr; Santán.
10. Aodh of Forenaghts; Coireall of Kilcurl; Comhghall of Bangor; Conlaodh Cráibhtheach.
11. Caoimhghin; Críodán son of Iollann; Fionnlugh; Molua Lobhar; Seanach Seanghabha.
12. Díoma Dubh; Earc Nasca; Lughaidh Oilithir.
13. Maol Dóid; Tighearnach Boircheach.
14. Maol Céadair; Mochuda.
15. Colmán of Oughaval; Colum of Monaincha; Damhnad; Fachtna of Kiltoom; Maodhóg of Ferns; Neamhnad; Sárán of Inis Mór.
16. Bréanainn of Clonfert; Cairneach; Duirtheach; Fiodhmhaine; Odhrán of Íseal Ciaráin; Tighearnach Boircheach.
17. Cadán of Bute.
18. Aghna; Bran Beag; Modhomhnóg Oilithir.
19. Ríceall.
20. Colmán of Longfordpass; Conall of Inishkeel; Eithearn.
21. Bairrfhionn of Drumcullen; Colmán Lobhar.
22. Aghna; Baoithín of Ennisboyne; Breacán of Inishmore; Conall of Inishkeel; Rónán of Dromiskin.
23. Srafán.
24. Aoidhbhe; Bearchán of Kilbraghan; Ingheana Fearghais.
25. Caol; Dúnchadh of Iona.
26. Beagán of Toureen; Colmán Stiallán.
27. Beagán of Toureen; Cillín of Tehallan; Comaigh; Eithearn.
28. Luchtighearn.
29. Briúinseach; Cuman of Ards; Daghán; Maol Tuile.
30. Saorghas.
31. Eoghan of Movilla; Tearnóg.

June

1. Cuimín Cadhan; Laobhán.
2. Aodhán of Kilmeage; Conall of Drumcliff.
3. Aifín; Brannabh son of Maonach; Caoimhghin; Glúnshalach; Moninne.
4. Faithleann; Molua son of Sineall; Searbhán.
5.
6. Coga of Kilcock; Iarlaithe of Tuam.
7. Colmán of Dromore; Fionnlugh.
8. Brón; Luaithrinn; Muirchú.
9. Baoithín of Iona; Buadán of Culdaff; Colum Cille.
10. Ainmhire; Foircheallán; Santán.
11. Mac Táil; Searbhan; Tochomhracht.

29. Caolán of Youghalarra; Comán son of Fionnbharr.
30. Cian; Cruachán; Maol Tuile of Dysart; Seachnasach.
31. Colmán of Longfordpass; Dallán Forghaill; Nadál; Papán.

August

1. Aruin; Beagán of Toureen; Brighid of Kildare; Colmán of Longfordpass; Cruachán; Damhán of Feamore; Dúileach; Latiaran; Libhréan of Inis Mór; Moríóg; Nathí of Taney; Soicheall; Subhach.
2. Cian; Comhghán of Cluain Connaidh; Mac Reithe.
3. Aodhán of Cluain Tarbh; Deirbhileadh; Feidhlimidh of Kilmore; Trea of Artrea.
4. Molua of Kyle.
5. Earnán of Cloonrallagh; Eiche; Libhear; Rónaid daughter of Séighín.
6. Crónán of Clondalkin; Earnán of Cloonrallagh; Eiche.
7.
8. Beoán of Feighcullen; Colmán of Inishbofin; Curcach daughter of Daol.
9. Colmán of Drumrat; Laobhán; Nathí of Achonry; Ríoghán.
10. Blán; Lobhrán; Mochuma of Drumbo.
11. Athracht of Killaraght; Athracht of Kintale; Lelia; Liadhain daughter of Diarmuid; Mac Reithe; Oireannán.
12. Caomhán Oilithir; Molaise of Aughris; Muireadhach of Killala; Séighín of Iona.
13. Íomhar; Momhaodhóg; Molaga of Singland.
14. Caomhán Oilithir; Fachtna of Ross Carbery.
15. Bearach; Mac Caorthainn of Clogher.
16. Daigh of Inishkeen.
17. Breacán son of Sárán; Earnán of Tory.
18. Colmán Cúile; Daigh of Inishkeen; Eirnín of Cluain Deochra.
19. Éanán of Drumraney; Mochta of Louth.
20. Coincheann of Killagh; Mothrianóg.
21. Seanach son of Aonghas.
22. Cuimín Cadhan; Seanán of Laraghbryan; Sineach of Killinny.
23. Eoghan of Ardstraw; Mogheanóg.
24. Fáilbhe of Rathvilly.
25. Michean.
26. Faolán of Strathfillan.
27. Caoimheall daughter of Caomhlugh; Maol Rubha; Usaille.
28. Feidhlimidh of Cashel.
29.
30. Crónán of Cloney; Fiachna / Fiachra; Lorn of Aghamore; Muadhán.
31. Aodh Deochain; Aodhán of Lindisfarne; Colmán of Kilmacduagh; Colum Tuama; Mochua of Darragh.

September

1. Neamhan; Sceallán.
2. Droine; Geintéan; Maine of Aghanagh; Seanán of Laraghbryan.
3. Ana; Balloin; Bláth; Mac Nise of Connor.
4. Comhghall of Carrowmore; Neas of Earnaidhe; Ultán of Ardbraccan.
5. Bricín; Eolang; Faithleann.
6. Giallán; Mac Cuilinn; Sciath.
7. Adhamhnán; Mac Cuilinn; Taoide.

8. Ciarán of Clonmacnoise; Eiche; Seanán of Laraghbryan.
9. Ciarán of Clonmacnoise.
10. Ailbhe of Emly; Ailbhe of Shancough; Finnian of Movilla; Mac Treana; Sceanbhán; Seanach Garbh.
11. Conamhail; Lorn of Kilcoony; Moshiona.
12. Ailbhe of Emly; Mac Laisre son of Conall; Molaise of Devenish.
13. Daghán; Ingheana Coluim.
14. Caomhán Breac of Russagh; Colmán of Myshall; Cormac of Cashel; Dallán Forghaill; Fíonán Cam; Ingheana Coluim.
15. Ainmhire; Cormac of Cashel.
16. Cobhthach of Achadh Maic; Críodán Ceartrannach; Feime; Laisréan of Durrow; Usaille.
17. Brocán of Cluain Iomarchair; Brocán Claon; Feime; Mac Earca; Riaghail.
18. Éanán of Drumraney; Feargna of Ceall Mhic an Fhile.
19.
20.
21. Sárán of Lissan.
22. Aodh son of Seanach; Colmán of Myshall.
23. Adhamhnán.
24. Caolchú; Ceallachán; Ingheana Cainnigh.
25. Ainmhire; Caolán of Annaghkeelaun; Colmán of Conry; Donnchadh; Eithne of Temple-etney; Fionnbharr of Cork.
26. Colmán of Lynally.
27. Fionnbharr of Cork.
28. Mac Dara; Scíre.
29. Colum Tuama; Greallán; Manchán of Lemanaghan.
30. Colmán of Clontibret; Ródán

October

1. Colmán Cille; Fiodhairle.
2. Giallán; Maoldubh Beag.
3. Nuadha.
4. Fíonán of Drumnid; Fíonán of Teach Oirthir.
5. Baothghalach; Sineach of Crohane.
6. Feathghna; Lughach.
7. Dubhthach of Iona; Dubhthach of Maca Lughair.
8. Ciarán; Maol Fithrigh.
9. Aodhán of Templeshanbo; Donnchadh; Fiontan son of Tál.
10. Fiontan Fionn.
11. Cainneach; Feargna of Ceall Mhic an Fhile; Foirtchearn; Lomán of Lough Gill; Mochaidhbheo.
12. Beag son of Dé; Beag Bile; Breacán of Inishmore; Diarmuid of Aireadh Seanaigh; Fiac; Mobhí Cláirineach.
13. Comhghán of Cluain Connaidh; Finnseach.
14. Colum of Inishkeen; Comadán.
15. Colmán of Cloyne; Cuán of Ahascragh; Molua son of Maonach.
16. Caoimhghin; Ciar of Kilkeary; Colmán of Connahy / Holdenstown / Kilroot; Riaghail.
17. Maonach of Dunleer.
18. Colmán of Kilclooney
19. Colmán Bán; Crónán of Tomgraney; Usaille.
20. Fiontan Maoldubh.
21. Anfadhán; Díoraidh; Munna of Taghmon.
22.
23. Dalbhach.
24. Caoide of Donaghedy; Earc of Míleac.
25. Caoide of Donaghedy; Conach; Dúthracht of Leamhchaill; Gormán; Laisréan of Holywood; Mac Cuill; Mearnóg of Kilmarnock.

26. Beoán of Meenan; Cruaidh; Dairí; Deirbhileadh; Meallán of Meenan; Odhrán Maighistir.
27. Abán; Colmán of Uí Fhiachrach; Earc of Donaghmore; Odhrán of Iona; Odhrán Maighistir; Sineach of Killiny.
28. Caoide of Donaghedy; Doirbhéan.
29. Cainnear of Kirkinner; Colmán of Colmanswell/Kilmacduagh; Earcnad; Lúireach.
30. Donnchadh; Feidhlimidh of Magheramorne.
31. Faolán of Aachen; Faolán of Kiltullagh.

November

1. Aodh of Foyran; Bigeall of Tulach; Brughach; Cairbre of Kilcarbry; Colmán of Ahamlish; Eiltín of Kinsale; Fiac; Lonán of Trevet; Maol Maodhóg.
2. Ainmhire; Aodhán of Kilmore; Dairí; Earc of Slane; Gall Cráibhtheach; Liobhrán; Lughaidh of Kilpatrick; Maol Maodhóg.
3. Brughach; Caomhán of Anatrim; Caomhlach; Corcanadan; Lapán of Clonatin; Lasair of Kilronan; Muirdheabhair of Dysert.
4. Tighearnach of Derryvella.
5. Cainne of Teach Cainne; Cainnear of Rinn Allaidh; Colmán of Dysart.
6. Aodh of Aghadooey; Feadhbhair.
7. Subhalach.
8. Bairrfhionn of Aughkiletaun; Colum of Culbrim; Maol Tuile.
9. Beinéan; Sárnad daughter of Aodh; Sineach of Kilrush.
10. Aodh of Rahugh; Ciarán of Tubbrid; Greallán; Osnad; Luchtighearn.
11. Cairbre of Coleraine; Crónán son of Sineall.
12. Angais; Beagnad of Kilbegnet; Brígh of Kilmoney; Cuimín Fada of Clonfert; Fionnchadh; Íomhar; Lonán of Killulagh; Meithean Chaol; Sineall of Cleenish; Fínghin.
13. Caillín; Colmán of Inishbofin/Oughtmama; Faoileann daughter of Eoghan; Fionnlugh; Lasair of Aghavea; Modhomhnóg; Ninnidh Láimhiodhan; Bairrfhionn of Midíne; Colmán Lobhar.
14. Colmán of Inch; Cuana of Eonish; Eór; Fachtna of Kiltoom; Gabhrán; Lorcán (Laurence).
15. Colmán of Oughtmama.
16. Aodh of Rahugh; Cionaodh; Curcach of Kilcorkey; Fiontan Maoldubh.
17. Buaidhbheo; Dúileach; Feilig.
18. Miodhan; Mochonóg Uamhach.
19. Cianán; Éadaoin.
20. Caoide of Churchtown; Fraochán.
21. Colmán Iomramha; Subhach.
22. Domhnall Ua hÉanna.
23.
24. Bearchán of Rough Island; Cianán; Colmán of Cloyne; Maine son of Eoghan.
25. Fíonán of Ray; Fionnchú.
26. Banbhán; Coibhdheanach.
27. Odhbha; Seachnall.
28. Acobhrán of Achadh Rathain; Cainneach of Achadh Rathain.
29. Bréanainn of Birr; Cianán.
30. Rónán of Dromiskin.

December

1. Mac Coinne.
2. Iotharnaisc.
3. Bearchán of Clonsast; Beoán of Ráith Osáin.